DOD'S
PARLIAMENTARY COMPANION
GUIDE TO THE
GENERAL ELECTION

The publishers would like to thank all the individuals who have spent time and care working with us to ensure that the entries in this book are correct, and everyone who has provided helpful advice and guidance during its publication.

No payment is either solicited or accepted for the inclusion of editorial entries in this publication. Every possible precaution has been taken to ensure that the information contained in this publication is accurate at the time of going to press and the publisher cannot accept any liability for errors or omissions, however caused.

DOD'S PARLIAMENTARY COMPANION GUIDE TO THE GENERAL ELECTION
EDITORS: Valerie Passmore, David Roe
DATABASE MANAGER: Kirsty Green-Armytage
MARKETING MANAGER: Rhodri Joyce
PRODUCTION MANAGER: Roy Hodgkinson
ADVERTISING SALES MANAGERS: Gordon Collier, Tim Burgess
IT MANAGER: Paul Currie
PUBLISHING DIRECTOR: Maria Farmery

Database typesetting by Dod's Parliamentary Communications
Printed in Great Britain by Unwin Brothers, The Gresham Press, Old Woking, Surrey

© 2005 Dod's Parliamentary Communications
Westminster Tower, 3 Albert Embankment, London SE1 7SP
Tel: 020 7091 7500 Fax: 020 7091 7555 E-mail: editorial@dods.co.uk
ISBN: 0 905702 57 3

Contents

The
Recruitment
specialists in
Public Affairs
and
Government Relations

Ellwood and Atfield specialise in recruiting communications professionals for organisations in the public, private and voluntary sectors.

The 2005 General Election

The parliament elected on 7 June 2001 could have continued until mid-2006, but expectation of an early election had built up throughout 2004 and the prime minister did nothing to dampen such expectation. When the new session of Parliament opened in November almost everyone at Westminster believed the election would be on 5 May 2005. But the programme of legislation contained in the Queen's Speech appeared ample for a full session rather than a foreshortened one. The prime minister clearly wanted to keep an option open to vary the date should some unforeseen circumstance arise, and parliamentary business was organised as if no election was anticipated. It is one of the curiosities of British general elections that the prime minister is under no obligation to confirm that date until the dissolution of parliament is announced. This need be only 17 working days before the election is held. It may also be viewed as curious that a government with a safe majority and a full legislative programme, and no great issue on which it wishes to seek the judgement of the electorate, should nevertheless inflict an early election on the country.

But these matters receive little public debate once battle has been joined. Our formal constitutional arrangements still imply that Parliament is primarily a consultative body to the Crown, and as such can be dissolved whenever the modern monarch (the prime minister) thinks it appropriate. In practice the prime minister chooses the date that he feels will give his party maximum advantage, while retaining flexibility in case of unforeseen events as long as possible. And Oppositions must always give every appearance of wanting an election as soon as possible to 'drive the rascals out' of office.

In accordance with constitutional propriety Tony Blair went to the Palace on the morning of Tuesday 5 April to ask the Queen to dissolve Parliament. Later that day Statements were made in Parliament indicating that it was hoped to complete the passage of 14 Bills in the following two days, adding these to the two that had already attained royal assent so far in the session. This meant that several Bills had to be abandoned, including the Identity Cards Bill, the Consumer Credit Bill, the Road Safety Bill, and the School Transport Bill, all of which had completed their Commons stages. Controversial clauses were dropped from other Bills in order to speed their passage, including incitement to religious hatred clauses in the Serious Crime and Police Bill and clauses relating to super casinos in the Gambling Bill. The Finance Bill implementing budget decisions was pruned severely, but still not enough for the liking of some members of the Opposition, who regretted the very attenuated four hours of scrutiny this Bill (still running to 106 clauses) received in the Commons.

The final Commons joust between Tony Blair and Michael Howard took place at question time on 6 April, with the Leader of the Opposition inviting Labour members to put their hands up if they were using a picture of the prime minister on their election addresses. Some foolishly did so, allowing Michael Howard to point out how few Labour MPs seemed enthusiastic about their party leader. Parliament was prorogued late afternoon on Thursday 7 April after two days of hectic legislative activity. Dissolution was on the following Monday, 11 April. This timing allowed for some to attend the funeral of the Pope in Rome on Friday the eighth.

The number of MPs retiring from the House was 86, including a crop of former senior Labour ministers. The number of MPs from Scotland had been 72, but following the advent of the Scottish parliament numbers were reduced to give Scotland a representation commensurate with that accorded to the rest of Britain. This resulted in re-drawn constituency boundaries in Scotland, and a reduction in the number of its MPs in the new parliament to 59, giving a 646-member House instead of the previous size of 659.

The campaign can be divided into the lengthy pre-dissolution period, often described as the phoney campaign, and the official campaign, a hectic three-week scramble up to polling day. During the phoney campaign the major parties vie with each other for advantage. In January a sitting Conservative MP, Robert Jackson, who had already announced he would retire at the next election, crossed the floor of the House to join the Labour party, and proceeded to make withering criticisms of his former Conservative colleagues. In the same month newspaper extracts from a forthcoming book portrayed animosity between the Chancellor and the prime minister; it seemed hard to conceal the antipathy that existed at the top of the Labour Party, and this caused public concern among several senior Labour MPs. Gordon Brown delivered his ninth budget on 16 March, with much emphasis on this being the thirteenth consecutive year of sustained economic growth. His proposals included help for pensioner council taxpayers and the extension of free public transport for pensioners. Michael Howard described it as a 'vote now pay later' budget. Polls showed that the public generally believed that whoever won the election taxes would indeed have to rise.

As the phoney campaign came to a close, furious argument erupted about plans for public spending. The Conservatives promised to spend less, but only £35 billion less by 2011/12. This was not actually a cut in spending, simply a less rapid increase than could be construed from Labour's plans. But Labour sought to discredit the Opposition by saying a cut of £35 billion would require the sacking of every teacher in the country. Polls showed the public preferred a rise in investment in public services to tax cuts, but also that over half the electorate believed the 'Conservatives would make further substantial cuts in public spending'. This was the background to the dismissal of Howard Flight as a Conservative candidate, following the publication of remarks he made at a private meeting of the 'Way Forward Group', saying that proposed savings had been 'sieved for what is politically acceptable'. Not only did Michael Howard sack him from the front-bench, but also had the party whip withdrawn on 25 March, thus preventing him from standing in the imminent election. Many saw this as rather brutal action, but Michael Howard stressed that he wanted to be 'totally straight with the British people'.

Another Conservative candidate was dismissed at much the same time because of an article he had written suggesting the EU had a Catholic agenda, but in his case the constituency association (of Slough) had to be suspended before a new candidate could be imposed.

A good deal of attention was also given to the techniques of campaigning being used during the phoney period. Both major parties attempted to identify key voters in marginal seats through using computer programmes and relevant databases. Supposedly 800,000 voters were crucial. Mail shots, e-mails and telephone calls were concentrated on these folk. Labour was reportedly sending out 1.5 million items of mail a month. On the day the election was announced 100,000 people received an e-mail from the prime minister. The Conservative Party employed a consultant who had been credited with success in political campaigning in Australia, Lynton Crosby. One of his techniques was known as 'dog whistle politics', meaning that a subject was seized on where it was believed a sharp and clear message could be sent to a section of the electorate, but effectively heard only by that particular group. Thus for example the Conservatives suddenly focused on the threat of travellers' encampments, a subject of high salience and concern to those who lived close to actual or threatened encampments. Later immigration and asylum were similarly treated.

The very low turnout in the 2001 election (under 60 per cent) had aroused considerable concern, and among the responses made were further changes designed to make postal voting easier. By 2005 it was estimated as many as 4 million people had postal votes (as opposed to some 700,000 in 1997 and perhaps 1.4 million in 2001). But considerable concern had also been expressed about the integrity of postal voting. On 4 April as the election was formally announced an election commissioner found six councillors in Birmingham guilty of vote rigging in the local elections held the previous year. Giving judgement he was very outspoken, saying this fraud 'would disgrace a banana republic', and that the Government appeared to be 'not simply in a state of complacency but one of denial' about the whole matter. In a Statement in Parliament Nick Raynsford, Minister for Local Government, denied that there was any complacency on the Government's part and emphasised the steps being taken to try and minimise fraud in the forthcoming election. Nevertheless throughout the campaign accusations rumbled on. It was reported that the Crown Prosecution Service was considering proceedings in some 39 other cases of alleged fraud. Numerous stories appeared in the media of votes denied or multiple votes being obtained. The possibilities of abuse, most of which have existed for many years, were highlighted. But an attempt to stop the whole election through a high court challenge was thrown out on 20 April. Very probably some legal actions will follow the election, in particular in narrowly won seats. It was clear that adjustments to procedures to safeguard confidence in the voting system were needed.

Of greater concern to some voters was the bias towards Labour that had appeared in the electoral system. Calculations showed that even if Labour and the Conservatives both won equal proportions of the popular vote, at 36.2 per cent, Labour could expect to win 370 seats and the Conservatives only 219. On a Conservative lead of 5 per cent in the vote, Labour would still remain the largest single party, while the Conservatives would need a lead of 9 per cent to become the largest single party. The main reasons for this were that Labour represents on average smaller seats than the Conservatives, a factor reinforced by the generally lower turnout in Labour-held seats. The last redistribution of seats in England, Wales and Northern Ireland was in 1997, but this was based on the population distribution prevailing in the 1991 census.

This bias in the electoral system reinforced the expectations of a Labour win. At the beginning of the campaign Peter Kellner extrapolated a Yougov poll in the Sunday Times as suggesting Labour would have 358 seats, the Conservatives 195 and Liberal Democrats 62, a prediction remarkably close to the final outcome. Though there was some movement during the campaign, at first giving the Conservatives greater hope, then snatching this away again, Labour's lead remained decisive. The Liberal Democrats as usual made a small gain in the polls. But greater interest focused on the apparent volatility of the electorate, with several polls showing up to a third of the electorate who expressed a voting preference also contemplating a change of mind before polling day. This undoubtedly contributed to the jitteriness of party leaders.

At the commencement of the campaign news came through of the collapse of Rover/MG with the likely loss of 10,000 jobs in a key part of the Midlands where there were several marginal seats. Older voters might have thought of the frenzied activity that would have greeted such an announcement in the 1960s or 1970s. But by 2005 the national mood was very different. Of course Government was expected to express concern, and to try and ease the situation. But no talk of a government-backed rescue plan emerged. It was clear that the Opposition would hardly treat the matter any differently from the Government. And its electoral impact was generally thought to be slight.

On 11 April the 7,000-word Conservative manifesto was published in pamphlet form, emblazoned on the cover with the slogan 'Are you thinking what we are thinking? It's time for action'. Among the promises made was a £500 a year ongoing cut in council tax bills for pensioners, and a £4 billion cut in taxes in the first budget. Curbing expenditure within government was emphasised with a contribution being made to this by cutting the number of MPs by 20 per cent, a proposal that attracted little attention in the campaign. Two days later came the 23,000-word Labour manifesto entitled 'Forward not back', published as a 112-page little red book. Much of this was a recitation of the achievements of the last eight years. At its launch Tony Blair was one of seven cabinet ministers standing at podiums, with other cabinet colleagues sat behind. In a signed preface the prime minister committed himself to his own political demise, writing, 'So now, I fight my last election as leader of my party and prime minister of our country.' This naturally prompted many questions during the campaign about the timing of such a departure, but to these no clear answer was given. Instead, and in order to counter the bad publicity that had earlier surrounded the Blair/Brown feud, a remarkable double act took place throughout the campaign, with the two appearing constantly together and forever being lavish in their praise of each other. Clearly this was meant to establish in the minds of voters that a vote for the Labour party was a vote for a Government to be led throughout the next parliament by Blair and perhaps later Brown.

The 16,000-word Liberal Democrat manifesto entitled the 'Real Alternative' was published in newspaper style format on 14 April. This proposed a 50p top rate of income tax, and the replacement of the council tax with a local income tax. The latter point drew questions at the manifesto launch which the party leader, Charles Kennedy, had some obvious difficulty in answering. Perhaps this was because the previous day his wife had given birth to their first child, an event that had understandably distracted him with a sleepless night!

Early in the election campaign a poll ranking the importance of issues to electors showed the national health service, taxation, education and law and order as the most important. In eighth place equal to Europe was Iraq. But during the campaign Iraq was the issue that would not go away. Tony Blair's decision to join the American led invasion had remained extremely controversial within his own party. And still the news from Iraq was not reassuring, as daily violence continued. In his Sedgefield constituency among the other 14 candidates standing was the father of a young British soldier killed in Iraq who won over 10 per cent of the vote, coming in at fourth place. In Bethnal Green and Bow Oona King's 10,000-plus majority was overturned by George Galloway, the former MP expelled from the Labour Party standing for his Respect party. Oona King had been a staunch supporter of Blair's Iraq policy in a constituency with a high concentration of Muslim voters, George Galloway his most outspoken opponent. Some Labour candidates reported hostility towards the prime minister on account of Iraq. In part it was Tony Blair's judgement that was called into question. But it was also the integrity with which the issue had been handled within government. Had the evidence of weapons of mass destruction been exaggerated? And how secure was the legal basis for going to war? A long-standing criticism had been the failure of the Government to publish in full the Attorney-General's advice on the legality of war in the absence of a specific UN resolution. However, a leak resulted in the government decision to publish the advice in full on 27 April. This showed that the summary published earlier had been much less equivocal than the full version. More surprising was the revelation that apart from Tony Blair, only Jack Straw as Foreign Secretary and Geoff Hoon as Secretary of State for Defence had seen the full version. When the cabinet discussed the matter the Attorney-General had been present, but apparently no ministers had requested a copy of the full written opinion.

Unsurprisingly this brought Iraq back as an issue to dominate news conferences and headlines for a few more days, something clearly unwelcome to the Government. Michael Howard called Tony Blair a 'liar', and Conservative advertisements were launched saying the prime minister had been 'prepared to lie to win an election'. Brian Sedgemore, a Labour MP standing down after 27 years in the House, resigned from Labour and joined the Liberal Democrats, calling on the electorate to give Tony Blair a 'bloody nose'. Tony Blair responded with the alarmist claim that it would only take one in ten of Labour's voters to abstain to let Howard into Downing Street by the back door. Labour launched a new slogan, 'If you value it, vote for it', with much emphasis on avoiding the bad old days of Conservative rule. Among Labour supporters there was talk of voting while 'holding one's nose'.

To the political cognoscenti the campaign had become quite interesting. But to many of the electorate it appeared confusing and boring. Argument seemed to centre on relatively minor policy differences between the major parties, while their leaders assailed each other's competence and integrity. There was little sense of a national debate about competing visions for the country, nor indeed any significant debate about a range of matters that seemed intrinsically far more important for future national well-being than the issues that dominated the headlines. Debate on pensions was on hold until a further review had reported. Europe was not an issue; after all there would be a referendum on Europe within the next year. Constitutional reform was likewise a marginal issue, despite the manifest incompleteness of the reform of the House of Lords. Was there any new thinking about how to solve the transport problem? Should nuclear power be revived? Election debate was almost oblivious to these issues.

One candidate died during the campaign, bringing to light the unexpected fact that in such circumstances, where ballot papers have already been printed and postal ballots distributed, the election has to be postponed. This meant that the sitting Conservative MP, Sir Patrick Cormack in Staffordshire South, had to await a by-election early in the new Parliament before he could return to Westminster.

As soon as the polls closed at 10 pm on 5 May the result of the joint BBC and ITV exit poll was announced. An overall Labour majority of 66 was predicted, exactly the figure that emerged the next day. Once again the safe Labour seat of Sunderland South was the first to declare, within 43 minutes of the polls closing, and faster by 15 seconds than in 2001. Turnout nation-wide had inched up, but remained at a historically very low level at 61.4 per cent. Labour's vote share fell, from 42 per cent in 2001 to 36 per cent, and this combined with the low turnout meant that Labour were returned to power with the actual support of only just over 21 per cent of the electorate. Never had a majority government been elected on such low figures. The Conservative share of the vote was almost identical to 2001. But the party won 33 more seats, including one in Scotland and three in Wales – both previously devoid of Conservative representation.

The Liberal Democrats vote share rose to 22.7 per cent and they were rewarded with 62 seats, their best performance since Labour had first formed a Government in 1923. In Northern Ireland the Democratic Unionists won nine seats, almost wiping out the Ulster Unionists who won one seat, with Sinn Fein winning five seats to the SDLP's three seats. Plaid Cymru finished with three seats in Wales, one fewer than in 2001, and the SNP gained six seats in Scotland, one more than in 2001.

The number of women MPs rose to 128, eight more than the previous highest total achieved in 1997. Labour with its policy of some all-female shortlists had the most with 98, the Conservatives had 17 and the Liberal Democrats ten. However, Labour lost one safe seat, Blaenau Gwent, where a female candidate was imposed, provoking a local Labour member of the Welsh Assembly, Peter Law, to stand as an independent. He won the seat with a 9,000-plus majority, overturning Labour's former 19,000 majority! Another independent, Richard Taylor, comfortably held his Wyre Forest seat, won first in 2001.

Tony Blair made a subdued return to Downing Street. A majority of 66 may seem quite comfortable from an historical perspective, but the number of openly rebellious Labour backbenchers made that look an insecure majority for radical new Labour legislation. Media reports suggested the prime minister had some difficulty in appointing his new government with several ministers resisting their proposed re-deployment. A number of backbenchers openly called for his departure to be sooner rather than later. Meanwhile Michael Howard announced that he would step down as Conservative leader, but not until a new procedure had been put in place for choosing his successor. Changes made while William Hague was leader had put the final choice in the hands of party members in the country; it was now deemed wiser to ensure MPs had a greater say in the final decision. So, unusually the leaders of both major parties have promised to depart before the next general election. The Conservatives can expect to have a new leader within a few months. The timing of Labour's change remains uncertain.

Donald Shell
Bristol University

GOVERNMENT AND OPPOSITION

The Cabinet

Prime Minister, First Lord of the Treasury and Minister for the Civil Service	**Tony Blair** MP
Deputy Prime Minister and First Secretary of State	**John Prescott** MP
Chancellor of the Exchequer	**Gordon Brown** MP
Secretary of State for Foreign and Commonwealth Affairs	**Jack Straw** MP
Secretary of State for Work and Pensions	**David Blunkett** MP
Secretary of State for Environment, Food and Rural Affairs	**Margaret Beckett** MP
Secretary of State for Transport and for Scotland	**Alistair Darling** MP
Secretary of State for Defence	**John Reid** MP
Leader of the House of Commons, Lord Privy Seal	**Geoffrey Hoon** MP
Secretary of State for Health	**Patricia Hewitt** MP
Secretary of State for Culture, Media and Sport	**Tessa Jowell** MP
Chief Whip	**Hilary Armstrong** MP
Secretary of State for the Home Department	**Charles Clarke** MP
Secretary of State for Northern Ireland and for Wales	**Peter Hain** MP
Minister without Portfolio and Labour Party Chair	**Ian McCartney** MP
Leader of the House of Lords and Lord President of the Council	**Baroness Amos**
Secretary of State for Constitutional Affairs and Lord Chancellor	**Lord Falconer of Thoroton**
Secretary of State for International Development	**Hilary Benn** MP
Secretary of State for Trade and Industry	**Alan Johnson** MP
Secretary of State for Education and Skills	**Ruth Kelly** MP
Chancellor of the Duchy of Lancaster	**John Hutton** MP
Chief Secretary to the Treasury	**Des Browne** MP
Minister of Communities and Local Government	**David Miliband** MP

Also attending Cabinet

Lords Chief Whip	**Lord Grocott**
Attorney General	**Lord Goldsmith**
Minister for Europe, Foreign and Commonwealth Office	**Douglas Alexander** MP

Departmental Ministers

Cabinet Office

Chancellor of the Duchy of Lancaster	Rt Hon **John Hutton** MP
Parliamentary Secretary	**Jim Murphy** MP

Department for Constitutional Affairs

Secretary of State for Constitutional Affairs and Lord Chancellor	Rt Hon **Lord Falconer of Thoroton**
Minister of State	Rt Hon **Harriet Harman** QC MP
Parliamentary Under-Secretaries of State	**Baroness Ashton of Upholland**
	Bridget Prentice MP

Department for Culture, Media and Sport

Secretary of State for Culture, Media and Sport	Rt Hon **Tessa Jowell** MP
Minister of State	Rt Hon **Richard Caborn** MP
Parliamentary Under-Secretaries of State	**David Lammy** MP
	James Purnell MP

Ministry of Defence

Secretary of State for Defence	Rt Hon Dr **John Reid** MP
Minister of State	Rt Hon **Adam Ingram** MP
Parliamentary Under-Secretaries of State	**Don Touhig** MP
	Lord Drayson

Office of the Deputy Prime Minister

Deputy Prime Minister and First Secretary of State	Rt Hon **John Prescott** MP
Ministers of State	Rt Hon **David Miliband** MP
	Yvette Cooper MP
	Phil Woolas MP
Parliamentary Under-Secretaries of State	**Jim Fitzpatrick** MP
	Baroness Andrews

Department for Education and Skills

Secretary of State for Education and Skills	Rt Hon **Ruth Kelly** MP
Ministers of State	Rt Hon **Jacqui Smith** MP
	Bill Rammell MP
	Rt Hon **Beverley Hughes** MP
Parliamentary Under-Secretaries of State	**Lord Adonis**
	Phil Hope MP
	Maria Eagle MP

Department for Environment, Food and Rural Affairs

Secretary of State for Environment, Food and Rural Affairs	Rt Hon **Margaret Beckett** MP
Minister of State	**Elliot Morley** MP
Parliamentary Under-Secretaries of State	**Ben Bradshaw** MP
	Jim Knight MP
	Lord Bach

Foreign and Commonwealth Office

Secretary of State for Foreign and Commonwealth Affairs (Foreign Secretary)	Rt Hon **Jack Straw** MP
Ministers of State	Rt Hon **Douglas Alexander** MP
	Dr **Kim Howells** MP
	Ian Pearson MP (also DTI)
Parliamentary Under-Secretary of State	**Lord Triesman**

Department of Health

Secretary of State for Health	Rt Hon **Patricia Hewitt** MP
Ministers of State	**Rosie Winterton** MP
	Rt Hon **Jane Kennedy** MP
	Lord Warner
Parliamentary Under-Secretaries of State	**Caroline Flint** MP
	Liam Byrne MP

Home Office

Secretary of State for the Home Department (Home Secretary)	Rt Hon **Charles Clarke** MP
Ministers of State	**Hazel Blears** MP
	Rt Hon **Baroness Scotland of Asthal** QC
	Tony McNulty MP
Parliamentary Under-Secretaries of State	**Paul Goggins** MP
	Fiona Mactaggart MP
	Andy Burnham MP

Department for International Development

Secretary of State for International Development	Rt Hon **Hilary Benn** MP
Parliamentary Under-Secretary of State	**Gareth Thomas** MP

Law Officers' Department

Attorney General	Rt Hon **Lord Goldsmith** QC
Solicitor General	**Mike O'Brien** MP
Advocate General	Dr **Lynda Clark** QC

Leader of the House of Commons

Leader of the House	Rt Hon **Geoffrey Hoon** MP
Deputy Leader	**Nigel Griffiths** MP

Leader of the House of Lords and Lord President of the Council

Leader	Rt Hon **Baroness Amos**

Minister without Portfolio

Minister without Portfolio	Rt Hon **Ian McCartney** MP

Northern Ireland Office

Secretary of State for Northern Ireland	Rt Hon **Peter Hain** MP
Ministers of State	**David Hanson** MP
	Rt Hon **Lord Rooker**
Parliamentary Under-Secretaries of State	**Angela Evans Smith** MP
	Shaun Woodward MP

Privy Council Office

Lord President of the Council	Rt Hon **Baroness Amos**

14% more enjoyable breakfasts. 14% more lingering kisses. 14% more spring in steps. 14% more whistling. 14% more politeness. 14% more "Good mornings." 14% more pleased bosses. 14% more "Hello honey I'm homes." 14% less dinners in dogs. Since introducing our new timetable punctuality has increased, you guessed it, by 14%.*

SOUTH WEST TRAINS
www.southwesttrains.co.uk

*Recorded by the Performance Department South West Trains from TRUST data.

Scotland Office

Secretary of State for Scotland	Rt Hon **Alistair Darling** MP
Parliamentary Under-Secretary of State	**David Cairns** MP

Department of Trade and Industry

Secretary of State for Trade and Industry	Rt Hon **Alan Johnson** MP
Ministers of State	Rt Hon **Alun Michael** MP
	Malcolm Wicks MP
	Ian Pearson MP (also FCO)
Parliamentary Under-Secretaries of State	**Gerry Sutcliffe** MP
	Barry Gardiner MP
	Lord Sainsbury of Turville
	Meg Munn MP

Department for Transport

Secretary of State for Transport	Rt Hon **Alistair Darling** MP
Minister of State	Dr **Stephen Ladyman** MP
Parliamentary Under-Secretaries of State	**Derek Twigg** MP
	Karen Buck MP

HM Treasury

Chancellor of the Exchequer	Rt Hon **Gordon Brown** MP
Chief Secretary to the Treasury	Rt Hon **Des Browne** MP
Paymaster General	Rt Hon **Dawn Primarolo** MP
Financial Secretary	**John Healey** MP
Economic Secretary	**Ivan Lewis** MP

Wales Office

Secretary of State for Wales	Rt Hon **Peter Hain** MP
Parliamentary Under-Secretary of State	**Nick Ainger** MP

Department for Work and Pensions

Secretary of State for Work and Pensions	Rt Hon **David Blunkett** MP
Ministers of State	Rt Hon **Margaret Hodge** MP
	Stephen Timms MP
Parliamentary Under-Secretaries of State	**Lord Hunt of Kings Heath**
	James Plaskitt MP
	Anne McGuire MP

Government Whips

HOUSE OF COMMONS

Chief Whip
Parliamentary Secretary to the Treasury

Rt Hon **Hilary Armstrong** MP

Deputy Chief Whip
Treasurer of HM Household

Bob Ainsworth MP

Whips
Comptroller of HM Household
Vice-Chamberlain of HM Household
Lords Commissioner of HM Treasury

Rt Hon **Thomas McAvoy** MP
John Heppell MP
Gillian Merron MP
Vernon Coaker MP
Tom Watson MP
David Watts MP
Joan Ryan MP

Assistant Whips

Frank Roy MP
Ian Cawsey MP
Alan Campbell MP
Claire Ward MP
Parmjit Dhanda MP
Tony Cunningham MP
Kevin Brennan MP

HOUSE OF LORDS

Chief Whip
Captain of the Honourable Corps of the Gentlemen-at-Arms

Rt Hon **Lord Grocott**

Deputy Chief Whip
Captain of the Queen's Bodyguard of the Yeoman of the Guard

Lord Davies of Oldham

Whips
Lords in Waiting

Lord Bassam of Brighton
Lord Evans of Temple Guiting
Lord McKenzie of Luton

Baronesses in Waiting

Baroness Crawley
Baroness Farrington of Ribbleton
Baroness Royall of Blaisdon

Alphabetical list of Ministers and Whips

ADONIS Lord — Parliamentary Under-Secretary of State, Department for Education and Skills

AINGER Nick — Parliamentary Under-Secretary of State, Wales Office

AINSWORTH Bob — Deputy Chief Whip

ALEXANDER Rt Hon Douglas — Minister of State, Foreign and Commonwealth Office

AMOS Rt Hon Baroness — Leader of the House of Lords and Lord President of the Council

ANDREWS Baroness — Parliamentary Under-Secretary of State, Office of the Deputy Prime Minister

ARMSTRONG Rt Hon Hilary — Chief Whip

ASHTON of UPHOLLAND Baroness — Parliamentary Under-Secretary of State, Department for Constitutional Affairs

BACH Lord — Parliamentary Under-Secretary of State, Department for Environment, Food and Rural Affairs

BASSAM of BRIGHTON Lord — Lords Whip

BECKETT Rt Hon Margaret — Secretary of State for Environment, Food and Rural Affairs

BENN Rt Hon Hilary — Secretary of State for International Development

BLAIR Rt Hon Tony — Prime Minister

BLEARS Hazel — Minister of State, Home Office

BLUNKETT Rt Hon David — Secretary of State for Work and Pensions

BRADSHAW Ben — Parliamentary Under-Secretary of State, Department for Environment, Food and Rural Affairs

BRENNAN Kevin — Assistant Whip

BROWN Rt Hon Gordon — Chancellor of the Exchequer

BROWNE Rt Hon Des — Chief Secretary to the Treasury

BUCK Karen — Parliamentary Under-Secretary of State, Department for Transport

BURNHAM Andy — Parliamentary Under-Secretary of State, Home Office

BYRNE Liam — Parliamentary Under-Secretary of State, Department of Health

CABORN Rt Hon Richard — Minister of State, Department for Culture, Media and Sport

CAIRNS David — Parliamentary Under-Secretary of State, Scotland Office

CAMPBELL Alan — Assistant Whip

CAWSEY Ian — Assistant Whip

CLARK Dr Lynda — Advocate General for Scotland

CLARKE Rt Hon Charles — Secretary of State for the Home Department (Home Secretary)

COAKER Vernon — Whip

COOPER Yvette — Minister of State, Office of the Deputy Prime Minister

CRAWLEY Baroness — Lords Whip

CUNNINGHAM Tony — Assistant Whip

DARLING Rt Hon Alistair — Secretary of State for Transport and for Scotland

DAVIES of OLDHAM Lord — Lords Deputy Chief Whip

DHANDA Parmjit — Assistant Whip

DRAYSON Lord — Parliamentary Under-Secretary of State, Ministry of Defence

EAGLE Maria — Parliamentary Under-Secretary of State, Department for Education and Skills

EVANS of TEMPLE GUITING Lord — Lords Whip

FALCONER of THOROTON Rt Hon Lord — Secretary of State for Constitutional Affairs and Lord Chancellor

FARRINGTON of RIBBLETON Baroness — Lords Whip

FITZPATRICK Jim — Parliamentary Under-Secretary of State, Office of the Deputy Prime Minister

FLINT Caroline — Parliamentary Under-Secretary of State, Department of Health

GARDINER Barry — Parliamentary Under-Secretary of State, Department of Trade and Industry

GOGGINS Paul — Parliamentary Under-Secretary of State, Home Office

GOLDSMITH Rt Hon Lord	Attorney General
GRIFFITHS Nigel	Deputy Leader of the House of Commons
GROCOTT Rt Hon Lord	Lords Chief Whip
HAIN Rt Hon Peter	Secretary of State for Northern Ireland and for Wales
HANSON David	Minister of State, Northern Ireland Office
HARMAN Rt Hon Harriet	Minister of State, Department for Constitutional Affairs
HEALEY John	Financial Secretary, HM Treasury
HEPPELL John	Whip
HEWITT Rt Hon Patricia	Secretary of State for Health
HODGE Rt Hon Margaret	Minister of State, Department for Work and Pensions
HOON Rt Hon Geoffrey	Leader of the House of Commons and Lord Privy Seal
HOPE Phil	Parliamentary Under-Secretary of State, Department for Education and Skills
HOWELLS Dr Kim	Minister of State, Foreign and Commonwealth Office
HUGHES Rt Hon Beverley	Minister of State, Department for Education and Skills
HUNT of KINGS HEATH Lord	Parliamentary Under-Secretary of State, Department for Work and Pensions
HUTTON Rt Hon John	Chancellor of the Duchy of Lancaster
INGRAM Rt Hon Adam	Minister of State, Ministry of Defence
JOHNSON Rt Hon Alan	Secretary of State for Trade and Industry
JOWELL Rt Hon Tessa	Secretary of State for Culture, Media and Sport
KELLY Rt Hon Ruth	Secretary of State for Education and Skills
KENNEDY Rt Hon Jane	Minister of State, Department of Health
KNIGHT Jim	Parliamentary Under-Secretary of State, Department for Environment, Food and Rural Affairs
LADYMAN Dr Stephen	Minister of State, Department for Transport
LAMMY David	Parliamentary Under-Secretary of State, Department for Culture, Media and Sport
LEWIS Ivan	Economic Secretary, HM Treasury
McAVOY Rt Hon Thomas	Whip
McCARTNEY Rt Hon Ian	Minister without Portfolio
McGUIRE Anne	Parliamentary Under-Secretary of State, Department for Work and Pensions
McKENZIE of LUTON Lord	Lords Whip
McNULTY Tony	Minister of State, Home Office
MACTAGGART Fiona	Parliamentary Under-Secretary of State, Home Office
MERRON Gillian	Whip
MICHAEL Rt Hon Alun	Minister of State, Department of Trade and Industry
MILIBAND Rt Hon David	Minister of State, Office of the Deputy Prime Minister
MORLEY Elliot	Minister of State, Department for Environment, Food and Rural Affairs
MUNN Meg	Parliamentary Under-Secretary of State, Department of Trade and Industry
MURPHY Jim	Parliamentary Secretary, Cabinet Office
O'BRIEN Mike	Solicitor General
PEARSON Ian	Minister of State, Foreign and Commonwealth Office and Department of Trade and Industry
PLASKITT James	Parliamentary Under-Secretary of State, Department for Work and Pensions
PRENTICE Bridget	Parliamentary Under-Secretary of State, Department for Constitutional Affairs
PRESCOTT Rt Hon John	Deputy Prime Minister and First Secretary of State
PRIMAROLO Rt Hon Dawn	Paymaster General, HM Treasury
PURNELL James	Parliamentary Under-Secretary of State, Department for Culture, Media and Sport
RAMMELL Bill	Minister of State, Department for Education and Skills
REID Rt Hon Dr John	Secretary of State for Defence

ROOKER Rt Hon Lord	Deputy Leader of the House of Lords; Minister of State, Northern Ireland Office
ROY Frank	Assistant Whip
ROYALL of BLAISDON Baroness	Lords Whip
RYAN Joan	Whip
SAINSBURY of TURVILLE Lord	Parliamentary Under-Secretary of State, Department of Trade and Industry
SCOTLAND of ASTHAL Rt Hon Baroness	Minister of State, Home Office
SMITH Angela Evans	Parliamentary Under-Secretary of State, Northern Ireland Office
SMITH Rt Hon Jacqui	Minister of State, Department for Education and Skills
STRAW Rt Hon Jack	Secretary of State for Foreign and Commonwealth Affairs (Foreign Secretary)
SUTCLIFFE Gerry	Parliamentary Under-Secretary of State, Department of Trade and Industry
THOMAS Gareth	Parliamentary Under-Secretary of State, Department for International Development
TIMMS Stephen	Minister of State, Department for Work and Pensions
TOUHIG Don	Parliamentary Under-Secretary of State, Ministry of Defence
TRIESMAN Lord	Parliamentary Under-Secretary of State, Foreign and Commonwealth Office
TWIGG Derek	Parliamentary Under-Secretary of State, Department for Transport
WARD Claire	Assistant Whip
WARNER Lord	Minister of State, Department of Health
WATSON Tom	Whip
WATTS David	Whip
WICKS Malcolm	Minister of State, Department of Trade and Industry
WINTERTON Rosie	Minister of State, Department of Health
WOODWARD Shaun	Parliamentary Under-Secretary of State, Northern Ireland Office
WOOLAS Phil	Minister of State, Office of the Deputy Prime Minister

Opposition

Conservatives (Official Opposition)

Shadow Cabinet

Leader of the Opposition	Rt Hon **Michael Howard** QC MP
Shadow Secretary of State for Defence and Deputy Leader	Rt Hon **Michael Ancram** MP
Shadow Secretary of State for Education and Skills	**David Cameron** MP
Shadow Home Secretary	Rt Hon **David Davis** MP
Shadow Secretary of State for Transport	**Alan Duncan** MP
Shadow Foreign Secretary	Dr **Liam Fox** MP
Shadow Leader of the House of Commons	**Christopher Grayling** MP
Shadow Chief Secretary to the Treasury	**Philip Hammond** MP
Shadow Secretary of State for Constitutional Affairs	**Oliver Heald** MP
Shadow Secretary of State for Health	**Andrew Lansley** MP
Shadow Secretary of State for Environment, Food and Rural Affairs	Rt Hon **Oliver Letwin** MP
Shadow Secretary of State for Northern Ireland	**David Lidington** MP
Chief Whip	Rt Hon **David Maclean** MP
Chairman of the Conservative Party	Rt Hon **Francis Maude** MP
Shadow Secretary of State for the Family and for Culture, Media and Sport	Rt Hon **Theresa May** MP
Shadow Secretary of State for International Development	**Andrew Mitchell** MP
Shadow Chancellor of the Exchequer	**George Osborne** MP
Shadow Secretary of State for Deregulation	Rt Hon **John Redwood** MP
Shadow Secretary of State for Work and Pensions	Rt Hon Sir **Malcolm Rifkind** MP
Shadow Secretary of State for Local Government Affairs and Communities	**Caroline Spelman** MP
Leader of the Opposition in the Lords	Rt Hon **Lord Strathclyde**
Shadow Secretary of State for Trade and Industry	**David Willetts** MP

Liberal Democrats

Shadow Cabinet

Leader	Rt Hon **Charles Kennedy** MP
Leader in the House of Lords	**Lord McNally**
Deputy Leader and Shadow Secretary of State for Foreign and Commonwealth Affairs	Rt Hon Sir **Menzies Campbell** MP
Shadow Chancellor of the Exchequer	Dr **Vincent Cable** MP
Shadow Home Secretary	**Mark Oaten** MP
Shadow Secretary of State for Health	Prof **Steve Webb** MP
Shadow Secretary of State for Education and Skills	**Edward Davey** MP
Shadow Secretary of State for Work and Pensions	**David Laws** MP
Shadow Office of the Deputy Prime Minister	**Simon Hughes** MP
Shadow Secretary of State for Environment and Rural Affairs	**Norman Baker** MP
Shadow Secretary of State for Defence	**Michael Moore** MP
Shadow Secretary of State for Trade and Industry	**Norman Lamb** MP
Shadow Secretary of State for Culture, Media and Sport	**Don Foster** MP
Shadow Secretary of State for Transport	**Tom Brake** MP
Shadow Secretary of State for International Development	**Andrew George** MP
Shadow Secretary of State for Scotland	**John Thurso** MP
Shadow Secretary of State for Northern Ireland and for Wales	**Lembit Öpik** MP
Spokesperson for Women and Older People	**Sandra Gidley** MP
Shadow Secretary of State for Communities and Local Government	**Sarah Teather** MP
Chair of the Parliamentary Party	**Matthew Taylor** MP
Chief Whip	**Andrew Stunell** MP

MEMBERS OF
PARLIAMENT

FUEL PROTESTS
IS ANYONE LISTENING?

We know that the current price of road diesel is a world problem.

But in the UK we have the EU's highest rate of tax. Hauliers are having to grapple with a daily change in fuel price. **You** try running a business when your raw material fluctuates in price so dramatically. Hauliers pay for it daily. But **their customers** pay them 60-90 days later. Even airline passengers pay a fuel surcharge **before** they get the service. **Small wonder there has been widespread talk of protest!** So what must hauliers have? **Simple – a level playing field for fuel.** At the very least they need price stability, so rates can catch up with costs.

We therefore suggest a regulator that automatically cuts in when the barrel price of oil exceeds a set rate thus reducing the tax. This would be paid for out of windfall oil revenues from the North Sea. And (dare we say it) the record profits posted by the oil companies.

One thing is certain. If world oil prices climb much higher then the very future of UK road haulage is at stake – and that means our way of life!

 The Road Haulage Association – Supporting the industry on which the UK depends www.rha.net

MPs' Biographies

Lab majority 7,427

ABBOTT, DIANE
Hackney North and Stoke Newington

Diane Julie Abbott. Born 27 September 1953; Daughter of late Reginald Abbott, welder, and late Mrs Julie Abbott, psychiatric nurse; Educated Harrow County Girls' Grammar School; Newnham College, Cambridge (BA history 1976); Married David Thompson 1991 (1 son) (marriage dissolved 1993). Administration trainee, Home Office 1976-78; Race relations officer, National Council for Civil Liberties 1978-80; Journalist, Thames Television 1980-82, TV AM 1982-84, freelance 1984-85; Principal press officer, Lambeth Council 1986-87; Equality officer, ACTT 1985-86; Member, RMT Parliamentary Campaigning Group 2002-; Westminster City Councillor 1982-86; Member Greater London Assembly advisory cabinet for women and equality 2000-

House of Commons: Member for Hackney North and Stoke Newington since 11 June 1987 general election. *Political interests:* Small Businesses. Jamaica, Africa

Member, Labour Party National Executive Committee 1994-97. First black female MP; *Recreations:* Reading, cinema

Diane Abbott, MP, House of Commons, London SW1A 0AA *Tel:* 020 7219 4330. *Constituency: Website:* www.hackney-labour.org.uk

Sinn Féin majority 19,315

ADAMS, GERRY
Belfast West

Gerry (Gerard) Adams. Born 6 October 1948; Son of late Gerard Adams and Annie Hannaway; Educated St Mary's Christian Brothers' School, Belfast; Married Colette McArdle 1971 (1 son). Bartender; Founder member of the civil rights movement

House of Commons: Member for Belfast West 1983-92, and since 1 May 1997 general election; Member, Northern Ireland Assembly 1981; Vice-President, Sinn Féin 1978-83, President 1983-; Member: Northern Ireland Forum 1996, new Northern Ireland Assembly for Belfast West 1998-

Member, PEN; *Publications: Before the Dawn, An Irish Voice, A Pathway to Peace, The Politics of Irish Freedom and Selected Writings, Falls Memories, Cage Eleven, The Street and Other Stories, An Irish Journal, Peace in Ireland – Towards a Lasting Peace; Hope and History* 2003; Thorr Peace Prize 1996; *Clubs:* Naomh Eoin; *Recreations:* Gaelic sports, Irish traditional music

Gerry Adams, MP, House of Commons, London SW1A 0AA *Tel:* 020 7219 8151. *Constituency:* 53 Falls Road, Belfast BT12 4PD *Tel:* 028 9022 3000 *E-mail:* sfwestbelfast@talk21.com

AFRIYIE, ADAM
Windsor

Adam Afriyie. Born 4 August 1965; Educated Addey and Stanhope, New Cross; Imperial College, London (BSc agricultural economics 1987). Managing director (now non-exec Chairman), Connect Support Services 1993-; Chairman (now non-exec), DeHavilland Information Services 1998-; Board member, Policy Exchange 2003-; Governor, Museum of London

House of Commons: Member for Windsor since 5 May 2005 general election

Con majority 10,292   Constituency branch chairman 1999-2004. National Trust; Trustee, Museum in Docklands 2003-; *Clubs:* Windsor and Eton Society; *Recreations:* Distance running

Adam Afriyie, MP, House of Commons, London SW1A 0AA *Tel:* 020 7219 8023. *Constituency:* 87 St Leonards Lane, Windsor SL4 3BZ *Tel:* 01753 678 983 *Website:* www.windsorconservatives.com

AINGER, NICK
Carmarthen West and South Pembrokeshire

Nick (Nicholas) Richard Ainger. Born 24 October 1949; Son of Richard John Wilkinson and Marjorie Isabel, née Dye; Educated Netherthorpe Grammar School, Staveley, Derbyshire; Married Sally Robinson 1976 (1 daughter). Marine and Port Services Ltd., Pembroke Dock 1977-92; Branch secretary, TGWU; Councillor, Dyfed County Council 1981-93; Vice-Chair, Dyfed County Council Labour Group 1989-92

House of Commons: Member for Pembroke 1992-97, and for Carmarthen West and

Lab majority 1,910   South Pembrokeshire since 1 May 1997 general election; Government Whip 2001-05; PPS to Secretaries of State for Wales: Ron Davies 1997-98, Alun Michael 1998-99, Paul Murphy 1999-2001; Parliamentary Under-Secretary of State, Wales Office 2005-. *Political interests:* Environment, Health. Ireland

British-Irish Interparliamentary Body 1993-2001; Member, Dyfed Wildlife Trust

Nick Ainger, MP, House of Commons, London SW1A 0AA *Tel:* 020 7219 2241 *Fax:* 020 7219 2690 *E-mail:* aingern@parliament.uk. *Constituency:* Ferry Lane Works, Ferry Lane, Pembroke Dock, Dyfed SA71 4RE *Tel:* 01646 684404 *Fax:* 01646 682954

AINSWORTH, BOB
Coventry North East

Bob (Robert) William Ainsworth. Born 19 June 1952; Son of late Stanley and Pearl Ainsworth; Educated Foxford Comprehensive School, Coventry; Married Gloria Sandall 1974 (2 daughters). Sheet metal worker; fitter with Jaguar Cars, Coventry 1971-91; Member, MSF: Shop steward 1974, Senior steward and secretary of joint shop stewards 1980-91, Union Branch President 1983-87; Councillor, Coventry City Council 1984-93, Deputy Leader 1988-91, Chair, Finance Committee 1989-92

House of Commons: Member for Coventry North East since 9 April 1992 general

Lab majority 14,222   election; Opposition Whip 1995-97; Government Whip 1997-2001; Deputy Chief Whip 2003-; Parliamentary Under-Secretary of State, Department of the Environment, Transport and the Regions 2001; Parliamentary Under-Secretary of State for Anti-drugs Co-ordination and Organised Crime, Home Office 2001-03. *Political interests:* Industry, Environment, Taxation. France, India, Pakistan, USA

PC 2005; *Clubs:* Bell Green Working Men's; Broad Street Rugby Football Old Boys'; *Recreations:* Walking, chess, reading, cycling

Bob Ainsworth, MP, House of Commons, London SW1A 0AA *Tel:* 020 7219 4047 *Fax:* 020 7219 2889 *E-mail:* ainsworthr@parliament.uk. *Constituency:* Office 3, 3rd Floor, Coventry Point, Market Way, Coventry, West Midlands CV1 1EA *Tel:* 024 7622 6707 *Fax:* 024 7655 3576

Con majority 15,921

AINSWORTH, PETER
East Surrey

Peter Michael Ainsworth. Born 16 November 1956; Son of late Lieutenant-Commander Michael Lionel Yeoward Ainsworth and Patricia Mary, née Bedford; Educated Bradfield College; Lincoln College, Oxford (MA English literature and language 1979); Married Claire Burnett 1981 (1 son 2 daughters). Research assistant to Sir John Stewart-Clark MEP 1979-81; Investment analyst, Laing & Cruickshank 1981-85; S G Warburg Securities 1985-92: Investment analyst 1985-87, Corporate finance 1987-92, Director 1990-92; Councillor, London Borough of Wandsworth 1986-94; Chair, Conservative Group on the Council 1990-92; Deputy Chair, Policy and Finance Committee

House of Commons: Member for East Surrey since 9 April 1992 general election; Assistant Government Whip 1996-97; Opposition Deputy Chief Whip 1997-98; PPS: to Jonathan Aitken as Chief Secretary to the Treasury 1994-95, to Virginia Bottomley as Secretary of State for National Heritage 1995-96; Member, Shadow Cabinet 1998-2002; Shadow Secretary of State for: Culture, Media and Sport 1998-2001, Environment, Food and Rural Affairs 2001-02. *Political interests:* Economic Policy, Environment

Member, The Bow Group 1983-. *Country Life* Country MP of the Year 1994; *Green* Magazine Campaigning MP of the Year 1994; *Clubs:* MCC; *Recreations:* Family, music, gardening

Peter Ainsworth, MP, House of Commons, London SW1A 0AA *Tel:* 020 7219 5078 *Fax:* 020 7219 2527 *E-mail:* info@peterainsworth.com. *Constituency:* 2 Hoskins Road, Oxted, Surrey RH8 9HT *Tel:* 01883 715782 *Fax:* 01883 730576

Lib Dem majority 4,148

ALEXANDER, DANNY
Inverness, Nairn, Badenoch and Strathspey

Daniel Alexander. Born 15 May 1972; Educated Lochaber High School, Fort William; St Anne's College, Oxford (BA philosophy, politics and economics 1993 MA); Engaged. Researcher, Campaign for Freedom of Information 1991; Press officer, European Movement 1996-97; Election aide to Jim Wallace MP 1997; Deputy director and head of communications, European Movement 1997-99; Head of communications: Britain in Europe campaign 1999-2003, Cairngorms National Park 2004-

House of Commons: Member for Inverness, Nairn, Badenoch and Strathspey since 5 May 2005 general election. *Political interests:* Highlands and Islands issues, housing, economic policy, Europe

Press officer, Scottish Liberal Democrats 1993-95. *Clubs:* Abernethy Angling Improvement Association; *Recreations:* Hill-walking, fishing, cricket, golf, reading, travel

Danny Alexander, MP, House of Commons, London SW1A 0AA
Tel: 020 7219 8328. *Constituency:* 32 Munro Place, Aviemore PH22 1TE
E-mail: danny@highlandlibdems.org.uk *Website:* www.highlandlibdems.org.uk

ALEXANDER, DOUGLAS
Paisley and Renfrewshire South

Douglas Garven Alexander. Born 26 October 1967; Son of Rev. Douglas N. Alexander and Dr. Joyce O. Alexander; Educated Park Mains High School, Erskine, Renfrewshire; Lester B. Pearson College, Vancouver, Canada; Edinburgh University (MA 1990, LLB 1993, Diploma in Legal Practice 1994); University of Pennsylvania, USA; Married Jacqueline Christian. Parliamentary researcher for Gordon Brown MP 1990-91; Solicitor: Brodies W.S. 1994-96, Digby Brown 1996-97; Member, TGWU

Lab majority 13,232

House of Commons: Contested Perth and Kinross 1995 by-election and Perth 1997 general election. Member for Paisley South 1997-2005, for Paisley and Renfrewshire South since 5 May 2005 general election; Minister for E-Commerce and Competitiveness, Department of Trade and Industry 2001-02; Cabinet Office 2002-04: Minister of State 2002-03, Minister for the Cabinet Office and Chancellor of the Duchy of Lancaster 2003-04; Minister of State for Trade, Investment and Foreign Affairs, Foreign and Commonwealth Office and Department of Trade and Industry 2004-05; Minister of State for Europe, Foreign and Commonwealth Office 2005-. *Political interests:* Constitutional Reform, Economic Policy, Employment

General election campaign co-ordinator 1999-2001. *Publications:* Co-author *New Scotland, New Britain*, 1999; PC 2005; *Recreations:* Running, angling

Rt Hon Douglas Alexander, MP, House of Commons, London SW1A 0AA *Tel:* 020 7219 1345 *E-mail:* alexanderd@parliament.uk. *Constituency:* 2014 Mile End Mill, Abbey Mill Business Centre, Paisley PA1 1JS *Tel:* 0141-561 0333 *Fax:* 0141-561 0334

ALLEN, GRAHAM
Nottingham North

Graham William Allen. Born 11 January 1953; Son of Bill and Edna Allen; Educated Forest Fields Grammar School, Nottingham; City of London Polytechnic (BA politics and economics); Leeds University (MA political sociology); Married Allyson (1 daughter). Warehouseman 1974; Labour Party research officer 1979-83; Local government officer 1983-84; National co-ordinator, Political Fund ballots 1984-86; GMBATU research and education officer 1986-87

Lab majority 12,171

House of Commons: Member for Nottingham North since 11 June 1987 general election; Government Whip 1997-2001; Shadow Minister for: Social Security 1991-92, Constitutional Affairs 1992-94, Media and Broadcasting 1994-95, Transport 1995-96, Environment 1996-97. *Political interests:* Economic Policy, Democratic Renewal. USA, Russia, China

Publications: Reinventing Democracy, 1995; *The Last Prime Minister*, 2001; *Clubs:* President Basford Hall Miners Welfare; Secretary, Lords and Commons Cricket XI; Member: Dunkirk Cricket, Bulwell Forest Golf; Vice-President Bulwell Cricket; *Recreations:* Playing and watching all sports, walking, cooking, oil painting

Graham Allen, MP, House of Commons, London SW1A 0AA *Tel:* 020 7219 5065. *Constituency: Tel:* 0115-979 2344

Con majority 8,959

AMESS, DAVID
Southend West

David Anthony Andrew Amess. Born 26 March 1952; Son of late James Amess and of Maud Amess; Educated St Bonaventure's Grammar School; Bournemouth College of Technology (BSc economics 1974); Married Julia Arnold 1983 (1 son 4 daughters). Junior school teacher 1970-71; Underwriter, Leslie Godwin Agency 1974-76; Accountancy personnel 1976-79; Senior consultant, Executemps Company Agency 1979-81; AA Recruitment Co 1981-87; Chair: Accountancy Solutions 1987-90, Accountancy Group 1990-96; Redbridge Council: Councillor 1982-86, Vice-chair, Housing Committee 1982-85

House of Commons: Contested Newham North West 1979 general election. Member for Basildon 1983-97, and for Southend West since 1 May 1997 general election; PPS to Parliamentary under secretaries, DHSS: Edwina Currie 1987-88, Lord Skelmersdale 1988, to Michael Portillo: as Minister of State Department of Transport 1988-90, at Department of Environment 1990-92, as Chief Secretary to the Treasury 1992-94, as Secretary of State for Employment 1994-95, for Defence 1995-97; Sponsored: Horses and Ponies Bill 1984-85, Members of Parliament (Minimum Age) Bill 1984-85, Horses, Ponies and Donkeys Bill 1987-88, Abortion (Right of Conscience) (Amendment) Bill 1988-89, British Nationality (Hon. Citizenship) Bill 1988-89, Adoption (Amendment) Bill 1989-90, Dogs Bill 1989-90, Pet Animals (Amendment) Bill 1990-91, Protection Against Cruel Tethering Act 1988, Human Fertilisation (Choice) Bill 1992-93, Voluntary Personal Security Cards Bill 1992-93, Football Matches (Violent and Disorderly Conduct) Bill 1992-93, Newly Qualified Drivers Bill 1993-94, Coercion in Family Planning (Prohibition) Bill 1994-95, Freezing of Human Embryos Bill 1995-96, Abortion (Amendment) Bill 1996-97, Reform of Quarantine Regulations Bill 1997-98, Voluntary Personal Security Cards Bill 1997-98, The Warm Homes Act 2000. *Political interests:* Health, Education, Transport, Environment, Pro-Life Movement. USA, European Union, Middle East, Far East, Pacific Basin

Hon. Secretary, Conservative Friends of Israel 1998-. Fairhaven Hospices, Salvation Army, RSPCA, Southend Fund; *Publications: The Basildon Experience*, 1995; Freeman, City of London; *Clubs:* Carlton, St Stephen's Constitutional; Kingswood Squash and Racketball; *Recreations:* Socialising, reading, writing, sports, modern music, keeping animals, gardening

David Amess, MP, House of Commons, London SW1A 0AA *Tel:* 020 7219 6387 *Fax:* 020 7219 2245 *E-mail:* amessd@parliament.uk. *Constituency:* Iveagh Hall, 67 Leigh Road, Leigh-on-Sea, Essex SS9 1JW *Tel:* 01702 472391 *Fax:* 01702 480677

Con majority 13,194

ANCRAM, MICHAEL
Devizes

Michael Andrew Foster Jude Kerr Ancram. Born 7 July 1945; Son of 12th Marquess of Lothian, KCVO, DL; succeeded his father 2004 as 13th Marquess of Lothian, 14th Earl of Lothian, 15th Earl of Ancram, Viscount of Briene, Lord Newbottle, Lord Jedburgh, Lord Kerr, 8th Baron Ker; Educated Ampleforth College; Christ Church, Oxford (BA history 1966, MA); Edinburgh University (LLB 1968); Married Lady Jane Fitzalan-Howard 1975 (2 daughters). Advocate, Scottish Bar 1970, QC(Scot) 1996; DL, Roxburgh, Ettrick and Lauderdale 1990-

House of Commons: Contested West Lothian 1970 general election. Member for Berwickshire and East Lothian February-October 1974, for Edinburgh South 1979-87 and for Devizes since 9 April 1992 general election; Frontbench Spokesperson for Constitutional Affairs, with overall responsibility for Scottish and Welsh issues 1997-98; Parliamentary Under-Secretary of State, Scottish Office 1983-87; Northern Ireland Office: Parliamentary Under-Secretary of State 1993-94, Minister of State 1994-97; Member, Shadow Cabinet 1997-; Deputy Chair, Conservative Party June-October 1998, Chair October 1998-2001; Deputy Leader of the Opposition 2001-; Shadow Secretary of State for: Foreign and Commonwealth Affairs 2001-05, International Affairs 2003-05, Defence 2005-. *Political interests:* Housing, Defence, Agriculture

Chair, Conservative Party in Scotland 1980-83; Contested leadership 2001; Member Conservative Policy Board 2001-. PC 1996; QC DL; *Recreations:* Skiing, photography, folksinging

Rt Hon Michael Ancram, MP, House of Commons, London SW1A 0AA
Tel: 020 7219 5072 *Fax:* 020 7219 2528 *E-mail:* ancramm@parliament.uk.
Constituency: 116 High Street, Marlborough, Wiltshire SN8 1LZ *Tel:* 01672 512675
Website: www.devizesconservatives.org.uk

Lab majority 5,335

ANDERSON, DAVID
Blaydon

David Anderson. Born 2 December 1953; Educated Maltby Grammar School; Durham Technical College (mining and mechanical engineering); Doncaster Technical College; Durham University; Married Eva 1973. Engineer National Coal Board mines 1969-89; Elderly care worker Newcastle upon Tyne social services 1989-2004; UNISON NEC board; MemberTUC general council

House of Commons: Member for Blaydon since 5 May 2005 general election

Trustee Durham Colliery Mechanics Trust; *Recreations:* Walking, travel, football, music, driving

David Anderson, MP, House of Commons, London SW1A 0AA
Tel: 020 7219 4348. *Constituency:* *E-mail:* dave.anderson@unison.co.uk

ANDERSON, JANET
Rossendale and Darwen

Janet Anderson. Born 6 December 1949; Daughter of late Tom Anderson, Labour Party agent, and late Ethel Pearson; Educated Kingsfield Comprehensive School, Bristol; Polytechnic of Central London (Diploma in bi-lingual business studies); University of Nantes; Married Vincent William Humphreys 1972 (2 sons 1 daughter) (divorced). Secretary, *The Scotsman* and *The Sunday Times* 1971-74; Personal assistant: to Barbara Castle as MP and MEP 1974-81, to Jack Straw MP 1981-87

Lab majority 3,676

House of Commons: Contested Rossendale and Darwen 1987 general election. Member for Rossendale and Darwen since 9 April 1992 general election; Opposition Spokeswoman for Women 1996-97; Opposition Whip 1995-96; Government Whip 1997-98; PPS to Margaret Beckett as Deputy Leader of the Labour Party 1992-93; Parliamentary Under-Secretary of State, Department for Culture, Media and Sport (Minister for Tourism, Film and Broadcasting) 1998-2001. *Political interests:* Footwear, Textile Industries, Quotas for Women, Health, Constitution, Employment, Home Affairs, Culture, Media and Sport. France, Cyprus, Italy

Parliamentary Labour Party Campaign Organiser 1988-90; Vice-Chair, Labour Campaign for Electoral Reform; Steering Committee Member, Labour Women's Network; Parliamentary Labour Party Representative, House of Commons Commission 1993-94; Secretary, Tribune Group 1993-96. Vice-President, Association of District Councils; *Clubs:* Rosemount Working Men's, Stacksteads; *Recreations:* Playing the piano, listening to opera

Janet Anderson, MP, House of Commons, London SW1A 0AA *Tel:* 020 7219 5375 *Fax:* 020 7219 2148 *E-mail:* andersonj@parliament.uk. *Constituency:* 731 Bacup Road, Waterfoot, Rossendale, Lancashire BB4 7EU *Tel:* 01706 220909

ARBUTHNOT, JAMES
North East Hampshire

James Norwich Arbuthnot. Born 4 August 1952; Son of late Sir John Sinclair-Wemyss Arbuthnot, 1st Bt, MBE, TD, MP for Dover 1950-64 and Lady Arbuthnot; Educated Wellesley House, Broadstairs; Eton College; Trinity College, Cambridge (BA law 1974); Married Emma Broadbent 1984 (1 son 3 daughters). Called to the Bar, Inner Temple 1975 and Lincoln's Inn 1977; Councillor, Royal Borough of Kensington and Chelsea 1978-87

Con majority 12,549

House of Commons: Contested Cynon Valley 1983 general election and 1984 by-election. Member for Wanstead and Woodford 1987-97 and for North East Hampshire since 1 May 1997 general election; Assistant Government Whip 1992-94; Opposition Chief Whip 1997-2001; PPS: to Archie Hamilton as Minister of State for the Armed Forces 1988-90, to Peter Lilley as Secretary of State for Trade and Industry 1990-92; Parliamentary Under-Secretary of State, Department of Social Security 1994-95; Minister of State for Procurement, Ministry of Defence 1995-97; Member, Shadow Cabinet 1997-2001; Shadow Secretary of State for Trade 2003-. *Political interests:* Taxation, Defence, Foreign Affairs, Law

Branch Chair, Putney Conservative Association 1975-77; Joint Deputy Chair, Chelsea Conservative Association 1980-82; President, Cynon Valley Conservative Association 1983-92. Heir presumptive to baronetcy; PC 1998; *Clubs:* Buck's; *Recreations:* Playing guitar, skiing, cooking

Rt Hon James Arbuthnot, MP, House of Commons, London SW1A 0AA *Tel:* 020 7219 4649 *E-mail:* arbuthnotj@parliament.uk. *Constituency:* North East Hampshire Conservative Association, 14a Butts Road, Alton, Hampshire GU34 1ND *Tel:* 01420 84122 *Fax:* 01420 84925 *Website:* www.nehants-conservatives.org.uk

Lab majority 13,443

ARMSTRONG, HILARY
North West Durham

Hilary Jane Armstrong. Born 30 November 1945; Daughter of late Ernest Armstrong, MP for Durham North West 1966-87, and of Hannah Armstrong; Educated Monkwearmouth Comprehensive School, Sunderland; West Ham College of Technology; Birmingham University (BSc sociology; Diploma in social work); Married Dr Paul Corrigan 1992. VSO teaching in Kenya 1967-69; Social worker, Newcastle Social Services 1970-73; Community worker, Southwick Neighbourhood Action Project 1973-75; Lecturer in community and youth work, Sunderland Polytechnic 1975-86; Secretary/Researcher for Ernest Armstrong MP (father) 1986-87; Chair, ASTMS Northern Division Council 1981-88; Councillor, Durham County Council 1985-88

House of Commons: Member for North West Durham since 11 June 1987 general election; Opposition Spokesperson on: Education 1988-92, Treasury and Economic Affairs 1994-95, The Environment and London 1995-97; Government Chief Whip (Parliamentary Secretary, HM Treasury) 2001-; PPS to John Smith, as Leader of the Opposition 1992-94; Minister of State, Department of the Environment, Transport and the Regions 1999-2001, (Minister for Local Government and Housing 1997-99, for Local Government and Regions 1999-2001). *Political interests:* Regional Development, World Development, Education, Environment. Central Africa, Kenya, South Africa, Tanzania, Uganda

Member: Labour Party National Executive Committee 1992-94, 1996-, Parliamentary Labour Party Parliamentary Committee. Vice-Chair, The British Council 1994-97; PC 1999; *Recreations:* Theatre, reading

Rt Hon Hilary Armstrong, MP, House of Commons, London SW1A 0AA
Tel: 020 7219 5076 *E-mail:* hilary@hilaryarmstrong.com. *Constituency:* North House, 17 North Terrace, Crook, Durham DL15 9AZ *Tel:* 01388 767065
Fax: 01388 767923

HOW SHOULD ENGLISHNESS BE EXPRESSED IN POLITICAL TERMS?

(David Blunkett, March 2005)

The English can have an English parliament ... I'll happily put up my hand for it.
Robin Cook, Power Inquiry, Feb 2005

An English parliament, on the same basis as the Scottish one, will be the minimum the English are likely to be satisfied with.
David Davis, Conservative Future article

Equality & parity of treatment of each nation within the UK will strengthen the Union; asymmetry where only Scotland has a parliament with all its huge political, financial and cultural advantages will tear the Union apart.

It is fanciful to think that an English parliament will be too dominant within the Union. The limits on each national parliament laid down by the UK government, exactly as they have been laid down for Scotland, will ensure no one country has any advantage.

70% of English people want their English affairs to be decided by English MPs only.* An English parliament alone will do that fairly - just like Scotland.

ARE YOU THINKING WHAT THE PEOPLE OF ENGLAND ARE THINKING?
ENGLAND FORWARD.
NOT BACK.

Covent Garden
St. George's Day 2005

*The Times/YouGov Poll, April 17th 2005

Campaign for an English Parliament
thecep.org.uk   07071 220234

Lab majority 2,438

ATKINS, CHARLOTTE
Staffordshire Moorlands

Charlotte Atkins. Born 24 September 1950; Daughter of Ronald and Jessie Atkins; Educated Colchester County High School, Essex; London School of Economics (BSc economics 1973); London University (MA area studies 1974); Married Gus Brain 1990 (1 daughter). Assistant community relations officer, Luton CRC 1974-76; Research officer/head of research, UCATT 1976-80; Research/political officer, AUEW (TASS) 1980-84; Press officer/parliamentary officer, COHSE/UNISON 1984-97; Member UNISON; Councillor, London Borough of Wandsworth 1982-86, Chief Whip and Deputy Leader of Labour Group 1983-86

House of Commons: Contested Eastbourne 1990 by-election. Member for Staffordshire Moorlands since 1 May 1997 general election; Assistant Government Whip 2002-04; PPS to Baroness Symons of Vernham Dean as Minister of State for Trade, Foreign and Commonwealth Office and Department of Trade and Industry and Deputy Leader of the House of Lords 2001-02; Parliamentary Under-Secretary of State, Department for Transport 2004-05. *Political interests:* Civil Liberties, Education, Employment, Health, Agriculture, Trade

Member: National Policy Forum to 1998, National Women's Committee to 1998; Vice-chair West Midlands Regional Group of Labour MPs to 2002. NSPCC; *Publications:* Various articles in *Chartist* on parliamentary and equality issues; co-author *How to Select or Reselect Your MP*; *Recreations:* Family activities, theatre, keeping fit, cycling, conservation

Charlotte Atkins, MP, House of Commons, London SW1A 0AA *Tel:* 020 7219 3591 *E-mail:* atkinsc@parliament.uk. *Constituency:* The former Police House, 15 Ravensclilte Road, Kidsgrove, Stoke on Trent ST7 4ET *Tel:* 01782 777661 *Fax:* 01782 777661

Con majority 5,020

ATKINSON, PETER
Hexham

Peter Landreth Atkinson. Born 19 January 1943; Son of Major Douglas and Amy Atkinson; Educated Cheltenham College; Married Brione Darley 1976 (2 daughters). Journalist: various weekly newspapers, freelance news agency 1961-68; *The Journal*, Newcastle upon Tyne 1968-72; reporter, later news editor *The Evening Standard* 1972-82; Director of public affairs, British Field Sports Society 1983-92; Councillor, London Borough of Wandsworth 1978-82; Member, Wandsworth Health Authority 1982-89; Councillor, Suffolk County Council 1989-92

House of Commons: Member for Hexham since 9 April 1992 general election; Opposition Whip: Agriculture, Scotland 1999-2000, Environment, Transport and the Regions 2000, Scotland, Social Security 2000-02, Home Office 2001-02; Opposition Whip 2003-; PPS: to Jeremy Hanley as Minister of State for the Armed Forces 1994, as Minister without Portfolio and Chair Conservative Party 1994-95, to Jeremy Hanley and Sir Nicholas Bonsor as Ministers of State, Foreign and Commonwealth Office 1995-96, to Lord Parkinson, as Chair Conservative Party 1997-99. *Political interests:* Agriculture, Industry. Overseas Territories, Eastern Europe, USA

Clubs: Albert Edward (Hexham), Northern Counties (Newcastle upon Tyne); Tynedale Rugby; *Recreations:* Shooting, gardening, racing

Peter Atkinson, MP, House of Commons, London SW1A 0AA *Tel:* 020 7219 4128 *Fax:* 020 7219 2775 *E-mail:* atkinsonp@parliament.co.uk. *Constituency:* 1 Meal Market, Hexham, Northumberland NE46 1NF *Tel:* 01434 603777 *Fax:* 01434 601659 *Website:* www.peteratkinson.com

AUSTIN, IAN
Dudley North

Ian Austin. Born 6 March 1965; Educated Dudley School; Married. Regional press officer, West Midlands Labour Party 1995-98; Deputy director of communications, Scottish Labour Party 1998-99; Special adviser to Gordon Brown as Chancellor of the Exchequer, HM Treasury 1999-2005; Dudley Borough councillor 1991-95

House of Commons: Member for Dudley North since 5 May 2005 general election

Ian Austin, MP, House of Commons, London SW1A 0AA *Tel:* 020 7219 4811. *Constituency: E-mail:* ianaustin@email.labour.org.uk

Lab majority 5,432

AUSTIN, JOHN
Erith and Thamesmead

John Eric Austin. Born 21 August 1944; Son of late Stanley Austin, electrician, and late Ellen Austin; Educated Glyn Grammar School, Epsom; Goldsmiths' College, London (Certificate in Community and Youth Work 1972); Bristol University (MSc policy studies 1990); Married Linda Walker 1965 (divorced 1988) (2 sons 1 daughter). Medical laboratory technician 1961-63; Labour Party organiser/agent 1963-70; Social/community worker, London Borough of Bexley 1972-74; Director, Bexley Council for Racial Equality 1974-92; Member, MSF (AMICUS); Chair, MSF Parliamentary Group 1998-2000; Councillor, London Borough of Greenwich 1970-94: Chair, Social Services Committee 1974-78, Deputy Leader 1981-82, Leader 1982-87, Mayor 1987-88, 1988-89

Lab majority 11,500

House of Commons: Contested Woolwich 1987, as John Austin-Walker. Member for Woolwich 1992-97, and for Erith and Thamesmead since 1 May 1997 general election (contested as John Austin-Walker). *Political interests:* Health, Social Services, Mental Health, Equal Opportunities, Environment, Foreign Affairs. Eastern Europe, Ireland, Kurdistan, Middle East

Member, Labour Friends of Bosnia 1994-; Chair, Socialist Campaign Group of MPs 1994-97; Member, Labour Friends of India 1996-; Joint Vice-Chair, London Regional Group of Labour MPs 1996-98, 1999 Treasurer, Labour First Past the Post Group 1997-. Chairman, Greenwich Community Health Council 1976-80; National Chairman, Association of Community Health Councils for England and Wales 1980-82; Vice-Chairman: Association of London Authorities (ALA) 1983-87, London Strategic Policy Unit 1985-87; Chairman: London Boroughs Emergency Planning Information Committee 1985-87, British Caribbean Association 1999-, London Ecology Unit 1985-87; Member, Political Committee CWS (Retail South East) 1987-93; Environment spokesperson for ALA 1992-94; Member, Executive Committee Inter-Parliamentary Union British Group 1996-, Vice-chair 2000-01, Chair 2001-; Vice-Chair, International Executive Parliamentary Association for Euro-Arab Co-operation 1997-; Co-Chair, Council for the Advancement of Arab British Understanding 1998-; Executive Committee, Commonwealth Parliamentary Association UK Branch, Member 1999-, Vice-chair 2004-; Board member, British Syria Society; Member, International Executive InterParliamentary Union 2003-; Trustee (unpaid) Greenwich MIND; Unpaid Director: London Marathon Charitable Trust, Grossness Engines Trust, Commonwealth Parliamentary Association; Trustee: Crossners Engines Trust, London Marathon Charitable Trust; Director British Syria Society; *Clubs:* St Patrick's Social (Plumstead), Northumberland Heath Working Men's (Erith), Woolwich Catholic; *Recreations:* Gardening, cookery, running (including marathons)

John Austin, MP, House of Commons, London SW1A 0AA *Tel:* 020 7219 5195 *Fax:* 020 7219 2706 *E-mail:* austinj@parliament.uk. *Constituency:* 301 Plumstead High Street, Plumstead, London SE18 1JX *Tel:* 020 8311 4444 *Fax:* 020 8311 6666

Con majority 8,782

BACON, RICHARD
South Norfolk

Richard Bacon. Born 3 December 1962; Educated King's School, Worcester; London School of Economics (BSc (Econ) politics and economics); Single. Investment banker Barclays 1986-89; Financial journalist Euromoney Publications plc 1993-94; Deputy director Management Consultancies Association 1994-96; Brunswick Public Relations 1996-99; Founder English Word Factory 1999-

House of Commons: Contested Vauxhall 1997 general election. Member for South Norfolk since 7 June 2001 general election. *Political interests:* Public Expenditure, Education, Health, Agriculture

Former chair Hammersmith Conservative Association; Co-founder Geneva Conservative general election voluntary agency. *Recreations:* Music, words

Richard Bacon, MP, House of Commons, London SW1A 0AA *Tel:* 020 7219 8301 *Fax:* 020 7219 1784. *Constituency:* Grasmere, Denmark Street, Diss, Norfolk IP22 4LE *Tel:* 01379 643728 *Fax:* 01379 642220 *E-mail:* reevet@parliament.uk

Lab/Co-op majority 10,894

BAILEY, ADRIAN
West Bromwich West

Adrian Bailey. Born 11 December 1945; Son of Edward Arthur Bailey, fitter and Sylvia Alice Bailey, née Bayliss; Educated Cheltenham Grammar School; Exeter University (BA economic history 1967) Loughborough College of Librarianship (postgraduate diploma in librarianship 1971); Married Jill Patricia Millard 1989 (1 stepson). Librarian, Cheshire County Council 1971-82; Political organiser, Co-operative Party 1982-2000; Contested Cheshire West 1979 European Parliament election; GMBATU 1982-2000; Sandwell Borough Council: Councillor 1991-, Chair finance 1992-97, Deputy leader 1997-2000

House of Commons: Contested South Worcester 1970 and Nantwich 1974 general elections, Wirral 1976 by-election. Member for West Bromwich West since 23 November 2000 by-election. *Political interests:* Co-operatives and Mutuals, Urban Regeneration, Animal Welfare (Anti Hunting with Dogs), Taxation, Economic Policy, Child Protection Policy

Secretary West Bromwich West constituency Labour Party 1993; Chair Parliamentary Group 2004. Action Aid, Redwings Horse Sanctuary, Staffs Bull Terrier Heritage Society, NSPCC; *Recreations:* football, swimming, walking

Adrian Bailey, MP, House of Commons, London SW1A 0AA *Tel:* 020 7219 6060 *Fax:* 020 7219 1202 *E-mail:* baileya@parliament.uk. *Constituency:* Terry Duffy House, Thomas Street, West Bromwich, West Midlands BR70 6NT *Tel:* 01215 691926 *Fax:* 01215 691936

Lab majority 12,116

BAIRD, VERA
Redcar

Vera Baird. Born 13 February 1951; Daughter of Jack Thomas and Alice Thomas, neé Marsland; Educated Chadderton Grammar School for Girls, Lancashire; Newcastle Polytechnic (LLB law 1972); Open University (BA literature and history 1983); London Guildhall University (MA modern history 2000); Married David John Taylor-Gooby 1972 (divorced 1978); married Robert Brian Baird 1978 (widowed 1979) (2 stepsons). Trainee solicitor 1972-73; Called to the Bar, Gray's Inn 1975; Barrister Newcastle and London 1975-; Visiting law fellow St Hilda's College, Oxford 1999; QC 2000; Bencher Gray's Inn 2004; Vice-president Newcastle Polytechnic Student Union 1971; TGWU 1982-; ISTC 2001-

House of Commons: Contested Berwick 1983 general election. Member for Redcar since 7 June 2001 general election. *Political interests:* Human Rights, Civil Liberties, Equal Opportunities, Criminal Law, Regional Development, Regeneration, Social Entrepreneurism. East and South Africa, Tanzania, Ethiopia, Burma, Falklands

Various constituency and branch offices local Labour Parties; Member Fabian Society; Vice-chair Society of Labour Lawyers. Jubilee 2000; Member: Criminal Bar Association, British Academy of Forensic Science; Gray's Inn advocacy trainer; Team leader Home Office gender and criminal justice legislation project; *Publications:* Co-author: *The Judiciary* (Justice) 1992, *Response to Runciman* (Society of Labour Lawyers) 1993, *Negotiated Justice* (Justice) 1993, *Economical with the Proof* (Tooks Court) 1993; *Rape in Court* (Society of Labour Lawyers) 1998; Co-author, *Defending Battered Women who Kill* 2002; *Profile of Millicent Fawcett* (Fawcett Society) 2002; Co-author, *The Last Resort*: A Study of The Criminal Cases Review Commission, 2003; QC; *Recreations:* Travel, reading, running

Vera Baird, MP, House of Commons, London SW1A 0AA *Tel:* 020 7219 8312 *Fax:* 020 7219 1790 *E-mail:* bairdv@parliament.uk. *Constituency:* Unit 12, Redcar Station Business Centre, Station Road, Redcar, Cleveland TS10 1RD *Tel:* 01642 471777 ext 312 *Fax:* 01642 484347

Lib Dem majority 8,474

BAKER, NORMAN
Lewes

Norman John Baker. Born 26 July 1957; Educated Royal Liberty School, Gidea Park; Royal Holloway College, London University (BA German 1978). Regional director, Our Price Records 1978-83; English as a foreign language teacher/lecturer 1985-97; Lib Dem environment campaigner, House of Commons 1989-90; Councillor: Lewes District Council 1987-99, Leader 1991-97, East Sussex County Council 1989-97

House of Commons: Contested Lewes 1992 general election. Member for Lewes since 1 May 1997 general election; Spokesperson for: Environment and Transport: Genetic modification and environment 1997-99, Animal Welfare 1997-, Millennium Dome 1998-2001, Transport 1998-99, Consumer Affairs and Broadcasting 1999-2001, Home Affairs 2001-02; Liberal Democrat Shadow Secretary of State for the Environment 2002-. *Political interests:* Civil Liberties, Environment. Tibet, Sweden

Publications: Various environmental texts; *Clubs:* Ronnie Scott's; *Recreations:* Walking, music

Norman Baker, MP, House of Commons, London SW1A 0AA *Tel:* 020 7219 2864 *Fax:* 020 7219 0445 *E-mail:* bakern@parliament.uk. *Constituency:* 204 High Street, Lewes, East Sussex BN7 2NS *Tel:* 01273 480281 *Fax:* 01273 480287

Con majority 10,797

BALDRY, TONY
Banbury

Tony (Antony) Brian Baldry. Born 10 July 1950; Son of Peter Baldry, consultant physician, and Oina, neé Paterson; Educated Leighton Park School, Reading; Sussex University (BA social science 1972, LLB 1973); Lincoln's Inn (barrister 1975); Married Catherine Weir 1979 (1 son 1 daughter) (divorced 1996); married Pippa Isbell 2001. TA Officer 1971-83; Honorary Colonel RLC (TA). Construction industry; Barrister specialising in construction law, general commercial law and international arbitration 1975-

House of Commons: Contested Thurrock 1979 general election. Member for Banbury since 9 June 1983 general election; PA to Margaret Thatcher 1974 general election, served in her private office March-October 1975; PPS: to Lynda Chalker as Minister of State, FCO 1985-87, to John Wakeham, as Lord Privy Seal 1987-88, as Leader of the House 1987-89, as Lord President of The Council 1988-89, as Secretary of State for Energy 1989-90; Parliamentary Under-Secretary of State: Department of Energy 1990, Department of Environment 1990-94, Foreign and Commonwealth Office 1994-95; Minister of State, Ministry of Agriculture, Fisheries and Food 1995-97. *Political interests:* Employment, Youth Affairs, Legal Affairs, Overseas Aid and Development, European Union, Childcare. Asia, Africa, Caribbean, North America, Middle East

Chair, Conservative Parliamentary Mainstream Group 1997-2001; Member executive committee 1992 Committee 2001-. Deputy Chair, Conservative Group for Europe 1981-83; Executive Committee Member, IPU British Group: 1997-, Treasurer 2000-; Robert Schumann Silver Medal 1978; Liveryman: Merchant Taylors Company, Stationers and Newspaper Makers Company, Arbitrators Company; *Clubs:* Carlton, Farmers'; *Recreations:* Walking, gardening, beagling

Tony Baldry, MP, House of Commons, London SW1A 0AA *Tel:* 020 7219 4476 *Fax:* 020 7219 5826 *E-mail:* baldryt@parliament.uk. *Constituency:* 16a North Bar, Banbury, Oxfordshire OX16 0TS *Tel:* 01295 262341 *Fax:* 01295 263140

Lab/Co-op majority 10,002

BALLS, ED
Normanton

Edward Michael Balls. Born 25 February 1967; Educated Nottingham High School; Keble College, Oxford (BA philosophy, politics and economics); John F Kennedy School of Government, Harvard (MPA); Married Yvette Cooper 1998. Teaching fellow Department of Economics, Harvard 1989-90; Economics leader writer and columnist Financial Times 1990-94; Economic adviser to Shadow Chancellor of Exchequer 1994-97; Secretary Labour Party Economic Policy Commission 1994-97; Economic adviser to Chancellor of Exchequer 1997-99; Chief Economic Adviser HM Treasury 1999-2004

House of Commons: Member for Normanton since 5 May 2005 general election

Publications: Co-editor, *Reforming Britain's Economic and Financial Policy*, 2002; World Bank Development Report, 1995; Contribution to academic journals including Scottish Journal of Political Economy, World Economics and reports by Social Justice Commission and Fabian Society; *Recreations:* Playing the violin and football with daughter Ellie and son Joe

Ed Balls, MP, House of Commons, London SW1A 0AA *Tel:* 020 7219 6299. *Constituency:* Ed Balls' Office, Former Queen's Street School, Normanton, West Yorkshire WF6 2DQ

BANKS, GORDON
Ochil and South Perthshire

Gordon Banks. Born 14 June 1955; Educated Lornshill Academy, Alloa; Glasgow College of Building (City and Guilds construction technology and concrete practice 1976); Stirling University (BA history and politics 2003); Married Lynda Nicol 1981. Chief buyer Barratt Developments 1976-86; Director Cartmore Building Supply Co Ltd 1986-; TGWU

House of Commons: Member for Ochil and South Perthshire since 5 May 2005 general election. *Political interests:* Economy, Europe, environment

Contested Mid Scotland and Fife regional list 2003 Scottish Parliament election; *Clubs:* Coeliac Society; *Recreations:* Guitar, songwriting, football, motor sport

Gordon Banks, MP, House of Commons, London SW1A 0AA *Tel:* 020 7219 8275. *Constituency:* 49-51 High St, Alloa *Tel:* 01259 214273 *E-mail:* ochilsp@btinternet.com

Lab majority 688

BARKER, GREGORY
Bexhill and Battle

Gregory Leonard George Barker. Born 8 March 1966; Educated Steyning Grammar School; Lancing College, West Sussex; Royal Holloway College, London University (BA modern history, economic history, politics 1987); Married Celeste Harrison 1992 (1 daughter 2 sons). Researcher Centre for Policy Studies 1987-89; Equity analyst Gerrard Vivian Gray 1988-90; Director International Pacific Securities 1990-97; Associate partner Brunswick Group Ltd 1997-98; Head investor communications Siberian Oil Company 1998-2000; Director Daric plc (Bartlett Merton) 1998-2001

House of Commons: Contested Eccles 1997 general election. Member for Bexhill and Battle since 7 June 2001 general election; Opposition Whip 2003-. *Political interests:* Environment, Education, Overseas Development. US, Germany, Russia, Australia

Chair: Shoreham Young Conservatives 1982-83, Holloway Conservative Society 1986-87; Vice-chair: Hammersmith Conservative Association 1993-95, Wandsworth and Tooting Conservative Association 1997-98. Associate Centre for Policy Studies 1988-; Member British-German Forum; Honourable Artillery Company; *Clubs:* Carlton, Bexhill Conservative Club; Bexhill Rowing Club; *Recreations:* Skiing, hunting, horse racing

Con majority 13,449

Gregory Barker, MP, House of Commons, London SW1A 0AA *Tel:* 020 7219 1852 *Fax:* 020 7219 1742 *E-mail:* barkerg@parliament.uk. *Constituency:* Bexhill and Battle Conservative Association, 6a Amherst Road, Bexhill on Sea, East Sussex TN40 1QJ *Tel:* 01424 219117 *Fax:* 01424 218367

BARLOW, CELIA
Hove

Celia Barlow. Born 28 September 1955; Educated King Edward High School for Girls, Birmingham; New Hall, Cambridge (MA archaeology and anthropology 1976); University College, Cardiff (postgrad diploma journalism 1978); Central St Martins (postgrad diploma independent film and video 1993); Married Robert Harvey Jaffa. Reporter *Telegraph and Argus*, Bradford 1979-82; Reporter, assistant editor Asia Television Hong Kong 1981-83; Regional journalist, assistant producer parliamentary 1983-95; Journalist, assistant producer, home news editor BBC TV News; Freelance video producer 1998-2000; Lecturer on video production 2000; NUJ 1977

Lab majority 420

House of Commons: Contested Chichester 2001 general election. Member for Hove since 5 May 2005 general election

Constituency secretary Chelsea 1993-95; Constituency chair Chichester 1998. *Publications:* Spray of Pearls (Gordon McGregor – paperback 1993)

Celia Barlow, MP, House of Commons, London SW1A 0AA *Tel:* 020 7219 5599. *Constituency: Tel:* 01273 721677 *E-mail:* celia@celia4hove.com

BARON, JOHN
Billericay

John Baron. Born 21 June 1959; Son of Raymond Arthur Ernest Baron and Kathleen Ruby (née Whittlestone); Educated Queens College, Taunton, Somerset; Jesus College, Cambridge (BA history and economics 1982); Royal Military College Sandhurst 1984; Married Thalia Anne Mayson, née Laird, architect (2 daughters). Captain Royal Regiment of Fusiliers 1984-87. Director: Henderson Private Investors Ltd 1987-99, Rothschild Asset Management 1999-2001

Con majority 11,206

House of Commons: Contested Basildon 1997 general election. Member for Billericay since 7 June 2001 general election; Shadow Spokesperson for Health 2002-03; Shadow Minister for: Health 2003, Public Services, Health and Education 2003-04, Health 2004-. *Political interests:* Health, Education, Law and Order, Charity and Voluntary Sector, Small Businesses, European Affairs

Numerous local charities; Director Two small Property Investment Companies; *Recreations:* Tennis, walking, history, family, cycling

John Baron, MP, House of Commons, London SW1A 0AA *Tel:* 020 7219 8138 *Fax:* 020 7219 1743 *E-mail:* baronj@parliament.uk. *Constituency:* 125 Bramble Tye, Noak Bridge, Basildon, Essex SS15 5GR *Tel:* 01268 520765 *Fax:* 01268 524009

Lib Dem majority
13,600

BARRETT, JOHN
Edinburgh West

John Andrew Barrett. Born 11 February 1954; Son of late Andrew Barrett, building contractor, and late Elizabeth Mary, née Benert, librarian; Educated Forrester High School, Edinburgh; Telford College, Edinburgh; Napier Polytechnic, Edinburgh; Married Carol Pearson 1975 (1 daughter). Director: ABC Productions 1985-, Edinburgh International Film Festival 1995-2001, The EDI Group 1997-99, Edinburgh and Borders Screen Industries Office 1997-2001, Edinburgh Filmhouse 1997-2001; Contested Linlithgow 1999 Scottish Parliament election; Edinburgh City Council: Councillor 1995-2001, Group transport spokesman 1999-2001, Group economic development spokesman 1995-99, Group chair 1997-2000, Convener Edinburgh West local development committee 2000-01

House of Commons: Member for Edinburgh West 2001-05, for new Edinburgh West since 5 May 2005 general election; Scottish Liberal Democrat Spokesperson on Cross Border Transport 2001-; Liberal Democrat Spokesperson on International Development 2002-. *Political interests:* Air and Rail Safety, Energy, Overseas Aid and Development, Environment, Pensions. Australia, Greece

Convener Lothian Region Liberal Democrats 1997-2000; Scottish Liberal Club: Chair 1995-2000, Vice-president 2000-; Election agent Donald Gorrie MP 1997. Member European Standing Committee B 2003-; *Clubs:* National Liberal; *Recreations:* Music, cinema, travel, meeting people

John Barrett, MP, House of Commons, London SW1A 0AA *Tel:* 020 7219 8224 *Fax:* 020 7219 1762 *E-mail:* barrettj@parliament.uk. *Constituency:* West Edinburgh Liberal Democrats, 1A Drum Brae Avenue, Edinburgh EH12 8TE *Tel:* 0131 339 0339 *Fax:* 0131 476 7101 *Website:* www.edinburghwestlibdems.org.uk

Lab majority 14,224

BARRON, KEVIN
Rother Valley

Kevin John Barron. Born 26 October 1946; Son of Richard Barron, retired and Edna Barron; Educated Maltby Hall Secondary Modern; Ruskin College, Oxford (Diploma in Labour studies 1977); Married Carol McGrath 1969 (1 son 2 daughters). National Coal Board 1962-83; AMICUS

House of Commons: Member for Rother Valley since 9 June 1983 general election; Opposition Spokesperson for: Energy 1988-92, Employment 1993-95, Health 1995-97; PPS to Neil Kinnock as Leader of the Opposition 1985-88; Sponsor private member's bill to ban advertising and promotion of tobacco products 1993, 94. *Political interests:* Energy, Environment, Home Affairs, Health, Intelligence and Security. Bulgaria

Chair, Yorkshire Regional Group of Labour MPs 1987-. One World Action; Thornberry Animal Sanctuary; BIBIC (British Institute for Brain Injured Children); Member: General Medical Council 1999-, Intelligence and Security Committee; PC 2001; *Recreations:* Family life, football, fly fishing, photography, walking

Rt Hon Kevin Barron, MP, House of Commons, London SW1A 0AA *Tel:* 020 7219 6306; 020 7219 4432 *Fax:* 020 7219 5952 *E-mail:* barronk@parliament.uk. *Constituency:* 9 Lordens Hill, Dinnington, Sheffield, South Yorkshire S25 2QE *Tel:* 01909 568611 *Fax:* 01909 569974

BATTLE, JOHN
Leeds West

John Dominic Battle. Born 26 April 1951; Son of John Battle, electrical engineer, and late Audrey Battle; Educated St Michael's College; Upholland College; Leeds University (BA English 1976); Married Mary Meenan 1977 (1 son 2 daughters). Research assistant 1979-83; National co-ordinator, Church Action on Poverty 1983-87; Member, AMICUS; Councillor, Leeds City Council 1980-87

Lab majority 12,810

House of Commons: Contested Leeds North West 1983 general election. Member for Leeds West since 11 June 1987 general election; Opposition Spokesperson for the Environment (Shadow Minister of Housing) 1992-94; Opposition Whip 1990; Shadow Minister for Housing 1993-94, Science and Technology 1994-95, Energy 1995-97; Minister of State: Department of Trade and Industry 1997-99, Foreign and Commonwealth Office 1999-2001. *Political interests:* Poverty and Wealth at Home and Abroad, Housing, Economic Policy, International Development, Science, Engineering

Joint Chair, British Trade International Board 1999-2001; *Publications: Tom McGuire*, 1992; PC 2002; *Recreations:* Folk music, poetry

Rt Hon John Battle, MP, House of Commons, London SW1A 0AA *Tel:* 020 7219 4201 *E-mail:* johnbattle@leedswest.freeserve.co.uk. *Constituency:* Unit 31, Whingate Business Park, Whingate, Leeds, West Yorkshire LS12 3AT *Tel:* 0113-231 0258 *Fax:* 0113-279 5850

BAYLEY, HUGH
City of York

Hugh Bayley. Born 9 January 1952; Son of Michael Bayley, architect, and Pauline Bayley; Educated Haileybury School; Bristol University (BSc politics 1974); York University (BPhil Southern African studies 1976); Married Fenella Jeffers 1984 (1 son 1 daughter). District officer, then National officer NALGO 1975-82; General secretary, International Broadcasting Trust 1982-86; York University 1986-92: Lecturer in social policy 1986-97, Research fellow in health economics 1987-92; TGWU 1975-82, BECTU 1982-, RMT 1992-2002; Councillor, Camden Borough Council 1980-86; York Health Authority 1988-90

Lab majority 10,472

House of Commons: Contested York 1987 general election. Member for York 1992-97, and for City of York since 1 May 1997 general election; PPS to Frank Dobson as Secretary of State for Health 1997-99; Parliamentary Under-Secretary of State, Department of Social Security 1999-2001. *Political interests:* Health, Economic Policy, Environment, International Development, Defence, Media, Electoral Reform. Africa

Member, Executive Committee: Inter-Parliamentary Union – UK Branch 1997-99 and 2001-, Commonwealth Parliamentary Association – UK Branch 1997-99, 2001-; Member: UK Delegation to the North Atlantic Assembly 1997-99, UK Delegation to NATO Parliamentary Assembly 2001-, UK Delegation to the Organisation for Security and Co-operation in Europe's Parliamentary Assembly 2001-; *Publications: The Nation's Health*, 1995

Hugh Bayley, MP, House of Commons, London SW1A 0AA *Tel:* 020 7219 6824 *Fax:* 020 7219 0346 *E-mail:* dellaganal@parliament.uk. *Constituency:* 59 Holgate Road, York YO24 4AA *Tel:* 01904 623713 *Fax:* 01904 623260

Lab majority 5,657

BECKETT, MARGARET
Derby South

Margaret Mary Beckett. Born 15 January 1943; Daughter of late Cyril Jackson, carpenter, and Winifred Jackson, teacher; Educated Notre Dame High School, Manchester and Norwich; Manchester College of Science and Technology; John Dalton Polytechnic; Married Lionel Arthur Beckett 1979 (2 stepsons). Student apprentice in metallurgy, AEI Manchester 1961-66; Experimental officer, Department of Metallurgy, Manchester University 1966-70; Industrial policy researcher, Labour Party 1970-74; Principal researcher, Granada Television 1979-83; Political adviser, Ministry of Overseas Development 1974; Member: T&GWU 1964-, NUJ, BECTU

House of Commons: Contested Lincoln February 1974 general election. Member for Lincoln October 1974-79, and for Derby South since 9 June 1983 general election; Assistant Government Whip 1975-76; PPS to Judith Hart as Minister of Overseas Development 1974-75; Parliamentary Under-Secretary of State, Department of Education and Science 1976-79; Shadow Minister, Social Security 1984-89; Shadow Chief Secretary to the Treasury 1989-92; Shadow Leader, House of Commons and Campaign Co-ordinator 1992-94; Deputy Leader, Labour Party and Opposition 1992-94; Leader of Opposition May-July 1994; Shadow Secretary of State for Health 1994-95; Shadow President of the Board of Trade 1995-97; President of the Board of Trade and Secretary of State for Trade and Industry 1997-98; President of the Council and Leader of the House of Commons 1998-2001; Secretary of State for Environment, Food and Rural Affairs 2001-. *Political interests:* Industry

Secretary, Traders Council and Labour Party 1968-70; Member: Labour Party National Executive Committee 1980-81, 1985-86, 1988-97, Fabian Society, Tribune Group, Socialist Education Committee, Labour Women's Action Committee, Derby Co-op Party, Socialist Environment and Resources Association. *Publications: The Need For Consumer Protection,* 1972; *The National Enterprise Board*; *The Nationalisation of Shipbuilding, Ship Repair and Marine Engineering; Relevant sections of Labour's Programme,* 1972/73; *Renewing the NHS,* 1995; *Vision for Growth @nr A New Industrial Strategy for Britain,* 1996; PC 1993; *Recreations:* Cooking, reading, caravanning

Rt Hon Margaret Beckett, MP, House of Commons, London SW1A 0AA
Tel: 020 7219 3584 *Fax:* 020 7219 4780.
Constituency: E-mail: beckettm@parliament.uk

BEGG, ANNE
Aberdeen South

Anne Begg. Born 6 December 1955; Daughter of David Begg, MBE, retired orthotist, and Margaret Catherine Begg, retired nurse; Educated Brechin High School; Aberdeen University (MA history and politics 1977); Aberdeen College of Education (Secondary Teaching Certificate 1978); Single. English and history teacher, Webster's High School, Kirriemuir 1978-88; English teacher, Arbroath Academy 1988-97; Member: Educational Institute of Scotland 1978-, EIS National Council 1990-95

Lab majority 1,348

House of Commons: Member for Aberdeen South 1997-2005, for new Aberdeen South since 5 May 2005 general election. *Political interests:* Disability, Broadcasting, Welfare Reform, Social Inclusion, Genetics

Member, Labour Party National Executive Committee 1998-99; PLP Member, Labour Party Policy Forum. Elected Member, General Teaching Council for Scotland 1994-97; Trustee, Aberdeen Safer Community Trust; Disabled Scot of the Year 1988; *Recreations:* Reading, cinema, theatre, public speaking

Anne Begg, MP, House of Commons, London SW1A 0AA *Tel:* 020 7219 2140 *Fax:* 020 7219 1264 *E-mail:* begga@parliament.uk. *Constituency:* 166 Market Street, Aberdeen AB11 5PP *Tel:* 01224 252704 *Fax:* 01224 252705

BEITH, ALAN
Berwick-upon-Tweed

Alan James Beith. Born 20 April 1943; Son of late James Beith, foreman packer, and Joan Beith; Educated King's School, Macclesfield; Nuffield College, Oxford (BA philosophy, politics and economics 1964); Balliol College, Oxford (BLitt, MA 1964); Married Barbara Jean Ward 1965 (died 1998) (1 son deceased 1 daughter); married Baroness Maddock 2001. Politics lecturer, Newcastle University 1966-73; Association of University Teachers; Councillor: Hexham RDC 1969-74, Tynedale DC 1974-75

Lib Dem majority 8,632

House of Commons: Contested Berwick-upon-Tweed 1970 general election. Member for Berwick-upon-Tweed since 8 November 1973 by-election; Liberal Spokesperson for Foreign Affairs 1985-87; Alliance Spokesperson on Foreign Affairs 1987; Liberal Treasury Spokesperson 1987; SLD Treasury Spokesperson 1988-89; Liberal Democrat: Treasury Spokesperson 1989-94, Home Affairs Spokesperson 1994-95, Spokesperson for: Police, Prison and Security Matters 1995-97, Home and Legal Affairs (Home Affairs) 1997-99, Cabinet Office 2001-02; Chief Whip, Liberal Party 1976-87. *Political interests:* Parliamentary and Constitutional Affairs, Architectural and Artistic Heritage. Canada, Scandinavia, Zimbabwe

Deputy Leader: Liberal Party 1985-88, Liberal Democrat 1992-2003. Diabetes UK; Member, Intelligence and Security Committee 1994-; Member Speaker's Committee on the Electoral Commission 2001-; Deputy chairman Review Committee of Privy Counsellors of the Anti-terrorism, Crime and Security Act 2002-; Representative, Council of Europe Assembly 1976-84; Member, Western European Union Assembly 1976-84; Trustee, Historic Chapels Trust, 1995-: Chair 2002-; *Publications:* Co-author *Case for Liberal Party and Alliance*, 1983; *Faith and Politics*, 1987; PC 1992; Hon. DCL, Newcastle University 1998; *Clubs:* National Liberal; *Recreations:* Music, walking, boating

Rt Hon Alan Beith, MP, House of Commons, London SW1A 0AA
Tel: 020 7219 3540 *Fax:* 020 7219 5890 *E-mail:* cheesemagn@parliament.uk.
Constituency: 54 Bondgate Within, Alnwick, Northumberland NE66 1JD
Tel: 01665 602901 *Fax:* 01665 605702

BELL, STUART
Middlesbrough

Lab majority 12,567

Stuart Bell. Born 16 May 1938; Son of late Ernest Bell, pitman and late Margaret Rose Bell; Educated Hookergate Grammar School; Council of Legal Education, Gray's Inn 1970; Married Margaret Bruce 1960 (1 son 1 daughter); married Margaret Allan 1980 (1 son). Barrister, called to the Bar, Gray's Inn 1970; Previously: colliery clerk, newspaper reporter, typist novelist; Conseil Juridique and International Lawyer Paris 1970-77; Member, General Municipal Boilermakers and Allied Trades Union; Councillor, Newcastle City Council 1980-83, Member: Finance, Health and Environment, Arts and Education Committee, Association of Metropolitan Authorities, Education Committee, Council of Local Education Authorities, Newcastle Area Health Authority (teaching)

House of Commons: Contested Hexham 1979 general election. Member for Middlesbrough since 9 June 1983 general election; Opposition Frontbench Spokesperson for: Northern Ireland 1984-87, Trade and Industry 1992-97; PPS to Roy Hattersley as Deputy Leader of Opposition 1983-84; Second Church Estates Commissioner 1997-. *Political interests:* Economic Policy, European Union, Middle East. USA, France

Member: Fabian Society, Society of Labour Lawyers. Member, House of Commons Commission 2000-; Founder member, British Irish Inter-Parliamentary Body 1990; Executive Member, British Group, Inter-Parliamentary Union 1992-95, Vice-Chair 1992-95; Vice-Chair, Interparliamentary Union; *Publications: Paris 69* 1973; *Days That Used to Be* 1975; *When Salem Came to the Boro* 1988; *Fabian Tract: How to Abolish the Lords* 1982; *Legal Tract: United States Customs Valuation* 1982; *The Children Act 1989 (annotated)* 1989; *Raising the Standard: The Case for First Past the Post* 1998; *Where Jenkins Went Wrong: A Further Case for First Past the Post* 1999; *Tony Really Loves Me* 2000; *Pathway to the Euro* 2002; *Binkie's Revolution* 2002; *The Honoured Society* 2003; *Lara's Theme* 2004; *Softly in the Dusk* 2004; *Kt* 2004; Freeman, City of London; *Clubs:* Beefsteak, Pratts; *Recreations:* Writing short stories, novels and feature articles

Sir Stuart Bell, MP, House of Commons, London SW1A 0AA *Tel:* 020 7219 3577 *Fax:* 020 7219 4873. *Constituency: Tel:* 01642 851252 *Fax:* 01642 850170
E-mail: contact@stuartbellmp.org *Website:* www.stuartbellmp.org

BELLINGHAM, HENRY
North West Norfolk

Con majority 9,180

Henry Campbell Bellingham. Born 29 March 1955; Educated Eton College; Magdalene College, Cambridge (BA 1978); Married Emma Whiteley 1993. Barrister, Middle Temple 1978-84; Company Director and Business Consultant 1997-2001
House of Commons: Member for Norfolk North West 1983-97. Contested Norfolk North West 1997 general election. Member for North West Norfolk since 7 June 2001 general election; PPS to Malcolm Rifkind MP 1991-97; Shadow Minister for: Trade and Industry 2002-03, Economic Affairs 2003-. *Political interests:* Small Businesses, Agriculture, Defence, Northern Ireland, Eastern Europe, Tourism

Chairman Conservative Council on Eastern Europe 1989-93. Trustee, Russian-European Trust 1994-; *Recreations:* Country sports, golf, cricket

Henry Bellingham, MP, House of Commons, London SW1A 0AA
Tel: 020 7219 8484 *Fax:* 020 7219 2844 *E-mail:* bellinghamh@parliament.uk.
Constituency: Greenland Fishery, Bridge Street, King's Lynn, Norfolk PE31 6BZ
Tel: 01553 773 023 *Fax:* 01485 600 292

BENN, HILARY
Leeds Central

Hilary James Wedgwood Benn. Born 26 November 1953; Son of Tony Benn and late Caroline Middleton De Camp; Educated Holland Park Comprehensive School; Sussex University (BA Russian and East European studies 1974); Married Rosalind Retey 1973 (died 1979); married Sally Christina Clark 1982 (3 sons, 1 daughter). Research officer and latterly head of policy and communications, MSF 1975-97; Special Adviser to David Blunkett, as Secretary of State for Education and Employment 1997-99; Member: AMICUS, GMB; Trustee, Unions 21; London Borough of Ealing: Councillor 1979-99, Deputy Leader 1986-90, Chair, Education Committee 1986-90

Lab majority 11,866

House of Commons: Contested Ealing North 1983 and 1987 general elections. Member for Leeds Central since 10 June 1999 by-election; Parliamentary Under-Secretary of State: Department for International Development 2001-02, for Community and Custodial Provision, Home Office 2002-03, Minister of State, Department for International Development 2003; Secretary of State for International Development 2003-. *Political interests:* International Development, Home Affairs, Education, Employment, Trade Unions, Environment, Urban Policy Member, Association of Metropolitan Authorities Education Committee 1986-90; Chair, Association of London Authorities Education Committee 1989-90; *Publications:* Contributor: *Beyond 2002: Long-term policies for Labour*, Profile Books 1999, *The Forces of Conservatism*, IPPR 1999; PC 2003; *Recreations:* Watching sport, gardening

Rt Hon Hilary Benn, MP, House of Commons, London SW1A 0AA
Tel: 020 7219 5770 *Fax:* 020 7219 2639 *E-mail:* bennh@parliament.uk.
Constituency: 2 Blenheim Terrace, Leeds, West Yorkshire LS2 9JG
Tel: 0113-244 1097 *Fax:* 0113-234 1176

BENTON, JOE
Bootle

Joseph Edward Benton. Born 28 September 1933; Son of late Thomas and Agnes Benton; Educated St Monica's Primary and Secondary School; Bootle Technical College; Married Doris Wynne 1959 (4 daughters). RAF national service 1955-57. Apprentice fitter and turner 1949; Personnel manager Pacific Steam Navigation Company; Girobank 1982-90; Member, RMT Parliamentary Campaigning Group 2002-; Sefton Borough Council: Councillor 1970-90, Leader, Labour Group 1985-90, Education spokesman 1977-86; JP, Bootle bench 1969

Lab majority 16,357

House of Commons: Member for Bootle since by-election 8 November 1990 by-election; Opposition Whip 1994-97. *Political interests:* Education, Housing, Local and Regional Government, Health

Recreations: Reading, listening to classical music, squash, swimming

Joe Benton, MP, House of Commons, London SW1A 0AA *Tel:* 020 7219 6973.
Constituency: 23A Oxford Road, Bootle, Liverpool L20 9HJ *Tel:* 0151-933 8432
Fax: 0151-933 4746

Taking a Risk – Sexual and Reproductive Health in Africa

When a poor woman in Africa becomes pregnant her life is at risk. In fact maternal mortality rates in Africa are the highest in the world and complications of pregnancy and childbirth the leading cause of death and disability for women of childbearing age. It is estimated that every year approximately 250,000 women die in Africa as a direct result of becoming pregnant.

A woman in sub-Saharan Africa has a lifetime risk of one in sixteen of dying from such complications, and in some African countries the risk is even as high as one in six. And there appears to be little sign that the situation is improving. In Kenya for instance, the figure for maternal deaths has risen instead of fallen over the last five years. In Ethiopia 90 per cent of all births are not attended by a trained midwife, while Sierra Leone has the highest maternal mortality rate in the world with 2,000 maternal deaths per 100,000 live births.

The situation is exacerbated by the prevalence of sexually transmitted infections and HIV/AIDS. With 76 percent of all young people living with HIV being female, the UN Secretary General has been moved to claim that HIV/AIDS in Sub-Saharan Africa has indeed a woman's face. Other diseases such as malaria also have devastating effects for pregnant women and their unborn children causing prenatal deaths, low birth weight and maternal anaemia. The poor health of a mother or her premature death not only has detrimental effects on the survival chances of infants, it impacts on the economic viability of families, perpetuating a vicious cycle of poverty. But simply by providing adequate and appropriate information on sexual and reproductive health and making services and supplies universally accessible, a substantial step could be made towards eliminating poverty in the region.

In 2000 the international community embarked on an ambitious plan to achieve eight Millennium Development Goals (MDGs) to tackle global poverty. Reviewing progress made so far in attaining those goals, an expert team presented its report "Investing in Development: A practical Plan to Achieve the Millennium Development Goals" to the UN Secretary General in January 2005. This report clearly identifies access to sexual and reproductive health information and services as vital to making headway in reducing global poverty. Yet the MDGs do not include a specific goal on sexual and reproductive health and the three goals directly related to sexual and reproductive health – reducing child mortality, improving maternal health and combating HIV/AIDS tuberculosis, malaria and other diseases – are those least likely to be met by the 2015 deadline, particularly in Sub-Saharan Africa.

African leaders are thus calling for the comprehensive provision of adequate and appropriate services for sexual and reproductive health. African Health Ministers have demanded that Africa's framework for economic and social recovery, the New Partnership for Africa's Development, incorporates sexual and reproductive health and the African Union has promised an action plan to provide the urgently needed information and services by October of this year. These concerns have been echoed in the Commission for Africa Report, published in March, which recommends that "African governments show strong leadership in promoting women's and men's right to sexual and reproductive health". But it is not African leaders alone who are called upon to act.

Within the next decade Africa will see the largest number of women of childbearing age ever. Unless there is greater access to contraception, antenatal care and skilled attendance at delivery, safe abortion and post-abortion care, maternal deaths in Sub-Saharan Africa will continue to rise.

Strong political commitment on the part of national governments and the international donor community is called for. In the UK, the Department for International Development (DFID) has underscored its commitment to upholding women's right to safe motherhood and has allocated £500 million annually over the next three years for the fight against HIV/AIDS and to promote sexual and reproductive health. The challenge now will be to ensure international commitment within the European Union and at the United Nations. Only thus can a cycle of poverty in Africa be broken and the tragic and unnecessary deaths of hundreds of thousands of mothers and infants each year be averted.

PROVIDING CHOICES IN REPRODUCTIVE HEALTHCARE

MARIE STOPES INTERNATIONAL

www.mariestopes.org.uk

BENYON, RICHARD
Newbury

Richard Benyon. Born 4 September 1960; Educated Bradfield College, Reading; Royal Agricultural College (diploma in real estate managment, land economy 1987); Married second Zoe Robinson 2004. Army 1980-85. Land agent chartered surveyor 1987-; Farmer 1990-; Newbury District Councillor 1991-95: Leader Conservative group 1994-95

House of Commons: Contested Newbury 1997 and 2001 general elections. Member

Con majority 3,460

for Newbury since 5 May 2005 general election. *Political interests:* Rural matters, social affairs. Africa, Northern Ireland

Vice chair, Citizens Advice 1994-; Berks Comm Foundation 1995-2000; Trustee: John Simons Trust 1986-, Mary Hare School For the Deaf 1999-; *Recreations:* walking, tennis, shooting, fishing

Richard Benyon, MP, House of Commons, London SW1A 0AA
Tel: 020 7219 8319. *Constituency:* West Berkshire Conservative Association, 6 Cheap Street, Newbury RG14 5DD *Tel:* 01635 40786 *Fax:* 01635 35151 *E-mail:* office@wbca.org.uk *Website:* www.wbca.org

BERCOW, JOHN
Buckingham

John Simon Bercow. Born 19 January 1963; Son of Brenda, neé Bailey, and late Charles Bercow; Educated Finchley Manorhill School; Essex University (BA government 1985); Married (1 son). Credit analyst, Hambros Bank 1987-88; Public affairs consultant, Rowland Sallingbury Casey, Public Affairs Arm of Saatchi & Saatchi Group 1988-95; Board director, Rowland Company 1994-95; Special adviser: to Jonathan Aitken as Chief Secretary to the Treasury 1995, to Virginia Bottomley as

Con majority 18,129

Secretary of State for National Heritage 1995-96; Lambeth Borough Council: Councillor, 1986-90, Deputy Leader, Conservative Opposition 1987-89

House of Commons: Contested Motherwell South 1987 and Bristol South 1992 general elections. Member for Buckingham since 1 May 1997 general election; Opposition Spokesman for: Education and Employment 1999-2000, Home Affairs 2000-01, Work and Pensions 2002; Shadow Chief Secretary to the Treasury 2001-02; Shadow Secretary of State for International Development 2003-04. *Political interests:* Education, Economic Policy, Small Businesses, Britain: EU relations, European Union. Israel, USA, Far East

Chair, University of Essex Conservative Association 1984-85; National Chair, Federation of Conservative Students 1986-87; Vice-Chair, Conservative Collegiate Forum 1987. Co-Director, Advanced Speaking and Campaigning Course; *Publications: Turning Scotland Around*, 1987; *Faster Moves Forward for Scotland*, 1987; *Aiming for the Heart of Europe: A Misguided Venture*, 1998; *Subsidiarity and the Illusion of Democratic Control*, 2003; *How Much Common Ground*, 2004; *Recreations:* Tennis, squash, reading, swimming, music

John Bercow, MP, House of Commons, London SW1A 0AA *Tel:* 020 7219 3462 *E-mail:* bercowj@parliament.uk. *Constituency:* Buckingham Constituency Conservative Association, Buckingham Road, Winslow, Buckingham, Buckinghamshire MK18 3DY *Tel:* 01296 714240 *Fax:* 01296 714273 *Website:* www.buckinghamconservative.co.uk

Con majority 11,997

BERESFORD, PAUL
Mole Valley

(Alexander) Paul Beresford. Born 6 April 1946; Son of Raymond and Joan Beresford; Educated Waimea College, Richmond, Nelson, New Zealand; Otago University, Dunedin, New Zealand; Married Julie Haynes (3 sons 1 daughter). Dental surgeon; Councillor, Wandsworth Borough Council 1978-94, Leader 1983-92

House of Commons: Member for Croydon Central 1992-97, and for Mole Valley since 1 May 1997 general election; Parliamentary Under-Secretary of State, Department of the Environment 1994-97. *Political interests:* Inner Cities, Housing, Education. Fiji, New Zealand, Samoa, Australia

Knighted 1990; BDS; *Recreations:* DIY, reading

Sir Paul Beresford, MP, House of Commons, London SW1A 0AA *Tel:* 020 7219 5139. *Constituency:* Mole Valley Conservative Association, 86 South Street, Dorking, Surrey RH4 2E2 *Tel:* 01306 883 312 *Fax:* 01306 885 194

Lab majority 7,873

BERRY, ROGER
Kingswood

Roger Leslie Berry. Born 4 July 1948; Son of Sydney and Mary Joyce Berry; Educated Dalton County Junior School; Huddersfield New College; Bristol University (BSc economics 1970); Sussex University (DPhil economics 1977); Married Alison Delyth 1996. Temporary lecturer in economics, School of African and Asian Studies, Sussex University 1973-74; Associate fellow, Institute of Development Studies, Sussex University 1973-74; Lecturer in economics: University of Papua New Guinea 1974-78, Bristol University 1978-92; Contested Bristol 1984 European Parliament election; Member, AMICUS (MSF) 1988-: chair parliamentary group 1997-98; Member, AUT 1978-; Avon County Council: Councillor 1981-92, Chair, Finance and Administration Committee 1983-86, Deputy Leader 1985-86, Leader, Labour Group 1986-92

House of Commons: Contested Weston-Super-Mare 1983 and Kingswood 1987 general elections. Member for Kingswood since 9 April 1992 general election. *Political interests:* Economic Policy, Disability, Third World, Local and Regional Government. Lithuania, Italy, China

Chair South and West Group of Labour MPs 1997-. *Publications:* Numerous journal and newspaper articles and pamphlets; Highland Park/Spectator Backbencher of the Year 1994; *Clubs:* Kingswood Labour; *Recreations:* Travel, food, cooking, gardening, reading

Dr Roger Berry, MP, House of Commons, London SW1A 0AA *Tel:* 020 7219 4106 *Fax:* 020 7219 2205 *E-mail:* berryr@parliament.uk. *Constituency:* PO Box 130, Fishponds, Bristol, Avon BS16 5FB *Tel:* 0117-956 1837 *Fax:* 0117-970 1363

Lab majority 15,967

BETTS, CLIVE
Sheffield Attercliffe

Clive James Charles Betts. Born 13 January 1950; Son of late Harold and late Nellie Betts; Educated King Edward VII School, Sheffield; Pembroke College, Cambridge (BA economics and politics 1971). Economist, Trades Union Congress 1971-73; Local government economist: Derbyshire County Council 1973-74, South Yorkshire County Council 1974-86, Rotherham Borough Council 1986-91; Member, TGWU; Sheffield City Council: Councillor 1976-92, Chairman: Housing Committee 1980-86, Finance Committee 1986-88, Deputy Leader 1986-87, Leader 1987-92

House of Commons: Contested Sheffield Hallam October 1974 and Louth 1979 general elections. Member for Sheffield Attercliffe since 9 April 1992 general election; Opposition Whip 1996-97; Assistant Government Whip 1997-98; Government Whip 1998-2001. *Political interests:* Economic Policy, Local and Regional Government, Housing. Europe

Member, Labour Leader's Campaign Team with responsibility for Environment and Local Government 1995-96; Member, Labour Housing Group. Vice-chair, Association of Metropolitan Authorities 1988-91; Chair, AMA Housing Committee 1985-89; Vice-president, LGA; Chair, South Yorkshire Pensions Authority 1989-92; *Recreations:* Supporting Sheffield Wednesday FC, playing squash, cricket, walking, real ale, scuba diving

Clive Betts, MP, House of Commons, London SW1A 0AA *Tel:* 020 7219 3588 *Fax:* 020 7219 2289 *E-mail:* bettsc@parliament.uk. *Constituency:* 2nd Floor, Barkers Pool House, Burgess Street, Sheffield, South Yorkshire S1 2HH *Tel:* 0114-273 4444 *Fax:* 0114-273 9666 *Website:* www.clivebetts.labour.co.uk

Con majority 4,419

BINLEY, BRIAN
Northampton South

Brian Binley. Born 1 May 1942; Educated Finedon Mulso C of E Secondary Modern; Married Jacqueline Denise 1985. Area manager Courage (central) Ltd 1976-79; National sales manager Phonatas Services Ltd 1980-87; General manager Tele Resources Ltd 1987-89; Managing director and founder BCC Marketing Services Ltd 1989-2001; Chair and founder Beechwood House Publishing Ltd 1993-2000; Chair BCC Marketing Services Ltd 2002-; Northamptonshire County Council: Shadow education vice-chair 1997-98, Finance portfolio holder and member of shadow cabinet 1998-, Chair finance and resources scrutiny committee 2001-

House of Commons: Member for Northampton South since 5 May 2005 general election. *Political interests:* Business, local government

National Young Conservatives organiser 1965-68; Agent, Kidderminster Conservative Association 1996-98. Freemason 1991-; Management committee member, The Lowdown Northampton 2004-; *Publications: Binley Directory of National Health Service Management,* Beechwood House 1993-; plus seven other directories; *Clubs:* Northampton Town and Country; Northampton Conservative; Carlton; *Recreations:* Northampton Town FC, Northamptonshire CCC, freemasonry, golf, opera, literature

Brian Binley, MP, House of Commons, London SW1A 0AA *Tel:* 020 7219 8298. *Constituency:* Agent: Brian Jarvis, White Lodge, 42 Billing Road, Northampton NN1 5DA *Tel:* 01604 250252 *Fax:* 01604 250252 *E-mail:* secretary@nsca.devlinfisher.net *Website:* www.northamptonsouthconservatives.com

Lab majority 7,084

BLACKMAN, LIZ
Erewash

Elizabeth Blackman. Born 26 September 1949; Educated Carlisle County High School for Girls; Prince Henry's Grammar School, Otley; Clifton College, Nottingham (BEd 1972); Married Derek Blackman (divorced 1999) (1 son 1 daughter). Head, Upper School, Bramcote Park Comprehensive, Nottingham; Member, GMB; Former Deputy Leader, Broxtowe Borough Council

House of Commons: Member for Erewash since 1 May 1997 general election; PPS to Geoff Hoon as Secretary of State for Defence 2000-05. *Political interests:* Education, Economy, Economic Regeneration and Economic Disenfranchisement, Health, Disability, Defence

Cancer Research, Natural Autistic Society, ME, Lupus Fibromyalgia; *Publications: Parliamentary Portions,* (charity recipe book) 1998; *Recreations:* Family, music, reading, gardening

Liz Blackman, MP, House of Commons, London SW1A 0AA *Tel:* 020 7219 2397 *Fax:* 020 7219 4837 *E-mail:* blackmanl@parliament.uk. *Constituency:* 23 Barratt Lane, Attenborough, Nottingham, Derbyshire NG9 6AD *Tel:* 0115-922 4380 *Fax:* 0115-943 1860

Lab majority 3,274

BLACKMAN-WOODS, ROBERTA
City of Durham

Roberta Blackman-Woods. Born 16 August 1957; Educated Ulster University (BSc social science 1979, PhD 1989); Married to Tim Blackman. Welfare rights officer, Newcastle City Council 1982-85; Lecturer in social policy 1985-95; Dean of labour studies, Ruskin College, Oxford 1995-2000; Professor of social policy and associate dean, Northumbria University 2000-; GMB

House of Commons: Member for City of Durham since 5 May 2005 general election. *Political interests:* Housing, education and regeneration

Former chair Newcastle East and Wallsend CLP; Chair City of Durham CLP. *Recreations:* Music

Roberta Blackman-Woods, MP, House of Commons, London SW1A 0AA *Tel:* 020 7219 4982. *Constituency: E-mail:* roberta@durhamlabour.org.uk

BLAIR, TONY
Sedgefield

Tony (Anthony Charles Lynton) Blair. Born 6 May 1953; Son of Leo Charles Lynton Blair and late Hazel Elisabeth Blair; Educated Durham Choristers School; Fettes College, Edinburgh; St John's College, Oxford (MA law 1974); Married Cherie Booth 1980 (3 sons 1 daughter). Called to the Bar, Lincoln's Inn 1976; Barrister specialising in trade union and industrial law 1976-83; Sponsored until March 1996 by Transport and General Workers' Union

Lab majority 18,457

House of Commons: Contested Beaconsfield by-election May 1982. Member for Sedgefield since 9 June 1983 general election; Opposition Spokesperson for: Treasury and Economic Affairs 1984-87, Trade and Industry 1987-88; Shadow Secretary of State for Energy 1988-89, Employment 1989-92, Shadow Home Secretary 1992-94; Leader, Labour Party 1994-; Leader of the Opposition 1994-97; Prime Minister, First Lord of the Treasury and Minister for the Civil Service May 1997-

Member, Parliamentary Labour Party Parliamentary Committee. *Publications: New Britain: My Vision of a Young Country*, 1996; PC 1994; Charlemagne Prize 1999; "Spectator" Parliamentarian of the Year 2002; Hon. DCL, Northumbria University 1995

Rt Hon Tony Blair, MP, House of Commons, London SW1A 0AA
Tel: 020 7219 3000. *Constituency:* Myrobella, Farfield Terrace, Trimdon Colliery, Trimdon Station, Durham TS29 6DT   *Tel:* 01429 882202
Website: www.sedgefieldlabour.org.uk

BLEARS, HAZEL
Salford

Hazel Anne Blears. Born 14 May 1956; Daughter of Arthur and Dorothy Blears; Educated Wardley Grammar School; Eccles VIth Form College; Trent Polytechnic (BA law 1977); Chester College of Law (Law Society part II 1978); Married Michael Halsall 1989. Trainee solicitor, Salford Council 1978-80; Private practice solicitor 1980-81; Solicitor: Rossendale Council 1981-83, Wigan Council 1983-85; Principal solicitor, Manchester City Council 1985-97; Branch Secretary, UNISON 1981-85; Member, TGWU; Councillor, Salford City Council 1984-92

Lab majority 7,945

House of Commons: Contested Tatton 1987, Bury South 1992 general elections. Member for Salford since 1 May 1997 general election; PPS to Alan Milburn: as Minister of State, Department of Health 1998, as Chief Secretary, HM Treasury January-October 1999; Department of Health 2001-03: Parliamentary Under-Secretary of State for: Health 2001-02, Public Health 2002-03; Minister of State (Crime Reduction, Policing, Community Safety and Counter-Terrorism), Home Office 2003-. *Political interests:* Employment, Health, Arts, Urban Regeneration

Vice-Chair North West Regional Group of Labour MPs 1997-98, Chair 1998-99; Member: North West Executive 1997-99, National Policy Forum 1997-2001, Leadership Campaign Team 1997-98; Labour Party Development Co-ordinator and Deputy to Ian McCartney 1998-2001; Leader Parliamentary Campaign Team 2003-. Trustee: Working Class Movement Library, Member Cooperative Action; *Publications: Making Healthcare Mutual*, Mutuo 2002; *Communities in Control*, Fabian Society 2003; PC 2005; *Recreations:* Dance, motorcycling

Hazel Blears, MP, House of Commons, London SW1A 0AA *Tel:* 020 7219 6595
Fax: 020 7219 0949 *E-mail:* blearsh@parliament.uk. *Constituency:* Jubilee House, 51 The Crescent, Salford, Greater Manchester M51 4WX *Tel:* 0161-925 0705
Fax: 0161-743 9173

Transforming Information into Intelligence

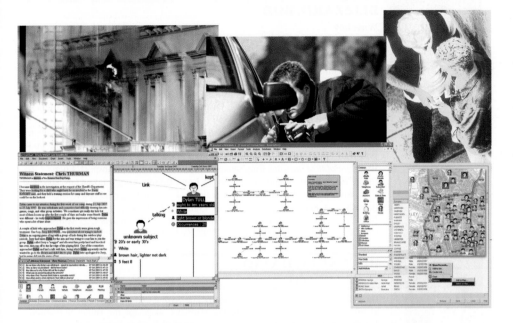

Reliable, secure, auditable and effective information sharing is key to multi-agency approaches to intelligence and crime. i2's range of software products enables agencies to use one simple query to search across multiple disparate databases. Information can then be visualised, analysed and shared effectively, allowing informed decision making and optimum allocation of resources.

By combining intelligent and intuitive access to all relevant information with the most capable and highest quality visualisation and analysis tools, i2's software solutions help deliver results against today's policing targets.

Used by every Police force in the UK, and recognised as the provider of the de-facto standard visual investigative analysis software worldwide, i2 provides its customers with effective software solutions to assist in the detection and prevention of crime.

A ChoicePoint® Company

For a copy of our preview CD, a demonstration or for more information, call us on **01223 728600** or visit our website at **www.i2group.com**

BLIZZARD, BOB
Waveney

Bob (Robert John) Blizzard. Born 31 May 1950; Son of late Arthur Blizzard, signwriter, and late Joan Blizzard; Educated Culford School, Bury St Edmunds; Birmingham University (BA 1971); Married Lyn Chance 1978 (1 son 1 daughter). Teacher: Gravesend Secondary School 1973-75, Head of English, Crayford Secondary School 1976-86, Head of English, Gorleston Secondary School 1986-97; Member: NUT, GMB; Waveney District Council: Councillor 1987-97, Leader 1991-97; Vice-Chair, SCEALA 1995-97

Lab majority 5,915

House of Commons: Member for Waveney since 1 May 1997 general election; PPS to: Baroness Hayman as Minister of State, Ministry of Agriculture, Fisheries and Food 1999-2001, Nick Brown as Minister of State, Department for Work and Pensions 2001-03. *Political interests:* Employment, Health, Education, Transport, Energy

Clubs: Royal Norfolk and Suffolk Yacht Club; Ronnie Scott's Jazz Club; 606 Jazz Club; *Recreations:* Walking, skiing, listening to jazz, watching cricket and rugby

Bob Blizzard, MP, House of Commons, London SW1A 0AA *Tel:* 020 7219 3880 *Fax:* 020 7219 3980 *E-mail:* blizzardb@parliament.uk. *Constituency:* 27 Milton Road East, Lowestoft, Suffolk NR32 1NT *Tel:* 01502 514913 *Fax:* 01502 580694

BLUNKETT, DAVID
Sheffield Brightside

David Blunkett. Born 6 June 1947; Son of late Arthur and Doris Blunkett; Educated Sheffield School for the Blind; Royal Normal College for the Blind; Shrewsbury Technical College; Sheffield Richmond College of Further Education (day release and evening courses); Sheffield University (BA political theory and institutions 1972); Huddersfield College of Education (PGCE 1973); Married Ruth Gwynneth Mitchell 1970 (3 sons) (divorced 1990). Office work, East Midlands Gas Board 1967-69; Tutor in industrial relations and politics, Barnsley College of Technology 1973-81; Shop steward GMB EMGB 1967-69; member, NATFHE 1973-87; member, UNISON 1973-; Councillor, Sheffield City Council 1970-1988, Chair, Social Services Committee 1976-80, Seconded as Leader 1980-87; Councillor, South Yorkshire County Council 1973-77; Chair, Race Relations Forum

Lab majority 13,644

House of Commons: Contested Sheffield Hallam February 1974 general election. Member for Sheffield Brightside since 11 June 1987 general election; Opposition Spokesperson for Environment (Local Government) 1988-92; Shadow Secretary of State for: Health 1992-94, Education 1994-95, Education and Employment 1995-97; Secretary of State for Education and Employment 1997-2001; Home Secretary 2001-04; Secretary of State for Work and Pensions 2005-. *Political interests:* Local and Regional Government, Education, Economic and Democratic Planning. France, USA

Member, Labour Party National Executive Committee 1983-98; Labour Party: Vice-Chair 1992-93, Chair 1993-94. Guide Dogs for the Blind; *Publications: Building from the Bottom,* 1983; *Democracy in Crisis – the Town Halls Respond,* 1987; *On a Clear Day –* (autobiography), 1995; updated 2002; *Politics and Progress,* 2001; PC 1997; *Recreations:* Walking, sailing, music, poetry

Rt Hon David Blunkett, MP, House of Commons, London SW1A 0AA *Tel:* 020 7219 4043 *Fax:* 020 7219 5903. *Constituency:* 4th Floor, Palatine Chambers, Pinstone Street, Sheffield, South Yorkshire S1 2HN *Tel:* 0114-273 5987 *Fax:* 0114-278 0384 *Website:* www.integer.org.uk/labour

There are two million people in the UK with sight problems. That means an average of 3,000 in every Parliamentary constituency.

Despite recent legislation blind and partially sighted people still face discrimination, social exclusion and poverty.

We consulted our 10,000 members on their priorities for change in the coming Parliament. They highlighted:

- Improved benefits to tackle poverty, social exclusion and the extra costs of transport and communication.

- Greater access to information in formats like large print, audio tape and braille.

- Improved civil rights to protect from discrimination in areas like employment, accessing goods and services, transport and voting.

We need your support to achieve change in these areas. Work with us to make a real difference to the lives of your blind and partially sighted constituents.

RNIB Campaigns Team
020 7391 2123
www.rnib.org.uk/campaigns

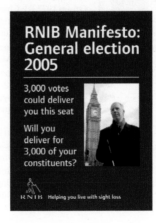

RNIB Manifesto: General election 2005

3,000 votes could deliver you this seat

Will you deliver for 3,000 of your constituents?

RNIB Helping you live with sight loss

R N I B   Helping you live with sight loss

Con majority 10,988

BLUNT, CRISPIN
Reigate

Crispin Jeremy Rupert Blunt. Born 15 July 1960; Son of Major-General Peter Blunt and Adrienne Blunt; Educated Wellington College; Royal Military Academy, Sandhurst; University College, Durham University (BA politics 1984); Cranfield Institute of Technology (MBA 1991); Married Victoria Jenkins 1990 (1 son 1 daughter). Army Officer 1979-90; Regimental duty 13th/18th Royal Hussars (QMO) in England, Germany and Cyprus. District agent, Forum of Private Business 1991-92; Political consultant, Politics International 1993; Special Adviser to Malcolm Rifkind: as Secretary of State for Defence 1993-95, as Foreign Secretary 1995-97

House of Commons: Contested West Bromwich East 1992 general election. Member for Reigate since 1 May 1997 general election; Opposition Spokesperson for Northern Ireland 2001-02; Opposition Whip 2004; Shadow Minister for Trade and Industry 2002-03. *Political interests:* Defence, Foreign Affairs, Environment, Energy *Clubs:* Royal Automobile; Reigate Priory Cricket; *Recreations:* Cricket

Crispin Blunt, MP, House of Commons, London SW1A 0AA *Tel:* 020 7219 2254 *Fax:* 020 7219 3373 *E-mail:* crispinbluntmp@parliament.uk. *Constituency:* Reigate Conservative Association, 86 South Street, Dorking, Surrey RH4 2EW *Tel:* 01306 888228 *Fax:* 01306 889444

Con majority 687

BONE, PETER
Wellingborough

Peter Bone. Born 19 October 1952; Educated Westcliff-on-Sea Grammar School, Essex; Married. Financial director Essex Electronics and Precision Engineering Group 1977-83; Chief executive High Tech Electronics Company 1983-90; Managing director international travel company; Councillor, Southend-on-Sea Borough Council 1977-86; Former Member Southern Airport Management Committee

House of Commons: Contested Islwyn 1992, Pudsey 1997 and Wellingborough 2001 general elections. Member for Wellingborough since 5 May 2005 general election

Deputy chair Southend West Conservative Association 1977-84; Press secretary Paul Channon MP 1982-84; Member National Union Executive Committee 1993-96; Former chair Islwyn Conservative Association; Former chair South Wales East Euro-Council; Founder member All Wales Conservative Policy Group (Think Tank). Contested Mid and West Wales 1994 European Parliament election; *Publications:* Contributor *Telegraph, The Times, Daily Express, Western Mail;* Numerous TV appearances and radio interviews; *Clubs:* Wellingborough Golf Club; *Recreations:* Ruuning marathons for charity

Peter Bone, MP, House of Commons, London SW1A 0AA *Tel:* 020 7219 8496. *Constituency:* Wellingborough Conservative Association, 21a High Road, Wellingborough, Northamptonshire NN8 4JZ *Tel:* 01933 271207 *Fax:* 01933 271207 *E-mail:* wrca@tory.org

BORROW, DAVID
South Ribble

David Stanley Borrow. Born 2 August 1952; Son of James Borrow, retired training officer, and Nancy Borrow, secretary; Educated Mirfield Grammar School, Mirfield; Lanchester Polytechnic (BA economics 1973); Single. Clerk to Merseyside Valuation Tribunal 1983-97; Member, UNISON; Former Branch Vice-Chair; Member, AEEU; Councillor, Preston Borough Council 1992-94, Leader 1992-94, 1995-97

Lab majority 2,184

House of Commons: Contested Wyre 1992 general election. Member for South Ribble since 1 May 1997 general election; PPS to Kim Howells as Minister of State: Department for Transport 2003-04, Department for Education and Skills 2004-. *Political interests:* Regional Development, Local and Regional Government, Aerospace, Small Businesses. Southern Africa

Member: Fabian Society, Co-operative Party. Member: European Standing Committee A 1998, European Standing Committee C 1999-

David Borrow, MP, House of Commons, London SW1A 0AA *Tel:* 020 7219 4126 *Fax:* 020 7219 4126 *E-mail:* borrowd@parliament.uk. *Constituency:* Crescent House, 2-6 Sandy Lane, Leyland, Lancashire PR25 2EB *Tel:* 01772 454727 *Fax:* 01772 422982

BOSWELL, TIMOTHY
Daventry

Timothy Eric Boswell. Born 2 December 1942; Son of late Eric Boswell and Joan Boswell; Educated Marlborough College; New College, Oxford (MA classics 1965, Diploma in agricultural economics 1966); Married Helen Delahay, née Rees 1969 (3 daughters). Conservative Research Department 1966-73; Head, Economic Section 1970-73; Farmer 1974-87; Leicestershire, Northamptonshire and Rutland County Branch of NFU, County Chairman 1983; Part-time Special Adviser to Minister of Agriculture 1984-86

Con majority 14,686

House of Commons: Contested Rugby February 1974 general election. Member for Daventry since 11 June 1987 general election; Opposition Spokesperson for: the Treasury June-December 1997, Trade and Industry December 1997-99, Education 1999-2001, Work and Pensions (People with Disabilities) 2001; Assistant Government Whip 1990-92; Government Whip 1992; PPS to Peter Lilley as Financial Secretary to Treasury 1989-90; Parliamentary Under-Secretary of State, Department for Education 1992-95; Parliamentary Secretary, Ministry of Agriculture, Fisheries and Food 1995-97; Shadow Minister for: Education and Skills (People with Disabilities) 2002-03, Home, Constitutional and Legal Affairs 2003-04, Home Affairs 2004, Work and Pensions and Welfare Reform 2004-. *Political interests:* Agriculture, Finance, European Union. Europe

Daventry Constituency Conservative Association Treasurer 1976-79, Chairman 1979-83. Member, Agricultural and Food Research Council 1988-90; *Clubs:* Farmers'; *Recreations:* Shooting

Timothy Boswell, MP, House of Commons, London SW1A 0AA
Tel: 020 7219 3520 *Fax:* 020 7219 4919 *E-mail:* hodgesm@parliament.uk.
Constituency: 2/3 Church Walk, Daventry, Northamptonshire NN11 4BL
Tel: 01327 703192 *Fax:* 01327 310263

BOTTOMLEY, PETER
Worthing West

Peter James Bottomley. Born 20 July 1944; Son of Sir James Bottomley, KCMG, HM Diplomatic Service, and Barbara Bottomley, social worker; Educated Comprehensive School, Washington DC; Westminster School, London; Trinity College, Cambridge (BA economics 1966, MA); Married Virginia Garnett (now MP as Virginia Bottomley) 1967 (1 son 2 daughters). Industrial sales, industrial relations, industrial economics; Member, TGWU

Con majority 9,379

House of Commons: Contested Greenwich, Woolwich West February and October 1974 general election. Member for Greenwich, Woolwich West by-election 1975-83, for Eltham 1983-97, and for Worthing West since 1 May 1997 general election; PPS: to Cranley Onslow as Minister of State, Foreign and Commonwealth Office 1982-83, to Norman Fowler as Secretary of State for Health and Social Security 1983-84; Parliamentary Under-Secretary of State: at Department of Employment 1984-86, at Department of Transport (Minister for Roads and Traffic) 1986-89, at Northern Ireland Office (Agriculture, Environment) 1989-90; PPS to Peter Brooke as Secretary of State for Northern Ireland September-November 1990. *Political interests:* Southern Africa, El Salvador, USA

President, Conservative Trade Unionists 1978-80. RIIA; Trustee, Christian Aid 1978-84; Fellow, Industry and Parliament Trust; Gold Medal, Institute of the Motor Industry 1988; Court Member, Drapers' Company; *Clubs:* Former Parliamentary swimming and occasional dinghy sailing champion

Peter Bottomley, MP, House of Commons, London SW1A 0AA *Tel:* 020 7219 5060 *Fax:* 020 7219 1212 *E-mail:* bottomleyp@parliament.uk.

BRADSHAW, BEN
Exeter

Ben (Benjamin) Peter James Bradshaw. Born 30 August 1960; Son of late Canon Peter Bradshaw and late Daphne Bradshaw, teacher; Educated Thorpe St Andrew School, Norwich; Sussex University (BA German 1982); Freiburg University, Germany; Partner. Award-winning BBC reporter and presenter 1986-97; BBC Berlin correspondent during fall of Berlin Wall 1989-91; Reporter for 'World At One' and 'World This Weekend' on BBC Radio 4 1991-97; Member, NUJ

Lab majority 7,665

House of Commons: Member for Exeter since 1 May 1997 general election; Introduced Pesticides Act (Private Member's Bill) 1998; PPS to John Denham as Minister of State, Department of Health 2000-01; Parliamentary Under-Secretary of State, Foreign and Commonwealth Office 2001-02; Parliamentary Secretary, Privy Council Office 2002-03; Parliamentary Under-Secretary of State, Department for Environment, Food and Rural Affairs 2003-: (Fisheries, Water and Nature Protection) 2003, (Minister for Nature Conservation and Fisheries) 2003-. *Political interests:* Foreign Affairs, Environment and Transport, Modernisation of Parliament. Europe – particularly Germany and Italy, USA

Labour Movement for Europe, Member: Labour Campaign for Electoral Reform, SERA, Christian Socialist Movement. *Publications:* Numerous for the BBC on domestic and foreign affairs; Argos Consumer Journalist of the Year 1989; Anglo-German Foundation Journalist of the Year 1990; Sony News Reporter Award 1993; Norfolk County Scholar; *Clubs:* Whipton Labour, Exeter; *Recreations:* Cycling, walking, cooking, music

Ben Bradshaw, MP, House of Commons, London SW1A 0AA *Tel:* 020 7219 6597 *Fax:* 020 7219 0950 *E-mail:* bradshawb@parliament.uk. *Constituency:* Labour HQ, 26B Clifton Hill, Exeter, Devon EX1 2DJ *Tel:* 01392 424464 *Fax:* 01392 425630 *Website:* www.exeter-labour.org.uk

BRADY, GRAHAM
Altrincham and Sale West

Graham Stuart Brady. Born 20 May 1967; Son of John Brady, accountant, and Maureen Brady, neé Birch, medical secretary; Educated Altrincham Grammar School; Durham University (BA law 1989); Married Victoria Lowther 1992 (1 son, 1 daughter). Shandwick PLC public relations consultancy 1989-90; Centre for Policy Studies 1990-92; Public affairs director, The Waterfront Partnership public relations and strategic public affairs consultancy 1992-97

Con majority 7,159

House of Commons: Member for Altrincham and Sale West since 1 May 1997 general election; Opposition Spokesman for: Employment 2000-01, Schools 2001-03; Opposition Whip (Trade and Industry, Cabinet Office) 2000; PPS to: Michael Ancram as Conservative Party Chairman 1999-2000, Michael Howard as Leader of the Opposition 2003-04; Shadow Minister for Europe 2004-. *Political interests:* Education, Health. Commonwealth, Far East, British Overseas Territories

Chairman, Durham University Conservative Association 1987-88; National Union Executive Committee 1988; Chairman, Northern Area Conservative Collegiate Forum 1987-89; Vice-Chairman, East Berkshire Conservative Association 1993-95. Friends of Rosie; *Publications: Towards an Employees' Charter – and Away From Collective Bargaining* (Centre for Policy Studies), 1991; *Recreations:* Family, gardening, reading

Graham Brady, MP, House of Commons, London SW1A 0AA *Tel:* 020 7219 4604 *Fax:* 020 7219 1649 *E-mail:* crowthers@parliament.uk. *Constituency:* Altrincham and Sale West Conservative Association, Thatcher House, Delahays Farm, Green Lane, Timperley, Cheshire WA15 8QW *Tel:* 0161-904 8828 *Fax:* 0161-904 8868

BRAKE, TOM
Carshalton and Wallington

Tom (Thomas Anthony) Brake. Born 6 May 1962; Son of Michael and Judy Brake; Educated Lycee International, St Germain-en-Laye, France; Imperial College, London (BSc physics 1983); Married Candida Goulden 1998 (1 daughter 1 son). Principal Consultant (IT), Cap Gemini; Councillor: London Borough of Hackney 1988-90, London Borough of Sutton 1994-98

Lib Dem majority 1,068

House of Commons: Contested Carshalton and Wallington 1992 general election. Member for Carshalton and Wallington since 1 May 1997 general election; Liberal Democrat Spokesperson for: Environment, Transport in London and Air Transport 1997-99, Environment, Transport, the Regions, Social Justice and London Transport 1999-2001; Transport, Local Government and the Regions 2001-02; Transport 2002-03; Liberal Democrat Whip 2000-04; Liberal Democrat Shadow Secretary of State for: International Development 2003-05, Transport 2005-. *Political interests:* Environment, Transport, Emergency Planning, International Development. France, Portugal, Russia, Australia

Oxfam; *Clubs:* Collingwood Athletic Club; *Recreations:* Sport, film, eating

Tom Brake, MP, House of Commons, London SW1A 0AA *Tel:* 020 7219 0924 *Fax:* 020 7219 6491. *Constituency:* Kennedy House, 5 Nightingale Road, Carshalton SM5 2DN *Tel:* 020 8255 8155 *Fax:* 020 8395 4453

BRAZIER, JULIAN
Canterbury

Julian William Hendy Brazier. Born 24 July 1953; Son of Lieutenant Colonel Peter Hendy Brazier, retired, and Patricia Audrey Helen, neé Stubbs; Educated Dragon School; Wellington College, Berks; Brasenose College, Oxford (Scholarship BA mathematics and philosophy 1975, MA); London Business School; Married Katherine Elizabeth Blagden 1984 (3 sons). TA 1972-82, 1989-92. Charter Consolidated Ltd 1975-84, economic research 1975-77, corporate finance 1977-81 and Secretary, executive committee of the Board 1981-84; Management consultant, H B Maynard International 1984-87

Con majority 7,471

House of Commons: Contested Berwick-upon-Tweed 1983 general election. Member for Canterbury since 11 June 1987 general election; Opposition Whip 2001-02; PPS to Gillian Shephard as: Minister of State, Treasury 1990-92, Secretary of State for Employment 1992-93; Shadow Minister for: Work and Pensions 2002-03, Home Affairs 2003, Foreign Affairs 2003-. *Political interests:* Defence, Foreign Affairs Economics, Law and Order, Families, Countryside. Middle East, South Africa, USA, Australia, New Zealand, Russia

President, Conservative Family Campaign 1995-2001; Vice-chair Conservative Party Listening to Churches Programme 2000-03. Friends of Canterbury Cathedral and Westminster Cathedral, Afghanaid, Red Cross Landmines Appeal, Royal British Legion; *Publications:* Co-author *Not Fit to Fight: The Cultural Subversion of the Armed Forces in Britain and America*, Social Affairs Unit 1999; Ten pamphlets on defence, social and economic issues (with Bow Group, Centre for Policy Studies and Conservative 2000); Territorial Decoration 1993; Highland Park/*The Spectator* Backbencher of the Year (jointly) 1996; TD; *Clubs:* Travellers; TD; *Recreations:* Cross-country running, science, philosophy

Julian Brazier, MP, House of Commons, London SW1A 0AA *Tel:* 020 7219 5178 *Fax:* 020 7219 0643. *Constituency:* 128A John Wilson Business Park, Whitstable, Kent CT5 3QT *Tel:* 01227 280277 *Fax:* 01227 280435

BREED, COLIN
South East Cornwall

Colin Edward Breed. Born 4 May 1947; Son of late Alfred and late Edith Violet Breed; Educated Torquay Boys Grammar School; Married Janet Courtiour 1968 (1 son 1 daughter). Manager, Midland Bank plc 1964-81; Managing director, Dartington and Co plc 1981-91; Director, Gemini Abrasives Ltd 1991-96; Councillor, Caradon District Council 1982-92; Mayor of Saltash 1989-90, 1995-96

Lib Dem majority 6,507

House of Commons: Member for South East Cornwall since 1 May 1997 general election; Liberal Democrat Spokesperson for: Competition and Consumer Affairs 1997-99, Competition 1999; Principal Spokesperson for Agriculture, Rural Affairs and Fisheries 1999-; Liberal Democrat Spokesperson for Environment, Food and Rural Affairs 2001-02; Liberal Democrat Spokesperson for Defence 2002-. *Political interests:* Cornwall, Rural Affairs, Conflict Resolution, Middle East

Christian Aid, Action Aid; Member, General Medical Council 1999-; Executive Committee Member, Council for Advancement of Arab-British Understanding; Chair, Princes Trust Volunteers (Devon); *Clubs:* St Mellion Golf and Country Club; *Recreations:* Watching sport, golf

Colin Breed, MP, House of Commons, London SW1A 0AA *Tel:* 020 7219 2588 *Fax:* 020 7219 5905 *E-mail:* colinbreedmp@aol.com. *Constituency:* Barras Street, Liskeard, Cornwall PL14 6AD *Tel:* 01579 342150 *Fax:* 01579 347019

Lab majority 8,167

BRENNAN, KEVIN
Cardiff West

Kevin Denis Brennan. Born 16 October 1959; Son of Michael John Brennan, retired steelworker and Beryl Marie, née Evans, school cook/cleaner; Educated St Alban's RC Comprehensive, Pontypool; Pembroke College, Oxford (BA philosophy, politics and economics 1982) (President Oxford Union 1982); University College of Wales, Cardiff (PGCE history 1985); Glamorgan University (MSc education management 1992); Married Amy Lynn Wack, poetry editor, 1988 (1 daughter). Cwmbran Community Press 1982-84: News editor, Volunteer organiser; Head of economics and business studies Radyr Comprehensive School 1985-94; Research officer to Rhodri Morgan MP 1995-99; Special adviser to Rhodri Morgan as First Minister National Assembly for Wales 2000-; NUT 1984-94; TGWU 1995-2001; Cardiff City Council: Vice-chair Finance 1991-92, Chair Finance 1993-96, Vice-chair Economic Development 1996-99, Chair Economic Scrutiny 1999-2001

House of Commons: Member for Cardiff West since 7 June 2001 general election; Assistant Government Whip 2005-; PPS to Alan Milburn as Chancellor of the Duchy of Lancaster 2004-05. *Political interests:* Economy, Constitutional Affairs. Ireland, Cyprus, Japan

Member: Fabian Society 1979-, Socialist Health Association, Bevan Foundation; Chair Cardiff West Constituency Labour Party 1998-2000; Executive Member Labour Campaign Electoral Reform. Chair Yes for Wales Cardiff 1997; *Clubs:* Canton Labour; *Recreations:* Rugby, golf, reading, cricket, music

Kevin Brennan, MP, House of Commons, London SW1A 0AA *Tel:* 020 7219 8156. *Constituency:* c/o Transport House, 1 Cathedral Road, Cardiff, South Glamorgan CF11 9SD *Tel:* 029 2022 3207 *Fax:* 029 2023 0422 *E-mail:* brennank@parliament.uk *Website:* www.cardiffwestlabour.fsnet.co.uk

Con majority 480

BROKENSHIRE, JAMES
Hornchurch

James Brokenshire. Born 1968; Educated Davenant Foundation Grammar School; Cambridge Centre for Sixth Form Studies; Exeter University (LLB law); Married to Catherine

House of Commons: Member for Hornchurch since 5 May 2005 general election. *Political interests:* Education, mobile phone masts, post office closures, law and order, health

James Brokenshire, MP, House of Commons, London SW1A 0AA *Tel:* 020 7219 8400. *Constituency:* 23 Butts Green Road, Hornchurch RM11 2JS *Tel:* 01708 443321 *Fax:* 01708 447592 *E-mail:* hornchurchca@tory.org *Website:* www.actionforhurnchurch.com

BROOKE, ANNETTE
Mid Dorset and Poole North

Annette Lesley Brooke. Born 7 June 1947; Daughter of Ernest Henry Kelly, bookbinder, and Edna Mabel Kelly; Educated Romford Technical College; London School of Ecnomics (BSc Econ 1968); Hughes Hall, Cambridge (Cert Ed 1969); Married Mike Brooke (2 daughters). Open University 1971-1991: Counsellor, Tutor: social sciences, economics; Various college posts: Reading, Aylesbury, Poole, Bournemouth; Head of economics Talbot Heath School Bournemouth 1984-94; Partner Broadstone Minerals; Owner Gemini shop Poole 1994-; Poole Borough Council 1986-2003: Councillor, Former member ALDC Standing Committee, Chair: Planning 1991-96, Education 1996-2000, Environmental Strategy Working Party 1995-97, Deputy leader ruling Liberal Democrat Group 1995-97, 1998-2000, Sheriff 1996-97, Mayor 1997-98, Deputy mayor 1998-99, Group leader 2000-01; Conference representative Mid Dorset and North Poole constituency

Lib Dem majority 5,482

House of Commons: Member for Mid Dorset and Poole North since 7 June 2001 general election; Liberal Democrat Spokesperson for: Home Affairs 2001-04, Children 2004-; Liberal Democrat Whip 2001-03. *Political interests:* Young People, Home Affairs. Sudan

Beveridge Group. Julia's House, Poole; Member European Standing Committee B 2001-02; *Recreations:* Gym, reading, shopping with daughters

Annette Brooke, MP, House of Commons, London SW1A 0AA
Tel: 020 7219 8473; 020 7219 8193 *Fax:* 020 7219 1898
E-mail: brookea@parliament.uk. *Constituency:* Broadstone Liberal Hall, 14 York Road, Broadstone, Dorset BH18 8ET *Tel:* 01202 693555; 01202 658420
Website: www.middorsetlib-dems.org.uk

BROWN, GORDON
Kirkcaldy and Cowdenbeath

Gordon Brown. Born 20 February 1951; Son of late Rev. Dr John Brown; Educated Kirkcaldy High School; Edinburgh University (MA 1972, PhD 1982); Married Sarah Macaulay 2000 (1 daughter deceased 1 son). Edinburgh University: Rector 1972-75, Temporary lecturer 1975-76; Lecturer in politics, Glasgow College of Technology 1976-80; Journalist, then editor, Scottish Television current affairs department 1980-83; Member, TGWU

Lab majority 18,216

House of Commons: Member for Dunfermline East 1983-2005, for Kirkcaldy and Cowdenbeath since 5 May 2005 general election; Opposition Front Bench Spokesman on Trade and Industry 1985-87; Shadow Spokesman for Trade and Industry 1989-92; Shadow Chief Secretary to The Treasury 1987-89; Shadow Chancellor of the Exchequer 1992-97; Chancellor of the Exchequer 1997-. *Political interests:* Economic Policy, Employment, Health, Social Security, Scotland

Member, Scottish Executive Labour Party 1977-83; Chairman, Labour Party in Scotland 1983-84; Former Member, Labour Party National Executive Committee; Head, General Election Campaign (Strategy) 1999-2001. Joint Hon Treasurer (ex-officio), Commonwealth Parliamentary Association (CPA) UK Branch 1997-99, Joint Hon Secretary 1999-; *Publications:* Co-editor *Values, Visions and Voices: An Anthology of Socialism*; Co-author *John Smith: Life and Soul of the Party*; *Maxton*; *Where There is Greed*; PC 1996; *The Spectator*/Highland Park Parliamentarian of the Year 1997; Channel 4 and *The House* Magazine Speechmaker of the Year 1999; *Recreations:* Tennis, football, reading, writing

Rt Hon Gordon Brown, MP, House of Commons, London SW1A 0AA
Tel: 020 7219 6345. *Constituency:* 318-324 High Street, Cowdenbeath,
Fife KY4 9QS *Tel:* 01383 611702 *Fax:* 01383 611703

Skanska – Keeping clients in mind and building a better Britain

2005 has continued where 2004 left off for the Private Finance Initiative (PFI) and Public Private Partnerships (PPP) in Britain. More schemes are coming to fruition and the quality of their design is increasing all the time. The emphasis continues to shift from just 'getting things done' towards a desire for more complete solutions to each project, ensuring the quality is to the end users' requirements, whether it be in the healthcare, education, defence, custodial or infrastructure sectors.

Skanska has been working hard to ensure that it balances the needs and priorities of all of its schemes' stakeholders. At its landmark PFI hospital schemes in the Midlands (Coventry and Derby) for example, Skanska's teams enter into regular dialogue with the NHS Trust, hospital staff and local residents, all of whom are affected by redevelopment works and all of whom are set to benefit from the result of our work. Moreover, Skanska employs community relations specialists on all of its large-scale schemes, not just in PFI/PPP, so that it ensures the best levels of consideration and co-operation with everyone involved in its drive to shape a better Britain.

Building better schemes – all the time

In July 2004, Skanska completed the redevelopment of the Ministry of Defence's Whitehall headquarters. At £352 million, it was the largest PFI/PPP scheme ever to be completed in the UK and was the result of a successful partnership between the MoD as client, Skanska as lead contractor and the other members of the supply chain. When Skanska unveiled the revitalised office environment a full two months ahead of schedule, it not only created a great new office but embraced a completely new way of operating. It was a showcase for PFI and a demonstration of

what could be achieved when the best parts of the public and private sectors combine.

Skanska is also Preferred Bidder on the £1 billion scheme to regenerate St Bartholomew's and The Royal London Hospitals – the largest PFI/PPP development ever to be procured in the UK. Skanska is taking a lead role in the design, construction, financing and operation of both hospitals – which will provide centres of clinical excellence in the City of London and healthcare facilities for the people of East London that will rival the best in Europe.

Attention to detail

Skanska's success can be attributed to several factors. First, an unwavering commitment to redeveloping Britain's social and economic infrastructure, of which its hospitals, schools, and prisons are core components. Second, a unique focus on its clients' requirements, ranging from the smallest fixtures and fittings, right through to buildings maintenance strategies that will continue well into the 21st Century.

Keeping in mind the benefits that can be offered to its clients and their end users, Skanska is looking forward to the continued progress of PFI/PPP under this new, revitalised government, which looks ready to commit to furthering the progress already set in place. Skanska's skills, expertise and experience in PFI/PPP, Prime Contracting and Highways Agency ECI contracting and many other initiatives, places it uniquely well in its market to deliver high quality infrastructure that is value for money for the British taxpayer.

The future looks bright for PFI and Skanska will ensure that its potential is fulfilled.

BROWN, LYN
West Ham

Lyn Brown. Born 13 April 1960; Living with partner. Founder London Library Development Board; Member: London Region Sports Board, London Arts Board, Museums, Libraries and Archives Council, London; UNISON

House of Commons: Member for West Ham since 5 May 2005 general election

Recreations: Walking and reading

Lyn Brown, MP, House of Commons, London SW1A 0AA *Tel:* 020 7219 6999.

Lab majority 9,801 *Constituency:* *E-mail:* lyn@lynbrown.org.uk

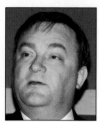

BROWN, NICK
Newcastle upon Tyne East and Wallsend

Nicholas H Brown. Born 13 June 1950; Educated Tunbridge Wells Technical High School; Manchester University (BA 1971). Proctor and Gamble advertising department; Legal adviser for northern region of GMBATU 1978-83; Councillor, Newcastle upon Tyne City Council 1980-83

House of Commons: Member for Newcastle upon Tyne East 1983-97, and for Newcastle upon Tyne East and Wallsend since 1 May 1997 general election; Opposition Frontbench Spokesperson for: Legal Affairs 1985-92, Treasury and Economic Affairs 1988-94; Opposition Spokesperson for Health 1994-95; Opposition Deputy Chief Whip 1995-97; Government Chief Whip 1997-98; Deputy to Margaret Beckett as Shadow Leader of the Commons 1992-94; Minister of Agriculture, Fisheries and Food 1998-2001; Minister of State for Work, Department of Work and Pensions 2001-03. *Political interests:* Australia, China, Japan, New Zealand, USA

Lab majority 7,565

PC 1997; Freeman, Newcastle 2001

Rt Hon Nick Brown, MP, House of Commons, London SW1A 0AA
Tel: 020 7219 4199 *Fax:* 020 7219 5941 *E-mail:* smithlu@parliament.uk.
Constituency: 1 Mosley Street, Newcastle upon Tyne, Tyne and Wear NE1 1YE
Tel: 0191-261 1408 *Fax:* 0191-261 1409

BROWN, RUSSELL
Dumfries and Galloway

Russell Brown. Born 17 September 1951; Son of late Howard Russell Brown and late Muriel Brown; Educated Annan Academy; Married Christine Calvert 1973 (2 daughters). Production supervisor ICI 1974-97; Member, TGWU 1974-: Branch Secretary and Branch Chair 1979-85; Councillor: Dumfries and Galloway Regional Council 1986-96, Annandale and Eskdale District Council 1988-96; Chair Public Protection Committee 1990-94; Councillor Dumfries and Galloway Unitary Council 1995-97; Member Dumfries and Galloway Tourist Board 1996-97

Lab majority 2,922

House of Commons: Member for Dumfries 1997-2005, for Dumfries and Galloway since 5 May 2005 general election; PPS to Leaders of the House of Lords: Lord Williams of Mostyn 2002-03, Baroness Amos 2003-. *Political interests:* Employment, Welfare State, Health and Safety Issues, Energy Policy. European Union

Cancer Research UK, Macmillan Cancer; *Recreations:* Sport (especially football)

Russell Brown, MP, House of Commons, London SW1A 0AA *Tel:* 020 7219 4429
Fax: 020 7219 0922. *Constituency:* 5 Friars Vennel, Dumfries DG1 2RQ
Tel: 01387 247902 *Fax:* 01387 247903 *E-mail:* russell@brownmp.new.labour.org.uk,
E-mail: vote4russell@email.labour.org.uk

BROWNE, DES
Kilmarnock and Loudoun

Des (Desmond) Henry Browne. Born 22 March 1952; Son of late Peter Browne, process worker, and of Maureen Browne, catering manageress; Educated Saint Michael's Academy, Kilwinning; Glasgow University (LLB 1975); Married Maura Taylor 1983 (2 sons). Qualified as solicitor 1976; Called to Scottish Bar 1993; Member UNISON

House of Commons: Contested Argyll and Bute 1992 general election. Member for

Lab majority 8,703

Kilmarnock and Loudoun 1997-2005, for new Kilmarnock and Loudon since 5 May 2005 general election; PPS to: Donald Dewar as Secretary of State for Scotland 1998-99, Adam Ingram as Minister of State, Northern Ireland Office 2000; Parliamentary Under-Secretary of State, Northern Ireland Office 2001-03; Minister of State for Work, Department for Work and Pensions 2003-04; Minister of State (Citizenship, Immigration and Nationality), Home Office 2004-05; Chief Secretary to the Treasury 2005-. *Political interests:* Legal Affairs, Human Rights, Disability, Education, Northern Ireland, Constitution, International Affairs. France, South Africa, Colombia, Rwanda, Burundi

Secretary, Scottish Labour Party Working Party on Prison System 1988-90. *Publications:* Briefing Paper for MPs on Criminal Justice (Scotland) Bill 1980; Report for Lord MacAulay's Working Party on the Prison System 1990; PC 2005; *Recreations:* Sports, football, tennis, swimming, reading, computing

Rt Hon Des Browne, MP, House of Commons, London SW1A 0AA
Tel: 020 7219 4501 *Fax:* 020 7219 2423 *E-mail:* browned@parliament.uk.
Constituency: Parliamentary Advice Centre, 32 Grange Street,
Kilmarnock KA1 2DD *Tel:* 01563 520267 *Fax:* 01563 539439

BROWNE, JEREMY
Taunton

Jeremy Browne. Born 17 May 1970; Educated Nottingham University (BA politics 1992); Married. Dewe Rogerson Ltd 1994-96; Liberal Democrat director of press and broadcasting 1997-2000; Edelman Worldwide 2000-02; ReputationInc 2003-04

House of Commons: Contested Enfield Southgate 1997 general election. Member for Taunton since 5 May 2005 general election

Lib Dem majority 573

Jeremy Browne, MP, House of Commons, London SW1A 0AA *Tel:* 020 7219 8478.
Constituency: Liberal Democrat Office, Castlemoat Chambers, Bath Place,
Taunton, Somerset TA1 4EP *Tel:* 01823 337874
E-mail: jeremy.browne@tauntonlibdems.org.uk
Website: www.tauntonlibdems.org.uk

BROWNING, ANGELA
Tiverton and Honiton

Angela Browning. Born 4 December 1946; Daughter of late Thomas and Linda Pearson; Educated Reading College of Technology; Bournemouth College of Technology; Married David Browning 1968 (2 sons). Teacher home economics, Adult Education 1968-74; Auxiliary nurse 1976-77; Self-employed consultant, manufacturing industry 1977-85; Management consultant specialising in training, corporate communications and finance 1985-94; Director, Small Business Bureau 1985-94; Chairman, Women Into Business 1988-92; Member, Department of Employment Advisory Committee for Women's Employment 1989-92

Con majority 11,051

House of Commons: Contested Crewe and Nantwich 1987 general election. Member for Tiverton 1992-97, and for Tiverton and Honiton since 1 May 1997 general election; Opposition Spokesperson on Education and Employment (Education and Disability) 1997-98; PPS to Michael Forsyth as Minister of State, Department of Employment 1993-94; Parliamentary Secretary, Ministry of Agriculture, Fisheries and Food 1994-97; Member, Shadow Cabinet 1999-2001: Shadow Secretary of State for Trade and Industry 1999-2000, Shadow Leader of the House 2000-01. *Political interests:* Small Businesses, Education (Special Needs), Mental Health, Learning Disabilities

Vice-chairman Conservative Party 2001-. National Autistic Society; Co-Chair The Women's National Commission 1995-97; Vice-President Institute of Sales and Marketing Management 1997-; *Recreations:* Theatre, supporting family of keen oarsmen, member of Thomas Hardy Society

Angela Browning, MP, House of Commons, London SW1A 0AA
Tel: 020 7219 5067 *Fax:* 020 7219 2557 *E-mail:* browningaf@parliament.uk.
Constituency: Tel: 01404 822103

BRUCE, MALCOLM
Gordon

Malcolm Bruce. Born 17 November 1944; Son of David Bruce, former agricultural merchant and hotelier, retired and Kathleen Elmslie Bruce; Educated Wrekin College, Shropshire; St Andrews University (MA economics and political science); Strathclyde University (MSc marketing); CPE and Inns of Court School of Law; Married Jane Wilson 1969 (divorced 1992) (1 son 1 daughter); married Rosemary Vetterlein 1998 (1 daughter 1 son). Trainee journalist, Liverpool Post 1966-67; Boots section buyer 1968-69; Research and information officer, NE Scotland Development Authority 1971-75; Director, Noroil Publishing House (UK) Ltd. 1975-81; Joint editor/publisher, Aberdeen Petroleum Publishing 1981-84; Member, NUJ

**Lib Dem majority
11,026**

House of Commons: Contested Angus North and Mearns October 1974, Aberdeenshire West 1979 general elections. Member for Gordon 1983-2005, for new Gordon since 5 May 2005 general election; Liberal Spokesperson for Energy 1985-87; Scottish Liberal Spokesperson for Education 1986-87; Alliance Spokesperson for Employment 1987; Liberal Spokesperson for Trade and Industry 1987-88; SLD Spokesperson for Natural Resources (energy and conservation) 1988-89; Liberal Democrat Spokesperson for: The Environment and Natural Resources 1989-90, Scottish Affairs 1990-92, Trade and Industry 1992-94, The Treasury 1994-99; Chair, Liberal Democrat Parliamentary Party 1999-2001; Liberal Democrat Shadow Secretary of State for: Environment, Food and Rural Affairs 2001-02, Trade and Industry 2003-05. *Political interests:* Energy, Gas Industry, Oil Industry, Industrial Policy, Trade Policy, Deaf Children, Scottish Home Rule and Federalism. USA, Canada, South Africa, Zimbabwe, Eastern Europe, the Balkans, Hungary, Czech Republic, Baltic States, Scandinavia

Leader Scottish: Social and Liberal Democrats 1988-89, Liberal Democrats 1989-92; President Scottish Liberal Democrats 2000-. National Deaf Children's Society; Rector, Dundee University 1986-89; Member, UK Delegation Parliamentary Assembly of the Council of Europe/Western European Union 2000-; Trustee Royal National Institute for the Deaf; *Recreations:* Golf, cycling, walking, theatre and music

Malcolm Bruce, MP, House of Commons, London SW1A 0AA *Tel:* 020 7219 6233 *Fax:* 020 7219 2334 *E-mail:* hendersonc@parliament.uk. *Constituency:* 71 High Street, Inverurie AB51 3QT *Tel:* 01467 623413 *Fax:* 01467 624994

BRYANT, CHRIS
Rhondda

Chris (Christopher) John Bryant. Born 11 January 1962; Son of Rees Bryant and Anne Gracie, née Goodwin; Educated Cheltenham College; Mansfield College, Oxford (BA English 1983, MA); Ripon College, Cuddesdon (MA CertTheol 1986); Single. Church of England: Ordained Deacon 1986, Priest 1987; Curate All Saints High Wycombe 1986-89; Diocesan youth chaplain Diocese of Peterborough 1989-91; Agent Holborn and St Pancras Labour Party 1991-93; Local government development officer Labour Party 1993-94; London manager Common Purpose 1994-96; Freelance author 1996-98; Head European Affairs BBC 1998-2000; GMB 1991-94; MSF 1994-; London Borough of Hackney: Councillor 1993-98, Chief whip 1994-95

Lab majority 16,242

House of Commons: Contested Wycombe 1997 general election. Member for Rhondda since 7 June 2001 general election. *Political interests:* Wales, European Affairs, Broadcasting, Information Economy. Spain, Latin America

Chair: Christian Socialist Movement 1993-98, Labour Movement for Europe 2002-. *Publications: Reclaiming The Ground*, Hodder and Stoughton 1993; *John Smith: An Appreciation*, Hodder and Stoughton 1994; *Possible Dreams*, Hodder and Stoughton 1995; *Stafford Cripps: The First Modern Chancellor*, Hodder and Stoughton 1997; *Glenda Jackson: The Biography*, HarperCollins 1999; *Clubs:* Ferndale RFC; *Recreations:* Swimming, theatre

Chris Bryant, MP, House of Commons, London SW1A 0AA *Tel:* 020 7219 8315 *Fax:* 020 7219 1792 *E-mail:* bryantc@parliament.uk. *Constituency:* 5 Cemetery Rd, Porth, Rhondda, Mid Glamorgan CF39 0LG *Tel:* 01443 687697 *Fax:* 01443 686405

BUCK, KAREN
Regent's Park and Kensington North

Karen Buck. Born 30 August 1958; Educated Chelmsford High School; London School of Economics (BSc Econ, MSc Econ, MA social policy and administration); Partner Barrie Taylor (1 son). Research and development worker, Outset (charity specialising in employment for disabled people) 1979-83; London Borough of Hackney: specialist officer developing services/employment for disabled people 1983-86, public health officer 1986-87; Labour Party Policy Directorate (Health) 1987-92; Labour Party Campaign Strategy Co-ordinator 1992-99; Member, TGWU; Councillor, Westminster City Council 1990-97; Member: Health Authority (late 1980s), Urban Regeneration Board; Chair, Westminster Early Years Development Partnership

Lab majority 6,131

House of Commons: Member for Regent's Park and Kensington North since 1 May 1997 general election; Parliamentary Under-Secretary of State, Department for Transport 2005-. *Political interests:* Housing, Urban Regeneration, Health Care, Welfare, Children

Chair, London Regional Group of Labour MPs 1999-. Everychild, Amnesty; *Recreations:* Music: rock, soul, jazz, opera

Karen Buck, MP, House of Commons, London SW1A 0AA *Tel:* 020 7219 1682 *Fax:* 020 7219 3664 *E-mail:* k.buck@rpkn-labour.co.uk. *Constituency:* The Labour Party, 4(G) Shirland Mews, London W9 3DY *Tel:* 020 8968 7999 *Fax:* 020 8960 0150

Lab majority 6,454

BURDEN, RICHARD
Birmingham Northfield

Richard Burden. Born 1 September 1954; Son of Kenneth Rodney Burden, engineer, and of late Pauline Burden, secretary; Educated Wallasey Technical Grammar School; Bramhall Comprehensive School; St John's College of Further Education, Manchester; York University (BA politics 1978); Warwick University (MA industrial relations 1979); Married Jane Slowey 2001 (1 stepson 2 stepdaughters). President, York University Students' Union 1976-77; NALGO: Branch Organiser, North Yorkshire 1979-81, West Midlands District Officer 1981-92; Member, TGWU 1979-; Sponsored by TGWU 1989-96

House of Commons: Contested Meriden 1987 general election. Member for Birmingham Northfield since 9 April 1992 general election; PPS to Jeffrey Rooker: as Minister of State and Deputy Minister, Ministry of Agriculture, Fisheries and Food (Minister for Food Safety) 1997-99, as Minister of State, Department of Social Security (Minister for Pensions) 1999-2001; Adviser on Motor Sports to Richard Caborn, as Minister of State for Sport 2002-. *Political interests:* Industrial Policy – especially Motor and Motorsport Industries, Middle East, Poverty, Health, Constitution, Electoral Reform, Regeneration, Regional Government. Middle East, Europe

Founder member, Bedale Labour Party 1980; Member, Labour Middle East Council, Vice-Chair 1994-95; Member, Co-operative Party; Chair, Labour Campaign for Electoral Reform 1996-98, Vice-Chair 1998-; Member, Fabian Society. Macmillan Cancer Relief; Founded Joint Action for Water Services (Jaws) 1985 to oppose water privatisation, Secretary 1985-90; *Publications: Tap Dancing – Water, The Environment and Privatisation,* 1988; *Clubs:* Kingshurst Labour, Austin Sports and Social, Austin Branch British Legion; 750 Motor, Historic Sports Car Club; *Recreations:* Cinema, motor racing

Richard Burden, MP, House of Commons, London SW1A 0AA *Tel:* 020 7219 2318 *Fax:* 020 7219 2170 *E-mail:* burdenr@parliament.uk. *Constituency:* Bournville College of Further Education, Bristol Road South, Birmingham, West Midlands B31 1JR *Tel:* 0121-475 9295 *Fax:* 0121-476 2400

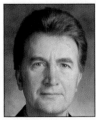

Lab majority 4,528

BURGON, COLIN
Elmet

Colin Burgon. Born 22 April 1948; Son of Thomas Burgon, tailoring worker, and Winifred Burgon, school secretary; Educated St Charles School, Leeds; St Michael's College, Leeds; City of Leeds and Carnegie College; Divorced (1 daughter). Teacher; Local government policy and research officer; Member, GMB

House of Commons: Contested Elmet 1987 and 1992 general elections. Member for Elmet since 1 May 1997 general election. *Political interests:* Youth Affairs, Planning Policy. USA, France, Italy, Spain

Former Secretary, Elmet Constituency Labour Party; Former Chair, Leeds Euro Constituency Labour Party. Member, CPRE; *Recreations:* Football (Leeds United), walking, the countryside, history (military and American Civil War)

Colin Burgon, MP, House of Commons, London SW1A 0AA *Tel:* 020 7219 6487. *Constituency:* 22A Main Street, Garforth, Leeds, West Yorkshire LS25 1AA *Tel:* 0113-287 5198 *Fax:* 0113-287 5958

BURNHAM, ANDY
Leigh

Andrew Murray Burnham. Born 7 January 1970; Son of Kenneth Roy Burnham, telecommunications engineer and Eileen Mary Burnham, neé Murray; Educated St Aelred's RC High School, Merseyside; Fitzwilliam College, Cambridge (BA English 1991, MA); Married Marie-France van Heel 2000 (1 son 1 daughter). Researcher to Tessa Jowell MP 1994-97; Parliamentary officer NHS Confederation 1997; Administrator Football Task Force 1997-98; Special adviser to Chris Smith as Secretary of State for Culture, Media, and Sport 1998-2001; TGWU 1995-; UNISON 2000-; Chair Supporters Direct 2002-

Lab majority 17,272

House of Commons: Member for Leigh since 7 June 2001 general election; PPS to: David Blunkett as Home Secretary 2003-04, Ruth Kelly as Secretary of State for Education and Skills 2004-05; Parliamentary Under-Secretary of State, Home Office 2005-. *Political interests:* Health, Sport, Media, Education, Crime

Member Co-operative Party. *Publications: Football in the Digital Age*, Mainstream Publishing 1999; *Supporters Direct @nr the changing face of the football business*, Frank Cass, 2000; *Clubs:* Lowton Labour Club; Leigh Catholic Club; *Recreations:* Football, cricket, rugby league, (Leigh RLFC, Everton FC)

Andy Burnham, MP, House of Commons, London SW1A 0AA *Tel:* 020 7219 8250 *E-mail:* grahamlm@parliament.uk. *Constituency:* 10 Market Street, Leigh, Greater Manchester WN7 1DS *Tel:* 01942 682353 *Fax:* 01942 682354

BURNS, SIMON
Chelmsford West

Simon Burns. Born 6 September 1952; Son of late Major B. S. Burns MC and Mrs Anthony Nash; Educated Christ the King School, Accra, Ghana; Stamford School; Worcester College, Oxford (BA history 1975); Married Emma Clifford 1982 (divorced) (1 son 1 daughter). Assistant to Sally Oppenheim, MP 1975-81; Director and company secretary, What to Buy for Business Ltd 1981-83; Conference organiser, Institute of Directors 1983-87

Con majority 9,620

House of Commons: Contested Alyn and Deeside 1983 general election. Member for Chelmsford 1987-97, and for Chelmsford West since 1 May 1997 general election; Opposition Spokesperson for: Social Security 1997-August 1998, Environment, Transport and the Regions (Planning, Housing and Construction) August 1998-99, Health 2001-03; Assistant Government Whip 1994-95; Government Whip 1995-96; PPS: to Timothy Eggar as Minister of State: at Department of Employment 1989-90, at Department of Education and Science 1990-92, at Department of Trade and Industry 1992-93; to Gillian Shephard as Minister of Agriculture, Fisheries and Food 1993-94; Parliamentary Under-Secretary of State, Department of Health 1996-97; Shadow Minister for: Health and Education 2001-04, Health 2004-. *Political interests:* Health. USA

Farleigh Hospice; Honorary PhD Anglia University; *Clubs:* Essex; *Recreations:* Photography, American politics, reading

Simon Burns, MP, House of Commons, London SW1A 0AA *Tel:* 020 7219 6811. *Constituency:* 88 Rectory Lane, Chelmsford, Essex CM1 1RF *Tel:* 01245 352872 *Fax:* 01245 344515

BURROWES, DAVID
Enfield Southgate

David John Barrington Burrowes. Born 12 June 1969; Educated Highgate School, London; Exeter University (LLB law 1991); Married Janet 1997. Assistant solicitor, Shepherd Harris and Co, Enfield 1995-2001; London Borough of Enfield: Councillor 1994, Corporate services lead spokesperson 1995-97, Education lead spokesperson 1997-99, Shadow cabinet member 1999-2000

House of Commons: Contested Edmonton 2001 general election. Member for Enfield Southgate since 5 May 2005 general election

Co-founder, Conservative Christian Fellowship 1990; Vice-chair, Exeter University Conservatives 1990-95; President and chair, Conservative Christian Fellowship 1990-95; Member, Enfield Southgate Conservative Association Executive 1995-98. *Publications:* Co-author *Moral Basis of Conservatism*, 1995

David Burrowes, MP, House of Commons, London SW1A 0AA
Tel: 020 7219 8144. *Constituency:* Esca House, 1 Chaseville Parade, Chaseville Park Road, Winchmore Hill, London N21 1PG *Tel:* 020 8360 0234 *Fax:* 020 8360 3915
E-mail: office@escatory.org *Website:* www.escatory.org

Con majority 1,747

BURSTOW, PAUL
Sutton and Cheam

Paul Kenneth Burstow. Born 13 May 1962; Son of Brian Burstow, tailor, and Sheila Burstow; Educated Glastonbury High School For Boys; Carshalton College of Further Education; South Bank Polytechnic (BA business studies); Married Mary Kemm. Buyer Allied Shoe Repairs; Printing company, Chiswick; Organising Secretary, Organisation of Social Democrat Councillors 1986; Political Secretary, Association of Liberal Democrat Councillors 1996-97; Councillor, London Borough of Sutton 1986-, Chair, Environment Services 1988-96, Deputy Leader 1994-99

House of Commons: Contested Sutton and Cheam 1992 general election. Member for Sutton and Cheam since 1 May 1997 general election; Liberal Democrat Spokesperson for: Disabled People 1997-98, Local Government (Social Services and Community Care) 1997-99, Local Government (Team Leader) 1997-99, Older People 1999-2003; Shadow Secretary of State for Health 2003-05. *Political interests:* Environment, Disability, Community Safety, Ageing

Former Member: SDP/Liberal Alliance, London Regional Liberal Democrat Executive; Member, Federal Policy Committee 1988-90. *Clubs:* National Liberal; *Recreations:* Cooking, reading, cycling, walking, keeping fit

Paul Burstow, MP, House of Commons, London SW1A 0AA *Tel:* 020 7219 1196.
Constituency: 312-314 High Street, Sutton, Surrey SM1 1PR *Tel:* 020 8288 6555
Fax: 020 8288 6550

Lib Dem majority 2,846

BURT, ALISTAIR
North East Bedfordshire

Alistair James Hendrie Burt. Born 25 May 1955; Son of James Hendrie Burt and Mina Christie Burt; Educated Bury Grammar School, Lancashire; St John's College, Oxford (BA jurisprudence 1977); Married Eve Alexandra Twite 1983 (1 son 1 daughter). Solicitor Private Practice 1980-98; Executive search consultant Whitehead Mann GKR 1997-2001; London Borough of Haringey 1982-84: Councillor, Conservative spokesman community affairs

Con majority 12,251

House of Commons: Member for Bury North 1983-97. Contested Bury North 1997 general election. Member for North East Bedfordshire since 7 June 2001 general election; Opposition Spokesperson for Education and Skills 2001-02; PPS to Kenneth Baker as Secretary of State for the Environment, for Education and Science and Chancellor of the Duchy of Lancaster 1985-90; Parliamentary Under-Secretary of State Department of Social Security 1992-95; Minister of State Department of Social Security and Minister for Disabled People 1995-97; Opposition Spokesperson for Education and Skills 2001-02; PPS to Leaders of the Opposition: Iain Duncan Smith 2002-03, Michael Howard 2003-. *Political interests:* Church Affairs, Trade and Industry, Third World, Foreign Affairs, Agriculture, Rural Affairs, Disability, Sport, Poverty, Social Affairs

Vice-President Tory Reform Group 1985-88; Chair Bow Group industry committee 1987-92. Chair Enterprise Forum 1998-2001; *Recreations:* Football, modern art, walking, outdoor leisure

Alistair Burt, MP, House of Commons, London SW1A 0AA *Tel:* 020 7219 8132 *Fax:* 020 7219 1740 *E-mail:* burta@parliament.uk. *Constituency:* Biggleswade Conservative Club, St Andrews Street, Biggleswade, Bedfordshire SG18 8BA *Tel:* 01767 313 385 *Fax:* 01767 316 697

BURT, LORELY
Solihull

Lorely Burt. Born 1957; Educated economics (BA); MBA; Married Richard. Formerly, Personnel management; Formerly, Prison Service; Director, Marketing consultancy company; Former founder, Licensed retail company; Councillor Dudley Metropolitan Borough Council

House of Commons: Contested Dudley South 2001 general election. Member for Solihull since 5 May 2005 general election

Lib Dem majority 279

Member Liberal Democrat: Federal Policy Committee, West Midlands regional executive. Contested West Midlands 2004 European Parliament election

Lorely Burt, MP, House of Commons, London SW1A 0AA *Tel:* 020 7219 8269. *Constituency:* *E-mail:* lorelyburt@solihull-libdems.org.uk

BUTLER, DAWN
Brent South

Dawn Butler. Born 3 November 1969; Single. GMB: National officer, Regional equality officer, Regional race officer; GMB

House of Commons: Member for Brent South since 5 May 2005 general election; executive officer, Job Centre, Civil Service 1993-96; recruitment officer and Black Women's Officer PCS 1996-97; national officer Race and Equality Officer GMB 1997-. *Political interests:* Poverty, unemployment, crime, health, children's welfare, equality, employment rights

Lab majority 11,326

New Statesman Most promising feminist under 35 (2002); *Recreations:* salsa dancing Dawn Butler, MP, House of Commons, London SW1A 0AA *Tel:* 020 7219 4385. *Constituency:* *E-mail:* dawnbutler@gmb.org.uk

BUTTERFILL, JOHN
Bournemouth West

Con majority 4,031

John Valentine Butterfill. Born 14 February 1941; Son of late George Thomas, Lloyd's broker, and late Elsie Amelia, neé Watts, Bank of England executive; Educated Caterham School; College of Estate Management, London (FRICS); Married Pamela Ross 1965 (1 son 3 daughters). Valuer, Jones Lang Wootton 1962-64; Senior executive, Hammerson Group 1964-69; Director, Audley Properties Ltd (Bovis Group) 1969-71; Managing Director, St Paul's Securities Group 1971-76; Senior partner, Curchod & Co. Chartered Surveyors 1977-92; President, European Property Associates 1980-2003; Contested London South Inner 1979 European Parliament election; Director: ISLEF Building and Construction Ltd 1985-91, Pavilion Services Group 1992-94

House of Commons: Contested Croydon North West 1981 by-election. Member for Bournemouth West since 9 June 1983 general election; PPS: to Cecil Parkinson: as Secretary of State for Energy 1988-89, as Secretary of State for Transport 1989-90, to Dr Brian Mawhinney as Minister of State, Northern Ireland Office 1991-92. *Political interests:* Trade and Industry, Tourism, Foreign Affairs, Environment, Housing, Health, Pensions. Spain, France, Germany, Scandinavia, Israel

Chair: Conservative Group for Europe 1989-92, Conservative Party Rules Committee 1997-; Member, Conservative Party Constitutional Committee 1998-; Vice-chair, Conservative Friends of Israel. PDSA, Action Research; Chairman of Trustees, Parliamentary Members' Fund 1977-2002; Parliamentary Contributory Pension Fund: Trustee 1977-2001, Chairman of Trustees 2001-; Kt 2004; *Recreations:* Skiing, tennis, bridge, music

Sir John Butterfill, MP, House of Commons, London SW1A 0AA
Tel: 020 7219 6383. *Constituency:* 135 Hankinson Road, Bournemouth, Dorset BH9 1HR *Tel:* 01202 776607 *Fax:* 01202 521481

BYERS, STEPHEN
North Tyneside

Lab majority 15,037

Stephen John Byers. Born 13 April 1953; Son of late Robert Byers, chief technician, RAF; Educated Chester City Grammar School; Chester College of Further Education; Liverpool Polytechnic (LLB); Single (1 son). Senior lecturer in law, Newcastle Polytechnic 1977-92; Member UNISON; North Tyneside Council: Councillor 1980-92, Chair, Education Committee 1982-85, Deputy Leader of the Council 1985-92

House of Commons: Contested Hexham 1983 general election. Member for Wallsend 1992-97, and for North Tyneside since 1 May 1997 general election; Opposition Spokesperson for Education and Employment 1995-97; Opposition Whip 1994-95; Minister of State, Department for Education and Employment (Minister for School Standards) 1997-98; Chief Secretary, HM Treasury July-December 1998; Secretary of State for Trade and Industry December 1998-2001; Secretary of State for Transport, Local Government and the Regions 2001-02

Member, Business and Technician Education Council 1985-89; Chair, Association of Metropolitan Authorities Education Committee 1990-92; Leader, Council of Local Education Authorities 1990-92; Chair, National Employers' Organisation for Teachers 1990-92; PC 1998

Rt Hon Stephen Byers, MP, House of Commons, London SW1A 0AA
Tel: 020 7219 4085 *Fax:* 020 7219 5041 *E-mail:* byerss@parliament.uk.
Constituency: 7 Palmersville, Great Lime Road, Forest Hall,
Newcastle upon Tyne NE12 9HW *Tel:* 0191-268 9111 *Fax:* 0191-268 9777

BYRNE, LIAM
Birmingham Hodge Hill

Liam Byrne. Born 2 October 1970; Educated Manchester University; Harvard University, USA (MBA); Married Sarah (2 sons 1 daughter). Andersen Consulting 1993; Leader of Labour Party's Office 1996-97; N M Rothschild 1997-99; eGS; Member National Executive, NVS

House of Commons: Member for Birmingham Hodge Hill since 15 July 2004 by-election; Parliamentary Under-Secretary of State, Department of Health 2005-. *Political interests:* Anti-Social Behaviour, Drugs, Social Policy

Lab majority 5,449

Adviser, 1997 general election campaign. Member, European Standing Committee B 2005-; *Publications: Cities of Enterprise, New Strategies for Full Employment;* Fellow, Social Market Foundation

Liam Byrne, MP, House of Commons, London SW1A 0AA *Tel:* 020 7219 6953. *Constituency: Tel:* 0121 747 9500; 0121 747 9504 *E-mail:* terrydavis@email.org.uk

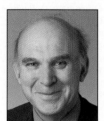

CABLE, VINCENT
Twickenham

(John) Vincent Cable. Born 9 May 1943; Son of late Leonard Cable and Edith Cable; Educated Nunthorpe Grammar School, York; Fitzwilliam College, Cambridge (President of Union) (BA natural science and economics 1966); Glasgow University (PhD international economics 1973); Widower (Dr Olympia Rebelo died 2001) (2 sons 1 daughter); married Rachel Wenbon Smith 2004. Finance officer, Kenya Treasury 1966-68; Economics lecturer, Glasgow University 1968-74; Diplomatic Service 1974-76; Deputy Director, Overseas Development Institute 1976-83; Special Adviser to John Smith as Secretary of State for Trade 1979; Special Adviser, Commonwealth General Secretary 1983-90; Adviser to World Commission on Environment and Development (Brundtland Commission) 1985-87; Group Planning, Shell 1990-93; Head economics programme, Chatham House 1993-95; Chief economist, Shell International 1995-97; Councillor (Labour), Glasgow City Council 1971-74

Lib Dem majority 9,965

House of Commons: Contested Glasgow Hillhead (Labour) 1970, York (SDP/Alliance) 1983 and 1987, Twickenham (Liberal Democrat) 1992 general elections. Member for Twickenham since 1 May 1997 general election; Liberal Democrat Spokesperson for the Treasury (EMU and The City) 1997-99; Principal Spokesperson for Trade and Industry 1999-2003; Shadow Chancellor of the Exchequer 2003-. *Political interests:* Economic Policy, Development, Policing, Energy, Environment. India, Russia, China, Nigeria, Kenya

Patron Shooting Star Hospice; Patron Shooting Star Trust; *Publications:* Wide variety of books and pamphlets including: *Protectionism and Industrial Decline,* 1983, *The New Giants: China and India,* 1994, *The World's New Fissures; The Politics of Identity* (Demos) 1995, *Globalisation and Global Governance,* 1999; Visiting fellow, Nuffield College, Oxford and at the London School of Economics (Centre for Global Governance); Former special professor of economics, Nottingham University 1999; Research fellow, international economics, Royal Institute of International Affairs; *Clubs:* British Legion Club, Twickenham; *Recreations:* Ballroom and Latin dancing, classical music, riding, walking

Dr Vincent Cable, MP, House of Commons, London SW1A 0AA
Tel: 020 7219 1106 *Fax:* 020 7219 1191 *E-mail:* cablev@parliament.uk.
Constituency: 2a Lion Road, Twickenham TW1 4JQ *Tel:* 020 8892 0215
Fax: 020 8892 0218

THE ASSOCIATION OF ANAESTHETISTS
of Great Britain & Ireland

Anaesthesia is the largest specialty within hospital medicine in the United Kingdom and the Association of Anaesthetists represents 90% of consultant and trainee anaesthetists in the UK. The Association not only offers professional advice to its members but has a respected record of producing national guidelines of good practice which are an essential component of clinical governance. It also organises a major educational programme for its members including large scientific meetings and smaller clinical seminars, as well as providing considerable funding to departments and individuals to pursue research in anaesthesia, critical care and pain medicine.

An effective and motivated anaesthetic workforce is essential not only to meet the nation's

elective and emergency surgical requirements but also to service the Intensive Care Units, the High Dependency Units, the Resuscitation Services, Pain Clinics and Obstetric Units. As well established team players many anaesthetists are also involved in healthcare management.

There is a major shortfall in the number of anaesthetists in the UK. More are being trained and the specialty is co-operating with the NHS Modernisation Agency in the development of non-medical Anaesthetic Practitioners to extend the Anaesthesia Team. However, a lack of anaesthetists may well be a limiting restriction to the expansion and improvement of NHS services and it is crucial that anaesthetists' contributions are appropriately respected and recognised. Anaesthetists undergo a 7 year postgraduate training programme before being eligible for a consultant post and it is important that the public, politicians and NHS management recognise that their skills are as equally complex and valuable as those of the surgeons with whom they work. The Association is concerned that the principle that has been established since the outset of the NHS in 1948 of equal pay for consultants in all specialties, may be breached by recent proposals from developing Independent Sector Treatment Centres. Recruitment and retention in this essential specialty must not be jeopardised for the profit of the private healthcare sector.

The Association and its members do, however, wish to contribute constructively to the exciting changes and challenges in the NHS. Reduced availability of both consultants and trainees with the introduction of the European Working Time Directive and the new Consultant Contract is a major threat

to continuation of emergency services as exist at the moment. The specialty will adapt, introducing innovative working practices and will also co-operate in the Hospital at Night initiatives particularly by sharing anaesthetists' core skills in identification and treatment of the acutely ill. The Association, however, does not believe that it will be possible to maintain the current number of hospital sites with full emergency medical services and a major rationalisation and restructuring is required. If standards are to be maintained or, indeed, improved, the public must understand that change is essential and that all their much loved local hospitals cannot continue in their current format. Sensible debate based on objective criteria rather than emotional response or media hype is required and it is important that our political colleagues grasp this formidable nettle.

The Association of Anaesthetists and its members are committed to playing their part in achieving the highest standards of healthcare for the population of the UK.

**The Association of Anaesthetists of Great Britain and Ireland
21 Portland Place
London W1B 1PY
020 7631 1650
www.aagbi.org**

CABORN, RICHARD
Sheffield Central

Richard George Caborn. Born 6 October 1943; Son of late George Caborn; Educated Hurlfield Comprehensive School; Granville College; Sheffield Polytechnic (engineering 1966); Married Margaret Hayes 1966 (1 son 1 daughter). Skilled engineer 1964-1979; MEP for Sheffield District 1979-84; Convenor of shop stewards AEEU

Lab majority 7,055

House of Commons: Member for Sheffield Central since 9 June 1983 general election; Opposition Spokesperson for: Trade and Industry 1988-90, with special responsibility for Regional Policy 1990-92, National Competitiveness and Regulation 1995-97; Minister of State: Department of the Environment, Transport and the Regions (Minister for the Regions, Regeneration and Planning) 1997-99, Department of Trade and Industry (Minister for Trade) 1999-2001; Department for Culture, Media and Sport (Minister for Sport) 2001-. *Political interests:* European Union, Trade Unions, Steel Industry. South Africa

Chair, Sheffield District Labour Party, served on Education Committee. Vice-President, Sheffield Trades Council 1968-79; Member, BBC Advisory Council 1975-78; Joint Chair, British Trade International Board 2000-01; Chair, European Parliament British Labour Party Group 1979-84; PC 1999; *Recreations:* Golf

Rt Hon Richard Caborn, MP, House of Commons, London SW1A 0AA
Tel: 020 7219 4211; 020 7219 6259 *Fax:* 020 7219 4866
E-mail: lawrences@parliament.uk. *Constituency:* 2nd Floor, Barkers Pool House, Burgess Street, Sheffield, South Yorkshire S1 2HF *Tel:* 0114-273 7947
Fax: 0114-275 3944 *Website:* www.integer.org.uk/labour

CAIRNS, DAVID
Inverclyde

(John) David Cairns. Born 7 August 1966; Educated Notre Dame High School, Greenock; Gregorian University, Rome; Franciscan Study Centre, Canterbury; Single. Priest 1991-94; Director Christian Socialist Movement 1994-97; Research assistant to Siobhan McDonagh MP 1997-2001; ISTC; London Borough of Merton 1998-2002: Councillor, Chief whip

Lab majority 11,259

House of Commons: Member for Greenock and Inverclyde 2001-05, for Inverclyde since 5 May 2005 general election; PPS to Malcolm Wicks as Minister of State, Department for Work and Pensions 2003-05; Parliamentary Under-Secretary of State, Scotland Office 2005-. *Political interests:* Defence, Employment, Welfare, Small Businesses

Member: Fabian Society, Christian Socialist Movement. Member European Standing Committee B 2003-

David Cairns, MP, House of Commons, London SW1A 0AA *Tel:* 020 7219 8242
Fax: 020 7219 1772 *E-mail:* cairnsd@parliament.uk. *Constituency:* The Parliamentary Office, 20 Union Street, Greenock PA16 8JL *Tel:* 01475 791820
Fax: 01475 791821

CALTON, PATSY
Cheadle

Patsy Calton. Born 19 September 1948; Daughter of late John and Joan Yeldon; Educated Wymondham College, Wymondham, Norfolk; University of Manchester Institute of Science and Technology (BSc biochemistry 1970); Manchester University (PGCE 1971); Married Clive Calton 1969 (2 daughters 1 son). Chemistry teacher Manchester Metropolitan Borough Council 1971-79; Human biology teacher Stockport Metropolitan Borough Council 1984-86; Chemistry teacher Stockport Metropolitan Borough Council 1987-89; Head of chemistry Cheshire County Council 1989-2001; NASUWT: Member 1993-2002, School representative 1998-2001, Associate Member 2002-; Stockport Metropolitan Borough Council: Councillor 1994-2002, Chair Environmental Health 1995-97, Deputy leader 1996-97, Chair Community Services 1997-99, Deputy leader 1998-2001, Chair Social Services 1999-2001

Lib Dem majority 4,020

House of Commons: Contested Cheadle 1992, 1997 general elections. Member for Cheadle since 7 June 2001 general election; Liberal Democrat Spokesperson for Northern Ireland 2001-02; Liberal Democrat Spokesperson for Health 2002-. *Political interests:* Environment, Transport, Community Services, Social Services, Science. Uganda, Cyprus

Chair Stockport Metropolitan Liberal Democrats 1993-96, 1997-2000; Member Liberal Democrat Federal Executive Committee 2001-. Stockport Cerebal Palsy Society; Chair, Travel Office Consumers' Panel; *Recreations:* Reading, gardening, running (London marathon 1999, 2001, 2002, 2003)

Patsy Calton, MP, House of Commons, London SW1A 0AA *Tel:* 020 7219 8471 *Fax:* 020 7219 1958 *E-mail:* caltonp@parliament.uk. *Constituency:* Hillson House, 3 Gill Bent Road, Cheadle Hulme, Cheadle, Stockport, Greater Manchester SK8 7LE *Tel:* 0161-486 1359 *Fax:* 0161-486 9005

CAMERON, DAVID
Witney

David Cameron. Born 9 October 1966; Son of Ian Donald and Mary Fleur Cameron; Educated Eton College, Windsor; Brasenose College, Oxford (BA philosophy, politics, economics 1988); Married Samantha Sheffield 1996 (1 son 1 daughter). Conservative Research Department 1988-92: Head of Political Section, member Prime Minister's Question Time briefing team; Special adviser to: Norman Lamont as Chancellor of the Exchequer 1992-93, Michael Howard as Home Secretary 1993-94; Director of corporate affairs Carlton Communications plc 1994-2001; Member NFU

Con majority 14,156

House of Commons: Contested Stafford 1997 general election. Member for Witney since 7 June 2001 general election; Shadow Minister for: Privy Council Office 2003, Local and Devolved Government Affairs 2004; Member Shadow Cabinet 2004-; Shadow Secretary of State for Education and Skills 2005-. *Political interests:* Economy, Home Affairs, European Affairs

Deputy Chairman Conservative Party 2003; Head of Policy Co-ordination Conservative Party 2004-. Oxfordshire Association for the Blind; Macmillan Nurses; SCCWID; *Recreations:* Tennis, bridge, cooking

David Cameron, MP, House of Commons, London SW1A 0AA *Tel:* 020 7219 3475 *E-mail:* camerond@parliament.uk. *Constituency:* 10 Bridge Street, Witney, Oxfordshire OX28 1HY *Tel:* 01993 702 302 *Fax:* 01993 776 639

campaigning to end animal experiments

Founded in 1898, the British Union for the Abolition of Vivisection (BUAV) is the leading British organisation campaigning against animal experimentation at a national and international level. The BUAV is committed to using all peaceful and legal means possible to end animal experiments and promote modern, non-animal research techniques.

As Chair of the European Coalition to End Animal Experiments, the BUAV is at the centre of anti-vivisection campaigning across Europe, liaising with key international groups and ensuring that laboratory animals are high on the European political agenda. In the UK, the BUAV regularly participates in the Parliamentary process, submitting evidence to consultations, committees and inquiries and working with MPs. Our primary campaigns include the use of primates in toxicology and research; animal testing for cosmetics and household products; and the European Union's REACH chemicals testing programme.

Further information on the BUAV's campaigns can be found on the Parliamentary website **www. politics.co.uk** *(search for "BUAV" under the "Opinion Formers" tab).* Our main website, **www.buav.org** carries in-depth additional information on these campaigns and all the issues surrounding animal experimentation.

For further information or assistance, contact our Parliamentary Officer on

0207 619 6970

BUAV: 16a Crane Grove, London N7 8NN. Email: info@buav.org Fax: 0207 700 0252

CAMPBELL, ALAN
Tynemouth

Alan Campbell. Born 8 July 1957; Son of Albert Campbell and Marian Campbell, neé Hewitt; Educated Blackfyne Secondary School, Consett; Lancaster University (BA politics); Leeds University (PGCE); Newcastle Polytechnic (MA history); Married Jayne Lamont (1 son 1 daughter). Whitley Bay High School 1980-89; Hirst High School, Ashington, Northumberland: teacher 1989-97, head of sixth form, head of department

Lab majority 4,143

House of Commons: Member for Tynemouth since 1 May 1997 general election; Assistant Government Whip 2005-; PPS to: Lord Macdonald of Tradeston as Minister for the Cabinet Office and Chancellor of the Duchy of Lancaster 2001-03, Adam Ingram as Minister of State, Ministry of Defence 2003-05. *Political interests:* Education, Constitutional Reform, Shipbuilding and Offshore Industries

Branch Secretary, Chair, Agent; Tynemouth Constituency Labour Party: Secretary, Campaign Co-ordinator; Hon. Secretary and Hon. Treasurer, Northern Group of Labour MPs 1999-; Member Seaside and Coastal Towns Group. *Recreations:* Family

Alan Campbell, MP, House of Commons, London SW1A 0AA *Tel:* 020 7219 6619 *Fax:* 020 7219 3006 *E-mail:* campbellal@parliament.uk. *Constituency:* 99 Howard Street, North Shields, Tyne and Wear NE30 1NA *Tel:* 0191-257 1927 *Fax:* 0191-257 6537

CAMPBELL, GREGORY
East Londonderry

Gregory Lloyd Campbell. Born 15 February 1953; Son of James Campbell and Martha Joyce, née Robinson; Educated Londonderry Technical College; Magee College (extra-mural certificate political studies 1982); Married Frances Patterson 1979 (1 son 3 daughters). Civil servant 1972-82, 1986-94; Self-employed businessman 1994-; Councillor Londonderry City Council 1981-

DUP majority 7,727

House of Commons: Contested Foyle 1983, 1987, 1992 and East Londonderry 1997 general elections. Member for East Londonderry since 7 June 2001 general election; Member: Northern Ireland Assembly 1982-86, Northern Ireland Forum for Political Dialogue 1996-98, New Northern Ireland Assembly 1998-2003, 2003-; Minister for Regional Development 2000-03. *Political interests:* Economic Development, Tourism, Employment, Enterprise, Trade and Industry

Spokesman for Security 1994; Whip 1998; Treasurer; Senior Party Officer. *Publications:* Various publications; *Discrimination: The Truth,* 1987; *Discrimination: Where Now?,* 1993; *Ulster's Verdict on the Joint Declaration,* 1994; *Working Toward 2000,* 1998; *Recreations:* Football, music, reading

Gregory Campbell, MP, House of Commons, London SW1A 0AA *Tel:* 020 7219 8495. *Constituency:* 25 Bushmills Road, Coleraine BT52 2BP *Tel:* 028 7032 7327 *Fax:* 028 7032 7328 *E-mail:* coleraine@dup.org.uk

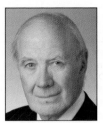

CAMPBELL, MENZIES
North East Fife

Lib Dem majority
12,571

(Walter) Menzies Campbell. Born 22 May 1941; Son of late George and Elizabeth Campbell; Educated Hillhead High School, Glasgow; Glasgow University (MA arts 1962, LLB law 1965); Stanford University, California (post graduate studies in international law 1966-67); Married Elspeth Mary Urquhart 1970. Called to the Bar (Scotland) 1968; QC (Scotland) 1982; Competed: 1964 (Tokyo) Olympics, 1966 Commonwealth Games (Jamaica); UK Athletics Team Captain 1965-66; UK 100 metres record holder 1967-74; Chair, Royal Lyceum Theatre Company, Edinburgh 1984-87

House of Commons: Contested Greenock and Port Glasgow February and October 1974, East Fife 1979, North East Fife 1983 general elections. Member for North East Fife 1987-2005, for new North East Fife since 5 May 2005 general election; Liberal Spokesperson for Arts, Broadcasting and Sport 1987-88; SLD Spokesperson for Defence, Sport 1988-89; Liberal Democrat Spokesperson for: Scotland (Legal Affairs, Lord Advocate) 1987-99, Defence and Disarmament, Sport 1989-94, Foreign Affairs and Defence, Sport 1994-97, Foreign Affairs (Defence and Europe) 1997-99; Principal Spokesperson for Defence and Foreign Affairs 1999-2001; Liberal Democrat Shadow Secretary of State for Foreign and Commonwealth Affairs 2001-. *Political interests:* Defence, Foreign Affairs, Legal Affairs, Sport, Arts. Middle East, North America

Chair Scottish Liberal Party 1975-77; Member Liberal Democrat Peel Group 2001-; Deputy Leader Liberal Democrat Party 2003-. Member: Board of the British Council 1998-2002, Council of the Air League 1999-; Member: North Atlantic Assembly 1989-, UK Delegation, Parliamentary Assembly of OSCE 1992-97, 1999-; CBE 1987; PC 1999; Kt 2004; Highland Park/*The Spectator* Member to Watch 1996; Channel 4 Opposition Politician of the Year 2004; The House Magazine Award 'Opposition Politician of the Year' 2004; D. Univ. (Glasgow) 2001; CBE QC; *Clubs:* Reform; CBE QC; *Recreations:* All sports, theatre, music

Rt Hon Sir Menzies Campbell, MP, House of Commons, London SW1A 0AA *Tel:* 020 7219 4446 *Fax:* 020 7219 0559 *E-mail:* nefifelibdem@cix.co.uk. *Constituency:* 16 Millbank, Cupar, Fife KY15 5EG *Tel:* 01334 656361 *Fax:* 01334 654045

CAMPBELL, RONNIE
Blyth Valley

Lab majority 8,527

Ronnie Campbell. Born 14 August 1943; Son of Ronnie and Edna Campbell; Educated Ridley High School, Blyth; Married Deidre McHale 1967 (5 sons, including twins 1 daughter). Miner 1958-86; NUM Lodge Secretary, Bates Colliery, Blyth 1982-86; NUM Sponsored MP; Councillor: Blyth Borough Council 1969-74, Blyth Valley Council 1974-88

House of Commons: Member for Blyth Valley since 11 June 1987 general election Chair, Northern Regional Group of Labour MPs 1999-. *Recreations:* Furniture restoration, stamp collecting, antiques

Ronnie Campbell, MP, House of Commons, London SW1A 0AA *Tel:* 020 7219 4216 *Fax:* 020 7219 4358 *E-mail:* ronniecampbellmp@btconnect.com. *Constituency:* 42 Renwick Road, Blyth, Northumberland NE24 2LQ *Tel:* 01670 363050; 01670 355192 *Fax:* 01670 363050

CARMICHAEL, ALISTAIR
Orkney and Shetland

Alistair (Alexander Morrison) Carmichael. Born 15 July 1965; Son of Alexander Calder Carmichael, farmer and Mina, née McKay; Educated Islay High School, Argyll; Aberdeen University: Scots law: (LLB 1992), (Dip LP 1993); Married Kathryn Jane Eastham 1987 (2 sons). Hotel manager 1984-89; Procurator fiscal depute Procurator Fiscal Service 1993-96; Solicitor private practice 1996-2001

Lib Dem majority
6,627

House of Commons: Contested Paisley South 1987 general election. Member for Orkney and Shetland since 7 June 2001 general election; Scottish Liberal Democrat Spokesperson on the Energy Review 2001-02; Liberal Democrat Deputy Spokesperson for: Northern Ireland 2002-, Home Affairs 2004-. *Political interests:* Transport, Agriculture, Fishing Industry, Criminal Justice, Energy

Member Liberal Democrat Federal Policy Committee 2004-. RNLI; Elder Church of Scotland 1995-; Director, Solicitors Will Aid (Scotland) Ltd; *Recreations:* Amateur dramatics, music

Alistair Carmichael, MP, House of Commons, London SW1A 0AA
Tel: 020 7219 8307 *Fax:* 020 7219 1787 *E-mail:* carmichaela@parliament.uk.
Constituency: Orkney:, 31 Broad Street, Kirkwall KW15 1DH *Tel:* 01856 876541
Fax: 01856 876162, Shetland:, 171 Commercial Street, Lerwick ZE1 0HX
Tel: 01595 690044

CARSWELL, DOUGLAS
Harwich

Douglas Carswell. Born 3 May 1971; Educated Charterhouse School, Godalming, Surrey; University of East Anglia (BA history 1993); King's College, London (MA 1994); Single. Corporate affairs manager, satellite television broadcaster, Italy 1997-99; Chief project officer INVESCO Asset Management 1999-2003

Con majority 920

House of Commons: Contested Sedgefield 2001 general election. Member for Harwich since 5 May 2005 general election. *Political interests:* Crime and policing, immigration, Britain's independence, education, NHS reform, local government finance reform, decentralisation

Press officer Conservative Central Office 1997; Policy Unit Conservative Party 2004-. *Publications: Direct Democracy*, 2002;*Paying for Localism*, 2004; *Clubs:* Clacton Conservative

Douglas Carswell, MP, House of Commons, London SW1A 0AA
Tel: 020 7219 8397. *Constituency:* 84 Station Road, Clacton-on-Sea,
Essex CO15 1SB *E-mail:* douglas.carswell@email.com
Website: www.harwichconservatives.com

If the UK is serious about tackling climate change it will grid connect Scotland's islands

Scotland's island regions could be connected to the UK electrical transmission grid at an annual cost of a few pence on the average domestic electricity consumer's bill.

With a capacity factor of over 50%, Burradale Windfarm in Shetland is probably the most productive windfarm in the world.

As Scotland's Northern and Western Isles command the UK's best renewable energy resources, this small outlay would provide the consumer with an astonishing level of return. The wind energy resources of Shetland and the Western Isles are amongst the best in the world. Cable connections to the Scottish Mainland are required to deliver this resource and would also provide the infrastructure necessary to facilitate the future exploitation of the Isles' equally impressive marine energy resource.

Wind energy is often criticised for being intermittent and needing back-up power sources. The geographical location of Scotland's islands means that the wind more-often-than-not blows there when the Mainland is calm and sometimes vice-versa. This means wind energy from one region can effectively provide a substantial part of the support needed to balance and maximise the integration of wind energy elsewhere in the UK.

The superior "load factors" or output efficiencies of turbines in the islands also gives more plentiful power for actual use. 2MW installed in the Islands can produce as much power over time as 3MW installed elsewhere. The development and connection of these world-class sources of green, renewable energy would add to the diversity and geographic spread of production, enhance the security of supply to the nation and ease growing development pressure in other more populous areas.

For the communities, local involvement and/or stake holdings can enhance the economic prosperity of the host regions and give a foundation for genuine community participation in, and acceptance of, large-scale windfarm developments.

In the Western Isles over 1350 MW is proposed mainly around AMEC's 700MW Barvas Moor project, Beinn Mhor Power's 400MW Muaith Eabhal Project and Scottish & Southern Energy's 250MW Pairc project.

In Shetland SSE has another 250MW project and Viking Energy Ltd has been established to develop a 300MW windfarm controlled by the Shetland community. Shetland has successfully accommodated Europe's largest oil terminal for the last 26 years and the unique Viking Energy concept hopes to replicate that success.

For the nation, the combined annual windfarm outputs from the two island groups plus Orkney would approach an astonishing 7,000 GW hours. This is equivalent to the domestic needs of 3.58 million people or 65% of Scotland's population. The combined outputs would provide 19.52% of the UK government's 10.4% renewable energy target for 2010 and would exceed the Scottish Executive's equivalent 18% target.

The combined outputs would importantly save 6.02 million tonnes of CO_2 emissions every year and could significantly improve the economics of those already approved UK grid upgrades.

The UK has been blessed with two island groups with pro-active local authorities seeking to supply over 2GW of power from clean, green, renewable energy.

The Government has recognised the contribution the islands can make in the recent announcement of its intention to cap transmission charges for island connections. This intention now needs to be delivered in a meaningful way.

Scotland's island communities want to make a huge contribution to the country's renewables targets. The Government needs to wake up to the vast resource on its doorstep and show leadership in making its delivery a reality.

**For further information contact
aaron.priest@sic.shetland.gov.uk
or dmckim@cne-siar.gov.uk**

CASH, WILLIAM
Stone

William Cash. Born 10 May 1940; Son of Paul Cash, MC (killed in action, 1944); Educated Stonyhurst College; Lincoln College, Oxford (MA); Married Bridget Mary Lee 1965 (2 sons 1 daughter). Solicitor, William Cash & Company

House of Commons: Member for Stafford 1984-97, and for Stone since 1 May 1997 general election; Shadow Attorney General 2001-03. *Political interests:* European Union, Trade and Industry, Media, Small Businesses, Heritage, Africa, Debt Relief. East Africa, Europe

Con majority 9,089

Chair, Friends of Bruges Group in the House of Commons 1989-. Member, Standing Committees on: Financial Services 1985-86, Banking 1986-87; Founder and Chair, The European Foundation; *Publications: Against a Federal Europe,* 1991; *Europe – The Crunch,* 1992; *AEA – The Associated European Area,* 2000; *Clubs:* Beefsteak, Carlton, Vincent's (Oxford); Secretary, Lords and Commons Cricket Club 1988-92; *Recreations:* Local history, cricket, jazz

William Cash, MP, House of Commons, London SW1A 0AA *Tel:* 020 7219 6330 *Fax:* 020 7219 3935. *Constituency:* 50 High Street, Stone, Staffordshire ST15 8AU *Tel:* 01785 811000 *Fax:* 01785 811000

CATON, MARTIN
Gower

Martin Philip Caton. Born 15 June 1951; Son of William John Caton and Pauline Joan Caton, retired shopkeepers; Educated Newport (Essex) Grammar School; Norfolk School of Agriculture; Aberystwyth College of Further Education (National Certificate in Agriculture, Higher National Certificate in Applied Biology); Married Bethan Evans 1996 (2 step daughters). Agriculture research, Welsh Plant Breeding Station, Aberystwyth 1972-84; Political researcher to David Morris MEP 1984-97; Member, GMB; Former Section Treasurer/Membership Secretary, IPCS; Councillor: Mumbles Community Council 1986-90, Swansea City Council 1988-95, City and County of Swansea 1995-97

Lab majority 6,703

House of Commons: Member for Gower since 1 May 1997 general election. *Political interests:* Environment, Planning, Education, European Union

Member: Socialist Environmental Resources Association, Socialist Health Association, Welsh Regional Group of Labour MPs, Former Vice-chair, Chair 2002-. *Recreations:* Reading, walking, theatre, thinking about gardening

Martin Caton, MP, House of Commons, London SW1A 0AA *Tel:* 020 7219 5111 *E-mail:* catonm@parliament.uk. *Constituency:* 26 Pontardulais Road, Gorseinon, Swansea, West Glamorgan SA4 4FE *Tel:* 01792 892100 *Fax:* 01792 892375

CAWSEY, IAN
Brigg and Goole

Ian Cawsey. Born 14 April 1960; Son of Arthur Henry Cawsey and Edith Morrison Cawsey; Educated Wintringham School; Married Linda Mary Kirman 1987 (1 son 2 daughters). Computing/IT work Imperial Foods and Seven Seas Health Care 1977-87 Personal assistant to Elliot Morley, MP 1987-97; Member: ISTC, GMB; Councillor, Humberside County Council 1989-96; Chair, Humberside Police Authority 1993-97; Leader, North Lincolnshire Council 1995-97

Lab majority 2,894

House of Commons: Member for Brigg and Goole since 1 May 1997 general election; Assistant Government Whip 2005-; PPS to: Lord Williams of Mostyn as Leader of the House of Lords 2001-02, David Miliband as: Minister of State, Department for Education and Skills 2002-04, Minister for the Cabinet Office 2005. *Political interests:* Police, Local and Regional Government, Animal Welfare. Poland

Member Fabian Society. Vice-President: Federation of Economic Development Authorities (FEDA), Broughton Ex-Servicemen's Association, Brigg Town FC; President, Goole AFC; Trustee, Jerry Green Foundation 2004-; *Clubs:* Kinsley Labour, Ashby Mill Road, Old Goole Working Men's Club; Brigg Town FC; *Recreations:* Football, playing in local 60s band 'The Moggies', playing in MP Band MP4

Ian Cawsey, MP, House of Commons, London SW1A 0AA *Tel:* 020 7219 5237 *Fax:* 020 7219 3047 *E-mail:* cawseyi@parliament.uk. *Constituency:* 7 Market Place, Brigg, Humberside DN20 8HA *Tel:* 01652 651327; 01405 767744 *Fax:* 01652 657132; 01405 767733

CHALLEN, COLIN
Morley and Rothwell

Colin Robert Challen. Born 12 June 1953; Son of Grenfell Stephen William Challen, quarry manager and Helen Mary Challen, neé Swift; Educated Norton Secondary School; Malton Grammar School; Hull University (BA philosophy 1982); Single. RAF 1971-74. Supplier accountant RAF 1971-74; Postman Post Office 1974-78; Printer and publisher self-employed 1982-94; Marketing development worker Humberside Co-operative Development Agency 1991-93; GPMU; Member GMB; Hull City Council: Councillor 1986-94, Labour group secretary 1991-94

Lab majority 12,343

House of Commons: Contested Beverley 1992 general election. Member for Morley and Rothwell since 7 June 2001 general election. *Political interests:* Economy, Environment, Pensions. Canada

Member Co-operative Party 1994-; Organiser Labour Party 1994-2000; Socialist Environment Resources Association (SERA) 1995-; Secretary: Morley South Labour Party 1998-2001, Leeds Co-operative Party 2000-;. *Publications: Price of Power: The Secret Funding of the Tory Party*, Vision London 1998; *Recreations:* Writing, art, rambling

Colin Challen, MP, House of Commons, London SW1A 0AA *Tel:* 020 7219 8260. *Constituency:* 2 Commercial Street, Morley, West Yorkshire LS27 8HY *Tel:* 0113 238 1312

Lab majority 3,724

CHAPMAN, BEN
Wirral South

Ben (James Keith) Chapman. Born 8 July 1940; Son of John Hartley and Elsie Vera Chapman; Educated Appleby Grammar School, Westmorland; Divorced (3 daughters); married Maureen Ann Byrne 1999. Pilot Officer, RAFVR 1959-61. Civil Servant: Ministry of Pensions and National Insurance 1958-62, Ministry of Aviation/BAA 1962-67, Rochdale Committee of Inquiry into Shipping 1967-70, Board of Trade 1970-74; First Secretary (Commercial) High Commission, Dar es Salaam, Tanzania 1974-78; First Secretary (Economic), High Commission, Accra, Ghana 1978-81; Assistant Secretary, Department of Trade and Industry 1981-87; Commercial Counsellor, Peking Embassy 1987-90; DTI North West: Director Merseyside and Deputy Regional Director 1991-93, Director Trade and Industry and Regional Director 1993-95; Director: On the Waterfront (Manchester) Ltd 1995-96, China Business Links Ltd 1995-97; Founder Consultant, Ben Chapman Associates 1995-97; Partner, The Pacific Practice 1996-97; Former Member, FDA; Member: UNISON, MSF, Amicus

House of Commons: Member for Wirral South since 27 February 1997 by-election; PPS to Richard Caborn: as Minister of State, Department of the Environment, Transport and the Regions (Minister for the Regions, Regeneration and Planning) 1997-99, as Minister of State, Department of Trade and Industry 1999-2001, as Minister of State (Minister for Sport), Department for Culture, Media and Sport 2001-. *Political interests:* Economic Development, Regional Development, Trade and Industry, Foreign Affairs. China, Pacific Rim, Turkey, Vietnam, Cuba

Fellow, Industry and Parliament Trust; *Recreations:* Opera, theatre, music, reading, walking

Ben Chapman, MP, House of Commons, London SW1A 0AA *Tel:* 020 7219 1143 *Fax:* 020 7219 1179 *E-mail:* chapmanb@parliament.uk. *Constituency:* 52 Bebington Road, New Ferry, Merseyside CH62 5BH *Tel:* 0151-643 8797 *Fax:* 0151-643 8546 *Website:* www.ben-chapman.org

Lab majority 2,926

CHAYTOR, DAVID
Bury North

David Michael Chaytor. Born 3 August 1949; Educated Bury Grammar School; London University (BA 1970, MPhil 1979); Leeds University (PGCE 1976); Married (1 son 2 daughters). Various lecturing posts 1973-82; Senior staff tutor, Manchester College of Adult Education 1983-90; Head, Department of Continuing Education, Manchester College of Arts and Technology 1990-97; Member, TGWU; Councillor, Calderdale Council 1982-97, Chair: Education Committee, Highways Committee, Economic Development Committee

House of Commons: Contested Calder Valley 1987 and 1992 general elections. Member for Bury North since 1 May 1997 general election. *Political interests:* Environment, Education, International Development, Transport. France, Albania, USA, Kazakhstan, Kirghizstan, Cameroon

Clubs: Rochdale Labour; Bury FC supporters club; *Recreations:* Walking, cycling, restoration of old buildings

David Chaytor, MP, House of Commons, London SW1A 0AA *Tel:* 020 7219 6625 *Fax:* 020 7219 0952 *E-mail:* chaytord@parliament.uk. *Constituency:* Bury North Constituency Labour Party, 14A Market Street, Bury, Greater Manchester BL9 0AJ *Tel:* 0161-764 2023 *Fax:* 0161-763 3410

CHOPE, CHRISTOPHER
Christchurch

Christopher Chope. Born 19 May 1947; Son of late Judge Robert Chope and of Pamela Chope, née Durell; Educated St Andrew's School, Eastbourne; Marlborough College; St Andrew's University (LLB 1970); Married Christine Mary Hutchinson 1987 (1 son 1 daughter). Barrister, Inner Temple 1972; Consultant, Ernst and Young 1992-98; Councillor, London Borough Wandsworth 1974-83, Chair, Housing Committee 1978-79, Leader of the Council 1979-83

Con majority 15,559

House of Commons: Member for Southampton Itchen 1983-92, and for Christchurch since 1 May 1997 general election; Opposition Spokesperson for: the Environment, Transport and the Regions 1997-98, Trade and Industry 1998-99, the Treasury 2001-02; PPS to Peter Brooke, as Minister of State, HM Treasury 1986; Parliamentary Under-Secretary of State: at Department of the Environment 1986-90, at Department of Transport (Minister for Roads and Traffic) 1990-92; Shadow Minister for: Transport 2002-03, Environment and Transport 2003-

Member, Executive Committee, Society of Conservative Lawyers 1983-86; Vice-Chair, Conservative Party 1997-98. Member: Health and Safety Commission 1992-97, Local Government Commission for England 1994-95; OBE 1982

Christopher Chope, MP, House of Commons, London SW1A 0AA
Tel: 020 7219 5808. *Constituency:* 18a Bargates, Christchurch, Dorset BH23 1QL
Tel: 01202 474949 *Fax:* 01202 475548 *E-mail:* jjamieson@conservatives.com

CLAPHAM, MICHAEL
Barnsley West and Penistone

Michael Clapham. Born 15 May 1943; Son of late Thomas Clapham, miner and Eva Ellen Clapham, née Winterbottom; Educated Darton Secondary Modern School; Barnsley Technical College; Leeds Polytechnic (BSc sociology 1973); Leeds University (PGCE 1974); Bradford University (MPhil industrial relations 1990); Married Yvonne Hallsworth 1965 (1 son 1 daughter). Miner 1958-69; Lecturer trade union studies, Whitwood FE College, Castleford 1974-77; Deputy Head, Comp Dept,

Lab majority 11,314

Yorkshire Area NUM 1977-83; Head, Industrial Relations NUM 1983-92; NUM: Member 1958-, Claims Officer 1977-83, Head, Industrial Relations Department 1983-; Member, UCATT 1994-; Chair: Barnsley Crime Prevention Partnership 1995-, Barnsley MAP- Anti-Racist Strategy Body; Hon Vice-President IOSH

House of Commons: Member for Barnsley West and Penistone since 9 April 1992 general election; PPS to Alan Milburn as Minister of State, Department of Health May-November 1997 (resigned over benefit cuts). *Political interests:* Coal Industry, Energy, Employment, Health, NATO, Eastern Europe. Tibet, Nepal, South Africa, Egypt, Bahrain, Eastern Europe

Member, Co-operative Party; Secretary, Higham Labour Party Branch 1981-83; Treasurer, Barnsley West and Penistone Constituency Labour Party 1983-92; Chair, Dodworth Labour Party Branch 1984-86. Member NATO Parliamentary Assembly 2000-; *Publications: The Case was made for Coal*, 1993 R Caherne; *The Miners and Clause IV*, 1994, Miners' Parliamentary Group; *Clubs:* Gilroyd Social Club; Dodworth Welfare Club; Wortley Hall; *Recreations:* Walking, gardening, reading

Michael Clapham, MP, House of Commons, London SW1A 0AA
Tel: 020 7219 0477 *Fax:* 020 7219 5015 *E-mail:* claphamm@parliament.uk.
Constituency: 18 Regent Street, Barnsley, South Yorkshire S70 2HG
Tel: 01226 731244 *Fax:* 01226 731259

FIRE BRIGADES UNION
PARLIAMENTARY GROUP

Our new Parliamentary Group aims to give a clearer and stronger voice to those who work in the fire service and the communities we serve

Key issues:

★ Campaign for national standards to underpin local fire and rescue plans

★ NO2 Fire Deaths campaign

★ Fight against regionalisation of emergency fire control rooms

★ Need to recruit more firefighters working the retained duty system

★ Fire service pensions ★ Health and safety

★ Professional fire service issues ★ Tackling assaults on firefighters

Chair Andrew Dismore MP
Vice-Chair Michael Clapham MP
Secretary John McDonnell MP

General Secretary: Matt Wrack · President: Ruth Winters

Fire Brigades Union
Bradley House
68 Coombe Road
Kingston Upon Thames
KT2 7AE
020 8541 1765
www.fbu.org.uk
info@fbu.org.uk

CLAPPISON, JAMES
Hertsmere

James Clappison. Born 14 September 1956; Son of late Leonard Clappison, farmer, and Dorothy Clappison; Educated St Peter's School, York; The Queen's College, Oxford (BA philosophy, politics and economics 1978); Married Helen Margherita Carter 1984 (1 son 3 daughters). Barrister 1981-; Contested Yorkshire South 1989 European Parliament election

Con majority 11,093

House of Commons: Contested Barnsley East 1987 general election, Bootle May and November 1990 by-elections. Member for Hertsmere since 9 April 1992 general election; Opposition Spokesperson for: Home Affairs (Crime, Immigration and Asylums) 1997-99, Education and Employment 1999-2000, Treasury 2000-01; PPS to Baroness Blatch: as Minister of State, Department for Education 1992-94, Home Office 1994-95; Parliamentary Under-Secretary of State, Department of the Environment 1995-97; Shadow Financial Secretary, HM Treasury 2000-01; Shadow Minister for Work 2001-02; Shadow Minister for the Treasury 2002. *Political interests:* Home Affairs, Economic Policy, Health, Education. Israel

Clubs: United Oxford and Cambridge University, Carlton; *Recreations:* Bridge, walking

James Clappison, MP, House of Commons, London SW1A 0AA
Tel: 020 7219 5027 *E-mail:* clappisonj@parliament.uk. *Constituency:* 104 High Street, London Colney, St Albans, Hertfordshire AL2 1QL *Tel:* 01727 828221 *Fax:* 01727 828044 *Website:* www.tory-herts.org

CLARK, GREG
Tunbridge Wells

Greg Clark. Born 1967; Married to Helen. Boston Consulting Group; Chief adviser, commercial policy BBC; Special adviser Ian Lang MP 1996-97; Director of policy Conservative Party 2001-

House of Commons: Member for Tunbridge Wells since 5 May 2005 general election. *Political interests:* Law and order, social deprivation, transport, health, housing development

Con majority 9,988

Greg Clark, MP, House of Commons, London SW1A 0AA *Tel:* 020 7219 6977. *Constituency:* Tunbridge Wells Conservative Association, 84 London Road, Tunbridge Wells, Kent TN1 1EA *Tel:* 01892 522581 *Fax:* 01892 522582 *E-mail:* greg@gregclark.co.uk *Website:* www.twconservatives.com

CLARK, KATY
North Ayrshire and Arran

Katy Clark. Born 3 July 1967. Solicitor; Head of membership legal services, UNISON; UNISON

House of Commons: Contested Galloway and Upper Nithsdale 2001 general election. Member for North Ayrshire and Arran since 5 May 2005 general election. *Political interests:* Policy development, equality, human rights

Lab majority 11,296

Katy Clark, MP, House of Commons, London SW1A 0AA *Tel:* 020 7219 4113. *Constituency:* Agent: Donald Reid, 7 Braehead Place, Saltcoats KA21 5LB *E-mail:* katy.clark@unison.co.uk

Lab majority 254

CLARK, PAUL
Gillingham

Paul Gordon Clark. Born 29 April 1957; Son of Gordon Thomas Clark, retired journalist, and of Sheila Gladys Clark, former Mayor of Gillingham; Educated Gillingham Grammar School; Keele University (BA economics and politics 1980); University of Derby (DMS 1997); Married Julie Hendrick 1980 (1 son 1 daughter). Centre manager, Trades Union Congress, National Education Centre 1986-97; AEEU: researcher to President and education officer 1980-86; Member: TUC, Amicus (Gillingham Branch); Councillor, Gillingham Borough Council 1982-90, Labour Group Leader 1988-90, Board Member of Thames Gateway Kent Partnership 2000-; Board Member Groundwork Medway/Swale 2001-

House of Commons: Contested Gillingham 1992 general election. Member for Gillingham since 1 May 1997 general election; Assistant Government Whip 2003-05; Joint PPS to Lord Irvine of Lairg as Lord Chancellor 1999-2001; PPS to Lord Falconer of Thoroton as Minister of State: Department for Transport, Local Government and the Regions 2001-02, Home Office 2002-03. *Political interests:* Education, Transport, Environment, Regeneration. Europe, Eastern Europe, South East Asia

Member: European Standing Committee A 1998, European Standing Committee B 1998-2000; *Clubs:* Anchorians Association; *Recreations:* Historic buildings, reading

Paul Clark, MP, House of Commons, London SW1A 0AA *Tel:* 020 7219 5207 *Fax:* 020 7219 2545 *E-mail:* clarkp@parliament.uk. *Constituency:* 62A Watling Street, Gillingham, Kent ME7 2YN *Tel:* 01634 574261 *Fax:* 01634 574276

Lab majority 3,653

CLARKE, CHARLES
Norwich South

Charles Rodway Clarke. Born 21 September 1950; Son of late Sir Richard Clarke, KCB, and Lady Brenda Clarke; Educated Highgate School, London; King's College, Cambridge (BA maths and economics 1973); Married Carol Pearson 1984 (2 sons). Part-time adult education maths lecturer, City Literary Institute 1981-83; Organiser, Community Challenge Conference, Gulbenkian Fund 1981-82; Researcher to Neil Kinnock, MP 1981-83; Chief of Staff to Neil Kinnock, MP 1983-92; Chief Executive, Quality Public Affairs 1992-97; Sabbatical President, Cambridge Students' Union 1971-72; Member, National Union of Students' Executive, President 1975-77; Councillor, London Borough of Hackney 1980-86, Chair, Housing Committee, Vice-Chair, Economic Development

House of Commons: Member for Norwich South since 1 May 1997 general election; Parliamentary Under-Secretary of State (School Standards), Department for Education and Employment 1998-99; Minister of State, Home Office 1999-2001; Labour Party Chair and Minister without Portfolio 2001-02; Secretary of State for Education and Skills 2002-04; Home Secretary 2004-

Chairman Labour Party Donations Committee 2002-. PC 2001; *Clubs:* Norwich Labour; *Recreations:* Chess, reading, walking

Rt Hon Charles Clarke, MP, House of Commons, London SW1A 0AA *Tel:* 020 7219 1194 *Fax:* 020 7219 0526. *Constituency:* Norwich Labour Party, 59 Bethel Street, Norwich NR2 1NL *Tel:* 01603 219902 *Fax:* 01603 663502

Prison Service succeeds in accessing further ESF Equal funding to research effective resettlement of offenders

Six years ago the Prison Service, North West Area, accessed European Social Funds for the first time and began to test for effective methods of working in resettling offenders in custody, trialling new and innovative approaches of working in partnership with other organisations in the prisons and in the communities.

The success of this project led the partnership to identify other research opportunities and in 2001, IMPACT (Innovation Means Prisons and Communities Together) first accessed ESF Equal funding to research and test for change, piloting new multi agency systems, to ensure that relevant professionals work with offenders at the appropriate stage. A second objective was to research stereotypical views of employers, designing and testing methods to increase the prospect of sustainable employment and then working with employers to combat discrimination and the barriers faced in the workplace. From the research, it has again been recognised that researching and testing new structures and systems is vital if we are to achieve the best that is possible with each individual offender and thereby the best prospect of reducing re offending, fewer victims and the opportunity to build safer communities

Clearly offenders cannot be treated as one group given the different offences and differing age and backgrounds. Inevitably there are offenders who are doubly disadvantaged in finding and sustaining employment, largely due to the stereotypical views of many employers; particularly for women, those with mental ill health, black and minority ethnic groups, those over 50 years of age and sex offenders.

In the next three years, IMPACT will use the new funding from EQUAL to test for change in those areas of double disadvantage, using action research to enable empowerment of offenders in custody, especially in those aspects that require offenders to take responsibility for the future for themselves and the communities in which they live.

The main themes for IMPACT will be to research current practice and test for change in the way in which we resettle:

- Women prisoners in custody, especially at the point of release and in the risk period, immediately post release
- Black and minority ethnic offenders in custody and immediately post release, testing for equality of opportunity
- Offenders over 50 years of age, empowering offenders to work with employers to test for change
- Juveniles and young offenders, testing for change through effective case management systems and supportive networks post release
- Sex offenders – creating business opportunities for those properly assessed within risk assessment procedures and motivated for training into self employment

The research will again be led by the Prison Service and will continue to use a multi agency approach, bringing together organisations from statutory, voluntary and private sector to develop those new approaches.

Key to this is the role of employers, trainers and educationalist. During the last three years the role of employers in the project has grown considerably and we now have large national employers working with us alongside medium and small employers. Employer involvement includes trialling new training systems pre release, providing individual training and employment placements pre and post release, working in pre release courses and business mentoring (for those offenders entering self employment).

Others, working in criminal justice in the EU, face similar problems in resettling offenders. IMPACT will continue to work with professionals in the EU to develop joint trials, undertaking parallel development, sharing findings and exchanging practical experiences.

Research findings will be disseminated across the EU with the aspiration that most will be mainstreamed into practice both in the prisons and the wider community, particularly those issues linked to the total economy, which are facing policy makers across the European Union.

For further information please contact:
Shelley Lockett
Tel: 01925 805291
Email: shelley.lockett@hmps.gsi.gov.uk

EUROPEAN UNION
European Social Fund

Con majority 12,974

CLARKE, KENNETH
Rushcliffe

Kenneth Clarke. Born 2 July 1940; Son of late Kenneth Clarke, watchmaker and jeweller, and Doris Clarke; Educated Nottingham High School; Gonville and Caius College, Cambridge (BA, LLB) (President, Cambridge Union 1963); Married Gillian Mary Edwards 1964 (1 son 1 daughter). Called to the Bar 1963; Member, Midland Circuit, practising from Birmingham; QC 1980; Non-executive Deputy Chair, Alliance UniChem 1997-; Director, Foreign & Colonial Investment Trust 1997-; Deputy Chair, British American Tobacco 1998-; Non-executive Chair: British American Racing (Holdings) Limited, Savoy Asset Management PLC; Director, Independent News and Media (UK)

House of Commons: Contested Mansfield Notts 1964 and 1966 general elections. Member for Rushcliffe since 18 June 1970 general election; Opposition Spokesperson for: Social Services 1974-76, Industry 1976-79; Assistant Government Whip 1972-74; Government Whip 1973-74; PPS to Solicitor General 1971-72; Parliamentary Secretary, Ministry of Transport 1979-80; Parliamentary Under-Secretary of State, Department of Transport 1980-82; Minister for Health 1982-85; Paymaster General and Employment Minister 1985-87; Chancellor, Duchy of Lancaster and Minister of Trade and Industry 1987-88; Secretary of State for: Health 1988-90, Education and Science 1990-92; Home Secretary 1992-93, Chancellor of the Exchequer 1993-97

Chair: Cambridge University Conservative Association 1961, Federation Conservative Students 1963-65; Contested leadership June 1997 and 2001. PC 1984; Hon. LLD: Nottingham University 1992, Huddersfield University 1992, Nottingham Trent University 1995; Honorary Fellow, Gonville and Caius College, Cambridge; Bencher, Grays Inn; QC; Liveryman, The Clockmakers Company; QC; *Clubs:* Garrick; QC; *Recreations:* Birdwatching, football, cricket, jazz, Formula 1 motor racing

Rt Hon Kenneth Clarke, MP, House of Commons, London SW1A 0AA
Tel: 020 7219 4528 *Fax:* 020 7219 4841 *E-mail:* clarkek@parliament.uk.
Constituency: Rushcliffe House, 17/19 Rectory Road, West Bridgford, Nottingham, Nottinghamshire NG2 6BE *Tel:* 0115-981 7224 *Fax:* 0115-981 7273

CLARKE, TOM
Coatbridge, Chryston and Bellshill

Thomas Clarke. Born 10 January 1941; Son of late James Clarke; Educated Columba High School, Coatbridge; Scottish College of Commerce. Assistant Director, Scottish Council for Educational Technology (Scottish Film Council) 1966-82; Member, GMB; Councillor: Coatbridge Town Council 1964-74, Monklands District Council 1974-82; Provost of Monklands 1974-82; JP 1972; President, Convention of Scottish Local Authorities 1978-80

Lab majority 19,519

House of Commons: Member for Coatbridge and Airdrie by-election 1982-83, for Monklands West 1983-97, for Coatbridge and Chryston 1997-2005, for Coatbridge, Chryston and Bellshill since 5 May 2005 general election; Principal Opposition Spokesperson for Development and Co-operation 1993-94; Author and Sponsor Disabled Persons (Services, Representation and Consultation) Act 1986; Shadow Minister for UK Personal Social Services 1987-92; Shadow Secretary of State for Scotland 1992-93, for International Development 1993-94; Shadow Cabinet Minister for Disabled People's Rights 1995-97; Minister of State (Film and Tourism), Department of National Heritage/for Culture, Media and Sport 1997-98. *Political interests:* Film Industry, Foreign Affairs, Civil Service, Local and Regional Government. Central America, Philippines, Africa, Asia, Eastern Europe, USA, Peru, South Africa, Indonesia

Disability, International Development, Film; Labour Member PAD Group to Iran, sponsored by Archbishop of Canterbury 1989; Led CPA delegations to Australia 2000; Observer Peruvian election 2001; Led IPU Rwanda 2002; Fellow, Industry and Parliament Trust; *Publications:* Director of award winning amateur film *Give us a Goal*, 1972; Joint chair, film review *A Bigger Picture*, 1998; CBE 1980; PC 1997; CBE; *Clubs:* Coatbridge Municipal Golf; CBE; *Recreations:* Films, walking, reading

Rt Hon Tom Clarke, MP, House of Commons, London SW1A 0AA
Tel: 020 7219 5007 *Fax:* 020 7219 6094 *E-mail:* clarket@parliament.uk.
Constituency: Municipal Buildings, Kildonan Street, Coatbridge ML5 3LF
Tel: 01236 600800 *Fax:* 01236 600808

CLEGG, NICK
Sheffield Hallam

Nicholas Clegg. Born 7 January 1967; Educated Westminster School; social anthropology, Cambridge University (MA 1989); political philosophy, Minnesota University, USA (1990); European affairs, College of Europe, Bruges, Belgium (diploma 1992); Married Miriam Gonzalez Durantez 2000. trainee journalist National Magazine, New York 1990; political consultant GJW Government Relations 1992-93; European Commission: official 1994-96; Adviser to vice-president Sir Leon Brittan European Commission 1996-99. MEP for East Midlands 1999-2004

Lib Dem majority 8,682

House of Commons: Member for Sheffield Hallam since 5 May 2005 general election. *Political interests:* trade and industry, education, globalisation

winner David Thomas prize, Financial Times 1993; *Recreations:* literature, theatre, mountaineering, skiing

Nick Clegg, MP, House of Commons, London SW1A 0AA *Tel:* 020 7219 6657.
Constituency: 85 Nethergreen Road, Sheffield S11 7EH *Tel:* 0114 230 9393
Fax: 0114 230 9614 *E-mail:* nickclegg@sheffieldhallam.org.uk

CLELLAND, DAVID
Tyne Bridge

David Gordon Clelland. Born 27 June 1943; Son of Archibald Clelland and Ellen Clelland, née Butchart; Educated Kelvin Grove Boys School, Gateshead; Gateshead Technical College; Hebburn Technical College; Charles Trevelyan Technical College (City and Guilds and electrical technician courses); Married Maureen Potts 1965 (2 daughters) (divorced). Electrical fitter 1964-81; Local Government Association Secretary 1981-85; AEEU: Shop steward 1967-81; Chair, Gateshead Council Recreation Committee 1976-84; Secretary, Association of Councillors 1981-86; Vice-chair, Gateshead Health Authority 1982-84; Gateshead Borough Council: Councillor 1982-86, Leader 1984-86

Lab majority 10,400

House of Commons: Member for Tyne Bridge since 5 December 1985 by-election; Opposition Whip 1995-97; Assistant Government Whip 1997-2001; Government Whip (Defence, International Development,   North East) 2001; Adviser on Greyhounds to Richard Caborn, as Minister of State for Sport 2002-. *Political interests:* Local and Regional Government, Home Affairs, Transport, Environment, Employment, Energy, Devolution, Constitutional Reform (House of Lords)

Northern Regional Group of Labour MPs: Hon. Secretary and Hon. Treasurer 1992-98, Vice-Chair 1999, Chair 2002-. *Recreations:* Golf, music, reading

David Clelland, MP, House of Commons, London SW1A 0AA *Tel:* 020 7219 3669 *Fax:* 020 7219 0328 *E-mail:* davidclellandmp@aol.com. *Constituency:* 19 Ravensworth Road, Dunston, Gateshead, Tyne and Wear NE11 9AB *Tel:* 01914 200300 *Fax:* 01914 200301

CLIFTON-BROWN, GEOFFREY
Cotswold

Geoffrey Clifton-Brown. Born 23 March 1953; Son of Robert and Elizabeth Clifton-Brown; Educated Eton College; Royal Agricultural College, Cirencester; Married Alexandra Peto-Shepherd 1979 (divorced 2003) (1 son 1 daughter). Graduate estate surveyor, Property Services Agency, Dorchester 1975; Investment surveyor, Jones Lang Wootton 1975-79; Managing director, own farming business in Norfolk 1979-

Con majority 9,688

House of Commons: Member for Cirencester and Tewkesbury 1992-97, and for Cotswold since 1 May 1997 general election; Opposition Spokesperson for: Environment, Food and Rural Affairs 2001, Transport, Local Government and the Regions 2001-02, Local Government, Housing and Planning 2002-03; Opposition Whip 1999-2001, 2004-; PPS to Douglas Hogg as Minister of Agriculture, Fisheries and Food 1995-97; Shadow Minister for: Local Government 2002-03, Local and Devolved Government 2003-04. *Political interests:* Economy, Taxation, Foreign Affairs, Environment, Agriculture. Brazil, France, Italy, China, Hong Kong

Chair, North Norfolk Constituency Association 1986-91. Member: Eastern Area Executive and Agricultural Committees 1986-91; *Publications: Privatisation of the State Pension @nr Secure Funded Provision for all* (Bow Group), 1996; Liveryman, The Worshipful Company of Farmers; Freeman, City of London; *Clubs:* Carlton, Farmers'; *Recreations:* Fishing, other rural pursuits

Geoffrey Clifton-Brown, MP, House of Commons, London SW1A 0AA *Tel:* 020 7219 5147 *Fax:* 020 7219 2550 *E-mail:* cliftonbrowng@parliament.uk. *Constituency:* 7 Rodney Road, Cheltenham, Gloucestershire GL50 1HX *Tel:* 01242 514551 *Fax:* 01242 514949 *Website:* www.cotswoldconservative.co.uk

CLWYD, ANN
Cynon Valley

Ann Clwyd. Born 21 March 1937; Daughter of Gwilym and Elizabeth Lewis; Educated Holywell Grammar School; The Queen's School, Chester; University College of Wales, Bangor; Married Owen Roberts 1963. Journalist; Broadcaster; MEP for Mid and West Wales 1979-84; Member: NUJ, TGWU

House of Commons: Contested Denbigh 1970 and Gloucester October 1974 general elections. Member for Cynon Valley since 3 May 1984 by-election; Opposition Spokesperson for: Employment 1993-94, Foreign Affairs 1994-95; Shadow Minister of Education and Women's Rights 1987-88; Shadow Secretary of State for: International Development 1989-92, Wales July-November 1992, National Heritage 1992-93; Assistant to John Prescott as Deputy Leader of Labour Party 1994-95. *Political interests:* Iraq, Turkey, Iran, Russia, Cambodia, Vietnam, East Timor

Member Labour Party National Executive Committee 1983-84; Chair Tribune Group 1986-87; Member Parliamentary Labour Party Parliamentary Committee 1997-, Deputy Chair 2001-. Member, Arts Council 1975-79; Vice-Chair, Welsh Arts Council 1975-79; Royal Commission on NHS 1976-79; Inter-Parliamentary Union: Executive committee member, British Group, Member, Human Rights Commission; Special Envoy to the Prime Minister on Human Rights in Iraq 2003; White Robe Gorsedd Member of Royal National Eisteddfod of Wales; PC 2004; *Spectator, House Magazine* and Channel Four Backbencher of the Year 2003; Hon. Fellow, University of North Wales; *Recreations:* Walking, boating

Ann Clwyd, MP, House of Commons, London SW1A 0AA *Tel:* 020 7219 6609 *Fax:* 020 7219 5943 *E-mail:* clwyda@parliament.uk. *Constituency:* 6 Dean Court, Aberdare, Mid Glamorgan CF44 7BN *Tel:* 01685 871394 *Fax:* 01685 883006

Lab majority 13,259

COAKER, VERNON
Gedling

Vernon Rodney Coaker. Born 17 June 1953; Son of Edwin Coaker; Educated Drayton Manor Grammar School, London; Warwick University (BA politics 1974); Trent Polytechnic (PGCE 1976); Married Jacqueline Heaton 1978 (1 son 1 daughter). Humanities teaching in Nottinghamshire: Manvers School 1976-82, Arnold Hill School 1982-89, Bramcote Park School 1989-95, Big Wood School 1995-97; Member: NUT, AEEU; Councillor, Rushcliffe Borough Council 1983-97

House of Commons: Member for Gedling since 1 May 1997 general election; Assistant Government Whip 2003-; PPS to: Stephen Timms: as Minister of State, Department of Social Security 1999, as Financial Secretary, HM Treasury 1999-2001, as Minister of State for School Standards, Department for Education and Skills 2001-02, as Minister of State for e-Commerce, Department of Trade and Industry 2002, Estelle Morris as Secretary of State for Education and Skills 2002, Tessa Jowell as Secretary of State for Culture, Media and Sport 2002-03. *Political interests:* Environment, Education, Welfare Reform, Foreign Policy, Sport. France, Kosovo, Macedonia, Angola

UNICEF; Member, European Standing Committee B 1998; *Recreations:* Sport, walking

Vernon Coaker, MP, House of Commons, London SW1A 0AA *Tel:* 020 7219 6627 *E-mail:* coakerv@parliament.uk. *Constituency:* 2A Parkyn Road, Daybrook, Nottingham, Nottinghamshire NG5 6BG *Tel:* 0115-920 4224 *Fax:* 0115-920 4500

Lab majority 3,811

Lab majority 9,163

COFFEY, ANN
Stockport

Ann Coffey. Born 31 August 1946; Daughter of late John Brown, MBE, Flight-Lieutenant, RAF, and of Marie Brown, nurse; Educated Nairn Academy; Bodmin and Bushey Grammar Schools; Polytechnic of South Bank, London (BSc sociology 1967); Walsall College of Education (Postgraduate Certificate in Education 1971); Manchester University (MSc psychiatric social work 1977); Married 1973 (divorced 1989) (1 daughter); married 1999. Trainee Social Worker, Walsall Social Services 1971-72; Social Worker: Birmingham 1972-73, Gwynedd 1973-74, Wolverhampton 1974-75, Stockport 1977-82, Cheshire 1982-88; Team Leader, Fostering, Oldham Social Services 1988-92; Member, USDAW; Stockport Metropolitan Borough Council: Councillor 1984-92, Leader of Labour Group 1988-92; Member, District Health Authority 1986-90

House of Commons: Contested Cheadle 1987 general election. Member for Stockport since 9 April 1992 general election; Opposition Spokeswoman on Health 1996-97; Opposition Whip 1995-96; Joint PPS to Tony Blair as Prime Minister 1997-98; PPS to Alistair Darling as Secretary of State for: Social Security/Work and Pensions 1998-2002, Transport 2002-, Scotland 2003-. *Political interests:* Children, Health

Recreations: Photography, drawing, cinema, swimming, reading

Ann Coffey, MP, House of Commons, London SW1A 0AA *Tel:* 020 7219 4546 *Fax:* 020 7219 0770 *E-mail:* coffeya@parliament.uk. *Constituency:* 207a Bramhall Lane, Stockport SK2 6JA *Tel:* 0161 483 2600; 0161 432 2188 *Fax:* 0161 483 1070

Lab majority 6,857

COHEN, HARRY
Leyton and Wanstead

Harry Cohen. Born 10 December 1949; Son of Emanuel and Anne Cohen; Educated George Gascoigne Secondary Modern; East Ham Technical College (part-time) Chartered Institute of Public Finance and Accountancy 1974; Birkbeck College, London University (MSc politics and administration 1995); Married Ellen Hussain 1978 (1 stepson 1 stepdaughter). Accountant and auditor, London Borough of Waltham Forest, Hackney and Haringey; Auditor, NALGO; Member, UNISON; Waltham Forest Borough Council: Councillor 1972-83, Chair, Planning Committee 1972-83, Secretary, Labour Group 1972-83; Member, Waltham Forest Area Health Authority 1972-83

House of Commons: Member for Leyton 1983-97, and for Leyton and Wanstead since 1 May 1997 general election. *Political interests:* Defence, Equality, Health, Transport, Ecology and Conservation, Animal Rights. Middle East, Central Europe, Eastern Europe, India, Pakistan, Bangladesh, Tibet

Vice-President, The Royal College of Midwives; Member, UK Delegation to North Atlantic Assembly 1992-; Chair, Sub-Committee for Economic Co-operation and Convergence with Central and Eastern Europe; Reserve, UK delegation to Organisation for Security and Co-operation in Europe 1997-2001; *Recreations:* Part-owner racing greyhound

Harry Cohen, MP, House of Commons, London SW1A 0AA *Tel:* 020 7219 6376; 020 7219 4137 *Fax:* 020 7219 0438 *E-mail:* cohenh@parliament.uk. *Constituency: Website:* www.harrycohen.labour.co.uk

CONNARTY, MICHAEL
Linlithgow and East Falkirk

Lab majority 11,202

Michael Connarty. Born 3 September 1947; Son of late Patrick and Elizabeth Connarty; Educated St Patrick's High School, Coatbridge; Stirling University (BA economics 1972); Glasgow University; Jordanhill College of Education (DCE 1975); Married Margaret Doran 1969 (1 son 1 daughter). President, Student Association, Stirling University 1970-71; Chair, Stirling Economic Development Co. 1987-90; Teacher economics and modern studies (secondary and special needs) 1975-92; Member: TGWU, EIS; Stirling District Council: Councillor 1977-90, Council leader 1980-90; JP 1977-90

House of Commons: Contested Stirling 1983 and 1987 general elections. Member for Falkirk East 1992-2005, for Linlithgow and East Falkirk since 5 May 2005 general election; PPS to Tom Clarke, as Minister of State, Department for Culture, Media and Sport (Film and Tourism) 1997-98. *Political interests:* Economy and Enterprise, International Development, European Union, Industry, Skills and Training, Youth Affairs, Crime, Drug Abuse, Small Businesses. Middle East, Latin America, Australia, USA

Member, Labour Party Scottish Executive Committee 1981-82, 1983-92; Chair, LP Scottish Local Government Committee 1988-90; Member, LP Local Government Committee (UK) 1989-91; Vice-Chair, COSLA Labour Group 1988-90; Chair, Stirlingshire Co-operative Party 1990-92; Vice-Chair, Scottish Group of Labour MPs 1996-98, Chair 1998-99. Board Member, Parliamentary Office of Science and Technology (POST) 1997-; Life Member: International Parliamentary Union 1992-, Commonwealth Parliamentary Association 1992-; British American Parliamentary Group 1992-; *Recreations:* Family, music (jazz and classical), reading, walking

Michael Connarty, MP, House of Commons, London SW1A 0AA

Tel: 020 7219 5071 *Fax:* 020 7219 2541 *E-mail:* connartym@parliament.uk.
Constituency: Room 8, 5 Kerse Road, Grangemouth FK3 8HQ *Tel:* 01324 474832
Fax: 01324 666811

Con majority 9,920

CONWAY, DEREK
Old Bexley and Sidcup

Derek Conway. Born 15 February 1953; Son of Leslie Conway, superintendent of parks and crematoria and Florence Conway, housewife; Educated Beacon Hill Boys' School; Gateshead Technical College; Newcastle upon Tyne Polytechnic; Married Colette Elizabeth Mary Lamb 1980 (2 sons 1 daughter). Territorial Decoration (Territorial Army). Former advertising manager; Regional Director and Principal Organiser National Fund for Research into Crippling Diseases 1974-83; Chief executive Cats Protection League 1998-2003; Member Transport and General Workers Union 1968-71; Gateshead Borough Council 1974-87: Councillor, Deputy group leader 1974-82; Tyne and Wear Metropolitan County Council: Councillor 1977-83, Leader 1979-82, Board Newcastle International Airport 1979-82; Member North of England Development Council 1979-83, Executive Board Washington Development Corporation 1979-83

House of Commons: Contested Durham October 1974, Newcastle upon Tyne East 1979 general elections. MP for Shrewsbury and Atcham 1983-97. Contested Shrewsbury 1997 general election. Member for Old Bexley and Sidcup since 7 June 2001 general election; Assistant government whip 1993-94; Government whip 1993-97; PPS: to Minister of State for Wales 1988-91, to Minister of State for Employment 1992-93. *Political interests:* Territorial Army, Defence, Voluntary Services, Animal Welfare, Foreign Affairs. Morocco, Caribbean

Member National Executive Committee 1971-81; National vice-chair Young Conservatives 1972-74; Member General Purposes Committee 1972-84; Vice-chair Conservative National Local Government Committee 1979-83; Chair: Gateshead Association, Northern Area Young Conservatives; Vice-chair Northern Area Conservatives. Cats Protection, Action for the Crippled Child; Board member Newcastle Airport 1979-82; British Youth Council; Board of Northern Arts; Member Institute of Directors; Inter-Parliamentary Union: Former executive member, Former leader UK delegation, Vice-president 92nd conference, Vice-chair 1991-93, Treasurer 2001-; Member Executive Committee: Commonwealth Parliamentary Association 2001-, British American Parliamentary Association 2001-; Territorial Army decoration; Freeman of City of London; *Recreations:* Walking, historical fiction

Derek Conway, MP, House of Commons, London SW1A 0AA *Tel:* 020 7219 8305 *E-mail:* conwayd@parliament.uk. *Constituency:* 19 Station Road, Sidcup DA15 7EB *Tel:* 020 8300 3471 *Fax:* 020 8300 9270

COOK, FRANK
Stockton North

Frank (Francis) Cook. Born 3 November 1935; Son of late James Cook; Educated Corby School, Sunderland; De La Salle College, Manchester; Institute of Education, Leeds; Married Patricia Lundrigan 1959 (divorced) (1 son 3 daughters). Previously: Schoolmaster, Gravedigger, Butlins Redcoat, Barman, Brewery hand, Gardener, Postman, Steel works transport manager; Construction, planning, field, cost engineer, project manager; Member and Sponsored by MSF

Lab majority 12,437

House of Commons: Member for Stockton North since 9 June 1983 general election; Opposition Whip 1987-92; Deputy Speaker Westminster Hall 1999-2001, 2002-. *Political interests:* Engineering, Peace and Disarmament, Alternative Energy, Expatriate Workers, Pensioners' Rights, Education, Ecology, Race Relations, Landmine Victim Support, Landmine Eradication Measures, Child Protection and Safety, Shooters' Rights. North Korea, South Korea, Turkey, Laos

RSPB; Member: NATO – Parliamentary Assembly 1987-2001, Vice-President 1998-2000; Organisation for Security and Co-operation in Europe Parliamentary Body 1991-2001; Trustee, Lucy Faithfull Foundation (for rehabilitation of sexual offenders); Fellow: Industry and Parliament Trust, Parliamentary Armed Services Trust; *Recreations:* Singing, climbing, fell-walking, swimming, supporting North East football

Frank Cook, MP, House of Commons, London SW1A 0AA *Tel:* 020 7219 4527 *Fax:* 020 7219 4303 *E-mail:* cookf@parliament.uk. *Constituency:* c/o The Health Centre, Queensway, Billingham, Teesside TS23 2LA *Tel:* 01642 643288 *Fax:* 01642 803271

COOK, ROBIN
Livingston

Robin (Robert) Finlayson Cook. Born 28 February 1946; Son of late Peter Cook; Educated Aberdeen Grammar School; Edinburgh University (MA English literature); Married Margaret Whitmore, medical consultant 1969 (2 sons) (divorced 1998); married Gaynor Regan, née Wellings 1998. Tutor-organiser, Workers' Educational Association 1970-74; Edinburgh Town Council: Councillor 1971-74, Chairman, Edinburgh Housing Committee 1973-74

Lab majority 13,097

House of Commons: Contested Edinburgh North 1970 general election. Member for Edinburgh Central 1974-83, for Livingston 1983-2005, for new Livingston since 5 May 2005 general election; Opposition Frontbench Spokesperson for: Treasury and Economic Affairs 1980-83, European and Community Affairs 1983-84; Spokesman on the City 1986-87; Shadow Secretary of State for: Health and Social Security 1987-92, Trade and Industry 1992-94, Foreign and Commonwealth Affairs 1994-97; Chair, NEC of Labour Party 1997; Secretary of State for Foreign and Commonwealth Affairs 1997-2001; Leader of the House of Commons and President of the Council 2001-03. *Political interests:* Welfare, Environment, Defence

Chair, Scottish Association of Labour Student Organisations 1966-67; Secretary, Edinburgh City Labour Party 1970-72; Labour Party Campaign Co-ordinator 1984-86; Former Member: Labour Party National Executive Committee, Labour Party National Policy Forum; Member Parliamentary Labour Party Parliamentary Committee 2001-. Member, House of Commons Commission 2001-03; Member, Executive Committee, Commonwealth Parliamentary Association (CPA) UK Branch 1999-; PC 1996; *The Spectator* Parliamentarian of the Year 1991, Debater of the Year 1996; *Recreations:* Reading, horse racing

Rt Hon Robin Cook, MP, House of Commons, London SW1A 0AA *Tel:* 020 7219 4431. *Constituency:* 4 Newyear Field Farm, Hawk Brae, Ladywell, Livingston EH54 6TW *Tel:* 01506 497961

Lab majority 6,084

COOPER, ROSIE
West Lancashire

Rosie Cooper. Born 5 September 1950; single. Concept Design Partnership & W Cooper Limited 1973-80; The Littlewoods Organisation 1980-2001: merchandiser 1980-92, (secondment as Lord Mayor of Liverpool 1992-93), PR manager 1994-95; group corporate communications manager 1995-99, project co-ordinator 1999-2001; member and vice-chair Liverpool Health Authority 1994-96; chair Women's Hospital 1996-2005; Equal Opportunities Commission 2001; board member Cosmopolitan Housing Association; director Merseyside Centre for Deaf People; trustee Roy Castle Foundation; Governor of several primary and secondary schools; USDAW; Lord Mayor of Liverpool 1992-93

House of Commons: Contested Liverpool Broadgreen 1992 general election. Member for West Lancashire since 5 May 2005 general election; Liverpool City Councillor 1973-2000; Lord Mayor, Liverpool 1992-93; Labour housing spokesperson Liverpool City Council 1999-2000; Labour candidate in 2004 European Parliament election for North West region

Recreations: theatre, music, cinema, community affairs

Rosie Cooper, MP, House of Commons, London SW1A 0AA *Tel:* 020 7219 5690. *Constituency:* *E-mail:* mick@jefferys106.freeserve.co.uk, *E-mail:* rosie.cooper@btinternet.com

Lab majority 15,246

COOPER, YVETTE
Pontefract and Castleford

Yvette Cooper. Born 20 March 1969; Daughter of Tony and June Cooper; Educated Eggars Comprehensive; Balliol College, Oxford (BA philosophy, politics and economics 1990); Harvard University (Kennedy Scholar 1991); London School of Economics (MSc economics 1995); Married Ed Balls 1998 (1 daughter 1 son). Economic researcher for John Smith MP 1990-92; Domestic policy specialist, Bill Clinton presidential campaign 1992; Policy adviser to Labour Treasury teams 1992-94; Economic columnist/Leader writer, *The Independent* 1995-97; Member, TGWU, GMB

House of Commons: Member for Pontefract and Castleford since 1 May 1997 general election; Parliamentary Under-Secretary of State for Public Health, Department of Health 1999-2002; Parliamentary Secretary, Lord Chancellor's Department 2002-03; Office of the Deputy Prime Minister: Parliamentary Under-Secretary of State 2003-05, Minister of State (Minister for Housing and Planning) 2005-. *Political interests:* Unemployment, Coal Industry, Poverty, Equal Opportunities. USA

Recreations: Swimming, painting, watching West Wing between Disney videos

Yvette Cooper, MP, House of Commons, London SW1A 0AA *Tel:* 020 7219 5080 *Fax:* 020 7219 0912 *E-mail:* coopery@parliament.uk. *Constituency:* 2 Wesley Street, Castleford, West Yorkshire WF10 1AE *Tel:* 01977 553388 *Fax:* 01977 551981

Anyone can do affordable housing

Like anything else, the provision of affordable housing can be learned over time. We should know. For over 100 years we have concentrated on nothing else. In fact, with a current development programme in excess of £420 million throughout the South East, and an allocation of over £25 million per year to the maintenance of our existing homes, you could say we know quite a lot. That's not to say that others can't learn too - it just depends whether you want to be part of their learning curve. To find out more about Southern Housing Group, visit **www.shgroup.org.uk** or call us on **08456 120 021**.

Southern Housing Group, Fleet House, 59-61 Clerkenwell Road, London EC1M 5LA

Southern Housing Group is a charitable housing association. Industrial & Provident Societies no: 27412R

SHGAD.CN.04/05.019

CORBYN, JEREMY
Islington North

Jeremy Corbyn. Born 26 May 1949; Son of David Benjamin and Naomi Loveday Jocelyn Corbyn; Educated Adams Grammar School, Newport, Shropshire; (3 sons); Former full-time organiser, National Union of Public Employees; Also worked for Tailor and Garment workers and AUEW; NUPE sponsored MP; Member, RMT Parliamentary Campaigning Group 2002-; Councillor, Haringey Borough Council 1974-84: Chair: Community Development 1975-78, Public Works 1978-79, Planning 1980-81

Lab majority 6,716

House of Commons: Member for Islington North since 9 June 1983 general election. *Political interests:* People of Islington, Defence, Welfare State, NHS, Campaigning for Socialism in the Community and against Racism, Anti-Imperialism and Internationalism, Transport Safety, Environment, Irish Affairs, Liberation Islington Local Agenda 21

Recreations: Running, railways

Jeremy Corbyn, MP, House of Commons, London SW1A 0AA *Tel:* 020 7219 3545. *Constituency:* 213a Blackstock Road, London N5 2LL *Tel:* 020 7226 5775 *Website:* www.northislington.freeserve.co.uk

COUSINS, JIM
Newcastle upon Tyne Central

James MacKay Cousins. Born 23 February 1944; Son of late Charles John Cousins, printing trade worker, and late Grace Ellen Cousins; Educated New College, Oxford; London School of Economics; Married Anne Elizabeth (2 sons, 1 stepson, 1 stepdaughter). Industrial relations and research worker in industry 1967-72; Research worker, urban affairs and city labour markets 1972-82; Lecturer, Sunderland Polytechnic 1982-87; Amicus-MSF; Councillor, Wallsend Borough Council 1969-73; Tyne and Wear County Council: Councillor 1973-86, Deputy leader 1981-86

Lab majority 3,982

House of Commons: Member for Newcastle upon Tyne Central since 11 June 1987 general election; Opposition Spokesperson for: Trade and Industry 1992-94, Foreign and Commonwealth Affairs 1994-95. *Political interests:* Financial Services. Czech Republic, Iran, Central Asian Republics

Chair, Northern Group of Labour MPs 1997-. *Recreations:* Composting

Jim Cousins, MP, House of Commons, London SW1A 0AA *Tel:* 020 7219 4204 *Fax:* 020 7219 6290. *Constituency:* 21 Portland Terrace, Newcastle upon Tyne, Tyne and Wear NE2 1QQ *Tel:* 0191-281 9888 *Fax:* 0191-281 3383 *E-mail:* jcousins@globalnet.co.uk

COX, GEOFFREY
Torridge and West Devon

Geoffrey Charles Cox. Born 30 April 1960; Educated King's College, Taunton; Downing College, Cambridge (BA English and law 1981); Married Patricia Margaret Jean Macdonald 1985. Barrister, Thomas More Chambers 1982-2001; Standing counsel of Mauritius 1996-2000; Member NFU

House of Commons: Contested Torridge and West Devon 2001 general election. Member for Torridge and West Devon since 5 May 2005 general election. *Political interests:* Agriculture, education, defence, legal and constitutional issues

Con majority 3,236

Recreations: Reading, walking dogs, swimming, countryside

Geoffrey Cox, MP, House of Commons, London SW1A 0AA *Tel:* 020 7219 4719. *Constituency:* Torridge & West Devon Conservative Association, Conservative Office, Bridge House, Fore Street, Okehampton EX20 1DL *Tel:* 01837 54151 *Fax:* 01837 54872 *E-mail:* geoffreycox.co.uk *Website:* www.geoffrey.co.uk

CRABB, STEPHEN
Preseli Pembrokeshire

Stephen Crabb. Born 20 January 1973; Educated Tasker Milward VC School, Haverfordwest; Bristol University (BSc politics 1995); London Business School (MBA 2004); Married Beatrice Alice Claude Odile Monnier 1996. Research assistant Andrew Rowe MP 1995-96; Parliamentary affairs officer National Council for Voluntary Youth Services 1996-98; London Chamber of Commerce: Campaigns executive 1998-2000, Campaigns manager 2000-02; Self-employed 2003-

Con majority 607

House of Commons: Contested Preseli Pembrokeshire 2001 general election. Member for Preseli Pembrokeshire since 5 May 2005 general election. *Political interests:* Crime, employment, air transport, young people

Chair North Southwark and Bermondsey Conservative Association 1998-2000. *Clubs:* Balfour; *Recreations:* Rugby, long distance running, cooking

Stephen Crabb, MP, House of Commons, London SW1A 0AA *Tel:* 020 7219 6518. *Constituency:* Winston Churchill House, 20 Upper Market Street, Haverfordwest SA61 1QA *Tel:* 01437 763527 *Fax:* 01437 766425 *E-mail:* office@pembrokeshireconservatives.com *Website:* www.pembrokeshire conservatives.com

CRAUSBY, DAVID
Bolton North East

David Crausby. Born 17 June 1946; Son of late Thomas Crausby, factory worker/club steward, and of Kathleen Crausby, cotton worker; Educated Derby Grammar School, Bury; Bury Technical College; Married Enid Noon 1965 (2 sons); Shop steward/works convenor, AEEU; Full-time works convenor 1978-97; Chair Amicus (AEEU) Group; Councillor, Bury Council 1979-92, Chair of Housing 1985-92

Lab majority 4,103

House of Commons: Contested Bury North 1987 and Bolton North East 1992 general elections. Member for Bolton North East since 1 May 1997 general election. *Political interests:* Industrial Relations, Pensions, Housing, Defence

Recreations: Football

David Crausby, MP, House of Commons, London SW1A 0AA *Tel:* 020 7219 4092 *Fax:* 020 7219 3713 *E-mail:* crausbyd@parliament.uk. *Constituency:* 570 Blackburn Road, Astley Bridge, Bolton, Greater Manchester BL1 6JN *Tel:* 01204 303340 *Fax:* 01204 304401

CREAGH, MARY
Wakefield

Lab majority 5,154

Mary Creagh. Born 2 December 1967; Educated Bishop Ullathorne RC Comprehensive, Coventry; Pembroke College, Oxford (BA modern langauges (French/Italian) 1990, MA); London School of Economics (MSc European studies 1997); Married Adam Pulham 2001. Stagaire Socialist group, European Parliament 1990; Assistant Stephen Hughes MEP 1991; Press officer: European Youth Forum 1991-95, London Enterprise Agency 1995-97; Lecturer in entrepreneurship Cranfield School of Management 1997-; GMB: Member 1991-95, 2003-, Chair Brussels branch 1992-95; Member UNISON 2004-; London Borough of Islington: Councillor 1998-2005, Leader Labour group 2000-04

House of Commons: Member for Wakefield since 5 May 2005 general election. *Political interests:* Europe, employment, social policy, disability issues, Irish community

Trustee Rathbone Training 1997-; Member: Oxfam 1995-, RNID 1996-, Ectopic Pregnancy Trust 2001-; *Recreations:* Family, yoga, cycling, swimming, food

Mary Creagh, MP, House of Commons, London SW1A 0AA *Tel:* 020 7219 6984. *Constituency:* Agent: Hazel Choucat, 23 Pinderfields Road, Wakefield WF1 3NQ *Tel:* 01924 369633

CRUDDAS, JON
Dagenham

Lab majority 7,605

Jonathan Cruddas. Born 7 April 1962; Son of John, sailor, and Pat, housewife, Cruddas; Educated Oaklands RC Comprehensive, Portsmouth; Warwick University 1981-88 (BSc, MA, PhD); University of Wisconsin, USA Visiting fellow 1987-88; Married Anna Mary Healy 1992 (1 son). Policy officer Labour Party Policy Directorate 1989-94; Chief assistant General Secretary Labour Party 1994-97; Deputy political secretary Prime Minister's political office Downing Street 1997-2001; TGWU 1989-2001: Branch secretary 1992-94

House of Commons: Member for Dagenham since 7 June 2001 general election. *Political interests:* Labour Law, Industrial Economy, Economic Regeneration

Clubs: Dagenham Working Men's, Dagenham Royal Naval Association; White Hart Dagenham Angling Society; *Recreations:* Golf, angling

Jon Cruddas, MP, House of Commons, London SW1A 0AA *Tel:* 020 7219 8161 *E-mail:* cruddasj@parliament.uk. *Constituency:* 10 Royal Parade, Church Street, Dagenham, Essex RM10 9XB *Tel:* 020 8984 7854

Lab majority 4,852

CRYER, ANN
Keighley

(Constance) Ann Cryer. Born 14 December 1939; Daughter of late Allen and Margaret Ann Place; Educated St John's Church of England Primary School; Spring Bank Secondary Modern, Darwen; Bolton Technical College (1955); Keighley Technical College (part-time) (1974); Married Bob Cryer, MP for Keighley and Bradford South 1963 (died 1994) (1 son John Cryer MP 1 daughter); Married Revd John G Hammersley 2003 (died 2004). Clerk: ICI Ltd 1955-60, GPO 1960-64; Personal assistant, Bob Cryer, MP, MEP 1974-94; Member: TGWU, ASLEF Parliamentary Group 2000-, RMT Parliamentary Group 2002-; Member, Darwen Borough Council 1962-65; JP, Bradford Bench, appointed 1996 (now on the supplemented list); Member Bradford Cathedral Council 2000-

House of Commons: Member for Keighley since 1 May 1997 general election. *Political interests:* Early Years Education, Health, Railways, Planning, Immigration, Human Rights of UK Asian Women – Campaigned against Forced Marriages. South Africa, Pakistan, Afghanistan, Palestine

Member, Co-operative Party 1965-; Chair, PLP CND Group 1997-. NSPCC; Member, Social Security Appeal Tribunal 1987-96; Delegate, Parliamentary Assembly of the Council of Europe 1997-2003; Member: Commonwealth Parliamentary Association 1997-, Equal Opportunities Committee 1998-2003 (Violence against women sub-committee), Culture and Education Committee 2000-03, Heritage Sub-committee, Media Sub-committee; Contributor to Canon Collins' Educational Trust for South Africa; *Publications:* Compiled *Boldness Be My Friend: Remembering Bob Cryer*, 1996; *Recreations:* Gardening, theatre, cinema, time with my six grandchildren, walking

Ann Cryer, MP, House of Commons, London SW1A 0AA *Tel:* 020 7219 5183 *E-mail:* rowenc@parliament.uk. *Constituency:* Bob Cryer House, 35 Devonshire Street, Keighley, West Yorkshire BD21 2BH *Tel:* 01535 210083 *Fax:* 01535 210085; 01535 670049

Lab majority 18,636

CUMMINGS, JOHN
Easington

John Scott Cummings. Born 6 July 1943; Son of late George and Mary Cummings, neé Cain; Educated Murton Council Infant, Junior, Senior Schools; Easington and Durham Technical Colleges 1958-62. Murton Colliery 1958-87, Colliery Electrician and Secretary 1967-87; Sponsored by NUM; Trustee NUM 1986-2000; Councillor, Easington Rural District Council 1970-73; Easington District Council: Councillor 1973-87, Chair 1975-76, Leader 1979-87; Member: Northumbrian Water Authority 1977-83, Peterlee and Aycliffe Development Corporation 1980-87

House of Commons: Member for Easington since 11 June 1987 general election; Opposition Whip (Northern and Overseas Development) 1994-97. *Political interests:* Energy, Environment, Coal Industry. Eastern Europe, Middle East, China

Chair, Northern Regional Group of Labour MPs 1999-. Member: Council of Europe 1992-, Western European Union 1992-; *Recreations:* Jack Russell terriers, walking, travel

John Cummings, MP, House of Commons, London SW1A 0AA *Tel:* 020 7219 5122. *Constituency:* Seaton Holme, Easington Village, Durham SR8 3BS *Tel:* 01915 273773

CUNNINGHAM, JAMES
Coventry South

James Cunningham. Born 4 February 1941; Son of Adam and Elizabeth Cunningham; Educated Columbia High School, Coatbridge; Tillycoultry College, Ruskin Courses (Labour Movement, Industrial Law); Married Marion Douglas Podmore 1985 (1 son 1 stepson 1 daughter 1 stepdaughter). Engineer Rolls Royce 1965-88; MSF shop steward 1968-88; Coventry City Council: Councillor 1972-92, Chair, Consumer Services Committee 1975-77, Vice-Chair: Finance Committee 1975-77, 1979-82, 1985-88, Leisure Committee 1975-77, Chair 1979-82, Vice-Chair, Transportation and Highways Committee 1983-85, Chief Whip, Labour Group 1985-87, Deputy Leader of the Council 1987-88, Leader of the Council 1988-92

Lab majority 6,255

House of Commons: Member for Coventry South East 1992-97, and for Coventry South since 1 May 1997 general election. *Political interests:* Economic Policy, European Union, Industrial Relations, NHS. USA, Eastern Europe, Russia

Coventry South East CLP: Secretary 1976-77, Chair 1977-79. *Recreations:* Walking, reading, historical buildings

James Cunningham, MP, House of Commons, London SW1A 0AA
Tel: 020 7219 6362 *Fax:* 020 7219 6362. *Constituency:* Rms 9-11 Palmer House, Palmer Lane, Burges, Coventry, West Midlands CV1 1HL *Tel:* 024 7655 3159
Fax: 024 7655 3159

CUNNINGHAM, TONY
Workington

Tony (Thomas Anthony) Cunningham. Born 16 September 1952; Son of late Daniel Cunningham, docker and Bessie Cunningham, neé Lister; Educated Workington Grammar School; Liverpool University (BA history and politics 1975); Didsbury College (PGCE 1976); TESL; Married Anne Margaret Gilmore 1984 (1 daughter 1 stepdaughter 1 stepson). Teacher: Alsager Comprehensive School 1976-80, Mikunguni Trade School, Zanzibar 1980-82, Netherhall School, Maryport 1983-94; Chief executive Human Rights NGO 1999-2000; MEP for Cumbria and North Lancashire 1994-99. Contested North West Region 1999 European Parliament election; NUT 1976-94: Local secretary 1985-94; AEEU 1993-; Allerdale Borough Council: Councillor 1987-94, Leader 1992-94

Lab majority 6,895

House of Commons: Member for Workington since 7 June 2001 general election; Assistant Government Whip 2005-; MEP Cumbria and North Lancashire 1994-99; PPS to Elliot Morley as Minister of State, Department for Environment, Food and Rural Affairs 2003-05. *Political interests:* Third World, Education, Tourism, Sport, Small Businesses. Sub Saharan Africa

Macmillan Nurses; Member European Standing Committee C; MEP Cumbria and North Lancashire 1994-99; *Clubs:* Station Road Working Men's, John Street; *Recreations:* Sport, running, reading, Workington RFC

Tony Cunningham, MP, House of Commons, London SW1A 0AA
Tel: 020 7219 8344 *Fax:* 020 7219 1947 *E-mail:* cunninghamt@parliament.uk.
Constituency: The Town Hall, Workington, Cumbria CA14 2RS *Tel:* 01900 65815
Fax: 01900 68348

Con majority 11,620

CURRY, DAVID
Skipton and Ripon

David Maurice Curry. Born 13 June 1944; Son of Thomas Harold and late Florence Joan Curry (neé Tyerman); Educated Ripon Grammar School; Corpus Christi College, Oxford (BA modern history 1966); Kennedy School of Government, Harvard University; Married Anne Helene Maude Roullet 1971 (1 son twin daughters). Newspaper Reporter, *Newcastle Journal* 1966-70; *Financial Times* 1970-79: world trade editor, international companies editor, Brussels correspondent, Paris correspondent ; Freelance journalist; MEP for North East Essex 1979-89; Vice-President, Local Government Association; Board Member British Association for Central and Eastern Europe

House of Commons: Contested Morpeth February and October 1974 general elections. Member for Skipton and Ripon since 11 June 1987 general election; Conservative Spokesperson European Parliament Budget Committee 1984-89; Ministry of Agriculture, Fisheries and Food: Parliamentary Secretary 1989-92, Minister of State 1992-93; Minister of State, Department of the Environment for: Local Government and Planning 1993-94, Local Government, Housing and Urban Regeneration 1994-97; Shadow Minister of Agriculture, Fisheries and Food June-November 1997; Member Shadow Cabinet 2003-04; Shadow Secretary of State for Local and Devolved Government Affairs 2003-04. *Political interests:* Agriculture, Foreign Affairs, Urban Issues and Local Government. Former Communist States in East and Central Europe, France

Chairman, Conservative Group for Europe. General rapporteur, EEC Budget for 1987; Director, British Association for Central and Eastern Europe; *Publications: The Conservative Tradition in Europe*, 1998; *Lobbying Government*, 1999; *The Sorcerer's apprentice: Government and Globalisation*, 2000; PC 1996; *Recreations:* Vegetable gardening, sailing

Rt Hon David Curry, MP, House of Commons, London SW1A 0AA
Tel: 020 7219 6202 *E-mail:* rapsonj@parliament.uk. *Constituency:* 19 Otley Street, Skipton, North Yorkshire BD23 1DY *Tel:* 01756 792092 *Fax:* 01756 798742

CURTIS-THOMAS, CLAIRE
Crosby

Claire Curtis-Thomas. Born 30 April 1958; Daughter of Joyce Curtis-Thomas; Educated Mynyddbach Comprehensive School For Girls, Swansea; Fareham Technical College, Hampshire (ONC mechanical engineering 1978); Cosham Technical College, Hampshire (HNC mechanical engineering 1980); University College of Wales, Cardiff (BSc mechanical engineering 1984); Aston University (MBA business administration 1996); Married Michael Jakub (1 son 2 daughters).

Lab majority 5,840

Research assistant, University College of Wales, Cardiff 1984-86; Shell Chemicals: Site mechnical engineer 1986-88, Head, UK Supply and Distribution Ltd 1988-90, Head, environmental strategy 1990-92; Birmingham City Council: Head of research and development laboratory 1992-93, Head of strategy and business planning 1993-95; Dean, Faculty of Business and Engineering, University of Wales College, Newport 1996-97; Member, TGWU; Councillor, Crewe and Nantwich Borough Council 1995-97

House of Commons: Member for Crosby since 1 May 1997 general election (Contested the seat as Claire Curtis-Tansley). *Political interests:* Economic Policy, Trade and Industry, Manufacturing and Engineering, Small Businesses. USA, India, South Africa, New Zealand

Member: Co-operative Party, Fabian Society, Labour Women's Network; Membership Secretary, Rossett and Marford Labour Party; Secretary, Eddisbury Constituency Labour Party; Vice-chair North West Regional Group of Labour MPs 2002-. Changed surname from Curtis-Tansley May 1997; Founder and president SETup (educational trust to promote science and engineering); *Recreations:* Family

Claire Curtis-Thomas, MP, House of Commons, London SW1A 0AA
Tel: 020 7219 4193 *Fax:* 020 7219 1540 *E-mail:* curtisthomasc@parliament.uk.
Constituency: The Minster, 16 Beach Lawn, Waterloo, Liverpool L22 8QA
Tel: 0151-928 7250 *Fax:* 0151-928 9325

DARLING, ALISTAIR
Edinburgh South West

Alistair Maclean Darling. Born 28 November 1953; Educated Loretto School; Aberdeen University (LLB 1976); Married Margaret McQueen Vaughan 1986 (1 son 1 daughter). Solicitor 1978-82; Advocate 1984-; Lothian Regional Council: Councillor 1982-87, Chair, Lothian Region Transport Committee 1986-87

House of Commons: Member for Edinburgh Central 1987-2005, for Edinburgh South

Lab majority 7,242

West since 5 May 2005 general election; Opposition Spokesman on Home Affairs 1988-92; Opposition Front Bench Spokesman on Treasury, Economic Affairs and the City 1992-96; Shadow Chief Secretary to the Treasury 1996-97; Sponsored Solicitors (Scotland) Act 1988 (Private Member's Bill); Chief Secretary to the Treasury 1997-98; Secretary of State for: Social Security/Work and Pensions 1998-2002, Transport 2002-, Scotland 2003-. *Political interests:* Transport, Education, Health, Economic Policy, Constitution

Member, Labour Party's Economic Commission 1994-97. PC 1997

Rt Hon Alistair Darling, MP, House of Commons, London SW1A 0AA
Tel: 020 7219 4584 *E-mail:* alistair.darling@dft.gsi.gov.uk. *Constituency:* 15A Stafford Street, Edinburgh EH3 7BU *Tel:* 0131-476 2552 *Fax:* 0131-467 3574

PUBLIC OWNERSHIP
THE RIGHT TRACK FOR OUR RAILWAY

TSSA – campaigning for an integrated, accountable and publicly controlled railway

Public ownership of rail deserves to be high on Labour's agenda

tssa
the union
for people
in transport
and travel

www.tssa.org.uk

DAVEY, EDWARD
Kingston and Surbiton

Edward Jonathon Davey. Born 25 December 1965; Son of late John George Davey, solicitor, and of late Nina Joan Davey (neé Stanbrook), teacher; Educated Nottingham High School; Jesus College, Oxford (College President) (BA philosophy, politics and economics 1988); Birkbeck College, London (MSc economics 1993); Single, no children. Senior economics adviser to Liberal Democrat MPs 1989-93; Management consultant, Omega Partners 1993-97; Director, Omega Partners Postal 1996-97

Lib Dem majority 8,966

House of Commons: Member for Kingston and Surbiton since 1 May 1997 general election; Liberal Democrat Spokesperson for: the Treasury (Public Spending and Taxation) 1997-99, Economy 1999-2001, London 2000-03, Office of the Deputy Prime Minister 2002-; London Whip 1997-2000; Liberal Democrat Shadow: Chief Secretary to the Treasury 2001-02, Secretary of State for Education and Skills 2005-. *Political interests:* Taxation, Economics, Internet, Employment, Environment, Modernisation of Parliament. Latin America

Chair, Costing Group (costing all policies for manifesto) 1992 and 1997 general elections; Member, Federal Policy Committee 1994-95; Liberal Democrat Policy Group (Economics, Tax and Benefits and Transport); Member, Association of Liberal Democrat Councillors. Patron: Jigsaw, Kingston Special Needs Project; Trustee, Kids Out; *Publications: Making MPs Work for our Money: Reforming Budget Scrutiny* (2000, Centre for Reform); Royal Humane Society Honourable Testimonial; Chief Constable London Transport Police Commendation; Royal Humane Society; *Clubs:* Member National Liberal Club, Surbiton; *Recreations:* Music, walking, swimming

Edward Davey, MP, House of Commons, London SW1A 0AA *Tel:* 020 7219 3512 *Fax:* 020 7219 0250 *E-mail:* daveye@parliament.uk. *Constituency:* Liberal Democrats, 21 Berrylands Road, Surbiton KT5 8QX *Tel:* 020 8288 0161 *Fax:* 020 8288 1090

Lab majority 15,359

DAVID, WAYNE
Caerphilly

Wayne David. Born 1 July 1957; Son of David Haydn David, teacher, and Edna Amelia, née Jones, housewife; Educated Cynffig Comprehensive School, Kenfig Hill, Glamorgan; University College, Cardiff (BA history and Welsh history 1979); University College, Swansea (economic history research 1979-82); University College, Cardiff (PGCE FE 1983); Married Catherine Thomas 1991. Teacher Brynteg Comprehensive School 1983-85; Tutor organiser Workers' Educational Association South Wales District 1985-89; Policy adviser youth policy Wales Youth Agency 1999-2001; MEP for South Wales 1989-94, South Wales Central 1994-99. Contested Rhondda 1999 National Assembly for Wales election; MSF1983-; AEEU 1998-; AMICUS 2004-; Cefn Cribwr Community Council 1985-91: Councillor, Chair 1986-87

House of Commons: Member for Caerphilly since 7 June 2001 general election; Team PPS, Ministry of Defence 2005. *Political interests:* European Affairs, Economy, Education. Poland, Bulgaria

Vice-president Socialist Group European Parliament 1994-98; Leader European Parliamentary Labour Party 1994-98; Ex-officio Member of Labour Party NEC 1994-98. UK Government link MP for Bulgaria; Vice-president Cardiff UN Association 1989-; *Publications:* Two pamphlets on the Future of Europe 1991 and 1993; Contributor: *The Future of Europe, Problems and Issues for the 21st Century,* 1996; Charles Morgan Prize in Welsh History 1979; Fellow Cardiff University 1995; *Clubs:* Bargoed Labour Club; *Recreations:* Music, playing the oboe

Wayne David, MP, House of Commons, London SW1A 0AA *Tel:* 020 7219 8152 *Fax:* 020 7219 1751 *E-mail:* davidw@parliament.uk. *Constituency:* Suite 5, St Fagans House, St Fagans Street, Caerphilly, Mid Glamorgan CF83 1FZ *Tel:* 029 2088 1061 *Fax:* 029 2088 1954

DAVIDSON, IAN
Glasgow South West

Ian Graham Davidson. Born 8 September 1950; Son of Graham Davidson and Elizabeth Crowe; Educated Jedburgh Grammar School; Galashiels Academy; Edinburgh University (MA); Jordanhill College; Married Morag Christine Anne Mackinnon 1978 (1 son 1 daughter). Sabbatical Chair National Association of Labour Students 1973-74; President Students' Association, Jordanhill College 1975-76; Researcher for Janey Buchan, MEP 1978-85; Project manager Community Service Volunteers 1985-92; Former chair MSF Parliamentary Group; Secretary: Trade Union Group of Labour MPs 1998-2002; Strathclyde Regional Council: Councillor 1978-92, Chair, Education Committee 1986-92

Lab/Co-op majority
13,896

House of Commons: Member for Glasgow Govan 1992-97, for Glasgow Pollok 1997-2005, for Glasgow South West since 5 May 2005 general election. *Political interests:* Local and Regional Government, Commonwealth, International Development, Local Economic Development, Defence, Co-operative Movement, Trade and Industry, Trade Unions, Shipbuilding, Europe, Poverty, Euro (Against). Africa, Europe, Scandinavia, The Commonwealth, USA, Japan, Germany, British Overseas Territories

Former Chair Kelvingrove Constituency Labour Party; Former Executive: Glasgow Labour Party, Strathclyde Regional Labour Party; Member Co-operative Party; Secretary: Tribune Group, Trade Union Group of Labour MPs 1998-2002; Chair Co-operative Parliamentary Group 1998-99; Founder and Chair Labour Against The Euro 2002-; Chair Scottish Regional Group of Labour MPs 2003-04. Chairman, COSLA Education Committee 1990-92; Member, New Europe Advisory Council; *Recreations:* Family, sport, distance running, swimming, rugby

Ian Davidson, MP, House of Commons, London SW1A 0AA *Tel:* 020 7219 3610 *Fax:* 020 7219 2238 *E-mail:* iandavidsonmp@parliament.uk. *Constituency:* 3 Kicmuir Drive, Glasgow G46 8BW *Tel:* 0141-883 8338 *Fax:* 0141-621 2154

DAVIES, DAVID
Monmouth

David Davies. Born 27 July 1970; Son of Peter and Kathleen Davies; Educated Bassaleg Comprehensive; Married. British Steel Corporation 1988-89; Youth hostel manager, USA; Work abroad, Australia: Picking grapes and tobacco, working on roads for Water Board, Being a rickshaw driver in a tourist resort 1989-91; Manager, Burrow Heath Ltd (forwarder and tea importers) 1991-99; AM for Monmouth constituency since 6 May 1999

Con majority 4,527

House of Commons: Contested Brigend 1997 general election. Member for Monmouth since 5 May 2005 general election; Spokesperson for: Local Government and Environment 1999-2000, Environment, Transport and Planning 2000-03; Education and Lifelong Learning 2003-; Chief Whip, Welsh Conservative Party 1999-2001; Deputy Leader/Business Secretary, Welsh Conservative Party 1999. *Political interests:* Non-Welsh speakers, Assembly finances. Sri Lanka, Australia, France

Organiser for anti-Assembly 'No' Campaign 1997; Campaign manager for Rod Richards as leader of Welsh Conservative Party 1998. St David's Foundation (Hospice Care); *Clubs:* Oriental (London); Chepstow Conservative; Abergavenny Conservative; Usk Conservative; Monmouth Conservative; *Recreations:* Surfing, long distance running, tennis, chess, reading

David Davies, MP, House of Commons, London SW1A 0AA *Tel:* 020 7219 8360. *Constituency: Tel:* 01291 672780 *E-mail:* david.davies@wales.gov.uk

FIRE BRIGADES UNION
PARLIAMENTARY GROUP

Our new Parliamentary Group aims to give a clearer and stronger voice to those who work in the fire service and the communities we serve

Key issues:

★ Campaign for national standards to underpin local fire and rescue plans

★ NO2 Fire Deaths campaign

★ Fight against regionalisation of emergency fire control rooms

★ Need to recruit more firefighters working the retained duty system

★ Fire service pensions ★ Health and safety

★ Professional fire service issues ★ Tackling assaults on firefighters

Chair Andrew Dismore MP
Vice-Chair Michael Clapham MP
Secretary John McDonnell MP

General Secretary: Matt Wrack · President: Ruth Winters

Fire Brigades Union
Bradley House
68 Coombe Road
Kingston Upon Thames
KT2 7AE
020 8541 1765
www.fbu.org.uk
info@fbu.org.uk

DAVIES, PHILIP
Shipley

Philip Andrew Davies. Born 5 January 1972; Educated Old Swinford Hospital School, Stourbridge; Huddersfield University (historical and political studies 1993); Married Deborah Gail Hemsley 1994. Asda Stores: Management training scheme 1995-97, Deputy customer services manager 1997, Customer relations manager 1997-98, Call centre manager 1998-99, Customer service project manager 2000-04, Marketing manager 2004-

Con majority 422

House of Commons: Contested Colne Valley 2001 general election. Member for Shipley since 5 May 2005 general election. *Political interests:* Law and order, Europe, education

Recreations: horseracing

Philip Davies, MP, House of Commons, London SW1A 0AA *Tel:* 020 7219 8264. *Constituency:* Shipley Conservatives Association, 76 Otley Road, Shipley BD18 3SA *Tel:* 01274 585830 *Fax:* 01274 531649 *E-mail:* philipdavies@shipleyconservatives.fsnet.co.uk

DAVIES, QUENTIN
Grantham and Stamford

Quentin Davies. Born 29 May 1944; Son of late Dr M I Davies, general practitioner, and the late Thelma Davies; Educated Dragon School, Oxford; Leighton Park; Gonville and Caius College, Cambridge (BA history 1966, MA); Harvard University, USA (Frank Knox Fellow); Married Chantal Tamplin 1983 (2 sons). HM Diplomatic Service 1967-74: 3rd Secretary, FCO 1967-69, 2nd Secretary, Moscow 1969-72, 1st Secretary, FCO 1972-74; Manager then assistant director, Morgan Grenfell & Co Ltd 1974-78; Director General and President, Morgan Grenfell France 1978-81; Director, Morgan Grenfell Co Ltd and certain group subsidiaries 1981-87, Consultant 1987-93; Consultant, National Westminster Securities plc 1993-99; Dewe Rogerson International 1987-94; Société Genérale d'Entreprises 1999-2000; Consultant Royal Bank of Scotland 1999-2002; Director: Vinci 2003-, Vinci UK 2003-, Lloyds of London

Con majority 7,445

House of Commons: Contested Birmingham Ladywood 1977 by-election. Member for Stamford and Spalding 1987-97, and for Grantham and Stamford since 1 May 1997 general election; Opposition Spokesperson for: Social Security 1998-99, the Treasury 1999-2000, Defence 2000-01; PPS to Angela Rumbold as Minister of State at: Department of Education and Science 1988-90, Home Office 1990-91; Shadow Minister for Pensions 1998-99; Shadow Paymaster General 1999-2000; Shadow Minister for Defence 2000-01; Shadow Secretary of State for Northern Ireland 2001-03. *Political interests:* Trade and Industry, Finance, Agriculture, Health, Welfare, Pensions, Overseas Development. Other EU, USA, Russia

Member of Executive Committee, Council for Economic Policy Research; *Publications: Britain and Europe: A Conservative View*, 1996; Liveryman, Goldsmiths' Company; *Clubs:* Beefsteak, Brooks's, Travellers', Grantham Conservative; *Recreations:* Reading, walking, skiing, travel

Quentin Davies, MP, House of Commons, London SW1A 0AA *Tel:* 020 7219 5518 *Fax:* 020 7219 2963 *E-mail:* daviesq@parliament.uk. *Constituency:* Conservative Office, North Street, Bourne, Lincolnshire *Tel:* 01778 421498 *Fax:* 01778 394443

Con majority 5,116

DAVIS, DAVID
Haltemprice and Howden

David Michael Davis. Born 23 December 1948; Son of late Ronald and Elizabeth Davis; Educated Bec Grammar School; Warwick University (BSc molecular science, computing science 1971); London Business School (MSc business studies 1973); Harvard Business School (AMP 1985); Married Doreen Cook 1973 (1 son 2 daughters). Joined Tate & Lyle 1974; Finance director, Manbré & Garton 1976-80; Managing director, Tate & Lyle Transport 1980-82; President, Redpath-Labatt joint venture 1982-84; Strategic planning director, Tate & Lyle 1984-87; Non-Executive director, Tate & Lyle 1987-90

House of Commons: Member for Boothferry 1987-97, and for Haltemprice and Howden since 1 May 1997 general election; Assistant Government Whip 1990-93; PPS to Francis Maude as Financial Secretary to Treasury 1988-90; Parliamentary Secretary, Office of Public Service and Science 1993-94; Minister of State, Foreign and Commonwealth Office 1994-97; Shadow Deputy Prime Minister with Shadow Ministerial responsibility for the Cabinet Office 2002-03; Shadow Secretary of State for Home, Constitutional and Legal Affairs 2003-04; Shadow Home Secretary 2003-. *Political interests:* Health, Law and Order, Industry, Agriculture

Contested leadership 2001; Party Chairman 2001-02; Member Conservative Policy Board 2001-. Member, Public Accounts Commission 1997-2001; *Publications: How to Turn Round a Company*, 1988; *The BBC Viewer's Guide to Parliament*, 1989; PC 1997; *Recreations:* Mountaineering, flying light aircraft, writing

Rt Hon David Davis, MP, House of Commons, London SW1A 0AA *Tel:* 020 7219 4710 *Fax:* 020 7219 5860 *E-mail:* davisd@parliament.uk. *Constituency:* Spaldington Court, Spaldington, Goole, Humberside DN14 7NG *Tel:* 01430 430365

Lab majority 1,421

DEAN, JANET
Burton

Janet Elizabeth Ann Dean. Born 28 January 1949; Daughter of late Harry and late Mary Gibson; Educated Winsford Verdin Grammar School; Married Alan Dean 1968 (deceased) (2 daughters). Bank clerk 1965-69; Clerk 1969-70; GMB; Member, South-East Staffordshire Health Authority 1981-90; Staffordshire County Council: Councillor 1981-97, Vice-Chair, Highways 1985-93, Vice-Chair, Social Services 1993-96; Councillor: East Staffordshire Borough Council 1991-97, Uttoxeter Town Council 1995-97; Mayor, East Staffordshire Borough Council 1996-97

House of Commons: Member for Burton since 1 May 1997 general election. *Political interests:* Health, Social Services, Education, Transport, Housing, Home Affairs, Hunting With Dogs (Against), Small Businesses

Vice-chair West Midlands Regional Group of Labour MPs 2002-; Rural Group of Labour MPs. Lupus UK; Member European Standing Committee A 1998-; Chair, Burton Breweries Charitable Trust; *Recreations:* Dress-making, reading

Janet Dean, MP, House of Commons, London SW1A 0AA *Tel:* 020 7219 6320 *Fax:* 020 7219 3010 *E-mail:* mcgirrc@parliament.uk. *Constituency:* Suite 13, First Floor, Cross Street Business Centre, Cross Street, Burton upon Trent, Staffordshire DE14 1EG *Tel:* 01283 509166 *Fax:* 01283 569964

Lab majority 9,302

DENHAM, JOHN
Southampton Itchen

John Yorke Denham. Born 15 July 1953; Son of Edward and Beryl Denham; Educated Woodroffe Comprehensive School, Lyme Regis; Southampton University (President, Student's Union 1976-77) (BSc chemistry); Married Ruth Eleanore Dixon 1979 (1 son 1 daughter) (divorced). Advice worker, Energy Advice Agency, Durham 1977-78; Transport campaigner, Friends of the Earth 1978-79; Head of Youth Affairs, British Youth Council 1979-83; Campaigner, War on Want 1984-88; Consultant to various voluntary organisations 1988-92; Member MSF; Hampshire County Council: Councillor 1981-89, Spokesperson on Education 1985-89; Southampton City Council: Councillor 1989-92, Chairman Housing Committee 1990-92

House of Commons: Member for Southampton Itchen since 9 April 1992 general election; Opposition Spokesperson for Social Security 1995-97; Department of Social Security: Parliamentary Under-Secretary of State 1997-98, Minister of State 1998-99; Minister of State: Department of Health 1999-2001, For Crime Reduction, Policing, Community Safety and Young People, Home Office 2001-03

PC 2000

Rt Hon John Denham, MP, House of Commons, London SW1A 0AA *Tel:* 020 7219 4515 *E-mail:* denhamj@parliament.uk. *Constituency:* 20-22 Southampton Street, Southampton, Hampshire SO15 2ED *Tel:* 023 8033 9807 *Fax:* 023 8033 9907 *Website:* www.johndenham.labour.co.uk

Lab majority 4,271

DHANDA, PARMJIT
Gloucester

Parmjit Singh Dhanda. Born 17 September 1971; Son of Balbir Singh Dhanda, driving instructor and Satvinder Kaur Dhanda, hospital cleaner; Educated Mellow Lane Comprehensive, Hayes, Middlesex; Nottingham University (BEng electronic engineering 1993, MSc information technology 1995); Married Rupinder Rai 2003. TUC Trainer; Assistant national organiser Connect 1998-; Member: USDAW 1999-, TGWU; London Borough of Hillingdon 1998-2001: Councillor, Member: Labour Party National Policy Forum representitive, Education and Skills Policy Commission

House of Commons: Member for Gloucester since 7 June 2001 general election; Assistant Government Whip 2005-; PPS to Stephen Twigg as Minister for School Standards 2004-05. *Political interests:* Science and Technology, Employment, European Affairs, Local and Regional Government. Indian Sub-continent, Europe

Agent general and local elections London Borough of Ealing 1996-98; Organiser Labour Party West London, Hampshire and Wiltshire 1996-98; Member: Fabian Society 1996-, Labour Housing Group 1996-, Co-operative Party 1996-, NEC working group on equal opportunities 1997-. Patron: Gloucestershire Action for Refugees and Asylum Seekers, Gloucestershire Inter Faith Group; Contested South East Region 1999 European Parliament election; Member: European Standing Committee A 2003-, European Standing Committee B 2003; *Publications:* Former writer for a football magazine; *Measuring distances using a gallium arsenide laser*, Nottingham University 1993; *Recreations:* Presenting newspaper review on satellite tv station, football, rugby, cricket, chess, writing

Parmjit Dhanda, MP, House of Commons, London SW1A 0AA *Tel:* 020 7219 8240 *Fax:* 020 7219 1771. *Constituency:* 1 Pullman Court, Great Western Road, Gloucester, Gloucestershire GL1 3ND *Tel:* 01452 311870 *Fax:* 01452 311874

DISMORE, ANDREW
Hendon

Andrew Dismore. Born 2 September 1954; Son of late Ian Dismore, hotelier, and Brenda Dismore; Educated Bridlington Grammar School; Warwick University (LLB 1975); London School of Economics (LLM 1976); Guildford College of Law 1978. Education Department, GMWU 1976-78; Solicitor: Robin Thomson and Partners 1978-95, Russell Jones and Walker 1995-; Member, GMB; Councillor, Westminster City Council 1982-97, Leader, Labour Group 1990-97

Lab majority 2,699

House of Commons: Member for Hendon since 1 May 1997 general election. *Political interests:* Social Security, Health, Civil Justice, Rights of Victims of Accidents and Crime, Middle East, Cyprus, Greece. Greece, Cyprus, Israel, Middle East, Indian Sub-Continent

Vice-chair: Friends of Israel, Friends of India. *Publications:* Various legal journals and articles; *Recreations:* Art, opera, travel, gardening

Andrew Dismore, MP, House of Commons, London SW1A 0AA
Tel: 020 7219 4026 *Fax:* 020 7219 1279 *E-mail:* andrewdismoremp@parliament.uk.
Constituency: Studio 4, Horwich Business Centre, 86 Lee Lane, Bolton BL6 7AE
Tel: 01204 693351 *Fax:* 01204 693383

DJANOGLY, JONATHAN
Huntingdon

Jonathan Simon Djanogly. Born 3 June 1965; Son of Sir Harry Djanogly CBE and Carol Djanogly; Educated University College School; Oxford Polytechnic (BA law and politics 1987); Guildford College of Law (law finals 1988); Married Rebecca Jane Silk 1991 (1 son 1 daughter). Partner: SJ Berwin Solicitors 1988-, Mail order retail business 1994-2002; Councillor Westminster City Council 1994-2001: Chairman: Traffic Committee 1995-96, Contracts 1996-97, Social Services Committee 1998-99, Environment Committee 1999-2000

Con majority 12,847

House of Commons: Contested Oxford East 1997 general election. Member for Huntingdon since 7 June 2001 general election; Shadow Minister for: Home, Constitutional and Legal Affairs 2004, Home Affairs 2004-. *Political interests:* Small Businesses, Trade, Environment, Rural Affairs, Transport, Planning

Chairman Oxford Polytechnic Conservative Association 1986-87; Vice-chairman Westminster North Conservative Association 1993-94. *Recreations:* Sport, arts, theatre, reading histories and biographies, Britain's countryside and heritage

Jonathan Djanogly, MP, House of Commons, London SW1A 0AA
Tel: 020 7219 2367 *Fax:* 020 7219 0476 *E-mail:* djanoglyj@parliament.uk.
Constituency: 8 Stukeley Road, Huntingdon, Cambridgeshire PE29 6XG
Tel: 01480 453062 *Fax:* 01480 453012

DOBBIN, JIM
Heywood and Middleton

Lab/Co-op majority
11,083

Jim Dobbin. Born 26 May 1941; Son of William Dobbin, miner, and Catherine Dobbin, neé McCabe, mill worker; Educated St Columba's High, Cowdenbeath; St Andrew's High, Kirkcaldy; Napier College, Edinburgh (BSc bacteriology, virology 1970); Married Pat Russell 1964 (2 sons 2 daughters). Microbiologist, NHS 1966-94; Member, MSF; Councillor, Rochdale Metropolitan Borough Council 1983-92, 1994-97; Chairman of Housing 1986-90, Leader of Labour Group 1994-96, Deputy Leader 1990-92, Leader of Council 1996-97

House of Commons: Contested Bury North 1992 general election. Member for Heywood and Middleton since 1 May 1997 general election. *Political interests:* Local and Regional Government, Health, Housing, Transport, Small Businesses. America (North and South), Spain, Africa

Chair, Rochdale District Labour Party 1980-81: Executive Member, Rochdale Constituency Labour Party 1986-87; Hon Treasurer, North West Regional Group of Labour MPs 1999-2004. Member European Standing Committee C 2002-; *Recreations:* Walking, football

Jim Dobbin, MP, House of Commons, London SW1A 0AA *Tel:* 020 7219 4530 *Fax:* 020 7219 2696 *E-mail:* dobbinj@parliament.uk. *Constituency:* 45 York Street, Heywood, Lancashire OL10 4NN *Tel:* 01706 361135 *Fax:* 01706 361137

DOBSON, FRANK
Holborn and St Pancras

Lab majority 4,787

Frank Dobson. Born 15 March 1940; Son of late James William Dobson, railwayman, and late Irene Dobson; Educated Archbishop Holgate's Grammar School, York; London School of Economics (BSc(Econ) 1962); Married Janet Mary Alker 1967 (1 daughter 2 sons). Worked at HQ of: CEGB 1962-70, Electricity Council 1970-75; Assistant Secretary, Office of Local Ombudsman 1975-79; RMT; Camden Borough Council: Councillor 1971-76, Leader of the Council 1973-75

House of Commons: Member for Holborn and St Pancras since 3 May 1979 general election; Opposition Spokesperson for Education 1981-83; Principal Opposition Spokesperson for: Energy 1989-92, Employment 1992-93, Transport and London 1993-94, Environment and London 1994-97; Shadow Health Minister 1983-87; Shadow Leader, House of Commons and Campaigns Co-ordinator 1987-89; Shadow: Energy Secretary 1989-92, Employment Secretary 1992-93, Transport Secretary 1993-94, Minister for London 1993-97, Environment Secretary 1994-97; Secretary of State for Health 1997-99. *Political interests:* Problems of Central London, Transport, Energy, Redistribution of Wealth, Government Reform. South Africa, Bangladesh

Coram's Field and Harmsworth Memorial Playground; Chair, Network South Africa 2004; PC 1997; *Clubs:* Covent Garden Community Centre; *Recreations:* Walking, theatre, watching cricket and football

Rt Hon Frank Dobson, MP, House of Commons, London SW1A 0AA *Tel:* 020 7219 5040 *Fax:* 020 7219 6956 *E-mail:* collinsb@parliament.uk. *Constituency:* 8 Camden Road, London NW1 9DP *Tel:* 020 7267 1676 *Fax:* 020 7482 3950

DODDS, NIGEL
Belfast North

Nigel Dodds. Born 20 August 1958; Son of Joseph Alexander Dodds, civil servant and Doreen Dodds, née McMahon; Educated Portora Royal School, Enniskillen; St John's College, Cambridge (BA law 1980); Queen's University, Belfast Institute of Professional Legal Studies (Cert PLS 1981); Married Dianne Harris 1985 (2 sons 1 daughter). Barrister 1981-; European Parliament Secretariat 1984-96; Member of Senate, Queens University Belfast 1985-93; Belfast City Council: Councillor 1985-, Chair Finance and Personnel Committee 1985-87, Lord Mayor Belfast 1988-89, Vice-President Association of Local Authorities of Northern Ireland 1989-90, Chair Health and Environment Committee 1989-91, Lord Mayor Belfast 1991-92, Chair Development Committee 1997-99

DUP majority 5,188

House of Commons: Member for Belfast North since 7 June 2001 general election; Chief Whip Democratic Unionist Party, House of Commons 2001-; Member: Northern Ireland Forum for Political Dialogue 1996-98, Northern Ireland Assembly 1998-: Minister for Social Development 1999-2000, 2001-02. *Political interests:* European Affairs, Constitution, Social Policy. USA, France

OBE 1997

Nigel Dodds, MP, House of Commons, London SW1A 0AA *Tel:* 020 7219 8419 *Fax:* 020 7219 1972 *E-mail:* doddsn@parliament.uk. *Constituency:* 210 Shore Road, Belfast BT15 3QB *Tel:* 028 9077 4774 *Fax:* 028 9077 7685

DOHERTY, PAT
West Tyrone

Pat Doherty. Born 18 July 1945; Married (2 sons 3 daughters). Site engineer 1975; Contested Donegal North East 1989 Dail general election, 1996 by-election and 1997 general election; Connaught/Ulster 1989 and 1994 European Parliament elections. Contested West Tyrone 1997 general election

House of Commons: Member for West Tyrone since 7 June 2001 general election. *Political interests:* Irish National Self-determination

Sinn Féin majority 5,005

Sinn Féin: Activist 1970-84; Director of Elections 1984-85; National organiser 1985-88; Vice-president 1988-, Leader of delegation to Dublin Forum for Peace and Reconciliation 1994-96, Member Castle Buildings talks team 1997-98, Spokesperson for Enterprise Trade and Investment 2000-. Founder member Local Credit Union 1992; New Northern Ireland Assembly 1998-: Member, Chair Enterprise, Trade and Investment Committee 1999-; *Recreations:* Walking, reading, building stone walls

Pat Doherty, MP, House of Commons, London SW1A 0AA *Tel:* 020 7219 3000. *Constituency:* 1A Melvin Road, Strabane BT82 9AE *Tel:* 028 7188 6464 *Fax:* 028 7188 0120

DUP majority 14,117

DONALDSON, JEFFREY
Lagan Valley

Jeffrey Mark Donaldson. Born 7 December 1962; Son of James and Sarah Anne Donaldson; Educated Kilkeel High School; Castlereagh College (Diploma, Electrical Engineering 1982); Married Eleanor Cousins 1987 (2 daughters). Ulster Defence Regiment 1980-85. Agent to Enoch Powell, MP 1983-84; Personal assistant to Sir James Molyneaux, MP 1984-85; Member, Northern Ireland Assembly 1985-86; Partner, financial services and estate agency business 1986-96; Member: Northern Ireland Forum 1996-98, Northern Ireland Assembly 2003-; Former Member, AEEU

House of Commons: Member for Lagan Valley since 1 May 1997 general election. (UUP member May 1997-January 2004, DUP Member from January 2004); Ulster Unionist Spokesperson for: Trade and Industry 1997-2000, Environment, Transport and the Regions 2000-01, Treasury 2001-02, Transport, Local Government and the Regions 2001-02, Work and Pensions 2001-03, Defence 2002-03, Trade and Industry 2002-03; Democratic Unionist Spokesperson for: Education 2004-, Defence 2004-; Member, Northern Ireland Assembly 1985-86, 2003-; Member, Northern Ireland Forum 1996-98. *Political interests:* Northern Ireland, Christian Values, Constitution, Transport, Defence. USA, South Africa, Israel

Honorary Secretary, Ulster Unionist Council 1988-2000, Vice-President 2000-03. Care and Tear Fund; *Recreations:* Hill-walking, reading, local history, church

Jeffrey Donaldson, MP, House of Commons, London SW1A 0AA *Tel:* 020 7219 3407 *Fax:* 020 7219 0696 *E-mail:* donaldsonjm@parliament.uk. *Constituency:* The Old Town Hall, 29 Castle Street, Lisburn BT27 4DH *Tel:* 028 9266 8001 *Fax:* 028 9267 1845

Lab majority 10,423

DONOHOE, BRIAN
Central Ayrshire

Brian Harold Donohoe. Born 10 September 1948; Son of late George and Catherine Donohoe; Educated Irvine Royal Academy; Kilmarnock Technical College (National certificate engineering 1972); Married Christine Pawson 1973 (2 sons). Apprentice engineer, Ailsa Shipyard 1965-70; Hunterston Nuclear Power Station 1977; ICI Organics Division, draughtsman 1977-81; NALGO District Officer 1981-92; Convenor, Political and Education Committee TASS 1969-81; Secretary, Irvine Trades Council 1973-82; Member, TGWU Parliamentary Campaigning Group 1992-; Chair: Cunninghame Industrial Development Committee 1975-85, North Ayrshire and Arran Local Health Council 1977-79

House of Commons: Member for Cunninghame South 1992-2005, for Central Ayrshire since 5 May 2005 general election. *Political interests:* Health, Local and Regional Government, Transport, Small Businesses. Singapore, Indonesia, Malaysia, USA, Taiwan

Treasurer, Cunninghame South Constituency Labour Party 1983-91; Chair, Scottish Group of Labour MPs 1997-98. Board Member Thrive; *Recreations:* Gardening

Brian Donohoe, MP, House of Commons, London SW1A 0AA *Tel:* 020 7219 6230 *Fax:* 020 7219 5388 *E-mail:* donohoeb@parliament.uk. *Constituency:* 17 Townhead, Irvine, Strathclyde KA12 0BL *Tel:* 01294 276844 *Fax:* 01294 313463

Lab majority 6,795

DORAN, FRANK
Aberdeen North

Frank Doran. Born 13 April 1949; Son of Francis Anthony and Betty Hedges Doran; Educated Ainslie Park Secondary School; Leith Academy; Dundee University (LLB 1975); Married Patricia Ann Govan 1967 (divorced) (2 sons). Solicitor 1977-88; Contested North-East Scotland, European Parliament election 1984; Member, GMB 1983-

House of Commons: Member for Aberdeen South 1987-92, for Aberdeen Central 1997-2005, for Aberdeen North since 5 May 2005 general election; Opposition Spokesperson for Energy 1988-92; PPS to Ian McCartney, MP: as Minister of State, Department of Trade and Industry (Competitiveness) 1997-99, as Minister of State, Cabinet Office 1999-2001. *Political interests:* Energy, Childcare, Families, Mental Health, Employment

Secretary: GMB Westminster Parliamentary Group, Trade Union Group of Labour MPs. *Clubs:* Aberdeen Trades Council; *Recreations:* Cinema, art, football, sport

Frank Doran, MP, House of Commons, London SW1A 0AA *Tel:* 020 7219 3481 *E-mail:* doranf@parliament.uk. *Constituency:* 166 Market Street, Aberdeen AB11 5PP *Tel:* 01224 252715 *Fax:* 01224 252716

Con majority 8,809

DORRELL, STEPHEN
Charnwood

Stephen James Dorrell. Born 25 March 1952; Son of late Philip Dorrell, Company Director; Educated Uppingham School; Brasenose College, Oxford (BA law 1973); Married Penelope Anne Taylor 1980 (3 sons 1 daughter). Director, family industrial clothing firm 1975-87, 1997-

House of Commons: Contested Kingston-upon-Hull East October 1974 general election. Member for Loughborough 1979-97, and for Charnwood since 1 May 1997 general election; Assistant Government Whip 1987-88; Government Whip 1988-90; PPS to Peter Walker as Secretary of State for Energy 1983-87; Parliamentary Under-Secretary of State, Department of Health 1990-92; Financial Secretary, HM Treasury 1992-94; Secretary of State for: National Heritage 1994-1995, Health 1995-97; Member, Shadow Cabinet 1997-98; Shadow Secretary of State for Education and Employment 1997-98. *Political interests:* Economics, Foreign Affairs

Chairman, Millennium Commission 1994-95; PC 1994; *Recreations:* Reading, theatre

Rt Hon Stephen Dorrell, MP, House of Commons, London SW1A 0AA *Tel:* 020 7219 4472 *Fax:* 020 7219 5838 *E-mail:* info@stephendorrell.org.uk. *Constituency:* 768 Melton Road, Thurmaston, Leicester, Leicestershire LE4 8BD *Tel:* 0116-260 8609 *Fax:* 0116-260 8700

Con majority 11,355

DORRIES, NADINE
Mid Bedfordshire

Nadine Dorries. Born 1958; Married to Paul. Nurse; Businesswoman; Adviser to Oliver Letwin MP

House of Commons: Contested Hazel Grove 2001 general election (as Nadine Bargery). Member for Mid Bedfordshire since 5 May 2005 general election. *Political interests:* Law and order, pensions, health, rural affairs

Nadine Dorries, MP, House of Commons, London SW1A 0AA *Tel:* 020 7219 4239. *Constituency:* Mid-Bedfordshire Conservative Association, St Michaels Close, High Street, Shefford, Bedfordshire SG17 5DD *Tel:* 01462 811992 *Fax:* 01462 811010 *E-mail:* admin@midbedsconservatives.com *Website:* www.midbedsconservatives.com

DOWD, JIM
Lewisham West

Jim Dowd. Born 5 March 1951; Son of late James and Elfriede Dowd; Educated Sedgehill Comprehensive School, London; London Nautical School. Apprentice telephone engineer, GPO (now BT) 1967-72; Station manager, Heron Petrol Stations Ltd. 1972-73; Telecommunications engineer, Plessey Company 1973-92; Member: POEU 1967-72, AMICUS (MSF) 1973-, GMB; London Borough of Lewisham: Councillor 1974-94, Deputy Leader 1984-86, Chair, Finance Committee, Deputy Mayor 1987, 1990, Mayor 1992; Member, Lewisham and North Southwark District Health Authority

Lab majority 9,932

House of Commons: Contested Beckenham 1983 and Lewisham West 1987 general elections. Member for Lewisham West since 9 April 1992 general election; Opposition Spokesperson on Northern Ireland 1995-97; Opposition Whip for London 1993-95; Government Whip 1997-2001. *Political interests:* NHS, Transport, Economic Policy, Industrial Policy, Environment, Housing, Animal Welfare, Human Rights, Education

Member, National Trust; *Clubs:* Bromley Labour Club; *Recreations:* Music, reading, theatre, Cornwall

Jim Dowd, MP, House of Commons, London SW1A 0AA *Tel:* 020 7219 4617 *Fax:* 020 7219 2686 *E-mail:* jimdowd.newlabour@care4free.net. *Constituency:* 43 Sunderland Road, Forest Hill, London SE23 2PS *Tel:* 020 8699 2001 *Fax:* 020 8291 5607

DREW, DAVID
Stroud

David Elliott Drew. Born 13 April 1952; Son of Ronald Montague Drew, company accountant, and late Maisie Joan Drew, hospital administrator; Educated Kingsfield School, Gloucestershire; Nottingham University (BA economics 1974); Birmingham University (PGCE 1976); Bristol Polytechnic (MA historical studies 1988); University of the West of England (MEd 1994); Married Anne Baker 1990 (2 sons 2 daughters). Economics and geography teacher, various schools in Warwickshire, Hertfordshire and Gloucestershire 1976-86; Lecturer, business education, Bristol Polytechnic/University of the West of England 1986-97; Member, NAS/UWT 1976-86; Branch secretary 1984-86; Member, NATFHE 1986-; Member, UNISON, then NUPE 1990-; Councillor: Stevenage Borough Council 1981-82, Stroud District Council 1987-95, Stonehouse Town Council 1987-, Gloucestershire County Council 1993-97

Lab/Co-op majority 350

House of Commons: Contested Stroud 1992 general election. Member for Stroud since 1 May 1997 general election. *Political interests:* Housing, Poverty, Planning, Environment, Education, Agriculture, Rural Affairs, Small Businesses. South Africa, Sudan, Bangladesh

Member: Co-op Party 1980-, Christian Socialist Movement, Labour Party Rural Revival, Labour Campaign for Electoral Reform; Treasurer, Gloucestershire County Labour Party 1987-93; Secretary, Stroud Constituency Labour Party 1992-93. Spent 20-25 days with MoD on "work experience" 1999 and 2002; *Publications:* Various IT related materials; *Clubs:* Bristol Rugby Football Club, Forest Green FC; *Recreations:* Reading, watching rugby, football

David Drew, MP, House of Commons, London SW1A 0AA *Tel:* 020 7219 6479 *Fax:* 020 7219 0910 *E-mail:* drewd@parliament.uk. *Constituency:* 5A Lansdown, Stroud, Gloucestershire G5 1BB *Tel:* 01453 752684 *Fax:* 01453 753756

DUDDRIDGE, JAMES
Rochford and Southend East

James Duddridge. Born 26 August 1971; Educated Crestwood School, Eastleigh; Huddersfield New College; Wells Blue School; Essex University (BA government 1993); Married Kathryn (Katy) Brigid Thompson 2004. Retail and merchant banking, Barclays Bank 1993-95; Barclays Bank Head Office 1995-96; Barclays Bank of Swaziland 1995-96; Sales director, Banque Belgolaise, Ivory Coast 1997-98; National sales manager, Barclays 1998; Account director and consultant, YouGov 2000-; Director, Okavango Ltd 2002-

Con majority 5,494

House of Commons: Contested Rother Valley 2001 general election. Member for Rochford and Southend East since 5 May 2005 general election. *Political interests:* African politics, pensions

Chair, Wells Young Conservatives 1989-91; Campaigns department, Conservative Central Office 1989-91; Chair, University of Essex Conservative Students 1990-91; Research assistant, Bernard Jenkin MP 1991-93; General election campaign manager, Stephen Shakespeare 1997; Executive Committee member Conservative Way Forward 2000-01; Adviser, Lady Miller Postal Services Bill 1999. *Recreations:* Running, cycling, Southampton FC, Southend United FC

James Duddridge, MP, House of Commons, London SW1A 0AA
Tel: 020 7219 6646. *Constituency:* Rochford and Southend East Conservative Association, Suite 1, Strand House, 742 Southchurch Street, Southend on Sea, Essex SS1 2PS *Tel:* 01702 600460 *Fax:* 01702 600460
E-mail: email@jamesduddridge.com *Website:* www.jamesduddridge.com

DUNCAN, ALAN
Rutland and Melton

Alan James Carter Duncan. Born 31 March 1957; Son of late Wing-Commander James Duncan, OBE, and Anne, née Carter; Educated Beechwood Park School, St Albans; Merchant Taylors' School, Northwood; St John's College, Oxford (BA philosophy, politics and economics 1979) (President, Oxford Union 1979); Harvard University (Kennedy Scholar). Graduate trainee, Shell International Petroleum 1979-81; Oil trader and adviser to governments and companies on oil supply, shipping and refining 1989-92; Visiting Fellow, St Antony's College, Oxford 2002-03

Con majority 12,930

House of Commons: Contested Barnsley West and Penistone 1987 general election. Member for Rutland and Melton since 9 April 1992 general election; Opposition Spokesman for: Health 1998-99, Trade and Industry 1999-2001, Foreign and Commonwealth Affairs 2001-03; PPS to Dr Brian Mawhinney: as Minister of State, Department of Health 1993-94, as Chairman Conservative Party 1995-97; Parliamentary Political Secretary to William Hague as Leader of the Conservative Party 1997-98; Shadow Secretary of State for: International Development 2003-05, Transport 2005-. *Political interests:* International Trade, International Economics, Social Security, Middle East

Vice-Chairman Conservative Party 1997-98. *Publications:* Co-author: (CPC pamphlet) *Bearing the Standard: Themes for a Fourth Term, 1991, Who Benefits? Reinventing Social Security, An End to Illusions, 1993, Saturn's Children: How the State Devours Liberty, Prosperity and Virtue, 1995; Beware Blair, 1997*; Liveryman, Merchant Taylors' Company; Freeman, City of London; *Clubs:* Beefsteak; *Recreations:* Shooting, skiing

Alan Duncan, MP, House of Commons, London SW1A 0AA *Tel:* 020 7219 5204
E-mail: duncana@parliament.uk. *Constituency: Tel:* 01664 566444
Fax: 01664 566555

Con majority 10,641

DUNCAN SMITH, IAIN
Chingford and Woodford Green

(George) Iain Duncan Smith. Born 9 April 1954; Son of late Group Captain W. G. G. Duncan Smith, DSO, DFC, and Pamela, neé Summers; Educated HMS Conway (Cadet School); Universita per Stranieri, Perugia, Italy; RMA Sandhurst; Dunchurch College of Management; Married Hon. Elizabeth Wynne Fremantle 1982 (2 sons 2 daughters). Commissioned, Scots Guards 1975; ADC to Major-General Sir John Acland, KCB, CBE, Commander of Commonwealth Monitoring Force in Zimbabwe 1979-81. GEC Marconi 1981; Director: Bellwinch Property 1988-89, Publishing Director Jane's Information Group 1989-92

House of Commons: Contested Bradford West 1987 general election. Member for Chingford 1992-97, and for Chingford and Woodford Green since 1 May 1997 general election; Member, Shadow Cabinet 1997-2003; Shadow Secretary of State for: Social Security 1997-99, Defence 1999-2001; Leader of the Opposition 2001-03; Leader, Conservative Party 2001-03. *Political interests:* Finance, Small Businesses, Transport, Defence, Environment

Vice-Chair, Fulham Conservative Association 1991; Chair Conservative Policy Board 2001-03. Haven House Foundation; *Publications:* Co-author *Who Benefits? Reinventing Social Security*; *Game, Set and Match?* (Maastricht); *Facing the Future* (Defence and Foreign and Commonwealth Affairs); *1994 and Beyond*; *A Response to Chancellor Kohl*; *A Race against time, Europe's growing vulnerablity to missile attack* 2002; *The Devil's Tune* (Robson Books) 2003; PC 2001; Freeman, City of London 1993; *Recreations:* Cricket, rugby, tennis, sport in general, painting, theatre, family

Rt Hon Iain Duncan Smith, MP, House of Commons, London SW1A 0AA *Tel:* 020 7219 2664. *Constituency:* 20A Station Road, Chingford, London E4 7BE *Tel:* 020 8524 4344

Con majority 2,027

DUNNE, PHILIP
Ludlow

Philip Dunne. Born 14 August 1958; Educated Eton College; Keble College, Oxford (BA philosophy, politics and economics 1980, MA); Married Domenica Margaret Anne Fraser 1989. Graduate trainee S.G. Warburg & Co Ltd 1980-88; Director of corporate development James Gulliver Associates 1988-90; Managing director Phoenix Securities and successor 1991-2001; Co-founder and chairman (non exec) Ottaker's plc 1987-; Chairman (non exec) Baronsmead VCT 4 plc 2001-; Partner Gatley Farms 1987-; NFU 1987-; South Shropshire District Council: Councillor 2001-, Member Standards Committee, Conservative group leader

House of Commons: Member for Ludlow since 5 May 2005 general election. *Political interests:* Agriculture, business (especially small business), economy, financial services, international affairs

Treasurer Ludlow Conservative Association 2001-02. Director: Juvenile Diabetes Research Foundation 1998-2005, Moor Park Charitable Trust 2001-; *Clubs:* Whites, Carlton; Church Stretton Golf Club; Kington Golf Club; *Recreations:* Country sports, skiing, shooting, travel

Philip Dunne, MP, House of Commons, London SW1A 0AA *Tel:* 020 7219 8474. *Constituency:* Ludlow Conservative Association, 54 Broad Street, Ludlow SY8 1GP *Tel:* 01584 872187 *Fax:* 01584 876345 *E-mail:* philipdunne@ludlowconservatives.com *Website:* www.philipdunne.com

DUNWOODY, GWYNETH
Crewe and Nantwich

Gwyneth Patricia Dunwoody. Born 12 December 1930; Daughter of late Morgan Phillips, sometime General Secretary of the Labour Party and late Baroness Phillips; Married Dr. John Elliott Orr Dunwoody 1954 (marriage dissolved 1975) (2 sons 1 daughter). Director, Film Production Association of GB 1970-74

House of Commons: Contested Exeter 1964 general election. Member for Exeter 1966-70, for Crewe February 1974-83, and for Crewe and Nantwich since 9 June 1983 general election; Opposition Front Bench Spokesman on: Foreign and Commonwealth Affairs 1979-80, NHS 1980-83, Parliamentary Campaigning and Information 1983-84; Opposition Spokesman on Transport 1984-85; Parliamentary Secretary to Board of Trade 1967-70; MEP 1975-79; Deputy Speaker, Westminster Hall 1999-2000. *Political interests:* Transport, NHS, Arts. Botswana, Central Africa, East Africa, Middle East

Labour Friends of Israel: Former Chair, President 1993-95, Life President 1995-. Vice-President, Socialist International Women; Vice-Chairman, European Parliament Social Affairs Committee; *Recreations:* Reading, listening to music

Gwyneth Dunwoody, MP, House of Commons, London SW1A 0AA
Tel: 020 7219 3490 *Fax:* 020 7219 6046. *Constituency:* 154 Nantwich Road, Crewe, Cheshire CW2 6BG *Tel:* 01270 589132 *Fax:* 01270 589135

Lab majority 7,078

DURKAN, MARK
Foyle

Mark Durkan. Born 26 June 1960; Son of late Brendan Durkan, police officer, and of Isobel Durkan; Educated St Patrick's Primary School, Derry; St Columb's College, Derry; Queen's University, Belfast; Married Jackie Green 1993. Deputy President, Union of Students in Ireland 1982-84; Parliamentary Assistant to John Hume MP 1984-98; Member: SDLP Talks Team, Brooke/Mayhew Talks 1991-92, Dublin Forum for Peace and Reconciliation 1994-96, Northern Ireland Forum for Political Dialogue 1996, SDLP Talks Team, Castle Buildings Talks 1996-98; MLA for Foyle since 25 June 1998: Minister of Finance and Personnel 1999 -2001, Deputy First Minister 2001-02; Councillor, Derry City Council 1993-2000; Member: Northern Ireland Housing Council 1993-95, Western Health and Social Services Council 1993-2000

House of Commons: Member for Foyle since 5 May 2005 general election

Chair SDLP 1990-95; Leader SDLP 2001-

Mark Durkan, MP, House of Commons, London SW1A 0AA *Tel:* 020 7219 5096. *Constituency:* 7B Messines Terrace, Racecourse Road, Derry BT48 7QZ *Tel:* 028 7136 0700 *Fax:* 028 7136 0808

SDLP majority 5,957

Lab majority 9,109

EAGLE, ANGELA
Wallasey

Angela Eagle. Born 17 February 1961; Daughter of André Eagle, printworker, and late Shirley Eagle, dressmaker and student; Educated Formby High School; St John's College, Oxford (BA philosophy, politics and economics); COHSE 1984-: first as a researcher, then as National Press Officer, currently as Parliamentary Liaison Officer; Member: COHSE, NUJ

House of Commons: Member for Wallasey since 9 April 1992 general election; Opposition Whip 1996-97; Parliamentary Under-Secretary of State: Department of the Environment, Transport and the Regions (Minister for Green Issues and Regeneration) 1997-98, Department of Social Security 1998-2001; Parliamentary Under-Secretary of State, Home Office 2001-02. *Political interests:* Economic Policy, NHS, Politics of Sport

Active at branch, women's section, general committee levels in Crosby Constituency 1978-80; Chairman: Oxford University Fabian Club 1980-83, National Conference of Labour Women 1991. *Publications:* Columnist and regular contributor to *Tribune*; *Recreations:* Chess, cricket, cinema

Angela Eagle, MP, House of Commons, London SW1A 0AA *Tel:* 020 7219 4074 *E-mail:* eaglea@parliament.uk. *Constituency:* 6 Manor Road, Liscard, Wallasey, Merseyside CH45 4JB *Tel:* 01925 574 913

Lab majority 7,193

EAGLE, MARIA
Liverpool Garston

Maria Eagle. Born 17 February 1961; Daughter of André Eagle, printworker, and late Shirley Eagle, dressmaker and student; Educated St Peter's Church of England Primary School, Formby; Formby High School (Comprehensive); Pembroke College, Oxford (BA philosophy, politics and economics 1983); College of Law, London (Common Professional Exam, Law Society Finals 1990). Voluntary sector 1983-90; Articles of clerkship, Brian Thompson & Partners, Liverpool 1990-92; Goldsmith Williams, Liverpool 1992-95; Senior Solicitor, Steven Irving & Co, Liverpool 1994-97; Member GMB

House of Commons: Contested Crosby 1992 general election. Member for Liverpool Garston since 1 May 1997 general election; PPS to John Hutton as Minister of State, Department of Health 1999-2001; Parliamentary Under-Secretary of State: (Minister for Disabled People), Department for Work and Pensions 2001-05, Department for Education and Skills 2005-. *Political interests:* Transport, Housing, Employment. Nicaragua, USA, Australia

Campaigns organiser Crosby 1993-96; Campaigns organiser, Press officer, Merseyside West Euro Constituency Labour Party 1983-84; Constituency Labour Party secretary, Press officer, political education officer 1983-85. Played cricket for Lancashire as a Junior; Played chess for England and Lancashire; *Publications:* Co-author *High Time or High Tide for Labour Women*; *Recreations:* Cinema, chess, cricket

Maria Eagle, MP, House of Commons, London SW1A 0AA *Tel:* 020 7219 5288 *Fax:* 020 7219 1157 *E-mail:* eaglem@parliament.uk. *Constituency:* Unit House, Speke Boulevard, Liverpool L24 9HZ *Tel:* 0151-448 1167 *Fax:* 0151-448 0976

EFFORD, CLIVE
Eltham

Clive Efford. Born 10 July 1958; Son of Stanley Efford, retired civil servant and Mary Agnes Elizabeth Christina Efford, neé Caldwell; Educated Walworth Comprehensive School; Southwark Further Education College; Married Gillian Vallins (3 daughters). Partner family-owned jewellery and watch repair business till 1987; Taxi driver 1987-97; Member, T&GWU; London Borough of Greenwich: Councillor 1986-98, Chair, Social Services, Health and Environment, Secretary Labour Group 1986-87; Chief Whip Labour Group 1990-91

Lab majority 3,276

House of Commons: Contested Eltham 1992 general election. Member for Eltham since 1 May 1997 general election; Presented two bills in Parliament on energy efficiency and energy conservation. *Political interests:* Welfare State, Health, Transport, Education, Environment, Local and Regional Government, Energy Conservation, Energy Efficiency, Energy from Waste, Waste Management, Recycling

Vice-chair London Group of Labour MPs 2001-02; Member Labour Friends of India. *Clubs:* Plumstead Co-op Club; CIU Club; Woolwich Catholic Club; *Recreations:* Football (FA Coachers Club)

Clive Efford, MP, House of Commons, London SW1A 0AA *Tel:* 020 7219 4057 *E-mail:* clive.efford@btinternet.com. *Constituency:* Westmount Road, Eltham, London SE9

ELLMAN, LOUISE
Liverpool Riverside

Louise Joyce Ellman. Born 14 November 1945; Daughter of late Harold and Anne Rosenberg; Educated Manchester High School for Girls; Hull University (BA sociology 1967); York University (MPhil social administration 1972); Married Geoffrey Ellman 1967 (1 son 1 daughter); Member, T&GWU; Councillor, Lancashire County Council 1970-97, Leader, County Labour Group 1977-97, Leader of Council 1981-97; Councillor, West Lancashire District Council 1974-87; Vice-Chair, Lancashire Enterprises 1982-97; Founder Chair, Northwest Regional Association 1991-92, Vice-Chair 1996-97

Lab/Co-op majority 10,214

House of Commons: Member for Liverpool Riverside since 1 May 1997 general election. *Political interests:* Regional Government, Local Government, Transport, Public Services, Arts, Middle East

Member, Co-op Party; Vice-chair Labour Friends of Israel

Louise Ellman, MP, House of Commons, London SW1A 0AA *Tel:* 020 7219 5210 *Fax:* 020 7219 2592 *E-mail:* ellmanl@parliament.uk. *Constituency:* First Floor, Threlfall Building, Trueman Street, Liverpool L3 2EX *Tel:* 0151-236 2969 *Fax:* 0151-236 4301

ELLWOOD, TOBIAS
Bournemouth East

Tobias Martin Ellwood. Born 12 August 1966; Educated Vienna International School, Austria; Loughborough University of Technology (BA design and technology 1990); City University Business School (MBA 1999); Single. Army officer, Royal Green Jackets 1991-96. Researcher to Tom King MP 1996-97; Senior business manager, London Stock Exchange 1999; Councillor, Dacorum Borough Council 1999

Con majority 5,244

House of Commons: Contested Worsley 2001 general election. Member for Bournemouth East since 5 May 2005 general election

Branch chair, Herts SW Conservative Association 1998. *Publications: Introduction to the Conservative Party*

Tobias Ellwood, MP, House of Commons, London SW1A 0AA *Tel:* 020 7219 4349. *Constituency:* Boscombe Conservative Club, Haviland Road West, Bournemouth, Dorset BH1 4JW *Tel:* 01202 397047 *Fax:* 01202 397047
E-mail: becaoffice@btconnect.com
Website: www.bournemouheastconservatives.com

ENGEL, NATASCHA
North East Derbyshire

Natascha Engel. Born 9 April 1967; Married. Local newspaper journalist; Translator; Editor *The Pensioner* newspaper; Volunteer: Amnesty International, Help the Aged; Member: GMB, GPMU

House of Commons: Member for North East Derbyshire since 5 May 2005 general election

Lab majority 10,065

Labour Party: national trade union policy co-ordinator, National trade union general election co-ordinator, Trade union political fund ballot co-ordinator, Trade Union Co-ordinating Committee (TUCC); Policy director The John Smith Institute; Organiser TUC Organising Academy. *Publications:* several pamphlets including 'Shop Stewards' Pocket Policy Guide', 'Trade Union Links with the Labour Party', 'Rights Won By Unions', 'Age of Regions', 'Learning to Organise'

Natascha Engel, MP, House of Commons, London SW1A 0AA *Tel:* 020 7219 4709. *Constituency:* 113 Saltergate, Chesterfield, Derbyshire SN40 1NF *Tel:* 01246 205642 *E-mail:* n.engel@btinternet.com

Lab majority 14,125

ENNIS, JEFFREY
Barnsley East and Mexborough

Jeffrey Ennis. Born 13 November 1952; Son of William, retired miner, and Jean Ennis; Educated Hemsworth Grammar School; Redland College, Bristol (CertEd, BEd 1975); Married Margaret Angela Knight 1980 (3 sons). Raw materials inspector, Lyons Bakery 1975-76; Primary teacher: Wolverhampton 1976-78, Hillsborough Primary School, Sheffield 1979-96; Member, TU 1975-; Representative, NASUWT at Hillsborough Primary 1979-96; Member, TGWU 1997-; Councillor, Barnsley Council 1980-96; Councillor, Barnsley Metropolitan Borough Council 1980-96, Deputy Leader 1988-95, Leader 1995-96; Chair, South Yorkshire Fire and Civil Defence Authority 1995-96

House of Commons: Member for Barnsley East from December 12, 1996 by-election-1997, and for Barnsley East and Mexborough since 1 May 1997 general election; PPS to Tessa Jowell: as Minister for Public Health, Department of Health 1997-99, as Minister of State, Department for Education and Employment (Minister for Employment, Welfare to Work and Equal Opportunities) 1999-2001. *Political interests:* Local and Regional Government, Environment, Education, Regeneration, Fire Service. Germany, Ukraine

Member, Co-operative Party. Member, British-Irish Inter-Parliamentary Body; *Clubs:* Member, British Legion; *Recreations:* Family activities, hill walking, sport, music, swimming, caravanning

Jeffrey Ennis, MP, House of Commons, London SW1A 0AA *Tel:* 020 7219 5008 *Fax:* 020 7219 2728 *E-mail:* ennisj@parliament.uk. *Constituency:* Dearne Town Hall, Goldthorpe, Rotherman, South Yorkshire S63 9EJ *Tel:* 01226 775080 *Fax:* 01226 775080

Lab majority 9,995

ETHERINGTON, BILL
Sunderland North

Bill (William) Etherington. Born 17 July 1941; Son of Marjorie and William Henderson Etherington; Educated Redby Infant and Junior School; Monkwearmouth Grammar School; Durham University (Certificate of Industrial Relations Studies); Married Irene Holton 1963 (2 daughters). Apprentice fitter, Austin & Pickersgill Shipyard 1957-63; Fitter, Dawdon Colliery 1963-83; Full-time official, NUM 1983-92; Member: AEU 1957-, NUM 1963-, National Executive Committee 1986-88, 1995-; Trustee, Mineworkers' Pension Scheme 1985-87; Representative, North Regional TUC 1985-92; NUM delegate, TUC 1990-91; Vice-President, North East Area NUM 1988-92; Member, RMT Parliamentary Campaigning Group 2002-04

House of Commons: Member for Sunderland North since 9 April 1992 general election. *Political interests:* Trades Union Legislation, Employment, Adult Education, Human Rights, Education, Equal Opportunities, NHS, Homelessness, Disability, Animal Welfare, Hunting With Dogs (Against), Fluoridation (Against)

Various posts, including local ward treasurer 1978-87; GMC delegate 1978-87; CLP Executive Committee member 1981-87. UK Delegation to Council of Europe and Western Europe Union: Member 1997-, Deputy Leader 2001-; *Clubs:* Kelloe Working Men's, Durham City; *Recreations:* Fell walking, motorcycling, watching soccer, local, industrial and transport history, reading

Bill Etherington, MP, House of Commons, London SW1A 0AA *Tel:* 020 7219 4603 *Fax:* 020 7219 1186. *Constituency:* 7 Bridge House, Bridge Street, Sunderland, Tyne and Wear SR1 1TE *Tel:* 0191-564 2489 *Fax:* 0191-564 2486

EVANS, NIGEL
Ribble Valley

Nigel Evans. Born 10 November 1957; Son of late Albert Evans, and of Betty Evans; Educated Dynevor School; University College of Wales, Swansea (BA politics 1979); Single. Management family retail newsagent and convenience store 1979-90; West Glamorgan County Council: Councillor 1985-91, Deputy Leader, Conservative Group 1990-91

Con majority 14,171

House of Commons: Contested Swansea West 1987 general election, Pontypridd 1989 by-election, Ribble Valley 1991 by-election. Member for Ribble Valley since 9 April 1992 general election; Opposition Spokesperson for: Constitutional Affairs (Scotland and Wales) 1997-99, Constitutional Affairs (Wales) 1999-2001; PPS: to David Hunt: as Secretary of State for Employment 1993-94, as Chancellor of the Duchy of Lancaster 1994-95; to Tony Baldry as Minister of State, Ministry of Agriculture, Fisheries and Food 1995-96; to William Hague as Secretary of State for Wales 1996-97; Shadow Secretary of State for Wales 2001-03. *Political interests:* Education, Small Businesses, US Elections, Local and Regional Government, Defence, Agriculture, International Politics, European Affairs, Telecommunications, Space. Caribbean, Central America, Europe, USA, Asia, Far East, Australia, Egypt, Bahrain, Grand Caymen, Gibraltar

Chairman, Conservative Welsh Parliamentary Candidates Policy Group 1990; President, Conservative North West Parliamentary Candidates Group 1991; Secretary, North West Conservative MPs 1992-97; Vice-chairman: (Wales), Conservative Party 1999-2001, Conservative Party (Conservatives Abroad) 2004-. Cancer, SCOPE; Has worked on three US presidential elections in New York, Florida and California; *Clubs:* Carlton, I.O.D., countryclubuk.com; *Recreations:* Tennis, swimming, running, theatre, cinema, arts

Nigel Evans, MP, House of Commons, London SW1A 0AA *Tel:* 020 7219 4165 *Fax:* 0870 131 3711 *E-mail:* nigelmp@hotmail.com. *Constituency:* 9 Railway View, Clitheroe, Lancashire BB7 2HA *Tel:* 01200 425939 *Fax:* 01200 422904

EVENNETT, DAVID
Bexleyheath and Crayford

David Anthony Evennett. Born 3 June 1949; Educated Buckhurst Hill County High School for Boys; London School of Economics: (BSc (Econ) economics 1971, MSc (Econ) politics 1972); Married Marilyn Smith 1975. Schoolmaster, Ilford County High School 1972-74; Marine insurance broker, Lloyds 1974-81; Member, Lloyds 1976-92; Director, Lloyds Underwriting Agency 1982-91; Commercial liaison manager, Bexley College 1997 – 2001; Freelance lecturer 2001-; Councillor, London

Con majority 4,551

Borough of Redbridge 1974-78

House of Commons: Contested Hackney South and Shoreditch 1979 general election. Member for Erith and Crayford 1983-97. Contested Bexleyheath and Crayford 1997 and 2001 general elections. Member for Bexleyheath and Crayford since 5 May 2005 general election; PPS to: Baroness Blatch as Minister of State for Education 1992-93, John Redwood as Secretary of State for Wales 1993-95, Baroness Blatch and David Maclean as Ministers of State, Home Office 1995-96, Gillian Shephard as Secretary of State for Education and Employment 1996-1997; Former vice-chair, House of Commons Motor Club. *Political interests:* Education, economy

Clubs: Bexleyheath Conservative Club; *Recreations:* Travel, reading, cinema

David Evennett, MP, House of Commons, London SW1A 0AA *Tel:* 020 7219 8403. *Constituency:* Bexleyheath and Crayford Conservative Association, 17 Church Road, Bexleyheath, Kent DA7 4DD *Tel:* 020 8303 4695 *Fax:* 020 8303 1497 *E-mail:* bexleyheath-crayford.tory.org *Website:* www.bexcrayconservatives.org.uk

Con majority 7,080

FABRICANT, MICHAEL
Lichfield

Michael Fabricant. Born 12 June 1950; Son of late Isaac Nathan Fabricant, and of Helena Fabricant, neé Freed; Educated Brighton, Hove and Sussex Grammar School, Brighton; Loughborough University (BSc economics and law 1973); Sussex University (MSc systems and econometrics 1974); Oxford University/London University/University of Southern California, Los Angeles, USA (PhD econometrics and economic forecasting 1975-78); Single. Economist and founder director, leading broadcast and communications group, manufacturing and commissioning electronics equipment to radio stations to 48 countries 1980-91; Adviser, Home Office on broadcasting matters; Staff, then freelance radio broadcaster and journalist 1968-80; Adviser to foreign governments on the establishment and management of radio stations, including the Russian Federation 1980-91; Has lived and worked extensively in Europe, Africa, the Far East, former Soviet Union, and the United States

House of Commons: Contested South Shields 1987 general election. Member for Mid-Staffordshire 1992-97, and for Lichfield since 1 May 1997 general election; PPS to Michael Jack as Financial Secretary to the Treasury 1996-97; Shadow Minister for: Trade and Industry 2003, Economic Affairs 2003-. *Political interests:* Trade and Industry, Foreign Affairs, Broadcasting and Media, Technology. Russia, Israel, USA, Australia, Eastern Europe

Chairman, Brighton Pavilion Conservative Association 1985-88; Member, Conservative Way Forward; Associate Member, European Research Group; Member, Conservative Against a Federal Europe. Cancer Research; Presented Bills to strengthen economic and political ties between UK, United States, Canada, Australia and New Zealand; Promoted legislation to encourage the flying of the Union Flag; Promoted legislation to force the Government to undertake and publish regular financial cost-benefit analyses of Britain's membership of the European Union; Member: Inter-Parliamentary Union, Commonwealth Parliamentary Association; *Clubs:* Rottingdean (Sussex); *Recreations:* Reading, music, fell-walking, skiing and listening to the Omnibus Edition of The Archers

Michael Fabricant, MP, House of Commons, London SW1A 0AA

Tel: 020 7219 5022 *E-mail:* www.michael.fabricant.mp.co.uk/contact.html.
Constituency: Tel: 01543 417868

Con majority 12,970

FALLON, MICHAEL
Sevenoaks

Michael Fallon. Born 14 May 1952; Son of late Martin Fallon, OBE, FRICS, and Hazel Fallon; Educated Epsom College, Surrey; St Andrews University (MA classics and ancient history 1974); Married Wendy Elisabeth Payne 1986 (2 sons). European Educational Research Trust 1974-75; Conservative Research Department 1975-79 (seconded to Opposition Whips Office, House of Lords 1975-77, EEC Desk Officer 1977-79); Secretary, Lord Home's Committee on Future of the House of Lords 1977-78; Joint Managing Director, European Consultants Ltd 1979-81; Assistant to Baroness Elles MEP 1979-83; Director, Quality Care Homes plc 1992-97; Chief Executive, Quality Care Developments Ltd 1996-97; Director: Just Learning Ltd 1996-, Bannatyne Fitness Ltd 1999-2000, Just Learning Holdings 2001-, Just Learning Development Ltd 2001-

House of Commons: Contested Darlington by-election March 1983. Member for Darlington 1983-92, and for Sevenoaks since 1 May 1997 general election; Opposition Frontbench Spokesperson for: Trade and Industry June-December 1997, the Treasury December 1997-98; Assistant Government Whip 1988-90; Government Whip (Lord Commissioner of HM Treasury) May-July 1990; PPS to Cecil Parkinson as Secretary of State for Energy 1987-88; Parliamentary Under-Secretary of State, Department of Education and Science 1990-92. *Political interests:* Constitution, Public Sector, Education, Energy

Member: Higher Education Funding Council 1992-97, Deregulation Task Force 1994-97, Advisory Council, Social Market Foundation 1994-2000; *Publications: Brighter Schools*, Social Market Foundation 1993; *Clubs:* Academy

Michael Fallon, MP, House of Commons, London SW1A 0AA *Tel:* 020 7219 6482 *Fax:* 020 7219 6791 *E-mail:* fallonm@parliament.uk. *Constituency:* 113 St John's Hill, Sevenoaks, Kent TN13 3PF *Tel:* 01732 452261

Lab majority 8,108

FARRELLY, PAUL
Newcastle-under-Lyme

(Christopher) Paul Farrelly. Born 2 March 1962; Son of late Thomas Farrelly and Anne Farrelly, née King; Educated Wolstanton County Grammar School; Marshlands Comprehensive, Newcastle-Under-Lyme; St Edmund Hall, Oxford (BA philosophy, politics and economics 1984); Married Victoria Jane Perry 1998 (1 son 1 daughter). Manager corporate finance division Barclays De Zoete Wedd Ltd 1984-90; Reuters Ltd 1990-95: Correspondent, News editor; Deputy city and business editor *Independent on Sunday* 1995-97; City editor *The Observer* 1997-2001; NUJ; MSF

House of Commons: Contested Chesham and Amersham 1997 general election. Member for Newcastle-under-Lyme since 7 June 2001 general election. *Political interests:* Education, Health, Employment, Trade and Industry, Regeneration, Investment, European Affairs, Pensions, Crime

Hornsey and Wood Green CLP: Secretary 1992-94, Vice-chair 1994-95; Newcastle-under-Lyme CLP 1998-: Campaign co-ordinator and organiser, Political education officer; Member Socialist Education Association. Member European Standing Committee B 2003-; *Clubs:* Holy Trinity Catholic Centre, Newcastle-Under-Lyme; Trentham RUFC, Finchley RFC; *Recreations:* Rugby, football, writing, biography, history, architecture

Paul Farrelly, MP, House of Commons, London SW1A 0AA *Tel:* 020 7219 8262 *Fax:* 020 7219 1986 *E-mail:* farrellyp@parliament.uk. *Constituency:* Waterloo Buildings, Dunkirk, Newcastle-under-Lyme, Staffordshire ST5 2SW *Tel:* 01782 715033

FARRON, TIM
Westmorland and Lonsdale

Timothy James Farron. Born 27 May 1970; Educated Lostock Hall High School, Preston, Lancashire; Runshaw Tertiary College, Leyland; Newcastle University (BA politics 1991); Married Rosie Alison Cantley 2000. Lancaster University: Adult education officer 1992-96, Student support officer 1996-98, Faculty administrator 1998-2002; Head of faculty administration, St Martin's College, (Ambleside, Lancaster, Carlisle) 2002-; Association of University Teachers 1995-; Group deputy leader, Lancashire County Council 1993-2000; Councillor: South Ribble Borough 1995-99, South Lakeland District 2004-

Lib Dem majority 267

House of Commons: Contested North West Durham 1992, South Ribble 1997 and Westmorland and Lonsdale 2001 general elections. Member for Westmorland and Lonsdale since 5 May 2005 general election. *Political interests:* Education, rural affairs, youth work, health, crime and policing, social care

Contested NW England 1999 European Parliament election; *Clubs:* President, Kendal and South Westmorland Liberal; Lib Dem Christian Forum; Cumbria Wildlife; Lakes Line User Group; *Recreations:* Fell walking, cycling, football, watching Blackburn Rovers, music

Tim Farron, MP, House of Commons, London SW1A 0AA *Tel:* 020 7219 8498. *Constituency:* The Cottage, Yard 2, Strichlandgate, Kendal, Cumbria LA9 4ND *Tel:* 01539 723403 *Fax:* 01539 723403 *E-mail:* timfarron@hotmail.com *Website:* www.timfarron.co.uk

FEATHERSTONE, LYNNE
Hornsey and Wood Green

Lynne Featherstone. Born 20 December 1951; Educated South Hampstead High School, London; Oxford Polytechnic (graphic design 1974); Married Stephen Featherstone 1982 (divorced 2002). Graphic designer, London and Australia 1974-77; Freelance designer 1977-80; Managing director, Inhouse Outhouse Design 1980-87; Strategic design consultant 1987-97; Councillor, Haringey Council: Leader of the Opposition, 1998-2003; Member Greater London Assembly 2000-: Chair, Assembly Committee on Transport 2003-

Lib Dem majority 2,395

House of Commons: Contested Hornsey and Wood Green 1997 and 2001 general elections. Member for Hornsey and Wood Green since 5 May 2005 general election. *Political interests:* Transport and policing

Vice-chair, Women Liberal Democrats; Member: Liberal Democrat Federal Executive; Association of Liberal Democrat Councillors; Parliamentary Candidates Association. *Publications:* Marketing and Communications Techniques for Architects (Longman) 1992; Daily Mail 'unsung hero' award 2002; Guardian political blog of the year 2004; *Recreations:* Writing poetry, film

Lynne Featherstone, MP, House of Commons, London SW1A 0AA *Tel:* 020 7219 8401. *Constituency:* 100 Uplands Road, London N8 9MJ *Tel:* 020 8340 5459 *Fax:* 020 8340 5459 *E-mail:* lynne@lynnefeatherstone.org *Website:* www.lynnefeatherstone.org

Lab majority 12,934

FIELD, FRANK
Birkenhead

Frank Field. Born 16 July 1942; Son of late Walter Field; Educated St Clement Danes Grammar School; Hull University (BSc economics 1963). Teacher in further education 1964-69; Director: Child Poverty Action Group 1969-79, Low Pay Unit 1974-80; Councillor, Hounslow Borough Council 1964-68

House of Commons: Contested Buckinghamshire South 1966 general election. Member for Birkenhead since 3 May 1979 general election; Opposition Spokesperson for Education 1980-81; Minister of State, Department of Social Security (Welfare Reform) 1997-98. *Political interests:* Poverty and Income Redistribution, Church Affairs. Poland

Publications: Publications on low pay, poverty and social issues since 1971; PC 1997; Two honorary doctorates; Two honorary fellowships

Rt Hon Frank Field, MP, House of Commons, London SW1A 0AA
Tel: 020 7219 5193 *Fax:* 020 7219 0601 *E-mail:* hendeyj@parliament.uk.

Con majority 8,095

FIELD, MARK
Cities of London and Westminster

Mark Christopher Field. Born 6 October 1964; Son of late Major Peter Charles Field and Ulrike Field, neé Peipe, housewife; Educated Reading School; St Edmund Hall, Oxford law (MA 1987) (JCR President); College of Law, Chester (solicitors' finals 1988); Married Michèle Louise Acton 1994. Trainee solicitor 1988-90; Solicitor Freshfields 1990-92; Employment consultant 1992-94; Kellyfield Consulting 1994-2001: Director and former Co-owner; Councillor Royal London Borough of Kensington and Chelsea 1994-2002

House of Commons: Contested Enfield North 1997 general election. Member for Cities of London and Westminster since 7 June 2001 general election; Opposition Whip 2003-04; Association/Ward Officer Kensington and Chelsea and Islington North Associations 1989-99; Member Standing Committees: Proceeds of Crime Act 2001-02, Enterprise Act 2001-02, Finance Act 2001-02, Licensing Act 2002-03, Housing Bill 2003-04; Shadow Minister for London 2003-. *Political interests:* Economy, Small Businesses, Employment, Culture, Media and Sport, Transport. USA, Germany, India, Israel, Syria

Parkinsons Disease Society; Royal National Institute for the Deaf; British Heart Foundation; *Publications:* Contributing Chapter to *A Blue Tomorrow* (Politicos 2001) and various articles for national newspapers on financial services, pensions and civil liberties issues; Freeman of Merchant Taylors Livery Company; Freeman of the City of London; *Clubs:* City of London Club; *Recreations:* Football, cricket, motor-racing, popular/rock music

Mark Field, MP, House of Commons, London SW1A 0AA *Tel:* 020 7219 8160
E-mail: fieldm@parliament.uk. *Constituency:* 90 Ebury Street, London SW1W 9QD
Tel: 020 7730 8181 *Fax:* 020 7730 4520

Lab majority 9,774

FISHER, MARK
Stoke-on-Trent Central

Mark Fisher. Born 29 October 1944; Son of late Sir Nigel Fisher, MC, MP 1950-83 and late Lady Gloria Flower; Educated Eton College; Trinity College, Cambridge (MA English literature 1966); Married Ingrid Hunt 1971 (divorced 1999) (2 sons 2 daughters). Documentary film producer and scriptwriter 1966-75; Principal, The Tattenhall Centre of Education 1975-83; Visiting Fellow, St Anthony's College, Oxford 2000-01; Member: NUT, MU; Staffordshire County Council: Councillor 1981-85, Chair, Libraries Committee 1981-83

House of Commons: Contested Leek 1979 general election. Member for Stoke-on-Trent Central since 9 June 1983 general election; Spokesperson on Arts and Media 1987-92; Frontbench Spokesperson for: The Citizen's Charter 1992-93, National Heritage 1993-97; Opposition Whip 1985-86; Parliamentary Under-Secretary of State: Department of National Heritage 1997, Department for Culture, Media and Sport 1997-98. *Political interests:* Urban Policy, Freedom of Information, Human Rights, Overseas Aid and Development, Broadcasting, Press, Cultural Policy, Arts. Hong Kong, Kashmir, Pakistan, Indonesia, Tunisia

Chair, Parliament First 2001-. Trustee: National Benevolent Fund for the Aged 1986-97, Education Extra 1992-97, Britten Pears Foundation 1998-, Estorick Foundation 2001-; *Publications: City Centres, City Cultures,* 1988; *Whose Cities?* (editor) 1991; *A New London,* 1992; Honorary Fellow: RIBA, Royal College of Art

Mark Fisher, MP, House of Commons, London SW1A 0AA *Tel:* 020 7219 4502 *Fax:* 020 7219 4894 *E-mail:* fisherm@parliament.uk. *Constituency:* Winton House, Stoke Road, Shelton, Stoke-on-Trent ST4 2RW *Tel:* 01782 848468 *Fax:* 01782 845658

Lab majority 7,129

FITZPATRICK, JIM
Poplar and Canning Town

Jim (James) Fitzpatrick. Born 4 April 1952; Son of James and Jean Fitzpatrick; Educated Holyrood Senior Secondary, Glasgow; Married Jane Lowe 1980 (1 son 1 daughter) (divorced). Trainee, Tytrak Ltd, Glasgow 1970-73; Driver, Mintex Ltd, London 1973-74; Firefighter, London Fire Brigade 1974-97; Member: National Executive Council, Fire Brigades Union, GPMU Parliamentary Group

House of Commons: Member for Poplar and Canning Town since 1 May 1997 general election; Assistant Government Whip 2001-02; Government Whip 2002-05; PPS to Alan Milburn as Secretary of State for Health 1999-2001; Parliamentary Under-Secretary of State, Office of the Deputy Prime Minister 2005-. *Political interests:* Poverty, Regeneration, Racism, Fire, Animal Welfare. Bangladesh

Barking Constituency Labour Party: Voluntary Agent 1986-91, Chair 1989-90; Member, London Labour Executive 1988-2000; Chair, Greater London Labour Party 1991-2000; Hon. Treasurer, London Regional Group of Labour MPs 1999-2001. Richard House Children's Hospice; Fire Brigade Long Service and Good Conduct Medal (20 years) 1994; *Clubs:* Hon President Millwall Rugby Football Club; Parliamentary football team; *Recreations:* Reading, TV/film, football, West Ham United FC

Jim Fitzpatrick, MP, House of Commons, London SW1A 0AA *Tel:* 020 7219 5085; 020 7219 6215 *Fax:* 020 7219 2776 *E-mail:* fitzpatrickj@parliament.uk.

FLELLO, ROBERT
Stoke-on-Trent South

Robert Charles Douglas Flello. Born 14 January 1966; Educated King's Norton Boys' School; University of Wales, Bangor (chemistry); Married. Executive officer Inland Revenue; Tax consultant Price Waterhouse; Manager Arthur Andersen; Director Platts Flello Ltd 2001-04; CEO Malachi Community Trust 2003-04; Member: TGWU, AEEU; Birmingham City councillor 2002-04

House of Commons: Member for Stoke-on-Trent South since 5 May 2005 general election. *Political interests:* Employment, crime, Treasury matters, transport

Lab majority 8,681

Chair Birminham Northfield CLP; Secretary Longbridge branch; Regional organiser 2004-05. *Recreations:* Running, motorbike riding, reading

Robert Flello, MP, House of Commons, London SW1A 0AA *Tel:* 020 7219 6744. *Constituency:* Agent: Mr Timothy Mullen, c/o 2A Stanton Road, Meir, Stoke-on-Trent ST3 6DD *Tel:* 01782 596803 *E-mail:* mail@robertflello.co.uk

FLINT, CAROLINE
Don Valley

Caroline Louise Flint. Born 20 September 1961; Daughter of late Wendy Flint (neé Beasley), clerical/shop employee; Educated Twickenham Girls School; Richmond Tertiary College; University of East Anglia (BA American history/literature and film studies); Marriage dissolved; married Phil Cole 2001 (1 son 1 daughter 1 stepson). Management trainee, GLC/ILEA 1984-85; Policy officer, ILEA 1985-87; Head, Women's Unit, National Union of Students 1988-89; Equal opportunities officer, Lambeth Council 1989-91; Welfare and staff development officer, Lambeth Council 1991-93; Senior researcher/Political officer, GMB Trade Union 1994-97; Member, GMB; Former shop steward: NALGO at GLC/LEA, GMB at Lambeth Council

Lab majority 8,598

House of Commons: Member for Don Valley since 1 May 1997 general election; Joint PPS to the Ministers of State, Foreign and Commonwealth Office 1999-2001; PPS to: Peter Hain as Minister of State: Department of Trade and Industry 2001, Foreign and Commonwealth Office 2001-02, John Reid as Minister without Portfolio and Party Chair 2002-03, John Reid as Leader of the House of Commons and President of the Council 2003; Parliamentary Under-Secretary of State (PUS), Home Office 2003-05: (Tackling Drugs, Reducing Organised and International Crime) 2003-04, (Reducing Organised and International Crime, Anti-Drugs Co-ordination and International and European Unit) 2004-05; PUS, Department of Health 2005-. *Political interests:* Employment, Education and Training, Childcare, Welfare to Work, Family Friendly Employment, Crime, Anti-Social Behaviour, House of Commons Modernisation, Education

National Women's Officer, Labour Students 1983-85; Executive Member, Labour Co-ordinating Committee 1984-85; Chair, Brentford and Isleworth Constituency Labour Party 1991-95; Branch Chair, Branch Secretary and GC Delegate; Facilitator, Labour National Policy Forums 1994-97; Associate Editor, *Renewal* 1995-2000; Member, Fabian Society; Member, Trade Union Group of Labour MPs. Member, GMB Group of MPs; Labour Party adviser to the Police Federation of England and Wales 1999; Member, Inter-Parliamentary Union 1997-; *Recreations:* Cinema, tennis, being with my family and friends

Caroline Flint, MP, House of Commons, London SW1A 0AA *Tel:* 020 7219 4407 *Fax:* 020 7219 1277 *E-mail:* flintc@parliament.uk. *Constituency:* Room 15, 115 St Sepulchre Gate West, Doncaster, South Yorkshire DN1 3AH *Tel:* 01302 366778 *Fax:* 01302 328833

Belief in Action

  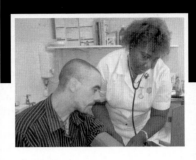

Throughout the UK, The Salvation Army is at the cutting edge of care in our churches and social service centres. Our mission takes us into the front line of the battle against the biggest social problems of the age.

Today our **services for homeless people** are offering individually tailored packages of care to people with a wide range of problems, including alcoholism and mental illness. Our **National Addiction Service** is combining scientific knowledge and professional care to help people break free from drugs.

Our Outreach and Resettlement Teams work in major cities to identify people sleeping rough. We build relationships with them as the first step towards offering longer-term programmes leading to resettlement in appropriate accommodation.

Our **residential and home care services** are giving older people the chance to retain their independence whilst receiving the care they need. Our **family and children's services** are working to help families stay together, while also supporting parents and children who are coping with family breakdown.

The Salvation Army is at the heart of almost every community. Through our network of 1000 centres across the UK, **we touch the lives of thousands of people,** often working in partnership with national and local government. At the same time we are innovators, constantly striving to raise our professional standards and the quality of our services so we can meet today's problems with tomorrow's solutions.

You can find out more about the work of The Salvation Army by visiting our website **www.salvationarmy.org.uk**

Or you can contact Jonathan Lomax, Public Affairs Officer, on **020 7367 4885** or email him at **jonathan.lomax@salvationarmy.org.uk**

Belief in Action

The Salvation Army is a registered charity.

FLYNN, PAUL
Newport West

Paul Flynn. Born 9 February 1935; Son of late James and late Kathleen Flynn; Educated St Illtyd's College, Cardiff; University College of Wales, Cardiff; Married 2nd Samantha Cumpstone 1985 (1 stepson, 1 stepdaughter and 1 son and 1 daughter (deceased) from previous marriage). Chemist, steel industry 1962-83; Broadcaster, Gwent Community Radio 1983-84; Research officer for Llewellyn Smith, as Labour MEP for South Wales 1984-87; Councillor: Newport Council 1972-81, Gwent County Council 1974-83

Lab majority 5,458

House of Commons: Contested Denbigh October 1974 general election. Member for Newport West since 11 June 1987 general election; Opposition Spokesman on: Health and Social Security 1988-89, Social Security 1989-90. *Political interests:* Health, Medicinal and Illegal Drugs, Social Security, Pensions, Animal Welfare, Devolution, Welsh Affairs, Constitutional Reform, Modernisation of Parliament. Baltic States, Eastern Europe, Hungary, Romania, Israel

Secretary, Welsh Group of Labour MPs 1997-. Board Member, Parliamentary Office of Science and Technology (POST) 1997-; Member, UK Delegation to Council of Europe and Western European Union 1997-; *Publications: Commons Knowledge. How to be a Backbencher*, 1997; *Baglu Mlaen (Staggering Forward)*, 1998; *Dragons Led by Poodles*, 1999; Campaign for Freedom of Information Award 1991; Highland Park/*The Spectator* Backbencher of the Year (jointly) 1996; *New Statesman* Best Website of an Elected Representative 2000-; *Recreations:* Local history, photography

Paul Flynn, MP, House of Commons, London SW1A 0AA *Tel:* 020 7219 3478 *Fax:* 020 7219 2433 *E-mail:* paulflynnmp@talk21.com.
Constituency: Tel: 01633 262348 *Fax:* 01633 760532

Lab majority 3,139

FOLLETT, BARBARA
Stevenage

(Daphne) Barbara Follett. Born 25 December 1942; Daughter of late William Vernon and late Charlotte Hubbard; Educated Sandford School, Addis Ababa, Ethiopia; Ellerslie Girls' High School, Cape Town; University of Cape Town (fine art); Open University (government); London School of Economics (BSc economic history 1993); Married Richard Turner 1963 (divorced 1971) (2 daughters); married Gerald Stonestreet 1971 (divorced 1974); married Les Broer 1974 (divorced 1985) (1 son); married Kenneth Martin Follett 1985 (1 stepson 1 stepdaughter). Part-time salesperson 1960-62: Ledger clerk, Barclays Bank of South Africa 1962-63; EFL teacher, Berlitz School of Languages 1964-66; Joint manager, fruit farm 1966-70; Acting regional secretary, South African Institute of Race Relations 1970-71; Regional manager, Kupugani 1971-74; National health education director, Kupugani 1975-78; Lecturer and assistant course organiser Centre for International Briefing 1980-84; Lecturer in cross-cultural communications 1985-87; Research associate, Institute of Public Policy Research 1993-96, Visiting Fellow 1993-; Director, EMILY's List UK 1993-; Member, Amicus/MSF

House of Commons: Contested Woking 1983, Epsom and Ewell 1987 general elections. Member for Stevenage since 1 May 1997 general election. *Political interests:* Economic and Industrial Policy, Gender, Race Relations, Overseas Aid and Development, International Development, Trade and Industry, Housing, Film Industry, Small Businesses. Africa, France

Member: Fabian Society, SERA; Chair, Eastern Regional Group of Labour MPs 1999-. One World Action; *Recreations:* Reading, Scrabble, photography, film, theatre and Star Trek

Barbara Follett, MP, House of Commons, London SW1A 0AA *Tel:* 020 7219 2649 *Fax:* 020 7219 1158 *E-mail:* barbara@barbara-follett.org.uk.
Constituency: Stevenage Labour Party, 4 Popple Way, Stevenage, Hertfordshire SG1 3TG *Tel:* 01438 222800 *Fax:* 01438 222292

Con majority 13,342

FORTH, ERIC
Bromley and Chislehurst

Eric Forth. Born 9 September 1944; Son of late William Forth and Aileen Forth; Educated Jordanhill College School, Glasgow; Glasgow University (MA politics and economics 1966); Married Linda St Clair 1967 (divorced 1994) (2 daughters); married Mrs Carroll Goff 1994 (1 stepson). Manager, industry (Ford, Deloitte, Dexion, Rank, Xerox) 1966-79; MEP for Birmingham North 1979-84; Councillor, Brentwood Urban District Council 1968-72

House of Commons: Contested Barking February and October 1974 general elections. Member for Mid Worcestershire 1983-97, and for Bromley and Chislehurst since 1 May 1997 general election; Joint Parliamentary Under-Secretary of State for Industry and Consumer Affairs, Department of Trade and Industry 1988-90; Joint Parliamentary Under-Secretary of State, Department of Employment 1990-92; Department for Education: Parliamentary Under-Secretary of State for Schools 1992-94, Minister of State 1994-95; Minister of State, Department for Education and Employment 1995-97; Shadow Leader of the House 2001-03; Member House of Commons Commission 2001-03. *Political interests:* Economic Policy, European Union, USA. Canada, USA, Australia, New Zealand

PC 1997; Channel 4 and *The House Magazine* Opposition Politician of the Year 2000; *Clubs:* Bromley Conservative; *Recreations:* Cinema, political biographies

Rt Hon Eric Forth, MP, House of Commons, London SW1A 0AA
Tel: 020 7219 6344. *Constituency:* Bromley and Chislehurst Conservative Association, 5 White Horse Hill, Chislehurst BR7 6DG *Tel:* 020 8295 2639

FOSTER, DON
Bath

Lib Dem majority
4,638

Don (Donald) Foster. Born 31 March 1947; Son of late John Anthony Foster, vicar and late Iris Edith Foster, neé Ellison; Educated Lancaster Royal Grammar School; Keele University (BSc physics and psychology 1969, CEd 1969); Bath University (MEd 1981); Married Victoria Jane Dorcas Pettegree 1968 (1 son 1 daughter). Science teacher, Sevenoaks School, Kent 1969-75; Science project director, Resources for Learning Development Unit, Avon LEA 1975-80; Education lecturer, Bristol University 1980-89; Management consultant, Pannell Kerr Forster 1989-92; Avon County Council: Councillor, Cabot Ward, Bristol 1981-89, Chair, Education Committee 1987-89

House of Commons: Contested (Liberal/Alliance) Bristol East 1987 general election. Member for Bath since 9 April 1992 general election; Spokesperson for: Education 1992-95, Education and Employment 1995-97; Principal Spokesperson for: Environment, Transport, the Regions and Social Justice 1999-2001, Transport, Local Government and the Regions 2001-02; Liberal Democrat Shadow Secretary of State for: Transport 2002-03, Culture, Media and Sport 2003-. *Political interests:* Education, Local and Regional Government, Transport. Africa, Israel, Central Europe

President, Liberal Democrat Youth and Students 1993-95. Water Aid; Executive, Association of County Councils 1985-89; Joint Hon. President, British Youth Council 1992-99; Vice-Chair, British Association for Central and Eastern Europe 1994-97; Trustee, Open School and Education Extra 1993-99; *Publications: Resource-based Learning in Science,* 1979; *Science With Gas,* 1981; Co-author: *Aspects of Science,* 1984, *Reading About Science,* 1984, *Nuffield Science,* 1986; *Teaching Science 11@nr13,* 1987; *From the Three Rs to the Three Cs,* 2003; Numerous educational and political articles and pamphlets; Hon. Fellow, Bath College of High Education 1995; *Clubs:* National Liberal; *Recreations:* Classical music, travel, sport

Don Foster, MP, House of Commons, London SW1A 0AA *Tel:* 020 7219 5001 *Fax:* 020 7219 2695 *E-mail:* fosterd@parliament.uk. *Constituency:* 31 James Street West, Bath, Avon BA1 2BT *Tel:* 01225 338973 *Fax:* 01225 463630

FOSTER, MICHAEL JABEZ
Hastings and Rye

Michael Jabez Foster. Born 26 February 1946; Son of Dorothy Foster; Educated Hastings Secondary; Hastings Grammar School; Leicester University (LLM 1995); Married Rosemary Kemp 1969 (2 sons). Solicitor's clerk 1963-72; Legal executive 1972-80; Solicitor 1980-; Member and Legal Adviser to GMB; Councillor: Hastings County Borough Council 1971-74, Hastings Borough Council 1973-79, 1983-87, East Sussex County Council 1973-77, 1981-97; Member: Sussex Police Authority, East Sussex Health Authority; DL, East Sussex 1993-

Lab majority 2,026

House of Commons: Contested Hastings February and October 1974 and 1979 general elections. Member for Hastings and Rye since 1 May 1997 general election; PPS: to Attorneys General John Morris 1999, Lord Williams of Mostyn 1999-2001, to Ross Cranston as Solicitor General 1999-2001, to Lord Goldsmith as Attorney General 2001-03, 2003- to Harriet Harman as Solicitor General 2001-03, 2003-. *Political interests:* Health and Poverty, Animal Welfare, Taxation, Employment. United Kingdom

Member: Society of Labour Lawyers, Christian Socialist Movement, Fabian Society. Member: Methodist Church, European Standing Committee A 1998-, Law Society, The Chartered Institute of Arbitrators, Mensa, European Standing Committee B 2003; Member, National Trust; DL; *Clubs:* Amherst Tennis Club; DL; *Recreations:* Lawn Tennis, Table Tennis

Michael Jabez Foster, MP, House of Commons, London SW1A 0AA *Tel:* 020 7219 1600 *Fax:* 020 7219 1393 *E-mail:* mp@1066.net. *Constituency:* Ellen Draper Centre, 84 Bohemia Road, St Leonards on Sea, East Sussex TN37 6RN *Tel:* 01424 460070 *Fax:* 01424 460072

FOSTER, MICHAEL JOHN
Worcester

Michael John Foster. Born 14 March 1963; Son of Brian William Foster, retired car worker, and Edna Foster, retired teacher; Educated Great Wyrley High School, Staffordshire; Wolverhampton Polytechnic (BA economics 1984); Wolverhampton University (PGCE 1995); Married Shauna Ogle 1985 (2 daughters 1 son). Financial planning and control department, Jaguar Cars Ltd: Financial analyst 1984-5, Senior analyst 1985-87, Manager 1989-91; Lecturer in accountancy, Worcester College of Technology 1991-97; Shop steward, TGWU 1986-88; Member, GMB, NATFHE

Lab majority 3,144

House of Commons: Member for Worcester since 1 May 1997 general election; Introduced Private Members' Bill to Ban Hunting With Dogs 1997; On School Crossing Patrols 2000, since incorporated into Transport Act 2000; PPS to Margaret Hodge, Department for Education and Skills, as: Minister of State for Lifelong Learning and Higher Education 2001-03, Minister of State for Children 2003-04; Team PPS, Department for Education and Skills 2004-. *Political interests:* Trade and Industry, Education and Training, Hunting With Dogs (Against), Small Businesses, Education

Agent, Mid Worcester 1992; Secretary, Constituency Labour Party, Worcester 1992-95. Acorns Hospice, St Richards Hospice; *Clubs:* Worcestershire County Cricket Club, House of Commons Soccer and Cricket Teams; *Recreations:* Sport, gardening

Michael John Foster, MP, House of Commons, London SW1A 0AA *Tel:* 020 7219 6379 *Fax:* 020 7219 6379 *E-mail:* fosterm@parliament.uk. *Constituency:* Arboretum Lodge, 24 Sansome Walk, Worcester, Worcestershire WR1 1LX *Tel:* 01905 26504

Con majority 6,016

FOX, LIAM
Woodspring

Liam Fox. Born 22 September 1961; Son of William Fox, teacher, and Catherine Fox; Educated St Bride's High School, East Kilbride; Glasgow University (MB, ChB 1983, MROGP 1989); Single no children. General practitioner; Divisional surgeon, St John's Ambulance

House of Commons: Contested Roxburgh and Berwickshire 1987 general election. Member for Woodspring since 9 April 1992 general election; Opposition Spokesperson for Constitutional Affairs, Scotland and Wales 1997-98; Frontbench Spokesperson for Constitutional Affairs, with overall responsibility for Scottish and Welsh issues 1998-99; Assistant Government Whip 1994-95; Government Whip 1995-96; PPS to Michael Howard as Home Secretary 1993-94; Parliamentary Under-Secretary of State, Foreign and Commonwealth Office 1996-97; Member Shadow Cabinet 1998-; Shadow: Secretary of State for Health 1999-2003, Foreign Secretary 2005-. *Political interests:* Health, Economic Policy, Foreign Affairs

Chair, West of Scotland Young Conservatives 1983; National Vice-Chair, Scottish Young Conservatives 1983-84; Secretary, West Country Conservative Members' Committee 1992-93; Co-chair Conservative Party 2003-05. President, Glasgow University Club 1982-83; Guest of US State Department, involving study of drug abuse problems in USA, and Republican Party campaigning techniques 1985; *Publications: Making Unionism Positive,* 1988; *Review of Health Reforms* (House of Commons Magazine), 1989; World Debating Competition, Toronto (Individual speaking prize) 1982; Best Speaker's Trophy, Glasgow University 1983; *Recreations:* Tennis, swimming, cinema, theatre

Dr Liam Fox, MP, House of Commons, London SW1A 0AA *Tel:* 020 7219 4198 *Fax:* 020 7219 2617. *Constituency:* 71 High Street, Nailsea BS48 1AW *Tel:* 01275 790090 *Fax:* 01275 790091

FRANCIS, HYWEL
Aberavon

David Hywel Francis. Born 6 June 1946; Son of David Francis, miners' union official and Catherine Francis, housewife; Educated Whitchurch Grammar School, Cardiff; University of Wales, Swansea (BA history 1968, PhD 1978); Married Mair Georgina Price 1968 (1 daughter 2 sons (1 deceased)). Organisation department assistant TUC 1971-72; Senior research assistant University of Wales, Swansea 1972-74; Department of Adult Continuing Education University of Wales, Swansea: Tutor and lecturer 1974-86, Director 1987-99, Professor 1992-99; Special adviser Secretary of State for Wales 1999-2000; Contested South Wales West 1999 National Assembly for Wales election; Fellow National Centre for Public Policy University of Wales, Swansea 2000-01; Member: AUT 1974-2001, ISTC 2000-

Lab majority 13,937

House of Commons: Member for Aberavon since 7 June 2001 general election; Introduced Carers (Equal Opportunities) Bill 2003. *Political interests:* Carers' Rights, Disability Rights, Citizenship, European Affairs, Lifelong Learning, Steel. France, India, Italy, Ireland, Cuba, South Africa

Member: Socialist Education Association 1999-, Co-operative Party 1999-. Cronfa Sam Francis; Member European Standing Committee B 2003-; Vice-president, Friends of Cyprus; Founder and trustee: Bevan Foundation Think-Tank 2000-, Paul Robeson Wales Trust; *Publications:* Co-author *The Fed: A history of the South Wales miners in the Twentieth Century*, Lawrence and Wishart 1980 reprint 1998; *Miners against Fascism*, Lawrence and Wishart 1984 reprint 2004; Co-editor *Communities and their Universities*, Lawrence and Wishart 1996; *Wales: A learning country* Welsh Centre for Lifelong Learning 1999; Member of the Gorsedd of the National Eisteddfod 1986; *Clubs:* Aberavon RFC, Briton Ferry Steel Cricket Club, Port Talbot Cricket Club; *Recreations:* Walking, cycling, swimming, cinema

Dr Hywel Francis, MP, House of Commons, London SW1A 0AA
Tel: 020 7219 8121 *Fax:* 020 7219 1734 *E-mail:* francish@parliament.uk.
Constituency: Eagle House, 2 Talbot Road, Port Talbot,
West Glamorgan SA13 1DH *Tel:* 01639 897660 *Fax:* 01639 891725

FRANCOIS, MARK
Rayleigh

Mark Gino Francois. Born 14 August 1965; Son of Reginald Charles Francois, engineer and Anna Maria Francois, née Carloni, cook; Educated Nicholas Comprehensive School, Basildon; Bristol University (BA history 1986); King's College, London (MA war studies 1987); Married Karen Thomas 2000. TA 1983-89, commissioned 1985. Management trainee Lloyds Bank 1987; Market Access International Public Affairs Consultancy 1988-95: Consultant, Director; Public affairs consultant Francois Associates 1996-2001; Basildon District Council 1991-95: Councillor, Vice-chair Housing 1992-95

Con majority 14,726

House of Commons: Contested Brent East 1997 general election. Member for Rayleigh since 7 June 2001 general election; Opposition Whip 2002-04; Shadow Minister for Economic Affairs 2004-. *Political interests:* Defence, Local and Regional Government , Housing, Environment

Member: Royal United Services Institute for Defence Studies 1991-, International Institute for Strategic Studies 1999-, European Standing Committee A 2002-, European Standing Committee B until 2003; *Clubs:* Carlton, Rayleigh Conservative; *Recreations:* Reading, sports, military history, travel

Mark Francois, MP, House of Commons, London SW1A 0AA *Tel:* 020 7219 8311
E-mail: mfrancois@rayleighconservatives.org.uk. *Constituency:* 25 Bellingham
Lane, Rayleigh, Essex SS6 7ED *Tel:* 01268 742 044 *Fax:* 01268 741 833

FRASER, CHRISTOPHER
South West Norfolk

Christopher Fraser. Born 25 October 1962; Educated Harrow College; Westminster University (BA). Chairman International Communications group of companies

House of Commons: Member for Mid Dorset and Poole North 1997-2001, for South West Norfolk since 5 May 2005 general election; PPS to Lord Strathclyde as Shadow Leader of the House of Lords 1999-2001. *Political interests:* SE Asia, Europe, USA, Canada, China, Australia

Con majority 10,086

Member: Inter-parliamentary Union 1997-2001, Commonwealth Parliamentary Association 1997-2001; Freeman, City of London; *Clubs:* Carlton, Athanaeum; *Recreations:* Golf, sailing, skiiing, riding

Christopher Fraser, MP, House of Commons, London SW1A 0AA *Tel:* 020 7219 6293. *Constituency:* Norfolk South West Conservative Association, Shirley House, 23 London Street, Swaffham, Norfolk PE37 7DD *Tel:* 01760 721241 *Fax:* 01760 721587 *E-mail:* swnca@tory.org

GALE, ROGER
North Thanet

Roger James Gale. Born 20 August 1943; Son of Richard Byrne Gale, solicitor, and Phyllis Mary Gale, neé Rowell; Educated Hardye's School, Dorchester; Guildhall School of Music and Drama (LGSM&D 1963); Married Wendy Bowman 1964 (divorced 1967); married Susan Linda Sampson 1971 (divorced 1980) (1 daughter); married Susan Gabrielle Marks 1980 (2 sons). Freelance broadcaster 1963-; Programme director, Radio Scotland 1965; Personal assistant to general manager, Universal Films 1971-72; Freelance reporter, BBC Radio London 1972-73; Producer: Radio 1 *Newsbeat*, BBC Radio 4 *Today* 1973-76; Director, BBC Children's Television 1976-79; Senior producer, Children's Television, Thames TV; Editor, Teenage Unit; Producer special projects, Thames TV 1979-83; Member: NUJ, Equity, BECTU

Con majority 7,634

House of Commons: Contested Birmingham Northfield by-election 1982. Member for North Thanet since 9 June 1983 general election; PPS to Ministers of State for the Armed Forces: Archibald Hamilton 1992-93, Jeremy Hanley 1993-94. *Political interests:* Education, Animal Welfare, Media, Broadcasting, Tourism, Leisure Industry, Licensed Trade. Cyprus, Cuba, Tunisia, Mongolia, Africa (Southern and Western)

Vice-Chairman, Holborn & St Pancras Conservative Association 1971-72; Member, Greater London Young Conservative Committee 1972-82; Vice-Chair Conservative Party 2001-03. Childrens' Country Holidays, Christian Childrens' Fund, Dogs Trust/Pathway, Animal Health Trust, Scouts; Hon. Associate, British Veterinary Association; Delegate, Council of Europe 1987-89; Delegate, Western European Union 1987-89; International Election Observer, Mongolia, South Africa, Mozambique, Ghana, The Gambia, Kenya, Macedonia; Fellow, Industry and Parliament Trust; Trustee: Children's Country Holidays Fund, 1st Margate (St John's) Scouts; RSPCA Richard Martin Award for Outstanding Contribution to Animal Welfare; Freeman, City of London; *Clubs:* Farmer's; Kent County Cricket, Royal Temple Yacht; *Recreations:* Swimming, sailing

Roger Gale, MP, House of Commons, London SW1A 0AA *Tel:* 020 7219 4087 *Fax:* 020 7219 6828 *E-mail:* galerj@parliament.uk. *Constituency:* The Old Forge, 215a Canterbury Road, Birchington, Kent CT7 9AH *Tel:* 01843 848588 *Fax:* 01843 844856

Respect majority 823

GALLOWAY, GEORGE
Bethnal Green and Bow

George Galloway. Born 16 August 1954; Son of George, engineer, and Sheila, neé Reilly, factory worker; Educated Charleston Primary; Harris Academy; Married Elaine Fyffe 1979 (divorced 1999) (1 daughter); married Dr Amineh Abu-Zayyad 2000. General labourer, Garden Works, Dundee 1972; Production worker, Michelin Tyres 1973; Labour organiser 1977-83; General secretary, War on Want 1983-87; Member, TGWU 1973-; Sponsored by TGWU 1987-96

House of Commons: Member for Glasgow Hillhead 1987-97, and for Glasgow Kelvin since 1 May 1997 general election; *Independent Labour Member October 2003-January 2004, RESPECT Member January 2004-05, for Bethnal Green and Bow since 5 May 2005 general election. *Political interests:* Foreign Affairs, Defence, Scotland

Labour Party organiser, Dundee East and West Constituencies 1977-83; Chair, Scottish Labour Party 1980-81. *Publications: Downfall: The Ceausescus and the Romanian Revolution* (jointly) 1989; *I'm Not The Only One*, 2004; Hilal-i-Quaid-Azam, the highest civil award in Pakistan for services to the restoration of democracy in Pakistan 1990; Hilal-i-Pakistan for services to the people of Kashmir 1996; Kashmir Centres Europe Kashmir Award for work, efforts, support and services to the Kashmir cause 1998; Spectator Magazine, Parliamentary Debater of the Year 2003; *Clubs:* Groucho; *Recreations:* Football, sport, films, music

George Galloway, MP, House of Commons, London SW1A 0AA
Tel: 020 7219 6940 *Fax:* 020 7219 2879 *E-mail:* gallowayg@parliament.uk.

Lab/Co-op majority 9,228

GAPES, MIKE
Ilford South

Mike (Michael) John Gapes. Born 4 September 1952; Son of Frank Gapes, retired postal worker, and Emily Gapes, retired office worker; Educated Buckhurst Hill County High School; Fitzwilliam College, Cambridge (MA economics 1975); Middlesex Polytechnic, Enfield (Diploma in industrial relations 1976); Married Frances Smith 1992 (3 daughters). Voluntary Service Overseas (VSO) Teacher, Swaziland 1971-72; Secretary, Cambridge Students' Union 1973-74; National Organisation of Labour Students: Vice-chair 1975-76, Chair 1976-77; National student organiser, Labour Party 1977-80; Research officer, Labour Party International Department 1980-88; Senior international officer, Labour Party 1988-92; Member, TGWU

House of Commons: Contested Ilford North 1983 general election. Member for Ilford South since 9 April 1992 general election; PPS: to Paul Murphy as Minister of State, Northern Ireland Office 1997-99, to Lord Rooker as Minister of State, Home Office 2001-02. *Political interests:* Defence, International Affairs, European Union, Economic Policy, Education

Deputy Chair, Parliamentary Labour Friends of Israel 1997-; Chair Co-op Party, Parliamentary Group 2000-01; Trade union liaison officer, London Group of Labour MPs 2001-; Member, Labour Friends of India. VSO, Oxfam, One World Action; Vice-President Council of European National Youth Committees 1977-79; Council Member Royal Institute of International Affairs 1996-99; Chair, Westminster Foundation for Democracy 2002; *Publications:* Contributor to several books and pamphlets; Fabian Society pamphlet: *After the Cold War*, 1990; *Clubs:* Vice-President, Ilford Football Club; West Ham United Supporters' Club; *Recreations:* My family and when I get time watching football at West Ham, blues and jazz music

Mike Gapes, MP, House of Commons, London SW1A 0AA *Tel:* 020 7219 6485
Fax: 020 7219 0978 *E-mail:* gapesm@parliament.uk.
Constituency: Website: www.mikegapes.org.uk

GARDINER, BARRY
Brent North

Lab majority 5,641

Barry Strachan Gardiner. Born 10 March 1957; Son of late John Flannegan Gardiner, general manager, Kelvin Hall, and of late Sylvia Strachan, doctor; Educated Haileybury College; St Andrews (MA philosophy 1983); Harvard University (J. F. Kennedy Scholarship 1983-84); Cambridge University (research 1984-87); Married Caroline Smith 1979 (3 sons 1 daughter). Partner, Mediterranean Average Adjusting Co 1987-97; Occasional Lecturer, The Academy of National Economy, Moscow 1992-96; Member: MSF, GMB; Cambridge City Council: Councillor 1988-94, Chair of Finance, Mayor 1992-93

House of Commons: Member for Brent North since 1 May 1997 general election; PPS to Beverley Hughes as Minister of State, Home Office 2002-04; Parliamentary Under-Secretary of State: Northern Ireland Office 2004-05, Department of Trade and Industry 2005-. *Political interests:* Economic Policy, Trade and Industry, Education, Foreign Affairs. India, Sri Lanka, Russia, Georgia

Member, Labour Finance and Industry Group; Chair, Labour Friends of India 1999-2002, Secretary 2002-04. *Publications:* Various articles relating to shipping and maritime affairs; Articles on Political Philosophy in the *Philosophical Quarterly*; Member, Shipwrights' Company; Freeman, City of London; *Clubs:* Royal Overseas League; *Recreations:* Walking, music, reading philosophy, bird-watching

Barry Gardiner, MP, House of Commons, London SW1A 0AA *Tel:* 020 7219 4046 *Fax:* 020 7219 2495 *E-mail:* gardinerb@parliament.uk.

GARNIER, EDWARD
Harborough

Con majority 3,892

Edward Henry Garnier. Born 26 October 1952; Son of late Colonel William d'Arcy Garnier, and Hon. Mrs Garnier; Educated Wellington College; Jesus College, Oxford 1971-74 (BA modern history 1974, MA); College of Law, London; Married Anna Caroline Mellows 1982 (2 sons 1 daughter). Barrister; Called to the Bar, Middle Temple 1976; QC 1995; Assistant Recorder 1998; Recorder 2000; Bencher, Middle Temple 2001

House of Commons: Contested Hemsworth 1987 general election. Member for Harborough since 9 April 1992 general election; PPS: to Alastair Goodlad and David Davis as Ministers of State, Foreign and Commonwealth Office 1994-95, to Sir Nicholas Lyell as Attorney-General and Sir Derek Spencer as Solicitor-General 1995-97, to Roger Freeman as Chancellor of the Duchy of Lancaster 1996-97; Shadow Minister, Lord Chancellor's Department 1997-99; Shadow Attorney General 1999-2001. *Political interests:* Agriculture, Defence, Foreign Affairs, Education, Constitutional Affairs

Treasurer, Macleod Group of Conservative MPs 1995-97; Society of Conservative Lawyers: Vice-chairman 2003, Chairman, Executive Committee 2003-. Secretary, Foreign Affairs Forum 1988-92, Vice-Chairman 1992-; Director, Great Britain-China Centre 1998-; *Publications:* Co-author *Bearing the Standard: Themes for a Fourth Term*, 1991; *Facing the Future*, 1993; Contributor to *Halsbury's Laws of England*, 4th edition 1985; Visiting Parliamentary Fellow, St Antony's College, Oxford 1996-97; QC; *Clubs:* Pratt's, Vincent's (Oxford); White's; QC; *Recreations:* Shooting, cricket, tennis, skiing, opera, biographical research

Edward Garnier, MP, House of Commons, London SW1A 0AA *Tel:* 020 7219 6524 *Fax:* 020 7219 2875 *E-mail:* garniere@parliament.uk. *Constituency:* 24 Nelson Street, Market Harborough, Leicestershire LE16 9AY *Tel:* 01858 464146 *Fax:* 01858 410013

postwatch

POSTWATCH, the watchdog for postal services

As MPs know from their postbags, mail remains a popular form of communication. Counterintuitively, the UK's mail market continues to grow year on year. Over 82 million items are on average delivered every day of the week apart from Sunday. This growth is despite the rise in e-mails, text messaging and mobile telephone calls.

Peter Carr
Chairman, Postwatch

With that amount of mail going through the system there are bound to be mistakes. When mistakes do happen it is helpful if customers let Royal Mail know. Customer feedback is one of the main ways Royal Mail finds where the problems are that need attention.

If Royal Mail or any other licensed postal operator does not deal with customer complaints satisfactorily, the customer can seek Postwatch's help. We are here to review how the operator has dealt with the case and where necessary to pursue apologies, explanations and recompense.

We operate through nine regional committees across the UK, with offices in Scotland, Wales, Northern Ireland and six regions across England. Each region monitors and investigates postal service provision and customer needs in their area. Postwatch is independent of the Government, the Regulator (Postcomm), the Royal Mail Group and all other postal operators.

Postwatch has a duty to assist and inform customers, we:

- advise and lobby the regulator (Postcomm), government, postal operators and other stakeholders on customer views and interests.
- campaign for improvements to postal and post office services.
- investigate proposed post office closures and oppose when necessary.
- negotiate and monitor Royal Mail's performance against service targets.
- advise the regulator on appropriate action should Royal Mail Group fail to meet performance targets, or breach any other licence conditions.
- investigate local and national postal problems.
- pursue and resolve individual complaints against licensed postal operators, with a view to resolving generic problems.
- ensure that customers are kept informed about key postal issues and market developments; and
- welcome a competitive business environment in which customer needs are put first.

To contact Postwatch call 0845 013 265, visit <u>www.postwatch.co.uk</u> or write to FREEPOST POSTWATCH

We look forward to helping you.

GAUKE, DAVID
South West Hertfordshire

David Michael Gauke. Born 8 October 1971; Educated Northgate High School, Ipswich; St Edmund Hall, Oxford St (BA law 1993, MA); College of Law, Chester (legal practice course 1995); Married Rachel Rank 2000. Parliamentary research assistant to Barry Legg MP 1993-94; Trainee solicitor and solicitor, Richards Butler 1995-99; Solicitor, Macfarlanes 1999-

House of Commons: Contested Brent East 2001 general election. Member for South West Hertfordshire since 5 May 2005 general election. *Political interests:* Financial services, education, Europe

Con majority 8,473

Committee member, National Association of Conservative Graduates 1997-98; Deputy chair, Brent East Conservative Association 1998-2000. Friends of Waters Meet 2004-; *Clubs:* Rickmansworth Conservative Club; *Recreations:* Football, cricket, country walks

David Gauke, MP, House of Commons, London SW1A 0AA *Tel:* 020 7219 5519. *Constituency:* South West Hertfordshire Conservative Association, Scots Bridge House, Scots Hill, Rickmansworth WD3 3BB *Tel:* 01923 771781 *Fax:* 01923 779471 *E-mail:* david@davidgauke.com *Website:* www.davidgauke.com

GEORGE, ANDREW
St Ives

Andrew Henry George. Born 2 December 1958; Son of Reginald Hugh George, horticulturist, and Diana May (neé Petherick), teacher and musician; Educated Helston Grammar School; Helston School; Sussex University (BA cultural and community studies 1980); University College, Oxford (MSc agricultural economics 1981); Married Jill Elizabeth Marshall 1987 (1 son 1 daughter). Charity worker for various rural community development bodies, Nottinghamshire 1981-85, Cornwall 1986-97; Deputy director Cornwall Rural Community Council 1994-97

Lib Dem majority 11,609

House of Commons: Contested St Ives 1992 general election. Member for St Ives since 1 May 1997 general election; Liberal Democrat Spokesperson for: Agriculture, Fisheries, Food and Rural Affairs (Fisheries) 1997-, Social Security (Disabilities) 1999-2001; Shadow Fisheries Minister 1997-99; Shadow Disabilities Minister 1999-2001; PPS to Charles Kennedy as Leader of the Liberal Democrat Party 2001-02; Liberal Democrat Shadow: Minister for Food and Rural Affairs 2002-05, Secretary of State for International Development 2005-. *Political interests:* Third World, Cornwall, Economic Development, Housing, Fishing Industry, Agriculture, Social Exclusion, Devolution, Small Nations, Racism, Domestic Violence, Immigration, Environment, Minority Groups. All small nations

Third world development, environmental, anti poverty, anti racial discrimination; Member: Cornwall Rural Housing Association, Penwith Credit Union; Trustee, TRELYA; *Publications: Cornwall at the Crossroads,* 1989; *A View from the Bottom Left-hand Corner,* Patten Press 2002; Plus other publications and articles; *Clubs:* Commons and Lords Cricket Club, Commons and Lords Rugby Club, Commons Football Team, Leedstown Cricket Club; *Recreations:* Cricket, football, rugby, tennis, swimming, writing, walking, Cornish culture, cycling, gardening, drawing, singing

Andrew George, MP, House of Commons, London SW1A 0AA *Tel:* 020 7219 4588 *Fax:* 020 7219 5572 *E-mail:* cooperu@parliament.uk. *Constituency:* Knights Yard, Belgravia Street, Penzance, Cornwall TR18 2EL *Tel:* 01736 360020 *Fax:* 01736 332866

Lab majority 7,946

GEORGE, BRUCE
Walsall South

Bruce Thomas George. Born 1 June 1942; Son of late Edgar Lewis George, former police officer and head of security, Wales National Coal Board and late Phyllis George; Educated Mountain Ash Grammar School; University of Wales (BA political theory and government 1964); Warwick University (MA comparative politics 1967); Married Lisa Toelle 1992. Assistant lecturer in politics, Glamorgan College of Technology 1964-66; Lecturer in politics, Manchester Polytechnic 1968-70; Senior lecturer in politics, Birmingham Polytechnic 1970-74; Tutor, Open University 1970-73; Visiting lecturer, Essex University 1983; Member GMB

House of Commons: Contested Southport 1970 general election. Member for Walsall South since 28 February 1974 general election. *Political interests:* Defence, International Affairs, Housing, Health, Social Services, Private Security, Small Businesses

Sister Dora Hospice, Walsall; Councillor, Council for Arms Control; Former Chair, Mediterranean Special Group; Chair, Political Committee, North Atlantic Assembly 1983-94; Parliamentary Assembly of Organisation for Security and Co-operation in Europe 1992-: Chair, General (First) Committee on Political Affairs and Security 1994-, Leader, UK Delegation 1997-, Vice-President 1999-2002, President 2002; Fellow, Industry and Parliament Trust; *Publications:* Numerous books and articles on defence, foreign affairs and the private security industry; Editor, *Jane's NATO Handbook 1989-90, 1990-91, 1991-92*; *Private Security*, 2000; *Labour Party and Defence*, 1992; PC 2001; Hon. Fellow, University of Wales, Swansea 2001; *Clubs:* Joint-Founder, House of Commons Football Club 1974; *Recreations:* Reading, supports Walsall Football Club

Rt Hon Bruce George, MP, House of Commons, London SW1A 0AA
Tel: 020 7219 4049; 020 7219 6610 *Fax:* 020 7219 3823
E-mail: georgeb@parliament.uk. *Constituency:* 34 Bridge Street, Walsall,
West Midlands WS1 1HQ *Tel:* 01922 724960 *Fax:* 01922 621844

Lab majority 7,993

GERRARD, NEIL
Walthamstow

Neil Gerrard. Born 3 July 1942; Son of late Francis and Emma Gerrard, primary school teachers; Educated Manchester Grammar School; Wadham College, Oxford (BA natural science 1964); Chelsea College, London (MED 1973); Polytechnic of South Bank (DPSE 1983); Married Marian Fitzgerald 1968 (divorced 1983) (2 sons). Secondary schoolteacher, Queen Elizabeth's School, Barnet 1965-68; Chemistry and IT lecturer, Hackney College 1968-92; Member, GMB; London Borough of Waltham Forest: Councillor 1973-90, Leader, Labour Group 1983-90, Leader of Council 1986-90

House of Commons: Contested Chingford 1979 general election. Member for Walthamstow since 9 April 1992 general election; PPS to: Dawn Primarolo as Financial Secretary, HM Treasury May-December 1997. *Political interests:* Housing, Planning, Race Relations, Foreign Affairs, HIV/AIDS, Refugees/Asylum, Criminal Justice, Disability. Middle East, Sri Lanka, Kashmir, India

Secretary, PLP Civil Liberties Group. *Recreations:* Theatre, cinema, reading, music, sport

Neil Gerrard, MP, House of Commons, London SW1A 0AA *Tel:* 020 7219 6368
Fax: 020 7219 4899 *E-mail:* gerrardn@parliament.uk. *Constituency:* 23 Orford
Road, Walthamstow, London E17 9NL

THE ROYAL BRITISH LEGION IN 2005 CAMPAIGNING FOR EX-SERVICE PEOPLE

Background

The Legion is Britain's largest ex-Service organisation, covering England and Wales and all of Ireland. It has 2,895 Branches, including 87 overseas, as well as 1,324 Womens' Section Branches. Total membership is 535,217, but the Legion represents the whole of the ex-Service community which numbers some 11 million. It provides financial assistance, nursing and respite care homes, employment for the disabled, small business advice and loans, resettlement training, free pensions advice and much more, all financed from public donations. It also provides a social focus for the ex-Service community in its branches, many of which have an affiliated club. In addition it is the de facto national custodian of Remembrance.

A campaigning organisation

The Legion has traditionally campaigned on behalf of its constituency to ensure their wellbeing. There have been numerous successes, notably the campaign in 1999/2000 for a £10,000 ex-gratia payment to survivors of Japanese PoW camps and their widows which has resulted in payments by the Government of over £230 million and the campaign for a meaningful commemoration of the 60th Anniversary of D Day in 2004, which also attained its objective.

The Legion is campaigning today on a number of issues, notably:

Gulf War Illnesses

- To ensure that the Government addresses its outstanding obligations to Gulf War veterans who have fallen ill since 1990/91.

- To seek further support for the recommendations of the Lloyd Inquiry into Gulf War Illnesses.

War Pensions and Compensation

- Monitoring the new Armed Forces Compensation Scheme to ensure that it is set up and implemented in accordance with the promises given to Parliament, Service personnel and their families.

- Contesting the criteria under which applications for War Pensions for service-attributable noise-induced hearing loss are assessed.

- Calling upon a remaining small number of Local Authorities to completely disregard War and War Widows Pensions when assessing applicants for Housing Benefit and Council Tax Rebate. It remains a Legion aim that there should be a statutory, national, full disregard funded by Central Government.

Other Campaigns

- The Legion supports campaigns by other organisations on behalf of pensioners, many of whom are ex-Service, where they are being financially penalised.

The Legion is seeking cross-party support for the benefit of veterans.

The Royal British Legion. Always on active service

The Royal British Legion, 48 Pall Mall, London SW1Y 5JY Tel: 020 7973 7265 Email: jlillies@britishlegion.org.uk

GIBB, NICK
Bognor Regis and Littlehampton

Nick (Nicolas) John Gibb. Born 3 September 1960; Son of late John McLean Gibb, civil engineer, and Eileen Mavern Gibb, retired schoolteacher; Educated Maidstone Boys' Grammar School; Roundhay School, Leeds; Thornes House School, Wakefield; Durham University (BA law 1981); Single. Chartered accountant, specialising in taxation, KPMG, London 1984-97

Con majority 7,822

House of Commons: Contested Stoke-on-Trent Central 1992 general election and Rotherham by-election 1994. Member for Bognor Regis and Littlehampton since 1 May 1997 general election; Opposition Spokesperson for: the Treasury December 1998-99, Trade and Industry (Energy, Regulation, Company Law, Competition) 1999-2001, Transport, Local Government and the Regions 2001. *Political interests:* Economics, Taxation, Education, Social Security. USA, Israel

Publications: Maintaining Momentum, Pamphlet on Tax Reform 1992; *Bucking the Market*, Pamphlet Opposing Membership of ERM 1990; *Duty to Repeal*, Pamphlet Calling for Abolition of Stamp Duty 1989; *Simplifying Taxes*, Pamphlet on Tax Reform 1987; *Recreations:* Long-distance running, skiing

Nick Gibb, MP, House of Commons, London SW1A 0AA *Tel:* 020 7219 6374 *Fax:* 020 7219 1395. *Constituency:* 110 London Road, Bognor Regis, West Sussex PO21 1BD *Tel:* 01243 826410 *Fax:* 01243 842076

GIBSON, IAN
Norwich North

Ian Gibson. Born 26 September 1938; Son of late William and Winifred Gibson; Educated Dumfries Academy; Edinburgh University (BSc genetics 1962, PhD); Married Elizabeth Frances Lubbock 1974 (2 daughters). University of East Anglia: lecturer 1965-71, senior lecturer 1971-97, dean of biology 1991-97; National Executive Committee, ASTMS/MSF 1972-96, AMICUS; Non-Executive Director Institute of Food Research; ESRC Science in Society Advisory Committee; Honorary Vice-President Royal Society Committee for Public Understanding of Science; Warwick University Faculty of Science Advisory Board; ESRC Innogen Centre Advisory Committee; Institute of Occupational Safety and Health

Lab majority 5,459

House of Commons: Contested Norwich North 1992. Member for Norwich North since 1 May 1997 general election; Chair: Parliamentary Office of Science and Technology 1998-2001, Editorial Board 'pH7' The Parliamentary Health Magazine. *Political interests:* Science, Technology, Health, Environment, Higher Education

Chair, MSF Parliamentary Group 1998-2000. Big C Charity Norwich, Leukaemia Research Fund, Cancer Research Campaign, Imperial Cancer Research Fund; Trustee, Covent Garden Cancer Research Trust; Patron: Humane Research Trust, Afrimed, Norfolk United Nations Association; Trustee, Radiation Research Trust; The House Magazine Award 'Backbencher of the Year' 2004; Honorary Professor, University of East Anglia 2003; e-politix Champion Award (Health) 2003; Engineering Council Professors Award 2004; *Clubs:* Chelsea Rotary Club; Football Supporters' Association; *Recreations:* Football

Dr Ian Gibson, MP, House of Commons, London SW1A 0AA *Tel:* 020 7219 1100 *Fax:* 020 7219 2799 *E-mail:* gibsoni@parliament.uk. *Constituency:* Norwich Labour Centre, 59 Bethel Street, Norwich, Norfolk NR1 1NL *Tel:* 01603 661144 *Fax:* 01603 663502 *Website:* www.norwich-labour-mps.org.uk

An Open Invitation to all Members of Parliament

The Parliamentary Link Scheme

The Royal Society of Chemistry invites you to join its **Parliamentary Link Scheme**. This pairs (i.e. links) you as an MP with a professional scientist who lives in your constituency. The **Link Scheme** is operated by the Society on an entirely voluntary basis.

It's designed to provide you with help on science. No strings attached.

The Society has a duty under its Royal Charter "to serve the public interest" and in this spirit it builds bridges and promotes dialogue between the scientific world and Parliament. The **Link Scheme** provides you with a point of contact for science. And more and more of the issues that you will face in the new Parliament will involve science in one way or another.

The biggest scientific event of the Parliamentary calendar which is held in the Palace of Westminster itself is called **Parliamentary Links Day** and all Members are invited to attend. This year the theme is the role of science in the G8 agenda and the European Union.

Dates for your diary:

Parliamentary Links Day 2005	**Tuesday 21 June 2005**
Chemistry Week 2005	**5–12 November 2005**
Parliamentary Links Day 2006	**Tuesday 27 June 2006**

For further details please contact:

Dr Stephen Benn
Parliamentary Affairs
020 7437 8656
020 7440 3310 FAX

BENNS@RSC.ORG

Royal Society of Chemistry
Burlington House
Piccadilly
LONDON W1J 0BA

You can also contact Ms Julie Smart at
smartj@rsc.org or parliament@rsc.org

GIDLEY, SANDRA
Romsey

Sandra Julia Gidley. Born 26 March 1957; Daughter of Frank Henry Rawson and Maud Ellen Rawson; Educated Eggars Grammar School, Alton, Hampshire; Afcent International, Brunssum, Netherlands; Windsor Girls School, Hamm, West Germany; Bath University (BPharm 1978); Married William Arthur Gidley 1979 (1 daughter 1 son). Pharmacist, Badham Chemists 1979-80; Pharmacy manager, G K Chemists 1980-81; Locum pharmacist 1982-92; Pharmacy manager, supermarkets 1992-2000; Councillor, Test Valley Borough Council 1995-2003; Mayor, Romsey Town 1997-98

Lib Dem majority
125

House of Commons: Member for Romsey since 4 May 2000 by-election; Liberal Democrat Spokesperson for: Health and Women's Issues 2001-02, Older People 2003-; Shadow Minister for Women 2003-. *Political interests:* Health, Education

Recreations: Photography, travel, theatre, badminton

Sandra Gidley, MP, House of Commons, London SW1A 0AA *Tel:* 020 7219 5986 *Fax:* 020 7219 2324 *E-mail:* gidleys@parliament.uk. *Constituency:* 3a Victoria Place, Love Lane, Romsey, Hampshire SO51 8DE *Tel:* 01794 511900 *Fax:* 01794 512538

GILDERNEW, MICHELLE
Fermanagh and South Tyrone

Michelle Gildernew. Born 28 March 1970; Educated St Josephs PS, Caledon; St Catherine's College, Armagh; University of Ulster, Coleraine; Married (1 son)

House of Commons: Member for Fermanagh and South Tyrone since 7 June 2001 general election; Head of London Office 1997-98; New Northern Ireland Assembly 1998-2002; Member Employment and Learning Committee; Deputy chair Social Development Committee 1999-; Member Centre Committee 2000-. *Political interests:* Housing, Rural Affairs, Education

Sinn Féin majority
4,582

Sinn Fein: Member: International Department, Inter-Party talks team, Former spokesperson women's issues, Press officer 1997; Head of London Office 1997-98; Spokesperson Social Development. *Clubs:* Aghaloo GFC

Michelle Gildernew, MP, House of Commons, London SW1A 0AA *Tel:* 020 7219 8162 *Fax:* 020 7219 6107. *Constituency:* 87 Main Street, Lisnaskea BT92 0JD *Tel:* 028 6772 3986 *Fax:* 028 6772 3643 *E-mail:* fstconstituency@fsmail.net

GILLAN, CHERYL
Chesham and Amersham

Cheryl Gillan. Born 21 April 1952; Daughter of late Adam Mitchell Gillan, company director, and late Mona Gillan; Educated Cheltenham Ladies' College; College of Law; Chartered Institute of Marketing; Married John Coates Leeming 1985. International Management Group 1977-84; Director, British Film Year 1984-86; Senior marketing consultant, Ernst and Young 1986-91; Contested Greater Manchester Central 1989 European Parliament election; Marketing director, Kidsons Impey 1991-93; Consultant PKF 1999-

Con majority 13,798

House of Commons: Member for Chesham and Amersham since 9 April 1992 general election; Opposition Spokesperson for: Trade and Industry 1997-98, Foreign and Commonwealth Affairs 1998-2001, International Development 1998-2001; Opposition Whip 2001-03; PPS to Viscount Cranborne, as Leader of the House of Lords and Lord Privy Seal 1994-95; Parliamentary Under-Secretary of State, Department of Education and Employment 1995-97; Shadow Minister for: Home, Constitutional and Legal Affairs 2003-04, Home Affairs 2004-. *Political interests:* Industry, Space, International Affairs, Defence, Education, Employment. Former Soviet Union, Europe, Hungary, Poland, USA, Japan, Pacific Rim, China

Chairman, Bow Group 1987-88. Member, Executive Committee, Commonwealth Parliamentary Association (CPA) UK Branch 1998-; UK Representative, British Islands and Mediterranean region on CPA Executive 1999-2004; Member, NATO Parliamentary Assembly 2003-; Member, Worshipful Company of Marketors; Freeman, City of London; *Clubs:* RAC; *Recreations:* Golf, music, gardening

Cheryl Gillan, MP, House of Commons, London SW1A 0AA *Tel:* 020 7219 4061 *Fax:* 020 7219 2762 *E-mail:* gillanc@parliament.uk. *Constituency:* 7B Hill Avenue, Amersham, Buckinghamshire HP6 5BD *Tel:* 01494 721577

GILROY, LINDA
Plymouth Sutton

Linda Gilroy. Born 19 July 1949; Daughter of late William and Gwendolen Jarvie; Educated Maynards, Exeter; Stirling High School; Edinburgh University (MA history 1971); Strathclyde University (postgraduate diploma, secretarial studies 1972); Married Bernard Gilroy 1986. Deputy director, Age Concern, Scotland 1972-79; Regional manager, Gas Consumers' Council 1979-96; Contested Devon and East Plymouth 1994 European Parliament election; Member, TGWU

Lab/Co-op majority 4,109

House of Commons: Contested South-East Cornwall 1992 general election. Member for Plymouth Sutton since 1 May 1997 general election; PPS to Nick Raynsford as Minister of State: Department for Transport, Local Government and the Regions 2001-02, Office of the Deputy Prime Minister 2002-. *Political interests:* Pensioners' Rights, Trade and Industry, Energy, Utility Regulation, Local and Regional Government, Small Businesses, Fair Trade. Turkey, Poland, New Zealand, Australia, America, Tanzania, Ghana

Member: National Policy Forum 2001-04, Health Policy Commission. *Recreations:* Theatre, swimming, walking

Linda Gilroy, MP, House of Commons, London SW1A 0AA *Tel:* 020 7219 4416 *Fax:* 020 7219 0987 *E-mail:* gilroyl@parliament.uk. *Constituency:* 65 Bretonside, Plymouth, Devon PL4 0BD *Tel:* 01752 226626 *Fax:* 01752 221645

GODSIFF, ROGER
Birmingham Sparkbrook and Small Heath

Roger Godsiff. Born 28 June 1946; Son of late George Godsiff, chargehand/fitter, and of Gladys Godsiff; Educated Catford Comprehensive School, London; Married Julia Brenda Morris 1977 (1 son 1 daughter). Banking 1965-70; Political Officer, APEX 1970-88; Senior research officer, GMB 1988-91; Member of and sponsored by GMB; London Borough of Lewisham: Councillor 1971-90, Labour Chief Whip 1974-77, Mayor 1977

Lab majority 3,289

House of Commons: Contested Birmingham Yardley 1983 general election. Member for Birmingham Small Heath 1992-97, and for Birmingham Sparkbrook and Small Heath since 1 May 1997 general election; Adviser on cricket to Richard Caborn, as Minister of State for Sport 2002-. *Political interests:* European Union, Foreign Affairs, Sport, Recreation, Immigration. Indian Sub-Continent, America, Middle East, Asia

Member, Co-operative Party. Member, Executive Committee, IPU 1999-; Chairman Charlton Athletic Community Trust; *Clubs:* Member, Charlton Athletic Supporters Club; *Recreations:* Sport in general, particularly football

Roger Godsiff, MP, House of Commons, London SW1A 0AA *Tel:* 020 7219 5191 *Fax:* 020 7219 2221 *E-mail:* godsiffr@parliament.uk. *Constituency:* 15D Lloyd Street, Small Heath, Birmingham, West Midlands B10 0LH *Tel:* 0121-772 2383 *Fax:* 0121-772 2383

GOGGINS, PAUL
Wythenshawe and Sale East

Paul Gerard Goggins. Born 16 June 1953; Son of John Goggins and late Rita Goggins; Educated St Bede's, Manchester; Ushaw College, Durham 1971-73; Birmingham Polytechnic (Certificate in Residential Care of Children and Young People 1976); Manchester Polytechnic (Certificate of Qualification in Social Work 1982); Married Wyn Bartley 1977 (2 sons 1 daughter). Child care worker, Liverpool Catholic Social Services 1974-75; Officer-in-Charge, local authority children's home, Wigan 1976-84; Project director, NCH Action For Children, Salford 1984-89; National director, Church Action On Poverty 1989-97; Member TGWU; Councillor, Salford City Council 1990-98

Lab majority 10,827

House of Commons: Member for Wythenshawe and Sale East since 1 May 1997 general election; PPS to: John Denham as Minister of State: Department of Social Security 1998-99, Department of Health 1999-2000; David Blunkett: as Secretary of State for Education and Employment 2000-01, as Home Secretary 2001-03; Parliamentary Under-Secretary of State (Correctional Services and Reducing Re-offending), Home Office 2003-. *Political interests:* Poverty, Unemployment, Housing, Transport, Global Poverty, Democratic Renewal, Community Regeneration

Recreations: Watching Manchester City football team, walking, singing

Paul Goggins, MP, House of Commons, London SW1A 0AA *Tel:* 020 7219 5865 *E-mail:* gogginsp@parliament.uk. *Constituency: Tel:* 0161-499 7900 *Fax:* 0161-499 7911

GOLDSWORTHY, JULIA
Falmouth and Camborne

Julia Goldsworthy. Born 10 September 1978; Educated Truro School, Cornwall; Fitzwilliam College, Cambridge (BA history 2000); Daiichi University of Economics, Japan (level 3 Japanese 2001); Birkbeck College, London (postgraduate certificate economics 2003); Single. Education researcher Truro College Business Centre 2004; Regeneration officer Carrick District Council 2004-

Lib Dem majority 1,886

House of Commons: Member for Falmouth and Camborne since 5 May 2005 general election. *Political interests:* Education, economic policy, housing

Senior political adviser to Liberal Democrat Parliamentary Party (economy and education) 2003-04. *Clubs:* Member: Falmouth Arts Club, Penzance Arts Club; *Recreations:* Gig rowing, playing clarinet

Julia Goldsworthy, MP, House of Commons, London SW1A 0AA
Tel: 020 7219 8210. *Constituency:* 75 Trelowarren Street, Camborne, Cornwall TR14 8AL *Tel:* 01209 716110 *E-mail:* jg@cantab.net
Website: www.falmouthandcambornelibdems.org

GOODMAN, HELEN
Bishop Auckland

Helen Goodman. Born 2 January 1958; Educated Lady Manners School, Bakewell; Somerville College, Oxford (BA philosophy, politics and economics 1979); Married Charles 1988. Research assistant Phillip Whitehead MP; Civil servant HM Treasury, ending as Head of Strategy Unit 1980-97; Director of Commission on Future of Multi Ethnic Britain 1998; Head of strategy Children's Society 1998-2002; Chief executive National Association of Toy and Leisure Libraries 2002-05; GMB

Lab majority 10,047

House of Commons: Member for Bishop Auckland since 5 May 2005 general election
Recreations: Cooking, family

Helen Goodman, MP, House of Commons, London SW1A 0AA
Tel: 020 7219 4346. *Constituency:* Labour North East office, 131 Bedford St, North Shields, Tyne and Wear NE29 6LA *Tel:* 0191 296 6012 *Fax:* 0191 257 0011
E-mail: helencgoodman@aol.com

GOODMAN, PAUL
Wycombe

Paul Alexander Cyril Goodman. Born 17 November 1959; Son of Abel Goodman and Irene Goodman, neé Rubens; Educated Cranleigh School, Surrey; York University (BA English literature 1981); Married Fiona Mary Ann Gill 1999. Public affairs executive Extel Consultancy 1984-85; Researcher Tom King MP 1985-87; Home news editor *Catholic Herald* 1990-91; Leader writer *Daily Telegraph* 1991-92; Reporter *Sunday Telegraph* 1992-95; *Daily Telegraph*: Comment editor 1995-2001, Leader writer 2001-02; Member National Union of Students Executive Committee 1981-83

Con majority 7,051

House of Commons: Member for Wycombe since 7 June 2001 general election; PPS to David Davis, MP as Chairman of the Conservative Party 2001-02; Shadow Minister for: Work and Pensions 2003, Disabled People 2003-04, Economic Affairs 2004, Work and Pensions and Welfare Reform 2004-. *Political interests:* Social Affairs. Kashmir

Chair Federation of Conservative Students 1983-84; Member policy unit Westminster Council 1988

Paul Goodman, MP, House of Commons, London SW1A 0AA *Tel:* 020 7219 5099 *Fax:* 020 7219 4614 *E-mail:* goodmanp@parliament.uk. *Constituency:* 150a West Wycombe Road, High Wycombe, Buckinghamshire HP12 3AE *Tel:* 01494 521777 *Fax:* 01494 510042 *Website:* www.wycombe.tory.org.uk

GOODWILL, ROBERT
Scarborough and Whitby

Robert Goodwill. Born 31 December 1956; Educated Bootham School, York; Newcastle University (BSc crop production 1979); Married Maureen Short 1987. Farmer 1979-; Contested Richmond and North Yorkshire 1994, Yorkshire (south) 1998 European Parliament elections; MEP for Yorkshire and the Humber 1999-2004: Vice-chair Conservative backbench committee 2001-04, Conservative environment spokesperson 2001-04; Member, then branch chair National Farmers Union

Con majority 1,245

House of Commons: Contested Redcar 1992 and North West Leicestershire 1997 general elections. Member for Scarborough and Whitby since 5 May 2005 general election. *Political interests:* Agriculture, fisheries, environment, transport

Patron, National Traction Engine Trust; *Clubs:* Sentinel Drivers, Farmers; *Recreations:* Steam ploughing, travel

Robert Goodwill, MP, House of Commons, London SW1A 0AA *Tel:* 020 7219 8268. *Constituency:* SWCA, 21 Muntriss Row, Scarborough, North Yorkshire YO11 2EW *Tel:* 01723 360621

GOVE, MICHAEL
Surrey Heath

Michael Gove. Born 26 August 1967; Educated Robert Gordon's College, Aberdeen; Lady Margaret Hall, Oxford University (BA English 1988); Married Sarah Rosemary Vine 2001. Reporter Aberdeen Press and Journal 1989; Researcher/reporter Scottish Television 1990-91; Reporter BBC News and Current Affairs 1991-96;*The Times*: writer and editor 1996-2005, writer 2005-; National Union of Journalists 1989-

House of Commons: Member for Surrey Heath since 5 May 2005 general election.

Con majority 10,845   *Political interests:* Education, crime, terrorism

Publications: Michael Portillo – The Future of the Right (Fourth Estate) 1995;*The Price of Peace* (ZPS) 2000

Michael Gove, MP, House of Commons, London SW1A 0AA *Tel:* 020 7219 6804. *Constituency:* Curzon House, Church Road, Windlesham GU20 6BH *Tel:* 01276 472468 *Fax:* 01276 451602 *E-mail:* michael@michaelgove.com *Website:* www.michaelgove.com

GRAY, JAMES
North Wiltshire

James Whiteside Gray. Born 7 November 1954; Son of late Very Revd John R. Gray and Dr Sheila Gray; Educated Glasgow High School; Glasgow University (MA history 1975); Christ Church, Oxford (history thesis 1975-77); Married Sarah Ann Beale 1980 (2 sons 1 daughter). Honourable Artillery Company (TA) 1978-84; Member, HAC Court of Assistants 2002-. Management trainee, P & O 1977-78; Broker, senior broker then department manager, Anderson Hughes & Co Ltd (Shipbrokers) 1978-84; Member, The Baltic Exchange 1978-92, Pro Bono Member 1997-; Managing director, GNI Freight Futures Ltd, Senior Manager, GNI Ltd (Futures Brokers) 1984-1992; Director: Baltic Futures Exchange 1989-91, Westminster Strategy 1995-96; Union of Country Sports Workers

Con majority 5,303

House of Commons: Contested Ross, Cromarty and Skye 1992 general election. Member for North Wiltshire since 1 May 1997 general election; Opposition Spokesman for: Defence 2001-02, Defra 2002-; Opposition Whip 2000-01; Special Adviser to Michael Howard, John Gummer as Secretaries of State for Environment 1991-95; Shadow Minister for: Environment, Food and Rural Affairs 2001-03, Environment and Transport 2003-. *Political interests:* Countryside, Agriculture, Defence, Scotland, Environment, Foreign Affairs. America, China, Mongolia, Sri Lanka

Deputy Chairman, Wandsworth Tooting Conservative Association 1994-96. International League for the Protection of Horses; Vice-President, HAC Saddle Club; Consultant, British Horse Industry Confederation 1995-2001; Member: Armed Forces Parliamentary Scheme (Army) 1998, Post Graduate Scheme 2000, Royal College of Defence Studies 2003; President: Chippenham Multiple Sclerosis Society, Association of British Riding Schools; Vice-chairman, Charitable Properties Association; *Publications: Financial Risk Management in the Shipping Industry*, 1985; *Futures and Options for Shipping*, 1987 (Winner of Lloyds of London Book Prize); *Shipping Futures*, 1990; Chapter in *Seaford House Papers*, 2004; Member, Honourable Artillery Company; Freeman, City of London 1978; *Clubs:* President, Chippenham Constitutional 2000-; Wootton Bassett Conservative; Pratt's; Member, Avon Vale Foxhounds; *Recreations:* Riding Horses

James Gray, MP, House of Commons, London SW1A 0AA *Tel:* 020 7219 6237 *Fax:* 020 7219 1163 *E-mail:* jamesgraymp@parliament.uk. *Constituency:* North Wilts Conservative Association, 44-45 Market Place, Chippenham, Wiltshire SN15 3HU *Tel:* 01249 652851 *Fax:* 01249 448582

Con majority 16,447

GRAYLING, CHRISTOPHER
Epsom and Ewell

Christopher Stephen Grayling. Born 1 April 1962; Educated Royal Grammar School, High Wycombe; Sidney Sussex College, Cambridge (BA history 1984); Married Susan Clare Dillistone 1987 (1 son 1 daughter). BBC News: Trainee 1985-86, Producer 1986-88; Programme editor Business Daily Channel 4 1988-91; Business development manager BBC Select 1991-93; Director: Charterhouse Prods Ltd 1993, Workhouse Ltd 1993-95, SSVC Group 1995-97; Change consultant and European marketing director Burson Marsteller 1997-2001; Councillor London Borough of Merton 1998-2002

House of Commons: Contested Warrington South 1997 general election. Member for Epsom and Ewell since 7 June 2001 general election; Shadow Spokesperson for Health 2002-03; Opposition Whip 2002; Shadow Minister for: Public Services, Health and Education 2003-04, Education 2004-05, Health 2005; Shadow Leader of the House of Commons 2005-. *Political interests:* Transport, Education, Health

Publications: The Bridgwater Heritage, 1983; *A Land Fit for Heroes,* 1985; *Just Another Star?,* co-author 1987; *Insight Guide to the Waterways of Europe,* co-author 1989; *Recreations:* Golf, cricket

Christopher Grayling, MP, House of Commons, London SW1A 0AA
Tel: 020 7219 8226 *E-mail:* graylingc@parliament.uk. *Constituency:* 212 Barnett Wood Lane, Ashtead, Surrey KT21 2DB *Tel:* 01372 271036 *Fax:* 01372 270906

Con majority 13,298

GREEN, DAMIAN
Ashford

Damian Howard Green. Born 17 January 1956; Son of Howard and late Audrey Green; Educated Reading School; Balliol College, Oxford (BA philosophy, politics and economics 1977, MA); President, Oxford Union 1977; Married Alicia Collinson 1988 (2 daughters). Financial journalist, BBC Radio 1978-82; Business producer, Channel 4 News 1982-84; News editor, business news, *The Times* 1984-85; Business editor, Channel 4 News, 1985-87; Programme presenter and city editor, *Business Daily* 1987-92; Special Adviser, Prime Minister's Policy Unit 1992-94; Public Affairs Consultant (Self-employed) 1995-97

House of Commons: Contested Brent East 1992 general election. Member for Ashford since 1 May 1997 general election; Opposition Spokesperson for: Education and Employment 1998-99, Environment 1999-2001; Shadow Secretary of State for: Education and Skills 2001-03, Transport 2003-04. *Political interests:* Economic Policy, Foreign Affairs, Media, Education, Employment, Rural Affairs. France, Italy

Vice-President, Tory Reform Group 1997-; Conservative Parliamentary Mainstream Group: Vice-chair 1997-2003, Chair 2003-. President, Find a Voice; *Publications: ITN Budget Fact Book,* 1984-85-86; *A Better BBC,* 1990; *The Cross-Media Revolution,* 1995; *Communities in the Countryside,* 1996; *Regulating the Media in the Digital Age,* 1997; *21st Century Conservatism,* 1998; *The Four Failures of the New Deal,* 1999; *Better Learning,* 2002; *More than Markets,* 2003; *Recreations:* Football, cricket, opera, cinema

Damian Green, MP, House of Commons, London SW1A 0AA *Tel:* 020 7219 3518 *Fax:* 020 7219 0904 *E-mail:* greend@parliament.uk. *Constituency:* c/o Hardy House, The Street, Bethenden, Ashford, Kent TN26 3AG *Tel:* 01233 820454 *Fax:* 01233 820111 *Website:* www.damiangreen.org.uk

GREENING, JUSTINE
Putney

Justine Greening. Born 30 April 1969; Educated Oakwood Comprehensive School, Rotherham, S Yorks; Thomas Rotherham College, Rotherham; Southampton University (BSc business economics and accounting 1990); London Business School (MBA 2000); Single. Audit assistant, PriceWaterhouse 1991-94; Audit assistant manager, Revisuisse PriceWaterhouse 1995-96; Finance manager, SmithKline Beecham, 1996-2001; Business strategy manager, GlaxoSmithKline, 2001-02; Sales and marketing finance manager, Centrica 2002-; Epping Town Council: Councillor 1999, Vice-chair finance and general planning committee 2000

Con majority 1,766

House of Commons: Contested Ealing, Acton and Shepherd's Bush 2001 general election. Member for Putney since 5 May 2005 general election

Epping Forest Conservative Association. *Publications:* 'A Wholly Healthy Britain' in *A Blue Tomorrow*, 2000; *Clubs:* Putney Society; Putney Music Society; Putney Rotary Club; *Recreations:* Swimming, cycling

Justine Greening, MP, House of Commons, London SW1A 0AA *Tel:* 020 7219 8300. *Constituency:* 3 Summerstown, London SW17 0BQ *Tel:* 020 8944 0378 *E-mail:* office@wandsworthconservatives.com *Website:* www.wandsworthconservatives.com

GREENWAY, JOHN
Ryedale

John Robert Greenway. Born 15 February 1946; Son of Bill and Kathleen Greenway; Educated Sir John Deane's Grammar School, Northwich; Hendon Police College; London College of Law; Married Sylvia Ann Gant 1974 (2 sons 1 daughter). Metropolitan Police Officer, stationed West End Central 1965-69; Insurance company representative 1970-72; Insurance broker and financial consultant 1973-; Chairman Register of Exercise Professionals; President Institute of Insurance Brokers; North Yorkshire County Council: Councillor 1985-87, Education and Schools Committees, Vice-chair, North Yorkshire Police Committee

Con majority 10,469

House of Commons: Member for Ryedale since 11 June 1987 general election; Opposition Spokesperson for: Home Affairs (Police, Criminal Policy, Constitution, Data Protection, Electoral Policy, Gambling and Licensing) 1997-2000, Culture, Media and Sport (Sports; Tourism) 2000-03; PPS to Baroness Trumpington, as Minister of State, Ministry of Agriculture, Fisheries and Food 1991-92. *Political interests:* Law and Order, Personal Finance, Agriculture, Broadcasting, Sales Promotion and Marketing, Tourism

Member, 92 Group. ActionAid; Patron Encephalitis Support Group; Member, Standing Committees 1997-98 to Consider: Data Protection Bill, Registration of Political Parties Bill, Special Immigration Appeals Commissioners Bill; Freedman of Information Bill 2000; Communications Bill 2003; Trustee National Playing Fields Association; Honorary Fellow, Chartered Insurance Institute; *Clubs:* President, York City FC; *Recreations:* Opera, music, wine, travel

John Greenway, MP, House of Commons, London SW1A 0AA *Tel:* 020 7219 6397 *Fax:* 020 7219 6059 *E-mail:* greenwayj@parliament.uk. *Constituency:* 109 Town Street, Old Malton, North Yorkshire YO17 0HD *Tel:* 01653 692023 *Fax:* 01653 696108

GRIEVE, DOMINIC
Beaconsfield

Dominic Charles Roberts Grieve. Born 24 May 1956; Son of late W. P. Grieve, MP 1964-83, and of late Evelyn Grieve, neé Mijouain; Educated Westminster School; Magdalen College, Oxford (BA modern history, 1978, MA 1989); Central London Polytechnic (Diploma in law 1980); Married Caroline Hutton 1990 (2 sons and 1 son deceased). Territorial Army 1981-83; Councillor, London Borough of Hammersmith and Fulham 1982-86

Con majority 15,253

House of Commons: Contested Norwood 1987 general election. Member for Beaconsfield since 1 May 1997 general election; Opposition Spokesperson for: Constitutional Affairs and Scotland 1999-2001, Home Office 2001-03; Shadow Attorney General 2003-. *Political interests:* Law and Order, Environment, Defence, Foreign Affairs, European Union, Constitution. France, Luxembourg

President, Oxford University Conservative Association 1977; Society of Conservative Lawyers: Chair Research Committee 1992-95, Chair Finance and General Purposes. Member, London Diocesan Synod of Church of England 1994-2000; Deputy Churchwarden; Member: National Trust, John Muir Trust; *Clubs:* Carlton; *Recreations:* Mountaineering, skiing, scuba diving, fell-walking, architecture and art

Dominic Grieve, MP, House of Commons, London SW1A 0AA *Tel:* 020 7219 6220 *Fax:* 020 7219 4803 *E-mail:* grieved@parliament.uk. *Constituency:* Disraeli House, 12 Aylesbury End, Beaconsfield, Buckinghamshire HP9 1LW *Tel:* 01494 673745 *Fax:* 01494 670428 *Website:* www.beaconsfield-conservatives.org.uk

GRIFFITH, NIA
Llanelli

Nia Griffith. Born 4 December 1956; Educated Oxford University BA modern languages (1979); University College of North Wales, Bangor (PGCE 1980); Divorced. Language teacher; Former education adviser; Former Estyn schools inspector; Head of languages Morriston Comprehensive School, Swansea; Chair Carmarthenshire Youth Project; Sheriff of Carmarthen 1997, Deputy mayor Carmarthen 1998

Lab majority 7,234

House of Commons: Member for Llanelli since 5 May 2005 general election; member Labour Party 1981-; Carmarthen Town Council: councillor 1987-, sheriff 1997, deputy mayor 1998; secretary Carmarthenshire County Labour Party 1994; former chair and agent Carmarthen West and South Pembrokeshire Constituency Labour Party. *Political interests:* Environment, Europe, community issues, cycle paths

Recreations: Arts, European cinema, music, cycling

Nia Griffith, MP, House of Commons, London SW1A 0AA *Tel:* 020 7219 6102. *Constituency:* 6 Queen Victoria Road, Llanelli SA15 2TL *E-mail:* griffithnia@aol.com

GRIFFITHS, NIGEL
Edinburgh South

Lab majority 405

Nigel Griffiths. Born 20 May 1955; Son of late Lionel Griffiths and of Elizabeth Griffiths; Educated Hawick High School; Edinburgh University (MA 1977); Moray House College of Education (1978); Married Sally McLaughlin 1979; City of Edinburgh District Council: Councillor 1980-87, Chair: Housing Committee, Decentralisation Committee 1986-87; Member: Edinburgh Festival Council 1984-87, Edinburgh Health Council 1982-87; Executive Member, Edinburgh Council of Social Service 1984-87

House of Commons: Member for Edinburgh South 1987-2005, for new Edinburgh South since 5 May 2005 general election; Opposition Spokesperson for Trade and Industry Specialising in International Trade and Consumer Affairs 1989-97; Opposition Whip 1987-89; Parliamentary Under-Secretary of State, Department of Trade and Industry 1997-: Competition and Consumer Affairs 1997-98, Small Business, Export Controls and Non-Proliferation 2001-03, Small Business and Enterprise 2003-04, Construction, Small Business and Enterprise 2004-05; Deputy Leader of the House of Commons 2005-. *Political interests:* Education, Housing, Health, Social Services, Disability, Scotland, Arts, Economic Policy, Small Businesses

President, EU Labour Club 1976-77; Member, Labour Party National Policy Forum 1999-. Secretary, Lothian Devolution Campaign 1978; Executive Member, Scottish Constitutional Convention 1988-90; Vice-President, Institute of Trading Standards Administration 1994-; Chair, Scottish Charities Kosovo Appeal 2000-; *Publications: Guide to Council Housing in Edinburgh*, 1981; *Council Housing on the Point of Collapse*, 1982; *Welfare Rights Survey*, 1981; *Welfare Rights Guide*, 1982, 1983, 1984, 1985, 1986; *Rights Guide for Mentally Handicapped People*, 1988; *300 Gains from the Labour Government*, 2000; *Recreations:* Travel, live entertainment, badminton, hill-walking and rock-climbing, architecture, reading, politics, scuba diving, flying

Nigel Griffiths, MP, House of Commons, London SW1A 0AA *Tel:* 020 7219 2424 *E-mail:* ngriffithsmp@parliament.uk. *Constituency:* 31 Minto Street, Edinburgh, EH9 2BT *Tel:* 0131-662 4520

GROGAN, JOHN
Selby

Lab majority 467

John Grogan. Born 24 February 1961; Son of late John Martin Grogan and late Maureen Grogan; Educated St Michael's College, Leeds; St John's College, Oxford (BA modern history and economics 1982); Single. Communications co-ordinator, Leeds City Council 1987-94; Contested York 1989 European Parliament election; Labour Party press officer, European Parliament, Brussels 1995; Self-employed conference organiser 1996-97; Member, GMB

House of Commons: Contested Selby 1987 and 1992 general elections. Member for Selby since 1 May 1997 general election. *Political interests:* Local and Regional Government, European Union, Economic Policy, Broadcasting, Sport, Liquor Licensing Reform, Small Businesses, Coal. Ukraine, Mongolia, Australia, New Zealand

Member: Fabian Society, Institute of Public Policy Research; John Smith Institute. *Clubs:* Yorkshire County Cricket Club; *Recreations:* Football, running, cinema

John Grogan, MP, House of Commons, London SW1A 0AA *Tel:* 020 7219 4403 *Fax:* 020 7219 2676 *E-mail:* groganj@parliament.uk. *Constituency:* 58 Gowthorpe, Selby, North Yorkshire YO8 4ET *Tel:* 01757 291152 *Fax:* 01757 291153

Does Construction Lack Substance on Sustainability?

We've all heard the one about the construction industry becoming sustainable haven't we? But did we really understand the message – and if so what are we doing about it?

Britain's commitment to reduce 60% of greenhouse gas emissions by 2050 saw Tony Blair declare that tackling global warming is 'unquestionably' an environmental priority and one that needs to be addressed at an international level. The Government has recently admitted that by 2010 the UK would only achieve a 14% cut in carbon dioxide emissions from 1990 levels, instead of the planned reduction of 20%.

So where does the UK construction industry fit into all of this. 50% of the UK problem can be apportioned directly to the buildings we live and work in. In very broad terms, there is a need to reduce (new build) CO_2 by a factor of four. The current (existing) stock will need to be refurbished to use around one third of what is currently the norm. This is a huge challenge.

The current public sector spend will result in buildings that are much better in terms of fossil fuel dependency but still fall short of what is really needed. We are effectively building projects that will need twice their 'carbon ration' by the year 2050. Yet surely we hope that today's new builds will last for at least 100 years.

Figures from The Alliance for Building Sustainability (TABS) show that £15bn a year is being spent on new construction - but will these new buildings deliver value – for hundreds of years? If we focus unduly on initial costs then the design team will be prevented from creating the sort of 'legacy' development that will best serve the organisation's purpose, and become a source of increasing pride, and asset value, into the longer term.

Buildings are far more central to the sustainability case than most people think. We are judged on our buildings, or at least perceived that the building we occupy provides to our values and beliefs.

However green or not our buildings are, at the moment this performance is invisible. We cannot see performance, just as we cannot see carbon dioxide emissions. We need credible labels to make performance visible. These are coming fast, and the Energy Performance in Buildings Directive will improve things enormously, but we do not need to wait for the EPBD before we proudly declare the CO_2 of our own buildings.

Fast Facts ...

- The UK is 1% of the world's population and yet we produce 2.3% of the world's CO_2
- In the UK, the biggest source of CO_2 is from burning fossil fuels - like coal, gas and oil – in power stations
- The UK has, in the form of wind power, the largest renewable energy resource in Europe

Con majority 9,685

GUMMER, JOHN
Suffolk Coastal

John Gummer. Born 26 November 1939; Son of late Canon Selwyn Gummer; Educated King's School, Rochester; Selwyn College, Cambridge (BA history 1961, MA 1971) (President of the Union 1962); Married Penelope Jane Gardner 1977 (2 sons 2 daughters). Former chairman, Siemssen Hunter Ltd; Since leaving office – Chairman, Sancroft International Ltd (corporate responsibility consultants); Chairman: Valpak Ltd, International Commission on Sustainable Consumption, Marine Stewardship Council; Director, Vivendi UK Ltd; Councillor, ILEA 1967-70

House of Commons: Contested Greenwich 1964 and 1966 general elections. Member for Lewisham West 1970-74, for Eye 1979-83, and for Suffolk Coastal since 9 June 1983 general election; Assistant Government Whip January 1981; Government Whip 1981-83; PPS: to Minister of Agriculture, Fisheries and Food 1971-72, to Secretary of State for Social Services 1979-81; Parliamentary Under-Secretary of State, Department of Employment 1983; Minister of State, Department of Employment 1983-84; Paymaster General 1984-85; Minister of State, Ministry of Agriculture, Fisheries and Food 1985-88; Minister for Local Government 1988-89; Minister of Agriculture, Fisheries and Food 1989-93; Secretary of State for the Environment 1993-97. *Political interests:* European Affairs, Environment

Chairman, Cambridge University Conservative Association 1961; Conservative Party: Vice-Chairman 1972-74, Chairman 1983-85; Chairman, Conservative Group for Europe 1997-2000. *Publications: When the Coloured People Come*; *The Permissive Society*; Co-author *The Christian Calendar*; *Faith in Politics* 1987; PC 1985

Rt Hon John Gummer, MP, House of Commons, London SW1A 0AA
Tel: 020 7219 4591 *Fax:* 020 7219 5906 *E-mail:* gummerj@parliament.uk.
Constituency: Suffolk Coastal Conservative Association, National Hall, Sun Lane, Woodbridge, Suffolk IP12 1EG *Tel:* 01394 380001 *Fax:* 01394 382570

Lab majority 13,498

GWYNNE, ANDREW
Denton and Reddish

Andrew John Gwynne. Born 4 June 1974; Educated Egerton Park Community High School, Denton; North East Wales Institute of Higher Education, Wrexham; Salford University (BA politics and contemporary history 1998); Married to Allison Louise Dennis. ICL 1990-92; National Computing Centre, Y2K team 1999-2000; Researcher Andrew Bennet MP 2000-01; European co-ordinator Arlene McCarthy MEP 2000-01; Amicus AEEU 2000-; Tameside MBC: Councillor 1996-, Chair of Denoton and Audenshaw district assembly 1998-2001, Chair of resources and community services scrutiny panel 2003-04

House of Commons: Member for Denton and Reddish since 5 May 2005 general election. *Political interests:* Education and skills, regeneration, local government, environment

Denton and Reddish Constituency Labour Party: Chair 1998-2004, Vice chair 1996-98. Supporter: Children's Society 2001-, WWF 2002-, National Trust 2003-; *Clubs:* Denton Labour Club

Andrew Gwynne, MP, House of Commons, London SW1A 0AA
Tel: 020 7219 4708. *Constituency:* Agent: Cllr Brenda Warrington, Denton and Reddish Labour Party, c/o Derek Bishop, 9 Hawthorn Road, Denton M34 3QP
E-mail: labour@andrewgwynne.co.uk *Website:* www.andrewgwynne.labour.co.uk, no constituency office

Con majority 17,807

HAGUE, WILLIAM
Richmond (Yorkshire)

William Jefferson Hague. Born 26 March 1961; Son of Nigel and Stella Hague; Educated Wath-on-Dearne Comprehensive School; Magdalen College, Oxford (philosophy, politics and economics 1979-82) (President, Oxford Union 1981); INSEAD Business School, France 1985-86; Married Ffion Jenkins 1997. Shell UK 1982-83; McKinsey and Company 1983-88; Political adviser to Sir Geoffrey Howe as Chancellor of the Exchequer and Leon Brittan as Chief Secretary to the Treasury 1983; Political and economic adviser JCB 2001-; Non-executive director AES Engineering 2001-; Member Political Council of Terra Firma Capital Partners 2001-

House of Commons: Contested Wentworth 1987 general election. Member for Richmond, Yorks. since 23 February 1989 by-election; PPS to Norman Lamont as Chancellor of the Exchequer 1990-93; Department of Social Security: Joint Parliamentary Under-Secretary of State, 1993-94, Minister of State, (Minister for Social Security and Disabled People) 1994-95; Secretary of State for Wales 1995-97; Leader of the Opposition 1997-2001; Leader, Conservative Party 1997-2001; Member Joint Committee on House of Lords Reform 2002-. *Political interests:* Agriculture, Economic Policy

President Oxford University Conservative Association 1981; Leader Conservative Party June 1997-2001. International Democrat Union, Global Alliance of Conservative, Christian Democrat and like-minded parties: Chairman 1999-2002, Deputy Chairman 2002-; *Publications: Speaking with Conviction*, Conservative Policy Forum, October 1998; *I will Give you Back your Country*, Conservative Policy Forum, September 2000; *Biography of William Pitt the Younger* (Due to be published 2004); PC 1995; *The Spectator*/Highland Park Parliamentarian of the Year 1998; *Clubs:* Beefsteak, Carlton, Buck's, Pratt's, Budokwai, Mark's; *Recreations:* Walking, sailing, cross country, skiing, judo

Rt Hon William Hague, MP, House of Commons, London SW1A 0AA
Tel: 020 7219 4611 *E-mail:* haguew@parliament.uk. *Constituency:* c/o 67 High Street, Northallerton, North Yorkshire DL7 8EG *Tel:* 01609 779093
Fax: 01609 778172

HAIN, PETER
Neath

Peter Hain. Born 16 February 1950; Son of Walter and Adelaine Hain; Educated Pretoria Boys High School, South Africa; Emanuel School, Wandsworth, London; Queen Mary College, London University (BSc economics and political science 1973); Sussex University (MPhil 1976); Married Patricia Western 1975 (divorced) (2 sons); married Elizabeth Haywood 2003; Head of research, Union of Communication Workers 1976-91; Member, GMB

Lab majority 12,710

House of Commons: Contested Putney 1983 and 1987 general elections. Member for Neath since by-election 4 April 1991 by-election; Opposition Spokesperson for Employment 1996-97; Opposition Whip 1995-96; Parliamentary Under-Secretary of State, Welsh Office 1997-99; Minister of State: Foreign and Commonwealth Office 1999-2001, Department of Trade and Industry (Minister for Energy and Competitiveness) 2001; Foreign and Commonwealth Office (Minister for Europe) 2001-02; Government representative European Union Convention 2002-; Secretary of State for Wales 2002-; Leader of the House of Commons and Lord Privy Seal 2003-05; Secretary of State for Northern Ireland 2005-. *Political interests:* Southern Africa

Leader, Young Liberals 1971-73; Member: Co-op, Fabians. *Publications:* 13 books including *Ayes to the Left: A future for socialism*, 1995; PC 2001; *Clubs:* Royal British Legion, Resolven; Resolven Rugby, Ynysygerwn Cricket; *Recreations:* Rugby, soccer, cricket, motor racing, rock and folk music

Rt Hon Peter Hain, MP, House of Commons, London SW1A 0AA
Tel: 020 7219 3925 *Fax:* 020 7219 3816 *E-mail:* hainp@parliament.uk.
Constituency: 39 Windsor Road, Neath, West Glamorgan SA11 1NB
Tel: 01639 630152 *Fax:* 01639 641196

HALL, MIKE
Weaver Vale

Michael Hall. Born 20 September 1952; Son of late Thomas Hall, maintenance engineer, and of late Veronica Hall, mail order clerk; Educated St Damian's Secondary Modern School; Padgate College of Higher Education (Teacher's Certificate 1977); North Cheshire College (BEd 1987); University College of Wales, Bangor (Diploma in Education 1989); Married Lesley Gosling 1975 (1 son). Scientific assistant, chemical industry 1969-73; Teacher of history and physical education, Bolton LEA 1977-85; Support teacher, Halton Community Assessment Team 1985-92; Warrington Borough Council: Councillor 1979-93; Chair: Environmental Health Committee 1981-84, Finance Sub-Committee 1984-85, Policy and Resources Committee 1985-92; Council Leader 1985-92

Lab majority 6,855

House of Commons: Member for Warrington South 1992-97, and for Weaver Vale since 1 May 1997 general election; Assistant Government Whip 1998-2001; PPS to: Ann Taylor as Leader of the House and President of the Council 1997-98, Secretaries of State for Health: Alan Milburn 2001-03, John Reid 2003-. *Political interests:* Poverty, Education, Local and Regional Government, Home Affairs, Health. Czech Republic

Mencap, Macmillan, RSPCA; *Clubs:* Lymm Lawn Tennis and Croquet, Owley Wood Sports and Social Club; *Recreations:* Tennis, walking, cooking, reading

Mike Hall, MP, House of Commons, London SW1A 0AA *Tel:* 020 7219 4001
E-mail: hallm@parliament.uk. *Constituency:* Room 17, Castle Park, Frodsham, Cheshire WA6 6UJ *Tel:* 01928 735000 *Fax:* 01928 735250

Learning for Life and Work – the key to success

Rewarding Learning

inside and outside the classroom

In Northern Ireland, the work of advising Government on what should be taught and assessed in the province's schools is carried out by the Council for the Curriculum, Examinations and Assessment (CCEA). As work begins to roll out the new curriculum, Robert Shilliday explains why Northern Ireland has chosen to introduce a new area into teaching and learning.

While our political leaders continue to strive to find an agreement that will take Northern Ireland forward, work has continued in key areas such as education to ensure we are ready for the challenges of the new century.

In June of last year the Minister for Education Barry Gardiner MP signalled he was accepting proposals from the Council for the Curriculum, Examinations and Assessment (CCEA) for what is taught and assessed in our schools.

Central to those arrangements is an exciting new curriculum area called Learning for Life and Work. Including education for employability, citizenship and personal, social and health education (PSHE), Learning for Life and Work seeks to equip young people with the knowledge and capabilities to succeed in their future education and the world of employment.

CCEA believes it is vital that this area is a central theme throughout each young person's education.

Business has long argued that schools and college-leavers lack the work-readiness skills that industry needs. Now is the chance to redress that balance.

As globalisation and technology shrink borders, we must work to broaden the horizons of our young people and prepare them for the opportunities and challenges they will encounter in both life and work.

Competing in the new economy will demand a partnership between business and education to stimulate curiosity, creativity and entrepreneurship amongst a new generation. If business is to profit from the Learning for Life and Work initiative, CCEA must work with them in helping teachers and schools to design and deliver it.

Therefore CCEA recognises that delivering learning for Life and Work will be a great challenge for teachers. Pilot projects in Education for Employability, Citizenship, and Personal Social and Heath Education are currently running in Northern Ireland Schools to help with the smooth introduction of these new areas. Both Entry level and GCSE Learning for Life and Work qualifications are being piloted this year.

CCEA is also working to draw together the support of government, employers and the wider community to help ensure that the content of Learning for Life and Work stimulates each young person's imagination and interest in key issues that affect their lives, including future career development.

The changes will be introduced in a phased manner from 2007 onwards.

Robert Shilliday is Communications Manager for the Council for the Curriculum, Examinations and Assessment.

www.cea.org.uk

HALL, PATRICK
Bedford

Patrick Hall. Born 20 October 1951; Son of Frank Hall, architect and Josie Hall, teacher; Educated Bedford Modern School; Birmingham University (BA geography 1970); Oxford Polytechnic (post graduate diploma town planning 1979). Local government planning officer Bedford 1975-91; Bedford Town Centre co-ordinator 1991-97; Member, NALGO 1974-97; Councillor, Bedfordshire County Council 1989-97; Member, North Bedfordshire Community Health Council 1988-97

Lab majority 3,383

House of Commons: Contested North Bedfordshire 1992 general election. Member for Bedford since 1 May 1997 general election

Hon. Secretary, Eastern Regional Group of Labour MPs 1999-. *Recreations:* Squash, gardens

Patrick Hall, MP, House of Commons, London SW1A 0AA *Tel:* 020 7219 3605 *Fax:* 020 7219 3987 *E-mail:* hallp@parliament.uk. *Constituency:* Broadway House, 4-6 The Broadway, Bedford, Bedfordshire MK40 2TE *Tel:* 01234 262699 *Fax:* 01234 272981

HAMILTON, DAVID
Midlothian

David Hamilton. Born 24 October 1950; Son of David Hamilton and Agnes Gardner; Educated Dalkeith High School; Married Jean Trench Macrae 1969 (2 daughters). Miner National Coal Board 1965-84; Employment training scheme supervisor Midlothian Council 1987-89; Placement and training officer Craigmillar Festival Society 1989-92; Chief executive Craigmillar Opportunities Trust 1992-2000; NUM 1965-87, 2001-: Delegate 1976-87, Joint union chair 1981-87, Chair numerous committees; TGWU 1987-2000; Member, RMT Parliamentary Campaigning Group 2002-; Councillor, Midlothian Council 1995-2000: Convenor Strategic Services Committee 1995-2000, Cabinet member Strategic Services Portfolio 2000-01; Convention of Scottish Local Authorities (COSLA): Chair Economic Development, Planning and Transport Committee 1997-99, Spokesman Economic Development and Tourism 1999-2001; Midlothian Chamber of Commerce -2002; Midlothian Enterprise Trust -2002; Midlothian Innovation Technology Trust 2002-

Lab majority 7,265

House of Commons: Member for Midlothian 2001-05, for new Midlothian since 5 May 2005 general election. *Political interests:* Economic Development, Transport, Social Inclusion. EU, USA, Gibraltar, Cyprus

Member, European Standing Committee A 2003-; *Clubs:* Dalkeith Miners Welfare; *Recreations:* Films, theatre

David Hamilton, MP, House of Commons, London SW1A 0AA *Tel:* 020 7219 8257 *Fax:* 020 7219 3606 *E-mail:* hamiltonda@parliament.uk. *Constituency:* PO Box 11, 95 High Street, Dalkeith *Tel:* 0131-654 1585 *Fax:* 0131-654 1586 *Website:* www.davidhamilton.labour.co.uk

HAMILTON, FABIAN
Leeds North East

Fabian Hamilton. Born 12 April 1955; Son of late Mario Uziell-Hamilton, solicitor, and Adrianne Uziell-Hamilton (Her Honour Judge Uziell-Hamilton); Educated Brentwood School, Brentwood, Essex; York University (BA social sciences); Married Rosemary Ratcliffe 1980 (1 son 2 daughters). Taxi driver 1978-79; graphic designer 1979-94; consultant and dealer, Apple Macintosh computer systems 1994-97; Member: SLADE 1978-82, NGA 1982-91, GPMU 1991-; Councillor, Leeds City Council 1987-98, Chair: Race Equality Committee 1988-94, Economic Development Committee 1994-96, Education Committee 1996-97

Lab majority 5,262

House of Commons: Contested Leeds North East 1992 general election. Member for Leeds North East since 1 May 1997 general election. *Political interests:* Education, Economic Development and Small Businesses, Racism, International Development, Alternative Fuels. Middle East, Europe, Southern Africa, Caribbean and Indian sub-continent, Cyprus

Member Co-op Party; Vice-chair Labour Friends of Israel. National Heart Research, St Gemmas Hospice, Childline; Trustee, National Heart Research Fund; Trustee National Heart Research Fund; *Recreations:* Film, opera, cycling, computers, photography

Fabian Hamilton, MP, House of Commons, London SW1A 0AA
Tel: 020 7219 3493 *Fax:* 020 7219 4945 *E-mail:* fabian@leedsne.co.uk.
Constituency: 6 Queenshill Approach, Leeds, West Yorkshire LS17 6AY
Tel: 0113-237 0022 *Fax:* 0113-237 0404

HAMMOND, PHILIP
Runnymede and Weybridge

Philip Hammond. Born 4 December 1955; Son of Bernard Lawrence Hammond, AMICE, retired civil engineer and local government officer; Educated Shenfield School, Brentwood, Essex; University College, Oxford (MA politics, philosophy and economics 1977); Married Susan Carolyn Williams-Walker 1991 (2 daughters 1 son). Assistant to Chair then marketing manager, Speywood Laboratories Ltd 1977-81; Director, Speywood Medical Ltd 1981-83; Established and ran medical equipment manufacturing and distribution companies 1983-94; Director, Castlemead Ltd 1984-; Director, various medical equipment manufacturing companies 1983-96; Partner, CMA Consultants 1993-95; Director, Castlemead Homes Ltd 1994-; Consultant to Government of Malawi 1995-97; Director, Consort Resources Ltd 1999-2003

Con majority 12,349

House of Commons: Contested Newham North East by-election 1994. Member for Runnymede and Weybridge since 1 May 1997 general election; Opposition Spokesperson for: Health and Social Services 1998-2001, Trade and Industry 2001-02; Shadow Minister: of State, Office of the Deputy Prime Minister 2002-03, for Local and Devolved Government Affairs 2003-05; Shadow Chief Secretary to the Treasury 2005-. *Political interests:* Economic Policy, International Trade, European Union, Defence, Social Security, Transport, Housing and Planning, Energy, Health. Latin America, Germany, Italy, Southern and Eastern Africa

East Lewisham Conservative Association: Executive Council Member 1982-89, Chair 1989-96; Member, Greater London Area Executive Council 1989-96; Vice-Chair, Greenwich and Lewisham Conservative Action Group 1993-94. White Lodge, Chertsey; Member, European Standing Committee B 1997-1998; *Clubs:* Carlton; *Recreations:* Travel, cinema, walking

Philip Hammond, MP, House of Commons, London SW1A 0AA
Tel: 020 7219 4055 *Fax:* 020 7219 5851 *E-mail:* hammondp@parliament.uk.
Constituency: Runnymede, Spelthorne and Weybridge, Conservative Association, 55 Cherry Orchard, Staines, Surrey TW18 2DQ *Tel:* 01784 453544
Fax: 01784 466109

Con majority 2,301

HAMMOND, STEPHEN
Wimbledon

Stephen William Hammond. Born 4 February 1962; Educated King Edward VI School, Southampton; Richard Hale School, Hertford; Queen Mary College, London University (BSc econ 1982); Married Sally Patricia Brodie 1991. Trainee analyst, Reed Stenhouse Investment Services 1983-85; Fund manager, Canada Life 1985-88; Stockbroker, UBS Philips and Drew 1988-91; Director UK equities, Dresdner Kleinwort Benson Securities 1991-98; Director Pan European research, Commerzbank Securities 1998; Merton Borough Council: Councillor 2002-, Environment spokesman 2002-04; Deputy group leader 2004-

House of Commons: Contested North Warwickshire 1997 and Wimbledon 2001 general elections. Member for Wimbledon since 5 May 2005 general election. *Political interests:* Health, financial affairs, transport, foreign affairs

Chair, Stevenage Conservatives 1991-94; Member, Eastern Area Executive 1992-94. Deputy chairman, Merton Citizens Advice Bureau 2000-; *Clubs:* Wimbledon Civic Forum; Wimbledon Society; Wimbledon Village Club; *Recreations:* Reading, sport, relaxing with family, cooking

Stephen Hammond, MP, House of Commons, London SW1A 0AA
Tel: 020 7219 8263. *Constituency:* Agent: Matt Sliver, 126 Arthur Road, Wimbledon, London SW19 8AA *Tel:* 020 8944 2905
E-mail: stephen.hammond@wimbledonconservatives.org.uk
Website: www.wimbledonconservatives.org.uk

Lib Dem majority 3,362

HANCOCK, MIKE
Portsmouth South

Mike (Michael) Thomas Hancock. Born 9 April 1946; Son of Thomas William Hancock and Margaret Eva Hancock (neé Cole); Married Jacqueline Elliott 1967 (1 son 1 daughter). Director, BBC Daytime; District Officer for Hampshire, Isle of Wight and Channel Islands Mencap 1989-97; Contested (Liberal Democrat) Wight and Hampshire South European Parliamentary election 1994; Councillor, Portsmouth City Council 1971-: Leader, Liberal Democrat Group 1989-97, Chair, Planning and Economic Development Committee; Councillor, Hampshire County Council 1973-97: Leader of the Opposition 1977-81, 1989-93, Leader 1993-97

House of Commons: Contested Portsmouth South (SDP) 1983, (SDP/Alliance) 1987 general elections. Member (SDP) for Portsmouth South 1984-87. Member for Portsmouth South since 1 May 1997 general election; Spokesperson for: Foreign Affairs, Defence and Europe (Defence) 1997-99; Environment, Transport, the Regions and Social Justice (Planning) 2000-01. *Political interests:* European Affairs, Defence, Sport

Member: Labour Party 1968-81, Social Democrat Party 1981-87, Liberal Democrat Party 1987-. Mencap, Save the Children, Animal Aid, NAVS, Christian Aid; Council of Europe, Western European Union, NATO; Trustee, Royal Marine Museum; *Publications: Council of Europe Report on International Abduction of children by one of the parents,* 2002; CBE 1992; CBE; *Recreations:* Supporter Portsmouth Football Club

Mike Hancock, MP, House of Commons, London SW1A 0AA *Tel:* 020 7219 5180
Fax: 020 7219 2496 *E-mail:* portsmouthldp@cix.co.uk. *Constituency:* 1A Albert Road, Southsea, Hampshire PO5 2SE *Tel:* 023 9286 1055 *Fax:* 023 9283 0530

Con majority 5,029

HANDS, GREG
Hammersmith and Fulham

Gregory Hands. Born 1965; Educated Dr Challoner's Grammar School, Bucks; Cambridge University (BA modern history, MA); Engaged to Irina. banker 1989-97; Hammersmith and Fulham Borough Council: Councillor 1998-: Leader Conservative group 1999-; Governor St Thomas' Primary School, Fulham; Member local police consultative group

House of Commons: Member for Hammersmith and Fulham since 5 May 2005 general election. *Political interests:* Environment, finance, foreign affairs, housing, criminal justice system. Eastern Europe

Recreations: cinema, playing football and tennis, local history

Greg Hands, MP, House of Commons, London SW1A 0AA *Tel:* 020 7219 5448. *Constituency:* 4 Greyhound Road, London W6 8NX *Tel:* 020 7385 1002 *Fax:* 020 7385 1711 *E-mail:* office@hfconservatives.com *Website:* www.hfconservatives.com

Lab majority 6,644

HANSON, DAVID
Delyn

David George Hanson. Born 5 July 1957; Son of Brian Hanson, retired fork lift driver and Glenda Hanson, retired wages clerk; Educated Verdin Comprehensive School, Winsford, Cheshire; Hull University (BA drama 1978, Certificate of Education 1980); Married Margaret Mitchell 1986 (2 sons 2 daughters). Vice-President, Hull University Students' Union 1978-79; Trainee, Co-operative Union 1980-81; Manager, Plymouth Co-operative 1981-82; Various posts with The Spastics Society 1982-89; Contested Cheshire West 1984 European Parliament election; Director, Re-Solv (The Society for the Prevention of Solvent Abuse) 1989-92; Member: T&G, MSF; Councillor: Vale Royal Borough Council 1983-91, Northwich Town Council 1987-91; Vale Royal Borough Council: Chair, Economic Development Committee 1988-89, Labour Leader 1989-91, Leader of Council

House of Commons: Contested Eddisbury 1983 and Delyn 1987 general elections. Member for Delyn since 9 April 1992 general election; Assistant Government Whip 1998-99; PPS to Alastair Darling as Chief Secretary to the Treasury 1997-98; Parliamentary Under-Secretary of State, Wales Office 1999-2001; PPS to Tony Blair as Prime Minister 2001-05; Minister of State, Northern Ireland Office 2005-. *Political interests:* Foreign Affairs, Health, Heritage, Local and Regional Government, Solvent Abuse, Treasury, Small Businesses. South Africa, Cyprus

Member, Leadership Campaign Team 1994-97. Re-Solv (Preventing Solvent Abuse); Flint Life Boats; Flint Abbeyfield Society; *Recreations:* Football, cinema, family

David Hanson, MP, House of Commons, London SW1A 0AA *Tel:* 020 7219 5064 *Fax:* 020 7219 2671 *E-mail:* hansond@parliament.uk. *Constituency:* 64 Chester Street, Flint CH6 5DH *Tel:* 01352 763159 *Fax:* 01352 730140

Lab majority 13,483

HARMAN, HARRIET
Camberwell and Peckham

Harriet Harman. Born 30 July 1950; Daughter of late John Bishop Harman, and of Anna Harman; Educated St Paul's Girls' School; York University (BA politics 1978); Married Jack Dromey 1982 (2 sons 1 daughter). Legal officer, National Council for Civil Liberties 1978-82

House of Commons: Member for Peckham 1982-1997, and for Camberwell and Peckham since 1 May 1997 general election; Spokesperson on Health 1987-92; Shadow Minister, Social Services 1984, 1985-87; Shadow Chief Secretary to the Treasury 1992-94; Shadow Secretary of State for: Employment 1994-95, Health 1995-96; Social Security 1996-97; Secretary of State for Social Security and Minister for Women 1997-98; Solicitor General, Law Officers' Department 2001-05; Minister of State, Department for Constitutional Affairs 2005-. *Political interests:* Women, Social Services, Provision for under 5s, Law, Domestic Violence, Civil Liberties

Member, Labour Party National Executive Committee 1993-98. Chair, Childcare Commission 1999-; PC 1997, QC 2001

Rt Hon Harriet Harman, MP, House of Commons, London SW1A 0AA
Tel: 020 7219 4218 *Fax:* 020 7219 4877 *E-mail:* harmanh@parliament.uk.
Constituency: Website: www.harrietharman.labour.co.uk

Con majority 2,049

HARPER, MARK
Forest of Dean

Mark Harper. Born 26 February 1970; Educated Headlands School, Swindon, Wiltshire Swindon College; Brasenose College, Oxford (BA philosophy, politics and economics 1991, MA); Married Margaret Whelan 1999. Auditor, KPMG 1991-95; Intel Corporation (UK) Ltd: Senior finance analyst 1995-97, Finance manager 1997-2000, Operations manager 2000-02; Own accountancy practice 2002-; Governor Newent Community School 2000-

House of Commons: Contested Forest of Dean 2001 general election. Member for Forest of Dean since 5 May 2005 general election. *Political interests:* Law and order, mobile phone masts, broadband

South Swindon Conservative Association: Treasurer 1993-98, Deputy chair 1998. *Recreations:* Walking the dogs, travel, cinema

Mark Harper, MP, House of Commons, London SW1A 0AA *Tel:* 020 7219 5056.
Constituency: 7 Rodney Street, Cheltenham, Gloucestershire GL50 1HX
Tel: 01594 542800 *Fax:* 01242 514949
E-mail: fod@gloucestershireconservatives.com

HARRIS, EVAN
Oxford West and Abingdon

Evan Harris. Born 21 October 1965; Son of Prof Frank Harris, CBE, former Dean of Medicine, Leicester University, and Brenda Harris, formerly scientific officer; Educated Liverpool Blue Coat Secondary School; Harvard High School, North Hollywood, USA; Wadham College, Oxford (BA physiology 1988); Oxford University Medical School (BM, BCh 1991); Divorced. NHS Hospital Doctor 1991-94; Public Health Registrar (Hon) 1994-97; BMA National Council 1994-97; Junior Doctors Committee Executive 1995-97

House of Commons: Member for Oxford West and Abingdon since 1 May 1997 general election; Spokesperson for: NHS 1997-99, Higher Education, Science and Women's Issues 1999-2001, Health 2001-03. *Political interests:* Health, Equality, Human Rights, Asylum, Science, Medical Ethics, Secularism. Israel, South Africa, USA

Member, Oxford West and Abingdon SDP and Lib Dem Executive Committee 1986-97; Hon. President, Lib Dems for Gay and Lesbian Rights 2000-. Member: Central Oxford Research Ethics Committee 1995-98, Oxford Diocesan Board of Social Responsibility 1998-, Medical Ethics Committee 2001-; Honorary Associate, National Secular Society 2001-; Member Industry and Parliament Trust 2001-; *Recreations:* TV, squash, bridge, chess

Dr Evan Harris, MP, House of Commons, London SW1A 0AA *Tel:* 020 7219 5128 *Fax:* 020 7219 2346 *E-mail:* harrise@parliament.uk. *Constituency:* The Old Jam Factory, 27 Park End Street, Oxford, Oxfordshire OX1 1HU *Tel:* 01865 245584 *Fax:* 01865 245589

Lib Dem majority 7,683

HARRIS, TOM
Glasgow South

Tom (Thomas) Harris. Born 20 February 1964; Son of Tom Harris, lorry/taxi driver, and Rita Harris, née Ralston, office clerk; Educated Garnock Academy, Kilbirnie, Ayrshire; Napier College, Edinburgh (HND journalism 1986); Married Carolyn Moffat 1998 (2 sons, 1 from previous marriage). Trainee reporter *East Kilbride News* 1986-88; Reporter *Paisley Daily Express* 1988-90; Press officer: Scottish Labour Party 1990-92, Strathclyde Regional Council 1993-96; Senior media officer Glasgow City Council 1996; Public relations manager East Ayrshire Council 1996-98; Chief public relations and marketing officer Strathclyde Passenger Transport Executive 1998-2001; NUJ 1984-97; UNISON 1997-; AMICUS 2004-

House of Commons: Member for Glasgow Cathcart 2001-05, for Glasgow South since 5 May 2005 general election; PPS to John Spellar as Minister of State, Northern Ireland Office 2003-. *Political interests:* Welfare Reform, Economy, Foreign Affairs, Northern Ireland. USA, Israel, Iraq

Member, Labour Friends of Israel. *Clubs:* Cathcart Labour Social; *Recreations:* Astronomy, cinema, hillwalking

Tom Harris, MP, House of Commons, London SW1A 0AA *Tel:* 020 7219 8237 *Fax:* 020 7219 1769 *E-mail:* tomharrismp@parliament.uk.
Constituency: Constituency Office, The Couper Institute, 86 Clarkston Road, Cathcart *Tel:* 0141 6376447 *Fax:* 0141 6379625

Lab majority 10,832

HARVEY, NICK
North Devon

Nick (Nicholas) Barton Harvey. Born 3 August 1961; Son of Frederick Harvey, civil servant, and Christine Harvey, teacher; Educated Queen's College, Taunton; Middlesex Polytechnic (BA business studies 1983); Married Kate Fox (1 daughter). President, Middlesex Polytechnic Students' Union 1981-82; Communications and marketing executive: Profile PR Ltd 1984-86, Dewe Rogerson Ltd 1986-91; Communications Consultant 1989-92; Former Member NUJ

Lib Dem majority
4,972

House of Commons: Contested Enfield Southgate (Liberal/Alliance) 1987 general election. Member for North Devon since 9 April 1992 general election; Liberal Democrat Spokesperson for: Transport 1992-94, Trade and Industry 1994-97, Constitution (English Regions) 1997-99; Principal Spokesperson for: Health 1999-2001, Culture, Media and Sport 2001-03. *Political interests:* Economics, European Union

National Vice-Chair, Union of Liberal Students 1981-82; Chair of Candidates Committee 1993-98; Chair of Campaigns and Communications 1994-99. Vice-President, Federation of Economic Development Authorities (FEDA) 2000-; Honorary Doctorate, Middlesex University 2000; *Recreations:* Travel, football, walking, music

Nick Harvey, MP, House of Commons, London SW1A 0AA *Tel:* 020 7219 6232 *Fax:* 020 7219 2683 *E-mail:* harveyn@parliament.uk. *Constituency:* 23 Castle Street, Barnstaple, Devon EX31 1DR *Tel:* 01271 328631 *Fax:* 01271 345664

HASELHURST, ALAN
Saffron Walden

Sir Alan Gordon Barraclough Haselhurst. Born 23 June 1937; Son of late John Haselhurst; Educated King Edward VI School, Birmingham; Cheltenham College; Oriel College, Oxford; Married Angela Margaret Bailey 1977 (2 sons 1 daughter). Secretary, Treasurer, Librarian, Oxford Union Society 1959-60; Executive chemicals and plastics industry 1960-70; Public affairs consultant 1974-97

Con majority 13,008

House of Commons: Member for Middleton and Prestwich 1970-February 1974, and for Saffron Walden from 7 July 1977 by-election; PPS to Mark Carlisle as Secretary of State, Education and Science 1979-81; Chair, Ways and Means and Deputy Speaker 1997-. *Political interests:* Education, Aerospace, Aviation, Youth Affairs, European Union, Agriculture, Community Development. USA, South Africa, Australia

President, Oxford University Conservative Association 1958; National Chair, Young Conservative Movement 1966-68; Deputy Chair, Conservative Group for Europe 1982-85. Chair, Commonwealth Youth Exchange Council 1978-81; Chair of Trustees, Community Projects Foundation 1986-97; Fellow, Industry and Parliament Trust 1979; *Publications: Occasionally Cricket,* Queen Anne Press 1999; *Eventually Cricket,* Queen Anne Press 2001; *Incidentally Cricket,* Queen Anne Press 2003; Knighted 1995; PC 1999; *Clubs:* MCC; Essex County Cricket Club, Executive Committee Member 1996-; *Recreations:* Hi-fi, watching cricket, gardening

Rt Hon Sir Alan Haselhurst, MP, House of Commons, London SW1A 0AA *Tel:* 020 7219 5214 *Fax:* 020 7219 5600 *E-mail:* haselhursta@parliament.uk. *Constituency:* The Old Armoury, Saffron Walden, Essex CB10 1JN *Tel:* 01799 506349 *Fax:* 01799 506047

Lab majority 13,934

HAVARD, DAI
Merthyr Tydfil and Rhymney

David Stewart Havard. Born 7 February 1950; Son of Eileen, former shop worker and family carer and late Edward (Ted) Havard, former miner; Educated Secondary modern school, Treharris; Grammar Technical, Quakers Yard, Edwardsville; Comprehensive school, Afon Taf; St Peter's College, Birmingham (Certificate in Education); Warwick University (MA industrial relations); Married Julia Watts 1986 (separated). Member Armed Forces Parliamentary Scheme (Army) 2002. MSF full time officer: Studies tutor 1971-75, Researcher 1975-79, Education 1975-82, Official 1989-, Delegation leader: Wales Labour Party, Conferences; Wales secretary; AMICUS

House of Commons: Member for Merthyr Tydfil and Rhymney since 7 June 2001 general election. *Political interests:* Education, Lifelong Learning, Health, Cancer and Blood, Industrial Relations and Working Conditions

Constituency Labour Party; Wales Labour Party Joint Policy Committee. Member European Standing Committee C; *Publications:* Contributor to academic publications on trade union and economic development; *Clubs:* Aberfan Social and Democratic; *Recreations:* Hillwalking, horse riding, birdwatching, Commons and Lords Rugby team

Dai Havard, MP, House of Commons, London SW1A 0AA *Tel:* 020 7219 8255 *Fax:* 020 7219 1449 *E-mail:* havardd@parliament.uk. *Constituency:* Room 3, First Floor, Venture Wales Building, Merthyr Tydfil Industrial Park, Pentrebach, Merthyr Tydfil, Mid Glamorgan CF48 4DR *Tel:* 01443 693924 *Fax:* 01443 692905

Con majority 15,780

HAYES, JOHN
South Holland and The Deepings

John Henry Hayes. Born 23 June 1958; Son of late Henry John and Lily Hayes; Educated Colfe's Grammar School, London; Nottingham University (BA politics, PGCE history/English 1977-82); Married Susan Hopewell 1997 (1 son). IT company 1983-99, (director 1986-97, non-executive director 1997-99); Councillor, Nottinghamshire County Council 1985-98, Conservative Spokesperson for Education 1988-97, Former Chair, County Conservative Group's Campaigns Committee

House of Commons: Contested Derby North East 1987, 1992 general elections. Member for South Holland and The Deepings since 1 May 1997 general election; Opposition Spokesperson for Education and Employment 2000-01; Opposition Pairing Whip 2001-02; Shadow Minister for: Agriculture 2002-03, Local and Devolved Government 2003-. *Political interests:* Education, Elections and Campaigning, Political Ideas and Philosophy, Local Government, Agriculture, Commerce and Industry, Welfare of the Elderly and Disabled, Disability. England, Italy, USA, Spain

Former Chair Young Conservatives; Vice-chair, Conservatives Against Federal Europe; Vice-chair Conservative Party 1999-2000; Member 1992 Group. Headway, various local charities in South Lincolnshire; *Publications: Representing Rural Britain – Blair's Bogus Claim*, Conservative Policy Forum 2000; *Answer the Question: Prime Ministerial Accountability and the Rule of Parliament*, Politica 2000; *Tony B. Liar*, Conservative Party 2001; *Clubs:* Carlton, Spalding; *Recreations:* The arts, many sports, gardening, antiques, history, good food and wine

John Hayes, MP, House of Commons, London SW1A 0AA *Tel:* 020 7219 1389 *Fax:* 020 7219 2273 *E-mail:* unterhaltera@parliament.uk. *Constituency:* 20 Station Street, Spalding, Lincolnshire PE11 1EB *Tel:* 01775 713905 *Fax:* 01775 713905

HEAL, SYLVIA
Halesowen and Rowley Regis

Sylvia Lloyd Heal. Born 20 July 1942; Daughter of late John Lloyd Fox, steelworker, and Ruby Fox; Educated Elfed Secondary Modern School, Buckley, North Wales; Coleg Harlech, University College of Wales, Swansea (BSc Econ 1968); Married Keith Heal 1965 (1 son 1 daughter). Medical records clerk 1957-63; Social worker: Department of Employment 1968-70, National Health Service 1980-90; National officer, Carers National Association 1992-97; Member, GMB; JP

Lab majority 4,337

House of Commons: Member for Mid Staffordshire 1990 by-election-1992. Member for Halesowen and Rowley Regis since 1 May 1997 general election; Shadow Minister of Health 1991-92; Deputy Shadow Minister for Women 1991-92; PPS to Secretaries of State for Defence: Lord Robertson of Port Ellen 1997-99, Geoffrey Hoon 1999-2000; First Deputy Chairman, Ways and Means and Deputy Speaker 2000-. *Political interests:* Health Education, Equal Opportunities

NATO Parliamentary Assembly 1997-2000; *Clubs:* London-Welsh Association, Rowley and Blackheath Labour Club, Halesowen Royal British Legion; *Recreations:* Walking, gardening, listening to male voice choirs

Sylvia Heal, MP, House of Commons, London SW1A 0AA *Tel:* 020 7219 2317 *Fax:* 020 7219 0956. *Constituency:* 119 Graingers Lane, Cradley Heath, West Midlands B64 6AH *Tel:* 01384 411521 *Fax:* 01384 413113

HEALD, OLIVER
North East Hertfordshire

Oliver Heald. Born 15 December 1954; Son of late J A Heald, chartered engineer and Joyce Heald, neé Pemberton, teacher; Educated Reading School; Pembroke College, Cambridge (MA law 1976); Married Christine Whittle 1979 (1 son 2 daughters). Barrister, Middle Temple 1977-

Con majority 9,138

House of Commons: Contested Southwark and Bermondsey 1987 general election. Member for North Hertfordshire 1992-97, and for North East Hertfordshire since 1 May 1997 general election; Opposition Spokesperson for: Home Affairs 2000-01, Health 2001-02; Opposition Whip 1997-2000; PPS: to Sir Peter Lloyd as Minister of State, Home Office 1994, to William Waldegrave as Minister of Agriculture, Fisheries and Food 1994-95; Parliamentary Under-Secretary of State, Department of Social Security 1995-97; Sponsored Private Member's Bill: Insurance Companies (Reserves) Act 1995; Shadow: Minister for Work and Pensions 2002-03, Leader of the House 2003-; Member House of Commons' Commission 2003-; Shadow Secretary of State for Constitutional Affairs 2004-. *Political interests:* Industrial Relations, Environment, Law and Order, Pensions

Chair, North Hertfordshire Conservative Association 1984-86; Vice-President, Southwark and Bermondsey Conservative Association 1988-93, President 1993-98, Patron 1998-. *Publications:* Co-author *Auditing the New Deal: What Figures for the Future*, Politeia 2004; *Recreations:* Sport, family

Oliver Heald, MP, House of Commons, London SW1A 0AA *Tel:* 020 7219 4505 *E-mail:* healdo@parliament.uk. *Constituency: Tel:* 01763 247640 *Fax:* 01763 247640 *Website:* www.oliverhealdmp.com

HEALEY, JOHN
Wentworth

John Healey. Born 13 February 1960; Son of Aidan Healey, prison service, and Jean Healey, teacher; Educated Lady Lumley's Comprehensive School, Pickering; St Peter's School, York; Christ's College, Cambridge (BA 1982); Married Jackie Bate 1993 (1 son). Journalist/deputy editor, *The House Magazine* 1983-84; Disability campaigner for three national charities 1984-90; Tutor, Open University Business School 1989-92; Campaigns manager, Issue Communications 1990-92; Head of communications, MSF Union 1992-94; Campaigns and communications director, TUC 1994-97; Member, GMB

Lab majority 15,056

House of Commons: Contested Ryedale 1992 general election. Member for Wentworth since 1 May 1997 general election; PPS to Gordon Brown as Chancellor of the Exchequer 1999-2001; Parliamentary Under-Secretary of State for Adult Skills, Department for Education and Skills 2001-02; Economic Secretary, HM Treasury 2002-. *Political interests:* Employment, Trade Unions, Economic Regeneration, Industrial Relations, Disability, Local and Regional Government

Rotherham Hospice; Bluebell Appeal for South Yorkshire Children's Hospice; *Recreations:* Family

John Healey, MP, House of Commons, London SW1A 0AA *Tel:* 020 7219 5170; 020 7219 2448 *Fax:* 020 7219 2451 *E-mail:* healeyj@parliament.uk. *Constituency:* 79 High Street, Walker Place, Rotherham, South Yorkshire S65 1UF *Tel:* 01709 875943 *Fax:* 01709 874207

HEATH, DAVID
Somerton and Frome

David William St John Heath. Born 16 March 1954; Son of Eric and Pamela Heath; Educated Millfield School, Street; St John's College, Oxford (MA physiological sciences 1976); City University (ophthalmic optics 1979); Married Caroline Netherton 1987 (1 son 1 daughter). Qualified optician in practice 1979-85; Parliamentary consultant, Worldwide Fund for Nature 1990-91; Consultant to various NGOs/Charities; Member, Audit Commission 1995-97; Councillor, Somerset County Council 1985-97, Leader of Council 1985-89; Chairman, Avon and Somerset Police Authority 1993-96

Lib Dem majority 812

House of Commons: Contested Somerton and Frome 1992 general election. Member for Somerton and Frome since 1 May 1997 general election; Spokesperson for: Foreign Affairs 1997-99, Agriculture, Rural Affairs and Fisheries 1999-2001, Work and Pensions 2001-02, Science 2001-03, Lord Chancellor's Department/Department for Constitutional Affairs 2002-, Home Office 2002-, Science 2004. *Political interests:* Education, Local and Regional Government, Rural Affairs, Environment, Home Affairs. Europe, France, Balkans

Member: Liberal Party National Executive 1988-89, Liberal Democrats Federal Executive 1990-92, 1993-95. Vice-Chair: Association of County Councils 1994-97, Committee of Local Police Authorities 1993-97; Member: Audit Commission 1994-97, Academic Council of Wilton Park 2002-; Member: Council of Local Authorities and Regions of Europe 1993-97, Parliamentary Assembly of the Organisation for Security and Co-operation in Europe (OSCE) 1997-; CBE 1989; CBE; *Clubs:* National Liberal; CBE; *Recreations:* Cricket, rugby football, until recently pig breeding

David Heath, MP, House of Commons, London SW1A 0AA *Tel:* 020 7219 6245 *Fax:* 020 7219 5939 *E-mail:* davidheath@davidheath.co.uk. *Constituency:* 14 Catherine Hill, Frome, Somerset BA11 1BZ *Tel:* 01373 473618 *Fax:* 01373 455152

HEATHCOAT-AMORY, DAVID
Wells

Con majority 3,040

David Heathcoat-Amory. Born 21 March 1949; Son of late Brigadier Roderick Heathcoat-Amory, MC; Educated Eton College; Christ Church College, Oxford (MA philosophy, politics and economics); Married Linda Adams 1978 (2 sons, 1 deceased 1 daughter). Qualified as chartered accountant 1974; Assistant finance director, British Technology Group 1980-83

House of Commons: Contested Brent South 1979 general election. Member for Wells since 9 June 1983 general election; Assistant Government Whip 1988-89; Government Whip July-October 1989; Deputy Chief Whip 1992-93; PPS: to Norman Lamont as Financial Secretary to the Treasury 1985-87, to Douglas Hurd as Home Secretary 1987-88; Parliamentary Under-Secretary of State: at Department of Environment 1989-90, at Department of Energy 1990-92; Minister of State, Foreign and Commonwealth Office 1993-94; Paymaster General 1994-96; Member, Shadow Cabinet 1997-2001; Shadow Chief Secretary to the Treasury 1997-2000; Shadow Secretary of State for Trade and Industry 2000-01. *Political interests:* Industrial Policy, Agriculture, Forestry, Arms Control, Energy, European Union

Treasurer, West Country Group of Conservative MPs 1983-85. Parliamentary representative European Union Convention 2002-04; PC 1996; *Recreations:* Fishing, shooting, music

Rt Hon David Heathcoat-Amory, MP, House of Commons, London SW1A 0AA *Tel:* 020 7219 3543 *E-mail:* heathcoat-amoryd@parliament.uk. *Constituency:* Priory Lodge, 7 Priory Road, Wells, Somerset BA5 1SR *Tel:* 01749 673146 *Fax:* 01749 670783

HEMMING, JOHN
Birmingham Yardley

Lib Dem majority 2,672

John Alexander Melvin Hemming. Born 16 March 1960; Educated King Edward's School, Birmingham; Magdalen College, Oxford (BA atomic, nuclear and theoretical physics 1981, MA); Married Christine Margaret Richard 1981. Senior partner, John Hemming and Company 1983; Member, Musicians' Union 1997; Councillor Birmingham City Council 1990-: Group leader 1998-

House of Commons: Contested Birmingham Hall Green 1983, Birmingham Small Heath 1987, Birmingham Yardley 1992, 1997 and 2001 general elections. Member for Birmingham Yardley since 5 May 2005 general election

John Hemming, MP, House of Commons, London SW1A 0AA *Tel:* 020 7219 4345. *Constituency:* 15 Chantry Road, Moseley, Birmingham B13 8DL *Tel:* 0121 722 3417 *E-mail:* john.hemming@jhc.co.uk

HENDERSON, DOUG
Newcastle upon Tyne North

Douglas Henderson. Born 9 June 1949; Son of John Henderson, railwayman, and Joy Henderson; Educated Waid Academy, Fife; Central College, Glasgow (economics); Strathclyde University, Glasgow (economics 1973); Married Janet Graham 1974 (divorced) (1 son); married Geraldine Daly 2002 (1 daughter). Apprentice, Rolls-Royce, Glasgow 1966-68; British Rail clerk, London 1969-70; Research officer GMWU, Glasgow 1973; Scottish organiser GMB 1975-85, Organiser Newcastle 1985-87

Lab majority 7,023

House of Commons: Member for Newcastle upon Tyne North since 11 June 1987 general election; Opposition Spokesperson on: Trade and Industry 1988-92, The Environment (Local Government) 1992-94, Citizen's Charter 1994-95, Home Affairs 1995-97; Minister of State (Europe), Foreign and Commonwealth Office 1997-98; Minister of State for the Armed Forces, Ministry of Defence 1998-99. *Political interests:* Economic Policy, Industrial Policy, Employment, IT Industry. former Soviet Union, USA, Middle East

Clubs: Lemington Labour, Newburn Memorial, Dinnington; Elswick Harriers, Cambuslang Harriers; *Recreations:* Athletics, mountaineering, cross-country skiing

Doug Henderson, MP, House of Commons, London SW1A 0AA
Tel: 020 7219 5017 *E-mail:* douglas@newcastle-north-clp.new.labour.org.uk.
Constituency: Tel: 0191-286 2024

Lab/Co-op majority
9,407

HENDRICK, MARK
Preston

Mark Phillip Hendrick. Born 2 November 1958; Son of Brian Francis Hendrick, timber worker, and Jennifer, née Chapman, clerk/typist; Educated Salford Grammar School; Liverpool Polytechnic (BSc electrical and electronic engineering 1982); Manchester University (MSc computer science 1985, CertEd 1992); Volkshochschule, Hanau, Germany ('Zertifikat Deutsch als Fremdsprache'); Single. Student engineer Ministry of Defence 1979; Werk student AEG Telefunken 1981; Science and Engineering Research Council 1982-84, 1985-88; Lecturer in electronics and software design, Stockport college 1990-94; MEP Lancashire Central 1994-99; Member Economic and Monetary Affairs and Industrial Policy committee 1994-99; Substitute: Foreign Affairs, Security and Defence Policy committee 1994-97, Member European Parliamentary Committee for Relations with Japan 1994-99; Environment, Public Health and Consumer Protection committee 1997-99; Member GMB; Councillor Salford City Council 1987-95; Representative Salford City Council as an alternate director Manchester Airport plc 1987-94; Vice-chair: planning committee 1987-94, management services committee 1990-94, policy committee 1992-94, education committee 1992-94; Hon vice-president Central and West Lancashire chamber of commerce and industry 1994-96, 2001-

House of Commons: Member for Preston since 23 November 2000 by-election; PPS to Margaret Beckett as Secretary of State for Environment, Food and Rural Affairs 2003-. *Political interests:* Foreign Affairs, Defence, European Affairs, Economic and Industrial Affairs, International Development. USA, Japan, Germany, Poland, Hungary

Branch secretary, Salford Co-operative Party 1984-94; Chair Eccles constituency Labour party 1990-94; Member, Preston and District Co-operative Party 1994-. RSPCA, CAFOD; *Publications: The euro and Co-operative Enterprise: Co-operating with the euro*, Co-operative Press Ltd 1998; *Changing States: A Labour Agenda for Europe*, Mandarin Paperbacks 1996; *Clubs:* Deepdale Labour; Penwortham Sports and Social; *Recreations:* football, boxing, chess

Mark Hendrick, MP, House of Commons, London SW1A 0AA *Tel:* 020 7219 4791 *Fax:* 020 7219 5220 *E-mail:* hendrickm@parliament.uk. *Constituency:* 6 Sedgwick Street, Preston, Lancashire PR1 1TP *Tel:* 01772 883575 *Fax:* 01772 887188

Con majority 15,921

HENDRY, CHARLES
Wealden

Charles Hendry. Born 6 May 1959; Son of late Charles W R Hendry and Margaret Anne Hendry; Educated Rugby School; Edinburgh University (BCom business studies 1981); Married Sallie Moores, née Smith 1995 (2 sons 1 stepson 1 stepdaughter). Account director Ogilvy and Mather PR 1982-88; Special adviser to: John Moore as Secretary of State for Social Services 1988, Antony Newton at Departments of Social Security and Trade and Industry 1988-90; at Burson-Marsteller: Senior counsellor public affairs 1990-92, Associate director public relations; Agenda Group: Chief executive 1999-01, Non-executive chair 2001- 04; Director, Incredi Bull Ideas 2003-

House of Commons: Contested Clackmannan 1983, Mansfield 1987 general elections. Member for High Peak 1992-1997. Contested High Peak 1997 general election. Member for Wealden since 7 June 2001 general election; Opposition Whip 2001-02; PPS: to William Hague and Lord Mackay of Ardbrecknish as Ministers of State, Department of Social Security 1994-95, to Gillian Shephard as Secretary of State for Education and Employment 1995; Vice-chair Conservative Party 1995-97; Shadow Minister for: Young People 2002-, Higher Education 2005-. *Political interests:* Trade and Industry, Youth Policy, Training, Urban Regeneration, Social Affairs, Housing, Homelessness, Rural Affairs, Agriculture. USA, Europe, Southern Africa

President Edinburgh University Conservative Association 1979-80; Vice-chair: Scottish Federation of Conservative Students 1980-81, Battersea Conservative Association 1981-83; Chief of staff Leader of Opposition 1997; Head of Business liaison, Conservative Party 1997-99; Deputy Chairman, Conservative Party 2003-. Member European Standing Committee B 1992-95; Joint honorary president British Youth Council 1992-97; Trustee: Drive for Youth 1989-98, UK Youth Parliament 2002-; *Recreations:* Tennis, skiing, family, opera, rugby, travel

Charles Hendry, MP, House of Commons, London SW1A 0AA *Tel:* 020 7219 8333 *E-mail:* hendryc@parliament.uk. *Constituency:* Wealden Conservative Association, The Granary, Bales Green Farm, Arlington, East Sussex BN27 6SH *Tel:* 01323 489289 *Website:* www.wealden.uk.com

Lab majority 13,904

HEPBURN, STEPHEN
Jarrow

Stephen Hepburn. Born 6 December 1959; Son of Peter and Margaret Hepburn; Educated Springfield Comprehensive, Jarrow; Newcastle University (BA politics). Labourer, South Tyneside Metropolitan Borough Council; Research assistant to Don Dixon MP; Member, UCATT; Councillor, South Tyneside Council 1985-, Deputy Leader 1990-97; Chair, Tyne & Wear Pensions 1989-97

House of Commons: Member for Jarrow since 1 May 1997 general election. *Political interests:* Small Businesses

St Clare's Hospice; *Clubs:* Neon CIU, Jarrow, Iona Catholic Club, Hebburn; President, Jarrow FC, Patron, Jarrow Roofing FC; *Recreations:* Sport

Stephen Hepburn, MP, House of Commons, London SW1A 0AA *Tel:* 020 7219 4134 *E-mail:* hepburns@parliament.uk. *Constituency:* 136/137 Tedco Business Centre, Jarrow, Tyne and Wear NE32 3DT *Tel:* 0191-420 0648 *Fax:* 0191-489 7531

Lab majority 6,939

HEPPELL, JOHN
Nottingham East

John Heppell. Born 3 November 1948; Son of late Robert Heppell, miner, and late Helen Heppell; Educated Rutherford Grammar School; South East Northumberland Technical College; Ashington Technical College; Married Eileen Golding 1974 (2 sons 1 daughter). Fitter: NCB 1964-70 and for number of firms in Nottingham area 1970-75; British Rail: Diesel fitter 1975-78, Workshop supervisor 1978-89; GMB; Councillor, Nottinghamshire County Council 1981-93; Assistant Whip 1982; Vice-Chair, Environment Committee 1983; Chair: East Midlands Airport 1985, Resources Committee 1986, Deputy Leader, Nottinghamshire County Council 1989-92; Former Chair, Equal Opportunities Committee; Former Chair, Greater Nottingham LRT Board; Former Vice-Chair, Policy Committee

House of Commons: Member for Nottingham East since 9 April 1992 general election; Government Whip 2001-; PPS to: Lord Richard as Lord Privy Seal and Leader of the House of Lords 1997-98, John Prescott as Deputy Prime Minister and Secretary of State for the Environment, Transport and the Regions 1998-2001. *Political interests:* Equal Opportunities, Transport, Local and Regional Government. India, Pakistan, Cyprus

Recreations: Walking, reading, swimming, birdwatching

John Heppell, MP, House of Commons, London SW1A 0AA *Tel:* 020 7219 4095 *Fax:* 020 7219 2969. *Constituency:* 9 Trinity Square, Nottingham, Nottinghamshire NG1 4AF *Tel:* 0115-947 4132 *Fax:* 0115-947 2029 *E-mail:* johnheppellmp@yahoo.co.uk

Con majority 11,309

HERBERT, NICK
Arundel and South Downs

Nick Herbert. Born 1963; Educated Haileybury, Hertford; Magdalene College, Cambridge (law and land economy). Political affairs British Field Sports Society 1990-96; Chief executive Business for Sterling 1998-2000; Director, Reform 2002-05 **House of Commons:** Contested Berwick-upon-Tweed 1997 general election. Member for Arundel and South Downs since 5 May 2005 general election. *Political interests:* Rural affairs, Europe, planning, law and order, public services, the economy *Recreations:* Watching cricket and rugby, racing, country sports, cinema, theatre, opera

Nick Herbert, MP, House of Commons, London SW1A 0AA *Tel:* 020 7219 3928. *Constituency: Tel:* 01903 816880 *Fax:* 01903 810348 *E-mail:* nick@nickherbert.com

HERMON, SYLVIA
North Down

Sylvia Hermon. Born 11 August 1955; Robert and Mary Paisley; Educated Dungannon High School for Girls; Aberstwyth University, Wales (law 1977); Part II Solicitors' Qualifying Examinations 1978; Married Sir John Hermon OBE QPM 1988 (2 sons). Lecturer European, international and constitutional law Queen's University, Belfast 1978-88

UUP majority 4,944

House of Commons: Member for North Down since 7 June 2001 general election; UUP Spokesperson for: Home Affairs 2001-, Trade and Industry 2001-02, Youth and Women's Issues 2001-, Culture, Media and Sport 2002-. *Political interests:* Policing, Human Rights, European Affairs, Health, Education

Author and committee member addressing Patten Report Criminal Justice Review 2000; Ulster Unionist Executive 1999; Constituency chair North Down Unionist Constituency Association 2001-03. *Publications: A Guide to EEC Law in Northern Ireland*, SLS Legal Publications (NI) 1986; *Recreations:* Fitness training, swimming, ornithology

Sylvia Hermon, MP, House of Commons, London SW1A 0AA *Tel:* 020 7219 8491 *Fax:* 020 7219 1969 *E-mail:* hermons@parliament.uk. *Constituency:* 17a Hamilton Road, Bangor BT20 4LF *Tel:* 028 9127 5858 *Fax:* 028 9127 5747

HESFORD, STEPHEN
Wirral West

Stephen Hesford. Born 27 May 1957; Son of Bernard and Nellie Hesford; Educated Urmston Grammar School; Bradford University (BSc social science 1978); Central London Polytechnic (LLM 1980); Married Elizabeth Anne Henshall 1984 (2 sons). Barrister 1981-97; Assistant to Joan Lestor, MP 1992-93; Branch Equal Opportunities Officer, GMB; Vice-Chair, North Manchester Community Health Council

Lab majority 1,097

House of Commons: Contested Suffolk South 1992 general election. Member for Wirral West since 1 May 1997 general election. *Political interests:* Economic Policy, Health, Social Services, Pensions, Education, Small Businesses. France

Member, Fabian Society; NEC Member, Socialist Health Association. ARCH Iniatives, Mencap, MIND, Word Development Movement, UKPHA; Member, European Standing Committee C 1999-; *Clubs:* Life Member, Lancashire Cricket Club; *Recreations:* Sport, music, reading

Stephen Hesford, MP, House of Commons, London SW1A 0AA *Tel:* 020 7219 6227 *Fax:* 020 7219 4953 *E-mail:* hesfords@parliament.uk. *Constituency:* 140 Ford Road, Upton, Wirral, Merseyside CH49 0TQ *Tel:* 0151-522 0531 *Fax:* 0151-522 0558 *Website:* www.poptel.org.uk/cfl/usr/w-wirral/

HEWITT, PATRICIA
Leicester West

Patricia Hope Hewitt. Born 2 December 1948; Daughter of Sir Lenox Hewitt, OBE and Lady Hope Hewitt; Educated Canberra Girls' Grammar School; Newnham College, Cambridge (BA English literature 1970); Married William Jack Birtles 1981 (1 son 1 daughter). Public relations officer, Age Concern 1971-73; National Council for Civil Liberties: Women's rights officer 1973-74, General Secretary 1974-83; To Neil Kinnock as Leader of the Opposition: Press secretary 1983-87, Policy co-ordinator 1987-89; Deputy director, Institute for Public Policy Research 1989-94; Director of research, Andersen Consulting (now Accenture) 1994-97; Member: MSF, TGWU; Chair, Council for Science and Technology

Lab majority 9,070

House of Commons: Contested Leicester East 1983 general election. Member for Leicester West since 1 May 1997 general election; Economic Secretary, HM Treasury 1998-99; Minister of State, Department of Trade and Industry (Minister for Small Business and E-Commerce) 1999-2001; Secretary of State for Trade and Industry, Minister for Women and Equality 2001-05; Secretary of State for Health 2005-. *Political interests:* Social Security, Employment, Family Policy, Information Technology. Australia, South Africa, India

Member: Labour Women's Advisory Committee 1976-82, Labour Campaign for Social Justice, Fabian Society. Various constituency charities and causes; Member, Secretary of State's Advisory Committee on the Employment of Women 1976-83; Vice-Chair: Commission on Social Justice 1992-94, British Council Board 1997-98; Advisory Board, International Human Rights League; Trustee, Institute for Public Policy Research 1995-98; *Publications:* Numerous, including books, pamphlets and articles for academic, specialist and popular journals. Also regular contributor on radio and television programmes; Visiting fellow, Nuffield College, Oxford; PC 2001; Honorary Fellow, London Business School; *Clubs:* New Parks Social Club; *Recreations:* Gardening, music, theatre

Rt Hon Patricia Hewitt, MP, House of Commons, London SW1A 0AA
Tel: 020 7219 4180 *E-mail:* hewittph@parliament.uk. *Constituency:* Janner House, Woodgate, Leicester, Leicestershire LE3 5GH *Tel:* 0116-251 6160
Fax: 0116-251 0482

HEYES, DAVID
Ashton under Lyne

David Alan Heyes. Born 2 April 1946; Son of Harold Heyes, police officer and Lilian Heyes, neé Crowe; Educated Blackley Technical High School, Manchester; Open University (BA social sciences 1987); Married Judith Egerton-Gallagher 1968 (1 son 1 daughter). Local Government Officer Manchester City Council 1962-74; Greater Manchester Council 1974-86, Oldham Metropolitan Borough Council 1987-90; Self-employed Computer graphics 1990-95; Development worker, Voluntary Action Manchester 1993-95; Deputy district manager Manchester Citizens Advice Bureau service 1995-2001; Member UNISON (formerly NALGO) 1962-; Oldham Metropolitan Borough Council: Councillor 1992-, Labour Group Secretary 1993-2000, Chair Personnel Committee 1994-2000, Vice-chair Policy Committee 1999-2000

Lab majority 13,952

House of Commons: Member for Ashton-Under-Lyne since 7 June 2001 general election. *Political interests:* Social Exclusion, Health, Education, Work and Pensions, Local and Regional Government

David Heyes, MP, House of Commons, London SW1A 0AA *Tel:* 020 7219 8129
Fax: 020 7219 1738 *E-mail:* heyesd@parliament.uk. *Constituency:* St. Michael's Court, St. Michael's Square, Stamford Street, Ashton-Under-Lyne OL6 6XN
Tel: 0161-331 9307 *Fax:* 0161-330 9420

Supportively SmokeFree

Liverpool's SmokeFree Bill* seeks powers to impose 100% restrictions on smoking in all enclosed workplaces in the City because...

Exemptions anticipated in the Government's forthcoming Health Bill...

- Won't protect workers in non-food pubs and clubs from the harmful health effects of second-hand smoke
- Won't provide the level playing field businesses want
- Could increase health inequalities in some of the most deprived wards in Liverpool - and England
- Would be difficult to enforce

Our campaign has cross party support in Liverpool City Council, overwhelming backing from the people of the city, employers and trade unions.

Please support Liverpool's Private Bill and urge the Government to introduce comprehensive smokefree legislation for all workplaces.*

*Liverpool City Council (Prohibition of Smoking in Places of Work) Bill

SmokeFree Liverpool

www.smokefreeliverpool.com

Liverpool 08

EUROPEAN CAPITAL OF CULTURE

HILL, KEITH
Streatham

Keith (Trevor) Hill. Born 28 July 1943; Son of Ernest Hill, printer, and late Ida Hill, textile machine operative; Educated City of Leicester Boys' Grammar School; Corpus Christi College, Oxford (MA philosophy, politics and economics 1965); University College of Wales, Aberystwyth (DipEd (Wales) 1966); Married Lesley Ann Sheppard 1972. Research assistant in politics, Leicester University 1966-68; Belgian government scholar, Brussels 1968-69; Lecturer in politics, Strathclyde University 1969-73; Research officer, Labour Party International Department 1974-76; Political Liaison Officer National Union of Rail, Maritime and Transport Workers (formerly NUR) 1976-92; Member RMT

Lab majority 7,466

House of Commons: Contested Blaby 1979 general election. Member for Streatham since 9 April 1992 general election; Assistant Government Whip 1998-99; Deputy Chief Whip (Treasurer of HM Household) 2001-03; PPS to Hilary Armstrong, as Minister of State (Minister for Local Government and Housing) 1997-98, Parliamentary Under-Secretary of State, Department of Environment, Transport and the Regions 1999-2001; Minister of State for Housing and Planning, Office of the Deputy Prime Minister 2003-05; PPS to Tony Blair as Prime Minister 2005-. *Political interests:* Transport, European Union, Environment. Europe, Africa

London Campaigner, Leadership Campaigns Team 1995; Hon. Secretary, London Group of Labour MPs 1997-98; Chair, Labour Movement for Europe 1997-98. Spires Centre, Streatham; Ace of Clubs, Clapham; *Publications: Belgium* in *European Political Parties* 1969; *Belgium: Political Change in A Segmented Society* in *Electoral Behaviour* 1974; PC 2003; *Recreations:* Walking, books, films, music

Rt Hon Keith Hill, MP, House of Commons, London SW1A 0AA
Tel: 020 7219 6980 *Fax:* 020 7219 2565 *E-mail:* hillk@parliament.uk.

HILLIER, MEG
Hackney South and Shoreditch

Meg Hillier. Born 14 February 1969; Educated St Hilda's College, Oxford (BA philosophy, politics and economics); City University, London (diploma in journalism); Married 1997. Reporter *South Yorkshire Times*; Petty officer P&O European Ferries 1992; PR officer Newlon Housing Group 1993;*Housing Today*: Reporter 1994, Features editor 1995; Freelance journalist 1998-2000; TGWU; London Borough of Islington: Councillor 1994-2002, Chair Neighbourhood Services 1995-97, Mayor 1998-99; GLA member for North East London 2000-04

Lab/Co-op majority 10,204

House of Commons: Member for Hackney South and Shoreditch since 5 May 2005 general election

Meg Hillier, MP, House of Commons, London SW1A 0AA *Tel:* 020 7219 5325.
Constituency: 88 Buck Road, London N1 4JE *Tel:* 07985 671385

HOBAN, MARK
Fareham

Mark Hoban. Born 31 March 1964; Son of Tom Hoban, general manager and Maureen Hoban, neé Orchard, housewife; Educated St Leonards RC Comprehensive School, Durham; London School of Economics (BSc Econ 1985); Married Fiona Jane Barrett 1994. Pricewaterhouse Coopers 1985-: Chartered accountant, Manager 1990-92, Senior manager 1992-2001

Con majority 11,702

House of Commons: Contested South Shields 1997 general election. Member for Fareham since 7 June 2001 general election; Opposition Whip 2002-03; Shadow Minister for: Public Services, Health and Education 2003-04, Education 2004-. *Political interests:* Economy, Trade and Industry, Education, Health

General election campaign manager 1987, 1992; Southampton Itchen Conservative Association: Treasurer 1989-91, Political vice-chair 1991-93; Finance officer Itchen, Test and Avon European Constituency Council 1993-95. Member European Standing Committee A 2001-; Liveryman Fruiterers' Company 2003-; Freeman, City of London 2003; *Recreations:* Cooking, reading, travel, entertaining

Mark Hoban, MP, House of Commons, London SW1A 0AA *Tel:* 020 7219 8228 *E-mail:* hobanm@parliament.co.uk. *Constituency:* 14 East Street, Fareham, Hampshire PO16 0BN *Tel:* 01329 233573 *Fax:* 01329 234197

HODGE, MARGARET
Barking

Margaret Eve Hodge. Born 8 September 1944; Daughter of Hans and Lisbeth Oppenheimer; Educated Bromley High School; Oxford High School; London School of Economics (BSc economics 1966); Married Andrew Watson 1968 (divorced 1978) (1 son 1 daughter); married Henry Hodge OBE 1978 (2 daughters). Teaching and market research 1966-73; Senior consultant, Price Waterhouse 1992-94; Member, TGWU; Councillor, London Borough of Islington 1973-94, Chair, Housing Committee 1975-79, Deputy Leader of Council 1981-82, Leader 1982-92

Lab majority 8,883

House of Commons: Member for Barking since 9 June 1994 by-election; Parliamentary Under-Secretary of State (Employment and Equal Opportunities), Department for Education and Employment 1998-2001; Department for Education and Skills 2001-05: Minister of State for: Lifelong Learning and Higher Education 2001-03, Lifelong Learning, Further and Higher Education 2003, Children, Young People and Families 2003-05; Minister of State (Work), Department for Work and Pensions 2005-. *Political interests:* Education, Local and Regional Government, Housing, Inner Cities, Democratic Reform, London Government

Member, Labour Party Local Government Committee 1983-92; Chair: London Group of Labour MPs 1995-98, Fabians 1997-98. Chair, Association of London Authorities 1984-92; Vice-Chair, AMA 1991-92; *Publications: Quality, Equality and Democracy*; *Beyond the Town Hall*; Fabian pamphlet on London Government, *Not Just the Flower Show*; Contributed chapters to a number of books as well as articles in numerous journals and newspapers; MBE 1978; PC 2003; Hon. Fellow, University of North London; Hon. DCL, City 1993; MBE; *Recreations:* Family, opera, piano, travel, cooking

Rt Hon Margaret Hodge, MP, House of Commons, London SW1A 0AA *Tel:* 020 7219 6666 *Fax:* 020 7219 3640 *E-mail:* haywoodmw@parliament.uk. *Constituency: Tel:* 020 8594 1333 *Fax:* 020 8594 1131

Lab majority 13,407

HODGSON, SHARON
Gateshead East and Washington West

Sharon Hodgson. Born 1 April 1966; Educated Heathfield Senior High School, Gateshead; Newcastle College (HEFC English 1997); TUC, National Education Centre (Open college network diploma in labour party organising 2000); Married Alan Hodgson 1990. Payroll/account clerk, Tyneside Safety Glass, Team Valley Trading Estate, Gateshead 1982-88; Northern Rock Building Society, Gosforth 1988-92; Payroll administrator, Burgess Microswitch, Team Valley Trading Estate, Gateshead 1992-94; Charity administrator, The Total Learning Challenge (Educational Charity), Newcastle 1998-99; Member: GMB 1999-; TGWU 2002-; Labour link co-ordinator, London, Unison 2002-

House of Commons: Member for Gateshead East and Washington West since 5 May 2005 general election. *Political interests:* Anti-social behaviour, regional regeneration (especially North East), education, employment and jobs, social inclusion, child care, transport, child poverty, trade justice/fair trade, welfare, pensions

Women's officer, Tyne Bridge CLP 1998-2000; Regional organiser, Labour North 1999-2000; Mitcham and Morden CLP: Constituency organiser 2000-02; Constituency secretary 2002-05. *Recreations:* Reading, cinema, cooking, shopping, travel, family

Sharon Hodgson, MP, House of Commons, London SW1A 0AA
Tel: 020 7219 5160. *Constituency: Tel:* 0191 4872844 *Fax:* 0191 4872844
E-mail: info@sharonhodgson.org *Website:* www.gatesheadwashingtonlp.org

Lab majority 9,977

HOEY, KATE
Vauxhall

Kate (Catharine) Letitia Hoey. Born 21 June 1946; Daughter of Thomas and Letitia Hoey; Educated Belfast Royal Academy; Ulster College of Physical Education (teaching diploma 1964); City of London College, London (BSc economics 1968); Single. Senior lecturer, Kingsway College 1976-85; Educational adviser to Arsenal Football Club 1985-89; Member, GMB; Councillor: Hackney Borough Council 1978-82, Southwark Borough Council 1988-89

House of Commons: Contested Dulwich 1983 and 1987 general elections. Member for Vauxhall since 15 June 1989 by-election; Member, Opposition team on Citizen's Charter and Women 1992-93; PPS to Frank Field as Minister of State, Department of Social Security 1997-98; Parliamentary Under-Secretary of State: Home Office (Metropolitan Police, European Union, Judicial Co-operation) 1998-99, Department for Culture, Media and Sport (Minister for Sport) 1999-2001. *Political interests:* Countryside, Sport, Foreign Affairs, Housing. Angola, Bosnia, Oman, Zimbabwe

Trustee: Royal National Lifeboat Institute Council, Outward Bound Trust; *Publications:* Occasional articles on sport in the press; *The Spectator*/Highland Park Debater of the Year Award 1998; University of Ulster Distinguished Graduate 2000; *Clubs:* Hon Vice-President Surrey County Cricket Club

Kate Hoey, MP, House of Commons, London SW1A 0AA *Tel:* 020 7219 5989
Fax: 020 7219 5985.

HOGG, DOUGLAS
Sleaford and North Hykeham

Douglas Martin Hogg. Born 5 February 1945; Son of late Baron Hailsham of St Marylebone, former Lord Chancellor who disclaimed his hereditary honours for life 1963 and was subsequently created a life peer; succeeded his father 2001 as 3rd Viscount Hailsham and 3rd Baron Hailsham; Educated Eton College; Christ Church, Oxford (MA history 1968) (President, Oxford Union 1966); Married Hon. Sarah Boyd-Carpenter (cr. Baroness Hogg, 1995) 1968 (qv) (1 son 1 daughter). Called to the Bar, Lincoln's Inn 1968 (Kennedy Law Scholar); QC 1990

Con majority 12,705

House of Commons: Member for Grantham 1979-97, and for Sleaford and North Hykeham since 1 May 1997 general election; Government Whip 1983-84; PPS to Leon Brittan as Chief Secretary to the Treasury 1982-83; Parliamentary Under-Secretary, Home Office 1986-89; Minister of State at: Department of Trade and Industry (Minister for Industry and Enterprise) 1989-90, Foreign and Commonwealth Office 1990-95; Minister of Agriculture, Fisheries and Food 1995-97 QC 1990; PC 1992

Rt Hon Douglas Hogg, MP, House of Commons, London SW1A 0AA
Tel: 020 7219 3444 *Fax:* 020 7219 4123
E-mail: hoggd@parliament.uk; edwardsa@parliament.uk. *Constituency:* Sleaford and North Hykeham Conservative Association, 6 Market Place, Sleaford, Lincolnshire NG34 7SD *Tel:* 01529 419000 *Fax:* 01529 419019

HOLLOBONE, PHILIP
Kettering

Philip Thomas Hollobone. Born 7 November 1964; Educated Dulwich College, London; Lady Margaret Hall, Oxford (BA modern history and economics 1987, MA); Married Donna Anne Cooksey 2001. Soldier and paratrooper, Territorial Army 1987-95. Investment bank analyst, various 1987-2000; Councillor: London Borough of Bromley 1990-94, Kettering District Council 2003-

Con majority 3,301

House of Commons: Contested Lewisham East 1997 and Kettering 2001 general elections. Member for Kettering since 5 May 2005 general election

Chairman Bromley and Chiselhurst Conservative Association 1999; Deputy chairman Kettering Conservative Association 2002-

Philip Hollobone, MP, House of Commons, London SW1A 0AA
Tel: 020 7219 8373. *Constituency:* 25 Montagu Street, Kettering NN16 8XG
Tel: 01536 512007 *Fax:* 01536 417423 *E-mail:* info@kettering-conservatives.org
Website: www.kettering-conservatives.org

HOLLOWAY, ADAM
Gravesham

Adam James Harold Holloway. Born 1965; Educated Cranleigh School, Surrey; Cambridge University (MA political science) Imperial College, London (MBA business). Commissioned, Grenadier Guards 1987-92. Presenter, World in Action, Granada TV 1992-93 Reporter, ITN 1993-97

Con majority 654

House of Commons: Member for Gravesham since 5 May 2005 general election

Trustee, Christian Aid 1997-2001 Trustee, Map Action 2002; *Clubs:* Gravesend Conservative Club Cavalry and Guards Club

Adam Holloway, MP, House of Commons, London SW1A 0AA
Tel: 020 7219 8402. *Constituency:* 190 Parrock Street, Gravesend, Kent
Tel: 01474 567715 *E-mail:* adamholloway@ntlworld

HOLMES, PAUL
Chesterfield

Paul Holmes. Born 16 January 1957; Son of Frank Holmes, plumber, and Dorothy, née Uttley, cutlery worker; Educated Firth Park School, Sheffield; York University (BA history 1978); Sheffield University (PGCE 1979); Married Raelene Palmer 1978 (2 daughters 1 son). History teacher Chesterfield 1979-84; Head of department Buxton 1984-90; Head of sixth form Buxton 1988-2000; Union Rep ATL 1989-99; NASUWT 1999-2001; Councillor Chesterfield Borough Council 1987-95, 1999-2003; Vice-president Local Government Association 2001-

Lib Dem majority 3,045

House of Commons: Member for Chesterfield since 7 June 2001 general election; Liberal Democrat Spokesperson for: Disability Issues 2001-02, Disability Issues and Work and Pensions 2002-. *Political interests:* Education, Health, Pensions, Law and Order, Human Rights, Constitutional Reform, International Affairs. Laos, Thailand, France, New Zealand, Ireland

Campaigner Local party; Election agent and organiser Tony Rogers 1992, 1997; Agent: Euro election 1994, Numerous Council elections. Mayor of Chesterfield Appeal; Ashgate Craft Special School, Pool Appeal; Ashgate Hospice; St Bernards Animal Sanctuary; Working with UNICEF on Campaign Against Child Exploitation; *Recreations:* Music, history, reading, archaeology

Paul Holmes, MP, House of Commons, London SW1A 0AA *Tel:* 020 7219 8158 *Fax:* 020 7219 1754 *E-mail:* holmesr@parliament.uk. *Constituency:* 69 West Bars, Chesterfield, Derbyshire S40 1BA *Tel:* 01246 234879 *Fax:* 01246 206333 *Website:* www.members.aol.com/liberaldems

HOOD, JIMMY
Lanark and Hamilton East

James Hood. Born 16 May 1948; Son of late William, miner, and Bridget Hood; Educated Lesmahagow Higher Grade School, Coatbridge College; Nottingham University; Married Marion Stewart McCleary 1967 (1 son 1 daughter). Mining engineer 1964-87; Member, NUM 1964-: Official 1973-87, Leader of Nottinghamshire striking miners in 1984-85 national miners' strike; Member, AEEU 1996-; Councillor, Newark and Sherwood District Council 1979-87

Lab majority 11,947

House of Commons: Member for Clydesdale 1987-2005, for Lanark and Hamilton East since 5 May 2005 general election. *Political interests:* NHS, Home Affairs, Agriculture, Environment, Energy, Housing, Education, Alcohol Abuse and Under-age Drinking, European Union, Defence

Member Scottish Parliamentary Group of Labour MPs; Member, Co-operative Party. Fellow, Industry and Parliament Trust; Armed Forces Parliamentary Scheme; *Recreations:* Gardening, reading, writing

Jimmy Hood, MP, House of Commons, London SW1A 0AA *Tel:* 020 7219 4585 *Fax:* 020 7219 5872 *E-mail:* hoodj@parliament.uk. *Constituency:* c/o Council Offices, South Vennel, Lanark ML11 7JT *Tel:* 01555 673177 *Fax:* 01555 673188

HOON, GEOFFREY
Ashfield

Geoff (Geoffrey) William Hoon. Born 6 December 1953; Son of Ernest and June Hoon; Educated Nottingham High School; Jesus College, Cambridge (BA law 1976, MA); Married Elaine Ann Dumelow 1981 (1 son 2 daughters). Lecturer in law, Leeds University 1976-82; Visiting professor of law, University of Louisville, USA 1980-81; Practising barrister 1982-84; MEP for Derbyshire 1984-94; Member TGWU

Lab majority 10,213

House of Commons: Member for Ashfield since 9 April 1992 general election; Opposition Spokesperson for Trade and Industry 1995-97; Opposition Whip 1994-95; Lord Chancellor's Department: Parliamentary Secretary 1997-98, Minister of State 1998-99; Minister of State, Foreign and Commonwealth Office 1999; Secretary of State for Defence 1999-2005; Lord Privy Seal and Leader of the House of Commons 2005-. *Political interests:* Economic Policy, European Union, Constitution, Defence. Europe, USA, Far East

NSPCC; Chair, European Parliament Delegation for relations with: China 1986-89, United States 1989-93; PC 1999; *Recreations:* Sport, football and running, cinema, music

Rt Hon Geoffrey Hoon, MP, House of Commons, London SW1A 0AA
Tel: 020 7219 2701 *Fax:* 020 7219 2428 *E-mail:* public@ministers.mod.uk.
Constituency: 8 Station Street, Kirkby-in-Ashfield, Nottinghamshire NG17 7AR
Tel: 01623 720399 *Fax:* 01623 720398

HOPE, PHIL
Corby

Phil (Philip) Ian Hope. Born 19 April 1955; Son of A. G. (Bob) Hope, former police commander, and Grace Hope; Educated Wandsworth Comprehensive, London; St Luke's College, Exeter University (BEd 1978); Married Allison Butt 1980 (1 son 1 daughter). Secondary school science teacher, Kettering School for Boys 1978-79; Youth policy adviser, National Council for Voluntary Organisations 1979-82; Head, Young Volunteer Resources Unit, National Youth Bureau 1982-85; Management/community work consultant, Framework 1985-97; Director, Framework in Print Publishing Co-operative; Member, NUT 1978-79; Member, MSF 1979-; Councillor, Kettering Borough Council 1983-87, Deputy Leader, Labour Group 1986-87; Councillor, Northamptonshire County Council 1993-97, Chair, Equal Opportunities Sub-Committee 1993-97, Chair, Labour Group 1993-97

Lab/Co-op majority 1,517

House of Commons: Contested Kettering 1992 general election. Member for Corby since 1 May 1997 general election; PPS to: Nick Raynsford as Minister of State, Department of the Environment, Transport and the Regions 1999-2001, John Prescott as Deputy Prime Minister and First Secretary of State 2001-03; Parliamentary Under-Secretary of State: Office of the Deputy Prime Minister 2003-05, Department for Education and Skills 2005-. *Political interests:* Youth Affairs, Social Inclusion, Community Regeneration

National Adviser on Youth Policy 1982-87; Member, Co-operative Party 1982-; Delegate to National Conference; Member, Labour Party Leadership Campaign Team 1997-99. Member: National Advisory Group on Personal, Social and Health Education (DfEE), Development Awareness Working Group (DfID); Member, Commonwealth Parliamentary Association 1997-; *Publications:* Author/co-author of many publications including: *Making the Best Use of Consultants*, 1993; *Education for Parenthood*, 1994; *Analysis and Action on Youth Health*, 1995; *Performance Appraisal*, 1995; *Clubs:* Corby Tennis Centre; *Recreations:* Tennis, juggling, gardening

Phil Hope, MP, House of Commons, London SW1A 0AA *Tel:* 020 7219 4075 *Fax:* 020 7219 2964 *E-mail:* hopep@parliament.uk. *Constituency:* 2nd Floor, Chisholm House, Queen's Square, Corby, Northamptonshire NN17 1PD *Tel:* 01536 443325 *Fax:* 01536 269462

RECOGNISING ACHIEVEMENT

OCR is one of the UK's leading examination boards which creates, designs and delivers all types of general and vocational qualifications.

If you want to know anything about:

- the design, construction and assessment of
    GCSEs
    VCEs
    A Levels
    Nationals
    GNVQs, NVQs
    Work-Related Learning
    Industry-leading IT Qualifications such as CLAiT and iPRO
    any other vocational qualifications

- the place of qualifications in the education system

- how examinations, tests and other assessments work

feel free to phone, write or email:

Bene't Steinberg, Group Director of Public Affairs,
1 Regent Street, Cambridge CB2 1GG
Tel: 01223 556003
steinberg.b@ucles.org.uk

www.ocr.org.uk

OCR (Oxford Cambridge and RSA Examinations) is a part of the
University of Cambridge Local Examination syndicate (UCLES).

UCLES is adopting a new name from July 2005, which expresses
more clearly what we do – Cambridge Assessment.

HOPKINS, KELVIN
Luton North

Kelvin Peter Hopkins. Born 22 August 1941; Son of late Professor Harold Horace Hopkins, FRS, physicist and mathematician, and Joan Avery Frost, medical secretary; Educated Queen Elizabeth's Grammar School, High Barnet; Nottingham University (BA politics, economics and mathematics with statistics); Married Patricia Langley 1965 (1 son 1 daughter). TUC Economic Department 1969-70, 1973-77; Policy and research officer, NALGO/UNISON 1977-94; Member, GMB; Delegate, Luton Trades Union Council; Councillor, Luton Borough 1972-76

Lab majority 6,487

House of Commons: Contested Luton North 1983 general election. Member for Luton North since 1 May 1997 general election; Adviser on Yachting to Richard Caborn, as Minister of State for Sport 2002-. *Political interests:* Economic Policy, Employment, Transport, Arts. France, Sweden

Vice-Chair, Central Region Labour Party 1995-96. Member, European Standing Committee B 1998-; *Publications:* Various NALGO publications; Hon. Fellow, Luton University 1993; *Clubs:* Luton Socialist, Lansdowne (Luton); Luton Town Football Club, UK Carrom Federation; *Recreations:* Music, photography, sailing on the Norfolk Broads

Kelvin Hopkins, MP, House of Commons, London SW1A 0AA *Tel:* 020 7219 6670 *Fax:* 020 7219 0957 *E-mail:* hopkinsk@parliament.uk. *Constituency:* 3 Union Street, Luton, Bedfordshire LU1 3AN *Tel:* 01582 488208 *Fax:* 01582 480990

HORAM, JOHN
Orpington

John Rhodes Horam. Born 7 March 1939; Son of Sydney and Catherine Horam; Educated Silcoates School, Wakefield; St Catharine's College, Cambridge (MA economics 1960); Married Judith Jackson 1987 (2 sons from previous marriage). Market research officer, Rowntree & Co. 1960-62; Leader and feature writer: *Financial Times* 1962-65, *The Economist* 1965-68; Managing director: Commodities Research Unit Ltd 1968-70, 1983-87, CRU Holdings Ltd. 1988-92; Deputy chair, CRU International Ltd 1992-95, 1997-

Con majority 4,947

House of Commons: Contested (Labour) Folkstone and Hythe 1966 general election. Member for Gateshead West 1970-83 (Labour 1970-81, SDP 1981-83). Contested Newcastle upon Tyne Central (SDP/Alliance) 1983 general election. Member for Orpington since 9 April 1992 general election; Labour Spokesperson for Economic Affairs 1979-81; SDP Spokesperson 1981-83; Parliamentary Under-Secretary of State, Department of Transport 1976-79; Parliamentary Secretary, Office of Public Service July-November 1995; Parliamentary Under-Secretary of State, Department of Health 1995-97. *Political interests:* Economic Policy, Transport, Health, Environment. France, Germany, USA

Friends of Animals League; Globe; *Publications: Making Britain Competitive*, 1993; *Clubs:* Orpington Conservative; *Recreations:* Opera, ballet, gardening, walking

John Horam, MP, House of Commons, London SW1A 0AA *Tel:* 020 7219 6328 *Fax:* 020 7219 3806 *E-mail:* horamj@parliament.uk. *Constituency:* 6 Sevenoaks Road, Orpington BR6 9JJ *Tel:* 01689 820347 *Fax:* 01689 890429

Lib Dem majority
2,303

HORWOOD, MARTIN
Cheltenham

Martin Horwood. Born 12 October 1962; Educated Cheltenham College; The Queen's College, Oxford (BA modern history 1984); Married Dr Shona Arora 1995. Account executive Ted Bates Advertising 1985-86; Director of development British Humanist Association 1986-88; Creative co-ordinator Help the Aged 1988-90; Donor marketing manager Oxfam 1990-95; Director of marketing and fundraising Oxfam (India) 1995-96; Director of fundraising Alzheimer's Society 1996-2001; Senior consultant then head of consultancy Target Direct Marketing 2001-; TGWU 1990-95; MSF/Amicus 1996-; Vale of White Horse District Council: Councillor 1991-95, Lib Dem group leader 1993-95

House of Commons: Contested Oxford East 1992 and Cities of London and Westminster 2001 general elections. Member for Cheltenham since 5 May 2005 general election. *Political interests:* Voluntary sector, sustainable development, environment

President Oxford Student Liberal Society 1983; Chair Union of Liberal Students 1984-85; Chair Liberal Information Network (LINk) 1987-90. Trustee Fight for Sight 2002-; Member: World Development Movement 1988-, Survival International 1992-, Alzheimer's Society 1996-, Amnesty International 1999-; *Recreations:* Cycling, drawing, astronomy, geneaology

Martin Horwood, MP, House of Commons, London SW1A 0AA
Tel: 020 7219 4704. *Constituency:* Cheltenham Liberal Democrats, 16 Hewlett Road, Cheltenham GL52 6AA *Tel:* 01242 225889
E-mail: cheltlibdems@yahoo.co.uk *Website:* www.cheltlibdems.org.uk

SNP majority 383

HOSIE, STEWART
Dundee East

Stewart Hosie. Born 3 January 1963; Educated Carnoustie High School; Bell Street Tech (HD computer studies); Married Shona Robison MSP 1997. Group IS manager MIH 1988-93; Systems analyst various organisations 1993-96; Year 200/EMU project manager Stakis Plc/Hilton 1996-2000; MSF 1992

House of Commons: Contested Kirkcaldy 1992 and 1997 general elections. Member for Dundee East since 5 May 2005 general election

Former SNP youth convener; SNP national secretary 1999-2003; Organisation convener 2003-. Contested Kirkcaldy 1999 Scottish Parliament election; *Recreations:* Football, hillwalking

Stewart Hosie, MP, House of Commons, London SW1A 0AA *Tel:* 020 7219 8164.
Constituency: 48 Grove Road, Broughty Ferry, Dundee DD5 1JN
E-mail: hosie@dundeesnp.org

HOWARD, MICHAEL
Folkestone and Hythe

Michael Howard. Born 7 July 1941; Son of late Bernard and Hilda Howard; Educated Llanelli Grammar School; Peterhouse, Cambridge (MA economics, LLB 1963); Married Sandra Paul 1975 (1 son 1 daughter and 1 step-son). Called to the Bar, Inner Temple 1964; QC 1982; Junior Counsel to the Crown 1980-82

Con majority 11,680

House of Commons: Contested Liverpool Edge Hill 1966 and 1970 general elections. Member for Folkestone and Hythe since 9 June 1983 general election; PPS to Sir Patrick Mayhew as Solicitor-General 1984-85; Parliamentary Under-Secretary of State, Trade and Industry 1985-87; Minister for: Local Government 1987-88, Water and Planning 1988-89, Housing and Planning 1989-90; Secretary of State for: Employment 1990-92, The Environment 1992-93, The Home Department 1993-97; Contested Leadership of the Conservative Party June 1997; Member, Shadow Cabinet 1997-99, 2001-; Shadow Secretary of State for Foreign and Commonwealth Affairs 1997-99; Shadow Chancellor of the Exchequer 2001-03; Leader of the Opposition 2003-; Leader, Conservative Party 2003-. *Political interests:* Home Affairs, Foreign Affairs. USA

Chair: Bow Group 1970, Coningsby Club 1972-73; Member Conservative Policy Board 2001-. PC 1990; "Spectator" Parliamentarian of the Year 2003; QC; *Clubs:* Carlton, Pratt's; QC; *Recreations:* Football and baseball

Rt Hon Michael Howard, MP, House of Commons, London SW1A 0AA
Tel: 020 7219 5383 *Fax:* 020 7219 0360 *E-mail:* howardm@parliament.uk.
Constituency: Folkestone and Hythe Conservative Association, 4 Westcliff Gardens, Folkestone, Kent CT20 1SP *Tel:* 01303 253524 *Fax:* 01303 251061

HOWARTH, DAVID
Cambridge

David Ross Howarth. Born 10 November 1958; Educated Queen Mary's Grammar School, Walsall; Clare College, Cambridge University (BA law 1981, MA, MPhil 1985) Yale Law School (LLM 1983); Married Edna Helen Murphy 1985. Fellow, Clare College, Cambridge University 1985; Law lecturer, Cambridge University 1988-; Cambridge City Council: Councillor 1987-2004, Leader of Liberal Democrats 1990-2004, Leader of Opposition 1992-2000, Leader of Council 2000-04

Lib Dem majority 4,339

House of Commons: Contested Cambridge 1992, 2001 and Peterborough 1997 general elections. Member for Cambridge since 5 May 2005 general election

Member, Federal Policy Committee 1989. *Publications: Textbook on Tort,*1995; Numerous articles in academic legal journals

David Howarth, MP, House of Commons, London SW1A 0AA *Tel:* 020 7219 8073.
Constituency: 40 Windsor Road, Cambridge, Cambridgeshire CB4 3JN
Tel: 01223 327553 *E-mail:* drh20@cam.ac.uk

HOWARTH, GEORGE
Knowsley North and Sefton East

George Howarth. Born 29 June 1949; Educated Schools in Huyton; Liverpool Polytechnic (BA social sciences 1977); Married Julie Rodgers 1977 (2 sons 1 daughter). Engineering apprentice 1966-70; Engineer 1970-75; Teacher 1975-80; Co-operative Development Services 1980-82; Chief executive Walm Co-operative Centre 1982-86; AEU; Chief executive, Wales TUC sponsored co-op. centre, Cardiff 1984-86; Councillor, Huyton Urban District Council 1971-75; Knowsley Borough Council: Councillor 1975-86, Deputy Leader 1982-83

Lab majority 16,269

House of Commons: Member Knowsley North 13 November 1986 by-election-1997, and for Knowsley North and Sefton East since 1 May 1997 general election; Opposition Spokesperson for: the Environment 1989-92; Environmental Protection 1993-94; Home Affairs 1994-97; Parliamentary Under-Secretary of State: Home Office (Minister for Fire and Emergency Planning, Liquor, Drugs and Elections) 1997-99, Northern Ireland Office 1999-2001. *Political interests:* Housing, Environment

Chair, Knowsley South Labour Party 1981-85; Secretary, Knowsley Borough District Labour Party 1977-80; Member, North West Region Executive, Labour Party 1981-84. *Recreations:* Coarse fishing, family, reading

George Howarth, MP, House of Commons, London SW1A 0AA
Tel: 020 7219 6902 *E-mail:* georgehowarthmp@hotmail.com. *Constituency:* 149 Cherryfield Drive, Kirkby, Merseyside L32 8SE *Tel:* 0151-546 9918
Fax: 0151-546 9918

HOWARTH, GERALD
Aldershot

Con majority 5,334

Gerald Howarth. Born 12 September 1947; Son of Mary and late James Howarth, retired company director; Educated Bloxham School, Banbury (Scholar); Southampton University (BA English 1969); Married Elizabeth Squibb 1973 (1 daughter 2 sons). Commissioned RAFVR 1968. Assistant manager, loan syndication Bank of America International Ltd 1971-77; European Arab Bank 1977-81: Manager and personal assistant to group managing director 1979, Manager, loan syndications 1980; Loan syndication manager responsible for arranging project and other loans in Africa, Middle East and South America, Standard Chartered Bank plc 1981-83; Joint managing director, Taskforce Communications 1993-95; Member, National Union of Seamen 1966; London Borough Council of Hounslow: Councillor 1982-83, Shadow Vice-chair, Environmental Planning Committee 1982-83, Member, Finance and General Purposes Committee

House of Commons: Member for Cannock and Burntwood 1983-92, and for Aldershot since 1 May 1997 general election; Opposition Spokesman on Defence 2002-03; PPS to Michael Spicer: as Parliamentary Under-Secretary of State, Department of Energy 1987-90, as Minister of State, Department of the Environment (Minister for Housing and Construction) 1990; to Sir George Young as Minister of State, Department of the Environment 1990-91, to Margaret Thatcher, MP December 1991-April 1992; Shadow Minister for Defence 2003-. *Political interests:* Aerospace, Aviation, Defence, Media, Privatisation. Germany, Russia, South Africa, Chile, Pakistan

Member, Greater London Area CPC Advisory Committee; Vice-Chairman, City Conservative Forum 1981-84; Founder Member, No Turning Back Group; Chairman, 92 Group of Conservative MPs 2001-. RNLI, ACET, RAF Benevolent Fund; Britannia Airways Parliamentary Pilot of the Year 1988; President, Air Display Association Europe; Fellow, Industry and Parliament Trust; *Publications:* Co-author *No Turning Back*, 1985, and further publications by the Group; *Clubs:* Aldershot Conservative, Liveryman, Guild of Air Pilots and Air Navigators; *Recreations:* Flying, tennis, DIY, family, livery companies

Gerald Howarth, MP, House of Commons, London SW1A 0AA *Tel:* 020 7219 5650 *Fax:* 020 7219 1198 *E-mail:* geraldhowarth@parliament.uk.
Constituency: Conservative Club, Victoria Road, Aldershot, Hampshire GU11 1JX *Tel:* 01252 323637 *Fax:* 01252 323637

Lab majority 13,191

HOWELLS, KIM
Pontypridd

Kim Scott Howells. Born 27 November 1946; Son of late Glanville Howells and of Joan Glenys Howells; Educated Mountain Ash Grammar School; Hornsey College of Art; Cambridge CAT (BA English and history 1974); Warwick University (PhD UK coal Industry (1937-57) 1979); Married Eirlys Davies 1983 (2 sons 1 daughter). Research officer, Coalfield History Project, University College of Wales, Swansea 1979-82; Freelance radio and television presenter and writer 1986-89; Research officer and newspaper editor, NUM South Wales Area 1982-89; Member GPMU

House of Commons: Member for Pontypridd since 23 February 1989 by-election; Opposition Spokesperson for: Development and Co-operation 1993-94, Foreign Affairs 1994, Home Affairs 1994-95, Trade and Industry 1995-97; Parliamentary Under-Secretary of State: Department for Education and Employment (Life-long Learning) 1997-98, Department of Trade and Industry 1998-2001 (Consumer and Corporate Affairs 1999-2000, Competition and Consumer Affairs 2000-2001); Parliamentary Under-Secretary of State (Minister for Tourism, Film and Broadcasting), Department for Culture, Media and Sport 2001-03; Minister of State: for Transport, Department for Transport 2003-04, Department for Education and Skills 2004-05, for the Middle East, Foreign and Commonwealth Office 2005-.
Political interests: Energy, Environment, Foreign Affairs, Transnational Broadcasting, Arts, Intellectural Property, Small Businesses. Germany, Italy, Latin America, Switzerland, USA, South Africa, Austria, Romania

Publications: Various, on 20th century industrial history and economics and politics of energy; Honorary Doctorate, Anglia Polytechnic University 1998; *Clubs:* Llantwit Fadre Cricket, Hopkinstown Cricket, Pontypridd Rugby Football, Pontypridd Cricket Club, British Mountaineering Council; *Recreations:* Writing, films, jazz, mountain climbing, painting, cycling

Dr Kim Howells, MP, House of Commons, London SW1A 0AA *Tel:* 020 7219 5813 *Fax:* 020 7219 5526 *E-mail:* raybouldc@parliament.uk. *Constituency:* 16 Tyfica Road, Pontypridd, Mid Glamorgan CF37 2DA *Tel:* 01443 402551 *Fax:* 01443 485628

Lab majority 7,625

HOYLE, LINDSAY
Chorley

Lindsay Harvey Hoyle. Born 10 June 1957; Son of Baron Hoyle (qv) and late Pauline Hoyle; Educated Anderton County Primary; Lords College, Bolton; Horwich FE; Bolton TIC (City & Guilds Construction); Married Catherine Swindley (2 daughters). Company director; Shop steward; Member, AMICUS (MSF); Councillor, Adlington Town Council 1980-98; Councillor, Chorley Borough Council 1980-98; Chair, Economic Development, Deputy Leader 1994-97; Mayor of Chorley 1997-98

House of Commons: Member for Chorley since 1 May 1997 general election. *Political interests:* Trade and Industry, Sport, Defence, Small Businesses, Agriculture. Gibraltar, Falkland Islands, British Overseas Territories

Armed Forces Parliamentary Scheme (Royal Marines) 1998-; Member, Cuerdon Valley Trust; *Clubs:* Member: Adlington Cricket Club, Chorley Cricket Club; *Recreations:* Cricket, Rugby League

Lindsay Hoyle, MP, House of Commons, London SW1A 0AA *Tel:* 020 7219 3515 *Fax:* 020 7219 3831 *E-mail:* wilsonp@parliament.uk. *Constituency:* 35-39 Market Street, Chorley, Lancashire PR7 2SW *Tel:* 01257 271555 *Fax:* 01257 277462

HUGHES, BEVERLEY
Stretford and Urmston

Lab majority 7,851

Beverley June Hughes. Born 30 March 1950; Daughter of late Norman Hughes and Doris Hughes; Educated Ellesmere Port Girls' Grammar School; Manchester University (BSc 1971, MSc 1978); Liverpool University (Diploma in applied social studies 1974); Married Thomas McDonald 1973 (2 daughters 1 son). Trainee probation officer, Merseyside 1971; Probation officer, Merseyside 1972; Manchester University: Research associate 1976; Lecturer 1981, Senior lecturer and head of department 1993-97; Member USDAW; Trafford Metropolitan Borough Council: Councillor 1986, Labour Group Deputy Leader 1990, Labour Group Leader 1992, Council Leader 1995-97; Director: Trafford Park Development Corporation 1992-97, Manchester Airport plc 1995-97

House of Commons: Member for Stretford and Urmston since 1 May 1997 general election; PPS to Hilary Armstrong as Minister of State, Department of the Environment, Transport and the Regions (Minister for Local Government and Housing) 1998-99; Parliamentary Under-Secretary of State, Department of the Environment, Transport and the Regions 1999-2001; Home Office 2001-04: Parliamentary Under-Secretary of State 2001-02, Minister of State 2002-04: for Citizenship, Immigration and Community Cohesion 2002-03, (Citizenship, Immigration and Counter Terrorism) 2003-04; Minister of State (Children), Department for Education and Skills 2005-. *Political interests:* Economic Regeneration, Investment, Local and Regional Government, Health and Community Care, Families, Regional Development, Education, Criminal Justice, Child Protection and Safety

Publications: Older People and Community Care: Critical Theory and Practice, 1995; Numerous academic and professional publications; PC 2004; *Recreations:* Jazz, fell-walking

Rt Hon Beverley Hughes, MP, House of Commons, London SW1A 0AA *Tel:* 020 7219 3611 *E-mail:* hughesb@parliament.uk. *Constituency:* c/o House of Commons, London SW1A 0AA *Tel:* 0161 749 9120 *Fax:* 0161 749 9121

Decisions that affect young lives

We give children their say

cafcass

Looking after children's interests in family courts

www.cafcass.gov.uk

HUGHES, SIMON
North Southwark and Bermondsey

Simon Henry Ward Hughes. Born 17 May 1951; Son of late James Henry Hughes and of Sylvia, née Ward; Educated Llandaff Cathedral School, Cardiff; Christ College, Brecon; Selwyn College, Cambridge (BA law 1973, MA); Inns of Court School of Law; College of Europe, Bruges (Certificate in Higher European Studies 1975); Single. Barrister Called to the Bar, Inner Temple 1974; In practice 1978-; GLC candidate 1981; Southwark Borough Council candidate 1982

Lib Dem majority
5,406

House of Commons: Member for Southwark and Bermondsey February 1983-97 by-election, and for North Southwark and Bermondsey since 1 May 1997 general election; Liberal Spokesperson for the Environment 1983-88; Alliance Spokesperson for Health January-June 1987; Spokesperson for: Education, Science and Training 1989-92, Environment and Natural Resources 1992-94, Urban Affairs and Young People 1994-97, Church of England 1988-97, Health and Social Welfare 1995-97, Health (Future of NHS) 1997-99; Principal Spokesperson for Home and Legal Affairs 1999-2003; Spokesperson for London 2003-; Liberal Democrat Deputy Whip 1989-99; Liberal Democrat Shadow Office of the Deputy Prime Minister 2005-. *Political interests:* Human Rights, Civil Liberties, Youth Affairs, Social Affairs, Housing, Environment. South Africa, Sierra Leone, Commonwealth, Peru

President, National League of Young Liberals 1986-92, Vice-President, Liberal Democrat Youth and Students 1983-86, President 1992-; Vice-Chair, Southwark and Bermondsey Liberal Association 1981-83; Former Chair, Liberal Party's Home Affairs Panel; Member, Association of Liberal Lawyers; President Liberal Democrat Party 2004-. London mayoral candidate 2002, 2004; Trainee, EEC Brussels 1976; Trainee and member Secretariat, Directorate and Commission on Human Rights, Council of Europe, Strasbourg 1976-77; Chair, Thames Festival Trust; *Publications:* Co-author *Human Rights in Western Europe – The Next 30 Years*, 1981; *The Prosecutorial Process in England and Wales*, 1981; *Across the Divide – Liberal Values for Defence and Disarmament*, 1986; *Pathways to Power*, 1992; *Who Goes Where – Asylum: Opportunity not Crisis*, 2002; Honorary Fellow, South Bank University; *Clubs:* Redriff (Rotherhithe); *Recreations:* Music, theatre, history, sport (Millwall and Hereford football clubs, Glamorgan county cricket club and Wales rugby football union), the countryside and open air

Simon Hughes, MP, House of Commons, London SW1A 0AA *Tel:* 020 7219 6256 *Fax:* 020 7219 6567 *E-mail:* simon@simonhughesmp.org.uk.
Constituency: Tel: 020 7403 2860 *Fax:* 020 7378 9670

NO GOOD FOOD SHOULD BE WASTED

FareShare is the national charity which redistributes good quality surplus food from the food and drink industry to homeless and disadvantaged people in the community.

We do this through a network of franchised depots run by local charitable groups in the community. We currently span 34 different cities, towns and boroughs across the UK and we provide an integrated service to the whole of the food chain, not just local stores and depots.

We are supported by the likes of Sainsbury's, Marks and Spencer, Pret A Manger, Kraft Foods and all the main food industry players. These companies have helped us install systems which ensure that our food handling capabilities are state of the art and that only food of maximum quality and freshness reaches the ultimate recipients.

Last year we were able to contribute food for over 3.3 million meals. We estimate that 12,000 homeless and other disadvantaged people have regular and nutritious food everyday because of our service.

The value of the service is estimated to be £5 million per year to our community members: local charitable organisations receiving the food are able to provide additional services to their clients with the resources this releases.

Our mission is to work with communities to relieve food poverty – the "No Good Food Should be Wasted" campaign is designed to

ensure valuable resources, currently wasted, are used to help us achieve this goal.

Our activity, socially inclusive and environmentally responsible, has led us to consider the issue of the "fit for purpose" product being wasted in other industrial sectors and in what quantities. Surely this can be diverted away from landfill, in the same way as we do with food, and used as originally intended?

DEFRA's recent review of the Waste Strategy shows that accurate and reliable data in this area is a concern. We seek commitment and support from Government and others to carry out research to identify these 'fit for purpose' resources and to develop models and techniques, in partnership with Government and other organisations to ensure their use becomes an integral part of the national Waste and Resource Strategy for the maximum benefit of society.

It will be a challenge but we have already shown through our work with the food industry that the rewards can be great both in the short term for our communities and in the longer term to the environment.

FareShare
Delivering Surplus Food to People in Need

To find out more about FareShare and support our campaign please visit our website www.fareshare.org.uk/whatdo/environment.html

Lib Dem majority
568

HUHNE, CHRIS
Eastleigh

Chris Huhne. Born 2 July 1954; Educated Westminster School 1967-71; French language and civilisation Sorbonne, Paris (certificate 1972); philosophy, politics and economics, Magdalen College, Oxford (BA, MA); Married Vicky Coumouzis 1984. freelance journalist 1975-76; trainee Liverpool Daily Post and Echo 1976-77; Brussels correspondent The Economist 1977-80; The Guardian: leader writer 1980-84; economics editor and columnist 1984-90; Independent on Sunday: economics and assistant editor 1990-91, Independent: business and city editor 1991-94; managing director and founder Sovereign Risk Ratings IBCA Ltd 1994-97; managing director and chief economist IBCA Ltd 1997-; MEP for South East 1999-2005: deputy leader EP Liberal Democrat Group; member National Union of Journalists

House of Commons: Contested Reading East 1983, Oxford West and Abingdon 1987 general elections. Member for Eastleigh since 5 May 2005 general election. *Political interests:* European single currency, economics, third world debt and development, Europe, electoral reform

Chair, Liberal Democrats public services policy commission; economic adviser, Liberal Democrats 1997. *Publications:* Co-author *Debt and Danger: The World Financial Crisis*, 1985; *Real World Economics: Essays on Imperfect and Fallible Governments*, 1990-91; *The Ecu Report: the Single European Currency*, 1991; Co-author *Both Sides of the Coin: the Case for the Euro and European Monetary Union*, 1999; Junior Financial Journalist of the Year 1981; Financial Journalist of the Year 1990; *Recreations:* family, football, cinema, history

Chris Huhne, MP, House of Commons, London SW1A 0AA *Tel:* 020 7219 4997. *Constituency:* Eastleigh Liberal Democrats, 109A Leigh Road, Eastleigh SO50 9DS *Tel:* 02380 620007 *Fax:* 02380 618245 *E-mail:* chuhneoffice@cix.co.uk *Website:* www.chrishuhnemep.org

Lab majority 5,062

HUMBLE, JOAN
Blackpool North and Fleetwood

(Jovanka) Joan Humble. Born 3 March 1951; Daughter of John Piplica and Dora Piplica; Educated Greenhead Grammar School, Keighley; Lancaster University (BA history 1972); Married Paul Humble 1972 (2 daughters). Civil servant, Department of Health and Social Security and Inland Revenue 1972-77; Housewife 1977-85; Member, TGWU; Councillor, Lancashire County Council 1985-97, Chair, Lancashire Social Services 1990-97; JP, Preston Bench

House of Commons: Member for Blackpool North and Fleetwood since 1 May 1997 general election. *Political interests:* Social Services, Education, Economic Regeneration, Small Businesses

Member: Co-operative Party, Christian Socialist Movement; Hon. Secretary, North West Regional Group of Labour MPs 1999-. Member, European Standing Committee A 1998; *Recreations:* Reading, gardening, cooking

Joan Humble, MP, House of Commons, London SW1A 0AA *Tel:* 020 7219 5025 *Fax:* 020 7219 2755 *E-mail:* sue@humblemp.freeserve.co.uk. *Constituency:* 216 Lord Street, Fleetwood, Lancashire FY7 6SW *Tel:* 01253 877346 *Fax:* 01253 777236

HUNT, JEREMY
South West Surrey

Jeremy Hunt. Born 1 November 1966; Educated Charterhouse, Surrey; Magdalen College, Oxford (BA philosophy, politics and economics 1988, MA). Management consultant, Outram Cullinan and co 1988-89 English teacher, Japan 1990-91 Founder/Managing director, Hot Courses Ltd 1991-

House of Commons: Member for South West Surrey since 5 May 2005 general election. *Political interests:* Education, Enterprise, Foreign Affairs

Con majority 5,711

Founder and Trustee, The Hotcourses Foundation 2004; *Recreations:* travel

Jeremy Hunt, MP, House of Commons, London SW1A 0AA *Tel:* 020 7219 6813. *Constituency:* SW Surrey Conservative Association, 2 Royal Parade, Tilford Road, Hindhead GO26 6TD *Tel:* 01428 604520 *Fax:* 01428 607498

E-mail: jeremy@localconservatives.org *Website:* www.localconservatives.org

HURD, NICK
Ruislip Northwood

Nicholas Hurd. Born 1962; Educated Eton College; Exeter College, Oxford (classics); Married Kim 1998. Flamings Bank (Brazil-based) 1995-99; Founder Small Business Network 2002; Director Band-X Ltd; Adviser Shadow Trade and Industry team Chief of staff, Tim Yeo MP 2003-

House of Commons: Member for Ruislip Northwood since 5 May 2005 general election. *Political interests:* Schools, hospitals, transport, environment

Con majority 8,910

Kensington and Chelsea borough champion for Steve Norris 2003. Trustee Greenhouse Schools Project; Mentor Princes Trust; *Recreations:* Sport, music

Nick Hurd, MP, House of Commons, London SW1A 0AA *Tel:* 020 7219 6648. *Constituency:* Ruislip-Northwood Conservative Association, 20b High Street, Northwood, Middlesex HA6 1BN *Tel:* 01923 822876 *Fax:* 01923 841514

E-mail: nick@nickhurd.com *Website:* www.nickhurd.com

HUTTON, JOHN
Barrow and Furness

John Hutton. Born 6 May 1955; Son of late George Hutton, salesman and general labourer, and Rosemary Hutton, orthoptist; Educated Westcliffe High School, Southend; Magdalen College, Oxford (BA law 1976, BCL 1978); Married Rosemary Caroline Little 1978 (divorced 1993) (3 sons 1 daughter and 1 son deceased). Research fellow, Magdalen College, Oxford 1980-81; Senior law lecturer, Newcastle Polytechnic 1981-92; Contested Cumbria and North Lancashire 1989 European Parliament election; Member GMB

Lab majority 6,037

House of Commons: Contested Penrith and the Border 1987 general election. Member for Barrow and Furness since 9 April 1992 general election; PPS to Margaret Beckett: as President of the Board of Trade and Secretary of State for Trade and Industry 1997-98, as President of the Council and Leader of the House of Commons 1998; Department of Health: Parliamentary Under-Secretary of State 1998-99, Minister of State for Health 1999-2005; Chancellor of the Duchy of Lancaster 2005-. *Political interests:* Defence, Welfare State, Home Affairs, Legal Affairs

St Mary's Hospice, Ulverston; RNLI; PC 2001; *Clubs:* Cemetery Cottages Workingmen's (Barrow-in-Furness); *Recreations:* Cricket, football, films, music, history

Rt Hon John Hutton, MP, House of Commons, London SW1A 0AA *Tel:* 020 7219 6228 *E-mail:* huttonj@parliament.uk. *Constituency:* 22 Hartington Street, Barrow-in-Furness, Cumbria LA14 5SL *Tel:* 01229 431204 *Fax:* 01229 432016

Lab majority 11,638

IDDON, BRIAN
Bolton South East

Brian Iddon. Born 5 July 1940; Son of late John Iddon and late Violet Iddon; Educated Christ Church Boys' School, Southport; Southport Technical College; Hull University (BSc chemistry 1961, PhD organic chemistry 1964, DSc 1981); Married Merrilyn-Ann Muncaster 1965 (divorced 1989) (2 daughters); married Eileen Harrison, née Barker 1995 (2 stepsons). Durham University: temporary lecturer 1964-65, senior demonstrator 1965-66 in organic chemistry; Salford University: lecturer 1966-78, senior lecturer 1978-86, reader 1986-97 in organic chemistry; Member, Association of University Teachers; Councillor, Bolton Metropolitan District Council 1977-98, Hon. Alderman 1998-, Housing Committee: Vice-Chair, 1980-82, Chair, 1986-96

House of Commons: Member for Bolton South East since 1 May 1997 general election. *Political interests:* Housing, Science and Technology, Health, Education (HE/FE in particular). Europe, Africa, India, Pakistan, Kashmir, Middle East

Member: North West Group of Labour MPs, Arts For Labour, Co-operative Party, Labour Middle East Council, Labour Friends of Remploy, Labour Housing Group, Labour PLP Keep The Link Group. Shelter, Amnesty International, Down's Syndrome Association, Cancer Research UK; Member: IPU, CPA; *Publications:* two books, research papers, research communications, major reviews, articles in magazines and a number of papers presented orally at conferences; Honorary Member, Society of Chemical Industry; *Clubs:* Honorary Membership, Derby Ward Labour Club; Member, Rumworth Labour Club; Our Lady of Lourdes Social Club; *Recreations:* Philately, gardening, cricket (spectator)

Dr Brian Iddon, MP, House of Commons, London SW1A 0AA *Tel:* 020 7219 4064; 020 7219 2096 *Fax:* 020 7219 2653 *E-mail:* iddonb@parliament.uk. *Constituency:* 60 St Georges Road, Bolton, Greater Manchester BL1 2DD *Tel:* 01204 371202 *Fax:* 01204 371374

Lab majority 12,732

ILLSLEY, ERIC
Barnsley Central

Eric Illsley. Born 9 April 1955; Son of John and Maud Illsley; Educated Barnsley Holgate Grammar School; Leeds University (LLB 1977); Married Dawn Webb 1978 (2 daughters). Yorkshire Area NUM: Compensation officer 1978-81, Assistant head of general department 1981-84, Head of general department and chief administration officer 1984-87; Member, MSF

House of Commons: Member for Barnsley Central since 11 June 1987 general election; Opposition Spokesperson for: Health 1994-95, Local Government 1995, Northern Ireland 1995-97; Labour Whip 1991-94. *Political interests:* Trade Unions, Mining, Energy, Social Security, Glass Industry. Australia, France

Secretary, Barnsley Constituency Labour Party 1981-83, Treasurer 1980-81; Secretary and election agent, Yorkshire South European Labour Party 1984-86; Member, Mining Group of MPs 1987-97; Hon. Treasurer, Yorkshire Regional Group of Labour MP 1997-. Member, Executive Committee: IPU 1997-, Commonwealth Parliamentary Association (CPA) UK Branch 1997-; *Recreations:* Gymnasium

Eric Illsley, MP, House of Commons, London SW1A 0AA *Tel:* 020 7219 3501 *Fax:* 020 7219 4863 *E-mail:* illsleye@parliament.uk. *Constituency:* 18 Regent Street, Barnsley, South Yorkshire S70 2HG *Tel:* 01226 730692 *Fax:* 01226 779429

INGRAM, ADAM
East Kilbride, Strathaven and Lesmahagow

Adam Paterson Ingram. Born 1 February 1947; Son of Bert Ingram, fitter, and Louisa Ingram; Educated Cranhill Senior Secondary School; Married Maureen McMahon 1970. Computer programmer/systems analyst 1967-77; Full-time trade union official 1977-87; Full-time union official, NALGO 1977-87; Member of Parliament supported by TGWU 1987-; District Councillor, East Kilbride 1980-87, Leader 1984-87

Lab majority 14,723

House of Commons: Contested Strathkelvin and Bearsden 1983 general election. Member for East Kilbride 1987-2005, for East Kilbride, Strathaven and Lesmahagow since 5 May 2005 general election; Opposition Spokesperson for: Social Security 1993-95, Trade and Industry 1995-97; Opposition Whip for Scottish Affairs and Treasury Matters 1988-89; PPS to Neil Kinnock as Leader of the Opposition 1988-92; Minister of State: Northern Ireland Office 1997-2001, for the Armed Forces, Ministry of Defence 2001-. *Political interests:* Energy, Aerospace, Defence, Northern Ireland. USA, Japan, Sub-Saharan, Africa

Chair, East Kilbride Constituency Labour Party 1981-85. Kilbryde Hospice; PC 1999; *Clubs:* Bridgeton Burns Club; *Recreations:* Fishing, cooking, reading

Rt Hon Adam Ingram, MP, House of Commons, London SW1A 0AA
Tel: 020 7219 4093 *E-mail:* adam_ingram@compuserve.com.
Constituency: Parliamentary Office, Civic Centre, East Kilbride G74 1AB
Tel: 01355 806016 *Fax:* 01355 806035,

IRRANCA-DAVIES, HUW
Ogmore

Huw Irranca-Davies. Born 22 January 1963; Son of Gerwin Davies and Teresa Davies, née Griffiths; Educated Gowerton Comprehensive School; Swansea Institute of Higher Education (MSc European leisure resort management); Married Joanna Irranca 1990 (3 sons). Leisure facility management; Senior lecturer and course director, business faculty, Swansea Institute of Higher Education 1996-2002; Member, GMB

Lab majority 13,703

House of Commons: Contested Brecon and Radnorshire 2001 general election. Member for Ogmore since 14 February 2002 by-election; PPS to Jane Kennedy as Minister of State: Northern Ireland Office 2003-04, Department for Work and Pensions 2004-. *Political interests:* Police Reform, Social Justice, European Union. Middle East, Northern Ireland

Vice-president, Neath Constituency Labour Party -2002; Secretary, Ystalyfera branch -2002. Tenovus (National Cancer Charity); Trustee and director, Charitable Trust (community regeneration); *Clubs:* Chair, Ogmore Valley Male Voice Choir; President, Maesteg Celtic Cricket Club; *Recreations:* Hill-walking, cycling, most sport, family

Huw Irranca-Davies, MP, House of Commons, London SW1A 0AA
Tel: 020 7219 4027 *Fax:* 020 7219 0134 *E-mail:* irrancadaviesh@parliament.uk.
Constituency: Tel: 01656 737777 *Fax:* 01656 737788

Con majority 12,459

JACK, MICHAEL
Fylde

(John) Michael Jack. Born 17 September 1946; Son of late Ralph Jack and Florence Edith Jack; Educated Bradford Grammar School; Bradford Technical College; Leicester University (BA economics 1968, MPhil transport economics 1970); Married Alison Jane Musgrave 1976 (2 sons). Manager transport and brands Proctor and Gamble 1971-75; PA to Lord Rayner 1975-76; Marks and Spencer 1975-80; Director, L. O. Jeffs Ltd (Part of Northern Foods from 1986) 1981-87; Member, Mersey Regional Health Authority 1984-87

House of Commons: Contested Newcastle Central February 1974. Member for Fylde since 11 June 1987 general election; Opposition Spokesperson for Health June-November 1997; PA to James Prior, MP 1979 general election; PPS to John Gummer: as Minister for Local Government 1988-89, as Minister of Agriculture, Fisheries and Food 1989-90; Joint Parliamentary Under-Secretary of State for Social Security 1990-92; Minister of State at: Home Office 1992-93, Ministry of Agriculture, Fisheries and Food 1993-95; Financial Secretary, HM Treasury 1995-97; Member, Shadow Cabinet 1997-98; Shadow Minister of Agriculture, Fisheries and Food November 1997-August 1998. *Political interests:* Economic Issues, Energy, Nuclear Industry, Horticulture, Sheltered Housing, Aerospace, Transport, Agriculture. China, USA, Italy

National Chair, Young Conservatives 1976;. Friends of Clifton Hospital; Friends of Trinity Hospice, Lytham St Annes; Nogal Players; Pear Tree School Kirham; Med Alert; Lytham St Annes Road Runners; Member: European Standing Committee C 1999-, Tax Law Rewrite Committee 1999-; PC 1997; Freeman, City of London; *Recreations:* Boule, motorsport, dinghy sailing, growing vegetables, running

Rt Hon Michael Jack, MP, House of Commons, London SW1A 0AA
Tel: 020 7219 5047 *Fax:* 020 7219 4129. *Constituency:* Universal, Fairfield, Bradshaw Lane, Greenhalgh, Lancashire PR4 3JA *Tel:* 01772 671533
Fax: 01772 671534 *E-mail:* fyldeconservatory@tory.org

Lab majority 3,729

JACKSON, GLENDA
Hampstead and Highgate

Glenda Jackson. Born 9 May 1936; Daughter of Harry and Joan Jackson; Educated West Kirby County Grammar School for Girls; RADA; Married Roy Hodges 1958 (divorced 1976) (1 son). Actress: Plays include: *The Idiot* 1962, *Love's Labour's Lost*, *Hamlet* 1965, *Three Sisters* 1967, *Hedda Gabler* 1975; Films include: *Women in Love*, *Mary, Queen of Scots*, *A Touch of Class*; Television includes *Elizabeth R* 1971; Member, Royal Shakespeare Company 1963-67, 1979-80; Member, Greater London Assembly advisory cabinet for homelessness 2000-

House of Commons: Member for Hampstead and Highgate since 9 April 1992 general election; Opposition Spokeswoman on Transport 1996-97; Parliamentary Under-Secretary of State, Department of the Environment, Transport and the Regions 1997-99; Resigned in July 1999 reshuffle. *Political interests:* Overseas Aid and Development, Housing, Environment

CBE 1978; Best film actress awards: Variety Clubs of Great Britain 1971, 1975, 1978, NY Film critics 1971, Oscar 1971, 1974; CBE; *Recreations:* Cooking, gardening, reading Jane Austen

Glenda Jackson, MP, House of Commons, London SW1A 0AA *Tel:* 020 7219 4008
Fax: 020 7219 2112.

JACKSON, STEWART
Peterborough

Con majority 2,740

Stewart James Jackson. Born 31 January 1965; Educated London Nautical School; Chatham House Grammar School, Ramsgate, Kent; Royal Holloway College, London University (BA economics and public administration 1988); Thames Valley University (MA human resource management 2001); Married Sarah O'Grady 1999. Business banking manager Lloyds Bank plc 1993-96; Retail branch manager Lloyds TSB Group 1996-98; Business services manager Aztec training and enterprise council for SW London 1998-2000; Business adviser – human resources Business Link for London 2000-; Member, Lloyds TSB Group Union 1989-98; London Borough of Ealing: Councillor 1990-98, Chair finance (grants) sub-committee 1993-94, Spokesperson housing 1994-96, planning 1996-98

House of Commons: Contested Brent South 1997 and Peterborough 2001 general elections. Member for Peterborough since 5 May 2005 general election. *Political interests:* Housing, planning, small business, environment

Deputy chair Ealing North Conservative Association 1998-2000. Board member, London City YMCA 1993-98; Lifesaver appeal, Peterborough 2001-; National Kidney Research Fund 2001-; *Publications:* Various articles in *Crossbow*, The Bow Group 1998-2000; *Clubs:* United and Cecil; Peterborough Conservative; *Recreations:* Reading, travel, theatre, cycling

Stewart Jackson, MP, House of Commons, London SW1A 0AA
Tel: 020 7219 8286. *Constituency:* Peterborough Conservative Association, 193 Dogsthorpe Road, Peterborough PE1 3AT *Tel:* 01733 343190 *Fax:* 01733 343150 *E-mail:* pboro@tory.org *Website:* www.peterboroughconservatives.com

JAMES, SIAN
Swansea East

Lab majority 11,249

Sian James. Born 24 June 1959; Educated University of Wales, Swansea (BA Welsh 1989); Married. Field officer National Federation of Young Farmers' Clubs 1990-91; Save the Children 1991-94; National Trust 1994-98; Securicor 1998-99; Lobbyist ATOC 1999-2003; Director, Welsh Women's Aid 2003-

House of Commons: Member for Swansea East since 5 May 2005 general election. *Political interests:* Social exclusion, public transport

Recreations: Reading, antiques

Sian James, MP, House of Commons, London SW1A 0AA *Tel:* 020 7219 6954. *Constituency:* 54 Caemawr Road, Morriston, Swansea SA6 7DX *Tel:* 01792 310333; 07792 069583 *E-mail:* sianjames@email.labour.org.uk

Con majority 10,903

JENKIN, BERNARD
North Essex

Bernard Jenkin. Born 9 April 1959; Son of Rt Hon. Baron Jenkin of Roding (qv); Educated Highgate School; William Ellis School; Corpus Christi College, Cambridge (BA English literature 1982) (President, Cambridge Union Society 1982); Married Anne Strutt 1988 (2 sons). Previously employed by: Ford Motor Co Ltd and 3i plc; Political Adviser to Leon Brittan MP 1986-88; Manager, Legal and General Ventures Ltd 1989-92; Adviser, Legal and General Group plc 1992-95; Chairman, Matching Parish Council 1985-87

House of Commons: Contested Glasgow Central 1987 general election. Member for North Colchester 1992-97, and for North Essex since 1 May 1997 general election; Opposition Spokesperson for: Constitutional Affairs, Scotland and Wales 1997-98, Environment, Transport and the Regions (Roads and Environment) 1998; PPS to Michael Forsyth as Secretary of State for Scotland 1995-97; Shadow Minister for Transport 1998-2001; Member, Shadow Cabinet 1999-2003; Shadow Secretary of State for: Defence 2001-03, The Regions 2003-. *Political interests:* Economic Policy, Trade, European Union, Defence, Foreign Affairs. USA, New Zealand, Singapore, Chile, France, Germany

Action Aid, BASC, National Trust, British Paralympic Association; Member, European Standing Committee B 1992-97; *Publications:* Co-author *Who Benefits: Reinventing Social Security*, 1993; *A Conservative Europe: 1994 and beyond*, 1994; *Fairer Business Rates*, 1996; *Clubs:* Colchester Conservative; *Recreations:* Sailing, music (especially opera), fishing, family, DIY

Bernard Jenkin, MP, House of Commons, London SW1A 0AA *Tel:* 020 7219 4029 *Fax:* 020 7219 5963 *E-mail:* jenkinb@parliament.uk. *Constituency:* North Essex Conservative Association, 107 High Street, Colchester, Essex CO1 1TH *Tel:* 01206 544114 *Fax:* 01206 544134 *Website:* www.northessex.tory.org.uk

Lab majority 2,569

JENKINS, BRIAN
Tamworth

Brian Jenkins. Born 19 September 1942; Son of late Hiram and Gladys Jenkins; Educated Kingsbury High School, Tamworth; Coventry College; Coleg Harlech; London School of Economics (BSc econ 1980); Wolverhampton Polytechnic (PGCE 1981); Married Joan Dix 1963 (1 son 1 daughter). Instrument mechanic, CEGB 1961-68; Industrial engineer, Jaguar Cars 1968-73; Percy Lane 1973-75; Student 1975-81; College lecturer: Isle of Man College 1981-83, Tamworth College 1983-96; GMB; Councillor, Tamworth Borough Council 1985-96, Mayor 1993-94

House of Commons: Contested South East Staffordshire 1992 general election. Member for South East Staffordshire 11 April 1996 by-election – 1997, and for Tamworth since 1 May 1997 general election; PPS: to Joyce Quin, as Minister of State, Home Office (Minister for Prisons, Probation and Europe) 1997-98, to Joyce Quin, Derek Fatchett and Tony Lloyd as Ministers of State, Foreign and Commonwealth Office 1998-99, to Joyce Quin, Geoff Hoon and Tony Lloyd as Ministers of State, Foreign and Commonwealth Office 1999, to Joyce Quin, as Minister of State and Deputy Minister, Ministry of Agriculture, Fisheries and Food 1999-2001. *Political interests:* Trade and Industry, Training, Housing. Europe, North America

Clubs: Tamworth Royal British Legion; *Recreations:* Music, reading, watching sport

Brian Jenkins, MP, House of Commons, London SW1A 0AA *Tel:* 020 7219 6622 *Fax:* 020 7219 0169 *E-mail:* jenkinsb@parliament.uk. *Constituency:* 31c Market Street, Tamworth, Staffordshire B79 7LR *Tel:* 01827 311957 *Fax:* 01827 311958

JOHNSON, ALAN
Hull West and Hessle

Alan Arthur Johnson. Born 17 May 1950; Son of Stephen Arthur and late Lillian May Johnson; Educated Sloane Grammar School, Chelsea; Married Judith Cox 1968 (divorced) (1 son 2 daughters); married Laura Jane Patient 1991 (1 son). Postman 1968-87; Local Officer, Slough UCW 1974-81; Union of Communication Workers: Branch Official 1976, Executive Council 1981-87, National Officer 1987-93, General Secretary 1993-95; Member, General Council, TUC 1993-95; Executive Member, Postal, Telegraph and Telephone International 1993-97; Director, Unity Bank Trust plc 1993-97; Joint General Secretary, Communication Workers Union 1995-97; Member, CWU

Lab majority 9,450

House of Commons: Member for Hull West and Hessle since 1 May 1997 general election; PPS to Dawn Primarolo: as Financial Secretary, HM Treasury 1997-99, as Paymaster General, HM Treasury 1999; Department of Trade and Industry 1999-2003: Parliamentary Under-Secretary of State (Competitiveness) 1999-2001, Minister of State 2001-03: Minister for Employment Relations and Regions 2001-02, Minister for Employment Relations, Industry and the Regions 2002-03; Minister of State for Lifelong Learning, Further and Higher Education, Department for Education and Skills 2003-04; Secretary of State for: Work and Pensions 2004-05, Trade and Industry 2005-. *Political interests:* Education, Electoral Reform, Employment, Post Office

Member: Eton and Slough Labour Party GMC 1976-87, Southern Regional Executive of Labour Party 1981-87, Member, Labour Party National Executive Committee 1995-97, Labour Campaign for Electoral Reform. Member, World Executive, Postal, Telegraph and Telephone International (PTTI) 1993-97; PC 2003; *Recreations:* Tennis, cooking, reading, Radio 4, music

Rt Hon Alan Johnson, MP, House of Commons, London SW1A 0AA
Tel: 020 7219 5227 *Fax:* 020 7219 5856 *E-mail:* johnsona@parliament.uk.
Constituency: Goodwin Resource Centre, Icehouse Road, Hull,
Humberside HU3 2HQ *Tel:* 01482 219211 *Fax:* 01482 219211

JOHNSON, BORIS
Henley

(Alexander) Boris de Pfeffel Johnson. Born 19 June 1964; Son of Stanley Patrick Johnson and Charlotte Johnson, neé Fawcett; Educated Eton College (King's Scholar); Balliol College, Oxford (Brackenbury Scholar in classics) (BA literae humaniores 1987); Married Marina Wheeler 1993 (2 sons 2 daughters). Trainee reporter: *Times, Wolverhampton Express, Star* 1987-88; *Daily Telegraph*: Leader and feature writer 1988-89, EC correspondent Brussels 1989-94, Assistant editor 1994-99; Political columnist *Spectator* 1994-95; Chief political commentator *Daily Telegraph*; Editor *Spectator* 1999-

Con majority 12,793

House of Commons: Contested Clwyd South 1997 general election. Member for Henley since 7 June 2001 general election; Shadow Minister for the Arts 2004

Vice-chairman (Campaigning), Conservative Party 2003-04. Member European Standing Committee B 2003-; *Publications:* Numerous radio and television broadcasts and publications *Friends, Voters, Countrymen,* 2001; *Lend Me Your Ears*; *What the Papers Say* Political Commentator of the Year 1997; Pagan Federation of Great Britain, National Journalist of the Year 1998; Editors' Editor of the Year 2003; British Press Awards, Columnist of the Year 2004; *Clubs:* Beefsteak; *Recreations:* Painting, poetry, tennis, skiing, rugby, cricket

Boris Johnson, MP, House of Commons, London SW1A 0AA *Tel:* 020 7219 8244.
Constituency: 8 Gorwell, Watlington, Oxfordshire OX49 5QE *Tel:* 01491 612 852
Fax: 01491 612 001 *E-mail:* soco@gorwell.fsbusiness.co.uk

Lab majority 7,351

JOHNSON, DIANA
Hull North

Diana Ruth Johnson. Born 25 July 1966; Educated Sir John Deans Sixth Form College, Cheshire; Northwich County Grammar School for Girls, Cheshire; Brunel University (BA modern history 1985); Queen Mary College, London University (LLB 1988); Council for Legal Education (law finals 1991); Living with partner. Law clerk family law firm, Philadelphia, USA 1989; Paralegal Herbert Smith Solicitors 1990; Law clerk immigration law firm, Hamilton, Ontario, Canada 1991; Volunteer/locum lawyer Tower Hamlets Law Centre 1993-95; Family lawyer McCormacks Solicitors 1994-95; Legal member Mental Health Act Commission 1995-98; Employment, immigration and education lawyer North Lewisham Law Centre 1995-99; Non-executive director Newham Healthcare Trust 1998-2001; Employment lawyer Paddington Law Centre 1999-; Member: MSF 1995-99, TGWU 1993-95, 1999-, UNISON; London Borough of Tower Hamlets: councillor 1994-2002, chair: social services 1997-2000, social services and health scrutiny panel

House of Commons: Member for Hull North since 5 May 2005 general election. *Political interests:* Employment rights, health, education, animal welfare

Constituency caseworker Mildred Gordon MP 1993; Member Co-operative party Labour Women's Network. *Recreations:* Cinema, walking, theatre

Diana Johnson, MP, House of Commons, London SW1A 0AA *Tel:* 020 7219 5647.
Constituency: 431 Beverley Road, Hull HU5 1LX
E-mail: diana.johnson@email.labour.org.uk

Con majority 133

JONES, DAVID
Clwyd West

David Ian Jones. Born 22 March 1952; Educated Ruabon Grammar School; London University College (LLB law 1973); Married Sara Eluned Tudor 1982. Senior partner David Jones & Company, Llandudno 1985-2005; AM for North Wales 2002-03

House of Commons: Contested Conwy 1997 and City of Chester 2001 general elections, member for Clwyd West since 5 May 2005 general election. *Political interests:* Law and order, constitution, Welsh affairs, countryside

Chair, Conwy Conservative Association 1998-99. Honorary life fellow, Cancer Research UK; Contested 1999 National Assembly for Wales election; *Recreations:* Travel

David Jones, MP, House of Commons, London SW1A 0AA *Tel:* 020 7219 8070.
Constituency: 3 Llewelyn Road, Colwyn Bay LL29 7AP *Tel:* 01492 530505
Fax: 01492 534157 *E-mail:* mail@clwydwest.org.uk *Website:* www.clwydwest.og.uk

Lab majority 12,204

JONES, HELEN
Warrington North

Helen Mary Jones. Born 24 December 1954; Daughter of late Robert Edward Jones and of Mary Scanlan; Educated St Werburgh's Primary School; Ursuline Convent, Chester; University College, London (BA); Chester College; Liverpool University (MEd); Manchester Metropolitan University; Married Michael Vobe 1988 (1 son). Teacher of English; Development officer, MIND; Justice and peace officer, Liverpool Archdiocese; Solicitor; Contested Lancashire Central 1984 European Parliament election; MSF: Labour Party Liaison Officer, North West Coast Region, Former Member: National Women's Committee, National Appeals Panel; Councillor, Chester City Council 1984-91

House of Commons: Contested Shropshire North 1983, Ellesmere Port and Neston 1987 general elections. Member for Warrington North since 1 May 1997 general election. *Political interests:* Education, Health

Recreations: Gardening, reading, cooking

Helen Jones, MP, House of Commons, London SW1A 0AA *Tel:* 020 7219 4048
E-mail: jonesh@parliament.uk. *Constituency:* Gilbert Wakefield House, 67 Bewsey Street, Warrington, Cheshire WA2 7JQ *Tel:* 01925 232480 *Fax:* 01925 232239

Lab majority 16,781

JONES, KEVAN
Durham North

Kevan Jones. Born 25 April 1964; Educated Portland Comprehensive, Worksop, Nottinghamshire; Newcastle upon Tyne Polytechnic (BA government and public policy); GMB: Political officer 1989-2001, Regional organiser 1992-99, Senior organiser 1999-2001; Newcastle City Council 1990-2001: Councillor, Former deputy leader, Group Council Cabinet member for Development, Chief whip, Chair: Public Health, Development and Transport

House of Commons: Member for Durham North since 7 June 2001 general election. *Political interests:* Regeneration, Transport, Employment, Regional Policy, Local and Regional Government, Defence

Parliamentary assistant N H Brown MP 1985-89; Northern Region Labour Party: Chair 1998-2000, Vice-chair 2000-. Member European Cities Environment Committee 1994-99; *Clubs:* Sacriston Workingmens Club; *Recreations:* Golf

Kevan Jones, MP, House of Commons, London SW1A 0AA *Tel:* 020 7219 8219
E-mail: kevanjonesmp@parliament.uk. *Constituency:* Co-operative Buildings, Plawsworth Road, Sacriston, Durham *Tel:* 0191 371 8834 *Fax:* 0191 371 8834

JONES, LYNNE
Birmingham Selly Oak

Lynne Jones. Born 26 April 1951; Daughter of late Stanley Stockton and of Jean Stockton; Educated Bartley Green Girls' Grammar School; Birmingham University (BSc 1972, PhD biochemistry 1979); Birmingham Polytechnic (Postgraduate diploma in housing studies 1987); Married (2 sons). Biochemistry research fellow, Birmingham University 1972-86; Housing association manager 1987-92; Member, MSF; Birmingham City Councillor 1980-94, Chair, Housing Committee 1984-87

Lab majority 8,851

House of Commons: Member for Birmingham Selly Oak since 9 April 1992 general election. *Political interests:* Economic Policy, Science, Social Security, Housing, Mental Health. Mozambique, Columbia

Oxfam; *Publications:* Regular columns in *Roof* magazine, Pensions Management; Contributions to: *Tribune*, Campaign Group News (available via own website); Spectator "Backbencher to Watch" 1998; *Recreations:* Family, cycling

Dr Lynne Jones, MP, House of Commons, London SW1A 0AA *Tel:* 020 7219 4190 *Fax:* 020 7219 3870 *E-mail:* jonesl@parliament.uk. *Constituency:* The Cotteridge Church, 24 Pershore Road South, Birmingham, West Midlands B30 3AS *Tel:* 0121-486 2808 *Fax:* 0121-486 2808

JONES, MARTYN
Clwyd South

Martyn Jones. Born 1 March 1947; Son of Vernon, engine driver, and Violet Jones; Educated Grove Park Grammar School, Wrexham; Liverpool College of Commerce; Liverpool Polytechnic (HND applied biology) 1966-67; Trent Polytechnic (MIBiol) 1968-69; Married Rhona Bellis 1974 (divorced 1991) (1 son 1 daughter). Microbiologist, Wrexham Lager Beer Co. 1969-June 1987; Member, TGWU 1974-; Vice-Chair, TGWU Parliamentary Group 2000-01; Chair TGWU Parliamentary Group 2001-02; Councillor, Clwyd County Council 1981-89

Lab majority 6,348

House of Commons: Member for Clwyd South West 1987-97, and for Clwyd South since 1 May 1997 general election; Opposition Spokesperson for Food, Agricultural and Rural Affairs 1994-95; Opposition Whip 1988-92. *Political interests:* Science, Ecology, Agriculture. Wales, Spain, USA

Chair, Clwyd County Party 1979-81; Member: Christian Socialist Movement, Socialist Environment and Resources Association, Fabian Society. Council Member: Royal College of Veterinary Surgeons, National Rifle Association; Vice-President, Federation of Economic Development Authorities (FEDA); *Recreations:* Backpacking, first aid, target shooting

Martyn Jones, MP, House of Commons, London SW1A 0AA *Tel:* 020 7219 3417 *Fax:* 020 7219 2815 *E-mail:* jonesst@parliament.uk. *Constituency:* Foundry Buildings, Gutter Hill, Johnstown, Wrexham, Clwyd LL4 1LU *Tel:* 01978 845938 *Fax:* 01978 843392

Complete post-election analysis

JOWELL, TESSA
Dulwich and West Norwood

Tessa Jowell. Born 17 September 1947; Daughter of Dr. Kenneth Palmer, and of Rosemary Palmer, radiographer; Educated St Margaret's School, Aberdeen; Aberdeen (MA), Edinburgh University; Goldsmith's College, London University; Married Roger Jowell 1970 (divorced 1977); married David Mills 1979 (1 son 1 daughter, 3 stepchildren). Child care officer, London Borough of Lambeth 1969-71; Psychiatric social worker, Maudsley Hospital 1972-74; Assistant director, MIND 1974-86; Director: Community care special action project, Birmingham 1987-90, Joseph Rowntree Foundation, Community Care Programme 1990-92; Senior visiting research fellow: Policy Studies Institute 1987-90, King's Fund Institute 1990-92; Member: TGWU, MSF; Councillor, London Borough of Camden 1971-86; Vice-Chair, then Chair, Social Services Committee of Association of Metropolitan Authorities 1978-86; Mental Health Act Commission 1985-90; Chair, Millennium Commission

Lab majority 8,807

House of Commons: Contested Ilford North 1978 by-election and 1979 general election. Member for Dulwich 1992-97, and for Dulwich and West Norwood since 1 May 1997 general election; Frontbench Opposition Spokesperson on: Women 1995-96, Health 1994-95, 1996-97; Opposition Whip 1994-95; Minister of State: Department of Health (Minister for Public Health) 1997-99, Department for Education and Employment (Minister for Employment, Welfare to Work and Equal Opportunities) 1999-2001; Minister for Women 1999-2001; Secretary of State for Culture, Media and Sport 2001-. *Political interests:* Italy

Homestart; Member: Central Council for Training and Education in Social Work 1983-89; Trustee Amelia Ward Prize Fund; *Publications:* Various articles on social policy; PC 1998; Visiting Fellow, Nuffield College, Oxford 1993-2003; *Recreations:* Gardening, family, reading

Rt Hon Tessa Jowell, MP, House of Commons, London SW1A 0AA
Tel: 020 7219 3409 *Fax:* 020 7219 2702 *E-mail:* jowellt@parliament.uk.
Constituency: 264 Rosendale Road, London SE24 9DL *Tel:* 020 8333 1372

JOYCE, ERIC
Falkirk

Eric Joyce. Born 13 October 1960; Son of late Leslie Robert Joyce and Sheila McKay, née Christie; Educated Perth Academy; Royal Military Academy, Sandhurst; Stirling University: (BA religious studies 1986); Bath University (MA education 1994); Keele University (MBA education 1995); Married Rosemary Jones 1991 (twin daughters). Private, Black Watch Regiment 1978-81; Officer 1987-99. Commission for Racial Equality 1999-2000; Member UNISON

Lab majority 13,475

House of Commons: Member for Falkirk West 2000-05, for Falkirk since 5 May 2005 general election; PPS to Mike O'Brien as Minister of State: Foreign and Commonwealth Office 2003-04, Department of Trade and Industry 2004-. *Political interests:* Foreign Affairs, International Development (especially Education Issues), Defence, Trade and Industry (especially Oil and Gas, GM Crops), Higher Education, Asylum and Immigration. Argentina, Turkey, USA, China

Executive Member, Fabian Society 1998-. *Publications: Arms and the Man – Renewing the Armed Services* (Fabian Society) 1997; *Now's the Hour: New Thinking for Holyrood* (Fabian Society) 1999; *Clubs:* Camelon Labour Club; *Recreations:* Climbing, judo, most sports

Eric Joyce, MP, House of Commons, London SW1A 0AA *Tel:* 020 7219 6210
Fax: 020 7219 2090 *E-mail:* ericjoycemp@parliament.uk. *Constituency:* The Studio, Burnfoot Lane, Falkirk FK1 5BH *Tel:* 01324 638919 *Fax:* 01324 679449,

They know violence against women is wrong....
now it is time to tell them what is right

Zero Tolerance
Making the Links with Gender Inequality

Find out more about Zero Tolerance educational interventions
www.zerotolerance.org.uk
t. 0131 221 9505
e. zerotolerance@btconnect.com

KAUFMAN, GERALD
Manchester Gorton

Gerald Bernard Kaufman. Born 21 June 1930; Son of Louis and Jane Kaufman; Educated Leeds Council Schools; Leeds Grammar School; The Queen's College, Oxford (MA philosophy, politics and economics 1953). Assistant general secretary, Fabian Society 1954-55; Political staff, *Daily Mirror* 1955-64; Political correspondent, *New Statesman* 1964-65; Parliamentary press liaison officer, Labour Party 1965-70; Member, GMB

Lab majority 5,808

House of Commons: Contested Bromley 1955 and Gillingham 1959 general elections. Member for Ardwick 1970-1983, and for Manchester Gorton since 9 June 1983 general election; Opposition Frontbench Spokesperson for the Environment 1979-80; Parliamentary Under-Secretary of State for the Environment 1974-75; Parliamentary Under-Secretary, Department of Industry 1975; Minister of State, Department of Industry 1975-79; Shadow Environment Secretary 1980-83; Shadow Home Secretary 1983-87; Shadow Foreign Secretary 1987-92

Member: Labour Party National Executive 1991-92, Fabian Society. Member, Royal Commission on Lords Reform February 1999-January 2000; *Publications:* Co-author, *How to Live Under Labour*, 1964; Editor, *The Left*, 1966; *To Build the Promised Land*, 1973; *How to Be a Minister*, 1980; Editor, *Renewal*, 1983; *My Life in the Silver Screen*, 1985; *Inside the Promised Land*, 1986; *Meet Me In St Louis*, 1994; *How to Be a Minister*, (updated and revised edition) 1997; PC 1978; Hilal-i-Pakistan 1999; Kt 2004; *Clubs:* President: Gorton and District Sunday Football League; *Recreations:* Cinema, theatre, opera, concerts, travel

Rt Hon Sir Gerald Kaufman, MP, House of Commons, London SW1A 0AA
Tel: 020 7219 5145 *Fax:* 020 7219 6825. *Constituency:* Gorton Sports and Social Club, Kirk Street, Manchester M18 8 *Tel:* 0161-248 0073 *Fax:* 0161-248 0073
E-mail: searsb@parliament.uk

KAWCZYNSKI, DANIEL
Shrewsbury and Atcham

Daniel Kawczynski. Born 24 January 1972; Educated St George's College, Weybridge; Stirling University (business studies with languages 1994); Married to Kate. Sales account manager telecommunications, BT, Cable & Wireless, Xerox
House of Commons: Contested Ealing Southall 2001 general election. Member for Shrewsbury and Atcham since 5 May 2005 general election

Con majority 1,808

Chairman Stirling University Conservative Association 1991. *Recreations:* Golf, tennis

Daniel Kawczynski, MP, House of Commons, London SW1A 0AA
Tel: 020 7219 6737. *Constituency:* Shrewsbury & Atcham West Conservative Association, Unit 1, Benbow Business Park, Harlescott Lane, Shrewsbury, Shropshire SY1 3FA *Tel:* 01743 465430 *E-mail:* DanielKawczynski@aol.com
Website: www.shrewsburyconservatives.org

KEEBLE, SALLY
Northampton North

Sally Keeble. Born 13 October 1951; Daughter of Sir Curtis Keeble, GCMG, and Lady Keeble; Educated Cheltenham Ladies' College; St Hugh's College, Oxford (BA theology 1973); University of South Africa (BA sociology 1981); Married Andrew Hilary Porter 1990 (1 son 1 daughter). Journalist: *Daily News*, Durban, South Africa 1973-79, *Birmingham Post* 1978-83; Press officer, Labour Headquarters 1983-84; Assistant director, External Relations, ILEA 1984-86; Head of communications, GMB 1986-90; Public affairs consultant 1995-97; Member: National Union of Journalists; Councillor, Southwark Council 1986-94, Leader 1990-93

Lab majority 3,960

House of Commons: Member for Northampton North since 1 May 1997 general election; PPS to Hilary Armstrong as Minister of State, Department of the Environment, Transport and the Regions (Minister for Local Government and Regions) 1999-2001; Parliamentary Under-Secretary of State: Department for Transport, Local Government and the Regions 2001-02, Department for International Development 2002-03. *Political interests:* Economic Policy, Home Affairs, Education, Local and Regional Government, Financial Services. North Africa, South Africa, USA

Publications: Citizens Look At Congress Profiles, 1971; *Flat Broke*, 1984; *Collectors Corner*, 1986; *Feminism, Infertility and New Reproductive Technologies*, 1994; *Conceiving Your Baby, How Medicine Can Help*, 1995; Honorary Fellow, South Bank University; *Recreations:* Antiques, walking, writing

Sally Keeble, MP, House of Commons, London SW1A 0AA *Tel:* 020 7219 4039 *Fax:* 020 7219 2642 *E-mail:* keebles@parliament.uk. *Constituency:* Unit 5, Barratt Building, Kingsthorpe Road, Northampton, Northamptonshire NN2 6EZ *Tel:* 01604 716275 *Fax:* 01604 716952

KEELEY, BARBARA
Worsley

Barbara Mary Keeley. Educated Mount St Mary's RC College, Leeds; Salford University (BSc politics and contemporary history); Married to Colin Huggett; GMB; Trafford Borough councillor 1995-2004

House of Commons: Member for Worsley since 5 May 2005 general election

Recreations: Jogging, swimming, keep fit, live music

Lab majority 9,368

Barbara Keeley, MP, House of Commons, London SW1A 0AA *Tel:* 020 7219 8025. *Constituency:* Worsley Labour Party, Emlyn Hall, Emlyn Street, Worsley M28 3JZ *E-mail:* barbara.keeley@btopenworld.com *Website:* www.barbarakeeley.co.uk

KEEN, ALAN
Feltham and Heston

Alan Keen. Born 25 November 1937; Son of late Jack and Gladys Keen; Educated St William Turner's School, Redcar, Cleveland; Married Ann Fox 1980 (now MP as Ann Keen) (2 sons 1 daughter). Part-time tactical scout (assessing opposition tactics) Middlesbrough FC 1967-85; Miscellaneous positions in private industry and commerce, mainly in the fire protection industry 1963-92; Member, GMB; Councillor, London Borough of Hounslow 1986-90

Lab/Co-op majority 6,820

House of Commons: Member for Feltham and Heston since 9 April 1992 general election. *Political interests:* Commerce, Industry, Foreign Affairs, Development, Democracy, Defence, Sport, Culture

Co-operative Party MPs 1992-; Secretary, Labour First Past the Post Group 1997-. Amnesty International, Shooting Star Trust; *Clubs:* Feltham Labour, Heston Catholic Social, Hanworth British Legion; *Recreations:* Playing and listening to music, Association football, athletics, cricket, jazz enthusiast

Alan Keen, MP, House of Commons, London SW1A 0AA *Tel:* 020 7219 2819 *Fax:* 020 7219 0985 *E-mail:* alankeenmp@parliament.uk. *Constituency:* Labour Party Office, Manor Place, Feltham TW14 9BT *Tel:* 020 8890 4489 *Fax:* 020 8893 2606

KEEN, ANN
Brentford and Isleworth

Ann Keen. Born 26 November 1948; Daughter of late John Fox, and of Ruby Fox; Educated Elfed Secondary Modern, Clwyd; Surrey University (PGCEA); Married Alan Keen (now MP) 1980 (2 sons 1 daughter). Registered Nurse 1976; Head, Faculty of Advanced Nursing, Queen Charlotte's College, Hammersmith 1992; General Secretary, Community and District Nursing Association 1994; Member, GMB

Lab majority 4,411

House of Commons: Contested Brentford and Isleworth 1987 and 1992 general elections. Member for Brentford and Isleworth since 1 May 1997 general election; PPS to: Frank Dobson as: Secretary of State for Health 1999, at HM Treasury 2000-01, Gordon Brown as Chancellor of the Exchequer 2001-. *Political interests:* Health, Child Poverty, International Development. South Africa, Cyprus

Hon. Professor of Nursing, Thames Valley University; CancerBACUP Paliamentary Figure of the Year; Fellowship Queen's Institute 2004; *Clubs:* Ewloe Social and Working Men's; Nurse/Physiotherapist, the House of Commons' Football Team; *Recreations:* Theatre, music, football

Ann Keen, MP, House of Commons, London SW1A 0AA *Tel:* 020 7219 5623 *Fax:* 020 7219 2233 *E-mail:* annkeenmp@parliament.uk. *Constituency:* Brentford and Isleworth Labour Party, 367 Chiswick High Road, London W4 4AG *Tel:* 020 8995 7289 *Fax:* 020 8742 1004

KEETCH, PAUL
Hereford

Paul Stuart Keetch. Born 21 May 1961; Son of late John Norton, engineer, and late Agnes (neé Hughes); Educated Hereford High School for Boys; Hereford Sixth Form College; Married Claire Elizabeth Baker 1991 (1 son). Self-employed business consultant 1979-95; Non-executive director, London Computer Company 1996-; Councillor, Hereford City Council 1983-86

Lib Dem majority 962

House of Commons: Member for Hereford since 1 May 1997 general election; Spokesperson for: Health 1997, Education and Employment (Employment and Training) 1997-99; Liberal Democrat Shadow Secretary of State for Defence 1999-2005. *Political interests:* National Heritage, Defence, Foreign Affairs. Former Soviet Union, Eastern Bloc countries, Eastern Europe

Joined Liberal Party 1975; Member Liberal Democrat Federal Executive Committee 2001-. NSPCC; OSCE Observer, Albanian Elections 1996; Adviser, Lithuanian Local and National Elections 1995, 1996; Member, Council of The Electoral Reform Society; *Clubs:* Hereford Liberal, Herefordshire Farmers', National Liberal; Herefordshire County Cricket Club; *Recreations:* Cricket (watching), swimming, entertaining friends at home, country walks with my wife and son

Paul Keetch, MP, House of Commons, London SW1A 0AA *Tel:* 020 7219 5163 *Fax:* 020 7219 1184 *E-mail:* paulkeetch@cix.co.uk. *Constituency:* 39 Widemarsh Street, Hereford, Hereford & Worcester HR4 9EA *Tel:* 01432 341483 *Fax:* 01432 378111

KELLY, RUTH
Bolton West

Ruth Maria Kelly. Born 9 May 1968; Daughter of Bernard James Kelly, pharmacist, and Gertrude Anne Kelly, teacher; Educated Sutton High School; Westminster School; Queen's College, Oxford (BA philosophy, politics and economics 1989); London School of Economics (MSc economics 1992); Married Derek John Gadd 1996 (1 son 3 daughters). Economics writer, *The Guardian* 1990-94; Deputy head, Inflation Report Division, Bank of England 1994-97; Member, MSF

Lab majority 2,064

House of Commons: Member for Bolton West since 1 May 1997 general election; PPS to Nick Brown as Minister of Agriculture, Fisheries and Food 1998-2001; HM Treasury 2001-04: Economic Secretary 2001-02, Financial Secretary 2002-04; Minister for the Cabinet Office 2004; Secretary of State for Education and Skills 2004-. *Political interests:* Economic Policy, European Affairs, Social Policy, Welfare Reform, Employment, Families. France, Spain

Bethnal Green and Stepney/Bow Constituency Labour Party: Treasurer 1994-96, Ward Secretary 1994-96; Bolton West Constituency Labour Party. *Publications:* Various Pamphlets on Finance and Taxation and family policy; PC 2004; *Recreations:* Walking, writing

Rt Hon Ruth Kelly, MP, House of Commons, London SW1A 0AA *Tel:* 020 7219 3496 *Fax:* 020 7219 2211 *E-mail:* kellyr@parliament.uk. *Constituency:* Studio 4, Horwich Business Centre, 86 Lee Lane, Horwich, Bolton, Greater Manchester BL7 7AE *Tel:* 01204 693351 *Fax:* 01204 693383

RECOGNISING ACHIEVEMENT

OCR is one of the UK's leading examination boards which creates, designs and delivers all types of general and vocational qualifications.

If you want to know anything about:

- the design, construction and assessment of
    GCSEs
    VCEs
    A Levels
    Nationals
    GNVQs, NVQs
    Work-Related Learning
    Industry-leading IT Qualifications such as CLAiT and iPRO
    any other vocational qualifications

- the place of qualifications in the education system

- how examinations, tests and other assessments work

feel free to phone, write or email:

Bene't Steinberg, Group Director of Public Affairs,
1 Regent Street, Cambridge CB2 1GG
Tel: 01223 556003
steinberg.b@ucles.org.uk

www.ocr.org.uk

KEMP, FRASER
Houghton and Washington East

Fraser Kemp. Born 1 September 1958; Son of William and Mary Kemp; Educated Washington Comprehensive; Married Patricia Mary Byrne 1989 (divorced) (2 sons 1 daughter). Civil servant 1975-81; Full-time branch secretary CPSA 1975-80; Member: GMB, AEEU

Lab majority 16,065

House of Commons: Member for Houghton and Washington East since 1 May 1997 general election; Assistant Government Whip 2001-05. *Political interests:* Technology, Motor Industry, Small Businesses. Australia

Full-time Labour Party organiser, Leicester 1981-84; Assistant regional organiser, East Midlands 1984-86; Regional secretary, West Midlands 1986-94; Secretary: National Annual Labour Party Conference Arrangements Committee 1993-96, Labour's National General Election Planning Group 1994-96; National Labour Party general election co-ordinator 1994-96; Secretary, Labour's NEC Campaigns and Elections Committee 1995-96. Patron, The Friends of Houghton Parish Church Trust; Member, Beamish Development Trust (North of England Open Air Museum); *Clubs:* Usworth and District Workmens and Institute (Washington); Hetton; Member, Houghton and Peterlee Athletics Club; *Recreations:* People

Fraser Kemp, MP, House of Commons, London SW1A 0AA *Tel:* 020 7219 5181 *Fax:* 020 7219 2536 *E-mail:* kempf@parliament.uk. *Constituency:* 14 Nesham Place, Church Street, Houghton-Le-Spring, Tyne and Wear DH5 8AG *Tel:* 0191-584 9266 *Fax:* 0191-584 8329

KENNEDY, CHARLES
Ross, Skye and Lochaber

Charles Peter Kennedy. Born 25 November 1959; Son of Ian Kennedy, crofter and Mary MacVarish MacEachen; Educated Lochaber High School, Fort William; Glasgow University (MA politics, philosophy and English 1982); Indiana University (1982-83); Married Sarah Gurling 2002. President, Glasgow University Union 1980-81; Winner, British Observer Mace Debating Tournament 1982; Journalist with BBC Highland, at Inverness 1982

Lib Dem majority 14,249

House of Commons: Member for Ross, Cromarty and Skye 1983-97, for Ross, Skye and Inverness West 1997-2005, for Ross, Skye and Lochaber since 5 May 2005 general election; Alliance Spokesman for Social Security 1987; SDP Spokesman for: Scotland and Social Security 1987-88, Trade and Industry 1988-89; Liberal Democrat Spokesman for: Health 1989-92, European Union Affairs 1992-97, Agriculture, Fisheries, Food and Rural Affairs 1997-99; Leader, Liberal Democrat Party 1999-. *Political interests:* Scotland, Social Policy, Broadcasting, European Union

Chair Glasgow University Social Democratic Club 1979-80; President Liberal Democrat Party 1990-94; Member Liberal Democrat: Federal Executive Committee, Policy Committee. Highland Hospice; Associate Member, Scottish Crofters Union;; *Publications: The Future of Politics,* 2000; *PC* 1999; *The Spectator* Member to Watch Award 1989; Channel 4 and *The House* Magazine, Political Humourist of the Year Award 1999; Doctorate Glasgow University 2001; *Clubs:* National Liberal; *Recreations:* Reading, writing, music, swimming, golf, journalism, broadcasting

Rt Hon Charles Kennedy, MP, House of Commons, London SW1A 0AA *Tel:* 020 7219 6226 *Fax:* 020 7219 4881 *E-mail:* rossldp@cix.co.uk. *Constituency:* 1a Montague Row, Inverness IV3 5DX *Tel:* 01463 714377 *Fax:* 01463 714380

KENNEDY, JANE
Liverpool Wavertree

Jane Kennedy. Born 4 May 1958; Daughter of Clifford Hodgson, engineer, and of Barbara Hodgson; Educated Haughton School, Darlington; Queen Elizabeth Sixth Form College; Liverpool University; Married Malcolm Kennedy 1977 (divorced 1998) (2 sons). Residential child care officer, Liverpool City Council (LCC) 1979-83; Care assistant, LCC Social Services 1983-88; Branch Secretary, NUPE 1983-88, Area Organiser 1988-92

Lab majority 5,173

House of Commons: Member for Liverpool Broadgreen 1992-97, and for Liverpool Wavertree since 1 May 1997 general election; Opposition Whip 1995-97; Assistant Government Whip 1997-98; Government Whip 1998-99; Parliamentary Secretary, Lord Chancellor's Department 1999-2001; Minister of State: Northern Ireland Office 2001-04, Department for Work and Pensions 2004-05, Department of Health 2005-. *Political interests:* Local and Regional Government, Public Services, Social Security, Foreign Affairs. Middle East and South East Asia

Chair, Labour Friends of Israel 1997-98. Oxfam; Fellow, Industry and Parliament Trust; PC 2003; *Recreations:* Walking, training Belgian Shepherd dogs, horse-riding

Rt Hon Jane Kennedy, MP, House of Commons, London SW1A 0AA *Tel:* 020 7219 4523 *E-mail:* jane.kennedy@parliament.uk. *Constituency:* 1st Floor, Threlfall Building, Trueman Street, Liverpool L3 2EX *Tel:* 0151-236 1117 *Fax:* 0151-236 0067

How would YOU cope with the loss of your sight?

There are two million people in the UK with sight problems. Many are unable to do the things most sighted people take for granted, such as shopping, going to work, meeting friends – all because they have not been given the right skills needed for living with sight loss.

These skills can only be obtained through appropriate rehabilitation training. However …

- 20% of local authorities do not provide any rehabilitation services at all.

- 30% of rehabilitation workers operating in the UK do not hold the necessary level of qualifications.

- UK-wide, there is a systemic shortfall of 800 rehabilitation workers.

What do we want Government to do about it?

- Introduce short-term measures to cover the shortfall in qualified rehabilitation workers.

- Undertake a strategic review of the provision of care services for visually impaired people.

- Commit to investing the necessary resources, ensuring that in future, blind and partially sighted people are guaranteed the right to independent living.

For further information about Guide Dogs' campaigning
tel 0118 983 8304 • **visit** www.guidedogs.org.uk
email rebecca.atherton@guidedogs.org.uk
Registered Charity No. 209617

Guide Dogs

Con majority 11,142

KEY, ROBERT
Salisbury

(Simon) Robert Key. Born 22 April 1945; Son of late Rt Rev. Maurice Key, former Bishop of Truro; Educated Salisbury Cathedral School; Sherborne School; Clare College, Cambridge (BA economics 1966, MA, CertEd 1967); Married Susan Priscilla Bright, née Irvine 1968 (1 son 2 daughters). Assistant master: Loretto School, Edinburgh 1967-69, Harrow School (economics department) 1969-83; Member, then Associate member, Association of Teachers and Lecturers 1967-; Vice-Chair, Wembley Branch ASTMS 1975-80

House of Commons: Contested Camden, Holborn and St Pancras South 1979 general election. Member for Salisbury since 9 June 1983 general election; Opposition Spokesperson for: Defence 1997-2001, Trade and Industry 2001-02, International Development 2002-03; Political Secretary to Edward Heath 1984-85; PPS: to Alick Buchanan-Smith as Minister of State for Energy 1985-87, to Christopher Patten: as Minister for Overseas Development 1987-89, as Secretary of State for the Environment 1989-90; Parliamentary Under-Secretary of State: at Department of the Environment 1990-92, at Department of National Heritage 1992-93 at Department of Transport (Minister for Roads and Traffic) 1993-94; Shadow Minister for: International Development 2002-03, Economic Affairs and for Environment and Transport 2004-. *Political interests:* Education, Arts, Foreign Affairs, Defence, Agriculture. France, Turkey, USA

Treasurer, Conservative Candidates' Association 1976-79; Chair, Harrow Central Conservative Association 1980-82; Vice-Chair, London Central Euro-Constituency 1980-82; Member: Conservative Party National Advisory Committee on Education 1979-82, Executive Committee National Union of Conservative Party 1980-83. Member: UK National Commission for UNESCO 1984-85, Medical Research Council 1989-90; Member, Executive Council, Inter Parliamentary Union British Branch 1986-90; Chair, Council for Education in the Commonwealth 1985-87; Substitute, UK Delegation to Council of Europe and Western Europe Union 1996-97; Founding Chairman, the Alice Trust for Autistic Children 1977-80; Council Member, Winston Churchill Memorial Trust 2004-; *Publications: Reforming our Schools,* 1988; *Clubs:* Garrick; *Recreations:* Singing, cooking, countryside

Robert Key, MP, House of Commons, London SW1A 0AA   *Tel:* 020 7219 6501 *Fax:* 020 7219 4865 *E-mail:* rob@robertkey.com. *Constituency:* The Morrison Hall, 12 Brown Street, Salisbury, Wiltshire SP1 1HE *Tel:* 01722 323050 *Fax:* 01722 327080 *Website:* www.salisburyconservatives.org

KHABRA, PIARA
Ealing Southall

Piara Singh Khabra. Born 20 November 1924; Educated Khalsa High School, Mahilpur, Punjab, India; Punjab University (BA social sciences 1951, BEd); Whitelands College, Putney (Diploma in Teaching 1968); Married Beulah Marian. Served Indian Armed Corps 1942-46. Clerical work, British Oxygen 1964-66; Class Teacher for Children aged 7-11, ILEA 1968-80; Community worker 1981-91; Chairman, Ealing law centre 1983-90; Member, MSF; Councillor, London Borough of Ealing 1978-82; JP 1977-

Lab majority 11,440

House of Commons: Member for Ealing Southall since 9 April 1992 general election. *Political interests:* Employment, Education, Race Relations, European Union, International Development. India

Member Quadripartite Committee 2000-2001; Member, Rajiv Ghandi Foundation; *Recreations:* Reading, watching football

Piara Khabra, MP, House of Commons, London SW1A 0AA *Tel:* 020 7219 5010; 020 7219 5918 *Fax:* 020 7219 5699 *E-mail:* miksj@parliament.uk. *Constituency:* 49-B The Broad Way, Southall UB1 1JY *Tel:* 020 8571 1003 *Fax:* 020 8571 1003

KHAN, SADIQ
Tooting

Sadiq Khan. Born 18 August 1970; Educated Ernest Bevin Secondary Comprehensive, London; North London University (LLB law 1992); College of Law (Law Society finals 1993); Married Saadiya Ahmad 1994. Christian Fisher Solicitors: Trainee solicitor 1993-95, Solicitor 1995-98, Partner 1998-2000; Equity partner Christian Fisher Khan Solicitors 2000-02; Equity partner and co-founder Christian Khan Solicitors 2002-04; Visiting lecturer University of North London and London Metropolitan University 1998-2004; Member: Amicus, UNISON, CWU; Wandsworth Borough Council: Councillor 1994-, Deputy leader Labour group 1996-2001; Governor Fircroft primary school

Lab majority 5,381

House of Commons: Member for Tooting since 5 May 2005 general election. *Political interests:* Social justice, crime, international affairs, public services

Founder Human Rights Lawyers Association; *Publications: Challenging Racism*, Lawrence and Wishart 2003*Police Misconduct (Legal Remedies)*, Legal Action Group 2005; Articles in various publications on legal matters; *Recreations:* Playing and watching sports, cinema, family, friends, local community

Sadiq Khan, MP, House of Commons, London SW1A 0AA *Tel:* 020 7219 6967. *Constituency:* Wandsworth Asian Centre, 57-59 Trinity Road, Tooting Bec, London SW17 7SD *Tel:* 020 8767 9660 *Fax:* 020 8772 4593 *E-mail:* tooting@email.org.uk *Website:* www.labourwandsworth.org.uk

KIDNEY, DAVID
Stafford

David Neil Kidney. Born 21 March 1955; Son of late Neil Bernard and Doris Kidney; Educated Longton High School; Sixth Form College, Stoke-on-Trent; Bristol University (LLB law 1976); Married Elaine Dickinson 1978 (1 son 1 daughter). Solicitor: Hanley, Stoke-on-Trent 1977-79, Stafford 1979-97; Member, MSF (now "AMICUS"); Councillor Stafford Borough Council 1987-97

Lab majority 2,121

House of Commons: Member for Stafford since 1 May 1997 general election; Team Parliamentary Private Secretary to Ministers of State, Department for Environment, Food and Rural Affairs 2002-03. *Political interests:* Children, Housing, Environment. Britain

Member, Society of Labour Lawyers. Bethany Project for Homeless; ASIST (Citizen Advocacy); Care Association South Staffordshire; Fellow, Industry and Parliament Trust; *Recreations:* Chess, bridge

David Kidney, MP, House of Commons, London SW1A 0AA *Tel:* 020 7219 6472 *Fax:* 020 7219 0919 *E-mail:* kidneyd@parliament.uk. *Constituency:* 1 Friars Terrace, Stafford ST17 4AU *Tel:* 01785 224444 *Fax:* 01785 250357 *Website:* www.staffordlab.freeserve.co.uk

KILFOYLE, PETER
Liverpool Walton

Peter Kilfoyle. Born 9 June 1946; Son of late Edward and Ellen Kilfoyle; Educated St Edward's College, Liverpool; Durham University; Christ's College, Liverpool; Married Bernadette Slater 1968 (2 sons 3 daughters). Labourer 1965-70, 1973-75; Student 1970-73; Teacher 1975-85; Member AMICUS

Lab majority 15,957

House of Commons: Member for Liverpool Walton since 4 July 1991 by-election; Opposition Spokesperson for: Education 1994-96, Education and Employment 1996-97; Opposition Whip 1992-94; Parliamentary Secretary: Office of Public Service 1997-98, Cabinet Office 1998-99; Parliamentary Under-Secretary of State, Ministry of Defence 1999-2000. *Political interests:* Foreign Affairs, Commonwealth, Employment, Education. Australia, Latin America, The Commonwealth

Labour Party organiser 1986-91. *Publications: Left Behind: Lessons from Labour's Heartlands* (Politico's), 2000; *Recreations:* Reading, music, spectator sport

Peter Kilfoyle, MP, House of Commons, London SW1A 0AA *Tel:* 020 7219 2591 *Fax:* 020 7219 2356 *E-mail:* kilfoylep@parliament.uk. *Constituency:* 69/71 County Road, Walton, Liverpool L4 3QD *Tel:* 0151-284 4150 *Fax:* 0151-284 4150

KIRKBRIDE, JULIE
Bromsgrove

Con majority 10,080

Julie Kirkbride. Born 5 June 1960; Daughter of late Henry Raymond Kirkbride and Barbara Kirkbride (neé Bancroft); Educated Highlands School, Halifax; Girton College, Cambridge (BA economics and history 1981, MA); Graduate School of Journalism, University of California 1982-83; Married Andrew Mackay MP 1997 (1 son). Researcher, Yorkshire Television 1983-86; Producer, BBC News and Current Affairs 1986-89; ITN 1989-92; Political correspondent, *Daily Telegraph* 1992-96; Social affairs editor, *Sunday Telegraph* 1996

House of Commons: Member for Bromsgrove since 1 May 1997 general election; Shadow Secretary of State for Culture, Media and Sport 2003-04. *Political interests:* Taxation, European Union, Social Security, Law and Order, Health

Vice-President, The Cambridge Union Society 1981. International Republican Institute Lecturer in Romania 1995; Member, Executive Committee: Commonwealth Parliamentary Association (CPA) UK Branch 1999-, Inter-Parliamentary Union 2001-; Rotary Foundation Scholar 1982-83; *Recreations:* Walking, opera

Julie Kirkbride, MP, House of Commons, London SW1A 0AA *Tel:* 020 7219 6417. *Constituency:* Conservative Association, 37 Worcester Road, Bromsgrove, Hereford & Worcester *Tel:* 01527 872135 *Fax:* 01527 575019 *E-mail:* office@bromsgrove-conservatives.org.uk

KNIGHT, GREG
Yorkshire East

Con majority 6,283

Greg (Gregory) Knight. Born 4 April 1949; Son of Albert George Knight, company director, and Isabel, née Bell; Educated Alderman Newton's Grammar School, Leicester; College of Law, London; College of Law, Guildford. Solicitor 1973-89, 1997-; Business consultant 1997-2001; Councillor Leicester City Council 1976-79; Leicestershire County Council 1977-83, Councillor, Chair: Haymarket Theatre Finance Committee 1979, Public Protection Committee 1981

House of Commons: Member for Derby North 1983-97. Contested Derby North 1997 general election. Member for Yorkshire East since 7 June 2001 general election; Assistant Government Whip 1989-90; Government Whip 1990-93; Government Deputy Chief Whip 1993-96; PPS to David Mellor QC: as Minister of State Foreign Office 1987-88, as Minister of State Health 1988-89; Minister of State Department of Trade and Industry 1996-97; Deputy Shadow Leader of the House 2002-03; Shadow Minister for: Culture, Media and Sport 2003, Environment and Transport 2003-. *Political interests:* Consumer Issues, Information Technology, Music, Arts, Home Affairs. USA

Chair: South Leicester Young Conservatives 1970-72, Leicester and Leicestershire Young Conservatives 1972-73; Vice-chair Conservative Parliamentary Candidates Association 1997-2001. Executive Committee Member, British-American Parliamentary Group 2001-; *Publications:* Co-author *Westminster Words* 1988; *Honourable Insults* 1990; *Parliamentary Sauce* 1993; *Right Honourable Insults* 1998; PC 1995; *Clubs:* Bridlington Conservative; *Recreations:* Classic and vintage cars, music

Rt Hon Greg Knight, MP, House of Commons, London SW1A 0AA *Tel:* 020 7219 8417 *E-mail:* secretary@gregknight.com. *Constituency:* 3 Tennyson Avenue, Bridlington YO15 2EU *Tel:* 01262 674074 *Website:* www.eyorksconservatives.com

Lab majority 1,812

KNIGHT, JIM
South Dorset

Jim Knight. Born 6 March 1965; Son of Philip John Knight, accountant and Hilary Jean Howlett, neé Harper, craftswoman; Educated Eltham College, London; Fitzwilliam College, Cambridge (BA geography, social and political sciences 1987); Married Anna Wheatley 1989 (1 daughter 1 son). Manager Central Studio Basingstoke 1988-90; Director: West Wiltshire Arts Centre Ltd 1990-91, Dentons Directories Ltd 1991-2001; Contested South West Region 1999 European Parliament election; MSF 1995-: Branch chair 1997-2001; AEEU 1998-; GMB 2001-; Frome Town Council: Councillor 1993-2001, Mayor 1998-2001; Mendip District Council: Councillor 1997-2001, Deputy leader 1999-2001, Labour group leader 1999-2001

House of Commons: Contested South Dorset 1997 general election. Member for South Dorset since 7 June 2001 general election; PPS at Department of Health 2003-05: to Rosie Winterton as Minister of State 2003-04, Team PPS 2004-05; Parliamentary Under-Secretary of State, Department for Environment, Food and Rural Affairs 2005-. *Political interests:* Foreign Policy, International Development, Families, Arts, Sport. Iran, Iraq, Taiwan, Turkey

Various posts Local constituency party 1990-. *Recreations:* Football, tennis, cooking, cycling

Jim Knight, MP, House of Commons, London SW1A 0AA *Tel:* 020 7219 8466 *Fax:* 020 7219 1976 *E-mail:* jimknightmp@parliament.uk. *Constituency:* 42 Southview Road, Weymouth, Dorset DT4 0JD *Tel:* 01305 759401

Lib Dem majority 3,731

KRAMER, SUSAN
Richmond Park

Susan Kramer. Born 21 July 1950; Educated St Paul's Girls' School, Hammersmith; St Hilda's College, Oxford (BA philosophy, politics and economics 1972 MA); Illinois University, USA (MBA business/finance 1982); Married John Davis Kramer 1972. Staff associate National Academy of Engineering 1972-73; Second vice-president Continental Bank, USA 1982-88; Vice-president corporate finance Citibank/Citicorp, USA 1988-92; Chief operating officer Future Water International 1992-95; Partner Kramer and Associates 1995-99; Board member CAIB Infrastructure Project Advisers 1997-99; Director: Infrastructure Capital Partners Ltd 1999-, Speciality Scanners Plc 2001-

House of Commons: Contested Dulwich and West Norwood 1997 general election. Member for Richmond Park since 5 May 2005 general election. *Political interests:* Environment, finance, transport

Chair Twickenham and Richmond Liberal Democrats 2001-02; Member: Women Liberal Democrats executive 1997-2000, London regiona executive 1997-2003, Liberal Democrat federal executive 2001-04. Vice-president Eve Appeal (ovarian cancer charity) 2003-; Contested London region 1999 European Parliament election and London mayoral election 2000; *Publications: Orange Book* chapter 'Harnessing the Markets to Achieve Environmental Goals', Profile Books 2004; *Clubs:* National Liberal; London Capital; *Recreations:* Dog walking, opera, theatre, reading, rowing

Susan Kramer, MP, House of Commons, London SW1A 0AA *Tel:* 020 7219 6531. *Constituency:* The Old Station Works, 119-123 Sandycombe Rd, Richmond TW9 2ER *Tel:* 020 8940 2994 *Fax:* 020 8940 2994 *E-mail:* susankramerppc:yahoo.co.uk *Website:* www.susankramer.org.uk

Nothing Works in Isolation

What a brilliant job UK livestock farmers have made of manufacturing the beautiful countryside which we all love and cherish.

I say UK farmers, but I should be more precise and lay much of the credit at the door of the sheep and cattle that have achieved this as a consequence of their daily activity. As with all the best things in life the product – the countryside, has been manufactured through a simplistic process – managed grazing – but behind that lies a complex balance of factors that, combined in the right proportions, work miracles but when isolated are ineffectual and weak.

What are the ingredients that make the recipe for a beautiful countryside? Firstly you need the tools to do the job – sheep and some cattle. For the livestock to be present they have to be economically viable for the person charged with their care. They also need to be kept healthy, which requires skill and experience and to be part of a tight management system – systems not learnt in a text book but enshrined in a mentality which has an instinctive understanding of livestock, flora and fauna.

So there we have it; for beautiful countryside you need the right mixture of healthy, economically viable livestock and skilled people in rural communities that are willing to look after them.

Of course determining the appropriate levels of each of these ingredients is an issue which generates various opinions and on which an increasing number of people profess to be expert. Sadly there are few – apart from those who actually do the job – who see the whole picture.

Environmentalists suffer from tunnel vision; retailers suffer from a ruthless streak unbecoming of those charged with selling the food upon which the nation depends; those choosing to invest their money in bricks and mortar, away from the urban sprawl, suffer from a total lack of understanding that rural communities won't survive if half of the houses are unoccupied for 75% of the time. All three categories are, I am sure, well intentioned from their own perspective but sadly ignorant of or unconcerned with the bigger picture.

Why can't an environmentalist understand that by de-stocking the hills all that happens is the countryside becomes wild and inaccessible to both man and beast? Why can't they understand that the few remaining animals will be blighted by ill health and disease as ticks become rampant on the abundance of bracken growing unchecked by livestock? Why can't they see that by seeking to ban the chemicals used to control those ticks and other parasites they make the situation worse?

As for the retailers – where do you start – incredibly efficient at what they do but at what cost to those who supply their raw materials? Is the word sustainable in their dictionary – I think not.

What hope for the rural communities that are slowly but surely being starved of the people that are their lifeblood? What hope indeed; money rules and whilst there is little money in sheep farming those that need to be in the countryside will always play second fiddle to those who just want to be there.

The ingredients in the countryside cake have taken a long time to balance. They are all totally dependant on each other and none of them works in isolation. The sheep industry and Government have a joint responsibility to ensure that the right balance is maintained.

NSA: In support of common sense and UK sheep farming

National Sheep Association
Malvern, WR13 6PH
enquiries@nationalsheep.org.uk
www.nationalsheep.org.uk

KUMAR, ASHOK
Middlesbrough South and East Cleveland

Ashok Kumar. Born 28 May 1956; Educated Rykenld School for Boys; Derby and District College of Art and Technology; Aston University (BSc chemical engineering 1978, MSc process analysis and development 1980, PhD fluid mechanics 1982). Research fellow, Imperial College, London 1982-85; Research scientist, British Steel 1985-97; Member: Association of University Teachers 1982-84, Steel and Industrial Managers' Union 1984-; Councillor, Middlesbrough Borough Council 1987-97

Lab majority 8,000

House of Commons: Member for Langbaurgh 1991 by-election – 1992, and for Middlesbrough South and East Cleveland since 1 May 1997 general election; PPS to Hilary Benn as: Minister of State, Department for International Development 2003, Secretary of State for International Development 2003-. *Political interests:* Trade and Industry, Education, Local and Regional Government, Small Businesses. Japan, USA, India, Korea, Kazakhstan, Bahrain

Chair Northern Regional Group of Labour MPs 2004-. Board Member, Parliamentary Office of Science and Technology (POST) 1997-; Vice-President, Federation of Economic Development Authorities (FEDA) 1997-; *Publications:* Articles in scientific and mathematical journals; *Clubs:* Marton Cricket Club; *Recreations:* Listening to music, reading history and philosophy books, playing badminton and cricket

Dr Ashok Kumar, MP, House of Commons, London SW1A 0AA
Tel: 020 7219 4460 *E-mail:* ashokkumarmp@parliament.uk. *Constituency:* 6-8 Wilson Street, Guisborough, Cleveland TS14 6NA *Tel:* 01287 610878 *Fax:* 01287 631894

LADYMAN, STEPHEN
South Thanet

Stephen John Ladyman. Born 6 November 1952; Son of Frank Ladyman, engineer, and of Winifred Ladyman; Educated Birkenhead Institute; Liverpool Polytechnic (BSc applied biology 1971-75); Strathclyde University (PhD for research into isotopic abundances in soil development 1975-79); Married Janet Baker 1994 (1 daughter 2 stepsons 1 stepdaughter). Computer manager, Pfizer Central Research; Member USDAW; Councillor, Thanet District Council 1995-99, Chair, Labour Group 1995-97, Chair, Finance Committee 1995-97

Lab majority 664

House of Commons: Contested Wantage 1987 general election. Member for South Thanet since 1 May 1997 general election; PPS to Adam Ingram as Minister of State for the Armed Forces, Ministry of Defence 2001-03; Liaison MP for the Netherlands; Parliamentary Under-Secretary of State for Health, Department of Health 2003-05; Minister of State, Department for Transport 2005-. *Political interests:* Environment, Economics, Industry, Science and Technology, Nuclear Power, Research, Defence, Small Businesses, Autism, Selective Education. Netherlands, China

Former Chair, Thanet South Constituency Labour Party; Member, Fabian Society. National Autistic Society; Member: European Standing Committee B 1997-99, European Standing Committee C 1999-2003; *Recreations:* Football, family, golf, house renovation

Dr Stephen Ladyman, MP, House of Commons, London SW1A 0AA
Tel: 020 7219 6946 *Fax:* 020 7219 6839 *E-mail:* ladymans@parliament.uk.
Constituency: 28 Newington Road, Ramsgate, Kent CT12 6EE *Tel:* 01843 852696 *Fax:* 01843 852689 *Website:* www.souththanetlp.freeserve.co.uk

LAING, ELEANOR
Epping Forest

Eleanor Laing. Born 1 February 1958; Daughter of late Matthew Pritchard and Betty, née McFarlane; Educated St Columba's School, Kilmacolm, Renfrewshire; Edinburgh University (BA, LLB) (First Woman President of Union); Married Alan Laing 1983 (divorced 2003) (1 son). Practised law in Edinburgh, City of London and industry; Special Adviser to John MacGregor: as Secretary of State for Education 1989-90, as Leader of the House of Commons 1990-92, as Secretary of State for Transport 1992-94

Con majority 14,358

House of Commons: Contested Paisley North 1987 general election. Member for Epping Forest since 1 May 1997 general election; Opposition Spokesperson for: Constitutional Affairs and Scotland 2000-01, Education and Skills 2001-03; Opposition Whip: (Constitutional, Education and Employment) 1999, (Social Security; Trade and Industry) 1999, (International Development; Trade and Industry; Wales) 1999-2000; Shadow Minister for: Children 2003, Women 2004-. *Political interests:* Education, Transport, Economic Policy, Constitution, Devolution. Australia, Gibraltar, USA, New Zealand

Recreations: Theatre, music, golf

Eleanor Laing, MP, House of Commons, London SW1A 0AA *Tel:* 020 7219 4203 *Fax:* 020 7219 0980. *Constituency:* Thatcher House, 4 Meadow Road, Loughton, Essex IG10 4HX *Tel:* 020 8508 6608 *Fax:* 020 8508 8099 *E-mail:* th@efca.tory.org.uk *Website:* www.efca.org.uk

LAIT, JACQUI
Beckenham

Jacqui Lait. Born 16 December 1947; Daughter of late Graham Lait and of Margaret Lait; Educated Paisley Grammar School; Strathclyde University (BA business 1967); Married Peter Jones 1974. Public relations, Jute Industries Ltd 1968-70; Visnews Ltd 1970-74; Government Information Service 1974-79; Parliamentary adviser, Chemical Industries Association 1980-84; Parliamentary consultant – own business 1984-92; Contested Strathclyde West 1984 European Parliament election; Chair, City and East London Family Health Services Authority 1987-91

Con majority 8,401

House of Commons: Contested Tyne Bridge 1985 by-election. Member for Hastings and Rye 1992-97, and for Beckenham since 20 November 1997 by-election; Opposition Spokesperson for Pensions 2000-01; Assistant Government Whip 1996-97; Opposition Whip 1999-2000; PPS: to Parliamentary Under-Secretaries of State, Department of Social Security 1994-95, to William Hague as Secretary of State for Wales 1995-96; Shadow Secretary of State for Scotland 2001-03; Shadow Minister for: Home, Constitutional and Legal Affairs 2003-04, Home Affairs 2004-. *Political interests:* Trade and Industry, European Union, Health. Australia, Europe, South Africa, USA

First woman in the Conservative Whips Office 1996-97; Chair, British Section, European Union of Women 1990-92; *Recreations:* Walking, swimming, theatre, food and wine

Jacqui Lait, MP, House of Commons, London SW1A 0AA *Tel:* 020 7219 1375 *Fax:* 020 7219 0141 *E-mail:* jacquilaitmp@parliament.uk. *Constituency:* c/o BCCA, 31 Beckenham Road, Beckenham BR3 4PR *Tel:* 020 8663 1425; 020 8663 1483 *Fax:* 020 8663 1483

LAMB, NORMAN
North Norfolk

Norman Peter Lamb. Born 16 September 1957; Son of late Hubert Horace Lamb, professor of climatology and Beatrice Moira Lamb, neé Milligan, nurse; Educated George Abbot School, Guildford, Surrey; Wymondham College, Wymondham, Norfolk; Leicester University (LLB 1980); Qualified as solicitor 1984; Married Mary Elizabeth Green 1984 (2 sons). Norwich City Council: Trainee solicitor 1982-84, Senior assistant solicitor 1984-85; Steele and Company Norfolk: Solicitor 1986-87; Partner Steele and Company Norfolk 1987-2001; Consultant 2001-; Norwich City Council: Councillor 1987-91, Group leader 1989-91

Lib Dem majority 10,606

House of Commons: Contested North Norfolk 1992, 1997 general elections. Member for North Norfolk since 7 June 2001 general election; Liberal Democrat Spokesperson for: International Development 2001-02, the Treasury 2002-; Liberal Democrat Shadow Secretary of State for Trade and Industry 2005-. *Political interests:* Employment, Social Affairs, Constitution, Environment, Housing. United States, South Africa

Chair Tottenham Liberals 1980-81; Norwich South Liberals 1985-87. Norfolk Air Ambulance; Member European Standing Committee A; *Publications: Remedies in the Employment Tribunal,* Sweet and Maxwell 1998; *Clubs:* Norwich City Football Club; *Recreations:* Walking, football

Norman Lamb, MP, House of Commons, London SW1A 0AA *Tel:* 020 7219 8480 *Fax:* 020 7219 1963 *E-mail:* normanlamb@hotmail.com. *Constituency:* 15 Market Place, North Walsham, Norfolk NR28 9BP *Tel:* 01692 403752 *Fax:* 01692 500818

LAMMY, DAVID
Tottenham

David Lammy. Born 19 July 1972; Son of Rosalind Lammy, council officer; Educated The King's School, Peterborough; School of Oriental and African Studies, London University (LLB 1993); Harvard Law School, USA (LLM 1997); Single. Barrister, 3 Serjeants Inn, Philip Naughton QC 1994-96; Attorney, Howard Rice Nemerovsky Canada Falk & Rabkin 1997-98; Barrister, D J Freeman 1998-2000; member Amicus; Member: Greater London Assembly 2000, Archbishops' Council 1999-2002

Lab majority 13,034

House of Commons: Member for Tottenham since 22 June 2000 by-election; PPS to Estelle Morris as Secretary of State for Education and Skills 2001-02; Parliamentary Under-Secretary of State: Department of Health 2002-03, Department for Constitutional Affairs 2003-05, Department for Culture, Media and Sport 2005-. *Political interests:* Health, Treasury (Regeneration), Arts and Culture, Education, International Development. USA, Caribbean, Latin America, Africa

Member: Fabian Society, Society of Labour Lawyers, Christian Socialist Movement. Trustee ActionAid; *Publications: Leading Together; Clubs:* Home House; The Honourable Society of Lincoln's Inn; *Recreations:* Film, live music, Spurs FC

David Lammy, MP, House of Commons, London SW1A 0AA *Tel:* 020 7219 0767 *Fax:* 020 7219 0357 *E-mail:* lammyd@parliament.uk.

LANCASTER, MARK
Milton Keynes North East

Con majority 1,665

Mark Lancaster. Born 12 May 1970; Educated Kimbolton School, Huntingdon; Royal Military Academy Sandhurst; Buckingham University (BSc business studies 1991);   Exeter University (MBA 1994); Married Katherine Elizabeth Reader 1995. Officer Royal Engineers 1988-90; Major Royal Engineers (TA) 1990-. Director, Kimbolton Fireworks Ltd 1990-; Councillor Huntingdon District Council 1990-99: Chair Leisure committee 1995-99

House of Commons: Contested Nuneaton 2001 general election. Member Milton Keynes North East since 5 May 2005 general election. *Political interests:* Defence, international development, commerce

Vice-chairman MKSNAP 2004-; *Publications:* Contributor, Pyrotechnics Principles and Practice, Chemical Publishing 1999; Territorial Decoration (TD) 2002; Member, Worshipful Company of Fanmakers; *Clubs:* United and Cecil Club; *Recreations:* Cricket, football, collecting classic British motorcycles

Mark Lancaster, MP, House of Commons, London SW1A 0AA *Tel:* 020 7219 8414. *Constituency:* 105 Queensway, Bletchley, Milton Keynes, Buckinghamshire MK2 2DN *Tel:* 01908 372038 *E-mail:* mark.lancaster@mkconservatives.com *Website:* www.mkconservatives.com

---

LANSLEY, ANDREW
South Cambridgeshire

Con majority 8,001

Andrew David Lansley. Born 11 December 1956; Son of Thomas Lansley, OBE, and Irene Lansley; Educated Brentwood School; Exeter University (BA politics 1979) (President, Guild of Students 1977-78); First marriage dissolved (3 daughters); married Sally Low 2001. Department of Industry (Department of Trade and Industry 1984-87) 1979-87; Private secretary to Secretary of State, at Department of Trade and Industry 1984-85; Principal Private Secretary, to Norman Tebbit as Chancellor of the Duchy of Lancaster 1985-87; Policy director, British Chambers of Commerce 1987-89; Deputy director-general, British Chambers of Commerce 1989-90; Director, Conservative Research Department 1990-95; Director, Public Policy Unit 1995-97; Vice-President, Local Government Association

House of Commons: Member for South Cambridgeshire since 1 May 1997 general election; Vice-chair Conservative Party 1998-99; Member, Shadow Cabinet 1999-2001; Shadow: Minister for the Cabinet Office and Policy Renewal 1999-2001, Chancellor of the Duchy of Lancaster 1999-2001, Secretary of State for Health 2003-; Member Shadow Cabinet 2004-. *Political interests:* Trade and Industry, Economic Policy, Small Businesses, Health, Local and Regional Government, Police, Film Industry. USA, Japan, Egypt, Israel, France, Germany, South Africa

Vice-Chairman, Conservative Party (with responsibility for Policy Renewal) 1998-99. *Publications: A Private Route,* 1988; Co-author *Conservatives and the Constitution,* 1997; *Do the right thing* – Why Conservatives must achieve greater fairness and diversity in candidate selection, 2002; *Extending the Reach,* 2003; CBE 1996; CBE; *Recreations:* Spending time with my children, films, biography, history, cricket

Andrew Lansley, MP, House of Commons, London SW1A 0AA *Tel:* 020 7219 2538 *Fax:* 020 7219 6835 *E-mail:* lansleya@parliament.uk. *Constituency:* 153 St Neots Road, Harwick, Cambridge, Cambridgeshire CB3 7QJ *Tel:* 01954 212707 *Fax:* 01954 211625

Ind majority 9,121

LAW, PETER
Blaenau Gwent

Peter Law. Born 1 April 1948; Son of late John (Jack) Law, master grocer, and late Rita Mary Law, housewife; Educated Llanfoist Primary School; Grofield Secondary Modern School; King Henry School; Nant-y-Glo Community College; Correspondence School; Open University (Public relations, social services); Married Patricia Bolter 1976 (5 children). Self-employed retail grocery 1964-87; Adviser in local government and public authorities 1987-99; Former Member, USDAW; Member: GMB, APEX, RMT, CWU; Councillor: Nantyglo and Blaenau Urban District Council 1970-74, Blaenau Gwent Borough Council 1974-96, Mayor 1988-89, Blaenau Gwent County Borough Council 1995-99; Justice of the Peace; Member: Gwent Police Authority, Gwent Magistrates Court Committee; Chair, Local Government Partnership Council 2000-

House of Commons: Member for Blaenau Gwent since 5 May 2005 general election; Secretary for Environment and Local Government 1999-2000; Secretary for Local Government 2000. *Political interests:* Social Justice, Health, Local Government, Economic Development, Environment

Former Treasurer, Chair, Secretary, Deputy agent, Local government election agent, Nant-y-Glo and Blaenau Gwent Constituency Labour Party; Leader, 'Yes' Campaign Blaenau Gwent 1997; Treasurer 'Yes for Wales' Gwent 1979 Referendum. Mencap; Member, The Institute of Public Relations; AM for Blaenau Gwent constituency since 6 May 1999; *Recreations:* Countryside walks, Land Rovers, forestry

Peter Law, MP, House of Commons, London SW1A 0AA *Tel:* 020 7219 4347. *Constituency:* 1 Bethcart Street, Ebbw Vale, Blaenau Gwent NP23 6HH *Tel:* 01495 304569 *Fax:* 01495 306908

Lib Dem majority 8,562

LAWS, DAVID
Yeovil

David Anthony Laws. Born 30 November 1965; Son of DA Laws and Mrs MT Davies; Educated St George's College, Weybridge, Surrey; King's College, Cambridge (BA economics 1987); Single. Vice-president JP Morgan and Company 1987-92; Barclays de Zoete Wedd Ltd 1992-94: Managing director, Head US Dollar and Sterling treasuries 1992-94

House of Commons: Contested Folkestone and Hythe 1997 general election. Member for Yeovil since 7 June 2001 general election; Liberal Democrat Spokesman for Defence 2001-02; Liberal Democrat Shadow: Chief Secretary to the Treasury 2002-05, Secretary of State for Work and Pensions 2005-. *Political interests:* Economy, Education, Pensions, Public Service Reform. Egypt, Jordan, France

Liberal Democrat Parliamentary Party: Economics adviser 1994-97, Director of Policy and Research 1997-99. Winner 1984 Observer Mace National Schools Debating Competition; *Recreations:* Running, rugby, reading, desert regions

David Laws, MP, House of Commons, London SW1A 0AA *Tel:* 020 7219 8413 *Fax:* 020 7219 8188 *E-mail:* lawsd@parliament.uk. *Constituency:* 94 Middle Street, Yeovil, Somerset BA20 1LT *Tel:* 01935 425 025 *Fax:* 01935 433 652

LAXTON, BOB
Derby North

Bob Laxton. Born 7 September 1944; Son of Alan and Elsie Laxton; Educated Woodlands Secondary School; Derby College of Art and Technology; Married (1 son from previous marriage). TU branch officer, Communication Workers' Union; Telecommunications engineer, BT plc 1961-; Member, Communication Workers' Union; Derby City Council: Councillor 1979-97, Council Leader 1986-88, 1994-97; Chair, East Midlands Local Government Association to 1997

Lab majority 3,757

House of Commons: Member for Derby North since 1 May 1997 general election; Member Trade and Industry Select Committee 1997-2001; PPS to Alan Johnson as Minister of State: Department of Trade and Industry 2001-03, Department for Education and Skills 2003-04, as Secretary of State for Work and Pensions 2004-. *Political interests:* Local and Regional Government, Education, Trade and Industry. Middle East, USA

Member Labour Middle East Council. Derbyshire Children's Friendship Group, 'Laurens' Link' (Family Drug Counselling Service), Derbyshire Branch National Osteoporosis Society; Labour Party Conference Debate, Local Government 1995; *Recreations:* Hill walking

Bob Laxton, MP, House of Commons, London SW1A 0AA *Tel:* 020 7219 4096 *Fax:* 020 7219 2329 *E-mail:* laxtonb@parliament.uk. *Constituency:* 1st Floor, Abbots Hill Chamber, Gower Street, Derby, Derbyshire DE! 2FS *Tel:* 01332 206699 *Fax:* 01332 206444

LAZAROWICZ, MARK
Edinburgh North and Leith

Marek Jerzy Lazarowicz. Born 8 August 1953; Son of Jerzy Witold Lazarowicz and Ivy Lazarowicz, neé Eacott; Educated St Benedicts School, London; St Andrews University (MA moral philosophy and medieval history 1976); Edinburgh University (LLB 1992); Diploma Legal Practice 1993; Married Caroline Elizabeth Johnston 1993 (1 daughter 3 sons). Organiser Scottish Education and Action for Development 1978-80; General secretary British Youth Council Scotland 1980-82; Organiser Scottish Education and Action for Development 1982-86; Advocate 1996-; TGWU 1978-; City of Edinburgh District Council 1980-96: Councillor, Leader of Council 1986-93; Councillor City of Edinburgh Council 1999-2001

Lab/Co-op majority 2,153

House of Commons: Contested Edinburgh Pentlands 1987 and 1992 general elections. Member for Edinburgh North and Leith 2001-05, for new Edinburgh North and Leith since 5 May 2005 general election. *Political interests:* Environment, Transport, Consumer Issues, Co-operative Issues, Constitution, Finance, Economy, Small Businesses

Member Co-operative Party; Chair Scottish Labour Party 1989-90; Member: Socialist Environment and Resources Association (SERA), SERA Parliamentary Group. *Publications:* Co-author *The Scottish Parliament: An Introduction*, T and T Clark 1999, 1st edition 1999, 2nd edition 2000, 3rd edition 2004; Various articles, papers and pamphlets on political and legal issues; *Recreations:* Jogging, walking, cycling

Mark Lazarowicz, MP, House of Commons, London SW1A 0AA *Tel:* 020 7219 8199 *E-mail:* mark@marklazarowicz.org.uk. *Constituency:* 86-88 Brunswick Street, Edinburgh EH7 5HU *Tel:* 0131 557 0577 *Fax:* 0131 557 5759

LEECH, JOHN
Manchester Withington

John Leech. Born 11 April 1971; Educated Manchester Grammar School; Loretto College; Brunel University (BA history and politics 1993); Single. Assistant restaurant manager McDonalds Restaurant Ltd 1995-97; Customer relations RAC Ltd 1998-; Manchester City Council: Deputy leader of the opposition 1998-, Deputy leader Liberal Democrats Group 2003-

House of Commons: Member for Manchester Withington since 5 May 2005 general election. *Political interests:* Housing, planning, transport

Lib Dem majority
667

Recreations: Amateur dramatics, football

John Leech, MP, House of Commons, London SW1A 0AA *Tel:* 020 7219 8353. *Constituency:* 53b Manley Road, Whalley Range, Manchester M16 8HP *Tel:* 0161-226 6542 *E-mail:* cllr.j.leech@manchester.gov.uk, Agent: John Cameron, Flat 24, Tatton Court, Egerton Road, Fallowfield *Tel:* 0161 224 9089; 0161 226 6542 *Website:* www.withingtonlibdems.org.uk

LEIGH, EDWARD
Gainsborough

Edward Julian Egerton Leigh. Born 20 July 1950; Son of late Sir Neville Leigh, KCVO, former Clerk to the Privy Council; Educated Oratory School, Berkshire; French Lycee, London; Durham University (BA history 1972) (President of Union); Married Mary Goodman 1984 (3 sons 3 daughters). Member: Conservative Research Department 1973-75, Private Office of Margaret Thatcher as Leader of the Opposition 1976-77; Barrister, Inner Temple 1977-; Fellow, Institute of Arbitrators 1999-; Councillor: Richmond Borough Council 1974-78, GLC 1977-81

Con majority 8,003

House of Commons: Contested Teesside, Middlesbrough October 1974 general election. Member for Gainsborough and Horncastle 1983-97, and for Gainsborough since 1 May 1997 general election; PPS to John Patten as Minister of State, Home Office 1990; Parliamentary Under-Secretary of State, Department of Trade and Industry 1990-93. *Political interests:* Defence, Foreign Affairs, Agriculture, Families

Former Chair Durham University Conservative Association; Member governing council Conservative Christian Fellowship. CAFOD; Chair, National Council for Civil Defence 1979-83; Director, Coalition For Peace Through Security 1981-83; Fellow, Industry and Parliament Trust; *Publications: Right Thinking*, 1982; *Onwards from Bruges*, 1989; *Choice and Responsibility – The Enabling State*, 1990; Knight of Honour and Devotion of the Sovereign Military Order of Malta; *Recreations:* Walking, reading

Edward Leigh, MP, House of Commons, London SW1A 0AA *Tel:* 020 7219 6480 *Fax:* 020 7219 4883 *E-mail:* leighe@parliament.uk. *Constituency:* 23 Queen Street, Market Rasen, Lincolnshire LN8 3EN *Tel:* 01673 844501; 01673 849003 *Fax:* 01673 844501; 01673 849003

LEPPER, DAVID
Brighton Pavilion

David Lepper. Born 15 September 1945; Son of late Harry Lepper, lorry driver, and late Maggie Lepper; Educated Gainsborough Secondary Modern, Richmond; Wimbledon Secondary School; Kent University (BA English and American literature 1968); Sussex University (PGCE, postgraduate certificate in media education 1992); Polytechnic of Central London (postgraduate diploma in film 1978); Married Jeane Stroud 1966 (1 son 1 daughter). Secondary school English and media studies teacher 1969-96; Member, NUT 1969-; Councillor, Brighton Council 1980-96: Council Leader 1986-97, Mayor 1993-94, Brighton and Hove Council 1996-97

Lab/Co-op majority 5,030

House of Commons: Contested Brighton Pavilion 1992 general election. Member for Brighton Pavilion since 1 May 1997 general election. *Political interests:* Environment and Housing, Leasehold Reform, Community and Economic Regeneration, Town Centre Issues, Cyprus, Small Businesses. France, Cyprus

Member: Fabian Society, Socialist Education Association, Socialist Health Association, SERA, Labour Animal Welfare Society. Alzheimer's Disease Society, Age Concern, ARDIS (Brighton); Fellow, Sussex University Society; Member: CPA 1997-, IPU; Trustee ARDIS (local dementia charity); *Publications: John Wayne*, 1986; Contributor to British Film Institute publications and other film journalism; *Clubs:* Brighton Trades and Labour; *Recreations:* Music, cinema, reading fiction and poetry, watching professional cycling

David Lepper, MP, House of Commons, London SW1A 0AA *Tel:* 020 7219 4421 *Fax:* 020 7219 5814. *Constituency:* John Saunders House, 179 Preston Road, Brighton, East Sussex BN1 6AG *Tel:* 01273 551532 *Fax:* 01273 550617

LETWIN, OLIVER
West Dorset

Oliver Letwin. Born 19 May 1956; Son of Professor William Letwin and late Dr Shirley Robin Letwin; Educated Eton College; Trinity College, Cambridge (BA history 1978, MA, PhD philosophy 1982); London Business School; Married Isabel Grace Davidson 1984 (1 son 1 daughter). Visiting fellow (Procter Fellow), Princeton University, USA 1980-81; Research fellow, Darwin College, Cambridge 1981-82; Special adviser to Sir Keith Joseph as Secretary of State for Education 1982-83; Special adviser, Prime Minister's Policy Unit 1983-86; N. M. Rothschild & Son, Merchant Bank 1986-2003: Manager 1986, Assistant Director 1987, Director 1991-2003, Managing Director 2003

Con majority 2,461

House of Commons: Contested Hackney North 1987, Hampstead and Highgate 1992 general elections. Member for West Dorset since 1 May 1997 general election; Opposition Spokesperson for: Constitutional Affairs, Scotland and Wales 1998-99, the Treasury 1999-2000; Shadow: Financial Secretary 1999-2000, Chief Secretary to the Treasury 2000-01, Home Secretary 2001-03, Secretary of State for Economic Affairs and Shadow Chancellor of the Exchequer 2003-05, Secretary of State for Environment, Food and Rural Affairs 2005-. *Political interests:* Economics, Employment, Education. Eastern Europe, Africa

Member, Conservative Disability Group. Joseph Weld Hospice; Member, European Standing Committee B 1998; *Publications: Ethics, Emotion and the Unity of the Self,* 1985; *Aims of Schooling,* 1986; *Privatising the World,* 1989; *Drift to Union,* 1989; *The Purpose of Politics,* 1999; Plus Articles and Reviews in learned and popular journals; PC 2002; *Recreations:* Ski-ing, sailing, tennis, reading, writing books

Rt Hon Oliver Letwin, MP, House of Commons, London SW1A 0AA *Tel:* 020 7219 4192 *Fax:* 020 7219 4405 *E-mail:* charlesa@parliament.uk. *Constituency:* Chapel House, Dorchester Road, Maiden Newton, Dorset DT2 0BG *Tel:* 01300 321188 *Fax:* 01300 321233

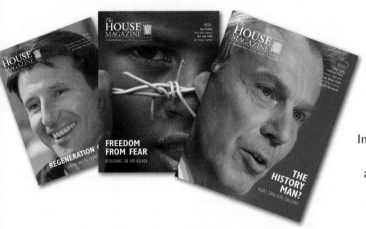

Lab majority 735

LEVITT, TOM
High Peak

Tom Levitt. Born 10 April 1954; Son of John and Joan Levitt; Educated Westwood High School, Leek; Lancaster University (BSc biological sciences 1975); Oxford University (PGCE 1976); Married Teresa Sledziewska 1983 (1 daughter). Teacher: Wiltshire County Council 1976-79, Gloucestershire County Council 1980-91; Contested Cotswolds 1989 European Parliament election; Supply teacher, Staffordshire County Council 1991-95; Sensory awareness trainer 1993-97; Consultant, Access for People With Sensory Impairments 1993-97; Member, NUT 1975-; School representative, NUT 1977-79, 1984-90; Local association president, NUT 1985; County division president, NUT 1988; Member: NUPE 1988-94, GMB 1995-; Councillor: Cirencester Town 1983-87, Stroud District 1990-92, Derbyshire County 1993-97, Vice-Chair, Education 1994-95

House of Commons: Contested Stroud 1987 and High Peak 1992 general elections. Member for High Peak since 1 May 1997 general election; PPS to: Barbara Roche as Minister of State: Home Office 1999-2001, Cabinet Office 2001-02, Office of the Deputy Prime Minister 2002-03, Secretaries of State for International Development: Baroness Amos 2003, Hilary Benn 2003-. *Political interests:* Disability, Education, Local and Regional Government, Quarrying, Voluntary Sector, Anti-Hunting. Western Europe, Poland

Member, SERA. RNID, Macmillan Cancer Relief; Member, Global Organisation of Parliamentarians Against Corruption; Trustee, Royal National Institute for Deaf People 1998-2003; *Publications:* Local Government Management Board: *Sound Policies*, 1994, *Sound Practice*, 1995, *Clear Access*, 1996; *Clubs:* Tideswell Cricket Club; *Recreations:* Cricket, walking, theatre

Tom Levitt, MP, House of Commons, London SW1A 0AA *Tel:* 020 7219 6599 *Fax:* 020 7219 0935 *E-mail:* tomlevittmp@parliament.uk. *Constituency:* 20 Hardwick Street, Buxton, Derbyshire SK17 6DH *Tel:* 01298 71111 *Fax:* 01298 71522

Lab majority 8,912

LEWIS, IVAN
Bury South

Ivan Lewis. Born 4 March 1967; Son of Joe and Gloria Lewis; Educated William Hulme Grammar School; Stand College; Bury Further Education College; Married Juliette Fox 1990 (2 sons). Co-ordinator, Contact Community Care Group 1986-89; Community care manager, Jewish Social Services 1989-92; Chief executive, Manchester Jewish Federation 1992-97; Member, MSF; Councillor, Bury Metropolitan Borough Council 1990-98; Chairman, Social Services Committee 1991-95

House of Commons: Member for Bury South since 1 May 1997 general election; PPS to Stephen Byers as Secretary of State for Trade and Industry 1999-2001; Parliamentary Under-Secretary of State, Department for Education and Skills: for Young People and Learning 2001-02, for Adult Learning and Skills 2002, for Young People and Adult Skills 2002-03, for Skills and Vocational Education 2003-05; Economic Secretary, HM Treasury 2005-. *Political interests:* Health, Crime, Education. Israel, USA

Chair, Bury South Labour Party 1991-96; Vice-Chair, Labour Friends of Israel 1997-2001. MENCAP; Trustee, Holocaust Educational Trust; *Recreations:* Keen supporter of Manchester City FC

Ivan Lewis, MP, House of Commons, London SW1A 0AA *Tel:* 020 7219 6404 *Fax:* 020 7219 6866. *Constituency:* 381 Bury New Road, Prestwich, Manchester M25 1AV *Tel:* 0161-773 5500 *Fax:* 0161-773 7959 *E-mail:* ivanlewis@fsnet.co.uk

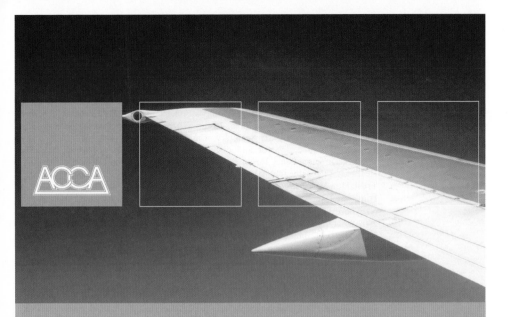

ABOUT ACCA

ACCA (The Association of Chartered Certified Accountants) is the largest global professional accountancy body, with 345,000 members and students in over 160 countries. Headquartered in London, we have an extensive network of over 70 staffed offices and other centres around the world. In the UK, we have 50,000 members (ACCA qualified accountants) and over 60,000 students.

We derive our strength as a leading global accountancy body from our statutory recognition in the UK, our open access and expertise in education and training. Our professional qualification is respected globally and our access to companies, governments, regulators and practitioners around the world give us a unique perspective on financial management and accountability in the public and private sectors.

OUR MEMBERS

ACCA members work in practising firms of accountants, commerce, industry and the public sector. We have members in senior government positions, across the Big Four accounting firms, in listed multinational companies and many are small business advisers and entrepreneurs.

OUR WORK

To complement our education and training of financial professionals, ACCA conducts research into and comments publicly on a wide range of business, financial and regulatory issues. We have in-house experts in tax, audit, financial reporting, corporate governance, education and lifelong learning, small business, public sector finance, pensions, debt management and corporate social responsibility.

Our member and student networks structure – with representatives in every constituency in the UK – ensures that ACCA is fully aware of the key issues affecting the accountancy profession and the business community at local, regional, national and international levels.

ACCA'S PUBLIC POLICY UNIT

Building productive links with UK Parliamentarians, the Government and its agencies and influencing policy development in the public interest are key priorities for ACCA.

Contact the Public Policy Unit for further information:
Andrew Silverman
Director – Communications and Public Affairs
tel: +44 (0)20 7059 7284 / mob: +44 (0)7715 367060
andrew.silverman@accaglobal.com

June Deasy
Public Affairs Manager
tel: +44 (0)20 7059 5751 / mob: +44 (0)7736 800393
june.deasy@accaglobal.com

Victoria Jonson
Senior Policy Adviser
tel: +44 (0)20 7059 5726 / mob: +44 (0)7803 146170
victoria.jonson@accaglobal.com

Con majority 6,551

LEWIS, JULIAN
New Forest East

Julian Murray Lewis. Born 26 September 1951; Son of Samuel Lewis and late Hilda Lewis; Educated Dynevor Grammar School, Swansea; Balliol College, Oxford (MA philosophy and politics 1977); St Antony's College, Oxford (DPhil strategic studies 1981). Seaman, HM Royal Naval Reserve 1979-82. Doctoral research (strategic studies) 1975-77, 1978-81; Secretary, Campaign for Representative Democracy 1977-78; Research director and director, Coalition for Peace Through Security 1981-85; Director, Policy Research Associates 1985-; Deputy director, Conservative Research Department 1990-96; Hon Vice-president, British Military Powerboat Trust; Hon Vice-president, Calshot Association

House of Commons: Contested Swansea West 1983 general election. Member for New Forest East since 1 May 1997 general election; Shadow Spokesman for Defence 2002-03; Opposition Whip 2001-02; Shadow Minister for: International Affairs 2003-04, the Cabinet Office 2004-. *Political interests:* Defence, Security, Foreign Affairs, European Affairs. Western Europe, Central and Eastern Europe, Russia

Treasurer, Oxford University Conservative Association 1971; Secretary, Oxford Union 1972; Honorary Vice-President, Greater London and West London Young Conservatives 1980s. Joint organiser of campaign against militant infiltration of the Labour Party 1977-78; Hon Vice-President, British Military Powerboat Trust; *Publications: Changing Direction: British Military Planning for Post-War Strategic Defence, 1942-1947,* 1988 (second edition 2003); *Who's Left? An Index of Labour MPs and Left-Wing Causes, 1985-1992,* 1992; *Labour's CND Cover-Up,* 1992; *The Liberal Democrats: The Character of Their Politics,* 1993; *What's Liberal? Liberal Democrat Quotations and Facts,* 1996; *Clubs:* Athenaeum, Hon president Totton Conservative; *Recreations:* History, fiction, films, music, photography

Dr Julian Lewis, MP, House of Commons, London SW1A 0AA *Tel:* 020 7219 4179. *Constituency:* New Forest East Conservative Association, 3 The Parade, Southampton Road, Cadnam, Hampshire SO40 2NG *Tel:* 023 8081 4817 *Website:* www.julianlewis.net

Con majority 8,469

LIDDELL-GRAINGER, IAN
Bridgwater

Ian Richard Peregrine Liddell-Grainger. Born 23 February 1959; Son of David Liddell-Grainger, farmer, and Ann Grainger; Educated Wellesley House School, Kent; Millfield School, Somerset; South of Scotland Agricultural College, Edinburgh (National Certificate of Agriculture); Married Jill Nesbitt 1959 (1 son 2 daughters). Major Fusiliers TA. Family farm Berwickshire 1980-85; Managing director property management and development companies group 1985-; Contested Tyne and Wear 1994 European Parliament election; Councillor: Tynedale District Council 1989-95, Northern Area Council 1992-95

House of Commons: Contested Torridge and Devon West 1997 general election. Member for Bridgwater since 7 June 2001 general election. *Political interests:* Business, Economy, Defence, Rural Affairs, Farming

Member Conservative agricultural forum; Chair Corbridge Branch Hexham Association 1992-94; President Tyne Bridge Conservative Association 1993-96. RNLI, Macmillans; Northern industrial representative European Parliament; Member House of Lords rural economy group; Adviser to chair: Foreign Affairs Select Committee, Defence Select Committee; *Recreations:* Walking, travel, skiing, family

Ian Liddell-Grainger, MP, House of Commons, London SW1A 0AA *Tel:* 020 7219 8149 *E-mail:* ianlg@parliament.uk. *Constituency:* 16 Northgate, Bridgwater, Somerset TA6 3EU *Tel:* 01278 458383 *Fax:* 01278 433613

LIDINGTON, DAVID
Aylesbury

David Lidington. Born 30 June 1956; Son of Roy and Rosa Lidington; Educated Haberdashers' Aske's School, Elstree; Sidney Sussex College, Cambridge (MA history, PhD); Married Helen Parry 1989 (4 sons). British Petroleum 1983-86; Rio Tinto Zinc 1986-87; Special Adviser to Douglas Hurd: at Home Office 1987-89, at Foreign and Commonwealth Office 1989-90; Senior Consultant, The Public Policy Unit 1991-92

Con majority 11,066

House of Commons: Contested Vauxhall 1987 general election. Member for Aylesbury since 9 April 1992 general election; Opposition Spokesperson for Home Affairs 1999-2001; PPS: to Michael Howard as Home Secretary 1994-97, to William Hague as Leader of the Opposition 1997-99; Shadow: Financial Secretary 2001-02, Minister for Agriculture and the Fisheries 2002, Secretary of State for: Environment, Food and Rural Affairs 2002-03, Northern Ireland 2003-. *Political interests:* Europe, Hong Kong

Various offices in: Cambridge University (Chairman), Enfield North Conservative Association; Conservative Christian Fellowship: Member governing council, Deputy chair board of directors. *Clubs:* Aylesbury Conservative; *Recreations:* History, choral singing, reading

David Lidington, MP, House of Commons, London SW1A 0AA   *Tel:* 020 7219 3432 *Fax:* 020 7219 2564   *E-mail:* davidlidingtonmp@parliament.uk.   *Constituency:* 100 Walton Street, Aylesbury, Buckinghamshire HP21 7QP   *Tel:* 01296 482102 *Fax:* 01296 398481

Con majority 11,393

LILLEY, PETER
Hitchin and Harpenden

Peter Bruce Lilley. Born 23 August 1943; Son of Arnold and Lillian (née Elliott) Lilley; Educated Dulwich College; Clare College, Cambridge (BA natural sciences and economic sciences 1965); Married Gail Ansell 1979. Economic adviser on underdeveloped countries 1966-72; Investment adviser on North Sea oil and other energy industries 1972-84; Consultant director, Conservative Research Department 1979-83; Partner, W Greenwell & Co 1979-86; Director: Great Western Resources Ltd 1985-87, Greenwell Montague Stockbrokers 1986-87 (Head, oil investment department); JP Morgan Fleming Claverhouse Investment Trust 1997-, Idox Plc 2002-; Member, School of Management Advisory Board, Southampton University 2002-

House of Commons: Contested Haringey, Tottenham October 1974 general election. Member for St Albans 1983-97, and for Hitchin and Harpenden since 1 May 1997 general election; Joint PPS: to Lord Bellwin, as Minister of State for Local Government, Department of the Environment and William Waldegrave as Parliamentary Under-Secretary of State, Department of Environment June-November 1984, to Nigel Lawson, as Chancellor of the Exchequer 1984-87; Economic Secretary to the Treasury 1987-89; Financial Secretary to the Treasury 1989-90; Secretary of State for: Trade and Industry 1990-92, Social Security 1992-97; Contested Leadership of the Conservative Party June 1997; Member, Shadow Cabinet 1997-99; Shadow Chancellor of the Exchequer 1997-98; Deputy Leader of the Opposition (with overall responsibility for development of party policy) 1998-99. *Political interests:* Economic Policy, European Union, Education, Race Relations. France

Chair, Bow Group 1973-75. Stairways (Mencap) Harpenden; Trustee, Parliamentary Contributory Pension Fund; Chairman, House of Commons Members Fund; *Publications: You Sincerely Want to Win? – Defeating Terrorism in Ulster*, 1972; *Lessons for Power*, 1974; Co-author, *Delusions of Income Policy*, 1977; Contributor, *End of the Keynesian Era*, 1980; *Thatcherism, the Next Generation*, 1989; *The Mais Lecture Benefits and Costs: Securing the Future of the Social Security*, 1993; *Patient Power*, (Demos) 2000; *Common Sense on Cannabis* (Social Market Foundation) 2001; *Taking Liberties* (Adam Smith Institute) 2002; *Save Our Pensions* (Social Market Foundation) 2003; PC 1990; *Clubs:* Carlton, Beefsteak

Rt Hon Peter Lilley, MP, House of Commons, London SW1A 0AA
Tel: 020 7219 4577 *Fax:* 020 7219 3840 *E-mail:* lilleyp@parliament.uk.
Constituency: Riverside House, 1 Place Farm, Wheathampstead,
Hertfordshire AL4 8SB *Tel:* 01582 834344 *Fax:* 01582 834884

LINTON, MARTIN
Battersea

Martin Linton. Born 11 August 1944; Son of Sydney Linton and late Karin Linton; Educated Christ's Hospital, Sussex; Pembroke College, Oxford (MA philosophy, politics and economics 1963-66); Université de Lyon; Married Kathy Stanley 1975 (died 1995) (2 daughters). Journalist on: *Daily Mail* 1966-71, *Financial Times* 1971, *Labour Weekly* 1971-79, *Daily Star* 1980-81, *The Guardian* 1981-97; Member: NUJ 1966-97, GMB; Councillor, London Borough of Wandsworth 1971-82, Chairman, Recreation Committee 1971-77

Lab majority 163

House of Commons: Member for Battersea since 1 May 1997 general election; PPS to: Baroness Blackstone as Minister of State (Minister for the Arts), Department for Culture, Media and Sport 2001-03, Peter Hain as Leader of the House of Commons 2003-. *Political interests:* Housing, Education, Culture, Political Finance, Voting Systems, Media-Politics Relations, Foreign Affairs. Sweden

Joined Labour Party 1968; Chairman, Constituency Labour Party 1994-96. Trinity Hospice; Treasurer, British Swedish Parliamentary Association; *Publications: Get Me Out Of Here*, 1980; *The Swedish Road to Socialism*, 1984; *Labour Can Still Win*, 1988; *The Guardian Guide to the House of Commons*, (editor) 1992; *What's wrong with first-past-the-post?*, 1993; *Money and Votes*, 1994; *Was It The Sun Wot Won It?*, 1995; Editor, *Guardian Election Guide*, 1997; *Making Votes Count*, 1998; *Beyond 2002*, 2000; *Recreations:* Playing music, watching football (Fulham FC)

Martin Linton, MP, House of Commons, London SW1A 0AA *Tel:* 020 7219 4619 *Fax:* 020 7219 5728. *Constituency:* Battersea Labour Party, 177 Lavender Hill, London SW11 5TE *Tel:* 020 7207 3060 *Fax:* 020 7207 3063 *Website:* www.labourwandsworth.org.uk/index.php

LLOYD, TONY
Manchester Central

Tony (Anthony) Joseph Lloyd. Born 25 February 1950; Son of late Sydney Lloyd, lithographic printer and Ciceley Lloyd, administrative officer; Educated Stretford Grammar School; Nottingham University (maths); Manchester Business School (business administration); Married Judith Ann Tear 1974 (1 son 3 daughters). University lecturer; GMB; Councillor, Trafford District Council 1979-84

Lab majority 9,776

House of Commons: Member for Stretford 1983-97, and for Manchester Central since 1 May 1997 general election; Opposition Spokesperson for: Transport 1988-89, Employment 1988-92, 1993-94, Education (responsible for co-ordinating policies on education and training) 1992-94, The Environment and London 1994-95, Foreign and Commonwealth Affairs 1995-97; Minister of State, Foreign and Commonwealth Office 1997-99. *Political interests:* Civil Liberties, Disarmament, Immigration, Race Relations, Industrial Policy, Human Rights, Overseas Aid and Development. Guatemala, Poland, the Balkans, Russia

Member Parliamentary Labour Party Parliamentary Committee 2001-. Leader, UK Delegation Parliamentary Assembly of the Council of Europe/Western European Union 2000-

Tony Lloyd, MP, House of Commons, London SW1A 0AA *Tel:* 020 7219 2678 *Fax:* 020 7219 2585 *E-mail:* contact@tonylloydmp.co.uk. *Constituency:* 10 Swan Street, Manchester M4 5JN *Tel:* 0161-819 2828 *Fax:* 0161-839 6875

LLWYD, ELFYN
Meirionnydd Nant Conwy

Elfyn Llwyd. Born 26 September 1951; Son of late Huw Meirion and Hefina Hughes; Educated Dyffryn Conwy School; Llanrwst Grammar School; University College of Wales, Aberystwyth (LLB law 1974); College of Law, Chester (Solicitor); Married Eleri Llwyd 1974 (1 son 1 daughter). Solicitor until 1997; President, Gwynedd Law Society 1990-91; Barrister, Gray's Inn 1997-

PlC majority 6,614

House of Commons: Member for Meirionnydd Nant Conwy since 9 April 1992 general election; Spokesperson for: Transport 1992-94, Trade and Industry 1992-94, Northern Ireland 1997-99, Housing 1997-, Local Government 1997-, Tourism 1997-, Home Affairs 1999-, Defence 2001-, Foreign Affairs 2004-; Plaid Cymru Parliamentary Whip 1995-2001; Leader, Plaid Cymru Parliamentary Party 1997-. *Political interests:* Civil Liberties, Agriculture, Tourism, Home Affairs. Spain, Scotland, USA, Wales, Greece

Member, Plaid Cymru Policy Cabinet 1994-, Parliamentary Leader 1997-. NSPCC, Children in Wales, Urdd Gobaith Cymru, Tenovus; Member, European Standing Committee B 2004-05; Chair, Dolgellau Hatchery Trust; *Clubs:* President: Estimaner Angling Association, Betws-y-Coed Football Club, Llanuwchllyn Football Club, Bala Rugby Club; Vice-President, Dolgellau Old Grammarians' Rugby Club; *Recreations:* Pigeon breeding, choral singing, rugby, fishing, cycling

Elfyn Llwyd, MP, House of Commons, London SW1A 0AA *Tel:* 020 7219 3555 *Fax:* 020 7219 2633 *E-mail:* llwyde@parliament.uk. *Constituency:* Adeiladau Glyndwr, Heol Glyndwr, Dolgellau, Gwynedd LL40 1BD *Tel:* 01341 422661 *Fax:* 01341 423990

LORD, MICHAEL
Central Suffolk and North Ipswich

Michael Lord. Born 17 October 1938; Son of late John Lord, schoolmaster; Educated William Hulme's Grammar School, Manchester; Christ's College, Cambridge (MA agriculture 1962); Married Jennifer Margaret Childs 1965 (1 son 1 daughter). Farmer and taught agriculture 1962-66; Director, Power Line Maintenance Ltd 1966-68; Founded Lords Tree Services Ltd 1968; Aboricultural Consultant 1983; North Bedfordshire Borough Council: Councillor 1974-77, Chair, Policy Commission 1974-77; Bedfordshire County Council: Councillor 1981-83, Chair, Further Education Committee 1981-83

Con majority 7,856

House of Commons: Contested Manchester Gorton 1979 general election. Member for Central Suffolk 1983-97, and for Central Suffolk and North Ipswich since 1 May 1997 general election; PPS to: John MacGregor, as Minister of Agriculture, Fisheries and Food 1984-85, as Chief Secretary to the Treasury 1985-87; Second Deputy Chairman, Ways and Means and Deputy Speaker 1997-. *Political interests:* Agriculture, Forestry, Environment

Cambridge Rugby Blue; Parliamentary delegate, The Council of Europe and the Western European Union 1987-91; Member, Executive Committee, Inter Parliamentary Union (IPU) British Group 1995-97; KB 2001; *Recreations:* Golf, sailing, gardening

Sir Michael Lord, MP, House of Commons, London SW1A 0AA *Tel:* 020 7219 5055 *Fax:* 020 7219 2931. *Constituency:* Central Suffolk and North Ipswich Conservative Association, 19 The Business Centre, Earl Soham, Woodbridge, Suffolk IP13 7SA *Tel:* 01728 685148 *Fax:* 01728 685157 *E-mail:* mail@centralsuffolk.co.uk

Con majority 8,183

LOUGHTON, TIM
East Worthing and Shoreham

Timothy Paul Loughton. Born 30 May 1962; Son of Reverend Michael Loughton and Pamela Dorothy Loughton; Educated The Priory School, Lewes, Sussex; Warwick University (BA classical civilisation 1983); Clare College, Cambridge (Research Mesopotamian archaeology 1983-84); Married Elizabeth Juliet MacLauchlan 1992 (1 son 2 daughters). Fund manager, Fleming Private Asset Management, City of London 1984-, Director 1992-2000; Formerly BIFU

House of Commons: Contested Sheffield Brightside 1992 general election. Member for East Worthing and Shoreham since 1 May 1997 general election; Opposition Spokesperson for: Environment, Transport and the Regions (Regeneration; Poverty; Regions; Housing) 2000-01, Health 2001-03; Shadow Minister for: Health and Education 2003, Children and the Family 2003-04, Children and for Health 2004-. *Political interests:* Finance, Foreign Affairs, Home Affairs, Education (Special Needs), Environmental Taxation, Environment and Housing, Disability, Animal Welfare, Health. Latin America, Middle East, Indian sub-continent

Chair Lewes Young Conservatives 1978; Vice-chair: Sussex Young Conservatives 1979, Lewes Constituency Conservative Association 1979, South East Area Young Conservatives 1980; Secretary Warwick University Conservative Association 1981-82; Member Cambridge University Conservative Association 1983-84; Member Bow Group 1985-92; Vice-chair Battersea Conservative Association 1990-91; Member London Area Conservative Executive Committee 1993-96; Life Vice-President Sheffield Brightside Constituency Association 1993-; Deputy Chair Battersea Constituency Conservative Association 1994-96; Executive Committee Member, Selsdon Group 1994-2003; Member Carlton Club Political Committee 1994-2004; Chair Conservative Disability Group 1998-. St Barnabas Hospice; General election PA to Tim Eggar MP 1987; Member: Burns committee Financial Services and Markets Bill 1999, Standing committee Financial Services and Markets Bill 1999-, Standing committee Local Government Bill 2000-, Homes Bill 2001-, Homelessness Bill 2001-, European Standing committee C 1999-2001; Lecturer, English Wine and Stock Exchange; Adoption and Children Bill November 2001-May 2002; Tobacco Advertising Bill 2003; Member: Royal Institute International Affairs, CPA, IPU; *Clubs:* Patron, Worthing Hockey; *Recreations:* Skiing, tennis, hockey, wine, archaeology

Tim Loughton, MP, House of Commons, London SW1A 0AA *Tel:* 020 7219 4471 *Fax:* 020 7219 0461 *E-mail:* loughtont@parliament.uk. *Constituency:* Haverfield House, 4 Union Place, Worthing BN11 1LG *Tel:* 01903 235168 *Fax:* 01903 219755

LOVE, ANDREW
Edmonton

Andrew Love. Born 21 March 1949; Son of late James Love and Olive Love; Educated Greenock High School; Strathclyde University (BSc physics); Association of Chartered Institute of Secretaries; Married Ruth Rosenthal 1983. Parliamentary Officer, Co-operative Party; Member (branch chairman 1980-83), TGWU; National Executive Member, NACO 1989-92; Councillor, London Borough of Haringey 1980-86

Lab/Co-op majority 8,075

House of Commons: Contested Edmonton 1992 general election. Member for Edmonton since 1 May 1997 general election; PPS to Jacqui Smith as Minister of State: Department of Health 2001-03, Department of Trade and Industry 2003-05. *Political interests:* Housing, Regeneration, Health, Mutuality, Small Businesses. France, Cyprus, Sri Lanka, Lebanon

Chair: Hornsey and Wood Green Labour Party 1987-89, Policy Committee, Greater London Labour Party 1990-94, Co-operative Parliamentary Group 1999-2001. Vice-patron: Helen Rollason Cancer Appeal, Heal Cancer Charity; Trustee, ICOF; *Clubs:* Royal Society of Arts; Muswell Hill Golf Club; *Recreations:* History, opera, cinema, golf

Andrew Love, MP, House of Commons, London SW1A 0AA *Tel:* 020 7219 6377 *Fax:* 020 7219 6623 *E-mail:* lovea@parliament.uk. *Constituency:* Broad House, 205 Fore Street, Edmonton, London N18 2TZ *Tel:* 020 8803 0574 *Fax:* 020 8807 1673

LUCAS, IAN
Wrexham

Ian Colin Lucas. Born 18 September 1960; Son of Colin Lucas, process engineer and Alice Lucas, cleaner; Educated Greenwell Comprehensive School, Gateshead; Royal Grammar School, Newcastle upon Tyne; New College, Oxford (BA jurisprudence 1982); College of Law, Christleton law (Solicitor's Final Exam 1983); Married Norah Anne Sudd 1986 (1 daughter 1 son). Russell-Cooke Potter and Chapman Solicitors: Articled clerk, assistant solicitor 1983-86; Solicitor's Admission 1985; Assistant Solicitor: Percy Hughes and Roberts 1986-87, Lees Moore and Price 1987-89, Roberts Moore Nicholas Jones 1989-92, DR Crawford 1992-97; Principal Crawford Lucas 1997-2000; Partner Stevens Lucas, Oswestry 2000-01; AMICUS/MSF 1996-; Member Gresford Community Council, Wrexham 1987-91

Lab majority 6,819

House of Commons: Contested Shropshire North 1997 general election. Member for Wrexham since 7 June 2001 general election. *Political interests:* Economy, European Affairs, Health, Education, Environment, Small Businesses. Germany, Japan, USA, India, Zimbabwe

Chair Wrexham Labour Party 1992-93; Vice-chair North Shropshire Labour Party 1993-2000; Society of Labour Lawyers 1996-; Fabian Society 2000-. *Recreations:* History, film, football, cricket, painting

Ian Lucas, MP, House of Commons, London SW1A 0AA *Tel:* 020 7219 8346 *Fax:* 020 7219 1948 *E-mail:* lucasi@parliament.uk. *Constituency:* 2 Mount Street, Wrexham LL13 8DN *Tel:* 01978 355 743 *Fax:* 01978 310 051

LUFF, PETER
Mid Worcestershire

Peter James Luff. Born 18 February 1955; Son of late Thomas Luff, master printer, and late Joyce Luff; Educated Windsor Grammar School; Corpus Christi College, Cambridge (BA economics 1976, MA); Married Julia Jenks 1982 (1 son 1 daughter). Research assistant to Peter Walker MP 1977-80; Head of private office to Edward Heath MP 1980-82; Company secretary, family stationery business, Luff & Sons Ltd to 1987; Account director, director and managing director, Good Relations Public Affairs Ltd 1982-87; Special Adviser to Lord Young of Graffham, Secretary of State for Trade and Industry 1987-89; Senior consultant, Lowe Bell Communications 1989-90; Assistant managing director, Good Relations Ltd 1990-92

Con majority 13,327

House of Commons: Contested Holborn and St Pancras 1987 general election. Member for Worcester 1992-97, and for Mid Worcestershire since 1 May 1997 general election; Opposition Whip 2000-: Home Office and Health 2000-01, Treasury, 2000-, Foreign Affairs 2001-02; Assistant Chief Whip 2002-; PPS: to Tim Eggar as Minister of State, Department of Trade and Industry 1993-96, to Lord Mackay of Clashfern as Lord Chancellor 1996-97, to Ann Widdecombe as Minister for Prisons, Home Office 1996-97. *Political interests:* Railways, Trade and Industry, Rural Affairs, Performing Arts, International Development. Hong Kong, Falkland Islands, Israel, India, Mongolia

Chairman, Conservative Parliamentary Friends of India 2001-. Water Aid, St Mungo's, Worcester Cathedral; Member, Joseph Rowntree Inquiry into Planning for Housing 1992-94; Member, Armed Forces Parliamentary Scheme (Royal Navy) 1996, 2002; Member, Executive Committee, Commonwealth Parliamentary Association; *Publications: Supporting Excellence – Funding Dance and Drama Students* (Bow Group), 1995; *Clubs:* Worcestershire County Cricket; *Recreations:* Steam railways, theatre, photography, shooting, diving

Peter Luff, MP, House of Commons, London SW1A 0AA *Tel:* 020 7219 5143
E-mail: luffjd@parliament.uk. *Constituency: Tel:* 01905 763952 *Fax:* 01905 761808

McAVOY, THOMAS
Rutherglen and Hamilton West

Thomas McLaughlin McAvoy. Born 14 December 1943; Son of late Edward McAvoy, steelworker, and late Frances McLaughlin McAvoy; Educated Secondary Schools; Married Eleanor Kerr 1968 (4 sons); Shop steward, AEU 1974-87; Chair, Rutherglen Community Council 1980-82; Councillor Strathclyde Regional Council 1982-87

Lab/Co-op majority 16,112

House of Commons: Member for Glasgow Rutherglen 1987-2005, for Ruitherglen and Hamilton West since 5 May 2005 general election; Opposition Whip 1991-93, 1996-97; Government Whip (Pairing Whip) 1997-. *Political interests:* Social Services. Ireland, USA

Member, Co-operative Party. PC 2003

Rt Hon Thomas McAvoy, MP, House of Commons, London SW1A 0AA
Tel: 020 7219 5009 *E-mail:* enquiries@tommymcavoy.org.uk. *Constituency:* 66 Hamilton Road, Rutherglen G73 3DQ *Tel:* 0141-647 5757 *Fax:* 0141-647 5456,

McCABE, STEVE
Birmingham Hall Green

Lab majority 5,714

Stephen James McCabe. Born 4 August 1955; Son of James and Margaret McCabe; Educated Port Glasgow, Senior Secondary; Moray House College, Edinburgh (Diploma in Social Studies 1977, Certificate Qualification Social Work 1977); Bradford University (MA social work 1986); Married Lorraine Lea Clendon 1991 (divorced) (1 son 1 daughter). Social work with young offenders 1977-85; Lecturer in social work NE Worcestershire College 1989-91; Part-time researcher British Association of Social Workers 1989-91; Part-time child protection social worker 1989-91; Central Council for Education in Social Work 1991-97; Member, MSF; Shop steward, NALGO 1978-82; Birmingham City Council: Councillor 1990-98, Chair, Transportation Committee 1993-96

House of Commons: Member for Birmingham Hall Green since 1 May 1997 general election; PPS to Charles Clarke as: Secretary of State for Education and Skills 2003-04, Home Secretary 2004-. *Political interests:* Community Care, Transport, Economic Issues, Police and Security Issues

Clubs: Local Cricket Club; *Recreations:* Reading, football, hill walking

Steve McCabe, MP, House of Commons, London SW1A 0AA *Tel:* 020 7219 4842; 020 7219 3509 *Fax:* 020 7219 0367 *E-mail:* mccabes@parliament.uk.
Constituency: c/o The Labour Party, Birmingham, West Midlands B5 7AF
Fax: 020 7219 0996

McCAFFERTY, CHRISTINE
Calder Valley

Lab majority 1,367

Chris (Christine) McCafferty. Born 14 October 1945; Daughter of late John and late Dorothy Livesley; Educated Whalley Range Grammar School For Girls, Manchester; Footscray High School, Melbourne, Australia; Married 1st, Michael McCafferty (1 son), married 2nd, David Tarlo. Welfare worker (Disabled), CHS Manchester 1963-70; Education welfare officer, Manchester Education Committee 1970-72; Registrar of marriages, Bury Registration District 1978-80; Project worker, Calderdale Well Woman Centre 1989-96; Member: NALGO 1967-81, MSF 1994-; Calderdale MBC: Councillor 1991-97, Chair, woman's advisory group 1991-93, disabilities advisory group 1991-93, adoption panel 1992-96; Member: Independent Education Appeals Panel 1991-97, Independent Advisory Panel 1991-97, Calderdale District Council 1991-, Hebden Royd Town Council 1991-95; Chair/Spokesperson, social services 1993-96; Executive of North Region Association for the Blind 1993-96; Member: West Yorkshire Police Authority 1994-97, West Yorkshire Police Complaints Committee 1994-97; Chair: Brighouse Police Community Forum 1994-97, Sowerby Bridge Police Community Forum 1994-97; Advisory Board, Queen Mary and Westfield College Public Policy Seminars

House of Commons: Member for Calder Valley since 1 May 1997 general election. *Political interests:* Health, Social Services, International Development. Gambia, India, Australia, Yemen

Member, Co-op Party 1990-. Director, Royd Regeneration Ltd; Trustee, Trades Club Building Hebden Bridge; Member, Political Advisory Committee, Environmental Industries Commission; Parliamentary Member, Council of Europe 1999; Member: Social Health and Family Committee, Sub Committee for Children; Parliamentary Member, Western European Union 1999-; Member, Rules and Procedures Committee; Trustee, Trades Club Building, Hebden Bridge 1992-; Director, Royd Regeneration Ltd 1996-; *Recreations:* Swimming, reading, caravanning

Christine McCafferty, MP, House of Commons, London SW1A 0AA
Tel: 020 7219 5026 *Fax:* 020 7219 7269 *E-mail:* mccafferty@btinternet.com.
Constituency: 15 Heptonstall Road, Hebden Bridge, West Yorkshire HX4 6AZ
Tel: 01422 843713 *Fax:* 01422 846713

McCARTHY, KERRY
Bristol East

Kerry McCarthy. Born 26 March 1965; Educated Denbigh High School, Luton; Luton Sixth Form College; Liverpool University (BA Russian, politics and linguistics); Law Society (CPE and final solicitors examinations 1994); Single. Legal assistant South Bedfordshire Magistrates Court 1986-88; Litigation assistant Neves Solicitors, Luton 1988-89; Trainee solicitor Wilde Sapte 1992-94; Legal manager Abbey National Treasury Services 1994-96; Senior counsel, debt markets Merril Lynch Europe Plc 1996-99; Lawyer The Labour Party 2001; Regional director Britain in Europe campaign 2003-04; Head of public policy The Waterfront Partnership 2004-05; TGWU 1994-2005; Luton Borough Council: Councillor 1995-2003, Chair of housing and cabinet member 1999-03; Director of London Luton Airport 1999-2003

Lab majority 8,621

House of Commons: Member for Bristol East since 5 May 2005 general election. *Political interests:* Economic policy, international trade/aid, crime and justice, community cohesion, transport

Chair Luton North Constituency Labour Party (CLP) 1994-96; Secretary Luton North CLP 1996-99; Vice-chair East of England regional board 1999-2005; National policy forum 1998-2005; Economic policy commission 1998-2005. *Clubs:* St George Labour; *Recreations:* Travel, scuba diving, F1 motor racing

Kerry McCarthy, MP, House of Commons, London SW1A 0AA
Tel: 020 7219 4510. *Constituency:* Agent: Pascal Mensah, 326a Church Road, Bristol BS5 8AJ *Tel:* 0117 941 2562 *E-mail:* east@bristollabourparty.org.uk
Website: www.bristollabourparty.org.uk/east

McCARTHY-FRY, SARAH
Portsmouth North

Sarah Louise McCarthy-Fry. Born 4 February 1955; Educated Portsmouth High School; Married Anthony McCarthy 1997. Accounts clerk FPT Industries Ltd 1985-88; GKN Aerospace and predecessors: Financial accountant 1988-2000, Financial analyst (Europe) 2000-03, Financial controller 2002-05; GMB 1985-92; GPMU 1992-98; TGWU 1998-2003 Amicus 20003-; Portsmouth City Council: Councillor 1994-2002, Deputy leader 1995-2000

Lab/Co-op majority 1,139

House of Commons: Member for Portsmouth North since 5 May 2005 general election. *Political interests:* Trade and Industry, social economy

Chair: South West Regional Labour Party 1996-97, South East Regional Labour Party 1998-2000. Contested Wight and Hants South 1994 and South East England 1999 European Parliament elections; *Recreations:* Tap dancing, dog walking

Sarah McCarthy-Fry, MP, House of Commons, London SW1A 0AA
Tel: 020 7219 6517. *Constituency:* Portsmouth Labour Party, Holbrook Road, Portsmouth, Hampshire PO1 1JB *Tel:* 023 9286 4976 *Fax:* 023 9229 6321
E-mail: contact@portsmouth-clp.new.labour.org.uk

Lab majority 18,149

McCARTNEY, IAN
Makerfield

Ian McCartney. Born 25 April 1951; Son of Hugh McCartney, Labour MP; Educated State Schools; Divorced (1 son deceased 2 daughters); married 2nd Ann Parkes, neé Kevan 1988. Secretary to Roger Stott MP 1979-87; TGWU: Branch secretary 1968, Shop steward 1970; Chair, TGWU Parliamentary Group; Wigan Borough Councillor 1982-87

House of Commons: Member for Makerfield since 11 June 1987 general election; Opposition Front Bench Spokesperson for: National Health Service 1992-94, Employment 1994-96, Education and Employment (Chief Employment Spokesperson) 1996-97; Minister of State: Department of Trade and Industry 1997-99, Cabinet Office 1999-2001; Minister of State for Pensions, Department for Work and Pensions 2001-03; Minister without Portfolio and Party Chair 2003-. *Political interests:* Local and Regional Government, Fire Service, Civil Defence, Health and Safety Issues, NHS, Social Services, Employment. Australia

Labour Party full-time officer 1973; Member, Labour Party National Executive Committee 1996-; Member, PLP General Election Campaign (Country) 1999-; Chair, Labour Party National Policy Forum 2002-; Member, Labour Party Joint Policy Commission. PC 1999; *Clubs:* Platt Bridge Labour; *Recreations:* Wigan Rugby League

Rt Hon Ian McCartney, MP, House of Commons, London SW1A 0AA
Tel: 020 7219 4503. *Constituency:* 1st Floor, Gerrard Winstanley House, Crawford Street, Wigan, Greater Manchester WN1 1NJ *Tel:* 01942 824029 *Fax:* 01942 492746

DUP majority 3,448

McCREA, WILLIAM
South Antrim

William (Robert Thomas) McCrea. Born 6 August 1948; Son of late Robert Thomas McCrea, farmer and of Sarah McCrea; Educated Cookstown Grammar School; Marietta Bible College, Ohio, USA (doctorate of divinity); Married Anne McKnight 1971 (2 sons 3 daughters). Civil Servant, Northern Ireland Department of Health and Social Services 1966-82; Member, Northern Ireland Assembly 1982-86; Member Northern Ireland Forum for Political Dialogue 1996-98; MLA for Mid Ulster 1998-; Magherafelt District Council: Councillor 1973-, Mayor 1977-81

House of Commons: MP for Mid Ulster 1983-97, for South Antrim September 2000-June 2001 and since 5 May 2005 general election. *Political interests:* Agriculture, Health, Elderly Issues, The Environment

Publications: In His Pathway

William McCrea, MP, House of Commons, London SW1A 0AA *Tel:* 020 7219 8525

Lab majority 12,560

McDONAGH, SIOBHAIN
Mitcham and Morden

Siobhain McDonagh. Born 20 February 1960; Daughter of Cumin and Breda McDonagh, née Doogue, retired builder and nurse; Educated Holy Cross Convent, New Malden; Essex University (BA government 1981); Single, no children. Clerical officer, DHSS 1981-83; Housing Benefits assistant 1983-84; Receptionist, Homeless Persons Unit, London Borough of Wandsworth 1984-86; Housing adviser 1986-88; Development co-ordinator, Battersea Church Housing Trust 1988-97; Member, GMB; Councillor, London Borough of Merton 1982-1997, Chair, Housing Committee 1990-95

House of Commons: Contested Mitcham and Morden 1987 and 1992 general elections. Member for Mitcham and Morden since 1 May 1997 general election. *Political interests:* Health, Housing, Quality of Life, Welfare Reform

Made first Conference Speech aged 23; Trustee Mitcham Garden Village; *Recreations:* Travel, friends, music

Siobhain McDonagh, MP, House of Commons, London SW1A 0AA
Tel: 020 7219 4678 *Fax:* 020 7219 0986 *E-mail:* mcdonaghs@parliament.uk.
Constituency: 1 Crown Road, Morden SM4 5DD *Tel:* 020 8542 4835
Fax: 020 8544 0377 *Website:* www.siobhainmcdonagh.org.uk

SDLP majority 1,235

McDONNELL, ALASDAIR
Belfast South

Alasdair McDonnell. Born 1 September 1949; Son of the late Charles McDonnell and the late Margaret, neé McIlhatton; Educated St McNissis College, Garron Tower; University College Dublin Medical School (MB, BCh, BAO 1975); Married Olivia Nugent 1998 (1 daughter 2 sons). Junior hospital doctor, Belfast 1975-79; Full-time GP 1979-99; Member, Northern Ireland Forum for Political Dialogue 1996; Part-time GP 1999-; MLA for Belfast South 1998-; Member, BMA; Councillor, Belfast City Council 1977-81, 1985-; Deputy Mayor of Belfast 1995-96; Chair, City Economic Development Sub-Committee 1997-99

House of Commons: Contested North Antrim 1970, Belfast South 1979 Westminster general election, 1982 by-election, 1983, 1987, 1992 and 1997 general elections. Member for Belfast South since 5 May 2005 general election. *Political interests:* Urban renewal, economic reconstruction, job creation, information technology, biotechnology. France, Germany, Netherlands, Atlantic Canada, USA

Deputy Leader, SDLP 2004-

Dr Alasdair McDonnell, MP, House of Commons, London SW1A 0AA
Tel: 020 7219 8528

Complete post-election analysis

McDONNELL, JOHN
Hayes and Harlington

Lab majority 10,847

John Martin McDonnell. Born 8 September 1951; Son of late Robert and Elsie McDonnell; Educated Great Yarmouth Grammar School, Burnley Technical College; Brunel University (BSc government and politics); Birkbeck College, London University (MSc politics and sociology); Married Cynthia Pinto 1995 (1 son 2 daughters). Shopfloor production worker 1968-73; Assistant head, social insurance department, National Union of Mineworkers 1977-78; Researcher, TUC 1978-82; Head of policy unit, London Borough of Camden 1985-87; Chief Executive: Association of London Authorities 1987-95, Association of London Government 1995-97; Former Shop Steward, UNISON; Co-ordinator, RMT Parliamentary Group 2002-; Chair PCS Parliamentary Group; Member: Justice Trade Unions Group, ASLEF Parliamentary Group; Co-ordinator Firefighters Parliamentary Support Group; GLC Councillor 1981-86: Chair Finance Committee, Deputy Leader

House of Commons: Member for Hayes and Harlington since 1 May 1997 general election. *Political interests:* Economics, Local and Regional Government, Irish Affairs, Environment, Aviation. Ireland, Kenya, Gambia, Tanzania, Punjab, Somalia, Nuloa Mountains

Member: Labour Party Animal Welfare Society, Labour Party Committee on Ireland, Labour Party CND; Chair: Labour Party Irish Society, Socialist Campaign Group of MPs; Member: UNISON Group, RMT Group. Harlington Hospice; Member, Friends of Ireland – Coalition in support of Belfast Agreement; Chair, Britain and Ireland Human Rights Centre; Member, London Wildlife Trust; *Publications:* Editor, *Labour Herald*; Contributor to: *Campaign Group News, Tribune, Red Pepper, Labour Briefing; Clubs:* Member: Hayes Irish Society, Hayes and Harlington Workingmen's, Hayes and Harlington History Society, Hayes and Harlington Community Centre; Hillingdon Outdoor Activities Centre; Wayfarer Sailing Association; Vice-president, Hayes Football Club; Patron, Hayes Cricket Club; *Recreations:* Sailing, football, cycling, gardening, theatre, cinema

John McDonnell, MP, House of Commons, London SW1A 0AA
Tel: 020 7219 6908 *E-mail:* office@john-mcdonnell.net. *Constituency:* Pump Lane, Hayes UB3 3NB *Tel:* 020 8569 0010 *Fax:* 020 8569 0109

FIRE BRIGADES UNION
PARLIAMENTARY GROUP

Our new Parliamentary Group aims to give a clearer and stronger voice to those who work in the fire service and the communities we serve

Key issues:

★ Campaign for national standards to underpin local fire and rescue plans

★ NO2 Fire Deaths campaign

★ Fight against regionalisation of emergency fire control rooms

★ Need to recruit more firefighters working the retained duty system

★ Fire service pensions ★ Health and safety

★ Professional fire service issues ★ Tackling assaults on firefighters

Chair Andrew Dismore MP
Vice-Chair Michael Clapham MP
Secretary John McDonnell MP

General Secretary: Matt Wrack · President: Ruth Winters

Fire Brigades Union
Bradley House
68 Coombe Road
Kingston Upon Thames
KT2 7AE
020 8541 1765
www.fbu.org.uk
info@fbu.org.uk

NO2
Fire Deaths
CAMPAIGNING TO KEEP YOU SAFE

MacDOUGALL, JOHN
Glenrothes

John William MacDougall. Born 8 December 1947; Son of William MacDougall, process worker and Barbara, housewife; Educated Templehall Secondary Modern School, Kirkcaldy, Fife; Rosyth Naval Dockyard College; Glenrothes Technical College; Fife College (Diploma industrial management); Married Cathy 1968 (1 son 1 daughter). Former board member Glenrothes Development Corporation; Member GMBA; Former chair Rosyth Dockyard and Naval Base Co-ordinating Committee; Former Leader Controlling Group COSLA; Fife Regional Council: Councillor 1982, Leader of Administration 1987-96, Chair Policy and Resources Committee 1989-96, Convener 1996-May 2001; Justice of the Peace

Lab majority 10,664

House of Commons: Member for Central Fife 2001-05, for Glenrothes since 5 May 2005 general election

CHAS, Kinross (childrens hospice); Former member: Scottish Broadcasting Authority, Scottish Constitutional Convention; Leader Inquiry into Financial Irregularities in European Community; Bureau Member Assembly of the European Regions 1992; Member Scottish Valuation Advisory Council 1992-96; Chair East of Scotland European Consortium 1993-96; Assembly of the European Regions: Former vice-president, Former treasurer; Member: Consultative Assembly British Section Council of European Municipalities, European Network Group COSLA; Founder member East of Scotland European Consortium; Alternate delegate Congress of Local and Regional Authorities of European Union; Convention of Scottish Local Authorities: Delegate, Member: Policy executive, European and International Affairs Committee; Delegate International Union of Local Authorities; Vice-president Development of CPMR/AER relations Assembly of the European Regions 1998-; Member: St Andrews University Court, St Andrews Joint Liaison Committee, Fife Economic Forum, Forth Road Bridge Joint Board; Alternate director East Neuk Ltd; Former chair and director Burntisland Initiative Recreational Trust Ltd; Chair and director Community Business Fife Ltd 1988-92; St Andrews Links Trust: Trustee 1996-98, Vice-chair 1998-2001; Director Fife Enterprise Ltd; Commonwealth Parliamentary Association; Inter Parliamentary Union; Honorary president: Fife Historic Buildings Trust, Wemyss Caves Preservation Trust; *Recreations:* Cycling, walking, sport

John MacDougall, MP, House of Commons, London SW1A 0AA
Tel: 020 7219 8233 *E-mail:* macdougallj@parliament.uk. *Constituency:* 5 Hanover Court, Glenrothes KY7 6SB

McFADDEN, PAT
Wolverhampton South East

Pat McFadden. Born 26 March 1965; Educated Holyrood Secondary School; Glasgow University; Edinburgh University; single. Former adviser to John Smith and Donald Dewar; Political Secretary, Prime Minister's Office 2002-05; Member TGWU

House of Commons: Member for Wolverhampton South East since 5 May 2005 general election

Recreations: Reading and sport

Lab majority 10,495

Pat McFadden, MP, House of Commons, London SW1A 0AA *Tel:* 020 7219 8024. *Constituency:* Campaign HQ, 39 Lichfield Street, Bilston WV14 0AJ
Tel: 0791 9247540

McFALL, JOHN
West Dunbartonshire

John McFall. Born 4 October 1944; Son of late John and Jean McFall; Educated Paisley College of Technology; Strathclyde University (BSc chemistry, MBA); Open University (BA education); Married (4 children). Mathematics and chemistry teacher; Assistant head teacher -1987

House of Commons: Member for Dumbarton 1987-2005, for West Dunbartonshire since 5 May 2005 general election; Opposition Spokesperson for Scottish Affairs (with responsibilities for Industry, Economic Affairs, Employment and Training, Home Affairs, Transport and Roads, Agriculture, Fisheries and Forestry) 1992-97; Opposition Whip 1989-91; Government Whip 1997-98; Parliamentary Under-Secretary of State, Northern Ireland Office 1998-99 (Minister for Education, Training and Employment, Health and Community Relations 1998-99, for Economy and Education 1999). *Political interests:* Defence, Education, Economic Policy, Co-operative Development. Latin America, Middle East, Romania

Lab/Co-op majority 12,553

Member, Co-operative Party. PC 2004; *Recreations:* Jogging, golf, reading
John McFall, MP, House of Commons, London SW1A 0AA *Tel:* 020 7219 3521 *E-mail:* mcfallj@parliament.uk. *Constituency:* 125 College Street, Dumbarton G82 1NH *Tel:* 01389 734214 *Fax:* 01389 761498

McGOVERN, JIM
Dundee West

James McGovern. Born 17 November 1956; Educated Lawside Academy, Dundee; Married to Norma. Glazier: Lynsey and Scott 1972-87, Dundee District Council 1987-97; GMB official 1997-; GMB; Elected representative Tayside Regional Council 1994-96

House of Commons: Member for Dundee West since 5 May 2005 general election
Recreations: Reading, gym, watching football

Lab majority 5,379

Jim McGovern, MP, House of Commons, London SW1A 0AA *Tel:* 020 7219 4938. *Constituency:* *E-mail:* jim.mcgovern@gmb.org.uk

McGRADY, EDDIE
South Down

Eddie (Edward) K McGrady. Born 3 June 1935; Son of late Michael and Lilian McGrady; Educated St Patrick's High School, Downpatrick; Institute of Chartered Accountants; Married Patricia Swail 1959 (2 sons 1 daughter). Partner M B McGrady & Co., Chartered Accountants (retired 1998); Downpatrick Urban District Council: Councillor 1961-73, Chair 1964-73; Down District Council: Councillor 1973-89, Chair 1975; Member Northern Ireland Policing Board 2002-

SDLP majority 9,140

House of Commons: Contested South Down in 1979 and 1983 general elections and 1986 by-election. Member for South Down since 11 June 1987 general election; Spokesperson for: Housing, Local Government, Environment; Chief Whip, SDLP 1979-; Member: Northern Ireland Assembly 1973, Minister for Co-ordination 1974, Northern Ireland Assembly 1982-86, Northern Ireland Forum 1996-98, Northern Ireland Assembly 1998-2002. *Political interests:* Northern Ireland, Constitutional Issues. Ireland, USA

Founder Member and First Chairman, SDLP 1970-72. *Clubs:* Saul GAC; *Recreations:* Walking, gardening
Eddie McGrady, MP, House of Commons, London SW1A 0AA *Tel:* 020 7219 4153 *E-mail:* e.mcgrady@sdlp.ie. *Constituency:* 32 Saul Street, Downpatrick BT30 6NQ *Tel:* 028 4461 2882 *Fax:* 028 4461 9574

Working with government on plastic cards and payments

APACS is the banking industry association for payments dealing with credit and debit cards, cheques, cash, automated payments and clearing issues. Its members are the UK's major banks, building societies and card companies.

APACS provides a central voice for the payments industry and a forum for its members to discuss non-competitive issues and to make industry-wide decisions on payments for the benefit of consumers and businesses. We are currently working with the Government and parliamentarians on a range of key consumer issues, some of which are set out below.

Transparency and marketing of credit card products

Card companies are committed to providing customers with clear and consistent information on their products to enable them to make the best borrowing decisions. The UK card industry has introduced the Summary Box on pre-contract material and the 2005 Banking Code includes guidelines on the Summary Box, wealth warnings, and the marketing of credit card cheques.

Data sharing and responsible lending

APACS members are committed to improving the quality of their lending decisions and assist with debt problems. The UK card industry has agreed to share full credit card data within the constraints of current legislation.

Anti-fraud activities

APACS co-ordinates a range of activities to tackle card fraud. One of the most visible recent initiatives has been the introduction of chip and PIN on credit and debits cards

which has been achieved hand-in-hand with the retail industry.

Internet safety and security

APACS remit includes internet banking and online payments. The industry works closely with law enforcement agencies in the UK and overseas to minimise online banking fraud. Card companies also take a hard line against online child abuse, campaigning to ensure that no UK company profits from child pornography on the Internet.

Payment Systems Task Force

APACS is a member of the Task Force chaired by the Office of Fair Trading and established in 2004 to identify, consider and resolve competition, efficiency and incentive issues relating to payment systems. APACS members have put together an implementation group to consider how a new faster service for telephone and Internet payments would work.

Future initiatives

APACS will seek to broaden and deepen its approach to transparency and responsible lending. APACS will campaign to see remaining obstacles to data sharing removed and to break down barriers between public and private sectors to allow better sharing of information on known fraudsters.

For further information

To find out more about any aspect of APACS' work please contact:

Sandra Quinn, Director of Corporate Communications
T: 020 7711 6234
E: sandra.quinn@apacs.org.uk

APACS

The UK Payments Association

McGUINNESS, MARTIN
Mid Ulster

Martin McGuinness. Born 23 May 1950; Educated Christian Brothers' Technical College. Sinn Fein Chief negotiator mid-1980s-; Member, Northern Ireland Assembly 1982, 1998-; Sinn Fein representative to the Dublin Forum for Peace and Reconciliation 1994-95; Minister for Education, Northern Ireland Assembly 1999-2003 (suspension)

House of Commons: Contested Foyle 1983, 1987 and 1992 general elections. Member for Mid Ulster since 1 May 1997 general election. *Political interests:* South Africa

Recreations: Cooking, walking, reading, fly fishing

Sinn Féin majority 10,976

Martin McGuinness, MP, House of Commons, London SW1A 0AA
Tel: 020 7219 8157. *Constituency:* 32 Burn Road, Cookstown BT80 8DN
Tel: 028 8676 5850 *Fax:* 028 8676 6734

McGUIRE, ANNE
Stirling

Anne Catherine McGuire. Born 26 May 1949; Daughter of late Albert Long, railway signalman, and late Agnes Long, shop worker; Educated Our Lady of St Francis Secondary School, Glasgow; Glasgow University (MA politics with history 1971); Notre Dame College of Education (Diploma in Secondary Education 1975); Married Len McGuire 1972 (1 son 1 daughter). Teacher, Supply, history/modern studies 1982-84; Development Worker/Senior Manager, Voluntary Sector, Community Service Volunteers 1984-93; Depute Director, Scottish Council for Voluntary Organisations 1993-97; National Executive, GMB 1987-91; Councillor, Strathclyde Regional Council 1980-82

Lab majority 4,767

House of Commons: Member for Stirling 1997-2005, for new Stirling since 5 May 2005 general election; Assistant Government Whip 1998-2001; Government Whip 2001-02; PPS to Donald Dewar as Secretary of State for Scotland December 1997-98; Parliamentary Under-Secretary of State: Scotland Office 2002-05, Department for Work and Pensions 2005-. *Political interests:* European Union, Rural Development, Urban Regeneration. USA, Germany

Member: Labour Party Scottish Executive 1984-97; Chair Labour Party Scotland 1992-93. Strathcarron Hospice; *Recreations:* Learning Gaelic, reading, walking

Anne McGuire, MP, House of Commons, London SW1A 0AA *Tel:* 020 7219 5014 *Fax:* 020 7219 2503 *E-mail:* mcguirea@parliament.uk. *Constituency:* 22 Viewfield Street, Stirling FK8 1UA *Tel:* 01786 446515 *Fax:* 01786 446513

Disability Rights Commission

Delivering Disability Equality

Since the Disability Rights Commission opened its doors five years ago we have begun to see a real change in the way that 10 million disabled people are treated throughout Britain. New legislation has strengthened disabled people's rights in housing, transport and created new tools to tackle institutional discrimination. We've supported successful legal cases – like Susan Archibald's – to defend and extend rights in the workplace and in services. Disabled people's expectations are rising and employers and service providers are beginning to take disability rights seriously.

Susan Archibald after winning a landmark House of Lords case strengthening employment rights for disabled people, courtesy of the Daily Record

There is still a long way to go. Disabled people are still twice as likely to be out of work and more likely to earn less and independent living is still a dream rather than a reality.

This Parliament offers unique opportunities to make major progress on equal citizenship for disabled people. Join us in delivering:

- welfare reform that delivers high quality support and better work opportunities

- firm progress on independent living – effective support to participate in society, and a future Commission for Equality and Human Rights that continues to be powerful, effective voice for all disabled people.

For more information contact our Parliamentary Affairs Team:
Caroline Ellis Tel: 020 7 543 7038. Caroline.Ellis@drc-gb.org
Neil Coyle. Tel: 0207 543 7039. Neil.Coyle@drc-gb.org
Textphone: 020 7543 7002. www.drc-gb.org

McINTOSH, ANNE
Vale of York

Anne Caroline Ballingall McIntosh. Born 20 September 1954; Daughter of Dr Alastair McIntosh, retired medical practitioner, and Mrs Grethe-Lise McIntosh; Educated Harrogate College; Edinburgh University (LLB 1977); Århus University, Denmark (European Law); Married John Harvey 1992. Trainee, EEC Competition Directorate 1978; Legal adviser, Didier and Associates, Brussels 1979-80; Apprentice, Scottish Bar, Edinburgh 1980-82; Admitted to Faculty of Advocates June 1982; Advocate, practising with Community Law Office, Brussels 1982-83; Adviser, European Democratic Group, principally on Transport, Youth Education, Culture, Tourism, Relations with Scandinavia, Austria and Yugoslavia 1983-89; MEP for Essex North East 1989-94, and for Essex North and Suffolk South 1994-99.

Con majority 13,712

House of Commons: Contested Workington, Cumbria 1987 general election. Member of Parliament for Vale of York since 1 May 1997 general election; Opposition Spokesperson for Culture, Media and Sport 2001-02; Shadow Minister for: Transport 2002-03, Environment and Transport 2003-. *Political interests:* Transport, Legal Affairs, Animal Welfare. Eastern Europe, Scandinavia

Advisory Board, National Eye Research (Yorkshire); Patron, Thirsk Museum Society; Member, European Standing Committee C 1999-2001; Member, European Parliament for: Essex North East 1989-94, Essex North and Suffolk South 1994-99; Assistant Whip, European Democratic Group 1989-92, Conservative Spokesman on Transport and Tourism 1992-99, Member, European People's Party 1992-99, Bureau Member 1994-97, Rapporteur on Air Transport, relations with third world countries and Trans-European Road Networks, EU Competition Policy, Air Transport Safety, Co-Chair, European Transport Safety Council 1994-99; President, Anglia Enterprise in Europe 1989-99; Fellow Industry and Parliament Trust 1995; Graduate Armed Forces Parliamentary Scheme, Royal Navy 2000; Honorary Doctorate of Laws Anglia Polytechnic University 1997; *Clubs:* Yorkshire Agricultural Society; Royal Over-seas League; Royal Automobile Club; *Recreations:* Swimming, walking, cinema

Anne McIntosh, MP, House of Commons, London SW1A 0AA *Tel:* 020 7219 3541 *Fax:* 020 7219 0972 *E-mail:* mcintosha@parliament.uk. *Constituency:* Vale of York Conservative Association, Thirsk Conservative Club, Thirsk YO7 1QS *Tel:* 01845 523835 *Fax:* 01845 527507

McISAAC, SHONA
Cleethorpes

Shona McIsaac. Born 3 April 1960; Daughter of Angus McIsaac, retired chief petty officer, and Isa, neé Nicol, school dinner lady; Educated SHAPE School, Belgium; Barne Barton Secondary Modern, Plymouth; Stoke Damerel High, Plymouth; Durham University (BSc geography 1981); Married Peter John Keith 1994. Senior sub-editor, *Chat*; Deputy chief-sub-editor, *Bella*; Chief sub-editor, *Woman*; Freelance food writer; Member, NUJ, USDAW; Councillor, London Borough of Wandsworth 1990-98

Lab majority 2,642

House of Commons: Member for Cleethorpes since 1 May 1997 general election; PPS to: Ministers of State, Northern Ireland Office: Adam Ingram 2000-01, Jane Kennedy 2001-03, Baroness Scotland of Asthal as Minister of State, Home Office 2003-. *Political interests:* Finance, Taxation, Benefits, Crime

Publications: Various non-political work-related publications; *Recreations:* Football, food, travel, cycling, archaeology of the UK, soap operas

Shona McIsaac, MP, House of Commons, London SW1A 0AA *Tel:* 020 7219 5801 *Fax:* 020 7219 3047 *E-mail:* mcisaacs@parliament.uk. *Constituency:* Immingham Resource Centre, Margaret Street, Immingham, Humberside DN40 1LE *Tel:* 01469 574324 *Fax:* 01469 510842

Con majority 12,036

MACKAY, ANDREW
Bracknell

Andrew James Mackay. Born 27 August 1949; Son of late Robert and Olive Mackay; Educated Solihull School; Married Diana Joy Kinchin 1974 (1 son 1 daughter) (divorced 1996); married Julie Kirkbride MP 1997 (1 son). Consultant to various public companies

House of Commons: Member for Birmingham Stechford 1977 by-election-1979. Member for Berkshire East 1983-97, and for Bracknell since 1 May 1997 general election; Assistant Government Whip 1992-94; Government Whip 1994-96; Deputy Chief Whip 1996-97; PPS to Tom King as Secretary of State: for Northern Ireland 1986-89, for Defence 1989-92; Sponsored Licensing (Retail Sales) Act 1988 (Private Member's Bill); Member, Shadow Cabinet 1997-2001; Shadow Secretary of State for Northern Ireland 1997-2001. *Political interests:* Foreign Affairs, Industry, Environment

Chair, Solihull Young Conservative 1971-74; Vice-Chair, Solihull Conservative Association 1971-74; Member, Conservative Party National Executive 1979-82; Deputy Chairman, Conservative Party 2004-. Chair, *Britain in Europe* Meriden Branch 1975 (Referendum); PC 1998; *Recreations:* Golf, tennis, good food, travel

Rt Hon Andrew Mackay, MP, House of Commons, London SW1A 0AA
Tel: 020 7219 2989 *Fax:* 020 7219 4123 *E-mail:* mackaya@parliament.uk.
Constituency: 10 Millbanke Court, Millbanke Way, Western Road, Bracknell, Berkshire RG12 1RP *Tel:* 01344 868286 *Website:* www.bracknellconservatives.com

Lab majority 3,338

McKECHIN, ANN
Glasgow North

Ann McKechin. Born 22 April 1961; Daughter of William McKechin and Anne McKechin (neé Coyle); Educated Sacred Heart High School, Paisley; Paisley Grammar School; Strathclyde University (LLB Scots law 1981); Single. Solicitor 1983-; Pacitti Jones Solicitors, Glasgow 1986-2000: Solicitor, Partner 1990-2000; Contested West of Scotland list 1999 Scottish Parliament election; T.G.W.U.

House of Commons: Member for Glasgow Maryhill 2001-05, for Glasgow North since 5 May 2005 general election; PPS to Jacqui Smith as Minister of State, Department of Trade and Industry 2005-. *Political interests:* International Development, Economics, Small Businesses. Rwanda, Africa

Glasgow Kelvin Labour Party: Constituency secretary 1995-98, Women's officer 2000-01. World Development Movement 1998-: Scottish representative 1998-2001, Council member 1999-; Member, Management Board, Mercycorps Scotland 2003-; Member Steering Committee of the WTO Parliamentary Conference; *Recreations:* Dancing, films, art history

Ann McKechin, MP, House of Commons, London SW1A 0AA *Tel:* 020 7219 8239
Fax: 020 7219 1770 *E-mail:* mckechina@parliament.uk.
Constituency: Tel: 0141-946 1300 *Fax:* 0141-946 1412

McKENNA, ROSEMARY
Cumbernauld, Kilsyth and Kirkintilloch East

Rosemary McKenna. Born 8 May 1941; Daughter of late Cornelius Harvey, publican, and late Mary Susan Crossan, chrome polisher and shopkeeper; Educated St Augustine's Comprehensive, Glasgow; Notre Dame College of Education (Diploma in Primary Education 1974); Married James Stephen McKenna 1963 (3 sons 1 daughter); Member AEEU, now AMICUS; Councillor, Cumbernauld and Kilsyth District Council 1984-96, Leader and Convenor of Policy and Resources 1984-88, Provost 1988-92, Leader 1992-94; Member: Cumbernauld Development Corporation 1985-97, Scottish Enterprise 1993-96, 1996-97

Lab majority 11,562

House of Commons: Member for Cumbernauld and Kilsyth 1997-2005, for Cumbernauld, Kilsyth and Kirkintilloch East since 5 May 2005 general election; Joint PPS to Ministers of State, Foreign and Commonwealth Office 1999-2001; PPS to Brian Wilson as Minister of State, Foreign and Commonwealth Office 2001. *Political interests:* Constitutional Reform, Democratic Renewal and Inclusive Politics, Libraries, Internet. France, USA

Chair, Constituency Party 1979-85; Member, Scottish Executive and National Local Government Committee 1994-98. Various; Member, Convention of Scottish Local Authorities 1984-96, Vice-President 1992-94, President 1994-96; Member, EU Committee of the Regions 1993-97; Chair, Ad-Hoc Committee on Equality Issues until 1997; Chair, Scotland Europa 1994-96; Chair, UK and European Standing Committees of Women Elected Members of the Council of European Municipalities and Regions 1995-98; Cumbernauld Theatre Trust 1984-95; CBE 1995; CBE; *Recreations:* Reading, family gatherings, travel

Rosemary McKenna, MP, House of Commons, London SW1A 0AA
Tel: 020 7219 4135 *Fax:* 020 7219 2544 *E-mail:* mckennar@parliament.uk.
Constituency: Lennox House, Lennox Road, Cumbernauld *Tel:* 01236 457788
Fax: 01236 457313

MACKINLAY, ANDREW
Thurrock

Andrew Mackinlay. Born 24 April 1949; Son of Daniel and Monica Mackinlay; Educated Salesian College, Chertsey, Surrey; Diploma in municipal administration 1968; Married Ruth Segar 1972 (2 sons 1 daughter). Local government officer with Surrey County Council 1965-75; NALGO Official 1975-92; Contested London South and Surrey East 1984 European Parliament election; Member: NALGO 1965-75; TGWU; Councillor, London Borough of Kingston upon Thames 1971-78

Lab majority 6,375

House of Commons: Contested Kingston-upon-Thames, Surbiton February and October 1974, Croydon Central 1983 and Peterborough 1987 general elections. Member for Thurrock since 9 April 1992 general election; Opposition Whip 1993-94. *Political interests:* Constitution, Devolution, Electoral Reform, Police, Ports Industry, River Thames, Transport, Channel Islands, Isle of Man, Irish Affairs, Elderly, Environment. Poland, Belgium, France, Baltic States, Czech/Slovak Republics, Hungary, Falkland Islands, Gibraltar, USA, Ireland

Member Parliamentary Labour Party Parliamentary Committee 2001-. Armed Forces Parliamentary Scheme (Royal Marines) 1997-98; Member, Parliamentary Delegation to OSCE; *Clubs:* Patron, Tilbury Football Club; *Recreations:* Visiting and studying First World War battlefields in France and Belgium, collecting Labour and Trade Union ephemera and memorabilia; non-league soccer, Ireland

Andrew Mackinlay, MP, House of Commons, London SW1A 0AA
Tel: 020 7219 6819 *E-mail:* mackinlaylabour@aol.com. *Constituency:* MPs Office, Civic Square, Tilbury, Essex RM18 8ZZ *Tel:* 01375 850359

Con majority 11,904

MACLEAN, DAVID
Penrith and The Border

David Maclean. Born 16 May 1953; Educated Fortrose Academy; Aberdeen University

House of Commons: Member for Penrith and The Border since 28 July 1983 by-election; Assistant Government Whip 1987-89; Government Whip 1988-89; Opposition Chief Whip 2001-03, 2003-; Parliamentary Secretary, Ministry of Agriculture, Fisheries and Food 1989-92; Minister of State: at Department of the Environment 1992-93, at Home Office 1993-97

PC 1995

Rt Hon David Maclean, MP, House of Commons, London SW1A 0AA
Tel: 020 7219 6494.

Con majority 10,753

McLOUGHLIN, PATRICK
West Derbyshire

Patrick Allan McLoughlin. Born 30 November 1957; Son of Patrick Alphonsos McLoughlin; Educated Cardinal Griffin Comprehensive School, Cannock; Staffordshire College of Agriculture; Married Lynne Patricia Newman 1984 (1 son 1 daughter). Agricultural worker 1974-79; Various positions with National Coal Board 1979-86; Councillor: Cannock Chase District Council 1980-87, Staffordshire County Council 1981-87

House of Commons: Contested Wolverhampton South East 1983 general election. Member for West Derbyshire since 8 May 1986 by-election; Assistant Government Whip 1995-96; Government Whip 1996-97; Opposition Pairing Whip 1997-98; Opposition Deputy Chief Whip 1998-; PPS: to Angela Rumbold as Minister of State, Department of Education 1987-88, to Lord Young of Graffham, as Secretary of State for Trade and Industry 1988-89; Parliamentary Under-Secretary of State, Department of Transport (Minister for Aviation and Shipping) 1989-92; Joint Parliamentary Under-Secretary of State, Department of Employment 1992-93; Parliamentary Under-Secretary of State for Trade and Technology, Department of Trade and Industry 1993-94. *Political interests:* Agriculture, Education

National Vice-Chair, Young Conservatives 1982-84

Patrick McLoughlin, MP, House of Commons, London SW1A 0AA
Tel: 020 7219 3511 *E-mail:* mcloughlinp@parliament.uk.
Constituency: Tel: 01332 558125 *Fax:* 01332 541509

SNP majority 1,441

MacNEIL, ANGUS
Na h-Eileanan An Iar

Angus MacNeil. Born 21 July 1970; Educated Castlebay Secondary School, Isle of Barra; Nicolson Institute, Stornoway, Isle of Lewis; Strathclyde University (BEng civil engineering 1992); Jordanhill College (PGCE primary teaching and bilingualism 1996); Married Jane Douglas 1998. Civil engineer Lilley Construction Ltd, Edinburgh 1992-93; Radio reporter BBC, Inverness 1993-95; Primary teacher Salen Primary School, Mull 1996-98; Gaelic development officer Lochaber 1998-99; Education lecturer part-time Inverness College 1999-

House of Commons: Contested Inverness East, Nairn and Lochaber 2001 general election. Member for Na h-Eileanan An Iar since 5 May 2005 general election

Convener Lochaber branch SNP 1999. Amnesty International; *Recreations:* Football, squash, shinty, sailing, boatbuilding and repair

Angus MacNeil, MP, House of Commons, London SW1A 0AA *Tel:* 020 7219 8476.
Constituency: 58 Tongasdale, Isle of Barra, Outer Hebrides HS9 5XW
E-mail: angus.macneil@gearasdan.freeserve.co.uk

Lab majority 4,730

McNULTY, TONY
Harrow East

Tony McNulty. Born 3 November 1958; Son of James Anthony McNulty, self-employed builder, and of Eileen McNulty; Educated Salvatorian College; Stanmore Sixth Form College; Liverpool University (BA political theory and institutions 1981); Virginia Polytechnic Institute and State University, USA (MA political science 1982); Married Christine Gilbert. Lecturer, Business School, Polytechnic/University of North London 1983-97; Member: T&G 1977-78, NUPE 1983-90, NATFHE 1983-97, AMICUS 1996-; Councillor, London Borough of Harrow 1986-97, Deputy Leader, Labour Group 1990-95, Leader 1995-97

House of Commons: Contested Harrow East 1992 general election. Member for Harrow East since 1 May 1997 general election; Assistant Government Whip 1999-2001; Government Whip 2001-02; PPS to David Blunkett as Secretary of State for Education and Employment with responsibility for post-16 provision 1997-99; Parliamentary Under-Secretary: Housing, Planning and Regeneration, Office of the Deputy Prime Minister 2002-03; Department for Transport 2003-04; Minister of State: Department for Transport 2004-05, Home Office 2005-. *Political interests:* Education, Health, Local and Regional Government, Regeneration, London. Ireland, France, Germany, India

Member: Socialist Educational Association, Fabian Society; Co-founder, Labour Friends of India; Member, Labour Friends of Israel. *Publications:* Various academic papers; *Clubs:* Wealdstone CIU; *Recreations:* Reading, theatre, rugby, cinema, football, gaelic games

Tony McNulty, MP, House of Commons, London SW1A 0AA *Tel:* 020 7219 4108 *Fax:* 020 7219 2417 *E-mail:* mcnultyt@parliament.uk. *Constituency:* 18 Byron Road, Wealdstone, Harrow HA3 7ST *Tel:* 020 8427 2100 *Fax:* 020 8424 2319

Lab majority 10,681

MacSHANE, DENIS
Rotherham

Denis MacShane. Born 21 May 1948; Educated Merton College, Oxford (MA modern history); London University (PhD international economics); Married Nathalie Pham 1987 (1 son 4 daughters). BBC producer 1969-77; Policy director, International Metal Workers' Federation 1980-92; Director, European Policy Institute 1992-94; President, National Union of Journalists 1978-79

House of Commons: Contested Solihull October 1974 general election. Member for Rotherham since 5 May 1994 by-election; PPS: to Joyce Quin, Derek Fatchett and Tony Lloyd as Ministers of State, Foreign and Commonwealth Office 1997-99, to Geoff Hoon as Minister of State, Foreign and Commonwealth Office 1999; Joint PPS to the Ministers of State for Foreign and Commonwealth Affairs 1999-2001-; Foreign and Commonwealth Office 2001-: Parliamentary Under-Secretary of State 2001-02, Minister of State 2002-. *Political interests:* International Economics, European Union, Manufacturing. Europe, East and South East Asia

Publications: Several books on international politics; *Recreations:* Family, walking

Dr Denis MacShane, MP, House of Commons, London SW1A 0AA
Tel: 020 7219 4060 *Fax:* 020 7219 6888 *E-mail:* macshaned@parliament.uk.
Constituency: 4 Hall Grove, Rotherham, South Yorkshire S60 2BS
Tel: 01709 367793 *Fax:* 01709 835622

Lab majority 7,851

MACTAGGART, FIONA
Slough

Fiona Mactaggart. Born 12 September 1953; Daughter of late Sir Ian Mactaggart and of late Rosemary Belhaven; Educated London University: King's College (BA English 1975), Goldsmiths' College (Postgraduate Teaching Certificate 1987), Institute of Education (MA 1993). Vice-President, National Secretary, National Union of Students 1978-81; Press and Public Relations Officer, National Council for Voluntary Organisations 1981; General Secretary, Joint Council for the Welfare of Immigrants 1982-86; Primary school teacher 1987-92; Public Relations Officer, private property company 1992; Lecturer in primary education, Institute of Education 1992-97; Former Member: TGWU 1982-86, NUJ, ASTMS 1981; Member: NUT 1987-92, AUT 1992-1997, GMB 1997-; London Borough of Wandsworth: Councillor 1986-90, Leader Labour Group 1988-90

House of Commons: Member for Slough since 1 May 1997 general election; PPS to Chris Smith as Secretary of State for Culture, Media and Sport December 1997-2001; Parliamentary Under-Secretary of State (Race Equality, Community Policy and Civil Renewal), Home Office 2003-. *Political interests:* Human Rights, Civil Liberties, Home Affairs, Education, Arts

Member, Fabian Society. *Recreations:* Walking, talking, reading, the arts, watching television

Fiona Mactaggart, MP, House of Commons, London SW1A 0AA
Tel: 020 7219 3416 *Fax:* 020 7219 0989 *E-mail:* mactaggartf@parliament.uk.
Constituency: 29 Church Street, Slough, Berkshire SL1 1PL *Tel:* 01753 518161
Fax: 01753 550293

Lab majority 7,948

MAHMOOD, KHALID
Birmingham Perry Barr

Khalid Mahmood. Born 1962. Former engineer; AEEU; Former adviser Danish International Trade Union; Birmingham City Council 1990-93: Councillor, Chair Race Relations

House of Commons: Member for Birmingham Perry Barr since 7 June 2001 general election; PPS to Tony McNulty as Minister of State, Department for Transport 2004-

Local Constituency Labour Party: Secretary, Vice-chair; Member: Socialist Health Association, Socialist Education Association; Labour Finance and Industry Group: National member, Midlands branch executive member

Khalid Mahmood, MP, House of Commons, London SW1A 0AA
Tel: 020 7219 8141. *Constituency:* Union of Students at UCE, Franchise Street, Birmingham B42 2SZ *Tel:* 0121-331 7744

Con majority 1,361

MAIN, ANNE
St Albans

Anne Main. Born 17 May 1957; Educated Bishop of Llandaff Secondary School, Cardiff; University College of Wales, Swansea (BA English 1978); Sheffield University (PGCE 1979); Married 1978, widowed 1991; married Andrew Jonathan Main 1995. Teaching and family 1979-80; Home-maker 1980-90; Carer for terminally ill husband 1990-91; Single parent and supply teacher 1991-95; NUT 1979-80; Councillor: Beaconsfield Parish Council 1999-2002, South Buckinghamshire District Council 2001-

House of Commons: Member for St Albans since 5 May 2005 general election. *Political interests:* Environment, education, health

Deputy branch chairman, Beaconsfield 2002-. Member: International League for the Protection of Horses 1999-, Berks, Oxon and Bucks Wildlife Trust 2001-; *Clubs:* Conservative Women's Club; St Albans Conservative; Beaconsfield Conservative; *Recreations:* Dog, art, reading, food and wine, exploring France

Anne Main, MP, House of Commons, London SW1A 0AA *Tel:* 020 7219 8270. *Constituency:* 104 High Street, London Colney, St Albans, Hertfordshire AL2 1QL *Tel:* 01727 825100 *Fax:* 01727 828404 *E-mail:* stalbans@tory-herts.org *Website:* www.stalbansconservatives.com

Lab majority 4,615

MALIK, SHAHID
Dewsbury

Shahid Malik. Born 24 November 1967; Educated London Polytechnic; Durham University Business School; Member: GMB, TGWU; Chair Urban Forum; Commissioner Commision for Racial Equality; Vice-chair UNESCO UK

House of Commons: Member for Dewsbury since 5 May 2005 general election

Governor Sheffield Hallam University

Shahid Malik, MP, House of Commons, London SW1A 0AA *Tel:* 020 7219 4727

MALINS, HUMFREY
Woking

Humfrey Jonathan Malins. Born 31 July 1945; Son of Rev P. Malins and late Lilian Joan Malins; Educated St John's School, Leatherhead; Brasenose College, Oxford (MA jurisprudence 1967); Married Lynda Petman 1979 (1 son 1 daughter). Deputy Metropolitan Stipendiary Magistrate 1992-97; Recorder of the Crown Court 1996-; Mole Valley District Council: Member 1973-82, Chairman, Housing Committee 1980-81

Con majority 6,612

House of Commons: Contested Liverpool Toxteth February and October 1974, East Lewisham 1979 general elections. Member for Croydon North West 1983-92, and for Woking since 1 May 1997 general election; Opposition Spokesperson for Home Affairs 2001-03; PPS: to Tim Renton as Minister of State, Home Office 1987-89, to Virginia Bottomley as Minister of State, Department of Health 1989-92; Shadow Minister for: Home Affairs 2003, Home, Constitutional and Legal Affairs 2003-04, Home Affairs 2004-. *Political interests:* Penal Affairs and Policy, Criminal Law Reform, European Union, Sport. Pakistan, Kashmir

Conservative Back Bench Legal Committee: Secretary 1983-86, Vice-Chair 1986-87. Chair, Trustees Immigration Advisory Service 1993-96; CBE 1997; CBE; *Clubs:* Vincents, Oxford, Walton Heath Golf, Richmond RFC; CBE; Captain, Parliamentary Golf Society; CBE; *Recreations:* Rugby, golf, gardening, family

Humfrey Malins, MP, House of Commons, London SW1A 0AA
Tel: 020 7219 4169; 020 7219 1189 *Fax:* 020 7219 2624
E-mail: malinsh@parliament.uk. *Constituency:* Woking Constituency Conservative Association, Churchill House, Chobham Road, Woking, Surrey GU21 4AA
Tel: 01483 773384 *Fax:* 01483 770060 *Website:* www.wcca.org.uk

MALLABER, JUDY
Amber Valley

Judy Mallaber. Born 10 July 1951; Daughter of late Kenneth Mallaber, librarian, and of late Margaret Joyce Mallaber, librarian; Educated North London Collegiate School; St Anne's College, Oxford (BA). Research officer, National Union of Public Employees 1975-85; Local government information unit 1985-96, Director 1987-95; Member, UNISON; Research Officer, NUPE 1975-85

House of Commons: Member for Amber Valley since 1 May 1997 general election.

Lab majority 5,275

Political interests: Economic Policy, Local and Regional Government, Education, Equal Opportunities, Employment

Labour Party posts include: Constituency Chair, Greater London Labour Party Regional Executive; Chair, Labour Research Department 1991-94; Vice-chair East Midlands Regional Group of Labour MPs 2002-. Advisory Council Member, Northern College for Adult Education, Barnsley; *Clubs:* Anvil, Ironville; *Recreations:* Cinema, theatre, reading, family and friends

Judy Mallaber, MP, House of Commons, London SW1A 0AA *Tel:* 020 7219 3428
E-mail: j.mallaber@btinternet.com. *Constituency:* Prospect House, Nottingham Road, Ripley, Derbyshire DE5 3AZ *Tel:* 01773 512792 *Fax:* 01773 742393

£11.6 billion

Some people think that the UK's clothing, footwear and textile industry has dwindled to insignificance, and is therefore not a priority for support.

We beg to differ.

Well over 40,000 businesses in the sector are working hard to meet the challenges of the global market. Together, they contribute £11.6 billion per year to the UK economy – around half the amount that Government spends on social services.

As their Sector Skills Council, we too are working hard – making sure that the clothing footwear and textile industry has access to appropriate training and adequate investment for skills.

To discover how many clothing, footwear and textile businesses are in your constituency, or to register your support for skills development for the sector, visit:

www.skillfast-uk.org/MPs

Tel: 0870 609 2889

Skillfast-UK, Richmond House,
Lawnswood Business Park, Redvers Close,
Leeds, LS16 6RD

skillfast-uk

The Sector Skills Council for apparel, footwear, textiles and related businesses.

MANN, JOHN
Bassetlaw

John Mann. Born 10 January 1960; Son of James Mann and Brenda Cleavin; Educated Bradford Grammar School; Manchester University (BA Econ 1982); Married Joanna White 1985 (2 daughters 1 son). Head research and education AEU 1988-90; National training officer TUC 1990-95; Liaison officer National Trade Union and Labour Party 1995-2000; Director Abraxas Communications Ltd 1998-2002; Contested East Midlands 1999 European Parliament election; AEEU 1985-; Councillor London Borough of Lambeth 1986-90

Lab majority 10,837

House of Commons: Member for Bassetlaw since 7 June 2001 general election. *Political interests:* Small Businesses, Training, Economic Regeneration, Sport

Publications: Labour and Youth: The Missing Generation, Fabian Society 1985; *Clubs:* IPD, YHA, Manton Miners; *Recreations:* Football, cricket, fellwalking

John Mann, MP, House of Commons, London SW1A 0AA *Tel:* 020 7219 8130 *Fax:* 020 7219 5965 *E-mail:* mannj@parliament.uk. *Constituency:* 68a Carlton Road, Worksop, Nottinghamshire S80 1PH *Tel:* 01909 506 200 *Fax:* 01909 532447 *Website:* www.johnmannmp.co.uk

MAPLES, JOHN
Stratford-on-Avon

John Maples. Born 22 April 1943; Educated Marlborough College; Downing College, Cambridge (BA law 1964, MA); Harvard Business School; Married Jane Corbin 1986 (1 son 1 daughter). Barrister at Law 1965-; Called to Bar 1965; Council member Royal Institute of International Affairs

Con majority 12,184

House of Commons: Member for Lewisham West 1983-92, and for Stratford-upon-Avon since 1 May 1997 general election; PPS to Norman Lamont as Chief Secretary to the Treasury 1987-90; Economic Secretary, Treasury 1990-92; Member, Shadow Cabinet 1997-2000; Shadow Secretary of State for: Health 1997-98, Defence 1998-99, Foreign and Commonwealth Affairs 1999-2000. *Political interests:* Foreign Affairs, Health, Economy. USA

Deputy Chair, Conservative Party 1994-95. Joint Vice-Chair, British-American Parliamentary International Group 1999-2003

John Maples, MP, House of Commons, London SW1A 0AA *Tel:* 020 7219 5495 *Fax:* 020 7219 2829 *E-mail:* maplesj@parliament.uk. *Constituency:* 3 Trinity Street, Stratford upon Avon, Warwickshire CV37 6BL *Tel:* 01789 292723 *Fax:* 01789 415866 *Website:* www.johnmaplesmp.com

MARRIS, ROB
Wolverhampton South West

Robert Marris. Born 8 April 1955; Son of Dr Charles Marris, radiologist, and Margaret Marris, JP; Educated St Edward's School, Oxford; University of British Columbia (BA sociology and history 1976, MA history 1979); Birmingham Polytechnic (law: Common Professional Examination 1983, Law Society Finals 1984); Partner Julia Pursehouse 1984. Firefighter British Columbia Forest Service 1974; Labourer Walter Derkaz and Company 1975; Trucker Eaton and Company 1977-79; Bus driver British Columbia Metro Transit 1979-82; Manby and Steward: Articled clerk 1985-87, Solicitor 1987-88; Solicitor Thompsons 1988-2001; TGWU 1985-

Lab majority 2,879

House of Commons: Member for Wolverhampton South West since 7 June 2001 general election. *Political interests:* Manufacturing, Industry, Transport, Environment. Canada

Foundation for Conductive Education; Member: New Democratic Party Canada 1980-82, European Standing Committee A 2003-, European Standing Committee B 2003; *Clubs:* Springvale Club, Bilston; Birmingham TUC; *Recreations:* Canadiana, football (Wolverhampton Wanderers FC)

Rob Marris, MP, House of Commons, London SW1A 0AA *Tel:* 020 7219 8342 *E-mail:* marrisr@parliament.uk. *Constituency:* 41 Bath Road, Wolverhampton, West Midlands WV1 4EW *Tel:* 01902 771166

MARSDEN, GORDON
Blackpool South

Gordon Marsden. Born 28 November 1953; Son of late George Henry Marsden and Joyce Marsden; Educated Stockport Grammar School; New College, Oxford (MA history 1976; London University (combined historical studies 1976-80); Harvard University 1978-79. Open University tutor/associate lecturer, arts faculty 1977-97; Public relations consultant 1980-85; Chief public affairs adviser to English Heritage 1984-85; Member, GMB/APEX

Lab majority 7,922

House of Commons: Contested Blackpool South 1992. Member for Blackpool South since 1 May 1997 general election; PPS to: Lord Irvine of Lairg as Lord Chancellor 2001-03, Tessa Jowell as Secretary of State for Culture, Media and Sport 2003-. *Political interests:* Heritage, Education, International Affairs, Social Affairs, Disability, Human Rights. USA, Russia, Caribbean, Eastern Europe

Joined Labour Party 1971; Joined Fabian Society 1975; Chairman, Young Fabians 1980-81; Fabian Society: Vice-Chair, Chair, Research and and Public Committee 1998-2000, Chair 2000-01. Member, Association of British Editors; Editor, *New Socialist* 1989-90; Judge, Ford Conservation Awards UK 1990-97; Board Member, Institute of Historical Research 1996-; President, British Resorts Association 1998-; Member, National Trust; Trustee, Dartmouth Street Trust; Board, History Today Trust; Advisory Board, Institute of Historical Research; *Publications: Victorian Values* (ed.) 1990; Contributor to *The History Debate*, 1990; *Victorian Values*, 2nd edition 1998; *Low Cost Socialism*, 1997; Contributor to *The English Question*, Fabian Society 2000; *International History of Censorship*, 2001; Gibbs Prize in History 1975; Kennedy Scholar, Harvard 1978-79; *Recreations:* Theatre, early music and medieval culture, swimming, heritage sites, architecture

Gordon Marsden, MP, House of Commons, London SW1A 0AA
Tel: 020 7219 1262 *Fax:* 020 7219 5859 *E-mail:* marsdeng@parliament.uk.
Constituency: 304 Highfield Road, Blackpool, Lancashire FY4 3JX
Tel: 01253 344143 *Fax:* 01253 344940

MARSHALL, DAVID
Glasgow East

David Marshall. Born 7 May 1941; Educated Larbert High School; Denny High School; Falkirk High School; Woodside Senior Secondary School, Glasgow; Married Christina Stewart 1968 (2 sons 1 daughter). Office worker; Shepherd; Tram and bus conductor; Member, TGWU 1960-; Chairman, TGWU Group of 33 MPs 1987-88; Councillor, Glasgow Corporation 1972-75; Strathclyde Regional Council: Councillor 1974-79, Chief Whip 1974-76, Member, Local Authorities Conditions of Service Advisory Board 1975-79; Chair: Manpower Committee of Convention of Scottish Local Authorities 1976-79, Manpower Committee 1978-79

Lab majority 13,507

House of Commons: Member for Glasgow Shettleston 1979-2005, for Glasgow East since 5 May 2005 general election; Sponsored Solvent Abuse (Scotland) Act as private member's bill 1983. *Political interests:* Aviation, Foreign Affairs, Poverty, Scottish Affairs, Transport

Labour Party Organiser, Glasgow 1969-71; Hon. Secretary and Hon. Treasurer, Scottish Group of Labour MPs 1981-2001. Vice-chair, Inter-Parliamentary Union (IPU) British Group 1994-97, Chair 1997-2000; Member, Executive Committee, Commonwealth Parliamentary Association (CPA) UK Branch 1997-99, Joint Vice-Chair 1999-2000; *Recreations:* Gardening, music

David Marshall, MP, House of Commons, London SW1A 0AA *Tel:* 020 7219 5134 *E-mail:* david@marshallmail.wanadoo.co.uk. *Constituency: Tel:* 0141-778 8125,

MARSHALL-ANDREWS, ROBERT
Medway

Bob (Robert) Graham Marshall-Andrews. Born 10 April 1944; Son of late Robin and late Eileen Marshall; Educated Mill Hill School; Bristol University (LLB 1966); Married Gillian Diana Elliott 1968 (1 son 1 daughter). Called to the Bar, Gray's Inn 1967, QC 1987, Bencher 1996; Recorder of the Crown Court 1982; Occasional novelist

Lab majority 213

House of Commons: Contested Richmond 1974 and Medway 1992. Member for Medway since 1 May 1997 general election. *Political interests:* Economic Policy, Environment, Civil Liberties, Parliamentary Democracy. East Africa, USA

Member, Society of Labour Lawyers. George Adamson Wildlife Preservation Trust; Trustee: George Adamson Wildlife Trust 1988-, Geffreye Museum 1990-; *Publications: Palace of Wisdom*, 1989/1990; *A Man Without Guilt* 2002; Observer Mace 1967; Spectacor Parliamentary Award 1997; QC; *Clubs:* Vice-President: Old Millhillians Rugby Club, Meoway Rugby Club; QC; *Recreations:* Theatre, reading, watching rugby, writing, walking, travel

Robert Marshall-Andrews, MP, House of Commons, London SW1A 0AA *Tel:* 020 7219 6920 *Fax:* 020 7219 2933 *E-mail:* marshallandrewsr@parliament.uk. *Constituency:* Moat House, 1 Castle Hill, Rochester, Kent ME1 1QQ *Tel:* 01634 814687 *Fax:* 01634 831294

Speaker majority
10,134

MARTIN, MICHAEL
Glasgow North East

Michael John Martin. Born 3 July 1945; Son of Michael Martin, merchant seaman and Mary McNeil, school cleaner; Educated St Patrick's Boys' School, Glasgow; Married Mary McLay 1966 (1 son 1 daughter). Metal worker, Rolls-Royce Engineering 1960-76; Full-time trades union official 1976-79; Shop Steward AUEW 1970-74; Trade union organiser, NUPE 1976-79; Member, AEEU (Craft Sector); Sponsored as MP by AEEU; Councillor: Glasgow Corporation 1973-74, Glasgow District Council 1974-79

House of Commons: Member for Glasgow Springburn 1979-2005, for Glasgow North East since 5 May 2005 general election; PPS to Denis Healey as Deputy Leader of the Labour Party 1980-83; First Deputy Chairman, Ways and Means (Deputy Speaker) 1997-2000; Speaker 2000-. *Political interests:* Trade and Industry, Drug Abuse, Industrial Relations, Equal Opportunities, Care of the Elderly, Human Rights. Italy, Canada, USA

Fellow, Industry and Parliament Trust; PC 2000; Honorary doctorate; *Recreations:* Hillwalking, folk music, local history, playing the Highland Pipes and member of the College of Piping

Rt Hon Michael Martin, MP, House of Commons, London SW1A 0AA *Tel:* 020 7219 5300/4111 *Fax:* 020 7219 6901. *Constituency: Tel:* 0141-762 2329 *Fax:* 0141-762 1519

Lab majority 5,695

MARTLEW, ERIC
Carlisle

Eric Anthony Martlew. Born 3 January 1949; Son of late George and Mary Jane Martlew; Educated Harraby School, Carlisle; Carlisle College; Married Elsie Barbara Duggan 1970. Nestlé Co. 1966-87: Laboratory technician, Personnel manager; Member: TGWU, GMB; Councillor, Carlisle County Borough Council 1972-74; Cumbria County Council: Councillor 1973-88, Chair 1983-85; East Cumbria Health Authority: Member 1975-88, Chairman 1977-79

House of Commons: Member for Carlisle since 11 June 1987 general election; Opposition Front Bench Spokesman on Defence, Disarmament and Arms Control with special responsibilities for the RAF 1992-95; Opposition Whip 1996-97; Shadow Defence Minister 1992-97; PPS: to Dr David Clark as Chancellor of the Duchy of Lancaster 1997-98, to Baroness Jay of Paddington as Lord Privy Seal, Leader of the Lords and Minister for Women 1998-2001. *Political interests:* Transport, Health, Social Services, Agriculture, Defence

Hon council member Rural Buildings Preservation Trust 1997-; Trustee, Parliamentary Pension Fund 1999-; *Recreations:* Photography, fell-walking, horse-racing, watching rugby league

Eric Martlew, MP, House of Commons, London SW1A 0AA *Tel:* 020 7219 4114 *Fax:* 020 7219 6898 *E-mail:* eric.martlewmp@email.labour.org.uk. *Constituency:* 3 Chatsworth Square, Carlisle, Cumbria CA1 1HB *Tel:* 01228 511395 *Fax:* 01228 819798

MATES, MICHAEL
East Hampshire

Michael John Mates. Born 9 June 1934; Son of Claude John Mates; Educated Blundell's School; King's College, Cambridge; Married Mary Rosamund Paton 1959 (divorced 1980) (2 sons 2 daughters); married Rosellen Bett 1982 (divorced 1995) (1 daughter). Army service 1954-74: 2nd Lieutenant RUR 1955; Queen's Dragoon Guards, RAC 1961, Major 1967, Lieutenant-Colonel 1973, Resigned commission 1974

Con majority 5,509

House of Commons: Member for Petersfield October 1974-83, East Hampshire since 9 June 1983 general election; Minister of State, Northern Ireland Office 1992-93. *Political interests:* Defence, Northern Ireland, Home Affairs

Wessex Children's Hospice Trust; Member, Intelligence Review Committee 2004; UK Delegate, NATO Parliamentary Assembly; PC 2004; Liveryman, Farriers' Company 1975, Master 1986-87; *Clubs:* MCC, Garrick; *Recreations:* Music

Rt Hon Michael Mates, MP, House of Commons, London SW1A 0AA
Tel: 020 7219 5166 *Fax:* 020 7219 4884 *E-mail:* matesm@parliament.uk.
Constituency: 14A Butts Road, Alton, Hampshire GU34 1ND *Tel:* 01420 84122

MAUDE, FRANCIS
Horsham

Francis Anthony Aylmer Maude. Born 4 July 1953; Son of late Baron Maude of Stratford-upon-Avon, PC (Life Peer), author and journalist, and late Lady Maude; Educated Abingdon School; Corpus Christi, Cambridge (MA history 1976) (Hulse Prize and Avory Studentship); College of Law (Forster Boulton Prize and Inner Temple Law Scholarship 1977); Married Christina Jane Hadfield 1984 (2 sons 3 daughters). Called to Bar, Inner Temple 1977; Practising barrister 1977-85; Head of global privatisation, Salomon Bros International 1992-93; Managing Director, global privatisation, Morgan Stanley & Co Ltd 1993-97; Chairman, Deregulation Task Force 1993-97; Non-executive Director: Asda Group plc 1993-99, Benfield Reinsurance Ltd 1994-99, Gartmore Shared Equity Trust 1997-99, Benfield Group plc 1999-, Deputy chair 2003-, Businesses for Sale Company plc 2000-2002; Chairman: Prestbury Holdings PLC, Jubilee Investment Trust plc, Incepta Group plc; Councillor, Westminster City Council 1978-84

Con majority 12,627

House of Commons: Member for North Warwickshire 1983-92, and for Horsham since 1 May 1997 general election; Government Whip 1985-87; PPS to Peter Morrison, as Minister of State for Employment 1984; Parliamentary Under-Secretary of State for Corporate and Consumer Affairs, Department of Trade and Industry 1987-89; Minister of State, Foreign and Commonwealth Office 1989-90; Financial Secretary to the Treasury 1990-92; Member, Shadow Cabinet 1997-2001; Shadow Secretary of State: for National Heritage 1997, for Culture, Media and Sport 1997-98; Shadow Chancellor of the Exchequer 1998-2000; Shadow Secretary of State for Foreign and Commonwealth Affairs 2000-01

Chairman Conservative Party 2005-. PC 1992; *Recreations:* Skiing, reading, opera

Rt Hon Francis Maude, MP, House of Commons, London SW1A 0AA
Tel: 020 7219 2494 *Fax:* 020 7219 0638 *E-mail:* francismaudemp@parliament.uk.
Constituency: Gough House, Madeira Avenue, Horsham, West Sussex RH12 1RL
Tel: 01403 242000 *Fax:* 01403 210600

THE ROYAL BRITISH LEGION IN 2005 CAMPAIGNING FOR EX-SERVICE PEOPLE

Background

The Legion is Britain's largest ex-Service organisation, covering England and Wales and all of Ireland. It has 2,895 Branches, including 87 overseas, as well as 1,324 Womens' Section Branches. Total membership is 535,217, but the Legion represents the whole of the ex-Service community which numbers some 11 million. It provides financial assistance, nursing and respite care homes, employment for the disabled, small business advice and loans, resettlement training, free pensions advice and much more, all financed from public donations. It also provides a social focus for the ex-Service community in its branches, many of which have an affiliated club. In addition it is the de facto national custodian of Remembrance.

A campaigning organisation

The Legion has traditionally campaigned on behalf of its constituency to ensure their wellbeing. There have been numerous successes, notably the campaign in 1999/2000 for a £10,000 ex-gratia payment to survivors of Japanese PoW camps and their widows which has resulted in payments by the Government of over £230 million and the campaign for a meaningful commemoration of the 60th Anniversary of D Day in 2004, which also attained its objective.

The Legion is campaigning today on a number of issues, notably:

Gulf War Illnesses

- To ensure that the Government addresses its outstanding obligations to Gulf War veterans who have fallen ill since 1990/91.
- To seek further support for the recommendations of the Lloyd Inquiry into Gulf War Illnesses.

War Pensions and Compensation

- Monitoring the new Armed Forces Compensation Scheme to ensure that it is set up and implemented in accordance with the promises given to Parliament, Service personnel and their families.
- Contesting the criteria under which applications for War Pensions for service-attributable noise-induced hearing loss are assessed.
- Calling upon a remaining small number of Local Authorities to completely disregard War and War Widows Pensions when assessing applicants for Housing Benefit and Council Tax Rebate. It remains a Legion aim that there should be a statutory, national, full disregard funded by Central Government.

Other Campaigns

- The Legion supports campaigns by other organisations on behalf of pensioners, many of whom are ex-Service, where they are being financially penalised.

The Legion is seeking cross-party support for the benefit of veterans.

The Royal British Legion. Always on active service

Registered Charity No: 219279

The Royal British Legion, 48 Pall Mall, London SW1Y 5JY Tel: 020 7973 7265 Email: jlillies@britishlegion.org.uk

MAY, THERESA
Maidenhead

Theresa Mary May. Born 1 October 1956; Daughter of late Rev Hubert Brasier and late Zaidee Brasier; Educated Wheatley Park Comprehensive School; St Hugh's College, Oxford (BA geography 1977, MA); Married Philip John May 1980. Association for Payment Clearing Services 1985-97: Various posts latterly senior adviser, international affairs; Councillor, London Borough of Merton 1986-94

Con majority 6,231

House of Commons: Contested North-West Durham 1992 general election and Barking 1994 by-election. Member for Maidenhead since 1 May 1997 general election; Opposition Spokeswoman for Education and Employment (schools, disabled people and women) 1998-99; Shadow Cabinet Spokeswoman for Women's Issues 1999-2001; Shadow Schools Minister 1998-99; Member Shadow Cabinet 1999-; Shadow Secretary of State for: Education and Employment 1999-2001, Transport, Local Government and the Regions 2001-02, Transport 2002, Environment and Transport 2003-04, the Family 2004-, Culture, Media and Sport 2005-. *Political interests:* Education, Disability, Local Government

Chairman, Conservative Disability Group 1997-98; Chairman, Conservative Party 2002-03. PC 2003; *Clubs:* Maidenhead Conservative; *Recreations:* Walking, cooking

Rt Hon Theresa May, MP, House of Commons, London SW1A 0AA
Tel: 020 7219 5206 *Fax:* 020 7219 1145 *E-mail:* mayt@parliament.uk.
Constituency: Maidenhead Conservative Association, 2 Castle End Farm, Ruscombe, Berkshire RG10 9XQ *Tel:* 0118 934 5433 *Fax:* 0118 934 5288

Lab majority 10,454

MEACHER, MICHAEL
Oldham West and Royton

Michael H Meacher. Born 4 November 1939; Son of late George H. Meacher; Educated Berkhamsted School, Hertfordshire; New College, Oxford (BA Greats 1962); London School of Economics (social administration Diploma 1963); Married Molly Christine Reid 1962 (divorced 1987) (2 sons 2 daughters); married Lucianne Sawyer, neé Craven 1988. Secretary, Danilo Dolci Trust 1964; Sembal research fellow in social gerontology, Essex University 1965-66; Lecturer in social administration: York University 1966-69, London School of Economics 1970; Visiting professor to Department of Sociology, Surrey University 1980-86; Member, UNISON

House of Commons: Contested Colchester 1966 general election and Oldham West 1968 by-election. Member for Oldham West 1970-97, and for Oldham West and Royton since 1 May 1997 general election; Principal Opposition Frontbench Spokesperson for: Health and Social Security 1983-87, Employment 1987-89, Social Security 1989-92, Overseas Development and Co-operation 1992-93, Citizen's Charter and Science 1993-94, Transport 1994-95, Education and Employment 1995-96, Environmental Protection 1996-97; Parliamentary Under-Secretary of State: Department of Industry 1974-75, Department of Health and Social Security 1975-76, Department of Trade 1976-79; Member, Shadow Cabinet 1983-97; Minister of State: Department of the Environment, Transport and the Regions (Minister for the Environment) 1997-2001, Department for Environment, Food and Rural Affairs (Environment) 2001-02, (Environment and Agri-Environment) 2002-03. *Political interests:* Economics and Social Policy, Redistribution of Income and Wealth, Industrial Democracy, Civil Liberties, Housing

Candidate for Deputy Leadership, Labour Party 1983; Member, Labour Party National Executive Committee 1983-89. Fellow, Industry and Parliament Trust; *Publications: The Care of Old People,* Fabian Society 1969; *Taken For A Ride: Special Residential Homes for the Elderly Mentally Infirm: A Study of Separatism in Social Policy,* 1972; *Socialism with a Human Face – the Political Economy in the 1980s,* 1982; *Diffusing Power – The key to Socialist Revival,* 1992; Numerous articles and pamphlets on social and economic policy; PC 1997; *Recreations:* Sport, music, reading

Rt Hon Michael Meacher, MP, House of Commons, London SW1A 0AA
Tel: 020 7219 4532; 020 7219 6461 *Fax:* 020 7219 5945
E-mail: massonm@parliament.uk. *Constituency:* 11 Church Lane, Oldham, Greater Manchester OL1 3AN *Tel:* 0161-626 5779 *Fax:* 0161-626 8572

MEALE, ALAN
Mansfield

Lab majority 11,365

(Joseph) Alan Meale. Born 31 July 1949; Son of late Albert Henry Meale, and of Elizabeth Meale; Educated St Joseph Roman Catholic School, Bishop Auckland; Durham University; Ruskin College, Oxford; Sheffield Hallam University; Married Diana Gilhespy 1983 (2 children). Author; editor; development officer; researcher for MPs Barbara Castle, Tony Benn, Dennis Skinner, Albert Booth; Parliamentary and political adviser to Michael Meacher as Principal Opposition Front Bench Spokesman on Health and Social Security 1984-87; National employment development officer, NACRO 1977-80; Assistant to Ray Buckton, General Secretary of ASLEF 1979-84; Former Deputy Leader, Local Authority

House of Commons: Member for Mansfield since 11 June 1987 general election; Opposition Whip 1992-94; PPS to John Prescott: as Deputy Leader of the Labour Party 1994-97, as Deputy Prime Minister and Secretary of State for the Environment, Transport and the Regions 1997-98; Parliamentary Under-Secretary of State, Department of the Environment, Transport and the Regions 1998-99; Adviser on horse racing to Richard Caborn, as Minister of State for Sport 2002-. *Political interests:* Home Affairs, Transport, Health, Social Security, Drug Abuse, Human Rights, Environment, Poverty, Sport, Unemployment, Media, Music. Cyprus

Chair, PLP East Midlands and Central Groups 1988-95; Former Vice-Chair, PLP Employment Committee; Member, Co-operative Party. Fellow and Postgraduate Fellow of the Industry and Parliament Trust; Founder, Former Chair, Executive Member, Parliamentary Beer Industries Committee; Governor Portland Training College; Chairman States Community Trust; Treasurer, CPA Cyprus Group (British Section); Former Executive Member: Commonwealth Parliamentary Association (CPA), Inter-Parliamentary Union (IPU); Member, UK Delegation Parliamentary Assembly of the Council of Europe/Western European Union 2000-; First Vice-President, COE CTTs Environment, Agriculture, Local and Regional Democracy 2001-; Chairman COE Sustainable Development 2002-04; Honorary Citizenship: of Morphou, Cyprus, of Mansfield, Ohio (USA); Honorary Senatorship of Louisiana (USA); Freeman, State of Louisiana, USA; Freeman, City of: Mansfield, Ohio, USA; Morphou, Cyprus; *Clubs:* Mansfield Town FC; *Recreations:* Reading, writing, arts, politics, sports, Mansfield Football Club, Cyprus

Alan Meale, MP, House of Commons, London SW1A 0AA *Tel:* 020 7219 4159 *E-mail:* enquiries@alanmeale.co.uk. *Constituency:* 5 Clumber Street, Mansfied, Nottinghamshire NG18 1NT *Tel:* 01623 660531 *Fax:* 01623 420495

MERCER, PATRICK
Newark

Con majority 6,464

Patrick John Mercer. Born 26 June 1956; Son of Rt Rev Eric Arthur John Mercer (Bishop of Exeter) and Rosemary, née Denby; Educated King's School, Chester; Exeter College, Oxford (MA modern history 1980); Royal Military Academy, Sandhurst (commission 1995); Married Catriona Jane Beaton (publisher) 1990 (1 son). The Worcestershire and Sherwood Foresters Regiment 1974-99: Second Lieutenant to Colonel (mentioned in Despatches 1982), gallantry commendation 1991. Regular Army Officer 1974-99: Head of strategy Army Training and Recruiting Agency, Commanding battalion in Bosnia, Canada, Tidworth, Operational service in the Balkans and Ulster; Reporter, BBC Radio 4 'Today' Programme 1999; Freelance journalist 2000-01; Member, King's College London mission to East Timor 2000; Governor, Tuxford Comprehensive School

House of Commons: Member for Newark since 7 June 2001 general election; Shadow Minister for Homeland Security 2003-. *Political interests:* Agriculture, Prisons, Defence, Northern Ireland. Ukraine, Russia, Israel, Serbia, Bosnia

Passed Staff College (psc) 1988; *Publications: Give Them a Volley and Charge*, Spellmount 1997; *Inkermann: The Soldier's Battle*, Osprey 1997; MBE 1993; OBE 1997; *Clubs:* Newark Working Men's, Newark Conservative, Army and Navy; *Recreations:* Painting, walking, bird-watching, history, country sports

Patrick Mercer, MP, House of Commons, London SW1A 0AA *Tel:* 020 7219 8477 *Fax:* 020 7219 1961 *E-mail:* millicanh@parliament.uk. *Constituency:* Newark and Retford Conservative Association, Belvedere, London Road, Newark, Nottinghamshire NG24 1TN *Tel:* 01636 612837 *Fax:* 01636 703 269

MERRON, GILLIAN
Lincoln

Lab majority 4,614

Gillian Merron. Born 12 April 1959; Daughter of late Harry Merron, factory store keeper and of late Bessie Merron, shop assistant; Educated Wanstead High School; Lancaster University (BSc management sciences 1981). Business development adviser 1982-85; Local government officer 1985-87; Full-time Official, National Union of Public Employees (now UNISON) 1987-95; Senior regional officer for Lincolnshire, UNISON 1995-97

House of Commons: Member for Lincoln since 1 May 1997 general election; Assistant Government Whip 2002-04; Government Whip 2004-; Sponsored, Football Sponsorship Levy Bill 1997; PPS: to Ministers of State, Ministry of Defence: Doug Henderson, MP (Minister for the Armed Forces) 1998-99, Baroness Symons of Vernham Dean (Minister for Defence Procurement) 1999-2001, to Dr John Reid as Secretary of State for Northern Ireland 2001-02. *Political interests:* Health, Exercise and Sport, Vocational Training, Transport

Constituency Party Officer; Vice-chair, Regional Labour Party Executive; Vice-chair, Central Region Group of Labour MPs 1997-99; Chair, East Midlands Regional Group of Labour MPs 1999-2002. Co-ordinated the Shadow Cabinet Central Region Campaign in General and European Elections 1992; Member, Armed Forces Parliamentary Scheme (RAF) 1997-98; Member, Standing Committee National Minimum Wage Bill, Northern Ireland Arms Decommissioning, Local Authority Tendering, New Northern Ireland Assembly (Elections) Order 1998- Football (Offences and Disorder) Bill Armed Forces Discipline Bill; Fellow-Elect, Industry and Parliament Trust Board Member, Westminster Foundation for Democracy 1998-2001; *Recreations:* Football, running, films, cycling

Gillian Merron, MP, House of Commons, London SW1A 0AA *Tel:* 020 7219 4031 *Fax:* 020 7219 0489 *E-mail:* merrong@parliament.uk. *Constituency:* Grafton House, 32 Newland, Lincoln, Lincolnshire LN1 1XJ *Tel:* 01522 888688 *Fax:* 01522 888686

MICHAEL, ALUN
Cardiff South and Penarth

Lab/Co-op majority
9,237

Alun Michael. Born 22 August 1943; Son of late Leslie Michael and of Elizabeth Michael; Educated Colwyn Bay Grammar School; Keele University (BA); Married Mary Crawley 1966 (2 sons 3 daughters). Journalist, *South Wales Echo* 1966-72; Youth Worker, Cardiff City Council 1972-74; Youth and Community Worker, South Glamorgan CC 1974-87; AM for Mid and West Wales region 1999-2000; Member, GMB; Former Member: TGWU, CYWU; Branch Secretary, National Union of Journalists 1967-70; General Secretary, Welsh Association of FE and Youth Service Officers 1973-75; JP, Cardiff 1972-; Chair, Cardiff Juvenile Bench 1986-87; Cardiff City Council: Councillor 1973-89, Past Chair: Finance Committee, Planning Committee, Economic Development Committee 1987-89

House of Commons: Member for Cardiff South and Penarth since 11 June 1987 general election; Opposition Spokesperson for: Welsh Affairs 1988-92, Home Affairs 1992-97; The Voluntary Sector 1994-97; Opposition Whip 1987-88; Minister of State, Home Office (Minister for Criminal Policy also responsible for Police and the Voluntary Sector) 1997-98; Secretary of State for Wales 1998-99; Minister of State, Department for Environment, Food and Rural Affairs: (Rural Affairs) 2001-02, (Rural Affairs and Urban Quality of Life) 2002-03, (Rural Affairs and Local Environmental Quality) 2003-05; Minister of State, Department of Trade and Industry 2005-. *Political interests:* Local and Regional Government, Housing, Youth Work, Juvenile Justice, Voluntary Sector, Community Development, Economic Development, Co-operative Development, Political Ideas and Philosophy. Germany, South Africa, Israel, Canada, Somalia, USA, Japan

Former Chair, Co-operative Group of MPs; Member, National Executive, Co-operative Party (representing Wales); Member, Christian Socialist Movement. YHA, NCH Action for Children, Marie Curie Homes, Prince's Trust, Citizens Advice Bureau, Community and Youth Organisations; Member: Commonwealth Parliamentary Association (CPA) (delegation to South Africa and Canada), Inter-Parliamentary Association (IPA); *Publications:* Contributor, *Restoring Faith in Politics*, 1966, *Challenges to a Challenging Faith*, 1995; Editor, *Tough on Crime and Tough on the Causes of Crime*, 1997, *Building the Future Together*, 1997; PC 1998; *Clubs:* Penarth Labour, Grange Stars (Cardiff), Earlswood (Cardiff); Penarth and Dinas Runners; *Recreations:* Long-distance walking, running, reading, opera, music

Rt Hon Alun Michael, MP, House of Commons, London SW1A 0AA
Tel: 020 7219 5980 *Fax:* 020 7219 5930 *E-mail:* alunmichaelmp@parliament.uk.
Constituency: PO Box 453, Cardiff, South Glamorgan CF11 9YN
Tel: 029 2022 3533 *Fax:* 029 2022 9936; 029 2022 9947

Lab majority 10,404

MILBURN, ALAN
Darlington

Alan Milburn. Born 27 January 1958; Son of Evelyn Metcalfe, former NHS secretary; Educated John Marlay School, Newcastle; Stokesley Comprehensive School; Lancaster University (BA history); Newcastle University; Partner, Ruth Briel (2 sons). Senior business development officer, North Tyneside Council 1990-92; Co-ordinator, Trade Union Studies Information Unit, Newcastle 1984-90; Co-ordinator, Sunderland Shipyards Campaign 1988-89; President, North East Region, MSF Union 1990-92

House of Commons: Member for Darlington since 9 April 1992 general election; Opposition Spokesperson for: Health 1995-96, Treasury and Economic Affairs (Shadow Economic Secretary) 1996-97; Minister of State, Department of Health 1997-98; Chief Secretary, HM Treasury December 1998-99; Secretary of State for Health 1999-2003; Chancellor of the Duchy of Lancaster 2004-05. *Political interests:* Economic Policy, Industry, Regional Policy, Crime, Health

Chair, Newcastle Central Constituency Labour Party 1988-90; Member, Northern Region Labour Party Executive Committee 1990-92. *Publications: Jobs and Industry, the North Can Make It,* 1986; *Plan for the North,* 1987; *The Case for Regional Government,* 1989; PC 1998; *Recreations:* Cricket, football, music, cinema

Rt Hon Alan Milburn, MP, House of Commons, London SW1A 0AA
Tel: 020 7219 3594 *Fax:* 020 7219 2689 *E-mail:* milburna@parliament.uk.
Constituency: 123 Victoria Road, Darlington, Durham DL1 5JH *Tel:* 01325 380366 *Fax:* 01325 381341

Lab majority 12,312

MILIBAND, DAVID
South Shields

David Wright Miliband. Born 15 July 1965; Son of Ralph Miliband and Marion, née Kozak; Educated Haverstock Comprehensive School; Corpus Christi College, Oxford (BA philosophy, politics and economics 1987); Massachusetts Institute of Technology (MSc political science 1989); Married Louise Shackelton 1998. Parliamentary officer National Council for Voluntary Organisations 1987-88; Research fellow Institute for Public Policy Research 1989-94; Secretary Commission on Social Justice 1992-94; Head of Policy Office, Leader of the Opposition 1994-97; Head of Prime Minister's Policy Unit 1997-2001; TGWU 1989-

House of Commons: Member for South Shields since 7 June 2001 general election; Minister of State for School Standards, Department for Education and Skills 2002-04; Minister for the Cabinet Office 2004-05; Minister of Communities and Local Govenment, Office of the Deputy Prime Minister 2005-. *Political interests:* Education, Employment

Secretary, Social Justice Commission; Founder Centre for European Reform; *Publications:* Editor *Reinventing the Left,* Polity Press 1994; Co-editor *Paying for Inequality,* Rivers Oram Press 1994; PC 2005; *Clubs:* Whiteleas Social, Cleadon Social; President, South Shields Football Club

Rt Hon David Miliband, MP, House of Commons, London SW1A 0AA
Tel: 020 7219 8320 *E-mail:* milibandd@parliament.uk. *Constituency:* South Shields Constituency Labour Party, Ede House, 143 Westoe Road, South Shields, Tyne and Wear NE33 3PD *Tel:* 0191 456 8910 *Fax:* 0191 456 5842

Photograph from BUAV undercover investigation

BUAV
campaigning to end animal experiments

Founded in 1898, the British Union for the Abolition of Vivisection (BUAV) is the leading British organisation campaigning against animal experimentation at a national and international level. The BUAV is committed to using all peaceful and legal means possible to end animal experiments and promote modern, non-animal research techniques.

As Chair of the European Coalition to End Animal Experiments, the BUAV is at the centre of anti-vivisection campaigning across Europe, liaising with key international groups and ensuring that laboratory animals are high on the European political agenda. In the UK, the BUAV regularly participates in the Parliamentary process, submitting evidence to consultations, committees and inquiries and working with MPs. Our primary campaigns include the use of primates in toxicology and research; animal testing for cosmetics and household products; and the European Union's REACH chemicals testing programme.

Further information on the BUAV's campaigns can be found on the Parliamentary website **www. politics.co.uk** *(search for "BUAV" under the "Opinion Formers" tab).* Our main website, **www.buav.org** carries in-depth additional information on these campaigns and all the issues surrounding animal experimentation.

For further information or assistance, contact our Parliamentary Officer on
0207 619 6970

BUAV: 16a Crane Grove, London N7 8NN. Email: info@buav.org Fax: 0207 700 0252

MILIBAND, ED
Doncaster North

Ed Miliband. Born 24 December 1969; Educated Oxford University; London School of Economics. HM Treasury: Special adviser to the Chancellor 1997-2002, Chairman of the Council of Economic Advisers 2004-05; teacher of economics Harvard University 2002-04; TGWU

House of Commons: Member for Doncaster North since 5 May 2005 general election
Ed Miliband, MP, House of Commons, London SW1A 0AA *Tel:* 020 7219 4778.
Lab majority 12,656   *Constituency: Tel:* 07913 809614 *E-mail:* milibanded@hotmail.com

MILLER, ANDREW
Ellesmere Port and Neston

Andrew Miller. Born 23 March 1949; Son of late Ernest and Daphne Miller; Educated Hayling Island Secondary School; Highbury Technical College; London School of Economics (diploma in industrial relations 1977); Married Frances Ewan (2 sons 1 daughter). Technician, Portsmouth Polytechnic, analyst in geology 1967-76; Regional official, MSF (formerly ASTMS) 1977-92; Member MSF 1968-

House of Commons: Member for Ellesmere Port and Neston since 9 April 1992 general election; Chair Leadership Campaign Team 1997-98; PPS to Ministers, Department of Trade and Industry 2001-; Member, First Steps Team working with the Foreign Office to promote relations with EU and prospective EU member states with specific responsibility for Hungary and Malta 2001-. *Political interests:* Industry, Economic Policy, Science and Technology, Communications and Information Technology, Pensions. Europe, China, USA, Malta, Hungary

Member: Labour Party, NW Regional Executive Committee 1984-92; President, Computing for Labour 1993-; Chair: Leadership Campaign Team 1997-98, North West Group of Labour MPs 1997-98; Member, Scientists for Labour 1997-. *Clubs:* Vice-President: Alvanley Cricket Club, Chester and Ellesmere Port Athletics Club; *Recreations:* Walking, photography, tennis, cricket

Andrew Miller, MP, House of Commons, London SW1A 0AA *Tel:* 020 7219 3580 *Fax:* 020 7219 3796 *E-mail:* millera@parliament.uk. *Constituency:* Whitby Hall Lodge, Stanney Lane, Ellesmere Port, Cheshire CH65 6QY *Tel:* 0151-357 3019 *Fax:* 0151-356 8226

Lab majority 6,486

MILLER, MARIA
Basingstoke

Maria Frances Lewis Miller. Born 26 March 1964; Educated Brynteg Comprehensive, Bridgend; London School of Economics (BSc economics 1985); Married Iain George Miller 1990. Advertising executive Grey Advertising Ltd 1985-90; Marketing manager Texaco 1990-94; Company director: Grey Advertising Ltd 1994-99, The Rowland Company 1999-2003

House of Commons: Contested Wolverhampton North East 2001 general election. Member for Basingstoke since 5 May 2005 general election. *Political interests:* Housing, education, media

Maria Miller, MP, House of Commons, London SW1A 0AA *Tel:* 020 7219 4238.
Constituency: Basingstoke Conservative Association, 149d Pack Lane, Basingstoke RG22 5HN *Tel:* 01256 322207 *Fax:* 01256 466236
E-mail: office@basingstokeconservatives.com
Website: www.basingstokeconservatives.com

Con majority 4,680

Doncaster... Catch us while you can!

Visit Doncaster today and be amazed by the incredible transformation changing the face of our emerging city. There is a real buzz about the place, a sense that you have to grab a piece of the action while you still can.

Where else in England is basing its regeneration on an international airport, a transport interchange and top 20 retail facilities, the largest education project in its country, a community stadium and is redeveloping its existing racecourse, conference and exhibition facilities?

To ensure our citizens are able to capture the benefits of our success, Doncaster's elected Mayor Martin Winter, is leading the transformation of the town into a successful city, with Doncaster Council undergoing a significant transformation that focuses on becoming a 'Winning Council'.

As one of the pilot authorities for Local Area Agreements, we are working with key partners such as the Doncaster Strategic Partnership to transform Doncaster into a place where you will want to work and live!

www.doncaster.gov.uk

Doncaster
discover the spirit

MILTON, ANNE
Guildford

Anne Milton. Born 1955; Educated Haywards Heath Grammar School, Sussex; St Bartholomew's Hospital, London; Married to Graham; Reigate Borough councillor 1999-2004

House of Commons: Member for Guildford since 5 May 2005 general election. *Political interests:* Affordable housing, transport, health

Vice-chairman Conservative Medical Society. *Recreations:* Running, gardening, reading, family

Con majority 347

Anne Milton, MP, House of Commons, London SW1A 0AA *Tel:* 020 7219 8392. *Constituency:* 15 London Road, Guildford, Surrey GU1 2AA *Tel:* 01483 300330 *Fax:* 01483 300321 *E-mail:* info@guildfordconservatives.com *Website:* www.guildfordconservatives.com

MITCHELL, ANDREW
Sutton Coldfield

Andrew John Bower Mitchell. Born 23 March 1956; Son of Sir David Mitchell, vintner and politician, and Pam Mitchell; Educated Rugby School; Jesus College, Cambridge (MA history 1978); President of the Union 1978; Married Sharon Denise Bennet 1985 (2 daughters). UN Peacekeeping Forces Cyprus: 1st Royal Tank Regiment (SSLC). International and corporate finance Lazard Brothers and Company Ltd 1979-87; Lazard Brothers: Consultant 1987-92, Director 1997-; Director: Miller Insurance Group 1997-2001, Financial Dynamics Holdings 1997-2002; Senior strategy adviser: Boots 1997-2000, Andersen Consulting/Accenture 1997-; Director Commer Group 1998-2002; Supervisory board member The Foundation 1999-; Member Islington Health Authority 1985-87

Con majority 12,283

House of Commons: Contested Sunderland South 1983 general election. Member for Gedling 1987-97. Contested Gedling 1997 general election. Member for Sutton Coldfield since 7 June 2001 general election; Assistant Government Whip 1992-93; Government Whip 1993-95; PPS: to William Waldegrave, Foreign and Commonwealth Office 1988-90, to John Wakeham as Secretary of State for Energy 1990-92; Vice-chair Conservative Party 1992-93; Parliamentary Under-Secretary of State Department of Social Security 1995-97; Shadow Minister for: Economic Affairs 2003-04, Home Affairs 2004-05; Shadow Secretary of State for International Development 2005-. *Political interests:* Health, Defence, Economy

Chair Cambridge University Conservative Association 1977; Islington North Conservatives 1983-85: President, Chair; Secretary One Nation Group of Conservative MPs 1989-92. Vice-chair Alexandra Rose Charity 1997-; President Norman Laud Association 2000-; Liveryman, Vintner's Company; *Clubs:* Carlton, Chair Coningsby 1984-85; *Recreations:* Music, windsurfing, skiing, walking

Andrew Mitchell, MP, House of Commons, London SW1A 0AA
Tel: 020 7219 8516. *Constituency:* Sutton Coldfield Conservative Association, 36 High Street, Sutton Coldfield, West Midlands B72 1UP *Tel:* 0121 354 2229 *Fax:* 0121 321 1762 *E-mail:* info@sutton-coldfield-tories.org.uk

MITCHELL, AUSTIN
Great Grimsby

Austin Vernon Mitchell. Born 19 September 1934; Son of Richard Vernon Mitchell, Dyer; Educated Woodbottom Council School; Bingley Grammar School; Manchester University (BA history 1956); Nuffield College, Oxford (MA, DPhil 1963); Married Patricia Dorothea Jackson (divorced) (2 daughters); married Linda Mary McDougall (1 son 1 daughter). Lecturer in history, Otago University, Dunedin, New Zealand 1959-63; Senior lecturer in politics, University of Canterbury, Christchurch, NZ 1963-67; Official fellow, Nuffield College, Oxford 1967-69; Journalist: Yorkshire Television 1969-71, BBC 1972, Yorkshire Television 1973-77; Political commentator, Sky Television's Target programme 1989-98; Associate editor, *The House Magazine*; GMB, NUJ

Lab majority 7,654

House of Commons: Member for Grimsby 1977-83 and for Great Grimsby since 9 June 1983 general election; Opposition Spokesperson for Trade and Industry 1988-89; Former Opposition Whip; PPS to John Fraser as Minister of State for Prices and Consumer Protection 1977-79. *Political interests:* Economics, Media, Fishing Industry, Agriculture, Poverty, Accountancy, Legal Reform, European Union, Electoral Reform, Constitutional Reform, Small Businesses. Canada, Iceland, New Zealand, France, Germany, China, Hong Kong, Nigeria

Member, Executive Council Fabian Society; Vice-chair Labour Campaign for Electoral Reform; Chair: Labour Euro-Safeguards Campaign, Labour Economic Policy Group. Harbour Place, Grimsby; Member: Hairdressing Council, Advisory Council, National Fishing Heritage Centre, Public Accounts Commission 1997-; Vice-President, Federation of Economic Development Authorities (FEDA); President, Debating Group; Member, Royal Institute of International Affairs; Joint Secretary, Esperanto Parliamentary Group; Fellow, Industry and Parliament Trust; *Publications: New Zealand Politics in Action 1962; Government by Party, 1966; Whigs in Opposition, 1815-30, 1969; Politics and People in New Zealand, 1970; Half Gallon Quarter Acre Pavlova @nr Paradise, 1974; Can Labour Win Again, 1979; Yes Maggie there is an Alternative; Westminster Man, 1982; The Case for Labour, 1983; Four Years in the Death of the Labour Party, 1983; Yorkshire Jokes 1988; Teach Thissen Tyke 1988; Britain, Beyond the Blue Horizon, 1989; Competitive Socialism, 1989; Election '45, 1995; Accounting for Change, 1993; Corporate Governance Matters, 1996; The Common Fisheries Policy, End or Mend?, 1996; Co-author Last Time: Labour's Lessons from the Sixties 1997; Farewell My Lords, 1999; Co-author Parliament in Pictures 1999; Pavlova Paradise Revisited 2002*; Order of New Zealand 1991; New Zealand Order of Merit for Services to New Zealand interests in the UK; *Recreations:* Photography, contemplating exercise

Austin Mitchell, MP, House of Commons, London SW1A 0AA *Tel:* 020 7219 4559 *Fax:* 020 7219 4843 *E-mail:* mitchellav@parliament.uk. *Constituency:* 15 New Cartergate, Grimsby, Humberside DN31 1RB *Tel:* 01472 342145 *Fax:* 01472 251484

MOFFATT, LAURA
Crawley

Laura Jean Moffatt. Born 9 April 1954; Daughter of Stanley and Barbara Field; Educated Hazelwick School, Crawley; Crawley College of Technology (pre nursing course); Married Colin Moffatt 1975 (3 sons). State Registered Nurse, Crawley Hospital (1975-97); Member, UNISON; Crawley Borough Council: Councillor 1984-96, Mayor 1989-90, Chair, Environmental Services 1987-96

House of Commons: Member for Crawley since 1 May 1997 general election; PPS to: Lord Irvine of Lairg as Lord Chancellor 2001-03, Lord Falconer of Thoroton as Secretary of State for Constitutional Affairs 2003-. *Political interests:* Health, Housing, Aerospace, Aviation, Defence, AIDS, Drug Abuse

NCH Action for Children, NSPCC; *Recreations:* Family, friends, walking, pets, swimming

Laura Moffatt, MP, House of Commons, London SW1A 0AA *Tel:* 020 7219 3619 *Fax:* 020 7219 0473 *E-mail:* moffattl@parliament.uk. *Constituency:* 6 The Broadway, Crawley, West Sussex RH10 1DS *Tel:* 01293 526005 *Fax:* 01293 527610 *Website:* www.lauramoffattmp.co.uk

Lab majority 37

MOLE, CHRIS
Ipswich

Chris Mole. Born 16 March 1958; Educated Dulwich College; University of Kent, Canterbury (BSc electronics 1979); Married Shona Gibb 1996 (2 sons). Technologist Plessey Research 1979-81; Research manager BT Labs 1981-98; Member Connect 1980-2001; Leader Suffolk County Council 1993-2001; Deputy leader EEDA 1998-2001

House of Commons: Member for Ipswich since 22 November 2001 by-election. *Political interests:* Local and Regional Government, European Affairs, Transport *Recreations:* Reading, films, music

Chris Mole, MP, House of Commons, London SW1A 0AA *Tel:* 020 7219 4158 *Fax:* 0870 1305681 *E-mail:* molec@parliament.uk. *Constituency:* 33 Silent Street, Ipswich, Suffolk IP1 1TF *Tel:* 01473 281559 *Fax:* 01473 217489 *Website:* www.ipswich-labour.org.uk

Lab majority 5,332

MOON, MADELEINE
Bridgend

Madeleine Moon. Born 27 March 1950; Educated Whinney Hill School; Durham Girls School; Married to Steve. Residential care home inspector Care Standards Inspectorate; Bridgend borough councillor 1991-; Former mayor of Porthcawl; Bridgend representative: Sports Council for Wales, Tourism South and West Wales; Chair British Resorts Association 1999-2001

House of Commons: Member for Bridgend since 5 May 2005 general election. *Political interests:* Environment, planning, partnerships

Madeleine Moon, MP, House of Commons, London SW1A 0AA *Tel:* 020 7219 4417. *Constituency:* *E-mail:* mmoonppc@aol.com

Lab majority 6,523

MOORE, MICHAEL
Berwickshire, Roxburgh and Selkirk

Michael Kevin Moore. Born 3 June 1965; Son of Reverend W. Haisley Moore, Church of Scotland minister, and Jill Moore, physiotherapist; Educated Strathallan School; Jedburgh Grammar School; Edinburgh University (MA politics and modern history 1987); Single. Research assistant to Archy Kirkwood, MP 1987-88; Coopers and Lybrand, Edinburgh 1988-97; Manager, Corporate Finance Practice 1993-97

House of Commons: Member for Tweeddale, Ettrick and Lauderdale 1997-2005, for Berwickshire, Roxburgh and Selkirk since 5 May 2005 general election; Spokesperson for: Scotland (Industry, Employment, Health and Environment) 1997-99, Transport 1999-2001, Scotland 2001; Liberal Democrat Shadow: Minister for Foreign Affairs 2001-05, Secretary of State for Trade and Industry 2005-. *Political interests:* Transport, Textiles, Europe, Corporate Social Responsibility, Foreign Affairs

Lib Dem majority 5,901

Campaign Chair, 1999 and 2003 Scottish Parliament elections; Parliamentary Group Convener 2000-01; Scottish MP representative Liberal Democrat Policy Committee 2001-02; Deputy Leader Scottish Liberal Democrats 2003-. Parliamentary Visiting Fellow, St Anthony's College, Oxford 2003-04; *Clubs:* Jed-Forest Rugby Club; *Recreations:* Rugby, hill-walking, music, films

Michael Moore, MP, House of Commons, London SW1A 0AA   *Tel:* 020 7219 2236 *Fax:* 020 7219 0263   *E-mail:* michaelmooremp@parliament.uk. *Constituency:* Parliamentary Office, 11 Island Street, Galashiels   *Tel:* 01896 663650 *Fax:* 01896 663655

MORAN, MARGARET
Luton South

Margaret Moran. Born 24 April 1955; Daughter of late Patrick (Jack) Moran, caretaker and of Mary, neé Murphy, home care worker; Educated St Ursula's, South London; St Mary's, Strawberry Hill, Twickenham; Birmingham University (BSocSc 1978). Director, Housing Association; Housing, local government, social services and education; Former national president, NALGO Housing Association Branch; TGWU; Councillor, London Borough of Lewisham 1984-97, Leader 1993-95, Chair, Housing Committee (6 years)

Lab majority 5,650

House of Commons: Contested Carshalton and Wallington 1992. Member for Luton South since 1 May 1997 general election; Assistant Government Whip 2003-05; PPS to: Gavin Strang as Minister of State (in Cabinet), Department of the Environment, Transport and the Regions (Minister for Transport) 1997-98, Dr Mo Mowlam as Minister for the Cabinet Office 1999-2001, Baroness Morgan of Huyton as Minister of State, Cabinet Office 2001, Barbara Roche as Minister of State for Women 2001-02, Andrew Smith as Secretary of State for Work and Pensions 2002-03. *Political interests:* Economy and Employment, Welfare, Housing and Urban Regeneration, Childcare, E-Issues. Northern Ireland, Kashmir, Spain, Bangladesh, Ireland

Member: Labour National Policy Forum, Labour Women's Network, Labour Housing Group. Save the Children Fund, Cancer Research Charities; Vice-Chair: Association of London Local Authorities, Association of Metropolitan Authorities; Chair, AMA Housing Committee; Citizensonline; *Publications:* Contributor: *Responding to the Global Public Health Challenge of Violence* Pfizer Journal; *Recreations:* Visiting historic sites, rambling, cinema

Margaret Moran, MP, House of Commons, London SW1A 0AA   *Tel:* 020 7219 5049 *Fax:* 020 7219 5094   *E-mail:* moranm@parliament.uk. *Constituency:* 93 Castle Street, Luton, Bedfordshire LU1 3AJ   *Tel:* 01582 731882   *Fax:* 01582 731885

MORDEN, JESSICA
Newport East

Jessica Morden. Born 29 May 1968; Educated Croefyceiliog Comprehensive School; Birmingham University. General secretary Welsh Labour Party; Member GMB

House of Commons: Member for Newport East since 5 May 2005 general election. *Political interests:* Economic development, anti-social behaviour

Recreations: Cinema, gym, cycling

Jessica Morden, MP, House of Commons, London SW1A 0AA *Tel:* 020 7219 6135. *Constituency:* *E-mail:* jessica_morden@new.labour.org.uk

Lab majority 6,838

MORGAN, JULIE
Cardiff North

Julie Morgan. Born 2 November 1944; Daughter of late Jack Edwards and Grace Edwards; Educated Dinas Powys Primary School; Howell's School, Llandaff, Cardiff; King's College, London University (BA English 1965); Manchester University; Cardiff University (Postgraduate Diploma in Social Administration, CQSW); Married Rhodri Morgan 1967 (now First Minister National Assembly for Wales) (1 son 2 daughters). Principal officer and development officer, West Glamorgan County Council 1983-87; Senior social worker, Barry Social Services 1985-87; Assistant director, Child Care, Barnados 1987-; Member, TGWU; Councillor: South Glamorgan Council 1985-96, Cardiff Council 1996; Member, Probation Committee

House of Commons: Contested Cardiff North 1992 general election. Member for Cardiff North since 1 May 1997 general election. *Political interests:* Equal Opportunities, Social Services, Childcare. Nicaragua, Ethiopia, Iran, India

Hon. Treasurer: Welsh Regional Group of Labour MPs 1999-, Parliamentary Labour Party Women's Group. *Recreations:* Swimming, walking

Julie Morgan, MP, House of Commons, London SW1A 0AA *Tel:* 020 7219 6960 *Fax:* 020 7219 0960 *E-mail:* morganj@parliament.uk. *Constituency:* Cardiff North Constituency Office, 17 Plasnewydd, Whitchurch, Cardiff, South Glamorgan CF14 1NR *Tel:* 029 2062 4166 *Fax:* 029 2062 3661

Lab majority 1,146

Lab majority 8,963

MORLEY, ELLIOT
Scunthorpe

Elliot Morley. Born 6 July 1952; Son of Anthony Morley and late Margaret Morley; Educated St Margaret's High School, Liverpool; Hull College of Education (BEd 1975); Married Patricia Hunt 1975 (1 son 1 daughter). Teacher Greatfield High School, Hull 1975-87; Former President, Hull Teachers Association; Hull City Council: Councillor 1979-86, Chair, City Transport Committee 1981-85, Former deputy traffic commissioner, NE Region; Member, NIJC of Municipal Bus Industries; Executive member, Federation of Public Passenger Employers 1981-86

House of Commons: Contested Beverley 1983 general election. Member for Glanford and Scunthorpe 1987-97, and for Scunthorpe since 1 May 1997 general election; Opposition Spokesperson for Food, Agriculture and Rural Affairs with special responsibility for animal welfare 1989-97; Parliamentary Secretary, Ministry of Agriculture, Fisheries and Food (Minister for Fisheries and the Countryside) 1997-2001; Department for Environment, Food and Rural Affairs 2001-: Parliamentary Under-Secretary 2001-03: (Minister for Fisheries and the Countryside) 2001-02, (Minister for Fisheries, Water and Nature Protection) 2002-03; Minister of State for Environment and Agri-Environment 2003-. *Political interests:* Education, Transport, Local and Regional Government, Green Issues, Countryside. Africa, Cyprus

Parliamentary Convener, Socialist Environmental Resources Association 1989-91; Steel Group of MPs. Vice-President: Federation of Economic Development Authorities (FEDA), Association of Drainage Authorities, Wildlife and Countryside Link; Former Council Member, British Trust for Ornithology; Trustee, Birds of the Humber Trust; Hon. Fellow, Lincolnshire and Humberside University; *Recreations:* Ornithology, travel, conservation, countryside issues, scuba-diving

Elliot Morley, MP, House of Commons, London SW1A 0AA *Tel:* 020 7219 3569 *E-mail:* emorleymp@aol.com. *Constituency:* Kinsley Labour Club, Cole Street, Scunthorpe, Humberside DN15 6QS *Tel:* 01724 842000 *Fax:* 01724 281734

Con majority 8,901

MOSS, MALCOLM
North East Cambridgeshire

Malcolm Douglas Moss. Born 6 March 1943; Son of late Norman Moss and Annie Moss, neé Gay; Educated Audenshaw Grammar School; St John's College, Cambridge (BA geography 1965, MA); Married Vivien Lorraine Peake 1965 (died 1997) (2 daughters); married Sonya Alexandra McFarlin, neé Evans 2000. Blundell's School: Assistant master 1966-68, Head of department, geography and economics 1968-70; Barwick Associates Ltd: Insurance consultant 1971-72, General manager 1972-74; Mandrake Associates Ltd: Co-Founder and director 1974-94, Managing director 1986-88; Chairman: Mandrake Group plc 1986-88, Mandrake Associates Ltd 1988-93; Wisbech Town Councillor 1979-87; Fenland District Councillor 1983-87; Cambridgeshire County Councillor 1985-87

House of Commons: Member for North East Cambridgeshire since 11 June 1987 general election; Opposition Spokesperson for: Northern Ireland November 1997-1999; Agriculture, Fisheries and Food 1999-2001, Local Government and the Regions 2001-02; Opposition Whip 1997; PPS: to Tristan Garel-Jones as Minister of State, Foreign and Commonwealth Office 1991-93, to Sir Patrick Mayhew as Secretary of State for Northern Ireland 1993-94; Parliamentary Under-Secretary of State, Northern Ireland Office 1994-97; Shadow Minister for: Transport 2002, Culture, Media and Sport 2002-03, Home, Constitutional and Legal Affairs 2003-04, Home Affairs 2004-. *Political interests:* Energy, Education, Housing, Small Businesses, Financial Services, Rural Development. France, Switzerland, USA, South Africa, Botswana

Larmor Award, St John's College; Trustee, Angles Theatre and Arts Centre, Wisbech; *Clubs:* Member, Lords and Commons: Ski Club, Tennis Club; *Recreations:* Amateur dramatics, gardening, skiing, tennis

Malcolm Moss, MP, House of Commons, London SW1A 0AA *Tel:* 020 7219 6933 *Fax:* 020 7219 1051 *E-mail:* mossm@parliament.uk. *Constituency:* 111 High Street, March, Cambridgeshire PE15 9LH *Tel:* 01354 656541 *Fax:* 01354 660417

Lab majority 1,501

MOUNTFORD, KALI
Colne Valley

Kali Mountford. Born 12 January 1954; Educated Crewe Grammar School for Girls; Crewe and Alsager College (DipHE) (BA philosophy, psychology, sociology 1988); (1 son 1 daughter); Member, CPSA 1975-97: Shop steward 1983-95, Branch secretary 1985-90, Regional secretary 1987-92, Department Employment Whitley Council Secretary 1988-95, Branch chair 1990-92, Trades Council Executive 1990-95; Councillor, Sheffield City Council 1992-96: Vice-Chair, Economic Development 1992-94, Chair, Personnel 1994-95, Deputy Chair, Finance 1995, Chair, Finance 1995-96

House of Commons: Member for Colne Valley since 1 May 1997 general election; PPS to Des Browne as Minister of State: Department for Work and Pensions 2003-04, Home Office 2004-. *Political interests:* Social Security, Employment, Textiles, Agriculture, Finance, Small Businesses

Member, Labour Party (Sheffield Brightside): General Management Committee 1985-95, Women's Officer 1989-91, Euro Constituency Vice-Chair 1989-91, Campaign Co-ordinator 1992, Recruitment Officer 1992-93. Member, Sheffield Race Equality Council 1993-95

Kali Mountford, MP, House of Commons, London SW1A 0AA *Tel:* 020 7219 4507 *Fax:* 020 7219 2906. *Constituency:* Civic Hall, 23 Carr Lane, Slaithwaite, Huddersfield, West Yorkshire HD7 5AG *Tel:* 01484 840100 *Fax:* 01484 840101

MUDIE, GEORGE
Leeds East

George Mudie. Born 6 February 1945; Educated Local state schools; Married (2 children). Trade Union Official; Former Leader, Leeds City Council

House of Commons: Member for Leeds East since 9 April 1992 general election; Opposition Whip 1994-97; Pairing and Accommodation Whip 1995-97; Deputy Chief Whip (Treasurer of HM Household) 1997-98; Parliamentary Under-Secretary of State (Lifelong Learning), Department for Education and Employment 1998-99

Lab majority 11,578   *Clubs:* Harehills Labour; *Recreations:* Watching football

George Mudie, MP, House of Commons, London SW1A 0AA *Tel:* 020 7219 5889. *Constituency:* 242 Brooklands Avenue, Leeds LS14 6NW

MULHOLLAND, GREGORY
Leeds North West

Gregory Thomas Mulholland. Born 31 August 1970; Educated St Ambrose College, Altrincham; York University (BA politics 1991, MA public administration and public policy 1995); Married Reagan Melita Hatton 2004. Account director, several leading agencies 1997-2002; Leeds City Council: Councillor 2003-, Lead member, corporate services 2004-

House of Commons: Member for Leeds North West since 5 May 2005 general election. *Political interests:* International development, public transport, social care

Lib Dem majority
1,877

Executive member, Edinburgh Central 2001; Vice-chair, Leeds North West 2003-. *Clubs:* LDWA, Adel War Memorial Association,; *Recreations:* Hillwalking, cinema, watching football and rugby league, skiing, travel

Gregory Mulholland, MP, House of Commons, London SW1A 0AA
Tel: 020 7219 5896. *Constituency:* Agent: Jim Spencer, 255a Otley Road, Leeds LS16 5LQ *Tel:* 0113 226 6825 *E-mail:* info@gregmulholland.org
Website: www.gregmulholland.org

MULLIN, CHRIS
Sunderland South

Chris Mullin. Born 12 December 1947; Son of Leslie and Teresa Mullin; Educated St Joseph's College, Ipswich; Hull University (LLB 1969); Married Nguyen Thi Ngoc 1987 (2 daughters). Author; Journalist; travelled extensively in Asia; BBC World Service 1974-78; *Tribune* 1978-84, editor 1982-84; Member: NUJ, MSF

House of Commons: Contested Devon North 1970, Kingston Upon Thames February 1974 general elections. Member for Sunderland South since 11 June 1987 general election; Parliamentary Under-Secretary of State: Department of the Environment, Transport and the Regions 1999-2001, Department for International Development 2001, Foreign and Commonwealth Office 2003-05. *Political interests:* Media Ownership, Justice. Cambodia, Tibet, Vietnam

Lab majority 11,059

Member Parliamentary Labour Party Parliamentary Committee 1997-99, 2001-. Chairman Medical Aid for Vietnam; *Publications: How to Select or Reselect your MP*, 1981; *The Tibetans*, 1981; *A Very British Coup*, 1982; *Error of Judgement*, 1986; *The Last Man Out of Saigon*, 1986; *The Year of the Fire Monkey*, 1991; Channel 4 and House Award for Questioner of the Year 1999; Hon. LLD, City University, London; *Recreations:* Walking, gardening

Chris Mullin, MP, House of Commons, London SW1A 0AA *Tel:* 020 7219 3440 *E-mail:* mullinc@parliament.uk. *Constituency:* 3 The Esplanade, Sunderland, Tyne and Wear SR2 7BQ *Tel:* Sunderland Office: 0191-567 2848 *Fax:* 0191-510 1063

Con majority 1,738

MUNDELL, DAVID
Dumfriesshire, Clydesdale and Tweeddale

David Gordon Mundell. Born 27 May 1962; Son of Doran Mundell, hotelier; Educated Lockerbie Academy; Edinburgh University (LLB 1984); Strathclyde University Business School (MBA 1991); Married Lynda Carmichael 1987 (2 sons 1 daughter). Corporate lawyer, Biggart Baillie & Gifford, Glasgow 1989-91; BT Scotland: Group legal adviser 1991-98, Head of national affairs 1998-99; MSP for South of Scotland region since 6 May 1999; Councillor: Annandale and Eskdale District Council 1984-86, Dumfries and Galloway Council 1986-87

House of Commons: Member for Dumfrieshire, Clydesdale and Tweeddale since 5 May 2005 general election. *Political interests:* Business, Commerce, Rural Affairs. USA

Contested Dumfries constituency 1999 Scottish Parliament election.

David Mundell, MP, House of Commons, London SW1A 0AA *Tel:* 020 7219 4895. *Constituency:* Dumfriesshire, Clydesdale and Tweeddale Conservative Association, Churchill House, 41a Castle Street, Dumfries DG1 1DU *Tel:* 01683 222745 *Fax:* 01683 222476 *E-mail:* david@davidmundell.com *Website:* www.davidmundell.com

Lab/Co-op majority 11,370

MUNN, MEG
Sheffield Heeley

Margaret Patricia Munn. Born 24 August 1959; Daughter of late Reginald Edward Munn, representative and Lillian Munn, née Seward, retired nurse tutor; Educated Rowlinson Comprehensive School, Sheffield; York University (BA languages 1981); Nottingham University (MA social work 1986); Certificate of Qualification in Social Work 1986; Certificate in Management Studies 1995; Diploma in Management Studies 1997; Married Dennis Bates 1989. Social work assistant, Berkshire County Council 1981-84; Nottinghamshire County Council: Social worker 1986-90, Senior social worker 1990-92; District manager, Barnsley Metropolitan Council 1992-96; Children's services manager, Wakefield Metropolitan District Council 1996-99; Assistant Director, City of York Council 1999-2000; UNISON 1981-96; Shop steward NALGO 1982-84; GMB 1997-; Councillor Nottingham City Council 1987-91

House of Commons: Member for Sheffield Heeley since 7 June 2001 general election; Team PPS, Department for Education and Skills 2003-04; PPS to Margaret Hodge as Minister of State, Department for Education and Skills 2004-05; Parliamentary Under-Secretary of State, Department of Trade and Industry 2005-. *Political interests:* Social Welfare, Social Affairs, Co-operative Issues, European Affairs, Small Businesses

Member Co-operative Party 1975-; Chair Women's Parliamentary Labour Party; Chair Co-operative Parliamentary Group 2005-. *Recreations:* Tennis, swimming, reading

Meg Munn, MP, House of Commons, London SW1A 0AA *Tel:* 020 7219 8316 *Fax:* 020 7219 1793 *E-mail:* munnm@parliament.uk. *Constituency:* 2nd Floor, Barkers Pool House, Burgess Street, Sheffield, South Yorkshire S1 2HF *Tel:* 0114 263 4004 *Fax:* 0114 263 4334

^{UK}VOICE

supporting people with learning disabilities who have experienced crime or abuse, their families, carers and professional workers

VOICE UK supports people with learning disabilities who have experienced crime or abuse. We also support families, carers and professional workers.

In recent years legislation has been introduced to support vulnerable people who are victims of crime. We urge you to continue to support the promotion of the rights of people with learning disabilities and other vulnerable victims of crime within the criminal justice system.

Thank you for your support in the past. We look forward to working for you in the future, and hope you will find time to attend the VOICE UK All Party Parliamentary Group meetings.

For more details about our work please go to:
www.voiceuk.org.uk

MURPHY, CONOR
Newry and Armagh

Conor Murphy. Born 1963; Educated St Colman's College, Newry; Queen's University, Belfast (MA Irish politics); Married. Project manager, South Armagh PoWs project; MLA for Newry and Armagh 1998-; Councillor, Newry and Mourne District Council 1989-97

House of Commons: Contested Newry and Armagh 2001 general election. Member for Newry and Armagh since 5 May 2005 general election

Sinn Féin majority
8,195

Sinn Féin group leader, Northern Ireland Assembly; Sinn Féin delegate Leeds Castle talks September 2004

Conor Murphy, MP, House of Commons, London SW1A 0AA *Tel:* 020 7219 8534. *Constituency:* Main Street, Camlough, Newry, Co Down *Tel:* 028 3083 9470 *Fax:* 028 3083 9423

MURPHY, DENIS
Wansbeck

Denis Murphy. Born 2 November 1948; Son of late John Murphy and of Josephine Murphy; Educated St Cuthberts Grammar School, Newcastle upon Tyne; Northumberland College (electrical engineering 1967); Married Nancy Moffat 1969 (separated) (1 son 1 daughter). Apprentice electrician 1965-69; Underground electrician, Ellington Colliery 1969-94; Member, National Union of Mineworkers (Craft Section) 1965-; General Secretary, Northumberland Colliery Mechanics Association 1989-97; Wansbeck District Council: Councillor 1990-97, Chair of Planning, Leader of Council 1994-97

Lab majority 10,581

House of Commons: Member for Wansbeck since 1 May 1997 general election. *Political interests:* Economic Development, Transport

Recreations: Cycling, walking

Denis Murphy, MP, House of Commons, London SW1A 0AA *Tel:* 020 7219 6474. *Constituency:* 94 Station Road, Ashington, Northumberland NE63 8RN *Tel:* 01670 523100 *Fax:* 01670 521655

MURPHY, JIM
East Renfrewshire

Jim (James) Murphy. Born 23 August 1967; Son of Jim Murphy, pipe-fitter, and Anne Murphy, secretary; Educated Bellarmine Secondary School, Glasgow; Milnerton High School, Cape Town; Strathclyde University; Married Claire Cook (1 daughter 1 son). President: NUS (Scotland) 1992-94, NUS 1994-96; Director, Endsleigh Insurance 1994-96; Project Manager, Scottish Labour Party 1996-97; Member, GMB

Lab majority 6,657

House of Commons: Member for Eastwood 1997-2005, for East Renfrewshire since 5 May 2005 general election; Assistant Government Whip 2002-03, Government Whip 2003-05; PPS to Helen Liddell as Secretary of State for Scotland 2001-02; Parliamentary Secretary, Cabinet Office 2005-. *Political interests:* Economy, International Affairs, Defence, Consumer Issues, Sport. Southern Africa, Middle East

Vice-Chair, Labour Friends of Israel 1997-01, Chair 2001-02; Member, Co-operative Party. *Clubs:* Bonnington Golf; *Recreations:* Football, travelling in Scotland, cinema, horse-racing, golf

Jim Murphy, MP, House of Commons, London SW1A 0AA *Tel:* 020 7219 4615 *Fax:* 020 7219 5657 *E-mail:* jimmurphy2005@parliament.uk. *Constituency:* 238 Ayr Road, Newton Mearns G77 6AA *Tel:* 0141 577 0100 *Fax:* 0141 616 3613

MURPHY, PAUL
Torfaen

Paul Peter Murphy. Born 25 November 1948; Son of late Ronald and late Marjorie Murphy; Educated St Francis School, Abersychan; West Monmouth School, Pontypool; Oriel College, Oxford (MA modern history); Single. Management trainee, CWS 1970-71; Lecturer in government, Ebbw Vale College of Further Education 1971-87; Member, TGWU; Torfaen Borough Council: Councillor 1973-87, Chair, Finance Committee 1976-86

Lab majority 14,791

House of Commons: Contested Wells 1979 general election. Member for Torfaen since 11 June 1987 general election; Opposition Spokesman on: Welsh Affairs 1988-94, Northern Ireland 1994-95, Foreign Affairs 1995, Defence, Disarmament and Arms Control 1995-97; Minister of State, Northern Ireland Office (Minister for Political Development) 1997-99; Secretary of State for Wales 1999-2002; Secretary of State for Northern Ireland 2002-05. *Political interests:* Local and Regional Government, Wales, Education, Housing, Foreign Affairs, Northern Ireland

Secretary, Torfaen Constituency Labour Party 1971-87; Chair, Welsh Group of Labour MPs 1996-97. Former Treasurer, Anglo-Austrian Society; Member, Royal Institute of International Affairs 1997-; Knight of St Gregory (Papal Award); PC 1999; KCMCO; Hon. Fellow, Oriel College, Oxford 2001; *Clubs:* Oxford and Cambridge Club; *Recreations:* Classical music, cooking

Rt Hon Paul Murphy, MP, House of Commons, London SW1A 0AA
Tel: 020 7219 3463 *E-mail:* hunta@parliament.uk. *Constituency:* 73 Upper Trosnant Street, Pontypool, Torfaen, Gwent NP4 8AU *Tel:* 01495 750078 *Fax:* 01495 752584

MURRISON, ANDREW
Westbury

Andrew William Murrison. Born 24 April 1961; Son of William Murrison and Marion Murrison, née Horn; Educated Harwich High School; The Harwich School; Bristol University medicine: (MB CHB 1984), (MD 1995); Cambridge Universty medicine (DPH 1996); Married Jennifer Jane Munden 1994 (5 daughters). Surgeon Commander Royal Navy 1981-2000. Principal Medical Officer HM Naval Base Portsmouth 1996-99; Staff Officer, Commander-In-Chief Fleet 1999-2000; Locum Consultant Occupational Physician Gloucestershire Royal Hospital and GP 2000-01; Research assistant Lord Freeman 2000-

Con majority 5,349

House of Commons: Member for Westbury since 7 June 2001 general election; Shadow Minister for: Public Services, Health and Education 2003-04, Health 2004-. *Political interests:* Health, Defence. Morocco

Bradford-on-Avon Preservation Trust, Independent Living Centre, Cancer Research UK; Lions; *Publications: Investors in Communities* (Bow Group) 2000; Gilbert Blane Medal 1994; *Clubs:* Warminster Conservative Club, Royal British Legion, Vice-president, Trowbridge White Ensign Association; *Recreations:* Sailing, skiing

Dr Andrew Murrison, MP, House of Commons, London SW1A 0AA
Tel: 020 7219 8337 *Fax:* 020 7219 1944 *E-mail:* murrisona@parliament.uk.
Constituency: Lovemead House, Roundstone Street, Trowbridge, Wiltshire BA14 8DG *Tel:* 01225 358584 *Fax:* 01225 358583

Lab/Co-op majority
8,962

NAYSMITH, DOUG
Bristol North West

Doug (John Douglas) Naysmith. Born 1 April 1941; Son of late James Naysmith and late Ina Vass; Educated Musselburgh Burgh School; George Heriots School, Edinburgh; Heriot-Watt University (biology); Edinburgh University (BSc zoology 1965, PhD surgical science 1970); Married Caroline Hill 1966 (separated) (1 son 1 daughter). Research assistant, Edinburgh University 1966-69; Post-doctoral fellow, Yale University, USA 1969-70; Research immunologist, Beecham Research Laboratories 1970-72; Bristol University: Research associate, Fellow, lecturer in immunology, Pathology Department 1972-92; Contested 1979 European Parliament election; Bristol University Administrator, Registrar's Office 1992-97; Past President and Secretary, Bristol AUT; Bristol City Council: Councillor 1981-98, Past Chair: Docks Committee, Health and Environmental Services Committee, Health Policy Committee, Port of Bristol Authority 1986-91; Past Labour Group Whip; Past member, Avon FPC; Past member, Bristol CHC

House of Commons: Contested Cirencester and Tewekesbury 1987, Bristol North West 1992 general elections. Member for Bristol North West since 1 May 1997 general election; Chair Bristol Co-operative Party 1990-97; Member Co-operative Party NEC 1994-96. *Political interests:* Health, Co-operative Development, Local and Regional Government, International Development, Science, Education, Ports and Shipping

Chair Bristol District Labour Party 1991-97; President Socialist Health Association 1991-97; National Vice-President Socialist Health Association 1997-2000; Co-operative Group of MPs 1997-. Member Council of Europe and WEU 1997-99; Past treasurer International Union of Immunology Societies; Past secretary European Federation of Immunology Societies; Member, Wildlife Trust; Trustee, Jenner Trust; *Publications:* Various scientific papers and book chapters; *Recreations:* Music, theatre, films, preserving paddle steamers

Dr Doug Naysmith, MP, House of Commons, London SW1A 0AA
Tel: 020 7219 4187 *Fax:* 020 7219 2602 *E-mail:* naysmithd@parliament.uk.
Constituency: Unit 6, Greenway Business Centre, Doncaster Road, Bristol, Avon BS10 5PY *Tel:* 0117-950 2385 *Fax:* 0117-950 5302

Con majority 3,893

NEWMARK, BROOKS
Braintree

Brooks Newmark. Born 8 May 1958; Educated Bedford School; Harvard College (BA history 1980); Worcester College, Oxford (politics postgraduate research 1980-82); Harvard Business School (MBA finance 1984); Married Lucy Keegan 1985. Vice-president, Lehman Brothers Inc 1984-87; Director, Newmark Brothers Ltd 1988-93; Principal, Stellican Ltd 1993-98; Partner, Apollo Management LP 1998

House of Commons: Contested Newcastle upon Tyne Central 1997 and Braintree 2001 general elections. Member for Braintree since 5 May 2005 general election

Chair, Southwark and Bermondsey Conservative Association 1990-93

Brooks Newmark, MP, House of Commons, London SW1A 0AA
Tel: 020 7219 8080. *Constituency:* Avenue Lodge, The Avenue, Witham,
Essex CM8 2DL *Tel:* 01376 512386 *Fax:* 01376 516475
E-mail: theoffice@braintreeconservatives.co.uk
Website: www.braintreeconservatives.co.uk

Lab majority 1,839

NORRIS, DAN
Wansdyke

Dan Norris. Born 28 January 1960; Son of David Norris and June Norris (neé Allen); Educated State schools; Sussex University (MSW). Former child protection officer; Member, GMB; Councillor: Bristol City Council 1989-92, 1995-97, Avon County Council 1994-96

House of Commons: Member for Wansdyke since 1 May 1997 general election; Assistant Government Whip 2001-03. *Political interests:* Freedom of Information, Child Protection and Safety, Animal Welfare

Member: Co-op Party, Labour Leader's Campaign Team with responsibility for Health 1998-99, General Election Campaign Team with responsibility for campaigning against the Liberal Democrats 1999-. Kidscape; Trustee, Snowdon Award Scheme; *Publications:* Various publications on prevention and reduction of violence; Hon. Fellow, School of Cultural and Community Studies, Sussex University; *Clubs:* Radstock Working Men's; *Recreations:* Photography

Dan Norris, MP, House of Commons, London SW1A 0AA *Tel:* 020 7219 6395. *Constituency: Tel:* 01454 857406 *Fax:* 01454 857382

Lib Dem majority 7,476

OATEN, MARK
Winchester

Mark Oaten. Born 8 March 1964; Son of Ivor and Audrey Oaten; Educated Queen's Comprehensive School, Watford; Hatfield Polytechnic (BA history, Diploma in International Public Relations 1986); Married Belinda Fordham 1992 (2 daughters). Director Oasis Radio, Hertfordshire 1988-97; Consultant Shandwick Public Affairs 1988-92; Managing Director Westminster Public Relations 1996-97; Managing Director Westminster Communications Ltd 1996-97; Councillor, Watford Borough Council 1986-94, Liberal Democrat Group Leader

House of Commons: Contested Watford 1992 general election. Member for Winchester since 1 May 1997 general election. (His two-vote victory was declared invalid and a by-election held on 20 November 1997 convincingly confirmed him in the seat); Liberal Democrat Spokesperson for: Social Security and Welfare (Disabled People) 1997-99, Foreign Affairs and Defence (Foreign Affairs) 1999-2000, Foreign Affairs and Defence (Europe) 2000-01, Cabinet Office 2001-03; PPS to Charles Kennedy as Leader of the Liberal Democrat Party 1999-2001; Liberal Democrat Shadow Home Secretary 2003-

Chair: Parliamentary Party 2001-, Liberal Democrat Peel Group 2001-. Member, European Standing Committee C 1999-2000; *Recreations:* Gardening, swimming

Mark Oaten, MP, House of Commons, London SW1A 0AA *Tel:* 020 7219 2703 *Fax:* 020 7219 2389 *E-mail:* oatenm@parliament.uk. *Constituency:* 13 City Road, Winchester, Hampshire SO23 8SD *Tel:* 01962 622212 *Fax:* 01962 863300

O'BRIEN, MIKE
North Warwickshire

Michael O'Brien. Born 19 June 1954; Son of late Timothy O'Brien and Mary O'Brien, neé Toomey; Educated St George's School; Blessed Edward Oldcorne School; North Staffs Polytechnic (BA history and politics, PGCE); Married Alison Joy Munro 1987 (2 daughters). Trainee solicitor 1977-80; Teacher training 1980-81; Lecturer in law, Colchester College of Further and Higher Education 1981-87; In practice as solicitor 1987-92; Branch secretary, NATFHE 1989-90

Lab majority 7,553

House of Commons: Contested Ruislip Northwood 1983 and North Warwickshire 1987 general elections. Member for North Warwickshire since 9 April 1992 general election; Opposition Spokesperson for Treasury and Economic Affairs 1995-96; Shadow Economic Secretary to the Treasury 1996-97; Parliamentary Under-Secretary of State, Home Office 1997-2001; Foreign and Commonwealth Office 2002-04: Parliamentary Under-Secretary of State 2002-03, Minister of State for Trade, Investment and Foreign Affairs (also DTI) 2003-04; Minister of State (Energy and E-Commerce), Department of Trade and Industry 2004-05; Solicitor General 2005-. *Political interests:* West Midlands Industry, Police, Coal Industry

Parliamentary Adviser to the Police Federation of England and Wales 1993-96; *Clubs:* Bedworth Ex Servicemen's, Woodend Workingmen's; Ansley Social Club; *Recreations:* Spending time with family

Mike O'Brien, MP, House of Commons, London SW1A 0AA *Tel:* 020 7219 6464. *Constituency:* 92 King Street, Bedworth, Warwickshire CV12 8JF *Tel:* 024 7631 5084

Con majority 6,195

O'BRIEN, STEPHEN
Eddisbury

Stephen Rothwell O'Brien. Born 1 April 1957; Son of David O'Brien, retired businessman and Rothy O'Brien, retired shopowner and nurse; Educated Loretto School, Mombasa, Kenya; Handbridge School, Chester; Heronwater School, Abergele, N Wales; Sedbergh School, Cumbria; Emmanuel College, Cambridge (law 1979, MA); College of Law, Chester (Professional Qualification 1980); Married Gemma Townshend 1986 (2 sons 1 daughter). Armed Forces Parliamentary Scheme (Army) 2001-03. Articles, Freshfields (Solicitors, City of London) 1981-83, Senior Managing Solicitor 1983-88; Redland plc 1988-98: Group secretary and director, Strategy and Corporate Affairs, Director of UK and overseas operations, Member, Group Executive Committee, Deputy chairman, Redland Tile and Brick (Northern Ireland 1995-98), Executive Director, Redland Clay Tile (Mexico1994-98); International business consultant 1998-

House of Commons: Member for Eddisbury since 22 July 1999 by-election; Opposition Whip 2001-02; Private Member's Bill, Honesty in Food Labelling 1999-2000, re-introduced 2002-03; PPS to: Francis Maude as Shadow Foreign Secretary 2000, Michael Ancram as Chairman Conservative Party 2000-01; Acting Director Office Leader of Conservative Party, Iain Duncan Smith 2001; Shadow: Financial Secretary to the Treasury 2002, Paymaster General 2002-03, Secretary of State for Industry 2003-. *Political interests:* Economy, Trade and Industry, Agriculture and the Rural Economy, Housing, Infrastructure, Transport, Northern Ireland, Foreign Affairs, Education, Constitutional Affairs. Ireland, East African countries, Australia, New Zealand, Mexico, USA

Chairman, Chichester Conservative Association 1998-99; Executive committee member, Westminster Candidates Association 1998-99; Special adviser, Conservative Business Liaison Unit (construction sector) 1998-2001; Member, National Membership Committee of the Conservative Party 1999-2001. St Luke's Hospice, Winsford; Founder Member, Brazil-UK Joint Business Council 1994; Council of Members, Scottish Business in the Community 1995-98; Member: British-Irish Inter-Parliamentary Body 2000-, International Parliamentary Union 1999-, Commonwealth Parliamentary Association 1999-; *Clubs:* Institute of Chartered Secretaries and Administrators, Law Society, Winsford Constitutional and Conservative, Cheshire Pitt Club; Vice-chairman, Ebernoe cricket club; *Recreations:* Music (piano), fell-walking, golf

Stephen O'Brien, MP, House of Commons, London SW1A 0AA
Tel: 020 7219 6315 *Fax:* 020 7219 0584 *E-mail:* obriens@parliament.uk.
Constituency: Eddisbury Conservative Association, 4 Church Walk, High Street, Tarporley, Cheshire CW6 0AJ *Tel:* 01829 733243 *Fax:* 01829 733243

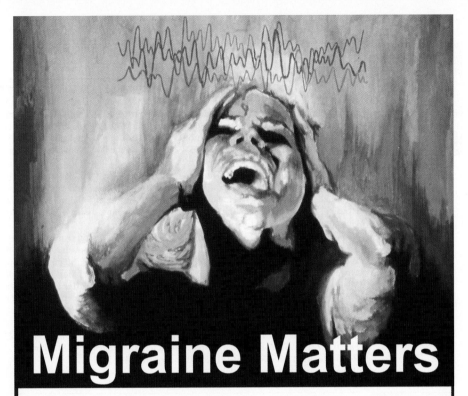

Migraine Matters

- 6 million people in the UK suffer from migraine.
- Migraine is classified by WHO as amongst the top 20 most disabling lifetime conditions.
- The cost to the UK economy is estimated at £1 billion per annum.
- In the UK, migraine is more prevalent than diabetes, epilepsy and asthma combined.

The Migraine Action Association is a registered charity providing information and support to migraine sufferers and their families, raising general awareness of the condition and funding specialist migraine clinics and further research.

The Association works closely with the All Party Parliamentary Group on Primary Headache Disorders to encourage better use of existing resources to improve the quality of care for migraine sufferers.

Visit www.migraine.org.uk or www.migraine4kids.org.uk

Migraine Action
ASSOCIATION

Migraine Action Association
6 Oakley Hay Lodge Business Park, Great Folds Road
Great Oakley, Northamptonshire NN18 9AS
Tel: 0870 050 5898   Fax: 01536 461444
E-mail: info@migraine.org.uk
Registered Charity No. 207783

O'HARA, EDWARD
Knowsley South

Edward O'Hara. Born 1 October 1937; Son of late Robert and Clara O'Hara, neé Davies; Educated Liverpool Collegiate School; Magdalen College, Oxford (MA literae humaniores 1962); Married Lillian Hopkins 1962 (2 sons 1 daughter). Lecturer/principal lecturer in higher education: C.F. Mott College 1970-75, City of Liverpool College of Higher Education 1975-85, Liverpool Polytechnic 1985-90; Member, Association of Teachers and Lecturers; Councillor, Knowsley Borough Council 1975-91

Lab majority 17,688

House of Commons: Member for Knowsley South since 27 September 1990 by-election; Deputy Speaker Westminster Hall 2001-. *Political interests:* Local and Regional Government, Regional Development, European Union, Education, Housing, Emergency Planning, Animal Welfare, Ageing Issues. CIS, Cyprus, Germany, Greece, Japan, USA

Member: Socialist Education Association, Co-operative Party, Fabian Society. Merseyside delegate to Régions Européenes de Tradition Industrielle 1989-90, Permanent Committee, Assembly of European Regions 1989-90, Member, Labour Movement in Europe 1990-, Council of Europe 1997-; Patron, Marilyn Houlton MND Trust 1991-; Community Development Foundation: Trustee 1992-, Chair 1997-; Vice-Chair, National Wild Flower Centre Development Trust 1996-; Patron Knowsley Arts Trust 1999-; *Recreations:* Theatre, literature, music (classical, jazz, folk – especially Rembetiko), watching soccer, Greek language and culture

Edward O'Hara, MP, House of Commons, London SW1A 0AA *Tel:* 020 7219 5232 *Fax:* 020 7219 4952 *E-mail:* oharae@parliament.uk. *Constituency:* 69 St. Mary's Road, Huyton L36 5SR *Tel:* 0151 489 8021 *Fax:* 0151 449 3873 *Website:* www.knowsleysouth.labour.co.uk

OLNER, BILL
Nuneaton

William John Olner. Born 9 May 1942; Son of late C. William Olner, coalminer, and late Lillian Olner; Educated Atherstone Secondary Modern School; North Warwickshire Technical College (City and Guilds Mechanical Engineering); Married Gillian Everitt 1962. Engineer; Skilled machinist, Rolls Royce, Coventry 1957-92; Apprenticed with Armstrong Siddeley Motors 1967-72; Member, AEU/AMICUS and branch secretary 1972-92; Nuneaton Borough Council: Councillor 1971-92, Chair, Planning Committee 1974-76, Deputy Leader 1980-82, Leader 1982-87, Chair, Policy and Resources Committee 1982-86, Mayor 1987-88, Chair, Environmental Health Committee 1990-92

Lab majority 2,280

House of Commons: Member for Nuneaton since 9 April 1992 general election. *Political interests:* Engineering, Local and Regional Government. France, USA, China, Ghana, Australia

Mary Ann Evans Hospice, Nuneaton; Joint Vice-Chair, Executive Committee, Commonwealth Parliamentary Association (CPA) UK Branch 1995-99, Member, 1999-; Freeman, City of Coventry; *Recreations:* Local Hospice Movement, walking, current affairs, television

Bill Olner, MP, House of Commons, London SW1A 0AA *Tel:* 020 7219 4154 *E-mail:* olnerb@parliament.uk. *Constituency:* 171 Queens Road, Nuneaton CV11 5NB *Tel:* 02476 642222 *Fax:* 02476 642223

ÖPIK, LEMBIT
Montgomeryshire

Lib Dem majority
7,173

Lembit Öpik. Born 2 March 1965; Son of Dr Uno Öpik and Liivi Öpik; Educated Royal Belfast Academical Institution; Bristol University (BA philosophy 1987) (President Union 1985-86); Single. Procter and Gamble Ltd: Brand assistant/Assistant brand manager 1988-91, Corporate training and organisation development manager 1991-96, Global human resources training manager 1996-97; Contested Northumbria 1994 European Parliament election; National Union of Students Executive 1987-88; Councillor, Newcastle upon Tyne City Council 1992

House of Commons: Contested Newcastle Central 1992 general election. Member for Montgomeryshire since 1 May 1997 general election; Spokesperson for: Welsh Affairs 1997-, Young People 1997-2002, Northern Ireland 2001-; Liberal Democrat Shadow Secretary of State for: Northern Ireland 1999-, Wales 2001-. *Political interests:* Transport, Education and Youth, Aerospace. Eastern Europe, China, Fiji

Member: Federal Executive Committee of Liberal Democrats 1991-, Federal Finance Administration Committee 1997-; Welsh Vice-President, Liberal Democrat Federal Party 1999-; Member, Federal Executive Committee 2001-; Leader: Welsh Liberal Democrat Parliamentary Party 2001-, Welsh Liberal Democrats 2001-. Hope House; Member, Welsh Grand Committee 1997-; *Publications:* Contributor to Patrick Moore's *2001 Astronomy Yearbook*; *Recreations:* Aviation, military history, astronomy, films

Lembit Öpik, MP, House of Commons, London SW1A 0AA *Tel:* 020 7219 1144 *Fax:* 020 7219 2210 *E-mail:* opikl@parliament.uk. *Constituency:* Montgomeryshire Liberal Democrats, 3 Park Street, Newtown, Powys SY16 1EE *Tel:* 01686 625527 *Fax:* 01686 628891 *Website:* www.montgomery.libdems.org

OSBORNE, GEORGE
Tatton

Con majority 11,731

George Gideon Oliver Osborne. Born 23 May 1971; Son of Sir Peter George Osborne Bt, founder and chairman Osborne and Little plc and Felicity Alexandra Osborne, née Loxton-Peacock, foodshop owner; Educated St Paul's School, London; Davidson College, North Carolina USA 1990; Magdalen College, Oxford (BA modern history 1993, MA); Married Frances Victoria Howell 1998 (1 son 1 daughter). Freelance journalist *Sunday* and *Daily Telegraph* 1993; Head of political section Conservative Research Department 1994-95; Special adviser Ministry of Agriculture, Fisheries and Food 1995-97; Political Office, 10 Downing Street 1997; Secretary Shadow Cabinet 1997-2001; Political secretary to William Hague MP as Leader of Opposition 1997-2001

House of Commons: Member for Tatton since 7 June 2001 general election; Opposition Whip 2003; Shadow: Minister for Economic Affairs 2003-04, Chief Secretary of the Treasury 2004-05, Chancellor of the Exchequer 2005-. *Political interests:* Economy, Taxation, Foreign Affairs, Education, Law and Order. USA, Hungary

Member Public Accounts Commission 2002-; Dean Rusk Scholarship 1990; Magdalen College Scholarship 1992; *Recreations:* Cinema, theatre, walking, observing American politics

George Osborne, MP, House of Commons, London SW1A 0AA *Tel:* 020 7219 8329; 020 7219 8214. *Constituency:* Tatton Conservative Association, Manchester Road, Knutsford, Cheshire WA16 0LT *Tel:* 01565 632181 *Fax:* 01565 632182 *E-mail:* contact@georgeosborne.co.uk

Macmillan cancer relief

Macmillan's Calls for **Action** for People Affected by Cancer

Whilst progress has been made in cancer care, there is still more to be done. Despite mortality rates falling, cancer has overtaken heart disease as the biggest killer disease in the UK – responsible for a quarter of all deaths. More people are also living longer with cancer. It is vital they and their families receive the right care and support when they need it.

Macmillan therefore calls on the new Parliament to help us persuade Government to:

1 Ensure cancer remains a top disease priority

■ Support this in practice by updating the NHS Cancer Plan; sustaining funding to build on progress for care and treatment; and improving the co-ordination of cancer services commissioning

2 Help families deal with the financial impact of cancer

■ Ensure every cancer patient is offered specialist benefits advice at the point of diagnosis

■ Change the law to make Disability Living Allowance and Attendance Allowance fairer for people with cancer

3 Develop Supportive and Palliative Care

■ Ensure joined-up provision of support and care from the point of diagnosis by health and social

care providers – with greater assistance to help people navigate the system

■ Commit adequate funding to implementing the National Institute of Clinical Excellence's Supportive and Palliative Care Guidance

4 Improve Treatment and Care

■ End the variations in treatment depending on where people live and the type of cancer they have

■ Provide adequate recruitment, training and retention of specialist medical staff and address the bottlenecks in diagnostic services and delays in radiotherapy treatment

■ Ensure greater collaboration between social and health care organisations and more assistance to help people to find their way through the system

5 Put patients' needs at the heart of planning and delivering cancer services

■ Treat cancer patients as individuals and offer them the opportunity to be involved in their own care and treatment

■ Involve cancer patients in the development and delivery of services at a strategic level through adequately funded Cancer Network User Partnership Groups

■ Ensure sustained funding for groups that teach people to manage their own care and treatment and self help and support groups

6 Ban smoking in all enclosed public places

■ Ban smoking in all enclosed public places and thereby encourage smokers to give up *and* protect others from the effects of secondhand smoke

If you have any questions about any aspects of Macmillan Cancer Relief's work, then please get in touch with:
Kevin Shinkwin Parliamentary Affairs Manager Tel: 020 7840 7868 Email: kshinkwin@macmillan.org.uk
Fiona Ferguson Parliamentary Affairs Officer Tel: 020 7840 4625 Email: fferguson@macmillan.org.uk

Macmillan CancerLine 0808 808 2020
www.macmillan.org.uk
Helping people living with cancer

Registered charity number: 261017

OSBORNE, SANDRA
Ayr, Carrick and Cumnock

Lab majority 9,997

Sandra Osborne. Born 23 February 1956; Daughter of Thomas Clark, labourer, and Isabella Clark, shop worker, meat factory worker, cleaner and laundry worker; Educated Camphill Senior Secondary, Paisley; Anniesland College; Jordanhill College; Strathclyde University (Diploma in community education 1990, Diploma in equality and discrimination 1991, MSc equality and discrimination 1992); Married Alastair Osborne 1982 (2 daughters); Member, TGWU; Former Branch Secretary, TGWU; Councillor, Kyle and Carrick District Council 1990-95; South Ayrshire Council: Councillor 1994-97, Convener, Community Services (Housing and Social Work) -1997

House of Commons: Member for Ayr 1997-2005, for Ayr, Carrick and Cumnock since 5 May 2005 general election; PPS to: Ministers of State for Scotland: Brian Wilson 1999-2001, George Foulkes 2001-02, Helen Liddell as Secretary of State for Scotland 2002-03. *Political interests:* Women, Housing, Poverty. All countries

Vice-chair, Scottish Regional Group of Labour MPs 1998-99, Chair 1999-. Member: European Standing Committee A until 2005, European Standing Committee B until 2003; *Recreations:* Reading and television

Sandra Osborne, MP, House of Commons, London SW1A 0AA *Tel:* 020 7219 6402 *E-mail:* osbornes@parliament.uk. *Constituency:* Constituency Office, Damside, Ayr KA8 8ER *Tel:* 01292 262906 *Fax:* 01292 885661,

OTTAWAY, RICHARD
Croydon South

Con majority 13,528

Richard Geoffrey James Ottaway. Born 24 May 1945; Son of late Professor Christopher Ottaway and of Grace Ottaway; Educated Backwell School, Somerset; Bristol University (LLB 1974); Married Nicola Kisch 1982. Officer in the Royal Navy 1961-70, Serving on: HMSs Beechampton, Nubian and Eagle 1967-70. Admitted solicitor 1977, specialising in international, maritime and commercial law; Partner, William A. Crump & Son 1981-87; Director, Coastal States Petroleum (UK) Ltd 1988-95

House of Commons: Member for Nottingham North 1983-87. Contested Nottingham North 1987 general election. Member for Croydon South since 9 April 1992 general election; Opposition Spokesperson for: Local Government and London 1997-99, Defence 1999-2000; Treasury 2000-01; Government Whip 1995-97; Opposition Whip June-November 1997; PPS: to Ministers of State, Foreign and Commonwealth Office 1985-87, to Michael Heseltine: as President of the Board of Trade and Secretary of State for Trade and Industry 1992-95, as Deputy Prime Minister and First Secretary of State 1995; Shadow Secretary of State for the Environment 2004. *Political interests:* Defence, Industry, Commerce, World Population. Malaysia, Singapore

Vice-chair Conservative Party (with responsibility for local government) 1998-99; Chair Executive Committee, Society of Conservative Lawyers 2000-03. London mayoral nominee 2002; *Publications:* Papers on international and maritime law, global pollution, London, privatisation, debt and international fraud; *Recreations:* Yacht racing, jazz

Richard Ottaway, MP, House of Commons, London SW1A 0AA
Tel: 020 7219 6392 *Fax:* 020 7219 2256 *E-mail:* ottawayrgj@parliament.uk.
Constituency: Croydon South Conservative Association, 36 Brighton Road, Purley, Surrey CR8 2LG *Tel:* 020 8660 0491 *Fax:* 020 8763 9686

OWEN, ALBERT
Ynys Môn

Albert Owen. Born 10 August 1959; Son of late William Owen and late Doreen, née Wood; Educated Holyhead County Comprehensive School, Anglesey; Coleg Harlech (Diploma industrial relations 1994); York University (BA politics 1997); Married Angela Margaret Magee 1983 (2 daughters). Merchant seafarer 1976-92; Welfare rights and employment adviser 1995-97; Centre manager Isle of Anglesey County Council 1997-; Contested Ynys Môn 1999 National Assembly for Wales election; RMT 1976-92: Health and safety officer 1985-87, Ferry sector national panel 1987-92; NUS 1992-97: Welfare officer 1992-94; UNISON 1997-2001; Town councillor 1997-99

Lab majority 1,242

House of Commons: Member for Ynys Môn since 7 June 2001 general election. *Political interests:* Welsh Affairs, Welfare, Economic Development. Ireland, Cyprus

Chair local branch 1987-92; Constituency Labour Party: Treasurer 1991-92, Vice-chair 1992-96; Press officer 1996-2000. Cancer Research; *Clubs:* Holyhead Sailing Club; *Recreations:* Cycling, walking, cooking, gardening

Albert Owen, MP, House of Commons, London SW1A 0AA *Tel:* 020 7219 8415 *Fax:* 020 7219 1951 *E-mail:* owena@parliament.uk. *Constituency:* 18/18a Thomas Street, Holyhead LL65 1RR *Tel:* 01407 765750 *Fax:* 01407 764336

PAICE, JIM
South East Cambridgeshire

Jim (James) Edward Thornton Paice. Born 24 April 1949; Son of late Edward Paice and of Winifred Paice; Educated Framlingham College; Writtle Agricultural College (National Diploma in Agriculture 1970); Married Ava Patterson 1973 (2 sons). Farm manager 1970-73; Farmer and contractor 1973-79; Training manager, later general manager, Framlingham Management and Training Services Ltd 1979-87, Non-executive director, 1987-89; Director, United Framlingham Farmers Ltd 1989-94; Suffolk Coastal District Council: Councillor 1976-87, Chair 1982-83

Con majority 8,624

House of Commons: Contested Caernarvon 1979 general election. Member for South East Cambridgeshire since 11 June 1987 general election; Opposition Spokesperson for: Agriculture, Fisheries and Food 1997-2001, Home Affairs 2001-03; PPS: to Baroness Trumpington, as Minister of State, Ministry of Agriculture, Fisheries and Food 1989-90, to John Selwyn Gummer: as Minister of Agriculture, Fisheries and Food 1990-93, as Secretary of State for the Environment 1993-94; Parliamentary Under-Secretary of State: Department of Employment 1994-95, Department for Education and Employment 1995-97; Shadow Minister for: Home, Constitutional and Legal Affairs 2003-04, Home Affairs 2004; Shadow Secretary of State for Agriculture, Fisheries and Food 2004-. *Political interests:* Small Businesses, Employment, Agriculture, Rural Affairs, Training, Waste Management. Europe, New Zealand

Game Conservancy Trust; UK delegate, EEC Council of Young Farmers 1974-78; Trustee Game Conservancy Trust; Fellow, Writtle University College; *Recreations:* Shooting, conservation

Jim Paice, MP, House of Commons, London SW1A 0AA *Tel:* 020 7219 4101 *Fax:* 020 7219 3804 *E-mail:* paicejet@parliament.uk. *Constituency:* Snailbridge House, The Moor, Fordham, Nr Ely, Cambridgeshire CB7 5LU *Tel:* 07638 721526 *Fax:* 07638 721526

DUP majority 17,965

PAISLEY, IAN
North Antrim

Ian Richard Kyle Paisley. Born 6 April 1926; Son of late Rev. J. Kyle Paisley; Educated Ballymena Model School; Ballymena Technical High School; South Wales Bible College; Reformed Presbyterian Theological College, Belfast; Married Eileen Emily Cassells 1956 (twin sons 3 daughters). Ordained 1946; Minister, Martyrs Memorial Free Presbyterian Church 1946-; Moderator, Free Presbyterian Church of Ulster 1951-; Founded *Protestant Telegraph* 1966; Member, Northern Ireland Assembly 1973-74; Co-chair, World Congress of Fundamentalists 1978; MEP for Northern Ireland 1979-2004; Elected to second Northern Ireland Assembly 1982; MP (Protestant Unionist) for Bannside, Co. Antrim, Parliament of Northern Ireland (Stormont) 1970-72; Leader of Opposition 1972; Member: Northern Ireland Forum 1996-98, Northern Ireland Assembly 1998-

House of Commons: Member for North Antrim since 18 June 1970 general election; Spokesman for Constitutional Affairs. *Political interests:* Foreign Affairs, Religious Affairs, Constitution

Leader (co-founder), Democratic Unionist Party 1971-. Member, Constitutional Convention 1975-76; Member: Rex Committee, Political Committee, European Parliament; *Publications:* Author of several publications; *Recreations:* History, Antiquarian book collecting

Rev Ian Paisley, MP, House of Commons, London SW1A 0AA *Tel:* 020 7219 3457. *Constituency:* 46 Hill Street, Ballymena BT43 6BH *Tel:* 028 2564 1421 *Fax:* 028 2564 1421

Lab majority 2,296

PALMER, NICK
Broxtowe

Nick (Nicholas) Palmer. Born 5 February 1950; Son of late Reginald and Irina Palmer; Educated International Schools, Vienna and Copenhagen; Copenhagen University (mathematics and computing 1967-72); Birkbeck College, London University (PhD mathematics 1975); Married Fiona Hunter 2000. Computing jobs with medical and pharmaceutical organisations; Head of internet services, Novartis, Switzerland 1995-97; Contested East Sussex and South Kent 1995 European Parliament election; Sponsor on fair trade issues for Department of Trade and Industry; Health and safety officer, MSF Brighton 1975-76

House of Commons: Contested Chelsea 1983 general election. Member for Broxtowe since 1 May 1997 general election; Team PPS, Department for Environment, Food and Rural Affairs 2003-. *Political interests:* Economy, Taxation, Fair Trade, Development, Animal Welfare. Scandinavia, Switzerland

National Executive Member, Labour Animal Welfare Society 1999-. Cats Protection League; Member, Danish 1975-77 and Swiss 1994-2004 Social Democrats; Worked on Draft Swiss Social Democrat Economic Programme; Member: European Standing Committee B 1998-05, European Standing Committee A 2005-; *Publications: The Comprehensive Guide to Board Wargaming*, 1977; *The Best of Board Wargaming*, 1980; *Beyond the Arcade*, 1984; *Parliamentary Portions*, 1998; *Recreations:* Postal and computer games

Dr Nick Palmer, MP, House of Commons, London SW1A 0AA *Tel:* 020 7219 2553 *Fax:* 020 7219 5205 *E-mail:* nickmp1@aol.com. *Constituency:* 23 Barratt Lane, Attenborough, Nottingham, Nottinghamshire NG9 6AD *Tel:* 0115-943 0721 *Fax:* 0115-943 1244 *Website:* www.broxtowelabour.org

PATERSON, OWEN
North Shropshire

Con majority 11,020

Owen William Paterson. Born 24 June 1956; Son of late Alfred Dobell Paterson and Cynthia Marian Paterson; Educated Radley College; Corpus Christi College, Cambridge (MA history 1978); Married Hon. Rose Ridley 1980 (2 sons 1 daughter). British Leather Co Ltd: Sales director 1985-93, Managing director 1993-99

House of Commons: Contested Wrexham 1992 general election. Member for North Shropshire since 1 May 1997 general election; Opposition Whip 2000-01: Agriculture, Culture, Media and Sport, Legal 2000-01, Agriculture, Culture and Sport, Legal Affairs 2001; PPS to Iain Duncan Smith as Leader of the Opposition 2001-03; Shadow Minister for Environment and Transport 2003-. *Political interests:* Trade, Industry, Agriculture, Foreign Affairs. Western and Eastern Europe, USA, China, India

Member: 92 Group 1997-, Conservative Friends of Israel 1997-, Conservative Way Forward 1997-, Conservative 2000 1997-; Vice-President, Conservatives Against a Federal Europe 1998-2001, Member, No Turning Back Group 1998-. Orthopaedic Institute Ltd, Gobowen, Ellesmere Community Care Centre Trust; Member: European Standing Committee A 1998-2001, Welsh Grand Committee 1998-2000; President, Cotance (European Tanners' Confederation) 1996-98; Member: World League For Freedom and Democracy 1997-, Inter-Parliamentary Union 1997-, Commonwealth Parliamentary Association 1997-; Member, Advisory Board, European Foundation 1998-; Liveryman, Leathersellers' Company; *Clubs:* Patron, Oswestry Cricket Club; Member, Shropshire Cricket Club

Owen Paterson, MP, House of Commons, London SW1A 0AA *Tel:* 020 7219 5185 *Fax:* 020 7219 3955 *E-mail:* patersono@parliament.uk. *Constituency:* Sambrook Hall, Noble Street, Wem, Shropshire SY4 5DT *Tel:* 01939 235222 *Fax:* 01939 232220

PEARSON, IAN
Dudley South

Lab majority 4,244

Ian Pearson. Born 5 April 1959; Son of late Phares and of Pauline Pearson; Educated Brierley Hill Grammar/Crestwood Comprehensive School; Balliol College, Oxford (BA philosophy, politics and economics 1980); Warwick University (MA industrial relations 1983, PhD industrial and business studies 1987); Married Annette Sandy 1988 (2 daughters 1 son). Deputy Director, Urban Trust 1987-88; Business and economic development consultant 1988-89; Joint chief executive, West Midlands Enterprise Board 1989-94; Member, TGWU; Councillor, Dudley Borough Council 1984-87

House of Commons: Member for Dudley West 15 December 1994 by-election-1997, and for Dudley South since 1 May 1997 general election; Assistant Government Whip 2001-02, Government Whip 2002; PPS to Geoffrey Robinson as Paymaster General, HM Treasury 1997-98; Parliamentary Under-Secretary of State, Northern Ireland Office 2002-05; Minister of State (Minister for Trade), Foreign and Commonwealth Office and Department of Trade and Industry 2005-. *Political interests:* Economic and Industrial Policy, Regional Development, Regeneration, Further and Higher Education. Central and Eastern Europe, India, USA, Canada

Local Government Policy Research Officer for the Labour Party 1985-87. Patron, Black Country Headway and Wordsley Kidney Patients Association; CAFOD; Chairman, Redhouse Cone Trust; *Publications: Universities and Innovation: Meeting the Challenge* 2000; *Clubs:* Stourbridge RFC, West Bromwich Albion FC; *Recreations:* Rugby, literature, architecture

Ian Pearson, MP, House of Commons, London SW1A 0AA *Tel:* 020 7219 6462 *Fax:* 020 7219 0390 *E-mail:* pearsoni@parliament.uk. *Constituency:* Suite 1, Grazebrook House, Peartree Lane, Dudley, West Midlands DY1 1HP *Tel:* 01384 455022 *Fax:* 01384 455045

Con majority 75

PELLING, ANDREW
Croydon Central

Andrew John Pelling. Born 20 August 1959; Educated Trinity School, Croydon; New College, Oxford (MA philosophy, politics and economics 1978). Head of debt syndicate Nomura International Plc 1986-94; Head of syndicate NatWest Markets 1994-97; Head of origination UFJ International plc 1997-; Croydon Council: Chairman, Education Committee 1988-94, Deputy leader, Conservative Group 1996-2002, Leader, Conservative Group 2002-

House of Commons: Member for Croydon Central since 5 May 2005 general election; GLA: London assembly member for Croydon and Sutton 2000-; Chair: Audit panel 2000-04, Budget committee 2004-. *Political interests:* Local and reformed government Deputy chairman, Croydon Central Conservatives 2001-02. *Clubs:* Reform, City University

Andrew Pelling, MP, House of Commons, London SW1A 0AA *Tel:* 020 7219 8472. *Constituency:* 36 Brighton Road, Purley, Surrey *Tel:* 020 8660 0491 *Website:* www.croydonconservatives.com

Con majority 499

PENNING, MIKE
Hemel Hempstead

Mike Penning. Born 28 September 1957; Educated Appleton School, Benfleet, Essex; King Edmund School, Rochford, Essex; Married to Angela. Soldier, Grenadier Guards 1974-81. Fire officer, Essex Fire and Rescue Services 1982-88; Freelance political journalist, Express Newspapers and News International 1988; Politics and journalism lecturer, UK and USA 1992; Media adviser and journalist, six Shadow Cabinet members; Former deputy chief press spokesperson, Conservative Central Office

House of Commons: Contested Thurrock 2001 general election. Member for Hemel Hempstead since 5 May 2005 general election. *Political interests:* Constitution, single currency (against)

Director, Conservatives Against a Federal Europe 1995; General election campaign manager, Rochford and Southend East 1997; Adviser, Conservative Back Bench Social Security Committee 1997; Member, Conservative Transport Policy Committee 1998-99; Member, Conservative Social Security Policy Committee 1998; Member, Conservative Family Campaign. *Recreations:* Rugby Union, Football

Mike Penning, MP, House of Commons, London SW1A 0AA *Tel:* 020 7219 8398. *Constituency:* Davidson House, 168 Queensway, Hemel Hempstead, Hertfordshire HP2 5NX *Tel:* 01442 255034 *Fax:* 01442 230918 *E-mail:* mike@penning4hemel.com *Website:* www.penning4hemel.com

Con majority 2,079

PENROSE, JOHN
Weston-Super-Mare

John David Penrose. Born 22 June 1964; Educated Ipswich School, Suffolk; Downing College, Cambridge (BA law 1986); Columbia University, USA (MBA 1991); Married Dido Mary Harding 1995. Risk manager, JP Morgan 1986-90; Management consultant, McKinsey and Company 1992-94; Commercial director, academic books, Thomson Publishing 1995-96; Managing director, schools publishing, Europe, Pearson PLC 1996-2000; Chairman, Logotron Ltd 2001-

House of Commons: Contested Ealing Southall 1997 and Weston-Super-Mare 2001 general elections. Member for Weston-Super-Mare since 5 May 2005 general election Treasurer, Leyton and Wanstead Conservative Association 1993-95. *Publications:* Members' Rights, The Bow Group 1997; *Clubs:* Weston-Super-Mare Conservative; Weston-Super-Mare Constitutional; Blagdon and District Beekeeping

John Penrose, MP, House of Commons, London SW1A 0AA *Tel:* 020 7219 8265. *Constituency:* 24-26 Alexandra Parade, Weston super Mare, Somerset BS23 1QX *Tel:* 01934 622894 *Fax:* 01934 632955
E-mail: john.penrose@weston-conservatives.co.uk
Website: www.weston-conservatives.co.uk

Lab majority 7,620

PICKING, ANNE
East Lothian

Anne Picking. Born 30 March 1958; Daughter of Frank and late Wilma Moffat; Educated Woodmill High Comprehensive School; Married David Adair Harold Picking 1984 (1 son). Fife Health Board: Nursing assistant 1975-77, Pupil nurse 1977-78, Enrolled nurse 1978-80; Northern Ireland Eastern Health and Social Service: Student nurse 1980-81, Staff nurse 1982-83; East Kent Community Health Care Trust 1984-: Staff nurse, Nursing sister; COHSE 1975-: Member NEC 1990-; UNISON 1975-: Member NEC 1999-2000, National President 1999-2000; Ashford Borough Council 1994-98: Chair Health Committee, Vice-chair Finance Committee, Group chair

House of Commons: Member for East Lothian 2001-05, for new East Lothian since 5 May 2005 general election. *Political interests:* Health, Social Justice, Economy, Small Businesses

Member NEC Labour Party. Member: European Standing Committee B 2003-, European Scrutiny Committee; *Clubs:* Prestonpans Labour, William Harvey Hospital Social; *Recreations:* Sailing, reading

Anne Picking, MP, House of Commons, London SW1A 0AA *Tel:* 020 7219 8220 *Fax:* 020 7219 1760 *E-mail:* pickinga@parliament.uk.
Constituency: Tel: 020 7219 8220 *Fax:* 020 7219 1760

PICKLES, ERIC
Brentwood and Ongar

Eric Pickles. Born 20 April 1952; Son of late Jack and Constance Pickles; Educated Greenhead Grammar School; Leeds Polytechnic; Married Irene 1976; Bradford Metropolitan District Council: Councillor 1979-91, Chairman: Social Services Committee 1982-84, Education Committee 1984-86, Leader of Conservative Group 1987-91; Member, Yorkshire Regional Health Authority 1982-90

Con majority 11,612

House of Commons: Member for Brentwood and Ongar since 9 April 1992 general election; Opposition Spokesperson for Social Security 1998-2001; Shadow: Minister for Transport 2001-02, Secretary of State for: Local Government and the Regions 2002-03, Local Government 2003-. *Political interests:* Housing, Health, Social Services, Local and Regional Government. Eastern Europe, India, Poland, USA

Member, Conservative Party National Union Executive Committee 1975-97; National Chairman, Young Conservatives 1980-81; Member, Conservative Party National Local Government Advisory Committee 1985-; Local Government Editor, Newsline 1990-; Deputy Leader, Conservative Group on Association of Metropolitan Authorities 1989-91; Vice-Chairman, Conservative Party 1993-97. Member, One Nation Forum 1987-91; Chair Joint Committee Against Racism 1982-87; *Clubs:* Carlton; *Recreations:* Films, opera, serious walking, golf

Eric Pickles, MP, House of Commons, London SW1A 0AA *Tel:* 020 7219 4428. *Constituency:* 19 Crown Street, Brentwood, Essex *Tel:* 01277 210725 *Fax:* 01277 202221 *E-mail:* boca@tory.org *Website:* www.tory.org/home/bocaweb

PLASKITT, JAMES
Warwick and Leamington

James Andrew Plaskitt. Born 23 June 1954; Son of late Ronald Edmund Plaskitt, and Phyllis Irene Plaskitt; Educated Pilgrim School, Bedford; University College, Oxford (MA philosophy, politics and economics 1976, MPhil); Single. Politics lecturer: University College 1977-78, Brunel University 1981-84, Christ Church, Oxford 1984-87; Business analyst 1984-97; Member, MSF; Councillor, Oxfordshire County Council 1985-97, Leader 1990-96

Lab majority 266

House of Commons: Contested Witney 1992 general election. Member for Warwick and Leamington since 1 May 1997 general election; Parliamentary Under-Secretary of State, Department for Work and Pensions 2005-. *Political interests:* Constitution, European Union, Education, Local and Regional Government, Welfare Reform, Economic Policy. All EU, USA

Publications: Contributor, *Beyond 2002 @nr A Programme for Labour's Second Term*, 1999

James Plaskitt, MP, House of Commons, London SW1A 0AA *Tel:* 020 7219 6207 *Fax:* 020 7219 4993 *E-mail:* plaskittj@parliament.uk. *Constituency:* First Floor, 2A Leam Terrace, Leamington Spa, Warwickshire CV31 1BB *Tel:* 01926 831151 *Fax:* 01926 338838

Lab majority 5,587

POPE, GREG
Hyndburn

Gregory Pope. Born 29 August 1960; Son of late Samuel Pope, ambulance officer, and of Sheila Pope; Educated St Mary's College Roman Catholic Grammar School, Blackburn; Hull University (BA politics 1981); Married Catherine Fallon 1985 (2 sons 1 daughter). Vice-President, Hull University Students Union 1981-82; Co-ordinator, Blackburn Trade Union Centre for the unemployed 1983-85; Paperworker, Star newspaper, Blackburn 1985-87; Local government officer, Lancashire County Council 1987-92; Councillor: Hyndburn Borough Council 1984-88, Blackburn Borough Council 1989-91

House of Commons: Contested Ribble Valley 1987 general election. Member for Hyndburn since 9 April 1992 general election; Opposition Whip 1995-97; Assistant Government Whip 1997-99; Government Whip 1999-2001. *Political interests:* Education, Housing, Foreign Affairs

Clubs: Accrington Old Band (CIU); *Recreations:* Walking, chess, music, watching Blackburn Rovers FC

Greg Pope, MP, House of Commons, London SW1A 0AA *Tel:* 020 7219 5842 *Fax:* 020 7219 0685 *E-mail:* popegj@parliament.uk. *Constituency:* 149 Blackburn Road, Accrington, Lancashire BB5 0AA *Tel:* 01254 382283 *Fax:* 01254 398089

Lab majority 7,059

POUND, STEPHEN
Ealing North

Stephen Pelham Pound. Born 3 July 1948; Son of Pelham Pound, journalist, and Dominica Pound, teacher; Educated Hertford Grammar School; London School of Economics (BSc economics 1979, Diploma in industrial relations 1981) (Sabbatical President of Union 1981-82); Married Maggie Griffiths 1976 (1 son 1 daughter). Armed Forces Parliamentary Scheme (Navy). Seaman 1964-66; Bus conductor 1966-68; Hospital porter 1969-79; Student 1979-84; Housing officer 1984-97; Branch Secretary, 640 Middlesex Branch, COHSE 1975-79; Branch Officer, T&GWU (ACTS) 1990-96; Councillor, London Borough of Ealing 1982-98, Mayor 1995-96

House of Commons: Member for Ealing North since 1 May 1997 general election. *Political interests:* Housing, Transport. Ireland

Labour Friends of India. Trustee, Charity of Wm Hobbayne (Hanwell); *Clubs:* St Joseph's Catholic Social, Hanwell; Fulham FC Supporters Club; *Recreations:* Watching football, playing cricket, snooker, jazz, gardening, collecting comics

Stephen Pound, MP, House of Commons, London SW1A 0AA *Tel:* 020 7219 1140 *Fax:* 020 7219 5982 *E-mail:* stevepoundmp@parliament.uk.
Constituency: Website: www.stephenpound.org.uk

PRENTICE, BRIDGET
Lewisham East

Bridget Prentice. Born 28 December 1952; Daughter of late James Corr, joiner, and of Bridget Corr, clerical worker; Educated Our Lady and St Francis School, Glasgow; Glasgow University (MA English literature and modern history 1973); London University (PGCE 1974); South Bank University (LLB 1992); Married Gordon Prentice (now MP) 1975 (divorced 2000). Rector's assessor, Glasgow University 1972-73; London Oratory School: English and history teacher 1974-86, Head of careers 1984-86; Head of careers, John Archer School 1986-88; London Borough of Hammersmith and Fulham: Councillor 1986-92, Chair: Public Services Committee 1987-90, Labour Group 1986-89; JP 1985-

Lab majority 6,751

House of Commons: Contested Croydon Central 1987 general election. Member for Lewisham East since 9 April 1992 general election; Opposition Whip 1995-97; Assistant Government Whip 1997-98, 2003-05; PPS to: Brian Wilson as Minister of State, Department of Trade and Industry (Minister for Trade) 1998-99, Lord Irvine of Lairg as Lord Chancellor 1999-2001; Parliamentary Under-Secretary of State, Department for Constitutional Affairs 2005-. *Political interests:* Education, Training, Constitutional Reform, Human Rights, Home Affairs. South Africa, USA

Chair, Fulham Constituency Labour Party 1982-85; Leadership Campaign Team Co-ordinator 1995-96. *Recreations:* Reading, music, crosswords, gardening, my cat, badminton (qualified coach), football

Bridget Prentice, MP, House of Commons, London SW1A 0AA *Tel:* 020 7219 3503 *Fax:* 020 7219 5581 *E-mail:* info@bridgetprenticemp.org.uk. *Constituency:* 82 Lee High Road, London SE13 5PF *Tel:* 020 8852 3995 *Fax:* 020 8852 2386; 020 7219 1286

PRENTICE, GORDON
Pendle

Gordon Prentice. Born 28 January 1951; Son of late William Prentice, and of late Esther Prentice; Educated George Heriot's School, Edinburgh; Glasgow University (MA politics and economics 1972); Married Bridget Corr 1975 (now MP as Bridget Prentice) (divorced 2000). Labour Party Policy Directorate 1982-92; Member, TGWU; London Borough of Hammersmith and Fulham: Councillor 1982-90, Deputy Leader, Labour Group 1982-84, Leader 1984-88

Lab majority 2,180

House of Commons: Member for Pendle since 9 April 1992 general election; PPS to Gavin Strang as Minister of State (in Cabinet), Department of the Environment, Transport and the Regions (Minister for Transport) May-December 1997. *Political interests:* Countryside, Agriculture, Manufacturing, Low Pay, Poverty, Regional Policy, Small Businesses. Pakistan, China, Korea, Australia, New Zealand, Canada

Member: Labour Party National Policy Forum 1999-2001, Parliamentary Labour Party Parliamentary Committee 2001-03. Executive Committee Member: Inter-Parliamentary Union (IPU) British Group, Member, British Delegation to Council of Europe and WEU 2001-; *Recreations:* Cooking, hillwalking

Gordon Prentice, MP, House of Commons, London SW1A 0AA *Tel:* 020 7219 4011 *E-mail:* prenticeg@parliament.uk. *Constituency:* 33 Carr Road, Nelson, Lancashire BB9 7JS *Tel:* 01282 695471 *Fax:* 01282 614097

PRESCOTT, JOHN
Hull East

John Leslie Prescott. Born 31 May 1938; Son of late John Herbert Prescott, railway controller and late Phyllis Prescott; Educated Ellesmere Port Secondary Modern School; Ruskin College, Oxford (DipEcon/Pol 1965); Hull University (BSc Econ 1968); Married Pauline Tilston 1961 (2 sons). Steward in the Merchant Navy 1955-63; Union Official, National Union of Seamen 1968-70; TU Official, National Union of Seamen, RMT (resigned 2002)

Lab majority 11,747

House of Commons: Contested Southport 1966 general election. Member for Kingston-upon-Hull East 1970-83 and for Hull East since 9 June 1983 general election; Opposition Frontbench Spokesperson for: Transport 1979-81, Regional Affairs and Devolution 1981-83; Shadow Secretary of State for Transport 1983-84; Employment 1984-87, Energy 1987-89, Transport 1988-93, Employment 1993-94; PPS to Peter Shore as Secretary of State for Trade 1974-76; Member, Shadow Cabinet 1983-97; Deputy Prime Minister 1997-; Secretary of State for the Environment, Transport and the Regions 1997-2001; First Secretary of State 2001-

Deputy Leader, Labour Party 1994-; Member: National Executive Committee of the Labour Party, Parliamentary Labour Party Parliamentary Committee; Deputy Leader, Labour Party National Executive Committee 1997-. Member, Council of Europe 1972-75; Delegate, EEC Parliamentary 1975; Leader, Labour Party Delegation to European Parliament 1976-79; PC 1994; North of England Zoological Society Gold Medal 1999; Priyadarshni Award 2002; *Recreations:* Jazz, theatre, music, aqua diving

Rt Hon John Prescott, MP, House of Commons, London SW1A 0AA
Tel: 020 7219 3618 *E-mail:* john.prescott@odpm.gsi.gov.uk. *Constituency:* 430 Holderness Road, Hull, Humberside HU9 3DW *Tel:* 01482 702698

PRICE, ADAM
Carmarthen East and Dinefwr

Adam Price. Born 23 September 1968; Son of Rufus and Angela Price; Educated Amman Valley Comprehensive School; Saarland University; Cardiff University (BA European community studies 1991); Single. Research associate University of Wales, Cardiff Department of City and Regional Planning 1991-93; Menter an Busnes: Project manager 1993-95, Executive manager 1995-96, Executive director 1996-98; Executive director Newidiem economic development consultancy 1998-

PlC majority 6,718

House of Commons: Contested Gower 1992 general election. Member for Carmarthen East and Dinefwr since 7 June 2001 general election; Plaid Cymru Spokesperson for: Economy and Taxation 2001-, Miners' Compensation 2001-, Regeneration 2001-, Trade and Industry 2001, Education and Skills 2001-04. *Political interests:* Economy, Regional Development, International Development, Culture, Education

Publications: Quiet Revolution? Language, Culture and Economy in the Nineties (Menter a Busnes) 1994; *The Diversity Dividend* (European Bureau for Lesser used Languages) 1996; *Rebuilding our Communities: A New Agenda for the Valleys*, 1993; Co-author *The other Wales: The Case for Objective 1 Funding Post 1999* (Institute of Welsh Affairs) 1998; *The Welsh Renaissance: Innovation and Inward Investment in Wales* (Regional Ind Research) 1992; *The Collective Entrepreneur* (Institute for Welsh Affairs); Spectator Inquisitor of the Year 2002; *Clubs:* Ammanford Working Men's Social; *Recreations:* Contemporary culture, good friends, good food, travel

Adam Price, MP, House of Commons, London SW1A 0AA *Tel:* 020 7219 8486
Fax: 020 7219 3705 *E-mail:* pricea@parliament.uk. *Constituency:* Plaid Cymru Office, 37 Wind Street, Ammanford SA18 3DN *Tel:* 01269 597 677
Fax: 01269 591 344

Belief in Action

Throughout the UK, The Salvation Army is at the cutting edge of care in our churches and social service centres. Our mission takes us into the front line of the battle against the biggest social problems of the age.

Today our **services for homeless people** are offering individually tailored packages of care to people with a wide range of problems, including alcoholism and mental illness. Our **National Addiction Service** is combining scientific knowledge and professional care to help people break free from drugs.

Our Outreach and Resettlement Teams work in major cities to identify people sleeping rough. We build relationships with them as the first step towards offering longer-term programmes leading to resettlement in appropriate accommodation.

Our **residential and home care services** are giving older people the chance to retain their independence whilst receiving the care they need. Our **family and children's services** are working to help families stay together, while also supporting parents and children who are coping with family breakdown.

The Salvation Army is at the heart of almost every community. Through our network of 1000 centres across the UK, **we touch the lives of thousands of people,** often working in partnership with national and local government. At the same time we are innovators, constantly striving to raise our professional standards and the quality of our services so we can meet today's problems with tomorrow's solutions.

You can find out more about the work of The Salvation Army by visiting our website **www.salvationarmy.org.uk**

Or you can contact Jonathan Lomax, Public Affairs Officer, on **020 7367 4885** or email him at **jonathan.lomax@salvationarmy.org.uk**

Belief in Action

The Salvation Army is a registered charity.

PRIMAROLO, DAWN
Bristol South

Dawn Primarolo. Born 2 May 1954; Educated Thomas Bennett Comprehensive School, Crawley; Bristol Polytechnic (BA social science 1984); Bristol University; Married 1972 (divorced) (1 son); married Thomas Ian Ducat 1990. Secretary 1972-73; Secretary and advice worker, Law Centre, East London; Secretary, Avon County Council 1975-78; Voluntary work 1978-81; Mature student 1981-87; Member UNISON; Councillor, Avon County Council 1985-87

Lab majority 11,142

House of Commons: Member for Bristol South since 11 June 1987 general election; Opposition Frontbench Spokesperson on: Health 1992-94, Treasury and Economic Affairs 1994-97; HM Treasury: Financial Secretary 1997-99, Paymaster General 1999-. *Political interests:* Education, Housing, Social Security, Health, Economic Policy, Equal Opportunities

Patron: Terence Higgins Trust, Knowle West Against Drugs, Children's Hospice South West; PC 2002

Rt Hon Dawn Primarolo, MP, House of Commons, London SW1A 0AA *Tel:* 020 7219 5202 *E-mail:* primarolod@parliament.uk. *Constituency:* PO Box 1002, Bristol, Avon BS99 1WH *Tel:* 0117-909 0063 *Fax:* 0117-909 0064 *Website:* www.dawnprimarolo.labour.co.uk

PRISK, MARK
Hertford and Stortford

Mark Michael Prisk. Born 12 June 1962; Son of Michael Raymond, chartered surveyor, and Irene June Prisk, née Pearce; Educated Truro School, Cornwall; Reading University (BSc land management 1983); Married Lesley Jane Titcomb 1989. Graduate surveyor Knight Frank 1983-85; Derrick Wade & Waters 1985-91; Senior surveyor 1985-89, Director 1989-91; Principal: The Mark Prisk Connection 1991-97, mp^2, consultancy 1997-2001

Con majority 13,097

House of Commons: Contested Newham North West 1992 and Wansdyke 1997 general elections. Member for Hertford and Stortford since 7 June 2001 general election; Opposition Whip 2004-; Shadow: Financial Secretary 2002-03, Paymaster General 2003-04. *Political interests:* Defence, Planning, Development, Small Businesses. Italy, China

Member Young Conservatives 1978-83; Chair Reading University Conservatives 1981-82; National vice-chair Federation of Conservative Students 1982-83; Deputy chair Hertfordshire Area 1999-2000. Founder East Hertfordshire Business Forum; Chair Hertfordshire Countryside Partnership; Creator Charter for Hertfordshire's Countryside; Parliamentary Chairman, First Defence 2002-04; Vice-President First Defence 2004-; *Publications: Eternal Vigilance, The Defence of a Free Society, First Defence,* 2003; *Clubs:* Saracens RFC, Middlesex CCC; *Recreations:* Music, piano, rugby, cricket, walking, running

Mark Prisk, MP, House of Commons, London SW1A 0AA *Tel:* 020 7219 6358 *Fax:* 020 7219 3826 *E-mail:* hunterj@parliament.uk. *Constituency:* Hertford and Stortford Conservatives, Unit 4, Swains Mill, Crane Mead, Ware, Hertfordshire SG12 9PY *Tel:* 01920 462 182 *Fax:* 01920 485 805

Con majority 942

PRITCHARD, MARK
The Wrekin

Mark Pritchard. Born 22 November 1966; Educated Afan Comprehensive School, Cymmer; Aylestone School, Hereford; London Guildhall University (MA marketing management); post-graduate diploma (marketing); Married Sondra 1997. Former parliamentary researcher; Director, marketing communications company; Councillor: Harrow Council, Woking Borough Council

House of Commons: Contested Warley 2001 general election. Member for The Wrekin since 5 May 2005 general election. *Political interests:* Rural affairs, defence, health, education, youth policy issues

Recreations: Walking, skiing, dogs, travel writing

Mark Pritchard, MP, House of Commons, London SW1A 0AA *Tel:* 020 7219 8494. *Constituency:*.The Wrekin Conservative Association, Sambrooke Hall, Noble Street, Wem SY4 5DT *Tel:* 01939 235222 *Fax:* 01939 232220 *E-mail:* info@markpritchard.com *Website:* www.markpritchard.com

Lab majority 4,941

PROSSER, GWYN
Dover

Gwyn Mathews Prosser. Born 27 April 1943; Son of late Glyn Prosser and of Doreen Prosser; Educated Dunvant Secondary Modern; Swansea Technical School; Swansea College of Technology (National Diploma, Mechanical Engineering, First Class Certificate of Competency, Marine Engineering); Married Rhoda McLeod 1972 (1 son 2 daughters). Merchant Navy cadet engineer 1960-64; Seagoing engineer, BP 1964-67, Blue Funnel 1967-71; Chief engineer, BR Shipping 1971-74; Test and guarantee engineer, Kincaid of Greenock 1974-77; Port engineer, Aramco, Saudi Arabia 1977-78; Chief engineer: Anscar 1978-79, Sealink Ferries at Dover 1979-92; Social survey interviewer, Civil Service 1993-96; Former member, NUMAST NEC; Political officer, MSF, South East Kent; Councillor, Dover District Council 1987-97; Kent County Council: Councillor 1989-97, Co-Chair, Economic Development and President, European Affairs 1993-97

House of Commons: Member for Dover since 1 May 1997 general election. *Political interests:* Transport, Shipping, Economic Development, Environment, Asylum, Immigration. Hungary

Organising opposition, Channel Tunnel Bill; Member, Parliamentary Assembly of: Council of Europe 1997-2001, Western European Union 1997-2001; Trustee, Numerous Local Charities; *Recreations:* Hill walking, swimming, awaiting revival of Welsh rugby

Gwyn Prosser, MP, House of Commons, London SW1A 0AA *Tel:* 020 7219 3704 *E-mail:* prosserg@parliament.uk. *Constituency:* 26 Coombe Valley Road, Dover CT17 0EP *Tel:* 01304 214484 *Fax:* 01304 214486

PUGH, JOHN
Southport

Lib Dem majority
3,838

John David Pugh. Born 28 June 1948; Son of James and Patricia Pugh; Educated Prescott Grammar School; Maidstone Grammar School; Durham University (BA philosophy 1971); (MA, MEd, MPhil, PhD logic); Married Annette Sangar 1971 (1 son 3 daughters). Merchant Taylors Boys School, Crosby 1983-: Teacher, Head of philosophy; Member ATL; Sefton Metropolitan Borough Council 1987-: Councillor, Group leader 1992-, Leader 2000-, Member: Local Joint Consultative Committee, Cabinet, Council, Joint Consultative Committee for Teaching Staff, Management Board Committee, Sefton Borough Partnership, Southport South Area Committee; Substitute member Social Services Ratification Committee; Former member Merseyside Police Authority; Member: North West Arts Board, Merseyside Partnership; Drector local airport

House of Commons: Member for Southport since 7 June 2001 general election; Liberal Democrat Spokesperson on Education 2002-. *Political interests:* Local and Regional Government, Elderly, Education, Transport

Former chair Southport Liberal Democrat Association. *Publications: Christian Understanding of God*, 1990; *Recreations:* Philosophy society Liverpool University, weightlifting, reading, football, computers

Dr John Pugh, MP, House of Commons, London SW1A 0AA *Tel:* 020 7219 8318 *Fax:* 020 7219 1794 *E-mail:* pughj@parliament.uk. *Constituency:* 35 Shakespeare Street, Southport, Lancashire PR8 5AB *Tel:* 01704 533555 *Fax:* 01704 884160

PURCHASE, KEN
Wolverhampton North East

Lab/Co-op majority
8,156

Kenneth Purchase. Born 8 January 1939; Son of late Albert Purchase, diecaster, and late Rebecca Purchase, cleaner; Educated Springfield Secondary Modern School; Wolverhampton Polytechnic (BA social science 1981); Married Brenda Sanders 1960 (2 daughters). Apprentice toolmaker, foundry industry 1956-60; Experimental component development, aerospace industry 1960-68; Toolroom machinist, motor industry 1968-76; Property division, Telford Development Corporation 1977-80; Housing Department, Walsall Metropolitan Borough Council 1981-82; Business Development Adviser, Black Country CDA Ltd 1982-92; Member, TGWU (ACTSS); Councillor: Wolverhampton County Borough Council 1970-74; Wolverhampton Metropolitan Borough Council 1973-90; Member: Wolverhampton Health Authority 1978-82, 1985-87, 1988-90, Wolverhampton Community Health Council 1990-92

House of Commons: Contested Wolverhampton North East 1987 general election. Member for Wolverhampton North East since 9 April 1992 general election; PPS to Robin Cook: as Foreign Secretary 1997-2001, as Leader of the House of Commons and President of the Council 2001-03. *Political interests:* Trade and Industry, Health, Education, Foreign Affairs, Small Businesses. Bahrain, Egypt, Cyprus, Saudi Arabia, Malta

Sponsored by Co-operative Party. *Recreations:* Listening to jazz

Ken Purchase, MP, House of Commons, London SW1A 0AA *Tel:* 020 7219 3602 *Fax:* 020 7219 2110 *E-mail:* kenpurchasemp@parliament.uk. *Constituency:* 492a Stafford Road, Wolverhampton WV10 6AN *Tel:* 01902 397698 *Fax:* 01902 397538

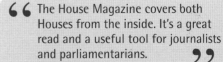

Lab majority 8,348

PURNELL, JAMES
Stalybridge and Hyde

James Purnell. Born 2 March 1970; Son of John Purnell, chartered accountant and Janet Purnell, teacher and civil servant; Educated Lycee International, St Gerrain en Laye, France; College Pierre et Marie Curie, Le Pecq, France; Royal Grammar School, Guildford; Balliol College, Oxford (BA philosophy, politics, economics 1991); Single. Researcher Tony Blair, Shadow Employment Secretary 1989-92; Strategy consultant Hydra Associates 1992-94; Research fellow media and communications project Institute for Public Policy Research 1994-95; Head corporate planning BBC 1995-97; Special adviser culture, media, sport and knowledge economy, Tony Blair, Prime Minister 1997-2001; Amicus – AEEU; London Borough of Islington: Councillor 1994-95, Chair Housing Committee, Chair Early Years Committee

House of Commons: Member for Stalybridge and Hyde since 7 June 2001 general election; Assistant Government Whip 2004-05; PPS to Ruth Kelly as: Financial Secretary, HM Treasury 2003-04, Minister for the Cabinet Office 2004; Parliamentary Under-Secretary of State, Department for Culture, Media and Sport 2005-. *Political interests:* Economy, Education, Housing, Culture, Poverty, Sport, Welfare, Employment, Pensions. Israel, India

Local Constituency Party: Former Ward secretary, Membership secretary, Treasurer, Delegate; Member: Co-operative Party, Fabian Society; Chair, Labour Friends of Israel 2002-. *Publications:* Various publications for IPPR; *Clubs:* Stalybridge Labour; Demon Eyes football team; *Recreations:* Football, cinema, theatre, golf

James Purnell, MP, House of Commons, London SW1A 0AA *Tel:* 020 7219 8166 *Fax:* 020 7219 1287 *E-mail:* purnellj@parliament.uk. *Constituency:* Hyde Town Hall, Market Street, Hyde, Cheshire SK14 1HL *Tel:* 0161-367 8077 *Fax:* 0161-367 0050

Lab majority 97

RAMMELL, BILL
Harlow

Bill Ernest Rammell. Born 10 October 1959; Son of William Ernest and Joan Elizabeth Rammell; Educated Burnt Mill Comprehensive, Harlow; University College of Wales, Cardiff (BA French and politics 1982); Married Beryl Jarhall 1983 (1 son 1 daughter). President, Cardiff University SU 1982-83; Management trainee, British Rail 1983-84; Regional officer, NUS 1984-87; Head of youth services, Basildon Council 1987-89; General manager, Kings College, London SU 1989-94; Senior university business manager, London University 1994-; Member, MSF; Councillor, Harlow Council 1985-97; Former Member, Local Government Information Unit

House of Commons: Member for Harlow since 1 May 1997 general election; Assistant Government Whip 2002; PPS to Tessa Jowell as Secretary of State for Culture, Media and Sport 2001-02; Parliamentary Under-Secretary of State, Foreign and Commonwealth Office 2002-05; Minister of State (Universities), Department for Education and Skills 2005-. *Political interests:* Education, Housing, Economic Policy, European Affairs, Media, Sport, Electoral Reform, Health. France, Sweden, USA, Germany, Hungary, Netherlands

Former Chair, CLP; Chair, Labour Movement for Europe 1999-. Member, European Standing Committee B 1998-; Vice-chair The European Movement 2001-; *Recreations:* Family, friends, sport, reading

Bill Rammell, MP, House of Commons, London SW1A 0AA *Fax:* 020 7219 2828 *E-mail:* rammellb@parliament.uk. *Constituency:* 1st Floor, Rooms 4-6, Market House, The High, Harlow, Essex CM20 1BL *Tel:* 01279 439706 *Fax:* 01279 425161

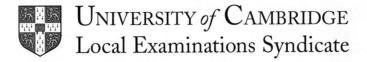

University *of* Cambridge
Local Examinations Syndicate

Should you wish to know anything about:

- University entrance tests
- Examinations, qualifications and assessment
- From primary to lifelong learning
- Vocational or general
- In the United Kingdom or around the world,

contact the largest assessment agency in Europe, a not-for-profit organisation recognised by governments around the world for its professional, rigorous and high standard assessments.

Feel free to phone, write or email at any time:

Bene't Steinberg, Group Director of Public Affairs,
1 Regent Street, Cambridge CB2 1GG.
01223 556003 (direct)
07803 727611 (mobile)
steinberg.b@ucles.org.uk

UCLES operates:

- OCR, one of the three main UK examination boards
- Cambridge International Examinations, which operates in 150 countries
- Cambridge English for Speakers of Other Languages

UCLES is adopting a new name from July 2005, which expresses more clearly what we do – Cambridge Assessment.

CAMBRIDGE ASSESSMENT

RANDALL, JOHN
Uxbridge

Alexander John Randall. Born 5 August 1955; Son of late Alec Albert Randall, company director, and of Joyce Margaret Randall (neé Gore); Educated Rutland House School, Hillingdon; Merchant Taylors School, Moor Park; School of Slavonic and East European Studies, London University (BA Serbo-Croat 1979); Married Katherine Frances Gray 1986 (2 sons 1 daughter). Randall's of Uxbridge: Sales assistant, Buyer, Director 1980-, Managing director 1988-97; Tour leader, Birdquest Holidays and Limosa Holidays as specialist ornithologist 1986-97

Con majority 6,171

House of Commons: Member for Uxbridge since 31 July 1997 by-election; Opposition Whip 2000-03: Social Security; Culture, Media and Sport 2000, Defence, Education and Employment 2000-2001, Home Office 2001, Foreign Affairs 2001-02, Transport 2002-03; Opposition Whip 2003-. *Political interests:* Environment, Trade and Industry, Foreign Affairs, Transport. Balkans, Russia

Hon. Treasurer, Uxbridge Conservative Association 1994, Chairman 1994-97. *Clubs:* Uxbridge Conservative; Member: Uxbridge Cricket Club, Uxbridge Rugby Football Club, Saracens Rugby Football Club, Middlesex County Cricket Club; *Recreations:* Local history, ornithology, theatre, opera, travel, music (plays piano), Uxbridge FC supporter, Cricket, Rugby

John Randall, MP, House of Commons, London SW1A 0AA *Tel:* 020 7219 3400 *Fax:* 020 7219 2590 *E-mail:* randallj@parliament.uk. *Constituency:* 36 Harefield Road, Uxbridge UB8 1PH *Tel:* 01895 239465 *Fax:* 01895 253105

RAYNSFORD, NICK
Greenwich and Woolwich

Nick (Wyvill Richard Nicolls) Raynsford. Born 28 January 1945; Son of late Wyvill and Patricia Raynsford; Educated Repton School; Sidney Sussex College, Cambridge (BA history 1966, MA); Chelsea School of Art (diploma in art and design 1972); Married Anne Jelley 1968 (3 daughters). Director, SHAC, the London Housing Aid Centre 1976-86; Member GMB; London Borough of Hammersmith and Fulham: Councillor 1971-75

Lab majority 10,146

House of Commons: Member for Fulham 1986 by-election -1987, for Greenwich 1992-97, and for Greenwich and Woolwich since 1 May 1997 general election; Opposition Spokesperson for: Transport and London 1993-94, Housing, Construction and London 1994-97; Former PPS to Roy Hattersley; Department of the Environment, Transport and the Regions 1997-2001: Parliamentary Under-Secretary of State 1997-99, Minister of State (Minister for Housing and Planning) 1999-2001; Minister of State (Minister for Local Government and the Regions), Department for Transport, Local Government and the Regions 2001-02; Office of the Deputy Prime Minister 2002-: Minister of State for: Local Government and the Regions 2002-03, Local and Regional Government 2003-05. *Political interests:* Housing, Social Policy, Transport, Environment. Europe

Publications: A Guide to Housing Benefit, 1982; Contributor to journals including *Building, Housing* and *New Statesman*; PC 2001; *Recreations:* Photography, walking, golf

Rt Hon Nick Raynsford, MP, House of Commons, London SW1A 0AA
Tel: 020 7219 2773 *Fax:* 020 7219 2619 *E-mail:* raynsfordn@parliament.uk.
Constituency: 32 Woolwich Road, London SE10 0JU *Tel:* 020 7219 5895
Fax: 020 7219 2619

Con majority 7,240

REDWOOD, JOHN
Wokingham

John Alan Redwood. Born 15 June 1951; Son of William and Amy Redwood (neé Champion); Educated Kent College, Canterbury; Magdalen College, Oxford (MA modern history 1971); St Antony's College, Oxford (DPhil modern history 1975); Married Gail Felicity Chippington 1974 (1 son 1 daughter) (divorced 2004). Fellow, All Souls College, Oxford 1972-87, 2003-; Tutor and lecturer 1972-73; Investment analyst, Robert Fleming & Co. 1974-77; N. M. Rothschild: Bank clerk 1977-78, Manager 1978-79, Assistant director 1979-80, Director, investment division 1980-83, Overseas corporate finance director and head of international (non-UK) privatisation 1986-87; Norcros plc: Non-executive director 1985-87, Chair 1987-89; Chair, Mabey Securities 1999-; Visiting professor Middlesex University Business School 2000-; Non-executive director, BNB plc 2001-; Chair, Concentric PLC 2003-; Councillor, Oxfordshire County Council 1973-77

House of Commons: Contested Southwark Peckham 1981 by-election. Member for Wokingham since 11 June 1987 general election; Department of Trade and Industry: Parliamentary Under-Secretary of State for Corporate Affairs 1989-90, Minister of State 1990-92; Minister of State, Department of the Environment (Minister for Local Government) 1992-93; Secretary of State for Wales 1993-95; Contested Leadership of Conservative Party 1995 and 1997; Member, Shadow Cabinet 1997-2000; Shadow Secretary of State for: Trade and Industry 1997-99, Environment, Transport and the Regions 1999-2000, Deregulation 2004-. *Political interests:* Popular Capitalism, European Affairs, Constitution, Euro, Transport, Economy, European Union. USA Chair, No Turning Back Group. Wokingham Hospital Macmillan Cancer Care Unit, Guide Dogs for the Blind; Adviser, Treasury and Civil Service Select Committee 1981; Head, Prime Minister's policy unit 1983-85; *Publications: Reason, Ridicule and Religion,* (Thames & Hudson) 1976; *Public Enterprise in Crisis,* (Blackwell) 1980; *Going for Broke,* (Blackwell) 1984; *Popular Capitalism,* (Routledge) 1987; *The Global Marketplace,* (HarperCollins) 1993; *Our Currency, Our Country,* (Penguin) 1997; Several books and articles, especially on wider ownership and popular capitalism; *The Death of Britain,* (Macmillan) 1999; *Stars and Strife,* (Macmillan) 2001; *Just Say No,* (Politicos) 2001; *Third Way Which Way?* (Middlesex) 2002; PC 1993; *Clubs:* Lords and Commons Cricket; *Recreations:* Village cricket, water sports

Rt Hon John Redwood, MP, House of Commons, London SW1A 0AA
Tel: 020 7219 4073 *Fax:* 020 7219 0377 *E-mail:* redwoodj@parliament.uk.
Constituency: 30 Rose Street, Wokingham, Berkshire RG40 3SU
Tel: 0118-962 9501 *Fax:* 0118-962 9323

Lab/Co-op majority
1,996

REED, ANDREW
Loughborough

Andy (Andrew) John Reed. Born 17 September 1964; Son of James Donald Reed and Margaret Ann Reed; Educated Riverside Junior, Birstall, Leicestershire; Stonehill High School, Birstall, Leicestershire; Longslade Community College, Birstall, Leicestershire; Leicester Polytechnic (BA public administration 1997); Married Sarah Elizabeth Chester 1992. Parliamentary assistant to Keith Vaz MP 1987-88; Urban regeneration, Leicester City Council 1988-90; Leicestershire County Council: economic development unit 1990-94, European affairs adviser 1994-97; NALGO 1988-: UNISON 1990-, Steward, Convenor, Executive, Leicestershire County Council, Conference Delegate, Service Conditions Officer; Councillor: Birstall Parish Council 1987-92, Charnwood Borough Council 1995-97, Chair, Economic Development 1995-97; Vice-chair, Loughborough Town Partnership 1995-97; Board Member, Business Link Loughborough 1995-99

House of Commons: Contested Loughborough 1992 general election. Member for Loughborough since 1 May 1997 general election; PPS: at Department for Culture, Media and Sport 2000-01, to Margaret Beckett as Secretary of State for Environment, Food and Rural Affairs 2001-03. *Political interests:* Economic Regeneration, Unemployment, Lifelong Learning, Education, Vocational Training, Sport, International Development, Co-operatives. South Africa, Germany, Ethiopia

Loughborough Constituency Labour Party: Chair 1988-92, Regional executive 1993-94; Member, East Midlands PLP; East Midlands Regional Group of Labour MPs: Vice-chair 1999-2002, Chair 2002-. *Clubs:* Leicester Rugby Football Club, Birstall Rugby Football Club: player and president; *Recreations:* Rugby, tennis, volleyball, any sport

Andrew Reed, MP, House of Commons, London SW1A 0AA *Tel:* 020 7219 3529 *Fax:* 020 7219 2405 *E-mail:* andy@andyreedmp.org.uk. *Constituency:* Unity House, Fennel Street, Loughborough, Leicestershire LE11 1UG *Tel:* 01509 261226 *Fax:* 01509 230579

Lab majority 6,320

REED, JAMIE
Copeland

Jamie Reed. Born 14 March 1973; Educated Whitehaven School; Manchester Metropolitan University (BA English 1994); Leicester University (MA mass communication 2000). Developing anti-racism network for sufferers of racism; GMB

House of Commons: Member for Copeland since 5 May 2005 general election

Recreations: American literature, modern history, football, fell walking, Whitehaven RLFC

Jamie Reed, MP, House of Commons, London SW1A 0AA *Tel:* 020 7219 4706

REID, ALAN
Argyll and Bute

Alan Reid. Born 7 August 1954; Son of James Reid and Catherine, née Steele; Educated Prestwick Academy; Ayr Academy; Strathclyde University (BSc maths 1975); Jordanhill College (teacher training qualification 1976); Bell College (computer data processing 1979); Single. Strathclyde Regional Council: Maths teacher 1976-77, Computer programmer 1977-85; Computer project programmer Glasgow University 1985-; EIS 1976-77; NALGO 1977-85; AUT 1985-; Renfrew District Council 1988-96: Councillor, Group secretary

Lib Dem majority 5,636

House of Commons: Contested Paisley South 1990 by-election, 1992 general election, Dumbarton 1997 general election. Member for Argyll and Bute 2001-05, for new Argyll and Bute since 5 May 2005 general election; Liberal Democrat Spokesperson for Scotland 2004-; Liberal Democrat Whip 2002-. *Political interests:* Environment, Employment, Fuel Tax, Health, Fishing Industry, Local Issues, Elderly, Farming, Rural Development, International Affairs

Scottish Liberal Democrats 1981-: Various posts, Vice-convener 1994-98, Member executive committee; Election agent George Lyon Scottish Parliament election 1999. *Recreations:* Chess, football, walking, reading, television

Alan Reid, MP, House of Commons, London SW1A 0AA *Tel:* 020 7219 8127 *Fax:* 020 7219 1737 *E-mail:* reida@parliament.uk. *Constituency:* 44 Hillfoot Street, Dunoon PA23 7DT *Tel:* 01369 704840 *Fax:* 01369 701212 *Website:* www.argyllandbute-libdems.org.uk

REID, JOHN
Airdrie and Shotts

John Reid. Born 8 May 1947; Son of late Thomas Reid, postman, and of Mary Reid, factory worker; Educated St Patrick's Senior Secondary School, Coatbridge; Stirling University (MA history 1978, PhD economic history 1987); Married Cathie McGowan 1969 (died 1998) (2 sons); Married Carine Adler 2002. Fellow Armed Forces Parliamentary Scheme. Scottish research officer, Labour Party 1979-83; Adviser to Neil Kinnock as Leader of the Labour Party 1983-85; Scottish organiser, Trade Unionists for Labour 1985-87; Member, TGWU

Lab majority 14,084

House of Commons: Member for Motherwell North 1987-97, for Hamilton North and Bellshill 1997-2005, for Airdrie and Shotts since 5 May 2005 general election; Deputy Shadow Spokesperson for Children 1989-90; Opposition Spokesperson for Defence, Disarmament and Arms Control 1990-97; Shadow Deputy Secretary of State for Defence 1995-97; Minister of State, Ministry of Defence (Minister for the Armed Forces) 1997-98; Minister of State, Department of the Environment, Transport and the Regions (Minister for Transport) 1998-99; Secretary of State for Scotland 1999-2001; Secretary of State for Northern Ireland 2001-02; Minister without Portfolio and Party Chair 2002-03; Leader of the House of Commons and President of the Council 2003; Secretary of State for Health 2003-05, Defence 2005-. *Political interests:* Foreign Affairs, Defence, Economy

Former Member Labour Party National Executive Committee. Fellow, Armed Services Parliamentary Scheme 1990-; PC 1998; *Recreations:* Football, crosswords

Rt Hon Dr John Reid, MP, House of Commons, London SW1A 0AA *Tel:* 020 7219 5945 *Fax:* 020 7219 5410. *Constituency:* Parliamentary Office, Montrose House, 154 Montrose Crescent, Hamilton *Tel:* 01698 454672 *Fax:* 01698 424732 *E-mail:* mezynskic@parliament.uk

Con majority 12,418

RIFKIND, MALCOLM
Kensington and Chelsea

Malcolm Rifkind. Born 21 June 1946; Educated George Watson's College, Edinburgh; Edinburgh University (LLB law, MSc); Married Edith Amalia Steinberg 1970. Lecturer, University College of Rhodesia 1967-68; Called to the Scottish Bar 1970; QC (Scotland) 1985; Member Edinburgh Town Council 1970-74

House of Commons: Contested Edinburgh Central 1970 general election. Member for Edinburgh Pentlands 1974-97. Contested Edinburgh Pentlands 1997 and 2001 general elections. Member for Kensington and Chelsea since 5 May 2005 general election; Opposition front bench spokesperson for Scottish Affairs 1975-76; Minister for Home Affairs and the Environment, Scottish Office 1979-82; Foreign and Commonwealth Office: Parliamentary Under-Secretary of State 1982-83, Minister of State 1983-86; Secretary of State for: Scotland 1986-90, Transport 1990-92, Defence 1992-95, Foreign and Commonwealth Affairs 1995-97; Shadow Secretary of State for Work and Pensions 2005-

Hon president, Scottish Young Conservatives 1976-77; Hon secretary, Federation of Conservative Students 1977-79. Privy Counsellor 1986; KCMG; *Clubs:* New Club, Pratt's

Rt Hon Sir Malcolm Rifkind, MP, House of Commons, London SW1A 0AA
Tel: 020 7219 5683. *Constituency:* 1A Chelsea Manor Street, London SW3 5RP
Tel: 020 7352 0102 *Fax:* 020 7351 5885 *E-mail:* kcca@btclick.com
Website: www.kcca.org.uk

Lab/Co-op majority
3,417

RIORDAN, LINDA
Halifax

Linda Riordan. Born 31 May 1953; Educated Bradford University; Married. Private secretary to Alice Mahon MP; Amicus; Calderdale Metropolitan Borough Councillor; Chair of the Ovenden Initiative; Non-executive director Calderdale and Huddersfield NHS Trust; Board member Pennine Housing 2000

House of Commons: Member for Halifax since 5 May 2005 general election

Recreations: Reading and swimming

Linda Riordan, MP, House of Commons, London SW1A 0AA *Tel:* 020 7219 5399

ROBATHAN, ANDREW
Blaby

Andrew Robert George Robathan. Born 17 July 1951; Son of late Douglas and Sheena Robathan (née Gimson); Educated Merchant Taylors' School, Northwood; Oriel College, Oxford (BA modern history 1973, MA); RMA, Sandhurst; Army Staff College (psc 1984); Married Rachael Maunder 1991 (1 son 1 daughter). Regular Army Officer, Coldstream Guards and SAS 1974-89; Rejoined Army for Gulf War January-April 1991. BP 1991-92; Councillor, London Borough of Hammersmith and Fulham 1990-92

Con majority 7,873

House of Commons: Member for Blaby since 9 April 1992 general election; PPS to Iain Sproat, as Minister of State, Department of National Heritage 1995-97; Shadow Minister for: Trade and Industry 2002-03, International Development 2003, Defence 2004-. *Political interests:* International Development, Environment, Transport, Defence, Northern Ireland, Conservation. Caucasus, Africa

Trustee, Halo Trust; Freeman, Merchant Taylors Company; Freeman, City of London; *Clubs:* Special Forces Club, Pratts; *Recreations:* Mountain walking, skiing, wild life, shooting

Andrew Robathan, MP, House of Commons, London SW1A 0AA
Tel: 020 7219 3459 *Fax:* 020 7219 3096. *Constituency:* Blaby Conservative Association, 35 Lutterworth Road, Blaby, Leicestershire LE8 4DW
Tel: 0116-277 9992 *Fax:* 0116-278 6664

ROBERTSON, ANGUS
Moray

Angus Robertson. Born 28 September 1969; Educated Broughton High School, Edinburgh; Aberdeen University (MA politics and international relations 1991); Partner. News editor Austrian Broadcasting Corporation 1991-99; Reporter BBC Austria 1992-99; Contributor: National Public Radio USA, Radio Telefís Eireann, Ireland, Deutsche Welle, Germany; Consultant in media skills, presentation skills and political affairs with Communications Skills International (CSI) 1994-2001; NUJ

SNP majority 5,676

House of Commons: Contested Midlothian 1999 Scottish Parliament election. Member for Moray 2001-05, for new Moray since 5 May 2005 general election; SNP Spokesperson for Foreign Affairs and Defence. *Political interests:* European Affairs, External Affairs, Defence, International Development, Youth Affairs, Foreign Affairs. Austria, Germany, Norway, Ireland, USA

Member National Executive Young Scottish Nationalists 1986; National organiser Federation of Student Nationalists 1988; Member SNP International Bureau; Deputy SNP spokesperson for Constitutional and External Affairs 1998-99; European policy adviser SNP Group Scottish Parliament. *Recreations:* Sport, current affairs, history, travel, socialising, cinema

Angus Robertson, MP, House of Commons, London SW1A 0AA
Tel: 020 7219 8259 *Fax:* 020 7219 1781. *Constituency:* Moray Parliamentary Office, 9 Wards Road, Elgin IV30 1NL *Tel:* 01343 551 111 *Fax:* 01343 556 355
E-mail: info@moraymp.org

ROBERTSON, HUGH
Faversham and Mid Kent

Hugh Michael Robertson. Born 9 October 1962; Son of George Patrick Robertson, headmaster, and June Miller Robertson, née McBryde; Educated King's School, Canterbury; Reading University (BSc land management 1985); Royal Military Academy Sandhurst (commissioned 1986); Married Anna Copson 2002. Army officer The Life Guards 1985-95. Army Officer 1985-95; Schroder Investment Management 1995-2001: Assistant director 1999-2001

Con majority 8,720

House of Commons: Member for Faversham and Mid Kent since 7 June 2001 general election; Opposition Spokesperson for Sport 2004-05; Opposition Whip 2002-04; Special adviser security Shadow Northern Ireland Secretary 1998-2001; Shadow Minister for Sport 2005-. *Political interests:* Defence, Foreign Affairs, Agriculture, Fruit Farming. China, Singapore, Middle East, Balkans, Syria

Armourers and Brasiers Prize 1986; Sultan of Brunei's Personal Order of Merit 1992; *Clubs:* Cavalry and Guards; Playing Member MCC, Member Chelsea FC; *Recreations:* Cricket, hockey, skiing

Hugh Robertson, MP, House of Commons, London SW1A 0AA
Tel: 020 7219 8230 *Fax:* 020 7219 1765 *E-mail:* robertsonh@parliament.uk.
Constituency: 8 Faversham Road, Lenham, Kent ME17 2PN *Tel:* 01622 850 574
Fax: 01622 850 294

ROBERTSON, JOHN
Glasgow North West

John Robertson. Born 17 April 1952; Educated Shawlands Academy; Langside College (ONC electrical engineering 1983); Stow College (HNC electrical engineering 1985); Married Eleanor Wilkins Munro 1973 (3 daughters). GPO/ Post Office/ British Telecom/ BT 1969-2000: technical officer 1973-87, special faults investigation officer 1987-91, customer service manager 1991-95, field manager 1995-99, local customer manager 1999-2000; Member: NCU/POEU/CWU 1969-90, STE/Connect 1991-; CWU/NCU: political and education officer, Glasglow Branch 1986-90; Connect: chair West of Scotland 1997-2000

Lab majority 10,093

House of Commons: Member for Glasgow Anniesland 2000-05, for Glasgow North West since 5 May 2005 general election. *Political interests:* Small Businesses

Chair Anniesland constituency Labour party 1995-2000; Former election agent to Donald Dewar MP, MSP; Secretary, Glasgow Group of MPs. Member European Standing Committee B until 2003; Commonwealth Parliamentary Association; International Parliamentary Union; *Clubs:* Cambus Athletic Football Club, Garrowhill Cricket Club; *Recreations:* reading, music, football, cricket

John Robertson, MP, House of Commons, London SW1A 0AA *Tel:* 020 7219 6964.
Constituency: 131 Dalsetter Avenue, Drumchapel, Glasgow G15 8TE
Tel: 0141 944 7298; 0141 944 7121 *E-mail:* jrmpoffice@btinternet.com
Website: www.johnrobertsonmp.co.uk

ROBERTSON, LAURENCE
Tewkesbury

Laurence Anthony Robertson. Born 29 March 1958; Son of James Robertson, former colliery electrician, and Jean Robertson (neé Larkin); Educated St James' Church of England Secondary School; Farnworth Grammar School; Bolton Institute of Higher Education (Management Services Diploma); Married Susan Lees 1989 (2 stepdaughters). Warehouse assistant 1976-77; Work study engineer 1977-83; Industrial management consultant 1983-89; Factory owner 1987-88; Charity fundraising, public relations and special events consultant 1988-

Con majority 9,892

House of Commons: Contested Makerfield 1987, Ashfield 1992 general elections. Member for Tewkesbury since 1 May 1997 general election; Opposition Whip 2001-03; Shadow Minister for: Trade and Industry 2003, Economic Affairs 2003-. *Political interests:* Overseas Aid, Constitution, European Affairs, Education, Economic Policy, Law and Order, Countryside, Northern Ireland. UK, USA, Ethiopia, other African countries

Former Member, Conservative 2000 Foundation; Former Member, Conservative Way Forward; Vice-Chair, Association of Conservative Clubs (ACC) 1997-2000. Overseas Aid charities; *Publications: Europe: the Case Against Integration*, 1991; *The Right Way Ahead*, 1995; *Recreations:* Horses and horseracing, golf, other sports (completed 6 marathons), reading, writing, countryside

Laurence Robertson, MP, House of Commons, London SW1A 0AA
Tel: 020 7219 4196 *Fax:* 020 7219 2325 *E-mail:* robertsonl@parliament.uk.
Constituency: Tewkesbury Conservative Association, Lloyds Bank Chambers, Abbey Terrace, Winchcombe, Gloucestershire GL54 5LL *Tel:* 01242 602388
Fax: 01242 604364

ROBINSON, GEOFFREY
Coventry North West

Geoffrey Robinson. Born 25 May 1938; Son of late Robert Norman Robinson and late Dorothy Jane Robinson; Educated Emanuel School, London; Clare College, Cambridge; Yale University, USA; Married Marie Elena Giorgio 1967 (1 daughter 1 son). Labour Party research assistant 1965-68; Senior executive, Industrial Reorganisation Corporation 1968-70; Financial controller, British Leyland 1970-72; Managing director, Leyland Innocenti 1972-73; Chief executive, Jaguar Cars Coventry 1974-75; Chief executive (unpaid), Triumph Motorcycles (Meriden) Ltd 1978-80; Director, West Midlands Enterprise Board 1982-85; Chief executive, TransTec plc 1986-97; Member, T&G

Lab majority 9,315

House of Commons: Member for Coventry North West since 4 March 1976 by-election; Opposition Front Bench Spokesman on: Science 1982-83, Trade and Industry and Regional Affairs 1983-87; Paymaster General, HM Treasury 1997-98. *Political interests:* Industry, Economic Policy, New Technology. France, Germany, Italy, USA

Publications: The Unconventional Minister: My Life in New Labour; *Recreations:* Motorcars, gardens, architecture, football

Geoffrey Robinson, MP, House of Commons, London SW1A 0AA
Tel: 020 7219 4504 *Fax:* 020 7219 0984 *E-mail:* geoffrey@newstatesman.co.uk.
Constituency: Transport House, Short Street, Coventry, West Midlands CV1 2LS
Tel: 024 7625 7870 *Fax:* 024 7625 7813

ROBINSON, IRIS
Strangford

Iris Robinson. Born 6 September 1949; Daughter of Joseph Collins and Mary McCartney; Educated Knockbreda Intermediate School; Castlereagh Technical College; Married Peter Robinson (later MP) 1970 (2 sons 1 daughter); Castlereagh Borough Council 1989-: Mayor Castlereagh 1992, 1995, 2000

House of Commons: Member for Strangford since 7 June 2001 general election; New Northern Ireland Assembly 1998-. *Political interests:* Health

DUP majority 13,049   Spokesperson Health, Social Services and Public Safety; Whip. MS; Chair Staff and Office Accommodation; Director: Ballybeen Square Regeneration Board, Tullycarnet Community Enterprises Ltd; Member: Dundonald International Icebowl Board, Central Services Committee; *Recreations:* Interior design

Iris Robinson, MP, House of Commons, London SW1A 0AA   *Tel:* 020 7219 8323 *Fax:* 020 7219 1797   *E-mail:* iris.robinson@ukgateway.net.
Constituency: Constituency Office, 2(B) James Street, Newtownards BT23 4DY *Tel:* 028 9182 7701   *Fax:* 028 9182 7703

ROBINSON, PETER
Belfast East

Peter David Robinson. Born 29 December 1948; Son of late David McCrea Robinson and Sheila Robinson; Educated Annadale Grammar School; Castlereagh College of Further Education; Married Iris Collins (later MP as Iris Robinson) 1970 (2 sons 1 daughter). Estate agent; Member, Northern Ireland Assembly 1982-86; Deputy Leader, Democratic Unionist Party: resigned 1987, re-elected 1988; Member: Northern Ireland Forum 1996-98, new Northern Ireland Assembly 1998-; Minister for Regional Development, Northern Ireland Assembly 1999-; Castlereagh Borough Council: Councillor 1977-, Alderman 1977, Deputy Mayor 1978, Mayor 1986

DUP majority 5,877

House of Commons: Member for Belfast East since 3 May 1979 general election (resigned seat December 1985 in protest against Anglo-Irish Agreement; re-elected 23 January 1986 by-election); Spokesman for Constitutional Affairs. *Political interests:* Housing, Shipbuilding, Community Care, Aerospace, Aviation, International Terrorism

Foundation Member, Ulster Democratic Unionist Party, Party Executive Member 1973-; Secretary, Central Executive Committee 1974-79; General Secretary 1975. Member, NI Sports Council; Hanwood Trust (Community Economic Initiative); *Publications: The North Answers Back; Capital Punishment for Capital Crime; Savagery and Suffering; Self-inflicted; Ulster the Prey; Ulster – The facts; Carson Man of Action; A War to be Won; It's Londonderry; Ulster in Peril; Give me Liberty; Hands off the UDR; Their cry was 'No Surrender'; IRA-Sinn Fein; The Union under Fire; Recreations:* Golf, bowling, breeding Koi carp

Peter Robinson, MP, House of Commons, London SW1A 0AA   *Tel:* 020 7219 3506 *Fax:* 020 7219 5854   *E-mail:* info@dup.org.uk.   *Constituency:* Strandtown Hall, 96 Belmont Road, Belfast BT4 3DE   *Tel:* 028 9047 3111   *Fax:* 028 9047 1797

ROGERSON, DAN
North Cornwall

Dan Rogerson. Born 23 July 1975; Educated University of Wales, Aberystwyth (BSc politics 1996); Married Heidi Lee Purser 1999. Research assistant Bedford Borough Council 1996-98; Administrative officer De Montfort University 1998-2002; Campaigns officer (Devon and Cornwall) Liberal Democrats 2002-04; UNISON 1996-97; Bedford Borough Council: Councillor 1999-2002, Deputy Group Leader 2000-02

Lib Dem majority 3,076

House of Commons: Contested North East Bedfordshire 2001 general election. Member for North Cornwall since 5 May 2005 general election. *Political interests:* Fighting post office closures, local services, local taxation

Member Association of Liberal Democrat Councillors 1998-. *Clubs:* Camping and Caravanning club; Camelford Liberal; St Lawrence's Social; *Recreations:* Blues music, collecting books of Liberal historical interest, reading

Dan Rogerson, MP, House of Commons, London SW1A 0AA *Tel:* 020 7219 4707. *Constituency:* 4 Tower St, Launceston, Cornwall PL15 8BQ *Tel:* 01566 772734 *E-mail:* danrogerson@dsl.pipex.com *Website:* www.danrogerson.org

ROONEY, TERRY
Bradford North

Terence Rooney. Born 11 November 1950; Son of late Eric and Frances Rooney; Educated Buttershaw Comprehensive School; Bradford College; Married Susanne Chapman 1969 (1 son 2 daughters). Commercial insurance broker; Welfare rights worker; Member: GPMU, UNISON; Bradford City Council: Councillor 1983-91, Chair, Labour Group 1988-91, Deputy Leader 1990-91

Lab majority 3,511

House of Commons: Member for Bradford North since 8 November 1990 by-election; PPS to: Michael Meacher as Minister of State: Department of the Environment, Transport and the Regions (Minister for the Environment) 1997-2001, Department for Environment, Food and Rural Affairs 2001-02, Keith Hill as Minister of State, Office of the Deputy Prime Minister 2003-. *Political interests:* Public Sector Housing, Poverty, Industrial Relations. Pakistan, India, Bangladesh

Campaign co-ordinator, Bradford West Labour Party in 1983 general election campaign; Hon. secretary, Yorkshire Regional Group of Labour MPs 1991-2001. Biasan; Member: Low Pay Unit, Unemployment Unit; Trustee, Bierley Community Association; *Recreations:* Crosswords, football, tennis

Terry Rooney, MP, House of Commons, London SW1A 0AA *Tel:* 020 7219 6407 *Fax:* 020 7219 5275 *E-mail:* rooneyt@parliament.uk. *Constituency:* 76 Kirkgate, Bradford, West Yorkshire BD1 1SZ *Tel:* 01274 777821 *Fax:* 01274 777817

Con majority 11,589

ROSINDELL, ANDREW
Romford

Andrew Richard Rosindell. Born 17 March 1966; Son of Frederick William Rosindell, tailor and Eileen Rosina Clark, pianist; Educated Marshalls Park Comprehensive School, Romford. Central Press Features London 1984-86; Freelance journalist 1986-97; Parliamentary researcher Vivian Bendall MP 1986-97; Director and International Director European Foundation 1997-2001; London Borough of Havering 1990-2002: Councillor, Member Standing Advisory Council on Religious Education 1990-2000, Vice-chairman Housing Committee 1996-97; Chairman North Romford Community Area Forum 1998-2002

House of Commons: Contested Glasgow Provan 1992 and Thurrock 1997 general elections. Member for Romford since 7 June 2001 general election. *Political interests:* British Overseas Territories, Foreign Affairs, European Affairs, Constitutional Affairs, Law and Order, Defence, Local and Regional Government, Dog issues, Gibraltar. Overseas Territories, Nordic countries, Australia, New Zealand, USA, Canada, Eastern Europe and the Gulf States

Chair: Romford Young Conservatives 1983-84, Greater London Young Conservatives 1987-88, National Young Conservatives 1993-94, Chase Cross Ward Romford 1988-99, Romford Conservative Association 1998-2001; International secretary Young Conservatives United Kingdom 1991-98; National Union Executive Committee Conservative Party: Member 1986-88, 1992-94; President Havering Park Ward Conservatives 2000-; Chairman Conservative Friends of Gibraltar 2002-; Member: Conservative Christian Fellowship; Vice-chairman Conservative Party 2004-. Chairman European Young Conservatives 1993-97; Executive Secretary International Young Democrat Union 1994-98; International Democrat Union Executive member 1998-2002, Chairman International Young Democrat Union 1998-2002; *Publications:* Co-author *Defending Our Great Heritage*, 1993; *Clubs:* Romford Conservative and Constitutional; Royal Air Forces Association; Romford Royal British Legion

Andrew Rosindell, MP, House of Commons, London SW1A 0AA
Tel: 020 7219 8475 *Fax:* 020 7219 1960 *E-mail:* andrew@rosindell.com.
Constituency: 85 Western Road, Romford, Essex RM1 3LS *Tel:* 01708 766700
Fax: 01708 707163 *Website:* www.andrew.rosindell.com

Lib Dem majority 442

ROWEN, PAUL
Rochdale

Paul John Rowen. Born 11 May 1955; Educated Bishop Henshaw RC Memorial High School, Rochdale; Nottingham University (BSc chemistry and geology 1976); PGCE 1977; Single. Science teacher Kimberley Comprehensive, Nottingham 1977-80; Head of chemistry St Albans RC High School, Oldham 1980-86; Head of science Our Lady's RC High School, Oldham 1986-90; Deputy headteacher Yorkshire Martyrs Catholic College, Bradford 1990; NUT National Union of Teachers 1977-86; Secondary Heads Association 1997; Rochdale Metropolitan Borough Council: Chair housing 1985-86, Leader Liberal Democrat Group 1990, Leader 1992-96

House of Commons: Contested Rochdale 2001 general election. Member for Rochdale since 5 May 2005 general election. *Political interests:* Education, housing, youth services, international development

Member ALDC Standing Committee 1996-99. *Recreations:* Hill-walking, travel, reading

Paul Rowen, MP, House of Commons, London SW1A 0AA *Tel:* 020 7219 8296.
Constituency: 144 Drake St, Rochdale, Lancashire *Tel:* 01706 355176
Fax: 01706 660295 *E-mail:* info@rochdalelibdems.org.uk
Website: www.rochdalelibdems.org.uk

ROY, FRANK
Motherwell and Wishaw

Frank Roy. Born 29 August 1958; Son of late James Roy, settler manager, and Esther McMahon, home-help; Educated St Joseph's High School, Motherwell; Our Lady's High School, Motherwell; Motherwell College (HNC marketing 1994); Glasgow Caledonian University (BA consumer and management studies 1994); Married Ellen Foy 1977 (1 son 1 daughter). Ravenscraig Steelworker 1977-91; Personal assistant to Helen Liddell, MP 1994-97; Member, GMB; Shop steward, ISTC 1983-90

Lab majority 15,222

House of Commons: Member for Motherwell and Wishaw 1997-2005, for new Motherwell and Wishaw since 5 May 2005 general election; Assistant Government Whip 2005-; PPS: to Helen Liddell as Minister of State, Scottish Office (Minister for Education) 1998-99, to Secretaries of State for Scotland: Dr John Reid 1999-2001, Helen Liddell 2001. *Political interests:* Employment, Social Welfare. Europe, USA

Parliamentary election agent to Dr Jeremy Bray 1987-92; Vice-President, Federation of Economic Development Authorities (FEDA); *Recreations:* Football, reading, music

Frank Roy, MP, House of Commons, London SW1A 0AA *Tel:* 020 7219 6467 *E-mail:* royf@parliament.uk. *Constituency:* Constituency Office, 265 Main Street, Wishaw *Tel:* 01698 303040 *Fax:* 01698 303060

RUANE, CHRIS
Vale of Clwyd

Chris Ruane. Born 18 July 1958; Son of late Michael Ruane, labourer, and Esther Ruane; Educated Ysgol Mair RC, Rhyl Primary; Blessed Edward Jones Comprehensive, Rhyl; University College of Wales, Aberystwyth (BSc (Econ) history and politics 1979); Liverpool University (PGCE 1980); Married Gill Roberts 1994 (2 daughters). Primary school teacher 1982-97, Deputy head 1991-97; National Union of Teachers: School Rep 1982-97, President, West Clwyd 1991, Vale of Clwyd 1997; Councillor, Rhyl Town Council 1988-99

Lab majority 4,669

House of Commons: Contested Clwyd North West 1992 general election. Member for Vale of Clwyd since 1 May 1997 general election; PPS to Peter Hain as Secretary of State for Wales 2002-. *Political interests:* Anti-Poverty, Education, Environment, Safe Communities. Belize

Member Labour Group of Seaside MPs 1997-. *Recreations:* Cooking, walking, reading, humour

Chris Ruane, MP, House of Commons, London SW1A 0AA *Tel:* 020 7219 6378 *Fax:* 020 7219 6090 *E-mail:* ruanec@parliament.uk. *Constituency:* 25 Kinmel Street, Rhyl, Clwyd LL18 1AH *Tel:* 01745 354626 *Fax:* 01745 334827

Lab majority 11,811

RUDDOCK, JOAN
Lewisham Deptford

Joan Ruddock. Born 28 December 1943; Daughter of late Kenneth Anthony and Eileen Anthony; Educated Pontypool Grammar School for Girls; Imperial College, London University (BSc botany 1965); Married Keith Ruddock 1963 (separated 1990, died 1996). Director: research and publications, Shelter, National Campaign for Homeless 1968-73, Oxford Housing Aid Centre 1973-77; Special programmes officer (MSC) for unemployed young people, Berkshire County Council 1977-79; Manager, Citizens Advice Bureau, Reading 1979-86; Member, TGWU

House of Commons: Contested Newbury 1979 general election. Member for Lewisham Deptford since 11 June 1987 general election; Opposition Spokesperson for: Transport 1989-92, Home Affairs 1992-94, Environmental Protection 1994-97; Private Members' Bill on flytipping – Control of Pollution Act (amendment) 1989; Parliamentary Under-Secretary of State for Women 1997-98; Promoted: Ten Minute Rule Bill 1999, Prophylactic Mastectomy Registry Presentation Bill 1999, Organic Food and Farming Targets Bill 1999, Sex Discrimination (Amendment) No. 2, Ten Minute Rule Bill 2002, Waste Bill, Private Members' Bill – Municipal Waste, Recycling Bill 2003, (Household Waste Recycling Act -2003). *Political interests:* Environment, Women, Foreign Affairs. Afghanistan, South Africa

Member, British Delegation to Council of Europe and Western European Union 1988-89; Inter-Parliamentary Union 2001-; Hon. Fellow: Goldsmith's College, London University; Laban Centre, London; *Recreations:* Travel, music, gardening

Joan Ruddock, MP, House of Commons, London SW1A 0AA *Tel:* 020 7219 6206 *Fax:* 020 7219 6045 *E-mail:* alexanderh@parliament.uk.

Con majority 9,930

RUFFLEY, DAVID
Bury St Edmunds

David Ruffley. Born 18 April 1962; Son of Jack Laurie Ruffley solicitor and Yvonne Grace, neé Harris; Educated Bolton Boys' School; Queens' College, Cambridge (BA law 1985); Single. Clifford Chance Solicitors, London 1985-91; Special adviser to Ken Clarke, MP as: Secretary of State for Education and Science 1991-92, Home Secretary 1992-93, Chancellor of the Exchequer 1993-96; Strategic Economic Consultant to the Conservative Party 1996-97

House of Commons: Member for Bury St Edmunds since 1 May 1997 general election; Opposition Whip 2004-. *Political interests:* Treasury, Home Affairs, Education, Broadcasting. USA, China, France

Unpaid adviser: to 'Catch 'em Young' young offenders project 1992, to Grant Maintained Schools Foundation 1996-97; Patron, Bury St Edmunds Town Trust; *Clubs:* Farmers' (Bury St Edmunds); The Suffolk Golf and Country Club; Bury St Edmunds Golf Club; *Recreations:* Football, cinema, golf, thinking

David Ruffley, MP, House of Commons, London SW1A 0AA *Tel:* 020 7219 2880 *Fax:* 020 7219 3998 *E-mail:* davidruffleymp@parliament.uk. *Constituency:* 1B Woolpit Business Park, Woolpit, Bury St Edmunds, Suffolk IP30 9UP *Tel:* 01359 244199 *Fax:* 01359 245002

RUSSELL, CHRISTINE
City of Chester

Lab majority 915

Christine Margaret Russell. Born 25 March 1945; Daughter of late John Alfred William Carr, farmer, and Phyllis Carr; Educated Spalding High School; London School of Librarianship; Polytechnic of North West London (Professional Librarianship Qualification, ALA 1970); Married Dr James Russell 1971 (divorced 1991) (1 son 1 daughter). Librarian: London Borough of Camden 1967-70, Glasgow University 1970-71, Dunbartonshire County Council 1971-73; Personal assistant to: Lyndon Harrison, MEP 1989-91, Brian Simpson, MEP 1992-94; Co-ordinator of Advocacy Project, MIND 1994-97; Member, GMB; JP 1980-; Chester City Council: Councillor 1980-97, Chair, Development Committee 1990-97

House of Commons: Member for City of Chester since 1 May 1997 general election. *Political interests:* Transport, Environment, Education, Urban Regeneration, Arts, International Development. Mozambique, South Africa, Middle East, Romania, Central America

Chester Constituency Labour Party: Agent 1986-95, Chair/President 1989-92. *Recreations:* Cinema, football, walking, art and architecture

Christine Russell, MP, House of Commons, London SW1A 0AA
Tel: 020 7219 6398 *Fax:* 020 7219 0943 *E-mail:* russellcm@parliament.uk.
Constituency: York House, York Street, Chester, Cheshire CH1 3LR
Tel: 01244 400174 *Fax:* 01244 400487

RUSSELL, BOB
Colchester

Lib Dem majority 6,277

Bob Russell. Born 31 March 1946; Son of late Ewart Russell and late Muriel Russell (neé Sawdy); Educated Myland Primary and St Helena Secondary Boys, Colchester; North-East Essex Technical College (Proficiency Certificate, National Council for the Training of Journalists 1966); Married Audrey Blandon 1967 (twin sons 1 daughter, 1 daughter deceased). Trainee reporter, *Essex County Standard* and *Colchester Gazette* 1963-66; News editor, *Braintree and Witham Times* 1966-68; Editor, *Maldon and Burnham Standard* 1968-69; Sub-editor: London *Evening News* 1969-72, London *Evening Standard* 1972-73; Press officer, BT Eastern Region 1973-85; Publicity information officer, Essex University 1986-97; Branch secretary, North-Essex, National Union of Journalists 1967-68; Councillor, Colchester Borough Council 1971-2002: Mayor 1986-87, Council Leader 1987-91

House of Commons: Member for Colchester since 1 May 1997 general election; Liberal Democrat Spokesperson for: Home and Legal Affairs 1997-99, Sport 1999-; Liberal Democrat Whip 1999-2002, 2003-. *Political interests:* Environment, Local and Regional Government, Sport, Transport, Animal Welfare, Voluntary Sector, Youth Organisations. St Helena

Member: Labour Party 1966, SDP May 1981, Liberal Democrats since formation. Colchester Stars Cycle Speedway; Honorary Alderman of Colchester; Journalists Prize, NEETC 1965; *Clubs:* Colchester United Football Club; *Recreations:* Local history, walking, camping, watching Colchester Utd FC

Bob Russell, MP, House of Commons, London SW1A 0AA *Tel:* 020 7219 5150
Fax: 020 7219 2365 *E-mail:* brooksse@parliament.uk. *Constituency:* Magdalen Hall, Wimpole Road, Colchester, Essex C01 2DE *Tel:* 01206 506600 *Fax:* 01206 506610

THE ROYAL BRITISH LEGION IN 2005 CAMPAIGNING FOR EX-SERVICE PEOPLE

Background

The Legion is Britain's largest ex-Service organisation, covering England and Wales and all of Ireland. It has 2,895 Branches, including 87 overseas, as well as 1,324 Womens' Section Branches. Total membership is 535,217, but the Legion represents the whole of the ex-Service community which numbers some 11 million. It provides financial assistance, nursing and respite care homes, employment for the disabled, small business advice and loans, resettlement training, free pensions advice and much more, all financed from public donations. It also provides a social focus for the ex-Service community in its branches, many of which have an affiliated club. In addition it is the de facto national custodian of Remembrance.

A campaigning organisation

The Legion has traditionally campaigned on behalf of its constituency to ensure their wellbeing. There have been numerous successes, notably the campaign in 1999/2000 for a £10,000 ex-gratia payment to survivors of Japanese PoW camps and their widows which has resulted in payments by the Government of over £230 million and the campaign for a meaningful commemoration of the 60th Anniversary of D Day in 2004, which also attained its objective.

The Legion is campaigning today on a number of issues, notably:

Gulf War Illnesses

- To ensure that the Government addresses its outstanding obligations to Gulf War veterans who have fallen ill since 1990/91.
- To seek further support for the recommendations of the Lloyd Inquiry into Gulf War Illnesses.

War Pensions and Compensation

- Monitoring the new Armed Forces Compensation Scheme to ensure that it is set up and implemented in accordance with the promises given to Parliament, Service personnel and their families.
- Contesting the criteria under which applications for War Pensions for service-attributable noise-induced hearing loss are assessed.
- Calling upon a remaining small number of Local Authorities to completely disregard War and War Widows Pensions when assessing applicants for Housing Benefit and Council Tax Rebate. It remains a Legion aim that there should be a statutory, national, full disregard funded by Central Government.

Other Campaigns

- The Legion supports campaigns by other organisations on behalf of pensioners, many of whom are ex-Service, where they are being financially penalised.

The Legion is seeking cross-party support for the benefit of veterans.

The Royal British Legion. Always on active service

Registered Charity No: 219279

The Royal British Legion, 48 Pall Mall, London SW1Y 5JY Tel: 020 7973 7265 Email: jlillies@britishlegion.org.uk

RYAN, JOAN
Enfield North

Joan Ryan. Born 8 September 1955; Daughter of Michael Joseph Ryan and Dolores Marie, neé Joyce; Educated St Josephs Secondary School, Notre Dame High School; City of Liverpool College (BA history, sociology 1979); Polytechnic of the South Bank (MSc sociology 1981); Married 2nd Martin Hegarty (1 son 1 daughter); Member: AEEU, NUT; Councillor, Barnet Council 1990-98, Deputy Leader 1994-98, Chair, Policy and Resources Committee 1994

Lab majority 1,920

House of Commons: Member for Enfield North since 1 May 1997 general election; Assistant Government Whip 2002-03, Government Whip 2003-; PPS to Andrew Smith: as Minister of State, Department for Education and Employment (Minister for Employment, Welfare to Work and Equal Opportunities) 1998-99, as Chief Secretary to the Treasury 1999-2002. *Political interests:* Investment, NHS, Local and Regional Government, Employment, Regeneration, Health. Cyprus, Ireland, Israel

Chair: Finchley Constituency Labour Party 1992-96, London North European Constituency 1994-97. Nightingale Community Hospice Trust; Trustee, Riders For Health; Patron, Nightingale Community Hospice Trust; *Recreations:* Swimming, reading, music, visiting historic buildings

Joan Ryan, MP, House of Commons, London SW1A 0AA *Tel:* 020 7219 6502 *Fax:* 020 7219 2335 *E-mail:* ryanj@parliament.uk. *Constituency:* 180 High Street, Enfield EN3 4EU *Tel:* 020 8805 9470 *Fax:* 020 8804 0754

SALMOND, ALEX
Banff and Buchan

Alex Elliot Anderson Salmond. Born 31 December 1954; Son of Robert and the late Mary Salmond; Educated Linlithgow Academy; St Andrew's University (MA economics and history); Married Moira French McGlashan 1981. Assistant agriculture and fisheries economist, Department of Agriculture and Fisheries (Scotland) 1978-80; Assistant economist, Royal Bank of Scotland 1980-82; Oil economist 1982-87; Economist 1984-87

SNP majority 11,837

House of Commons: Member for Banff and Buchan 1987-2005, MSP for Banff and Buchan 1999-2001, member for new Banff and Buchan since 5 May 2005 general election; Parliamentary Spokesperson for: Constitution, Economy, Trade and Industry, Fishing 1992-97, Constitution; Fishing 1997-, Treasury 2001-. *Political interests:* Fishing Industry, Agriculture, Energy, Third World, Scottish Economy. Europe

SNP National Executive: Member 1981-, Vice-chair 1985-87, Deputy Leader 1987, Senior Vice-convener 1988-90, National convener 1990-2000, 2004-; Leader Westminster Parliamentary Group 2001-04. Hon. Vice-President, Scottish Centre for Economic and Social Research; Visiting Professor of Economics, Strathclyde University; *Recreations:* Golf, reading, football

Alex Salmond, MP, House of Commons, London SW1A 0AA *Tel:* 020 7219 3494 *E-mail:* mp@alexsalmond.net. *Constituency:* 17 Maiden Street, Peterhead AB42 1EE *Tel:* 01779 470444 *Fax:* 01779 474460

SALTER, MARTIN
Reading West

Martin John Salter. Born 19 April 1954; Son of Raymond and Naomi Salter; Educated Grammar school; Sussex University; Married Natalie O'Toole. Co-ordinator, Reading Centre for the Unemployed 1986-86; Regional manager, Co-operative Home Services housing association 1987-96; Member, TGWU; Former shop steward: TGWU, UCATT; Reading Borough Council: Councillor 1984-96, Chair Leisure Committee 1986-88, Deputy Leader 1987-96

Lab majority 4,682

House of Commons: Contested Reading East 1987 general election. Member for Reading West since 1 May 1997 general election; Parliamentary Adviser on shooting and fishing to Richard Caborn, as Minister of State for Sport 2002-. *Political interests:* Environment, Local and Regional Government, Housing, Northern Ireland, Human Rights. India, Pakistan, Ireland

Member, Co-operative Party; Organiser, Network of Labour Councils in South 1987-94; Joint Vice-Chair, South and West Group of Labour MPs 1997-98; Chair, South East Regional Group of Labour MPs 1998-; Representative, South East PLP Campaign Team 1999-. Secretary, Punjab Human Rights Sub Group; Vice-President, Supporters Trust, Reading Football Club; *Publications:* Various articles in national and local press, Fabian Review and Punch; *Clubs:* Reading and District Angling Association and other Fishing Clubs; *Recreations:* Angling, walking, football

Martin Salter, MP, House of Commons, London SW1A 0AA *Tel:* 020 7219 5079 *Fax:* 020 7219 2749 *E-mail:* salterm@parliament.uk. *Constituency:* 413 Oxford Road, Reading, Berkshire RG30 1HA *Tel:* 0118-954 6782 *Fax:* 0118-954 6784

SANDERS, ADRIAN
Torbay

Adrian Mark Sanders. Born 25 April 1959; Son of John Sanders, insurance official, and of late Helen, nurse; Educated Torquay Boys' Grammar School; Married Alison Nortcliffe 1992. Parliamentary officer, Liberal Democrat Whips' Office 1989-90; Association of Liberal Democrat Councillors 1990-92; Policy officer, National Council for Voluntary Organisations 1992-93; Worked for Paddy Ashdown, MP and Party Leader 1992-93, organised his tour of Britain 1993; Southern Association of Voluntary Action Groups for Europe 1993-97; Contested Devon and East Plymouth 1994 European Parliament election; Councillor, Torbay Borough Council 1984-86

Lib Dem majority 2,029

House of Commons: Contested Torbay 1992 general election. Member for Torbay since 1 May 1997 general election; Spokesperson for: Housing 1997-2001, Environment, Transport, the Regions and Social Justice 1999-2001, Transport, Local Government and the Regions (Local Government) 2001-02; Liberal Democrat Spokesperson for Tourism 2002-; Liberal Democrat Whip 1997-2001. *Political interests:* Local and Regional Government, Voluntary Sector, Tourism. USA

Vice-President, National League of Young Liberals 1985; Political secretary, Devon and Cornwall Regional Liberal Party 1983-84; Information officer, Association of Liberal Councillors 1986-89. Member: CPA, IPU, British American Parliamentary Group; *Clubs:* Paignton Club; *Recreations:* Football

Adrian Sanders, MP, House of Commons, London SW1A 0AA *Tel:* 020 7219 6304 *Fax:* 020 7219 3963 *E-mail:* asanders@cix.co.uk. *Constituency:* 69 Belgrave Road, Torquay, Devon TQ2 5HZ *Tel:* 01803 200036 *Fax:* 01803 200031

SARWAR, MOHAMMED
Glasgow Central

Mohammad Sarwar. Born 18 August 1952; Son of Mohammad Abdullah and Rushida Abdullah; Educated University of Faisalabad, Pakistan (BA political science); Married Perveen Sarwar 1976 (3 sons 1 daughter). Director, United Wholesale Ltd 1983-97; Member, GMB; Councillor: Glasgow District Council 1992-95, Glasgow City Council 1995-97

House of Commons: Member for Glasgow Govan 1997-2005, for Glasgow Central since 5 May 2005 general election. *Political interests:* Housing, Employment, Economic Policy, Devolution, International Affairs, International Development, British Shipbuilding, Pensioners' Rights, Senior Citizens. Pakistan, Middle East, Developing World

Member: Scottish Labour Executive 1994-97, Scottish Labour Gala Fund-raising Dinner Organising Committee; Constituency Labour Party: Former Branch Chair, Membership Secretary, Trades Union Liaison Officer; Scottish Regional Group of Labour MPs: Former Vice-chair, Chair 2002-. Scottish Conference, Racism Debate 1994; BBC Scotland, Frontline Scotland 1995; BBC Newsnight 1995; Several appearances Reporting Scotland 1995-96; *Recreations:* Family and friends, charitable work, abseiling

Mohammed Sarwar, MP, House of Commons, London SW1A 0AA
Tel: 020 7219 5024; 020 7219 0547 *Fax:* 020 7219 5898. *Constituency:* 247 Paisley Road West, Glasgow G51 1NE *Tel:* 0141-427 5250 *Fax:* 0141-427 5938

Lab majority 8,531

SCOTT, LEE
Ilford North

Lee Scott. Born 6 April 1956; Educated Clarkes College, Ilford, Essex; Married Estelle Dorenne Kins 1987. Director, Scott and Fishell 1972-1982; Sales executive: Toshiba 1982-84, ITT 1984-86, NKR 1986-88; Campaign director/provincial director, United Jewish Israel Appeal 1988-98; Director, Scott Associates 1998-; London Borough of Redbridge: Councillor 1998-, Cabinet member for regeneration and the community 2002

House of Commons: Contested Waveney 2001 general election. Member for Ilford North since 5 May 2005 general election. *Political interests:* Middle East affairs, trade and industry, community issues

Deputy chair (political), Ilford North CC 1998-99; Essex area chairman, Conservative Friends of Israel 2001-. Committee member, Victim Support Redbridge 1999-; *Recreations:* Music, reading, sport

Lee Scott, MP, House of Commons, London SW1A 0AA *Tel:* 020 7219 8326. *Constituency:* 9 Sevenways Parade, Gants Hill, Ilford, Essex IG2 6XH *Tel:* 020 8551 4333 *Fax:* 020 8551 7693 *E-mail:* leescott@tory.org

Con majority 1,653

SEABECK, ALISON
Plymouth Devonport

Alison Seabeck. Born 20 February 1954; Amicus – MSF: Member, Secretary of South Thames community branch
House of Commons: Member for Plymouth Devonport since 5 May 2005 general election
Recreations: Travelling, swimming
Alison Seabeck, MP, House of Commons, London SW1A 0AA *Tel:* 020 7219 6431. *Constituency: Tel:* 0117 9447133 *E-mail:* alisonseabeck@yahoo.co.uk

Lab majority 8,103

SELOUS, ANDREW
South West Bedfordshire

Andrew Edmund Armstrong Selous. Born 27 April 1962; Son of Commander Gerald Selous, and Miranda Selous, née Casey; Educated London School of Economics (BSc Econ industry and trade 1984); Married Harriet Victoria Marston 1993 (3 daughters). TA officer Honourable Artillery Company, Royal Regiment of Fusiliers 1981-94. Director CNS Electronics Ltd 1988-94; Underwriter Great Lakes Re (UK) plc 1991-

House of Commons: Contested Sunderland North 1997 general election. Member for South West Bedfordshire since 7 June 2001 general election; Opposition Whip 2004; PPS to Michael Ancram as Shadow Foreign Secretary 2004. *Political interests:* Trade and Industry, Social Affairs, Families, Defence, Homelessness

Con majority 8,277

Bow Group 1982-; Chairman, Conservative Christian Fellowship 2001-. Community Family Trusts; *Publications: Lessons from the Frontline*, private pamphlet for CCF 1997; *Clubs:* Leighton Buzzard Conservative, Dunstable Conservative; *Recreations:* Family, walking, tennis, bridge

Andrew Selous, MP, House of Commons, London SW1A 0AA *Tel:* 020 7219 8134 *Fax:* 020 7219 1741 *E-mail:* selousa@parliament.uk. *Constituency:* 6c Princes Street, Dunstable, Bedfordshire LU6 1LF *Tel:* 01582 662 821 *Fax:* 01582 476 619

SHAPPS, GRANT
Welwyn Hatfield

Grant V Shapps. Born 14 September 1968; Educated Watford Boys Grammar School; Manchester Polytechnic (HND business and finance 1989); Married Belinda-Jo Goldstone 1998. Sales executive Nashua Gestetner 1989-90; Director Printhouse Corporation 1990-2000; Chair Printhouse plc 2000

House of Commons: Contested North Southwark and Bermondsey 1997 and Welwyn Hatfield 2001 general elections. Member for Welwyn Hatfield since 5 May 2005 general election

Con majority 5,946

Branch chair Barnhill, Brent North 1995-99; Member: Conservative Friends of Israel 1995, Selsdon Group 1996, Conservative Foreign Affairs Forum 1996; Vice-president North Southwark and Bermondsey Association 1997. *Publications: What's Right for 21st Century* (Printhouse Publishing), 2001

Grant Shapps, MP, House of Commons, London SW1A 0AA *Tel:* 020 7219 8497. *Constituency:* Welwyn Hatfield Conservative Association, Maynard House, The Common, Hatfield, Hertfordshire AL10 0NF *Tel:* 01707 262632 *Fax:* 08717 333 825; 01707 263892 *E-mail:* grant@shapps.com *Website:* www.shapps.com

SHAW, JONATHAN
Chatham and Aylesford

Jonathan Rowland Shaw. Born 3 June 1966; Son of Alan James Shaw and Les Percival; Educated Vinters Boys School, Maidstone; West Kent College of Further Education (Diploma in Social Care); Bromley College (Certificate in Social Services 1990); Married Sue Gurmin 1990 (1 son 1 daughter). Social worker, Kent Council; Member, UNISON; Councillor, Rochester 1993-98, Chair, Community Development Committee 1995

Lab majority 2,332

House of Commons: Member for Chatham and Aylesford since 1 May 1997 general election. *Political interests:* Community Development, Economic Development, Housing, Welfare

Member, Fabian Society. *Recreations:* All music especially folk music, reading, walking, family

Jonathan Shaw, MP, House of Commons, London SW1A 0AA *Tel:* 020 7219 6919 *Fax:* 020 7219 0938 *E-mail:* shawj@parliament.uk. *Constituency:* 411 High Street, Chatham, Kent ME4 4NM *Tel:* 01634 811573 *Fax:* 01634 811006

SHEERMAN, BARRY
Huddersfield

Barry John Sheerman. Born 17 August 1940; Son of late Albert William and Florence Sheerman; Educated Hampton Grammar School; Kingston Technical College; London School of Economics (BSc economics 1965); Kingston University (MSc 1967); Married Pamela Elizabeth Brenchley 1965 (1 son 3 daughters). Lecturer, University College of Wales, Swansea 1966-79; Member, AUT, MSF; Member Loughor and Lliw Valley Unitary District Council 1972-79

Lab/Co-op majority 8,351

House of Commons: Contested Taunton October 1974 general election. Member for Huddersfield East 1979-83, for Huddersfield since 9 June 1983 general election; Opposition Spokesperson for: Employment and Education 1983-88, Home Affairs 1988-92, Disabled People's Rights 1992-94; Shadow Minister for: Education and Employment 1983-87, Home Affairs deputy to Roy Hattersley 1987-92, Disability 1992-94. *Political interests:* Trade, Industry, Finance, Further Education, Education, Economy. European Union, South America, USA

Member, Co-operative Party; Chair, Labour Forum for Criminal Justice. National Children's Centre; Chair, Cross-Party Advisory Group on Preparation for EMU 1998-; Vice-Chair, Joint Pre-Legislative Committee Investigating the Financial Services and Markets Bill 1998-; Chair, Interparle (Parliamentary Communication Across Europe) 1997-; World Bank Business Partnership for Development Global Road Safety Partnership (GRSP); Chair, National Educational Research and Development Trust; Fellow, Industry and Parliament Trust; Director and Trustee, National Children's Centre; *Publications:* Co-author, *Harold Laski: A Life on the Left*, 1993; *Clubs:* Member, Royal Commonwealth Club; *Recreations:* Walking, biography, films

Barry Sheerman, MP, House of Commons, London SW1A 0AA *Tel:* 020 7219 5037 *Fax:* 020 7219 2404 *E-mail:* sheermanb@parliament.uk. *Constituency:* Labour Party, 6 Cross Church Street, Huddersfield, West Yorkshire HD1 2PT *Tel:* 01484 451382 *Fax:* 01484 451334

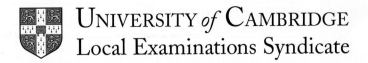

University *of* Cambridge
Local Examinations Syndicate

Should you wish to know anything about:

* University entrance tests
* Examinations, qualifications and assessment
* From primary to lifelong learning
* Vocational or general
* In the United Kingdom or around the world,

contact the largest assessment agency in Europe, a not-for-profit organisation recognised by governments around the world for its professional, rigorous and high standard assessments.

Feel free to phone, write or email at any time:

Bene't Steinberg, Group Director of Public Affairs,
1 Regent Street, Cambridge CB2 1GG.
01223 556003 (direct)
07803 727611 (mobile)
steinberg.b@ucles.org.uk

UCLES operates:

* OCR, one of the three main UK examination boards
* Cambridge International Examinations, which operates in 150 countries
* Cambridge English for Speakers of Other Languages

UCLES is adopting a new name from July 2005, which expresses more clearly what we do – Cambridge Assessment.

CAMBRIDGE ASSESSMENT

SHEPHERD, RICHARD
Aldridge-Brownhills

Richard Charles Scrimgeour Shepherd. Born 6 December 1942; Son of late Alfred Shepherd and Davida Sophia, neé Wallace; Educated London School of Economics; John Hopkins School of Advanced International Studies (MSc economics). Director, retail food business in London Underwriter, Lloyd's 1974-94

House of Commons: Contested Nottingham East February 1974 general election. Member for Aldridge-Brownhills since 3 May 1979 general election; Personal assistant to Edward Taylor MP (Glasgow Cathcart) October 1974 general election; Introduced four Private Member's Bills: The Crown Immunity Bill 1986, Protection of Official Information Bill 1988, The Referendum Bill 1992, Public Interest Disclosure Bill

Member, South East Economic Planning Council 1970-74; The Spectator's Award as: Backbencher of the Year 1987, Parliamentarian of the Year 1995; Campaign for Freedom of Information 1988; *Clubs:* Beefsteak, Chelsea Arts

Richard Shepherd, MP, House of Commons, London SW1A 0AA
Tel: 020 7219 5004. *Constituency:* 82 Walsall Road, Aldridge, Walsall,
West Midlands WS9 0JW *Tel:* 01922 451449 *Fax:* 01922 458078

Con majority 5,507

SHERIDAN, JIM
Paisley and Renfrewshire North

James Sheridan. Born 24 November 1952; Educated St Pius Secondary School; Married Jean McDowell 1977 (1 son 1 daughter). Print room assistant Beaverbrook Newspapers 1967-70; Semi-skilled painter Barcley Curle 1970-74; M/C operator Bowater Containers 1974-79; Semi-skilled painter Yarrow Shipbuilders 1982-84; Material handler Pilkington Optronics 1984-99; TGWU 1984-: Convener 1984-99, Stand down official 1998-99; Renfrewshire Council: Councillor 1999-, Vice-convener Social Work, Chair Scrutiny Board

House of Commons: Member for West Renfrewshire 2001-05, for Paisley and Renfrewshire North since 5 May 2005 general election. *Political interests:* Foreign Affairs, Defence, Employment, Welfare, Social Affairs

Clubs: Inchinnan Community Association; *Recreations:* Keep fit, golf, football

Jim Sheridan, MP, House of Commons, London SW1A 0AA *Tel:* 020 7219 8314.
Constituency: 21 John Wood Street, Port Glasgow PA14 5HU *Tel:* 01475 791826
Fax: 01475 791829 *E-mail:* jim@james-sheridan-mp.org.uk

Lab majority 11,001

SHORT, CLARE
Birmingham Ladywood

Clare Short. Born 15 February 1946; Daughter of late Frank and Joan Short; Educated St Francis JI School, Handsworth; St Paul's Grammar, Birmingham; Keele University; Leeds University (BA political science 1968); Married Andrew Moss 1964 (divorced 1971) (1 son); married Alex Lyon (MP 1966-83) 1982 (died 1993). Civil servant, Home Office 1970-75; Director: AFFOR – Community organisation concerned with race and urban deprivation in Handsworth 1976-77, Youth Aid 1979-83, Unemployment unit 1981-83; Member, UNISON

Lab majority 6,801

House of Commons: Member for Birmingham Ladywood since 9 June 1983 general election; Opposition Spokesperson for: Employment 1985-88, Social Security 1989-91; Opposition Frontbench Spokesperson for: Environmental Protection 1992-93, Women 1993-95; Principal Opposition Spokesperson for Transport 1995-96; Shadow Minister for Overseas Development 1996-97; Secretary of State for International Development 1997-2003. *Political interests:* Unemployment, Race Relations, Immigration, Low Pay, Home Affairs, Northern Ireland, Women

Member, Labour Party National Executive Committee 1988-98. Chair, Human Rights Committee of Socialist International 1996-98; PC 1997; *Recreations:* Swimming, family, friends

Rt Hon Clare Short, MP, House of Commons, London SW1A 0AA
Tel: 020 7219 4148 *Fax:* 020 7219 2586.

SIMMONDS, MARK
Boston and Skegness

Mark Jonathan Mortlock Simmonds. Born 12 April 1964; Son of Neil Mortlock Simmonds, teacher, and Mary Griffith Simmonds, née Morgan, teacher; Educated Worksop College, Nottinghamshire; Trent Polytechnic (BSc urban estate surveying 1986); Married Lizbeth Josefina Hanomancin-Garcia 1994 (2 daughters, 1 son). Surveyor Savills 1986-88; Partner Strutt and Parker 1988-96; Director Hillier Parker 1997-99; Chairman Mortlock Simmonds Brown 1999-; London Borough of Wandsworth 1990-94: Councillor, Chairman: Property Committee 1991-92, Housing Committee 1992-94

Con majority 5,907

House of Commons: Contested Ashfield 1997 general election. Member for Boston and Skegness since 7 June 2001 general election; Shadow Minister for: Public Services, Health and Education 2003-04, Education 2004, Foreign Affairs 2004-. *Political interests:* Economy, Education, Agriculture, Foreign Affairs. Latin America *Clubs:* Naval and Military; Honky Tonk Cricket; *Recreations:* Reading, history, rugby, tennis, family

Mark Simmonds, MP, House of Commons, London SW1A 0AA *Tel:* 020 7219 6254 *Fax:* 020 7219 1746 *E-mail:* simmondsm@parliament.uk. *Constituency:* The Conservative Association, Main Ridge West, Boston, Lincolnshire PE21 6QQ
Tel: 01205 751414 *Fax:* 01205 751414

Lab majority 9,575

SIMON, SIÔN
Birmingham Erdington

Siôn Llewelyn Simon. Born 23 December 1968; Son of Jeffrey Simon and Anne Loverini Owen, née Jones; Educated Handsworth Grammar School, Birmingham; Magdalen College, Oxford (BA philosophy, politics and economics 1990); Divorced (2 daughters 1 son). Research assistant George Robertson MP 1990-93; Senior manager Guinness PLC 1993-95; Freelance 1995-97; Labour Party general election HQ 1997; Columnist *Daily Telegraph* 1997-Oct 2001; Associate editor *The Spectator* 1997-; Columnist: *Daily Express* 1998, *News of the World* 2000-01; TGWU 1990-96, AEEU 1997-, NUJ 1997-

House of Commons: Member for Birmingham Erdington since 7 June 2001 general election. *Political interests:* Social Democracy, Urban Regeneration, Crime, European Affairs. USA, Italy, France, Japan, Australia, Spain

Siôn Simon, MP, House of Commons, London SW1A 0AA *Tel:* 020 7219 8140 *Fax:* 020 7219 5856 *E-mail:* simons@parliament.uk. *Constituency:* 50a Reservoir Road, Erdington, Birmingham, West Midlands B23 6DG *Tel:* 0121 373 1147 *Fax:* 0121 382 6347

Lab majority 7,486

SIMPSON, ALAN
Nottingham South

Alan Simpson. Born 20 September 1948; Son of Reg and Marjorie Simpson; Educated Bootle Grammar School; Nottingham Trent Polytechnic (BSc economics 1971); Divorced (2 sons 1 daughter). President, Students' Union, Nottingham Polytechnic 1969-70; Assistant General Secretary, Nottingham Council of Voluntary Service 1970-74; set up first pilot project for the national non-custodial treatment of offenders programme 1971-74; Community worker, Inner city anti-vandalism project 1974-78; Research Officer, Nottingham Racial Equality Council 1979-92; Member, UNISON

House of Commons: Contested Nottingham South in 1987 general election. Member for Nottingham South since 9 April 1992 general election; Adviser on tennis to Richard Caborn, as Minister of State for Sport 2002-. *Political interests:* Environment, Economics, Disarmament, Food Safety, GM Issues, Fuel Poverty

Board Member, Tribune Newspaper 1996-; Vice-chair Socialist Campaign of Labour MPs: Secretary, 1995-2001, Treasurer SCG 2001-02; Chair, Labour Against the War 2001-. Action Aid; *Publications:* Books on: common security, community development, housing, employment, policing policies, Europe, racism; 1999 Green Ribbon Award, Environment Back Bencher of the Year; *Recreations:* Tennis, cricket, football (also a lifelong supporter of Everton FC), vegetarian cooking, music (eclectic taste), reading

Alan Simpson, MP, House of Commons, London SW1A 0AA *Tel:* 020 7219 4534 *E-mail:* simpsona@parliament.uk. *Constituency:* Vernon House, 18 Friar Lane, Nottingham, Nottinghamshire NG1 6DQ *Tel:* 0115-956 0460 *Fax:* 0115-956 0445

SIMPSON, DAVID
Upper Bann

David Simpson. Born 16 February 1959; Educated Birches Primary School; Killicomaine High School; College of Business Studies, Belfast. MLA for Upper Bann 2003-; Councillor, Craigavon Borough Council 2001-

House of Commons: Member for Upper Bann since 5 May 2005 general election

Vice-President, DUP; Vice-Chairman: DUP Victims Committee, DUP Council Association; Chairman, Upper Bann Constituency Association

DUP majority 5,298

David Simpson, MP, House of Commons, London SW1A 0AA *Tel:* 020 7219 8533. *Constituency:* 13 Thomas St, Portadown, Craigavon *Tel:* 028 383 2234 *Fax:* 028 383 2123

SIMPSON, KEITH
Mid Norfolk

Keith Robert Simpson. Born 29 March 1949; Son of Harry Simpson and Jean Betty, neé Day; Educated Thorpe Grammar School, Norfolk; Hull University (BA history 1970); King's College, University of London (PGCE 1965); Married Pepita Hollingsworth 1984 (1 son). London University OTC 1970-72; Honorary Colonel Royal Military Police T.A.. Senior lecturer in war studies, RMA Sandhurst 1973-86; Head of foreign affairs and defence section, Conservative Research Department 1987-88; Special adviser to George Younger and Tom King as Secretaries of State for Defence 1988-90; Director, Cranfield Security Studies Institute, Cranfield University 1991-97

Con majority 7,560

House of Commons: Contested Plymouth Devonport 1992 general election. Member for Mid Norfolk since 1 May 1997 general election; Opposition Spokesperson for: Defence 1998-99, Environment, Food and Rural Affairs 2001-02; Opposition Whip 1999-2001: Home Office, Culture, Media and Sport: Wales 1999, Treasury, Health 1999-2000, Home Office, International Development 2000, Health, Treasury 2000-01; Shadow Minister for Defence 2002-. *Political interests:* Foreign Affairs, Defence, Education, Farming, Countryside. USA, Germany, France, Poland

National Vice-chair, Federation of Conservative Students 1971-72. Macmillan Cancer Relief; Member, European Standing Committee A 1998; *Publications: The Old Contemptibles*, 1981; Joint Editor *A Nations in Arms*, 1985; *History of the German Army*, 1985; Editor *The War the Infantry Knew 1914-1919*, 1986; *Recreations:* Walking dogs, reading, visiting restaurants, cinema, collecting and consuming malt whiskies, observing ambitious people

Keith Simpson, MP, House of Commons, London SW1A 0AA *Tel:* 020 7219 4053 *Fax:* 020 7219 0975 *E-mail:* keithsimpsonmp@parliament.uk. *Constituency:* Mid Norfolk Conservative Association, The Stable, Church Farm, Attlebridge, Norfolk NR9 5ST *Tel:* 01603 865763 *Fax:* 01603 865762

SINGH, MARSHA
Bradford West

Marsha Singh. Born 11 October 1954; Son of Harbans Singh and late Kartar Kaur; Educated Belle Vue Boys Upper School; Loughborough University (BA languages, politics and economics of modern Europe 1976); Married Sital Kaur 1971 (widowed 2001) (1 son 1 daughter). Senior development manager, Bradford Community Health 1990-97; Member, UNISON

House of Commons: Member for Bradford West since 1 May 1997 general election.

Lab majority 3,026   *Political interests:* European Union, Health, Education, Small Businesses. Palestine, Pakistan/Kashmir, India, Middle East, Europe

Chair: Bradford West Labour Party 1986-91, 1996-97, District Labour Party 1992. *Recreations:* Chess, bridge, reading

Marsha Singh, MP, House of Commons, London SW1A 0AA *Tel:* 020 7219 4516 *Fax:* 020 7219 0965. *Constituency:* Bradford West Constituency Office, 2nd Floor, 76 Kirkgate, Bradford, West Yorkshire BD1 1HY *Tel:* 01274 402220 *Fax:* 01274 402211

SKINNER, DENNIS
Bolsover

Dennis Skinner. Born 11 February 1932; Son of Edward Skinner; Educated Tupton Hall Grammar School; Ruskin College, Oxford; Married Mary Parker 1960 (1 son 2 daughters). Miner 1949-70; President, Derbyshire Miners 1966-70; Clay Cross UDC 1960-70; County Councillor, Derbyshire 1964-70; Former President, Derbyshire UDC Association

House of Commons: Member for Bolsover since 18 June 1970 general election.

Lab majority 18,437   *Political interests:* Inland Waterways, Energy, Economic Policy, Environment, Anti-Common Market, Third World

President, North East Derbyshire Constituency Labour Party 1968-71; Member, Labour Party National Executive Committee 1978-92, 1994-98, 1999-; Vice-Chair, Labour Party 1987-88, Chair 1988-89. Former Member, Scarsdale Valuation Panel; *Recreations:* Cycling, tennis, athletics (watching)

Dennis Skinner, MP, House of Commons, London SW1A 0AA *Tel:* 020 7219 5107 *Fax:* 020 7219 0028. *Constituency:* 1 Elmhurst Close, South Normanton, Derbyshire *Tel:* 01773 581027

SLAUGHTER, ANDY
Ealing, Acton and Shepherd's Bush

Andrew Francis Slaughter. Born 29 September 1960; Educated Exeter University. Barrister specialising in criminal, housing and personal injury law; Amicus; London Borough of Hammersmith and Fulham: Councillor 1986-, Deputy council leader 1991-96, Council leader 1996-

House of Commons: Contested Uxbridge 1997 by-election. Member for Ealing, Acton and Shepherd's Bush since 5 May 2005 general election. *Political interests:*

Lab majority 5,520   International affairs, housing, education

Andy Slaughter, MP, House of Commons, London SW1A 0AA *Tel:* 020 7219 4990. *Constituency:* 143 Becklow Road, London W12 9HH *E-mail:* andy@andyslaughter.com

Lab majority 963

SMITH, ANDREW
Oxford East

Andrew David Smith. Born 1 February 1951; Son of late David E. C. Smith and Georgina H. J. Smith; Educated Reading Grammar School; St John's College, Oxford (BA 1972, BPhil economics, politics, sociology 1974); Married Valerie Lambert 1976 (1 son). Member relations officer, Oxford and Swindon Co-op Society 1979-87; Member, Union Shop, Distributive and Allied Workers; Oxford City Councillor 1976-87; Chairman: Recreation and Amenities Committee 1980-83, Planning Committee 1985-87

House of Commons: Contested Oxford East 1983. Member for Oxford East since 11 June 1987 general election; Opposition Spokesman on Education 1988-92; Opposition Frontbench Spokesman on Treasury and Economic Affairs 1992-96; Shadow Chief Secretary to the Treasury 1994-96; Shadow Secretary of State for Transport 1996-97; Minister of State, Department for Education and Employment (Minister for Employment, Welfare to Work and Equal Opportunities) 1997-99; Chief Secretary to the Treasury 1999-2002; Secretary of State for Work and Pensions 2002-04. *Political interests:* Car Industry, Education, Retail Industry, Transport, Employment. Europe

Member, Labour Party Economy Policy Commission; Member Parliamentary Labour Party Parliamentary Committee 1999-2002. Pathway Shelter Workshop; PC 1997; Hon. Doctorate, Oxford Brookes University; *Clubs:* Blackbird Leys Community Association; President Blackbird Leys Boys and Girls Football Club

Rt Hon Andrew Smith, MP, House of Commons, London SW1A 0AA
Tel: 020 7219 4512 *Fax:* 020 7219 2965. *Constituency:* 21 Templars Square, Cowley, Oxford, Oxfordshire OX4 3UZ *Tel:* 01865 772893 *Fax:* 01865 772916
E-mail: andrewsmith.mp@virgin.net

Lab/Co-op majority 11,243

SMITH, ANGELA
Sheffield Hillsborough

Angela Smith. Born 16 August 1961; Educated Nottingham University; Newnham College, Cambridge (PhD); Amicus; Sheffield City Council: Councillor, Cabinet member for education; Member Regional Education and Skills Commission; Chair 14-19 Board, Sheffield First for Learning and Work

House of Commons: Member for Sheffield Hillsborough since 5 May 2005 general election

Angela Smith, MP, House of Commons, London SW1A 0AA *Tel:* 020 7219 6713.
Constituency: E-mail: angelasmith@sheffieldlabourparty.co.uk

SMITH, ANGELA EVANS
Basildon

Angela Evans Smith. Born 7 January 1959; Daughter of Patrick Evans, factory worker, and Emily, neé Russell, supervisor of church pre-school; Educated Chalvedon Comprehensive, Basildon; Leicester Polytechnic (BA public administration); Married Nigel Smith 1978. Trainee accountant, London Borough of Newham 1982-83; League Against Cruel Sports, finally head of political and public relations 1983-95; Research assistant to Alun Michael MP 1995-97; Member: TGWU, AEEU; Essex County Council: Councillor 1989-97, Chief Whip 1993-96, Lead Spokesperson, Fire and Public Protection Committee 1993-96

Lab majority 3,142

House of Commons: Contested Southend West 1987 general election. Member for Basildon since 1 May 1997 general election; Assistant Government Whip 2001-02; Joint PPS to Paul Boateng as Minister of State, Home Office 1999-2001; Parliamentary Under-Secretary of State, Northern Ireland Office 2002-. *Political interests:* Home Affairs, Animal Welfare, International Development, Employment. Cuba, Germany, USA

Angela Evans Smith, MP, House of Commons, London SW1A 0AA
Tel: 020 7219 6273 *Fax:* 020 7219 0926 *E-mail:* flackk@parliament.uk.
Constituency: Cornwallis House, Howard Chase, Basildon, Essex SS14 1DL
Tel: 01268 284830 *Fax:* 01268 284831

SMITH, GERALDINE
Morecambe and Lunesdale

Geraldine Smith. Born 29 August 1961; Daughter of John and Ann Smith; Educated Morecambe High School; Lancaster and Morecambe College (Diploma business studies 1978); Single. Postal officer 1980-97; Member, Communication Workers Union 1980-: positions including North West area administration representative 1994-97; Councillor, Lancaster City Council 1991-97; Chair: Coastal Protection, Economic Development and Tourism Policy

Lab majority 4,768

House of Commons: Member for Morecambe and Lunesdale since 1 May 1997 general election. *Political interests:* Economic Regeneration, Tourism, Public/Private Partnerships, Small Businesses. Ireland, Eastern Europe

Various positions including constituency secretary; North West Regional Group of Labour MPs: Former Vice-chair, Chair 2002-. Member, European Standing Committee C 1999-2002; UK substitute delegate, Council of Europe 1999-; Delegate to the Council of Europe; *Recreations:* Playing chess, walking and campaigning

Geraldine Smith, MP, House of Commons, London SW1A 0AA *Tel:* 020 7219 5816
Fax: 020 7219 0977 *E-mail:* smithg@parliament.uk. *Constituency:* Morecambe and Lunesdale CLP, Labour Party Offices, 26-28 Victoria Street, Morecambe, Lancashire LA4 4AJ *Tel:* 01524 411367 *Fax:* 01524 411369

Founded in 1957, the Captive Animals' Protection Society (CAPS) is a leading UK-based organisation working on behalf of animals used in entertainment.

Our campaigns to end the use of all animals in circuses have highlighted the miserable lives of these animals - transported from town to town and forced to perform tricks, often through cruelty.

Our investigators obtain the hard evidence required to expose animal suffering. Political lobbying by CAPS since 1957 has persuaded over 200 local authorities across Britain to ban animal circuses from council-owned land. We also lobby for a national ban on the use of animals in circuses. MPs from the three main parties have served as Patrons of CAPS throughout our history.

Working with other organisations, CAPS has exposed the suffering created by pet fairs, illegal animal markets selling exotic animals such as birds and reptiles. We have lobbied for the law to be strictly enforced to end these 'animal jumble sales'.

The cruelty and conservation con of zoos is becoming more widely recognised because of our work. CAPS investigations have exposed the unnatural conditions animals are confined to in zoos and how some animals are forced to perform circus-style tricks. Real conservation involves protecting animals' natural habitats, not confining them to captivity.

Education is important, if we are to end animal cruelty, and each year we send out hundreds of free information packs and deal with enquiries from students and teachers. We have recently added a charity wing to take our education work forward.

The Captive Animals' Protection Society, PO Box 573, Preston, PR1 9WW
Tel/Fax: 0845 330 3911 E-mail: info@captiveanimals.org
Website: www.captiveanimals.org

SMITH, JACQUI
Redditch

Jacqui (Jacqueline) Smith. Born 3 November 1962; Daughter of Michael L. Smith, headteacher, and Jill Smith, retired teacher; Educated Dyson Perrins High School, Malvern, Worcs; Hertford College, Oxford University (BA philosophy, politics and economics 1984); Worcester College of Higher Education (PGCE 1986); Married Richard Timney 1987 (2 sons). Economics teacher, Arrow Vale High School, Redditch 1986-88; Teacher, Worcester Sixth Form College 1988-90; Head of economics, GNVQ co-ordinator, Haybridge High School, Hagley 1990-97; Member: NUT, GMB; Councillor, Redditch Borough Council 1991-97

Lab majority 2,716

House of Commons: Member for Redditch since 1 May 1997 general election; Parliamentary Under-Secretary of State, Department for Education and Employment 1999-2001; Minister of State for: Community, Department of Health 2001-03, Minister of State for Industry and the Regions and Deputy Minister for Women and Equality, Department of Trade and Industry 2003-05; Minister of State (Schools), Department for Education and Skills 2005-. *Political interests:* Industry, Education and Training, Economic Policy, Social Services

Member, British East-West Centre; Member, Worcester Nature Conservation Trust; PC 2003; *Recreations:* Family, football, theatre

Rt Hon Jacqui Smith, MP, House of Commons, London SW1A 0AA
Tel: 020 7219 5190 *E-mail:* smithjj@parliament.uk. *Constituency:* Unit 16, 1st Floor, Greenlands Business Centre, Studley Road, Redditch,
Hereford & Worcester B98 7HD *Tel:* 01527 523355 *Fax:* 01527 523355

SMITH, JOHN
Vale of Glamorgan

John William Patrick Smith. Born 17 March 1951; Son of John and Margaret Smith; Educated Penarth Grammar School; Gwent College of Higher Education; University College of Wales, Cardiff (BSc economics); Married Kathleen Mulvaney 1971 (2 sons 1 daughter). RAF 1967-71. Carpenter and joiner, Vale Borough Council 1971-76; Mature student 1976-81; University tutor (UCC) 1981-85; Senior lecturer in business studies 1985-89; Campaign manager, Gwent Image Partnership, chief executive 1992-; Member: MSF 1970-, TASS, NATFHE, AUT, NUPE, UCATT; Vale of Glamorgan Borough Council: Councillor 1979-91, Opposition Finance and Housing Spokesperson 1979-87, Labour Group Secretary 1981-83, Labour Group Leader 1983-88

Lab majority 1,808

House of Commons: Contested Vale of Glamorgan 1987 general election. Member for Vale of Glamorgan 1989-92 and since 1 May 1997 general election; PPS to Roy Hattersley as Deputy Leader of Labour Party 1989-92; Contributed to: Trade Union Bill, Armed Forces Bill, Barry Old Harbour Bill, Seat Belt Regulation; PPS to Dr John Reid: as Minister of State, Ministry of Defence (Minister for the Armed Forces) 1997-98, Department of the Environment, Transport and the Regions (Minister of Transport) 1998-99. *Political interests:* Economic Development, Industrial Relations, Transport Safety, Defence, Deep Vein Thrombosis in Air Travellers

Chair, Young Socialists 1967-94; Member: Vale of Glamorgan CLP 1972-, Welsh Executive 1985-89, 1996-; Chair, Wales Labour Party 1988-89; Member, National Policy Forum 1996; Former Vice-chair, Welsh Parliamentary Labour Party. Advisory Council on Transport Safety 1989-92; Member: Commonwealth Parliamentary Association (CPA), UK Delegation to North Atlantic Assembly; *Recreations:* Reading, walking, camping, boating

John Smith, MP, House of Commons, London SW1A 0AA *Tel:* 020 7219 3589
Fax: 020 7219 0939 *E-mail:* smithj@parliament.uk. *Constituency:* 115 High Street, Barry, South Glamorgan *Tel:* 01446 743769 *Fax:* 01446 747921

What's special about the Institute of Education? A lot!

The Institute of Education is the only college of the University of London dedicated entirely to education and education-related areas of social science. Our expertise ranges from early years to higher education, from health promotion to international development.

The Institute is widely recognised as a world leader in educational research. At any one time, over 300 staff are engaged in more than 100 funded research projects and are in demand as speakers, consultants and collaborative partners throughout the world.

Nearly 6,500 postgraduates study at the Institute. Over two-thirds are studying for master's and other advanced degrees; about a quarter are training to be teachers; and the rest are undertaking research degrees.

With such dynamic figures as Sydney Webb and Basil Bernstein in our history, it's no wonder that the Institute is a high profile forum for international debate, hosting dynamic conferences and lectures involving leading figures in the world of education and politics.

World-leading research centres based at the Institute include the Centre for Longitudinal Studies, which carries out the renowned British birth cohort studies; the Thomas Coram Research Unit, which studies children and families; and the ESRC-funded Teaching and Learning Research Programme. We are partners in all four of the national research centres established by the DfES, three of which are based at the Institute.

So if you need to know about education, get in touch!

INSTITUTE OF EDUCATION
UNIVERSITY OF LONDON

020 7612 6459
info@ioe.ac.uk
www.ioe.ac.uk

SMITH, ROBERT
West Aberdeenshire and Kincardine

Robert Smith. Born 15 April 1958; Son of late Sir (William) Gordon Smith, Bt, VRD, and of Diana Lady Smith; Educated Merchant Taylors' School, Northwood; Aberdeen University (BSc); Married Fiona Anne Cormack MD 1993 (3 daughters). Family estate manager until 1997; Councillor, Aberdeenshire Council 1995-97; JP 1997

House of Commons: Contested (SDP/Liberal Alliance) Aberdeen North 1987 general election. Member for West Aberdeenshire and Kincardine 1997-2005, for new West Aberdeenshire and Kincardine since 5 May 2005 general election; Spokesperson for Scotland 1999-2001; Liberal Democrat Whip 1999-2001, Deputy Chief Whip 2001-. *Political interests:* Electoral Reform, Offshore Oil and Gas Industry, Rural Affairs

General Council Assessor, Aberdeen University 1994-98; Director, Grampian Transport Museum 1995-97; Vice-convener, Grampian Joint Police Board 1995-97; Member, Electoral Reform Society; Member, European Standing Committee A 2000-01; Bt; *Clubs:* Royal Yacht Squadron, Royal Thames Yacht; Bt; *Recreations:* Hill-walking, sailing

Sir Robert Smith, MP, House of Commons, London SW1A 0AA
Tel: 020 7219 3531 *Fax:* 020 7219 4526. *Constituency:* 6 Dee Street, Banchory, Kincardineshire, AB31 5ST *Tel:* 01330 820330 *Fax:* 01330 820338
E-mail: bobsmith@cix.co.uk

Lib Dem majority
7,471

SNELGROVE, ANNE
South Swindon

Anne Snelgrove. Born 7 August 1957; Educated Bracknell Ranelagh School; King Alfred's College, Winchester; City University, London; Married; Amicus
House of Commons: Member for South Swindon since 5 May 2005 general election
Recreations: Gardening, cinema, reading
Anne Snelgrove, MP, House of Commons, London SW1A 0AA
Tel: 020 7219 6963. *Constituency:* South Swindon Labour Party, 13 Bath Road, Swindon SN1 4AS *Tel:* 01793 615444

Lab/Co-op majority
1,353

SOAMES, NICHOLAS
Mid Sussex

Nicholas Soames. Born 12 February 1948; Son of late Baron and Lady Soames; Educated Eton College; Married Catherine Weatherall 1981 (divorced 1988) (1 son), married Serena Smith 1993 (1 daughter 1 son). Lieutenant, 11th Hussars 1967-72. Equerry to Prince of Wales 1970-72; Stockbroker 1972-74; PA to: Sir James Goldsmith 1974-76, US Senator Mark Hatfield 1976-78; Assistant director, Sedgwick Group 1979-81; Council of RUSI

Con majority 5,890

House of Commons: Contested Dumbartonshire Central 1979 general election. Member for Crawley 1983-97, and for Mid Sussex since 1 May 1997 general election; PPS: to John Gummer as Minister of State for Employment and Chairman of the Conservative Party 1984-86; to Nicholas Ridley as Secretary of State for the Environment 1987-89; Joint Parliamentary Secretary, Ministry of Agriculture, Fisheries and Food 1992-94; Minister of State for the Armed Forces, Ministry of Defence 1994-97; Shadow Secretary of State for Defence 2003-05; Member Shadow Cabinet 2004-05. *Political interests:* Defence, Foreign Affairs, Trade and Industry, Aerospace, Aviation, Agriculture and Countryside matters

Trustee, Amber Foundation; President Rare Birds Survival Trust; *Clubs:* White's, Turf, Pratt's; *Recreations:* Country pursuits

Nicholas Soames, MP, House of Commons, London SW1A 0AA
Tel: 020 7219 4184 *Fax:* 020 7219 2998 *E-mail:* soamesn@parliament.uk.
Constituency: 5 Hazelgrove Road, Haywards Heath, West Sussex RH16 3PH
Tel: 01444 452590 *Fax:* 01444 415766

SOULSBY, PETER
Leicester South

Peter Alfred Soulsby. Born 27 December 1948; Educated Minchinden School, Southgate; Leicester University, BEd (City of Leicester College); Married Alison Prime 1969. Special educational needs teacher 1973-90; British Waterways: Board member 1998-, Vice-chair 2000-; TGWU; Leicester City Council: Councillor 1973-2003, Council leader 1981-94, 1995-99; Chaired Leicester City Challenge Project 1994-98; Former member Audit Commission; Permanent member Beacon Council Advisory Panel

Lab majority 3,717

House of Commons: Contested Leicester South 2004 by-election. Member for Leicester South since 5 May 2005 general election

Election agent to Jim Marshall in 1997 and 2001 general elections. Kt 1999; *Recreations:* Inland waterways

Sir Peter Soulsby, MP, House of Commons, London SW1A 0AA
Tel: 020 7219 8332. *Constituency:* 131a Evington Road, Leicester LE2 1QJ
Tel: 0116-220 8284 *E-mail:* leicestersouth.labour@ntlworld.com

SOUTHWORTH, HELEN
Warrington South

Helen Mary Southworth. Born 13 November 1956; Educated Larkhill Convent School; Lancaster University (BA); Married Edmund Southworth (1 son). Director, Age Concern (St Helens); Non-executive director, St Helens and Knowsley Health Authority; Representative on the Community Health Council for 8 years; Member, MSF; Councillor, St Helens Borough Council 1994-98, Chair, Leisure Committee 1994-96; Non-executive Member, St Helens and Knowsley Health Authority

Lab majority 3,515

House of Commons: Contested Wirral South general election 1992. Member for Warrington South since 1 May 1997 general election; PPS to Paul Boateng as: Financial Secretary to the Treasury 2001-02, Chief Secretary to the Treasury 2002-. *Political interests:* Health, Housing, Democracy, Small Businesses. Denmark, Sweden, Finland

Trustee, History of Parliament Trust; *Publications:* Co-author, *National Standards for Day Care Provision*; *Recreations:* Family, gardening, painting, walking the dog

Helen Southworth, MP, House of Commons, London SW1A 0AA
Tel: 020 7219 3568 *Fax:* 020 7219 2115 *E-mail:* southworthh@parliament.uk.
Constituency: 33 Cairo Street, Warrington, Cheshire WA1 1EH *Tel:* 01925 240002 *Fax:* 01925 632614

SPELLAR, JOHN
Warley

John Francis Spellar. Born 5 August 1947; Son of late William David Spellar, and of Phyllis Kathleen Spellar; Educated Dulwich College, London; St Edmund's Hall, Oxford (BA philosophy, politics and economics 1969); Married Anne Rosalind Wilmot 1981 (1 daughter); National Officer, Electrical, Electronic, Telecommunication and Plumbing Union 1969-97

Lab majority 10,147

House of Commons: Contested Bromley 1970 general election. Member for Birmingham Northfield from 28 October 1982 by-election to June 1983. Contested Birmingham Northfield 1987 general election. Member for Warley West 1992-97, and for Warley since 1 May 1997 general election; Opposition Spokesperson for: Northern Ireland 1994-95, Defence, Disarmament and Arms Control 1995-97; Opposition Whip 1992-94; Ministry of Defence: Parliamentary Under-Secretary of State 1997-99, Minister of State for the Armed Forces 1999-2001; Minister of State (Minister for Transport), Department of Transport, Local Government and the Regions 2001-02; Minister of State for Transport, Department for Transport 2002-03; Minister of State, Northern Ireland Office 2003-05. *Political interests:* Energy, Electronics Industry, Motor Industry, Construction Industry. Australia, Israel, USA

PC 2001; *Clubs:* Rowley Regis and Blackheath Labour; *Recreations:* Gardening

Rt Hon John Spellar, MP, House of Commons, London SW1A 0AA
Tel: 020 7219 0674; 020 7219 5800 *Fax:* 020 7219 2113
E-mail: spellarj@parliament.uk. *Constituency:* Brandhall Labour Club, Tame Road, Oldbury, West Midlands B68 0JT *Tel:* 0121 423 2933

SPELMAN, CAROLINE
Meriden

Con majority 7,009

Caroline Alice Spelman. Born 4 May 1958; Daughter of late Marshall and Helen Margaret Cormack; Educated Herts and Essex Grammar School for Girls; Queen Mary College, London University (BA European studies 1980); Married Mark Spelman 1987 (2 sons 1 daughter). Sugar Beet commodity secretary, National Farmers Union 1981-84; Deputy director, International Confederation of European Beetgrowers, Paris 1984-89; Research fellow, Centre for European Agricultural Studies 1989-93; Director, Spelman, Cormack and Associates, Food and Biotechnology Consultancy 1989-

House of Commons: Contested Bassetlaw 1992 general election. Member for Meriden since 1 May 1997 general election; Opposition Spokesperson for: Health 1999-2001, Women's Issues 1999; Opposition Whip (Agriculture; Environment, Transport and the Regions) 1998-99; Shadow: Secretary of State for International Development 2001-03, Minister for Women 2001-04, Secretary of State for: the Environment 2003-04, Local and Devolved Government Affairs 2004-. *Political interests:* Environment, Agriculture, International Development. France, Germany, India, Pakistan

Co-opted member executive committee Conservative Women's National Council; Member board of directors governing council Conservative Christian Fellowship. Trustee of Domestic Violence Refuge (MABL) and Drug Rehabilitation Charity (WELCOME); Board Member, Parliamentary Office of Science and Technology (POST) 1997-2001; Trustee Snowdon Awards Scheme for Disabled; *Publications: A Green and Pleasant Land*, Bow Group Paper 1994; *Clubs:* Parliamentary Choir; Member: Lords and Commons Ski Club, Lords and Commons Tennis Club; *Recreations:* Tennis, skiing, cooking, gardening

Caroline Spelman, MP, House of Commons, London SW1A 0AA
Tel: 020 7219 4189 *Fax:* 020 7219 0378 *E-mail:* spelmanc@parliament.uk.
Constituency: 2 Manor Road, Solihull, West Midlands B91 2BH *Tel:* 0121-711 2955
Fax: 0121-711 2955

Con majority 2,475

SPICER, MICHAEL
West Worcestershire

(William) Michael Hardy Spicer. Born 22 January 1943; Son of late Brigadier L. H. Spicer; Educated Wellington College; Emmanuel College, Cambridge (MA economics 1964); Married Patricia Ann Hunter 1967 (1 son 2 daughters). Assistant to editor The Statist 1964-66; Conservative Research Department 1966-68; Director, Conservative Systems Research Centre 1968-70, Managing director, Economic Models Limited 1970-80

House of Commons: Contested Easington 1966 and 1970 general elections. Member for South Worcestershire 1974-97, and for West Worcestershire since 1 May 1997 general election; PPS to Sally Oppenheim as Minister for Trade and Consumer Affairs 1979-81; Parliamentary Under-Secretary of State for Transport 1984-87; Aviation Minister 1985-87; Parliamentary Under-Secretary of State, Department of Energy 1987-90; Minister of State, Housing and Planning, Department of Environment 1990. *Political interests:* Economic Policy. USA

Conservative Party: Vice-Chair 1981-83, Deputy Chair 1983-84, Board member 2001-. Chairman, European Research Group 1992-2001; Joint chairman, Congress of Democracy; Chairman, Parliamentary and Scientific Committee 1996-99; *Publications: A Treaty Too Far: A New Policy For Europe,* 1992; *The Challenge from the East: The Rebirth of the West,* 1996; Six novels; Knighted 1996; *Clubs:* Pratts, Garrick; *Recreations:* Tennis, writing novels, painting, bridge

Sir Michael Spicer, MP, House of Commons, London SW1A 0AA *Tel:* 020 7219 6250. *Constituency:* 209a Worcester Road, Malvern Link, Malvern, Worcestershire WR14 1SP *Tel:* 01684 573469 *Fax:* 01684 575280

Con majority 8,201

SPINK, BOB
Castle Point

Bob (Robert) M Spink. Born 1 August 1948; Son of George, panel beater, and Brenda; Educated Holycroft School, Keighley; Manchester University, Cranfield University (PhD, CDipAF, BSc engineering, MSc industrial engineering); Married Janet Mary Barham 1968 (divorced) (3 sons 1 daughter). RAF 1964-66 (invalided). Engineer EMI Electronics Ltd 1966-77; Industrial and management consultant 1977-80; Director and co-owner Seafarer Navigation International Ltd 1980-84; Management consultant Harold Whitehead and Partners 1984-92; Director: Bournemouth International Airport plc 1989-93, Harold Whitehead and Partners 1997-; Member 1966-75: DATA, TASS, AUEW; Dorset County Council 1985-93: Councillor, Member Dorset Police Authority 1985-93, Deputy group leader 1989-90, Chair Education Policy Committee 1989-93

House of Commons: Member for Castle Point 1992-1997. Contested Castle Point 1997 general election. Member for Castle Point since 7 June 2001 general election; PPS: to Ann Widdecombe as Minister of State for Employment 1994-95, as Minister of State Home Office 1995-97, to John Watts as Minister of State for Railways, Roads and Local Transport, Department of Transport 1997; Private member's bill on: Underage drinking, Over development in the South East. *Political interests:* Employment, Trade and Industry, Education, Elderly, Britain's Sovereignty

Parliamentary Office of Science and Technology: Board member 1993-97, Director; *Recreations:* Marathons, pottery, gardening

Dr Bob Spink, MP, House of Commons, London SW1A 0AA *Tel:* 020 7219 8468 *Fax:* 020 7219 1956 *E-mail:* spinkr@parliament.uk.

Con majority 8,909

SPRING, RICHARD
West Suffolk

Richard Spring. Born 24 September 1946; Son of late H. J. A. Spring and of late Marjorie Watson-Morris; Educated Rondebosch, Cape; University of Cape Town; Magdalene College, Cambridge; Married Hon. Jane Henniker-Major 1979 (divorced 1993) (1 son 1 daughter). Merrill Lynch Ltd 1971-86, Vice-President 1976-86; Deputy managing director, Hutton International Associates 1986-88; Executive director, Shearson Lehman Hutton 1988-90; Managing director, Xerox Furman Selz 1990-92

House of Commons: Contested Ashton-under-Lyne 1983 general election. Member for Bury St Edmunds 1992-97, and for West Suffolk since 1 May 1997 general election; Opposition Spokesperson for: Culture, Media and Sport November 1997-2000, Foreign Affairs 2000-03; PPS: to Sir Patrick Mayhew as Secretary of State for Northern Ireland 1994-95, to Tim Eggar, as Minister for Trade and Industry 1995-96, to Nicholas Soames and James Arbuthnot as Ministers of State, Ministry of Defence 1996-97; Shadow Minister for: International Affairs 2003-04, Economic Affairs 2004-. *Political interests:* Europe, South Africa, USA, Middle East, China, Pacific Rim

Various offices in Westminster Conservative Association 1976-87, including CPC Chair 1990; Vice-Chair, Conservative Industrial Fund 1993-96. Governer, Westminster Foundation for Democracy; *Publications:* Contributed to *Fairer Business Rates* Conservative Backbench Committee on Smaller Businesses, July 1996; *Clubs:* Boodle's; *Recreations:* Country pursuits, tennis, swimming

Richard Spring, MP, House of Commons, London SW1A 0AA *Tel:* 020 7219 5192. *Constituency:* 4a Exeter Road, Newmarket, Suffolk CB8 8LT *Tel:* 01638 669391 *Fax:* 01638 669410

Lab majority 11,562

SQUIRE, RACHEL
Dunfermline and West Fife

Rachel Squire. Born 13 July 1954; Daughter of Louise Anne Squire; Educated Godolphin and Latymer Girls' School; Durham University (BA anthropology 1975); Birmingham University (CQSW 1978); Married Allan Lee Mason 1984. Social worker, Birmingham City Council 1975-81; Area officer, NUPE: Liverpool 1981-82, Ayrshire 1982-83, Renfrewshire 1983-85, All of Scotland Education Officer 1985-92; Trade union official 1981-92; Member, UNISON

House of Commons: Member for Dunfermline West 1992-2005, for Dunfermline and West Fife since 5 May 2005 general election; PPS to Ministers of State, Department for Education and Employment: Stephen Byers 1997-98, Estelle Morris 1998-2001. *Political interests:* Defence, NHS, Community Care, Foreign Affairs. Scandinavia, Europe, Former Eastern Bloc, Russia, Korea

Head, Scottish Labour Party's Task Force on Community Care 1993-97; Member, Labour Movement in Europe; Chair, Scottish Policy Forum, Labour Party 1998-2002. Labour Representative, Commission on Future of Scotland's Voluntary Sector; Fellow, Industry and Parliament Trust (BAe); Member, National Trust (Scotland); Fellow (Navy), Armed Forces Parliamentary Scheme 1993-94, 2001-; *Recreations:* Archaeology, reading, cooking

Rachel Squire, MP, House of Commons, London SW1A 0AA *Tel:* 020 7219 5144. *Constituency:* Parliamentary Office, Music Hall Lane, Dunfermline KY12 7NG *Tel:* 01383 622889 *Fax:* 01383 623500, *E-mail:* west.fife.labour@ukf.net

STANLEY, JOHN
Tonbridge and Malling

Con majority 13,352

John P Stanley. Born 19 January 1942; Educated Repton School; Lincoln College, Oxford; Married Susan Giles 1968 (1 son 1 daughter 1 son deceased). Conservative Research Department 1967-68; Research Associate, Institute for Strategic Studies 1968-69; Rio Tinto-Zinc Corp. Ltd 1969-79

House of Commons: Contested Newton 1970 general election. Member for Tonbridge and Malling since 28 February 1974 general election; PPS to Margaret Thatcher as Leader of the Opposition 1976-79; Minister for Housing and Construction 1979-83; Minister for the Armed Forces 1983-87; Minister of State, Northern Ireland Office 1987-88

Member, Executive Committee, Commonwealth Parliamentary Association (CPA) UK Branch 1999-; PC 1984; Knighted 1988; *Recreations:* Music and the arts, sailing

Rt Hon Sir John Stanley, MP, House of Commons, London SW1A 0AA *Tel:* 020 7219 4506. *Constituency:* 91 High Street, West Malling, Maidstone, Kent ME19 6NA *Tel:* 01732 842794 *Fax:* 01732 873960

STARKEY, PHYLLIS
Milton Keynes South West

Lab majority 4,010

Phyllis Margaret Starkey. Born 4 January 1947; Daughter of late Dr John and Catherine Hooson Williams; Educated Perse School for Girls, Cambridge; Lady Margaret Hall, Oxford (BA biochemistry 1970); Clare Hall, Cambridge (PhD 1974); Married Hugh Walton Starkey 1969 (2 daughters). Research scientist: Strangeways Laboratory, Cambridge 1974-81, Sir William Dunn School of Pathology, Oxford 1981-84; University lecturer in obstetrics, Oxford University and fellow, Somerville College 1984-93; Science policy administrator, Biotechnology and Biological Sciences Research Council 1993-97; Parliamentary fellow, St Antony's College, Oxford 1997-98; Member: AUT 1974-93, AMICUS (MSF) 1992-, PTC 1993-97; Oxford City Council: Councillor 1983-97, Leader 1990-93, Chair of Transport 1985-88, Chair of Finance 1988-90, 1993-96

House of Commons: Member for Milton Keynes South West since 1 May 1997 general election; Team PPS, Foreign and Commonwealth Office 2001-02; PPS to Denis MacShane as Minister of State, Foreign and Commonwealth Affairs 2002-. *Political interests:* Science, Health, Environment and Transport, Local Democracy and Regional Devolution, Foreign Affairs, Middle East. Palestine, France, North Africa, Middle East

South East Regional Group of Labour MPs: Vice-Chair 1998-2003, Chair 2003-. Oxfam; Chair, Local Government Information Unit 1992-97; Representative of Labour Councillors on National Policy Forum 1995-97; Board Member, Parliamentary Office of Science and Technology (POST) 1997-, Chair 2002-; Trustee, Theatres Trust; *Publications:* Seventy scientific papers 1977-96; K M Stott Prize, Newnham College, Cambridge 1974; *Recreations:* Gardening, cinema, walking, family

Dr Phyllis Starkey, MP, House of Commons, London SW1A 0AA *Tel:* 020 7219 0456; 020 7219 6427 *Fax:* 020 7219 6865. *Constituency:* The Labour Hall, Newport Road, New Bradwell, Milton Keynes MK13 0AA *Tel:* 01908 225522 *Fax:* 01908 320731 *Website:* www.phylilisstarkey.labour.co.uk

Con majority 1,947

STEEN, ANTHONY
Totnes

Anthony David Steen. Born 22 July 1939; Son of late Stephen Steen; Educated Westminster School; Grays Inn; London University; Married Carolyn Padfield 1966 (1 son 1 daughter). Called to the Bar 1962; Barrister, Gray's Inn; Youth leader and social worker; Founder, Task Force (Young helping the old) with Government grant 1964, First Director 1964-68; As community worker initiated Young Volunteer Force, Government Urban Development Foundation, First Director 1968-74; Lecturer in law, Ghana High Commission and Council of Legal Education 1964-67; Ministry of Defence Court Martials Defence Counsel; Adviser to Federal and Provincial Canadian Governments on unemployment and youth problems 1970-71

House of Commons: Member for Liverpool Wavertree 1974-83, for South Hams 1983-97, and for Totnes since 1 May 1997 general election; PPS to Peter Brooke as Secretary of State for National Heritage 1992-94. *Political interests:* Urban and Rural Regeneration, Community Care, Youth Affairs, Conservation, Heritage, Fishing Industry, Agriculture, Deregulation and Scrutiny of EU Directives, Affordable Housing, Environmental Pollution and Social and Community Work. Middle East, St Helena, West Indies

Appointed by the Prime Minister to generate new activity amongst MPs in constituency work 1994; Conservative Central Office Co-ordinator for Critical Seats 1982-87; Joint National Chairman, Impact 80s Campaign 1980-82; Chair, Minority Party Unit 1999-2000. Member, Council for Christians and Jews; Trustee of: Education Extra, Dartington International Summer School, Taskforce Trust; *Publications: New Life for Old Cities*, 1981; *Tested Ideas for Political Success*, 1983, 7th ed, 1993; *Public Land Utilisation Management Schemes (PLUMS)*, 1988; *Clubs:* Royal North Cape, Royal Automobile; Lords and Commons Cycle, Lords and Commons Tennis; *Recreations:* Piano playing, cycling and tennis

Anthony Steen, MP, House of Commons, London SW1A 0AA *Tel:* 020 7219 5045 *Fax:* 020 7219 6586 *E-mail:* steena@parliament.uk. *Constituency:* TCCA, Station Road, Totnes, Devon TQ9 5HW *Tel:* 01803 866064 *Fax:* 01803 867286

Lab majority 12,886

STEWART, IAN
Eccles

Ian Stewart. Born 28 August 1950; Son of John and Helen; Educated Calder St Secondary, Blantyre; Alfred Turner Secondary Modern, Irlam, nr Manchester; Stretford Technical College 1966-69; Manchester Metropolitan University (MPhil Management of Change in progress); Married Merilyn Holding 1968 (2 sons 1 daughter). Regional full-time officer, Transport and General Workers Union for 20 years; Member, Transport and General Workers 1966-

House of Commons: Member for Eccles since 1 May 1997 general election; PPS: to Ministers of State, Department of Trade and Industry: Brian Wilson 2001-03, Stephen Timms 2003-04, to Stephen Timms as Financial Secretary, HM Treasury 2004-. *Political interests:* Employment, Education and Training, Economics, Trade and Industry, Investment, Regional Development, Information Technology, Democracy, International Affairs, Small Businesses. EU, Central and Eastern Europe, China, USA, Commonwealth

Founder, European Foundation for Social Partnership and Continuing Training Initiatives; Secretary, House of Commons Football Team; Member: Society of International Industrial Relations, UK China Forum (Industry Group); Executive Member, Great Britain-China Centre; *Publications: Youth Unemployment and Government Training Strategies,* 1981; Visiting fellow, Salford University; *Recreations:* Tai-Chi, painting, research into philosophical religious and life systems, scientific and medical developments

Ian Stewart, MP, House of Commons, London SW1A 0AA *Tel:* 020 7219 6175 *Fax:* 020 7219 0903 *E-mail:* ianstewartmp@parliament.uk. *Constituency:* Eccles Parliamentary Office, Eccles Town Hall, Church Street, Eccles, Greater Manchester M30 0EL *Tel:* 0161-707 4688 *Fax:* 0161-789 8065

Lab majority 706

STOATE, HOWARD
Dartford

Howard Geoffrey Stoate. Born 14 April 1954; Son of late Alvan Stoate, engineer, and late Maisie Stoate, teacher; Educated Kingston Grammar School; King's College, London University (MBBS 1974, MSc, DRCOG, FRCGP); Married Deborah Dunkerley 1979 (2 sons). Junior hospital doctor 1977-81; GP, Bexley Heath 1982-; GP tutor, Queen Mary's Hospital, Sidcup 1989-; Chair, Bexley Ethics Research Committee 1995-97; Member: MPU, MSF; Councillor, Dartford Borough Council 1990-99, Chair, Finance and Corporate Business 1995-99

House of Commons: Contested Old Bexley and Sidcup 1987, Dartford 1992 general elections. Member for Dartford since 1 May 1997 general election; PPS to: John Denham as Minister of State, Home Office 2001-03, Estelle Morris as Minister of State, Department for Culture, Media and Sport 2003-. *Political interests:* Health, Education, Environment, Home Affairs. Spain

Vice-Chair, DCLP 1984-91; Chair, LP Branch 1985-97; Vice-Chair, Dartford Fabian Society. Vice-Chair, Regional Graduate Education Board 1997-; Member, British Medical Association; *Publications:* Many medical publications, particularly on health screening; *All's Well that Starts Well – A Strategy for Children's Health,* Fabian Society, 2002; *Clubs:* Emsworth Sailing Club; *Recreations:* Running, sailing, reading, music, car building

Dr Howard Stoate, MP, House of Commons, London SW1A 0AA *Tel:* 020 7219 4571 *Fax:* 020 7219 6820. *Constituency:* Civic Centre, Home Gardens, Dartford, Kent DA1 1DR *Tel:* 01322 343234 *Fax:* 01322 343235 *E-mail:* hstoate@hotmail.com

STRANG, GAVIN
Edinburgh East

Gavin Steel Strang. Born 10 July 1943; Son of James S. Strang, tenant farmer; Educated Morrison's Academy; Edinburgh University (BSc 1964); Churchill College, Cambridge University (DipAgriSci 1965); Edinburgh University (PhD 1968); Married Bettina Morrison, neé Smith 1973 (1 son, 2 stepsons). Member, Tayside Economic Planning Consultative Group 1966-68; Scientist, Agricultural Research Council 1968-70; Member, TGWU

Lab majority 6,202

House of Commons: Member for Edinburgh East 1970-97, for Edinburgh East and Musselburgh 1997-2005, and for Edinburgh East since 5 May 2005 general election; Opposition Frontbench Spokesperson for: Agriculture 1979-82, Employment 1987-89, Food, Agriculture and Rural Affairs 1992-97; Parliamentary Under-Secretary of State for Energy February-October 1974; Parliamentary Secretary to Ministry of Agriculture 1974-79; Minister of State (in Cabinet), Department of the Environment, Transport and the Regions (Minister for Transport) 1997-98. *Political interests:* Agriculture, Transport, Fishing Industry, AIDS. Europe

PC 1997; *Recreations:* Swimming, golf, watching football, walking in the countryside

Rt Hon Gavin Strang, MP, House of Commons, London SW1A 0AA
Tel: 020 7219 5155 *E-mail:* daviesk@parliament.uk. *Constituency:* 54 Portobello High Street, Edinburgh EH15 1DA *Tel:* 0131-669 6002

STRAW, JACK
Blackburn

Jack (John Whitaker) Straw. Born 3 August 1946; Son of Walter Arthur Straw; Educated Brentwood School; Leeds University (LLB 1967); Inns of Court School of Law 1972; Married Alice Perkins 1978 (1 son 1 daughter). President, National Union of Students 1969-71; Called to the Bar, Inner Temple 1972; Practised as Barrister 1972-74; Special adviser: to Barbara Castle, MP as Secretary of State for Social Services 1974-76, to Peter Shore, MP as Secretary of State for the Environment 1976-77; Member, staff of Granada Television *World in Action* 1977-79; Elected Master of Bench of the Inner Temple 1997; Member, GMB; Councillor, Islington Borough Council 1971-78; ILEA: Member 1971-74, Deputy Leader 1973

Lab majority 8,009

House of Commons: Contested Tonbridge and Malling February 1974 general election. Member for Blackburn since 3 May 1979 general election; Opposition Front Bench Spokesman on: Treasury and Economic Affairs 1980-83, Environment 1983-87; Shadow Education Secretary 1987-92; Shadow Environment Secretary 1992-94; Shadow Home Secretary 1994-97; Home Secretary 1997-2001; Foreign Secretary 2001-. *Political interests:* Education, Taxation, Economic Policy, Local and Regional Government, Police, European Union

Member, Labour Party National Executive Committee 1994-95. Joint Vice-Chair, British-American Parliamentary International Group 1999-; *Publications: Policy and Ideology*, 1993; PC 1997; Visiting fellow, Nuffield College, Oxford 1990-98; Hon. LLD, Leeds University 1999; *Clubs:* Hon Vice-President Blackburn Rovers FC 1998; *Recreations:* Cooking, walking, music, watching Blackburn Rovers

Rt Hon Jack Straw, MP, House of Commons, London SW1A 0AA
Tel: 020 7219 5070. *Constituency:* Richmond Chambers, Richmond Road, Blackburn, Lancashire BB1 7AS *Tel:* 01254 52317 *Fax:* 01254 682213

STREETER, GARY
South West Devon

Gary Streeter. Born 2 October 1955; Son of Kenneth Victor, farmer, and Shirley Streeter; Educated Tiverton Grammar School; King's College, London (LLB 1977); Married Janet Vanessa Stevens 1978 (1 son 1 daughter). Solicitor; Partner, Foot and Bowden, Plymouth 1984-98, specialist in company and employment law; Plymouth City Council: Councillor 1986-92, Chairman, Housing Committee 1989-91

Con majority 10,141

House of Commons: Member for Plymouth Sutton 1992-97, and for South West Devon since 1 May 1997 general election; Opposition Spokesperson for: Foreign Affairs 1997-98, Europe 1997-98; Assistant Government Whip 1995-96; PPS: to Sir Derek Spencer as Solicitor General 1993-95, to Sir Nicholas Lyell as Attorney-General 1994-95; Parliamentary Secretary, Lord Chancellor's Department 1996-97; Shadow Secretary of State for International Development 1998-2001; Shadow Minister for Foreign Affairs 2003-. *Political interests:* Law and Order, Family Moral and Social Affairs, Developing World

Chair board of directors governing council Conservative Christian Fellowship; Vice-Chair Conservative Party 2001-02. *Recreations:* Watching cricket and rugby, family

Gary Streeter, MP, House of Commons, London SW1A 0AA *Tel:* 020 7219 4070
Fax: 020 7219 2414 *E-mail:* mail@garystreeter.co.uk.
Constituency: Tel: 01752 335666 *Fax:* 01752 338401
Website: www.garystreeter.co.uk

STRINGER, GRAHAM
Manchester Blackley

Graham Stringer. Born 17 February 1950; Son of late Albert Stringer, railway clerk, and Brenda Stringer, shop assistant; Educated Moston Brook High School; Sheffield University (BSc chemistry 1971); Married Kathryn Carr 1999 (1 son 1 stepson 1 stepdaughter). Analytical chemist; Chair of Board, Manchester Airport plc 1996-97; Branch officer and shop steward, MSF; Councillor, Manchester City Council 1979-98, Leader 1984-96

Lab majority 12,027

House of Commons: Member for Manchester Blackley since 1 May 1997 general election; Government Whip 2001-02; Parliamentary Secretary, Cabinet Office 1999-2001. *Political interests:* Urban Regeneration, House of Lords Reform, Revitalising Local Democracy, New Aviation and Airports

Hon. RNCM; *Clubs:* Member: Manchester Tennis and Racquet Club, Cheetham Hill Cricket Club

Graham Stringer, MP, House of Commons, London SW1A 0AA
Tel: 020 7219 6055 *E-mail:* stringerg@parliament.uk. *Constituency:* Constituency Office, 4th Floor, Mancat Moston Campus, Ashley Lane, Manchester M9 4WU
Tel: 0161-202 6600 *Fax:* 0161-202 6626

STUART, GISELA
Birmingham Edgbaston

Gisela Gschaider Stuart. Born 26 November 1955; Daughter of late Martin Gschaider and Liane Krompholz; Educated Realschule Vilsbiburg; Manchester Polytechnic; London University (LLB); Married Robert Scott Stuart 1980 (divorced 2000) (2 sons). Deputy Director, London Book Fair 1983; Translator; Lawyer and lecturer, Worcester College of Technology and Birmingham University 1992-1997; Member, AMICUS

Lab majority 2,349

House of Commons: Member for Birmingham Edgbaston since 1 May 1997 general election; PPS to Paul Boateng as Minister of State, Home Office 1998-99; Parliamentary Under-Secretary of State, Department of Health 1999-2001; Parliamentary representative Convention on Future of Europe 2002-05. *Political interests:* Pension Law, Constitutional Reform, European Union

Publications: The Making of Europe's Constitution Fabia Society 2003

Gisela Stuart, MP, House of Commons, London SW1A 0AA *Tel:* 020 7219 5051 *E-mail:* stuartg@parliament.uk. *Constituency: Tel:* 0121-428 5011 *Fax:* 0121-428 5073

STUART, GRAHAM
Beverley and Holderness

Graham Charles Stuart. Born 12 March 1962; Educated Glenalmond College, Perthshire; Selwyn College, Cambridge (BA law/philosophy 1985); Married Anne Crawshaw. Sole proprietor Go Enterprises 1984; Managing director CSL Publishing Ltd 1987; Director Marine Publishing Co Ltd 1999-; Cambridge City Council: Councillor 1998, Leader Conservative Group 2000

Con majority 2,580

House of Commons: Contested Cambridge 2001 general election. Member for Beverley and Holderness since 5 May 2005 general election.

Graham Stuart, MP, House of Commons, London SW1A 0AA *Tel:* 020 7219 4340. *Constituency:* 9 Cross Street, Beverley HU17 9AX *Tel:* 01482 881316 *Fax:* 01482 861667 *E-mail:* tory@bevhold.fsnet.co.uk *Website:* www.beverleyandholdernessconservatives.com

STUNELL, ANDREW
Hazel Grove

Lib Dem majority 7,748

(Robert) Andrew Stunell. Born 24 November 1942; Son of late Robert George Stunell and Trixie Stunell; Educated Surbiton Grammar School; Manchester University (architecture RIBA Pt. II exemption 1963); Liverpool Polytechnic; Married Gillian Chorley 1967 (3 sons 2 daughters). Architectural assistant: CWS Manchester 1965-67, Runcorn New Town 1967-81; Freelance architectural assistant 1981-85; Various posts including political secretary, Association of Liberal Democrat Councillors (ALDC) 1985-97, Head of Service 1989-96; Member, NALGO: New Towns Whitley Council 1977-81; Councillor: Chester City Council 1979-90, Cheshire County Council 1981-91, Stockport Metropolitan Borough Council 1994-2002

House of Commons: Contested City of Chester 1979, 1983, 1987, Hazel Grove 1992 general elections. Member for Hazel Grove since 1 May 1997 general election; Liberal Democrat Spokesperson for Energy 1997-; Deputy Chief Whip 1997-2001; Chief Whip 2001-. *Political interests:* Local Democracy and Regional Devolution, Third World, Race Relations, Energy, Climate Change. All

Various local and national party offices 1977-; Member: Liberal Democrat Federal Executive Committee 2001-, Liberal Democrat Federal Conference Committee 2001-. Vice-chair, Association of County Councils 1985-90; Vice-president, Local Government Association 1997-; *Publications: Life In The Balance*, 1986; *Budgeting For Real*, 1984, 2nd edition 1994, 3rd edition 1999; *Thriving In The Balance*, 1995; *Open Active & Effective*, 1995; *Local Democracy Guaranteed*, 1996; *Energy – Clean and Green to 2050*, 1999; *Nuclear Waste-Cleaning up the Mess*, 2001; OBE 1995; OBE; *Recreations:* Theoretical astronomy, camping, table tennis

Andrew Stunell, MP, House of Commons, London SW1A 0AA *Tel:* 020 7219 5223 *Fax:* 020 7219 2302 *E-mail:* stunella@parliament.uk. *Constituency:* Liberal Democrat HQ, 68A Compstall Road, Romiley, Stockport, Greater Manchester SK6 4DE *Tel:* 0161-406 7070 *Fax:* 0161-494 2425

SUTCLIFFE, GERRY
Bradford South

Lab majority 9,167

Gerry Sutcliffe. Born 13 May 1953; Son of Henry and Margaret Sutcliffe; Educated Cardinal Hinsley Grammar School, Bradford; Married Maria Holgate 1972 (3 sons). Salesperson 1969-72; Display advertising, *Bradford Telegraph and Argus* 1972-75; Field printers, Bradford 1975-80; Deputy Branch Secretary, SOGAT/GPMU 1980-94; Member: Yorkshire and Humberside Trade Union Friends of Labour, Regional TUC; Bradford City Council: Councillor 1982-94, Leader 1992-94

House of Commons: Member for Bradford South since 9 June 1994 by-election; Assistant Government Whip 1999-2001; Government Whip 2000-03; PPS to Harriet Harman as Secretary of State for Social Security and Minister for Women 1997-98; PPS to Stephen Byers: as Chief Secretary, HM Treasury July-December 1998, as Secretary of State for Trade and Industry 1999; Parliamentary Under-Secretary of State, Department of Trade and Industry 2003-: Employment Relations, Competition and Consumers 2003-04, Employment Relations, Consumers and Postal Services 2004-. *Political interests:* Employment, Local and Regional Government. Pakistan, Bangladesh, India, European Union

Member, Regional Labour Party Executive; Vice-chair, Yorkshire Regional Group of Labour MPs 1997-. *Recreations:* Sport, music

Gerry Sutcliffe, MP, House of Commons, London SW1A 0AA *Tel:* 020 7219 3247 *Fax:* 020 7219 1227 *E-mail:* sutcliffeg@parliament.uk. *Constituency:* 3rd Floor, 76 Kirkgate, Bradford, West Yorkshire BD1 1SZ *Tel:* 01274 400007 *Fax:* 01274 400020

Con majority 17,285

SWAYNE, DESMOND
New Forest West

Desmond Angus Swayne. Born 20 August 1956; Son of George Joseph Swayne and Elisabeth McAlister Swayne, neé Gibson; Educated Drumley House, Ayrshire; Bedford School; St Mary's College, St Andrews University (MA theology 1980); Married Moira Cecily Teek 1987 (1 son 2 daughters). Major, Territorial Army. Schoolmaster, 'A' level economics: Charterhouse 1980-81, Wrekin College 1982-87; Manager, Risk Management Systems, Royal Bank of Scotland 1988-96

House of Commons: Contested Pontypridd 1987, West Bromwich West 1992 general elections. Member for New Forest West since 1 May 1997 general election; Opposition Spokesperson for: Health 2001, Defence 2001-02; Opposition Whip 2002-03; Shadow Minister for: International Affairs 2003-04, Northern Ireland 2004; PPS to Michael Howard as Leader of the Opposition 2004-

TD; *Clubs:* Cavalry and Guards; Serpentine Swimming Club; *Recreations:* Territorial Army

Desmond Swayne, MP, House of Commons, London SW1A 0AA *Tel:* 020 7219 4886 *E-mail:* desmondswayne@hotmail.com. *Constituency:* 4 Cliff Crescent, Marine Drive, Barton-on-Sea, New Milton, Hampshire BH25 7EB *Tel:* 01425 629844 *Fax:* 01425 621898 *Website:* www.desmondswaynemp.com

Lib Dem majority 4,061

SWINSON, JO
East Dunbartonshire

Jo Swinson. Born 5 February 1980; Educated Douglas Academy, Milngavie, Glasgow; London School of Economics (BSc management 2000); Single. Marketing executive Viking FM 2000-02; Marketing manager Spaceandpeople Ltd 2002-04; Development officer UK Public Health Association Scotland 2004-; Councillor, Milngavie Community Council 2003-

House of Commons: Contested Hull East 2001 general election. Member for East Dunbartonshire since 5 May 2005. *Political interests:* Corporate social responsibility, equality

Liberal Democrat Youth and Students (LDYS): Secretary 1998-99, Vice-chair 1999-2000, Vice-chair campaigns 2000; Vice-chair: Haltemprice and Howden Liberal Democrats 2000, Gender Balance Taskforce 2003. Trustee, Help a Local Child 2001-02; Contested Strathkelvin and Bearsden 2003 Scottish Parliament election; *Recreations:* Hiking, gym, salsa dancing, reading

Jo Swinson, MP, House of Commons, London SW1A 0AA *Tel:* 020 7219 8088. *Constituency:* 20 Keystone Quadrant, Milngavie GG2 6LL *Tel:* 0141 956 6673 *Fax:* 0141 563 7919 *E-mail:* jo@joswinson.org.uk *Website:* www.joswinson.org.uk

SWIRE, HUGO
East Devon

Hugo George William Swire. Born 30 November 1959; Son of late H R Swire and of Marchioness Townshend, neé Montgomerie; Educated St Aubyns; Eton College; St Andrews University; Royal Military Academy Sandhurst; Married Sasha Nott 1996 (2 daughters). Commissioned 1st Battalion Grenadier Guards 1979-83; Joint managing director International News Services and Prospect Films 1983-85; Financial consultant Streets Financial Ltd 1985-87; Head of development National Gallery 1988-92; Sotheby's: Deputy director 1992-97, Director 1997-2003

Con majority 7,936

House of Commons: Contested Greenock and Inverclyde 1997 general election. Member for East Devon since 7 June 2001 general election; Opposition Whip 2003-04; PPS to Theresa May as chairman of the Conservative Party 2003; Shadow Minister for the Arts 2004-. *Political interests:* Arts, Tourism, Field Sports, Agriculture, Architectural Heritage, Defence, Foreign Affairs, Rural Affairs, Northern Ireland, Housing. United Arab Emirates, Lebanon, Oman, Slovenia

Secretary Conservative Middle East Council. Children's hospice, South West; Member European Standing Committee C; Advisory Committee, The Airey Neave Trust; *Clubs:* White's, Pratt's, Beefsteak; *Recreations:* Country pursuits, skiing, tennis, gardening, reading, travel, arts

Hugo Swire, MP, House of Commons, London SW1A 0AA *Tel:* 020 7219 8173
Fax: 020 7219 1895. *Constituency:* 45 Imperial Road, Exmouth, Devon EX8 1DQ
Tel: 01395 264 251 *Fax:* 01395 272 205
E-mail: office@eastdevonconservatives.org.uk
Website: www.eastdevonconservatives.org.uk

SYMS, ROBERT
Poole

Robert Andrew Raymond Syms. Born 15 August 1956; Son of Raymond Syms, builder, and Mary Syms, teacher; Educated Colston's School, Bristol; Married Nicola Guy 1991 (divorced 1999); married Fiona Mellersh 2000 (1 daughter 1 son). Director, family building, plant hire and property group, based in Chippenham, Wiltshire 1978-; Councillor: North Wiltshire District Council 1983-87, Wiltshire County Council 1985-97; Member, Wessex Regional Health Authority 1988-90

Con majority 5,988

House of Commons: Contested Walsall North 1992 general election. Member for Poole since 1 May 1997 general election; Opposition Spokesperson for Environment, Transport and Regions 1999-2001; Opposition Whip 2003; PPS to Michael Ancram as Chair Conservative Party 1999-2000; Shadow Minister for Local and Devolved Government Affairs 2003-. *Political interests:* Economic Policy, Constitution, Local and Regional Government. USA, most of English speaking world

North Wiltshire Conservative Association: Treasurer 1982-84, Deputy Chair 1983-84, Chair 1984-86; Vice-Chair Conservative Party 2001-03. Member, Calne Development Project Trust 1986-97; *Recreations:* Reading, music

Robert Syms, MP, House of Commons, London SW1A 0AA *Tel:* 020 7219 4601.
Constituency: Poole Conservative Association, 38 Sandbanks Road, Poole,
Dorset BH14 8BX *Tel:* 01202 739922 *Fax:* 01202 739944 *E-mail:* dhector@tory.org

TAMI, MARK
Alyn and Deeside

Mark Richard Tami. Born 3 October 1962; Son of Michael John Tami and Patricia Tami; Educated Enfield Grammar School; Swansea University (BA history 1985); Married Sally Ann Daniels 1994 (2 sons). AEEU: Head of research and communications 1992-99, Head of policy 1999-2001; Member AEEU 1986-; Member TUC General Council 1999-2001

House of Commons: Member for Alyn and Deeside since 7 June 2001 general

Lab majority 8,378   election. *Political interests:* Manufacturing, Aerospace, Small Businesses

Treasurer, Labour Friends of Australia. Member European Standing Committee B 2003-; *Publications:* Co-author *Votes for All*, Fabian Society pamphlet, 2000; *Clubs:* Glamorgan County Cricket; *Recreations:* Football (Norwich City), cricket, fishing, antiques

Mark Tami, MP, House of Commons, London SW1A 0AA *Tel:* 020 7219 8174 *Fax:* 020 7219 1943 *E-mail:* tamim@parliament.uk. *Constituency:* Deeside Enterprise Centre, Rowleys Drive, Shotton, Deeside CH5 1PP *Tel:* 01244 819854 *Fax:* 01244 823548

TAPSELL, PETER
Louth and Horncastle

Peter H B Tapsell. Born 1 February 1930; Son of late Eustace Tapsell and late Jessie Tapsell (neé Hannay); Educated Tonbridge School; Merton College, Oxford (BA modern history 1953, MA); Diploma in Economics 1954; Married The Hon. Cecilia Hawke, daughter of 9th Baron Hawke 1963 (divorced 1971) (1 son deceased); married Gabrielle Mahieu 1974. Subaltern Army national service in Middle East 1948-50; Royal Sussex Regiment. Personal Assistant to Prime Minister (Anthony

Con majority 9,896   Eden) 1955; Member, London Stock Exchange 1957-90; Adviser to central banks and international companies 1960-; Partner, James Capel and Co 1960-90

House of Commons: Contested Wednesbury February 1957 by-election. Member for Nottingham West 1959-64, for Horncastle 1966-83, for Lindsey East 1983-97, and for Louth and Horncastle since 1 May 1997 general election; Opposition Frontbench Spokesperson for: Foreign and Commonwealth Affairs 1976-77, Treasury and Economic Affairs 1977-78. *Political interests:* Foreign Affairs, Economics and Finance. Third World

Longest serving Conservative MP; Member: Trilateral Commission 1979-98, Business Advisory Council of the UN, International Investment Advisory Board to Brunei Government 1976-83; Hon Deputy Chair, Mitsubishi Trust Oxford Foundation; Brunei Dato 1971; Hon Life Member 6th Squadron RAF 1971; Knighted 1985; Spectator Backbencher of the Year 1993; Honorary Postmaster, Merton College, Oxford 1953; Honorary Fellow, Merton College, Oxford 1989; *Clubs:* Athenaeum, Carlton, Hurlingham; *Recreations:* Overseas travel, walking in mountains, reading, history

Sir Peter Tapsell, MP, House of Commons, London SW1A 0AA *Tel:* 020 7219 4477 *Fax:* 020 7219 0976. *Constituency:* Cannon Street House, Cannon Street, Louth, Lincolnshire *Tel:* 01507 609840 *Fax:* 01507 608091

TAYLOR, DARI
Stockton South

Dari (Daria Jean) Taylor. Born 13 December 1944; Daughter of late Daniel Jones, MP for Burnley 1959-83, and late Phyllis Jones; Educated Ynyshir Girls' School; Burnley Municipal College; Nottingham University (BA politics); Durham University (MA social policy); Married David E Taylor 1970 (1 daughter). Assistant lecturer, Basford College of Further Education 1970-71; Lecturer, Westbridgeford College of Further Education 1971-81; Lecturer (PT), North Tyneside College of Further Education 1986-87; General Municipal and Boilermakers 1990: Research Support 1990, Regional Education Officer, Northern Region 1993-97; Regional/Local Representative NATFHE; Member, General Municipal and Boilermakers (GMB); Trade Union Support and Information Unit; Councillor, Sunderland Metropolitan Council 1986-97

Lab majority 6,139

House of Commons: Member for Stockton South since 1 May 1997 general election; PPS to: Parliamentary Under Secretaries Lewis Moonie and Lord Bach, Ministry of Defence 2001-03, Hazel Blears as Minister of State, Home Office 2003-. *Political interests:* Economic Policy, Industry, Education, Housing, Defence. Europe, Africa, USA

Leadership Campaign Team. *Recreations:* Choral singing, walking, travelling

Dari Taylor, MP, House of Commons, London SW1A 0AA *Tel:* 020 7219 4608 *Fax:* 020 7219 6876 *E-mail:* webstera@parliament.uk. *Constituency:* 109 Lanehouse Road, Thornaby on Tees TS17 8AB *Tel:* 01642 604546 *Fax:* 01642 608395

TAYLOR, DAVID
North West Leicestershire

David Leslie Taylor. Born 22 August 1946; Son of late Leslie Taylor, civil servant, and Eileen Mary Taylor, retired postal worker; Educated Ashby-de-la-Zouch Boys Grammar School; Leicester Polytechnic and Lanchester Polytechnic (Chartered Public Finance Accountant 1970); Open University (BA maths and computing 1974); Married Pamela Caunt 1969 (4 daughters 1 son deceased). Accountant and Computer Manager, Leicestershire County Council 1977-97; Department steward and auditor, NALGO (now UNISON) 1985-97; Councillor, North West Leicestershire District Council 1981-87, 1992-95; Councillor, Heather Parish Council 1987-2003, Chair 1996-97, 2001-02; JP, Ashby-de-la-Zouch 1985-

Lab/Co-op majority 4,477

House of Commons: Contested North West Leicestershire 1992 general election. Member for North West Leicestershire since 1 May 1997 general election. *Political interests:* Housing, Low Pay, Rural Affairs, Environment, Safer Communities (Crime), Small Businesses. France

Member, Labour Campaign for Electoral Reform. *Clubs:* Ibstock Working Mens; Coalville Labour; Hugglescote Working Mens; Ibstock Town Cricket; President, Heather Sparkenhoe Cricket Club; *Recreations:* Running, Cycling

David Taylor, MP, House of Commons, London SW1A 0AA *Tel:* 020 7219 4567 *Fax:* 020 7219 6808 *E-mail:* taylordl@parliament.uk. *Constituency:* Labour Office, 17 Hotel Street, Coalville, Leicestershire LE67 3EQ *Tel:* 01530 814372 *Fax:* 01530 813833

Con majority 7,727

TAYLOR, IAN
Esher and Walton

Ian Colin Taylor. Born 18 April 1945; Son of late Horace Stanley Taylor and late Beryl Harper; Educated Whitley Abbey School, Coventry; Keele University (BA economics, politics and modern history 1967); London School of Economics (research scholar 1967-69); Married Hon Carole Alport 1974 (2 sons). Hill Samuel & Co 1969-71; Stirling & Co 1971-75; Banque Pommier, Paris 1975-76; Shenley International Finance 1976-80; Director, Mathercourt Securities Ltd 1980-91; Corporate Finance Consultant; Executive Director, Interregnum PLC; Director: Next Fifteen Group PLC, Screen PLC, Radioscape Ltd, Speed-Trap Ltd

House of Commons: Contested Coventry South East 1974 general election. Member for Esher 1987-97, and for Esher and Walton since 1 May 1997 general election; Opposition Spokesperson for Northern Ireland June-November 1997; PPS to William Waldegrave as: Minister of State, Foreign and Commonwealth Office 1988-90, as Secretary of State for Health 1990-92, as Chancellor of the Duchy of Lancaster, Minister for Public Services and Science 1992-94; Parliamentary Under Secretary of State, Department of Trade and Industry (Minister for Science and Technology) 1994-97. *Political interests:* European Union, Economy, Science and Technology. Former Soviet Union, France, Germany, Middle East, Scandinavia, USA

National Chair, Federation of Conservative Students 1968-69; Chair, European Union of Christian Democratic and Conservative Students 1969-70; Member, Conservative National Union Executive and other national committees 1966-75, 1990-95; National Chair, Conservative Group for Europe 1985-88; Vice-Chair, Association of Conservative Clubs 1988-92; Chair: Conservative Foreign and Commonwealth Council 1990-95, Tory Europe Network 2003-. Various constituency charities, Help the Aged (Research into Ageing), Princess Alice Hospice (Esher); Member, Finance Bill Standing Committees 1987-94; Board Member, Parliamentary Office of Science and Technology (POST) 1997-; Council Member, Parliamentary Information Technology Committee; Director, EURIM (European Informatics Market) 1999-; Chair: European Movement 2001-, Tory Europe Network 2002-; Adviser, Broadband Stakeholders Group 2002-04; Trustee: Painshill Park Trust 1998-, Centre of the Cell 2004-; *Publications: Fair Shares for all the Workers*, 1988; *Releasing the Community Spirit – The Active Citizen*, 1990; *A Community of Employee Shareholders*, 1992; *The Positive Europe*, 1993; *Escaping the Protectionist Trap*, 1995; *Net-Working*, 1996; *Conservative Tradition in Europe*, 1996; *Science, Government and Society*, 1998; *Restoring the Balance*, 2000; *Full Steam Ahead*, 2001; *Federal Britain in a Federal Europe*, 2001; *Europe: Our Case*, 2002; *Shaping The New Europe – The British Opportunity (EUW) 2002; Twin Towers: Europe and America (TEN) 2003; Corporate Social Responsibility – Should Business be Socially Aware (TRG) 2003*; MBE 1974; MBE; Worshipful Company of Information Technologists 1998-; MBE; *Clubs:* Buck's, IOD, Commonwealth; MBE; *Recreations:* Country walks, shooting, cigars, opera

Ian Taylor, MP, House of Commons, London SW1A 0AA *Tel:* 020 7219 5221 *Fax:* 020 7219 5492 *E-mail:* taylori@parliament.uk. *Constituency:* Cheltonian House, Portsmouth Road, Esher, Surrey KT10 9SD *Tel:* 01372 469105 *Fax:* 01372 469091 *Website:* www.esherwalton.com

TAYLOR, MATTHEW
Truro and St Austell

Matthew Owen John Taylor. Born 3 January 1963; Son of Ken Taylor, TV author, and Jill Taylor, née Black; Educated Treliske School, Truro; University College School, London; Lady Margaret Hall, Oxford (BA politics, philosophy and economics 1986, MA); Single. Sabbatical President, Oxford University Student Union 1985-86; Economic policy researcher, Parliamentary Liberal Party, attached to David Penhaligan MP 1986-87

Lib Dem majority
7,403

House of Commons: Member for Truro 12 March 1987 by-election -1997 and for Truro and St Austell since 1 May 1997 general election; Liberal Spokesperson for Energy 1987-88; Liberal Democrat Spokesperson for: England (Local Government, Housing and Transport) 1988-89, Trade and Industry 1989-90, Education 1990-92, Citizen's Charter 1992-94; Principal Spokesperson for: Environment 1994-97, the Environment and Transport 1997-99, Economy 1999-2003; Chair Liberal Democrat Parliamentary Party 2003-

Chair, Liberal Democrat Campaigns and Communications 1989-95

Matthew Taylor, MP, House of Commons, London SW1A 0AA *Tel:* 020 7219 6686 *Fax:* 020 7219 4903 *E-mail:* bucknalls@parliament.uk. *Constituency:* Liberal Democrats, 10 South Street, St Austell, Cornwall PL25 5BH *Tel:* 01726 63443 *Fax:* 01726 68457

TAYLOR, RICHARD
Wyre Forest

Richard Thomas Taylor. Born 7 July 1934; Son of Thomas Taylor, cotton spinner and Mabel Taylor, née Hickley; Educated The Leys School, Cambridge; Clare College, Cambridge (BA natural sciences 1956); Westminster Medical School (BChir 1959, MB 1960); Married Elizabeth Ann Brett 1962 (divorced 1986) (2 daughters 1 son); married Christine Helen Miller 1990 (1 daughter). Medical officer RAF 1961-64. House physician and surgeon 1959-61; St Stephen's Hospital, London: Senior house physician 1964-65, Medical registrar 1965-66; Westminster Hospital: Medical registrar 1966-67, Senior medical registrar 1967-72; Consultant in general medicine with special interest in rheumatology Kidderminster General Hospital and Droitwich Centre for Rheumatic Diseases 1972-95; BMA 1959-2001

Ind KHHC majority
5,250

House of Commons: Member for Wyre Forest since 7 June 2001 general election. *Political interests:* National Health Service

UNICEF; Worcester Wildlife Trust; *Publications:* Papers on drug treatment of rheumatic diseases etc in various medical journals 1968-73; *Recreations:* Family, ornithology, gardening, classic cars

Dr Richard Taylor, MP, House of Commons, London SW1A 0AA
Tel: 020 7219 4598 *Fax:* 020 7219 1967 *E-mail:* pricemah@parliament.uk.
Constituency: Gavel House, 137 Franche Road, Kidderminster DY11 5AP
Tel: 01562 753333

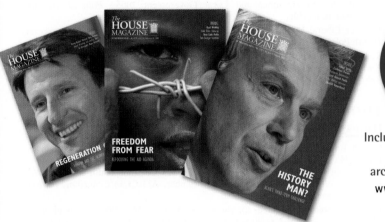

TEATHER, SARAH
Brent East

Sarah Teather. Born 1 June 1974; Educated St John's College, Cambridge (BA pharmacology). Policy Analyst, Macmillan Fund for Cancer Relief; Councillor, London Borough of Islington 2002-03

House of Commons: Contested Finchley and Golders Green 2001 general election. Member for Brent East since 18 September 2003 by-election; Liberal Democrat Spokesperson for: Health 2004, London 2004-; Liberal Democrat Shadow Secretary of State for Communities and Local Government 2005-. *Political interests:* Environment, Health

Lib Dem majority
2,712

Member Liberal Democrat National Policy Committee; Chair Liberal Democrat Health Policy Working Group

Sarah Teather, MP, House of Commons, London SW1A 0AA *Tel:* 020 7219 8147 *E-mail:* teathers@parliament.uk. *Constituency:* 82 Walm Lane, London NW2 4R *Tel:* 020 8459 0455 *Fax:* 020 8830 3280 *Website:* www.brentlibdems.org.uk

THOMAS, GARETH
Harrow West

Gareth Richard Thomas. Born 15 July 1967; Educated Hatch End High School; Lowlands College; University College of Wales, Aberystwyth (BSc (Econ) politics 1988); King's College, London (MA imperial and Commonwealth studies 1996); University of Greenwich (PGCE 1992); Member, AMICUS; Councillor, Harrow 1990-97, Labour Group Whip 1996-96

House of Commons: Member for Harrow West since 1 May 1997 general election; Member Environmental Audit Select Committee 1997-99; PPS to Charles Clarke: as Minister of State, Home Office 1999-2001, as Minister without Portfolio and Party Chair 2001-02, as Secretary of State for Education and Skills 2002-03; Sponsored Private Member's Bill, Industrial and Provident Societies Bill 2002; Parliamentary Under-Secretary of State, Department for International Development 2003-. *Political interests:* Energy, Mutuals, Health, Environment. Europe, Norway, India, Sri Lanka, Pakistan

Lab/Co-op majority
2,028

Member: Fabian Society, SERA; Chair Co-operative Party 2000-. Vice-Chair, Association of Local Government Social Services Committee; *Publications: At the Energy Crossroads* Policies for a Low Carbon Economy, Fabian Society, June 2001; *From Margins to Mainstream – Making Social Resposibility Part of Corporate Culture*, 2002; *Clubs:* United Services Club, Pinner; *Recreations:* Canoeing, running, rugby union

Gareth Thomas, MP, House of Commons, London SW1A 0AA *Tel:* 020 7219 4243 *E-mail:* thomasgr@parliament.uk. *Constituency:* 132 Blenheim Road, West Harrow HA2 7AA *Tel:* 020 8861 6300

Taking a Risk – Sexual and Reproductive Health in Africa

When a poor woman in Africa becomes pregnant her life is at risk. In fact maternal mortality rates in Africa are the highest in the world and complications of pregnancy and childbirth the leading cause of death and disability for women of childbearing age. It is estimated that every year approximately 250,000 women die in Africa as a direct result of becoming pregnant.

A woman in sub-Saharan Africa has a lifetime risk of one in sixteen of dying from such complications, and in some African countries the risk is even as high as one in six. And there appears to be little sign that the situation is improving. In Kenya for instance, the figure for maternal deaths has risen instead of fallen over the last five years. In Ethiopia 90 per cent of all births are not attended by a trained midwife, while Sierra Leone has the highest maternal mortality rate in the world with 2,000 maternal deaths per 100,000 live births.

The situation is exacerbated by the prevalence of sexually transmitted infections and HIV/AIDS. With 76 percent of all young people living with HIV being female, the UN Secretary General has been moved to claim that HIV/AIDS in Sub-Saharan Africa has indeed a woman's face. Other diseases such as malaria also have devastating effects for pregnant women and their unborn children causing prenatal deaths, low birth weight and maternal anaemia. The poor health of a mother or her premature death not only has detrimental effects on the survival chances of infants, it impacts on the economic viability of families, perpetuating a vicious cycle of poverty. But simply by providing adequate and appropriate information on sexual and reproductive health and making services and supplies universally accessible, a substantial step could be made towards eliminating poverty in the region.

In 2000 the international community embarked on an ambitious plan to achieve eight Millennium Development Goals (MDGs) to tackle global poverty. Reviewing progress made so far in attaining those goals, an expert team presented its report "Investing in Development: A practical Plan to Achieve the Millennium Development Goals" to the UN Secretary General in January 2005. This report clearly identifies access to sexual and reproductive health information and services as vital to making headway in reducing global poverty. Yet the MDGs do not include a specific goal on sexual and reproductive health and the three goals directly related to sexual and reproductive health – reducing child mortality, improving maternal health and combating HIV/AIDS tuberculosis, malaria and other diseases – are those least likely to be met by the 2015 deadline, particularly in Sub-Saharan Africa.

African leaders are thus calling for the comprehensive provision of adequate and appropriate services for sexual and reproductive health. African Health Ministers have demanded that Africa's framework for economic and social recovery, the New Partnership for Africa's Development, incorporates sexual and reproductive health and the African Union has promised an action plan to provide the urgently needed information and services by October of this year. These concerns have been echoed in the Commission for Africa Report, published in March, which recommends that "African governments show strong leadership in promoting women's and men's right to sexual and reproductive health". But it is not African leaders alone who are called upon to act.

Within the next decade Africa will see the largest number of women of childbearing age ever. Unless there is greater access to contraception, antenatal care and skilled attendance at delivery, safe abortion and post-abortion care, maternal deaths in Sub-Saharan Africa will continue to rise.

Strong political commitment on the part of national governments and the international donor community is called for. In the UK, the Department for International Development (DFID) has underscored its commitment to upholding women's right to safe motherhood and has allocated £500 million annually over the next three years for the fight against HIV/AIDS and to promote sexual and reproductive health. The challenge now will be to ensure international commitment within the European Union and at the United Nations. Only thus can a cycle of poverty in Africa be broken and the tragic and unnecessary deaths of hundreds of thousands of mothers and infants each year be averted.

MARIE STOPES INTERNATIONAL
www.mariestopes.org.uk

Lab majority 484

THORNBERRY, EMILY
Islington South and Finsbury

Emily Thornberry. Born 27 July 1960; Educated Kent University, Canterbury (BA law 1982); Married Christopher Nugee 1992. Member Mike Mansfield's Chambers: Tooks Court 1985; Member TGWU (ACTS) 1985

House of Commons: Member for Islington South and Finsbury since 5 May 2005 general election

Member Labour Party's London Regional Board 2000. Campaigns director in sabbatical year 1998-99; *Recreations:* Family, cycling, travel

Emily Thornberry, MP, House of Commons, London SW1A 0AA
Tel: 020 7219 5676. *Constituency:* 65 Barnsbury Street, Islington, London N1 1EK
Tel: 0207 6078373 *E-mail:* emily@islingtonlabour.org.uk

Lib Dem majority 8,168

THURSO, JOHN
Caithness, Sutherland and Easter Ross

John Archibald Sinclair Thurso. Born 10 September 1953; Son of late Robin, 2nd Viscount Thurso and Margaret, née Robertson; succeeded his father 1995 as 3rd Viscount Thurso and 6th Bt of Ulbster; Educated Eton College; Westminster Technical College (HCIMA membership exam 1974); Married Marion Ticknor, née Sage 1976 (2 sons 1 daughter). Director: Lancaster Hotel 1981-85, Cliveden House Ltd 1985-93; Non-executive director, Savoy Hotel plc 1993-98; Managing director Fitness and Leisure Holdings Ltd 1995-2001; Chair: Thurso Fisheries Ltd 1995-, Scrabster Harbour Trust 1996-2001; Director: Profile Recruitment and Management Ltd 1996-2002, Walker Greenbank plc 1997-2002, Anton Mosiman Ltd 1997-2002; Deputy Chairman, Millennium and Copthorn's Hotels plc 2002-

House of Commons: Member for Caithness, Sutherland and Easter Ross 2001-05, for new Caithness, Sutherland and Easter Ross since 5 May 2005 general election; Liberal Democrat Lords spokesperson for: Tourism 1996-99, Food 1998-99; Scottish Liberal Democrat Spokesperson on Tourism 2001-; Liberal Democrat Spokesperson for Scotland 2001-03; Liberal Democrat Whip 2001-02; Liberal Democrat Shadow Secretary of State for Transport and Scotland 2003-. *Political interests:* Tourism, House of Lords Reform

Member Liberal Democrat Party Federal Policy Committee 1999-2001. First former hereditary member of House of Lords to become an MP; *Publications: Tourism Tomorrow*, 1998; Liveryman Innholders' Company 1997; Freeman City of London 1991; *Clubs:* Brook's, New Edinburgh

John Thurso, MP, House of Commons, London SW1A 0AA *Tel:* 020 7219 8154
Fax: 020 7219 3797 *E-mail:* thursoj@parliament.uk. *Constituency:* Thurso East Mains, Thurso KW14 8HN *Tel:* 01847 892600

Lab majority 13,155

TIMMS, STEPHEN
East Ham

Stephen Timms. Born 29 July 1955; Son of late Ronald James Timms, engineer, and of Margaret Joyce Timms, retired school teacher; Educated Farnborough Grammar School, Hampshire; Emmanuel College, Cambridge (MA mathematics 1977, MPhil operational research 1978); Married Hui-Leng Lim 1986. Computer and telecommunications industry; Logica Ltd 1978-86; Ovum Ltd 1986-94; Member, MSF; London Borough of Newham: Councillor 1984-97, Leader of the Council 1990-94, Former Chair, Economic Development Committee, Chair, Planning Committee 1987-90; Board Member, East London Partnership (now East London Business Alliance) 1990-; Stratford Development Partnership 1992-94; Chair, Race Education and Employment Forum

House of Commons: Member for Newham North East from 9 June 1994 by-election-1997, and for East Ham since 1 May 1997 general election; PPS to Andrew Smith as Minister of State, Department for Education and Employment 1997-98; Joint PPS to Marjorie Mowlam, as Secretary of State for Northern Ireland 1998; Parliamentary Under-Secretary of State, Department of Social Security 1998-99, Minister of State 1999; Financial Secretary, HM Treasury 1999-2001; Minister of State: For School Standards, Department for Education and Skills 2001-02, For Energy, E-Commerce and Postal Services, Department of Trade and Industry 2002-04; Financial Secretary, HM Treasury 2004-05; Minister of State (Pensions), Department for Work and Pensions 2005-. *Political interests:* Economic Policy, Urban Regeneration, Telecommunications, Employment, Christian Socialism Joint Vice-Chair, Christian Socialist Movement 1995-98. *Publications: Broadband Communications: The Commercial Impact*, 1987; Honorary doctorate

Stephen Timms, MP, House of Commons, London SW1A 0AA *Tel:* 020 7219 4000 *Fax:* 020 7219 2949 *E-mail:* stephen@stephentimmsmp.org.uk. *Constituency: Website:* www.stephentimmsmp.org.uk

Lab majority 6,652

TIPPING, PADDY
Sherwood

Paddy Tipping. Born 24 October 1949; Son of late Ernest Tipping, newsagent, and late Margaret Tipping, clerk; Educated Hipperholme Grammar School; Nottingham University (BA philosophy 1972, MA applied social science 1978); Married Irene Margaret Quinn 1970 (2 daughters). Social worker, Nottingham and Nottinghamshire 1972-79; Project Leader, Church of England Children's Society, Nottingham 1979-83; Member, UNISON; Councillor, Nottinghamshire County Council 1981-93; Director: Nottinghamshire Co-operative Development Agency 1983-93, Nottingham Development Enterprise 1987-93

House of Commons: Contested Rushcliffe 1987 general election. Member for Sherwood since 9 April 1992 general election; PPS to Jack Straw as Home Secretary 1997-99; Parliamentary Secretary, Privy Council Office 1999-2001. *Political interests:* Local and Regional Government, Energy, Education, Police, Workers' Co-operatives, Rural Affairs, Agriculture, Environment. Former Soviet Union

Member, Co-operative Party; Chair: Central Region Group of Labour MPs 1997-2001, East Midlands Group of Labour MPs until 1999. Member: Industry and Parliament Trust, Armed Forces Parliamentary Trust; *Clubs:* Clipstone Miners' Welfare; *Recreations:* Family, gardening, running, walking

Paddy Tipping, MP, House of Commons, London SW1A 0AA *Tel:* 020 7219 5044 *Fax:* 020 7219 3641. *Constituency:* Sherwood Parliamentary Office, 1st Floor, Council Offices, Watnall Road, Hucknall, Nottinghamshire NG15 7LA *Tel:* 0115-964 0314 *Fax:* 0115-968 1639

Look in to our world of financial education

Institute of Financial Services (*ifs*)

◆ Internationally recognized qualifications for the industry and consumers
◆ Training and accreditation services
◆ Tailored solutions for industry

institute of
financial services

School of Finance

T 01227 818609
W www.ifslearning.com

The *ifs* is the official brand of The Chartered Institute of Bankers, a registered charity.

TODD, MARK
South Derbyshire

Mark Wainwright Todd. Born 29 December 1954; Son of Matthew and Viv Todd; Educated Sherborne School; Emmanuel College, Cambridge (BA history 1976); Married Sarah Margaret Dawson 1979 (1 son). Longman Group, latterly Addison Wesley Longman 1977-96: Managing Director: Longman Industry and Public Service Management 1988-92, Longman Cartermill 1990-92, Director: Information Technology 1992-94, Operations 1994-96; ASTMS (now AMICUS), union chairman at employers; Cambridge City Council 1980-92: Deputy Leader 1982-87, Leader of Council 1987-90

Lab majority 4,495

House of Commons: Member for South Derbyshire since 1 May 1997 general election; PPS to Baroness Symons of Vernham Dean as Deputy Leader of the Lords and Minister of State, FCO and DTI 2002-. *Political interests:* Business, Economics, Local and Regional Government, Environment, Agriculture, Transport. Europe, Third World

Director, Cambridge and District Co-operative Society 1986-89; *Recreations:* Reading, cinema

Mark Todd, MP, House of Commons, London SW1A 0AA *Tel:* 020 7219 3549 *Fax:* 020 7219 4935 *E-mail:* toddm@parliament.uk. *Constituency:* 37 Market Street, Church Gresley, Swadlincote, Derbyshire DE11 9PR *Tel:* 01283 551573 *Fax:* 01283 210640

TOUHIG, DON
Islwyn

Don (James Donnelly) Touhig. Born 5 December 1947; Son of late Michael and Catherine Touhig; Educated St Francis School, Abersychan; Mid Gwent College; Married Jennifer Hughes 1968 (2 sons 2 daughters). Journalist 1968-76; Editor, Free Press of Monmouthshire 1976-90; General manager and editor in chief, Free Press Group of Newspapers 1988-92; General manager (business development), Bailey Group 1992-93, Bailey Print 1993-95; Member, TGWU; Councillor, Gwent County Council 1973-95; Chair, Finance Committee 1992-94

Lab/Co-op majority 15,740

House of Commons: Contested Richmond and Barnes 1992 general election. Member for Islwyn since 16 February 1995 by-election; Assistant Government Whip 1999-2001; Public Interest Disclosure (Private Member's Bill) 1995; PPS to Gordon Brown as Chancellor of the Exchequer 1997-99; Parliamentary Under-Secretary of State: Wales Office 2001-05, Ministry of Defence 2005-. *Political interests:* Treasury, Employment, Health, Education, Local and Regional Government

Hon. Secretary, Welsh Regional Group of Labour MPs 1995-99; Member, Labour Leadership Campaign Team (responsible for Devolution in Wales) 1996-97; Member, Co-Operative Party; Chair, Co-operative Parliamentary Group 1999. St David's Foundation; Member, European Standing Committee B 1995-96; Trustee, Medical Council on Alcoholism; Papal Knight of the Order of St Sylvester; *Recreations:* Reading, cooking for family and friends, music, walking

Don Touhig, MP, House of Commons, London SW1A 0AA *Tel:* 020 7219 6435 *Fax:* 020 7219 2070 *E-mail:* touhigd@parliament.uk. *Constituency:* 6 Woodfieldside Business Park, Penmaen Road, Pontllanfraith, Blackwood, Gwent NP12 2DG *Tel:* 01495 231990 *Fax:* 01495 231959

Time for recognition

As we commemorate 60 years since the end of the second world war, RNID is fighting for justice for veterans deafened during and since that conflict, right up to the Iraq war. Our campaign seeks fair compensation for all ex servicemen and women whose hearing has been damaged while serving in the armed forces.

- British veterans have to experience a very high level of hearing loss in order to qualify for compensation. This is much higher than in other countries.

- Scientists agree that the system is unfair.

In 1996 Tony Blair described the system as **"shabby and mean-minded"** (Hansard, 5 Dec 1996: Column 1200).

Yet this injustice has not been put right.

Please support RNID's campaign for justice for deafened veterans. For more information, please contact Mark Morris on **020 7296 8063** or **mark.morris@rnid.org.uk**, or Chris Underwood on **020 7296 8248** or **chris.underwood@rnid.org.uk**

www.rnid.org.uk

RNID ● ❙❙❙
for deaf and hard of hearing people

TREDINNICK, DAVID
Bosworth

Con majority 5,319

David Tredinnick. Born 19 January 1950; Son of Stephen Victor Tredinnick and Evelyn Mabel, neé Wates; Educated Eton College; Mons Officer Cadet School; Graduate School of Business; Cape Town University (MBA 1975); St John's College, Oxford (MLitt 1987); Married Rebecca Shott 1983 (1 son 1 daughter). 2nd Lieutenant Grenadier Guards 1968-71. Trainee, E. B. Savory Milln & Co. (Stockbrokers) 1972-73; Account executive, Quadrant Int. 1974; Salesman, Kalle Infotech UK 1976; Sales manager, Word Right Word Processing 1977-78; Consultant, Baird Communications NY 1978-79; Marketing manager, QI Europe Ltd 1979-81; Manager, Malden Mitcham Properties 1981-87

House of Commons: Contested Cardiff South and Penarth 1983 general election. Member for Bosworth since 11 June 1987 general election; PPS to Sir Wyn Roberts as Minister of State, Welsh Office 1991-94. *Political interests:* Complementary and Alternative Medicine, Health Care, Diet and Nutrition, Foreign Affairs, Home Affairs, Police, Law and Order, Environment. Eastern Europe

Chair, British Atlantic Group of Young Politicians 1989-91; Future of Europe Trust 1991-95; *Recreations:* Golf, skiing, tennis, windsurfing, sailing

David Tredinnick, MP, House of Commons, London SW1A 0AA
Tel: 020 7219 4514 *Fax:* 020 7219 4901 *E-mail:* tredinnickd@parliament.uk.
Constituency: Bosworth Conservative Association, 10a Priory Walk, Hinckley, Leicestershire LE10 1BZ *Tel:* 01455 635741 *Fax:* 01455 612023

TRICKETT, JON
Hemsworth

Lab majority 13,481

Jon Trickett. Born 2 July 1950; Son of Laurence and Rose Trickett; Educated Roundhay School, Leeds; Hull University (BA politics); Leeds University (MA political sociology); Married Sarah Balfour 1993 (1 son 2 daughters). Plumber/builder 1974-86; Member, GMB Union; Member, RMT Parliamentary Campaigning Group 2002-; Leeds City Council: Councillor 1984-96, Chair: Finance Committee 1985-88, Housing Committee 1988-89, Leader of the Council 1989-96

House of Commons: Member for Hemsworth since 1 February 1996 by-election; PPS to Peter Mandelson: as Minister without Portfolio 1997-98, as Secretary of State for Trade and Industry July-December 1998. *Political interests:* Economic Policy, Finance, Industry, Sport. Middle East, France, USA

Clubs: British Cycling Federation; Member: British Cycling Federation, West Riding Sailing Club; Hon Life Member, Cyclists' Touring Club; *Recreations:* Cycle racing, windsurfing

Jon Trickett, MP, House of Commons, London SW1A 0AA *Tel:* 020 7219 5074
Fax: 020 7219 2133 *E-mail:* trickettj@parliament.uk. *Constituency:* 18 Market Street, Hemsworth, Pontefract, West Yorkshire WF9 5LB *Tel:* 01977 722290
Fax: 01977 722290

Lab majority 5,870

TRUSWELL, PAUL
Pudsey

Paul Anthony Truswell. Born 17 November 1955; Son of John Truswell, retired foundryman, and Olive Truswell, retired cleaner; Educated Firth Park Comprehensive School; Leeds University (BA history 1977); Married Suzanne Evans (2 sons). Journalist, Yorkshire Post Newspapers 1977-88; Local government officer, Wakefield MDC 1988-97; Member: UNISON, NUJ; Councillor, Leeds City Council 1982-97; Member: Leeds Eastern Health Authority 1982-90, Leeds Community Health Council 1990-92, Leeds Family Health Services Authority 1992-96

House of Commons: Member for Pudsey since 1 May 1997 general election. *Political interests:* Health, Social Services, Environment

Clubs: Civil Service, Guiseley Factory Workers; *Recreations:* Cinema, cricket, tennis, badminton, photography

Paul Truswell, MP, House of Commons, London SW1A 0AA *Tel:* 020 7219 3504 *Fax:* 020 7219 2252. *Constituency:* 10A Greenside, Pudsey, West Yorkshire LS28 8PU *Tel:* 0113-229 3553 *Fax:* 0113-229 3800

Con majority 12,978

TURNER, ANDREW
Isle of Wight

Andrew John Turner. Born 24 October 1953; Son of Eustace Albert Turner, schoolmaster, and Joyce Mary Turner, née Lowe, schoolmistress; Educated Rugby School; Keble College, Oxford (BA geography 1976, MA 1981); Birmingham University (PGCE 1977); Henley Management College; Single. Teacher economics and geography comprehensive schools 1977-84; Conservative Research Department specialist: education, trade and industry 1984-86; Special Adviser Secretary of State for Social Services 1986-88; Director Grant-Maintained Schools Foundation 1988-97; Contested Birmingham East 1994 European Parliament election; Education consultant 1997-2001; Deputy Director, Education Unit, Institute of Economic Affairs 1998-2000; Head of policy and resources, education department, London Borough of Southwark 2000-01; Councillor Oxford City Council 1979-96; Sheriff of Oxford 1994-95

House of Commons: Contested Hackney South and Shoreditch 1992 and Isle of Wight 1997 general elections. Member for Isle of Wight since 7 June 2001 general election; Sponsored Animal Welfare (Journey to Slaughter) Bill 2001. *Political interests:* Education, Social Services, Economy, Constitution

Party worker ward and constituency level; Campaign co-ordinator DHSS Ministers general election 1987; Appointee party education policy groups for general elections: 1987, 1992,   2001; Vice-president Association of Conservative Clubs 2002-; Vice-chairman (Campaigning), Conservative Party 2003-. *Clubs:* United Oxford and Cambridge University; *Recreations:* Walking, old movies, avoiding gardening

Andrew Turner, MP, House of Commons, London SW1A 0AA *Tel:* 020 7219 8490. *Constituency:* 24 The Mall, Carisbrooke Road, Newport PO30 1BW *Tel:* 01983 530808 *Fax:* 01983 822266 *E-mail:* mail@islandmp.com *Website:* www.islandmp.com

TURNER, DES
Brighton Kemptown

Des (Desmond Stanley) Turner. Born 17 July 1939; Son of late Stanley M. M. Turner and of Elsie Turner; Educated Luton Grammar School; Imperial College, London (BSc botany 1961, MSc biochemistry 1962); University College, London (PhD biochemistry 1972); Brighton Polytechnic (PGCE); Married Lynne Rogers 1997 (1 daughter from previous marriage). Medical researcher; Teacher; Partner in independent brewery; Past Member: AUT, TGWU, NUT; Member, MSF (AMICUS); Councillor: East Sussex County Council 1985-96, Brighton Borough Council 1994-96, Brighton and Hove Unitary Council 1996-99

Lab majority 2,737

House of Commons: Contested Mid-Sussex 1979 general election. Member for Brighton Kemptown since 1 May 1997 general election. *Political interests:* Health, Social Services, Employment, Disability, Housing, Science Policy, Animal Welfare, Fuel Poverty and Renewable Energy. Europe, Peru

Shelter, Age Concern, Brighton Housing Trust, Terence Higgins Trust, NSPCC; Parliamentary observer: Albanian elections 1997, Bosnian elections 1998; Member, Brighton Housing Trust; *Publications:* Research papers and reviews; R. D. Lawrence Memorial Fellow, British Diabetic Association 1970-72; *Clubs:* Polytechnic Fencing Club, Brighton Marina Yacht Club; *Recreations:* Sailing, fencing

Dr Des Turner, MP, House of Commons, London SW1A 0AA *Tel:* 020 7219 4024 *E-mail:* turnerd@parliament.uk. *Constituency:* 179 Preston Road, Brighton, East Sussex BN1 6AG *Tel:* 01273 330610 *Fax:* 01273 500966

TURNER, NEIL
Wigan

Neil Turner. Born 16 September 1945; Educated Carlisle Grammar School; Married Susan 1971 (1 son). Quantity surveyor, Fairclough Builders (later AMEC) 1967-94; Operations manager, North Shropshire District Council 1995-97; Member, MSF; Councillor, Wigan County Borough Council 1972-74; Wigan Metropolitan Borough Council: Councillor 1975-2000, Vice-Chair, Highways and Works Committee 1978-80, Chair 1980-97, Chair, Best Value Review Panel 1998-99

Lab majority 11,767

House of Commons: Contested Oswestry 1970 general election. Member for Wigan since 23 September 1999 by-election; PPS to Ian McCartney as: Minister of State, Department for Work and Pensions 2001-03, Minister without Portfolio and Party Chair 2003-. *Political interests:* Local and Regional Government, Housing

Former Member, Sale Young Socialists. Vice-Chair, Public Services Committee, Association of Metropolitan Authorities 1987-95, Chair 1995-97; Vice-Chair, Local Government Association Quality Panel 1997-98, Chair 1998-99; *Recreations:* Keen follower of Wigan Rugby League Club, naval history

Neil Turner, MP, House of Commons, London SW1A 0AA *Tel:* 020 7219 4494 *E-mail:* turnern@parliament.uk. *Constituency:* Gerrard Winstanley House, Crawford Street, Wigan, Greater Manchester WN1 1NG *Tel:* 01942 242047 *Fax:* 01942 828008

TWIGG, DEREK
Halton

Derek Twigg. Born 9 July 1959; Son of Kenneth and Irene Twigg; Educated Bankfield High School, Widnes; Halton College of Further Education; Married Mary Cassidy 1988 (1 son 1 daughter). Civil servant, Department for Education and Employment 1975-96; Political consultant 1996-; PCS: Branch secretary, Branch chair 1978-84; Member GMB; Councillor, Cheshire County Council 1981-85; Halton Borough Council: Councillor 1983-97, Chair of Housing 1988-93, Chair of Finance 1993-96, Education Spokesperson 1996-97

Lab majority 14,606

House of Commons: Member for Halton since 1 May 1997 general election; Assistant Government Whip 2002-03, Government Whip 2003-04; PPS: to Helen Liddell: as Minister of State, Department of the Environment, Transport and the Regions (Minister for Transport) 1999, as Minister of State, Department of Trade and Industry (Minister for Energy and Competitiveness in Europe) 1999-2001; to Stephen Byers as Secretary of State for Transport, Local Government and the Regions 2001-02; Parliamentary Under-Secretary of State: Department for Education and Skills 2004-05, Department for Transport 2005-. *Political interests:* Economy, Education, Health and Poverty, Housing. Greece

Member, European Standing Committee B 1997-98; *Recreations:* Various sporting activities, hill walking, military history

Derek Twigg, MP, House of Commons, London SW1A 0AA *Tel:* 020 7219 3554 *E-mail:* twiggd@parliament.uk. *Constituency:* F2 Moor Lane Business Centre, Moor Lane, Widnes, Cheshire WA8 7AQ *Tel:* 0151-424 7030 *Fax:* 0151-495 3800 *Website:* www.haltonlabourparty.org.uk

TYRIE, ANDREW
Chichester

Andrew Tyrie. Born 15 January 1957; Son of the late Derek and Patricia Tyrie; Educated Felstead School, Essex; Trinity College, Oxford (BA philosophy, politics and economics 1979 MA); College of Europe, Bruges (Diploma in economics 1980); Wolfson College, Cambridge (MPhil international relations 1981). Group head office, British Petroleum 1981-83; Adviser to Chancellors of the Exchequer: Nigel Lawson 1986-89, John Major 1989-90, Fellow, Nuffield College, Oxford 1990-91; Senior economist, European Bank for Reconstruction and Development 1992-97

Con majority 10,860

House of Commons: Contested Houghton and Washington 1992 general election. Member for Chichester since 1 May 1997 general election; Shadow: Financial Secretary 2003-04, Paymaster General 2004-. *Political interests:* European Union, Economic Policy

Member, Public Accounts Commission 1997-; Member, Inter-Parliamentary Union; *Publications:* Various works on economic and monetary union in Europe and other European issues; *The Prospects for Public Spending*, 1996; *Reforming the Lords: a Conservative Approach*, 1998; *Sense on EMU*, 1998; Co-author *Leviathan at Large: The New Regulator for the Financial Markets*, 2000; *Mr Blair's Poodle: An Agenda for Reviving the House of Commons*, 2000; *Back from the Brink*, 2001; Co-author, *Statism by Stealth: New Labour, New Collectivism*, 2002; *Axis of Instability: America, Britain and the New World Order after Iraq*, 2003; *Clubs:* MCC, RAC, Chichester Yacht Club, Goodwood Golf and Country Clubs, The Garrick; *Recreations:* Golf

Andrew Tyrie, MP, House of Commons, London SW1A 0AA *Tel:* 020 7219 6371 *Fax:* 020 7219 0625 *E-mail:* tyriea@parliament.uk. *Constituency:* Chichester Conservative Association, 145 St Pancras, Chichester, West Sussex PO19 4LH *Tel:* 01243 783519 *Fax:* 01243 536848

Lab majority 5,778

USSHER, KITTY
Burnley

Kitty Ussher. Born 18 March 1971; Educated Balliol College, Oxford (BA philosophy, politics and economics 1993 MA); Birkbeck College, London (MSc economics 1998); Married Peter John Colley 1999. Secretary Paul Boateng MP 1993-94; Researcher Martin O'Neill MP, Kim Howells MP, Adam Ingram MP 1994-97; Economist: Economist Intelligence Unit 1997-98, Centre for European Reform 1998-2000; Chief economist Britain in Europe 2000-01; Special adviser Patricia Hewitt and Department of Trade and Industry 2001-04; Amicus; Lambeth London Borough Council: Councillor 1998-2002, Chair environment scrutiny committee 2000-01, Chair finance scrutiny committee 2001-02

House of Commons: Member for Burnley since 5 May 2005 general election. *Political interests:* Economic policy, industrial policy, regional policy

Publications: Spectre of Tax Harmonisation?, Centre for European Reform 2000; *Recreations:* Hill walking, nice food

Kitty Ussher, MP, House of Commons, London SW1A 0AA *Tel:* 020 7219 4702. *Constituency:* Burnley Labour Party, 2 Victoria Road, Burnley, Lancashire BB11 1DD *Tel:* 01282 423001 *Fax:* 01282 839623 *E-mail:* kitty@burnleylabour.org.uk *Website:* www.burnleylabour.org.uk

Con majority 8,017

VAIZEY, ED
Wantage

Edward Vaizey. Born 5 June 1969; Educated Merton College, Oxford. Barrister specialising in family law and child care; Director and partner Consolidated Communications; Freelance journalist

House of Commons: Contested Bristol East 1997 general election. Member for Wantage since 5 May 2005 general election. *Political interests:* Farming, housing development, transport, hunting

Election aide to Iain Duncan Smith 2001 general election. Trustee the Trident Trust (work experience for children); *Publications:* Editor:*A Blue Tomorrow*, Politicos 2002,*Blue Books*, Politicos

Ed Vaizey, MP, House of Commons, London SW1A 0AA *Tel:* 020 7219 6991. *Constituency:* Wantage Conservative Association, Orchard House, Portway OX12 9BU *Tel:* 01235 769090 *Fax:* 01235 224833 *E-mail:* ed@wantageconservatives.com *Website:* www.wantageconservatives.com

Con majority 9,833

VARA, SHAILESH
North West Cambridgeshire

Shailesh Vara. Born 4 September 1960; Educated Aylesbury Grammar School; Brunel University (LLB law); Guildford College of Law (Solicitors Professional Examinations); Single. Solicitor, Richards Butler, Hong Kong 1989-90; Senior legal adviser and business consultant, London First 1998-99; Solicitor, CMS Cameron McKenna; Vice-President, Small Business Bureau

House of Commons: Contested Birmingham Ladywood 1997 and Northampton South 2001 general elections. Member for North West Cambridgeshire since 5 May 2005 general election

Vice-chair, local association 1991-97; Member, Conservative Lawyers 1991; PA general election, Oliver Letwin MP 1992; Vice-chair, Greater London Area CPC 1994-97; Member, National Union 1996-98; Member executive committees, Association of Conservative Party Candidates 1998. *Publications:* Contributor: Conservative Lawyers, Greater London Area CPC

Shailesh Vara, MP, House of Commons, London SW1A 0AA *Tel:* 020 7219 4703. *Constituency:* North West Cambridgeshire Conservative Association, The Barn, Hawthorn Farm, Ashton, Stamford PE9 3BA *Tel:* 01780 749379 *Fax:* 01780 783770 *E-mail:* svara@shaileshvara.com *Website:* www.shaileshvara.com

Lab majority 15,876

VAZ, KEITH
Leicester East

Keith Vaz. Born 26 November 1956; Son of Merlyn Verona Vaz, mother and teacher; Educated St Joseph's Convent, Aden; Latymer Upper School, Hammersmith; Gonville and Caius College, Cambridge (BA law 1979, MA 1987, MCFI 1988); College of Law, London; Married Maria Fernandes 1993 (1 son, 1 daughter). Articled clerk, Richmond Council 1980-82; Solicitor 1982; Senior solicitor, Islington LBC 1982-85; Contested Surrey West 1984 European Parliament election; Solicitor: Highfields and Belgrave Law Centre 1985-87, North Leicester Advice Centre 1986-87; Contested Surrey West 1994 European Parliament elections; Member, UNISON 1985-

House of Commons: Contested Richmond and Barnes 1983 general election. Member for Leicester East since 11 June 1987 general election; Opposition Front Bench Spokesman on: The Environment 1992-97; PPS to: John Morris as Attorney General 1997-99, Solicitors General Lord Falconer of Thoroton 1997-98, Ross Cranston 1998-99; Parliamentary Secretary, Lord Chancellor's Department 1999; Minister of State, Foreign and Commonwealth Office (Minister for Europe) 1999-2001. *Political interests:* Education, Legal Services, Local and Regional Government, Race Relations, Urban Policy, Small Businesses. India, Pakistan, Yemen, Bangladesh, Oman

Chair: Labour Party Race Action Group 1983-, Unison Group 1990-99; Tribune Group: Vice-chair 1992, Treasurer 1994; Labour Party Regional Executive 1994-96. Member, Standing Committees on: Immigration Bill 1987-88, Legal Aid Bill 1988, Children's Bill 1988-89, Football Spectators Bill 1989, National Health Service and Community Care Bill 1989-90, Courts and Legal Services Bill 1990, Armed Forces Bill 1990-91, Promoter, Race Relations Remedies Act 1994; Governor, Commonwealth Institute 1998-99; Board Member, The British Council 1999-; Member, Executive Committee Inter-Parliamentary Union 1993-94; *Publications:* Co-author *Law Reform Now*, 1996; *Clubs:* Safari (Leicester); *Recreations:* Tennis

Keith Vaz, MP, House of Commons, London SW1A 0AA *Tel:* 020 7219 6419 *Fax:* 020 7219 5743. *Constituency:* 144 Uppingham Road, Leicester, Leicestershire LE5 0QF *Tel:* 0116-212 2028

VIGGERS, PETER
Gosport

Con majority 5,730

Peter J Viggers. Born 13 March 1938; Son of late John Sidney Viggers and Evelyn Viggers; Educated Portsmouth Grammar School; Trinity Hall, Cambridge (history and law 1961, MA); College of Law, Guildford 1967; Married Dr Jennifer Mary McMillan 1968 (2 sons 1 daughter). National service RAF pilot 1956-58; Territorial Army Officer 1962-67. Solicitor 1967; Chair and director of companies in banking, oil, hotels, textiles, pharmaceuticals, venture capital 1970-79; Member Council of Lloyd's of London 1992-95; Chair: Tracer Petroleum Corporation 1996-98, Lloyd's Pension Fund 1996-

House of Commons: Member for Gosport since 28 February 1974 general election; PPS: to Sir Ian Percival as Solicitor General 1979-83, to Peter Rees as Chief Secretary to the Treasury 1983-85; Parliamentary Under-Secretary of State (Industry Minister), Northern Ireland Office 1986-89. *Political interests:* Finance, Trade and Industry, Defence, Local Hospitals. Japan, South East Asia, USA, China, Central and Eastern Europe

Chair, Cambridge University Conservative Association 1960. Warrior Preservation Trust; Member: European Standing Committee A 1998-, European Standing Committee B until 2003; UK Delegate, North Atlantic Assembly 1981-86, 1992-; Chair: Sub-Committee on Central and Eastern Europe 1999-2000, Political Committee 2000-; Fellow Industry and Parliament Trust; Trustee Royal Navy Submarine Museum Appeal; *Publications: Reserve Forces,* RUSI Journal, 2003; *Clubs:* Boodle's; President, Gosport Conservative; House of Commons Yacht Club: Member, Commodore 1982-83, Admiral 1997-99; *Recreations:* Beagling, opera, travel

Peter Viggers, MP, House of Commons, London SW1A 0AA *Tel:* 020 7219 5081 *Fax:* 020 7219 3985. *Constituency:* Gosport Conservative Association, 167 Stoke Road, Gosport, Hampshire PO12 1SE *Tel:* 023 9258 8400 *Fax:* 023 9252 7624 *E-mail:* peter.viggers@btconnect.com

VILLIERS, THERESA
Chipping Barnet

Con majority 5,960

Theresa Villiers. Born 5 March 1968; Educated Sarum Hall School, Francis Holland School, London; law Bristol University (LLB 1990); Jesus College, Oxford University (BCL 1991); Inns of Court School of Law (1992); Married Sean Wilken 1999. barrister Lincoln's Inn 1994-95; lecturer in law King's College, London University 1995-99; MEP for London 1999-2005: EP Conservatives: deputy leader 2001-03

House of Commons: Member for Chipping Barnet since 5 May 2005 general election. *Political interests:* Economic policy, economic and monetary union, business, deregulation, transport, information technology, media, animal welfare, Cyprus

Publications: European Tax harmonisation: The Impending Threat; co-author Waiver, Variation and Estoppel (Chancery Wiley Law Publications 1998)

Theresa Villiers, MP, House of Commons, London SW1A 0AA *Tel:* 020 7219 4705

Lab majority 741

VIS, RUDI
Finchley and Golders Green

Rudi (Rudolf) Jan Vis. Born 4 April 1941; Son of late Laurens Vis, insurance broker, and late Helena Vis; Educated High School, Alkmaar, The Netherlands; University of Maryland, USA (BSc economics 1970); London School of Economics (MSc economics 1972); Brunel University (PhD economics 1976); Married Joan Hanin 1982 (divorced) (1 son); married Jacqueline Suffling 2001 (twin sons). Dutch armed services 1960-64. Administrator US Air Force, Madrid 1964-66; Night manager, Hotel Fleissis, Amsterdam 1966; University of Maryland, USA 1966-70; Principal lecturer, economics, North East London Polytechnic/University of East London 1971-97; Member: NATFHE 1971-94, AMICUS (MSF) 1994-; Councillor, London Borough of Barnet 1986-98

House of Commons: Member for Finchley and Golders Green since 1 May 1997 general election. *Political interests:* Finance, European Union, Economics, Defence, Elderly, Small Businesses. All

Member: Co-op Party 1971-, SERA 1986-, Labour Movement in Europe 1997-, European Movement 1999-. Independent Panel for Special Education Advice (IPSEA); Member: Howard League for Penal Reform 1986-, European Standing Committee A 1998-, Finchley Society 1998-, Council for the Advancement of Arab-British Understanding 2000-; Member: Council of Europe, Western European Union; Member College Farm Finchley; Hon. Doctorate, Schiller International University 1997; *Recreations:* Walking through London

Dr Rudi Vis, MP, House of Commons, London SW1A 0AA *Tel:* 020 7219 4562 *Fax:* 020 7219 0565 *E-mail:* visr@parliament.uk. *Constituency:* Labour Party Constituency Office, 38 Church Lane, London N2 8DT *Tel:* 020 8883 0411 *Fax:* 020 8883 0411

Con majority 11,509

WALKER, CHARLES
Broxbourne

Charles Walker. Born 11 September 1967; Educated American School of London; Oregon University, USA (BSc politics and American history 1990); Married Fiona Jane Newman 1995. Communications director, CSQ Plc 1997-2001; Director: Blue Arrow Ltd 1999-2001, LSM Processing Ltd 2002-04, Debitwise 2004; Amicus; Wandsworth Borough Councillor 2002-

House of Commons: Contested Ealing North 2001 general election. Member for Broxbourne since 5 May 2005 general election. *Political interests:* Employment, taxation, the economy

Vice chairman: Lewisham East Conservatives 1992-93, Battersea Conservatives 2002-03. *Recreations:* Fishing, watching cricket

Charles Walker, MP, House of Commons, London SW1A 0AA *Tel:* 020 7219 4701. *Constituency:* 76 High Street, Hoddesdon, Hertfordshire EN11 8ET *Tel:* 01992 479972 *Fax:* 01992 479973 *E-mail:* broxbourne@tory.org *Website:* www.broxbourneconservatives.com

WALLACE, BEN
Lancaster and Wyre

Benjamin Wallace. Born 15 May 1970; Educated Millfield School, Somerset; Royal Military Academy, Sandhurst 1989; Married Liza 2001. Army officer, Scots Guards 1990-98. Ski instructor, Austrian National Ski School 1988-89; EU and overseas director, Qinetiq 2003-

House of Commons: Member for Lancaster and Wyre since 5 May 2005 general election. *Political interests:* Defence, health, security, Europe

Con majority 4,171

Recreations: Sailing, skiing, racing, motorsport

Ben Wallace, MP, House of Commons, London SW1A 0AA *Tel:* 020 7219 5804. *Constituency:* Redman House, 8 King's Arcade, Lancaster, Lancashire LA1 1LE *Tel:* 01524 32027 *Fax:* 01524 847518 *E-mail:* lancasterwyre@tory.org

WALLEY, JOAN
Stoke-on-Trent North

Joan Lorraine Walley. Born 23 January 1949; Daughter of late Arthur and late Mary Emma Walley; Educated Biddulph Grammar School; Hull University (BA social administration); University College of Wales, Swansea (Diploma in community work development); Married Jan Ostrowski 1981 (2 sons). Alcoholics recovery project 1970-73; Local government officer: Swansea City Council 1974-78, Wandsworth Council 1978-79; NACRO development officer 1979-82; Member, UNISON; Lambeth Council: Councillor 1981-85, Chair, Health and Consumer Services Committee

Lab majority 10,036

House of Commons: Member for Stoke-on-Trent North since 11 June 1987 general election; Opposition Spokesperson on: Environmental Protection and Development 1988-90, Transport 1990-95. *Political interests:* Environment, Health, Small Businesses. Eastern Europe

Member: SERA, SEA. Member, Armed Forces Parliamentary Scheme (RAF); *Clubs:* Fegg Hayes Sports and Social; *Recreations:* Walking, swimming, music, football

Joan Walley, MP, House of Commons, London SW1A 0AA *Tel:* 020 7219 4524 *Fax:* 020 7219 4397 *E-mail:* walleyj@parliament.uk. *Constituency:* Unit 5, Burslem Enterprise Centre, Moorland Road, Burslem, Stoke-on-Trent ST6 1JN *Tel:* 01782 577900 *Fax:* 01782 836462

Con majority 2,244

WALTER, ROBERT
North Dorset

Robert Walter. Born 30 May 1948; Educated Lord Weymouth School, Warminster; Aston University, Birmingham (BSc 1971); Married Sally Middleton 1970 (died 1995) (2 sons 1 daughter); married Barbara Gorna 2000. Former Farmer; Sheep farm, South Devon; Director and Vice-President, Aubrey G Lanston and Co 1986-97; Member, London Stock Exchange 1983-86; Visiting lecturer in East-West trade, Westminster University

House of Commons: Contested Bedwelty 1979. Member for North Dorset since 1 May 1997 general election; Opposition Spokesperson for Constitutional Affairs (Wales) 1999-2001. *Political interests:* Agriculture, Health

Chair: Aston University Conservative Association 1967-69, Westbury Constituency Young Conservative 1973-76, Conservative Foreign Affairs Forum 1986-88, Member: Carlton Club Political Committee 1991-99, National Union Executive Committee 1992-95, Conservative Group for Europe: Chair 1992-95, Vice-President 1997-2000. Member, European Standing Committee B 1998-; Former Chairman, European Democrat Forum; Member: British-Irish Inter-Parliamentary Body 1997, Assembly of Western European Union 2001-, Parliamentary Assembly of Council of Europe 2001-; Liveryman, Worshipful Company of Needlemakers 1983; Freeman, City of London 1983; *Recreations:* Sailing

Robert Walter, MP, House of Commons, London SW1A 0AA *Tel:* 020 7219 6981 *Fax:* 020 7219 2608 *E-mail:* walterr@parliament.uk. *Constituency:* The Stables, White Cliff Gardens, Blandford Forum, Dorset DT11 7BU *Tel:* 0845 123 2785 *Fax:* 01258 459 614

Lab majority 407

WALTHO, LYNDA
Stourbridge

Lynda Waltho. Born 19 May 1960; Educated Keele University; PGCE University of Central England; Married Steve. Principal adviser to Neena Gill MEP; Assistant to Sylvia Heal MP; Member GMB

House of Commons: Member for Stourbridge since 5 May 2005 general election. *Political interests:* Education, childcare, economy

Regional organiser West Midlands Labour Party. *Recreations:* Walking, reading, listening to music, cinema

Lynda Waltho, MP, House of Commons, London SW1A 0AA *Tel:* 020 7219 6749. *Constituency:* Lynda Waltho Campaign Centre, Stourbridge Labour Club, The Lawns, Hagley Road, Stourbridge *Tel:* 07875 771365, *Website:* lynda_waltho@new.labour.org.uk

Lab majority 1,148

WARD, CLAIRE
Watford

Claire Margaret Ward. Born 9 May 1972; Daughter of Frank and Catherine Ward; Educated Loreto College, St Albans, Hertfordshire; University of Hertfordshire (LLB 1993); Brunel University (MA Britain and the European Union 1994); College of Law, London; Married. Part-time clerical and secretarial work 1985-95; Trainee Solicitor 1995-98; Solicitor 1998-; Member, TGWU 1987-; Winner: South East TUC Mike Perkins Memorial Award for Young Trade Unionists 1989, TGWU National Youth Award 1990; Delegate, TGWU Biennial Delegate Conference 1991; Councillor, Elstree and Boreham Wood Town Council 1994-97, Mayor 1996-97, Former Vice-chair, Leisure and Entertainments Committee

House of Commons: Member for Watford since 1 May 1997 general election; Assistant Government Whip 2005-; PPS to John Hutton as Minister of State, Department of Health 2001-05. *Political interests:* Transport, Education, Employment, Home Affairs, Culture, Media, Sport. St Lucia

Member, Co-operative Party and CRS Ltd 1987-; Youth Representative, Labour Party National Executive Committee 1991-95; Chair: Boreham Wood Branch Labour Party 1991-97, Hertsmere Constituency Labour Party 1992-96; Member, Central Region Executive Committee 1993; Member: London Region CRS Political Committee 1993-2001, Co-operative Party Parliamentary Panel 1994-95; Member, Labour Party National Policy Commissions on: Democracy and Citizenship 1992-95, Social Policy 1992-95, Equalities 1992-95, Environment 1992-95; Member: Fabian Society, Society of Labour Lawyers. Youngest Labour Woman MP; Patron, Young European Movement; *Clubs:* Reform; *Recreations:* Cinema, reading, restaurants, Watford Football Club

Claire Ward, MP, House of Commons, London SW1A 0AA *Tel:* 020 7219 4910 *Fax:* 020 7219 0468 *E-mail:* wardc@parliament.uk. *Constituency:* 270 St Albans Road, Watford, Hertfordshire WD24 6PE *Tel:* 01923 213579 *Fax:* 01923 213595

WAREING, ROBERT
Liverpool West Derby

Lab majority 15,225

Robert Nelson Wareing. Born 20 August 1930; Son of late Robert and Florence Patricia Wareing; Educated Ranworth Square Council School, Liverpool; Alsop High School, Liverpool; Bolton College of Education (Teacher's Certificate 1957); External student, London University (BSc economics 1956); Married Betty Coward 1962 (died 1989). RAF 1948-50. Local government officer, Liverpool Corporation 1946-48, 1950-56; Lecturer: Brooklyn Technical College 1957-59, Wigan and District Mining and Technical College 1959-63, Liverpool College of Commerce 1963-64, Liverpool City Institute of Further Education 1964-72; Principal lecturer/deputy head adult education, Central Liverpool College of FE 1972-83; Member: AMICUS, RMT Parliamentary Campaigning Group 2002-; Merseyside County Council: Councillor 1981-86, Chairman, Economic Development Committee 1981-83, Chief Whip, Labour Group 1981-83

House of Commons: Contested Berwick-upon-Tweed 1970 general election and Liverpool Edge Hill 1979 by-election and 1979 general election. Member for Liverpool, West Derby since 9 June 1983 general election; Assistant Opposition Whip 1987-92. *Political interests:* Economic and Foreign Affairs, Regional Economic Policy, Disability, Tranquilliser Addiction, Motor Industry, Airports Policy. Russia, Yugoslavia, Germany, Latin America, Eastern Europe, Far East

President, Liverpool District Labour Party 1972-73, 1974-81. Disablement Income Group; Vice-President, AMA 1984-97; *Clubs:* Royal Navy Club, Kirkby, Merseyside; *Recreations:* Watching soccer, concert-going, ballet, motoring, travel

Robert Wareing, MP, House of Commons, London SW1A 0AA *Tel:* 020 7219 3482 *Fax:* 020 7219 6187 *E-mail:* wareingr@parliament.uk. *Constituency:* 74a Mill Lane, West Derby, Liverpool L12 7JB *Tel:* 0151-256 9111 *Fax:* 0151-226 0285

WATERSON, NIGEL
Eastbourne

Con majority 1,124

Nigel Christopher Waterson. Born 12 October 1950; Son of late James Waterson and Katherine Mahon; Educated Leeds Grammar School; The Queen's College, Oxford (BA law 1971, MA); Married Gisela Guettler 1979 (divorced); married Bernadette Anne O'Halloran 1989 (divorced); married Dr Barbara Judge 1999. Solicitor; Barrister; Founder and senior partner of law firm, Waterson Hicks; Research assistant to Sally Oppenheim, MP 1972-73; Councillor, London Borough of Hammersmith and Fulham 1974-78

House of Commons: Contested Islington South and Finsbury 1979 general election. Member for Eastbourne since 9 April 1992 general election; Opposition Spokesperson for: Local Government and Housing 1999-2001, Trade and Industry 2001-02; Opposition Whip: Social Security, Health, Legal, Lord Chancellor; Eastern 1997-98, Home Office, Culture, Media and Sport 1998-99; PPS to: Gerry Malone as Minister of State, Department of Health 1995-96, Michael Heseltine as Deputy Prime Minister 1996-97; Shadow Minister for Pensions 2003-. *Political interests:* Health, Foreign Affairs, Tourism, Shipping, Energy. USA, Greece, France

President, Oxford University Conservative Association 1970; Chair, Bow Group 1986-87; Chair: Hammersmith Conservative Association 1987-90, Hammersmith and Fulham Joint Management Committee 1988-90; Member, CPC Advisory Committee 1986-90; Hon. Patron, Bow Group 1993-95. Patron, Eastbourne Multiple Sclerosis; Member: IPU, CPA; *Clubs:* Eastbourne Constitutional; Sussex County Cricket Club; *Recreations:* Sailing, reading, music, walking on the Downs

Nigel Waterson, MP, House of Commons, London SW1A 0AA *Tel:* 020 7219 4576 *Fax:* 020 7219 2561 *E-mail:* watersonn@parliament.uk. *Constituency:* Eastbourne Conservative Association, 179 Victoria Drive, Eastbourne, East Sussex BN20 8QJ *Tel:* 01323 720776 *Fax:* 01323 410994

WATKINSON, ANGELA
Upminster

Angela Eileen Watkinson. Born 18 November 1941; Daughter of Edward John Ellicott and Maisie Eileen Ellicott, née Thompson; Educated Wanstead County High School; Anglia University (HNC public administration 1989); Married Roy Michael Watkinson 1961 (1 son 2 daughters). Bank of New South Wales 1958-64; Family career break 1964-76; Special school secretary Essex County Council 1976-88; London Borough of Barking and Dagenham: Clerk to school governing bodies 1988, Committee clerk 1988-89; Committee manager Basildon District Council 1989-94; Councillor, Group secretary, Committee chair: London Borough of Havering 1994-98, Essex County Council 1997-2001

Con majority 6,042

House of Commons: Member for Upminster since 7 June 2001 general election; Opposition Whip 2002-04; Shadow Minister for: Health and Education 2004, Education 2004-. *Political interests:* Education, Law and Order, Families, European Affairs, Constitution, Local and Regional Government. Sweden, USA

Secretary: Upminster Ward 1988-93, Emerson Park Ward 1993-96: Chair 1996-2001; Upminster Conservative Association: Executive member 1988-99, Executive officer 1997-99; Billericay Conservative Association: Executive Member 1997-2001, Vice-president 1999-; Member: Monday Club 1996-2001, Conservative Councillors Association 1998-, Conservative Way Forward Group 1998-, Conservative Christian Fellowship 1999-, Conservative Friends of Israel 2001-. St Luke's Hospice; Subscriber European Foundation 1998-; *Recreations:* Working, family, reading, music, dining, crosswords, visiting stately homes and gardens, animal sanctuaries

Angela Watkinson, MP, House of Commons, London SW1A 0AA
Tel: 020 7219 8470 *Fax:* 020 7219 1957 *E-mail:* watkinsona@parliament.uk.
Constituency: 23 Butts Green Road, Hornchurch, Essex RM11 2JS
Tel: 01708 475252 *Fax:* 01708 470495

WATSON, TOM
West Bromwich East

Tom Watson. Born 8 January 1967; Son of Anthony Watson, social worker, and Linda Watson, née Pearce, social worker; Educated King Charles I, Kidderminster; Married Siobhan Corby 2001. Marketing officer Save the City of Wells 1987-88; Account executive advertising agency 1988-90; Development officer, Labour Party 1993-97; AEEU 1995-: Member, National political officer 1997-

Lab majority 11,652

House of Commons: Member for West Bromwich East since 7 June 2001 general election; Assistant Government Whip 2004-05; Government Whip 2005-; PPS to Dawn Primarolo as Paymaster General, HM Treasury 2003-04. *Political interests:* Industry, Manufacturing, Law and Order, Small Businesses. USA, Japan, Australia

Labour Party: National Development Officer (Youth) 1993-97, Former research assistant, National Co-ordinator Labour Campaign for First Past the Post 1997-; Director: Tribune 2000-, Policy Network 2000-. Cystic Fibrosis Trust; *Publications:* Co-author *Votes for All*, Fabian Society pamphlet 2000; *Clubs:* West Bromwich Labour, Friar Park Labour; *Recreations:* Supporter of Kidderminster Harriers FC, walking

Tom Watson, MP, House of Commons, London SW1A 0AA *Tel:* 020 7219 8335
E-mail: watsont@parliament.uk. *Constituency:* 1 Thomas Street, West Bromwich, West Midlands B70 6NT *Tel:* 0121-569 1904 *Fax:* 0121-553 1898

HOME BUILDERS FEDERATION

Meeting housing needs and aspirations

The UK is currently suffering from a housing affordability crisis which is preventing many people from meeting their aspirations to become home-owners. A YouGov survey for the HBF in April 2005 found that 95% of people think buying a first home is financially difficult.

The root of this crisis is an underlying long-term shortage of supply. Increasing supply to bring it into better equilibrium with demand is the only way to ensure sustainable affordability.

The British people recognise this. 72% agree that Britain needs more homes. It was also the central conclusion of the Barker Review, the most comprehensive review of house-building for 60 years, which stated that the current low rate of house building is not a realistic option. It estimated an additional 70,000 – 120,000 private homes are needed per year in England alone.

Members of the **Home Builders Federation** (HBF), the principal trade federation for private sector house builders and voice of the house building industry in England and Wales, want to respond to the market and build the right number and types of homes to meet people's needs, in the right locations. In order to achieve this goal we need a policy framework which allows us to get the fundamentals of housing supply right.

One immediate priority for this Parliament is to ensure that planning policy enables house builders to deliver the homes the UK needs. At present, the Planning Policy Guidance for Housing (PPG3) does not take sufficient account of key demographic trends and factors such as the need for different densities and parking provision in different market contexts. As Kate Barker recommended, PPG3 should therefore be rigorously reviewed, with stakeholder and panel scrutiny of the evidence base weighing up the policy costs and benefits and facilitating flexibility on the ground.

The **Home Builders Federation's** 300 members account for over 80% of all new houses built in England and Wales in any one year, and include companies of all sizes, ranging from multi national household names through regionally based businesses to small companies. We look forward to working with the Government on making progress towards implementing the recommendations of the Barker Review. The long-term health of the housing market and the stability of the British economy depends on it.

For more information:

John Slaughter
Director of External Affairs
Home Builders Federation
020 7960 1604
john.slaughter@hbf.co.uk

WATTS, DAVID
St Helens North

David Leonard Watts. Born 26 August 1951; Son of Leonard and Sarah Watts; Educated Seel Road Secondary Modern School; Married Avril Davies 1972 (2 sons). Labour Party organiser; Research assistant to Angela Eagle MP 1992-93 and John Evans MP 1993-97; Shop steward, United Biscuits AEU; St Helens MBC: Councillor 1979-97, Deputy Leader 1990-93, Leader 1993-97; Chair: Education Development Committee 1979-83, Economic Development Committee 1983-90

Lab majority 13,962

House of Commons: Member for St Helens North since 1 May 1997 general election; Government Whip 2005-; PPS to: John Spellar: as Minister of State for the Armed Forces, Ministry of Defence 1999-2001, as Minister of Transport, Department for Transport, Local Government and the Regions 2001-02, as Minister of State, Department for Transport 2002-03, John Prescott as Deputy Prime Minister 2003-05. *Political interests:* Regional Policy, Education, Training

PLP North West Regional Group: Vice-chair 1999-2000, Chair 2000-01. Vice-chair, Association of Metropolitan Authorities; UK President, Euro Group of Industrial Regions 1989-93; *Recreations:* Watching football and rugby, reading

David Watts, MP, House of Commons, London SW1A 0AA *Tel:* 020 7219 6325 *E-mail:* wattsd@parliament.uk. *Constituency:* Ann Ward House, 1 Milk Street, St Helens, Merseyside WA10 1PX *Tel:* 01744 623416 *Fax:* 01744 623417

WEBB, STEVE
Northavon

Steve (Steven) John Webb. Born 18 July 1965; Son of Brian and Patricia Webb; Educated Dartmouth High School, Birmingham; Hertford College, Oxford (BA philosophy, politics and economics 1983, MA); Married Helen Edwards 1993 (1 daughter 1 son). Researcher then programme director, Institute for Fiscal Studies 1986-95; Professor of social policy, University of Bath 1995-

House of Commons: Member for Northavon since 1 May 1997 general election; Spokesperson for Social Security and Welfare (Pensions) 1997-99; Principal Spokesperson for Social Security 1999-2001; Liberal Democrat Shadow Secretary of State for: Work and Pensions 2001-05, Health 2005-. *Political interests:* Social Affairs, Welfare, Third World, Internet

Lib Dem majority 11,033

Member: Liberal Democrat Tax and Benefits Working Group, Liberal Democrat Costings Group, Liberal Democrat Policy Committee. Member, Commission on Social Justice; Specialist Adviser to Social Security Select Committee; *Publications:* Include: *Beyond The Welfare State*, 1990, Co-author *For Richer, For Poorer*, 1994, *Inequality in the UK*, 1997

Prof Steve Webb, MP, House of Commons, London SW1A 0AA *Tel:* 020 7219 4378 *Fax:* 020 7219 1110 *E-mail:* stevewebb@cix.co.uk. *Constituency:* Poole Court, Poole Court Drive, Yate, Bristol, Avon BS37 5PP *Tel:* 01454 322100

Belief in Action

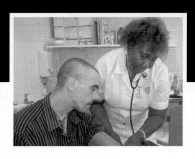

Throughout the UK, The Salvation Army is at the cutting edge of care in our churches and social service centres. Our mission takes us into the front line of the battle against the biggest social problems of the age.

Today our **services for homeless people** are offering individually tailored packages of care to people with a wide range of problems, including alcoholism and mental illness. Our **National Addiction Service** is combining scientific knowledge and professional care to help people break free from drugs.

Our Outreach and Resettlement Teams work in major cities to identify people sleeping rough. We build relationships with them as the first step towards offering longer-term programmes leading to resettlement in appropriate accommodation.

Our **residential and home care services** are giving older people the chance to retain their independence whilst receiving the care they need. Our f**amily and children's services** are working to help families stay together, while also supporting parents and children who are coping with family breakdown.

The Salvation Army is at the heart of almost every community. Through our network of 1000 centres across the UK, **we touch the lives of thousands of people,** often working in partnership with national and local government. At the same time we are innovators, constantly striving to raise our professional standards and the quality of our services so we can meet today's problems with tomorrow's solutions.

You can find out more about the work of The Salvation Army by visiting our website **www.salvationarmy.org.uk**

Or you can contact Jonathan Lomax, Public Affairs Officer, on **020 7367 4885** or email him at **jonathan.lomax@salvationarmy.org.uk**

Belief in Action

WEIR, MIKE
Angus

Michael Fraser Weir. Born 24 March 1957; Son of James Gordon Weir, electrician, and Elizabeth Mary, née Fraser, hospital cook; Educated Arbroath High School; Aberdeen University (LLB 1979); Married Anne Elizabeth Jack 1985 (2 daughters). Solicitor: Charles Wood and Son 1981-83, Myers and Wills 1983-84; Solicitor and partner J and DG Shiell 1984-2001; Angus District Council 1984-88: Councillor, Convener General Purposes Committee 1984-88

SNP majority 1,601

House of Commons: Contested Aberdeen South 1987 general election. Member for Angus 2001-05, for new Angus since 5 May 2005 general election; SNP Spokesperson for: Trade and Industry, Health, Environment. *Political interests:* Disability, European Affairs, Rural Affairs, Health, Education, Employment, Legal Affairs, International Development

Various posts Local party. Law Society of Scotland 1981; *Recreations:* History, organic gardening

Mike Weir, MP, House of Commons, London SW1A 0AA *Tel:* 020 7219 8125 *Fax:* 020 7219 1746 *E-mail:* weirm@parliament.uk. *Constituency:* SNP Office, 16 Brothock Bridge, Arbroath *Tel:* 01241 874522 *Fax:* 01241 879350

WHITEHEAD, ALAN
Southampton Test

Alan Patrick Vincent Whitehead. Born 15 September 1950; Educated Isleworth Grammar School, Isleworth, Middlesex; Southampton University (BA politics and philosophy 1973, PhD political science 1976); Married Sophie Wronska 1979 (1 son 1 daughter). Director, Outset 1979-83, Deputy 1976-79; Director, BIIT 1983-92; Professor of public policy, Southampton Institute 1992-97; Member, UNISON (formerly NUPE); Councillor, Southampton City Council 1980-92, Leader 1984-92

Lab majority 7,018

House of Commons: Contested Southampton Test 1983, 1987, 1992 general elections. Member for Southampton Test since 1 May 1997 general election; Joint PPS to David Blunkett as Secretary of State for Education and Employment 1999-2000; PPS to Baroness Blackstone as Minister for Education and Employment 1999-2001; Parliamentary Under-Secretary of State, Department for Transport, Local Government and the Regions 2001-02. *Political interests:* Environment, Local and Regional Government, Higher Education, Education, Constitution, Transport, Energy. Poland, France, Estonia, Lithuania

Member, Labour Party National Policy Forum 1999-2001. Director, Southampton Environment Centre; *Publications:* Various chapters, articles and papers including: Co-author *TUPE – the EU's Revenge on the Iron Lady*, 1994; *Spain, European Regions and City States*, 1995; *Rational Actors and Irrational Structures*, 1995; *Local Government Finance – Accountancy or Accountability?*, 1995; Joint editor, *Beyond 2002: Long-Term Policies for Labour;* Visiting professor, Southampton Institute 1997-; *Recreations:* Football (playing and watching), writing, tennis

Dr Alan Whitehead, MP, House of Commons, London SW1A 0AA *Tel:* 020 7219 6338 *Fax:* 020 7219 0918 *E-mail:* whiteheada@parliament.uk. *Constituency:* Southampton Labour Party, 20-22 Southampton Street, Southampton, Hampshire SO15 1ED *Tel:* 023 8023 1942 *Fax:* 023 8023 1943 *Website:* www.southampton-labour.org.uk

Con majority 12,573

WHITTINGDALE, JOHN
Maldon and Chelmsford East

John Flasby Lawrance Whittingdale. Born 16 October 1959; Son of late John Whittingdale and of Margaret Whittingdale; Educated Sandroyd School, Wiltshire; Winchester College; University College, London (BSc economics 1982); Married Ancilla Murfitt 1990 (1 son 1 daughter). Head, political section, Conservative research department 1982-84; Special adviser to Secretary of State for Trade and Industry 1984-87; Manager, N. M. Rothschild & Sons 1987; Political secretary to Margaret Thatcher as Prime Minister 1988-90; Private secretary to Margaret Thatcher 1990-92

House of Commons: Member for South Colchester and Maldon 1992-97, and for Maldon and Chelmsford East since 1 May 1997 general election; Opposition Spokesperson for the Treasury (Tax, VAT and Duties; EU Budget and other EU Issues) 1998-99; Opposition Whip 1997-98; PPS to Eric Forth: as Minister of State for Education 1994-95, as Minister of State for Education and Employment 1994-96; Parliamentary private secretary to William Hague as Leader of the Opposition 1999-2001; Shadow Secretary of State for: Trade and Industry 2001-02, Culture, Media and Sport 2002-03, Agriculture, Fisheries and Food 2003-04, Culture, Media and Sport 2004-. *Political interests:* Broadcasting and Media. Israel, USA, Korea, Malaysia, Japan

Member: 92 Group, No Turning Back Group. *Publications: New Policies for the Media,* 1995; OBE 1990; OBE; *Clubs:* Essex; OBE; *Recreations:* Cinema, music

John Whittingdale, MP, House of Commons, London SW1A 0AA
Tel: 020 7219 3557 *Fax:* 020 7219 2522 *E-mail:* jwhittingdale.mp@tory.org.uk.
Constituency: Maldon and East Chelmsford Conservative Association, 120B High Street, Maldon, Essex CM9 5ET *Tel:* 01621 855663 *Fax:* 01621 855217

Lab majority 13,888

WICKS, MALCOLM
Croydon North

Malcolm Wicks. Born 1 July 1947; Son of Arthur Wicks and of late Daisy Wicks; Educated Elizabeth College, Guernsey; North West London Polytechnic; London School of Economics (BSc sociology); Married Margaret Baron 1968 (1 son 2 daughters). Fellow, Department of Social Administration, York University 1968-70; Research worker, Centre for Environmental Studies 1970-72; Lecturer in social administration, Brunel University 1970-74; Social policy analyst, Urban Deprivation Unit, Home Office 1974-77; Lecturer in social policy, Civil Service College 1977-78; Research director and secretary, Study Commission on the Family 1978-83; Director, Family Policy Studies Centre 1983-92; TGWU

House of Commons: Contested Croydon North West 1987 general election. Member for Croydon North West 1992-97, and for Croydon North since 1 May 1997 general election; Opposition Spokesperson for Social Security 1995-97; Parliamentary Under-Secretary of State (Lifelong Learning), Department for Education and Employment 1999-2001; Department for Work and Pensions 2001-05: Parliamentary Under-Secretary of State (Work) 2001-03, Minister of State for Pensions 2003-05; Minister of State (Minister for Energy), Department of Trade and Industry 2005-. *Political interests:* Social Policy, Welfare State, Education. Australia, Europe, New Zealand

Publications: Several publications and articles on social policy and welfare including: *Old and Cold: hypothermia and social policy*, 1978; Co-author *Government and Urban Poverty*, 1983; *A Future for All: do we need a welfare state?* 1987; Co-author *Family Change and Future Policy*, 1990; *A New Agenda* (IPPR), 1993; *Clubs:* Ruskin House Labour (Croydon); *Recreations:* Music, walking, gardening, very occasional white water rafting

Malcolm Wicks, MP, House of Commons, London SW1A 0AA *Tel:* 020 7219 4418 *Fax:* 020 7219 2795 *E-mail:* wicksm@parliament.uk. *Constituency:* 84 High Street, Thornton Heath, Croydon CR7 8LF *Tel:* 020 8665 1214 *Fax:* 020 8683 0179

BG Group

Though the UK is expected to be a net importer of natural gas in 2005 or 2006, BG Group is aiming to increase its production from the North Sea from next year. And we will be one of the UK Continental Shelf's most active explorers in 2005, with plans to drill six to nine wells. There has been a mindset of inevitable decline in the UK oil and gas business. Here at BG we are challenging that mindset. We're also developing a new terminal in Milford Haven, Wales, to import liquefied natural gas and intend to play an important role in securing Britain's energy supply

Natural gas. It's our business   www.bg-group.com

Here today, Here tomorrow

COR020

Con majority 14,856

WIDDECOMBE, ANN
Maidstone and The Weald

Ann Noreen Widdecombe. Born 4 October 1947; Daughter of late James Murray Widdecombe CB, OBE, retired Director General in Ministry of Defence, and of Rita Widdecombe; Educated La Sainte Union Convent, Bath; Birmingham University (BA Latin 1969); Lady Margaret Hall, Oxford (BA philosophy, politics and economics 1972, MA); Single. With Unilever in marketing 1973-75; Senior administrator, London University 1975-1987; Member, Association of University Teachers 1978-83; Councillor, Runnymede District Council 1976-78

House of Commons: Contested Burnley 1979, Plymouth Devonport 1983 general elections. Member for Maidstone 1987-97, and for Maidstone and The Weald since 1 May 1997 general election; Introduced Abortion Amendment Bill 1988-89; PPS to Tristan Garel-Jones as Minister of State, Foreign and Commonwealth Office 1990; Joint Parliamentary Under-Secretary of State, Department of Social Security 1990-93; Department of Employment: Joint Parliamentary Under-Secretary of State 1993-94, Minister of State 1994-95; Minister of State, Home Office 1995-97; Member, Shadow Cabinet 1998-2001; Shadow Secretary of State for Health 1998-99; Shadow Home Secretary 1999-2001. *Political interests:* Abortion, Health, Defence, Prisons. Singapore

Vice-chair, National Association of Conservative Graduates 1974-76. LIFE; ZOCS (Zambian Open Community Schools); Member, Gas Consumers Council 1984-86; *Publications:* Various publications including *A Layman's Guide to Defence*, 1984; *Outspoken and Inspired*, 1999; *The Clematis Tree*, 2000; *An Act of Treachery*, 2002; PC 1997; Highland Park/*The Spectator* Minister of the Year 1996; Talk Radio, Straight Talker of the Year 1997; *Clubs:* The Carlton; *Recreations:* Reading, researching Charles II's escape, writing

Rt Hon Ann Widdecombe, MP, House of Commons, London SW1A 0AA *Tel:* 020 7219 5091 *Fax:* 020 7219 2413 *E-mail:* widdecombea@parliament.uk. *Constituency:* 3 Albion Place, Maidstone, Kent ME14 5DY *Tel:* 01622 752463 *Fax:* 01622 844330 *Website:* www.annwiddecombemp.com

Con majority 13,187

WIGGIN, BILL
Leominster

William David Wiggin. Born 4 June 1966; Son of Sir Jerry Wiggin and Mrs Rosie Dale Harris; Educated Eton College; University College of North Wales (BA economics 1988); Married Camilla Chilvers 1999. Trader UBS 1991-93; Associate director currency options sales Dresdner Kleinwort Benson 1994-98; Manager structured products Commerzbank 1998-; Contested North West region 1999 European Parliament election

House of Commons: Contested Burnley 1997 general election. Member for Leominster since 7 June 2001 general election; Shadow: Minister for Environment, Food and Rural Affairs 2003, Secretary of State for Wales 2003-. *Political interests:* Defence, Agriculture, Treasury, Environment

Vice-chair Hammersmith and Fulham Conservative Association 1995-97. Trustee, Violet Eveson Charitable Trust; Freeman of City of London; Goldsmiths Company; *Clubs:* Hurlingham, Annabels, Pratt's; *Recreations:* Motorcycles, diving, fencing, country sports

Bill Wiggin, MP, House of Commons, London SW1A 0AA *Tel:* 020 7219 1777 *E-mail:* billwigginmp@parliament.uk. *Constituency:* 8 Corn Square, Leominster, Hereford & Worcester HR6 8LR *Tel:* 01568 612 565 *Fax:* 01568 610 320

When it comes to question time make sure you've got all the answers. For accurate and detailed information call our Parliamentary line on 08707 540106. So the next time you talk about animal welfare, it will be as good as hearing it from the horse's mouth. www.rspca.org.uk

RSPCA

Speak authoritatively on animal welfare

Con majority 6,508

WILLETTS, DAVID
Havant

David Lindsay Willetts. Born 9 March 1956; Son of John and Hilary Willetts; Educated King Edward's School, Birmingham; Christ Church, Oxford (BA philosophy, politics and economics 1978); Married Hon. Sarah Butterfield 1986 (1 son 1 daughter). HM Treasury 1978-84; Private secretary to Financial Secretary 1981-82; Principal, Monetary Policy Division 1982-84; Prime Minister's Downing Street Policy Unit 1984-86; Director of Studies, Centre for Policy Studies 1987-92; Consultant director, Conservative Research Department 1987-92; Director: Retirement Security Ltd 1988-94, Electra Corporate Ventures Ltd 1988-94; Visiting Fellow, Nuffield College, Oxford 1999-; Member, Global Commission on Ageing 2000-; Member: Lambeth and Lewisham Family Practitioners' Committee 1987-90, Parkside Health Authority 1988-90, Social Security Advisory Committee 1989-92

House of Commons: Member for Havant since 9 April 1992 general election; Opposition Spokesman on Education and Employment (Employment) 1997-98; Assistant Government Whip 1994-95; Government Whip July-November 1995; PPS to Sir Norman Fowler as Chairman of Conservative Party 1993-94; Parliamentary Secretary, Office of Public Service 1995-96; Paymaster General, Office of Public Service July-December 1996; Shadow Secretary of State for: Education and Employment 1998-99, Social Security 1999-2001, Work and Pensions 2001-05, and Welfare Reform 2004-05, Trade and Industry 2005-. *Political interests:* Economic Policy, Health, Social Security, Education. USA, Germany

Chair, Conservative Research Department 1997; Member Conservative Policy Board 2001-; Head of Policy Co-ordination Conservative Party 2003-04. *Publications: Modern Conservatism*, 1992; *Civic Conservatism*, 1994; *Blair's Gurus*, 1996; *Why Vote Conservative*, 1997; *Welfare to Work*, 1998; *After the Landslide*, 1999; *Browned-off: What's Wrong with Gordon Brown's Social Policy* 2000; Co-author *Tax Credits: Do They Add Up?* 2002; *Left Out, Left Behind*, 2003; *Old Europe? Demographic Change and Pension Reform*, 2003; *Clubs:* Hurlingham; *Recreations:* Swimming, reading, cycling

David Willetts, MP, House of Commons, London SW1A 0AA *Tel:* 020 7219 4570 *Fax:* 020 7219 2567 *E-mail:* willettsd@parliament.uk. *Constituency:* c/o Havant Conservative Association, 19 South Street, Havant, Hampshire PO9 1BU *Tel:* 023 9249 9746 *Fax:* 023 9249 8753

WILLIAMS, ALAN
Swansea West

Alan John Williams. Born 14 October 1930; Son of Emlyn Williams, coal miner; Educated Cardiff High School; Cardiff College of Technology (BSc economics, London 1954); University College, Oxford (BA philosophy, politics and economics); Married Patricia Rees 1957 (2 sons 1 daughter). Lecturer in economics, Welsh College of Advanced Technology; Member, Association of Teachers at Technical Institutes, affiliated to NUT 1958-; Member, Transport Salaried Staff Association (TSSA)

Lab majority 4,269

House of Commons: Contested Poole 1959 general election. Member for Swansea West since 15 October 1964 general election; Opposition Spokesman on: Industry 1970-71, Higher Education 1971-72, Consumer Affairs 1973-74; Opposition Frontbench Spokesperson for: Wales 1979-80, Industry and Consumer Affairs 1979-87, The Civil Service 1980-83; PPS to Edward Short as Postmaster General 1966-67; Parliamentary Under-Secretary of State, Department of Economic Affairs 1967-69; Joint Parliamentary Secretary, Ministry of Technology 1969-70; Minister of State for: Prices and Consumer Protection 1974-76, Industry 1976-79; Deputy Shadow Leader of the House and Campaigns Co-ordinator 1983-87; Shadow Secretary of State for Wales 1987-88; Father of the House 2005-. *Political interests:* Regional Policy, Industrial Policy, Employment, Micro-Technology

Member: Fabian Society, Co-operative Party; Chair, Welsh Parliamentary Labour Group 1966-67. Swansea Spastics Society; Member: Public Accounts Committee 1990-, Lord Chancellor's Advisory Council on Committee Records 1995-; Chairman, Public Accounts Commission 1997-; Council of Europe and Western European 1966-67; Chair, Welsh Branch of British-Russia Centre 1995-2001; Member, North Atlantic Alliance 1997-2001; PC January 1977; Freeman, City of Swansea; *Clubs:* Clyne Golf; *Recreations:* Golf

Rt Hon Alan Williams, MP, House of Commons, London SW1A 0AA
Tel: 020 7219 3449 *Fax:* 020 7219 6943 *E-mail:* batchelore@parliament.uk.
Constituency: Alexandra House, 42 High Street, Swansea,
West Glamorgan SA1 1LM *Tel:* 01792 655097 *Fax:* 01792 655097

WILLIAMS, BETTY
Conwy

Lab majority 3,081

Betty Williams. Born 31 July 1944; Daughter of late Griffith Williams and of Elizabeth Williams; Educated Ysgol Dyffryn Nantlle, Penygroes; Normal College, Bangor (BA communications 1995); Evan Glyn Williams (2 sons). Secretarial 1961-71; Freelance journalist/media researcher 1995-97; Member, T&GWU; Councillor: Arfon Borough Council 1970-91 (mayor 1990-91), Gwynned County Council 1976-93; Former Member: Gwynedd Health Authority, Snowdonia National Park Committee (Northern)

House of Commons: Contested Caernarfon 1983, Conwy 1987 and 1992 general elections. Member for Conwy since 1 May 1997 general election. *Political interests:* Social Services, Health, Health Education, Environmental Health, Consumer Issues, Education (Special Needs), Railways, Small Businesses. Malta, Romania, India, Poland

Welsh Regional Group of Labour MPs: Vice-chair 2002-03, Chair 2003-. Ty Gobaith Hospice Hope House; Former Member: Gas Consumers' Council for Wales, Electricity Consultative Committee; Deacon, Seion C Talysarn; Commonwealth Parliamentary Association; Inter-Parliamentary Union; Hon President, Tyddyn Bach Trust; Hon Fellow University of Wales, Bangor 2000; HTV Student of the Year; National Eisteddfod Prize for video production; John Evans Memorial Prize; Y Cymro Prize 1994-95; *Recreations:* Eisteddfodau, opera, hymn singing festivals, sheep dog trials

Betty Williams, MP, House of Commons, London SW1A 0AA *Tel:* 020 7219 5052 *Fax:* 020 7219 2759 *E-mail:* bettywilliamsmp@parliament.uk. *Constituency: Tel:* 01248 680 097

PlC majority 5,209

WILLIAMS, HYWEL
Caernarfon

Hywel Williams. Born 14 May 1953; Son of Robert Williams and Jennie Page Williams, shopkeepers; Educated Glan y Môr School, Pwllheli; University of Wales: Cardiff (BSc psychology 1974), Bangor (CQSW social work 1979); Divorced (3 daughters). Social worker: Mid Glamorgan County Council 1974-76, Gwynedd County Council 1976-84; North Wales Social Work Practice Centre University of Wales Bangor 1985-94: Project worker 1985-94, Head of centre 1991-94; Freelance lecturer consultant and author Social work and social policy 1994-; Contested Clwyd South 1999 National Assembly for Wales election; NALGO 1974-84; NUPE 1974-84; UCAC 1984-94

House of Commons: Member for Caernarfon since 7 June 2001 general election; Plaid Cymru Spokesperson for: Work and Pensions 2001-, Social Security 2001-, Health 2001-, Disability 2001-, International Development 2004-. *Political interests:* Social Affairs, Social Security, Social Work, Language Issues, Kurdish Issues. Turkey

Policy developer Social security and policy for older people Plaid Cymru 1999-; Plaid Cymru policy cabinet 1999-. Christian Aid, North Wales Air Ambulance; Member: Welsh Committee Central Council for Education and Training in Social Work, European Standing Committee B 2002-04; *Publications: Social Work in Action in the 1980s STI* (Contributor); *Geirfa Gwaith Cymdeithasol/ A Social Work Vocabulary,* University of Wales Press 1988; *Geirfa Gwaith Plant/ Child Care Terms,* University of Wales Press 1993 (General Editor); *Gwaith Cymdeithasol a'r Iaith Gymraeg/ Social Work and the Welsh Language,* University of Wales Press/CCETSW; *Llawlyfr Hyfforddi a Hyfforddwyr/ An Index of Trainers and Training,* AGWC 1994; *Gofal – Pecyn Adnoddau a Hyfforddi Gofal yn y Gymuned yng Nghymru/ A Training and Resource Pack for Community Care in Wales,* CCETSW Cymru 1998; Contributor, *Speaking the Invisible,* National Assembly for Wales 2002; *Recreations:* Reading, cinema, walking, kite flying

Hywel Williams, MP, House of Commons, London SW1A 0AA *Tel:* 020 7219 5021 *Fax:* 020 7219 3705 *E-mail:* williamshy@parliament.uk. *Constituency:* 8 Castle Street, Caernarfon, Gwynedd *Tel:* 01286 672 076 *Fax:* 01286 672 003

Lib Dem majority 219

WILLIAMS, MARK
Ceredigion

Mark Fraser Williams. Born 24 March 1966; Educated Richard Hale School, Hertford; Universty College of Wales, Aberystwyth (BSc politics and economics 1987); Plymouth University (PGCE primary education 1993); Married Helen Refna Wyatt 1997. Teacher: Madron Daniel School, Cornwall 1993-96, Forches Cross School, Barnstaple, Devon 1996-2000; Deputy head teacher, Llangorse Church in Wales School nr Brecon 2000; Member, NASUWT, (National Association of Schoolmasters/Union of Women Teachers) 1993

House of Commons: Contested Monmouth 1997 general election, Ceredigion 2000 by-election and 2001 general election. Member for Ceredigion since 5 May 2005 general election. *Political interests:* Education, rural affairs

Research assistant, Liberal/Liberal Democrat Peers 1987-92; Member, Welsh Liberal Democrats Executive 1991-92; Constituency assistant, Geraint Howells MP 1987-92; President, Ceredigion Liberal Democrats 1998-2000; Member, Welsh Liberal Democrats Campaign Committee 2000. *Recreations:* Reading, political biographies, gardening, fresh air

Mark Williams, MP, House of Commons, London SW1A 0AA *Tel:* 020 7219 8469. *Constituency: Tel:* 01970 615880 *Fax:* 01970 615880

WILLIAMS, ROGER

Brecon and Radnorshire

Roger Hugh Williams. Born 22 January 1948; Educated Christ College; Cambridge University (BA agriculture 1969); Married Penelope James 1973 (1 daughter 1 son). Farmer 1969-; Contested Carmarthen West and South Pembrokeshire 1999 National Assembly for Wales election; Former chair Brecon and Radnorshire NFU; Member Farmers Union of Wales; Councillor Powys County Council 1981-2001; Brecon Beacons National Park 1985-: Councillor, Chair 1991-95

Lib Dem majority
3,905

House of Commons: Member for Brecon and Radnorshire since 7 June 2001 general election; Liberal Democrat Spokesperson for Rural Affairs 2002-; Liberal Democrat Whip 2004-. *Political interests:* Agriculture, Education, Economic Development

Recreations: Sport, walking, nature conservation

Roger Williams, MP, House of Commons, London SW1A 0AA *Tel:* 020 7219 8145 *E-mail:* brecrad@cix.co.uk. *Constituency:* 4 Watergate, Brecon, Powys LD3 9AN *Tel:* 01874 625 739 *Fax:* 01874 625 635

WILLIAMS, STEPHEN

Bristol West

Stephen Roy Williams. Born 11 October 1966; Educated Mountain Ash Comprehensive School; Bristol University (BA history 1988); Single. Graduate trainee up to supervisor, Coopers and Lybrand, Bristol 1988-95; Tax manager: Kraft Jacobs Suchard Ltd, Cheltenham Head Office 1995, Grant Thornton, Cheltenham Head Office 1996-98, Grant Thornton, Bristol Office 1998-; Deputy Leader/Group Chair Liberal Democrat Group, Avon Council 1993-96; Bristol City Council: Councillor 1995-99, Leader Liberal Democrat Group/Shadow Council Leader 1995-97

Lib Dem majority
5,128

House of Commons: Contested Bristol South 1997 and Bristol West 2001 general elections. Member for Bristol West since 5 May 2005 general election. *Political interests:* Taxation, education, preventative health care, transport, civil rights, arts, Europe

Chair, Bristol University SDP/Liberal Club 1986-87; Constituency secretary, Cynon Valley SDP 1986-88. *Recreations:* Art galleries, historic sites, theatre, cinema, eating out, swimming, playing pool, gym

Stephen Williams, MP, House of Commons, London SW1A 0AA *Tel:* 020 7219 8416. *Constituency:* Flat 6, 14 Portland Street, Kingsdown, Bristol, Avon BS2 8HL *Tel:* 0117 944 1714 *E-mail:* stevewilliams@cix.co.uk

WILLIS, PHIL
Harrogate and Knaresborough

Phil (Philip George) Willis. Born 30 November 1941; Son of late George Willis, postman, and of late Norah, nurse; Educated Burnley Grammar School; City of Leeds and Carnegie College (Cert Ed 1963); Birmingham University (BPhil education 1978); Married Heather Sellars 1974 (1 son 1 daughter). Head teacher, Ormesby School, Cleveland 1978-82; Head teacher, John Smeaton Community High School, Leeds 1983-97; Member, Secondary Heads Association; Harrogate Borough Council: Councillor 1988-99, first Liberal Democrat Leader 1990-97; North Yorkshire County Council: Councillor 1993-97, Deputy Group Leader 1993-97

Lib Dem majority 10,429

House of Commons: Member for Harrogate and Knaresborough since 1 May 1997 general election; Liberal Democrat Spokesperson for Education and Employment (Further, Higher and Adult Education) 1997-99; Principal Spokesperson for: Education and Employment 1999-2000; North, Midlands and Wales Whip 1997-99; Liberal Democrat Shadow Secretary of State for Education and Skills 2000-05. *Political interests:* Inclusive Education, Health, Local and Regional Government, Northern Ireland, Gibraltar, Ireland

Member, Association of Liberal Democrat Councillors. National Children's Homes, St Michael's Hospice, Harrogate; Times Educational Supplement 'Man of the Year' 2002; *Clubs:* Leeds United Football Club; *Recreations:* Theatre, music, dance (especially ballet), football (Leeds United)

Phil Willis, MP, House of Commons, London SW1A 0AA *Tel:* 020 7219 5709 *Fax:* 020 7219 0971 *E-mail:* johnfox@cix.co.uk. *Constituency:* Ashdown House, Station Parade, Harrogate, North Yorkshire HG1 5BR *Tel:* 01423 528888 *Fax:* 01423 505700

WILLOTT, JENNY
Cardiff Central

Jennifer Nancy Willott. Born 29 May 1974; Educated Wimbledon High School; Uppingham School;; St Mary's College, Durham (BA classics 1996); London School of Economics (MSc Econ development studies 1997); Single. Researcher and proposal writer, Adithi NGO, Bihar, India 1995; Head of office, Lembit Öpik MP 1997-2000; Researcher, Lib Dem group, National Assembly for Wales 2000-01; Project administrator, Barnado's, Derwen project 2001; Head of advocacy, UNICEF UK 2001-03; Area manager, Victim Support Wales 2003-; London Borough of Merton councillor 1998-2000

Lib Dem majority 5,593

House of Commons: Contested Cardiff Central 2001 general election. Member for Cardiff Central since 5 May 2005 general election. *Political interests:* International development, foreign affairs, children's issues, crime and disorder

Unicef UK; Shelter; *Recreations:* Travelling, music, reading

Jenny Willott, MP, House of Commons, London SW1A 0AA *Tel:* 020 7219 8418. *Constituency:* 133 City Road, Roath, Cardiff CF24 *Tel:* 029 2049 2227 *Fax:* 029 2047 1168 *E-mail:* jenny@jennywillott.com *Website:* www.jennywillott.com

WILLS, MICHAEL
North Swindon

Michael David Wills. Born 20 May 1952; Son of late Stephen Wills and Elizabeth Wills; Educated Haberdashers Aske's, Elstree; Clare College, Cambridge (BA history 1973); Married Jill Freeman 1984 (3 sons 2 daughters). Third secretary later second secretary, HM Diplomatic Service 1976-80; Researcher, later producer, London Weekend Television 1980-84; Director, Juniper Productions TV production company 1984-97; Member, TGWU

Lab majority 2,571

House of Commons: Member for North Swindon since 1 May 1997 general election; Parliamentary Under-Secretary of State: Department of Trade and Industry (Minister for Small Firms, Trade and Industry) 1999, Department for Education and Employment 1999-2001; Parliamentary Secretary, Lord Chancellor's Department 2001-02; Parliamentary Under-Secretary of State, Home Office 2002-03: for Criminal Justice System IT 2002, (Information Technology in the Criminal Justice System) 2003

Chair, Non-Ministerial Cross-Party Advisory Group on Preparation for the EMU 1998-

Michael Wills, MP, House of Commons, London SW1A 0AA *Tel:* 020 7219 4399 *E-mail:* willsm@parliament.uk. *Constituency: Tel:* 020 7219 4399

WILSHIRE, DAVID
Spelthorne

David Wilshire. Born 16 September 1943; Educated Kingswood School, Bath; Fitzwilliam College, Cambridge (BA geography 1965, MA); Married Margaret Weeks 1967 (separated 2000) (1 son, 1 daughter deceased). Built up own group of small businesses; Worked for MEPs 1979-85; Partner, Western Political Research Services 1979-2000; Co-director, Political Management Programme, Brunel University 1985-90; Partner, Moorlands Research Services 2000-; Wansdyke District Council: Councillor 1976-87, Leader 1981-87; Councillor Avon County Council 1977-81

Con majority 9,936

House of Commons: Member for Spelthorne since 11 June 1987 general election; Opposition Whip 2001-; PPS: to Alan Clark as Minister for Defence Procurement 1991-92, to Peter Lloyd as Minister of State, Home Office 1992-94. *Political interests:* Foreign Affairs, Aviation, Political Process, Northern Ireland

The Compassionate Friends; Member, British-Irish Inter-Parliamentary Body 1990-2001; Treasurer, IPU British Branch 1997-2000; Substitute Member, Assembly of Council of Europe 1997-2001; Vice-Chairman, CPA UK Branch 1998-99; Executive Committee Member, British-American Parliamentary Group 2001-; *Publications: Scene from the Hill*; *Recreations:* Gardening, wine and cider-making

David Wilshire, MP, House of Commons, London SW1A 0AA *Tel:* 020 7219 3534 *Fax:* 020 7219 5852. *Constituency:* 55 Cherry Orchard, Staines, Middlesex TW8 2DQ *Tel:* 01784 450822 *Fax:* 01784 466109

WILSON, ROBERT
Reading East

Robert Wilson. Born 1965; Educated Reading University; Married Jane. Entrepreneur in health and communications; Adviser to David Davis MP; Councillor Reading Borough Council 1992-96, 2004-

House of Commons: Member for Reading East since 5 May 2005 general election. *Political interests:* Crime, education, immigration

Conservative campaign manager 1992 general elction campaign

Con majority 475

Robert Wilson, MP, House of Commons, London SW1A 0AA *Tel:* 020 7219 6519. *Constituency:* Reading East Conservative Association, 12a South View Park, Marsack Street, Caversham, Reading, Berkshire RG4 5AF *Tel:* 0118-375 9785 *Fax:* 0118-375 9786 *E-mail:* office@readingeastconservatives.com *Website:* www.readingeastconservatives.com

WILSON, SAMMY
East Antrim

Sammy Wilson. Born 4 April 1953; Son of Alexander and Mary Wilson. Head of economics, Grammar School; MLA for Belfast East 1998-2003, and for East Antrim 2003-; East Belfast City Council: Councillor 1981-, Lord Mayor 1986; Member, Northern Ireland Policing Board 2001-

House of Commons: Member for East Antrim since 5 May 2005 general election; Member Northern Ireland Forum for Political Dialogue 1996

DUP majority 7,304

Sammy Wilson, MP, House of Commons, London SW1A 0AA *Tel:* 020 7219 8523

WINNICK, DAVID
Walsall North

David Winnick. Born 26 June 1933; Son of late E. G. and Rose Winnick; Educated Secondary school; London School of Economics (diploma social administration 1974); Married Bengisu Rona 1968 (divorced 1984). Administrative Employee; Association of Professional, Executive, Clerical & Computer Staff (APEX): Member of Executive Council 1978-88, Vice-President 1983-88; Councillor: Willesden Borough Council 1959-64, Brent Borough Council 1964-66

House of Commons: Contested Harwich 1964 general election. Member for Croydon South 1966-70. Contested Croydon Central October 1974 general election and Walsall North 1976 by-election. Member for Walsall North since 3 May 1979 general election

British Co-Chair, British-Irish Inter-Parliamentary Body 1997-

Lab majority 6,640

David Winnick, MP, House of Commons, London SW1A 0AA *Tel:* 020 7219 5003 *Fax:* 020 7219 0257 *E-mail:* winnickd@parliament.uk. *Constituency:* Bellamy House, Wilkes Street, Willenhall WV13 2BS *Tel:* 01902 605020 *Fax:* 01902 637372

Con majority 8,246

WINTERTON, ANN
Congleton

(Jane) Ann Winterton. Born 6 March 1941; Daughter of late Joseph Robert and Ellen Jane Hodgson; Educated Erdington Grammar School for Girls; Married Nicholas Winterton (now MP, later Sir) 1960 (2 sons 1 daughter)

House of Commons: Member for Congleton since 9 June 1983 general election; Opposition Spokesman for National Drug Strategy 1998-2001; Shadow Minister for Agriculture and Fisheries 2001-02. *Political interests:* Textile Industries, Pharmaceutical and Chemical Industries, Agriculture, Transport, Fisheries. Austria, Namibia, South Africa, USA

Member, West Midlands Conservative Women's Advisory Committee 1969-71. Joint Master, South Staffordshire Hunt 1959-64; Representative, Organisation for Security and Co-operation in Europe; Fellow, Industry and Parliament Trust; *Recreations:* Cinema, theatre, music, tennis, riding, skiing

Ann Winterton, MP, House of Commons, London SW1A 0AA *Tel:* 020 7219 3585 *Fax:* 020 7219 6886 *E-mail:* wintertona@parliament.uk. *Constituency:* Riverside, Mountbatten Way, Congleton, Cheshire CW12 1DY *Tel:* 01260 278866 *Fax:* 01260 271212

Con majority 9,401

WINTERTON, NICHOLAS
Macclesfield

Nicholas Winterton. Born 31 March 1938; Son of late Norman Harry Winterton; Educated Bilton Grange Preparatory School; Rugby School; Married Ann Hodgson (now MP as Ann Winterton) 1960 (2 sons 1 daughter). Army national service 1957-59. Sales executive trainee, Shell-Mex BP Ltd 1959-60; Sales and general manager, Stevens & Hodgson Ltd 1960-71; Warwickshire County Council: Councillor 1967-72, Chair, County Youth Service Sub-Committee 1969-72, Deputy Chair, Education Committee 1970-72

House of Commons: Contested Newcastle-under-Lyme October 1969 by-election and 1970 general election. Member for Macclesfield since 30 September 1971 by-election; Deputy Speaker Westminster Hall 1999-2001, 2002-; Chairman: Health Select Committee 1990-92, Procedure Committee 1997-; Member, Speaker's Panel of Chairmen, Modernisation and Liaison Committee. *Political interests:* Local and Regional Government, NHS, Sport, Recreation, Paper Industries, Textile Industries, Foreign Affairs, Media, Pharmaceutical and Chemical Industries. South Africa, Indonesia, Taiwan, USA, Denmark, Sweden, Austria, Namibia, Zimbabwe

Multiple Sclerosis, Riding for the Disabled, Friends of the Pallotti Day Care Centre, Friends of the Rossendale Trust, NSPCC, Crossroads Association; Chair, Executive Committee of Anglo/Austrian Society 1999-2000; Hon. Vice-President: National Association of Master Bakers, Confectioners and Caterers, The Royal College of Midwives; Vice-President, National Association of Local Councils; Hon Member Macclesfield and District Lions Club; Member of Council, League for Exchange of Commonwealth Teachers 1979-92; Member, Executive Committee: Commonwealth Parliamentary Association (CPA) UK Branch 1997-, Inter-Parliamentary Union, UK Branch; Fellow, Industry and Parliament Trust -2001; Knight Bachelor 2002; Past Upper Bailiff and Member of the Court of Assistants, Worshipful Company of Weavers; Freeman, City of London; Freeman, Borough of Macclesfield; *Clubs:* Cavalry and Guards, Lighthouse, Old Boys and Park Green Macclesfield; Hon. Vice-president: Bollington Bowling Club, Bollington Cricket Club, Macclesfield Cricket Club, Prince Albert Angling Society; President: Macclesfield Hockey Club, New Century Bowman, Macclesfield Satellite Swimming Club, Disley Amalgamated Sports Club; Hon life member Macclesfield Rugby Union Football Club; Hon Vice-president, Poynton Sports Club; *Recreations:* Squash, tennis, swimming, jogging, skiing

Sir Nicholas Winterton, MP, House of Commons, London SW1A 0AA
Tel: 020 7219 4402 *Fax:* 020 7219 6886. *Constituency:* Macclesfield Conservative and Unionist Association, West Bank Road, Macclesfield, Cheshire SK10 3DU
Tel: 01625 422848 *Fax:* 01625 617066 *E-mail:* mca@tory.org.uk

Lab majority 9,802

WINTERTON, ROSIE
Doncaster Central

Rosie Winterton. Born 10 August 1958; Daughter of Gordon Winterton, teacher, and late Valerie Winterton, teacher; Educated Doncaster Grammar School; Hull University (BA history 1979). Constituency personal assistant to John Prescott, MP 1980-86; Parliamentary officer: Southwark Council 1986-88, Royal College of Nursing 1988-90; Managing Director, Connect Public Affairs 1990-94; Head of private office of John Prescott as Deputy Leader of Labour Party 1994-97; Branch Officer, TGWU 1998-99; Member: NUJ, TGWU

House of Commons: Member for Doncaster Central since 1 May 1997 general election; Parliamentary Secretary, Lord Chancellor's Department 2001-03; Minister of State, Department of Health 2003-. *Political interests:* Regional Policy, Employment, Transport, Housing, Home Affairs

Member, Labour Party Strategic Campaign Committee; Representative, PLP on the National Policy Forum of the Labour Party. Leader, Leadership Campaign Team 1998-99; Chair, Transport and General Workers' Parliamentary Group 1998-99; Former Member, Standing Committees: Local Government Finance (Supplementary Credit Approvals) Bill, Regional Development Agencies Bill; Member Standing Committees: Transport Bill January 2000, Finance Bill April 2000; Intelligence and Security Committee January 2000-; *Clubs:* Doncaster Trades and Labour, Intake Social, Doncaster Catholic; *Recreations:* Sailing, reading

Rosie Winterton, MP, House of Commons, London SW1A 0AA *Tel:* 020 7219 0925 *Fax:* 020 7219 4581 *E-mail:* wintertonr@parliament.uk. *Constituency:* Guildhall Advice Centre, Old Guildhall Yard, Doncaster, South Yorkshire DN1 1QW *Tel:* 01302 735241 *Fax:* 01302 735242

SNP majority 1,521

WISHART, PETER
Perth and North Perthshire

Peter Wishart. Born 9 March 1962; Son of late Alex Wishart, former dockyard worker and Nan Irvine, retired teacher; Educated Queen Anne High School, Dunfermline, Fife; Moray House College of Education (Dip CommEd 1984); Married Carrie Lindsay 1990 (separated 2003) (1 son). Musician Big Country 1981; Community worker Central Region 1984-85; Musician Runrig 1985-2001; Musicians Union 1985-

House of Commons: Member for North Tayside 2001-05, for Perth and North Perthshire since 5 May 2005 general election; SNP Spokesperson for: Transport 2001-, Rural Affairs 2001-, Culture, Media and Sport 2001-; SNP Chief Whip 2001-. *Political interests:* Drugs Issues, Justice and Equality, Arts and Culture. Scandinavia, Germany

Member: National Council 1997-, NEC 1999-; Executive vice-convener fundraising SNP 1999-2001. Member, European Standing Committee B 2005-; *Recreations:* Music, hillwalking, travel

Peter Wishart, MP, House of Commons, London SW1A 0AA *Tel:* 020 7219 8303 *E-mail:* wishartp@parliament.uk. *Constituency:* 35 Perth Street, Blairgowrie PH10 6DL *Tel:* 01250 876 576 *Fax:* 01250 876 991

DIAGNOSTICS: faster decision making, better outcomes

In today's health service faster and better decision making, leading to better outcomes, is expected. Our government wants it, patients deserve it. Doctors and nurses want the best technology to support patient care and patients want the best treatment. Everyone wants to know their taxes are being used wisely!

Diagnostic tests play a crucial role in identifying the presence of disease, as well in monitoring treatment. They can provide early signs of a disease, and rapid access to results can facilitate earlier treatment and reduce hospital stay. But what do we know about diagnostic tests, when they are useful, and how the results improve outcomes?

Here are some examples of how tests can help improve both the efficiency and effectiveness of our health services:

1) Brain natriuretic peptide (BNP) tests can help diagnose heart failure earlier, and more effectively, by targeting those who would normally have to go to hospital for an expensive 'echo' test (for which there can be long waiting times); they also help manage patients with heart failure more effectively

2) Regular access to glycated haemoglobin tests helps to show the effectiveness of diabetics care, whilst urine albumin tests provide early signs of complications of the disease

3) Glucose tests can help detect the UK's 'Missing Million' diabetics. Early and effective treatment reduces the onset of secondary complications such as blindness and kidney disease

4) Cholesterol is one of a number of risk factors for coronary heart disease; early recognition of an increased cholesterol in the blood and appropriate therapy can reduce that risk

Investment in tests like those highlighted above can reduce the overall cost of healthcare whilst also improving outcomes.

More information on these and many other tests can be obtained from a website recently launched in 2004 by the Association for Clinical Biochemistry, Lab Tests Online UK, to be found at www.labtestsonline.org.uk.

The Association for Clinical Biochemistry trains clinical scientists to specialize in ensuring that biochemical testing can make effective contributions to effective healthcare delivery. Currently, UK investment in laboratory diagnostics is the second lowest amongst our EC partners. The Association provides guidelines on the use of tests and contributes to ongoing research and development in new tests by publishing widely, including its own journal and books. Wider dialogue on all these issues are welcomed via its offices.

Association for Clinical Biochemistry
130–132 Tooley Street, London SE1 2TU
Tel 020 7403 8001
info@acb.org.uk
www.acb.org.uk

The Association for Clinical Biochemistry

WOOD, MIKE
Batley and Spen

Mike Wood. Born 3 March 1946; Son of late Rowland L. Wood, foundry worker, and Laura M. Wood, retired cleaner; Educated Nantwich and Acton Grammar School, Nantwich, Cheshire; Salisbury/Wells Theological College (Cert Theol 1974); Leeds University (CQSW 1981); Leeds Metropolitan University (BA history and politics 1989); Married 2nd Christine O'Leary 1999 (1 son 1 daughter from previous marriage; 2 stepdaughters). Probation officer, social worker, community worker 1965-97; Trade unionist 1962-; Member: UNISON, GMB; Kirklees Metropolitan District Council: Councillor 1980-88, Deputy Leader of Council 1986-87

Lab majority 5,788

House of Commons: Contested Hexham 1987 general election. Member for Batley and Spen since 1 May 1997 general election. *Political interests:* Poverty, Housing, Transport, Environmental Issues and World Development, Small Businesses. France, Indian Sub-continent

Member, Labour Friends of India. Kirkwood Hospice, Huddersfield; *Publications: Probation Hostel Directory*, 1980; *Recreations:* Sport, music, ornithology, walking

Mike Wood, MP, House of Commons, London SW1A 0AA *Tel:* 020 7219 4125. *Constituency:* Tom Myer's House, 9 Cross Crown Street, Cleckheaton BD19 3HW *Tel:* 01274 335233 *Fax:* 01274 335235

WOODWARD, SHAUN
St Helens South

Shaun Anthony Woodward. Born 26 October 1958; Son of Dennis George Woodward and Joan Lillian, neé Nunn; Educated Bristol Grammar School; Jesus College, Cambridge (MA English literature); Married Camilla Davan Sainsbury 1987 (1 son 3 daughters). BBC TV News and Current Affairs 1982-98; Director of communications, Conservative Party 1991-92; Member, AEEU

Lab majority 9,309

House of Commons: Member for Witney 1 May 1 1997 general election-June 2001 (Conservative May 1997-December 1999, Labour December 1999-June 2001) and Member for St Helens South since 7 June 2001 general election; Opposition Frontbench Spokesperson for Environment, Transport and the Regions 1999; Parliamentary Under-Secretary of State, Northern Ireland Office 2005-. *Political interests:* Finance, Environment, Education, Culture, Children's Issues, European Affairs, Race Relations and Civil Rights, Regeneration, International Development, Speaker's Advisory Committee on Works of Art. USA, France, Germany, Italy, China and Australia

Director: English National Opera 1998-2001, Marine Stewardship Council 1998-2001; Former Member, Foundation Board, RSC; Trustee, Childline; Vice-President, St Helens District Council for Voluntary Service; Honorary President, St Helens Millennium Centre; *Publications:* Co-author: *Tranquillisers*, 1983, *Ben: The Story of Ben Hardwick*, 1984, *Drugwatch*, 1985; Visiting professor, Queen Mary and Westfield College, London University; Visiting fellow, John F. Kennedy School of Government, Harvard University; *Recreations:* Opera, tennis, reading, gardening, architecture

Shaun Woodward, MP, House of Commons, London SW1A 0AA *Tel:* 020 7219 2680 *Fax:* 020 7219 0979 *E-mail:* shaunwoodwardmp@email.labour.org.uk. *Constituency:* 1st Floor, Century House, Hardshaw Street, St Helens, Merseyside WA10 1QW *Tel:* 01744 24226 *Fax:* 01744 24306

The HOUSE MAGAZINE

For the inside track on the new Parliament

only £195 a year

Includes access to the fully searchable online archive of past issues at: www.housemag.co.uk

The House Magazine is the unique weekly publication for the Houses of Parliament and all those with an interest in policy and legislation.

Published every week that Parliament is in session, you will receive:

- Unrivalled insight into the previous week's parliamentary business as well as a comprehensive look ahead to the coming week's agenda in both the House of Commons and House of Lords
- Focus on key policy topics with exclusive contributions from senior government figures and relevant opposition MPs as well as leading industry experts
- Interviews with key figures in public life, industry and the media
- In-depth profiles of leading parliamentarians
- Insightful news and analysis about domestic and international politics

> " The House Magazine has become an important source of information and a great asset to Westminster life. "
>
> **The Prime Minister, Tony Blair MP**

> " The House Magazine covers both Houses from the inside. It's a great read and a useful tool for journalists and parliamentarians. "
>
> **Sky News Political Editor Adam Boulton**

For a free sample copy and information on how to subscribe please visit www.housemag.co.uk or call 020 7091 7510

Lab majority 3,590

WOOLAS, PHIL
Oldham East and Saddleworth

Philip James Woolas. Born 11 December 1959; Son of Dennis and Maureen Woolas; Educated Nelson Grammar School; Walton Lane High School; Nelson and Colne College; Manchester University (BA philosophy 1981); Married Tracey Allen 1988 (2 sons). President, National Union of Students 1984-86; BBC Newsnight producer 1988-90; Channel 4 News producer 1990; Head of communication, GMB 1991-97; Member, GMB

House of Commons: Contested Littleborough and Saddleworth by-election 1995. Member for Oldham East and Saddleworth since 1 May 1997 general election; Assistant Government Whip 2001-02; Government Whip 2002-03; PPS to Lord Macdonald of Tradeston, as Minister of State for Transport, Department of the Environment, Transport and the Regions (Minister for Transport) 1999-2001; Deputy Leader of the House of Commons, Privy Council Office 2003-05; Minister of State (Minister for Local Government), Office of the Deputy Prime Minister 2005-. *Political interests:* Employment, Economics, Media, Trade and Industry, Benzodiazipines. Kashmir and Jammu

Chair, Tribune Newspaper 1997-2001; Deputy Leader, Leadership Campaign Team 1997-99. Beat the Benzos; RTS Award for Political Coverage 1990; *Clubs:* Lancashire County Cricket Club, Manchester United Football Club; *Recreations:* Photography

Phil Woolas, MP, House of Commons, London SW1A 0AA *Tel:* 020 7219 1149 *Fax:* 020 7219 0992 *E-mail:* woolasp@parliament.uk. *Constituency:* 11 Church Lane, Oldham, Greater Manchester OL1 3AN *Tel:* 0161-624 4248 *Fax:* 0161-626 8572

Lab majority 3,055

WRIGHT, ANTHONY DAVID
Great Yarmouth

Anthony David Wright. Born 12 August 1954; Son of late Arthur Wright and of Jean Wright; Educated Hospital Secondary modern school, Great Yarmouth; City and Guilds Mechanical Engineer apprentice 1969-73; Married Barbara Fleming 1988 (1 son 1 daughter 1 stepdaughter). Engineering apprentice 1970-74; Engineer 1974-83; Labour Party organiser/agent 1983-97; Member: AMICUS, GMB; Great Yarmouth Borough Council: Councillor 1980-82, 1986-98, Leader of Council 1996-97

House of Commons: Member for Great Yarmouth since 1 May 1997 general election; PPS to Ruth Kelly as Financial Secretary to the Treasury 2002-03. *Political interests:* Local and Regional Government, Trade and Industry. Cyprus

Member European Standing Committee C 1999-; Director Seachange Trust 1995-

Anthony David Wright, MP, House of Commons, London SW1A 0AA *Tel:* 020 7219 3447 *Fax:* 020 7219 2304 *E-mail:* wrighta@parliament.uk. *Constituency:* 21 Euston Road, Great Yarmouth, Norfolk NR30 1DZ *Tel:* 01493 332291 *Fax:* 01493 332189

Belief in Action

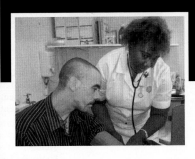

Throughout the UK, The Salvation Army is at the cutting edge of care in our churches and social service centres. Our mission takes us into the front line of the battle against the biggest social problems of the age.

Today our **services for homeless people** are offering individually tailored packages of care to people with a wide range of problems, including alcoholism and mental illness. Our **National Addiction Service** is combining scientific knowledge and professional care to help people break free from drugs.

Our Outreach and Resettlement Teams work in major cities to identify people sleeping rough. We build relationships with them as the first step towards offering longer-term programmes leading to resettlement in appropriate accommodation.

Our **residential and home care services** are giving older people the chance to retain their independence whilst receiving the care they need. Our f**amily and children's services** are working to help families stay together, while also supporting parents and children who are coping with family breakdown.

The Salvation Army is at the heart of almost every community. Through our network of 1000 centres across the UK, **we touch the lives of thousands of people,** often working in partnership with national and local government. At the same time we are innovators, constantly striving to raise our professional standards and the quality of our services so we can meet today's problems with tomorrow's solutions.

You can find out more about the work of The Salvation Army by visiting our website **www.salvationarmy.org.uk**

Or you can contact Jonathan Lomax, Public Affairs Officer, on **020 7367 4885** or email him at **jonathan.lomax@salvationarmy.org.uk**

Belief in Action

The Salvation Army is a registered charity.

WRIGHT, DAVID
Telford

David Wright. Born 22 December 1966; Son of Kenneth William Wright and Heather Wright, neé Wynn; Educated Wrockwardine Wood Comprehensive School, Telford, Shropshire; New College, Telford, Shropshire; Wolverhampton Polytechnic (BA humanities 1988); Married Lesley Insole 1996. Housing strategy manager Sandwell Metropolitan Borough Council 1988-2001; Member TGWU 1988-; Councillor Wrekin District Council 1989-97; Oakengates Town Council 1989-2000: Councillor, Former chair

Lab majority 5,406

House of Commons: Member for Telford since 7 June 2001 general election; PPS to Rosie Winterton as Minister of State, Department of Health 2004-. *Political interests:* Development of Housing and Regeneration Strategy, Regional Development, Sports Development, Hunting With Dogs (Against), Poverty. France, USA

Various former positions: Wrekin and Telford Constituency Labour Parties, Oakengates Branch Labour Party. National Canine Defence League; *Clubs:* Member: Wrockwardine Wood and Trench Labour, Dawley Social; *Recreations:* Football (Telford United and Shrewsbury Town), local history, visiting medieval towns

David Wright, MP, House of Commons, London SW1A 0AA *Tel:* 020 7219 8331 *Fax:* 020 7219 1979 *E-mail:* wrightda@parliament.uk. *Constituency:* 35B High Street, Dawley, Telford, Shropshire TF4 2EX *Tel:* 01952 507747 *Fax:* 01952 506064

WRIGHT, IAIN
Hartlepool

Iain Wright. Born 9 May 1972; Educated Manor Comprehensive School, Hartlepool; Tiffany (2 sons 1 daughter). Chartered accountant; Accountant OneNorthEast regional development agency; Member GMB; Councillor Hartlepool Borough Council 2002-05: Cabinet member for performance management

House of Commons: Member for Hartlepool since 30 October 2004 by-election

Member, European Standing Committee A 2005-

Lab majority 7,478

Iain Wright, MP, House of Commons, London SW1A 0AA *Tel:* 020 7219 5587. *Constituency:* 23 South Road, Hartlepool, Cleveland TS26 9HD *Tel:* 01429 224403

WRIGHT, JEREMY
Rugby and Kenilworth

Jeremy Wright. Born 24 October 1972; Educated Taunton School, Somerset; Trinity School, New York City, USA; Exeter University (LLB law 1995); Inns of Court School of Law (Bar vocational course 1996); Married Yvonne Annette Salter 1998. Barrister, specialising in criminal law 1996-

House of Commons: Member for Rugby and Kenilworth since 5 May 2005 general election. *Political interests:* Criminal justice, education, foreign affairs

Con majority 1,556

Chairman, Warwick and Leamington Conservative Association 2002-03. Member and former scholar and congressional intern, English Speaking Union 1992-; *Recreations:* Travel, golf, James Bond films

Jeremy Wright, MP, House of Commons, London SW1A 0AA *Tel:* 020 7219 8299. *Constituency:* Alberta Buildings, Alberta Street, Rugby, Warwickshire CV21 2RS *Tel:* 01788 542677 *Fax:* 01788 569735 *E-mail:* jeremy@jeremywright.co.uk *Website:* www.jeremywright.co.uk

Lab majority 9,227

WRIGHT, TONY WAYLAND
Cannock Chase

Anthony Wayland Wright. Born 11 March 1948; Son of Frank and Maud Wright; Educated Desborough Primary School; Kettering Grammar School; London School of Economics (BSc economics 1970); Harvard University (Kennedy Scholar 1970-71); Balliol College, Oxford (DPhil 1973); Married Moira Elynwy Phillips 1973 (3 sons and 1 son deceased). Lecturer in politics, University College of North Wales, Bangor 1973-75; School of Continuing Studies, Birmingham University: Lecturer, Senior lecturer, Reader in politics 1975-92; AUT; Chair, South Birmingham Community Health Council 1983-85

House of Commons: Contested Kidderminster 1979 general election. Member for Cannock and Burntwood 1992-97, and for Cannock Chase since 1 May 1997 general election; PPS to Lord Irvine of Lairg as Lord Chancellor 1997-98. *Political interests:* Education, Health, Environment, Constitution

Executive Member, Fabian Society. *Publications:* Include: *G. D. H. Cole and Socialist Democracy*, 1979; *Local Radio and Local Democracy*, 1982; *British Socialism*, 1983; *Socialisms: Theories and Practices*, 1986; *R. H. Tawney*, 1987; *Matters of Death and Life: A Study of Bereavement Support in Hospitals*, 1988; *Consuming Public Services*, 1990 (editor); *Contemporary Political Ideologies*, 1993 (editor); *Subjects and Citizens*, 1993; *Socialisms: Old and New*, 1996; *The People's Party*, 1997; *Who Can I Complain To?*, 1997; *Why Vote Labour?*, 1997; Joint Editor, *The Political Quarterly*; *The New Social Democracy*, 1999 (joint editor); *The British Political Process*, 2000 (editor); *The English Question*, 2000 (joint editor); *British Politics: A Very Short Introduction*, 2003; Hon professor, Birmingham University 1999-; *Recreations:* Tennis, football, secondhand bookshops, walking, gardening

Dr Tony Wayland Wright, MP, House of Commons, London SW1A 0AA
Tel: 020 7219 5029; 020 7219 5583   *Fax:* 020 7219 2665
E-mail: wrightt@parliament.uk.   *Constituency:* 6A Hallcourt Crescent, Cannock, Staffordshire WS11 3AB   *Tel:* 01543 467810   *Fax:* 01543 467811

Lab majority 79

WYATT, DEREK
Sittingbourne and Sheppey

Derek Wyatt. Born 4 December 1949; Son of late Reginald and Margaret Wyatt; Educated Westcliff County High School; Colchester Royal Grammar School; St Luke's College, Exeter (Certificate of Education 1971); Open University (BA art and architecture 1978); St Catherine's College, Oxford (research 1981-82); University of California, Berkeley (management 2002); Married Joanna Willett (1 daughter 1 son). Director and a Publisher, William Heinemann 1986-88; Head of Programmes, Wire TV 1994-95; Director, Computer Channel, BSkyB 1995-97; Councillor, London Borough of Haringey 1994-96, Chairman, Alexandra Palace and Parks 1994-96

House of Commons: Member for Sittingbourne and Sheppey since 1 May 1997 general election; Adviser on Rugby Union to Richard Caborn, as Minister of State for Sport 2002-. *Political interests:* Venture Capital, Internet, British Council, Foreign Affairs, Media, Money Laundering. Southern Africa, Middle East, China

Demelza House Children's Hospice; Founder Oxford Internet Institute 2000; Trustee Major Stanley's, Oxford University 1993-; Fellow: Industry and Parliament Trust (Motorola) 1998-2001, Parliament Voluntary Sector Trust (Raleigh International) 1999-2001; *Publications:* 6 books to date including: *Wisecracks From The Movies*, 1987, *Rugby DisUnion*, 1995, Co-author *Rugby Revolution*, 2003; UNO Special Commendation 1987; United Nations Commendation (Apartheid in Sport) 1987; Worshipful Company of Information Technologists; Freeman, City of London; *Clubs:* RAC, Vincents (Oxford); Charlton Athletic FC, Penguin International RFC (Executive); Played Rugby for Oxford University, Barbarians and England; *Recreations:* Reading, sport, writing, travel, jazz

Derek Wyatt, MP, House of Commons, London SW1A 0AA *Tel:* 020 7219 5238 *Fax:* 020 7219 5520 *E-mail:* wyattd@parliament.uk. *Constituency:* 5 London Road, Sittingbourne, Kent ME10 1NQ *Tel:* 01795 477277 *Fax:* 01795 479558

Con majority 6,606

YEO, TIM
South Suffolk

Timothy Stephen Kenneth Yeo. Born 20 March 1945; Son of late Dr Kenneth John Yeo and Norah Margaret Yeo; Educated Charterhouse; Emmanuel College, Cambridge (MA history 1968); Married Diane Helen Pickard 1970 (1 son 1 daughter). Cambridge University Air Squadron 1964-67. Assistant treasurer, Bankers Trust Company 1970-73; Director: Worcester Engineering Co. Ltd 1975-86, The Spastics Society 1980-83, Univent plc 1995-, Genus plc 2002-

House of Commons: Contested Bedwelty February 1974 general election. Member for South Suffolk since 9 June 1983 general election; Opposition Spokesperson for Environment, Transport and the Regions (Local Government, Regions, Planning and Housing) 1997-98; PPS to Douglas Hurd: as Home Secretary 1988-89, as Foreign and Commonwealth Secretary 1989-90; Joint Parliamentary Under-Secretary of State at: Department of the Environment 1990-92, Department of Health 1992-93; Minister of State for Environment and Countryside, Department of the Environment 1993-94; Shadow Minister of Agriculture, Fisheries and Food 1998-2001; Shadow Secretary of State for: Culture, Media and Sport 2001-02, Trade and Industry 2002-03, Public Services, Health and Education 2003-04, Environment and Transport 2004-05. *Political interests:* Health, Economic Policy, Unemployment, Charity Reform, Rural Affairs

Vice-Chair, Conservative Party (with responsibility for Local Government) 1998. The Childrens Trust; Golf Correspondent Country Life 1994-; Trustee, Tanzania Development Trust 1980-97; Fellow, Industry and Parliament Trust; *Publications:* Public Accountancy and Aquisition of Charities 1983; *Clubs:* Royal St George's (Sandwich), Royal and Ancient Golf Club of St Andrews, MCC, Sunningdale Golf; Captain, Parliamentary Golfing Society 1991-95; *Recreations:* Golf, skiing

Tim Yeo, MP, House of Commons, London SW1A 0AA *Tel:* 020 7219 6366 *Fax:* 020 7219 4857 *E-mail:* timyeomp@parliament.uk. *Constituency:* 43 High Street, Hadleigh, Suffolk IP7 5AB *Tel:* 01473 823435 *Fax:* 01473 823536

YOUNG, GEORGE
North West Hampshire

George Young. Born 16 July 1941; Son of Sir George Young, 5th Bt, CMG, and Elizabeth Young, neé Knatchbull-Hugessen; Educated Eton College; Christ Church, Oxford (BA philosophy, politics and economics 1963, MA); Surrey University (MPhil economics 1971); Married Aurelia Nemon-Stuart 1964 (2 sons 2 daughters). Economic adviser, Post Office 1969-74; Councillor, London Borough of Lambeth 1968-71; GLC Councillor for Ealing 1970-73; Chair, Acton Housing Association 1972-79

Con majority 13,264

House of Commons: Member for Ealing Acton 1974-97, and for North West Hampshire since 1 May 1997 general election; Opposition Whip 1976-79; Government Whip July-November 1990; Parliamentary Under-Secretary of State at: Department of Health and Social Services 1979-81, Department of Environment 1981-86; Department of Environment: Minister for Housing and Planning 1990-93, Minister for Housing, Inner Cities and Construction 1993-94; Financial Secretary, HM Treasury 1994-95; Secretary of State for Transport 1995-97; Member, Shadow Cabinet 1997-2000; Shadow Secretary of State for Defence 1997-98; Shadow Leader of the House of Commons 1998-99; Shadow Chancellor of the Duchy of Lancaster 1998-99; Shadow Leader of the House of Commons and Constitutional Affairs 1999-2000. *Political interests:* Housing, Disability, Health Education, Constitutional Reform

6th Baronet, created 1813, succeeded his father 1960; Trustee, Guinness Trust 1986-90; *Publications: Tourism – Blessing or Blight,* 1970; PC 1993; *Recreations:* Bicycling, opera

Rt Hon Sir George Young, MP, House of Commons, London SW1A 0AA
Tel: 020 7219 6665 *Fax:* 020 7219 2566 *E-mail:* sirgeorge@sirgeorgeyoung.org.uk.
Constituency: 2 Church Close, Andover, Hampshire SP10 1DP *Tel:* 01264 401401
Fax: 01264 391155

YOUNGER-ROSS, RICHARD
Teignbridge

Richard Alan Younger-Ross. Born 29 January 1953; Son of late Arthur George Ross and Patricia Ross; Educated Walton-on-Thames Secondary Modern School; Ewell Technical College (HNC building construction 1976); Married Susan Younger 1982. Architectural assistant various architectural practices 1970-90; Design consultant self-employed 1990-2001

Lib Dem majority 6,215

House of Commons: Contested Chislehurst 1987 and Teignbridge 1992, 1997 general elections. Member for Teignbridge since 7 June 2001 general election; Liberal Democrat Spokesperson for Office of the Deputy Prime Minister 2004-; Liberal Democrat Whip 2002-03, 2004-. *Political interests:* Economy, Trade and Industry. USA, Kurdistan

Organising vice-chair NLYL 1979; Parliamentary researcher 1981; Secretary-general YLM 1981-82; Economics spokesperson south west 1994-97. Member European Standing Committee C; *Recreations:* Cooking, riding, folk music, gardening, football (Arsenal FC)

Richard Younger-Ross, MP, House of Commons, London SW1A 0AA
Tel: 020 7219 8479 *E-mail:* yrossr@parliament.uk. *Constituency:* 70 Queen Street, Newton Abbot, Devon TQ12 2ER *Tel:* 01626 202626 *Fax:* 01626 202016

New MPs

(123 MPs who did not serve in the 2001 Parliament, four of whom had been MPs in earlier Parliaments)

AFRIYIE, Adam	Con	Windsor
ALEXANDER, Danny	Lib Dem	Inverness, Nairn, Badenoch and Strathspey
ANDERSON, David	Lab	Blaydon
AUSTIN, Ian	Lab	Dudley North
BALLS, Ed	Lab/Co-op	Normanton
BANKS, Gordon	Lab	Ochil and South Perthshire
BARLOW, Celia	Lab	Hove
BENYON, Richard	Con	Newbury
BINLEY, Brian	Con	Northampton South
BLACKMAN-WOODS, Roberta	Lab	City of Durham
BONE, Peter	Con	Wellingborough
BROKENSHIRE, James	Con	Hornchurch
BROWN, Lyn	Lab	West Ham
BROWNE, Jeremy	Lib Dem	Taunton
BURROWES, David	Con	Enfield Southgate
BURT, Lorely	Lib Dem	Solihull
BUTLER, Dawn	Lab	Brent South
CARSWELL, Douglas	Con	Harwich
CLARK, Greg	Con	Tunbridge Wells
CLARK, Katy	Lab	North Ayrshire and Arran
CLEGG, Nick	Lib Dem	Sheffield Hallam
COOPER, Rosie	Lab	West Lancashire
COX, Geoffrey	Con	Torridge and West Devon
CRABB, Stephen	Con	Preseli Pembrokeshire
CREAGH, Mary	Lab	Wakefield
DAVIES, David	Con	Monmouth
DAVIES, Philip	Con	Shipley
DORRIES, Nadine	Con	Mid Bedfordshire
DUDDRIDGE, James	Con	Rochford and Southend East
DUNNE, Philip	Con	Ludlow
DURKAN, Mark	SDLP	Foyle
ELLWOOD, Tobias	Con	Bournemouth East
ENGEL, Natascha	Lab	North East Derbyshire
EVENNETT, David*	Con	Bexleyheath and Crayford
FARRON, Tim	Lib Dem	Westmorland and Lonsdale
FEATHERSTONE, Lynne	Lib Dem	Hornsey and Wood Green
FLELLO, Robert	Lab	Stoke-on-Trent South
FRASER, Christopher*	Con	South West Norfolk
GAUKE, David	Con	South West Hertfordshire
GOLDSWORTHY, Julia	Lib Dem	Falmouth and Camborne
GOODMAN, Helen	Lab	Bishop Auckland

* MP in earlier Parliament

GOODWILL, Robert	*Con*	Scarborough and Whitby
GOVE, Michael	*Con*	Surrey Heath
GREENING, Justine	*Con*	Putney
GRIFFITH, Nia	*Lab*	Llanelli
GWYNNE, Andrew	*Lab*	Denton and Reddish
HAMMOND, Stephen	*Con*	Wimbledon
HANDS, Greg	*Con*	Hammersmith and Fulham
HARPER, Mark	*Con*	Forest of Dean
HEMMING, John	*Lib Dem*	Birmingham Yardley
HERBERT, Nick	*Con*	Arundel and South Downs
HILLIER, Meg	*Lab/Co-op*	Hackney South and Shoreditch
HODGSON, Sharon	*Lab*	Gateshead East and Washington West
HOLLOBONE, Philip	*Con*	Kettering
HOLLOWAY, Adam	*Con*	Gravesham
HORWOOD, Martin	*Lib Dem*	Cheltenham
HOSIE, Stewart	*SNP*	Dundee East
HOWARTH, David	*Lib Dem*	Cambridge
HUHNE, Chris	*Lib Dem*	Eastleigh
HUNT, Jeremy	*Con*	South West Surrey
HURD, Nick	*Con*	Ruislip Northwood
JACKSON, Stewart	*Con*	Peterborough
JAMES, Sian	*Lab*	Swansea East
JOHNSON, Diana	*Lab*	Hull North
JONES, David	*Con*	Clwyd West
KAWCZYNSKI, Daniel	*Con*	Shrewsbury and Atcham
KEELEY, Barbara	*Lab*	Worsley
KHAN, Sadiq	*Lab*	Tooting
KRAMER, Susan	*Lib Dem*	Richmond Park
LANCASTER, Mark	*Con*	Milton Keynes North East
LAW, Peter	*Ind*	Blaenau Gwent
LEECH, John	*Lib Dem*	Manchester Withington
McCARTHY, Kerry	*Lab*	Bristol East
McCARTHY-FRY, Sarah	*Lab/Co-op*	Portsmouth North
McCREA, William*	*DUP*	South Antrim
McDONNELL, Alasdair	*SDLP*	Belfast South
McFADDEN, Pat	*Lab*	Wolverhampton South East
McGOVERN, Jim	*Lab*	Dundee West
MacNEIL, Angus	*SNP*	Na h-Eileanan An Iar
MAIN, Anne	*Con*	St Albans
MALIK, Shahid	*Lab*	Dewsbury
MILIBAND, Ed	*Lab*	Doncaster North
MILLER, Maria	*Con*	Basingstoke
MILTON, Anne	*Con*	Guildford
MOON, Madeleine	*Lab*	Bridgend
MORDEN, Jessica	*Lab*	Newport East
MULHOLLAND, Gregory	*Lib Dem*	Leeds North West

* MP in earlier Parliament

MUNDELL, David	*Con*	Dumfriesshire, Clydesdale and Tweeddale
MURPHY, Conor	*Sinn Féin*	Newry and Armagh
NEWMARK, Brooks	*Con*	Braintree
PELLING, Andrew	*Con*	Croydon Central
PENNING, Mike	*Con*	Hemel Hempstead
PENROSE, John	*Con*	Weston-Super-Mare
PRITCHARD, Mark	*Con*	The Wrekin
REED, Jamie	*Lab*	Copeland
RIFKIND, Malcolm*	*Con*	Kensington and Chelsea
RIORDAN, Linda	*Lab/Co-op*	Halifax
ROGERSON, Dan	*Lib Dem*	North Cornwall
ROWEN, Paul	*Lib Dem*	Rochdale
SCOTT, Lee	*Con*	Ilford North
SEABECK, Alison	*Lab*	Plymouth Devonport
SHAPPS, Grant	*Con*	Welwyn Hatfield
SIMPSON, David	*DUP*	Upper Bann
SLAUGHTER, Andy	*Lab*	Ealing, Acton and Shepherd's Bush
SMITH, Angela	*Lab/Co-op*	Sheffield Hillsborough
SNELGROVE, Anne	*Lab/Co-op*	South Swindon
SOULSBY, Peter	*Lab*	Leicester South
STUART, Graham	*Con*	Beverley and Holderness
SWINSON, Jo	*Lib Dem*	East Dunbartonshire
THORNBERRY, Emily	*Lab*	Islington South and Finsbury
USSHER, Kitty	*Lab*	Burnley
VAIZEY, Ed	*Con*	Wantage
VARA, Shailesh	*Con*	North West Cambridgeshire
VILLIERS, Theresa	*Con*	Chipping Barnet
WALKER, Charles	*Con*	Broxbourne
WALLACE, Ben	*Con*	Lancaster and Wyre
WALTHO, Lynda	*Lab*	Stourbridge
WILLIAMS, Mark	*Lib Dem*	Ceredigion
WILLIAMS, Stephen	*Lib Dem*	Bristol West
WILLOTT, Jenny	*Lib Dem*	Cardiff Central
WILSON, Robert	*Con*	Reading East
WILSON, Sammy	*DUP*	East Antrim
WRIGHT, Jeremy	*Con*	Rugby and Kenilworth

* MP in earlier Parliament

Defeated MPs

(50: 36 Labour, 4 Conservative, 5 Lib Dem, 3 UUP, 1 Plaid Cymru, 1 SNP)

ATHERTON, Candy	*Lab*	Falmouth and Camborne
BEARD, Nigel	*Lab*	Bexleyheath and Crayford
BEGGS, Roy	*UUP*	East Antrim
BRADLEY, Keith	*Lab*	Manchester Withington
BRADLEY, Peter	*Lab*	The Wrekin
BURNSIDE, David	*UUP*	South Antrim
CAMPBELL, Anne	*Lab*	Cambridge
CASALE, Roger	*Lab*	Wimbledon
CLARK, Helen	*Lab*	Peterborough
CLARKE, Tony	*Lab*	Northampton South
COLLINS, Tim	*Con*	Westmorland and Lonsdale
COLMAN, Tony	*Lab*	Putney
COTTER, Brian	*Lib Dem*	Weston-Super-Mare
CRYER, John	*Lab*	Hornchurch
DAVEY, Valerie	*Lab*	Bristol West
DAVIES, Geraint	*Lab*	Croydon Central
DOUGHTY, Sue	*Lib Dem*	Guildford
DUNCAN, Peter	*Con*	Galloway and Upper Nithsdale
EDWARDS, Huw	*Lab*	Monmouth
EWING, Annabelle	*SNP*	Perth
FITZSIMONS, Lorna	*Lab*	Rochdale
FLOOK, Adrian	*Con*	Taunton
GILL, Parmjit	*Lib Dem*	Leicester South
GREEN, Matthew	*Lib Dem*	Ludlow
HENDERSON, Ivan	*Lab*	Harwich
HURST, Alan	*Lab*	Braintree
JOHNSON, Melanie	*Lab*	Welwyn Hatfield
JONES, Jon Owen	*Lab*	Cardiff Central
KING, Andy	*Lab*	Rugby and Kenilworth
KING, Oona	*Lab*	Bethnal Green and Bow
LESLIE, Christopher	*Lab*	Shipley
LUKE, Iain	*Lab*	Dundee East
LYONS, John	*Lab*	Strathkelvin and Bearsden
MACDONALD, Calum	*Lab*	Western Isles
McWALTER, Tony	*Lab*	Hemel Hempstead
PERHAM, Linda	*Lab*	Ilford North
POLLARD, Kerry	*Lab*	St Albans
POND, Chris	*Lab*	Gravesham
QUINN, Lawrie	*Lab*	Scarborough and Whitby
RENDEL, David	*Lib Dem*	Newbury
ROCHE, Barbara	*Lab*	Hornsey and Wood Green
SAWFORD, Phil	*Lab*	Kettering
STEWART, David	*Lab*	Inverness East, Nairn and Lochaber

STINCHCOMBE, Paul	*Lab*	Wellingborough
TAYLOR, John Mark	*Con*	Solihull
THOMAS, Gareth	*Lab*	Clwyd West
THOMAS, Simon	*PlC*	Ceredigion
TRIMBLE, David	*UUP*	Upper Bann
TWIGG, Stephen	*Lab*	Enfield Southgate
WHITE, Brian	*Lab*	Milton Keynes North East

Retiring MPs

(86, of whom 24 given life peerages)

ADAMS, Irene*	*Lab*	Paisley North
ALLAN, Richard	*Lib Dem*	Sheffield Hallam
ANDERSON, Donald*	*Lab*	Swansea East
ATKINSON, David	*Con*	Bournemouth East
BANKS, Tony*	*Lab*	West Ham
BARNES, Harry	*Lab*	North East Derbyshire
BENNETT, Andrew	*Lab*	Denton and Reddish
BEST, Harold	*Lab*	Leeds North West
BOATENG, Paul	*Lab*	Brent South
BOTTOMLEY, Virginia*	*Con*	South West Surrey
BURNETT, John	*Lib Dem*	Torridge and West Devon
CAPLIN, Ivor	*Lab*	Hove
CHAPMAN, Sydney	*Con*	Chipping Barnet
CHIDGEY, David*	*Lib Dem*	Eastleigh
CLARK, Lynda*	*Lab*	Edinburgh Pentlands
COLEMAN, Iain	*Lab*	Hammersmith and Fulham
CORSTON, Jean*	*Lab*	Bristol East
COX, Tom	*Lab*	Tooting
CRAN, James	*Con*	Beverley and Holderness
CRANSTON, Ross	*Lab*	Dudley North
CUNNINGHAM, Jack*	*Lab*	Copeland
DALYELL, Tam	*Lab*	Linlithgow
DAVIES, Denzil	*Lab*	Llanelli
DAWSON, Hilton	*Lab*	Lancaster and Wyre
DROWN, Julia	*Lab*	South Swindon
FLIGHT, Howard	*Con*	Arundel and South Downs
FOSTER, Derek*	*Lab*	Bishop Auckland
FOULKES, George*	*Lab*	Carrick, Cumnock and Doon Valley
GRIFFITHS, Jane	*Lab*	Reading East
GRIFFITHS, Win	*Lab*	Bridgend
HAWKINS, Nick	*Con*	Surrey Heath

* Awarded life peerages in dissolution honours

HINCHLIFFE, David	Lab	Wakefield
HOWARTH, Alan*	Lab	Newport East
HUGHES, Kevin	Lab	Doncaster North
HUME, John	SDLP	Foyle
HUNTER, Andrew	DUP	Basingstoke
JACKSON, Helen	Lab	Sheffield Hillsborough
JACKSON, Robert	Con	Wantage
JAMIESON, David	Lab	Plymouth Devonport
JONES, Nigel*	Lib Dem	Cheltenham
KIRKWOOD, Archy*	Lib Dem	Roxburgh and Berwickshire
LAWRENCE, Jackie	Lab	Preseli Pembrokeshire
LEWIS, Terry	Lab	Worsley
LIDDELL, Helen	Lab	Airdrie and Shotts
McNAMARA, Kevin	Lab	Hull North
McWILLIAM, John	Lab	Blaydon
MAHON, Alice	Lab	Halifax
MALLON, Séamus	SDLP	Newry and Armagh
MARSDEN, Paul	Lib Dem	Shrewsbury and Atcham
MAWHINNEY, Brian*	Con	North West Cambridgeshire
MOONIE, Lewis*	Lab	Kirkcaldy
MORRIS, Estelle*	Lab	Birmingham Yardley
NORMAN, Archie	Con	Tunbridge Wells
O'BRIEN, William	Lab	Normanton
O'NEILL, Martin*	Lab	Ochil
ORGAN, Diana	Lab	Forest of Dean
PAGE, Richard	Con	South West Hertfordshire
PICKTHALL, Colin	Lab	West Lancashire
PIKE, Peter	Lab	Burnley
PORTILLO, Michael	Con	Kensington and Chelsea
QUIN, Joyce	Lab	Gateshead East and Washington West
RAPSON, Syd	Lab	Portsmouth North
ROE, Marion	Con	Broxbourne
ROSS, Ernie	Lab	Dundee West
SAVIDGE, Malcolm	Lab	Aberdeen North
SAYEED, Jonathan	Con	Mid Bedfordshire
SEDGEMORE, Brian	Lab	Hackney South and Shoreditch
SHEPHARD, Gillian*	Con	South West Norfolk
SHIPLEY, Debra	Lab	Stourbridge
SMITH, Chris*	Lab	Islington South and Finsbury
SMITH, Llewellyn	Lab	Blaenau Gwent
SMYTH, Martin	UUP	Belfast South
SOLEY, Clive*	Lab	Ealing, Acton and Shepherd's Bush
STEINBERG, Gerry	Lab	City of Durham
STEVENSON, George	Lab	Stoke-on-Trent South
TAYLOR, Ann*	Lab	Dewsbury
TAYLOR, Teddy	Con	Rochford and Southend East

* Awarded life peerages in dissolution honours

TONGE, Jenny*	*Lib Dem*	Richmond Park
TREND, Michael	*Con*	Windsor
TURNER, Dennis*	*Lab*	Wolverhampton South East
TYLER, Paul*	*Lib Dem*	North Cornwall
TYNAN, Bill	*Lab*	Hamilton South
WILKINSON, John	*Con*	Ruislip Northwood
WILSON, Brian	*Lab*	Cunninghame North
WORTHINGTON, Tony	*Lab*	Clydebank and Milngavie
WRAY, James	*Lab*	Glasgow Baillieston

* Awarded life peerages in dissolution honours

Women MPs

(128, compared with 118 after 2001 election)

ABBOTT, Diane	*Lab*	Hackney North and Stoke Newington
ANDERSON, Janet	*Lab*	Rossendale and Darwen
ARMSTRONG, Hilary	*Lab*	North West Durham
ATKINS, Charlotte	*Lab*	Staffordshire Moorlands
BAIRD, Vera	*Lab*	Redcar
BARLOW, Celia	*Lab*	Hove
BECKETT, Margaret	*Lab*	Derby South
BEGG, Anne	*Lab*	Aberdeen South
BLACKMAN, Liz	*Lab*	Erewash
BLACKMAN-WOODS, Roberta	*Lab*	City of Durham
BLEARS, Hazel	*Lab*	Salford
BROOKE, Annette	*Lib Dem*	Mid Dorset and Poole North
BROWN, Lyn	*Lab*	West Ham
BROWNING, Angela	*Con*	Tiverton and Honiton
BUCK, Karen	*Lab*	Regent's Park and Kensington North
BURT, Lorely	*Lib Dem*	Solihull
BUTLER, Dawn	*Lab*	Brent South
CALTON, Patsy	*Lib Dem*	Cheadle
CLARK, Katy	*Lab*	North Ayrshire and Arran
CLWYD, Ann	*Lab*	Cynon Valley
COFFEY, Ann	*Lab*	Stockport
COOPER, Rosie	*Lab*	West Lancashire
COOPER, Yvette	*Lab*	Pontefract and Castleford
CREAGH, Mary	*Lab*	Wakefield
CRYER, Ann	*Lab*	Keighley
CURTIS-THOMAS, Claire	*Lab*	Crosby
DEAN, Janet	*Lab*	Burton
DORRIES, Nadine	*Con*	Mid Bedfordshire
DUNWOODY, Gwyneth	*Lab*	Crewe and Nantwich

EAGLE, Angela	*Lab*	Wallasey
EAGLE, Maria	*Lab*	Liverpool Garston
ELLMAN, Louise	*Lab/Co-op*	Liverpool Riverside
ENGEL, Natascha	*Lab*	North East Derbyshire
FEATHERSTONE, Lynne	*Lib Dem*	Hornsey and Wood Green
FLINT, Caroline	*Lab*	Don Valley
FOLLETT, Barbara	*Lab*	Stevenage
GIDLEY, Sandra	*Lib Dem*	Romsey
GILDERNEW, Michelle	*Sinn Féin*	Fermanagh and South Tyrone
GILLAN, Cheryl	*Con*	Chesham and Amersham
GILROY, Linda	*Lab/Co-op*	Plymouth Sutton
GOLDSWORTHY, Julia	*Lib Dem*	Falmouth and Camborne
GOODMAN, Helen	*Lab*	Bishop Auckland
GREENING, Justine	*Con*	Putney
GRIFFITH, Nia	*Lab*	Llanelli
HARMAN, Harriet	*Lab*	Camberwell and Peckham
HEAL, Sylvia	*Lab*	Halesowen and Rowley Regis
HERMON, Sylvia	*UUP*	North Down
HEWITT, Patricia	*Lab*	Leicester West
HILLIER, Meg	*Lab/Co-op*	Hackney South and Shoreditch
HODGE, Margaret	*Lab*	Barking
HODGSON, Sharon	*Lab*	Gateshead East and Washington West
HOEY, Kate	*Lab*	Vauxhall
HUGHES, Beverley	*Lab*	Stretford and Urmston
HUMBLE, Joan	*Lab*	Blackpool North and Fleetwood
JACKSON, Glenda	*Lab*	Hampstead and Highgate
JAMES, Sian	*Lab*	Swansea East
JOHNSON, Diana	*Lab*	Hull North
JONES, Helen	*Lab*	Warrington North
JONES, Lynne	*Lab*	Birmingham Selly Oak
JOWELL, Tessa	*Lab*	Dulwich and West Norwood
KEEBLE, Sally	*Lab*	Northampton North
KEELEY, Barbara	*Lab*	Worsley
KEEN, Ann	*Lab*	Brentford and Isleworth
KELLY, Ruth	*Lab*	Bolton West
KENNEDY, Jane	*Lab*	Liverpool Wavertree
KIRKBRIDE, Julie	*Con*	Bromsgrove
KRAMER, Susan	*Lib Dem*	Richmond Park
LAING, Eleanor	*Con*	Epping Forest
LAIT, Jacqui	*Con*	Beckenham
McCAFFERTY, Christine	*Lab*	Calder Valley
McCARTHY, Kerry	*Lab*	Bristol East
McCARTHY-FRY, Sarah	*Lab/Co-op*	Portsmouth North
McDONAGH, Siobhain	*Lab*	Mitcham and Morden
McGUIRE, Anne	*Lab*	Stirling
McINTOSH, Anne	*Con*	Vale of York
McISAAC, Shona	*Lab*	Cleethorpes

McKECHIN, Ann	*Lab*	Glasgow North
McKENNA, Rosemary	*Lab*	Cumbernauld, Kilsyth and Kirkintilloch East
MACTAGGART, Fiona	*Lab*	Slough
MAIN, Anne	*Con*	St Albans
MALLABER, Judy	*Lab*	Amber Valley
MAY, Theresa	*Con*	Maidenhead
MERRON, Gillian	*Lab*	Lincoln
MILLER, Maria	*Con*	Basingstoke
MILTON, Anne	*Con*	Guildford
MOFFATT, Laura	*Lab*	Crawley
MOON, Madeleine	*Lab*	Bridgend
MORAN, Margaret	*Lab*	Luton South
MORDEN, Jessica	*Lab*	Newport East
MORGAN, Julie	*Lab*	Cardiff North
MOUNTFORD, Kali	*Lab*	Colne Valley
MUNN, Meg	*Lab/Co-op*	Sheffield Heeley
OSBORNE, Sandra	*Lab*	Ayr, Carrick and Cumnock
PICKING, Anne	*Lab*	East Lothian
PRENTICE, Bridget	*Lab*	Lewisham East
PRIMAROLO, Dawn	*Lab*	Bristol South
RIORDAN, Linda	*Lab/Co-op*	Halifax
ROBINSON, Iris	*DUP*	Strangford
RUDDOCK, Joan	*Lab*	Lewisham Deptford
RUSSELL, Christine	*Lab*	City of Chester
RYAN, Joan	*Lab*	Enfield North
SEABECK, Alison	*Lab*	Plymouth Devonport
SHORT, Clare	*Lab*	Birmingham Ladywood
SMITH, Angela	*Lab/Co-op*	Sheffield Hillsborough
SMITH, Angela Evans	*Lab*	Basildon
SMITH, Geraldine	*Lab*	Morecambe and Lunesdale
SMITH, Jacqui	*Lab*	Redditch
SNELGROVE, Anne	*Lab/Co-op*	South Swindon
SOUTHWORTH, Helen	*Lab*	Warrington South
SPELMAN, Caroline	*Con*	Meriden
SQUIRE, Rachel	*Lab*	Dunfermline and West Fife
STARKEY, Phyllis	*Lab*	Milton Keynes South West
STUART, Gisela	*Lab*	Birmingham Edgbaston
SWINSON, Jo	*Lib Dem*	East Dunbartonshire
TAYLOR, Dari	*Lab*	Stockton South
TEATHER, Sarah	*Lib Dem*	Brent East
THORNBERRY, Emily	*Lab*	Islington South and Finsbury
USSHER, Kitty	*Lab*	Burnley
VILLIERS, Theresa	*Con*	Chipping Barnet
WALLEY, Joan	*Lab*	Stoke-on-Trent North
WALTHO, Lynda	*Lab*	Stourbridge
WARD, Claire	*Lab*	Watford
WATKINSON, Angela	*Con*	Upminster

WIDDECOMBE, Ann	Con	Maidstone and The Weald
WILLIAMS, Betty	Lab	Conwy
WILLOTT, Jenny	Lib Dem	Cardiff Central
WINTERTON, Ann	Con	Congleton
WINTERTON, Rosie	Lab	Doncaster Central

MPs' Political Interests

The interests listed are supplied by MPs themselves

Abortion
Widdecombe, Ann	Con

Accountancy
Mitchell, Austin	Lab

Aerospace
Borrow, David	Lab
Crabb, Stephen	Con
Haselhurst, Alan	Con
Howarth, Gerald	Con
Ingram, Adam	Lab
Jack, Michael	Con
Moffatt, Laura	Lab
Öpik, Lembit	Lib Dem
Robinson, Peter	DUP
Soames, Nicholas	Con
Tami, Mark	Lab

Africa
Cash, William	Con
Duddridge, James	Con

Ageing
Burstow, Paul	Lib Dem

Agriculture and Rural Affairs
Ancram, Michael	Con
Atkins, Charlotte	Lab
Atkinson, Peter	Con
Bacon, Richard	Con
Bellingham, Henry	Con
Boswell, Timothy	Con
Brazier, Julian	Con
Breed, Colin	Lib Dem
Burt, Alistair	Con
Carmichael, Alistair	Lib Dem
Clifton-Brown, Geoffrey	Con
Curry, David	Con
Davies, Quentin	Con
Davis, David	Con
Djanogly, Jonathan	Con
Drew, David	Lab/Co-op
Evans, Nigel	Con
Garnier, Edward	Con
George, Andrew	Lib Dem
Gildernew, Michelle	Sinn Féin
Gray, James	Con
Green, Damian	Con
Greenway, John	Con
Hague, William	Con
Haselhurst, Alan	Con

Hayes, John	Con
Heath, David	Lib Dem
Heathcoat-Amory, David	Con
Hoey, Kate	Lab
Hood, Jimmy	Lab
Hoyle, Lindsay	Lab
Jones, Martyn	Lab
Key, Robert	Con
Leigh, Edward	Con
Liddell-Grainger, Ian	Con
Llwyd, Elfyn	PlC
Lord, Michael	Con
Luff, Peter	Con
McGuire, Anne	Lab
McLoughlin, Patrick	Con
Martlew, Eric	Lab
Mercer, Patrick	Con
Mitchell, Austin	Lab
Morley, Elliot	Lab
Moss, Malcolm	Con
Mountford, Kali	Lab
O'Brien, Stephen	Con
Paice, Jim	Con
Paterson, Owen	Con
Prentice, Gordon	Lab
Robertson, Hugh	Con
Ruane, Chris	Lab
Salmond, Alex	SNP
Simmonds, Mark	Con
Simpson, Keith	Con
Smith, Robert	Lib Dem
Soames, Nicholas	Con
Spelman, Caroline	Con
Strang, Gavin	Lab
Swire, Hugo	Con
Taylor, David	Lab/Co-op
Tipping, Paddy	Lab
Todd, Mark	Lab
Walter, Robert	Con
Weir, Mike	SNP
Wiggin, Bill	Con
Williams, Roger	Lib Dem
Winterton, Ann	Con
Yeo, Tim	Con

Air Transport
Haselhurst, Alan	Con
Howarth, Gerald	Con
McDonnell, John	Lab
Marshall, David	Lab
Moffatt, Laura	Lab

Robinson, Peter	DUP
Soames, Nicholas	Con
Wareing, Robert	Lab
Wilshire, David	Con

Alternative Energy
Cook, Frank	Lab
Hamilton, Fabian	Lab

Animal Welfare
Cawsey, Ian	Lab
Cohen, Harry	Lab
Conway, Derek	Con
Fitzpatrick, Jim	Lab
Flynn, Paul	Lab
Foster, Michael Jabez	Lab
Gale, Roger	Con
Johnson, Diana	Lab
McIntosh, Anne	Con
Norris, Dan	Lab
Palmer, Nick	Lab
Russell, Bob	Lib Dem
Smith, Angela Evans	Lab
Villiers, Theresa	Con

Anti-Common Market
Goodwill, Robert	Con
Skinner, Dennis	Lab

Anti-Hunting
Bailey, Adrian	Lab/Co-op
Foster, Michael John	Lab
Levitt, Tom	Lab
Vaizey, Ed	Con
Wright, David	Lab

Anti-Imperialism and Internationalism
Corbyn, Jeremy	Lab

Anti-Social Behaviour
Byrne, Liam	Lab
Hodgson, Sharon	Lab
Morden, Jessica	Lab

Architectural and Artistic Heritage
Beith, Alan	Lib Dem
Swire, Hugo	Con

Arms Control
Heathcoat-Amory, David	Con

Arts and Culture

Blears, Hazel	*Lab*
Campbell, Menzies	*Lib Dem*
Dunwoody, Gwyneth	*Lab*
Ellman, Louise	*Lab/Co-op*
Field, Mark	*Con*
Hopkins, Kelvin	*Lab*
Howells, Kim	*Lab*
Key, Robert	*Con*
Knight, Greg	*Con*
Knight, Jim	*Lab*
Lammy, David	*Lab*
Linton, Martin	*Lab*
Luff, Peter	*Con*
Mactaggart, Fiona	*Lab*
Price, Adam	*PlC*
Purnell, James	*Lab*
Russell, Christine	*Lab*
Swire, Hugo	*Con*
Ward, Claire	*Lab*
Wishart, Peter	*SNP*
Woodward, Shaun	*Lab*

Asylum and Immigration

Gerrard, Neil	*Lab*
Harris, Evan	*Lib Dem*
Prosser, Gwyn	*Lab*

Benefits

McIsaac, Shona	*Lab*

Benzodiazipines

Woolas, Phil	*Lab*

Biotechnology

McDonnell, Alasdair	*SDLP*

British Council

Wyatt, Derek	*Lab*

British Overseas Territories

Rosindell, Andrew	*Con*

Broadband

Harper, Mark	*Con*

Broadcasting and Media

Begg, Anne	*Lab*
Bryant, Chris	*Lab*
Fabricant, Michael	*Con*
Fisher, Mark	*Lab*
Gale, Roger	*Con*
Greenway, John	*Con*
Grogan, John	*Lab*
Howells, Kim	*Lab*
Kennedy, Charles	*Lib Dem*
Ruffley, David	*Con*
Whittingdale, John	*Con*

Business

Binley, Brian	*Con*
Liddell-Grainger, Ian	*Con*
Mundell, David	*Con*
Todd, Mark	*Lab*
Villiers, Theresa	*Con*

Cancer and Blood

Havard, Dai	*Lab*

Charity and Voluntary Sector

Baron, John	*Con*
Yeo, Tim	*Con*

Child Poverty

Hodgson, Sharon	*Lab*
Keen, Ann	*Lab*

Child Protection

Bailey, Adrian	*Lab/Co-op*
Norris, Dan	*Lab*

Childcare

Baldry, Tony	*Con*
Doran, Frank	*Lab*
Flint, Caroline	*Lab*
Hodgson, Sharon	*Lab*
Moran, Margaret	*Lab*
Morgan, Julie	*Lab*
Waltho, Lynda	*Lab*

Children

Buck, Karen	*Lab*
Coffey, Ann	*Lab*
Kidney, David	*Lab*
Willott, Jenny	*Lib Dem*

Christian Socialism

Timms, Stephen	*Lab*

Christian Values

Donaldson, Jeffrey	*DUP*

Citizenship

Francis, Hywel	*Lab*

Civil Defence

McCartney, Ian	*Lab*

Civil Justice

Dismore, Andrew	*Lab*

Civil Liberties

Atkins, Charlotte	*Lab*
Baird, Vera	*Lab*
Baker, Norman	*Lib Dem*
Harman, Harriet	*Lab*
Hughes, Simon	*Lib Dem*

Lloyd, Tony	*Lab*
Llwyd, Elfyn	*PlC*
Mactaggart, Fiona	*Lab*
Marshall-Andrews, Robert	*Lab*
Meacher, Michael	*Lab*
Williams, Stephen	*Lib Dem*

Civil Service

Clarke, Tom	*Lab*

Climate Change

Stunell, Andrew	*Lib Dem*

Co-operative Issues

Bailey, Adrian	*Lab/Co-op*
Davidson, Ian	*Lab/Co-op*
Lazarowicz, Mark	*Lab/Co-op*
McFall, John	*Lab/Co-op*
Munn, Meg	*Lab/Co-op*
Naysmith, Doug	*Lab/Co-op*

Coal

Clapham, Michael	*Lab*
Cooper, Yvette	*Lab*
Cummings, John	*Lab*
O'Brien, Mike	*Lab*

Commerce and Industry

Hayes, John	*Con*
Keen, Alan	*Lab/Co-op*
Ottaway, Richard	*Con*

Commonwealth

Davidson, Ian	*Lab/Co-op*
Kilfoyle, Peter	*Lab*

Community Care

McCabe, Steve	*Lab*
Robinson, Peter	*DUP*
Squire, Rachel	*Lab*
Steen, Anthony	*Con*

Community Development

Griffith, Nia	*Lab*
Michael, Alun	*Lab/Co-op*
Scott, Lee	*Con*
Shaw, Jonathan	*Lab*

Community Safety

Burstow, Paul	*Lib Dem*

Community Services

Calton, Patsy	*Lib Dem*

Complementary and Alternative Medicine

Tredinnick, David	*Con*

Conflict Resolution
Breed, Colin   Lib Dem

Conservation
Robathan, Andrew   Con
Steen, Anthony   Con

Constitutional Affairs
Anderson, Janet   Lab
Brennan, Kevin   Lab
Browne, Des   Lab
Burden, Richard   Lab
Darling, Alistair   Lab
Dodds, Nigel   DUP
Donaldson, Jeffrey   DUP
Fallon, Michael   Con
Garnier, Edward   Con
Grieve, Dominic   Con
Hoon, Geoffrey   Lab
Laing, Eleanor   Con
Lamb, Norman   Lib Dem
Lazarowicz, Mark   Lab/Co-op
McGrady, Eddie   SDLP
Mackinlay, Andrew   Lab
Paisley, Ian   DUP
Plaskitt, James   Lab
Redwood, John   Con
Robertson, Laurence   Con
Rosindell, Andrew   Con
Syms, Robert   Con
Turner, Andrew   Con
Watkinson, Angela   Con
Whitehead, Alan   Lab
Wright, Tony Wayland   Lab

Constitutional Reform
Alexander, Douglas   Lab
Campbell, Alan   Lab
Dobson, Frank   Lab
Holmes, Paul   Lib Dem
McKenna, Rosemary   Lab
Prentice, Bridget   Lab
Stuart, Gisela   Lab
Young, George   Con

Construction Industry
Spellar, John   Lab

Consumer Issues
Knight, Greg   Con
Lazarowicz, Mark   Lab/Co-op
Murphy, Jim   Lab
Williams, Betty   Lab

Cornwall
Breed, Colin   Lib Dem
George, Andrew   Lib Dem

Corporate Social Responsibility
Moore, Michael   Lib Dem
Swinson, Jo   Lib Dem

Crime
Burnham, Andy   Lab
Crabb, Stephen   Con
Flello, Robert   Lab
Flint, Caroline   Lab
Gove, Michael   Con
Khan, Sadiq   Lab
Lewis, Ivan   Lab
McCarthy, Kerry   Lab
McIsaac, Shona   Lab
Milburn, Alan   Lab
Simon, Siôn   Lab
Wilson, Robert   Con

Criminal Justice
Carmichael, Alistair   Lib Dem
Hands, Greg   Con
Wright, Jeremy   Con

Criminal Law
Baird, Vera   Lab
Malins, Humfrey   Con

Cyprus
Dismore, Andrew   Lab
Lepper, David   Lab/Co-op
Villiers, Theresa   Con

Deaf Children
Bruce, Malcolm   Lib Dem

Decentralisation
Carswell, Douglas   Con

Deep Vein Thrombosis in Air Travellers
Smith, John   Lab

Defence
Ancram, Michael   Con
Arbuthnot, James   Con
Bayley, Hugh   Lab
Bellingham, Henry   Con
Blackman, Liz   Lab
Blunt, Crispin   Con
Brazier, Julian   Con
Cairns, David   Lab
Campbell, Menzies   Lib Dem
Cohen, Harry   Lab
Conway, Derek   Con
Cook, Robin   Lab
Corbyn, Jeremy   Lab
Cox, Geoffrey   Con
Crausby, David   Lab

Davidson, Ian   Lab/Co-op
Donaldson, Jeffrey   DUP
Duncan Smith, Iain   Con
Evans, Nigel   Con
Francois, Mark   Con
Galloway, George   Respect
Gapes, Mike   Lab/Co-op
Garnier, Edward   Con
George, Bruce   Lab
Gillan, Cheryl   Con
Gray, James   Con
Grieve, Dominic   Con
Hammond, Philip   Con
Hancock, Mike   Lib Dem
Hendrick, Mark   Lab/Co-op
Hoon, Geoffrey   Lab
Howarth, Gerald   Con
Hoyle, Lindsay   Lab
Hutton, John   Lab
Ingram, Adam   Lab
Jenkin, Bernard   Con
Jones, Kevan   Lab
Joyce, Eric   Lab
Keen, Alan   Lab/Co-op
Keetch, Paul   Lib Dem
Key, Robert   Con
Lancaster, Mark   Con
Leigh, Edward   Con
Lewis, Julian   Con
Liddell-Grainger, Ian   Con
McFall, John   Lab/Co-op
Martlew, Eric   Lab
Mercer, Patrick   Con
Mitchell, Andrew   Con
Moffatt, Laura   Lab
Murphy, Jim   Lab
Murrison, Andrew   Con
Ottaway, Richard   Con
Prisk, Mark   Con
Pritchard, Mark   Con
Reid, John   Lab
Robathan, Andrew   Con
Robertson, Angus   SNP
Robertson, Hugh   Con
Rosindell, Andrew   Con
Selous, Andrew   Con
Sheridan, Jim   Lab
Simpson, Keith   Con
Smith, John   Lab
Soames, Nicholas   Con
Squire, Rachel   Lab
Swire, Hugo   Con
Taylor, Dari   Lab
Viggers, Peter   Con
Vis, Rudi   Lab
Wallace, Ben   Con
Widdecombe, Ann   Con
Wiggin, Bill   Con

Democracy

Allen, Graham	Lab
Goggins, Paul	Lab
Hodge, Margaret	Lab
Keen, Alan	Lab/Co-op
McKenna, Rosemary	Lab
Southworth, Helen	Lab

Deregulation

Villiers, Theresa	Con

Developing World

Streeter, Gary	Con

Development

Cable, Vincent	Lib Dem
Keen, Alan	Lab/Co-op
Palmer, Nick	Lab
Prisk, Mark	Con

Devolution

Davies, David	Con
Flynn, Paul	Lab
Laing, Eleanor	Con
Mackinlay, Andrew	Lab
Sarwar, Mohammed	Lab

Diet and Nutrition

Tredinnick, David	Con

Disability

Begg, Anne	Lab
Berry, Roger	Lab
Blackman, Liz	Lab
Browne, Des	Lab
Burstow, Paul	Lib Dem
Creagh, Mary	Lab
Francis, Hywel	Lab
Griffiths, Nigel	Lab
Healey, John	Lab
Levitt, Tom	Lab
Marsden, Gordon	Lab
May, Theresa	Con
Turner, Des	Lab
Wareing, Robert	Lab
Weir, Mike	SNP
Young, George	Con

Disarmament

Cook, Frank	Lab
Lloyd, Tony	Lab
Simpson, Alan	Lab

Domestic Violence

Harman, Harriet	Lab

Drugs Issues

Byrne, Liam	Lab
Martin, Michael	Speaker
Meale, Alan	Lab
Wishart, Peter	SNP

E-Issues

Moran, Margaret	Lab

Eastern Europe

Bellingham, Henry	Con
Clapham, Michael	Lab

Ecology and Conservation

Cohen, Harry	Lab
Jones, Martyn	Lab

Economic Issues

Blunkett, David	Lab
Campbell, Gregory	DUP
Chapman, Ben	Lab
Follett, Barbara	Lab
George, Andrew	Lib Dem
Hamilton, David	Lab
Hamilton, Fabian	Lab
Hendrick, Mark	Lab/Co-op
Jack, Michael	Con
McCabe, Steve	Lab
Murphy, Denis	Lab
Owen, Albert	Lab
Pearson, Ian	Lab
Prosser, Gwyn	Lab
Shaw, Jonathan	Lab
Smith, John	Lab
Wareing, Robert	Lab
Williams, Roger	Lib Dem

Economic Policy

Ainsworth, Peter	Con
Alexander, Danny	Lib Dem
Alexander, Douglas	Lab
Allen, Graham	Lab
Bailey, Adrian	Lab/Co-op
Battle, John	Lab
Bayley, Hugh	Lab
Bell, Stuart	Lab
Bercow, John	Con
Berry, Roger	Lab
Betts, Clive	Lab
Brown, Gordon	Lab
Cable, Vincent	Lib Dem
Clappison, James	Con
Cunningham, James	Lab
Curtis-Thomas, Claire	Lab
Darling, Alistair	Lab
Dowd, Jim	Lab
Eagle, Angela	Lab
Forth, Eric	Con

Fox, Liam	Con
Gapes, Mike	Lab/Co-op
Gardiner, Barry	Lab
Goldsworthy, Julia	Lib Dem
Green, Damian	Con
Grogan, John	Lab
Hague, William	Con
Hammond, Philip	Con
Henderson, Doug	Lab
Hesford, Stephen	Lab
Hoon, Geoffrey	Lab
Hopkins, Kelvin	Lab
Horam, John	Con
Jenkin, Bernard	Con
Jones, Lynne	Lab
Keeble, Sally	Lab
Kelly, Ruth	Lab
Laing, Eleanor	Con
Lansley, Andrew	Con
Lilley, Peter	Con
McCarthy, Kerry	Lab
McFall, John	Lab/Co-op
Mallaber, Judy	Lab
Marshall-Andrews, Robert	Lab
Milburn, Alan	Lab
Miller, Andrew	Lab
Plaskitt, James	Lab
Primarolo, Dawn	Lab
Rammell, Bill	Lab
Robertson, Laurence	Con
Robinson, Geoffrey	Lab
Sarwar, Mohammed	Lab
Skinner, Dennis	Lab
Smith, Jacqui	Lab
Spicer, Michael	Con
Straw, Jack	Lab
Syms, Robert	Con
Taylor, Dari	Lab
Timms, Stephen	Lab
Trickett, Jon	Lab
Tyrie, Andrew	Con
Ussher, Kitty	Lab
Villiers, Theresa	Con
Willetts, David	Con
Yeo, Tim	Con

Economics and Finance

Blackman, Liz	Lab
Brennan, Kevin	Lab
Cameron, David	Con
Challen, Colin	Lab
Clifton-Brown, Geoffrey	Con
Connarty, Michael	Lab
Davey, Edward	Lib Dem
David, Wayne	Lab
Dorrell, Stephen	Con
Field, Mark	Con
Gibb, Nick	Con

Stewart, Ian	Lab	Crabb, Stephen	Con	Blunt, Crispin	Con
Stoate, Howard	Lab	Creagh, Mary	Lab	Brown, Russell	Lab
Straw, Jack	Lab	Davey, Edward	Lib Dem	Bruce, Malcolm	Lib Dem
Taylor, Dari	Lab	Dhanda, Parmjit	Lab	Cable, Vincent	Lib Dem
Tipping, Paddy	Lab	Doran, Frank	Lab	Carmichael, Alistair	Lib Dem
Touhig, Don	Lab/Co-op	Eagle, Maria	Lab	Clapham, Michael	Lab
Turner, Andrew	Con	Etherington, Bill	Lab	Clelland, David	Lab
Twigg, Derek	Lab	Farrelly, Paul	Lab	Cummings, John	Lab
Vaz, Keith	Lab	Field, Mark	Con	Dobson, Frank	Lab
Waltho, Lynda	Lab	Flello, Robert	Lab	Doran, Frank	Lab
Ward, Claire	Lab	Flint, Caroline	Lab	Gilroy, Linda	Lab/Co-op
Watkinson, Angela	Con	Foster, Michael Jabez	Lab	Heathcoat-Amory, David	Con
Watts, David	Lab	Gillan, Cheryl	Con	Hood, Jimmy	Lab
Weir, Mike	SNP	Green, Damian	Con	Howells, Kim	Lab
Whitehead, Alan	Lab	Healey, John	Lab	Illsley, Eric	Lab
Wicks, Malcolm	Lab	Henderson, Doug	Lab	Ingram, Adam	Lab
Willetts, David	Con	Hewitt, Patricia	Lab	Jack, Michael	Con
Williams, Betty	Lab	Hodgson, Sharon	Lab	Moss, Malcolm	Con
Williams, Mark	Lib Dem	Hopkins, Kelvin	Lab	Salmond, Alex	SNP
Williams, Roger	Lib Dem	Johnson, Alan	Lab	Skinner, Dennis	Lab
Williams, Stephen	Lib Dem	Jones, Kevan	Lab	Spellar, John	Lab
Willis, Phil	Lib Dem	Kelly, Ruth	Lab	Stunell, Andrew	Lib Dem
Wilson, Robert	Con	Khabra, Piara	Lab	Thomas, Gareth	Lab/Co-op
Woodward, Shaun	Lab	Kilfoyle, Peter	Lab	Tipping, Paddy	Lab
Wright, Jeremy	Con	Lamb, Norman	Lib Dem	Waterson, Nigel	Con
Wright, Tony Wayland	Lab	Letwin, Oliver	Con		

Elections and Campaigning

Hayes, John	Con	McDonnell, Alasdair	SDLP	**Engineering**	
		Mallaber, Judy	Lab	Battle, John	Lab
Electoral Reform		Miliband, David	Lab	Cook, Frank	Lab
Burden, Richard	Lab	Mountford, Kali	Lab	Olner, Bill	Lab
Huhne, Chris	Lib Dem	Paice, Jim	Con		
Johnson, Alan	Lab	Reid, Alan	Lib Dem	**Enterprise**	
Mackinlay, Andrew	Lab	Roy, Frank	Lab	Campbell, Gregory	DUP
Smith, Robert	Lib Dem	Ryan, Joan	Lab	Fraser, Christopher	Con
		Sarwar, Mohammed	Lab	Hunt, Jeremy	Con
Electronics Industry		Sheridan, Jim	Lab		
Spellar, John	Lab	Smith, Andrew	Lab	**Environment**	
		Smith, Angela Evans	Lab	Ainger, Nick	Lab
Emergency Planning		Spink, Bob	Con	Ainsworth, Bob	Lab
Brake, Tom	Lib Dem	Stewart, Ian	Lab	Ainsworth, Peter	Con
O'Hara, Edward	Lab	Sutcliffe, Gerry	Lab	Amess, David	Con
		Timms, Stephen	Lab	Armstrong, Hilary	Lab
Employment		Touhig, Don	Lab/Co-op	Austin, John	Lab
Alexander, Douglas	Lab	Turner, Des	Lab	Baker, Norman	Lib Dem
Anderson, Janet	Lab	Walker, Charles	Con	Banks, Gordon	Lab
Atkins, Charlotte	Lab	Ward, Claire	Lab	Barker, Gregory	Con
Benn, Hilary	Lab	Weir, Mike	SNP	Barrett, John	Lib Dem
Blears, Hazel	Lab	Williams, Alan	Lab	Barron, Kevin	Lab
Blizzard, Bob	Lab	Winterton, Rosie	Lab	Bayley, Hugh	Lab
Brown, Gordon	Lab	Woolas, Phil	Lab	Benn, Hilary	Lab
Brown, Russell	Lab			Blunt, Crispin	Con
Butler, Dawn	Lab	**Employment Law**		Bradshaw, Ben	Lab
Cairns, David	Lab	Johnson, Diana	Lab	Brake, Tom	Lib Dem
Campbell, Gregory	DUP			Burstow, Paul	Lib Dem
Clapham, Michael	Lab	**Energy**		Butterfill, John	Con
Clelland, David	Lab	Barrett, John	Lib Dem	Cable, Vincent	Lib Dem
		Barron, Kevin	Lab	Calton, Patsy	Lib Dem
		Blizzard, Bob	Lab	Caton, Martin	Lab

Challen, Colin	Lab	Ruane, Chris	Lab	Hendrick, Mark	Lab/Co-op
Chaytor, David	Lab	Ruddock, Joan	Lab	Hermon, Sylvia	UUP
Clark, Paul	Lab	Russell, Christine	Lab	Kelly, Ruth	Lab
Clelland, David	Lab	Russell, Bob	Lib Dem	Lewis, Julian	Con
Clifton-Brown, Geoffrey	Con	Salter, Martin	Lab	Lucas, Ian	Lab
Coaker, Vernon	Lab	Simpson, Alan	Lab	Mole, Chris	Lab
Cook, Robin	Lab	Skinner, Dennis	Lab	Moore, Michael	Lib Dem
Cummings, John	Lab	Spelman, Caroline	Con	Munn, Meg	Lab/Co-op
Davey, Edward	Lib Dem	Starkey, Phyllis	Lab	Rammell, Bill	Lab
Davies, David	Con	Stoate, Howard	Lab	Redwood, John	Con
Djanogly, Jonathan	Con	Taylor, David	Lab/Co-op	Robertson, Angus	SNP
Dowd, Jim	Lab	Teather, Sarah	Lib Dem	Robertson, Laurence	Con
Drew, David	Lab/Co-op	Thomas, Gareth	Lab/Co-op	Rosindell, Andrew	Con
Duncan Smith, Iain	Con	Todd, Mark	Lab	Simon, Siôn	Lab
Efford, Clive	Lab	Truswell, Paul	Lab	Watkinson, Angela	Con
Ennis, Jeffrey	Lab	Walley, Joan	Lab	Weir, Mike	SNP
Francois, Mark	Con	Whitehead, Alan	Lab	Woodward, Shaun	Lab
Gibson, Ian	Lab	Wiggin, Bill	Con		
Goodwill, Robert	Con	Wood, Mike	Lab		
Gray, James	Con	Woodward, Shaun	Lab	**European Union**	
Grieve, Dominic	Con	Wright, Tony Wayland	Lab	Baldry, Tony	Con
Griffith, Nia	Lab			Bell, Stuart	Lab
Gummer, John	Con	**Environmental Health**		Bercow, John	Con
Gwynne, Andrew	Lab	Williams, Betty	Lab	Boswell, Timothy	Con
Hands, Greg	Con			Caborn, Richard	Lab
Heald, Oliver	Con	**Equal Opportunities**		Cash, William	Con
Heath, David	Lib Dem	Austin, John	Lab	Caton, Martin	Lab
Hill, Keith	Lab	Baird, Vera	Lab	Connarty, Michael	Lab
Hood, Jimmy	Lab	Butler, Dawn	Lab	Cunningham, James	Lab
Horam, John	Con	Clark, Katy	Lab	Forth, Eric	Con
Horwood, Martin	Lib Dem	Cohen, Harry	Lab	Gapes, Mike	Lab/Co-op
Howarth, George	Lab	Cooper, Yvette	Lab	Godsiff, Roger	Lab
Howells, Kim	Lab	Etherington, Bill	Lab	Grieve, Dominic	Con
Hughes, Simon	Lib Dem	Follett, Barbara	Lab	Grogan, John	Lab
Hurd, Nick	Con	Harris, Evan	Lib Dem	Hammond, Philip	Con
Jackson, Glenda	Lab	Heal, Sylvia	Lab	Harvey, Nick	Lib Dem
Jackson, Stewart	Con	Heppell, John	Lab	Haselhurst, Alan	Con
Kidney, David	Lab	Mallaber, Judy	Lab	Heathcoat-Amory, David	Con
Kramer, Susan	Lib Dem	Martin, Michael	Speaker	Hill, Keith	Lab
Ladyman, Stephen	Lab	Morgan, Julie	Lab	Hoon, Geoffrey	Lab
Lamb, Norman	Lib Dem	Primarolo, Dawn	Lab	Irranca-Davies, Huw	Lab
Lazarowicz, Mark	Lab/Co-op	Swinson, Jo	Lib Dem	Jenkin, Bernard	Con
Lepper, David	Lab/Co-op			Kennedy, Charles	Lib Dem
Lord, Michael	Con	**Euro**		Khabra, Piara	Lab
Loughton, Tim	Con	Huhne, Chris	Lib Dem	Kirkbride, Julie	Con
Lucas, Ian	Lab	Redwood, John	Con	Lait, Jacqui	Con
McCrea, William	DUP	Villiers, Theresa	Con	Lilley, Peter	Con
McDonnell, John	Lab			McGuire, Anne	Lab
Mackay, Andrew	Con	**European Affairs**		MacShane, Denis	Lab
Main, Anne	Con	Baron, John	Con	Malins, Humfrey	Con
Marris, Rob	Lab	Bryant, Chris	Lab	O'Hara, Edward	Lab
Marshall-Andrews, Robert	Lab	Cameron, David	Con	Plaskitt, James	Lab
Moon, Madeleine	Lab	David, Wayne	Lab	Singh, Marsha	Lab
Prosser, Gwyn	Lab	Dhanda, Parmjit	Lab	Straw, Jack	Lab
Randall, John	Con	Dodds, Nigel	DUP	Stuart, Gisela	Lab
Raynsford, Nick	Lab	Francis, Hywel	Lab	Taylor, Ian	Con
Reid, Alan	Lib Dem	Gummer, John	Con	Tyrie, Andrew	Con
Robathan, Andrew	Con	Hancock, Mike	Lib Dem	Vis, Rudi	Lab

Expatriate Workers
Cook, Frank   *Lab*

Fair Trade
Hodgson, Sharon   *Lab*
Palmer, Nick   *Lab*

Family Policy
Brazier, Julian   *Con*
Doran, Frank   *Lab*
Flint, Caroline   *Lab*
Hewitt, Patricia   *Lab*
Hughes, Beverley   *Lab*
Kelly, Ruth   *Lab*
Knight, Jim   *Lab*
Leigh, Edward   *Con*
Selous, Andrew   *Con*
Streeter, Gary   *Con*
Watkinson, Angela   *Con*

Farming
Liddell-Grainger, Ian   *Con*
Robertson, Hugh   *Con*
Simpson, Keith   *Con*
Vaizey, Ed   *Con*

Field Sports
Swire, Hugo   *Con*

Film Industry
Clarke, Tom   *Lab*

Finance
Boswell, Timothy   *Con*
Davies, Quentin   *Con*
Duncan Smith, Iain   *Con*
Hammond, Stephen   *Con*
Hands, Greg   *Con*
Kramer, Susan   *Lib Dem*
Lazarowicz, Mark   *Lab/Co-op*
Loughton, Tim   *Con*
McIsaac, Shona   *Lab*
Mountford, Kali   *Lab*
Sheerman, Barry   *Lab/Co-op*
Trickett, Jon   *Lab*
Viggers, Peter   *Con*
Vis, Rudi   *Lab*
Woodward, Shaun   *Lab*

Financial Services
Cousins, Jim   *Lab*
Dunne, Philip   *Con*
Gauke, David   *Con*
Keeble, Sally   *Lab*
Moss, Malcolm   *Con*

Fire
Fitzpatrick, Jim   *Lab*

Fire Service
Ennis, Jeffrey   *Lab*
McCartney, Ian   *Lab*

Fishing Industry
Carmichael, Alistair   *Lib Dem*
George, Andrew   *Lib Dem*
Mitchell, Austin   *Lab*
Reid, Alan   *Lib Dem*
Salmond, Alex   *SNP*
Steen, Anthony   *Con*
Strang, Gavin   *Lab*
Winterton, Ann   *Con*

Food Safety
Simpson, Alan   *Lab*

Footwear
Anderson, Janet   *Lab*

Foreign Affairs
Arbuthnot, James   *Con*
Austin, John   *Lab*
Blunt, Crispin   *Con*
Bradshaw, Ben   *Lab*
Brazier, Julian   *Con*
Burt, Alistair   *Con*
Butterfill, John   *Con*
Campbell, Menzies   *Lib Dem*
Chapman, Ben   *Lab*
Clarke, Tom   *Lab*
Clifton-Brown, Geoffrey   *Con*
Coaker, Vernon   *Lab*
Conway, Derek   *Con*
Curry, David   *Con*
Dorrell, Stephen   *Con*
Fabricant, Michael   *Con*
Fox, Liam   *Con*
Fraser, Christopher   *Con*
Galloway, George   *Respect*
Gapes, Mike   *Lab/Co-op*
Gardiner, Barry   *Lab*
Garnier, Edward   *Con*
George, Bruce   *Lab*
Gerrard, Neil   *Lab*
Gillan, Cheryl   *Con*
Godsiff, Roger   *Lab*
Gray, James   *Con*
Green, Damian   *Con*
Grieve, Dominic   *Con*
Hammond, Stephen   *Con*
Hands, Greg   *Con*
Hanson, David   *Lab*
Harris, Tom   *Lab*
Hendrick, Mark   *Lab/Co-op*
Hoey, Kate   *Lab*
Howard, Michael   *Con*
Howells, Kim   *Lab*

Hunt, Jeremy   *Con*
Jenkin, Bernard   *Con*
Joyce, Eric   *Lab*
Keen, Alan   *Lab/Co-op*
Keetch, Paul   *Lib Dem*
Kennedy, Jane   *Lab*
Key, Robert   *Con*
Knight, Jim   *Lab*
Leigh, Edward   *Con*
Lewis, Julian   *Con*
Loughton, Tim   *Con*
Mackay, Andrew   *Con*
Maples, John   *Con*
Marsden, Gordon   *Lab*
Marshall, David   *Lab*
Moore, Michael   *Lib Dem*
Murphy, Jim   *Lab*
Murphy, Paul   *Lab*
Osborne, George   *Con*
Paisley, Ian   *DUP*
Paterson, Owen   *Con*
Pope, Greg   *Lab*
Purchase, Ken   *Lab/Co-op*
Randall, John   *Con*
Reid, John   *Lab*
Robertson, Angus   *SNP*
Robertson, Hugh   *Con*
Rosindell, Andrew   *Con*
Ruddock, Joan   *Lab*
Sarwar, Mohammed   *Lab*
Sheridan, Jim   *Lab*
Simmonds, Mark   *Con*
Simpson, Keith   *Con*
Soames, Nicholas   *Con*
Squire, Rachel   *Lab*
Starkey, Phyllis   *Lab*
Tapsell, Peter   *Con*
Tredinnick, David   *Con*
Waterson, Nigel   *Con*
Willott, Jenny   *Lib Dem*
Wilshire, David   *Con*
Wright, Jeremy   *Con*
Wyatt, Derek   *Lab*

Forestry
Heathcoat-Amory, David   *Con*
Lord, Michael   *Con*

Freedom of Information
Fisher, Mark   *Lab*
Norris, Dan   *Lab*

Fuel Tax
Reid, Alan   *Lib Dem*

Gas Industry
Bruce, Malcolm   *Lib Dem*

Genetics
Begg, Anne | Lab

Gibraltar
Willis, Phil | Lib Dem

Glass Industry
Illsley, Eric | Lab

Globalisation
Clegg, Nick | Lib Dem

GM Issues
Joyce, Eric | Lab
Simpson, Alan | Lab

Green Issues
Morley, Elliot | Lab

Health
Ainger, Nick | Lab
Amess, David | Con
Anderson, Janet | Lab
Atkins, Charlotte | Lab
Austin, John | Lab
Bacon, Richard | Con
Baron, John | Con
Barron, Kevin | Lab
Bayley, Hugh | Lab
Benton, Joe | Lab
Blackman, Liz | Lab
Blears, Hazel | Lab
Blizzard, Bob | Lab
Brady, Graham | Con
Brokenshire, James | Con
Brown, Gordon | Lab
Buck, Karen | Lab
Burden, Richard | Lab
Burnham, Andy | Lab
Burns, Simon | Con
Butterfill, John | Con
Clapham, Michael | Lab
Clappison, James | Con
Clark, Greg | Con
Coffey, Ann | Lab
Cohen, Harry | Lab
Cryer, Ann | Lab
Darling, Alistair | Lab
Davies, Quentin | Con
Davis, David | Con
Dean, Janet | Lab
Dismore, Andrew | Lab
Dobbin, Jim | Lab/Co-op
Donohoe, Brian | Lab
Dorries, Nadine | Con
Efford, Clive | Lab
Farrelly, Paul | Lab
Farron, Tim | Lib Dem

Flynn, Paul | Lab
Foster, Michael Jabez | Lab
Fox, Liam | Con
George, Bruce | Lab
Gibson, Ian | Lab
Gidley, Sandra | Lib Dem
Grayling, Christopher | Con
Griffiths, Nigel | Lab
Hall, Mike | Lab
Hammond, Stephen | Con
Hanson, David | Lab
Harris, Evan | Lib Dem
Havard, Dai | Lab
Hermon, Sylvia | UUP
Hesford, Stephen | Lab
Heyes, David | Lab
Hoban, Mark | Con
Holmes, Paul | Lib Dem
Horam, John | Con
Hughes, Beverley | Lab
Hurd, Nick | Con
Iddon, Brian | Lab
Johnson, Diana | Lab
Jones, Helen | Lab
Kawczynski, Daniel | Con
Keen, Ann | Lab
Kirkbride, Julie | Con
Lait, Jacqui | Con
Lammy, David | Lab
Lansley, Andrew | Con
Lewis, Ivan | Lab
Love, Andrew | Lab/Co-op
Lucas, Ian | Lab
McCafferty, Christine | Lab
McCrea, William | DUP
McDonagh, Siobhain | Lab
McNulty, Tony | Lab
Main, Anne | Con
Maples, John | Con
Martlew, Eric | Lab
Meale, Alan | Lab
Merron, Gillian | Lab
Milburn, Alan | Lab
Milton, Anne | Con
Mitchell, Andrew | Con
Moffatt, Laura | Lab
Murrison, Andrew | Con
Naysmith, Doug | Lab/Co-op
Picking, Anne | Lab
Pickles, Eric | Con
Primarolo, Dawn | Lab
Pritchard, Mark | Con
Purchase, Ken | Lab/Co-op
Reid, Alan | Lib Dem
Robinson, Iris | DUP
Ryan, Joan | Lab
Singh, Marsha | Lab
Southworth, Helen | Lab

Starkey, Phyllis | Lab
Stoate, Howard | Lab
Teather, Sarah | Lib Dem
Thomas, Gareth | Lab/Co-op
Touhig, Don | Lab/Co-op
Tredinnick, David | Con
Truswell, Paul | Lab
Turner, Des | Lab
Twigg, Derek | Lab
Wallace, Ben | Con
Walley, Joan | Lab
Walter, Robert | Con
Waterson, Nigel | Con
Weir, Mike | SNP
Widdecombe, Ann | Con
Willetts, David | Con
Williams, Betty | Lab
Williams, Stephen | Lib Dem
Willis, Phil | Lib Dem
Wright, Tony Wayland | Lab
Yeo, Tim | Con

Health and Safety
Brown, Russell | Lab
McCartney, Ian | Lab

Health Education
Heal, Sylvia | Lab
Williams, Betty | Lab
Young, George | Con

Heritage
Cash, William | Con
Hanson, David | Lab
Keetch, Paul | Lib Dem
Marsden, Gordon | Lab
Steen, Anthony | Con

Highlands and Islands
Alexander, Danny | Lib Dem

HIV/AIDS
Gerrard, Neil | Lab
Moffatt, Laura | Lab
Strang, Gavin | Lab

Home Affairs
Barron, Kevin | Lab
Benn, Hilary | Lab
Brooke, Annette | Lib Dem
Cameron, David | Con
Clappison, James | Con
Clelland, David | Lab
Dean, Janet | Lab
Hall, Mike | Lab
Heath, David | Lib Dem
Hood, Jimmy | Lab
Howard, Michael | Con

Hutton, John	Lab	Hughes, Simon	Lib Dem
Keeble, Sally	Lab	Iddon, Brian	Lab
Knight, Greg	Con	Jack, Michael	Con
Llwyd, Elfyn	PlC	Jackson, Glenda	Lab
Loughton, Tim	Con	Jackson, Stewart	Con
Mactaggart, Fiona	Lab	Jenkins, Brian	Lab
Mates, Michael	Con	Jones, Lynne	Lab
Meale, Alan	Lab	Kidney, David	Lab
Prentice, Bridget	Lab	Lamb, Norman	Lib Dem
Ruffley, David	Con	Leech, John	Lib Dem
Short, Clare	Lab	Linton, Martin	Lab
Smith, Angela Evans	Lab	Love, Andrew	Lab/Co-op

Harris, Evan Lib Dem
Hermon, Sylvia UUP
Holmes, Paul Lib Dem
Hughes, Simon Lib Dem
Lloyd, Tony Lab
Mactaggart, Fiona Lab
Marsden, Gordon Lab
Martin, Michael Speaker
Meale, Alan Lab
Prentice, Bridget Lab
Salter, Martin Lab

Hutton, John	Lab
Keeble, Sally	Lab
Knight, Greg	Con
Llwyd, Elfyn	PlC
Loughton, Tim	Con
Mactaggart, Fiona	Lab
Mates, Michael	Con
Meale, Alan	Lab
Prentice, Bridget	Lab
Ruffley, David	Con
Short, Clare	Lab
Smith, Angela Evans	Lab
Stoate, Howard	Lab
Tredinnick, David	Con
Ward, Claire	Lab
Winterton, Rosie	Lab

Homelessness
Selous, Andrew — Con

Horticulture
Jack, Michael — Con

House of Lords Reform
Stringer, Graham — Lab
Thurso, John — Lib Dem

Housing
Alexander, Danny	Lib Dem
Ancram, Michael	Con
Battle, John	Lab
Benton, Joe	Lab
Beresford, Paul	Con
Betts, Clive	Lab
Blackman-Woods, Roberta	Lab
Buck, Karen	Lab
Butterfill, John	Con
Clark, Greg	Con
Crausby, David	Lab
Dean, Janet	Lab
Dobbin, Jim	Lab/Co-op
Dowd, Jim	Lab
Drew, David	Lab/Co-op
Eagle, Maria	Lab
Francois, Mark	Con
George, Andrew	Lib Dem
George, Bruce	Lab
Gerrard, Neil	Lab
Gildernew, Michelle	Sinn Féin
Goggins, Paul	Lab
Goldsworthy, Julia	Lib Dem
Griffiths, Nigel	Lab
Hands, Greg	Con
Hendry, Charles	Con
Hodge, Margaret	Lab
Hoey, Kate	Lab
Hood, Jimmy	Lab
Howarth, George	Lab

McDonagh, Siobhain	Lab
Meacher, Michael	Lab
Michael, Alun	Lab/Co-op
Miller, Maria	Con
Milton, Anne	Con
Moffatt, Laura	Lab
Moss, Malcolm	Con
Murphy, Paul	Lab
O'Brien, Stephen	Con
O'Hara, Edward	Lab
Osborne, Sandra	Lab
Pickles, Eric	Con
Pope, Greg	Lab
Pound, Stephen	Lab
Primarolo, Dawn	Lab
Purnell, James	Lab
Rammell, Bill	Lab
Raynsford, Nick	Lab
Robinson, Peter	DUP
Rooney, Terry	Lab
Rowen, Paul	Lib Dem
Salter, Martin	Lab
Sarwar, Mohammed	Lab
Shaw, Jonathan	Lab
Slaughter, Andy	Lab
Southworth, Helen	Lab
Taylor, Dari	Lab
Taylor, David	Lab/Co-op
Turner, Des	Lab
Turner, Neil	Lab
Twigg, Derek	Lab
Vaizey, Ed	Con
Winterton, Rosie	Lab
Wood, Mike	Lab
Young, George	Con

Housing and Urban Regeneration
Moran, Margaret — Lab
Wright, David — Lab

Human Rights
Baird, Vera	Lab
Browne, Des	Lab
Clark, Katy	Lab
Etherington, Bill	Lab
Fisher, Mark	Lab

Immigration and Race Relations
Cryer, Ann	Lab
Godsiff, Roger	Lab
Lloyd, Tony	Lab
Prosser, Gwyn	Lab
Short, Clare	Lab

Industrial Democracy
Meacher, Michael — Lab

Industrial Economy
Cruddas, Jon — Lab

Industrial Policy
Bruce, Malcolm	Lib Dem
Dowd, Jim	Lab
Heathcoat-Amory, David	Con
Henderson, Doug	Lab
Lloyd, Tony	Lab
Ussher, Kitty	Lab
Williams, Alan	Lab

Industrial Relations and Working Conditions
Crausby, David	Lab
Cunningham, James	Lab
Havard, Dai	Lab
Heald, Oliver	Con
Healey, John	Lab
Martin, Michael	Speaker
Rooney, Terry	Lab
Smith, John	Lab

Industry
Ainsworth, Bob	Lab
Atkinson, Peter	Con
Beckett, Margaret	Lab
Connarty, Michael	Lab
Davis, David	Con
Gillan, Cheryl	Con
Keen, Alan	Lab/Co-op
Ladyman, Stephen	Lab
Mackay, Andrew	Con
Marris, Rob	Lab
Milburn, Alan	Lab
Miller, Andrew	Lab

Ottaway, Richard	*Con*	
Paterson, Owen	*Con*	
Robinson, Geoffrey	*Lab*	
Sheerman, Barry	*Lab/Co-op*	
Smith, Jacqui	*Lab*	
Taylor, Dari	*Lab*	
Trickett, Jon	*Lab*	
Watson, Tom	*Lab*	

Information Economy
Bryant, Chris — *Lab*

Information Technology
Henderson, Doug	*Lab*
Hewitt, Patricia	*Lab*
Knight, Greg	*Con*
McDonnell, Alasdair	*SDLP*
Miller, Andrew	*Lab*
Villiers, Theresa	*Con*

Infrastructure
O'Brien, Stephen — *Con*

Inland Waterways
Skinner, Dennis — *Lab*

Inner Cities
Beresford, Paul	*Con*
Hodge, Margaret	*Lab*

Intellectual Property
Howells, Kim — *Lab*

Intelligence and Security
Barron, Kevin — *Lab*

International Aid and Development
Battle, John	*Lab*
Bayley, Hugh	*Lab*
Benn, Hilary	*Lab*
Brake, Tom	*Lib Dem*
Chaytor, David	*Lab*
Connarty, Michael	*Lab*
Davidson, Ian	*Lab/Co-op*
Follett, Barbara	*Lab*
Hamilton, Fabian	*Lab*
Hendrick, Mark	*Lab/Co-op*
Keen, Ann	*Lab*
Khabra, Piara	*Lab*
Knight, Jim	*Lab*
Lammy, David	*Lab*
Luff, Peter	*Con*
McCafferty, Christine	*Lab*
McKechin, Ann	*Lab*
Naysmith, Doug	*Lab/Co-op*
Price, Adam	*PlC*
Robathan, Andrew	*Con*

Robertson, Angus	*SNP*	
Russell, Christine	*Lab*	
Sarwar, Mohammed	*Lab*	
Smith, Angela Evans	*Lab*	
Spelman, Caroline	*Con*	

International Economics
Duncan, Alan	*Con*
MacShane, Denis	*Lab*

International Terrorism
Robinson, Peter — *DUP*

International Trade
Duncan, Alan	*Con*
Hammond, Philip	*Con*
Kawczynski, Daniel	*Con*
McCarthy, Kerry	*Lab*

Internet
Davey, Edward	*Lib Dem*
McKenna, Rosemary	*Lab*
Webb, Steve	*Lib Dem*
Wyatt, Derek	*Lab*

Investment
Farrelly, Paul	*Lab*
Hughes, Beverley	*Lab*
Ryan, Joan	*Lab*
Stewart, Ian	*Lab*

Irish Affairs
Creagh, Mary	*Lab*
Doherty, Pat	*Sinn Féin*
McDonnell, John	*Lab*

Justice
McCarthy, Kerry	*Lab*
Michael, Alun	*Lab/Co-op*
Mullin, Chris	*Lab*
Wishart, Peter	*SNP*

Kurdish Issues
Williams, Hywel — *PlC*

Labour Law
Cruddas, Jon — *Lab*

Language Issues
Williams, Hywel — *PlC*

Law
Arbuthnot, James	*Con*
Harman, Harriet	*Lab*

Law and Order
Baron, John	*Con*
Brazier, Julian	*Con*

Brokenshire, James	*Con*	
Clark, Greg	*Con*	
Davies, Philip	*Con*	
Davis, David	*Con*	
Dorries, Nadine	*Con*	
Farron, Tim	*Lib Dem*	
Greenway, John	*Con*	
Grieve, Dominic	*Con*	
Harper, Mark	*Con*	
Heald, Oliver	*Con*	
Herbert, Nick	*Con*	
Holmes, Paul	*Lib Dem*	
Jones, David	*Con*	
Kirkbride, Julie	*Con*	
Osborne, George	*Con*	
Robertson, Laurence	*Con*	
Rosindell, Andrew	*Con*	
Streeter, Gary	*Con*	
Watkinson, Angela	*Con*	
Watson, Tom	*Lab*	
Willott, Jenny	*Lib Dem*	

Learning Disabilities
Browning, Angela — *Con*

Leasehold Reform
Lepper, David — *Lab/Co-op*

Legal Affairs
Baldry, Tony	*Con*
Browne, Des	*Lab*
Campbell, Menzies	*Lib Dem*
Cox, Geoffrey	*Con*
Hutton, John	*Lab*
McIntosh, Anne	*Con*
Vaz, Keith	*Lab*

Leisure
Gale, Roger	*Con*
Godsiff, Roger	*Lab*
Winterton, Nicholas	*Con*

Libraries
McKenna, Rosemary — *Lab*

Licensed Trade
Grogan, John — *Lab*

Lifelong Learning
Francis, Hywel	*Lab*
Havard, Dai	*Lab*
Reed, Andrew	*Lab/Co-op*

Local and Regional Government
Benton, Joe	*Lab*
Berry, Roger	*Lab*
Betts, Clive	*Lab*
Binley, Brian	*Con*

Blunkett, David	Lab	Stunell, Andrew	Lib Dem	Villiers, Theresa	Con
Borrow, David	Lab	Sutcliffe, Gerry	Lab	Ward, Claire	Lab
Carswell, Douglas	Con	Syms, Robert	Con	Woolas, Phil	Lab
Cawsey, Ian	Lab	Tipping, Paddy	Lab	Wyatt, Derek	Lab
Clarke, Tom	Lab	Todd, Mark	Lab		
Clelland, David	Lab	Touhig, Don	Lab/Co-op	**Medical Ethics**	
Davidson, Ian	Lab/Co-op	Turner, Neil	Lab	Harris, Evan	Lib Dem
Dhanda, Parmjit	Lab	Vaz, Keith	Lab		
Dobbin, Jim	Lab/Co-op	Watkinson, Angela	Con	**Medicinal and Illegal Drugs**	
Donohoe, Brian	Lab	Whitehead, Alan	Lab	Flynn, Paul	Lab
Efford, Clive	Lab	Willis, Phil	Lib Dem		
Ellman, Louise	Lab/Co-op	Winterton, Nicholas	Con	**Mental Health**	
Ennis, Jeffrey	Lab	Wright, Anthony David	Lab	Austin, John	Lab
Evans, Nigel	Con			Browning, Angela	Con
Foster, Don	Lib Dem	**Local Economic Development**		Doran, Frank	Lab
Fraser, Christopher	Con	Davidson, Ian	Lab/Co-op	Jones, Lynne	Lab
Gilroy, Linda	Lab/Co-op				
Grogan, John	Lab			**Micro-Technology**	
Gwynne, Andrew	Lab	**Local Issues**		Williams, Alan	Lab
Hall, Mike	Lab	Reid, Alan	Lib Dem		
Hanson, David	Lab	Rogerson, Dan	Lib Dem	**Middle East**	
Hayes, John	Con	Viggers, Peter	Con	Bell, Stuart	Lab
Healey, John	Lab			Breed, Colin	Lib Dem
Heath, David	Lib Dem			Burden, Richard	Lab
Heppell, John	Lab	**London**		Dismore, Andrew	Lab
Heyes, David	Lab	Dobson, Frank	Lab	Duncan, Alan	Con
Hodge, Margaret	Lab	Hodge, Margaret	Lab	Ellman, Louise	Lab/Co-op
Hughes, Beverley	Lab	McNulty, Tony	Lab	Scott, Lee	Con
Jones, Kevan	Lab			Starkey, Phyllis	Lab
Keeble, Sally	Lab	**Low Pay**			
Kennedy, Jane	Lab	Prentice, Gordon	Lab	**Mining**	
Kumar, Ashok	Lab	Short, Clare	Lab	Illsley, Eric	Lab
Lansley, Andrew	Con	Taylor, David	Lab/Co-op		
Laxton, Bob	Lab			**Mobile Phone Masts**	
Levitt, Tom	Lab			Brokenshire, James	Con
McCartney, Ian	Lab	**Manufacturing and Engineering**		Harper, Mark	Con
McDonnell, John	Lab	Curtis-Thomas, Claire	Lab		
McNulty, Tony	Lab	MacShane, Denis	Lab	**Modernisation of Parliament**	
Mallaber, Judy	Lab	Marris, Rob	Lab	Bradshaw, Ben	Lab
May, Theresa	Con	Prentice, Gordon	Lab	Davey, Edward	Lib Dem
Michael, Alun	Lab/Co-op	Tami, Mark	Lab		
Mole, Chris	Lab	Watson, Tom	Lab	**Money Laundering**	
Morley, Elliot	Lab			Wyatt, Derek	Lab
Murphy, Paul	Lab	**Media**			
Naysmith, Doug	Lab/Co-op	Bayley, Hugh	Lab	**Motor Industry**	
O'Hara, Edward	Lab	Burnham, Andy	Lab	Kemp, Fraser	Lab
Olner, Bill	Lab	Cash, William	Con	Smith, Andrew	Lab
Pelling, Andrew	Con	Field, Mark	Con	Spellar, John	Lab
Pickles, Eric	Con	Fisher, Mark	Lab	Wareing, Robert	Lab
Plaskitt, James	Lab	Fraser, Christopher	Con		
Pugh, John	Lib Dem	Gale, Roger	Con	**Music**	
Russell, Bob	Lib Dem	Green, Damian	Con	Knight, Greg	Con
Ryan, Joan	Lab	Howarth, Gerald	Con		
Salter, Martin	Lab	Linton, Martin	Lab	**Mutuality**	
Sanders, Adrian	Lib Dem	Miller, Maria	Con	Love, Andrew	Lab/Co-op
Starkey, Phyllis	Lab	Mitchell, Austin	Lab		
Straw, Jack	Lab	Mullin, Chris	Lab	**Mutuals**	
Stringer, Graham	Lab	Rammell, Bill	Lab	Thomas, Gareth	Lab/Co-op

National Health Service
Corbyn, Jeremy	Lab
Cunningham, James	Lab
Dowd, Jim	Lab
Dunwoody, Gwyneth	Lab
Eagle, Angela	Lab
Hood, Jimmy	Lab
McCartney, Ian	Lab
Ryan, Joan	Lab
Squire, Rachel	Lab
Taylor, Richard	Ind KHHC
Winterton, Nicholas	Con

NATO
Clapham, Michael	Lab

New Technology
Robinson, Geoffrey	Lab

Northern Ireland
Bellingham, Henry	Con
Browne, Des	Lab
Donaldson, Jeffrey	DUP
Harris, Tom	Lab
Ingram, Adam	Lab
McGrady, Eddie	SDLP
Mates, Michael	Con
Mercer, Patrick	Con
Murphy, Paul	Lab
Robathan, Andrew	Con
Salter, Martin	Lab
Short, Clare	Lab
Willis, Phil	Lib Dem
Wilshire, David	Con

Nuclear Industry
Jack, Michael	Con
Ladyman, Stephen	Lab

Oil and Gas Industry
Bruce, Malcolm	Lib Dem
Smith, Robert	Lib Dem

Overseas Aid and Development
Baldry, Tony	Con
Barker, Gregory	Con
Barrett, John	Lib Dem
Fisher, Mark	Lab
Follett, Barbara	Lab
Jackson, Glenda	Lab
Robertson, Laurence	Con

Paper Industries
Winterton, Nicholas	Con

Parliamentary and Constitutional Affairs
Beith, Alan	Lib Dem

Parliamentary Democracy
Marshall-Andrews, Robert	Lab

Partnerships
Moon, Madeleine	Lab

Penal Affairs and Policy
Malins, Humfrey	Con

Pensions
Barrett, John	Lib Dem
Challen, Colin	Lab
Crausby, David	Lab
Davies, Quentin	Con
Dorries, Nadine	Con
Duddridge, James	Con
Flynn, Paul	Lab
Heald, Oliver	Con
Hesford, Stephen	Lab
Hodgson, Sharon	Lab
Holmes, Paul	Lib Dem
Laws, David	Lib Dem
Miller, Andrew	Lab
Stuart, Gisela	Lab

People of Islington
Corbyn, Jeremy	Lab

Personal Finance
Greenway, John	Con

Pharmaceutical and Chemical Industries
Winterton, Ann	Con

Planning
Burgon, Colin	Lab
Caton, Martin	Lab
Cryer, Ann	Lab
Djanogly, Jonathan	Con
Drew, David	Lab/Co-op
Gerrard, Neil	Lab
Herbert, Nick	Con
Jackson, Stewart	Con
Leech, John	Lib Dem
Moon, Madeleine	Lab
Prisk, Mark	Con

Police and Security Issues
Cable, Vincent	Lib Dem
Cawsey, Ian	Lab
Hermon, Sylvia	UUP
Irranca-Davies, Huw	Lab
Lansley, Andrew	Con
McCabe, Steve	Lab
Mackinlay, Andrew	Lab

O'Brien, Mike	Lab
Straw, Jack	Lab
Tipping, Paddy	Lab
Tredinnick, David	Con

Policy Development
Clark, Katy	Lab

Political Finance
Linton, Martin	Lab

Political Ideas and Philosophy
Hayes, John	Con

Political Process
Wilshire, David	Con

Popular Capitalism
Redwood, John	Con

Post Office
Brokenshire, James	Con
Johnson, Alan	Lab
Rogerson, Dan	Lib Dem

Poverty
Battle, John	Lab
Burden, Richard	Lab
Cooper, Yvette	Lab
Drew, David	Lab/Co-op
Field, Frank	Lab
Fitzpatrick, Jim	Lab
Goggins, Paul	Lab
Hall, Mike	Lab
Marshall, David	Lab
Mitchell, Austin	Lab
Osborne, Sandra	Lab
Prentice, Gordon	Lab
Purnell, James	Lab
Rooney, Terry	Lab
Ruane, Chris	Lab
Wood, Mike	Lab
Wright, David	Lab

Private Security
George, Bruce	Lab

Privatisation
Howarth, Gerald	Con

Pro-Life Movement
Amess, David	Con

Provision for under 5s
Harman, Harriet	Lab

Public Expenditure
Bacon, Richard	Con

Public Sector
Fallon, Michael — Con

Public Services
Ellman, Louise — Lab/Co-op
Kennedy, Jane — Lab
Khan, Sadiq — Lab
Laws, David — Lib Dem

Public/Private Partnerships
Smith, Geraldine — Lab

Quality of Life
McDonagh, Siobhain — Lab

Quarrying
Levitt, Tom — Lab

Quotas for Women
Anderson, Janet — Lab

Race Relations and Civil Rights
Fitzpatrick, Jim — Lab
Follett, Barbara — Lab
Gerrard, Neil — Lab
Hamilton, Fabian — Lab
Khabra, Piara — Lab
Lilley, Peter — Con
Lloyd, Tony — Lab
Short, Clare — Lab
Stunell, Andrew — Lib Dem
Vaz, Keith — Lab

Railways
Cryer, Ann — Lab
Luff, Peter — Con

Redistribution of Wealth
Dobson, Frank — Lab
Meacher, Michael — Lab

Regeneration
Bailey, Adrian — Lab/Co-op
Baird, Vera — Lab
Blackman-Woods, Roberta — Lab
Blears, Hazel — Lab
Buck, Karen — Lab
Clark, Paul — Lab
Cruddas, Jon — Lab
Ennis, Jeffrey — Lab
Farrelly, Paul — Lab
Fitzpatrick, Jim — Lab
Gwynne, Andrew — Lab
Healey, John — Lab
Hendry, Charles — Con
Hodgson, Sharon — Lab
Hope, Phil — Lab/Co-op
Hughes, Beverley — Lab

Humble, Joan — Lab
Jones, Kevan — Lab
Lammy, David — Lab
Lepper, David — Lab/Co-op
Love, Andrew — Lab/Co-op
McGuire, Anne — Lab
McNulty, Tony — Lab
Mann, John — Lab
Pearson, Ian — Lab
Reed, Andrew — Lab/Co-op
Russell, Christine — Lab
Ryan, Joan — Lab
Simon, Siôn — Lab
Smith, Geraldine — Lab
Steen, Anthony — Con
Stringer, Graham — Lab
Timms, Stephen — Lab

Regional Policy
Armstrong, Hilary — Lab
Baird, Vera — Lab
Borrow, David — Lab
Chapman, Ben — Lab
Hughes, Beverley — Lab
Jones, Kevan — Lab
Milburn, Alan — Lab
O'Hara, Edward — Lab
Pearson, Ian — Lab
Prentice, Gordon — Lab
Price, Adam — PlC
Stewart, Ian — Lab
Ussher, Kitty — Lab
Watts, David — Lab
Williams, Alan — Lab
Winterton, Rosie — Lab
Wright, David — Lab

Regulatory Issues
Gilroy, Linda — Lab/Co-op

Religious Affairs
Burt, Alistair — Con
Field, Frank — Lab
Paisley, Ian — DUP

Research
Ladyman, Stephen — Lab

Retail Industry
Smith, Andrew — Lab

Rural Affairs
Benyon, Richard — Con
Dorries, Nadine — Con
Farron, Tim — Lib Dem
Fraser, Christopher — Con

Herbert, Nick — Con
Mundell, David — Con
Pritchard, Mark — Con
Williams, Mark — Lib Dem

Safe Communities
Taylor, David — Lab/Co-op

Sales Promotion and Marketing
Greenway, John — Con

Science and Technology
Battle, John — Lab
Calton, Patsy — Lib Dem
Dhanda, Parmjit — Lab
Gibson, Ian — Lab
Harris, Evan — Lib Dem
Iddon, Brian — Lab
Jones, Lynne — Lab
Jones, Martyn — Lab
Ladyman, Stephen — Lab
Miller, Andrew — Lab
Naysmith, Doug — Lab/Co-op
Starkey, Phyllis — Lab
Taylor, Ian — Con
Turner, Des — Lab

Scottish Affairs
Brown, Gordon — Lab
Galloway, George — Respect
Gray, James — Con
Griffiths, Nigel — Lab
Kennedy, Charles — Lib Dem
Marshall, David — Lab
Salmond, Alex — SNP

Security
Lewis, Julian — Con
Wallace, Ben — Con

Senior Citizens
Martin, Michael — Speaker
Pugh, John — Lib Dem
Spink, Bob — Con
Vis, Rudi — Lab

Shipbuilding and Offshore Industries
Campbell, Alan — Lab
Robinson, Peter — DUP

Shipping
Prosser, Gwyn — Lab
Waterson, Nigel — Con

Skills and Training
Connarty, Michael — Lab

Small Businesses

Abbott, Diane	*Lab*
Baron, John	*Con*
Bellingham, Henry	*Con*
Bercow, John	*Con*
Borrow, David	*Lab*
Browning, Angela	*Con*
Cairns, David	*Lab*
Cash, William	*Con*
Cunningham, Tony	*Lab*
Curtis-Thomas, Claire	*Lab*
Djanogly, Jonathan	*Con*
Dobbin, Jim	*Lab/Co-op*
Donohoe, Brian	*Lab*
Duncan Smith, Iain	*Con*
Dunne, Philip	*Con*
Evans, Nigel	*Con*
Field, Mark	*Con*
Foster, Michael John	*Lab*
Fraser, Christopher	*Con*
Gilroy, Linda	*Lab/Co-op*
Hepburn, Stephen	*Lab*
Hesford, Stephen	*Lab*
Hoyle, Lindsay	*Lab*
Humble, Joan	*Lab*
Jackson, Stewart	*Con*
Kemp, Fraser	*Lab*
Kumar, Ashok	*Lab*
Lansley, Andrew	*Con*
Lepper, David	*Lab/Co-op*
Love, Andrew	*Lab/Co-op*
Lucas, Ian	*Lab*
McKechin, Ann	*Lab*
Mann, John	*Lab*
Moss, Malcolm	*Con*
Mountford, Kali	*Lab*
Munn, Meg	*Lab/Co-op*
Paice, Jim	*Con*
Picking, Anne	*Lab*
Prisk, Mark	*Con*
Purchase, Ken	*Lab/Co-op*
Robertson, John	*Lab*
Singh, Marsha	*Lab*
Smith, Geraldine	*Lab*
Southworth, Helen	*Lab*
Tami, Mark	*Lab*
Taylor, David	*Lab/Co-op*
Vaz, Keith	*Lab*
Vis, Rudi	*Lab*
Walley, Joan	*Lab*
Watson, Tom	*Lab*
Wood, Mike	*Lab*

Social Affairs

Benyon, Richard	*Con*
Byrne, Liam	*Lab*
Dodds, Nigel	*DUP*
Goodman, Paul	*Con*
Hendry, Charles	*Con*
Heyes, David	*Lab*
Hodgson, Sharon	*Lab*
Hughes, Simon	*Lib Dem*
Irranca-Davies, Huw	*Lab*
James, Sian	*Lab*
Kelly, Ruth	*Lab*
Kennedy, Charles	*Lib Dem*
Lamb, Norman	*Lib Dem*
McCarthy, Kerry	*Lab*
Marsden, Gordon	*Lab*
Munn, Meg	*Lab/Co-op*
Picking, Anne	*Lab*
Raynsford, Nick	*Lab*
Selous, Andrew	*Con*
Sheridan, Jim	*Lab*
Simon, Siôn	*Lab*
Webb, Steve	*Lib Dem*
Wicks, Malcolm	*Lab*
Williams, Hywel	*PlC*

Social Deprivation

Clark, Greg	*Con*

Social Economy

McCarthy-Fry, Sarah	*Lab/Co-op*

Social Security

Brown, Gordon	*Lab*
Dismore, Andrew	*Lab*
Duncan, Alan	*Con*
Flynn, Paul	*Lab*
Gibb, Nick	*Con*
Hammond, Philip	*Con*
Hewitt, Patricia	*Lab*
Illsley, Eric	*Lab*
Jones, Lynne	*Lab*
Kennedy, Jane	*Lab*
Kirkbride, Julie	*Con*
Meale, Alan	*Lab*
Mountford, Kali	*Lab*
Primarolo, Dawn	*Lab*
Willetts, David	*Con*
Williams, Hywel	*PlC*

Social Services

Austin, John	*Lab*
Calton, Patsy	*Lib Dem*
Dean, Janet	*Lab*
George, Bruce	*Lab*
Griffiths, Nigel	*Lab*
Harman, Harriet	*Lab*
Hesford, Stephen	*Lab*
Humble, Joan	*Lab*
McAvoy, Thomas	*Lab/Co-op*
McCafferty, Christine	*Lab*
McCartney, Ian	*Lab*
Martlew, Eric	*Lab*

Morgan, Julie	*Lab*
Pickles, Eric	*Con*
Smith, Jacqui	*Lab*
Truswell, Paul	*Lab*
Turner, Andrew	*Con*
Turner, Des	*Lab*
Williams, Betty	*Lab*

Social Welfare

Farron, Tim	*Lib Dem*
Mulholland, Gregory	*Lib Dem*
Munn, Meg	*Lab/Co-op*
Roy, Frank	*Lab*

Social Work

Williams, Hywel	*PlC*

Solvent Abuse

Hanson, David	*Lab*

Southern Africa

McGuinness, Martin	*Sinn Féin*

Space

Gillan, Cheryl	*Con*

Sport

Burnham, Andy	*Lab*
Campbell, Menzies	*Lib Dem*
Coaker, Vernon	*Lab*
Cunningham, Tony	*Lab*
Eagle, Angela	*Lab*
Godsiff, Roger	*Lab*
Grogan, John	*Lab*
Hancock, Mike	*Lib Dem*
Hoey, Kate	*Lab*
Hoyle, Lindsay	*Lab*
Knight, Jim	*Lab*
Malins, Humfrey	*Con*
Mann, John	*Lab*
Merron, Gillian	*Lab*
Murphy, Jim	*Lab*
Purnell, James	*Lab*
Rammell, Bill	*Lab*
Reed, Andrew	*Lab/Co-op*
Russell, Bob	*Lib Dem*
Trickett, Jon	*Lab*
Winterton, Nicholas	*Con*
Wright, David	*Lab*

Steel Associated Metals/Materials

Caborn, Richard	*Lab*
Francis, Hywel	*Lab*

Sustainable Development

Horwood, Martin	*Lib Dem*

Taxation

Ainsworth, Bob	Lab
Arbuthnot, James	Con
Bailey, Adrian	Lab/Co-op
Clifton-Brown, Geoffrey	Con
Davey, Edward	Lib Dem
Foster, Michael Jabez	Lab
Gibb, Nick	Con
Kirkbride, Julie	Con
McIsaac, Shona	Lab
Osborne, George	Con
Palmer, Nick	Lab
Straw, Jack	Lab
Walker, Charles	Con
Williams, Stephen	Lib Dem

Technology

Fabricant, Michael	Con
Gibson, Ian	Lab
Kemp, Fraser	Lab

Telecommunications

Timms, Stephen	Lab

Territorial Army

Conway, Derek	Con

Terrorism

Gove, Michael	Con

Textile Industries

Anderson, Janet	Lab
Moore, Michael	Lib Dem
Mountford, Kali	Lab
Winterton, Ann	Con
Winterton, Nicholas	Con

Thames

Mackinlay, Andrew	Lab

Third World

Berry, Roger	Lab
Burt, Alistair	Con
Cunningham, Tony	Lab
George, Andrew	Lib Dem
Salmond, Alex	SNP
Skinner, Dennis	Lab
Stunell, Andrew	Lib Dem
Webb, Steve	Lib Dem

Tourism

Bellingham, Henry	Con
Butterfill, John	Con
Campbell, Gregory	DUP
Cunningham, Tony	Lab
Fraser, Christopher	Con
Gale, Roger	Con
Greenway, John	Con

Llwyd, Elfyn	PlC
Sanders, Adrian	Lib Dem
Smith, Geraldine	Lab
Swire, Hugo	Con
Thurso, John	Lib Dem
Waterson, Nigel	Con

Town Centre Issues

Lepper, David	Lab/Co-op

Trade and Industry

Bruce, Malcolm	Lib Dem
Burt, Alistair	Con
Butterfill, John	Con
Campbell, Gregory	DUP
Cash, William	Con
Chapman, Ben	Lab
Clegg, Nick	Lib Dem
Curtis-Thomas, Claire	Lab
Davies, Quentin	Con
Fabricant, Michael	Con
Farrelly, Paul	Lab
Follett, Barbara	Lab
Foster, Michael John	Lab
Gardiner, Barry	Lab
Gilroy, Linda	Lab/Co-op
Hendry, Charles	Con
Hoban, Mark	Con
Hoyle, Lindsay	Lab
Jenkins, Brian	Lab
Joyce, Eric	Lab
Kumar, Ashok	Lab
Lait, Jacqui	Con
Lansley, Andrew	Con
Laxton, Bob	Lab
Luff, Peter	Con
McCarthy-Fry, Sarah	Lab/Co-op
Martin, Michael	Speaker
O'Brien, Stephen	Con
Purchase, Ken	Lab/Co-op
Randall, John	Con
Scott, Lee	Con
Selous, Andrew	Con
Soames, Nicholas	Con
Spink, Bob	Con
Stewart, Ian	Lab
Viggers, Peter	Con
Woolas, Phil	Lab
Wright, Anthony David	Lab
Younger-Ross, Richard	Lib Dem

Trade Unions

Benn, Hilary	Lab
Caborn, Richard	Lab
Etherington, Bill	Lab
Healey, John	Lab
Illsley, Eric	Lab

Training

Hendry, Charles	Con
Jenkins, Brian	Lab
Mann, John	Lab
Merron, Gillian	Lab
Paice, Jim	Con
Prentice, Bridget	Lab
Reed, Andrew	Lab/Co-op
Watts, David	Lab

Tranquilliser Addiction

Wareing, Robert	Lab

Transport

Amess, David	Con
Blizzard, Bob	Lab
Brake, Tom	Lib Dem
Calton, Patsy	Lib Dem
Carmichael, Alistair	Lib Dem
Chaytor, David	Lab
Clark, Greg	Con
Clark, Paul	Lab
Clelland, David	Lab
Cohen, Harry	Lab
Darling, Alistair	Lab
Dean, Janet	Lab
Djanogly, Jonathan	Con
Dobbin, Jim	Lab/Co-op
Dobson, Frank	Lab
Donaldson, Jeffrey	DUP
Donohoe, Brian	Lab
Dowd, Jim	Lab
Duncan Smith, Iain	Con
Dunwoody, Gwyneth	Lab
Eagle, Maria	Lab
Efford, Clive	Lab
Ellman, Louise	Lab/Co-op
Featherstone, Lynne	Lib Dem
Field, Mark	Con
Flello, Robert	Lab
Foster, Don	Lib Dem
Goggins, Paul	Lab
Goodwill, Robert	Con
Grayling, Christopher	Con
Hamilton, David	Lab
Hammond, Philip	Con
Hammond, Stephen	Con
Heppell, John	Lab
Hill, Keith	Lab
Hodgson, Sharon	Lab
Hopkins, Kelvin	Lab
Horam, John	Con
Hurd, Nick	Con
James, Sian	Lab
Jones, Kevan	Lab
Kramer, Susan	Lib Dem
Laing, Eleanor	Con
Lazarowicz, Mark	Lab/Co-op

Leech, John	*Lib Dem*	Goggins, Paul	*Lab*	Hodgson, Sharon	*Lab*
McCabe, Steve	*Lab*	Reed, Andrew	*Lab/Co-op*	Kelly, Ruth	*Lab*
McCarthy, Kerry	*Lab*	Short, Clare	*Lab*	McDonagh, Siobhain	*Lab*
McIntosh, Anne	*Con*	Yeo, Tim	*Con*	Moran, Margaret	*Lab*
Marris, Rob	*Lab*			Owen, Albert	*Lab*
Marshall, David	*Lab*	**Urban Issues and Local**		Plaskitt, James	*Lab*
Meale, Alan	*Lab*	**Government**		Shaw, Jonathan	*Lab*
Merron, Gillian	*Lab*	Curry, David	*Con*	Sheridan, Jim	*Lab*
Milton, Anne	*Con*	Fisher, Mark	*Lab*	Webb, Steve	*Lib Dem*
Mole, Chris	*Lab*	Vaz, Keith	*Lab*		
Moore, Michael	*Lib Dem*			**Welfare State**	
Morley, Elliot	*Lab*	**US Elections**		Brown, Russell	*Lab*
Mulholland, Gregory	*Lib Dem*	Evans, Nigel	*Con*	Corbyn, Jeremy	*Lab*
Murphy, Denis	*Lab*			Efford, Clive	*Lab*
O'Brien, Stephen	*Con*	**USA**		Hutton, John	*Lab*
Öpik, Lembit	*Lib Dem*	Forth, Eric	*Con*	Wicks, Malcolm	*Lab*
Pound, Stephen	*Lab*				
Prosser, Gwyn	*Lab*	**Venture Capital**		**Welfare to Work**	
Pugh, John	*Lib Dem*	Wyatt, Derek	*Lab*	Flint, Caroline	*Lab*
Randall, John	*Con*				
Raynsford, Nick	*Lab*	**Victims of Accidents and Crime**		**West Midlands Industry**	
Redwood, John	*Con*	Dismore, Andrew	*Lab*	O'Brien, Mike	*Lab*
Robathan, Andrew	*Con*				
Russell, Christine	*Lab*	**Voluntary Sector**		**Women**	
Russell, Bob	*Lib Dem*	Conway, Derek	*Con*	Harman, Harriet	*Lab*
Smith, Andrew	*Lab*	Fraser, Christopher	*Con*	Osborne, Sandra	*Lab*
Strang, Gavin	*Lab*	Horwood, Martin	*Lib Dem*	Ruddock, Joan	*Lab*
Todd, Mark	*Lab*	Levitt, Tom	*Lab*		
Vaizey, Ed	*Con*	Michael, Alun	*Lab/Co-op*	**Work and Pensions**	
Villiers, Theresa	*Con*	Russell, Bob	*Lib Dem*	Heyes, David	*Lab*
Ward, Claire	*Lab*	Sanders, Adrian	*Lib Dem*		
Whitehead, Alan	*Lab*			**World Development**	
Williams, Stephen	*Lib Dem*	**Voting Systems**		Armstrong, Hilary	*Lab*
Winterton, Ann	*Con*	Linton, Martin	*Lab*		
Winterton, Rosie	*Lab*			**World Population**	
Wood, Mike	*Lab*	**Wales**		Ottaway, Richard	*Con*
		Bryant, Chris	*Lab*		
		Jones, David	*Con*	**Youth Affairs**	
Transport Safety		Murphy, Paul	*Lab*	Baldry, Tony	*Con*
Barrett, John	*Lib Dem*	Owen, Albert	*Lab*	Brooke, Annette	*Lib Dem*
Smith, John	*Lab*			Burgon, Colin	*Lab*
		Waste		Connarty, Michael	*Lab*
Treasury		Paice, Jim	*Con*	Crabb, Stephen	*Con*
Flello, Robert	*Lab*			Haselhurst, Alan	*Con*
Hanson, David	*Lab*	**Welfare**		Hendry, Charles	*Con*
Ruffley, David	*Con*	Begg, Anne	*Lab*	Hope, Phil	*Lab/Co-op*
Touhig, Don	*Lab/Co-op*	Buck, Karen	*Lab*	Hughes, Simon	*Lib Dem*
Wiggin, Bill	*Con*	Cairns, David	*Lab*	Michael, Alun	*Lab/Co-op*
		Coaker, Vernon	*Lab*	Pritchard, Mark	*Con*
Unemployment		Cook, Robin	*Lab*	Robertson, Angus	*SNP*
Cooper, Yvette	*Lab*	Davies, Quentin	*Con*	Rowen, Paul	*Lib Dem*
		Harris, Tom	*Lab*	Steen, Anthony	*Con*

MPs by Age (Ages as at 5 May 2005)

Name	Age	Name	Age	Name	Age
KHABRA, Piara	80	SHEERMAN, Barry	64	MARSHALL-ANDREWS, Robert	61
PAISLEY, Ian	79	VIS, Rudi	64	MICHAEL, Alun	61
TAPSELL, Peter	75	WINTERTON, Ann	64	RUDDOCK, Joan	61
DUNWOODY, Gwyneth	74	BINLEY, Brian	63	STRANG, Gavin	61
KAUFMAN, Gerald	74	CAMPBELL, Menzies	63	WILSHIRE, David	61
WAREING, Robert	74	DOBBIN, Jim	63	AUSTIN, John	60
WILLIAMS, Alan	74	ETHERINGTON, Bill	63	BOTTOMLEY, Peter	60
SKINNER, Dennis	73	HOPKINS, Kelvin	63	BRUCE, Malcolm	60
BENTON, Joe	71	HOWARD, Michael	63	CURRY, David	60
WINNICK, David	71	McKENNA, Rosemary	63	DAVIES, Quentin	60
FLYNN, Paul	70	MARSHALL, David	63	FISHER, Mark	60
MATES, Michael	70	STANLEY, John	63	FORTH, Eric	60
MITCHELL, Austin	70	WATKINSON, Angela	63	HODGE, Margaret	60
TAYLOR, Richard	70	WILLIS, Phil	63	HOGG, Douglas	60
COOK, Frank	69	YOUNG, George	63	KEY, Robert	60
McGRADY, Eddie	69	ATKINSON, Peter	62	LAXTON, Bob	60
CLWYD, Ann	68	BECKETT, Margaret	62	LINTON, Martin	60
JACKSON, Glenda	68	BEITH, Alan	62	McFALL, John	60
HASELHURST, Alan	67	BOSWELL, Timothy	62	MORGAN, Julie	60
KEEN, Alan	67	FIELD, Frank	62	MUDIE, George	60
O'HARA, Edward	67	FOLLETT, Barbara	62	RAYNSFORD, Nick	60
VIGGERS, Peter	67	GEORGE, Bruce	62	RUSSELL, Christine	60
WINTERTON, Nicholas	67	GERRARD, Neil	62	TAYLOR, Dari	60
BELL, Stuart	66	HEAL, Sylvia	62	TAYLOR, Ian	60
GIBSON, Ian	66	JENKINS, Brian	62	WILLIAMS, Betty	60
HORAM, John	66	MAPLES, John	62	YEO, Tim	60
LORD, Michael	66	MOSS, Malcolm	62	ANCRAM, Michael	59
PRESCOTT, John	66	OLNER, Bill	62	ARMSTRONG, Hilary	59
PURCHASE, Ken	66	PROSSER, Gwyn	62	BAILEY, Adrian	59
ROBINSON, Geoffrey	66	SHEPHERD, Richard	62	BERESFORD, Paul	59
CRYER, Ann	65	SPICER, Michael	62	COOK, Robin	59
DOBSON, Frank	65	STUNELL, Andrew	62	DOHERTY, Pat	59
GUMMER, John	65	CABLE, Vincent	61	ELLMAN, Louise	59
MEACHER, Michael	65	CABORN, Richard	61	FOSTER, Michael Jabez	59
STEEN, Anthony	65	CAMPBELL, Ronnie	61	GREENWAY, John	59
TURNER, Des	65	CLAPHAM, Michael	61	HANCOCK, Mike	59
BUTTERFILL, John	64	CLELLAND, David	61	HEYES, David	59
CASH, William	64	COUSINS, Jim	61	LEPPER, David	59
CHAPMAN, Ben	64	CUMMINGS, John	61	McCAFFERTY, Christine	59
CLARKE, Kenneth	64	GALE, Roger	61	MALINS, Humfrey	59
CLARKE, Tom	64	HILL, Keith	61	MARTIN, Michael	59
CUNNINGHAM, James	64	LILLEY, Peter	61	OTTAWAY, Richard	59
IDDON, Brian	64	McAVOY, Thomas	61	RUSSELL, Bob	59
NAYSMITH, Doug	64				

SHORT, Clare	59	DORAN, Frank	56	STRINGER, Graham	55
TURNER, Neil	59	HEATHCOAT-AMORY,		TIPPING, Paddy	55
WOOD, Mike	59	David	56	TREDINNICK, David	55
BARRON, Kevin	58	HEPPELL, John	56	WYATT, Derek	55
BREED, Colin	58	HEWITT, Patricia	56	ATKINS, Charlotte	54
BROWNING, Angela	58	HOOD, Jimmy	56	BAIRD, Vera	54
COFFEY, Ann	58	KEEN, Ann	56	BALDRY, Tony	54
CRAUSBY, David	58	KNIGHT, Greg	56	BATTLE, John	54
FOSTER, Don	58	LOVE, Andrew	56	BLIZZARD, Bob	54
FRANCIS, Hywel	58	McCREA, William	56	BROWN, Gordon	54
GODSIFF, Roger	58	MACKINLAY, Andrew	56	BROWN, Nick	54
HOEY, Kate	58	MacSHANE, Denis	56	CLARKE, Charles	54
HOWELLS, Kim	58	MARTLEW, Eric	56	COOPER, Rosie	54
INGRAM, Adam	58	MILLER, Andrew	56	DAVIDSON, Ian	54
JACK, Michael	58	MURPHY, Denis	56	DOWD, Jim	54
JONES, Martyn	58	MURPHY, Paul	56	FABRICANT, Michael	54
KILFOYLE, Peter	58	PAICE, Jim	56	HAMILTON, David	54
RIFKIND, Malcolm	58	POUND, Stephen	56	HARMAN, Harriet	54
SPRING, Richard	58	PUGH, John	56	HUMBLE, Joan	54
STARKEY, Phyllis	58	ROBINSON, Peter	56	JOHNSON, Alan	54
STRAW, Jack	58	SIMPSON, Alan	56	JONES, Lynne	54
TAYLOR, David	58	SIMPSON, Keith	56	KRAMER, Susan	54
BLUNKETT, David	57	SOULSBY, Peter	56	LEIGH, Edward	54
BROOKE, Annette	57	SPINK, Bob	56	McCARTNEY, Ian	54
BURGON, Colin	57	WALLEY, Joan	56	McGUINNESS, Martin	54
CHOPE, Christopher	57	WALTER, Robert	56	PRENTICE, Gordon	54
CONNARTY, Michael	57	AINGER, Nick	55	ROONEY, Terry	54
HOWARTH, Gerald	57	ANDERSON, Janet	55	SMITH, Andrew	54
JOWELL, Tessa	57	BETTS, Clive	55	SMITH, John	54
LAIT, Jacqui	57	BLACKMAN, Liz	55	STEWART, Ian	54
LAW, Peter	57	CHAYTOR, David	55	TRICKETT, Jon	54
MacDOUGALL, John	57	COHEN, Harry	55	WATERSON, Nigel	54
MULLIN, Chris	57	CORBYN, Jeremy	55	WHITEHEAD, Alan	54
REID, John	57	EVENNETT, David	55	AMESS, David	53
SOAMES, Nicholas	57	GILROY, Linda	55	BAYLEY, Hugh	53
SPELLAR, John	57	HAIN, Peter	55	BROWN, Russell	53
TOUHIG, Don	57	HAVARD, Dai	55	BROWNE, Des	53
WICKS, Malcolm	57	HENDERSON, Doug	55	CATON, Martin	53
WIDDECOMBE, Ann	57	HOWARTH, George	55	DORRELL, Stephen	53
WILLIAMS, Roger	57	HUGHES, Beverley	55	DREW, David	53
WRIGHT, Tony Wayland	57	LLOYD, Tony	55	FEATHERSTONE,	
ADAMS, Gerry	56	McDONNELL, Alasdair	55	Lynne	53
BERRY, Roger	56	McGUIRE, Anne	55	FITZPATRICK, Jim	53
CALTON, Patsy	56	MACKAY, Andrew	55	GILLAN, Cheryl	53
DAVIS, David	56	MEALE, Alan	55	HALL, Patrick	53
DEAN, Janet	56	MOON, Madeleine	55	HUGHES, Simon	53
DONOHOE, Brian	56	PALMER, Nick	55	JONES, David	53
		ROBINSON, Iris	55	KEEBLE, Sally	53

LEWIS, Julian	53	HOON, Geoffrey	51	BURT, Alistair	49
LLWYD, Elfyn	53	LAZAROWICZ, Mark	51	GREEN, Damian	49
McDONNELL, John	53	LEVITT, Tom	51	GRIFFITHS, Nigel	49
MALLABER, Judy	53	MACLEAN, David	51	HAMMOND, Philip	49
PICKLES, Eric	53	MACTAGGART, Fiona	51	HERMON, Sylvia	49
REDWOOD, John	53	MARSDEN, Gordon	51	HUTTON, John	49
ROBATHAN, Andrew	53	MAUDE, Francis	51	McCABE, Steve	49
ROBERTSON, John	53	MOFFATT, Laura	51	MITCHELL, Andrew	49
WATTS, David	53	MOUNTFORD, Kali	51	OSBORNE, Sandra	49
AINSWORTH, Bob	52	PRIMAROLO, Dawn	51	RANDALL, John	49
ALLEN, Graham	52	RIORDAN, Linda	51	ROWEN, Paul	49
ARBUTHNOT, James	52	SALTER, Martin	51	RYAN, Joan	49
BONE, Peter	52	SEABECK, Alison	51	SCOTT, Lee	49
BORROW, David	52	STOATE, Howard	51	STREETER, Gary	49
BURNS, Simon	52	SUTCLIFFE, Gerry	51	STUART, Gisela	49
BYERS, Stephen	52	THURSO, John	51	TIMMS, Stephen	49
CAMPBELL, Gregory	52	TURNER, Andrew	51	TRUSWELL, Paul	49
CLIFTON-BROWN, Geoffrey	52	WILLIAMS, Hywel	51	WILLETTS, David	49
CONWAY, Derek	52	BELLINGHAM, Henry	50	AINSWORTH, Peter	48
CUNNINGHAM, Tony	52	BURDEN, Richard	50	BLEARS, Hazel	48
ENNIS, Jeffrey	52	DISMORE, Andrew	50	CLAPPISON, James	48
FALLON, Michael	52	GALLOWAY, George	50	CLARK, Paul	48
GAPES, Mike	52	GRAY, James	50	DUNCAN, Alan	48
GARNIER, Edward	52	HAMILTON, Fabian	50	GARDINER, Barry	48
HALL, Mike	52	HEALD, Oliver	50	GIDLEY, Sandra	48
LADYMAN, Stephen	52	HOPE, Phil	50	GOODWILL, Robert	48
MORLEY, Elliot	52	HUHNE, Chris	50	GRIEVE, Dominic	48
PRENTICE, Bridget	52	ILLSLEY, Eric	50	GRIFFITH, Nia	48
SARWAR, Mohammed	52	JONES, Helen	50	HOLMES, Paul	48
SHERIDAN, Jim	52	KIDNEY, David	50	KUMAR, Ashok	48
WILLS, Michael	52	LUFF, Peter	50	LANSLEY, Andrew	48
WILSON, Sammy	52	McCARTHY-FRY, Sarah	50	LETWIN, Oliver	48
YOUNGER-ROSS, Richard	52	McINTOSH, Anne	50	LIDINGTON, David	48
		MARRIS, Rob	50	McGOVERN, Jim	48
ABBOTT, Diane	51	MORAN, Margaret	50	MAY, Theresa	48
ANDERSON, David	51	O'BRIEN, Mike	50	MERCER, Patrick	48
BARRETT, John	51	PLASKITT, James	50	O'BRIEN, Stephen	48
BENN, Hilary	51	REID, Alan	50	PATERSON, Owen	48
BLAIR, Tony	51	SALMOND, Alex	50	SOUTHWORTH, Helen	48
BRAZIER, Julian	51	SINGH, Marsha	50	SWAYNE, Desmond	48
CHALLEN, Colin	51	SQUIRE, Rachel	50	SYMS, Robert	48
COAKER, Vernon	51	TODD, Mark	50	TYRIE, Andrew	48
DARLING, Alistair	51	WRIGHT, Anthony David	50	VAZ, Keith	48
DENHAM, John	51	MILTON, Anne	49/50	WEIR, Mike	48
DUNCAN SMITH, Iain	51	BANKS, Gordon	49	BURT, Lorely	47/48
GOGGINS, Paul	51	BARLOW, Celia	49	BAKER, Norman	47
HEATH, David	51	BEGG, Anne	49	BLACKMAN-WOODS, Roberta	47

CAMPBELL, Alan	47	BROWN, Lyn	45	HAMMOND, Stephen	43
CURTIS-THOMAS, Claire	47	CAWSEY, Ian	45	HARVEY, Nick	43
DAVID, Wayne	47	COX, Geoffrey	45	KEETCH, Paul	43
EVANS, Nigel	47	GOODMAN, Paul	45	RUFFLEY, David	43
GOODMAN, Helen	47	HEALEY, John	45	SELOUS, Andrew	43
HANSON, David	47	HEMMING, John	45	SMITH, Angela	43
HESFORD, Stephen	47	HENDRY, Charles	45	SMITH, Geraldine	43
HOYLE, Lindsay	47	HEPBURN, Stephen	45	STUART, Graham	43
KENNEDY, Jane	47	JAMES, Sian	45	WISHART, Peter	43
LAING, Eleanor	47	KENNEDY, Charles	45	HURD, Nick	42/43
LAMB, Norman	47	McDONAGH, Siobhain	45	MAHMOOD, Khalid	42/43
McLOUGHLIN, Patrick	47	McISAAC, Shona	45	BACON, Richard	42
MAIN, Anne	47	MANN, John	45	BERCOW, John	42
MILBURN, Alan	47	MUNN, Meg	45	BRAKE, Tom	42
MOLE, Chris	47	NORRIS, Dan	45	BURSTOW, Paul	42
PENNING, Mike	47	OWEN, Albert	45	DONALDSON, Jeffrey	42
PICKING, Anne	47	PELLING, Andrew	45	FOSTER, Michael John	42
ROBERTSON, Laurence	47	RAMMELL, Bill	45	FRASER, Christopher	42
SMITH, Robert	47	SWIRE, Hugo	45	HORWOOD, Martin	42
SNELGROVE, Anne	47	TWIGG, Derek	45	HOSIE, Stewart	42
SPELMAN, Caroline	47	WHITTINGDALE, John	45	IRRANCA-DAVIES, Huw	42
DORRIES, Nadine	46/47	WOOLAS, Phil	45	LOUGHTON, Tim	42
BUCK, Karen	46	BENYON, Richard	44	MUNDELL, David	42
DODDS, Nigel	46	BLUNT, Crispin	44	PRISK, Mark	42
DUNNE, Philip	46	BRADSHAW, Ben	44	ROBERTSON, Hugh	42
EFFORD, Clive	46	DURKAN, Mark	44	SMITH, Jacqui	42
GEORGE, Andrew	46	EAGLE, Angela	44	TAMI, Mark	42
HAYES, John	46	EAGLE, Maria	44	TAYLOR, Matthew	42
HENDRICK, Mark	46	GIBB, Nick	44	HERBERT, Nick	41/42
HOWARTH, David	46	GROGAN, John	44	MURPHY, Conor	41/42
JENKIN, Bernard	46	HAGUE, William	44	HARRIS, Tom	41
KEMP, Fraser	46	JOYCE, Eric	44	HOBAN, Mark	41
LIDDELL-GRAINGER, Ian	46	KIRKBRIDE, Julie	44	JONES, Kevan	41
McNULTY, Tony	46	LUCAS, Ian	44	MILLER, Maria	41
MERRON, Gillian	46	McKECHIN, Ann	44	OATEN, Mark	41
NEWMARK, Brooks	46	MURRISON, Andrew	44	SIMMONDS, Mark	41
PEARSON, Ian	46	POPE, Greg	44	AUSTIN, Ian	40
ROY, Frank	46	SLAUGHTER, Andy	44	FIELD, Mark	40
RUANE, Chris	46	THORNBERRY, Emily	44	HOLLOBONE, Philip	40
SANDERS, Adrian	46	VARA, Shailesh	44	JACKSON, Stewart	40
SIMPSON, David	46	WALTHO, Lynda	44	JOHNSON, Boris	40
SMITH, Angela Evans	46	BRYANT, Chris	43	KNIGHT, Jim	40
WINTERTON, Rosie	46	CRUDDAS, Jon	43	McCARTHY, Kerry	40
WOODWARD, Shaun	46	FARRELLY, Paul	43	McFADDEN, Pat	40
BARON, John	45	FLINT, Caroline	43	ÖPIK, Lembit	40
BRENNAN, Kevin	45	FOX, Liam	43	PENROSE, John	40
		GRAYLING, Christopher	43	REED, Andrew	40

HANDS, Greg	39/40	WRIGHT, David	38	CARSWELL, Douglas	34
HOLLOWAY, Adam	39/40	CLARK, Greg	37/38	DAVIES, David	34
WILSON, Robert	39/40	ALEXANDER, Douglas	37	FARRON, Tim	34
AFRIYIE, Adam	39	BRADY, Graham	37	KHAN, Sadiq	34
BARKER, Gregory	39	CLARK, Katy	37	LANCASTER, Mark	34
CARMICHAEL, Alistair	39	CREAGH, Mary	37	LEECH, John	34
DAVEY, Edward	39	GOVE, Michael	37	MacNEIL, Angus	34
DJANOGLY, Jonathan	39	MALIK, Shahid	37	MULHOLLAND,	
FLELLO, Robert	39	MURPHY, Jim	37	Gregory	34
FRANCOIS, Mark	39	THOMAS, Gareth	37	USSHER, Kitty	34
HARRIS, Evan	39	VILLIERS, Theresa	37	WALLACE, Ben	34
HODGSON, Sharon	39	WALKER, Charles	37	DAVIES, Philip	33
LAWS, David	39	BROKENSHIRE, James	36/37	DHANDA, Parmjit	33
MILIBAND, David	39	COOPER, Yvette	36	DUDDRIDGE, James	33
MOORE, Michael	39	GREENING, Justine	36	GAUKE, David	33
ROSINDELL, Andrew	39	HILLIER, Meg	36	KAWCZYNSKI, Daniel	33
WEBB, Steve	39	KELLY, Ruth	36	OSBORNE, George	33
WILLIAMS, Mark	39	MORDEN, Jessica	36	ALEXANDER, Danny	32
BALLS, Ed	38	PRICE, Adam	36	CRABB, Stephen	32
CAIRNS, David	38	SHAPPS, Grant	36	LAMMY, David	32
CAMERON, David	38	SIMON, Siôn	36	REED, Jamie	32
CLEGG, Nick	38	BURNHAM, Andy	35	WARD, Claire	32
ELLWOOD, Tobias	38	BURROWES, David	35	WRIGHT, Iain	32
ENGEL, Natascha	38	BUTLER, Dawn	35	WRIGHT, Jeremy	32
HUNT, Jeremy	38	GILDERNEW, Michelle	35	GWYNNE, Andrew	30
JOHNSON, Diana	38	HARPER, Mark	35	TEATHER, Sarah	30
LEWIS, Ivan	38	MILIBAND, Ed	35	WILLOTT, Jenny	30
PRITCHARD, Mark	38	PURNELL, James	35	ROGERSON, Dan	29
SHAW, Jonathan	38	ROBERTSON, Angus	35	GOLDSWORTHY, Julia	26
WATSON, Tom	38	VAIZEY, Ed	35	SWINSON, Jo	25
WIGGIN, Bill	38	BROWNE, Jeremy	34		
WILLIAMS, Stephen	38	BYRNE, Liam	34	Information not supplied	
				KEELEY, Barbara	

GENERAL ELECTION
POLLING RESULTS

Parties with seats in the House of Commons

Con	Conservative	Pl C	Plaid Cymru
DUP	Democratic Unionist Party	Respect	Respect – The Unity Coalition
Ind KHHC	Independent Kidderminster Hospital and Health Concern	SDLP	Social Democratic and Labour Party
		SF	Sinn Féin
Lab	Labour	SNP	Scottish National Party
Lab/Co-op	Labour Co-operative	Speaker	The Speaker
Lib Dem	Liberal Democrat	UUP	Ulster Unionist Party

Parties with candidates in the General Election

AFC Alliance for Change; **Alliance** Alliance; **Anti-CF** Anti-Corruption Forum; **AP** Alternative Party; **Baths** Save the Bristol North Baths Party; **BMG** Blair Must Go Party; **BNP** British National Party; **BPP** British Public Party; **Bridges** Build Duddon and Morecambe Bridges; **Burnley** Burnley First Independent; **CAP** Community Action Party; **CD** Christian Democratic Party; **CG** Community Group; **Clause 28** Clause 28 Children's Protection Christian Democrats; **CMEP** Church of the Militant Elvis Party; **Comm** Communist Party; **Comm GB** Communist Party of Great Britain; **Common Good** The Common Good; **Community** Community; **CP** Civilisation Party; **CPA** Christian People's Alliance; **CRD** Campaigning for Real Democracy; **Croydon** Croydon Pensions Alliance; **Currency** Virtue Currency Cognitive Appraisal Party; **DCSP** Direct Customer Service Party; **DDTP** Death, Dungeons and Taxes Party; **Dem Lab** Democratic Labour Party; **Dem Soc All** Democratic Socialist Alliance – People Before Profit; **DWSB** Defend the Welfare State against Blairism; **EC** Extinction Club; **EDP** English Democratic Party; **EEP** English Parliamentary Party; **Eng Dem** English Democrats Party; **England** English Democrats – Putting England First; **FDP** Fancy Dress Party; **FFUK** familiesfirst.uk.net; **Fit** Fit Party For Integrity And Trust; **Forum** Open Forum; **Forward Wales** Forward Wales Party; **FP** Freedom Party; **Free** Free Party; **Free Scot** Free Scotland Party; **GBB** Get Britain Back Party; **Green Soc** Alliance for Green Socialism; **Greens** Green Party; **Honesty** Demanding Honesty in Politics and Whitehall; **IOW** Isle of Wight Party; **IP** Imperial Party; **Iraq** "Iraq War, Not In My Name"; **IWCA** Independent Working Class Association; **IZB** Islam Zinda Baad Platform; **Jam** Jam Wrestling Party; **JLDP** John Lillburne Democratic Party; **JP** Justice Party; **LCA** Legalise Cannabis Alliance; **LEDP** Lower Excise Duty Party; **LG** Life of Latgale; **Lib** Liberal; **LibP** Liberated Party; **Local** Local Community Party; **Loony** Official Monster Raving Loony Party; **Marxist** Marxist Party; **Masts** Removal of Tetra masts in Cornwall; **MC** The Millennium Council; **Meb Ker** Mebyon Kernow (the party for Cornwall); **MNP** Motorcycle News Party; **Mus** Muslim Party; **NACVP** Newcastle Academy with Christian Values Party; **NEP** New English Party; **New Brit** New Britain Party; **NF** National Front; **NIUP** Northern Ireland Unionist Party; **NIWC** Northern Ireland Women's Coalition; **NMB** New Millennium Bean Party; **Northern** Northern Progress For You; **OCV** Operation Christian Vote; **Online** Seeks a Worldwide Online Participatory Directory; **Paisley** Pride in Paisley Party; **PDP** Progressive Democratic Party; **PHF** People of Horsham First; **PJP** People's Justice Party; **Power** Max Power Party; **PPS** Pensioners' Party Scotland; **Pro-Euro Con** Pro Euro Conservative Party; **Progress** Peace and Progress Party; **ProLife** Pro-Life Alliance; **Protest** Protest Vote Party; **PRTYP** Personality And Rational Thinking? Yes! Party; **Publican** Publican Party – Free to Smoke (Pubs); **PUP** Progressive Unionist Party; **Qari** Qari; **RA** Residents Association; **Reform 2000** Reform 2000; **Respect** Respect – The Unity Coalition; **RMGB** Residents and Motorists of Great Britain; **RNRL** Rock 'N' Roll Loony Party; **RP** Rate Payer; **SA** Socialist Alliance; **SAP** Socialist Alternative Party; **Scot Lab** Scottish Labour; **Scot Senior** Scottish Senior Citizens Party; **Senior** Senior Citizens Party; **SFRP** Scottish Freedom Referendum Party; **Silent** Silent Majority Party; **SLP** Socialist Labour Party; **SNH** Safeguard The National Health Service; **Soc EA** Socialist Environmental Alliance; **Soc Unity** Socialist Unity Network; **Socialist** Socialist; **SOS** SOS! Voters against Overdevelopment of Northampton; **SSCUP** Scottish Senior Citizens' Unity Party; **SSP** Scottish Socialist Party; **St Albans** St Albans Party; **Stuckist** Stuckist Party; **Sun Rad** Sunrise Radio; **SUP** Scottish Unionist Party; **TCP** CountrySide Party; **telepath** telepathicpartnership.com; **TEPK** Tigers Eye the Party for Kids; **TGP** Grey Party; **Third** Third Way; **TP** Their Party; **TPP** The Peace Party – non-violence, justice, environment; **UKC** UK Community Issues Party; **UKIP** UK Independence Party; **UKP** United Kingdom Pathfinders; **UKPP** UK Pensioners' Party; **UKUP** United Kingdom Unionist Party; **UPP** Unrepresented Peoples Party; **UTW** Ulster Third Way; **Veritas** Veritas; **Vote Dream** Vote for yourself rainbow dream ticket; **Wessex Reg** Wessex Regionalists; **Work** The People's Choice Making Politicians Work; **World Rev** World Revolutionary Party; **WP** Workers' Party; **WRP** Workers' Revolutionary Party; **XPP** Xtraordinary People Party; **YPB** Your Party (Banbury).

ABERAVON

		%	+/-%
*Francis, H. (Lab)	18,077	60.1	-3.1
Waller, C. (Lib Dem)	4,140	13.8	4.0
Evans, P. (PlC)	3,545	11.8	2.0
Rees-Mogg, A. (Con)	3,064	10.2	2.6
Wright, W. (Veritas)	768	2.6	0.0
la Vey, M. (Greens)	510	1.7	0.0
Lab majority	13,937	46.30	
Electorate	51,080		
Turnout	30,104	58.94	

Lab hold (3.6% from Lab to Lib Dem)

ABERDEEN NORTH
(New Scottish constituency)

		%	+/-%
*Doran, F. (Lab)	15,557	42.5	
Delaney, S. (Lib Dem)	8,762	23.9	
Stewart, K. (SNP)	8,168	22.3	
Anderson, D. (Con)	3,456	9.4	
Connon, J. (SSP)	691	1.9	
Lab majority	6,795	18.55	
Electorate	65,714		
Turnout	36,634	55.75	

Lab hold (9.3% from Lab to Lib Dem)

ABERDEEN SOUTH
(New Scottish constituency)

		%	+/-%
*Begg, A. (Lab)	15,272	36.7	
Harris, V. (Lib Dem)	13,924	33.5	
Whyte, S. (Con)	7,134	17.1	
Watt, M. (SNP)	4,120	9.9	
Reeki, R. (Greens)	768	1.9	
Munro, D. (SSP)	403	1.0	
Lab majority	1,348	3.24	
Electorate	67,012		
Turnout	41,621	62.11	

Lab hold (3.1% from Lab to Lib Dem)

WEST ABERDEENSHIRE AND KINCARDINE
(New Scottish constituency)

		%	+/-%
*Smith, R. (Lib Dem)	19,285	46.3	
Johnstone, A. (Con)	11,814	28.4	
Barrowman, J. (Lab)	5,470	13.1	
Little, C. (SNP)	4,700	11.3	
Grant, L. (SSP)	379	0.9	
Lib Dem majority	7,471	17.94	
Electorate	65,548		
Turnout	41,648	63.54	

Lib Dem hold (2.3% from Con to Lib Dem)

AIRDRIE AND SHOTTS
(New Scottish constituency)

		%	+/-%
*Reid, J. (Lab)	19,568	59.0	
Balfour, M. (SNP)	5,484	16.5	
Watt, H. (Lib Dem)	3,792	11.4	
Cottis, S. (Con)	3,271	9.9	
Coats, F. (SSP)	706	2.1	
Rowan, J. (Ind)	337	1.0	
Lab majority	14,084	42.48	
Electorate	61,955		
Turnout	33,158	53.52	

Lab hold (1.5% from SNP to Lab)

ALDERSHOT

		%	+/-%
*Howarth, G. (Con)	20,572	42.7	0.6
Collett, A. (Lib Dem)	15,238	31.7	4.0
Linsley, H. (Lab)	9,895	20.6	-4.6
Rumsey, D. (UKIP)	1,182	2.5	0.7
Cowd, G. (Eng Dem)	701	1.5	0.0
Hope, H. (Loony)	553	1.2	0.3
Con majority	5,334	11.08	
Electorate	78,553		
Turnout	48,141	61.28	

Con hold (1.7% from Con to Lib Dem)

ALDRIDGE-BROWNHILLS

		%	+/-%
*Shepherd, R. (Con)	18,744	47.4	-2.8
Phillips, J. (Lab)	13,237	33.5	-6.8
Sheward, R. (Lib Dem)	4,862	12.3	3.7
Vaughan, W. (BNP)	1,620	4.1	0.0
Eardley, G. (UKIP)	1,093	2.8	0.0
Con majority	5,507	13.92	
Electorate	61,761		
Turnout	39,556	64.05	

Con hold (2.0% from Lab to Con)

ALTRINCHAM AND SALE WEST

		%	+/-%
*Brady, G. (Con)	20,569	46.4	0.3
Stockton, J. (Lab)	13,410	30.3	-9.2
Chappell, I. (Lib Dem)	9,595	21.7	7.2
Peart, G. (UKIP)	736	1.7	0.0
Con majority	7,159	16.16	
Electorate	67,247		
Turnout	44,310	65.89	

Con hold (4.7% from Lab to Con)

ALYN AND DEESIDE

		%	+/-%
*Tami, M. (Lab)	17,331	48.8	-3.5
Hale, L. (Con)	8,953	25.2	-1.0
Brighton, P. (Lib Dem)	6,174	17.4	4.5
Coombs, R. (PlC)	1,320	3.7	0.4
Crawford, W. (UKIP)	918	2.6	1.2
Armstrong-Braun, K. (Forward Wales)	378	1.1	0.0
Kilshaw, J. (Ind)	215	0.6	-0.1
Davies, G. (Comm)	207	0.6	0.0
Lab majority	8,378	23.60	
Electorate	58,939		
Turnout	35,496	60.22	

Lab hold (1.2% from Lab to Con)

AMBER VALLEY

		%	+/-%
*Mallaber, J. (Lab)	21,593	45.6	-6.3
Shaw, G. (Con)	16,318	34.4	-1.2
Smith, K. (Lib Dem)	6,225	13.1	0.7
Snell, P. (BNP)	1,243	2.6	0.0
Stevenson, A. (Veritas)	1,224	2.6	0.0
Price, H. (UKIP)	788	1.7	0.0
Lab majority	5,275	11.13	
Electorate	75,376		
Turnout	47,391	62.87	

Lab hold (2.6% from Lab to Con)

* Member of last parliament

ANGUS

(New Scottish constituency)

		%	+/-%
*Weir, M. (SNP)	12,840	33.7	
Bushby, S. (Con)	11,239	29.5	
Bradley, D. (Lab)	6,850	18.0	
Rennie, S. (Lib Dem)	6,660	17.5	
Manley, A. (SSP)	556	1.5	
SNP majority	1,601	4.20	
Electorate	63,093		
Turnout	38,145	60.46	

SNP hold (1.3% from Con to SNP)

EAST ANTRIM

		%	+/-%
Wilson, S. (DUP)	15,766	49.6	13.6
*Beggs, R. (UUP)	8,462	26.6	-9.8
Neeson, S. (Alliance)	4,869	15.3	2.9
O'Connor, D. (SDLP)	1,695	5.3	-2.0
McKeown, J. (Sinn Féin)	828	2.6	0.1
Kerr, D. (Vote Dream)	147	0.5	0.0
DUP majority	7,304	22.99	
Electorate	58,335		
Turnout	31,767	54.46	

DUP gain (0.0%)

NORTH ANTRIM

		%	+/-%
*Paisley, I. (DUP)	25,156	54.8	4.9
McGuigan, P. (Sinn Féin)	7,191	15.7	5.9
McCune, R. (UUP)	6,637	14.5	-6.5
Farren, S. (SDLP)	5,585	12.2	-4.7
Dunlop, J. (Alliance)	1,357	3.0	0.4
DUP majority	17,965	39.12	
Electorate	74,450		
Turnout	45,926	61.69	

DUP hold (0.0%)

SOUTH ANTRIM

		%	+/-%
McCrea, W. (DUP)	14,507	38.2	3.5
*Burnside, D. (UUP)	11,059	29.1	-7.9
McClelland, N. (SDLP)	4,706	12.4	0.3
Cushinan, H. (Sinn Féin)	4,407	11.6	2.2
Ford, D. (Alliance)	3,278	8.6	4.2
DUP majority	3,448	9.08	
Electorate	66,931		
Turnout	37,957	56.71	

DUP gain (0.0%)

ARGYLL AND BUTE

(New Scottish constituency)

		%	+/-%
*Reid, A. (Lib Dem)	15,786	36.5	
McGrigor, J. (Con)	10,150	23.5	
Manson, C. (Lab)	9,696	22.4	
Strong, I. (SNP)	6,716	15.5	
Henderson, D. (SSP)	881	2.0	
Lib Dem majority	5,636	13.04	
Electorate	67,325		
Turnout	43,229	64.21	

Lib Dem hold (1.9% from Con to Lib Dem)

ARUNDEL AND SOUTH DOWNS

		%	+/-%
Herbert, N. (Con)	24,752	49.8	-2.4
Deedman, D. (Lib Dem)	13,443	27.1	4.7
Whitlam, S. (Lab)	8,482	17.1	-3.6
Moffat, A. (UKIP)	2,700	5.4	0.7
Stack, M. (Protest)	313	0.6	0.0
Con majority	11,309	22.76	
Electorate	72,535		
Turnout	49,690	68.50	

Con hold (3.6% from Con to Lib Dem)

ASHFIELD

		%	+/-%
*Hoon, G. (Lab)	20,433	48.6	-9.5
Inglis-Jones, G. (Con)	10,220	24.3	-0.1
Johnson, W. (Lib Dem)	5,829	13.9	2.6
Adkins, R. (Ind)	2,292	5.5	0.0
Allsop, K. (Ind)	1,900	4.5	0.8
Hemstock, S. (Veritas)	1,108	2.6	0.0
Grenfell, E. (Ind)	269	0.6	0.0
Lab majority	10,213	24.29	
Electorate	73,403		
Turnout	42,051	57.29	

Lab hold (4.7% from Lab to Con)

ASHFORD

		%	+/-%
*Green, D. (Con)	26,651	51.6	4.1
Whitaker, V. (Lab)	13,353	25.8	-6.3
Took, C. (Lib Dem)	8,308	16.1	1.0
Boden, R. (Greens)	1,753	3.4	0.6
Stroud, B. (UKIP)	1,620	3.1	0.6
Con majority	13,298	25.73	
Electorate	79,493		
Turnout	51,685	65.02	

Con hold (5.2% from Lab to Con)

ASHTON UNDER LYNE

		%	+/-%
*Heyes, D. (Lab)	21,211	57.4	-5.1
Brown, G. (Con)	7,259	19.6	0.6
Jones, L. (Lib Dem)	5,108	13.8	2.0
Jones, A. (BNP)	2,051	5.6	1.0
Whittaker, J. (UKIP)	768	2.1	0.0
Crossfield, J. (Local)	570	1.5	0.0
Lab majority	13,952	37.74	
Electorate	72,000		
Turnout	36,967	51.34	

Lab hold (2.8% from Lab to Con)

AYLESBURY

		%	+/-%
*Lidington, D. (Con)	25,253	49.1	1.8
Jones, P. (Lib Dem)	14,187	27.6	0.6
Khaliel, M. (Lab)	9,540	18.5	-4.7
Adams, C. (UKIP)	2,479	4.8	2.3
Con majority	11,066	21.50	
Electorate	82,428		
Turnout	51,459	62.43	

Con hold (0.6% from Lib Dem to Con)

AYR, CARRICK AND CUMNOCK

(New Scottish constituency)

		%	+/-%
*Osborne, S. (Lab)	20,433	45.4	
Jones, M. (Con)	10,436	23.2	
Waugh, C. (Lib Dem)	6,341	14.1	

* Member of last parliament

Brodie, C. (SNP)	5,932	13.2	
Steele, M. (SSP)	554	1.2	
McDaid, J. (Scot Lab)	395	0.9	
McCormack, B. (UKIP)	365	0.8	
Lab majority	9,997	22.19	
Electorate	73,448		
Turnout	45,048	61.33	

Lab hold (2.2% from Lab to Con)

CENTRAL AYRSHIRE
(New Scottish constituency)

		%	+/-%
*Donohoe, B. (Lab)	19,905	46.4	
Clark, G. (Con)	9,482	22.1	
Kennedy, I. (Lib Dem)	6,881	16.1	
Hanif, J. (SNP)	4,969	11.6	
Morton, D. (SSP)	820	1.9	
Cochrane, R. (SLP)	468	1.1	
Groves, J. (UKIP)	346	0.8	
Lab majority	10,423	24.31	
Electorate	68,643		
Turnout	42,871	62.46	

Lab hold (0.7% from Con to Lab)

NORTH AYRSHIRE AND ARRAN
(New Scottish constituency)

		%	+/-%
Clark, K. (Lab)	19,417	43.9	
Connell, S. (Con)	8,121	18.4	
Gurney, T. (SNP)	7,938	18.0	
White, G. (Lib Dem)	7,264	16.4	
Turbett, C. (SSP)	780	1.8	
Pursley, J. (UKIP)	382	0.9	
McDaid, L. (SLP)	303	0.7	
Lab majority	11,296	25.55	
Electorate	73,737		
Turnout	44,205	59.95	

Lab hold (2.7% from Lab to Con)

BANBURY

		%	+/-%
*Baldry, T. (Con)	26,382	46.9	1.8
Sibley, L. (Lab)	15,585	27.7	-7.3
Patrick, Z. (Lib Dem)	10,076	17.9	2.0
Duckmanton, A. (Greens)	1,590	2.8	0.3
Heimann, D. (UKIP)	1,241	2.2	0.9
Starkey, J. (NF)	918	1.6	0.0
Rowe, C. (YPB)	417	0.7	0.0
Con majority	10,797	19.21	
Electorate	87,168		
Turnout	56,209	64.48	

Con hold (4.5% from Lab to Con)

BANFF AND BUCHAN
(New Scottish constituency)

		%	+/-%
*Salmond, A. (SNP)	19,044	51.2	
Wallace, S. (Con)	7,207	19.4	
Anderson, E. (Lib Dem)	4,952	13.3	
Okasha, R. (Lab)	4,476	12.0	
Ross, V. (OCV)	683	1.8	
Kemp, K. (UKIP)	442	1.2	
Will, S. (SSP)	412	1.1	
SNP majority	11,837	31.81	
Electorate	65,570		
Turnout	37,216	56.76	

SNP hold (2.2% from Con to SNP)

BARKING

		%	+/-%
*Hodge, M. (Lab)	13,826	47.8	-13.1
Prince, K. (Con)	4,943	17.1	-5.9
Barnbrook, R. (BNP)	4,916	17.0	10.6
Wickenden, T. (Lib Dem)	3,211	11.1	1.4
Jones, T. (UKIP)	803	2.8	0.0
Cleeland, L. (Greens)	618	2.1	0.0
Panton, D. (Ind)	530	1.8	0.0
Saxby, M. (WRP)	59	0.2	0.0
Lab majority	8,883	30.73	
Electorate	57,658		
Turnout	28,906	50.13	

Lab hold (3.6% from Lab to Con)

BARNSLEY CENTRAL

		%	+/-%
*Illsley, E. (Lab)	17,478	61.1	-8.6
Crompton, M. (Lib Dem)	4,746	16.6	1.9
Morel, P. (Con)	3,813	13.3	0.2
Broadley, G. (BNP)	1,403	4.9	0.0
Wood, D. (Ind)	1,175	4.1	0.0
Lab majority	12,732	44.49	
Electorate	60,592		
Turnout	28,615	47.23	

Lab hold (5.2% from Lab to Lib Dem)

BARNSLEY EAST AND MEXBOROUGH

		%	+/-%
*Ennis, J. (Lab)	20,779	62.9	-4.6
Brook, S. (Lib Dem)	6,654	20.2	4.3
Abbott, C. (Con)	4,853	14.7	2.3
Robinson, T. (SLP)	740	2.2	0.0
Lab majority	14,125	42.77	
Electorate	66,941		
Turnout	33,026	49.34	

Lab hold (4.4% from Lab to Lib Dem)

BARNSLEY WEST AND PENISTONE

		%	+/-%
*Clapham, M. (Lab)	20,372	55.3	-3.3
Watkinson, C. (Con)	9,058	24.6	1.8
Brelsford, A. (Lib Dem)	7,422	20.1	1.5
Lab majority	11,314	30.70	
Electorate	66,985		
Turnout	36,852	55.02	

Lab hold (2.5% from Lab to Con)

BARROW AND FURNESS

		%	+/-%
*Hutton, J. (Lab)	17,360	47.6	-8.1
Dorman, W. (Con)	11,323	31.0	0.7
Rabone, B. (Lib Dem)	6,130	16.8	4.6
Beach, A. (UKIP)	758	2.1	0.3
Bell, T. (Bridges)	409	1.1	0.0
Greaves, B. (Veritas)	306	0.8	0.0
Young, H. (Ind)	207	0.6	0.0
Lab majority	6,037	16.54	
Electorate	61,883		
Turnout	36,493	58.97	

Lab hold (4.4% from Lab to Con)

* Member of last parliament

BASILDON

		%	+/-%
*Smith, A. (Lab)	18,720	43.4	-9.3
Powell, A. (Con)	15,578	36.1	2.3
Thompson, M. (Lib Dem)	4,473	10.4	1.3
Colgate, E. (BNP)	2,055	4.8	0.0
Blythe, A. (UKIP)	1,143	2.7	-0.8
Copping, V. (Greens)	662	1.5	0.0
Gandy, K. (Eng Dem)	510	1.2	0.0
Lab/Co-op majority	3,142	7.28	
Electorate	73,912		
Turnout	43,141	58.37	

Lab/Co-op hold (5.8% from Lab/Co-op to Con)

BASINGSTOKE

		%	+/-%
Miller, M. (Con)	19,955	41.5	-1.2
Harvey, P. (Lab)	15,275	31.7	-9.1
Smith, J. (Lib Dem)	9,952	20.7	6.7
Effer, P. (UKIP)	1,044	2.2	-0.3
Shirley, D. (Greens)	928	1.9	0.0
Robertson, R. (BNP)	821	1.7	0.0
Macnair, R. (MC)	148	0.3	0.0
Con majority	4,680	9.73	
Electorate	76,404		
Turnout	48,123	62.98	

Con hold (4.0% from Lab to Con)

BASSETLAW

		%	+/-%
*Mann, J. (Lab)	22,847	56.6	1.3
Sheppard, J. (Con)	12,010	29.8	-0.5
Dobbie, D. (Lib Dem)	5,485	13.6	0.9
Lab majority	10,837	26.86	
Electorate	69,389		
Turnout	40,342	58.14	

Lab hold (0.9% from Con to Lab)

BATH

		%	+/-%
*Foster, D. (Lib Dem)	20,101	43.9	-6.6
Dawson, S. (Con)	15,463	33.7	4.6
Ajderian, H. (Lab)	6,773	14.8	-0.9
Lucas, E. (Greens)	2,494	5.4	2.3
Crowder, R. (UKIP)	770	1.7	0.2
Cobbe, P. (Ind)	177	0.4	0.0
Walker, G. (Ind)	58	0.1	0.0
Lib Dem majority	4,638	10.12	
Electorate	66,824		
Turnout	45,836	68.59	

Lib Dem hold (5.6% from Lib Dem to Con)

BATLEY AND SPEN

		%	+/-%
*Wood, M. (Lab)	17,974	45.8	-4.0
Light, R. (Con)	12,186	31.1	-5.7
Bentley, N. (Lib Dem)	5,731	14.6	4.3
Auty, C. (BNP)	2,668	6.8	0.0
Lord, C. (Greens)	649	1.7	0.1
Lab majority	5,788	14.76	
Electorate	62,948		
Turnout	39,208	62.29	

Lab hold (0.8% from Con to Lab)

BATTERSEA

		%	+/-%
*Linton, M. (Lab)	16,569	40.4	-9.9
Schofield, D. (Con)	16,406	40.0	3.4
Bhatti, N. (Lib Dem)	6,006	14.6	2.5
Charlton, H. (Greens)	1,735	4.2	0.0
Jones, T. (UKIP)	333	0.8	0.0
Lab majority	163	0.40	
Electorate	69,548		
Turnout	41,049	59.02	

Lab hold (6.7% from Lab to Con)

BEACONSFIELD

		%	+/-%
*Grieve, D. (Con)	24,126	55.4	2.7
Chapman, P. (Lib Dem)	8,873	20.4	-1.3
Sobel, A. (Lab)	8,422	19.4	-2.4
Fagan, J. (UKIP)	2,102	4.8	1.0
Con majority	15,253	35.05	
Electorate	68,083		
Turnout	43,523	63.93	

Con hold (2.0% from Lib Dem to Con)

BECKENHAM

		%	+/-%
*Lait, J. (Con)	22,183	45.3	0.1
Curran, L. (Lab)	13,782	28.2	-6.2
Foulger, J. (Lib Dem)	10,862	22.2	6.1
Cartwright, J. (UKIP)	1,301	2.7	0.9
Reed, R. (Ind)	836	1.7	0.0
Con majority	8,401	17.16	
Electorate	74,738		
Turnout	48,964	65.51	

Con hold (3.1% from Lab to Con)

BEDFORD

		%	+/-%
*Hall, P. (Lab)	17,557	41.7	-6.2
Fuller, R. (Con)	14,174	33.7	0.9
Headley, M. (Lib Dem)	9,063	21.5	5.7
Conquest, P. (UKIP)	995	2.4	1.3
McCready, J. (Ind)	283	0.7	-1.7
Lab majority	3,383	8.04	
Electorate	70,629		
Turnout	42,072	59.57	

Lab hold (3.6% from Lab to Con)

MID BEDFORDSHIRE

		%	+/-%
Dorries, N. (Con)	23,345	46.3	-3.6
Chapman, M. (Lib Dem)	11,990	23.8	7.4
Lindsay, M. (Lab)	11,351	22.5	-8.5
Joselyn, R. (UKIP)	1,372	2.7	0.0
Foley, B. (Greens)	1,292	2.6	0.0
Martin, H. (Veritas)	769	1.5	0.0
Ali, S. (Ind)	301	0.6	0.0
Con majority	11,355	22.52	
Electorate	73,768		
Turnout	50,420	68.35	

Con hold (2.6% from Con to Lib Dem)

NORTH EAST BEDFORDSHIRE

		%	+/-%
*Burt, A. (Con)	24,725	49.9	2.5
White, K. (Lab)	12,474	25.2	-4.9
Rutherford, S. (Lib Dem)	10,320	20.9	1.1
May, J. (UKIP)	1,986	4.0	1.3

* Member of last parliament

Con majority	12,251	24.75
Electorate	72,757	
Turnout	49,505	68.04

Con hold (3.7% from Lab to Con)

SOUTH WEST BEDFORDSHIRE

		%	+/-%
*Selous, A. (Con)	22,114	48.3	6.1
Still, J. (Lab)	13,837	30.2	-10.2
Strange, A. (Lib Dem)	7,723	16.9	2.1
Wise, T. (UKIP)	1,923	4.2	1.5
Benett, I. (Ind)	217	0.5	0.0
Con majority	8,277	18.07	
Electorate	74,096		
Turnout	45,814	61.83	

Con hold (8.2% from Lab to Con)

BELFAST EAST

		%	+/-%
*Robinson, P. (DUP)	15,152	49.2	6.6
Empey, R. (UUP)	9,275	30.1	6.9
Long, N. (Alliance)	3,746	12.2	-3.7
Devenny, D. (Sinn Féin)	1,029	3.3	0.0
Muldoon, M. (SDLP)	844	2.7	0.4
Greer, A. (Con)	434	1.4	-0.8
Bell, J. (WP)	179	0.6	0.3
Gilby, L. (Vote Dream)	172	0.6	0.0
DUP majority	5,877	19.06	
Electorate	53,176		
Turnout	30,831	57.98	

DUP hold (0.0%)

BELFAST NORTH

		%	+/-%
*Dodds, N. (DUP)	13,935	45.6	4.8
Kelly, G. (Sinn Féin)	8,747	28.6	3.4
Maginness, A. (SDLP)	4,950	16.2	-4.8
Cobain, F. (UUP)	2,154	7.1	-4.9
Hawkins, M. (Alliance)	438	1.4	0.0
Delaney, M. (WP)	165	0.5	-0.1
Gilby, L. (Vote Dream)	151	0.5	0.0
DUP majority	5,188	16.99	
Electorate	52,853		
Turnout	30,540	57.78	

DUP hold (0.0%)

BELFAST SOUTH

		%	+/-%
McDonnell, A. (SDLP)	10,339	32.3	1.7
Spratt, J. (DUP)	9,104	28.4	0.0
McGimpsey, M. (UUP)	7,263	22.7	-22.1
Maskey, A. (Sinn Féin)	2,882	9.0	1.4
Rice, G. (Alliance)	2,012	6.3	0.9
Gilby, L. (Vote Dream)	235	0.7	0.0
Lynn, P. (WP)	193	0.6	0.1
SDLP majority	1,235	3.86	
Electorate	52,668		
Turnout	32,028	60.81	

SDLP gain (0.0%)

BELFAST WEST

		%	+/-%
*Adams, G. (Sinn Féin)	24,348	70.5	4.4
Attwood, A. (SDLP)	5,033	14.6	-4.4
Dodds, D. (DUP)	3,652	10.6	4.1

McGimpsey, C. (UUP)	779	2.3	-4.0
Lowry, J. (WP)	432	1.3	-0.6
Gilby, L. (Vote Dream)	154	0.5	0.0
Kennedy, L. (Ind)	147	0.4	0.0
Sinn Féin majority	19,315	55.91	
Electorate	53,831		
Turnout	34,545	64.17	

Sinn Féin hold (0.0%)

BERWICK-UPON-TWEED

		%	+/-%
*Beith, A. (Lib Dem)	19,052	52.8	1.4
Elliott, M. (Con)	10,420	28.9	0.8
Reynolds, G. (Lab)	6,618	18.3	0.6
Lib Dem majority	8,632	23.92	
Electorate	56,944		
Turnout	36,090	63.38	

Lib Dem hold (0.3% from Con to Lib Dem)

BERWICKSHIRE, ROXBURGH AND SELKIRK

(New Scottish constituency)		%	+/-%
*Moore, M. (Lib Dem)	18,993	41.9	
Lamont, J. (Con)	13,092	28.8	
Held, S. (Lab)	7,206	15.9	
Orr, A. (SNP)	3,885	8.6	
Hein, J. (Lib Dem)	916	2.0	
McIver, G. (SSP)	695	1.5	
Neilson, P. (UKIP)	601	1.3	
Lib Dem majority	5,901	13.00	
Electorate	71,702		
Turnout	45,388	63.30	

Lib Dem hold (5.9% from Lib Dem to Con)

BETHNAL GREEN AND BOW

		%	+/-%
*Galloway, G. (Respect)	15,801	35.9	0.0
*King, O. (Lab)	14,978	34.0	-16.4
Bakth, S. (Con)	6,244	14.2	-10.1
Dulu, S. (Lib Dem)	4,928	11.2	-4.3
Foster, J. (Greens)	1,950	4.4	0.1
Etefia, E. (AFC)	68	0.2	0.0
Pugh, C. (ND)	38	0.1	0.0
Respect majority	823	1.87	
Electorate	85,950		
Turnout	44,007	51.20	

Respect gain (0.0%)

BEVERLEY AND HOLDERNESS

		%	+/-%
Stuart, G. (Con)	20,434	40.7	-0.6
McManus, G. (Lab)	17,854	35.6	-4.1
Willie, B. (Lib Dem)	9,578	19.1	3.2
Marriott, O. (UKIP)	2,336	4.7	1.5
Con majority	2,580	5.14	
Electorate	77,460		
Turnout	50,202	64.81	

Con hold (1.7% from Lab to Con)

BEXHILL AND BATTLE

		%	+/-%
*Barker, G. (Con)	24,629	52.6	4.5
Varrall, M. (Lib Dem)	11,180	23.9	-0.8
Jones, M. (Lab)	8,457	18.1	-1.4
Smith, A. (UKIP)	2,568	5.5	-2.3

* Member of last parliament

BEXHILL AND BATTLE *continued*

Con majority	13,449	28.72
Electorate	69,676	
Turnout	46,834	67.22

Con hold (2.6% from Lib Dem to Con)

BEXLEYHEATH AND CRAYFORD		%	+/-%
Evennett, D. (Con)	19,722	46.3	6.4
*Beard, N. (Lab)	15,171	35.6	-7.9
Raval, D. (Lib Dem)	5,144	12.1	1.0
Dunford, J. (UKIP)	1,302	3.1	1.1
Lee, J. (BNP)	1,241	2.9	-0.6
Con majority	4,551	10.69	
Electorate	65,025		
Turnout	42,580	65.48	

Con gain (7.2% from Lab to Con)

BILLERICAY		%	+/-%
*Baron, J. (Con)	25,487	52.2	4.8
Dodds, A. (Lab)	14,281	29.2	-7.2
Hibbs, M. (Lib Dem)	6,471	13.2	-0.6
Robinson, B. (BNP)	1,435	2.9	0.0
Callaghan, S. (UKIP)	1,184	2.4	0.1
Con majority	11,206	22.94	
Electorate	79,537		
Turnout	48,858	61.43	

Con hold (6.0% from Lab to Con)

BIRKENHEAD		%	+/-%
*Field, F. (Lab)	18,059	65.0	-5.5
Kelly, S. (Lib Dem)	5,125	18.4	5.6
Morton, H. (Con)	4,602	16.6	-0.1
Lab majority	12,934	46.55	
Electorate	57,097		
Turnout	27,786	48.66	

Lab hold (5.5% from Lab to Lib Dem)

BIRMINGHAM EDGBASTON		%	+/-%
*Stuart, G. (Lab)	16,465	43.8	-5.3
Alden, D. (Con)	14,116	37.5	0.9
Dixon, M. (Lib Dem)	5,185	13.8	1.8
Beck, P. (Greens)	1,116	3.0	0.0
White, S. (UKIP)	749	2.0	0.0
Lab majority	2,349	6.24	
Electorate	64,893		
Turnout	37,631	57.99	

Lab hold (3.1% from Lab to Con)

BIRMINGHAM ERDINGTON		%	+/-%
*Simon, S. (Lab)	16,810	53.0	-3.8
Elvidge, V. (Con)	7,235	22.8	-1.4
Evans, J. (Lib Dem)	5,027	15.8	4.1
Ebanks, S. (BNP)	1,512	4.8	0.0
Hepburn, R. (UKIP)	746	2.4	0.7
Williams, T. (NF)	416	1.3	-0.9
Lab majority	9,575	30.16	
Electorate	64,951		
Turnout	31,746	48.88	

Lab hold (1.2% from Lab to Con)

BIRMINGHAM HALL GREEN		%	+/-%
*McCabe, S. (Lab)	16,304	47.2	-7.4
Hughes, E. (Con)	10,590	30.7	-3.8
Harmer, R. (Lib Dem)	6,682	19.4	10.5
Melhuish, D. (UKIP)	960	2.8	0.6
Lab majority	5,714	16.55	
Electorate	57,222		
Turnout	34,536	60.35	

Lab hold (1.8% from Lab to Con)

BIRMINGHAM HODGE HILL		%	+/-%
*Byrne, L. (Lab)	13,822	48.6	-15.2
Davies, N. (Lib Dem)	8,373	29.5	21.4
Thomas, D. (Con)	3,768	13.3	-6.7
Adams, D. (BNP)	1,445	5.1	1.7
Duffen, A. (UKIP)	680	2.4	1.4
Begg, A. (Progress)	329	1.2	0.0
Lab majority	5,449	19.18	
Electorate	53,903		
Turnout	28,417	52.72	

Lab hold (18.3% from Lab to Lib Dem)

BIRMINGHAM LADYWOOD		%	+/-%
*Short, C. (Lab)	17,262	51.9	-17.0
Khan, A. (Lib Dem)	10,461	31.5	23.3
Stroud, P. (Con)	3,515	10.6	-0.7
Nazemi Afshar, L. (UKIP)	2,008	6.0	5.1
Lab majority	6,801	20.46	
Electorate	70,977		
Turnout	33,246	46.84	

Lab hold (20.1% from Lab to Lib Dem)

BIRMINGHAM NORTHFIELD		%	+/-%
*Burden, R. (Lab)	15,419	49.7	-6.3
Ford, V. (Con)	8,965	28.9	-0.7
Sword, T. (Lib Dem)	4,171	13.4	2.2
Cattall, M. (BNP)	1,278	4.1	0.0
Chant, G. (UKIP)	641	2.1	0.2
Rodgers, R. (Common Good)	428	1.4	0.0
Houldey, L. (SAP)	120	0.4	0.0
Sweeney, F. (WRP)	34	0.1	0.0
Lab majority	6,454	20.78	
Electorate	54,868		
Turnout	31,056	56.60	

Lab hold (2.8% from Lab to Con)

BIRMINGHAM PERRY BARR		%	+/-%
*Mahmood, K. (Lab)	18,269	47.0	0.4
Hunt, J. (Lib Dem)	10,321	26.5	3.6
Khan, N. (Con)	6,513	16.7	-6.4
Naseem, M. (Respect)	2,173	5.6	0.0
Clair, R. (SLP)	890	2.3	-1.8
Balu, B. (UKIP)	745	1.9	1.0
Lab majority	7,948	20.43	
Electorate	70,126		
Turnout	38,911	55.49	

Lab hold (1.6% from Lab to Lib Dem)

* Member of last parliament

BIRMINGHAM SELLY OAK

		%	+/-%
*Jones, L. (Lab)	19,226	46.1	-6.4
Tildesley, J. (Con)	10,375	24.9	-1.8
Brighton, R. (Lib Dem)	9,591	23.0	6.7
Smith, B. (Greens)	1,581	3.8	0.5
Burnett, R. (UKIP)	967	2.3	0.9
Lab majority	8,851	21.21	
Electorate	70,162		
Turnout	41,740	59.49	

Lab hold (2.3% from Lab to Con)

BIRMINGHAM SPARKBROOK AND SMALL HEATH

		%	+/-%
*Godsiff, R. (Lab)	13,787	36.1	-21.4
Yaqoob, S. (Respect)	10,498	27.5	0.0
Hussain, T. (Lib Dem)	7,727	20.2	7.0
Mirza, S. (SA)	3,480	9.1	-1.7
Brookes, J. (UKIP)	1,342	3.5	1.8
Jamieson, I. (Greens)	855	2.2	0.0
Chaudhary, A. (Ind)	503	1.3	-0.5
Lab majority	3,289	8.61	
Electorate	73,721		
Turnout	38,192	51.81	

Lab hold (0.0%)

BIRMINGHAM YARDLEY

		%	+/-%
Hemming, J. (Lib Dem)	13,648	46.4	8.0
Innes, J. (Lab)	10,976	37.3	-9.6
Uppal, P. (Con)	2,970	10.1	-3.0
Purcell, R. (BNP)	1,523	5.2	0.0
Yaqub, M. (UKIP)	314	1.1	0.0
Lib Dem majority	2,672	9.08	
Electorate	50,975		
Turnout	29,431	57.74	

Lib Dem gain (8.8% from Lab to Lib Dem)

BISHOP AUCKLAND

		%	+/-%
Goodman, H. (Lab)	19,065	50.0	-8.8
Foote Wood, C. (Lib Dem)	9,018	23.7	7.9
Bell, R. (Con)	8,736	22.9	0.2
Hopson, M. (UKIP)	1,309	3.4	0.0
Lab majority	10,047	26.35	
Electorate	67,534		
Turnout	38,128	56.46	

Lab hold (8.4% from Lab to Lib Dem)

BLABY

		%	+/-%
*Robathan, A. (Con)	22,487	45.5	-0.9
Morgan, D. (Lab)	14,614	29.6	-3.8
Stephenson, J. (Lib Dem)	9,382	19.0	1.6
Robinson, M. (BNP)	1,704	3.5	0.6
Young, D. (UKIP)	1,201	2.4	0.0
Con majority	7,873	15.94	
Electorate	75,444		
Turnout	49,388	65.46	

Con hold (1.5% from Lab to Con)

BLACKBURN

		%	+/-%
*Straw, J. (Lab)	17,562	42.0	-12.1
Ameen, I. (Con)	9,553	22.9	-8.3
Melia, A. (Lib Dem)	8,608	20.6	12.5

Holt, N. (BNP)	2,263	5.4	0.0
Murray, C. (Ind)	2,082	5.0	4.0
Baxter, D. (UKIP)	954	2.3	-0.7
Carter, G. (Greens)	783	1.9	0.0
Lab majority	8,009	19.16	
Electorate	73,494		
Turnout	41,805	56.88	

Lab hold (1.9% from Lab to Con)

BLACKPOOL NORTH AND FLEETWOOD

		%	+/-%
*Humble, J. (Lab)	20,620	47.6	-3.1
Williamson, G. (Con)	15,558	35.9	-1.4
Bate, S. (Lib Dem)	5,533	12.8	3.1
Hopwood, R. (UKIP)	1,579	3.7	1.4
Lab majority	5,062	11.69	
Electorate	74,975		
Turnout	43,290	57.74	

Lab hold (0.9% from Lab to Con)

BLACKPOOL SOUTH

		%	+/-%
*Marsden, G. (Lab)	19,375	50.5	-3.8
Winstanley, M. (Con)	11,453	29.9	-3.1
Holt, D. (Lib Dem)	5,552	14.5	3.9
Goodwin, R. (BNP)	1,113	2.9	0.0
Porter, J. (UKIP)	849	2.2	0.1
Lab majority	7,922	20.66	
Electorate	73,529		
Turnout	38,342	52.15	

Lab hold (0.3% from Lab to Con)

BLAENAU GWENT

		%	+/-%
Law, P. (Ind)	20,505	58.2	0.0
Jones, M. (Lab)	11,384	32.3	-39.8
Thomas, B. (Lib Dem)	1,511	4.3	-5.0
Price, J. (PlC)	843	2.4	-8.8
Lee, P. (Con)	816	2.3	-5.2
Osborne, P. (UKIP)	192	0.5	0.0
Ind majority	9,121	25.87	
Electorate	53,301		
Turnout	35,251	66.14	

Ind gain (0.0%)

BLAYDON

		%	+/-%
Anderson, D. (Lab)	20,120	51.5	-3.3
Maughan, P. (Lib Dem)	14,785	37.9	4.1
Luckhurst, D. (Con)	3,129	8.0	-3.4
Endacott, N. (UKIP)	1,019	2.6	0.0
Lab majority	5,335	13.66	
Electorate	62,413		
Turnout	39,053	62.57	

Lab hold (3.7% from Lab to Lib Dem)

BLYTH VALLEY

		%	+/-%
*Campbell, R. (Lab)	19,659	55.0	-4.8
Reid, J. (Lib Dem)	11,132	31.1	6.7
Windridge, M. (Con)	4,982	13.9	-2.0
Lab majority	8,527	23.84	
Electorate	63,640		
Turnout	35,773	56.21	

Lab hold (5.7% from Lab to Lib Dem)

* Member of last parliament

BOGNOR REGIS AND LITTLEHAMPTON

		%	+/-%
*Gibb, N. (Con)	18,183	44.6	-0.6
O'Neill, G. (Lab)	10,361	25.4	-5.3
McDougall, S. (Lib Dem)	8,927	21.9	4.3
Lithgow, A. (UKIP)	3,276	8.0	3.5
Con majority	7,822	19.20	
Electorate	65,591		
Turnout	40,747	62.12	

Con hold (2.4% from Lab to Con)

BOLSOVER

		%	+/-%
*Skinner, D. (Lab)	25,217	65.2	-3.4
Hawksworth, D. (Lib Dem)	6,780	17.5	5.6
Imam, H. (Con)	6,702	17.3	-2.2
Lab majority	18,437	47.64	
Electorate	67,568		
Turnout	38,699	57.27	

Lab hold (4.5% from Lab to Lib Dem)

BOLTON NORTH EAST

		%	+/-%
*Crausby, D. (Lab)	16,874	45.7	-8.6
Brierley, P. (Con)	12,771	34.6	1.9
Killeya, A. (Lib Dem)	6,044	16.4	6.1
Epsom, K. (UKIP)	640	1.7	0.0
Ainscow, A. (Veritas)	375	1.0	0.0
Lowe, L. (SLP)	207	0.6	-0.5
Lab majority	4,103	11.12	
Electorate	67,394		
Turnout	36,911	54.77	

Lab hold (5.3% from Lab to Con)

BOLTON SOUTH EAST

		%	+/-%
*Iddon, B. (Lab)	18,129	56.9	-4.9
Dunleavy, D. (Con)	6,491	20.4	-3.8
Harasiwka, F. (Lib Dem)	6,047	19.0	7.5
Bates, F. (UKIP)	840	2.6	0.0
Jones, D. (Veritas)	343	1.1	0.0
Lab majority	11,638	36.54	
Electorate	63,697		
Turnout	31,850	50.00	

Lab hold (0.6% from Lab to Con)

BOLTON WEST

		%	+/-%
*Kelly, R. (Lab)	17,239	42.5	-4.5
Allott, P. (Con)	15,175	37.4	3.8
Perkins, T. (Lib Dem)	7,241	17.9	-0.5
Ford, M. (UKIP)	524	1.3	0.0
Ford, M. (Veritas)	290	0.7	0.0
Griggs, K. (XPP)	74	0.2	0.0
Lab majority	2,064	5.09	
Electorate	63,836		
Turnout	40,543	63.51	

Lab hold (4.2% from Lab to Con)

BOOTLE

		%	+/-%
*Benton, J. (Lab)	19,345	75.5	-2.1
Newby, C. (Lib Dem)	2,988	11.7	3.1
Moustafa, W. (Con)	1,580	6.2	-1.8
Nutall, P. (UKIP)	1,054	4.1	0.0
Glover, P. (SAP)	655	2.6	0.0

Lab majority	16,357	63.84
Electorate	53,700	
Turnout	25,622	47.71

Lab hold (2.6% from Lab to Lib Dem)

BOSTON AND SKEGNESS

		%	+/-%
*Simmonds, M. (Con)	19,329	46.2	3.3
Kenny, P. (Lab)	13,422	32.1	-9.6
Horsnell, R. (UKIP)	4,024	9.6	7.8
Riley, A. (Lib Dem)	3,649	8.7	-3.7
Russell, W. (BNP)	1,025	2.5	0.0
Petz, M. (Greens)	420	1.0	-0.3
Con majority	5,907	14.11	
Electorate	71,212		
Turnout	41,869	58.79	

Con hold (6.4% from Lab to Con)

BOSWORTH

		%	+/-%
*Tredinnick, D. (Con)	20,212	42.6	-1.9
Herd, R. (Lab)	14,893	31.4	-8.0
Moore, J. (Lib Dem)	10,528	22.2	5.9
Walker, D. (UKIP)	1,866	3.9	0.0
Con majority	5,319	11.20	
Electorate	71,596		
Turnout	47,499	66.34	

Con hold (3.1% from Lab to Con)

BOURNEMOUTH EAST

		%	+/-%
Ellwood, T. (Con)	16,925	45.0	1.7
Garratt, A. (Lib Dem)	11,681	31.1	-2.6
Stokes, D. (Lab)	7,191	19.1	-0.7
Collier, T. (UKIP)	1,802	4.8	1.7
Con majority	5,244	13.95	
Electorate	63,426		
Turnout	37,599	59.28	

Con hold (2.2% from Lib Dem to Con)

BOURNEMOUTH WEST

		%	+/-%
*Butterfill, J. (Con)	14,057	41.4	-1.4
Renaut, R. (Lib Dem)	10,026	29.6	4.4
Williams, D. (Lab)	7,824	23.1	-5.8
Maclaire-Hillier, M. (UKIP)	2,017	6.0	2.8
Con majority	4,031	11.88	
Electorate	63,658		
Turnout	33,924	53.29	

Con hold (2.9% from Con to Lib Dem)

BRACKNELL

		%	+/-%
*Mackay, A. (Con)	25,412	49.7	3.1
Keene, A. (Lab)	13,376	26.2	-6.9
Glendon, L. (Lib Dem)	10,128	19.8	2.7
Pearson, V. (UKIP)	1,818	3.6	1.0
Roberts, D. (Ind)	407	0.8	0.0
Con majority	12,036	23.53	
Electorate	80,657		
Turnout	51,141	63.41	

Con hold (5.0% from Lab to Con)

BRADFORD NORTH

		%	+/-%
*Rooney, T. (Lab)	14,622	42.5	-7.2
Ward, D. (Lib Dem)	11,111	32.3	12.5

* Member of last parliament

Khong, T. (Con)	5,569	16.2	-7.9
Cromie, L. (BNP)	2,061	6.0	1.4
Schofield, S. (Greens)	560	1.6	-0.1
Yildiz, U. (Respect)	474	1.4	0.0
Lab majority	3,511	10.21	
Electorate	64,515		
Turnout	34,397	53.32	

Lab hold (9.9% from Lab to Lib Dem)

BRADFORD SOUTH

		%	+/-%
*Sutcliffe, G. (Lab)	17,954	49.1	-6.7
Carter, G. (Con)	8,787	24.0	-4.3
Doyle, M. (Lib Dem)	5,334	14.6	4.0
Lewthwaite, J. (BNP)	2,862	7.8	0.0
Curtis, D. (Greens)	695	1.9	0.0
Smith, J. (UKIP)	552	1.5	-0.7
Muchewicz, T. (Veritas)	421	1.2	0.0
Lab majority	9,167	25.04	
Electorate	67,576		
Turnout	36,605	54.17	

Lab hold (1.2% from Lab to Con)

BRADFORD WEST

		%	+/-%
*Singh, M. (Lab)	14,570	40.1	-7.9
Rashid, H. (Con)	11,544	31.7	-5.4
Ali, M. (Lib Dem)	6,620	18.2	11.9
Cromie, P. (BNP)	2,525	6.9	0.0
Darr, P. (Greens)	1,110	3.1	-3.9
Lab majority	3,026	8.32	
Electorate	67,356		
Turnout	36,369	54.00	

Lab hold (1.3% from Lab to Con)

BRAINTREE

		%	+/-%
Newmark, B. (Con)	23,597	44.5	3.2
*Hurst, A. (Lab)	19,704	37.1	-4.8
Turner, P. (Lib Dem)	7,037	13.3	2.0
Abbott, J. (Greens)	1,308	2.5	0.0
Lord, R. (UKIP)	1,181	2.2	0.7
Nolan, B. (Ind)	228	0.4	0.0
Con majority	3,893	7.34	
Electorate	80,458		
Turnout	53,055	65.94	

Con gain (4.0% from Lab to Con)

BRECON AND RADNORSHIRE

		%	+/-%
*Williams, R. (Lib Dem)	17,182	44.8	8.0
Davies, A. (Con)	13,277	34.6	-0.2
Veale, L. (Lab)	5,755	15.0	-6.4
Gwynfor, M. (PlC)	1,404	3.7	0.2
Phillips, E. (UKIP)	723	1.9	0.7
Lib Dem majority	3,905	10.18	
Electorate	55,171		
Turnout	38,341	69.49	

Lib Dem hold (4.1% from Con to Lib Dem)

BRENT EAST

		%	+/-%
*Teather, S. (Lib Dem)	14,764	47.5	37.0
Qureshi, Y. (Lab)	12,052	38.8	-24.4
Kwarteng, K. (Con)	3,193	10.3	-7.9
Ali, S. (Greens)	905	2.9	-1.8
Weininger, M. (Ind)	115	0.4	0.0
Weiss, R. (Vote Dream)	39	0.1	0.0

Lib Dem majority	2,712	8.73	
Electorate	56,227		
Turnout	31,068	55.25	

Lib Dem gain (30.7% from Lab to Lib Dem)

BRENT NORTH

		%	+/-%
*Gardiner, B. (Lab)	17,420	48.8	-10.6
Blackman, B. (Con)	11,779	33.0	3.7
Hughes, H. (Lib Dem)	5,672	15.9	4.6
Ahmad, B. (Progress)	685	1.9	0.0
Weiss, R. (Vote Dream)	126	0.4	0.0
Lab majority	5,641	15.81	
Electorate	60,148		
Turnout	35,682	59.32	

Lab hold (7.1% from Lab to Con)

BRENT SOUTH

		%	+/-%
Butler, D. (Lab)	17,501	58.8	-14.5
Allie, J. (Lib Dem)	6,175	20.8	9.9
Saha, R. (Con)	4,485	15.1	2.5
Langley, R. (Greens)	957	3.2	0.0
Wallace, S. (Ind)	297	1.0	0.0
Fernandez, R. (Ind)	288	1.0	0.0
Weiss, R. (Vote Dream)	61	0.2	0.0
Lab majority	11,326	38.05	
Electorate	56,508		
Turnout	29,764	52.67	

Lab hold (12.2% from Lab to Lib Dem)

BRENTFORD AND ISLEWORTH

		%	+/-%
*Keen, A. (Lab)	18,329	39.8	-12.5
Northcote, A. (Con)	13,918	30.3	1.1
Dakers, A. (Lib Dem)	10,477	22.8	9.3
Hunt, J. (Greens)	1,652	3.6	0.6
Andrews, P. (Community)	1,118	2.4	0.0
Stoneman, M. (NF)	523	1.1	0.0
Lab majority	4,411	9.59	
Electorate	84,366		
Turnout	46,017	54.54	

Lab hold (6.8% from Lab to Con)

BRENTWOOD AND ONGAR

		%	+/-%
*Pickles, E. (Con)	23,609	53.5	15.5
Stollar, G. (Lib Dem)	11,997	27.2	11.6
Adams, J. (Lab)	6,579	14.9	2.3
Gulleford, S. (UKIP)	1,805	4.1	2.7
Appleton, A. (Ind)	155	0.4	0.0
Con majority	11,612	26.30	
Electorate	64,496		
Turnout	44,145	68.45	

Con hold (1.9% from Lib Dem to Con)

BRIDGEND

		%	+/-%
Moon, M. (Lab)	16,410	43.4	-9.1
Baker, H. (Con)	9,887	26.1	0.8
Warren, P. (Lib Dem)	7,949	21.0	6.6
Clubb, G. (PlC)	2,527	6.7	-0.5
Spink, J. (Greens)	595	1.6	0.0
Rajan, K. (UKIP)	491	1.3	0.0
Lab majority	6,523	17.23	
Electorate	63,936		
Turnout	37,859	59.21	

Lab hold (5.0% from Lab to Con)

* Member of last parliament

BRIDGWATER

		%	+/-%
*Liddell-Grainger, I. (Con)	21,240	44.2	3.7
Burchell, M. (Lab)	12,771	26.6	-0.2
Main, J. (Lib Dem)	10,940	22.7	-7.3
Wienstein, R. (UKIP)	1,767	3.7	0.9
Graham, C. (Greens)	1,391	2.9	0.0
Con majority	8,469	17.60	
Electorate	75,790		
Turnout	48,109	63.48	

Con hold (2.0% from Lab to Con)

BRIGG AND GOOLE

		%	+/-%
*Cawsey, I. (Lab)	19,257	45.2	-3.7
Bean, M. (Con)	16,363	38.4	-0.8
Johnson, G. (Lib Dem)	5,690	13.4	4.1
Martin, S. (UKIP)	1,268	3.0	1.3
Lab majority	2,894	6.80	
Electorate	67,364		
Turnout	42,578	63.21	

Lab hold (1.4% from Lab to Con)

BRIGHTON KEMPTOWN

		%	+/-%
*Turner, D. (Lab)	15,858	39.9	-7.9
Symes, J. (Con)	13,121	33.0	-2.2
Pepper, M. (Lib Dem)	6,560	16.5	6.2
Williams, S. (Greens)	2,800	7.1	3.8
Chamberlain-Webber, J. (UKIP)			
	758	1.9	0.5
O'Reilly, C. (TPP)	172	0.4	0.0
McLeod, J. (SLP)	163	0.4	-0.5
Cooke, E. (Ind)	127	0.3	0.0
Clarke, P. (SAP)	113	0.3	0.0
Dobbs, G. (Ind)	47	0.1	0.0
Lab majority	2,737	6.89	
Electorate	65,985		
Turnout	39,719	60.19	

Lab hold (2.8% from Lab to Con)

BRIGHTON PAVILION

		%	+/-%
*Lepper, D. (Lab/Co-op)	15,427	35.5	-13.2
Weatherley, M. (Con)	10,397	23.9	-1.1
Taylor, K. (Greens)	9,530	21.9	12.6
Thorpe, H. (Lib Dem)	7,171	16.5	3.4
Crisp-Comotto, K. (UKIP)	508	1.2	0.3
Greenstein, T. (Green Soc)	188	0.4	0.0
Fyvie, I. (SLP)	152	0.4	-1.1
Rooke, C. (Ind)	122	0.3	0.0
Jago, K. (Ind)	44	0.1	0.0
Lab/Co-op majority	5,030	11.55	
Electorate	68,087		
Turnout	43,539	63.95	

Lab/Co-op hold (6.1% from Lab/Co-op to Con)

BRISTOL EAST

		%	+/-%
McCarthy, K. (Lab)	19,152	45.9	-9.1
James, P. (Lib Dem)	10,531	25.2	8.1
Manning, J. (Con)	8,787	21.1	-0.7
Krishna-Das, A. (Greens)	1,586	3.8	1.1
Smith, J. (UKIP)	1,132	2.7	1.3
North, P. (Respect)	532	1.3	0.0

Lab majority	8,621	20.66
Electorate	68,096	
Turnout	41,720	61.27

Lab hold (8.6% from Lab to Lib Dem)

BRISTOL NORTH WEST

		%	+/-%
*Naysmith, D. (Lab/Co-op)	22,192	46.7	-5.4
Watson, A. (Con)	13,230	27.9	-0.9
Hoyle, B. (Lib Dem)	9,545	20.1	4.2
Lees, C. (UKIP)	1,132	2.4	-0.1
Blundell, M. (EDP)	828	1.7	0.0
Jones, G. (SAP)	565	1.2	0.0
Lab/Co-op majority	8,962	18.87	
Electorate	77,703		
Turnout	47,492	61.12	

Lab/Co-op hold (2.3% from Lab/Co-op to Con)

BRISTOL SOUTH

		%	+/-%
*Primarolo, D. (Lab)	20,778	49.1	-7.8
Barnard, K. (Lib Dem)	9,636	22.8	7.9
Hill, G. (Con)	8,466	20.0	-2.3
Bolton, C. (Greens)	2,127	5.0	2.0
Dent, M. (UKIP)	1,321	3.1	1.9
Lab majority	11,142	26.32	
Electorate	70,835		
Turnout	42,328	59.76	

Lab hold (7.9% from Lab to Lib Dem)

BRISTOL WEST

		%	+/-%
Williams, S. (Lib Dem)	21,987	38.3	9.4
*Davey, V. (Lab)	16,859	29.4	-7.5
Martin, D. (Con)	15,429	26.9	-1.9
Quinnell, J. (Greens)	2,163	3.8	0.3
Muir, S. (UKIP)	439	0.8	-0.1
Kennedy, B. (SLP)	329	0.6	-0.5
Reid, D. (Baths)	190	0.3	0.0
Lib Dem majority	5,128	8.93	
Electorate	81,382		
Turnout	57,396	70.53	

Lib Dem gain (8.4% from Lab to Lib Dem)

BROMLEY AND CHISLEHURST

		%	+/-%
*Forth, E. (Con)	23,583	51.1	1.6
Reeves, R. (Lab)	10,241	22.2	-6.4
Brooks, P. (Lib Dem)	9,368	20.3	1.4
Hooper, D. (UKIP)	1,475	3.2	0.3
Garrett, A. (Greens)	1,470	3.2	0.0
Con majority	13,342	28.92	
Electorate	71,173		
Turnout	46,137	64.82	

Con hold (4.0% from Lab to Con)

BROMSGROVE

		%	+/-%
*Kirkbride, J. (Con)	24,387	51.0	-0.7
Jones, D. (Lab)	14,307	29.9	-4.0
Haswell, S. (Lib Dem)	7,197	15.1	3.2
Buckingham, P. (UKIP)	1,919	4.0	1.6
Con majority	10,080	21.08	
Electorate	70,762		
Turnout	47,810	67.56	

Con hold (1.6% from Lab to Con)

* Member of last parliament

BROXBOURNE

		%	+/-%
Walker, C. (Con)	21,878	53.9	-0.3
Bolden, J. (Lab)	10,369	25.5	-4.9
Porrer, A. (Lib Dem)	4,973	12.2	1.3
Emerson, A. (BNP)	1,929	4.8	2.5
Harvey, M. (UKIP)	1,479	3.6	1.4
Con majority	11,509	28.33	
Electorate	68,106		
Turnout	40,628	59.65	

Con hold (2.3% from Lab to Con)

BROXTOWE

		%	+/-%
*Palmer, N. (Lab)	20,457	41.9	-6.7
Seely, B. (Con)	18,161	37.2	0.6
Watts, D. (Lib Dem)	7,837	16.1	1.4
Anderson, P. (Greens)	896	1.8	0.0
Wolfe, P. (UKIP)	695	1.4	0.0
Hockney, D. (Veritas)	590	1.2	0.0
Gregory, M. (Ind)	170	0.4	0.0
Lab majority	2,296	4.70	
Electorate	71,121		
Turnout	48,806	68.62	

Lab hold (3.6% from Lab to Con)

BUCKINGHAM

		%	+/-%
*Bercow, J. (Con)	27,748	57.4	3.8
Greene, D. (Lab)	9,619	19.9	-4.3
Croydon, L. (Lib Dem)	9,508	19.7	-0.3
Williams, D. (UKIP)	1,432	3.0	0.8
Con majority	18,129	37.53	
Electorate	70,265		
Turnout	48,307	68.75	

Con hold (4.1% from Lab to Con)

BURNLEY

		%	+/-%
Ussher, K. (Lab)	14,999	38.5	-10.9
Birtwistle, G. (Lib Dem)	9,221	23.7	7.5
Brooks, H. (Burnley)	5,786	14.8	0.0
Miah, Y. (Con)	4,206	10.8	-10.1
Starr, L. (BNP)	4,003	10.3	-1.0
Slater, J. (Ind)	392	1.0	0.0
McDowell, R. (UKIP)	376	1.0	-1.4
Lab majority	5,778	14.82	
Electorate	65,869		
Turnout	38,983	59.18	

Lab hold (9.2% from Lab to Lib Dem)

BURTON

		%	+/-%
*Dean, J. (Lab)	19,701	41.1	-7.9
Pepper, A. (Con)	18,280	38.2	-0.4
Johnson, S. (Lib Dem)	6,236	13.0	3.4
Russell, J. (BNP)	1,840	3.8	0.0
Lancaster, P. (UKIP)	913	1.9	-0.2
Buxton, B. (Veritas)	912	1.9	0.0
Lab majority	1,421	2.97	
Electorate	78,556		
Turnout	47,882	60.95	

Lab hold (3.7% from Lab to Con)

BURY NORTH

		%	+/-%
*Chaytor, D. (Lab)	19,130	43.1	-8.1
Nuttall, D. (Con)	16,204	36.5	-0.1
Davison, W. (Lib Dem)	6,514	14.7	2.6
Clough, S. (BNP)	1,790	4.0	0.0
Silver, P. (UKIP)	476	1.1	0.0
O'Neill, R. (SLP)	172	0.4	0.0
Upton, I. (Veritas)	153	0.3	0.0
Lab majority	2,926	6.58	
Electorate	72,268		
Turnout	44,439	61.49	

Lab hold (4.0% from Lab to Con)

BURY SOUTH

		%	+/-%
*Lewis, I. (Lab)	19,741	50.4	-8.8
Williams, A. (Con)	10,829	27.7	0.8
D'Albert, V. (Lib Dem)	6,968	17.8	3.9
Greenhalgh, J. (UKIP)	1,059	2.7	0.0
Hossack, Y. (Ind)	557	1.4	0.0
Lab majority	8,912	22.76	
Electorate	66,898		
Turnout	39,154	58.53	

Lab hold (4.8% from Lab to Con)

BURY ST EDMUNDS

		%	+/-%
*Ruffley, D. (Con)	24,332	46.2	2.8
Monaghan, D. (Lab)	14,402	27.4	-11.1
Chappell, D. (Lib Dem)	10,423	19.8	5.9
Howlett, J. (UKIP)	1,859	3.5	1.9
Manning, G. (Greens)	1,603	3.1	0.0
Con majority	9,930	18.87	
Electorate	79,658		
Turnout	52,619	66.06	

Con hold (7.0% from Lab to Con)

CAERNARFON

		%	+/-%
*Williams, H. (PlC)	12,747	45.5	1.2
Eaglestone, M. (Lab)	7,538	26.9	-5.4
ab Owain, M. (Lib Dem)	3,508	12.5	6.3
Opperman, G. (Con)	3,483	12.4	-2.7
Williams, E. (UKIP)	723	2.6	0.7
PlC majority	5,209	18.60	
Electorate	46,393		
Turnout	27,999	60.35	

PlC hold (3.3% from Lab to PlC)

CAERPHILLY

		%	+/-%
*David, W. (Lab)	22,190	56.6	-1.6
Whittle, L. (PlC)	6,831	17.4	-3.6
Watson, S. (Con)	5,711	14.6	3.2
Ali, A. (Lib Dem)	3,861	9.8	0.5
Beard, G. (Forward Wales)	636	1.6	0.0
Lab majority	15,359	39.15	
Electorate	66,939		
Turnout	39,229	58.60	

Lab hold (1.0% from PlC to Lab)

CAITHNESS, SUTHERLAND AND EASTER ROSS

(New Scottish constituency)		%	+/-%
*Thurso, J. (Lib Dem)	13,957	50.5	
Jamieson, A. (Lab)	5,789	20.9	
Shirron, K. (SNP)	3,686	13.3	
Ross, A. (Con)	2,835	10.3	
Campbell, G. (Ind)	848	3.1	
Ivory, L. (SSP)	548	2.0	

* Member of last parliament

CAITHNESS, SUTHERLAND AND EASTER ROSS

continued

Lib Dem majority	8,168	29.53
Electorate	46,837	
Turnout	27,663	59.06

Lib Dem hold (7.6% from Lab to Lib Dem)

CALDER VALLEY

		%	+/-%
*McCafferty, C. (Lab)	18,426	38.6	-4.1
Truss, L. (Con)	17,059	35.7	-0.5
Ingleton, L. (Lib Dem)	9,027	18.9	2.9
Gregory, J. (BNP)	1,887	4.0	0.0
Palmer, P. (Greens)	1,371	2.9	0.7
Lab majority	1,367	2.86	
Electorate	71,325		
Turnout	47,770	66.98	

Lab hold (1.8% from Lab to Con)

CAMBERWELL AND PECKHAM

		%	+/-%
*Harman, H. (Lab)	18,933	65.3	-4.3
Porter, R. (Lib Dem)	5,450	18.8	5.5
Lee, J. (Con)	2,841	9.8	-1.1
Ingram, P. (Greens)	1,172	4.0	0.8
Penhallow, D. (UKIP)	350	1.2	0.0
Sharkey, M. (SLP)	132	0.5	-0.3
Kulkarni, S. (WRP)	113	0.4	0.1
Lab majority	13,483	46.51	
Electorate	55,739		
Turnout	28,991	52.01	

Lab hold (4.9% from Lab to Lib Dem)

CAMBRIDGE

		%	+/-%
Howarth, D. (Lib Dem)	19,152	43.9	18.9
*Campbell, A. (Lab)	14,813	34.0	-11.1
Lyon, I. (Con)	7,193	16.5	-6.5
Lucas-Smith, M. (Greens)	1,245	2.9	-0.4
Davies, H. (UKIP)	569	1.3	0.1
Woodcock, T. (Respect)	477	1.1	0.0
Forscey-Moore, S. (Ind)	60	0.1	0.0
Wilkinson, G. (Ind)	60	0.1	0.0
Lib Dem majority	4,339	9.96	
Electorate	70,154		
Turnout	43,596	62.10	

Lib Dem gain (15.0% from Lab to Lib Dem)

NORTH EAST CAMBRIDGESHIRE

		%	+/-%
*Moss, M. (Con)	24,181	47.5	-0.6
Costain, F. (Lab)	15,280	30.0	-4.8
Dean, A. (Lib Dem)	8,693	17.1	3.1
Baynes, L. (UKIP)	2,723	5.4	2.9
Con majority	8,901	17.50	
Electorate	85,079		
Turnout	50,877	59.80	

Con hold (2.1% from Lab to Con)

NORTH WEST CAMBRIDGESHIRE

		%	+/-%
Vara, S. (Con)	22,504	45.8	-4.0
Orhan, A. (Lab)	12,671	25.8	-5.6
Souter, J. (Lib Dem)	11,232	22.9	7.1
Brown, R. (UKIP)	2,685	5.5	3.5

Con majority	9,833	20.03
Electorate	79,694	
Turnout	49,092	61.60

Con hold (0.8% from Lab to Con)

SOUTH CAMBRIDGESHIRE

		%	+/-%
*Lansley, A. (Con)	23,676	45.0	0.7
Dickson, A. (Lib Dem)	15,675	29.8	2.9
Wilson, S. (Lab)	10,189	19.4	-4.9
Page, R. (UKIP)	1,556	3.0	1.2
Saggers, S. (Greens)	1,552	3.0	0.5
Con majority	8,001	15.20	
Electorate	77,022		
Turnout	52,648	68.35	

Con hold (1.1% from Con to Lib Dem)

SOUTH EAST CAMBRIDGESHIRE

		%	+/-%
*Paice, J. (Con)	26,374	47.1	2.9
Chatfield, J. (Lib Dem)	17,750	31.7	4.8
Ross, F. (Lab)	11,936	21.3	-5.1
Con majority	8,624	15.38	
Electorate	85,901		
Turnout	56,060	65.26	

Con hold (1.0% from Con to Lib Dem)

CANNOCK CHASE

		%	+/-%
*Wright, T. (Lab)	22,139	51.3	-4.8
Collard, I. (Con)	12,912	29.9	-0.1
Pinkett, J. (Lib Dem)	5,934	13.8	-0.1
Jenkins, R. (UKIP)	2,170	5.0	0.0
Lab majority	9,227	21.38	
Electorate	75,194		
Turnout	43,155	57.39	

Lab hold (2.3% from Lab to Con)

CANTERBURY

		%	+/-%
*Brazier, J. (Con)	21,113	44.4	2.9
Hilton, A. (Lab)	13,642	28.7	-8.2
Barnard-Langston, J. (Lib Dem)	10,059	21.1	3.3
Meaden, G. (Greens)	1,521	3.2	1.2
Moore, J. (UKIP)	926	2.0	0.2
van de Benderskum, R. (LCA)	326	0.7	0.0
Con majority	7,471	15.70	
Electorate	72,046		
Turnout	47,587	66.05	

Con hold (5.6% from Lab to Con)

CARDIFF CENTRAL

		%	+/-%
Willott, J. (Lib Dem)	17,991	49.8	13.1
*Jones, J. (Lab)	12,398	34.3	-4.3
Mohindra, G. (Con)	3,339	9.2	-6.7
Grigg, R. (PlC)	1,271	3.5	-1.3
Hughes, F. (UKIP)	386	1.1	0.0
Hughes, F. (UKIP)	383	1.1	0.4
Savoury, A. (Ind)	168	0.5	0.0
Beany, C. (NMB)	159	0.4	0.0
Taylor-Dawson, C. (Vote Dream)	37	0.1	0.0

* Member of last parliament

Lib Dem majority 5,593 15.48
Electorate 61,001
Turnout 36,132 59.23
Lib Dem gain (8.7% from Lab/Co-op to Lib Dem)

CARDIFF NORTH

		%	+/-%
*Morgan, J. (Lab)	17,707	39.0	-6.9
Morgan, J. (Con)	16,561	36.5	4.9
Dixon, J. (Lib Dem)	8,483	18.7	3.4
Rowlands, J. (PlC)	1,936	4.3	-1.5
Hulston, D. (UKIP)	534	1.2	-0.2
Hobbs, A. (Forward Wales)	138	0.3	0.0
Taylor-Dawson, C. (Vote Dream)	1	0.0	0.0
Lab majority	1,146	2.53	
Electorate	64,341		
Turnout	45,360	70.50	

Lab hold (5.9% from Lab to Con)

CARDIFF SOUTH AND PENARTH

		%	+/-%
*Michael, A. (Lab/Co-op)	17,447	47.3	-8.9
Green, V. (Con)	8,210	22.2	0.4
Cox, G. (Lib Dem)	7,529	20.3	7.6
Toby, J. (PlC)	2,023	5.5	-0.1
Matthews, J. (Greens)	729	2.0	0.0
Tuttle, J. (UKIP)	522	1.4	0.0
Bartlett, D. (SAP)	269	0.7	0.0
Taylor, A. (Ind)	104	0.3	0.0
Taylor-Dawson, C. (Vote Dream)	79	0.2	0.0
Lab/Co-op majority	9,237	25.02	
Electorate	65,710		
Turnout	36,912	56.17	

Lab/Co-op hold (4.7% from Lab/Co-op to Con)

CARDIFF WEST

		%	+/-%
*Brennan, K. (Lab)	15,729	45.5	-9.0
Baker, S. (Con)	7,562	21.9	0.5
Goldsworthy, A. (Lib Dem)	6,060	17.5	4.5
McEvoy, N. (PlC)	4,316	12.5	2.8
Callan, J. (UKIP)	727	2.1	0.8
Taylor-Dawson, C. (Vote Dream)	167	0.5	0.0
Lab majority	8,167	23.63	
Electorate	59,847		
Turnout	34,561	57.75	

Lab hold (4.8% from Lab to Con)

CARLISLE

		%	+/-%
*Martlew, E. (Lab)	17,019	48.1	-3.1
Mitchelson, M. (Con)	11,324	32.0	-2.8
Tweedie, S. (Lib Dem)	5,916	16.7	5.0
Cochrane, S. (UKIP)	792	2.2	0.0
Gibson, L. (LCA)	343	1.0	-0.6
Lab majority	5,695	16.09	
Electorate	59,508		
Turnout	35,394	59.48	

Lab hold (0.1% from Lab to Con)

CARMARTHEN EAST AND DINEFWR

		%	+/-%
*Price, A. (PlC)	17,561	45.9	3.5
Hendry, R. (Lab)	10,843	28.3	-7.3
Davies, S. (Con)	5,235	13.7	0.8
Hughes, J. (Lib Dem)	3,719	9.7	2.3
Squires, M. (UKIP)	661	1.7	0.0
Whitworth, S. (LCA)	272	0.7	0.0
PlC majority	6,718	17.54	
Electorate	53,484		
Turnout	38,291	71.59	

PlC hold (5.4% from Lab to PlC)

CARMARTHEN WEST AND SOUTH PEMBROKESHIRE

		%	+/-%
*Ainger, N. (Lab)	13,953	36.9	-4.7
Morris, D. (Con)	12,043	31.8	2.5
Dixon, J. (PlC)	5,582	14.7	-3.9
Allen, J. (Lib Dem)	5,399	14.3	5.5
MacDonald, J. (UKIP)	545	1.4	0.0
Daszak, A. (LCA)	237	0.6	0.0
Turner, N. (ND)	104	0.3	0.0
Lab majority	1,910	5.04	
Electorate	56,245		
Turnout	37,863	67.32	

Lab hold (3.6% from Lab to Con)

CARSHALTON AND WALLINGTON

		%	+/-%
*Brake, T. (Lib Dem)	17,357	40.3	-4.7
Andrew, K. (Con)	16,289	37.8	4.0
Theobald, A. (Lab)	7,396	17.2	-1.2
Day, F. (UKIP)	1,111	2.6	1.4
Steel, B. (Greens)	908	2.1	0.6
Lib Dem majority	1,068	2.48	
Electorate	67,844		
Turnout	43,061	63.47	

Lib Dem hold (4.4% from Lib Dem to Con)

CASTLE POINT

		%	+/-%
*Spink, B. (Con)	22,118	48.3	3.7
Akehurst, L. (Lab)	13,917	30.4	-11.7
Sandbach, J. (Lib Dem)	4,719	10.3	2.5
Hamper, N. (UKIP)	3,431	7.5	4.3
Willis, I. (Greens)	1,617	3.5	0.0
Con majority	8,201	17.91	
Electorate	69,480		
Turnout	45,802	65.92	

Con hold (7.7% from Lab to Con)

CENTRAL AYRSHIRE – see under Ayrshire

CENTRAL SUFFOLK AND NORTH IPSWICH – see under Suffolk

CEREDIGION

		%	+/-%
Williams, M. (Lib Dem)	13,130	36.5	9.7
*Thomas, S. (PlC)	12,911	35.9	-2.4
Harrison, J. (Con)	4,455	12.4	-7.1
Davies, A. (Lab)	4,337	12.1	-3.4
Bradney, D. (Greens)	846	2.4	0.0
Sheridan, I. (Veritas)	268	0.8	0.0

* Member of last parliament

CEREDIGION *continued*

Lib Dem majority	219	0.61
Electorate	53,493	
Turnout	35,947	67.20

Lib Dem gain (6.0% from PlC to Lib Dem)

CHARNWOOD

		%	+/-%
*Dorrell, S. (Con)	23,571	46.6	-1.7
Robinson, R. (Lab)	14,762	29.2	-3.0
King, S. (Lib Dem)	9,057	17.9	1.7
Holders, A. (BNP)	1,737	3.4	0.0
Bye, J. (UKIP)	1,489	2.9	-0.4
Con majority	8,809	17.40	
Electorate	76,274		
Turnout	50,616	66.36	

Con hold (0.7% from Lab to Con)

CHATHAM AND AYLESFORD

		%	+/-%
*Shaw, J. (Lab)	18,387	43.7	-4.6
Jobson, A. (Con)	16,055	38.2	0.8
Enever, D. (Lib Dem)	5,744	13.7	1.8
King, J. (UKIP)	1,226	2.9	0.4
Russell, M. (England)	668	1.6	0.0
Lab majority	2,332	5.54	
Electorate	70,515		
Turnout	42,080	59.68	

Lab hold (2.7% from Lab to Con)

CHEADLE

		%	+/-%
*Calton, P. (Lib Dem)	23,189	48.9	6.5
Day, S. (Con)	19,169	40.4	-1.9
Miller, M. (Lab)	4,169	8.8	-5.2
Cavanagh, V. (UKIP)	489	1.0	-0.3
Chadfield, R. (BNP)	421	0.9	0.0
Lib Dem majority	4,020	8.47	
Electorate	68,123		
Turnout	47,437	69.63	

Lib Dem hold (4.2% from Con to Lib Dem)

CHELMSFORD WEST

		%	+/-%
*Burns, S. (Con)	22,946	45.0	2.5
Robinson, S. (Lib Dem)	13,326	26.1	2.9
Kennedy, R. (Lab)	13,236	25.9	-3.5
Wedon, K. (UKIP)	1,544	3.0	1.4
Con majority	9,620	18.84	
Electorate	82,489		
Turnout	51,052	61.89	

Con hold (0.2% from Con to Lib Dem)

CHELTENHAM

		%	+/-%
Horwood, M. (Lib Dem)	18,122	41.5	-6.2
Gearson, V. (Con)	15,819	36.3	1.1
Evans, C. (Lab)	4,988	11.4	-0.6
Hodges, R. (Ind)	2,651	6.1	5.8
Bessant, K. (Greens)	908	2.1	0.3
Warry, N. (UKIP)	608	1.4	0.2
Hanks, D. (Loony)	525	1.2	0.0
Lib Dem majority	2,303	5.28	
Electorate	71,541		
Turnout	43,621	60.97	

Lib Dem hold (3.6% from Lib Dem to Con)

CHESHAM AND AMERSHAM

		%	+/-%
*Gillan, C. (Con)	25,619	54.4	3.9
Ford, J. (Lib Dem)	11,821	25.1	0.8
Huq, R. (Lab)	6,610	14.0	-4.7
Wilkins, N. (Greens)	1,656	3.5	1.1
Samuel-Camps, D. (UKIP)	1,391	3.0	-0.1
Con majority	13,798	29.30	
Electorate	69,217		
Turnout	47,097	68.04	

Con hold (1.5% from Lib Dem to Con)

CITY OF CHESTER

		%	+/-%
*Russell, C. (Lab)	17,458	38.9	-9.6
Offer, P. (Con)	16,543	36.8	3.7
Jones, M. (Lib Dem)	9,818	21.9	7.2
Weddell, A. (UKIP)	776	1.7	-0.3
Abrams, E. (Eng Dem)	308	0.7	0.0
Lab majority	915	2.04	
Electorate	69,785		
Turnout	44,903	64.34	

Lab hold (6.7% from Lab to Con)

CHESTERFIELD

		%	+/-%
*Holmes, P. (Lib Dem)	20,875	47.3	-0.5
Rich, S. (Lab)	17,830	40.4	-1.6
Kreling, M. (Con)	3,605	8.2	0.0
Brady, C. (UKIP)	997	2.3	0.0
Jerram, I. (Eng Dem)	814	1.8	0.0
Lib Dem majority	3,045	6.90	
Electorate	74,007		
Turnout	44,121	59.62	

Lib Dem hold (0.5% from Lab to Lib Dem)

CHICHESTER

		%	+/-%
*Tyrie, A. (Con)	25,302	48.3	1.3
Hilliar, A. (Lib Dem)	14,442	27.6	3.4
Austin, J. (Lab)	9,632	18.4	-3.1
Denny, D. (UKIP)	3,025	5.8	1.0
Con majority	10,860	20.72	
Electorate	78,645		
Turnout	52,401	66.63	

Con hold (1.1% from Con to Lib Dem)

CHINGFORD AND WOODFORD GREEN

		%	+/-%
*Duncan Smith, I. (Con)	20,555	53.2	5.0
Wright, S. (Lab)	9,914	25.7	-7.7
Beanse, J. (Lib Dem)	6,832	17.7	2.2
McGough, M. (UKIP)	1,078	2.8	0.0
White, B. (Ind)	269	0.7	0.0
Con majority	10,641	27.53	
Electorate	61,386		
Turnout	38,648	62.96	

Con hold (6.4% from Lab to Con)

CHIPPING BARNET

		%	+/-%
Villiers, T. (Con)	19,744	46.6	0.2
Coakley-Webb, P. (Lab)	13,784	32.5	-7.5
Hooker, S. (Lib Dem)	6,671	15.7	2.2
Poppy, A. (Greens)	1,199	2.8	0.0
Kaye, V. (UKIP)	924	2.2	0.0
Weiss, R. (Vote Dream)	59	0.1	0.0

* Member of last parliament

Con majority	5,960	14.06
Electorate	66,143	
Turnout	42,381	64.07

Con hold (3.9% from Lab to Con)

CHORLEY

		%	+/-%
*Hoyle, L. (Lab)	25,131	50.7	-1.6
Mallett, S. (Con)	17,506	35.3	0.6
Wilson-Fletcher, A. (Lib Dem)			
	6,932	14.0	2.8
Lab majority	7,625	15.38	
Electorate	78,838		
Turnout	49,569	62.87	

Lab hold (1.1% from Lab to Con)

CHRISTCHURCH

		%	+/-%
*Chope, C. (Con)	28,208	54.7	-0.4
Coman, L. (Lib Dem)	12,649	24.5	-3.2
King, J. (Lab)	8,051	15.6	0.5
Hughes, D. (UKIP)	2,657	5.2	3.2
Con majority	15,559	30.17	
Electorate	74,109		
Turnout	51,565	69.58	

Con hold (1.4% from Lib Dem to Con)

CITIES OF LONDON AND WESTMINSTER –
see under London and Westminster

CITY OF CHESTER – see under Chester

CITY OF DURHAM – see under Durham

CITY OF YORK – see under York

CLEETHORPES

		%	+/-%
*McIsaac, S. (Lab)	18,889	43.3	-6.3
Vickers, M. (Con)	16,247	37.3	0.9
Lowis, G. (Lib Dem)	6,437	14.8	2.8
Hardie, W. (UKIP)	2,016	4.6	2.5
Lab majority	2,642	6.06	
Electorate	70,746		
Turnout	43,589	61.61	

Lab hold (3.6% from Lab to Con)

CLWYD SOUTH

		%	+/-%
*Jones, M. (Lab)	14,808	45.0	-6.4
Biggins, T. (Con)	8,460	25.7	0.9
Burnham, D. (Lib Dem)	5,105	15.5	5.3
Strong, M. (PlC)	3,111	9.5	-2.4
Humphreys, A. (Forward Wales)			
	803	2.4	0.0
Powell, N. (UKIP)	644	2.0	0.3
Lab majority	6,348	19.28	
Electorate	52,353		
Turnout	32,931	62.90	

Lab hold (3.6% from Lab to Con)

VALE OF CLWYD

		%	+/-%
*Ruane, C. (Lab)	14,875	46.0	-4.0
Elphick, F. (Con)	10,206	31.6	-0.6
Jewkes, E. (Lib Dem)	3,820	11.8	2.4
Jones, M. (PlC)	2,309	7.2	0.0
Young, M. (Ind)	442	1.4	0.0
Khambatta, E. (UKIP)	375	1.2	-0.1
Ditchfield, J. (LCA)	286	0.9	0.0

* Member of last parliament

Lab majority	4,669	14.45
Electorate	51,982	
Turnout	32,313	62.16

Lab hold (1.7% from Lab to Con)

CLWYD WEST

		%	+/-%
Jones, D. (Con)	12,909	36.3	0.7
*Thomas, G. (Lab)	12,776	35.9	-2.9
Taylor, F. (Lib Dem)	4,723	13.3	1.9
Williams, E. (PlC)	3,874	10.9	-2.0
Nicholson, W. (UKIP)	512	1.4	0.1
James, J. (Ind)	507	1.4	0.0
Keenan, P. (SLP)	313	0.9	0.0
Con majority	133	0.37	
Electorate	55,642		
Turnout	35,614	64.01	

Con gain (1.8% from Lab to Con)

COATBRIDGE, CHRYSTON AND BELLSHILL

(New Scottish constituency)		%	+/-%
*Clarke, T. (Lab)	24,725	64.5	
Ross, D. (SNP)	5,206	13.6	
Ackland, R. (Lib Dem)	4,605	12.0	
Paterson, L. (Con)	2,775	7.2	
Kinloch, J. (SSP)	1,033	2.7	
Lab majority	19,519	50.90	
Electorate	67,385		
Turnout	38,344	56.90	

Lab hold (1.8% from Lab to SNP)

COLCHESTER

		%	+/-%
*Russell, B. (Lib Dem)	21,145	47.1	4.5
Bentley, K. (Con)	14,868	33.1	3.2
Bruni, L. (Lab)	8,886	19.8	-5.2
Lib Dem majority	6,277	13.98	
Electorate	79,010		
Turnout	44,899	56.83	

Lib Dem hold (0.6% from Con to Lib Dem)

COLNE VALLEY

		%	+/-%
*Mountford, K. (Lab)	17,536	35.9	-4.5
Throup, M. (Con)	16,035	32.8	2.3
Wilson, E. (Lib Dem)	11,822	24.2	-0.7
Fowler, B. (BNP)	1,430	2.9	0.0
Hedges, L. (Greens)	1,295	2.7	0.4
Martinek, H. (Veritas)	543	1.1	0.0
Mumford, I. (Loony)	259	0.5	0.0
Lab majority	1,501	3.07	
Electorate	74,121		
Turnout	48,920	66.00	

Lab hold (3.4% from Lab to Con)

CONGLETON

		%	+/-%
*Winterton, A. (Con)	21,189	45.4	-0.9
Milton, N. (Lab)	12,943	27.7	-2.8
Key, E. (Lib Dem)	12,550	26.9	5.3
Con majority	8,246	17.66	
Electorate	72,770		
Turnout	46,682	64.15	

Con hold (0.9% from Lab to Con)

CONWY

		%	+/-%
*Williams, B. (Lab)	12,479	37.1	-4.7
Bebb, G. (Con)	9,398	27.9	4.2
Roberts, G. (Lib Dem)	6,723	20.0	3.1
Rowlinson, P. (PlC)	3,730	11.1	-5.4
Killock, J. (Greens)	512	1.5	0.0
Jones, D. (SLP)	324	1.0	0.0
Khambatta, K. (UKIP)	298	0.9	-0.2
Evans, T. (LCA)	193	0.6	0.0
Lab majority	3,081	9.15	
Electorate	53,987		
Turnout	33,657	62.34	

Lab hold (4.5% from Lab to Con)

COPELAND

		%	+/-%
Reed, J. (Lab)	17,033	50.5	-1.3
Whiteside, C. (Con)	10,713	31.7	-5.8
Hollowell, F. (Lib Dem)	3,880	11.5	0.8
Caley-Knowles, E. (UKIP)	735	2.2	0.0
Earley, B. (Ind)	734	2.2	0.0
Mossop, A. (Eng Dem)	662	2.0	0.0
Lab majority	6,320	18.72	
Electorate	54,206		
Turnout	33,757	62.28	

Lab hold (2.2% from Con to Lab)

CORBY

		%	+/-%
*Hope, P. (Lab/Co-op)	20,913	43.1	-6.2
Griffith, A. (Con)	19,396	40.0	2.7
Radcliffe, D. (Lib Dem)	6,184	12.7	2.7
Gillman, I. (UKIP)	1,278	2.6	0.8
Carey, S. (SLP)	499	1.0	-0.6
Morris, J. (Ind)	257	0.5	0.0
Lab/Co-op majority	1,517	3.13	
Electorate	73,000		
Turnout	48,527	66.48	

Lab/Co-op hold (4.5% from Lab/Co-op to Con)

NORTH CORNWALL

		%	+/-%
Rogerson, D. (Lib Dem)	23,842	42.6	-9.4
Formosa, M. (Con)	20,766	37.1	3.3
Acton, D. (Lab)	6,636	11.9	2.1
Campbell Bannerman, D. (UKIP)			
	3,063	5.5	1.0
Cole, D. (Meb Ker)	1,351	2.4	0.0
Eastwood, A. (Veritas)	324	0.6	0.0
Lib Dem majority	3,076	5.49	
Electorate	86,841		
Turnout	55,982	64.46	

Lib Dem hold (6.4% from Lib Dem to Con)

SOUTH EAST CORNWALL

		%	+/-%
*Breed, C. (Lib Dem)	24,986	46.7	0.8
Gray, A. (Con)	18,479	34.6	-1.0
Binley, C. (Lab)	6,069	11.4	-1.1
Lucas, D. (UKIP)	2,693	5.0	1.2
Sandercock, G. (Meb Ker)	769	1.4	-0.9
Assheton-Salton, A. (Veritas)			
	459	0.9	0.0
Lib Dem majority	6,507	12.17	
Electorate	80,704		
Turnout	53,455	66.24	

Lib Dem hold (0.9% from Con to Lib Dem)

COTSWOLD

		%	+/-%
*Clifton-Brown, G. (Con)	23,326	49.3	-1.1
Beckerlegge, P. (Lib Dem)			
	13,638	28.8	4.6
Dempsey, M. (Lab)	8,457	17.9	-4.7
Buckley, R. (UKIP)	1,538	3.3	0.4
Derieg, J. (Ind)	392	0.8	0.0
Con majority	9,688	20.46	
Electorate	71,039		
Turnout	47,351	66.65	

Con hold (2.8% from Con to Lib Dem)

COVENTRY NORTH EAST

		%	+/-%
*Ainsworth, B. (Lab)	21,178	56.9	-4.1
Birdi, J. (Con)	6,956	18.7	-0.1
Field, R. (Lib Dem)	6,123	16.5	5.3
Nellist, D. (SAP)	1,874	5.0	0.0
Sootheran, P. (UKIP)	1,064	2.9	0.0
Lab majority	14,222	38.24	
Electorate	70,225		
Turnout	37,195	52.97	

Lab hold (2.0% from Lab to Con)

COVENTRY NORTH WEST

		%	+/-%
*Robinson, G. (Lab)	20,942	48.2	-3.2
Connell, B. (Con)	11,627	26.8	0.9
Anderson, I. (Lib Dem)	7,932	18.3	4.6
Clarke, D. (BNP)	1,556	3.6	0.0
List, S. (UKIP)	766	1.8	0.2
Downes, N. (SAP)	615	1.4	0.0
Lab majority	9,315	21.44	
Electorate	73,180		
Turnout	43,438	59.36	

Lab hold (2.1% from Lab to Con)

COVENTRY SOUTH

		%	+/-%
*Cunningham, J. (Lab)	18,649	45.8	-4.4
Wheeler, H. (Con)	12,394	30.5	0.9
McKee, V. (Lib Dem)	7,228	17.8	3.6
Windsor, R. (SAP)	1,097	2.7	0.0
Brown, W. (UKIP)	829	2.0	0.0
Rogers, I. (Ind)	344	0.9	-0.6
Rooney, J. (FFUK)	144	0.4	0.0
Lab majority	6,255	15.37	
Electorate	68,884		
Turnout	40,685	59.06	

Lab hold (2.6% from Lab to Con)

CRAWLEY

		%	+/-%
*Moffatt, L. (Lab)	16,411	39.1	-10.2
Smith, H. (Con)	16,374	39.0	6.8
Sheard, R. (Lib Dem)	6,503	15.5	2.8
Trower, R. (BNP)	1,277	3.0	0.0
Walters, R. (UKIP)	935	2.2	-0.7
Burnham, R. (Dem Soc All)	263	0.6	0.0
Khan, A. (JP)	210	0.5	-0.2
Lab majority	37	0.09	
Electorate	71,911		
Turnout	41,973	58.37	

Lab hold (0.0%)

* Member of last parliament

CREWE AND NANTWICH

		%	+/-%
*Dunwoody, G. (Lab)	21,240	48.8	-5.5
Moore-Dutton, E. (Con)	14,162	32.6	2.1
Roberts, P. (Lib Dem)	8,083	18.6	5.1
Lab majority	7,078	16.28	
Electorate	72,472		
Turnout	43,485	60.00	

Lab hold (3.8% from Lab to Con)

CROSBY

		%	+/-%
*Curtis-Thomas, C. (Lab)	17,463	48.3	-6.9
Jones, D. (Con)	11,623	32.1	-0.4
Murray, J. (Lib Dem)	6,298	17.4	6.3
Whittaker, J. (UKIP)	454	1.3	0.0
Bottoms, G. (Comm)	199	0.6	0.0
Braid, D. (Clause 28)	157	0.4	0.0
Lab majority	5,840	16.14	
Electorate	54,255		
Turnout	36,194	66.71	

Lab hold (3.3% from Lab to Con)

CROYDON CENTRAL

		%	+/-%
Pelling, A. (Con)	19,974	40.8	2.3
*Davies, G. (Lab)	19,899	40.7	-6.6
Hargreaves, J. (Lib Dem)	6,384	13.0	1.8
Edwards, I. (UKIP)	1,066	2.2	1.0
Golberg, B. (Greens)	1,036	2.1	0.0
Bowness, M. (Veritas)	304	0.6	0.0
Cartwright, J. (Loony)	193	0.4	-0.5
Stears, J. (Work)	101	0.2	0.0
Con majority	75	0.15	
Electorate	80,825		
Turnout	48,957	60.57	

Con gain (4.4% from Lab to Con)

CROYDON NORTH

		%	+/-%
*Wicks, M. (Lab)	23,555	53.7	-9.8
Ahmad, T. (Con)	9,667	22.1	-1.2
Gee-Turner, A. (Lib Dem)	7,560	17.2	6.8
Khan, S. (Greens)	1,248	2.9	0.0
Pearce, H. (UKIP)	770	1.8	0.3
Gibson, P. (Croydon)	394	0.9	0.0
McKenzie, W. (Veritas)	324	0.7	0.0
Rasheed, F. (Ind)	197	0.5	0.0
Chambers, M. (Work)	132	0.3	0.0
Lab majority	13,888	31.67	
Electorate	83,796		
Turnout	43,847	52.33	

Lab hold (4.3% from Lab to Con)

CROYDON SOUTH

		%	+/-%
*Ottaway, R. (Con)	25,320	51.8	2.6
Smith, P. (Lab)	11,792	24.1	-5.8
Lawman, S. (Lib Dem)	10,049	20.6	2.3
Feisenberger, J. (UKIP)	1,054	2.2	-0.1
Dare, G. (Veritas)	497	1.0	0.0
Samuel, M. (Work)	185	0.4	0.0
Con majority	13,528	27.67	
Electorate	76,872		
Turnout	48,897	63.61	

Con hold (4.2% from Lab to Con)

CUMBERNAULD, KILSYTH AND KIRKINTILLOCH EAST

(New Scottish constituency)

		%	+/-%
*McKenna, R. (Lab)	20,251	51.8	
Hepburn, J. (SNP)	8,689	22.2	
O'Donnell, H. (Lib Dem)	5,817	14.9	
Boswell, J. (Con)	2,718	7.0	
O'Neill, W. (SSP)	1,141	2.9	
Elliott, P. (OCV)	472	1.2	
Lab majority	11,562	29.58	
Electorate	64,748		
Turnout	39,088	60.37	

Lab hold (1.1% from Lab to SNP)

CYNON VALLEY

		%	+/-%
*Clwyd, A. (Lab)	17,074	64.1	-1.5
Benney, G. (PlC)	3,815	14.3	-3.1
Phelps, M. (Lib Dem)	2,991	11.2	1.8
Dunn, A. (Con)	2,062	7.7	0.2
Davies, S. (UKIP)	705	2.7	0.0
Lab majority	13,259	49.76	
Electorate	45,369		
Turnout	26,647	58.73	

Lab hold (0.8% from PlC to Lab)

DAGENHAM

		%	+/-%
*Cruddas, J. (Lab)	15,446	50.1	-7.2
White, M. (Con)	7,841	25.4	-0.3
Kempton, J. (Lib Dem)	3,106	10.1	-0.2
Rustem, L. (BNP)	2,870	9.3	4.3
Batten, G. (UKIP)	1,578	5.1	0.0
Lab majority	7,605	24.66	
Electorate	60,141		
Turnout	30,841	51.28	

Lab hold (3.4% from Lab to Con)

DARLINGTON

		%	+/-%
*Milburn, A. (Lab)	20,643	52.4	-3.9
Frieze, A. (Con)	10,239	26.0	-4.3
Adamson, R. (Lib Dem)	7,269	18.5	7.5
Hoodless, J. (UKIP)	730	1.9	0.0
Davies, D. (Veritas)	507	1.3	0.0
Lab majority	10,404	26.41	
Electorate	65,281		
Turnout	39,388	60.34	

Lab hold (0.2% from Con to Lab)

DARTFORD

		%	+/-%
*Stoate, H. (Lab)	19,909	42.6	-5.4
Johnson, G. (Con)	19,203	41.1	0.5
Bucklitsch, P. (Lib Dem)	5,036	10.8	2.3
Croucher, M. (UKIP)	1,407	3.0	0.8
Tibby, M. (NEP)	1,224	2.6	0.0
Lab majority	706	1.51	
Electorate	74,028		
Turnout	46,779	63.19	

Lab hold (2.9% from Lab to Con)

* Member of last parliament

DAVENTRY

		%	+/-%
*Boswell, T. (Con)	31,206	51.6	2.4
Hammond, A. (Lab)	16,520	27.3	-4.9
Saul, H. (Lib Dem)	9,964	16.5	0.4
Mahoney, B. (UKIP)	1,927	3.2	0.8
Wilkins, B. (Veritas)	822	1.4	0.0
Con majority	14,686	24.30	
Electorate	88,758		
Turnout	60,439	68.09	

Con hold (3.6% from Lab to Con)

DELYN

		%	+/-%
*Hanson, D. (Lab)	15,540	45.7	-5.8
Bell, J. (Con)	8,896	26.2	-0.5
Jones, T. (Lib Dem)	6,089	17.9	2.5
Thomas, P. (PlC)	2,524	7.4	0.9
Crawford, M. (UKIP)	533	1.6	0.0
Williams, N. (Ind)	422	1.2	0.0
Lab majority	6,644	19.54	
Electorate	52,766		
Turnout	34,004	64.44	

Lab hold (2.7% from Lab to Con)

DENTON AND REDDISH

		%	+/-%
Gwynne, A. (Lab)	20,340	57.4	-7.8
Story, A. (Con)	6,842	19.3	-0.3
Seabourne, A. (Lib Dem)	5,814	16.4	4.0
Edgar, J. (BNP)	1,326	3.7	0.0
Price, G. (UKIP)	1,120	3.2	0.4
Lab majority	13,498	38.08	
Electorate	68,267		
Turnout	35,442	51.92	

Lab hold (3.8% from Lab to Con)

DERBY NORTH

		%	+/-%
*Laxton, B. (Lab)	19,272	44.0	-6.9
Aitken-Davies, R. (Con)	15,515	35.4	0.4
Beckett, J. (Lib Dem)	7,209	16.5	2.4
Bardoe, M. (Veritas)	958	2.2	0.0
Medgyesy, M. (UKIP)	864	2.0	0.0
Lab majority	3,757	8.57	
Electorate	68,173		
Turnout	43,818	64.27	

Lab hold (3.6% from Lab to Con)

DERBY SOUTH

		%	+/-%
*Beckett, M. (Lab)	19,683	45.4	-11.1
Care, L. (Lib Dem)	14,026	32.3	13.1
Brackenbury, D. (Con)	8,211	18.9	-5.3
Black, D. (UKIP)	845	2.0	0.0
Leeming, F. (Veritas)	608	1.4	0.0
Lab majority	5,657	13.04	
Electorate	70,397		
Turnout	43,373	61.61	

Lab hold (12.1% from Lab to Lib Dem)

NORTH EAST DERBYSHIRE

		%	+/-%
Engel, N. (Lab)	21,416	49.3	-6.3
Johnson, D. (Con)	11,351	26.1	-0.4
Snowdon, T. (Lib Dem)	8,812	20.3	2.5
Perkins, K. (UKIP)	1,855	4.3	0.0
Lab majority	10,065	23.17	
Electorate	70,981		
Turnout	43,434	61.19	

Lab hold (3.0% from Lab to Con)

SOUTH DERBYSHIRE

		%	+/-%
*Todd, M. (Lab)	24,823	44.5	-6.2
Spencer, S. (Con)	20,328	36.4	0.8
Newton-Cook, D. (Lib Dem)	7,600	13.6	3.5
Joines, D. (BNP)	1,797	3.2	0.0
Spalton, R. (Veritas)	1,272	2.3	0.0
Lab majority	4,495	8.05	
Electorate	85,049		
Turnout	55,820	65.63	

Lab hold (3.5% from Lab to Con)

WEST DERBYSHIRE

		%	+/-%
*McLoughlin, P. (Con)	24,378	47.7	-0.3
Menon, D. (Lab)	13,625	26.6	-6.8
Dring, R. (Lib Dem)	11,408	22.3	6.7
Cruddas, M. (UKIP)	1,322	2.6	1.3
Delves, N. (Loony)	405	0.8	-0.1
Kyslun, M. (Ind)	5	0.0	-0.7
Con majority	10,753	21.03	
Electorate	73,865		
Turnout	51,143	69.24	

Con hold (3.2% from Lab to Con)

DEVIZES

		%	+/-%
*Ancram, M. (Con)	27,253	48.5	1.3
Hornby, F. (Lib Dem)	14,059	25.0	3.0
Charity, S. (Lab)	12,519	22.3	-2.6
Wood, A. (UKIP)	2,315	4.1	1.3
Con majority	13,194	23.50	
Electorate	86,168		
Turnout	56,146	65.16	

Con hold (0.8% from Con to Lib Dem)

EAST DEVON

		%	+/-%
*Swire, H. (Con)	23,075	46.9	-0.6
Dumper, T. (Lib Dem)	15,139	30.7	0.5
Court, J. (Lab)	7,598	15.4	-1.2
McNamee, C. (UKIP)	3,035	6.2	0.5
Way, C. (Ind)	400	0.8	0.0
Con majority	7,936	16.11	
Electorate	71,000		
Turnout	49,247	69.36	

Con hold (0.5% from Con to Lib Dem)

NORTH DEVON

		%	+/-%
*Harvey, N. (Lib Dem)	23,840	45.9	1.7
Fraser, O. (Con)	18,868	36.3	-1.8
Cann, M. (Lab)	4,656	9.0	-1.2
Browne, J. (UKIP)	2,740	5.3	0.2
Knight, R. (Greens)	1,826	3.5	1.1
Lib Dem majority	4,972	9.57	
Electorate	76,203		
Turnout	51,930	68.15	

Lib Dem hold (1.8% from Con to Lib Dem)

* Member of last parliament

SOUTH WEST DEVON

		%	+/-%
*Streeter, G. (Con)	21,906	44.8	-2.0
Evans, J. (Lib Dem)	11,765	24.1	5.7
Mavin, C. (Lab)	11,545	23.6	-8.0
Williams, H. (UKIP)	3,669	7.5	4.3
Con majority	10,141	20.74	
Electorate	71,307		
Turnout	48,885	68.56	

Con hold (3.9% from Con to Lib Dem)

TORRIDGE AND WEST DEVON

		%	+/-%
Cox, G. (Con)	25,013	42.7	2.7
Walter, D. (Lib Dem)	21,777	37.2	-5.0
Richards, R. (Lab)	6,001	10.2	-0.5
Jackson, M. (UKIP)	3,790	6.5	1.7
Christie, P. (Greens)	2,003	3.4	1.1
Con majority	3,236	5.52	
Electorate	83,489		
Turnout	58,584	70.17	

Con gain (3.8% from Lib Dem to Con)

DEWSBURY

		%	+/-%
Malik, S. (Lab)	15,807	41.0	-9.6
Warsi, S. (Con)	11,192	29.0	-1.2
Hill, K. (Lib Dem)	5,624	14.6	2.6
Exley, D. (BNP)	5,066	13.1	8.7
Smithson, B. (Greens)	593	1.5	0.0
Girvan, A. (Ind)	313	0.8	0.0
Lab majority	4,615	11.96	
Electorate	62,243		
Turnout	38,595	62.01	

Lab hold (4.2% from Lab to Con)

DON VALLEY

		%	+/-%
*Flint, C. (Lab)	19,418	52.7	-2.0
Duguid, A. (Con)	10,820	29.4	0.7
Arnold, S. (Lib Dem)	6,626	18.0	6.8
Lab majority	8,598	23.32	
Electorate	66,993		
Turnout	36,864	55.03	

Lab hold (1.3% from Lab to Con)

DONCASTER CENTRAL

		%	+/-%
*Winterton, R. (Lab)	17,617	51.3	-7.8
Wilson, P. (Lib Dem)	7,815	22.8	9.8
Kerner, S. (Con)	6,489	18.9	-4.8
Wilkinson, J. (BNP)	1,239	3.6	0.0
Simmons, A. (UKIP)	1,191	3.5	0.7
Lab majority	9,802	28.53	
Electorate	65,731		
Turnout	34,351	52.26	

Lab hold (8.8% from Lab to Lib Dem)

DONCASTER NORTH

		%	+/-%
Miliband, E. (Lab)	17,531	55.5	-7.6
Drake, M. (Con)	4,875	15.4	0.8
Pickett, D. (Lib Dem)	3,800	12.0	1.4
Williams, M. (CG)	2,365	7.5	0.0
Haggan, L. (BNP)	1,506	4.8	0.0
Nixon, R. (UKIP)	940	3.0	0.7
Cassidy, M. (England)	561	1.8	0.0

Lab majority	12,656	40.08	
Electorate	61,741		
Turnout	31,578	51.15	

Lab hold (4.2% from Lab to Con)

MID DORSET AND POOLE NORTH

		%	+/-%
*Brooke, A. (Lib Dem)	22,000	48.7	6.7
Hayes, S. (Con)	16,518	36.6	-4.5
Murray, P. (Lab)	5,221	11.6	-3.9
King, A. (UKIP)	1,420	3.1	1.7
Lib Dem majority	5,482	12.14	
Electorate	65,924		
Turnout	45,159	68.50	

Lib Dem hold (5.6% from Con to Lib Dem)

NORTH DORSET

		%	+/-%
*Walter, R. (Con)	23,714	44.9	-1.8
Gasson, E. (Lib Dem)	21,470	40.7	1.9
Yarwood, J. (Lab)	4,596	8.7	-2.5
Frampton Hobbs, R. (UKIP)			
	1,918	3.6	1.5
Arliss, R. (Greens)	1,117	2.1	0.0
Con majority	2,244	4.25	
Electorate	74,286		
Turnout	52,815	71.10	

Con hold (1.9% from Con to Lib Dem)

SOUTH DORSET

		%	+/-%
*Knight, J. (Lab)	20,231	41.6	-0.3
Matts, E. (Con)	18,419	37.9	-3.7
Oakes, G. (Lib Dem)	7,647	15.7	1.3
Chalker, H. (UKIP)	1,571	3.2	1.2
Hamilton, V. (LCA)	282	0.6	0.0
Parkes, B. (Respect)	219	0.5	0.0
Kirkwood, A. (PRTYP)	107	0.2	0.0
Bex, C. (Wessex Reg)	83	0.2	0.0
Marchesi, D. (SLP)	25	0.1	0.0
Lab majority	1,812	3.73	
Electorate	70,668		
Turnout	48,584	68.75	

Lab hold (1.7% from Con to Lab)

WEST DORSET

		%	+/-%
*Letwin, O. (Con)	24,763	46.5	1.9
McGuinness, J. (Lib Dem)	22,302	41.9	0.1
Roberts, D. (Lab)	4,124	7.8	-5.8
Guest, L. (UKIP)	1,084	2.0	0.0
Greene, S. (Greens)	952	1.8	0.0
Con majority	2,461	4.62	
Electorate	69,764		
Turnout	53,225	76.29	

Con hold (0.9% from Lib Dem to Con)

DOVER

		%	+/-%
*Prosser, G. (Lab)	21,680	45.3	-3.5
Watkins, P. (Con)	16,739	35.0	-2.3
Hook, A. (Lib Dem)	7,607	15.9	4.5
Wiltshire, M. (UKIP)	1,252	2.6	0.1
Matcham, V. (Ind)	606	1.3	0.0

* Member of last parliament

DOVER *continued*

Lab majority	4,941	10.32
Electorate	70,884	
Turnout	47,884	67.55

Lab hold (0.6% from Lab to Con)

NORTH DOWN

		%	+/-%
*Hermon, S. (UUP)	16,268	50.4	-5.6
Weir, P. (DUP)	11,324	35.1	0.0
Alderdice, D. (Alliance)	2,451	7.6	0.0
Logan, L. (SDLP)	1,009	3.1	-0.3
Robertson, J. (Con)	822	2.6	0.4
Carter, C. (Ind)	211	0.7	-0.5
McCrory, J. (Sinn Féin)	205	0.6	-0.2
UUP majority	4,944	15.31	
Electorate	59,748		
Turnout	32,290	54.04	

UUP hold (0.0%)

SOUTH DOWN

		%	+/-%
*McGrady, E. (SDLP)	21,557	44.8	-1.6
Ruane, C. (Sinn Féin)	12,417	25.8	6.0
Wells, J. (DUP)	8,815	18.3	3.3
Nesbitt, D. (UUP)	4,775	9.9	-7.7
Crozier, J. (Alliance)	613	1.3	0.0
SDLP majority	9,140	18.97	
Electorate	73,668		
Turnout	48,177	65.40	

SDLP hold (0.0%)

DUDLEY NORTH

		%	+/-%
Austin, I. (Lab)	18,306	44.2	-7.9
Hillas, I. (Con)	12,874	31.1	-3.4
Lewis, G. (Lib Dem)	4,257	10.3	1.6
Darby, S. (BNP)	4,022	9.7	5.0
Davis, M. (UKIP)	1,949	4.7	0.0
Lab majority	5,432	13.12	
Electorate	68,766		
Turnout	41,408	60.22	

Lab hold (2.3% from Lab to Con)

DUDLEY SOUTH

		%	+/-%
*Pearson, I. (Lab)	17,800	45.3	-4.5
Longhi, M. (Con)	13,556	34.5	3.4
Bramall, J. (Lib Dem)	4,808	12.2	-2.7
Salvage, J. (BNP)	1,841	4.7	0.0
Benion, A. (BNP)	1,271	3.2	0.9
Lab majority	4,244	10.81	
Electorate	65,228		
Turnout	39,276	60.21	

Lab hold (4.0% from Lab to Con)

DULWICH AND WEST NORWOOD

		%	+/-%
*Jowell, T. (Lab)	19,059	45.4	-9.5
Mitchell, J. (Lib Dem)	10,252	24.4	9.2
Humphreys, K. (Con)	9,200	21.9	-0.8
Jones, J. (Greens)	2,741	6.5	1.5
Atkinson, R. (UKIP)	290	0.7	0.0
Heather, D. (Veritas)	241	0.6	0.0
Rose, A. (SLP)	149	0.4	0.0
Weleminsky, J. (Fit)	57	0.1	0.0

* Member of last parliament

Lab majority	8,807	20.97
Electorate	72,232	
Turnout	41,989	58.13

Lab hold (9.4% from Lab to Lib Dem)

DUMFRIES AND GALLOWAY

(New Scottish constituency)

		%	+/-%
*Brown, R. (Lab)	20,924	41.1	
*Duncan, P. (Con)	18,002	35.4	
Henderson, D. (SNP)	6,182	12.2	
Legg, K. (Lib Dem)	4,259	8.4	
Schofield, J. (Greens)	745	1.5	
Dennis, J. (SSP)	497	1.0	
Smith, M. (OCV)	282	0.6	
Lab majority	2,922	5.74	
Electorate	74,273		
Turnout	50,891	68.52	

Lab hold (2.7% from Con to Lab)

DUMFRIESSHIRE, CLYDESDALE AND TWEEDDALE

(New Scottish constituency)

		%	+/-%
Mundell, D. (Con)	16,141	36.2	
Marshall, S. (Lab)	14,403	32.3	
Kenton, P. (Lib Dem)	9,046	20.3	
Wood, A. (SNP)	4,075	9.1	
MacTavish, S. (SSP)	521	1.2	
Lee, T. (UKIP)	430	1.0	
Con majority	1,738	3.90	
Electorate	66,045		
Turnout	44,616	67.55	

Con gain (8.0% from Lab to Con)

EAST DUNBARTONSHIRE

(New Scottish constituency)

		%	+/-%
Swinson, J. (Lib Dem)	19,533	41.8	
*Lyons, J. (Lab)	15,472	33.1	
Jack, D. (Con)	7,708	16.5	
Sagan, C. (SNP)	2,716	5.8	
Page, P. (SSP)	419	0.9	
Lib Dem majority	4,061	8.69	
Electorate	64,763		
Turnout	46,724	72.15	

Lib Dem gain (7.5% from Lab to Lib Dem)

WEST DUNBARTONSHIRE

(New Scottish constituency)

		%	+/-%
*McFall, J. (Lab/Co-op)	21,600	51.9	
Chalmers, T. (SNP)	9,047	21.8	
Walker, N. (Lib Dem)	5,999	14.4	
Murdoch, C. (Con)	2,679	6.4	
Robertson, L. (SSP)	1,708	4.1	
Maher, B. (UKIP)	354	0.9	
Dawson, M. (OCV)	202	0.5	
Lab/Co-op majority	12,553	30.18	
Electorate	67,805		
Turnout	41,589	61.34	

Lab/Co-op hold (38.0% from SNP to Lab/Co-op)

DUNDEE EAST

(New Scottish constituency)

		%	+/-%
Hosie, S. (SNP)	14,708	37.2	
*Luke, I. (Lab)	14,325	36.2	

Bustin, C. (Con)	5,061	12.8
Sneddon, C. (Lib Dem)	4,498	11.4
Duke, H. (SSP)	537	1.4
Low, D. (UKIP)	292	0.7
Allison, D. (Ind)	119	0.3
SNP majority	383	0.97
Electorate	63,335	
Turnout	39,540	62.43

SNP gain (1.1% from Lab to SNP)

DUNDEE WEST
(New Scottish constituency)

		%	+/-%
McGovern, J. (Lab)	16,468	44.6	
Fitzpatrick, J. (SNP)	11,089	30.0	
Garry, N. (Lib Dem)	5,323	14.4	
McKinley, C. (Con)	3,062	8.3	
McFarlane, J. (SSP)	994	2.7	
Lab majority	5,379	14.56	
Electorate	65,857		
Turnout	36,936	56.09	

Lab hold (4.0% from Lab to SNP)

DUNFERMLINE AND WEST FIFE
(New Scottish constituency)

		%	+/-%
*Squire, R. (Lab)	20,111	47.4	
Herbert, D. (Lib Dem)	8,549	20.2	
Chapman, D. (SNP)	8,026	18.9	
Smillie, R. (Con)	4,376	10.3	
Archibald, S. (SSP)	689	1.6	
Borland, I. (UKIP)	643	1.5	
Lab majority	11,562	27.27	
Electorate	70,775		
Turnout	42,394	59.90	

Lab hold (6.5% from Lab to Lib Dem)

CITY OF DURHAM

		%	+/-%
Blackman-Woods, R. (Lab)			
	20,928	47.2	-8.9
Woods, C. (Lib Dem)	17,654	39.8	16.1
Rogers, B. (Con)	4,179	9.4	-7.9
Martin, A. (Veritas)	1,603	3.6	0.0
Lab majority	3,274	7.38	
Electorate	71,441		
Turnout	44,364	62.10	

Lab hold (12.5% from Lab to Lib Dem)

DURHAM NORTH

		%	+/-%
*Jones, K. (Lab)	23,932	64.1	-3.1
Latham, P. (Lib Dem)	7,151	19.2	5.1
Watson, M. (Con)	6,258	16.8	-2.0
Lab majority	16,781	44.94	
Electorate	67,506		
Turnout	37,341	55.32	

Lab hold (4.1% from Lab to Lib Dem)

NORTH WEST DURHAM

		%	+/-%
*Armstrong, H. (Lab)	21,312	53.9	-8.6
Ord, A. (Lib Dem)	7,869	19.9	5.0
Devlin, J. (Con)	6,463	16.4	-4.5
Stelling, W. (Ind)	3,865	9.8	0.0

* Member of last parliament

Lab majority	13,443	34.03
Electorate	68,130	
Turnout	39,509	57.99

Lab hold (6.8% from Lab to Lib Dem)

EALING, ACTON AND SHEPHERD'S BUSH

		%	+/-%
Slaughter, A. (Lab)	16,579	41.8	-12.3
Gough, J. (Con)	11,059	27.9	2.8
Malcolm, G. (Lib Dem)	9,986	25.2	8.6
Burgess, G. (Greens)	1,999	5.1	0.0
Lab majority	5,520	13.93	
Electorate	70,454		
Turnout	39,623	56.24	

Lab hold (7.5% from Lab to Con)

EALING NORTH

		%	+/-%
*Pound, S. (Lab)	20,956	45.1	-10.6
Curtis, R. (Con)	13,897	29.9	0.6
Fruzza, F. (Lib Dem)	9,148	19.7	8.5
Outten, A. (Greens)	1,319	2.8	0.5
Lambert, R. (UKIP)	692	1.5	0.0
Malindine, D. (Veritas)	495	1.1	0.0
Lab majority	7,059	15.18	
Electorate	78,298		
Turnout	46,507	59.40	

Lab hold (5.6% from Lab to Con)

EALING SOUTHALL

		%	+/-%
*Khabra, P. (Lab)	22,937	48.8	1.3
Bakhai, N. (Lib Dem)	11,497	24.4	14.4
Nicholson, M. (Con)	10,147	21.6	3.3
Edwards, S. (Greens)	2,175	4.6	0.1
Bilku, M. (WRP)	289	0.6	0.0
Lab majority	11,440	24.32	
Electorate	83,738		
Turnout	47,045	56.18	

Lab hold (6.6% from Lab to Lib Dem)

EASINGTON

		%	+/-%
*Cummings, J. (Lab)	22,733	71.4	-5.5
ord, C. (Lib Dem)	4,097	12.9	2.5
Nicholson, L. (Con)	3,400	10.7	0.3
McDonald, I. (BNP)	1,042	3.3	0.0
Robinson, D. (SLP)	583	1.8	-0.7
Lab majority	18,636	58.50	
Electorate	61,084		
Turnout	31,855	52.15	

Lab hold (4.0% from Lab to Lib Dem)

EAST ANTRIM – see under Antrim

EAST DEVON – see under Devon

EAST DUNBARTONSHIRE – see under Dunbartonshire

EAST HAM

		%	+/-%
*Timms, S. (Lab)	21,326	53.9	-19.2
Khaliq Mian, A. (Respect)	8,171	20.7	0.0
Macken, S. (Con)	5,196	13.1	-3.5
Haigh, A. (Lib Dem)	4,296	10.9	3.9
Bamber, D. (CPA)	580	1.5	

EAST HAM *continued*

Lab majority	13,155	33.25
Electorate	78,104	
Turnout	39,569	50.66

Lab hold (0.0%)

EAST HAMPSHIRE – see under Hampshire

EAST KILBRIDE, STRATHAVEN AND LESMAHAGOW

(New Scottish constituency)

		%	+/-%
*Ingram, A. (Lab)	23,264	48.7	
Edwards, D. (SNP)	8,541	17.9	
Oswald, J. (Lib Dem)	7,904	16.6	
Lewis, T. (Con)	4,776	10.0	
Robb, K. (Greens)	1,575	3.3	
Gentle, R. (Ind)	1,513	3.2	
Houston, J. (Ind)	160	0.3	
Lab majority	14,723	30.84	
Electorate	75,132		
Turnout	47,733	63.53	

Lab hold (0.8% from SNP to Lab)

EAST LONDONDERRY – see under Londonderry

EAST LOTHIAN – see under Lothian

EAST RENFREWSHIRE – see under Renfrewshire

EAST SURREY – see under Surrey

EAST WORTHING AND SHOREHAM – see under Worthing

EASTBOURNE

		%	+/-%
*Waterson, N. (Con)	21,033	43.5	-0.6
Lloyd, S. (Lib Dem)	19,909	41.1	1.9
Jones, A. (Lab)	5,268	10.9	-2.4
Meggs, A. (UKIP)	1,233	2.6	0.5
Gross, C. (Greens)	949	2.0	0.0
Con majority	1,124	2.32	
Electorate	74,628		
Turnout	48,392	64.84	

Con hold (1.2% from Con to Lib Dem)

EASTLEIGH

		%	+/-%
Huhne, C. (Lib Dem)	19,216	38.6	-2.1
Burns, C. (Con)	18,648	37.5	3.2
Watt, C. (Lab)	10,238	20.6	-1.4
Murphy, C. (UKIP)	1,669	3.4	1.6
Lib Dem majority	568	1.14	
Electorate	76,844		
Turnout	49,771	64.77	

Lib Dem hold (2.6% from Lib Dem to Con)

ECCLES

		%	+/-%
*Stewart, I. (Lab)	19,702	56.9	-7.6
Matuk, T. (Con)	6,816	19.7	-1.0
Brophy, J. (Lib Dem)	6,429	18.6	3.7
Reeve, P. (UKIP)	1,685	4.9	0.0
Lab majority	12,886	37.21	
Electorate	69,006		
Turnout	34,632	50.19	

Lab hold (3.3% from Lab to Con)

EDDISBURY

		%	+/-%
*O'Brien, S. (Con)	21,181	46.4	0.1
Green, M. (Lab)	14,986	32.8	-3.2
Crotty, J. (Lib Dem)	8,182	17.9	2.2
Roxborough, S. (UKIP)	1,325	2.9	1.0
Con majority	6,195	13.56	
Electorate	72,249		
Turnout	45,674	63.22	

Con hold (1.6% from Lab to Con)

EDINBURGH EAST

(New Scottish constituency)

		%	+/-%
*Strang, G. (Lab)	15,899	40.0	
Mackenzie, G. (Lib Dem)	9,697	24.4	
Tymkewycz, S. (SNP)	6,760	17.0	
Brown, M. (Con)	4,093	10.3	
Gillespie, C. (Greens)	2,266	5.7	
Grant, C. (SSP)	868	2.2	
Harris, B. (DDTP)	89	0.2	
Clifford, P. (ND)	37	0.1	
Lab majority	6,202	15.62	
Electorate	64,826		
Turnout	39,709	61.25	

Lab hold (8.5% from Lab to Lib Dem)

EDINBURGH NORTH AND LEITH

(New Scottish constituency)

		%	+/-%
*Lazarowicz, M. (Lab/Co-op)	14,597	34.2	
Crockart, M. (Lib Dem)	12,444	29.2	
Whyte, I. (Con)	7,969	18.7	
Hutchison, D. (SNP)	4,344	10.2	
Sydenham, M. (Greens)	2,482	5.8	
Scott, B. (SSP)	804	1.9	
Lab/Co-op majority	2,153	5.05	
Electorate	68,038		
Turnout	42,640	62.67	

Lab/Co-op hold (8.3% from Lab/Co-op to Lib Dem)

EDINBURGH SOUTH

(New Scottish constituency)

		%	+/-%
*Griffiths, N. (Lab)	14,188	33.2	
MacLaren, M. (Lib Dem)	13,783	32.3	
Brown, G. (Con)	10,291	24.1	
Sutherland, G. (SNP)	2,635	6.2	
Burgess, S. (Greens)	1,387	3.3	
Robertson, M. (SSP)	414	1.0	
Lab majority	405	0.95	
Electorate	60,993		
Turnout	42,698	70.00	

Lab hold (6.5% from Lab to Lib Dem)

EDINBURGH SOUTH WEST

(New Scottish constituency)

		%	+/-%
*Darling, A. (Lab)	17,476	39.8	
Buchan, G. (Con)	10,234	23.3	
Clark, S. (Lib Dem)	9,252	21.1	
Elliot-Cannon, N. (SNP)	4,654	10.6	
Blair-Fish, J. (Greens)	1,520	3.5	
Smith, P. (SSP)	585	1.3	
Boys, W. (UKIP)	205	0.5	

* Member of last parliament

Lab majority 7,242 16.49
Electorate 67,135
Turnout 43,926 65.43
Lab hold (0.7% from Lab to Con)

EDINBURGH WEST

(New Scottish constituency)		%	+/-%
*Barrett, J. (Lib Dem)	22,417	49.5	
Brogan, D. (Con)	8,817	19.5	
Ghaleigh, N. (Lab)	8,433	18.6	
Cleland, S. (SNP)	4,124	9.1	
Spindler, A. (Greens)	964	2.1	
Clark, G. (SSP)	510	1.1	
Lib Dem majority	13,600	30.05	
Electorate	65,741		
Turnout	45,265	68.85	

Lib Dem hold (6.7% from Con to Lib Dem)

EDMONTON

		%	+/-%
*Love, A. (Lab/Co-op)	18,456	53.2	-5.7
Zetter, L. (Con)	10,381	29.9	-0.9
Kilbane-Dawe, I. (Lib Dem)			
	4,162	12.0	5.0
Armstrong, N. (Greens)	889	2.6	0.0
Rolph, G. (UKIP)	815	2.4	1.2
Lab/Co-op majority	8,075	23.27	
Electorate	58,764		
Turnout	34,703	59.05	

Lab/Co-op hold (2.4% from Lab/Co-op to Con)

ELLESMERE PORT AND NESTON

		%	+/-%
*Miller, A. (Lab)	20,371	48.4	-6.9
Hogg, M. (Con)	13,885	33.0	3.9
Cooke, S. (Lib Dem)	6,607	15.7	4.1
Crocker, H. (UKIP)	1,206	2.9	0.9
Lab majority	6,486	15.42	
Electorate	68,249		
Turnout	42,069	61.64	

Lab hold (5.4% from Lab to Con)

ELMET

		%	+/-%
*Burgon, C. (Lab)	22,260	47.2	-0.8
Millard, A. (Con)	17,732	37.6	-1.3
Kirk, M. (Lib Dem)	5,923	12.6	1.7
Andrews, T. (BNP)	1,231	2.6	0.0
Lab majority	4,528	9.60	
Electorate	68,514		
Turnout	47,146	68.81	

Lab hold (0.3% from Con to Lab)

ELTHAM

		%	+/-%
*Efford, C. (Lab)	15,381	43.6	-9.3
Drury, S. (Con)	12,105	34.3	2.2
Gerrard, I. (Lib Dem)	5,669	16.1	3.9
Elms, J. (UKIP)	1,024	2.9	0.8
Roberts, B. (BNP)	979	2.8	0.0
Graham, A. (Ind)	147	0.4	-0.3
Lab majority	3,276	9.28	
Electorate	57,236		
Turnout	35,305	61.68	

Lab hold (5.7% from Lab to Con)

ENFIELD NORTH

		%	+/-%
*Ryan, J. (Lab)	18,055	44.3	-2.4
de Bois, N. (Con)	16,135	39.6	-1.1
Radford, S. (Lib Dem)	4,642	11.4	2.6
Farr, T. (BNP)	1,004	2.5	0.9
Robbens, G. (UKIP)	750	1.8	0.7
Burns, P. (Ind)	163	0.4	-0.2
Lab majority	1,920	4.71	
Electorate	66,460		
Turnout	40,749	61.31	

Lab hold (0.6% from Lab to Con)

ENFIELD SOUTHGATE

		%	+/-%
Burrowes, D. (Con)	18,830	44.6	6.0
*Twigg, S. (Lab)	17,083	40.5	-11.4
Kakoulakis, Z. (Lib Dem)	4,724	11.2	4.2
Doughty, T. (Greens)	1,083	2.6	1.0
Hall, B. (UKIP)	490	1.2	0.5
Con majority	1,747	4.14	
Electorate	63,613		
Turnout	42,210	66.35	

Con gain (8.7% from Lab to Con)

EPPING FOREST

		%	+/-%
*Laing, E. (Con)	23,783	53.0	3.9
Charalambous, B. (Lab)	9,425	21.0	-8.2
Heavens, M. (Lib Dem)	8,279	18.5	-0.1
Leppert, J. (BNP)	1,728	3.9	0.0
Smith, A. (UKIP)	1,014	2.3	-0.8
Tibrook, R. (Eng Dem)	631	1.4	0.0
Con majority	14,358	32.01	
Electorate	72,776		
Turnout	44,860	61.64	

Con hold (6.1% from Lab to Con)

EPSOM AND EWELL

		%	+/-%
*Grayling, C. (Con)	27,146	54.4	6.3
Lees, J. (Lib Dem)	10,699	21.5	-0.7
Mansell, C. (Lab)	10,265	20.6	-5.9
Kefford, P. (UKIP)	1,769	3.6	0.2
Con majority	16,447	32.97	
Electorate	75,515		
Turnout	49,879	66.05	

Con hold (3.5% from Lib Dem to Con)

EREWASH

		%	+/-%
*Blackman, L. (Lab)	22,472	44.5	-4.8
Simmonds, D. (Con)	15,388	30.4	-4.5
Garnett, M. (Lib Dem)	7,073	14.0	2.5
Kilroy-Silk, R. (Veritas)	2,957	5.9	0.0
Graham, S. (BNP)	1,319	2.6	1.4
Kingscott, G. (UKIP)	941	1.9	0.4
Seerius, R. (Loony)	287	0.6	-0.3
Bishop, D. (CMEP)	116	0.2	0.0
Lab majority	7,084	14.01	
Electorate	78,376		
Turnout	50,553	64.50	

Lab hold (0.1% from Lab to Con)

* Member of last parliament

ERITH AND THAMESMEAD

		%	+/-%
*Austin, J. (Lab)	20,483	54.4	-4.9
Bromby, C. (Con)	8,983	23.9	-1.9
Toole, S. (Lib Dem)	5,088	13.5	2.1
Ravenscroft, B. (BNP)	1,620	4.3	0.0
Thomas, B. (UKIP)	1,477	3.9	0.0
Lab majority	11,500	30.54	
Electorate	72,058		
Turnout	37,651	52.25	

Lab hold (1.5% from Lab to Con)

ESHER AND WALTON

		%	+/-%
*Taylor, I. (Con)	21,882	45.7	-3.3
Marsh, M. (Lib Dem)	14,155	29.6	7.1
Taylor, R. (Lab)	9,309	19.4	-4.2
Collignon, B. (UKIP)	1,582	3.3	-1.6
Chinnery, C. (Loony)	608	1.3	0.0
Cutler, R. (SLP)	342	0.7	0.0
Con majority	7,727	16.14	
Electorate	76,926		
Turnout	47,878	62.24	

Con hold (5.2% from Con to Lib Dem)

NORTH ESSEX

		%	+/-%
*Jenkin, B. (Con)	22,811	47.6	0.1
Hughes, E. (Lab)	11,908	24.8	-6.6
Raven, J. (Lib Dem)	9,831	20.5	3.0
Fox, C. (Greens)	1,718	3.6	0.0
Curtis, G. (UKIP)	1,691	3.5	-0.1
Con majority	10,903	22.73	
Electorate	73,037		
Turnout	47,959	65.66	

Con hold (3.4% from Lab to Con)

EXETER

		%	+/-%
*Bradshaw, B. (Lab)	22,619	41.1	-8.7
Cox, P. (Con)	14,954	27.2	-0.3
Underwood, J. (Lib Dem)	11,340	20.6	8.2
Danks, M. (Lib)	2,214	4.0	-0.9
Brenan, T. (Greens)	1,896	3.4	1.1
Fitzgeorge-Parker, M. (UKIP)			
	1,854	3.4	1.3
Stuart, J. (Ind)	191	0.4	0.0
Lab majority	7,665	13.92	
Electorate	84,964		
Turnout	55,068	64.81	

Lab hold (4.2% from Lab to Con)

FALKIRK

(New Scottish constituency)

		%	+/-%
*Joyce, E. (Lab)	23,264	50.9	
Love, L. (SNP)	9,789	21.4	
Chomczuck, C. (Lib Dem)	7,321	16.0	
Potts, D. (Con)	4,538	9.9	
Quinlan, D. (SSP)	838	1.8	
Lab majority	13,475	29.45	
Electorate	76,784		
Turnout	45,750	59.58	

Lab hold (0.4% from Lab to SNP)

FALMOUTH AND CAMBORNE

		%	+/-%
Goldsworthy, J. (Lib Dem)			
	16,747	34.9	10.4
*Atherton, C. (Lab)	14,861	31.0	-8.6
Crossley, A. (Con)	12,644	26.3	-3.6
Mahon, M. (UKIP)	1,820	3.8	1.0
Mudd, D. (Ind)	961	2.0	0.0
Holmes, P. (Lib)	423	0.9	-0.5
Wasley, H. (Meb Ker)	370	0.8	-1.1
Gifford, P. (Veritas)	128	0.3	0.0
Smith, R. (Masts)	61	0.1	0.0
Lib Dem majority	1,886	3.93	
Electorate	71,509		
Turnout	48,015	67.15	

Lib Dem gain (9.5% from Lab to Lib Dem)

FAREHAM

		%	+/-%
*Hoban, M. (Con)	24,151	49.7	2.7
Carr, J. (Lab)	12,449	25.6	-6.0
de Ste-Croix, R. (Lib Dem)			
	10,551	21.7	3.0
Mason-Apps, P. (UKIP)	1,425	2.9	0.4
Con majority	11,702	24.09	
Electorate	72,599		
Turnout	48,576	66.91	

Con hold (4.3% from Lab to Con)

FAVERSHAM AND MID KENT

		%	+/-%
*Robertson, H. (Con)	21,690	49.7	4.1
Bradstock, A. (Lab)	12,970	29.7	-5.7
Naghi, D. (Lib Dem)	7,204	16.5	3.0
Thompson, R. (UKIP)	1,152	2.6	0.6
Davidson, N. (Loony)	610	1.4	0.0
Con majority	8,720	19.99	
Electorate	66,411		
Turnout	43,626	65.69	

Con hold (4.9% from Lab to Con)

FELTHAM AND HESTON

		%	+/-%
*Keen, A. (Lab/Co-op)	17,741	47.6	-11.6
Bowen, M. (Con)	10,921	29.3	5.1
Khalsa, S. (Lib Dem)	6,177	16.6	2.8
Kemp, G. (NF)	975	2.6	0.0
Anstis, E. (Greens)	815	2.2	0.0
Mullett, L. (UKIP)	612	1.6	0.0
Prachar, W. (Ind)	41	0.1	0.0
Lab/Co-op majority	6,820	18.29	
Electorate	75,391		
Turnout	37,282	49.45	

Lab/Co-op hold (8.4% from Lab/Co-op to Con)

FERMANAGH AND SOUTH TYRONE

		%	+/-%
*Gildernew, M. (Sinn Féin)	18,638	38.2	4.1
Foster, A. (DUP)	14,056	28.8	0.0
Elliott, T. (UUP)	8,869	18.2	-15.9
Gallagher, T. (SDLP)	7,230	14.8	-3.9
Sinn Féin majority	4,582	9.39	
Electorate	67,174		
Turnout	48,793	72.64	

Sinn Féin hold (0.0%)

* Member of last parliament

NORTH EAST FIFE
(New Scottish constituency)

		%	+/-%
*Campbell, M. (Lib Dem)	20,088	52.1	
Scott-Hayward, M. (Con)	7,517	19.5	
King, A. (Lab)	4,920	12.8	
Campbell, R. (SNP)	4,011	10.4	
Park, J. (Greens)	1,071	2.8	
Pickard, D. (UKIP)	533	1.4	
Ferguson, J. (SSP)	416	1.1	
Lib Dem majority	12,571	32.60	
Electorate	62,057		
Turnout	38,556	62.13	

Lib Dem hold (3.2% from Con to Lib Dem)

FINCHLEY AND GOLDERS GREEN

		%	+/-%
*Vis, R. (Lab)	17,487	40.5	-5.8
Mennear, A. (Con)	16,746	38.8	1.0
Garden, S. (Lib Dem)	7,282	16.9	4.8
Lynch, N. (Greens)	1,136	2.6	-0.5
Jacobs, J. (UKIP)	453	1.1	0.3
Weiss, R. (Vote Dream)	110	0.3	0.0
Lab majority	741	1.71	
Electorate	69,808		
Turnout	43,214	61.90	

Lab hold (3.4% from Lab to Con)

FOLKESTONE AND HYTHE

		%	+/-%
*Howard, M. (Con)	26,161	53.9	8.9
Carroll, P. (Lib Dem)	14,481	29.9	-2.3
Tomison, M. (Lab)	6,053	12.5	-7.7
Dawe, H. (Greens)	688	1.4	0.0
Holdsworth, P. (UKIP)	619	1.3	-1.4
Jug, T. (Loony)	175	0.4	0.0
Hylton-Potts, R. (GBB)	153	0.3	0.0
Leon-Smith, G. (Senior)	151	0.3	0.0
Dunn, S. (Progress)	22	0.1	0.0
Con majority	11,680	24.08	
Electorate	70,914		
Turnout	48,503	68.40	

Con hold (5.6% from Lib Dem to Con)

FOREST OF DEAN

		%	+/-%
Harper, M. (Con)	19,474	40.9	2.1
Owen, I. (Lab)	17,425	36.6	-6.8
Coleman, C. (Lib Dem)	8,185	17.2	4.3
Hill, P. (UKIP)	1,140	2.4	0.9
Tweedie, S. (Greens)	991	2.1	-0.7
Reeve, A. (Ind)	300	0.6	0.0
Morgan, G. (EEP)	125	0.3	0.0
Con majority	2,049	4.30	
Electorate	67,225		
Turnout	47,640	70.87	

Con gain (4.5% from Lab to Con)

FOYLE

		%	+/-%
Durkan, M. (SDLP)	21,119	46.3	-3.9
McLaughlin, M. (Sinn Féin)			
	15,162	33.2	6.7
Hay, W. (DUP)	6,557	14.4	-0.8
McCann, E. (Soc EA)	1,649	3.6	0.0
Storey, E. (UUP)	1,091	2.4	-4.5
Reel, B. (Vote Dream)	31	0.1	0.0

SDLP majority	5,957	13.06
Electorate	69,207	
Turnout	45,609	65.90

SDLP hold (0.0%)

FYLDE

		%	+/-%
*Jack, M. (Con)	24,287	53.4	1.1
Parbury, W. (Lab)	11,828	26.0	-4.8
Winlow, B. (Lib Dem)	7,748	17.0	2.3
Akeroyd, T. (Lib)	1,647	3.6	0.0
Con majority	12,459	27.38	
Electorate	75,703		
Turnout	45,510	60.12	

Con hold (3.0% from Lab to Con)

GAINSBOROUGH

		%	+/-%
*Leigh, E. (Con)	20,040	43.9	-2.3
Heath, A. (Lib Dem)	12,037	26.4	-0.3
Knight, J. (Lab)	11,744	25.7	-1.4
Pearson, S. (UKIP)	1,860	4.1	0.0
Con majority	8,003	17.52	
Electorate	70,733		
Turnout	45,681	64.58	

Con hold (1.0% from Con to Lib Dem)

GATESHEAD EAST AND WASHINGTON WEST

		%	+/-%
Hodgson, S. (Lab)	20,997	60.6	-7.6
Hindle, F. (Lib Dem)	7,590	21.9	7.0
Martin, L. (Con)	4,812	13.9	-0.9
Batty, J. (UKIP)	1,269	3.7	1.5
Lab majority	13,407	38.67	
Electorate	61,421		
Turnout	34,668	56.44	

Lab hold (7.3% from Lab to Lib Dem)

GEDLING

		%	+/-%
*Coaker, V. (Lab)	20,329	46.1	-5.0
Soubry, A. (Con)	16,518	37.5	-0.8
Poynter, R. (Lib Dem)	6,070	13.8	3.2
Margerison, A. (UKIP)	741	1.7	0.0
Johnson, D. (Veritas)	411	0.9	0.0
Lab majority	3,811	8.65	
Electorate	68,917		
Turnout	44,069	63.95	

Lab hold (2.1% from Lab to Con)

GILLINGHAM

		%	+/-%
*Clark, P. (Lab)	18,621	41.2	-3.3
Butcher, T. (Con)	18,367	40.7	1.6
Stamp, A. (Lib Dem)	6,734	14.9	1.3
Mackinlay, C. (UKIP)	1,191	2.6	0.4
Bryan, G. (Ind)	254	0.6	0.0
Lab majority	254	0.56	
Electorate	72,223		
Turnout	45,167	62.54	

Lab hold (2.4% from Lab to Con)

* Member of last parliament

VALE OF GLAMORGAN

		%	+/-%
*Smith, J. (Lab)	19,481	41.2	-4.3
Cairns, A. (Con)	17,673	37.3	2.3
Hooper, M. (Lib Dem)	6,140	13.0	0.8
Shaw, B. (PlC)	2,423	5.1	-1.2
Suchorzewski, R. (UKIP)	840	1.8	0.8
Langford, K. (Lib)	605	1.3	0.0
Mules, P. (SLP)	162	0.3	0.0
Lab majority	1,808	3.82	
Electorate	68,657		
Turnout	47,324	68.93	

Lab hold (3.3% from Lab to Con)

GLASGOW CENTRAL

(New Scottish constituency)

		%	+/-%
*Sarwar, M. (Lab)	13,518	48.2	
Nelson, I. (Lib Dem)	4,987	17.8	
Kidd, B. (SNP)	4,148	14.8	
Sullivan, R. (Con)	1,757	6.3	
Masterton, G. (Greens)	1,372	4.9	
Gordon, M. (SSP)	1,110	4.0	
Hamilton, W. (BNP)	671	2.4	
Johnson, I. (SLP)	255	0.9	
Greig, T. (OCV)	139	0.5	
McKenzie, E. (Comm GB)	80	0.3	
Lab majority	8,531	30.43	
Electorate	64,053		
Turnout	28,037	43.77	

Lab hold (7.4% from Lab to Lib Dem)

GLASGOW EAST

(New Scottish constituency)

		%	+/-%
*Marshall, D. (Lab)	18,775	60.7	
McNeill, L. (SNP)	5,268	17.0	
Jackson, D. (Lib Dem)	3,665	11.9	
Thomson, C. (Con)	2,135	6.9	
Savage, G. (SSP)	1,096	3.5	
Lab majority	13,507	43.66	
Electorate	64,130		
Turnout	30,939	48.24	

Lab hold (1.5% from Lab to SNP)

GLASGOW NORTH

(New Scottish constituency)

		%	+/-%
*McKechin, A. (Lab)	11,001	39.4	
Rodger, A. (Lib Dem)	7,663	27.5	
McLean, K. (SNP)	3,614	12.9	
Pope, B. (Con)	2,441	8.7	
Bartos, M. (Greens)	2,135	7.7	
Tarlton, N. (SSP)	1,067	3.8	
Lab majority	3,338	11.96	
Electorate	55,419		
Turnout	27,921	50.38	

Lab hold (8.7% from Lab to Lib Dem)

GLASGOW NORTH EAST

(New Scottish constituency)

		%	+/-%
*Martin, M. (Speaker)	15,153	53.3	
McLaughlin, J. (SNP)	5,019	17.7	
Kelly, D. (SLP)	4,036	14.2	
Campbell, G. (SSP)	1,402	4.9	
Houston, D. (SUP)	1,266	4.5	
McLean, S. (BNP)	920	3.2	
Chambers, J. (Ind)	622	2.2	
Speaker majority	10,134	35.66	
Electorate	62,042		
Turnout	28,418	45.80	

Speaker hold (6.6% from Speaker to SNP)

GLASGOW NORTH WEST

(New Scottish constituency)

		%	+/-%
*Robertson, J. (Lab)	16,748	49.2	
Graham, P. (Lib Dem)	6,655	19.5	
Hendry, G. (SNP)	4,676	13.7	
Roxburgh, M. (Con)	3,262	9.6	
Wardrop, M. (Greens)	1,333	3.9	
Irwin, A. (SSP)	1,108	3.3	
Muir, C. (SLP)	279	0.8	
Lab majority	10,093	29.63	
Electorate	61,880		
Turnout	34,061	55.04	

Lab hold (6.8% from Lab to Lib Dem)

GLASGOW SOUTH

(New Scottish constituency)

		%	+/-%
*Harris, T. (Lab)	18,153	47.2	
Sanderson, A. (Lib Dem)	7,321	19.1	
MacLean, F. (SNP)	4,860	12.7	
McAlpine, J. (Con)	4,836	12.6	
Allan, K. (Greens)	1,692	4.4	
Stevenson, R. (SSP)	1,303	3.4	
Entwistle, D. (SLP)	266	0.7	
Lab majority	10,832	28.19	
Electorate	68,837		
Turnout	38,431	55.83	

Lab hold (4.9% from Lab to Lib Dem)

GLASGOW SOUTH WEST

(New Scottish constituency)

		%	+/-%
*Davidson, I. (Lab/Co-op)	18,653	60.2	
Dornan, J. (SNP)	4,757	15.4	
Gordon, K. (Lib Dem)	3,593	11.6	
Brady, S. (Con)	1,786	5.8	
Baldassara, K. (SSP)	1,666	5.4	
McConnachie, A. (Ind)	379	1.2	
Shaw, V. (SLP)	143	0.5	
Lab/Co-op majority	13,896	44.86	
Electorate	62,005		
Turnout	30,977	49.96	

Lab/Co-op hold (0.2% from SNP to Lab/Co-op)

GLENROTHES

(New Scottish constituency)

		%	+/-%
*MacDougall, J. (Lab)	19,395	51.9	
Beare, J. (SNP)	8,731	23.4	
Riches, E. (Lib Dem)	4,728	12.7	
Don, B. (Con)	2,651	7.1	
Rodger, G. (PPS)	716	1.9	
Balfour, M. (SSP)	705	1.9	
Smith, P. (UKIP)	440	1.2	

* Member of last parliament

Lab majority	10,664	28.54
Electorate	66,563	
Turnout	37,366	56.14

Lab hold (2.7% from Lab to SNP)

GLOUCESTER

		%	+/-%
*Dhanda, P. (Lab)	23,138	44.7	-1.1
James, P. (Con)	18,867	36.4	-1.3
Hilton, J. (Lib Dem)	7,825	15.1	0.9
Phipps, G. (UKIP)	1,116	2.2	0.5
Meloy, B. (Greens)	857	1.7	0.0
Lab majority	4,271	8.24	
Electorate	82,500		
Turnout	51,803	62.79	

Lab hold (0.1% from Con to Lab)

GORDON

(New Scottish constituency)

		%	+/-%
*Bruce, M. (Lib Dem)	20,008	45.0	
Brotchie, I. (Lab)	8,982	20.2	
Atkinson, P. (Con)	7,842	17.7	
Strathdee, J. (SNP)	7,098	16.0	
Paterson, T. (SSP)	508	1.1	
Lib Dem majority	11,026	24.81	
Electorate	71,925		
Turnout	44,438	61.78	

Lib Dem hold (3.7% from Lab to Lib Dem)

GOSPORT

		%	+/-%
*Viggers, P. (Con)	19,268	44.8	1.1
Williams, R. (Lab)	13,538	31.5	-5.6
Roberts, R. (Lib Dem)	7,145	16.6	1.5
Bowles, J. (UKIP)	1,825	4.2	1.3
Smith, A. (Greens)	1,258	2.9	0.0
Con majority	5,730	13.32	
Electorate	71,119		
Turnout	43,034	60.51	

Con hold (3.4% from Lab to Con)

GOWER

		%	+/-%
*Caton, M. (Lab)	16,786	42.5	-4.9
Murray, M. (Con)	10,083	25.5	-2.0
Tregoning, N. (Lib Dem)	7,291	18.4	6.4
Caiach, S. (PlC)	3,089	7.8	-2.5
Lewis, R. (UKIP)	1,264	3.2	0.0
Griffiths, R. (Greens)	1,029	2.6	1.0
Lab majority	6,703	16.95	
Electorate	60,925		
Turnout	39,542	64.90	

Lab hold (1.4% from Lab to Con)

GRANTHAM AND STAMFORD

		%	+/-%
*Davies, Q. (Con)	22,109	46.9	0.8
Selby, I. (Lab)	14,664	31.1	-5.2
O'Connor, P. (Lib Dem)	7,838	16.6	2.2
Rising, S. (UKIP)	1,498	3.2	0.0
Brown, B. (Eng Dem)	774	1.6	0.0
Andrews, J. (CRD)	264	0.6	0.0
Con majority	7,445	15.79	
Electorate	74,074		
Turnout	47,147	63.65	

Con hold (3.0% from Lab to Con)

GRAVESHAM

		%	+/-%
Holloway, A. (Con)	19,739	43.7	4.9
*Pond, C. (Lab)	19,085	42.2	-7.7
Parmenter, B. (Lib Dem)	4,851	10.7	1.5
Coates, G. (UKIP)	850	1.9	-0.2
Nickerson, C. (Ind)	654	1.5	0.0
Con majority	654	1.45	
Electorate	68,705		
Turnout	45,179	65.76	

Con gain (6.3% from Lab to Con)

GREAT GRIMSBY

		%	+/-%
*Mitchell, A. (Lab)	15,512	47.1	-10.9
Taylor, G. (Con)	7,858	23.8	0.7
de Fraitas, A. (Lib Dem)	6,356	19.3	0.3
Fyfe, S. (BNP)	1,338	4.1	0.0
Grant, M. (UKIP)	1,239	3.8	0.0
Brookes, D. (Greens)	661	2.0	0.0
Lab majority	7,654	23.22	
Electorate	63,711		
Turnout	32,964	51.74	

Lab hold (5.8% from Lab to Con)

GREAT YARMOUTH

		%	+/-%
*Wright, A. (Lab)	18,850	45.6	-4.8
Fox, M. (Con)	15,795	38.2	-0.9
Newton, S. (Lib Dem)	4,585	11.1	2.7
Poole, B. (UKIP)	1,759	4.3	2.2
Skipper, M. (LCA)	389	0.9	0.0
Lab majority	3,055	7.38	
Electorate	68,887		
Turnout	41,378	60.07	

Lab hold (2.0% from Lab to Con)

GREENWICH AND WOOLWICH

		%	+/-%
*Raynsford, N. (Lab)	17,527	49.2	-11.3
Le Breton, C. (Lib Dem)	7,381	20.7	5.1
Craig, A. (Con)	7,142	20.1	0.8
Sharman, D. (Greens)	1,579	4.4	0.0
Bushell, G. (Eng Dem)	1,216	3.4	0.0
Gain, S. (UKIP)	709	2.0	-0.1
Nagalingam, P. (Ind)	61	0.2	0.0
Lab majority	10,146	28.49	
Electorate	64,033		
Turnout	35,615	55.62	

Lab hold (8.2% from Lab to Lib Dem)

GUILDFORD

		%	+/-%
Milton, A. (Con)	22,595	43.8	2.3
*Doughty, S. (Lib Dem)	22,248	43.1	0.5
Landles, K. (Lab)	5,054	9.8	-3.9
Pletts, J. (Greens)	811	1.6	0.0
Haslam, M. (UKIP)	645	1.3	-0.3
Morris, J. (TPP)	166	0.3	0.0
Lavin, V. (Ind)	112	0.2	0.0
Con majority	347	0.67	
Electorate	75,566		
Turnout	51,631	68.33	

Con gain (0.9% from Lib Dem to Con)

* Member of last parliament

HACKNEY NORTH AND STOKE NEWINGTON

		%	+/-%
*Abbott, D. (Lab)	14,268	48.6	-12.5
Blanchard, J. (Lib Dem)	6,841	23.3	9.2
Hurer, E. (Con)	4,218	14.4	-0.6
Borris, M. (Greens)	2,907	9.9	2.5
Vail, D. (Ind)	602	2.1	0.0
Sen, N. (SLP)	296	1.0	-1.5
Barrow, N. (Loony)	248	0.8	0.0
Lab majority	7,427	25.28	
Electorate	59,260		
Turnout	29,380	49.58	

Lab hold (10.8% from Lab to Lib Dem)

HACKNEY SOUTH AND SHOREDITCH

		%	+/-%
Hillier, M. (Lab/Co-op)	17,048	52.9	-11.3
Bayliss, H. (Lib Dem)	6,844	21.2	6.7
Moss, J. (Con)	4,524	14.0	0.3
Dan Lyan, I. (Greens)	1,779	5.5	0.0
Ryan, D. (Respect)	1,437	4.5	0.0
Rae, B. (Lib)	313	1.0	0.0
Goldman, M. (Comm)	200	0.6	-0.2
Leff, J. (WRP)	92	0.3	-0.2
Lab/Co-op majority	10,204	31.65	
Electorate	64,818		
Turnout	32,237	49.73	

Lab/Co-op hold (9.0% from Lab/Co-op to Lib Dem)

HALESOWEN AND ROWLEY REGIS

		%	+/-%
*Heal, S. (Lab)	19,243	46.6	-6.4
Jones, L. (Con)	14,906	36.1	1.8
Turner, M. (Lib Dem)	5,204	12.6	2.2
Sinclair, N. (UKIP)	1,974	4.8	2.4
Lab majority	4,337	10.49	
Electorate	65,748		
Turnout	41,327	62.86	

Lab hold (4.1% from Lab to Con)

HALIFAX

		%	+/-%
Riordan, L. (Lab/Co-op)	16,579	41.8	-7.2
Hopkins, K. (Con)	13,162	33.2	-0.7
Taylor, M. (Lib Dem)	7,100	17.9	3.4
Wallace, G. (BNP)	2,627	6.6	0.0
Holmes, T. (NF)	191	0.5	0.0
Lab/Co-op majority	3,417	8.62	
Electorate	64,861		
Turnout	39,659	61.14	

Lab/Co-op hold (3.3% from Lab/Co-op to Con)

HALTEMPRICE AND HOWDEN

		%	+/-%
*Davis, D. (Con)	22,792	47.5	4.2
Neal, J. (Lib Dem)	17,676	36.8	-2.1
Hart, E. (Lab)	6,104	12.7	-3.0
Mainprize, J. (BNP)	798	1.7	0.0
Lane, P. (UKIP)	659	1.4	-0.8
Con majority	5,116	10.65	
Electorate	68,471		
Turnout	48,029	70.15	

Con hold (3.2% from Lib Dem to Con)

HALTON

		%	+/-%
*Twigg, D. (Lab)	21,460	62.8	-6.4
Bloom, C. (Con)	6,854	20.1	1.5
Barlow, R. (Lib Dem)	5,869	17.2	4.9
Lab majority	14,606	42.73	
Electorate	64,379		
Turnout	34,183	53.10	

Lab hold (3.9% from Lab to Con)

HAMMERSMITH AND FULHAM

		%	+/-%
Hands, G. (Con)	22,407	45.4	5.6
Smallman, M. (Lab)	17,378	35.2	-9.1
Bullion, A. (Lib Dem)	7,116	14.4	2.6
Harrold, F. (Greens)	1,933	3.9	0.7
Fisher, G. (UKIP)	493	1.0	0.2
Con majority	5,029	10.20	
Electorate	79,082		
Turnout	49,327	62.37	

Con gain (7.4% from Lab to Con)

EAST HAMPSHIRE

		%	+/-%
*Mates, M. (Con)	24,273	45.7	-2.0
Bright, R. (Lib Dem)	18,764	35.3	5.4
Broughton, M. (Lab)	8,519	16.0	-3.6
Samuel-Camps, D. (UKIP)	1,583	3.0	0.2
Con majority	5,509	10.37	
Electorate	58,673		
Turnout	53,139	90.57	

Con hold (3.7% from Con to Lib Dem)

NORTH EAST HAMPSHIRE

		%	+/-%
*Arbuthnot, J. (Con)	25,407	53.7	0.5
Carew, A. (Lib Dem)	12,858	27.2	4.2
McGrath, K. (Lab)	7,630	16.1	-3.8
Birch, P. (UKIP)	1,392	2.9	-0.9
Con majority	12,549	26.54	
Electorate	72,939		
Turnout	47,287	64.83	

Con hold (1.8% from Con to Lib Dem)

NORTH WEST HAMPSHIRE

		%	+/-%
*Young, G. (Con)	26,005	50.7	0.6
Tod, M. (Lib Dem)	12,741	24.9	3.6
Mumford, M. (Lab)	10,594	20.7	-4.8
Sumner, P. (UKIP)	1,925	3.8	0.5
Con majority	13,264	25.87	
Electorate	79,763		
Turnout	51,265	64.27	

Con hold (1.5% from Con to Lib Dem)

HAMPSTEAD AND HIGHGATE

		%	+/-%
*Jackson, G. (Lab)	14,615	38.3	-8.6
Wauchope, P. (Con)	10,886	28.5	3.9
Fordham, E. (Lib Dem)	10,293	27.0	6.4
Berry, S. (Greens)	2,013	5.3	0.6
Nielsen, M. (UKIP)	275	0.7	-0.2
Weiss, R. (Vote Dream)	91	0.2	0.0
Lab majority	3,729	9.77	
Electorate	68,737		
Turnout	38,173	55.53	

Lab hold (6.2% from Lab to Con)

* Member of last parliament

HARBOROUGH

		%	+/-%
*Garnier, E. (Con)	20,536	42.9	-1.8
Hope, J. (Lib Dem)	16,644	34.7	1.4
Evans, P. (Lab)	9,222	19.2	-0.7
King, M. (UKIP)	1,520	3.2	1.2
Con majority	3,892	8.12	
Electorate	74,583		
Turnout	47,922	64.25	

Con hold (1.6% from Con to Lib Dem)

HARLOW

		%	+/-%
*Rammell, B. (Lab)	16,453	41.4	-6.4
Halfon, R. (Con)	16,356	41.2	6.4
Spenceley, L. (Lib Dem)	5,002	12.6	-0.8
Felgate, J. (UKIP)	981	2.5	-0.6
Bennett, A. (Veritas)	941	2.4	0.0
Lab majority	97	0.24	
Electorate	63,500		
Turnout	39,733	62.57	

Lab hold (0.0%)

HARROGATE AND KNARESBOROUGH

		%	+/-%
*Willis, P. (Lib Dem)	24,113	56.3	0.7
Punyer, M. (Con)	13,684	31.9	-2.7
Ferris, L. (Lab)	3,627	8.5	1.1
Royston, C. (UKIP)	845	2.0	0.2
Banner, C. (BNP)	466	1.1	0.0
Allman, J. (AFC)	123	0.3	0.0
Lib Dem majority	10,429	24.33	
Electorate	65,622		
Turnout	42,858	65.31	

Lib Dem hold (1.7% from Con to Lib Dem)

HARROW EAST

		%	+/-%
*McNulty, T. (Lab)	23,445	46.1	-9.2
Ashton, D. (Con)	18,715	36.8	4.7
Nandhra, P. (Lib Dem)	7,747	15.2	2.7
Cronin, P. (UKIP)	916	1.8	0.0
Lab majority	4,730	9.31	
Electorate	84,033		
Turnout	50,823	60.48	

Lab hold (6.9% from Lab to Con)

HARROW WEST

		%	+/-%
*Thomas, G. (Lab/Co-op)	20,298	42.5	-7.1
Freer, M. (Con)	18,270	38.3	1.8
Noyce, C. (Lib Dem)	8,188	17.1	4.3
Cronin, J. (UKIP)	576	1.2	0.1
Daver, B. (Ind)	427	0.9	0.0
Lab/Co-op majority	2,028	4.25	
Electorate	74,228		
Turnout	47,759	64.34	

Lab/Co-op hold (4.5% from Lab/Co-op to Con)

HARTLEPOOL

		%	+/-%
*Wright, I. (Lab)	18,251	51.5	-7.6
Dunn, J. (Lib Dem)	10,773	30.4	15.4
Vigar, A. (Con)	4,058	11.5	-9.4
Harrison, F. (SLP)	373	1.1	-1.3
Hobbs, J. (Ind)	288	0.8	0.0
Springer, G. (UKIP)	275	0.8	0.0
Headbanger, S. (Loony)	162	0.5	0.0
Lab majority	7,478	21.10	
Electorate	68,776		
Turnout	35,436	51.52	

Lab hold (11.5% from Lab to Lib Dem)

HARWICH

		%	+/-%
Carswell, D. (Con)	21,235	42.1	1.9
*Henderson, I. (Lab)	20,315	40.3	-5.3
Tully, K. (Lib Dem)	5,913	11.7	3.2
Titford, J. (UKIP)	2,314	4.6	-0.5
Tipple, J. (Respect)	477	1.0	0.0
Humphrey, C. (ND)	154	0.3	0.0
Con majority	920	1.83	
Electorate	80,474		
Turnout	50,408	62.64	

Con gain (3.6% from Lab to Con)

HASTINGS AND RYE

		%	+/-%
*Foster, M. (Lab)	18,107	42.1	-5.0
Coote, M. (Con)	16,081	37.4	0.8
Stevens, R. (Lib Dem)	6,479	15.1	4.7
Grant, T. (UKIP)	1,098	2.6	0.3
Phillips, S. (Greens)	1,032	2.4	0.7
Ord-Clarke, J. (Loony)	207	0.5	0.0
Lab majority	2,026	4.71	
Electorate	63,437		
Turnout	43,004	67.79	

Lab hold (2.9% from Lab to Con)

HAVANT

		%	+/-%
*Willetts, D. (Con)	18,370	44.4	0.5
Bogle, S. (Lab)	11,862	28.7	-4.9
Bentley, A. (Lib Dem)	8,358	20.2	1.7
Dawes, T. (Greens)	1,006	2.4	0.5
Harris, S. (UKIP)	998	2.4	1.0
Johnson, I. (BNP)	562	1.4	0.0
Thomas, R. (Veritas)	195	0.5	0.0
Con majority	6,508	15.74	
Electorate	68,545		
Turnout	41,351	60.33	

Con hold (2.7% from Lab to Con)

HAYES AND HARLINGTON

		%	+/-%
*McDonnell, J. (Lab)	19,009	58.7	-7.0
Worrall, R. (Con)	8,162	25.2	1.1
Ball, J. (Lib Dem)	3,174	9.8	3.8
Hazel, T. (BNP)	830	2.6	0.4
Haley, M. (UKIP)	552	1.7	0.0
Outten, B. (Greens)	442	1.4	0.0
Goddard, P. (Ind)	220	0.7	0.0
Lab majority	10,847	33.49	
Electorate	57,493		
Turnout	32,389	56.34	

Lab hold (4.0% from Lab to Con)

HAZEL GROVE

		%	+/-%
*Stunell, A. (Lib Dem)	19,355	49.5	-2.6
White, A. (Con)	11,607	29.7	-0.4
Graystone, A. (Lab)	6,834	17.5	1.3
Ryan, K. (UKIP)	1,321	3.4	1.7

* Member of last parliament

HAZEL GROVE *continued*

Lib Dem majority	7,748	19.81
Electorate	64,376	
Turnout	39,117	60.76

Lib Dem hold (1.1% from Lib Dem to Con)

HEMEL HEMPSTEAD

		%	+/-%
Penning, M. (Con)	19,000	40.3	1.9
*McWalter, T. (Lab)	18,501	39.3	-7.3
Grayson, R. (Lib Dem)	8,089	17.2	4.4
Newton, B. (UKIP)	1,518	3.2	1.1
Con majority	499	1.06	
Electorate	73,095		
Turnout	47,108	64.45	

Con gain (4.6% from Lab/Co-op to Con)

HEMSWORTH

		%	+/-%
*Trickett, J. (Lab)	21,630	58.8	-6.6
Mortimer, J. (Con)	8,149	22.2	1.1
Hall-Matthews, D. (Lib Dem)			
	5,766	15.7	4.4
Burdon, J. (UKIP)	1,247	3.4	0.0
Lab majority	13,481	36.64	
Electorate	67,339		
Turnout	36,792	54.64	

Lab hold (3.9% from Lab to Con)

HENDON

		%	+/-%
*Dismore, A. (Lab)	18,596	44.5	-8.0
Evans, R. (Con)	15,897	38.0	3.7
Boethe, N. (Lib Dem)	5,831	13.9	2.4
Williams, D. (Greens)	754	1.8	0.0
Smallman, M. (UKIP)	637	1.5	0.5
Weiss, R. (Vote Dream)	68	0.2	0.0
Stewart, M. (PDP)	56	0.1	0.0
Lab majority	2,699	6.45	
Electorate	71,764		
Turnout	41,839	58.30	

Lab hold (5.9% from Lab to Con)

HENLEY

		%	+/-%
*Johnson, B. (Con)	24,894	53.5	7.4
Turner, D. (Lib Dem)	12,101	26.0	-1.0
Saeed, K. (Lab)	6,862	14.8	-6.4
Stevenson, M. (Greens)	1,518	3.3	0.7
Gray-Fisk, D. (UKIP)	1,162	2.5	-0.7
Con majority	12,793	27.49	
Electorate	68,538		
Turnout	46,537	67.90	

Con hold (4.2% from Lib Dem to Con)

HEREFORD

		%	+/-%
*Keetch, P. (Lib Dem)	20,285	43.3	2.4
Taylor, V. (Con)	19,323	41.2	2.5
Calver, T. (Lab)	4,800	10.2	-4.9
Lunt, B. (Greens)	1,052	2.2	-0.4
Kingsley, C. (UKIP)	1,030	2.2	-0.5
Morton, P. (Ind)	404	0.9	0.0
Lib Dem majority	962	2.05	
Electorate	71,813		
Turnout	46,894	65.30	

Lib Dem hold (0.1% from Lib Dem to Con)

HERTFORD AND STORTFORD

		%	+/-%
*Prisk, M. (Con)	25,074	50.5	5.8
Henry, R. (Lab)	11,977	24.1	-8.7
Lucas, J. (Lib Dem)	9,129	18.4	-1.5
Hart, P. (Greens)	1,914	3.9	0.0
Sodey, D. (UKIP)	1,026	2.1	-0.6
Lemay, D. (Veritas)	572	1.2	0.0
Con majority	13,097	26.36	
Electorate	73,394		
Turnout	49,692	67.71	

Con hold (7.2% from Lab to Con)

NORTH EAST HERTFORDSHIRE

		%	+/-%
*Heald, O. (Con)	22,402	47.3	3.2
Harrop, A. (Lab)	13,264	28.0	-8.4
Coleman, I. (Lib Dem)	10,147	21.4	4.2
Hitchman, D. (UKIP)	1,561	3.3	1.0
Con majority	9,138	19.29	
Electorate	72,190		
Turnout	47,374	65.62	

Con hold (5.8% from Lab to Con)

SOUTH WEST HERTFORDSHIRE

		%	+/-%
Gauke, D. (Con)	23,494	46.9	2.6
Featherstone, E. (Lib Dem)			
	15,021	30.0	3.7
Cross, K. (Lab)	10,466	20.9	-6.1
Rodden, C. (UKIP)	1,107	2.2	0.4
Con majority	8,473	16.92	
Electorate	73,170		
Turnout	50,088	68.45	

Con hold (0.5% from Con to Lib Dem)

HERTSMERE

		%	+/-%
*Clappison, J. (Con)	22,665	53.2	5.4
Tebb, K. (Lab)	11,572	27.2	-8.8
Davies, J. (Lib Dem)	7,817	18.4	3.2
Dry, J. (SLP)	518	1.2	0.3
Con majority	11,093	26.06	
Electorate	67,572		
Turnout	42,572	63.00	

Con hold (7.1% from Lab to Con)

HEXHAM

		%	+/-%
*Atkinson, P. (Con)	17,605	42.4	-2.2
Graham, K. (Lab)	12,585	30.3	-8.3
Duffield, A. (Lib Dem)	10,673	25.7	10.7
Riddell, I. (Eng Dem)	521	1.3	0.0
Davison, T. (IP)	129	0.3	0.0
Con majority	5,020	12.09	
Electorate	60,374		
Turnout	41,513	68.76	

Con hold (3.1% from Lab to Con)

HEYWOOD AND MIDDLETON

		%	+/-%
*Dobbin, J. (Lab/Co-op)	19,438	49.8	-7.9
Pathmarajah, S. (Con)	8,355	21.4	-6.2
Lavin, C. (Lib Dem)	7,261	18.6	7.4
Aronsson, G. (BNP)	1,855	4.8	0.0
Burke, P. (Lib)	1,377	3.5	0.9
Whittaker, J. (UKIP)	767	2.0	0.0

* Member of last parliament

Lab/Co-op majority	11,083	28.38
Electorate	71,510	
Turnout	39,053	54.61

Lab/Co-op hold (0.9% from Lab/Co-op to Con)

HIGH PEAK

		%	+/-%
*Levitt, T. (Lab)	19,809	39.6	-7.0
Bingham, A. (Con)	19,074	38.2	0.9
Godwin, M. (Lib Dem)	10,000	20.0	3.9
Schwartz, M. (UKIP)	1,106	2.2	0.0
Lab majority	735	1.47	
Electorate	75,275		
Turnout	49,989	66.41	

Lab hold (3.9% from Lab to Con)

HITCHIN AND HARPENDEN

		%	+/-%
*Lilley, P. (Con)	23,627	49.9	2.5
Hedges, H. (Lib Dem)	12,234	25.8	7.8
Orrett, P. (Lab)	10,499	22.2	-10.4
Saunders, J. (UKIP)	828	1.8	0.4
Rigby, P. (Ind)	199	0.4	-0.4
Con majority	11,393	24.04	
Electorate	67,207		
Turnout	47,387	70.51	

Con hold (2.7% from Con to Lib Dem)

HOLBORN AND ST PANCRAS

		%	+/-%
*Dobson, F. (Lab)	14,857	43.2	-10.6
Fraser, J. (Lib Dem)	10,070	29.3	11.3
James, M. (Con)	6,482	18.9	2.0
Oliver, A. (Greens)	2,798	8.1	2.1
Weiss, R. (Vote Dream)	152	0.4	0.0
Lab majority	4,787	13.93	
Electorate	68,237		
Turnout	34,359	50.35	

Lab hold (11.0% from Lab to Lib Dem)

HORNCHURCH

		%	+/-%
Brokenshire, J. (Con)	16,355	42.9	0.6
*Cryer, J. (Lab)	15,875	41.6	-4.9
Green, N. (Lib Dem)	2,894	7.6	-0.7
Moore, I. (BNP)	1,313	3.4	0.0
Webb, L. (UKIP)	1,033	2.7	0.2
Brown, M. (RA)	395	1.0	0.0
Williamson, G. (Third)	304	0.8	0.3
Con majority	480	1.26	
Electorate	59,773		
Turnout	38,169	63.86	

Con gain (2.7% from Lab to Con)

HORNSEY AND WOOD GREEN

		%	+/-%
Featherstone, L. (Lib Dem)			
	20,512	43.3	17.6
*Roche, B. (Lab)	18,117	38.3	-11.6
Forrest, P. (Con)	6,014	12.7	-3.0
Forbes, J. (Greens)	2,377	5.0	0.0
Freshwater, R. (UKIP)	310	0.7	0.0
Lib Dem majority	2,395	5.06	
Electorate	76,621		
Turnout	47,330	61.77	

Lib Dem gain (14.6% from Lab to Lib Dem)

* Member of last parliament

HORSHAM

		%	+/-%
*Maude, F. (Con)	27,240	50.0	-1.5
Sharpley, R. (Lib Dem)	14,613	26.8	2.3
Chishti, R. (Lab)	9,320	17.1	-3.1
Miller, H. (UKIP)	2,552	4.7	1.8
Duggan, J. (PJP)	416	0.8	0.0
Jeremiah, M. (PHF)	354	0.7	0.0
Con majority	12,627	23.17	
Electorate	80,974		
Turnout	54,495	67.30	

Con hold (1.9% from Con to Lib Dem)

HOUGHTON AND WASHINGTON EAST

		%	+/-%
*Kemp, F. (Lab)	22,310	64.3	-8.9
Greenfield, M. (Lib Dem)	6,245	18.0	5.5
Devenish, T. (Con)	4,772	13.8	-0.5
Richardson, J. (BNP)	1,367	3.9	0.0
Lab majority	16,065	46.30	
Electorate	67,089		
Turnout	34,694	51.71	

Lab hold (7.2% from Lab to Lib Dem)

HOVE

		%	+/-%
Barlow, C. (Lab)	16,786	37.5	-8.4
Boles, N. (Con)	16,366	36.5	-1.8
Elgood, P. (Lib Dem)	8,002	17.9	8.8
Ballam, A. (Greens)	2,575	5.8	2.5
Bower, S. (UKIP)	575	1.3	0.4
O'Keefe, P. (Respect)	268	0.6	0.0
Dobbs, B. (Ind)	95	0.2	0.1
Franklin, R. (Silent)	78	0.2	0.0
Ralfe, B. (Ind)	51	0.1	0.0
Lab majority	420	0.94	
Electorate	69,939		
Turnout	44,796	64.05	

Lab hold (3.3% from Lab to Con)

HUDDERSFIELD

		%	+/-%
*Sheerman, B. (Lab/Co-op)	16,341	46.8	-6.5
Bone, E. (Lib Dem)	7,990	22.9	7.9
Meacock, D. (Con)	7,597	21.7	-3.1
Stewart-Turner, J. (Greens)	1,651	4.7	1.2
Hanson, K. (BNP)	1,036	3.0	0.0
Quarmby, T. (Ind)	325	0.9	0.0
Lab/Co-op majority	8,351	23.90	
Electorate	61,723		
Turnout	34,940	56.61	

Lab/Co-op hold (7.2% from Lab/Co-op to Lib Dem)

HULL EAST

		%	+/-%
*Prescott, J. (Lab)	17,609	56.8	-7.8
Sloan, A. (Lib Dem)	5,862	18.9	4.0
Lindsay, K. (Con)	4,038	13.0	-0.8
Siddle, A. (BNP)	1,022	3.3	0.0
Toker, J. (Lib)	1,018	3.3	0.0
Morris, G. (Veritas)	750	2.4	0.0
Noon, R. (Ind)	334	1.1	0.0
Muir, L. (SLP)	207	0.7	-2.0
Wagner, C. (LCA)	182	0.6	0.0

HULL EAST *continued*

Lab majority	11,747	37.87
Electorate	65,407	
Turnout	31,022	47.43

Lab hold (5.9% from Lab to Lib Dem)

HULL NORTH

		%	+/-%
Johnson, D. (Lab)	15,364	51.9	-5.2
Healy, D. (Lib Dem)	8,013	27.1	7.4
Rivlin, L. (Con)	3,822	12.9	-4.2
Deane, M. (Greens)	858	2.9	0.0
Wainwright, B. (BNP)	766	2.6	0.0
Robinson, T. (Veritas)	389	1.3	0.0
Veasey, C. (Northern)	193	0.7	0.0
Wagner, C. (LCA)	179	0.6	-1.1
Lab majority	7,351	24.85	
Electorate	62,590		
Turnout	29,584	47.27	

Lab hold (6.3% from Lab to Lib Dem)

HULL WEST AND HESSLE

		%	+/-%
*Johnson, A. (Lab)	15,305	55.0	-3.4
Nolan, D. (Lib Dem)	5,855	21.1	6.0
Woods, K. (Con)	5,769	20.7	0.2
Wallis, S. (Veritas)	889	3.2	0.0
Lab majority	9,450	33.97	
Electorate	61,494		
Turnout	27,818	45.24	

Lab hold (4.7% from Lab to Lib Dem)

HUNTINGDON

		%	+/-%
*Djanogly, J. (Con)	26,646	50.8	0.9
Huppert, J. (Lib Dem)	13,799	26.3	2.5
Sartain, S. (Lab)	9,821	18.7	-4.1
Norman, D. (UKIP)	2,152	4.1	0.7
Con majority	12,847	24.51	
Electorate	83,843		
Turnout	52,418	62.52	

Con hold (0.8% from Con to Lib Dem)

HYNDBURN

		%	+/-%
*Pope, G. (Lab)	18,136	46.0	-8.7
Mawdsley, J. (Con)	12,549	31.8	-1.4
Greene, B. (Lib Dem)	5,577	14.1	4.5
Jackson, C. (BNP)	2,444	6.2	0.0
Whittaker, J. (UKIP)	743	1.9	-0.7
Lab majority	5,587	14.16	
Electorate	67,086		
Turnout	39,449	58.80	

Lab hold (3.7% from Lab to Con)

ILFORD NORTH

		%	+/-%
Scott, L. (Con)	18,781	43.7	3.1
*Perham, L. (Lab)	17,128	39.8	-6.0
Gayler, M. (Lib Dem)	5,896	13.7	2.0
Cross, A. (UKIP)	902	2.1	0.2
Levin, M. (Ind)	293	0.7	0.0
Con majority	1,653	3.84	
Electorate	70,718		
Turnout	43,000	60.80	

Con gain (4.6% from Lab to Con)

ILFORD SOUTH

		%	+/-%
*Gapes, M. (Lab/Co-op)	20,856	48.9	-10.8
Metcalfe, S. (Con)	11,628	27.2	1.5
Lake, M. (Lib Dem)	8,761	20.5	9.3
Rana, K. (BPP)	763	1.8	0.0
Taylor, C. (UKIP)	685	1.6	-1.8
Lab/Co-op majority	9,228	21.61	
Electorate	79,639		
Turnout	42,693	53.61	

Lab/Co-op hold (6.1% from Lab/Co-op to Con)

INVERCLYDE

(New Scottish constituency)

		%	+/-%
*Cairns, D. (Lab)	18,318	50.8	
McMillan, S. (SNP)	7,059	19.6	
Herbison, D. (Lib Dem)	6,123	17.0	
Fraser, G. (Con)	3,692	10.2	
Landels, D. (SSP)	906	2.5	
Lab majority	11,259	31.19	
Electorate	59,291		
Turnout	36,098	60.88	

Lab hold (2.5% from Lab to SNP)

INVERNESS, NAIRN, BADENOCH AND STRATHSPEY

(New Scottish constituency)

		%	+/-%
Alexander, D. (Lib Dem)	17,830	40.3	
*Stewart, D. (Lab)	13,682	30.9	
Thompson, D. (SNP)	5,992	13.5	
Rowantree, R. (Con)	4,579	10.4	
MacLeod, D. (Greens)	1,065	2.4	
Lawson, D. (Publican)	678	1.5	
Macdonald, G. (SSP)	429	1.0	
Lib Dem majority	4,148	9.37	
Electorate	69,636		
Turnout	44,255	63.55	

Lib Dem gain (6.0% from Lab to Lib Dem)

IPSWICH

		%	+/-%
*Mole, C. (Lab)	18,336	43.8	-7.5
West, P. (Con)	13,004	31.1	0.5
Atkins, R. (Lib Dem)	8,464	20.2	5.0
West, A. (UKIP)	1,134	2.7	1.1
Kay, J. (Eng Dem)	641	1.5	0.0
Wainman, S. (Ind)	299	0.7	0.0
Lab majority	5,332	12.73	
Electorate	68,825		
Turnout	41,878	60.85	

Lab hold (4.0% from Lab to Con)

ISLE OF WIGHT

		%	+/-%
*Turner, A. (Con)	32,717	49.0	9.2
Rowlands, A. (Lib Dem)	19,739	29.5	-5.8
Chiverton, M. (Lab)	11,484	17.2	1.9
Tarrant, M. (UKIP)	2,352	3.5	0.2
Corby, E. (Ind)	551	0.8	-1.4
Con majority	12,978	19.42	
Electorate	109,046		
Turnout	66,843	61.30	

Con hold (7.5% from Lib Dem to Con)

* Member of last parliament

ISLINGTON NORTH

		%	+/-%
*Corbyn, J. (Lab)	16,118	51.2	-10.7
Willoughby, L. (Lib Dem)	9,402	29.9	10.9
Talbot, N. (Con)	3,740	11.9	1.1
Nott, J. (Greens)	2,234	7.1	0.9
Lab majority	6,716	21.32	
Electorate	58,427		
Turnout	31,494	53.90	

Lab hold (10.8% from Lab to Lib Dem)

ISLINGTON SOUTH AND FINSBURY

		%	+/-%
Thornberry, E. (Lab)	12,345	39.9	-14.1
Fox, B. (Lib Dem)	11,861	38.3	10.2
McLean, M. (Con)	4,594	14.8	1.2
Humphreys, J. (Greens)	1,471	4.8	0.0
Theophanides, P. (UKIP)	470	1.5	0.0
Gardner, A. (Loony)	189	0.6	0.0
Gidden, C. (Ind)	31	0.1	-0.9
Lab majority	484	1.56	
Electorate	57,748		
Turnout	30,961	53.61	

Lab hold (12.1% from Lab to Lib Dem)

ISLWYN

		%	+/-%
*Touhig, D. (Lab/Co-op)	19,687	63.8	2.2
Criddle, J. (PlC)	3,947	12.8	0.9
Dillon, L. (Lib Dem)	3,873	12.6	-0.7
Howells, P. (Con)	3,358	10.9	2.9
Lab/Co-op majority	15,740	51.00	
Electorate	50,595		
Turnout	30,865	61.00	

Lab/Co-op hold (0.7% from PlC to Lab/Co-op)

JARROW

		%	+/-%
*Hepburn, S. (Lab)	20,554	60.5	-5.6
Schardt, B. (Lib Dem)	6,650	19.6	4.5
Jack, L. (Con)	4,807	14.2	-0.5
Badger, A. (UKIP)	1,567	4.6	2.5
Nettleship, R. (SNH)	400	1.2	0.0
Lab majority	13,904	40.92	
Electorate	61,814		
Turnout	33,978	54.97	

Lab hold (5.1% from Lab to Lib Dem)

KEIGHLEY

		%	+/-%
*Cryer, A. (Lab)	20,720	44.7	-3.5
Poulsen, K. (Con)	15,868	34.3	-4.7
Fekri, N. (Lib Dem)	5,484	11.8	0.9
Griffin, N. (BNP)	4,240	9.2	0.0
Lab majority	4,852	10.48	
Electorate	68,229		
Turnout	46,312	67.88	

Lab hold (0.6% from Con to Lab)

KENSINGTON AND CHELSEA

		%	+/-%
Rifkind, M. (Con)	18,144	57.9	3.4
Kingsley, J. (Lib Dem)	5,726	18.3	2.5
Atkinson, C. (Lab)	5,521	17.6	-5.6
Stephenson, J. (Greens)	1,342	4.3	0.2
Eilorat, M. (UKIP)	395	1.3	-0.2
Bovill, A. (Ind)	107	0.3	0.0
Adams, E. (Green Soc)	101	0.3	0.0

* Member of last parliament

Con majority	12,418	39.63	
Electorate	62,662		
Turnout	31,336	50.01	

Con hold (0.5% from Lib Dem to Con)

KETTERING

		%	+/-%
Hollobone, P. (Con)	25,401	45.7	2.2
*Sawford, P. (Lab)	22,100	39.7	-5.0
Aron, R. (Lib Dem)	6,882	12.4	2.2
Clark, R. (UKIP)	1,263	2.3	0.6
Con majority	3,301	5.93	
Electorate	81,887		
Turnout	55,646	67.95	

Con gain (3.6% from Lab to Con)

KILMARNOCK AND LOUDOUN

(New Scottish constituency)

		%	+/-%
*Browne, D. (Lab)	20,976	47.3	
Coffey, D. (SNP)	12,273	27.7	
Smith, G. (Con)	5,026	11.3	
Lang, K. (Lib Dem)	4,945	11.1	
Kerr, H. (SSP)	833	1.9	
Robertson, R. (UKIP)	330	0.7	
Lab majority	8,703	19.61	
Electorate	72,851		
Turnout	44,383	60.92	

Lab hold (5.5% from Lab to SNP)

KINGSTON AND SURBITON

		%	+/-%
*Davey, E. (Lib Dem)	25,397	51.1	-9.1
Davis, K. (Con)	16,431	33.0	4.8
Parrott, N. (Lab)	6,553	13.2	4.4
Thornton, B. (UKIP)	657	1.3	0.4
Hayball, J. (SLP)	366	0.7	0.1
Henson, D. (Veritas)	200	0.4	0.0
Weiss, R. (Vote Dream)	146	0.3	0.0
Lib Dem majority	8,966	18.02	
Electorate	72,671		
Turnout	49,750	68.46	

Lib Dem hold (7.0% from Lib Dem to Con)

KINGSWOOD

		%	+/-%
*Berry, R. (Lab)	26,491	47.0	-7.8
Inksip, O. (Con)	18,618	33.1	4.7
Brewer, G. (Lib Dem)	9,089	16.1	1.4
Knight, J. (UKIP)	1,444	2.6	0.5
Burnside, D. (Ind)	669	1.2	0.0
Lab majority	7,873	13.98	
Electorate	84,400		
Turnout	56,311	66.72	

Lab hold (6.3% from Lab to Con)

KIRKCALDY AND COWDENBEATH

(New Scottish constituency)

		%	+/-%
*Brown, G. (Lab)	24,278	58.1	
Bath, A. (SNP)	6,062	14.5	
Cole-Hamilton, A. (Lib Dem)			
	5,450	13.0	
Randall, S. (Con)	4,308	10.3	
West, S. (SSP)	666	1.6	
Adams, P. (UKIP)	516	1.2	
Parker, J. (Scot Senior)	425	1.0	
Kwantes, E. (Ind)	47	0.1	
Sargent, P. (Ind)	44	0.1	
Lab majority	18,216	43.58	
Electorate	71,606		
Turnout	41,796	58.37	

Lab hold (1.8% from SNP to Lab)

KNOWSLEY NORTH AND SEFTON EAST

		%	+/-%
*Howarth, G. (Lab)	23,461	63.3	-3.4
Clucas, F. (Lib Dem)	7,192	19.4	5.6
Purewal, N. (Con)	5,064	13.7	-2.6
McDermott, M. (BNP)	872	2.4	0.0
Whatham, S. (SLP)	464	1.3	-0.3
Lab majority	16,269	43.91	
Electorate	70,403		
Turnout	37,053	52.63	

Lab hold (4.5% from Lab to Lib Dem)

KNOWSLEY SOUTH

		%	+/-%
*O'Hara, E. (Lab)	24,820	68.1	-3.2
Smithson, D. (Lib Dem)	7,132	19.6	6.6
Leadsom, A. (Con)	4,492	12.3	0.7
Lab majority	17,688	48.53	
Electorate	70,726		
Turnout	36,444	51.53	

Lab hold (4.9% from Lab to Lib Dem)

LAGAN VALLEY

		%	+/-%
*Donaldson, J. (DUP)	23,289	54.7	41.3
McCrea, B. (UUP)	9,172	21.5	-35.0
Close, S. (Alliance)	4,316	10.1	-6.5
Butler, P. (Sinn Féin)	3,197	7.5	1.6
Lewsley, P. (SDLP)	2,598	6.1	-1.4
DUP majority	14,117	33.16	
Electorate	70,742		
Turnout	42,572	60.18	

DUP gain (38.3% from UUP to DUP)

LANARK AND HAMILTON EAST

(New Scottish constituency)

		%	+/-%
*Hood, J. (Lab)	20,072	46.1	
Grieve, F. (Lib Dem)	8,125	18.6	
Wilson, J. (SNP)	7,746	17.8	
Pettigrew, R. (Con)	5,576	12.8	
Reilly, D. (SSP)	802	1.8	
Mackay, D. (UKIP)	437	1.0	
McFarlane, D. (Ind)	416	1.0	
Mawhinney, R. (OCV)	415	1.0	
Lab majority	11,947	27.41	
Electorate	73,736		
Turnout	43,589	59.11	

Lab hold (5.9% from Lab to Lib Dem)

WEST LANCASHIRE

		%	+/-%
Cooper, R. (Lab)	20,746	48.1	-6.4
Doran, A. (Con)	14,662	34.0	2.0
Kemp, R. (Lib Dem)	6,059	14.0	2.5
Freeman, A. (UKIP)	871	2.0	0.0
Garrett, S. (Eng Dem)	525	1.2	0.0
Braid, D. (Clause 28)	292	0.7	0.0
Lab majority	6,084	14.10	
Electorate	74,777		
Turnout	43,155	57.71	

Lab hold (4.2% from Lab to Con)

LANCASTER AND WYRE

		%	+/-%
Wallace, B. (Con)	22,266	42.8	0.6
Sacks, A. (Lab)	18,095	34.8	-8.3
Langhorn, S. (Lib Dem)	8,453	16.2	6.0
Barry, J. (Greens)	2,278	4.4	1.3
Mander, J. (UKIP)	969	1.9	0.5
Con majority	4,171	8.01	
Electorate	80,739		
Turnout	52,061	64.48	

Con gain (4.5% from Lab to Con)

LEEDS CENTRAL

		%	+/-%
*Benn, H. (Lab)	17,526	60.1	-6.9
Coleman, R. (Lib Dem)	5,660	19.4	6.2
Cattell, B. (Con)	3,865	13.2	-1.0
Collett, M. (BNP)	1,201	4.1	0.0
Sewards, P. (UKIP)	494	1.7	-1.2
Dear, M. (Ind)	189	0.7	0.0
Taiwo, O. (Ind)	126	0.4	0.0
Fitzgerald, J. (AFC)	125	0.4	0.0
Lab majority	11,866	40.66	
Electorate	62,939		
Turnout	29,186	46.37	

Lab hold (6.5% from Lab to Lib Dem)

LEEDS EAST

		%	+/-%
*Mudie, G. (Lab)	17,799	59.2	-3.8
Tear, A. (LG)	6,221	20.7	7.2
Ponniah, D. (Con)	5,557	18.5	-1.0
Socrates, P. (Ind)	500	1.7	1.2
Lab majority	11,578	38.49	
Electorate	54,691		
Turnout	30,077	54.99	

Lab hold (5.5% from Lab to Lib Dem)

LEEDS NORTH EAST

		%	+/-%
*Hamilton, F. (Lab)	18,632	44.9	-4.2
Lobley, M. (Con)	13,370	32.2	0.9
Brown, J. (Lib Dem)	8,427	20.3	4.4
Foote, C. (Green Soc)	1,038	2.5	0.0
Lab majority	5,262	12.69	
Electorate	63,304		
Turnout	41,467	65.50	

Lab hold (2.6% from Lab to Con)

LEEDS NORTH WEST

		%	+/-%
Mulholland, G. (Lib Dem)	16,612	37.2	10.2
Blake, J. (Lab)	14,735	33.0	-9.0

* Member of last parliament

Lee, G. (Con)	11,510	25.7	-3.8
Hemingway, M. (Greens)	1,128	2.5	0.0
Knowles, A. (England)	545	1.2	0.0
Sutton, J. (Green Soc)	181	0.4	0.0
Lib Dem majority	1,877	4.20	
Electorate	71,644		
Turnout	44,711	62.41	

Lib Dem gain (9.6% from Lab to Lib Dem)

LEEDS WEST

		%	+/-%
*Battle, J. (Lab)	18,704	55.5	-6.7
Finlay, D. (Lib Dem)	5,894	17.5	7.0
Metcalfe, T. (Con)	4,807	14.3	-1.4
Blackburn, D. (Greens)	2,519	7.5	-0.6
Day, J. (BNP)	1,166	3.5	0.0
Sewards, D. (UKIP)	628	1.9	-0.5
Lab majority	12,810	37.99	
Electorate	62,882		
Turnout	33,718	53.62	

Lab hold (6.9% from Lab to Lib Dem)

LEICESTER EAST

		%	+/-%
*Vaz, K. (Lab)	24,015	58.1	0.6
Fernandes, S. (Con)	8,139	19.7	-4.8
Cooper, S. (Lib Dem)	7,052	17.1	4.8
Brown, C. (Veritas)	1,666	4.0	0.0
Smalley, V. (SLP)	434	1.1	-1.0
Lab majority	15,876	38.44	
Electorate	66,383		
Turnout	41,306	62.22	

Lab hold (2.7% from Con to Lab)

LEICESTER SOUTH

		%	+/-%
Soulsby, P. (Lab)	16,688	39.4	-15.1
*Gill, P. (Lib Dem)	12,971	30.6	13.4
McElwee, M. (Con)	7,549	17.8	-5.3
Ridley, Y. (Respect)	2,720	6.4	0.0
Follett, M. (Greens)	1,379	3.3	0.4
Roseblade, K. (Veritas)	573	1.4	0.0
Roberts, D. (SLP)	315	0.7	-0.9
Lord, P. (Ind)	216	0.5	0.0
Lab majority	3,717	8.76	
Electorate	72,310		
Turnout	42,411	58.65	

Lab hold (14.3% from Lab to Lib Dem)

LEICESTER WEST

		%	+/-%
*Hewitt, P. (Lab)	17,184	51.7	-2.5
Richardson, S. (Con)	8,114	24.4	-0.8
Haq, Z. (Lib Dem)	5,803	17.5	2.2
Forse, G. (Greens)	1,571	4.7	1.5
Score, S. (SAP)	552	1.7	0.0
Lab majority	9,070	27.30	
Electorate	62,389		
Turnout	33,224	53.25	

Lab hold (0.9% from Lab to Con)

NORTH WEST LEICESTERSHIRE

		%	+/-%
*Taylor, D. (Lab/Co-op)	21,449	45.5	-6.6
Le Page, N. (Con)	16,972	36.0	2.1
Keyes, R. (Lib Dem)	5,682	12.1	1.7
Blunt, J. (UKIP)	1,563	3.3	1.1
Potter, C. (BNP)	1,474	3.1	0.0

Lab/Co-op majority	4,477	9.50	
Electorate	70,519		
Turnout	47,140	66.85	

Lab/Co-op hold (4.3% from Lab/Co-op to Con)

LEIGH

		%	+/-%
*Burnham, A. (Lab)	23,097	63.3	-1.2
Wedderburn, L. (Con)	5,825	16.0	-2.2
Crowther, D. (Lib Dem)	4,962	13.6	0.8
Franzen, I. (CAP)	2,189	6.0	0.0
Hampson, T. (LCA)	415	1.1	0.0
Lab majority	17,272	47.34	
Electorate	72,473		
Turnout	36,488	50.35	

Lab hold (0.5% from Con to Lab)

LEOMINSTER

		%	+/-%
*Wiggin, B. (Con)	25,407	52.1	3.1
Williams, C. (Lib Dem)	12,220	25.0	-1.7
Bell, P. (Lab)	7,424	15.2	-1.6
Norman, F. (Greens)	2,191	4.5	0.9
Venables, P. (UKIP)	1,551	3.2	-0.2
Con majority	13,187	27.03	
Electorate	63,121		
Turnout	48,793	77.30	

Con hold (2.4% from Lib Dem to Con)

LEWES

		%	+/-%
*Baker, N. (Lib Dem)	24,376	52.4	-4.0
Love, R. (Con)	15,902	34.2	-0.8
Black, R. (Lab)	4,169	9.0	1.7
Murray, S. (Greens)	1,071	2.3	0.0
Petley, J. (UKIP)	1,034	2.2	0.8
Lib Dem majority	8,474	18.20	
Electorate	67,073		
Turnout	46,552	69.40	

Lib Dem hold (1.6% from Lib Dem to Con)

LEWISHAM DEPTFORD

		%	+/-%
*Ruddock, J. (Lab)	16,902	55.6	-9.4
Blango, C. (Lib Dem)	5,091	16.8	5.0
Cartlidge, J. (Con)	3,773	12.4	0.0
Johnson, D. (Greens)	3,367	11.1	4.6
Page, I. (SAP)	742	2.4	0.0
Holland, D. (UKIP)	518	1.7	0.0
Lab majority	11,811	38.86	
Electorate	59,018		
Turnout	30,393	51.50	

Lab hold (7.2% from Lab to Lib Dem)

LEWISHAM EAST

		%	+/-%
*Prentice, B. (Lab)	14,263	45.8	-7.9
Cleverly, J. (Con)	7,512	24.1	0.3
Thomas, R. (Lib Dem)	6,787	21.8	5.4
Baker, A. (Greens)	1,243	4.0	0.0
Tarling, A. (UKIP)	697	2.2	1.0
Franklin, B. (NF)	625	2.0	0.0
Lab majority	6,751	21.69	
Electorate	59,135		
Turnout	31,127	52.64	

Lab hold (4.1% from Lab to Con)

* Member of last parliament

LEWISHAM WEST

		%	+/-%
*Dowd, J. (Lab)	16,611	52.0	-9.0
Feakes, A. (Lib Dem)	6,679	20.9	7.5
McAnuff, E. (Con)	6,396	20.0	-2.3
Long, N. (Greens)	1,464	4.6	0.0
Winton, J. (UKIP)	773	2.4	0.9
Lab majority	9,932	31.11	
Electorate	58,349		
Turnout	31,923	54.71	

Lab hold (8.3% from Lab to Lib Dem)

LEYTON AND WANSTEAD

		%	+/-%
*Cohen, H. (Lab)	15,234	45.8	-12.2
Khan, M. (Lib Dem)	8,377	25.2	9.2
Foster, J. (Con)	7,393	22.2	2.5
Gunstock, A. (Greens)	1,523	4.6	1.5
Jones, N. (UKIP)	591	1.8	0.7
Robertson, M. (Ind)	155	0.5	0.0
Lab majority	6,857	20.61	
Electorate	60,444		
Turnout	33,273	55.05	

Lab hold (10.7% from Lab to Lib Dem)

LICHFIELD

		%	+/-%
*Fabricant, M. (Con)	21,274	48.6	-0.5
Gardner, N. (Lab)	14,194	32.5	-6.1
Jackson, I. (Lib Dem)	6,804	15.6	4.9
McKenzie, M. (UKIP)	1,472	3.4	1.7
Con majority	7,080	16.19	
Electorate	65,565		
Turnout	43,744	66.72	

Con hold (2.8% from Lab to Con)

LINCOLN

		%	+/-%
*Merron, G. (Lab)	16,724	45.4	-8.5
McCartney, K. (Con)	12,110	32.9	1.7
Gabriel, L. (Lib Dem)	6,715	18.2	5.6
Smith, N. (UKIP)	1,308	3.6	1.3
Lab majority	4,614	12.52	
Electorate	65,203		
Turnout	36,857	56.53	

Lab hold (5.1% from Lab to Con)

LINLITHGOW AND EAST FALKIRK

(New Scottish constituency)

		%	+/-%
*Connarty, M. (Lab)	22,121	47.7	
Guthrie, G. (SNP)	10,919	23.5	
Glenn, S. (Lib Dem)	7,100	15.3	
Veitch, M. (Con)	5,486	11.8	
Hendry, A. (SSP)	763	1.6	
Lab majority	11,202	24.15	
Electorate	76,739		
Turnout	46,389	60.45	

Lab hold (1.2% from Lab to SNP)

LIVERPOOL GARSTON

		%	+/-%
*Eagle, M. (Lab)	18,900	54.0	-7.4
Keaveney, P. (Lib Dem)	11,707	33.5	10.4
Rudd, A. (Con)	3,424	9.8	-5.7
Kearney, K. (UKIP)	780	2.2	0.0
Oatley, D. (WRP)	163	0.5	0.0

Lab majority	7,193	20.57	
Electorate	63,669		
Turnout	34,974	54.93	

Lab hold (8.9% from Lab to Lib Dem)

LIVERPOOL RIVERSIDE

		%	+/-%
*Ellman, L. (Lab/Co-op)	17,951	57.6	-13.8
Marbrow, R. (Lib Dem)	7,737	24.8	8.1
Howatson, G. (Con)	2,843	9.1	0.7
Cranie, P. (Greens)	1,707	5.5	0.0
Marshall, B. (SLP)	498	1.6	0.0
Irving, A. (UKIP)	455	1.5	0.0
Lab/Co-op majority	10,214	32.75	
Electorate	75,171		
Turnout	31,191	41.49	

Lab/Co-op hold (11.0% from Lab/Co-op to Lib Dem)

LIVERPOOL WALTON

		%	+/-%
*Kilfoyle, P. (Lab)	20,322	72.8	-5.1
Reid, K. (Lib Dem)	4,365	15.6	1.1
Buckle, S. (Con)	1,655	5.9	-0.1
Moran, J. (UKIP)	1,108	4.0	2.4
Wood, D. (Lib)	480	1.7	0.0
Lab majority	15,957	57.13	
Electorate	62,044		
Turnout	27,930	45.02	

Lab hold (3.1% from Lab to Lib Dem)

LIVERPOOL WAVERTREE

		%	+/-%
*Kennedy, J. (Lab)	18,441	52.4	-10.3
Eldridge, C. (Lib Dem)	13,268	37.7	13.3
Steen, J. (Con)	2,331	6.6	-3.0
Bill, M. (UKIP)	660	1.9	0.8
Theys, G. (SLP)	244	0.7	-0.4
Filby, P. (Dem Soc All)	227	0.7	0.0
Lab majority	5,173	14.71	
Electorate	69,189		
Turnout	35,171	50.83	

Lab hold (11.8% from Lab to Lib Dem)

LIVERPOOL WEST DERBY

		%	+/-%
*Wareing, R. (Lab)	19,140	62.8	-3.4
Radford, S. (Lib)	3,606	11.8	-3.1
Garrett, P. (Con)	2,567	8.4	0.4
Andersen, K. (SLP)	698	2.3	0.0
Baden, P. (UKIP)	538	1.8	0.0
Lab majority	15,225	49.98	
Electorate	64,591		
Turnout	30,464	47.16	

Lab hold (2.7% from Lab to Lib Dem)

LIVINGSTON

(New Scottish constituency)

		%	+/-%
*Cook, R. (Lab)	22,657	51.1	
Constance, A. (SNP)	9,560	21.6	
Dundas, C. (Lib Dem)	6,832	15.4	
Ross, A. (Con)	4,499	10.2	
Nimmo, S. (SSP)	789	1.8	
Lab majority	13,097	29.54	
Electorate	76,353		
Turnout	44,337	58.07	

Lab hold (1.2% from Lab to SNP)

* Member of last parliament

LLANELLI

		%	+/-%
Griffith, N. (Lab)	16,592	46.9	-1.6
Baker, N. (PlC)	9,358	26.5	-4.4
Phillips, A. (Con)	4,844	13.7	4.2
Rees, K. (Lib Dem)	4,550	12.9	4.4
Lab majority	7,234	20.47	
Electorate	55,678		
Turnout	35,344	63.48	

Lab hold (1.4% from PlC to Lab)

CITIES OF LONDON AND WESTMINSTER

		%	+/-%
*Field, M. (Con)	17,260	47.3	1.0
Lloyd, H. (Lab)	9,165	25.1	-8.0
Rossi, M. (Lib Dem)	7,306	20.0	4.7
Smith, T. (Greens)	1,544	4.2	0.4
Merton, C. (UKIP)	399	1.1	-0.3
Haw, B. (Ind)	298	0.8	0.0
McLachlan, J. (CPA)	246	0.7	0.0
Harris, D. (Veritas)	218	0.6	0.0
Cass, J. (Ind)	51	0.1	0.0
Con majority	8,095	22.19	
Electorate	72,577		
Turnout	36,487	50.27	

Con hold (4.5% from Lab to Con)

EAST LONDONDERRY

		%	+/-%
*Campbell, G. (DUP)	15,225	42.9	10.7
McClarty, D. (UUP)	7,498	21.1	-6.3
Dallat, J. (SDLP)	6,077	17.1	-3.7
Leonard, B. (Sinn Féin)	5,709	16.1	0.5
Boyle, Y. (Alliance)	924	2.6	-1.5
Samuel, M. (Ind)	71	0.2	0.0
DUP majority	7,727	21.76	
Electorate	58,861		
Turnout	35,504	60.32	

DUP hold (0.0%)

EAST LOTHIAN

(New Scottish constituency)

		%	+/-%
*Picking, A. (Lab)	18,983	41.5	
Butler, C. (Lib Dem)	11,363	24.8	
Stevenson, B. (Con)	7,315	16.0	
McLennan, P. (SNP)	5,995	13.1	
Collie, M. (Greens)	1,132	2.5	
Galbraith, G. (SSP)	504	1.1	
Robb, E. (UKIP)	306	0.7	
Thompson, W. (OCV)	178	0.4	
Lab majority	7,620	16.65	
Electorate	70,989		
Turnout	45,776	64.48	

Lab hold (7.5% from Lab to Lib Dem)

LOUGHBOROUGH

		%	+/-%
*Reed, A. (Lab/Co-op)	19,098	41.4	-8.4
Morgan, N. (Con)	17,102	37.1	1.7
Smith, G. (Lib Dem)	8,258	17.9	5.1
Sherratt, B. (UKIP)	1,094	2.4	0.3
McVay, J. (Veritas)	588	1.3	0.0
Lab/Co-op majority	1,996	4.33	
Electorate	72,351		
Turnout	46,140	63.77	

Lab/Co-op hold (5.0% from Lab/Co-op to Con)

LOUTH AND HORNCASTLE

		%	+/-%
*Tapsell, P. (Con)	21,744	46.6	-1.9
Hodgkiss, F. (Lab)	11,848	25.4	-6.1
Martin, F. (Lib Dem)	9,480	20.3	0.2
Pain, C. (UKIP)	3,611	7.7	0.0
Con majority	9,896	21.20	
Electorate	75,313		
Turnout	46,683	61.99	

Con hold (2.1% from Lab to Con)

LUDLOW

		%	+/-%
Dunne, P. (Con)	20,979	45.1	5.7
*Green, M. (Lib Dem)	18,952	40.7	-2.5
Knowles, N. (Lab)	4,974	10.7	-2.7
Gaffney, J. (Greens)	852	1.8	-0.2
Zucherman, M. (UKIP)	783	1.7	-0.3
Con majority	2,027	4.36	
Electorate	64,572		
Turnout	46,540	72.07	

Con gain (4.1% from Lib Dem to Con)

LUTON NORTH

		%	+/-%
*Hopkins, K. (Lab)	19,062	48.7	-8.0
Hall, H. (Con)	12,575	32.1	0.9
Jack, L. (Lib Dem)	6,081	15.5	5.8
Brown, C. (UKIP)	1,255	3.2	0.8
Gurney, K. (Forum)	149	0.4	0.0
Lab majority	6,487	16.58	
Electorate	68,175		
Turnout	39,122	57.38	

Lab hold (4.5% from Lab to Con)

LUTON SOUTH

		%	+/-%
*Moran, M. (Lab)	16,610	42.7	-12.5
Stay, R. (Con)	10,960	28.2	-1.3
Hussain, Q. (Lib Dem)	8,778	22.6	11.7
Lawman, C. (UKIP)	957	2.5	1.0
Scheimann, M. (Greens)	790	2.0	0.0
Ilyas, M. (Respect)	725	1.9	0.0
Lynn, A. (WRP)	98	0.3	0.0
Lab majority	5,650	14.52	
Electorate	71,949		
Turnout	38,918	54.09	

Lab hold (5.6% from Lab to Con)

MACCLESFIELD

		%	+/-%
*Winterton, N. (Con)	22,628	49.6	0.7
Carter, S. (Lab)	13,227	29.0	-4.1
O'Brien, C. (Lib Dem)	8,918	19.6	1.5
Scott, J. (Veritas)	848	1.9	0.0
Con majority	9,401	20.61	
Electorate	72,267		
Turnout	45,621	63.13	

Con hold (2.4% from Lab to Con)

MAIDENHEAD

		%	+/-%
*May, T. (Con)	23,312	50.8	5.8
Newbound, K. (Lib Dem)	17,081	37.3	-0.2
Pritchard, J. (Lab)	4,144	9.0	-6.1
Rait, T. (BNP)	704	1.5	0.0
Lewis, D. (UKIP)	609	1.3	-0.4

* Member of last parliament

MAIDENHEAD *continued*

Con majority	6,231	13.59
Electorate	63,978	
Turnout	45,850	71.67

Con hold (3.0% from Lib Dem to Con)

MAIDSTONE AND THE WEALD

		%	+/-%
*Widdecombe, A. (Con)	25,670	52.7	3.0
Breeze, B. (Lab)	10,814	22.2	-4.8
Corney, M. (Lib Dem)	10,808	22.2	2.3
Robertson, A. (UKIP)	1,463	3.0	0.9
Con majority	14,856	30.47	
Electorate	74,054		
Turnout	48,755	65.84	

Con hold (3.9% from Lab to Con)

MAKERFIELD

		%	+/-%
*McCartney, I. (Lab)	22,494	63.2	-5.3
Ranger, K. (Con)	4,345	12.2	-5.4
Beswick, T. (Lib Dem)	3,789	10.7	-0.8
Franzen, P. (CAP)	2,769	7.8	0.0
Shambley, D. (BNP)	1,221	3.4	0.0
Atherton, G. (UKIP)	962	2.7	0.0
Lab majority	18,149	51.01	
Electorate	69,039		
Turnout	35,580	51.54	

Lab hold (0.0% from Con to Lab)

MALDON AND CHELMSFORD EAST

		%	+/-%
*Whittingdale, J. (Con)	23,732	51.5	2.2
Tibballs, S. (Lab)	11,159	24.2	-5.9
Lambert, M. (Lib Dem)	9,270	20.1	4.2
Pryke, J. (UKIP)	1,930	4.2	1.6
Con majority	12,573	27.28	
Electorate	69,502		
Turnout	46,091	66.32	

Con hold (4.1% from Lab to Con)

MANCHESTER BLACKLEY

		%	+/-%
*Stringer, G. (Lab)	17,187	62.3	-6.7
Donaldson, I. (Lib Dem)	5,160	18.7	7.3
Ahmed, A. (Con)	3,690	13.4	-1.0
Bullock, R. (UKIP)	1,554	5.6	0.0
Lab majority	12,027	43.59	
Electorate	60,229		
Turnout	27,591	45.81	

Lab hold (7.0% from Lab to Lib Dem)

MANCHESTER CENTRAL

		%	+/-%
*Lloyd, T. (Lab)	16,993	58.1	-10.6
Ramsbottom, M. (Lib Dem)	7,217	24.7	9.0
Jackson, T. (Con)	2,504	8.6	-0.4
Durrant, S. (Greens)	1,292	4.4	0.5
Kemp, R. (NF)	421	1.4	0.0
O'Connor, D. (UKIP)	382	1.3	0.0
Whittaker, J. (UKIP)	272	0.9	0.0
Sinclair, R. (SLP)	183	0.6	-1.2
Lab majority	9,776	33.41	
Electorate	69,656		
Turnout	29,264	42.01	

Lab hold (9.8% from Lab to Lib Dem)

MANCHESTER GORTON

		%	+/-%
*Kaufman, G. (Lab)	15,480	53.2	-9.6
Afzal, Q. (Lib Dem)	9,672	33.2	11.9
Byrne, A. (Con)	2,848	9.8	-0.2
Beaman, G. (UKIP)	783	2.7	1.0
Waller, D. (WRP)	181	0.6	0.0
Key, M. (RP)	159	0.6	0.0
Lab majority	5,808	19.94	
Electorate	64,696		
Turnout	29,123	45.02	

Lab hold (10.8% from Lab to Lib Dem)

MANCHESTER WITHINGTON

		%	+/-%
Leech, J. (Lib Dem)	15,872	42.4	20.4
*Bradley, K. (Lab)	15,205	40.6	-14.3
Bradley, K. (Con)	3,919	10.5	-4.8
Candeland, B. (Greens)	1,595	4.3	-0.1
Gutfreund-Walmsley, R. (UKIP)	424	1.1	0.0
Benett, I. (Ind)	243	0.7	0.0
Zalzala, Y. (Ind)	153	0.4	0.0
Reed, R. (TP)	47	0.1	0.0
Lib Dem majority	667	1.78	
Electorate	67,781		
Turnout	37,458	55.26	

Lib Dem gain (17.3% from Lab to Lib Dem)

MANSFIELD

		%	+/-%
*Meale, A. (Lab)	18,400	48.1	-9.1
Wright, A. (Con)	7,035	18.4	-8.8
Rickersey, S. (Ind)	6,491	17.0	0.0
Shelley, R. (Lib Dem)	5,316	13.9	-1.8
Harvey, M. (Veritas)	1,034	2.7	0.0
Lab majority	11,365	29.69	
Electorate	69,131		
Turnout	38,276	55.37	

Lab hold (0.1% from Lab to Con)

MEDWAY

		%	+/-%
*Marshall-Andrews, R. (Lab)	17,333	42.2	-6.8
Reckless, M. (Con)	17,120	41.7	2.5
Juby, G. (Lib Dem)	5,152	12.5	3.2
Oakley, B. (UKIP)	1,488	3.6	1.1
Lab majority	213	0.52	
Electorate	67,251		
Turnout	41,093	61.10	

Lab hold (4.6% from Lab to Con)

MEIRIONNYDD NANT CONWY

		%	+/-%
*Llwyd, E. (PlC)	10,597	51.3	1.7
Jones, R. (Lab)	3,983	19.3	-3.4
Munford, D. (Con)	3,402	16.5	-2.3
Fawcett, A. (Lib Dem)	2,192	10.6	1.7
Wykes, F. (UKIP)	466	2.3	0.0
PlC majority	6,614	32.04	
Electorate	33,443		
Turnout	20,640	61.72	

PlC hold (2.5% from Lab to PlC)

* Member of last parliament

MERIDEN

		%	+/-%
*Spelman, C. (Con)	22,416	48.2	0.5
Brown, J. (Lab)	15,407	33.1	-6.1
Laitenen, W. (Lib Dem)	7,113	15.3	4.2
Brookes, D. (UKIP)	1,567	3.4	1.3
Con majority	7,009	15.07	
Electorate	77,342		
Turnout	46,503	60.13	

Con hold (3.3% from Lab to Con)

MERTHYR TYDFIL AND RHYMNEY

		%	+/-%
*Havard, D. (Lab)	18,129	60.5	-1.3
Rees, C. (Lib Dem)	4,195	14.0	6.5
Turner, N. (PlC)	2,972	9.9	-4.8
Berry, R. (Con)	2,680	8.9	1.8
Greer, N. (Forward Wales)	1,030	3.4	0.0
Parry, G. (UKIP)	699	2.3	0.0
Marsden, I. (SLP)	271	0.9	-1.3
Lab majority	13,934	46.48	
Electorate	54,579		
Turnout	29,976	54.92	

Lab hold (3.9% from Lab to Lib Dem)

MID BEDFORDSHIRE – see under Bedfordshire

MID DORSET AND POOLE NORTH – see under Dorset

MID NORFOLK – see under Norfolk

MID SUSSEX – see under Sussex

MID ULSTER – see under Ulster

MID WORCESTERSHIRE – see under Worcestershire

MIDDLESBROUGH

		%	+/-%
*Bell, S. (Lab)	18,562	57.8	-9.8
Michna, J. (Lib Dem)	5,995	18.7	8.2
Flynn-Macleod, C. (Con)	5,263	16.4	-2.8
Armes, R. (BNP)	819	2.6	0.0
Landers, M. (UKIP)	768	2.4	0.0
Elder, J. (Ind)	503	1.6	0.0
Arnott, D. (Ind)	230	0.7	0.0
Lab majority	12,567	39.10	
Electorate	65,924		
Turnout	32,140	48.75	

Lab hold (9.0% from Lab to Lib Dem)

MIDDLESBROUGH SOUTH AND EAST CLEVELAND

		%	+/-%
*Kumar, A. (Lab)	21,945	50.2	-5.1
Brooks, M. (Con)	13,945	31.9	-2.1
Minns, C. (Lib Dem)	6,049	13.8	3.2
Groves, G. (BNP)	1,099	2.5	0.0
Bull, C. (UKIP)	658	1.5	0.0
Lab majority	8,000	18.31	
Electorate	71,883		
Turnout	43,696	60.79	

Lab hold (1.5% from Lab to Con)

MIDLOTHIAN

(New Scottish constituency)

		%	+/-%
*Hamilton, D. (Lab)	17,153	45.5	
Mackintosh, F. (Lib Dem)	9,888	26.2	
Beattie, C. (SNP)	6,400	17.0	
McGill, I. (Con)	3,537	9.4	
Gilfillan, N. (SSP)	726	1.9	
Lab majority	7,265	19.27	
Electorate	60,644		
Turnout	37,704	62.17	

Lab hold (7.0% from Lab to Lib Dem)

MILTON KEYNES NORTH EAST

		%	+/-%
Lancaster, M. (Con)	19,674	39.3	1.2
*White, B. (Lab)	18,009	35.9	-6.0
Carr, J. (Lib Dem)	9,789	19.5	1.8
Phillips, M. (UKIP)	1,400	2.8	0.6
Richardson, G. (Greens)	1,090	2.2	0.0
Vyas, A. (Ind)	142	0.3	0.0
Con majority	1,665	3.32	
Electorate	78,758		
Turnout	50,104	63.62	

Con gain (3.6% from Lab to Con)

MILTON KEYNES SOUTH WEST

		%	+/-%
*Starkey, P. (Lab)	20,862	42.8	-6.7
Stewart, I. (Con)	16,852	34.6	0.4
Stuart, N. (Lib Dem)	7,909	16.2	5.6
Harlock, G. (UKIP)	1,750	3.6	1.7
Francis, A. (Greens)	1,336	2.7	0.6
Lab majority	4,010	8.23	
Electorate	82,228		
Turnout	48,709	59.24	

Lab hold (3.6% from Lab to Con)

MITCHAM AND MORDEN

		%	+/-%
*McDonagh, S. (Lab)	22,489	56.4	-4.0
Shellhorn, A. (Con)	9,929	24.9	0.8
Christie-Smith, J. (Lib Dem)	5,583	14.0	3.9
Walsh, T. (Greens)	1,395	3.5	1.1
Roberts, A. (Veritas)	286	0.7	0.0
Alagaratnam, R. (ND)	186	0.5	0.0
Lab majority	12,560	31.50	
Electorate	65,172		
Turnout	39,868	61.17	

Lab hold (2.4% from Lab to Con)

MOLE VALLEY

		%	+/-%
*Beresford, P. (Con)	27,060	54.8	4.2
Butt, N. (Lib Dem)	15,063	30.5	1.5
Bi, F. (Lab)	5,310	10.8	-5.9
Payne, D. (UKIP)	1,475	3.0	0.2
Meekins, R. (Veritas)	507	1.0	0.0
Con majority	11,997	24.28	
Electorate	68,181		
Turnout	49,415	72.48	

Con hold (1.4% from Lib Dem to Con)

* Member of last parliament

MONMOUTH

		%	+/-%
Davies, D. (Con)	21,396	46.9	5.0
*Edwards, H. (Lab)	16,869	37.0	-5.8
Hobson, P. (Lib Dem)	5,852	12.8	1.4
Clark, J. (PlC)	993	2.2	-0.2
Bufton, J. (UKIP)	543	1.2	-0.3
Con majority	4,527	9.92	
Electorate	63,093		
Turnout	45,653	72.36	

Con gain (5.4% from Lab to Con)

MONTGOMERYSHIRE

		%	+/-%
*Öpik, L. (Lib Dem)	15,419	51.2	1.8
Baynes, S. (Con)	8,246	27.4	-0.5
Tinline, D. (Lab)	3,454	11.5	-0.4
ap Gwynn, E. (PlC)	2,078	6.9	0.1
Easton, C. (UKIP)	900	3.0	0.3
Lib Dem majority	7,173	23.83	
Electorate	46,766		
Turnout	30,097	64.36	

Lib Dem hold (1.2% from Con to Lib Dem)

MORAY

(New Scottish constituency)

		%	+/-%
*Robertson, A. (SNP)	14,196	36.6	
Halcro-Johnston, J. (Con)	8,520	22.0	
Hutchens, K. (Lab)	7,919	20.4	
Gorn, L. (Lib Dem)	7,460	19.2	
Anderson, N. (SSP)	698	1.8	
SNP majority	5,676	14.63	
Electorate	66,463		
Turnout	38,793	58.37	

SNP hold (4.1% from Con to SNP)

MORECAMBE AND LUNESDALE

		%	+/-%
*Smith, G. (Lab)	20,331	48.8	-0.7
Airey, J. (Con)	15,563	37.4	0.0
Stone, A. (Lib Dem)	5,741	13.8	4.6
Lab majority	4,768	11.45	
Electorate	67,775		
Turnout	41,635	61.43	

Lab hold (0.4% from Lab to Con)

MORLEY AND ROTHWELL

		%	+/-%
*Challen, C. (Lab)	20,570	48.4	-8.6
Vineall, N. (Con)	8,227	19.4	-6.2
Golton, S. (Lib Dem)	6,819	16.1	1.9
Finnigan, R. (Ind)	4,608	10.8	0.0
Beverley, C. (BNP)	2,271	5.3	0.0
Lab majority	12,343	29.05	
Electorate	72,248		
Turnout	42,495	58.82	

Lab hold (1.2% from Lab to Con)

MOTHERWELL AND WISHAW

(New Scottish constituency)

		%	+/-%
*Roy, F. (Lab)	21,327	57.5	
MacQuarrie, I. (SNP)	6,105	16.5	
Snowden, C. (Lib Dem)	4,464	12.0	
Finnie, P. (Con)	3,440	9.3	
McEwan, G. (SSP)	1,019	2.8	
Carter, D. (Free)	384	1.0	
Thompson, C. (OCV)	370	1.0	

		%
Lab majority	15,222	41.02
Electorate	66,987	
Turnout	37,109	55.40

Lab hold (2.4% from SNP to Lab)

NA H-EILEANAN AN IAR

(previously Western Isles)

		%	+/-%
MacNeil, A. (SNP)	6,213	44.9	8.1
*Macdonald, C. (Lab)	4,772	34.5	-10.5
Davis, J. (Lib Dem)	1,096	7.9	1.5
Hargreaves, J. (OCV)	1,048	7.6	0.0
Maciver, A. (Con)	610	4.4	-5.1
Telfer, J. (SSP)	97	0.7	-1.5
SNP majority	1,441	10.41	
Electorate	21,576		
Turnout	13,836	64.13	

SNP gain (9.3% from Lab to SNP)

NEATH

		%	+/-%
*Hain, P. (Lab)	18,835	52.6	-8.1
Owen, A. (PlC)	6,125	17.1	-1.3
Waye, S. (Lib Dem)	5,112	14.3	4.8
Davies, H. (Con)	4,136	11.6	2.1
Jay, S. (Greens)	658	1.8	0.0
Brienza, G. (Ind)	360	1.0	0.0
Tabram, P. (LCA)	334	0.9	0.0
Falconer, H. (Respect)	257	0.7	0.0
Lab majority	12,710	35.49	
Electorate	57,607		
Turnout	35,817	62.17	

Lab hold (3.4% from Lab to PlC)

NEW FOREST EAST

		%	+/-%
*Lewis, J. (Con)	21,975	48.6	6.1
Dash, B. (Lib Dem)	15,424	34.1	0.7
Roberts, S. (Lab)	5,492	12.1	-9.5
Davies, K. (UKIP)	2,344	5.2	2.7
Con majority	6,551	14.48	
Electorate	68,633		
Turnout	45,235	65.91	

Con hold (2.7% from Lib Dem to Con)

NEW FOREST WEST

		%	+/-%
*Swayne, D. (Con)	26,004	56.5	0.7
Kaushik, M. (Lib Dem)	8,719	18.9	-6.9
Hurne, J. (Lab)	7,590	16.5	1.8
Lawrence, B. (UKIP)	1,917	4.2	0.4
Richards, J. (Greens)	1,837	4.0	0.0
Con majority	17,285	37.52	
Electorate	69,232		
Turnout	46,067	66.54	

Con hold (3.8% from Lib Dem to Con)

NEWARK

		%	+/-%
*Mercer, P. (Con)	21,946	48.0	1.6
Reece, J. (Lab)	15,482	33.9	-3.6
Thompstone, S. (Lib Dem)	7,276	15.9	2.7
Creasy, C. (UKIP)	992	2.2	0.0
Con majority	6,464	14.15	
Electorate	72,249		
Turnout	45,696	63.25	

Con hold (2.6% from Lab to Con)

*Member of last parliament

NEWBURY

		%	+/-%
Benyon, R. (Con)	26,771	49.0	5.5
*Rendel, D. (Lib Dem)	23,311	42.6	-5.6
Van Nooijen, O. (Lab)	3,239	5.9	-1.0
McMahon, D. (UKIP)	857	1.6	0.2
Cornish, N. (Ind)	409	0.8	0.0
Singleton, B. (Ind)	86	0.2	0.0
Con majority	3,460	6.33	
Electorate	75,903		
Turnout	54,673	72.03	

Con gain (5.5% from Lib Dem to Con)

NEWCASTLE-UNDER-LYME

		%	+/-%
*Farrelly, P. (Lab)	18,053	45.4	-8.0
Lefroy, J. (Con)	9,945	25.0	-2.6
Johnson, T. (Lib Dem)	7,528	18.9	3.4
Nixon, D. (UKIP)	1,436	3.6	2.1
Dawson, J. (BNP)	1,390	3.5	0.0
Dobson, A. (Greens)	918	2.3	0.0
Harvey-Lover, M. (Veritas)	518	1.3	0.0
Lab majority	8,108	20.38	
Electorate	68,414		
Turnout	39,788	58.16	

Lab hold (2.7% from Lab to Con)

NEWCASTLE UPON TYNE CENTRAL

		%	+/-%
*Cousins, J. (Lab)	16,211	45.1	-9.8
Stone, G. (Lib Dem)	12,229	34.1	12.4
Morton, W. (Con)	5,749	16.0	-5.3
Hulm, J. (Greens)	1,254	3.5	0.0
Harding, C. (NACVP)	477	1.3	0.0
Lab majority	3,982	11.09	
Electorate	62,734		
Turnout	35,920	57.26	

Lab hold (11.1% from Lab to Lib Dem)

NEWCASTLE UPON TYNE EAST AND WALLSEND

		%	+/-%
*Brown, N. (Lab)	17,462	55.1	-8.0
Ord, D. (Lib Dem)	9,897	31.2	11.6
Dias, N. (Con)	3,532	11.2	-0.7
Hopwood, W. (SAP)	582	1.8	0.0
Levy, M. (Comm GB)	205	0.7	0.0
Lab majority	7,565	23.88	
Electorate	56,900		
Turnout	31,678	55.67	

Lab hold (9.8% from Lab to Lib Dem)

NEWCASTLE UPON TYNE NORTH

		%	+/-%
*Henderson, D. (Lab)	19,224	50.0	-10.1
Beadle, R. (Lib Dem)	12,201	31.7	12.3
Hudson, N. (Con)	6,022	15.7	-4.8
Lab majority	7,023	18.27	
Electorate	64,599		
Turnout	38,444	59.51	

Lab hold (11.2% from Lab to Lib Dem)

NEWPORT EAST

		%	+/-%
Morden, J. (Lab)	14,389	45.2	-9.5
Townsend, E. (Lib Dem)	7,551	23.7	9.7
Collings, M. (Con)	7,459	23.4	0.3
Asghar, M. (PlC)	1,221	3.8	-1.0
Thomas, R. (UKIP)	945	3.0	1.7
Screen, L. (SLP)	260	0.8	-0.5
Lab majority	6,838	21.49	
Electorate	54,956		
Turnout	31,825	57.91	

Lab hold (9.6% from Lab to Lib Dem)

NEWPORT WEST

		%	+/-%
*Flynn, P. (Lab)	16,021	44.8	-7.9
Morgan, W. (Con)	10,563	29.6	3.4
Flanagan, N. (Lib Dem)	6,398	17.9	6.2
Salkeld, T. (PlC)	1,278	3.6	-3.6
Moelwyn Hughes, H. (UKIP)	848	2.4	0.9
Varley, P. (Greens)	540	1.5	0.0
Arjomand, S. (Ind)	84	0.2	0.0
Lab majority	5,458	15.27	
Electorate	60,287		
Turnout	35,732	59.27	

Lab hold (5.6% from Lab to Con)

NEWRY AND ARMAGH

		%	+/-%
Murphy, C. (Sinn Féin)	20,965	41.4	10.4
Bradley, D. (SDLP)	12,770	25.2	-12.2
Berry, P. (DUP)	9,311	18.4	-1.0
Kennedy, D. (UUP)	7,025	13.9	1.6
Markey, G. (Ind)	625	1.2	0.0
Sinn Féin majority	8,195	16.16	
Electorate	72,448		
Turnout	50,696	69.98	

Sinn Féin gain (0.0%)

MID NORFOLK

		%	+/-%
*Simpson, K. (Con)	23,564	43.1	-1.7
Zeichner, D. (Lab)	16,004	29.2	-6.8
Clifford-Jackson, V. (Lib Dem)	12,988	23.7	9.2
Fletcher, S. (UKIP)	2,178	4.0	1.4
Con majority	7,560	13.81	
Electorate	81,738		
Turnout	54,734	66.96	

Con hold (2.6% from Lab to Con)

NORTH NORFOLK

		%	+/-%
*Lamb, N. (Lib Dem)	31,515	53.5	10.8
Dale, I. (Con)	20,909	35.5	-6.3
Harris, P. (Lab)	5,447	9.2	-4.1
Agnew, S. (UKIP)	978	1.7	0.6
Appleyard, J. (Ind)	116	0.2	0.0
Lib Dem majority	10,606	17.99	
Electorate	80,784		
Turnout	58,965	72.99	

Lib Dem hold (8.6% from Con to Lib Dem)

NORTH WEST NORFOLK

		%	+/-%
*Bellingham, H. (Con)	25,471	50.3	1.8
Welfare, D. (Lab)	16,291	32.2	-9.6
Higginson, S. (Lib Dem)	7,026	13.9	5.5
Stone, M. (UKIP)	1,861	3.7	2.3

* Member of last parliament

NORTH WEST NORFOLK *continued*

Con majority	9,180	18.12
Electorate	82,171	
Turnout	50,649	61.64

Con hold (5.7% from Lab to Con)

SOUTH NORFOLK

		%	+/-%
*Bacon, R. (Con)	26,399	44.8	2.6
Mack, I. (Lib Dem)	17,617	29.9	0.0
Morgan, J. (Lab)	13,262	22.5	-2.0
Tye, P. (UKIP)	1,696	2.9	1.4
Con majority	8,782	14.89	
Electorate	85,896		
Turnout	58,974	68.66	

Con hold (1.3% from Lib Dem to Con)

SOUTH WEST NORFOLK

		%	+/-%
Fraser, C. (Con)	25,881	47.0	-5.2
Morgan, C. (Lab)	15,795	28.7	-5.9
Pond, A. (Lib Dem)	10,207	18.5	7.8
Hall, D. (UKIP)	2,738	5.0	2.4
Hayes, K. (Ind)	506	0.9	0.0
Con majority	10,086	18.30	
Electorate	88,260		
Turnout	55,127	62.46	

Con hold (0.3% from Lab to Con)

NORMANTON

		%	+/-%
Balls, E. (Lab/Co-op)	19,161	51.2	-4.9
Percy, A. (Con)	9,159	24.5	-2.5
Butterworth, S. (Lib Dem)	6,357	17.0	2.4
Aveyard, J. (BNP)	1,967	5.3	0.0
Harrop, M. (Ind)	780	2.1	0.0
Lab/Co-op majority	10,002	26.73	
Electorate	65,129		
Turnout	37,424	57.46	

Lab/Co-op hold (1.2% from Lab/Co-op to Con)

NORTH ANTRIM – see under Antrim

NORTH AYRSHIRE AND ARRAN – see under Ayrshire

NORTH CORNWALL – see under Cornwall

NORTH DEVON – see under Devon

NORTH DORSET – see under Dorset

NORTH DOWN – see under Down

NORTH EAST BEDFORDSHIRE – see under Bedfordshire

NORTH EAST CAMBRIDGESHIRE – see under Cambridgeshire

NORTH EAST DERBYSHIRE – see under Derbyshire

NORTH EAST FIFE – see under Fife

NORTH EAST HAMPSHIRE – see under Hampshire

NORTH EAST HERTFORDSHIRE – see under Hertfordshire

NORTH ESSEX – see under Essex

NORTH SHROPSHIRE – see under Shropshire

NORTH SOUTHWARK AND BERMONDSEY – see under Southwark

NORTH SWINDON – see under Swindon

NORTH THANET – see under Thanet

NORTH TYNESIDE – see under Tyneside

NORTH WARWICKSHIRE – see under Warwickshire

NORTH WEST CAMBRIDGESHIRE – see under Cambridgeshire

NORTH WEST DURHAM – see under Durham

NORTH WEST HAMPSHIRE – see under Hampshire

NORTH WEST LEICESTERSHIRE – see under Leicestershire

NORTH WILTSHIRE – see under Wiltshire

NORTHAMPTON NORTH

		%	+/-%
*Keeble, S. (Lab)	16,905	40.2	-9.2
Collins, D. (Con)	12,945	30.8	0.4
Simpson, A. (Lib Dem)	10,317	24.5	6.8
Howsam, J. (UKIP)	1,050	2.5	1.1
Withrington, P. (SOS)	495	1.2	0.0
Otchie, A. (CPA)	336	0.8	0.0
Lab majority	3,960	9.42	
Electorate	73,926		
Turnout	42,048	56.88	

Lab hold (4.8% from Lab to Con)

NORTHAMPTON SOUTH

		%	+/-%
Binley, B. (Con)	23,818	43.7	2.6
*Clarke, T. (Lab)	19,399	35.6	-7.3
Barron, K. (Lib Dem)	8,327	15.3	2.8
Clark, D. (UKIP)	1,032	1.9	-0.5
Green, A. (Veritas)	508	0.9	0.0
Harrisson, J. (SOS)	437	0.8	0.0
Percival, J. (Loony)	354	0.7	0.0
Fitzpatrick, F. (Ind)	346	0.6	0.0
Webb, T. (CPA)	260	0.5	0.0
Con majority	4,419	8.11	
Electorate	89,722		
Turnout	54,481	60.72	

Con gain (4.9% from Lab to Con)

NORTHAVON

		%	+/-%
*Webb, S. (Lib Dem)	30,872	52.3	-0.1
Butt, C. (Con)	19,839	33.6	-1.1
Gardener, P. (Lab)	6,277	10.6	-0.9
Blake, A. (UKIP)	1,032	1.8	0.4
Pinder, A. (Greens)	922	1.6	0.0
Beacham, T. (Ind)	114	0.2	0.0
Lib Dem majority	11,033	18.68	
Electorate	81,800		
Turnout	59,056	72.20	

Lib Dem hold (0.5% from Con to Lib Dem)

* Member of last parliament

NORWICH NORTH

		%	+/-%
*Gibson, I. (Lab)	21,097	44.9	-2.6
Tumbridge, J. (Con)	15,638	33.3	-1.3
Whitmore, R. (Lib Dem)	7,616	16.2	1.4
Holmes, A. (Greens)	1,252	2.7	0.9
Youles, J. (UKIP)	1,122	2.4	1.4
Holden, B. (Ind)	308	0.7	0.2
Lab majority	5,459	11.61	
Electorate	76,992		
Turnout	47,033	61.09	

Lab hold (0.6% from Lab to Con)

NORWICH SOUTH

		%	+/-%
*Clarke, C. (Lab)	15,904	37.7	-7.8
Aalders-Dunthorne, A. (Lib Dem)	12,251	29.0	6.4
Little, A. (Con)	9,567	22.7	-2.1
Ramsay, A. (Greens)	3,101	7.4	4.0
Ahlstrom, V. (UKIP)	597	1.4	0.3
Constable, C. (Eng Dem)	466	1.1	0.0
Barnard, D. (LCA)	219	0.5	-0.9
Blackwell, R. (WRP)	85	0.2	0.0
Lab majority	3,653	8.66	
Electorate	70,409		
Turnout	42,190	59.92	

Lab hold (7.1% from Lab to Lib Dem)

NOTTINGHAM EAST

		%	+/-%
*Heppell, J. (Lab)	13,787	45.8	-13.1
Ghazni, I. (Lib Dem)	6,848	22.8	9.7
Thornton, J. (Con)	6,826	22.7	-1.6
Baxter, A. (Greens)	1,517	5.0	0.0
Ellwood, A. (UKIP)	740	2.5	0.0
Radcliff, P. (Soc Unity)	373	1.2	0.0
Lab majority	6,939	23.06	
Electorate	60,634		
Turnout	30,091	49.63	

Lab hold (11.4% from Lab to Lib Dem)

NOTTINGHAM NORTH

		%	+/-%
*Allen, G. (Lab)	17,842	58.7	-5.8
Patel, P. (Con)	5,671	18.7	-5.1
Ball, T. (Lib Dem)	5,190	17.1	6.5
Marriott, I. (UKIP)	1,680	5.5	0.0
Lab majority	12,171	40.06	
Electorate	61,894		
Turnout	30,383	49.09	

Lab hold (0.3% from Lab to Con)

NOTTINGHAM SOUTH

		%	+/-%
*Simpson, A. (Lab)	16,506	47.4	-7.1
Mattu, S. (Con)	9,020	25.9	-1.3
Sutton, T. (Lib Dem)	7,961	22.9	6.3
Browne, K. (UKIP)	1,353	3.9	2.2
Lab majority	7,486	21.49	
Electorate	68,921		
Turnout	34,840	50.55	

Lab hold (2.9% from Lab to Con)

NUNEATON

		%	+/-%
*Olner, B. (Lab)	19,945	44.1	-8.1
Pawsey, M. (Con)	17,665	39.0	4.3
Asghar, A. (Lib Dem)	5,884	13.0	1.9
Tyson, K. (UKIP)	1,786	3.9	1.9
Lab majority	2,280	5.04	
Electorate	73,440		
Turnout	45,280	61.66	

Lab hold (6.2% from Lab to Con)

OCHIL AND SOUTH PERTHSHIRE

(New Scottish constituency)		%	+/-%
Banks, G. (Lab)	14,645	31.4	
*Ewing, A. (SNP)	13,957	29.9	
Smith, E. (Con)	10,021	21.5	
Whittingham, C. (Lib Dem)	6,218	13.3	
Baxter, G. (Greens)	978	2.1	
Campbell, I. (SSP)	420	0.9	
Bushby, D. (UKIP)	275	0.6	
Kelly, M. (Free Scot)	183	0.4	
Lab majority	688	1.47	
Electorate	70,731		
Turnout	46,697	66.02	

Lab hold (0.2% from Lab to SNP)

OGMORE

		%	+/-%
*Irranca-Davies, H. (Lab)	18,295	60.4	-1.6
Radford, J. (Lib Dem)	4,592	15.2	2.4
Lloyd-Nesling, N. (Con)	4,243	14.0	2.9
Williams, J. (PlC)	3,148	10.4	-3.6
Lab majority	13,703	45.26	
Electorate	52,349		
Turnout	30,278	57.84	

Lab hold (2.0% from Lab to Lib Dem)

OLD BEXLEY AND SIDCUP

		%	+/-%
*Conway, D. (Con)	22,191	49.8	4.4
Moore, G. (Lab)	12,271	27.5	-9.9
O'Hare, N. (Lib Dem)	6,564	14.7	1.0
Barnbrook, M. (UKIP)	2,015	4.5	1.1
Sayers, C. (BNP)	1,227	2.8	0.0
Peters, G. (Ind)	304	0.7	0.0
Con majority	9,920	22.26	
Electorate	68,227		
Turnout	44,572	65.33	

Con hold (7.2% from Lab to Con)

OLDHAM EAST AND SADDLEWORTH

		%	+/-%
*Woolas, P. (Lab)	17,968	41.4	2.8
Dawson, T. (Lib Dem)	14,378	33.2	0.6
Chapman, K. (Con)	7,901	18.2	2.1
Treacy, M. (BNP)	2,109	4.9	-6.4
Nield, V. (UKIP)	873	2.0	0.5
O#Grady, P. (Ind)	138	0.3	0.0
Lab majority	3,590	8.28	
Electorate	75,680		
Turnout	43,367	57.30	

Lab hold (1.1% from Lib Dem to Lab)

* Member of last parliament

OLDHAM WEST AND ROYTON

		%	+/-%
*Meacher, M. (Lab)	18,452	49.1	-2.0
Moore, S. (Con)	7,998	21.3	3.6
Bodsworth, S. (Lib Dem)	7,519	20.0	7.6
Corbett, A. (BNP)	2,606	6.9	-9.5
Short, D. (UKIP)	987	2.6	0.0
Lab majority	10,454	27.83	
Electorate	70,496		
Turnout	37,562	53.28	

Lab hold (2.8% from Lab to Con)

ORKNEY AND SHETLAND

		%	+/-%
*Carmichael, A. (Lib Dem)	9,138	51.5	10.2
Meade, R. (Lab)	2,511	14.2	-6.4
Nairn, F. (Con)	2,357	13.3	-5.4
Mowat, J. (SNP)	1,833	10.3	-4.5
Aberdein, J. (SSP)	992	5.6	1.0
Dyble, S. (UKIP)	424	2.4	0.0
Cruickshank, P. (LCA)	311	1.8	0.0
Nugent, B. (Free Scot)	176	1.0	0.0
Lib Dem majority	6,627	37.35	
Electorate	33,048		
Turnout	17,742	53.69	

Lib Dem hold (8.3% from Lab to Lib Dem)

ORPINGTON

		%	+/-%
*Horam, J. (Con)	26,718	48.8	5.0
Maines, C. (Lib Dem)	21,771	39.8	-3.6
Bird, E. (Lab)	4,914	9.0	-1.9
Greenhough, J. (UKIP)	1,331	2.4	0.5
Con majority	4,947	9.04	
Electorate	78,276		
Turnout	54,734	69.92	

Con hold (4.3% from Lib Dem to Con)

OXFORD EAST

		%	+/-%
*Smith, A. (Lab)	15,405	36.9	-12.5
Goddard, S. (Lib Dem)	14,442	34.6	11.1
Morris, V. (Con)	6,992	16.7	-2.0
Sanders, J. (Greens)	1,813	4.3	0.6
Blair, H. (Ind)	1,485	3.6	3.4
Leen, M. (IWCA)	892	2.1	0.0
Gardner, P. (UKIP)	715	1.7	0.3
Mylvaganam, P. (Ind)	46	0.1	0.0
Lab majority	963	2.30	
Electorate	72,234		
Turnout	41,790	57.85	

Lab hold (11.8% from Lab to Lib Dem)

OXFORD WEST AND ABINGDON

		%	+/-%
*Harris, E. (Lib Dem)	24,336	46.3	-1.6
McLean, A. (Con)	16,653	31.7	1.6
Bance, A. (Lab)	8,725	16.6	-1.1
Lines, T. (Greens)	2,091	4.0	1.2
Watney, M. (UKIP)	795	1.5	0.6
Lib Dem majority	7,683	14.61	
Electorate	80,195		
Turnout	52,600	65.59	

Lib Dem hold (1.6% from Lib Dem to Con)

PAISLEY AND RENFREWSHIRE NORTH

(New Scottish constituency)

		%	+/-%
*Sheridan, J. (Lab)	18,697	45.7	
Wilson, B. (SNP)	7,696	18.8	
Hutton, L. (Lib Dem)	7,464	18.3	
Lardner, P. (Con)	5,566	13.6	
McGregor, A. (SSP)	646	1.6	
McGavigan, K. (SLP)	444	1.1	
Pearson, J. (UKIP)	372	0.9	
Lab majority	11,001	26.91	
Electorate	63,076		
Turnout	40,885	64.82	

Lab hold (1.3% from Lab to SNP)

PAISLEY AND RENFREWSHIRE SOUTH

(New Scottish constituency)

		%	+/-%
*Alexander, D. (Lab)	19,904	52.6	
McCartin, E. (Lib Dem)	6,672	17.6	
Doig, A. (SNP)	6,653	17.6	
Begg, T. (Con)	3,188	8.4	
Hogg, I. (SSP)	789	2.1	
Matthew, G. (Paisley)	381	1.0	
Rodgers, R. (Ind)	166	0.4	
Broadbent, H. (SLP)	107	0.3	
Lab majority	13,232	34.95	
Electorate	60,181		
Turnout	37,860	62.91	

Lab hold (6.2% from Lab to Lib Dem)

PENDLE

		%	+/-%
*Prentice, G. (Lab)	15,250	37.1	-7.6
Ellison, J. (Con)	13,070	31.8	-2.1
Anwar, S. (Lib Dem)	9,528	23.2	9.4
Boocock, T. (BNP)	2,547	6.2	1.2
Cannon, G. (UKIP)	737	1.8	-1.0
Lab majority	2,180	5.30	
Electorate	64,917		
Turnout	41,132	63.36	

Lab hold (2.7% from Lab to Con)

PENRITH AND THE BORDER

		%	+/-%
*Maclean, D. (Con)	24,046	51.3	-3.6
Walker, G. (Lib Dem)	12,142	25.9	4.2
Boaden, M. (Lab)	8,958	19.1	0.6
Robinson, W. (UKIP)	1,187	2.5	0.4
Gibson, M. (LCA)	549	1.2	-0.8
Con majority	11,904	25.39	
Electorate	70,922		
Turnout	46,882	66.10	

Con hold (3.9% from Con to Lib Dem)

PERTH AND NORTH PERTHSHIRE

(New Scottish constituency)

		%	+/-%
*Wishart, P. (SNP)	15,469	33.7	
Taylor, D. (Con)	13,948	30.4	
Maughan, D. (Lab)	8,601	18.7	
Campbell, G. (Lib Dem)	7,403	16.1	
Stott, P. (SSP)	509	1.1	
SNP majority	1,521	3.31	
Electorate	70,895		
Turnout	45,930	64.79	

SNP hold (3.9% from SNP to Con)

* Member of last parliament

PETERBOROUGH

		%	+/-%
Jackson, S. (Con)	17,364	42.1	4.2
*Clark, H. (Lab)	14,624	35.5	-9.7
Sandford, N. (Lib Dem)	6,876	16.7	2.2
Herdman, M. (UKIP)	1,242	3.0	0.6
Blackham, T. (NF)	931	2.3	0.0
Potter, M. (MNP)	167	0.4	0.0
Con majority	2,740	6.65	
Electorate	67,499		
Turnout	41,204	61.04	

Con gain (6.9% from Lab to Con)

PLYMOUTH DEVONPORT

		%	+/-%
Seabeck, A. (Lab)	18,612	44.3	-14.0
Cuming, R. (Con)	10,509	25.0	-2.1
Jolly, J. (Lib Dem)	8,000	19.0	8.2
Wakeham, B. (UKIP)	3,324	7.9	5.6
Greene, K. (Ind)	747	1.8	0.0
Hawkins, R. (SLP)	445	1.1	0.3
Staunton, T. (Respect)	376	0.9	0.0
Lab majority	8,103	19.29	
Electorate	72,848		
Turnout	42,013	57.67	

Lab hold (6.0% from Lab to Con)

PLYMOUTH SUTTON

		%	+/-%
*Gilroy, L. (Lab/Co-op)	15,497	40.6	-10.2
Colvile, O. (Con)	11,388	29.8	-1.7
Gillard, K. (Lib Dem)	8,685	22.7	8.4
Cumming, R. (UKIP)	2,392	6.3	3.8
Hawkins, R. (SLP)	230	0.6	-0.3
Lab/Co-op majority	4,109	10.76	
Electorate	67,202		
Turnout	38,192	56.83	

Lab/Co-op hold (4.2% from Lab/Co-op to Con)

PONTEFRACT AND CASTLEFORD

		%	+/-%
*Cooper, Y. (Lab)	20,973	63.7	-6.1
Jones, S. (Con)	5,727	17.4	-0.2
Paxton, W. (Lib Dem)	3,942	12.0	4.6
Cass, S. (BNP)	1,835	5.6	0.0
Hague, B. (Green Soc)	470	1.4	0.0
Lab majority	15,246	46.27	
Electorate	61,871		
Turnout	32,947	53.25	

Lab hold (3.0% from Lab to Con)

PONTYPRIDD

		%	+/-%
*Howells, K. (Lab)	20,919	52.8	-7.2
Powell, M. (Lib Dem)	7,728	19.5	8.7
Edwards, Q. (Con)	5,321	13.4	0.1
Richards, J. (PlC)	4,420	11.2	-2.6
Bevan, D. (UKIP)	1,013	2.6	1.0
Griffiths, R. (Comm)	233	0.6	0.0
Lab majority	13,191	33.28	
Electorate	65,074		
Turnout	39,634	60.91	

Lab hold (7.9% from Lab to Lib Dem)

POOLE

		%	+/-%
*Syms, R. (Con)	17,571	43.4	-1.8
Plummer, M. (Lib Dem)	11,583	28.6	3.1
Brown, D. (Lab)	9,376	23.1	-3.7
Barnes, J. (UKIP)	1,436	3.5	1.1
Pirnie, P. (BNP)	547	1.4	0.0
Con majority	5,988	14.78	
Electorate	64,178		
Turnout	40,513	63.13	

Con hold (2.4% from Con to Lib Dem)

POPLAR AND CANNING TOWN

		%	+/-%
*Fitzpatrick, J. (Lab)	15,628	40.1	-21.1
Archer, T. (Con)	8,499	21.8	2.0
Rahman, O. (Respect)	6,573	16.9	0.0
Ludlow, J. (Lib Dem)	5,420	13.9	2.8
McGrenera, T. (Greens)	955	2.5	0.0
Hoque, A. (Ind)	815	2.1	0.0
Smith, T. (Veritas)	650	1.7	0.0
Ademolake, S. (CPA)	470	1.2	0.0
Lab majority	7,129	18.27	
Electorate	61,768		
Turnout	39,010	63.16	

Lab hold (11.6% from Lab to Con)

PORTSMOUTH NORTH

		%	+/-%
McCarthy-Fry, S. (Lab/Co-op)	15,412	40.9	-9.8
Mordaunt, P. (Con)	14,273	37.8	1.1
Lawson, G. (Lib Dem)	6,684	17.7	7.4
Smith, M. (UKIP)	1,348	3.6	2.1
Lab/Co-op majority	1,139	3.02	
Electorate	62,884		
Turnout	37,717	59.98	

Lab/Co-op hold (5.5% from Lab/Co-op to Con)

PORTSMOUTH SOUTH

		%	+/-%
*Hancock, M. (Lib Dem)	17,047	42.2	-2.4
Dinenage, C. (Con)	13,685	33.9	4.8
Button, M. (Lab)	8,714	21.6	-2.3
Pierson, D. (UKIP)	928	2.3	1.5
Lib Dem majority	3,362	8.33	
Electorate	70,969		
Turnout	40,374	56.89	

Lib Dem hold (3.6% from Lib Dem to Con)

PRESELI PEMBROKESHIRE

		%	+/-%
Crabb, S. (Con)	14,106	36.6	3.2
Hayman, S. (Lab)	13,499	35.0	-6.4
Smith, D. (Lib Dem)	4,963	12.9	2.3
Mathias, M. (PlC)	4,752	12.3	-0.4
Carver, J. (UKIP)	498	1.3	0.4
Scott-Cato, M. (Greens)	494	1.3	0.0
Bowen, T. (SLP)	275	0.7	-0.5
Con majority	607	1.57	
Electorate	55,502		
Turnout	38,587	69.52	

Con gain (4.8% from Lab to Con)

* Member of last parliament

PRESTON

		%	+/-%
*Hendrick, M. (Lab/Co-op)	17,210	50.5	-6.5
Bryce, F. (Con)	7,803	22.9	-0.1
Parkinson, W. (Lib Dem)	5,701	16.7	3.6
Lavalette, M. (Respect)	2,318	6.8	0.0
Boardman, E. (UKIP)	1,049	3.1	0.0
Lab/Co-op majority	9,407	27.60	
Electorate	63,351		
Turnout	34,081	53.80	

Lab/Co-op hold (3.2% from Lab/Co-op to Con)

PUDSEY

		%	+/-%
*Truswell, P. (Lab)	21,261	45.8	-2.3
Singleton, P. (Con)	15,391	33.1	-2.5
Keeley, J. (Lib Dem)	8,551	18.4	4.2
Daniel, D. (UKIP)	1,241	2.7	0.6
Lab majority	5,870	12.64	
Electorate	70,411		
Turnout	46,444	65.96	

Lab hold (0.1% from Con to Lab)

PUTNEY

		%	+/-%
Greening, J. (Con)	15,497	42.4	4.0
*Colman, T. (Lab)	13,731	37.5	-8.9
Ambache, J. (Lib Dem)	5,965	16.3	2.7
Magnum, K. (Greens)	993	2.7	0.0
Gahan, A. (UKIP)	388	1.1	0.1
Con majority	1,766	4.83	
Electorate	61,498		
Turnout	36,574	59.47	

Con gain (6.5% from Lab to Con)

RAYLEIGH

		%	+/-%
*Francois, M. (Con)	25,609	55.4	5.3
Ware-Lane, J. (Lab)	10,883	23.6	-7.2
Cumberland, S. (Lib Dem)	7,406	16.0	0.6
Davies, J. (UKIP)	2,295	5.0	1.3
Con majority	14,726	31.88	
Electorate	71,996		
Turnout	46,193	64.16	

Con hold (6.3% from Lab to Con)

READING EAST

		%	+/-%
Wilson, R. (Con)	15,557	35.4	3.5
Page, T. (Lab)	15,082	34.4	-10.4
Howson, J. (Lib Dem)	10,619	24.2	5.7
White, R. (Greens)	1,548	3.5	1.1
Lamb, D. (UKIP)	849	1.9	0.7
Lloyd, J. (Ind)	135	0.3	0.0
Hora, R. (Ind)	122	0.3	0.1
Con majority	475	1.08	
Electorate	72,806		
Turnout	43,912	60.31	

Con gain (7.0% from Lab to Con)

READING WEST

		%	+/-%
*Salter, M. (Lab)	18,940	45.0	-8.1
Cameron, E. (Con)	14,258	33.9	1.8
Gaines, D. (Lib Dem)	6,663	15.8	3.0
Williams, P. (UKIP)	1,180	2.8	0.8
Windisch, A. (Greens)	921	2.2	0.0
Boyle, D. (Veritas)	141	0.3	0.0

Lab majority	4,682	11.12
Electorate	69,011	
Turnout	42,103	61.01

Lab hold (5.0% from Lab to Con)

REDCAR

		%	+/-%
*Baird, V. (Lab)	19,968	51.4	-8.9
Swales, I. (Lib Dem)	7,852	20.2	7.6
Lehrle, J. (Con)	6,954	17.9	-7.2
McGlade, C. (Ind)	2,379	6.1	0.0
Harris, A. (BNP)	985	2.5	0.0
Walker, E. (UKIP)	564	1.5	0.0
Taylor, J. (SLP)	159	0.4	-1.6
Lab majority	12,116	31.18	
Electorate	66,947		
Turnout	38,861	58.05	

Lab hold (8.3% from Lab to Lib Dem)

REDDITCH

		%	+/-%
*Smith, J. (Lab)	18,012	44.7	-0.9
Lumley, K. (Con)	15,296	38.0	-1.0
Hicks, N. (Lib Dem)	5,602	13.9	3.6
Ison, J. (UKIP)	1,381	3.4	0.0
Lab majority	2,716	6.74	
Electorate	64,121		
Turnout	40,291	62.84	

Lab hold (0.0% from Con to Lab)

REGENT'S PARK AND KENSINGTON NORTH

		%	+/-%
*Buck, K. (Lab)	18,196	44.7	-9.9
Bradshaw, J. (Con)	12,065	29.7	2.7
Martins, R. (Lib Dem)	7,569	18.6	6.0
Miller, P. (Greens)	1,985	4.9	1.5
Perrin, P. (UKIP)	456	1.1	0.2
Boufas, R. (CP)	227	0.6	0.0
Dharamsey, A. (Ind)	182	0.5	0.3
Lab majority	6,131	15.07	
Electorate	55,824		
Turnout	40,680	72.87	

Lab hold (6.3% from Lab to Con)

REIGATE

		%	+/-%
*Blunt, C. (Con)	20,884	49.0	1.2
Kulka, J. (Lib Dem)	9,896	23.2	2.1
Townend, S. (Lab)	8,896	20.9	-6.6
Wraith, J. (UKIP)	1,921	4.5	1.8
Green, H. (EDP)	600	1.4	0.0
Selby, M. (Ind)	408	1.0	0.0
Con majority	10,988	25.79	
Electorate	65,719		
Turnout	42,605	64.83	

Con hold (0.5% from Con to Lib Dem)

EAST RENFREWSHIRE

(previously Eastwood)

		%	+/-%
*Murphy, J. (Lab)	20,815	43.9	-3.7
Cook, R. (Con)	14,158	29.9	1.1
MacDonald, G. (Lib Dem)	8,659	18.3	5.4
Bhutta, O. (SNP)	3,245	6.9	-1.7
Henderson, I. (SSP)	528	1.1	-0.6

* Member of last parliament

Lab majority	6,657	14.04
Electorate	65,714	
Turnout	47,405	72.14

Lab hold (2.4% from Lab to Con)

RHONDDA

		%	+/-%
*Bryant, C. (Lab)	21,198	68.1	-0.3
Jones, L. (PlC)	4,956	15.9	-5.2
Roberts, K. (Lib Dem)	3,264	10.5	6.0
Stuart-Smith, P. (Con)	1,730	5.6	1.0
Lab majority	16,242	52.14	
Electorate	51,041		
Turnout	31,148	61.03	

Lab hold (2.5% from PlC to Lab)

SOUTH RIBBLE

		%	+/-%
*Borrow, D. (Lab)	20,428	43.0	-3.4
Fullbrook, L. (Con)	18,244	38.4	0.3
Alcock, M. (Lib Dem)	7,634	16.1	0.6
Jones, K. (UKIP)	1,205	2.5	0.0
Lab majority	2,184	4.60	
Electorate	75,357		
Turnout	47,511	63.05	

Lab hold (1.8% from Lab to Con)

RIBBLE VALLEY

		%	+/-%
*Evans, N. (Con)	25,834	51.9	0.4
Young, J. (Lib Dem)	11,663	23.4	-5.2
Davenport, J. (Lab)	10,924	22.0	2.0
Henry, K. (UKIP)	1,345	2.7	0.0
Con majority	14,171	28.48	
Electorate	75,692		
Turnout	49,766	65.75	

Con hold (2.8% from Lib Dem to Con)

RICHMOND PARK

		%	+/-%
Kramer, S. (Lib Dem)	24,011	46.7	-1.0
Forgione, M. (Con)	20,280	39.5	1.9
Butler, J. (Lab)	4,768	9.3	-2.0
Page, J. (Greens)	1,379	2.7	0.2
Dul, P. (UKIP)	458	0.9	0.2
Flower, P. (CPA)	288	0.6	0.0
Harrison, M. (Ind)	83	0.2	-0.1
Weiss, R. (Vote Dream)	63	0.1	0.0
Meacock, R. (Ind)	44	0.1	0.0
Lib Dem majority	3,731	7.26	
Electorate	70,555		
Turnout	51,374	72.81	

Lib Dem hold (1.4% from Lib Dem to Con)

RICHMOND (YORKSHIRE)

		%	+/-%
*Hague, W. (Con)	26,722	59.1	0.2
Foster, N. (Lab)	8,915	19.7	-2.2
Bell, J. (Lib Dem)	7,982	17.7	-0.3
Rowe, L. (Greens)	1,581	3.5	0.0
Con majority	17,807	39.40	
Electorate	69,521		
Turnout	45,200	65.02	

Con hold (1.2% from Lab to Con)

ROCHDALE

		%	+/-%
Rowen, P. (Lib Dem)	16,787	41.1	6.2
*Fitzsimons, L. (Lab)	16,345	40.0	-9.2

		%	+/-%
Hussain, K. (Con)	4,270	10.5	-2.9
Adams, D. (BNP)	1,773	4.3	0.0
Whittaker, J. (UKIP)	499	1.2	0.0
Chatterjee, S. (Greens)	448	1.1	-0.8
Salim, M. (IZB)	361	0.9	0.0
Faulkner, C. (Veritas)	353	0.9	0.0
Lib Dem majority	442	1.08	
Electorate	69,894		
Turnout	40,836	58.43	

Lib Dem gain (7.7% from Lab to Lib Dem)

ROCHFORD AND SOUTHEND EAST

		%	+/-%
Duddridge, J. (Con)	17,874	45.3	-8.3
Grindrod, F. (Lab)	12,380	31.4	-3.4
Longley, G. (Lib Dem)	5,967	15.1	7.7
Croft, J. (UKIP)	1,913	4.9	0.0
Vaughan, A. (Greens)	1,328	3.4	0.7
Con majority	5,494	13.92	
Electorate	71,186		
Turnout	39,462	55.44	

Con hold (2.4% from Con to Lab)

ROMFORD

		%	+/-%
*Rosindell, A. (Con)	21,560	59.1	6.1
Mullane, M. (Lab)	9,971	27.3	-9.0
Seeff, G. (Lib Dem)	3,066	8.4	0.4
McCaffrey, J. (BNP)	1,088	3.0	1.8
Murray, T. (UKIP)	797	2.2	0.7
Con majority	11,589	31.77	
Electorate	58,571		
Turnout	36,482	62.29	

Con hold (7.5% from Lab to Con)

ROMSEY

		%	+/-%
*Gidley, S. (Lib Dem)	22,465	44.7	-2.3
Nokes, C. (Con)	22,340	44.4	2.3
Stevens, M. (Lab)	4,430	8.8	0.6
Wigley, M. (UKIP)	1,076	2.1	0.6
Lib Dem majority	125	0.25	
Electorate	72,177		
Turnout	50,311	69.71	

Lib Dem hold (2.3% from Lib Dem to Con)

ROSS, SKYE AND LOCHABER

(New Scottish constituency)		%	+/-%
*Kennedy, C. (Lib Dem)	19,100	58.7	
Conniff, C. (Lab)	4,851	14.9	
Hodgson, J. (Con)	3,275	10.1	
Will, M. (SNP)	3,119	9.6	
Jardine, D. (Greens)	1,097	3.4	
Anderson, P. (UKIP)	500	1.5	
McLeod, A. (SSP)	412	1.3	
Grant, M. (Ind)	184	0.6	
Lib Dem majority	14,249	43.79	
Electorate	50,507		
Turnout	32,538	64.42	

Lib Dem hold (11.3% from Lab to Lib Dem)

* Member of last parliament

ROSSENDALE AND DARWEN

		%	+/-%
*Anderson, J. (Lab)	19,073	42.9	-5.8
Adams, N. (Con)	15,397	34.7	-2.1
Carr, M. (Lib Dem)	6,670	15.0	0.4
Wentworth, A. (BNP)	1,736	3.9	0.0
McIver, G. (Greens)	821	1.9	0.0
Duthie, D. (UKIP)	740	1.7	0.0
Lab majority	3,676	8.27	
Electorate	72,207		
Turnout	44,437	61.54	

Lab hold (1.8% from Lab to Con)

ROTHER VALLEY

		%	+/-%
*Barron, K. (Lab)	21,871	55.4	-6.7
Phillips, C. (Con)	7,647	19.4	-2.3
Bristow, P. (Lib Dem)	6,272	15.9	3.4
Casss, N. (BNP)	2,020	5.1	0.0
Brown, G. (UKIP)	1,685	4.3	0.5
Lab majority	14,224	36.01	
Electorate	67,973		
Turnout	39,495	58.10	

Lab hold (2.2% from Lab to Con)

ROTHERHAM

		%	+/-%
*MacShane, D. (Lab)	15,840	52.8	-11.1
Gordon, T. (Lib Dem)	5,159	17.2	6.6
Rotherham, L. (Con)	4,966	16.6	-2.8
Guest, M. (BNP)	1,986	6.6	0.0
Cutts, D. (UKIP)	1,122	3.7	1.3
Penycate, D. (Greens)	905	3.0	1.1
Lab majority	10,681	35.63	
Electorate	54,410		
Turnout	29,978	55.10	

Lab hold (8.8% from Lab to Lib Dem)

RUGBY AND KENILWORTH

		%	+/-%
Wright, J. (Con)	23,447	41.2	1.5
*King, A. (Lab)	21,891	38.4	-6.6
Allanach, R. (Lib Dem)	10,143	17.8	4.0
Thurley, J. (UKIP)	911	1.6	0.1
Hadland, B. (Ind)	299	0.5	0.0
Pallikaropoulos, L. (Ind)	258	0.5	0.0
Con majority	1,556	2.73	
Electorate	83,303		
Turnout	56,949	68.36	

Con gain (4.0% from Lab to Con)

RUISLIP NORTHWOOD

		%	+/-%
Hurd, N. (Con)	18,939	47.7	-1.0
Cox, M. (Lib Dem)	10,029	25.3	6.0
Riley, A. (Lab)	8,323	21.0	-7.5
Lee, G. (Greens)	892	2.3	0.3
Edward, I. (NF)	841	2.1	0.0
Courtenay, R. (UKIP)	646	1.6	0.0
Con majority	8,910	22.46	
Electorate	60,774		
Turnout	39,670	65.27	

Con hold (3.5% from Con to Lib Dem)

RUNNYMEDE AND WEYBRIDGE

		%	+/-%
*Hammond, P. (Con)	22,366	51.4	2.7
Greenwood, P. (Lab)	10,017	23.0	-5.9
Bolton, H. (Lib Dem)	7,771	17.9	1.5

Micklethwait, T. (UKIP)	1,719	4.0	0.8
Gilman, C. (Greens)	1,180	2.7	-0.2
Collett, A. (Loony)	358	0.8	0.0
Osman, K. (UKC)	113	0.3	0.0
Con majority	12,349	28.37	
Electorate	74,172		
Turnout	43,524	58.68	

Con hold (4.3% from Lab to Con)

RUSHCLIFFE

		%	+/-%
*Clarke, K. (Con)	27,899	49.5	2.0
Gamble, E. (Lab)	14,925	26.5	-7.5
Khan, K. (Lib Dem)	9,813	17.4	3.8
Anthony, S. (Greens)	1,692	3.0	0.7
Faithfull, M. (UKIP)	1,358	2.4	-0.2
Moss, D. (Veritas)	624	1.1	0.0
Con majority	12,974	23.04	
Electorate	79,913		
Turnout	56,311	70.47	

Con hold (4.8% from Lab to Con)

RUTHERGLEN AND HAMILTON WEST

(New Scottish constituency)		%	+/-%
*McAvoy, T. (Lab/Co-op)	24,054	55.6	
Robertson, I. (Lib Dem)	7,942	18.4	
Park, M. (SNP)	6,023	13.9	
Crerar, P. (Con)	3,621	8.4	
Bonnar, B. (SSP)	1,164	2.7	
Murdoch, J. (UKIP)	457	1.1	
Lab/Co-op majority	16,112	37.24	
Electorate	73,998		
Turnout	43,261	58.46	

Lab/Co-op hold (5.4% from Lab/Co-op to Lib Dem)

RUTLAND AND MELTON

		%	+/-%
*Duncan, A. (Con)	25,237	51.2	3.1
Arnold, L. (Lab)	12,307	25.0	-4.8
Hudson, G. (Lib Dem)	9,153	18.6	0.8
Baker, P. (UKIP)	1,554	3.2	0.6
Shelley, D. (Veritas)	696	1.4	0.0
Pender, H. (Ind)	337	0.7	0.0
Con majority	12,930	26.24	
Electorate	75,823		
Turnout	49,284	65.00	

Con hold (4.0% from Lab to Con)

RYEDALE

		%	+/-%
*Greenway, J. (Con)	21,251	48.2	1.0
Beever, G. (Lib Dem)	10,782	24.4	-11.6
Blanchard, P. (Lab)	9,148	20.7	6.0
Feaster, S. (UKIP)	1,522	3.5	1.4
Clarke, J. (Lib)	1,417	3.2	0.0
Con majority	10,469	23.73	
Electorate	67,770		
Turnout	44,120	65.10	

Con hold (6.3% from Lib Dem to Con)

SAFFRON WALDEN

		%	+/-%
*Haselhurst, A. (Con)	27,263	51.4	2.5
Tealby-Watson, E. (Lib Dem)			
	14,255	26.9	1.9

* Member of last parliament

Nandanwa, S. (Lab)	8,755	16.5	-6.1
Brown, R. (Eng Dem)	1,412	2.7	0.0
Tyler, R. (UKIP)	860	1.6	-1.9
Hackett, T. (Veritas)	475	0.9	0.0
Con majority	13,008	24.53	
Electorate	77,600		
Turnout	53,020	68.32	

Con hold (0.3% from Lib Dem to Con)

SALFORD

		%	+/-%
*Blears, H. (Lab)	13,007	57.6	-7.5
Owen, N. (Lib Dem)	5,062	22.4	6.2
Cash, L. (Con)	3,440	15.2	-0.1
Duffy, L. (UKIP)	1,091	4.8	0.0
Lab majority	7,945	35.15	
Electorate	53,294		
Turnout	22,600	42.41	

Lab hold (6.9% from Lab to Lib Dem)

SALISBURY

		%	+/-%
*Key, R. (Con)	25,961	47.8	1.2
Denton-White, R. (Lib Dem)			
	14,819	27.3	-2.8
Moody, C. (Lab)	9,457	17.4	-0.1
Howard, F. (UKIP)	2,290	4.2	0.5
Soutar, H. (Greens)	1,555	2.9	0.8
Holme, J. (Ind)	240	0.4	0.0
Con majority	11,142	20.51	
Electorate	80,385		
Turnout	54,322	67.58	

Con hold (2.0% from Lib Dem to Con)

SCARBOROUGH AND WHITBY

		%	+/-%
Goodwill, R. (Con)	19,248	41.0	1.4
*Quinn, L. (Lab)	18,003	38.4	-8.8
Exley-Moore, T. (Lib Dem)	7,495	16.0	7.6
Dixon, J. (Greens)	1,214	2.6	0.4
Abbott, P. (UKIP)	952	2.0	0.0
Con majority	1,245	2.65	
Electorate	73,806		
Turnout	46,912	63.56	

Con gain (5.1% from Lab to Con)

SCUNTHORPE

		%	+/-%
*Morley, E. (Lab)	17,355	53.1	-6.6
Sturdy, J. (Con)	8,392	25.7	-3.2
Poole, N. (Lib Dem)	5,556	17.0	7.6
Baxendale, D. (UKIP)	1,361	4.2	3.1
Lab majority	8,963	27.44	
Electorate	62,669		
Turnout	32,664	52.12	

Lab hold (1.7% from Lab to Con)

SEDGEFIELD

		%	+/-%
*Blair, T. (Lab)	24,429	58.9	-6.0
Lockwood, A. (Con)	5,972	14.4	-6.5
Browne, R. (Lib Dem)	4,935	11.9	2.9
Keys, R. (Ind)	4,252	10.3	0.0
Brown, W. (UKIP)	646	1.6	-0.9
Farrell, M. (SDLP)	253	0.6	0.0
Luckhurst-Matthews, F. (Veritas)			
	218	0.5	0.0
Abraham, B. (Ind)	209	0.5	0.0

Maroney, B. (Loony)	157	0.4	0.0
Cockburn, J. (BMG)	103	0.3	0.0
Pattinson, T. (Senior)	97	0.2	0.0
Gilham, C. (UKPP)	82	0.2	0.0
John, H. (Ind)	68	0.2	0.0
Barker, J. (Ind)	45	0.1	0.0
Brennan, J. (Ind)	17	0.0	0.0
Lab majority	18,457	44.49	
Electorate	66,666		
Turnout	41,483	62.23	

Lab hold (0.3% from Con to Lab)

SELBY

		%	+/-%
*Grogan, J. (Lab)	22,623	43.1	-2.0
Menzies, M. (Con)	22,156	42.2	1.4
Cuthbertson, I. (Lib Dem)	7,770	14.8	3.7
Lab majority	467	0.89	
Electorate	78,111		
Turnout	52,549	67.27	

Lab hold (1.7% from Lab to Con)

SEVENOAKS

		%	+/-%
*Fallon, M. (Con)	22,437	51.8	2.4
Abbotts, B. (Lib Dem)	9,467	21.9	0.2
Stanley, T. (Lab)	9,101	21.0	-4.6
Dobson, R. (UKIP)	1,309	3.0	0.3
Marshall, J. (Eng Dem)	751	1.7	0.0
Ellis, M. (UKP)	233	0.5	0.0
Con majority	12,970	29.96	
Electorate	65,109		
Turnout	43,298	66.50	

Con hold (1.1% from Lib Dem to Con)

SHEFFIELD ATTERCLIFFE

		%	+/-%
*Betts, C. (Lab)	22,250	60.1	-7.7
Moore, K. (Lib Dem)	6,283	17.0	2.8
Critchlow, T. (Con)	5,329	14.4	-0.8
Arnott, J. (UKIP)	1,680	4.5	1.7
Jones, B. (BNP)	1,477	4.0	0.0
Lab majority	15,967	43.13	
Electorate	67,815		
Turnout	37,019	54.59	

Lab hold (5.2% from Lab to Lib Dem)

SHEFFIELD BRIGHTSIDE

		%	+/-%
*Blunkett, D. (Lab)	16,876	68.5	-8.4
Harston, J. (Lib Dem)	3,232	13.1	4.4
Clark, T. (Con)	2,205	9.0	-1.2
Hartigan, C. (BNP)	1,537	6.2	0.0
Clark, J. (UKIP)	779	3.2	1.8
Lab majority	13,644	55.40	
Electorate	51,379		
Turnout	24,629	47.94	

Lab hold (6.4% from Lab to Lib Dem)

SHEFFIELD CENTRAL

		%	+/-%
*Caborn, R. (Lab)	14,950	49.9	-11.6
Qadar, A. (Lib Dem)	7,895	26.3	6.6
George, S. (Con)	3,094	10.3	-0.6
Little, B. (Greens)	1,808	6.0	2.7
Bowler, M. (Respect)	1,284	4.3	0.0
Payne, M. (BNP)	539	1.8	0.0
Arnott, C. (UKIP)	415	1.4	0.5

* Member of last parliament

SHEFFIELD CENTRAL *continued*

Lab majority	7,055	23.53
Electorate	59,862	
Turnout	29,985	50.09

Lab hold (9.1% from Lab to Lib Dem)

SHEFFIELD HALLAM

		%	+/-%
Clegg, N. (Lib Dem)	20,710	51.2	-4.2
Pitfield, S. (Con)	12,028	29.8	-1.3
Hussain, M. (Lab)	5,110	12.6	0.2
Cole, R. (Greens)	1,331	3.3	0.0
Cordle, S. (CPA)	441	1.1	0.0
James, N. (UKIP)	438	1.1	0.0
Senior, I. (BNP)	369	0.9	0.0
Lib Dem majority	8,682	21.48	
Electorate	59,606		
Turnout	40,427	67.82	

Lib Dem hold (1.5% from Lib Dem to Con)

SHEFFIELD HEELEY

		%	+/-%
*Munn, M. (Lab/Co-op)	18,405	54.0	-3.0
Ross, C. (Lib Dem)	7,035	20.6	-2.1
Crawshaw, A. (Con)	4,987	14.6	0.4
Beatson, J. (BNP)	1,314	3.9	0.0
Unwin, R. (Greens)	1,312	3.9	1.6
Suter, M. (UKIP)	775	2.3	0.4
Dunnell, M. (SAP)	265	0.8	0.0
Lab/Co-op majority	11,370	33.35	
Electorate	59,748		
Turnout	34,093	57.06	

Lab/Co-op hold (0.5% from Lab/Co-op to Lib Dem)

SHEFFIELD HILLSBOROUGH

		%	+/-%
*Smith, A. (Lab)	23,477	51.2	-5.7
Commons, J. (Lib Dem)	12,234	26.7	4.1
Doyle-Price, J. (Con)	6,890	15.0	-3.3
Wright, D. (BNP)	2,010	4.4	0.0
Patterson, M. (UKIP)	1,273	2.8	0.5
Lab majority	11,243	24.50	
Electorate	75,706		
Turnout	45,884	60.61	

Lab hold (4.9% from Lab to Lib Dem)

SHERWOOD

		%	+/-%
*Tipping, P. (Lab)	22,824	48.4	-5.8
Laughton, B. (Con)	16,172	34.3	0.5
Harris, P. (Lib Dem)	6,384	13.6	1.6
Dawkins, M. (UKIP)	1,737	3.7	0.0
Lab majority	6,652	14.12	
Electorate	75,913		
Turnout	47,117	62.07	

Lab hold (3.2% from Lab to Con)

SHIPLEY

		%	+/-%
Davies, P. (Con)	18,608	39.0	-1.9
*Leslie, C. (Lab)	18,186	38.2	-5.8
Briggs, J. (Lib Dem)	7,018	14.7	3.9
Linden, T. (BNP)	2,000	4.2	0.0
Deakin, Q. (Greens)	1,665	3.5	0.5
Crabtree, D. (Iraq)	189	0.4	0.0

Con majority	422	0.89
Electorate	69,575	
Turnout	47,666	68.51

Con gain (2.0% from Lab to Con)

SHREWSBURY AND ATCHAM

		%	+/-%
Kawczynski, D. (Con)	18,960	37.7	0.3
Ion, M. (Lab)	17,152	34.1	-10.5
Burt, R. (Lib Dem)	11,487	22.8	10.5
Lewis, P. (UKIP)	1,349	2.7	-0.6
Bullard, E. (Greens)	1,138	2.3	0.4
Gollins, J. (Ind)	126	0.3	-0.3
Harris, N. (Online)	84	0.2	0.0
Con majority	1,808	3.59	
Electorate	73,193		
Turnout	50,296	68.72	

Con gain (5.4% from Lab to Con)

NORTH SHROPSHIRE

		%	+/-%
*Paterson, O. (Con)	23,061	49.6	0.9
Samuels, S. (Lab)	12,041	25.9	-9.3
Bourne, S. (Lib Dem)	9,175	19.7	7.0
Smith, I. (UKIP)	2,233	4.8	2.3
Con majority	11,020	23.69	
Electorate	73,477		
Turnout	46,510	63.30	

Con hold (5.1% from Lab to Con)

SITTINGBOURNE AND SHEPPEY

		%	+/-%
*Wyatt, D. (Lab)	17,051	41.8	-4.0
Henderson, G. (Con)	16,972	41.6	5.1
Nelson, J. (Lib Dem)	5,183	12.7	-1.4
Dean, S. (UKIP)	926	2.3	0.5
Young, M. (Loony)	479	1.2	-0.6
Cassidy, D. (Veritas)	192	0.5	0.0
Lab majority	79	0.19	
Electorate	62,950		
Turnout	40,803	64.82	

Lab hold (4.5% from Lab to Con)

SKIPTON AND RIPON

		%	+/-%
*Curry, D. (Con)	25,100	49.7	-2.7
English, P. (Lib Dem)	13,480	26.7	0.6
Baptie, P. (Lab)	9,393	18.6	1.2
Bannister, I. (UKIP)	2,274	4.5	0.4
Leakey, R. (Currency)	274	0.5	0.0
Con majority	11,620	23.00	
Electorate	76,485		
Turnout	50,521	66.05	

Con hold (0.0%)

SLEAFORD AND NORTH HYKEHAM

		%	+/-%
*Hogg, D. (Con)	26,855	50.3	0.6
Bull, K. (Lab)	14,150	26.5	-5.5
Harding-Price, D. (Lib Dem)	9,710	18.2	2.0
Croft, G. (UKIP)	2,682	5.0	2.8
Con majority	12,705	23.79	
Electorate	79,612		
Turnout	53,397	67.07	

Con hold (3.1% from Lab to Con)

* Member of last parliament

SLOUGH

		%	+/-%
*Mactaggart, F. (Lab)	17,517	47.2	-11.0
Gunn, S. (Con)	9,666	26.1	-0.1
McCann, T. (Lib Dem)	5,739	15.5	4.9
Khan, A. (Respect)	1,632	4.4	0.0
Howard, G. (UKIP)	1,415	3.8	1.9
Wood, D. (Greens)	759	2.1	0.0
Janik, P. (Ind)	367	1.0	0.0
Lab majority	7,851	21.16	
Electorate	71,595		
Turnout	37,095	51.81	

Lab hold (5.5% from Lab to Con)

SOLIHULL

		%	+/-%
Burt, L. (Lib Dem)	20,896	39.9	14.0
*Taylor, J. (Con)	20,617	39.4	-6.0
Vaughan, R. (Lab)	8,058	15.4	-10.2
Carr, D. (BNP)	1,752	3.4	0.0
Moore, A. (UKIP)	990	1.9	-0.3
Lib Dem majority	279	0.53	
Electorate	77,910		
Turnout	52,313	67.15	

Lib Dem gain (10.0% from Con to Lib Dem)

SOMERTON AND FROME

		%	+/-%
*Heath, D. (Lib Dem)	23,759	44.1	0.4
Allen, C. (Con)	22,947	42.6	0.2
Pestell, J. (Lab)	5,865	10.8	-0.8
Lukins, W. (UKIP)	1,047	1.9	0.2
Beaman, C. (Veritas)	484	0.9	0.0
Lib Dem majority	812	1.50	
Electorate	77,806		
Turnout	54,102	69.53	

Lib Dem hold (0.1% from Con to Lib Dem)

SOUTH ANTRIM – see under Antrim

SOUTH CAMBRIDGESHIRE – see under Cambridgeshire

SOUTH DERBYSHIRE – see under Derbyshire

SOUTH DORSET – see under Dorset

SOUTH DOWN – see under Down

SOUTH EAST CAMBRIDGESHIRE – see under Cambridgeshire

SOUTH EAST CORNWALL – see under Cornwall

SOUTH HOLLAND AND THE DEEPINGS

		%	+/-%
*Hayes, J. (Con)	27,544	57.1	1.7
Woodings, L. (Lab)	11,764	24.4	-7.0
Jarvis, S. (Lib Dem)	6,244	12.9	2.6
Corney, J. (UKIP)	1,950	4.0	1.2
Poll, P. (Ind)	747	1.6	0.0
Con majority	15,780	32.71	
Electorate	77,453		
Turnout	48,249	62.29	

Con hold (4.3% from Lab to Con)

SOUTH NORFOLK – see under Norfolk

SOUTH RIBBLE – see under Ribble

SOUTH SHIELDS

		%	+/-%
*Miliband, D. (Lab)	18,269	60.5	-2.7
Psallidas, S. (Lib Dem)	5,957	19.7	2.9
Lewis, R. (Con)	5,207	17.2	0.4
Afshari-Naderi, N. (Ind)	773	2.6	1.7
Lab majority	12,312	40.76	
Electorate	59,403		
Turnout	30,206	50.85	

Lab hold (2.8% from Lab to Lib Dem)

SOUTH STAFFORDSHIRE – see under Staffordshire

SOUTH SUFFOLK – see under Suffolk

SOUTH SWINDON – see under Swindon

SOUTH THANET – see under Thanet

SOUTH WEST BEDFORDSHIRE – see under Bedfordshire

SOUTH WEST DEVON – see under Devon

SOUTH WEST HERTFORDSHIRE – see under Hertfordshire

SOUTH WEST NORFOLK – see under Norfolk

SOUTH WEST SURREY – see under Surrey

SOUTHAMPTON ITCHEN

		%	+/-%
*Denham, J. (Lab)	20,871	48.3	-6.2
Drummond, F. (Con)	11,569	26.8	-0.6
Goodall, D. (Lib Dem)	9,162	21.2	6.2
Rose, K. (UKIP)	1,623	3.8	1.8
Lab majority	9,302	21.52	
Electorate	78,818		
Turnout	43,225	54.84	

Lab hold (2.8% from Lab to Con)

SOUTHAMPTON TEST

		%	+/-%
*Whitehead, A. (Lab)	17,845	42.7	-9.8
MacLoughlin, S. (Con)	10,827	25.9	0.4
Sollitt, S. (Lib Dem)	10,368	24.8	6.7
Spottiswoode, J. (Greens)	1,482	3.6	0.0
Day, P. (UKIP)	1,261	3.0	1.1
Lab majority	7,018	16.80	
Electorate	72,833		
Turnout	41,783	57.37	

Lab hold (5.1% from Lab to Con)

SOUTHEND WEST

		%	+/-%
*Amess, D. (Con)	18,408	46.2	-0.1
Wexham, P. (Lib Dem)	9,449	23.7	-1.2
Etienne, J. (Lab)	9,072	22.8	-2.3
Sampson, C. (UKIP)	1,349	3.4	-0.3
Velmurgan, M. (Ind)	745	1.9	0.0
Moss, J. (England)	701	1.8	0.0
Anslow, D. (Power)	106	0.3	0.0
Con majority	8,959	22.49	
Electorate	64,915		
Turnout	39,830	61.36	

Con hold (0.6% from Lib Dem to Con)

* Member of last parliament

SOUTHPORT

		%	+/-%
*Pugh, J. (Lib Dem)	19,093	46.3	2.6
Bigley, M. (Con)	15,255	37.0	0.6
Brant, P. (Lab)	5,277	12.8	-3.8
Durrance, T. (UKIP)	749	1.8	0.5
Givens, B. (YPB)	589	1.4	0.0
Forster, H. (Veritas)	238	0.6	0.0
Lib Dem majority	3,838	9.32	
Electorate	67,977		
Turnout	41,201	60.61	

Lib Dem hold (1.0% from Con to Lib Dem)

NORTH SOUTHWARK AND BERMONDSEY

		%	+/-%
*Hughes, S. (Lib Dem)	17,874	47.1	-9.9
McNeill, K. (Lab)	12,468	32.9	2.0
Branch, D. (Con)	4,752	12.5	4.9
Poorun, S. (Greens)	1,137	3.0	1.0
Robson, L. (UKIP)	791	2.1	1.4
Winnett, P. (NF)	704	1.9	0.2
Lawanson, S. (CPA)	233	0.6	0.0
Lib Dem majority	5,406	14.24	
Electorate	77,084		
Turnout	37,959	49.24	

Lib Dem hold (5.9% from Lib Dem to Lab)

SPELTHORNE

		%	+/-%
*Wilshire, D. (Con)	21,620	50.5	5.4
Dibble, K. (Lab)	11,684	27.3	-10.0
James, S. (Lib Dem)	7,318	17.1	2.4
Browne, C. (UKIP)	1,968	4.6	1.7
Schwark, C. (UKC)	239	0.6	0.0
Con majority	9,936	23.20	
Electorate	69,650		
Turnout	42,829	61.49	

Con hold (7.7% from Lab to Con)

ST ALBANS

		%	+/-%
Main, A. (Con)	16,953	37.3	2.1
*Pollard, K. (Lab)	15,592	34.3	-11.2
Green, M. (Lib Dem)	11,561	25.4	7.5
Evans, R. (UKIP)	707	1.6	0.2
Girsman, J. (St Albans)	430	1.0	0.0
Reynolds, M. (Ind)	219	0.5	0.0
Con majority	1,361	2.99	
Electorate	64,595		
Turnout	45,462	70.38	

Con gain (6.6% from Lab to Con)

ST HELENS NORTH

		%	+/-%
*Watts, D. (Lab)	22,329	56.9	-4.3
Beirne, J. (Lib Dem)	8,367	21.3	3.7
Oakley, P. (Con)	7,410	18.9	0.1
Hall, S. (UKIP)	1,165	3.0	0.0
Lab majority	13,962	35.55	
Electorate	69,834		
Turnout	39,271	56.23	

Lab hold (4.0% from Lab to Lib Dem)

ST HELENS SOUTH

		%	+/-%
*Woodward, S. (Lab)	19,345	54.5	4.8
Spencer, B. (Lib Dem)	10,036	28.3	5.2
Riley, U. (Con)	4,602	13.0	-0.9
Nightingale, M. (UKIP)	847	2.4	1.4
Perry, M. (SLP)	643	1.8	-2.6
Lab majority	9,309	26.24	
Electorate	65,441		
Turnout	35,473	54.21	

Lab hold (0.2% from Lab to Lib Dem)

ST IVES

		%	+/-%
*George, A. (Lib Dem)	25,577	50.7	-0.9
Mitchell, C. (Con)	13,968	27.7	-3.5
Dooley, M. (Lab)	6,583	13.1	-0.3
Faulkner, M. (UKIP)	2,551	5.1	1.2
Slack, K. (Greens)	1,738	3.5	0.0
Lib Dem majority	11,609	23.03	
Electorate	74,716		
Turnout	50,417	67.48	

Lib Dem hold (1.3% from Con to Lib Dem)

STAFFORD

		%	+/-%
*Kidney, D. (Lab)	19,889	43.7	-4.3
Chambers, D. (Con)	17,768	39.0	2.4
Stamp, B. (Lib Dem)	6,390	14.0	4.6
Goode, F. (UKIP)	1,507	3.3	-1.9
Lab majority	2,121	4.66	
Electorate	70,359		
Turnout	45,554	64.75	

Lab hold (3.3% from Lab to Con)

STAFFORDSHIRE MOORLANDS

		%	+/-%
*Atkins, C. (Lab)	18,126	41.0	-8.0
Hayes, M. (Con)	15,688	35.5	0.1
Fisher, J. (Lib Dem)	6,927	15.7	1.8
Povey, S. (UKIP)	3,512	7.9	6.2
Lab majority	2,438	5.51	
Electorate	69,136		
Turnout	44,253	64.01	

Lab hold (4.1% from Lab to Con)

SOUTH STAFFORDSHIRE – By-election pending due to death of Jo Harrison, Lib Dem candidate

STALYBRIDGE AND HYDE

		%	+/-%
*Purnell, J. (Lab)	17,535	49.7	-5.8
Boardman, L. (Con)	9,187	26.0	-1.8
Bingham, V. (Lib Dem)	5,532	15.7	2.2
Byrne, N. (BNP)	1,399	4.0	0.0
Smee, M. (Greens)	1,088	3.1	0.0
Whittaker, J. (UKIP)	573	1.6	-1.6
Lab majority	8,348	23.64	
Electorate	66,013		
Turnout	35,314	53.50	

Lab hold (2.0% from Lab to Con)

STEVENAGE

		%	+/-%
*Follett, B. (Lab)	18,003	42.9	-9.0
Freeman, G. (Con)	14,864	35.5	3.7
Davies, J. (Lib Dem)	7,610	18.2	4.0
Peebles, V. (UKIP)	1,305	3.1	0.0
Losonczi, A. (Ind)	152	0.4	-0.4

* Member of last parliament

Lab majority	3,139	7.49	
Electorate	66,889		
Turnout	41,934	62.69	

Lab hold (6.4% from Lab to Con)

STIRLING

(New Scottish constituency)

		%	+/-%
*McGuire, A. (Lab)	15,729	36.0	
Kerr, S. (Con)	10,962	25.1	
Holdsworth, K. (Lib Dem)	9,052	20.7	
McGlinchey, F. (SNP)	5,503	12.6	
Illingworth, D. (Greens)	1,302	3.0	
Sheret, R. (SSP)	458	1.1	
McDonald, J. (Ind)	261	0.6	
Willis, M. (OCV)	215	0.5	
Desmond, M. (UKIP)	209	0.5	
Lab majority	4,767	10.91	
Electorate	64,554		
Turnout	43,691	67.68	

Lab hold (4.2% from Lab to Con)

STOCKPORT

		%	+/-%
*Coffey, A. (Lab)	18,069	50.5	-8.1
Berridge, E. (Con)	8,906	24.9	-1.0
Floodgate, L. (Lib Dem)	7,832	21.9	6.4
Simpson, R. (UKIP)	964	2.7	0.0
Lab majority	9,163	25.62	
Electorate	65,593		
Turnout	35,771	54.53	

Lab hold (3.5% from Lab to Con)

STOCKTON NORTH

		%	+/-%
*Cook, F. (Lab)	20,012	54.9	-8.5
Baldwin, H. (Con)	7,575	20.8	-1.3
Hughes, N. (Lib Dem)	6,869	18.9	7.0
Hughes, K. (BNP)	986	2.7	0.0
Lab majority	12,437	34.14	
Electorate	63,271		
Turnout	36,428	57.57	

Lab hold (3.6% from Lab to Con)

STOCKTON SOUTH

		%	+/-%
*Taylor, D. (Lab)	21,480	47.8	-5.2
Gaddas, J. (Con)	15,341	34.2	1.7
Barker, M. (Lib Dem)	7,171	16.0	2.4
Allison, S. (UKIP)	931	2.1	0.0
Lab majority	6,139	13.67	
Electorate	71,286		
Turnout	44,923	63.02	

Lab hold (3.4% from Lab to Con)

STOKE-ON-TRENT CENTRAL

		%	+/-%
*Fisher, M. (Lab)	14,760	52.9	-7.8
Redfern, J. (Lib Dem)	4,986	17.9	3.2
Baroudy, E. (Con)	4,823	17.3	-1.5
Coleman, M. (BNP)	2,178	7.8	0.0
Bonfiglio, J. (UKIP)	914	3.3	0.0
Cessford, J. (SAP)	246	0.9	0.0
Lab majority	9,774	35.02	
Electorate	57,643		
Turnout	27,907	48.41	

Lab hold (5.5% from Lab to Lib Dem)

STOKE-ON-TRENT NORTH

		%	+/-%
*Walley, J. (Lab)	16,191	52.6	-5.3
Browning, B. (Con)	6,155	20.0	1.2
Jebb, H. (Lib Dem)	4,561	14.8	2.9
Cartlidge, S. (BNP)	2,132	6.9	0.0
Braithwaite, E. (UKIP)	696	2.3	0.0
Taylor, I. (Veritas)	689	2.2	0.0
Chesters, H. (Ind)	336	1.1	-10.2
Lab majority	10,036	32.63	
Electorate	58,422		
Turnout	30,760	52.65	

Lab hold (3.3% from Lab to Con)

STOKE-ON-TRENT SOUTH

		%	+/-%
Flello, R. (Lab)	17,727	46.9	-6.9
Deaville, M. (Con)	9,046	23.9	-0.7
Martin, A. (Lib Dem)	5,894	15.6	2.5
Leat, M. (BNP)	3,305	8.7	5.0
Benson, N. (UKIP)	1,043	2.8	0.0
Allen, G. (Veritas)	805	2.1	0.0
Lab majority	8,681	22.95	
Electorate	70,612		
Turnout	37,820	53.56	

Lab hold (3.1% from Lab to Con)

STONE

		%	+/-%
*Cash, W. (Con)	22,733	48.3	-0.7
Davis, M. (Lab)	13,644	29.0	-6.8
Stevens, R. (Lib Dem)	9,111	19.4	4.3
Nattrass, M. (UKIP)	1,548	3.3	0.0
Con majority	9,089	19.32	
Electorate	70,359		
Turnout	47,036	66.85	

Con hold (3.1% from Lab to Con)

STOURBRIDGE

		%	+/-%
Waltho, L. (Lab)	17,089	41.0	-6.2
Coad, D. (Con)	16,682	40.0	2.4
Bramall, C. (Lib Dem)	6,850	16.4	4.3
Mau, D. (UKIP)	1,087	2.6	0.7
Lab majority	407	0.98	
Electorate	64,479		
Turnout	41,708	64.68	

Lab hold (4.3% from Lab to Con)

STRANGFORD

		%	+/-%
*Robinson, I. (DUP)	20,921	56.5	13.7
McGimpsey, G. (UUP)	7,872	21.3	-19.0
McCarthy, K. (Alliance)	3,332	9.0	2.3
Boyle, J. (SDLP)	2,496	6.7	0.6
Dick, T. (Con)	1,462	4.0	0.0
Kennedy, D. (Sinn Féin)	949	2.6	0.4
DUP majority	13,049	35.24	
Electorate	69,040		
Turnout	37,032	53.64	

DUP hold (0.0%)

* Member of last parliament

STRATFORD-ON-AVON

		%	+/-%
*Maples, J. (Con)	28,652	49.2	-1.1
Juned, S. (Lib Dem)	16,468	28.3	-0.5
Blackmore, R. (Lab/Co-op)			
	10,145	17.4	0.7
Cottam, H. (UKIP)	1,621	2.8	0.6
Davies, M. (Greens)	1,354	2.3	0.2
Con majority	12,184	20.92	
Electorate	84,591		
Turnout	58,240	68.85	

Con hold (0.3% from Con to Lib Dem)

STREATHAM

		%	+/-%
*Hill, K. (Lab)	18,950	46.7	-10.2
Sanders, D. (Lib Dem)	11,484	28.3	10.0
Sproule, J. (Con)	7,238	17.8	-0.1
Collins, S. (Greens)	2,245	5.5	1.1
Gittings, T. (UKIP)	396	1.0	0.0
Colvill, W. (World Rev)	127	0.3	0.0
Stone, P. (Ind)	100	0.3	0.0
West, R. (Ind)	40	0.1	0.0
Acheng, S. (Ind)	35	0.1	0.0
Lab majority	7,466	18.38	
Electorate	79,193		
Turnout	40,615	51.29	

Lab hold (10.1% from Lab to Lib Dem)

STRETFORD AND URMSTON

		%	+/-%
*Hughes, B. (Lab)	19,417	51.0	-10.2
Hinds, D. (Con)	11,566	30.4	3.3
Bhatti, F. (Lib Dem)	5,323	14.0	4.0
Krantz, M. (Respect)	950	2.5	0.0
McManus, M. (UKIP)	845	2.2	0.0
Lab majority	7,851	20.61	
Electorate	61,979		
Turnout	38,101	61.47	

Lab hold (6.7% from Lab to Con)

STROUD

		%	+/-%
*Drew, D. (Lab/Co-op)	22,527	39.6	-6.9
Carmichael, N. (Con)	22,177	39.0	1.6
Hirst, P. (Lib Dem)	8,026	14.1	3.2
Whiteside, M. (Greens)	3,056	5.4	1.9
Noble, E. (UKIP)	1,089	1.9	0.3
Lab/Co-op majority	350	0.62	
Electorate	79,748		
Turnout	56,875	71.32	

Lab/Co-op hold (4.3% from Lab/Co-op to Con)

CENTRAL SUFFOLK AND NORTH IPSWICH

		%	+/-%
*Lord, M. (Con)	22,333	43.9	-0.5
MacDonald, N. (Lab)	14,477	28.5	-8.6
Houseley, A. (Lib Dem)	10,709	21.1	4.9
West, J. (UKIP)	1,754	3.5	1.1
Wolfe, M. (Greens)	1,593	3.1	0.0
Con majority	7,856	15.44	
Electorate	76,271		
Turnout	50,866	66.69	

Con hold (4.0% from Lab to Con)

SUFFOLK COASTAL

		%	+/-%
*Gummer, J. (Con)	23,415	44.6	1.2
Rowe, D. (Lab)	13,730	26.1	-8.6
Young, D. (Lib Dem)	11,637	22.1	3.9
Curtis, R. (UKIP)	2,020	3.8	0.2
Whitlow, P. (Greens)	1,755	3.3	0.0
Con majority	9,685	18.43	
Electorate	77,423		
Turnout	52,557	67.88	

Con hold (4.9% from Lab to Con)

SOUTH SUFFOLK

		%	+/-%
*Yeo, T. (Con)	20,471	42.0	0.6
Pollard, K. (Lib Dem)	13,865	28.5	3.5
Craig, K. (Lab)	11,917	24.5	-5.7
Carver, J. (UKIP)	2,454	5.0	1.6
Con majority	6,606	13.56	
Electorate	67,799		
Turnout	48,707	71.84	

Con hold (1.5% from Con to Lib Dem)

WEST SUFFOLK

		%	+/-%
*Spring, R. (Con)	21,682	49.1	1.5
Jefferys, M. (Lab)	12,773	28.9	-8.6
Graves, A. (Lib Dem)	7,573	17.1	5.3
Smith, I. (UKIP)	2,177	4.9	1.8
Con majority	8,909	20.15	
Electorate	72,856		
Turnout	44,205	60.67	

Con hold (5.0% from Lab to Con)

SUNDERLAND NORTH

		%	+/-%
*Etherington, B. (Lab)	15,719	54.4	-8.3
Daughton, S. (Con)	5,724	19.8	1.9
Hollern, J. (Lib Dem)	4,277	14.8	2.7
Herron, N. (Ind)	2,057	7.1	2.0
Hiles, D. (BNP)	1,136	3.9	1.6
Lab majority	9,995	34.57	
Electorate	58,146		
Turnout	28,913	49.72	

Lab hold (5.1% from Lab to Con)

SUNDERLAND SOUTH

		%	+/-%
*Mullin, C. (Lab)	17,982	58.6	-5.3
Oliver, R. (Con)	6,923	22.5	2.5
Kane, G. (Lib Dem)	4,492	14.6	2.8
Guynan, D. (BNP)	1,166	3.8	2.0
Warner, R. (Loony)	149	0.5	-0.5
Lab majority	11,059	36.01	
Electorate	62,256		
Turnout	30,712	49.33	

Lab hold (3.9% from Lab to Con)

EAST SURREY

		%	+/-%
*Ainsworth, P. (Con)	27,659	56.2	3.7
Pursehouse, J. (Lib Dem)	11,738	23.8	-0.6
Bridge, J. (Lab)	7,288	14.8	-4.3
Ston, A. (UKIP)	2,158	4.4	0.5
Matthews, W. (LCA)	410	0.8	0.0
Con majority	15,921	32.32	
Electorate	73,948		
Turnout	49,253	66.60	

Con hold (2.1% from Lib Dem to Con)

* Member of last parliament

SURREY HEATH

		%	+/-%
Gove, M. (Con)	24,642	51.5	1.8
Harper, R. (Lib Dem)	13,797	28.8	3.2
Lowe, C. (Lab)	7,989	16.7	-4.7
Smith, S.	1,430	3.0	-0.3
Con majority	10,845	22.66	
Electorate	76,090		
Turnout	47,858	62.90	

Con hold (0.7% from Con to Lib Dem)

SOUTH WEST SURREY

		%	+/-%
Hunt, J. (Con)	26,420	50.4	5.1
Cordon, S. (Lib Dem)	20,709	39.5	-4.0
Sleigh, T. (Lab)	4,150	7.9	-0.8
Clark, T. (UKIP)	958	1.8	-0.6
Platt, G. (Veritas)	172	0.3	0.0
Con majority	5,711	10.90	
Electorate	72,977		
Turnout	52,409	71.82	

Con hold (4.6% from Lib Dem to Con)

MID SUSSEX

		%	+/-%
*Soames, N. (Con)	23,765	48.0	1.9
Tierney, S. (Lib Dem)	17,875	36.1	5.0
Fromant, R. (Lab)	6,280	12.7	-6.3
Piggott, H. (UKIP)	1,574	3.2	0.7
Con majority	5,890	11.90	
Electorate	72,114		
Turnout	49,494	68.63	

Con hold (1.6% from Con to Lib Dem)

SUTTON AND CHEAM

		%	+/-%
*Burstow, P. (Lib Dem)	19,768	47.1	-1.7
Willis, R. (Con)	16,922	40.4	2.4
Shukla, A. (Lab)	4,954	11.8	-1.4
Weiss, R. (Vote Dream)	288	0.7	0.0
Lib Dem majority	2,846	6.79	
Electorate	63,319		
Turnout	41,932	66.22	

Lib Dem hold (2.0% from Lib Dem to Con)

SUTTON COLDFIELD

		%	+/-%
*Mitchell, A. (Con)	24,308	52.5	2.1
Pocock, R. (Lab)	12,025	26.0	-1.2
Drury, C. (Lib Dem)	7,710	16.7	-2.4
Shorrock, S. (UKIP)	2,275	4.9	2.2
Con majority	12,283	26.52	
Electorate	72,995		
Turnout	46,318	63.45	

Con hold (1.6% from Lab to Con)

SWANSEA EAST

		%	+/-%
James, S. (Lab)	17,457	56.6	-8.6
Speht, R. (Lib Dem)	6,208	20.1	9.9
Bland, E. (Con)	3,103	10.1	0.0
Couch, C. (PlC)	2,129	6.9	-4.6
Holloway, K. (BNP)	770	2.5	0.0
Jenkins, T. (UKIP)	674	2.2	0.7
Young, T. (Greens)	493	1.6	0.1
Lab majority	11,249	36.48	
Electorate	58,813		
Turnout	30,834	52.43	

Lab hold (9.3% from Lab to Lib Dem)

SWANSEA WEST

		%	+/-%
*Williams, A. (Lab)	13,833	41.8	-6.9
Kinzett, R. (Lib Dem)	9,564	28.9	12.4
Abdel-Haq, M. (Con)	5,285	16.0	-3.0
Roberts, H. (PlC)	2,150	6.5	-4.1
Shrewsbury, M. (Greens)	738	2.2	0.3
Ford, M. (UKIP)	609	1.8	-0.2
Williams, R. (SAP)	288	0.9	0.0
Pank, S. (LCA)	218	0.7	0.0
Lab majority	4,269	12.90	
Electorate	57,946		
Turnout	33,086	57.10	

Lab hold (9.6% from Lab to Lib Dem)

NORTH SWINDON

		%	+/-%
*Wills, M. (Lab)	19,612	43.7	-9.2
Tomlinson, J. (Con)	17,041	38.0	4.3
Evemy, M. (Lib Dem)	6,831	15.2	3.7
Tingey, R. (UKIP)	998	2.2	0.3
Newman, A. (Soc Unity)	208	0.5	0.0
Reynolds, E. (Ind)	195	0.4	0.0
Lab majority	2,571	5.73	
Electorate	73,636		
Turnout	44,885	60.96	

Lab hold (6.7% from Lab to Con)

SOUTH SWINDON

		%	+/-%
Snelgrove, A. (Lab/Co-op)			
	17,534	40.3	-11.0
Buckland, R. (Con)	16,181	37.2	2.8
Stebbing, S. (Lib Dem)	7,322	16.8	4.9
Hughes, B. (Greens)	1,234	2.8	0.0
Halden, S. (UKIP)	955	2.2	0.6
Hayward, A. (Ind)	193	0.4	0.0
Williams, J. (Ind)	53	0.1	0.0
Lab majority	1,353	3.11	
Electorate	72,267		
Turnout	43,472	60.15	

Lab hold (6.9% from Lab to Con)

TAMWORTH

		%	+/-%
*Jenkins, B. (Lab)	18,801	43.0	-6.0
Pincher, C. (Con)	16,232	37.1	-0.5
Bennion, P. (Lib Dem)	6,175	14.1	2.4
Eston, P. (Veritas)	1,320	3.0	0.0
Simpson, T. (UKIP)	1,212	2.8	1.1
Lab majority	2,569	5.87	
Electorate	71,675		
Turnout	43,740	61.03	

Lab hold (2.8% from Lab to Con)

TATTON

		%	+/-%
*Osborne, G. (Con)	21,447	51.8	3.7
Madders, J. (Lab)	9,716	23.5	-3.8
Arnold, A. (Lib Dem)	9,016	21.8	3.2
Bowler, D. (UKIP)	996	2.4	0.5
Gibson, M. (Ind)	239	0.6	0.0
Con majority	11,731	28.33	
Electorate	64,140		
Turnout	41,414	64.57	

Con hold (3.7% from Lab to Con)

* Member of last parliament

TAUNTON

		%	+/-%
Browne, J. (Lib Dem)	25,764	43.3	2.0
*Flook, A. (Con)	25,191	42.3	0.6
Govier, A. (Lab)	7,132	12.0	-3.0
Miles, H. (UKIP)	1,441	2.4	0.4
Lib Dem majority	573	0.96	
Electorate	85,466		
Turnout	59,528	69.65	

Lib Dem gain (0.7% from Con to Lib Dem)

TEIGNBRIDGE

		%	+/-%
*Younger-Ross, R. (Lib Dem)			
	27,808	45.7	1.3
Johnson, S. (Con)	21,593	35.5	-3.9
Sherwood, C. (Lab)	6,931	11.4	-1.0
Colman, T. (UKIP)	3,881	6.4	2.6
Wills, R. (Lib)	685	1.1	0.0
Lib Dem majority	6,215	10.21	
Electorate	88,674		
Turnout	60,898	68.68	

Lib Dem hold (2.6% from Con to Lib Dem)

TELFORD

		%	+/-%
*Wright, D. (Lab)	16,506	48.3	-6.3
Kyriazis, S. (Con)	11,100	32.5	5.0
Jenkins, I. (Lib Dem)	4,941	14.4	1.5
McCartney, T. (UKIP)	1,659	4.9	1.3
Lab majority	5,406	15.80	
Electorate	59,277		
Turnout	34,206	57.71	

Lab hold (5.7% from Lab to Con)

TEWKESBURY

		%	+/-%
*Robertson, L. (Con)	22,339	49.2	3.1
Cameron, A. (Lib Dem)	12,447	27.4	1.1
Mannan, C. (Lab)	9,179	20.2	-6.7
Rendell, R. (Greens)	1,488	3.3	0.0
Con majority	9,892	21.76	
Electorate	72,145		
Turnout	45,453	63.00	

Con hold (1.0% from Lib Dem to Con)

NORTH THANET

		%	+/-%
*Gale, R. (Con)	21,699	49.6	-0.7
Johnston, I. (Lab)	14,065	32.2	-2.2
Barnard, M. (Lib Dem)	6,279	14.4	3.4
Stocks, T. (UKIP)	1,689	3.9	1.5
Con majority	7,634	17.46	
Electorate	72,734		
Turnout	43,732	60.13	

Con hold (0.8% from Lab to Con)

SOUTH THANET

		%	+/-%
*Ladyman, S. (Lab)	16,660	40.4	-5.3
MacGregor, M. (Con)	15,996	38.8	-2.3
Voizey, G. (Lib Dem)	5,431	13.2	3.8
Farage, N. (UKIP)	2,079	5.0	3.8
Green, H. (Greens)	888	2.2	0.0
Kinsella, M. (Ind)	188	0.5	-1.5
Lab majority	664	1.61	
Electorate	63,436		
Turnout	41,242	65.01	

Lab hold (1.5% from Lab to Con)

THE WREKIN – see under Wrekin

THURROCK

		%	+/-%
*Mackinlay, A. (Lab)	20,636	47.2	-9.3
Hague, G. (Con)	14,261	32.6	2.9
Palmer, E. (Lib Dem)	4,770	10.9	0.6
Geri, N. (BNP)	2,526	5.8	0.0
Jackson, C. (UKIP)	1,499	3.4	0.0
Lab majority	6,375	14.59	
Electorate	79,545		
Turnout	43,692	54.93	

Lab hold (6.1% from Lab to Con)

TIVERTON AND HONITON

		%	+/-%
*Browning, A. (Con)	27,838	47.9	0.8
Nation, D. (Lib Dem)	16,787	28.9	-7.0
Bentley, F. (Lab)	7,944	13.7	1.7
Edwards, R. (UKIP)	2,499	4.3	2.0
Collins, R. (Lib)	1,701	2.9	1.9
Matthews, C. (Greens)	1,399	2.4	0.6
Con majority	11,051	19.00	
Electorate	83,375		
Turnout	58,168	69.77	

Con hold (3.9% from Lib Dem to Con)

TONBRIDGE AND MALLING

		%	+/-%
*Stanley, J. (Con)	24,357	52.9	3.5
Hayman, V. (Lab)	11,005	23.9	-6.1
Barstow, J. (Lib Dem)	8,980	19.5	1.6
Waller, D. (UKIP)	1,721	3.7	1.0
Con majority	13,352	28.99	
Electorate	68,444		
Turnout	46,063	67.30	

Con hold (4.8% from Lab to Con)

TOOTING

		%	+/-%
Khan, S. (Lab)	17,914	43.1	-11.0
Bethell, J. (Con)	12,533	30.2	3.7
Dearden, S. (Lib Dem)	8,110	19.5	4.7
Vitelli, S. (Greens)	1,695	4.1	-0.6
Zaidi, A. (Respect)	700	1.7	0.0
McDonald, S. (UKIP)	424	1.0	0.0
Perkin, I. (Ind)	192	0.5	0.0
Lab majority	5,381	12.95	
Electorate	70,504		
Turnout	41,568	58.96	

Lab hold (7.4% from Lab to Con)

TORBAY

		%	+/-%
*Sanders, A. (Lib Dem)	19,317	40.8	-9.7
Wood, M. (Con)	17,288	36.6	0.2
Pedrick-Friend, D. (Lab)	6,972	14.7	5.3
Booth, G. (UKIP)	3,726	7.9	4.7
Lib Dem majority	2,029	4.29	
Electorate	76,474		
Turnout	47,303	61.86	

Lib Dem hold (4.9% from Lib Dem to Con)

TORFAEN

		%	+/-%
*Murphy, P. (Lab)	20,472	56.9	-5.2
Ramsey, N. (Con)	5,681	15.8	-0.1

*　Member of last parliament

Watkins, V. (Lib Dem)	5,678	15.8	4.6
Preece, A. (PlC)	2,242	6.2	-1.5
Rowlands, D. (UKIP)	1,145	3.2	1.3
Turner-Thomas, R. (Ind)	761	2.1	0.0
Lab majority	14,791	41.11	
Electorate	60,669		
Turnout	35,979	59.30	

Lab hold (2.5% from Lab to Con)

TORRIDGE AND WEST DEVON – see under Devon

TOTNES

		%	+/-%
*Steen, A. (Con)	21,112	41.7	-2.8
Treleaven, M. (Lib Dem)	19,165	37.9	0.7
Burns, V. (Lab)	6,185	12.2	0.0
Knapman, R. (UKIP)	3,914	7.7	1.6
Thompson, M. (Ind)	199	0.4	0.0
Con majority	1,947	3.85	
Electorate	74,744		
Turnout	50,575	67.66	

Con hold (1.7% from Con to Lib Dem)

TOTTENHAM

		%	+/-%
*Lammy, D. (Lab)	18,343	57.9	-9.5
Hoban, W. (Lib Dem)	5,309	16.8	7.3
MacDougall, W. (Con)	4,278	13.5	-0.4
Alder, J. (Respect)	2,014	6.4	0.0
McAskie, P. (Greens)	1,457	4.6	0.0
Durrani, J. (SLP)	263	0.8	0.0
Lab majority	13,034	41.16	
Electorate	66,231		
Turnout	31,664	47.81	

Lab hold (8.4% from Lab to Lib Dem)

TRURO AND ST AUSTELL

		%	+/-%
*Taylor, M. (Lib Dem)	24,089	46.7	-1.6
Kemp, F. (Con)	16,686	32.4	0.1
Mackenzie, C. (Lab)	6,991	13.6	-0.1
Noakes, D. (UKIP)	2,736	5.3	2.0
Jenkin, C. (Meb Ker)	1,062	2.1	-0.2
Lib Dem majority	7,403	14.36	
Electorate	80,256		
Turnout	51,564	64.25	

Lib Dem hold (0.8% from Lib Dem to Con)

TUNBRIDGE WELLS

		%	+/-%
Clark, G. (Con)	21,083	49.6	0.7
Murphy, L. (Lib Dem)	11,095	26.1	1.5
Jedrzejewski, J. (Lab)	8,736	20.6	-2.7
Webb, V. (UKIP)	1,568	3.7	0.4
Con majority	9,988	23.51	
Electorate	64,630		
Turnout	42,482	65.73	

Con hold (0.4% from Con to Lib Dem)

TWICKENHAM

		%	+/-%
*Cable, V. (Lib Dem)	26,696	51.7	2.9
Maynard, P. (Con)	16,731	32.4	-1.1
Whitington, B. (Lab)	5,868	11.4	-2.5

Gower, H. (Greens)	1,445	2.8	-0.1
Orchard, D. (UKIP)	766	1.5	0.3
Gilbert, B. (Ind)	117	0.2	0.0
Weiss, R. (Vote Dream)	64	0.1	0.0
Lib Dem majority	9,965	19.28	
Electorate	72,015		
Turnout	51,687	71.77	

Lib Dem hold (2.0% from Con to Lib Dem)

TYNE BRIDGE

		%	+/-%
*Clelland, D. (Lab)	16,151	61.2	-9.3
Boyle, C. (Lib Dem)	5,751	21.8	9.5
Fairhead, T. (Con)	2,962	11.2	-2.1
Scott, K. (BNP)	1,072	4.1	0.0
Russell, J. (Respect)	447	1.7	0.0
Lab majority	10,400	39.42	
Electorate	53,565		
Turnout	26,383	49.25	

Lab hold (9.4% from Lab to Lib Dem)

TYNEMOUTH

		%	+/-%
*Campbell, A. (Lab)	20,143	47.0	-6.2
McIntyre, M. (Con)	16,000	37.3	3.9
Finlay, C. (Lib Dem)	6,716	15.7	4.0
Lab majority	4,143	9.67	
Electorate	64,023		
Turnout	42,859	66.94	

Lab hold (5.1% from Lab to Con)

NORTH TYNESIDE

		%	+/-%
*Byers, S. (Lab)	22,882	62.0	-7.5
McLellan, D. (Con)	7,845	21.2	6.7
Ferguson, G. (Lib Dem)	6,212	16.8	4.4
Lab majority	15,037	40.71	
Electorate	64,634		
Turnout	36,939	57.15	

Lab hold (7.1% from Lab to Con)

WEST TYRONE

		%	+/-%
*Doherty, P. (Sinn Féin)	16,910	38.9	-1.9
Deeny, C. (Ind)	11,905	27.4	0.0
Buchanan, T. (DUP)	7,742	17.8	0.0
McMenamin, E. (SDLP)	3,949	9.1	-19.7
Hussey, D. (UUP)	2,981	6.9	-23.6
Sinn Féin majority	5,005	11.51	
Electorate	60,286		
Turnout	43,487	72.13	

Sinn Féin hold (0.0%)

MID ULSTER

		%	+/-%
*McGuinness, M. (Sinn Féin)	21,641	47.6	-3.4
McCrea, I. (DUP)	10,665	23.5	-7.7
McGlone, P. (SDLP)	7,922	17.4	0.7
Armstrong, B. (UUP)	4,853	10.7	0.0
Donnelly, F. (WP)	345	0.8	-0.3
Sinn Féin majority	10,976	24.16	
Electorate	62,666		
Turnout	45,426	72.49	

Sinn Féin hold (0.0%)

* Member of last parliament

UPMINSTER

		%	+/-%
*Watkinson, A. (Con)	16,820	48.5	3.0
Darvill, K. (Lab)	10,778	31.1	-10.8
Truesdale, P. (Lib Dem)	3,128	9.0	-0.4
Ower, R. (RA)	1,455	4.2	0.0
Roberts, C. (BNP)	1,174	3.4	0.0
Hindle, A. (UKIP)	701	2.0	-1.2
Collins, M. (Greens)	543	1.6	0.0
Durant, D. (Third)	78	0.2	0.0
Con majority	6,042	17.42	
Electorate	55,075		
Turnout	34,677	62.96	

Con hold (6.9% from Lab to Con)

UPPER BANN

		%	+/-%
Simpson, D. (DUP)	16,679	37.6	8.1
*Trimble, D. (UUP)	11,381	25.6	-7.9
O'Dowd, J. (Sinn Féin)	9,305	21.0	-0.2
Kelly, D. (SDLP)	5,747	12.9	-2.0
Castle, A. (Alliance)	955	2.2	0.0
French, T. (WP)	355	0.8	-0.2
DUP majority	5,298	11.93	
Electorate	72,402		
Turnout	44,422	61.35	

DUP gain (0.0%)

UXBRIDGE

		%	+/-%
*Randall, J. (Con)	16,840	49.0	1.9
Marshall, R. (Lab)	10,669	31.0	-9.8
Mahmood, T. (Lib Dem)	4,544	13.2	3.0
Le May, C. (BNP)	763	2.2	0.0
Young, S. (Greens)	725	2.1	0.0
Kerby, R. (UKIP)	553	1.6	-0.2
Shaw, P. (NF)	284	0.8	0.0
Con majority	6,171	17.95	
Electorate	57,878		
Turnout	34,378	59.40	

Con hold (5.8% from Lab to Con)

VALE OF CLWYD – see under Clwyd

VALE OF GLAMORGAN – see under Glamorgan

VALE OF YORK – see under York

VAUXHALL

		%	+/-%
*Hoey, K. (Lab)	19,744	52.9	-6.3
Anglin, C. (Lib Dem)	9,767	26.2	6.0
Heckels, E. (Con)	5,405	14.5	1.0
Summers, T. (Greens)	1,705	4.6	0.1
McWhirter, R. (UKIP)	271	0.7	0.0
Lambert, D. (Socialist)	240	0.6	0.0
Polenceus, J. (Eng Dem)	221	0.6	0.0
Lab majority	9,977	26.71	
Electorate	79,637		
Turnout	37,353	46.90	

Lab hold (6.1% from Lab to Lib Dem)

WAKEFIELD

		%	+/-%
Creagh, M. (Lab)	18,802	43.3	-6.6
Shelbrooke, A. (Con)	13,648	31.5	0.8
Ridgway, D. (Lib Dem)	7,063	16.3	3.9
Rowe, G. (BNP)	1,328	3.1	0.0
Hardcastle, D. (Greens)	1,297	3.0	0.4

		%	+/-%
Upex, J. (UKIP)	467	1.1	-0.6
McEnhill, A. (England)	356	0.8	0.0
Griffiths, M. (SAP)	319	0.7	0.0
Sheridan, L. (SLP)	101	0.2	-1.3
Lab majority	5,154	11.88	
Electorate	73,118		
Turnout	43,381	59.33	

Lab hold (3.7% from Lab to Con)

WALLASEY

		%	+/-%
*Eagle, A. (Lab)	20,085	54.8	-6.1
Fraser, L. (Con)	10,976	29.9	2.0
Pemberton, J. (Lib Dem)	4,770	13.0	1.8
Griffiths, P. (UKIP)	840	2.3	0.0
Lab majority	9,109	24.84	
Electorate	63,764		
Turnout	36,671	57.51	

Lab hold (4.0% from Lab to Con)

WALSALL NORTH

		%	+/-%
*Winnick, D. (Lab)	15,990	47.8	-10.3
Lucas, I. (Con)	9,350	28.0	-1.1
Taylor, D. (Lib Dem)	4,144	12.4	3.4
Locke, W. (BNP)	1,992	6.0	0.0
Lenton, A. (UKIP)	1,182	3.5	1.0
Smith, P. (Dem Lab)	770	2.3	0.0
Lab majority	6,640	19.86	
Electorate	63,268		
Turnout	33,428	52.84	

Lab hold (4.6% from Lab to Con)

WALSALL SOUTH

		%	+/-%
*George, B. (Lab)	17,633	49.9	-9.0
Sabar, K. (Con)	9,687	27.4	-3.1
Asmal, M. (Lib Dem)	3,240	9.2	2.4
Bennett, D. (UKIP)	1,833	5.2	2.4
Smith, K. (BNP)	1,776	5.0	0.0
Fazal, N. (Respect)	1,146	3.3	0.0
Lab majority	7,946	22.50	
Electorate	60,370		
Turnout	35,315	58.50	

Lab hold (3.0% from Lab to Con)

WALTHAMSTOW

		%	+/-%
*Gerrard, N. (Lab)	17,323	50.3	-11.9
Ahmed, F. (Lib Dem)	9,330	27.1	12.5
Wright, J. (Con)	6,254	18.2	0.1
Brock, R. (UKIP)	810	2.4	1.5
Taaffe, N. (SAP)	727	2.1	-0.2
Lab majority	7,993	23.21	
Electorate	63,079		
Turnout	34,444	54.60	

Lab hold (12.2% from Lab to Lib Dem)

WANSBECK

		%	+/-%
*Murphy, D. (Lab)	20,315	55.2	-2.6
Reed, S. (Lib Dem)	9,734	26.4	3.7
Scrope, G. (Con)	5,515	15.0	2.2
Best, N. (Greens)	1,245	3.4	0.8
Lab majority	10,581	28.75	
Electorate	63,096		
Turnout	36,809	58.34	

Lab hold (3.1% from Lab to Lib Dem)

* Member of last parliament

WANSDYKE

		%	+/-%
*Norris, D. (Lab)	20,686	40.6	-6.2
Watt, C. (Con)	18,847	37.0	1.5
Coleshill, G. (Lib Dem)	10,050	19.7	5.3
Sandell, P. (UKIP)	1,129	2.2	0.9
Parkes, G. (Ind)	221	0.4	0.0
Lab majority	1,839	3.61	
Electorate	70,359		
Turnout	50,933	72.39	

Lab hold (3.9% from Lab to Con)

WANTAGE

		%	+/-%
Vaizey, E. (Con)	22,354	43.1	3.4
Crawford, A. (Lib Dem)	14,337	27.6	-0.4
McDonald, M. (Lab)	12,464	24.0	-4.2
Twine, A. (Greens)	1,332	2.6	0.4
Tolstoy-Miloslavsky, N. (UKIP)	798	1.5	-0.4
Lambourne, G. (Eng Dem)	646	1.2	0.0
Con majority	8,017	15.44	
Electorate	76,156		
Turnout	51,931	68.19	

Con hold (1.9% from Lib Dem to Con)

WARLEY

		%	+/-%
*Spellar, J. (Lab)	17,462	54.4	-6.1
Bissell, K. (Con)	7,315	22.8	0.0
Ferguson, T. (Lib Dem)	4,277	13.3	2.8
Smith, S. (BNP)	1,761	5.5	0.0
Connigale, M. (SLP)	637	2.0	-4.2
Matthews, D. (UKIP)	635	2.0	0.0
Lab majority	10,147	31.62	
Electorate	56,171		
Turnout	32,087	57.12	

Lab hold (3.1% from Lab to Con)

WARRINGTON NORTH

		%	+/-%
*Jones, H. (Lab)	21,632	53.5	-8.2
Ferryman, A. (Con)	9,428	23.3	0.5
Walker, P. (Lib Dem)	7,699	19.1	5.6
Kirkham, J. (UKIP)	1,086	2.7	0.7
Hughes, M. (CAP)	573	1.4	0.0
Lab majority	12,204	30.19	
Electorate	73,352		
Turnout	40,418	55.10	

Lab hold (4.4% from Lab to Con)

WARRINGTON SOUTH

		%	+/-%
*Southworth, H. (Lab)	18,972	40.5	-8.7
Bruce, F. (Con)	15,457	33.0	0.0
Marks, I. (Lib Dem)	11,111	23.7	7.4
Kelley, G. (UKIP)	804	1.7	0.3
Kennedy, P. (Ind)	453	1.0	0.0
Lab majority	3,515	7.51	
Electorate	75,724		
Turnout	46,797	61.80	

Lab hold (4.4% from Lab to Con)

WARWICK AND LEAMINGTON

		%	+/-%
*Plaskitt, J. (Lab)	22,238	40.6	-8.2
Whiteside, C. (Con)	21,972	40.1	2.5
Forbes, L. (Lib Dem)	8,119	14.8	3.7
Davison, I. (Greens)	1,534	2.8	0.0
Warwick, G. (UKIP)	921	1.7	0.5
Lab majority	266	0.49	
Electorate	81,205		
Turnout	54,784	67.46	

Lab hold (5.3% from Lab to Con)

NORTH WARWICKSHIRE

		%	+/-%
*O'Brien, M. (Lab)	22,561	48.1	-6.0
Gibb, I. (Con)	15,008	32.0	-0.4
Roodhouse, J. (Lib Dem)	6,212	13.2	1.9
MacKenzie, M. (BNP)	1,910	4.1	0.0
Campbell, I. (UKIP)	1,248	2.7	0.5
Lab majority	7,553	16.09	
Electorate	75,435		
Turnout	46,939	62.22	

Lab hold (2.8% from Lab to Con)

WATFORD

		%	+/-%
*Ward, C. (Lab)	16,575	33.6	-11.7
Brinton, S. (Lib Dem)	15,427	31.2	13.8
Miraj, A. (Con)	14,634	29.6	-3.7
Rackett, S. (Greens)	1,466	3.0	1.0
Wright, K. (UKIP)	1,292	2.6	1.5
Lab majority	1,148	2.32	
Electorate	76,280		
Turnout	49,394	64.75	

Lab hold (12.8% from Lab to Lib Dem)

WAVENEY

		%	+/-%
*Blizzard, B. (Lab)	22,505	45.3	-5.4
Aldous, P. (Con)	16,590	33.4	0.8
Bromley, N. (Lib Dem)	7,497	15.1	3.7
Aylett, B. (UKIP)	1,861	3.8	1.4
Elliott, G. (Greens)	1,200	2.4	0.3
Lab majority	5,915	11.91	
Electorate	77,138		
Turnout	49,653	64.37	

Lab hold (3.1% from Lab to Con)

WEALDEN

		%	+/-%
*Hendry, C. (Con)	28,975	52.1	2.3
Wigley, S. (Lib Dem)	13,054	23.5	-0.3
Rose, D. (Lab)	9,360	16.8	-3.5
Salmon, J. (Greens)	2,150	3.9	1.5
Riddle, K. (UKIP)	2,114	3.8	0.9
Con majority	15,921	28.61	
Electorate	82,261		
Turnout	55,653	67.65	

Con hold (1.3% from Lib Dem to Con)

WEAVER VALE

		%	+/-%
*Hall, M. (Lab)	18,759	47.6	-4.9
Mackie, A. (Con)	11,904	30.2	2.3
Griffiths, T. (Lib Dem)	7,723	19.6	5.2
Swinscoe, B. (UKIP)	1,034	2.6	1.2

* Member of last parliament

WEAVER VALE *continued*

Lab majority	6,855	17.39
Electorate	69,072	
Turnout	39,420	57.07

Lab hold (3.6% from Lab to Con)

WELLINGBOROUGH

		%	+/-%
Bone, P. (Con)	22,674	42.8	0.6
*Stinchcombe, P. (Lab)	21,987	41.5	-5.3
Church, R. (Lib Dem)	6,147	11.6	2.3
Wrench, J. (UKIP)	1,214	2.3	0.6
Alex, N. (Veritas)	749	1.4	0.0
Dickson, A. (Lib Dem)	234	0.4	0.0
Con majority	687	1.30	
Electorate	79,679		
Turnout	53,005	66.52	

Con gain (3.0% from Lab to Con)

WELLS

		%	+/-%
*Heathcoat-Amory, D. (Con)			
	23,071	43.6	-0.2
Munt, T. (Lib Dem)	20,031	37.8	-0.5
Whittle, D. (Lab)	8,288	15.7	0.2
Reed, S. (UKIP)	1,575	3.0	0.8
Con majority	3,040	5.74	
Electorate	77,842		
Turnout	52,965	68.04	

Con hold (0.2% from Lib Dem to Con)

WELWYN HATFIELD

		%	+/-%
Shapps, G. (Con)	22,172	49.6	9.2
*Johnson, M. (Lab)	16,226	36.3	-6.9
Bedford, S. (Lib Dem)	6,318	14.1	0.1
Con majority	5,946	13.30	
Electorate	65,617		
Turnout	44,716	68.15	

Con gain (8.1% from Lab to Con)

WENTWORTH

		%	+/-%
*Healey, J. (Lab)	21,225	59.6	-7.9
Hughes, M. (Con)	6,169	17.3	-1.5
Orrell, K. (Lib Dem)	4,800	13.5	2.7
Pygott, J. (BNP)	1,798	5.1	0.0
Wilkinson, J. (UKIP)	1,604	4.5	1.6
Lab majority	15,056	42.30	
Electorate	63,561		
Turnout	35,596	56.00	

Lab hold (3.2% from Lab to Con)

WEST ABERDEENSHIRE AND KINCARDINE –
see under Aberdeenshire

WEST BROMWICH EAST

		%	+/-%
*Watson, T. (Lab)	19,741	55.6	-0.3
Bromwich, R. (Con)	8,089	22.8	-3.2
Garrett, I. (Lib Dem)	4,386	12.4	-1.5
Butler, C. (BNP)	2,329	6.6	0.0
Grey, S. (UKIP)	607	1.7	-0.9
Sambrook, J. (SLP)	200	0.6	-1.2
Macklin, M. (Ind)	160	0.5	0.0

* Member of last parliament

Lab majority	11,652	32.81
Electorate	60,565	
Turnout	35,512	58.63

Lab hold (1.5% from Con to Lab)

WEST BROMWICH WEST

		%	+/-%
*Bailey, A. (Lab/Co-op)	18,951	54.3	-6.5
Harker, M. (Con)	8,057	23.1	-2.0
Smith, M. (Lib Dem)	3,583	10.3	3.5
Lloyd, J. (BNP)	3,456	9.9	5.4
Walker, K. (UKIP)	870	2.5	0.9
Lab/Co-op majority	10,894	31.20	
Electorate	66,752		
Turnout	34,917	52.31	

Lab/Co-op hold (2.2% from Lab/Co-op to Con)

WEST DERBYSHIRE – see under Derbyshire

WEST DORSET – see under Dorset

WEST DUNBARTONSHIRE – see under
Dunbartonshire

WEST HAM

		%	+/-%
Brown, L. (Lab)	15,840	51.2	-18.7
German, L. (Respect)	6,039	19.5	0.0
Whitbread, C. (Con)	3,618	11.7	-4.7
Sugden, A. (Lib Dem)	3,364	10.9	3.5
Lithgow, J. (Greens)	894	2.9	-1.2
Hammond, S. (CPA)	437	1.4	0.0
Mayhew, H. (UKIP)	409	1.3	-0.9
Alcantara, G. (Veritas)	365	1.2	0.0
Lab majority	9,801	31.65	
Electorate	62,184		
Turnout	30,966	49.80	

Lab hold (0.0%)

WEST LANCASHIRE – see under Lancashire

WEST SUFFOLK – see under Suffolk

WEST TYRONE – see under Tyrone

WEST WORCESTERSHIRE – see under
Worcestershire

WESTBURY

		%	+/-%
*Murrison, A. (Con)	24,749	44.5	2.4
Hames, D. (Lib Dem)	19,400	34.9	3.3
Gibby, P. (Lab)	9,640	17.3	-4.1
Williams, L. (UKIP)	1,815	3.3	0.8
Con majority	5,349	9.62	
Electorate	83,039		
Turnout	55,604	66.96	

Con hold (0.4% from Con to Lib Dem)

WESTMORLAND AND LONSDALE

		%	+/-%
Farron, T. (Lib Dem)	22,569	45.5	5.1
*Collins, T. (Con)	22,302	44.9	-2.0
Reardon, J. (Lab)	3,796	7.7	-3.3
Gibson, R. (UKIP)	660	1.3	0.2
Kemp, A. (Ind)	309	0.6	0.0
Lib Dem majority	267	0.54	
Electorate	69,363		
Turnout	49,636	71.56	

Lib Dem gain (3.6% from Con to Lib Dem)

WESTON-SUPER-MARE

		%	+/-%
Penrose, J. (Con)	19,804	40.3	1.6
*Cotter, B. (Lib Dem)	17,725	36.1	-3.4
Egan, D. (Lab)	9,169	18.7	-1.1
Spencer, P. (UKIP)	1,207	2.5	1.1
Courtney, C. (BNP)	778	1.6	0.0
Human, W. (Ind)	225	0.5	0.0
Hemingway-Arnold, P. (Honesty)			
	187	0.4	0.0
Con majority	2,079	4.23	
Electorate	74,900		
Turnout	49,095	65.55	

Con gain (2.5% from Lib Dem to Con)

WIGAN

		%	+/-%
*Turner, N. (Lab)	18,901	55.1	-6.6
Coombes, J. (Con)	7,134	20.8	0.0
Capstick, D. (Lib Dem)	6,051	17.7	2.9
Whittaker, J. (UKIP)	1,166	3.4	0.0
Williams, K. (CAP)	1,026	3.0	0.0
Lab majority	11,767	34.33	
Electorate	64,267		
Turnout	34,278	53.34	

Lab hold (3.3% from Lab to Con)

NORTH WILTSHIRE

		%	+/-%
*Gray, J. (Con)	26,282	46.9	1.4
Fox, P. (Lib Dem)	20,979	37.4	-0.8
Nash, D. (Lab)	6,794	12.1	-2.2
Dowdney, N. (UKIP)	1,428	2.6	0.5
Allnatt, P. (Ind)	578	1.0	0.0
Con majority	5,303	9.46	
Electorate	80,896		
Turnout	56,061	69.30	

Con hold (1.1% from Lib Dem to Con)

WIMBLEDON

		%	+/-%
Hammond, S. (Con)	17,886	41.2	4.6
*Casale, R. (Lab)	15,585	35.9	-9.8
Gee, S. (Lib Dem)	7,868	18.1	5.1
Barrow, G. (Greens)	1,374	3.2	0.7
Mills, A. (UKIP)	408	0.9	-0.1
Coverdale, C. (Ind)	211	0.5	0.0
Wilson, A. (TEPK)	50	0.1	0.0
Weiss, R. (Vote Dream)	22	0.1	0.0
Con majority	2,301	5.30	
Electorate	63,714		
Turnout	43,404	68.12	

Con gain (7.2% from Lab to Con)

WINCHESTER

		%	+/-%
*Oaten, M. (Lib Dem)	31,225	50.6	-3.9
Hollingbery, G. (Con)	23,749	38.5	0.2
Davies, P. (Lab)	4,782	7.8	1.8
Abbott, D. (UKIP)	1,321	2.1	1.0
Pendragon, A. (Ind)	581	0.9	0.0
Lib Dem majority	7,476	12.12	
Electorate	85,810		
Turnout	61,658	71.85	

Lib Dem hold (2.1% from Lib Dem to Con)

WINDSOR

		%	+/-%
Afriyie, A. (Con)	21,646	49.5	2.3
Wood, A. (Lib Dem)	11,354	26.0	-0.2
Muller, M. (Lab)	8,339	19.1	-5.0
Black, D. (UKIP)	1,098	2.5	0.0
Wall, D. (Greens)	1,074	2.5	0.0
Hooper, P. (Ind)	182	0.4	0.0
Con majority	10,292	23.56	
Electorate	68,290		
Turnout	43,693	63.98	

Con hold (1.2% from Lib Dem to Con)

WIRRAL SOUTH

		%	+/-%
*Chapman, B. (Lab)	16,892	42.5	-4.9
Cross, C. (Con)	13,168	33.2	-1.6
Holbrook, S. (Lib Dem)	8,568	21.6	3.8
Scott, D. (UKIP)	616	1.6	0.0
Jones, L. (Ind)	460	1.2	0.0
Lab majority	3,724	9.38	
Electorate	58,834		
Turnout	39,704	67.48	

Lab hold (1.7% from Lab to Con)

WIRRAL WEST

		%	+/-%
*Hesford, S. (Lab)	17,543	42.6	-4.7
McVey, E. (Con)	16,446	39.9	2.7
Clarke, J. (Lib Dem)	6,652	16.1	0.6
Moore, J. (UKIP)	429	1.0	0.0
Taylor, R. (AP)	163	0.4	0.0
Lab majority	1,097	2.66	
Electorate	61,050		
Turnout	41,233	67.54	

Lab hold (0.0%)

WITNEY

		%	+/-%
*Cameron, D. (Con)	26,571	49.3	4.3
Leffman, L. (Lib Dem)	12,415	23.1	2.7
Gray, T. (Lab)	11,845	22.0	-6.8
Dossett-Davies, R. (Greens)			
	1,682	3.1	0.9
Wesson, P. (UKIP)	1,356	2.5	1.0
Con majority	14,156	26.28	
Electorate	78,053		
Turnout	53,869	69.02	

Con hold (0.8% from Lib Dem to Con)

WOKING

		%	+/-%
*Malins, H. (Con)	21,838	47.4	1.4
Lee, A. (Lib Dem)	15,226	33.1	2.8
Blagbrough, E. (Lab)	7,507	16.3	-4.0
Davies, M. (UKIP)	1,324	2.9	-0.5
Osman, M. (UKC)	150	0.3	0.0
Con majority	6,612	14.36	
Electorate	72,676		
Turnout	46,045	63.36	

Con hold (0.7% from Con to Lib Dem)

* Member of last parliament

WOKINGHAM

		%	+/-%
*Redwood, J. (Con)	22,174	48.1	2.0
Bray, P. (Lib Dem)	14,934	32.4	0.0
Black, D. (Lab)	6,991	15.2	-2.2
Carstairs, F. (UKIP)	994	2.2	0.1
Owen, T. (Loony)	569	1.2	-0.8
Colborne, R. (BNP)	376	0.8	0.0
Hall, M. (telepath)	34	0.1	0.0
Con majority	7,240	15.71	
Electorate	68,614		
Turnout	46,072	67.15	

Con hold (1.0% from Lib Dem to Con)

WOLVERHAMPTON NORTH EAST

		%	+/-%
*Purchase, K. (Lab/Co-op)	17,948	54.5	-5.8
Robson, A. (Con)	9,792	29.7	1.1
Jackson, D. (Lib Dem)	3,845	11.7	3.8
Simpson, L. (UKIP)	1,371	4.2	1.0
Lab/Co-op majority	8,156	24.75	
Electorate	60,595		
Turnout	32,956	54.39	

Lab/Co-op hold (3.5% from Lab/Co-op to Con)

WOLVERHAMPTON SOUTH EAST

		%	+/-%
McFadden, P. (Lab)	16,790	59.4	-8.0
Fairbairn, J. (Con)	6,295	22.3	0.5
Murray, D. (Lib Dem)	3,682	13.0	4.3
Simmons, K. (UKIP)	1,484	5.3	0.0
Lab majority	10,495	37.15	
Electorate	54,047		
Turnout	28,251	52.27	

Lab hold (4.3% from Lab to Con)

WOLVERHAMPTON SOUTH WEST

		%	+/-%
*Marris, R. (Lab)	18,489	44.4	-3.9
Verma, S. (Con)	15,610	37.5	-2.3
Ross, C. (Lib Dem)	5,568	13.4	5.0
Hope, D. (UKIP)	1,029	2.5	0.8
Mullins, E. (BNP)	983	2.4	0.0
Lab majority	2,879	6.91	
Electorate	67,096		
Turnout	41,679	62.12	

Lab hold (0.8% from Lab to Con)

WOODSPRING

		%	+/-%
*Fox, L. (Con)	21,587	41.8	-1.9
Bell, M. (Lib Dem)	15,571	30.2	5.9
Stevens, C. (Lab)	11,249	21.8	-3.8
Lewis, R. (Greens)	1,309	2.5	-0.1
Butcher, A. (UKIP)	1,269	2.5	1.5
Howson, M. (BNP)	633	1.2	0.0
Con majority	6,016	11.65	
Electorate	71,662		
Turnout	51,618	72.03	

Con hold (3.9% from Con to Lib Dem)

WORCESTER

		%	+/-%
*Foster, M. (Lab)	19,421	41.9	-6.7
Harper, M. (Con)	16,277	35.1	-0.5
Dhonau, M. (Lib Dem)	7,557	16.3	3.7
Chamings, R. (UKIP)	1,113	2.4	-0.9
Roberts, M. (BNP)	980	2.1	0.0
Lennard, C. (Greens)	921	2.0	0.0
Dowson, P. (Ind)	119	0.3	0.0
Lab majority	3,144	6.78	
Electorate	72,384		
Turnout	46,388	64.09	

Lab hold (3.1% from Lab to Con)

MID WORCESTERSHIRE

		%	+/-%
*Luff, P. (Con)	24,783	51.5	0.4
Gregson, M. (Lab)	11,456	23.8	-3.6
Rowley, M. (Lib Dem)	9,796	20.4	1.6
Eaves, A. (UKIP)	2,092	4.4	1.6
Con majority	13,327	27.69	
Electorate	71,546		
Turnout	48,127	67.27	

Con hold (2.0% from Lab to Con)

WEST WORCESTERSHIRE

		%	+/-%
*Spicer, M. (Con)	20,959	45.4	-0.6
Wells, T. (Lib Dem)	18,484	40.0	6.1
Bhatti, Q. (Lab)	4,945	10.7	-3.3
Bovey, C. (UKIP)	1,590	3.4	-0.1
Victory, M. (Greens)	1,099	2.3	-0.2
Con majority	2,475	5.26	
Electorate	66,999		
Turnout	47,077	70.27	

Con hold (3.4% from Con to Lib Dem)

WORKINGTON

		%	+/-%
*Cunningham, T. (Lab)	19,554	49.2	-6.3
Pattinson, J. (Con)	12,659	31.9	2.3
Clarkson, K. (Lib Dem)	5,815	14.6	2.2
Richardson, M. (UKIP)	1,328	3.3	0.0
Peacock, J. (LCA)	381	1.0	-1.5
Lab majority	6,895	17.35	
Electorate	61,441		
Turnout	39,737	64.68	

Lab hold (4.3% from Lab to Con)

WORSLEY

		%	+/-%
Keeley, B. (Lab)	18,859	51.0	-6.1
Evans, G. (Con)	9,491	25.7	1.9
Clayton, R. (Lib Dem)	6,902	18.7	1.2
Gill, B. (UKIP)	1,694	4.6	0.0
Lab majority	9,368	25.36	
Electorate	69,534		
Turnout	36,946	53.13	

Lab hold (4.0% from Lab to Con)

EAST WORTHING AND SHOREHAM

		%	+/-%
*Loughton, T. (Con)	19,548	43.9	0.7
Yates, D. (Lab)	11,365	25.5	-3.4
Doyle, J. (Lib Dem)	10,844	24.4	1.4
Jelf, R. (UKIP)	2,109	4.7	2.0
Baldwin, C. (LCA)	677	1.5	-0.6
Con majority	8,183	18.37	
Electorate	72,302		
Turnout	44,543	61.61	

Con hold (2.1% from Lab to Con)

* Member of last parliament

WORTHING WEST

		%	+/-%
*Bottomley, P. (Con)	21,383	47.6	0.1
Potter, C. (Lib Dem)	12,004	26.7	0.2
Bignell, A. (Lab)	8,630	19.2	-2.3
Cross, T. (UKIP)	2,374	5.3	0.8
Baldwin, C. (LCA)	550	1.2	0.0
Con majority	9,379	20.87	
Electorate	71,780		
Turnout	44,941	62.61	

Con hold (0.0% from Con to Lib Dem)

THE WREKIN

		%	+/-%
Pritchard, M. (Con)	18,899	42.0	3.5
*Bradley, P. (Lab)	17,957	39.9	-7.2
Tomlinson, B. (Lib Dem)	6,608	14.7	3.3
Lawson, B. (UKIP)	1,590	3.5	0.5
Con majority	942	2.09	
Electorate	67,291		
Turnout	45,054	66.95	

Con gain (5.4% from Lab to Con)

WREXHAM

		%	+/-%
*Lucas, I. (Lab)	13,993	46.1	-7.0
Rippeth, T. (Lib Dem)	7,174	23.6	6.5
Coffey, T. (Con)	6,079	20.0	-2.4
Owen, S. (PlC)	1,744	5.7	-0.2
Walker, J. (BNP)	919	3.0	0.0
Williams, J. (Forward Wales)	476	1.6	0.0
Lab majority	6,819	22.44	
Electorate	48,016		
Turnout	30,385	63.28	

Lab hold (6.7% from Lab to Lib Dem)

WYCOMBE

		%	+/-%
*Goodman, P. (Con)	20,331	45.8	3.4
Wassell, J. (Lab)	13,280	29.9	-5.5
Oates, J. (Lib Dem)	8,780	19.8	2.7
Davis, R. (UKIP)	1,735	3.9	1.6
Fitton, D. (Ind)	301	0.7	0.1
Con majority	7,051	15.87	
Electorate	71,464		
Turnout	44,427	62.17	

Con hold (4.4% from Lab to Con)

WYRE FOREST

		%	+/-%
*Taylor, R. (Ind KHHC)	18,739	39.9	-18.2
Garnier, M. (Con)	13,489	28.7	9.7
Bayliss, M. (Lab)	10,716	22.8	0.7
Oborski, F. (Lib)	2,666	5.7	0.0
Lee, R. (UKIP)	1,074	2.3	1.5
Priest, B. (Loony)	303	0.6	0.0
Ind KHHC majority	5,250	11.17	
Electorate	73,192		
Turnout	46,987	64.20	

Ind KHHC hold (13.9% from Ind KHHC to Con)

WYTHENSHAWE AND SALE EAST

		%	+/-%
*Goggins, P. (Lab)	18,878	52.2	-7.8
Meehan, J. (Con)	8,051	22.3	-1.8
Firth, A. (Lib Dem)	7,766	21.5	9.1
Ford, W. (UKIP)	1,120	3.1	0.0
Worthington, L. (SAP)	369	1.0	0.0

Lab majority	10,827	29.92	
Electorate	71,766		
Turnout	36,184	50.42	

Lab hold (3.0% from Lab to Con)

YEOVIL

		%	+/-%
*Laws, D. (Lib Dem)	25,658	51.4	7.2
Jenkins, I. (Con)	17,096	34.3	-1.8
Rolfe, C. (Lab)	5,256	10.5	-4.2
Livings, G. (UKIP)	1,903	3.8	1.5
Lib Dem majority	8,562	17.15	
Electorate	77,668		
Turnout	49,913	64.26	

Lib Dem hold (4.5% from Con to Lib Dem)

YNYS MÔN

		%	+/-%
*Owen, A. (Lab)	12,278	34.6	-0.4
Wyn, E. (PlC)	11,036	31.1	-1.5
Rogers, P. (Ind)	5,216	14.7	14.1
Roach, J. (Con)	3,915	11.0	-11.5
Green, S. (Lib Dem)	2,418	6.8	-1.3
Gill, E. (UKIP)	367	1.0	0.0
Evans, T. (LCA)	232	0.7	0.0
Lab majority	1,242	3.50	
Electorate	52,512		
Turnout	35,462	67.53	

Lab hold (0.6% from PlC to Lab)

CITY OF YORK

		%	+/-%
*Bayley, H. (Lab)	21,836	46.9	-5.4
Booth, C. (Con)	11,364	24.4	0.9
Waller, A. (Lib Dem)	10,166	21.8	4.1
D'Agorne, A. (Greens)	2,113	4.5	1.5
Jackson, R. (UKIP)	832	1.8	0.6
Curran, K. (Ind)	121	0.3	0.0
Fleck, D. (DDTP)	93	0.2	0.0
Hinkles, A. (Ind)	72	0.2	0.0
Lab majority	10,472	22.47	
Electorate	75,555		
Turnout	46,597	61.67	

Lab hold (3.1% from Lab to Con)

VALE OF YORK

		%	+/-%
*McIntosh, A. (Con)	26,025	51.7	0.0
Scott, D. (Lab)	12,313	24.4	-1.4
Wilcock, J. (Lib Dem)	12,040	23.9	3.7
Con majority	13,712	27.22	
Electorate	76,000		
Turnout	50,378	66.29	

Con hold (0.7% from Lab to Con)

YORKSHIRE EAST

		%	+/-%
*Knight, G. (Con)	21,215	45.2	-0.6
Hoddinott, E. (Lab)	14,932	31.8	-3.2
Wastling, J. (Lib Dem)	9,075	19.3	4.8
Tressider, C. (UKIP)	1,703	3.6	-0.2
Con majority	6,283	13.39	
Electorate	76,648		
Turnout	46,925	61.22	

Con hold (1.3% from Lab to Con)

* Member of last parliament

State of the parties

	2005 General Election	*2001 General Election*
Labour*	355	412
Conservative	197	166
Liberal Democrat	62	52
Democratic Unionist Party	9	5
Scottish National Party	6	5
Sinn Fein	5	4
Social Democratic Labour Party	3	3
Plaid Cymru	3	4
Independent	2	1
Ulster Unionist Party	1	6
Respect	1	
The Speaker	1	1
Total	**645†**	**659**

*Includes 29 Labour/Co-operative MPs, excludes Speaker
†By-election pending in South Staffordshire

Share of the vote

	Seats	*Gains*	*Losses*	*Net*	*Votes*	*% of votes*	*+/– %*
Lab	356‡	0	47	–47	9,556,183	35.2	–5.5
Con	197	36	3	+33	8,772,598	32.3	0.6
Lib Dem	62	16	5	+11	5,982,045	22	3.7
DUP	9	4	0	+4	241,856	0.9	0.2
SNP	6	2	0	+2	412,267	1.5	–0.3
SF	5	1	0	+1	174,530	0.6	–0.1
PlC	3	0	1	–1	174,838	0.6	–0.1
SDLP	3	1	1	0	125,626	0.5	–0.1
UUP	1	0	5	–5	127,314	0.5	–0.3
Respect	1	1	0	1	68,065	0.3	0.3
Ind KHHC	1	0	0	0	18,739	0.1	0.0
UKIP	0	0	0	0	618,898	2.3	0.8
Green	0	0	0	0	257,758	1	0.4
BNP	0	0	0	0	192,850	0.7	0.5
Scot Soc	0	0	0	0	43,514	0.2	–0.1
Scottish Grn	0	0	0	0	25,760	0.1	0.1
Liberal	0	0	0	0	19,068	0.1	0.0
Others	1	1	0	1	251,646	0.9	0.0
Turnout					**27,132,327**	**61.3**	**2.0**

‡Includes Speaker

Share of the vote by region

Eastern

	Seats	Gain	Loss	Net	Votes	%	+/– %
Conservative	40	6	0	6	1,147,180	43.3	1.5
Labour	13	0	7	–7	790,372	29.8	–7.0
Lib Dem	3	1	0	1	578,741	21.8	4.3
UKIP	0	0	0	0	83,112	3.1	0.9
Green	0	0	0	0	25,396	1	0.4
BNP	0	0	0	0	9,673	0.4	0.4
Eng Dems	0	0	0	0	3,809	0.1	0.1
Veritas	0	0	0	0	2,757	0.1	0.1
Respect	0	0	0	0	1,679	0.1	0.1
Nat Front	0	0	0	0	931	0	0.0
Cannabis	0	0	0	0	608	0	0.0
Soc Labour	0	0	0	0	518	0	0.0
St Alban	0	0	0	0	430	0	0.0
Open Forum	0	0	0	0	366	0	0.0
Workers Rev	0	0	0	0	183	0	0.0
Motorbike	0	0	0	0	167	0	0.0
Max	0	0	0	0	106	0	0.0
Others	0	0	0	0	3,785	0.3	–0.4
Turnout					**2,649,813**	**63.6**	**1.9**

East Midlands

	Seats	Gain	Loss	Net	Votes	%	+/– %
Labour	25	0	3	–3	779,943	38.6	–6.5
Conservative	18	3	0	3	747,438	37	–0.3
Lib Dem	1	0	0	0	372,041	18.4	3.0
UKIP	0	0	0	0	63,798	3.2	2.1
Veritas	0	0	0	0	16,388	0.8	0.8
BNP	0	0	0	0	10,299	0.5	0.4
Green	0	0	0	0	7,475	0.4	0.2
Respect	0	0	0	0	2,720	0.1	0.1
Ashfield	0	0	0	0	2,292	0.1	0.1
Eng Dems	0	0	0	0	1,588	0.1	0.1
Soc Labour	0	0	0	0	1,482	0.1	–0.2
Loony	0	0	0	0	1,046	0.1	0.1
SOS	0	0	0	0	932	0	0.0
Christian PA	0	0	0	0	596	0	0.0
Soc Alt	0	0	0	0	552	0	0.0
Soc Unity	0	0	0	0	373	0	0.0
Free Dems	0	0	0	0	264	0	0.0
Elvis	0	0	0	0	116	0	0.0
Others	0	0	0	0	10,738	0.6	0.3
Turnout					**2,020,081**	**62.8**	**2.0**

London

	Seats	Gain	Loss	Net	Votes	%	+/– %
Labour	44	0	11	–11	1,135,687	38.9	–8.4
Conservative	21	8	0	8	931,966	31.9	1.4
Lib Dem	8	2	0	2	638,533	21.9	4.4
Respect	1	1	0	1	40,735	1.4	1.4

Green	0	0	0	0	78,595	2.7	1.0
UKIP	0	0	0	0	42,956	1.5	0.5
BNP	0	0	0	0	19,028	0.7	0.2
Nat Front	0	0	0	0	3,952	0.1	0.1
Veritas	0	0	0	0	3,580	0.1	0.1
Christian PA	0	0	0	0	2,254	0.1	0.1
Res Ass	0	0	0	0	1,850	0.1	0.1
Soc Alt	0	0	0	0	1,469	0.1	0.0
Eng Dems	0	0	0	0	1,437	0	0.0
Yourself	0	0	0	0	1,289	0	0.0
Soc Labour	0	0	0	0	1,206	0	−0.3
Community	0	0	0	0	1,118	0	0.0
Brit Public	0	0	0	0	763	0	0.0
Peace	0	0	0	0	685	0	0.0
Workers Rev	0	0	0	0	680	0	0.0
Loony	0	0	0	0	630	0	0.0
Peoples	0	0	0	0	418	0	0.0
Croydon	0	0	0	0	394	0	0.0
Third Way	0	0	0	0	382	0	0.0
Liberal	0	0	0	0	313	0	0.0
Socialist	0	0	0	0	240	0	0.0
Civil	0	0	0	0	227	0	0.0
Communist	0	0	0	0	200	0	0.0
AGS	0	0	0	0	101	0	0.0
Change	0	0	0	0	68	0	0.0
Integrity	0	0	0	0	57	0	0.0
Progressive	0	0	0	0	56	0	0.0
Tiger's Eye	0	0	0	0	50	0	0.0
Others	0	0	0	0	6,660	0.5	0.2
Turnout					**2,917,579**	**58.2**	**2.9**

North East

	Seats	Gain	Loss	Net	Votes	%	+/− %
Labour	28	0	0	0	580,453	52.9	−6.5
Lib Dem	1	0	0	0	256,295	23.3	6.6
Conservative	1	0	0	0	214,414	19.5	−1.8
UKIP	0	0	0	0	11,703	1.1	0.3
BNP	0	0	0	0	9,672	0.9	0.8
Green	0	0	0	0	2,787	0.3	0.0
Veritas	0	0	0	0	2,328	0.2	0.2
Nat Front	0	0	0	0	1,250	0.1	0.1
Soc Labour	0	0	0	0	1,115	0.1	−0.5
Soc Alt	0	0	0	0	582	0.1	0.1
Eng Dems	0	0	0	0	521	0	0.0
Newcastle	0	0	0	0	477	0	0.0
Loony	0	0	0	0	468	0	0.0
Respect	0	0	0	0	447	0	0.0
Save NHS	0	0	0	0	400	0	0.0
Communist	0	0	0	0	205	0	0.0
Imper Party	0	0	0	0	129	0	0.0
Blair Go	0	0	0	0	103	0	0.0
OAPs	0	0	0	0	97	0	0.0
Pensioners	0	0	0	0	82	0	0.0
Others	0	0	0	0	14,673	1.5	0.9
Turnout					**1,098,201**	**57.2**	**0.8**

North West

	Seats	Gain	Loss	Net	Votes	%	+/– %
Labour	61	0	3	–3	1,327,668	45	–5.7
Conservative	9	1	1	0	846,195	28.7	–0.6
Lib Dem	6	3	0	3	629,250	21.3	4.6
UKIP	0	0	0	0	62,831	2.1	1.2
BNP	0	0	0	0	31,529	1.1	0.4
Green	0	0	0	0	10,012	0.3	–0.1
Liberal	0	0	0	0	7,110	0.2	0.0
Community	0	0	0	0	6,553	0.2	0.2
Respect	0	0	0	0	3,268	0.1	0.1
Soc Labour	0	0	0	0	3,109	0.1	–0.3
Veritas	0	0	0	0	2,906	0.1	0.1
Cannabis	0	0	0	0	1,688	0.1	0.1
Eng Dems	0	0	0	0	1,495	0.1	0.1
Soc Alt	0	0	0	0	1,024	0	0.0
Your Party	0	0	0	0	589	0	0.0
Local Comm	0	0	0	0	570	0	0.0
Clause 28	0	0	0	0	449	0	0.0
Nat Front	0	0	0	0	421	0	0.0
Bridges	0	0	0	0	409	0	0.0
Prog Lab	0	0	0	0	382	0	0.0
IZB Platform	0	0	0	0	361	0	0.0
Workers Rev	0	0	0	0	344	0	0.0
Dem Socs	0	0	0	0	227	0	0.0
Communist	0	0	0	0	199	0	0.0
Alternative	0	0	0	0	163	0	0.0
Resolve	0	0	0	0	159	0	0.0
Xtra People	0	0	0	0	74	0	0.0
Their	0	0	0	0	47	0	0.0
Others	0	0	0	0	11,753	0.6	0.3
Turnout					**2,950,785**	**57.1**	**1.2**

South East

	Seats	Gain	Loss	Net	Votes	%	+/– %
Conservative	58	5	0	5	1,754,259	45	2.1
Labour	19	0	3	–3	951,323	24.4	–5.0
Lib Dem	6	0	2	–2	990,477	25.4	1.7
UKIP	0	0	0	0	122,257	3.1	0.6
Green	0	0	0	0	52,410	1.3	0.5
BNP	0	0	0	0	3,740	0.1	0.1
Eng Dems	0	0	0	0	3,366	0.1	0.1
Loony	0	0	0	0	3,080	0.1	0.0
Cannabis	0	0	0	0	1,963	0.1	0.1
Respect	0	0	0	0	1,900	0	0.0
New England	0	0	0	0	1,224	0	0.0
Veritas	0	0	0	0	1,207	0	0.0
Nat Front	0	0	0	0	918	0	0.0
Workers	0	0	0	0	892	0	0.0
Soc Labour	0	0	0	0	657	0	–0.1
English Ind	0	0	0	0	654	0	0.0
UK Com	0	0	0	0	502	0	0.0
Rock Loony	0	0	0	0	479	0	0.0
Your Party	0	0	0	0	417	0	0.0

	Seats	Gain	Loss	Net	Votes	%	+/– %
Horsham	0	0	0	0	354	0	0.0
Peace	0	0	0	0	338	0	0.0
Protest	0	0	0	0	313	0	0.0
Dem Socs	0	0	0	0	263	0	0.0
UK Path	0	0	0	0	233	0	0.0
Justice	0	0	0	0	210	0	0.0
AGS	0	0	0	0	188	0	0.0
Britian Back	0	0	0	0	153	0	0.0
OAPs	0	0	0	0	151	0	0.0
Millennium	0	0	0	0	148	0	0.0
Soc Alt	0	0	0	0	113	0	0.0
Silent	0	0	0	0	78	0	0.0
Telepathic	0	0	0	0	34	0	0.0
Peace	0	0	0	0	22	0	0.0
Others	0	0	0	0	7,282	0.4	0.1
Turnout					**3,901,605**	**64.3**	**2.7**

South West

	Seats	Gain	Loss	Net	Votes	%	+/– %
Conservative	22	3	1	2	985,346	38.6	0.1
Lib Dem	16	3	2	1	831,134	32.6	1.4
Labour	13	0	3	–3	582,520	22.8	–3.5
UKIP	0	0	0	0	95,492	3.7	1.2
Green	0	0	0	0	33,012	1.3	0.5
Liberal	0	0	0	0	5,023	0.2	0.0
Mebyon Kern	0	0	0	0	3,552	0.1	0.0
BNP	0	0	0	0	1,958	0.1	0.1
Veritas	0	0	0	0	1,395	0.1	0.1
Respect	0	0	0	0	1,098	0	0.0
Soc Labour	0	0	0	0	1,029	0	–0.1
Eng Dems	0	0	0	0	828	0	0.0
Soc Alt	0	0	0	0	565	0	0.0
Loony	0	0	0	0	525	0	0.0
Cannabis	0	0	0	0	282	0	0.0
Soc Unity	0	0	0	0	208	0	0.0
Save Baths	0	0	0	0	190	0	0.0
Honesty	0	0	0	0	187	0	0.0
Eng Parl	0	0	0	0	125	0	0.0
PARTY	0	0	0	0	107	0	0.0
Wessex	0	0	0	0	83	0	0.0
Masts	0	0	0	0	61	0	0.0
Others	0	0	0	0	8,564	0.5	0.3
Turnout					**2,553,284**	**66.6**	**1.7**

West Midlands

	Seats	Gain	Loss	Net	Votes	%	+/– %
Labour	39	0	4	–4	932,993	38.9	–6.1
Conservative	15	4	1	3	835,282	34.8	0.1
Lib Dem	3	2	1	1	446,570	18.6	3.8
Ind Kid Hosp	1	0	0	0	18,739	0.8	–0.4
UKIP	0	0	0	0	75,302	3.1	1.3
BNP	0	0	0	0	42,581	1.8	1.5
Green	0	0	0	0	14,611	0.6	0.2

					Votes	%	+/− %
Respect	0	0	0	0	13,817	0.6	0.6
Veritas	0	0	0	0	4,244	0.2	0.2
Soc Alt	0	0	0	0	3,952	0.2	0.2
Liberal	0	0	0	0	2,666	0.1	0.1
Soc Labour	0	0	0	0	1,727	0.1	−0.2
Dem Lab	0	0	0	0	770	0	0.0
Common Good	0	0	0	0	428	0	0.0
Nat Front	0	0	0	0	416	0	−0.1
Peace	0	0	0	0	329	0	0.0
Loony	0	0	0	0	303	0	0.0
Fam First	0	0	0	0	144	0	0.0
World	0	0	0	0	84	0	0.0
Workers Rev	0	0	0	0	34	0	0.0
Others	0	0	0	0	2,548	0.2	−0.4
Turnout					**2,397,540**	**61.4**	**2.8**

Yorkshire and Humberside

	Seats	Gain	Loss	Net	Votes	%	+/− %
Labour	44	0	3	−3	958,006	43.6	−5.0
Conservative	9	2	0	2	640,582	29.1	−1.1
Lib Dem	3	1	0	1	454,705	20.7	3.6
BNP	0	0	0	0	61,090	2.8	2.6
UKIP	0	0	0	0	32,291	1.5	−0.4
Green	0	0	0	0	26,316	1.2	0.3
Veritas	0	0	0	0	4,239	0.2	0.2
Liberal	0	0	0	0	2,435	0.1	0.1
Comm Group	0	0	0	0	2,365	0.1	0.1
Respect	0	0	0	0	1,758	0.1	0.1
AGS	0	0	0	0	1,689	0.1	0.1
Eng Dems	0	0	0	0	1,462	0.1	0.1
Soc Labour	0	0	0	0	1,048	0	−0.4
Soc Alt	0	0	0	0	584	0	0.0
Christian PA	0	0	0	0	441	0	0.0
Cannabis	0	0	0	0	361	0	0.0
Virtue	0	0	0	0	274	0	0.0
Loony	0	0	0	0	259	0	0.0
Change	0	0	0	0	248	0	0.0
N Progress	0	0	0	0	193	0	0.0
Nat Front	0	0	0	0	191	0	0.0
Iraq	0	0	0	0	189	0	0.0
Death	0	0	0	0	93	0	0.0
Others	0	0	0	0	8,543	0.4	0.1
Turnout					**2,199,362**	**58.7**	**1.9**

Seats which changed parties

Changes are from the 2001 general election; thus Brent East is shown as changing parties, although the Liberal Democrats gained it from Labour in a by-election; similarly Leicester South does not appear as a change in party as a by-election gain was reversed at the general election. Lagan Valley is listed as the sitting MP changed his party during the course of the last parliament

	2001	*2005*
Antrim East	UUP	DUP
Antrim South	UUP	DUP
Belfast South	UUP	SDLP
Bethnal Green and Bow	Labour	Respect
Bexleyheath and Crayford	Labour	Conservative
Birmingham Yardley	Labour	Liberal Democrat
Blaenau Gwent	Labour	Independent
Braintree	Labour	Conservative
Brent East	Labour	Liberal Democrat
Bristol West	Labour	Liberal Democrat
Cambridge	Labour	Liberal Democrat
Cardiff Central	Labour	Liberal Democrat
Ceredigion	Plaid Cymru	Liberal Democrat
Clwyd West	Labour	Conservative
Croydon Central	Labour	Conservative
Dumfriesshire, Clydesdale and Tweeddale	Labour*	Conservative
Dundee East	Labour*	Scottish National Party
Enfield Southgate	Labour	Conservative
Falmouth and Camborne	Labour	Liberal Democrat
Forest of Dean	Labour	Conservative
Gravesham	Labour	Conservative
Guildford	Liberal Democrat	Conservative
Hammersmith and Fulham	Labour	Conservative
Harwich	Labour	Conservative
Hemel Hempstead	Labour	Conservative
Hornchurch	Labour	Conservative
Hornsey and Wood Green	Labour	Liberal Democrat
Ilford North	Labour	Conservative
Inverness, Nairn, Badenoch and Strathspey	Labour*	Liberal Democrat
Kettering	Labour	Conservative
Lagan Valley	UUP	DUP
Lancaster and Wyre	Labour	Conservative
Leeds North West	Labour	Liberal Democrat
Ludlow	Liberal Democrat	Conservative
Manchester Withington	Labour	Liberal Democrat
Milton Keynes North East	Labour	Conservative
Monmouth	Labour	Conservative
Na h-Eileannan An Iar (previously Western Isles)	Labour	SNP
Newbury	Liberal Democrat	Conservative
Newry and Armagh	SDLP	Sinn Fein
Northampton South	Labour	Conservative
Peterborough	Labour	Conservative
Preseli Pembrokeshire	Labour	Conservative
Putney	Labour	Conservative

Reading East	Labour	Conservative
Rochdale	Labour	Liberal Democrat
Rugby and Kenilworth	Labour	Conservative
St Albans	Labour	Conservative
Scarborough and Whitby	Labour	Conservative
Shipley	Labour	Conservative
Shrewsbury and Atcham	Labour	Conservative
Solihull	Conservative	Liberal Democrat
Taunton	Conservative	Liberal Democrat
Torridge and West Devon	Liberal Democrat	Conservative
Upper Bann	UUP	DUP
Wellingborough	Labour	Conservative
Welwyn Hatfield	Labour	Conservative
Westmorland and Lonsdale	Conservative	Liberal Democrat
Weston-Super-Mare	Liberal Democrat	Conservative
Wimbledon	Labour	Conservative
The Wrekin	Labour	Conservative

*Notional holder after boundary changes in Scottish constituencies since the 2001 general election.

Results in vulnerable Labour seats

		% Maj 2001	Result	Swing
1	Dumfries and Galloway*	0.3	Lab hold	2.7% Con to Lab
2	South Dorset	0.3	Lab hold	1.7% Con to Lab
3	Braintree	0.7	Con gain	4.0% Lab to Con
4	Monmouth	0.9	Con gain	5.4% Lab to Con
5	Lancaster and Wyre	0.9	Con gain	4.5% Lab to Con
6	Kettering	1.2	Con gain	3.6% Lab to Con
7	Dundee East*	1.3	SNP gain	1.1% Lab to SNP
8	Northampton South	1.7	Con gain	4.9% Lab to Con
9	Ochil and South Perthshire*	1.8	Lab hold	0.2% Lab to SNP
10	Cardiff Central	1.9	Lib Dem gain	8.7% Lab to Lib Dem
11	Ynys Môn	2.4	Lab hold	0.6% PlC to Lab
12	Inverness, Nairn, Badenoch and Strathspey*	2.7	Lib Dem gain	6.0% Lab to Lib Dem
13	Welwyn Hatfield	2.8	Con gain	8.1% Lab to Con
14	Shipley	3.1	Con gain	2.0% Lab to Con
15	Clwyd West	3.2	Con gain	1.8% Lab to Con
16	Bexleyheath and Crayford	3.6	Con gain	7.2% Lab to Con
17	North East Milton Keynes	3.9	Con gain	3.6% Lab to Con
18	Hornchurch	4.2	Con gain	2.7% Lab to Con
19	Selby	4.3	Lab hold	1.7% Lab to Con
20	Hammersmith and Fulham	4.5	Con gain	7.4% Lab to Con

* Notional majority following boundary changes.

Results in vulnerable Conservative seats

		% Maj 2001	Result	Swing
1	Taunton	0.4	Lib Dem gain	0.7% Con to Lib Dem
2	Orpington	0.5	Con hold	4.3% Lib Dem to Con
3	Boston and Skegness	1.3	Con hold	6.4% Lab to Con
4	Beverley and Holderness	1.7	Con hold	1.7% Lab to Con
5	South West Surrey	1.7	Con hold	4.6% Lib Dem to Con
6	South West Bedfordshire	1.8	Con hold	8.2% Lab to Con
7	Basingstoke	1.8	Con hold	4.0% Lab to Con
8	Castle Point	2.5	Con hold	7.7% Lab to Con
9	West Dorset	2.9	Con hold	0.9% Lib Dem to Con
10	Upminster	3.7	Con hold	6.9% Lab to Con
11	Haltemprice and Howden	4.3	Con hold	3.2% Lib Dem to Con
12	Isle of Wight	4.5	Con hold	7.5% Lib Dem to Con
13	Canterbury	4.6	Con hold	5.6% Lab to Con
14	Eastbourne	4.8	Con hold	1.2% Con to Lib Dem
15	Bury St Edmunds	5.0	Con hold	7.0% Lab to Con
16	Bosworth	5.1	Con hold	3.1% Lab to Con
17	Wells	5.4	Con hold	0.2% Lib Dem to Con
18	Hexham	6.0	Con hold	3.1% Lab to Con
19	Uxbridge	6.3	Con hold	5.8% Lab to Con
20	Chipping Barnet	6.4	Con hold	3.9% Lab to Con

Results in vulnerable Liberal Democrat seats

		% Maj 2001	Result	Swing
1	Cheadle	0.1	Lib Dem hold	4.2% Con to Lib Dem
2	Weston-Super-Mare	0.7	Con gain	2.5% Lib Dem to Con
3	North Norfolk	0.9	Lib Dem hold	8.6% Con to Lib Dem
4	Mid Dorset and Poole North	0.9	Lib Dem hold	5.6% Con to Lib Dem
5	Guildford	1.1	Con gain	0.9% Lib Dem to Con
6	Somerton and Frome	1.3	Lib Dem hold	0.1% Con to Lib Dem
7	Brecon and Radnorshire	2.0	Lib Dem hold	4.1% Con to Lib Dem
8	Torridge and West Devon	2.1	Con gain	3.8% Lib Dem to Con
9	Hereford	2.2	Lib Dem hold	0.1% Lib Dem to Con
10	Ludlow	3.8	Con gain	4.1% Lib Dem to Con

Seats by percentage majority

				%	Majority
1	Joe Benton	Lab	Bootle	63.84	16,357
2	John Cummings	Lab	Easington	58.50	18,636
3	Peter Kilfoyle	Lab	Liverpool Walton	57.13	15,957
4	Gerry Adams	Sinn Féin	Belfast West	55.91	19,315
5	David Blunkett	Lab	Sheffield Brightside	55.40	13,644
6	Chris Bryant	Lab	Rhondda	52.14	16,242
7	Ian McCartney	Lab	Makerfield	51.01	18,149
8	Don Touhig	Lab/Co-op	Islwyn	51.00	15,740
9	Tom Clarke	Lab	Coatbridge, Chryston and Bellshill	50.90	19,519
10	Robert Wareing	Lab	Liverpool West Derby	49.98	15,225
11	Ann Clwyd	Lab	Cynon Valley	49.76	13,259
12	Edward O'Hara	Lab	Knowsley South	48.53	17,688
13	Dennis Skinner	Lab	Bolsover	47.64	18,437
14	Andy Burnham	Lab	Leigh	47.34	17,272
15	Frank Field	Lab	Birkenhead	46.55	12,934
16	Harriet Harman	Lab	Camberwell and Peckham	46.51	13,483
17	Dai Havard	Lab	Merthyr Tydfil and Rhymney	46.48	13,934
18	Fraser Kemp	Lab	Houghton and Washington East	46.30	16,065
19	Hywel Francis	Lab	Aberavon	46.30	13,937
20	Yvette Cooper	Lab	Pontefract and Castleford	46.27	15,246
21	Huw Irranca-Davies	Lab	Ogmore	45.26	13,703
22	Kevan Jones	Lab	Durham North	44.94	16,781
23	Ian Davidson	Lab/Co-op	Glasgow South West	44.86	13,896
24	Eric Illsley	Lab	Barnsley Central	44.49	12,732
25	Tony Blair	Lab	Sedgefield	44.49	18,457
26	George Howarth	Lab	Knowsley North and Sefton East	43.91	16,269
27	Charles Kennedy	Lib Dem	Ross, Skye and Lochaber	43.79	14,249
28	David Marshall	Lab	Glasgow East	43.66	13,507
29	Graham Stringer	Lab	Manchester Blackley	43.59	12,027
30	Gordon Brown	Lab	Kirkcaldy and Cowdenbeath	43.58	18,216
31	Clive Betts	Lab	Sheffield Attercliffe	43.13	15,967
32	Jeffrey Ennis	Lab	Barnsley East and Mexborough	42.77	14,125
33	Derek Twigg	Lab	Halton	42.73	14,606
34	John Reid	Lab	Airdrie and Shotts	42.48	14,084
35	John Healey	Lab	Wentworth	42.30	15,056
36	David Lammy	Lab	Tottenham	41.16	13,034
37	Paul Murphy	Lab	Torfaen	41.11	14,791
38	Frank Roy	Lab	Motherwell and Wishaw	41.02	15,222
39	Stephen Hepburn	Lab	Jarrow	40.92	13,904
40	David Miliband	Lab	South Shields	40.76	12,312
41	Stephen Byers	Lab	North Tyneside	40.71	15,037
42	Hilary Benn	Lab	Leeds Central	40.66	11,866
43	Ed Miliband	Lab	Doncaster North	40.08	12,656
44	Graham Allen	Lab	Nottingham North	40.06	12,171
45	Malcolm Rifkind	Con	Kensington and Chelsea	39.63	12,418
46	David Clelland	Lab	Tyne Bridge	39.42	10,400
47	William Hague	Con	Richmond (Yorkshire)	39.40	17,807
48	Wayne David	Lab	Caerphilly	39.15	15,359
49	Ian Paisley	DUP	North Antrim	39.12	17,965
50	Stuart Bell	Lab	Middlesbrough	39.10	12,567

				%	Majority
51	Joan Ruddock	*Lab*	Lewisham Deptford	38.86	11,811
52	Sharon Hodgson	*Lab*	Gateshead East and Washington West	38.67	13,407
53	George Mudie	*Lab*	Leeds East	38.49	11,578
54	Keith Vaz	*Lab*	Leicester East	38.44	15,876
55	Bob Ainsworth	*Lab*	Coventry North East	38.24	14,222
56	Andrew Gwynne	*Lab*	Denton and Reddish	38.08	13,498
57	Dawn Butler	*Lab*	Brent South	38.05	11,326
58	John Battle	*Lab*	Leeds West	37.99	12,810
59	John Prescott	*Lab*	Hull East	37.87	11,747
60	David Heyes	*Lab*	Ashton under Lyne	37.74	13,952
61	John Bercow	*Con*	Buckingham	37.53	18,129
62	Desmond Swayne	*Con*	New Forest West	37.52	17,285
63	Alistair Carmichael	*Lib Dem*	Orkney and Shetland	37.35	6,627
64	Thomas McAvoy	*Lab/Co-op*	Rutherglen and Hamilton West	37.24	16,112
65	Ian Stewart	*Lab*	Eccles	37.21	12,886
66	Pat McFadden	*Lab*	Wolverhampton South East	37.15	10,495
67	Jon Trickett	*Lab*	Hemsworth	36.64	13,481
68	Brian Iddon	*Lab*	Bolton South East	36.54	11,638
69	Sian James	*Lab*	Swansea East	36.48	11,249
70	Chris Mullin	*Lab*	Sunderland South	36.01	11,059
71	Kevin Barron	*Lab*	Rother Valley	36.01	14,224
72	Michael Martin	*Speaker*	Glasgow North East	35.66	10,134
73	Denis MacShane	*Lab*	Rotherham	35.63	10,681
74	David Watts	*Lab*	St Helens North	35.55	13,962
75	Peter Hain	*Lab*	Neath	35.49	12,710
76	Iris Robinson	*DUP*	Strangford	35.24	13,049
77	Hazel Blears	*Lab*	Salford	35.15	7,945
78	Dominic Grieve	*Con*	Beaconsfield	35.05	15,253
79	Mark Fisher	*Lab*	Stoke-on-Trent Central	35.02	9,774
80	Douglas Alexander	*Lab*	Paisley and Renfrewshire South	34.95	13,232
81	Bill Etherington	*Lab*	Sunderland North	34.57	9,995
82	Neil Turner	*Lab*	Wigan	34.33	11,767
83	Frank Cook	*Lab*	Stockton North	34.14	12,437
84	Hilary Armstrong	*Lab*	North West Durham	34.03	13,443
85	Alan Johnson	*Lab*	Hull West and Hessle	33.97	9,450
86	John McDonnell	*Lab*	Hayes and Harlington	33.49	10,847
87	Tony Lloyd	*Lab*	Manchester Central	33.41	9,776
88	Meg Munn	*Lab/Co-op*	Sheffield Heeley	33.35	11,370
89	Kim Howells	*Lab*	Pontypridd	33.28	13,191
90	Stephen Timms	*Lab*	East Ham	33.25	13,155
91	Jeffrey Donaldson	*DUP*	Lagan Valley	33.16	14,117
92	Christopher Grayling	*Con*	Epsom and Ewell	32.97	16,447
93	Tom Watson	*Lab*	West Bromwich East	32.81	11,652
94	Louise Ellman	*Lab/Co-op*	Liverpool Riverside	32.75	10,214
95	John Hayes	*Con*	South Holland and The Deepings	32.71	15,780
96	Joan Walley	*Lab*	Stoke-on-Trent North	32.63	10,036
97	Menzies Campbell	*Lib Dem*	North East Fife	32.60	12,571
98	Peter Ainsworth	*Con*	East Surrey	32.32	15,921
99	Elfyn Llwyd	*PlC*	Meirionnydd Nant Conwy	32.04	6,614
100	Eleanor Laing	*Con*	Epping Forest	32.01	14,358
101	Mark Francois	*Con*	Rayleigh	31.88	14,726
102	Alex Salmond	*SNP*	Banff and Buchan	31.81	11,837
103	Andrew Rosindell	*Con*	Romford	31.77	11,589
104	Malcolm Wicks	*Lab*	Croydon North	31.67	13,888
105	Lyn Brown	*Lab*	West Ham	31.65	9,801

				%	Majority
106	Meg Hillier	Lab/Co-op	Hackney South and Shoreditch	31.65	10,204
107	John Spellar	Lab	Warley	31.62	10,147
108	Siobhain McDonagh	Lab	Mitcham and Morden	31.50	12,560
109	Adrian Bailey	Lab/Co-op	West Bromwich West	31.20	10,894
110	David Cairns	Lab	Inverclyde	31.19	11,259
111	Vera Baird	Lab	Redcar	31.18	12,116
112	Jim Dowd	Lab	Lewisham West	31.11	9,932
113	Adam Ingram	Lab	East Kilbride, Strathaven and Lesmahagow	30.84	14,723
114	Margaret Hodge	Lab	Barking	30.73	8,883
115	Michael Clapham	Lab	Barnsley West and Penistone	30.70	11,314
116	John Austin	Lab	Erith and Thamesmead	30.54	11,500
117	Ann Widdecombe	Con	Maidstone and The Weald	30.47	14,856
118	Mohammed Sarwar	Lab	Glasgow Central	30.43	8,531
119	Helen Jones	Lab	Warrington North	30.19	12,204
120	John McFall	Lab/Co-op	West Dunbartonshire	30.18	12,553
121	Christopher Chope	Con	Christchurch	30.17	15,559
122	Siôn Simon	Lab	Birmingham Erdington	30.16	9,575
123	John Barrett	Lib Dem	Edinburgh West	30.05	13,600
124	Michael Fallon	Con	Sevenoaks	29.96	12,970
125	Paul Goggins	Lab	Wythenshawe and Sale East	29.92	10,827
126	Alan Meale	Lab	Mansfield	29.69	11,365
127	John Robertson	Lab	Glasgow North West	29.63	10,093
128	Rosemary McKenna	Lab	Cumbernauld, Kilsyth and Kirkintilloch East	29.58	11,562
129	Robin Cook	Lab	Livingston	29.54	13,097
130	John Thurso	Lib Dem	Caithness, Sutherland and Easter Ross	29.53	8,168
131	Eric Joyce	Lab	Falkirk	29.45	13,475
132	Cheryl Gillan	Con	Chesham and Amersham	29.30	13,798
133	Colin Challen	Lab	Morley and Rothwell	29.05	12,343
134	John Stanley	Con	Tonbridge and Malling	28.99	13,352
135	Eric Forth	Con	Bromley and Chislehurst	28.92	13,342
136	Denis Murphy	Lab	Wansbeck	28.75	10,581
137	Gregory Barker	Con	Bexhill and Battle	28.72	13,449
138	Charles Hendry	Con	Wealden	28.61	15,921
139	John MacDougall	Lab	Glenrothes	28.54	10,664
140	Rosie Winterton	Lab	Doncaster Central	28.53	9,802
141	Nick Raynsford	Lab	Greenwich and Woolwich	28.49	10,146
142	Nigel Evans	Con	Ribble Valley	28.48	14,171
143	Jim Dobbin	Lab/Co-op	Heywood and Middleton	28.38	11,083
144	Philip Hammond	Con	Runnymede and Weybridge	28.37	12,349
145	Charles Walker	Con	Broxbourne	28.33	11,509
146	George Osborne	Con	Tatton	28.33	11,731
147	Tom Harris	Lab	Glasgow South	28.19	10,832
148	Michael Meacher	Lab	Oldham West and Royton	27.83	10,454
149	Peter Luff	Con	Mid Worcestershire	27.69	13,327
150	Richard Ottaway	Con	Croydon South	27.67	13,528
151	Mark Hendrick	Lab/Co-op	Preston	27.60	9,407
152	Iain Duncan Smith	Con	Chingford and Woodford Green	27.53	10,641
153	Boris Johnson	Con	Henley	27.49	12,793
154	Elliot Morley	Lab	Scunthorpe	27.44	8,963
155	Jimmy Hood	Lab	Lanark and Hamilton East	27.41	11,947
156	Michael Jack	Con	Fylde	27.38	12,459
157	Patricia Hewitt	Lab	Leicester West	27.30	9,070
158	John Whittingdale	Con	Maldon and Chelmsford East	27.28	12,573
159	Rachel Squire	Lab	Dunfermline and West Fife	27.27	11,562
160	Anne McIntosh	Con	Vale of York	27.22	13,712

				%	*Majority*
161 Bill Wiggin	Con	Leominster		27.03	13,187
162 Jim Sheridan	Lab	Paisley and Renfrewshire North		26.91	11,001
163 John Mann	Lab	Bassetlaw		26.86	10,837
164 Ed Balls	Lab/Co-op	Normanton		26.73	10,002
165 Kate Hoey	Lab	Vauxhall		26.71	9,977
166 James Arbuthnot	Con	North East Hampshire		26.54	12,549
167 Andrew Mitchell	Con	Sutton Coldfield		26.52	12,283
168 Alan Milburn	Lab	Darlington		26.41	10,404
169 Mark Prisk	Con	Hertford and Stortford		26.36	13,097
170 Helen Goodman	Lab	Bishop Auckland		26.35	10,047
171 Dawn Primarolo	Lab	Bristol South		26.32	11,142
172 Eric Pickles	Con	Brentwood and Ongar		26.30	11,612
173 David Cameron	Con	Witney		26.28	14,156
174 Alan Duncan	Con	Rutland and Melton		26.24	12,930
175 Shaun Woodward	Lab	St Helens South		26.24	9,309
176 James Clappison	Con	Hertsmere		26.06	11,093
177 George Young	Con	North West Hampshire		25.87	13,264
178 Peter Law	Ind	Blaenau Gwent		25.87	9,121
179 Crispin Blunt	Con	Reigate		25.79	10,988
180 Damian Green	Con	Ashford		25.73	13,298
181 Ann Coffey	Lab	Stockport		25.62	9,163
182 Katy Clark	Lab	North Ayrshire and Arran		25.55	11,296
183 David Maclean	Con	Penrith and The Border		25.39	11,904
184 Barbara Keeley	Lab	Worsley		25.36	9,368
185 Diane Abbott	Lab	Hackney North and Stoke Newington		25.28	7,427
186 Gerry Sutcliffe	Lab	Bradford South		25.04	9,167
187 Alun Michael	Lab/Co-op	Cardiff South and Penarth		25.02	9,237
188 Diana Johnson	Lab	Hull North		24.85	7,351
189 Angela Eagle	Lab	Wallasey		24.84	9,109
190 Malcolm Bruce	Lib Dem	Gordon		24.81	11,026
191 Alistair Burt	Con	North East Bedfordshire		24.75	12,251
192 Ken Purchase	Lab/Co-op	Wolverhampton North East		24.75	8,156
193 Jon Cruddas	Lab	Dagenham		24.66	7,605
194 Alan Haselhurst	Con	Saffron Walden		24.53	13,008
195 Jonathan Djanogly	Con	Huntingdon		24.51	12,847
196 Angela Smith	Lab	Sheffield Hillsborough		24.50	11,243
197 Phil Willis	Lib Dem	Harrogate and Knaresborough		24.33	10,429
198 Piara Khabra	Lab	Ealing Southall		24.32	11,440
199 Brian Donohoe	Lab	Central Ayrshire		24.31	10,423
200 Timothy Boswell	Con	Daventry		24.30	14,686
201 Geoffrey Hoon	Lab	Ashfield		24.29	10,213
202 Paul Beresford	Con	Mole Valley		24.28	11,997
203 Martin McGuinness	Sinn Féin	Mid Ulster		24.16	10,976
204 Michael Connarty	Lab	Linlithgow and East Falkirk		24.15	11,202
205 Mark Hoban	Con	Fareham		24.09	11,702
206 Michael Howard	Con	Folkestone and Hythe		24.08	11,680
207 Peter Lilley	Con	Hitchin and Harpenden		24.04	11,393
208 Alan Beith	Lib Dem	Berwick-upon-Tweed		23.92	8,632
209 Barry Sheerman	Lab/Co-op	Huddersfield		23.90	8,351
210 Nick Brown	Lab	Newcastle upon Tyne East and Wallsend		23.88	7,565
211 Ronnie Campbell	Lab	Blyth Valley		23.84	8,527
212 Lembit Öpik	Lib Dem	Montgomeryshire		23.83	7,173
213 Douglas Hogg	Con	Sleaford and North Hykeham		23.79	12,705
214 John Greenway	Con	Ryedale		23.73	10,469
215 Owen Paterson	Con	North Shropshire		23.69	11,020

				%	Majority
216	James Purnell	*Lab*	Stalybridge and Hyde	23.64	8,348
217	Kevin Brennan	*Lab*	Cardiff West	23.63	8,167
218	Mark Tami	*Lab*	Alyn and Deeside	23.60	8,378
219	Adam Afriyie	*Con*	Windsor	23.56	10,292
220	Andrew Mackay	*Con*	Bracknell	23.53	12,036
221	Richard Caborn	*Lab*	Sheffield Central	23.53	7,055
222	Greg Clark	*Con*	Tunbridge Wells	23.51	9,988
223	Michael Ancram	*Con*	Devizes	23.50	13,194
224	Caroline Flint	*Lab*	Don Valley	23.32	8,598
225	Andrew Love	*Lab/Co-op*	Edmonton	23.27	8,075
226	Austin Mitchell	*Lab*	Great Grimsby	23.22	7,654
227	Neil Gerrard	*Lab*	Walthamstow	23.21	7,993
228	David Wilshire	*Con*	Spelthorne	23.20	9,936
229	Francis Maude	*Con*	Horsham	23.17	12,627
230	Natascha Engel	*Lab*	North East Derbyshire	23.17	10,065
231	John Heppell	*Lab*	Nottingham East	23.06	6,939
232	Kenneth Clarke	*Con*	Rushcliffe	23.04	12,974
233	Andrew George	*Lib Dem*	St Ives	23.03	11,609
234	David Curry	*Con*	Skipton and Ripon	23.00	11,620
235	Sammy Wilson	*DUP*	East Antrim	22.99	7,304
236	Robert Flello	*Lab*	Stoke-on-Trent South	22.95	8,681
237	John Baron	*Con*	Billericay	22.94	11,206
238	Ivan Lewis	*Lab*	Bury South	22.76	8,912
239	Nick Herbert	*Con*	Arundel and South Downs	22.76	11,309
240	Bernard Jenkin	*Con*	North Essex	22.73	10,903
241	Michael Gove	*Con*	Surrey Heath	22.66	10,845
242	Nadine Dorries	*Con*	Mid Bedfordshire	22.52	11,355
243	Bruce George	*Lab*	Walsall South	22.50	7,946
244	David Amess	*Con*	Southend West	22.49	8,959
245	Hugh Bayley	*Lab*	City of York	22.47	10,472
246	Nick Hurd	*Con*	Ruislip Northwood	22.46	8,910
247	Ian Lucas	*Lab*	Wrexham	22.44	6,819
248	Derek Conway	*Con*	Old Bexley and Sidcup	22.26	9,920
249	Mark Field	*Con*	Cities of London and Westminster	22.19	8,095
250	Sandra Osborne	*Lab*	Ayr, Carrick and Cumnock	22.19	9,997
251	Gregory Campbell	*DUP*	East Londonderry	21.76	7,727
252	Laurence Robertson	*Con*	Tewkesbury	21.76	9,892
253	Bridget Prentice	*Lab*	Lewisham East	21.69	6,751
254	Mike Gapes	*Lab/Co-op*	Ilford South	21.61	9,228
255	John Denham	*Lab*	Southampton Itchen	21.52	9,302
256	David Lidington	*Con*	Aylesbury	21.50	11,066
257	Alan Simpson	*Lab*	Nottingham South	21.49	7,486
258	Jessica Morden	*Lab*	Newport East	21.49	6,838
259	Nick Clegg	*Lib Dem*	Sheffield Hallam	21.48	8,682
260	Geoffrey Robinson	*Lab*	Coventry North West	21.44	9,315
261	Tony Wayland Wright	*Lab*	Cannock Chase	21.38	9,227
262	Jeremy Corbyn	*Lab*	Islington North	21.32	6,716
263	Lynne Jones	*Lab*	Birmingham Selly Oak	21.21	8,851
264	Peter Tapsell	*Con*	Louth and Horncastle	21.20	9,896
265	Fiona Mactaggart	*Lab*	Slough	21.16	7,851
266	Iain Wright	*Lab*	Hartlepool	21.10	7,478
267	Julie Kirkbride	*Con*	Bromsgrove	21.08	10,080
268	Patrick McLoughlin	*Con*	West Derbyshire	21.03	10,753
269	Tessa Jowell	*Lab*	Dulwich and West Norwood	20.97	8,807
270	John Maples	*Con*	Stratford-on-Avon	20.92	12,184

					%	Majority
271	Peter Bottomley	Con	Worthing West		20.87	9,379
272	Richard Burden	Lab	Birmingham Northfield		20.78	6,454
273	Gary Streeter	Con	South West Devon		20.74	10,141
274	Andrew Tyrie	Con	Chichester		20.72	10,860
275	Gordon Marsden	Lab	Blackpool South		20.66	7,922
276	Kerry McCarthy	Lab	Bristol East		20.66	8,621
277	Beverley Hughes	Lab	Stretford and Urmston		20.61	7,851
278	Harry Cohen	Lab	Leyton and Wanstead		20.61	6,857
279	Nicholas Winterton	Con	Macclesfield		20.61	9,401
280	Maria Eagle	Lab	Liverpool Garston		20.57	7,193
281	Robert Key	Con	Salisbury		20.51	11,142
282	Nia Griffith	Lab	Llanelli		20.47	7,234
283	Clare Short	Lab	Birmingham Ladywood		20.46	6,801
284	Geoffrey Clifton-Brown	Con	Cotswold		20.46	9,688
285	Khalid Mahmood	Lab	Birmingham Perry Barr		20.43	7,948
286	Paul Farrelly	Lab	Newcastle-under-Lyme		20.38	8,108
287	Richard Spring	Con	West Suffolk		20.15	8,909
288	Shailesh Vara	Con	North West Cambridgeshire		20.03	9,833
289	Hugh Robertson	Con	Faversham and Mid Kent		19.99	8,720
290	Gerald Kaufman	Lab	Manchester Gorton		19.94	5,808
291	David Winnick	Lab	Walsall North		19.86	6,640
292	Andrew Stunell	Lib Dem	Hazel Grove		19.81	7,748
293	Des Browne	Lab	Kilmarnock and Loudoun		19.61	8,703
294	David Hanson	Lab	Delyn		19.54	6,644
295	Andrew Turner	Con	Isle of Wight		19.42	12,978
296	William Cash	Con	Stone		19.32	9,089
297	Alison Seabeck	Lab	Plymouth Devonport		19.29	8,103
298	Oliver Heald	Con	North East Hertfordshire		19.29	9,138
299	Martyn Jones	Lab	Clwyd South		19.28	6,348
300	Vincent Cable	Lib Dem	Twickenham		19.28	9,965
301	David Hamilton	Lab	Midlothian		19.27	7,265
302	Tony Baldry	Con	Banbury		19.21	10,797
303	Nick Gibb	Con	Bognor Regis and Littlehampton		19.20	7,822
304	Liam Byrne	Lab	Birmingham Hodge Hill		19.18	5,449
305	Jack Straw	Lab	Blackburn		19.16	8,009
306	Peter Robinson	DUP	Belfast East		19.06	5,877
307	Angela Browning	Con	Tiverton and Honiton		19.00	11,051
308	Eddie McGrady	SDLP	South Down		18.97	9,140
309	David Ruffley	Con	Bury St Edmunds		18.87	9,930
310	Doug Naysmith	Lab/Co-op	Bristol North West		18.87	8,962
311	Simon Burns	Con	Chelmsford West		18.84	9,620
312	Jamie Reed	Lab	Copeland		18.72	6,320
313	Steve Webb	Lib Dem	Northavon		18.68	11,033
314	Hywel Williams	PlC	Caernarfon		18.60	5,209
315	Frank Doran	Lab	Aberdeen North		18.55	6,795
316	John Gummer	Con	Suffolk Coastal		18.43	9,685
317	Keith Hill	Lab	Streatham		18.38	7,466
318	Tim Loughton	Con	East Worthing and Shoreham		18.37	8,183
319	Ashok Kumar	Lab	Middlesbrough South and East Cleveland		18.31	8,000
320	Christopher Fraser	Con	South West Norfolk		18.30	10,086
321	Alan Keen	Lab/Co-op	Feltham and Heston		18.29	6,820
322	Doug Henderson	Lab	Newcastle upon Tyne North		18.27	7,023
323	Jim Fitzpatrick	Lab	Poplar and Canning Town		18.27	7,129
324	Norman Baker	Lib Dem	Lewes		18.20	8,474
325	Henry Bellingham	Con	North West Norfolk		18.12	9,180

				%	Majority
326	Andrew Selous	Con	South West Bedfordshire	18.07	8,277
327	Edward Davey	Lib Dem	Kingston and Surbiton	18.02	8,966
328	Norman Lamb	Lib Dem	North Norfolk	17.99	10,606
329	John Randall	Con	Uxbridge	17.95	6,171
330	Robert Smith	Lib Dem	West Aberdeenshire and Kincardine	17.94	7,471
331	Bob Spink	Con	Castle Point	17.91	8,201
332	Ann Winterton	Con	Congleton	17.66	8,246
333	Ian Liddell-Grainger	Con	Bridgwater	17.60	8,469
334	Adam Price	PlC	Carmarthen East and Dinefwr	17.54	6,718
335	Edward Leigh	Con	Gainsborough	17.52	8,003
336	Malcolm Moss	Con	North East Cambridgeshire	17.50	8,901
337	Roger Gale	Con	North Thanet	17.46	7,634
338	Angela Watkinson	Con	Upminster	17.42	6,042
339	Stephen Dorrell	Con	Charnwood	17.40	8,809
340	Mike Hall	Lab	Weaver Vale	17.39	6,855
341	Tony Cunningham	Lab	Workington	17.35	6,895
342	Madeleine Moon	Lab	Bridgend	17.23	6,523
343	Jacqui Lait	Con	Beckenham	17.16	8,401
344	David Laws	Lib Dem	Yeovil	17.15	8,562
345	Nigel Dodds	DUP	Belfast North	16.99	5,188
346	Martin Caton	Lab	Gower	16.95	6,703
347	David Gauke	Con	South West Hertfordshire	16.92	8,473
348	Alan Whitehead	Lab	Southampton Test	16.80	7,018
349	Anne Picking	Lab	East Lothian	16.65	7,620
350	Kelvin Hopkins	Lab	Luton North	16.58	6,487
351	Steve McCabe	Lab	Birmingham Hall Green	16.55	5,714
352	John Hutton	Lab	Barrow and Furness	16.54	6,037
353	Alistair Darling	Lab	Edinburgh South West	16.49	7,242
354	Gwyneth Dunwoody	Lab	Crewe and Nantwich	16.28	7,078
355	Michael Fabricant	Con	Lichfield	16.19	7,080
356	Conor Murphy	Sinn Féin	Newry and Armagh	16.16	8,195
357	Graham Brady	Con	Altrincham and Sale West	16.16	7,159
358	Claire Curtis-Thomas	Lab	Crosby	16.14	5,840
359	Ian Taylor	Con	Esher and Walton	16.14	7,727
360	Hugo Swire	Con	East Devon	16.11	7,936
361	Eric Martlew	Lab	Carlisle	16.09	5,695
362	Mike O'Brien	Lab	North Warwickshire	16.09	7,553
363	Andrew Robathan	Con	Blaby	15.94	7,873
364	Paul Goodman	Con	Wycombe	15.87	7,051
365	Barry Gardiner	Lab	Brent North	15.81	5,641
366	David Wright	Lab	Telford	15.80	5,406
367	Quentin Davies	Con	Grantham and Stamford	15.79	7,445
368	David Willetts	Con	Havant	15.74	6,508
369	John Redwood	Con	Wokingham	15.71	7,240
370	Julian Brazier	Con	Canterbury	15.70	7,471
371	Gavin Strang	Lab	Edinburgh East	15.62	6,202
372	Jenny Willott	Lib Dem	Cardiff Central	15.48	5,593
373	Ed Vaizey	Con	Wantage	15.44	8,017
374	Michael Lord	Con	Central Suffolk and North Ipswich	15.44	7,856
375	Andrew Miller	Lab	Ellesmere Port and Neston	15.42	6,486
376	Jim Paice	Con	South East Cambridgeshire	15.38	8,624
377	Lindsay Hoyle	Lab	Chorley	15.38	7,625
378	James Cunningham	Lab	Coventry South	15.37	6,255
379	Sylvia Hermon	UUP	North Down	15.31	4,944
380	Paul Flynn	Lab	Newport West	15.27	5,458

				%	*Majority*
381	Andrew Lansley	Con	South Cambridgeshire	15.20	8,001
382	Stephen Pound	Lab	Ealing North	15.18	7,059
383	Caroline Spelman	Con	Meriden	15.07	7,009
384	Karen Buck	Lab	Regent's Park and Kensington North	15.07	6,131
385	Richard Bacon	Con	South Norfolk	14.89	8,782
386	Kitty Ussher	Lab	Burnley	14.82	5,778
387	Robert Syms	Con	Poole	14.78	5,988
388	Mike Wood	Lab	Batley and Spen	14.76	5,788
389	Jane Kennedy	Lab	Liverpool Wavertree	14.71	5,173
390	Angus Robertson	SNP	Moray	14.63	5,676
391	Evan Harris	Lib Dem	Oxford West and Abingdon	14.61	7,683
392	Andrew Mackinlay	Lab	Thurrock	14.59	6,375
393	Jim McGovern	Lab	Dundee West	14.56	5,379
394	Margaret Moran	Lab	Luton South	14.52	5,650
395	Julian Lewis	Con	New Forest East	14.48	6,551
396	Chris Ruane	Lab	Vale of Clwyd	14.45	4,669
397	Humfrey Malins	Con	Woking	14.36	6,612
398	Matthew Taylor	Lib Dem	Truro and St Austell	14.36	7,403
399	Simon Hughes	Lib Dem	North Southwark and Bermondsey	14.24	5,406
400	Greg Pope	Lab	Hyndburn	14.16	5,587
401	Patrick Mercer	Con	Newark	14.15	6,464
402	Paddy Tipping	Lab	Sherwood	14.12	6,652
403	Mark Simmonds	Con	Boston and Skegness	14.11	5,907
404	Rosie Cooper	Lab	West Lancashire	14.10	6,084
405	Theresa Villiers	Con	Chipping Barnet	14.06	5,960
406	Jim Murphy	Lab	East Renfrewshire	14.04	6,657
407	Liz Blackman	Lab	Erewash	14.01	7,084
408	Bob Russell	Lib Dem	Colchester	13.98	6,277
409	Roger Berry	Lab	Kingswood	13.98	7,873
410	Tobias Ellwood	Con	Bournemouth East	13.95	5,244
411	Andy Slaughter	Lab	Ealing, Acton and Shepherd's Bush	13.93	5,520
412	Frank Dobson	Lab	Holborn and St Pancras	13.93	4,787
413	Ben Bradshaw	Lab	Exeter	13.92	7,665
414	James Duddridge	Con	Rochford and Southend East	13.92	5,494
415	Richard Shepherd	Con	Aldridge-Brownhills	13.92	5,507
416	Keith Simpson	Con	Mid Norfolk	13.81	7,560
417	Dari Taylor	Lab	Stockton South	13.67	6,139
418	David Anderson	Lab	Blaydon	13.66	5,335
419	Theresa May	Con	Maidenhead	13.59	6,231
420	Stephen O'Brien	Con	Eddisbury	13.56	6,195
421	Tim Yeo	Con	South Suffolk	13.56	6,606
422	Greg Knight	Con	Yorkshire East	13.39	6,283
423	Peter Viggers	Con	Gosport	13.32	5,730
424	Grant Shapps	Con	Welwyn Hatfield	13.30	5,946
425	Ian Austin	Lab	Dudley North	13.12	5,432
426	Mark Durkan	SDLP	Foyle	13.06	5,957
427	Alan Reid	Lib Dem	Argyll and Bute	13.04	5,636
428	Margaret Beckett	Lab	Derby South	13.04	5,657
429	Michael Moore	Lib Dem	Berwickshire, Roxburgh and Selkirk	13.00	5,901
430	Sadiq Khan	Lab	Tooting	12.95	5,381
431	Alan Williams	Lab	Swansea West	12.90	4,269
432	Chris Mole	Lab	Ipswich	12.73	5,332
433	Fabian Hamilton	Lab	Leeds North East	12.69	5,262
434	Paul Truswell	Lab	Pudsey	12.64	5,870
435	Gillian Merron	Lab	Lincoln	12.52	4,614

				%	Majority
436	Colin Breed	Lib Dem	South East Cornwall	12.17	6,507
437	Annette Brooke	Lib Dem	Mid Dorset and Poole North	12.14	5,482
438	Mark Oaten	Lib Dem	Winchester	12.12	7,476
439	Peter Atkinson	Con	Hexham	12.09	5,020
440	Ann McKechin	Lab	Glasgow North	11.96	3,338
441	Shahid Malik	Lab	Dewsbury	11.96	4,615
442	David Simpson	DUP	Upper Bann	11.93	5,298
443	Bob Blizzard	Lab	Waveney	11.91	5,915
444	Nicholas Soames	Con	Mid Sussex	11.90	5,890
445	John Butterfill	Con	Bournemouth West	11.88	4,031
446	Mary Creagh	Lab	Wakefield	11.88	5,154
447	Joan Humble	Lab	Blackpool North and Fleetwood	11.69	5,062
448	Liam Fox	Con	Woodspring	11.65	6,016
449	Ian Gibson	Lab	Norwich North	11.61	5,459
450	David Lepper	Lab/Co-op	Brighton Pavilion	11.55	5,030
451	Pat Doherty	Sinn Féin	West Tyrone	11.51	5,005
452	Geraldine Smith	Lab	Morecambe and Lunesdale	11.45	4,768
453	David Tredinnick	Con	Bosworth	11.20	5,319
454	Richard Taylor	Ind KHHC	Wyre Forest	11.17	5,250
455	Judy Mallaber	Lab	Amber Valley	11.13	5,275
456	David Crausby	Lab	Bolton North East	11.12	4,103
457	Martin Salter	Lab	Reading West	11.12	4,682
458	Jim Cousins	Lab	Newcastle upon Tyne Central	11.09	3,982
459	Gerald Howarth	Con	Aldershot	11.08	5,334
460	Anne McGuire	Lab	Stirling	10.91	4,767
461	Jeremy Hunt	Con	South West Surrey	10.90	5,711
462	Ian Pearson	Lab	Dudley South	10.81	4,244
463	Linda Gilroy	Lab/Co-op	Plymouth Sutton	10.76	4,109
464	David Evennett	Con	Bexleyheath and Crayford	10.69	4,551
465	David Davis	Con	Haltemprice and Howden	10.65	5,116
466	Sylvia Heal	Lab	Halesowen and Rowley Regis	10.49	4,337
467	Ann Cryer	Lab	Keighley	10.48	4,852
468	Angus MacNeil	SNP	Na h-Eileanan An Iar	10.41	1,441
469	Michael Mates	Con	East Hampshire	10.37	5,509
470	Gwyn Prosser	Lab	Dover	10.32	4,941
471	Richard Younger-Ross	Lib Dem	Teignbridge	10.21	6,215
472	Terry Rooney	Lab	Bradford North	10.21	3,511
473	Greg Hands	Con	Hammersmith and Fulham	10.20	5,029
474	Roger Williams	Lib Dem	Brecon and Radnorshire	10.18	3,905
475	Don Foster	Lib Dem	Bath	10.12	4,638
476	David Howarth	Lib Dem	Cambridge	9.96	4,339
477	David Davies	Con	Monmouth	9.92	4,527
478	Glenda Jackson	Lab	Hampstead and Highgate	9.77	3,729
479	Maria Miller	Con	Basingstoke	9.73	4,680
480	Alan Campbell	Lab	Tynemouth	9.67	4,143
481	Andrew Murrison	Con	Westbury	9.62	5,349
482	Colin Burgon	Lab	Elmet	9.60	4,528
483	Ann Keen	Lab	Brentford and Isleworth	9.59	4,411
484	Nick Harvey	Lib Dem	North Devon	9.57	4,972
485	David Taylor	Lab/Co-op	North West Leicestershire	9.50	4,477
486	James Gray	Con	North Wiltshire	9.46	5,303
487	Sally Keeble	Lab	Northampton North	9.42	3,960
488	Michelle Gildernew	Sinn Féin	Fermanagh and South Tyrone	9.39	4,582
489	Ben Chapman	Lab	Wirral South	9.38	3,724
490	Danny Alexander	Lib Dem	Inverness, Nairn, Badenoch and Strathspey	9.37	4,148

				%	Majority
491 John Pugh	*Lib Dem*	Southport		9.32	3,838
492 Tony McNulty	*Lab*	Harrow East		9.31	4,730
493 Clive Efford	*Lab*	Eltham		9.28	3,276
494 Betty Williams	*Lab*	Conwy		9.15	3,081
495 John Hemming	*Lib Dem*	Birmingham Yardley		9.08	2,672
496 William McCrea	*DUP*	South Antrim		9.08	3,448
497 John Horam	*Con*	Orpington		9.04	4,947
498 Stephen Williams	*Lib Dem*	Bristol West		8.93	5,128
499 Peter Soulsby	*Lab*	Leicester South		8.76	3,717
500 Sarah Teather	*Lib Dem*	Brent East		8.73	2,712
501 Jo Swinson	*Lib Dem*	East Dunbartonshire		8.69	4,061
502 Charles Clarke	*Lab*	Norwich South		8.66	3,653
503 Vernon Coaker	*Lab*	Gedling		8.65	3,811
504 Linda Riordan	*Lab/Co-op*	Halifax		8.62	3,417
505 Roger Godsiff	*Lab*	Birmingham Sparkbrook and Small Heath		8.61	3,289
506 Bob Laxton	*Lab*	Derby North		8.57	3,757
507 Patsy Calton	*Lib Dem*	Cheadle		8.47	4,020
508 Mike Hancock	*Lib Dem*	Portsmouth South		8.33	3,362
509 Marsha Singh	*Lab*	Bradford West		8.32	3,026
510 Phil Woolas	*Lab*	Oldham East and Saddleworth		8.28	3,590
511 Janet Anderson	*Lab*	Rossendale and Darwen		8.27	3,676
512 Parmjit Dhanda	*Lab*	Gloucester		8.24	4,271
513 Phyllis Starkey	*Lab*	Milton Keynes South West		8.23	4,010
514 Edward Garnier	*Con*	Harborough		8.12	3,892
515 Brian Binley	*Con*	Northampton South		8.11	4,419
516 Mark Todd	*Lab*	South Derbyshire		8.05	4,495
517 Patrick Hall	*Lab*	Bedford		8.04	3,383
518 Ben Wallace	*Con*	Lancaster and Wyre		8.01	4,171
519 Helen Southworth	*Lab*	Warrington South		7.51	3,515
520 Barbara Follett	*Lab*	Stevenage		7.49	3,139
521 Anthony David Wright	*Lab*	Great Yarmouth		7.38	3,055
522 Roberta Blackman-Woods	*Lab*	City of Durham		7.38	3,274
523 Brooks Newmark	*Con*	Braintree		7.34	3,893
524 Angela Evans Smith	*Lab/Co-op*	Basildon		7.28	3,142
525 Susan Kramer	*Lib Dem*	Richmond Park		7.26	3,731
526 Rob Marris	*Lab*	Wolverhampton South West		6.91	2,879
527 Paul Holmes	*Lib Dem*	Chesterfield		6.90	3,045
528 Des Turner	*Lab*	Brighton Kemptown		6.89	2,737
529 Ian Cawsey	*Lab*	Brigg and Goole		6.80	2,894
530 Paul Burstow	*Lib Dem*	Sutton and Cheam		6.79	2,846
531 Michael John Foster	*Lab*	Worcester		6.78	3,144
532 Jacqui Smith	*Lab*	Redditch		6.74	2,716
533 Stewart Jackson	*Con*	Peterborough		6.65	2,740
534 David Chaytor	*Lab*	Bury North		6.58	2,926
535 Andrew Dismore	*Lab*	Hendon		6.45	2,699
536 Richard Benyon	*Con*	Newbury		6.33	3,460
537 Gisela Stuart	*Lab*	Birmingham Edgbaston		6.24	2,349
538 Shona McIsaac	*Lab*	Cleethorpes		6.06	2,642
539 Philip Hollobone	*Con*	Kettering		5.93	3,301
540 Brian Jenkins	*Lab*	Tamworth		5.87	2,569
541 David Heathcoat-Amory	*Con*	Wells		5.74	3,040
542 Russell Brown	*Lab*	Dumfries and Galloway		5.74	2,922
543 Michael Wills	*Lab*	North Swindon		5.73	2,571

			%	*Majority*
544 Jonathan Shaw	*Lab*	Chatham and Aylesford	5.54	2,332
545 Geoffrey Cox	*Con*	Torridge and West Devon	5.52	3,236
546 Charlotte Atkins	*Lab*	Staffordshire Moorlands	5.51	2,438
547 Dan Rogerson	*Lib Dem*	North Cornwall	5.49	3,076
548 Gordon Prentice	*Lab*	Pendle	5.30	2,180
549 Stephen Hammond	*Con*	Wimbledon	5.30	2,301
550 Martin Horwood	*Lib Dem*	Cheltenham	5.28	2,303
551 Michael Spicer	*Con*	West Worcestershire	5.26	2,475
552 Graham Stuart	*Con*	Beverley and Holderness	5.14	2,580
553 Ruth Kelly	*Lab*	Bolton West	5.09	2,064
554 Lynne Featherstone	*Lib Dem*	Hornsey and Wood Green	5.06	2,395
555 Mark Lazarowicz	*Lab/Co-op*	Edinburgh North and Leith	5.05	2,153
556 Bill Olner	*Lab*	Nuneaton	5.04	2,280
557 Nick Ainger	*Lab*	Carmarthen West and South Pembrokeshire	5.04	1,910
558 Justine Greening	*Con*	Putney	4.83	1,766
559 Joan Ryan	*Lab*	Enfield North	4.71	1,920
560 Michael Jabez Foster	*Lab*	Hastings and Rye	4.71	2,026
561 Nick Palmer	*Lab*	Broxtowe	4.70	2,296
562 David Kidney	*Lab*	Stafford	4.66	2,121
563 Oliver Letwin	*Con*	West Dorset	4.62	2,461
564 David Borrow	*Lab*	South Ribble	4.60	2,184
565 Philip Dunne	*Con*	Ludlow	4.36	2,027
566 Andrew Reed	*Lab/Co-op*	Loughborough	4.33	1,996
567 Mark Harper	*Con*	Forest of Dean	4.30	2,049
568 Adrian Sanders	*Lib Dem*	Torbay	4.29	2,029
569 Gareth Thomas	*Lab/Co-op*	Harrow West	4.25	2,028
570 Robert Walter	*Con*	North Dorset	4.25	2,244
571 John Penrose	*Con*	Weston-Super-Mare	4.23	2,079
572 Gregory Mulholland	*Lib Dem*	Leeds North West	4.20	1,877
573 Mike Weir	*SNP*	Angus	4.20	1,601
574 David Burrowes	*Con*	Enfield Southgate	4.14	1,747
575 Julia Goldsworthy	*Lib Dem*	Falmouth and Camborne	3.93	1,886
576 David Mundell	*Con*	Dumfriesshire, Clydesdale and Tweeddale	3.90	1,738
577 Alasdair McDonnell	*SDLP*	Belfast South	3.86	1,235
578 Anthony Steen	*Con*	Totnes	3.85	1,947
579 Lee Scott	*Con*	Ilford North	3.84	1,653
580 John Smith	*Lab*	Vale of Glamorgan	3.82	1,808
581 Jim Knight	*Lab*	South Dorset	3.73	1,812
582 Dan Norris	*Lab*	Wansdyke	3.61	1,839
583 Daniel Kawczynski	*Con*	Shrewsbury and Atcham	3.59	1,808
584 Albert Owen	*Lab*	Ynys Môn	3.50	1,242
585 Mark Lancaster	*Con*	Milton Keynes North East	3.32	1,665
586 Peter Wishart	*SNP*	Perth and North Perthshire	3.31	1,521
587 Anne Begg	*Lab*	Aberdeen South	3.24	1,348
588 Phil Hope	*Lab/Co-op*	Corby	3.13	1,517
589 Anne Snelgrove	*Lab*	South Swindon	3.11	1,353
590 Kali Mountford	*Lab*	Colne Valley	3.07	1,501
591 Sarah McCarthy-Fry	*Lab/Co-op*	Portsmouth North	3.02	1,139
592 Anne Main	*Con*	St Albans	2.99	1,361
593 Janet Dean	*Lab*	Burton	2.97	1,421
594 Christine McCafferty	*Lab*	Calder Valley	2.86	1,367
595 Jeremy Wright	*Con*	Rugby and Kenilworth	2.73	1,556
596 Stephen Hesford	*Lab*	Wirral West	2.66	1,097
597 Robert Goodwill	*Con*	Scarborough and Whitby	2.65	1,245
598 Julie Morgan	*Lab*	Cardiff North	2.53	1,146

				%	Majority
599	Tom Brake	*Lib Dem*	Carshalton and Wallington	2.48	1,068
600	Claire Ward	*Lab*	Watford	2.32	1,148
601	Nigel Waterson	*Con*	Eastbourne	2.32	1,124
602	Andrew Smith	*Lab*	Oxford East	2.30	963
603	Mark Pritchard	*Con*	The Wrekin	2.09	942
604	Paul Keetch	*Lib Dem*	Hereford	2.05	962
605	Christine Russell	*Lab*	City of Chester	2.04	915
606	George Galloway	*Respect*	Bethnal Green and Bow	1.87	823
607	Douglas Carswell	*Con*	Harwich	1.83	920
608	John Leech	*Lib Dem*	Manchester Withington	1.78	667
609	Rudi Vis	*Lab*	Finchley and Golders Green	1.71	741
610	Stephen Ladyman	*Lab*	South Thanet	1.61	664
611	Stephen Crabb	*Con*	Preseli Pembrokeshire	1.57	607
612	Emily Thornberry	*Lab*	Islington South and Finsbury	1.56	484
613	Howard Stoate	*Lab*	Dartford	1.51	706
614	David Heath	*Lib Dem*	Somerton and Frome	1.50	812
615	Gordon Banks	*Lab*	Ochil and South Perthshire	1.47	688
616	Tom Levitt	*Lab*	High Peak	1.47	735
617	Adam Holloway	*Con*	Gravesham	1.45	654
618	Peter Bone	*Con*	Wellingborough	1.30	687
619	James Brokenshire	*Con*	Hornchurch	1.26	480
620	Chris Huhne	*Lib Dem*	Eastleigh	1.14	568
621	Paul Rowen	*Lib Dem*	Rochdale	1.08	442
622	Robert Wilson	*Con*	Reading East	1.08	475
623	Mike Penning	*Con*	Hemel Hempstead	1.06	499
624	Lynda Waltho	*Lab*	Stourbridge	0.98	407
625	Stewart Hosie	*SNP*	Dundee East	0.97	383
626	Jeremy Browne	*Lib Dem*	Taunton	0.96	573
627	Nigel Griffiths	*Lab*	Edinburgh South	0.95	405
628	Celia Barlow	*Lab*	Hove	0.94	420
629	John Grogan	*Lab*	Selby	0.89	467
630	Philip Davies	*Con*	Shipley	0.89	422
631	Anne Milton	*Con*	Guildford	0.67	347
632	David Drew	*Lab/Co-op*	Stroud	0.62	350
633	Mark Williams	*Lib Dem*	Ceredigion	0.61	219
634	Paul Clark	*Lab*	Gillingham	0.56	254
635	Tim Farron	*Lib Dem*	Westmorland and Lonsdale	0.54	267
636	Lorely Burt	*Lib Dem*	Solihull	0.53	279
637	Robert Marshall-Andrews	*Lab*	Medway	0.52	213
638	James Plaskitt	*Lab*	Warwick and Leamington	0.49	266
639	Martin Linton	*Lab*	Battersea	0.40	163
640	David Jones	*Con*	Clwyd West	0.37	133
641	Sandra Gidley	*Lib Dem*	Romsey	0.25	125
642	Bill Rammell	*Lab*	Harlow	0.24	97
643	Derek Wyatt	*Lab*	Sittingbourne and Sheppey	0.19	79
644	Andrew Pelling	*Con*	Croydon Central	0.15	75
645	Laura Moffatt	*Lab*	Crawley	0.09	37

Constituencies' Whereabouts

Constituencies in England do not necessarily fall within a single county, as they did before local government re-organisation in the late 1990s. County names for English seats are as they applied when current constituencies boundaries were established before the 1997 general election. Thus, for instance, 'Avon', 'Cleveland' and 'Humberside' appear, although they have since been abolished.

Constituencies in Scotland are allocated to regions used by the Scottish Parliament. Asterisked constituencies fall substantially within the region indicated, but not entirely

Aberavon	South Wales West
Aberdeen North	North East Scotland
Aberdeen South	North East Scotland
West Aberdeenshire and Kincardine	North East Scotland
Airdrie and Shotts	Central Scotland
Aldershot	Hampshire
Aldridge-Brownhills	West Midlands
Altrincham and Sale West	Greater Manchester
Alyn and Deeside	North Wales
Amber Valley	Derbyshire
Angus*	North East Scotland
East Antrim	N Ireland
North Antrim	N Ireland
South Antrim	N Ireland
Argyll and Bute*	Highlands and Islands
Arundel and South Downs	West Sussex
Ashfield	Nottinghamshire
Ashford	Kent
Ashton under Lyne	Greater Manchester
Aylesbury	Buckinghamshire
Ayr, Carrick and Cumnock	South Scotland
Central Ayrshire	South Scotland
North Ayrshire and Arran*	West of Scotland
Banbury	Oxfordshire
Banff and Buchan	North East Scotland
Barking	Outer London
Barnsley Central	South Yorkshire
Barnsley East and Mexborough	South Yorkshire
Barnsley West and Penistone	South Yorkshire
Barrow and Furness	Cumbria
Basildon	Essex
Basingstoke	Hampshire
Bassetlaw	Nottinghamshire
Bath	Avon
Batley and Spen	West Yorkshire
Battersea	Inner London
Beaconsfield	Buckinghamshire
Beckenham	Outer London
Bedford	Bedfordshire
Mid Bedfordshire	Bedfordshire
North East Bedfordshire	Bedfordshire
South West Bedfordshire	Bedfordshire
Belfast East	N Ireland
Belfast North	N Ireland
Belfast South	N Ireland
Belfast West	N Ireland
Berwickshire, Roxburgh and Selkirk	South Scotland
Berwick-upon-Tweed	Northumberland
Bethnal Green and Bow	Inner London
Beverley and Holderness	Humberside
Bexhill and Battle	East Sussex
Bexleyheath and Crayford	Outer London
Billericay	Essex
Birkenhead	Merseyside
Birmingham Edgbaston	West Midlands
Birmingham Erdington	West Midlands
Birmingham Hall Green	West Midlands
Birmingham Hodge Hill	West Midlands
Birmingham Ladywood	West Midlands
Birmingham Northfield	West Midlands
Birmingham Perry Barr	West Midlands
Birmingham Selly Oak	West Midlands
Birmingham Sparkbrook and Small Heath	West Midlands
Birmingham Yardley	West Midlands
Bishop Auckland	Durham
Blaby	Leicestershire
Blackburn	Lancashire
Blackpool North and Fleetwood	Lancashire
Blackpool South	Lancashire
Blaenau Gwent	South Wales East
Blaydon	Tyne and Wear
Blyth Valley	Northumberland
Bognor Regis and Littlehampton	West Sussex
Bolsover	Derbyshire
Bolton North East	Greater Manchester
Bolton South East	Greater Manchester
Bolton West	Greater Manchester
Bootle	Merseyside
Boston and Skegness	Lincolnshire

Bosworth	Leicestershire
Bournemouth East	Dorset
Bournemouth West	Dorset
Bracknell	Berkshire
Bradford North	West Yorkshire
Bradford South	West Yorkshire
Bradford West	West Yorkshire
Braintree	Essex
Brecon and Radnorshire	Mid and West Wales
Brent East	Outer London
Brent North	Outer London
Brent South	Outer London
Brentford and Isleworth	Outer London
Brentwood and Ongar	Essex
Bridgend	South Wales West
Bridgwater	Somerset
Brigg and Goole	Humberside
Brighton Kemptown	East Sussex
Brighton Pavilion	East Sussex
Bristol East	Avon
Bristol North West	Avon
Bristol South	Avon
Bristol West	Avon
Bromley and Chislehurst	Outer London
Bromsgrove	Hereford & Worcester
Broxbourne	Hertfordshire
Broxtowe	Nottinghamshire
Buckingham	Buckinghamshire
Burnley	Lancashire
Burton	Staffordshire
Bury North	Greater Manchester
Bury South	Greater Manchester
Bury St Edmunds	Suffolk
Caernarfon	North Wales
Caerphilly	South Wales East
Caithness, Sutherland and Easter Ross	Highlands and Islands
Calder Valley	West Yorkshire
Camberwell and Peckham	Inner London
Cambridge	Cambridgeshire
North East Cambridgeshire	Cambridgeshire
North West Cambridgeshire	Cambridgeshire
South Cambridgeshire	Cambridgeshire
South East Cambridgeshire	Cambridgeshire
Cannock Chase	Staffordshire
Canterbury	Kent
Cardiff Central	South Wales Central
Cardiff North	South Wales Central
Cardiff South and Penarth	South Wales Central
Cardiff West	South Wales Central
Carlisle	Cumbria

Carmarthen East and Dinefwr	Mid and West Wales
Carmarthen West and South Pembrokeshire	Mid and West Wales
Carshalton and Wallington	Outer London
Castle Point	Essex
Ceredigion	Mid and West Wales
Charnwood	Leicestershire
Chatham and Aylesford	Kent
Cheadle	Greater Manchester
Chelmsford West	Essex
Cheltenham	Gloucestershire
Chesham and Amersham	Buckinghamshire
City of Chester	Cheshire
Chesterfield	Derbyshire
Chichester	West Sussex
Chingford and Woodford Green	Outer London
Chipping Barnet	Outer London
Chorley	Lancashire
Christchurch	Dorset
Cities of London and Westminster	Inner London
Cleethorpes	Humberside
Clwyd South	North Wales
Vale of Clwyd	North Wales
Clwyd West	North Wales
Coatbridge, Chryston and Bellshill	Central Scotland
Colchester	Essex
Colne Valley	West Yorkshire
Congleton	Cheshire
Conwy	North Wales
Copeland	Cumbria
Corby	Northamptonshire
North Cornwall	Cornwall
South East Cornwall	Cornwall
Cotswold	Gloucestershire
Coventry North East	West Midlands
Coventry North West	West Midlands
Coventry South	West Midlands
Crawley	West Sussex
Crewe and Nantwich	Cheshire
Crosby	Merseyside
Croydon Central	Outer London
Croydon North	Outer London
Croydon South	Outer London
Cumbernauld, Kilsyth and Kirkintilloch East*	Central Scotland
Cynon Valley	South Wales Central
Dagenham	Outer London
Darlington	Durham
Dartford	Kent
Daventry	Northamptonshire
Delyn	North Wales

Denton and Reddish	Greater Manchester
Derby North	Derbyshire
Derby South	Derbyshire
North East Derbyshire	Derbyshire
South Derbyshire	Derbyshire
West Derbyshire	Derbyshire
Devizes	Wiltshire
East Devon	Devon
North Devon	Devon
South West Devon	Devon
Torridge and West Devon	Devon
Dewsbury	West Yorkshire
Don Valley	South Yorkshire
Doncaster Central	South Yorkshire
Doncaster North	South Yorkshire
Mid Dorset and Poole North	Dorset
North Dorset	Dorset
South Dorset	Dorset
West Dorset	Dorset
Dover	Kent
North Down	N Ireland
South Down	N Ireland
Dudley North	West Midlands
Dudley South	West Midlands
Dulwich and West Norwood	Inner London
Dumfries and Galloway	South Scotland
Dumfriesshire, Clydesdale and Tweeddale	South Scotland
East Dunbartonshire*	West of Scotland
West Dunbartonshire	West of Scotland
Dundee East	North East Scotland
Dundee West	North East Scotland
Dunfermline and West Fife	Mid Scotland and Fife
City of Durham	Durham
Durham North	Durham
North West Durham	Durham
Ealing, Acton and Shepherd's Bush	Outer London
Ealing North	Outer London
Ealing Southall	Outer London
Easington	Durham
East Ham	Outer London
East Kilbride, Strathaven and Lesmahagow*	Central Scotland
Eastbourne	East Sussex
Eastleigh	Hampshire
Eccles	Greater Manchester
Eddisbury	Cheshire
Edinburgh East	Lothians
Edinburgh North and Leith	Lothians
Edinburgh South	Lothians

Edinburgh South West	Lothians
Edinburgh West	Lothians
Edmonton	Outer London
Ellesmere Port and Neston	Cheshire
Elmet	West Yorkshire
Eltham	Inner London
Enfield North	Outer London
Enfield Southgate	Outer London
Epping Forest	Essex
Epsom and Ewell	Surrey
Erewash	Derbyshire
Erith and Thamesmead	Outer London
Esher and Walton	Surrey
North Essex	Essex
Exeter	Devon
Falkirk	Central Scotland
Falmouth and Camborne	Cornwall
Fareham	Hampshire
Faversham and Mid Kent	Kent
Feltham and Heston	Outer London
Fermanagh and South Tyrone	N Ireland
North East Fife	Mid Scotland and Fife
Finchley and Golders Green	Outer London
Folkestone and Hythe	Kent
Forest of Dean	Gloucestershire
Foyle	N Ireland
Fylde	Lancashire
Gainsborough	Lincolnshire
Gateshead East and Washington West	Tyne and Wear
Gedling	Nottinghamshire
Gillingham	Kent
Vale of Glamorgan	South Wales Central
Glasgow Central	Glasgow
Glasgow East	Glasgow
Glasgow North	Glasgow
Glasgow North East	Glasgow
Glasgow North West	Glasgow
Glasgow South	Glasgow
Glasgow South West	Glasgow
Glenrothes	Mid Scotland and Fife
Gloucester	Gloucestershire
Gordon	North East Scotland
Gosport	Hampshire
Gower	South Wales West
Grantham and Stamford	Lincolnshire
Gravesham	Kent
Great Grimsby	Humberside
Great Yarmouth	Norfolk
Greenwich and Woolwich	Inner London
Guildford	Surrey

Hackney North and Stoke Newington	Inner London
Hackney South and Shoreditch	Inner London
Halesowen and Rowley Regis	West Midlands
Halifax	West Yorkshire
Haltemprice and Howden	Humberside
Halton	Cheshire
Hammersmith and Fulham	Inner London
East Hampshire	Hampshire
North East Hampshire	Hampshire
North West Hampshire	Hampshire
Hampstead and Highgate	Inner London
Harborough	Leicestershire
Harlow	Essex
Harrogate and Knaresborough	North Yorkshire
Harrow East	Outer London
Harrow West	Outer London
Hartlepool	Cleveland
Harwich	Essex
Hastings and Rye	East Sussex
Havant	Hampshire
Hayes and Harlington	Outer London
Hazel Grove	Greater Manchester
Hemel Hempstead	Hertfordshire
Hemsworth	West Yorkshire
Hendon	Outer London
Henley	Oxfordshire
Hereford	Hereford & Worcester
Hertford and Stortford	Hertfordshire
North East Hertfordshire	Hertfordshire
South West Hertfordshire	Hertfordshire
Hertsmere	Hertfordshire
Hexham	Northumberland
Heywood and Middleton	Greater Manchester
High Peak	Derbyshire
Hitchin and Harpenden	Hertfordshire
Holborn and St Pancras	Inner London
Hornchurch	Outer London
Hornsey and Wood Green	Outer London
Horsham	West Sussex
Houghton and Washington East	Tyne and Wear
Hove	East Sussex
Huddersfield	West Yorkshire
Hull East	Humberside
Hull North	Humberside
Hull West and Hessle	Humberside
Huntingdon	Cambridgeshire
Hyndburn	Lancashire
Ilford North	Outer London
Ilford South	Outer London

Inverclyde	West of Scotland
Inverness, Nairn, Badenoch and Strathspey	Highlands and Islands
Ipswich	Suffolk
Isle of Wight	Isle of Wight
Islington North	Inner London
Islington South and Finsbury	Inner London
Islwyn	South Wales East
Jarrow	Tyne and Wear
Keighley	West Yorkshire
Kensington and Chelsea	Inner London
Kettering	Northamptonshire
Kilmarnock and Loudoun*	Central Scotland
Kingston and Surbiton	Outer London
Kingswood	Avon
Kirkcaldy and Cowdenbeath	Mid Scotland and Fife
Knowsley North and Sefton East	Merseyside
Knowsley South	Merseyside
Lagan Valley	N Ireland
Lanark and Hamilton East*	South Scotland
West Lancashire	Lancashire
Lancaster and Wyre	Lancashire
Leeds Central	West Yorkshire
Leeds East	West Yorkshire
Leeds North East	West Yorkshire
Leeds North West	West Yorkshire
Leeds West	West Yorkshire
Leicester East	Leicestershire
Leicester South	Leicestershire
Leicester West	Leicestershire
North West Leicestershire	Leicestershire
Leigh	Greater Manchester
Leominster	Hereford & Worcester
Lewes	East Sussex
Lewisham Deptford	Inner London
Lewisham East	Inner London
Lewisham West	Inner London
Leyton and Wanstead	Outer London
Lichfield	Staffordshire
Lincoln	Lincolnshire
Linlithgow and East Falkirk*	Lothians
Liverpool Garston	Merseyside
Liverpool Riverside	Merseyside
Liverpool Walton	Merseyside
Liverpool Wavertree	Merseyside
Liverpool West Derby	Merseyside
Livingston	Lothians

Llanelli	Mid and West Wales
East Londonderry	N Ireland
East Lothian*	South Scotland
Loughborough	Leicestershire
Louth and Horncastle	Lincolnshire
Ludlow	Shropshire
Luton North	Bedfordshire
Luton South	Bedfordshire
Macclesfield	Cheshire
Maidenhead	Berkshire
Maidstone and The Weald	Kent
Makerfield	Greater Manchester
Maldon and Chelmsford East	Essex
Manchester Blackley	Greater Manchester
Manchester Central	Greater Manchester
Manchester Gorton	Greater Manchester
Manchester Withington	Greater Manchester
Mansfield	Nottinghamshire
Medway	Kent
Meirionnydd Nant Conwy	Mid and West Wales
Meriden	West Midlands
Merthyr Tydfil and Rhymney	South Wales East
Middlesbrough	Cleveland
Middlesbrough South and East Cleveland	Cleveland
Midlothian*	Lothians
Milton Keynes North East	Buckinghamshire
Milton Keynes South West	Buckinghamshire
Mitcham and Morden	Outer London
Mole Valley	Surrey
Monmouth	South Wales East
Montgomeryshire	Mid and West Wales
Moray*	Highlands and Islands
Morecambe and Lunesdale	Lancashire
Morley and Rothwell	West Yorkshire
Motherwell and Wishaw	Central Scotland
Na h-Eileanan An Iar	Highlands and Islands
Neath	South Wales West
New Forest East	Hampshire
New Forest West	Hampshire
Newark	Nottinghamshire
Newbury	Berkshire
Newcastle-under-Lyme	Staffordshire
Newcastle upon Tyne Central	Tyne and Wear
Newcastle upon Tyne East and Wallsend	Tyne and Wear
Newcastle upon Tyne North	Tyne and Wear
Newport East	South Wales East
Newport West	South Wales East

Newry and Armagh	N Ireland
Mid Norfolk	Norfolk
North Norfolk	Norfolk
North West Norfolk	Norfolk
South Norfolk	Norfolk
South West Norfolk	Norfolk
Normanton	West Yorkshire
Northampton North	Northamptonshire
Northampton South	Northamptonshire
Northavon	Avon
Norwich North	Norfolk
Norwich South	Norfolk
Nottingham East	Nottinghamshire
Nottingham North	Nottinghamshire
Nottingham South	Nottinghamshire
Nuneaton	Warwickshire
Ochil and South Perthshire	Mid Scotland and Fife
Ogmore	South Wales West
Old Bexley and Sidcup	Outer London
Oldham East and Saddleworth	Greater Manchester
Oldham West and Royton	Greater Manchester
Orkney and Shetland	Highlands and Islands
Orpington	Outer London
Oxford East	Oxfordshire
Oxford West and Abingdon	Oxfordshire
Paisley and Renfrewshire North	West of Scotland
Paisley and Renfrewshire South	West of Scotland
Pendle	Lancashire
Penrith and The Border	Cumbria
Perth and North Perthshire*	Mid Scotland and Fife
Peterborough	Cambridgeshire
Plymouth Devonport	Devon
Plymouth Sutton	Devon
Pontefract and Castleford	West Yorkshire
Pontypridd	South Wales Central
Poole	Dorset
Poplar and Canning Town	Inner London
Portsmouth North	Hampshire
Portsmouth South	Hampshire
Preseli Pembrokeshire	Mid and West Wales
Preston	Lancashire
Pudsey	West Yorkshire
Putney	Inner London
Rayleigh	Essex
Reading East	Berkshire
Reading West	Berkshire
Redcar	Cleveland

Redditch	Hereford & Worcester
Regent's Park and Kensington North	Inner London
Reigate	Surrey
East Renfrewshire	West of Scotland
Rhondda	South Wales Central
South Ribble	Lancashire
Ribble Valley	Lancashire
Richmond Park	Outer London
Richmond (Yorkshire)	North Yorkshire
Rochdale	Greater Manchester
Rochford and Southend East	Essex
Romford	Outer London
Romsey	Hampshire
Ross, Skye and Lochaber	Highlands and Islands
Rossendale and Darwen	Lancashire
Rother Valley	South Yorkshire
Rotherham	South Yorkshire
Rugby and Kenilworth	Warwickshire
Ruislip Northwood	Outer London
Runnymede and Weybridge	Surrey
Rushcliffe	Nottinghamshire
Rutherglen and Hamilton West*	Central Scotland
Rutland and Melton	Leicestershire
Ryedale	North Yorkshire
Saffron Walden	Essex
St Albans	Hertfordshire
St Helens North	Merseyside
St Helens South	Merseyside
St Ives	Cornwall
Salford	Greater Manchester
Salisbury	Wiltshire
Scarborough and Whitby	North Yorkshire
Scunthorpe	Humberside
Sedgefield	Durham
Selby	North Yorkshire
Sevenoaks	Kent
Sheffield Attercliffe	South Yorkshire
Sheffield Brightside	South Yorkshire
Sheffield Central	South Yorkshire
Sheffield Hallam	South Yorkshire
Sheffield Heeley	South Yorkshire
Sheffield Hillsborough	South Yorkshire
Sherwood	Nottinghamshire
Shipley	West Yorkshire
Shrewsbury and Atcham	Shropshire
North Shropshire	Shropshire
Sittingbourne and Sheppey	Kent
Skipton and Ripon	North Yorkshire

Sleaford and North Hykeham	Lincolnshire
Slough	Berkshire
Solihull	West Midlands
Somerton and Frome	Somerset
South Holland and The Deepings	Lincolnshire
South Shields	Tyne and Wear
Southampton Itchen	Hampshire
Southampton Test	Hampshire
Southend West	Essex
Southport	Merseyside
North Southwark and Bermondsey	Inner London
Spelthorne	Surrey
Stafford	Staffordshire
Staffordshire Moorlands	Staffordshire
South Staffordshire	Staffordshire
Stalybridge and Hyde	Greater Manchester
Stevenage	Hertfordshire
Stirling	Mid Scotland and Fife
Stockport	Greater Manchester
Stockton North	Cleveland
Stockton South	Cleveland
Stoke-on-Trent Central	Staffordshire
Stoke-on-Trent North	Staffordshire
Stoke-on-Trent South	Staffordshire
Stone	Staffordshire
Stourbridge	West Midlands
Strangford	N Ireland
Stratford-on-Avon	Warwickshire
Streatham	Inner London
Stretford and Urmston	Greater Manchester
Stroud	Gloucestershire
Central Suffolk and North Ipswich	Suffolk
Suffolk Coastal	Suffolk
South Suffolk	Suffolk
West Suffolk	Suffolk
Sunderland North	Tyne and Wear
Sunderland South	Tyne and Wear
East Surrey	Surrey
Surrey Heath	Surrey
South West Surrey	Surrey
Mid Sussex	West Sussex
Sutton and Cheam	Outer London
Sutton Coldfield	West Midlands
Swansea East	South Wales West
Swansea West	South Wales West
North Swindon	Wiltshire
South Swindon	Wiltshire
Tamworth	Staffordshire
Tatton	Cheshire
Taunton	Somerset

Teignbridge	Devon
Telford	Shropshire
Tewkesbury	Gloucestershire
North Thanet	Kent
South Thanet	Kent
Thurrock	Essex
Tiverton and Honiton	Devon
Tonbridge and Malling	Kent
Tooting	Inner London
Torbay	Devon
Torfaen	South Wales East
Totnes	Devon
Tottenham	Outer London
Truro and St Austell	Cornwall
Tunbridge Wells	Kent
Twickenham	Outer London
Tyne Bridge	Tyne and Wear
Tynemouth	Tyne and Wear
North Tyneside	Tyne and Wear
West Tyrone	N Ireland
Mid Ulster	N Ireland
Upminster	Outer London
Upper Bann	N Ireland
Uxbridge	Outer London
Vauxhall	Inner London
Wakefield	West Yorkshire
Wallasey	Merseyside
Walsall North	West Midlands
Walsall South	West Midlands
Walthamstow	Outer London
Wansbeck	Northumberland
Wansdyke	Avon
Wantage	Oxfordshire
Warley	West Midlands
Warrington North	Cheshire
Warrington South	Cheshire
Warwick and Leamington	Warwickshire
North Warwickshire	Warwickshire
Watford	Hertfordshire
Waveney	Suffolk
Wealden	East Sussex
Weaver Vale	Cheshire
Wellingborough	Northamptonshire
Wells	Somerset
Welwyn Hatfield	Hertfordshire
Wentworth	South Yorkshire
West Bromwich East	West Midlands
West Bromwich West	West Midlands
West Ham	Outer London
Westbury	Wiltshire
Westmorland and Lonsdale	Cumbria
Weston-Super-Mare	Avon
Wigan	Greater Manchester
North Wiltshire	Wiltshire
Wimbledon	Outer London
Winchester	Hampshire
Windsor	Berkshire
Wirral South	Merseyside
Wirral West	Merseyside
Witney	Oxfordshire
Woking	Surrey
Wokingham	Berkshire
Wolverhampton North East	West Midlands
Wolverhampton South East	West Midlands
Wolverhampton South West	West Midlands
Woodspring	Avon
Worcester	Hereford & Worcester
Mid Worcestershire	Hereford & Worcester
West Worcestershire	Hereford & Worcester
Workington	Cumbria
Worsley	Greater Manchester
East Worthing and Shoreham	West Sussex
Worthing West	West Sussex
The Wrekin	Shropshire
Wrexham	North Wales
Wycombe	Buckinghamshire
Wyre Forest	Hereford & Worcester
Wythenshawe and Sale East	Greater Manchester
Yeovil	Somerset
Ynys Môn	North Wales
City of York	North Yorkshire
Vale of York	North Yorkshire
Yorkshire East	Humberside

PARTY MANIFESTOS

Labour Party

ECONOMY

Labour's economic record is unprecedented – the highest employment ever, longest period of uninterrupted growth in modern history, lowest sustained interest and inflation rates for a generation.Our economic policies will build on the platform of stability and growth in three ways:entrenching a low-debt/high-employment economy which generates investment in public services; supporting enterprise and wealth creation by making Britain the best place to do business; and helping every part of Britain and every person in Britain to contribute to and gain from the strength of our economy. And as we work globally to tackle climate change we recognise the challenge and the opportunity of achieving sustainable development at home.

The new Labour case

Our economic record has finally laid to rest the view that Labour could not be trusted with the economy. We are winning the argument that economic dynamism and social justice must go hand in hand. In the future the countries that do best will be those with a shared purpose about the long-term changes and investments they need to make – and have the determination to equip their people for that future. So, we approach new challenges with a progressive strategy for growth. In our third term we will build new ladders of social mobility and advancement on the firm foundations of stability, investment and growth.

Low debt and high employment

In the last eight years we have pioneered a British way to economic stability.Our economyhas grown in everyquarter with this Government. Interest rates have averaged 5.3 per cent since 1997, saving mortgage payers on average nearly £4,000 per year compared to the Tory years.

Only with Labour, which constructed this framework, will this continue. We will maintain our inflation target at two per cent. We will continue to meet our fiscal rules: over the economic cycle, we will borrow only to invest, and keep net debt at a stable and prudent level.

Public spending and taxation

The longest period of uninterrupted economic growth in modern times has enabled the Government to deliver the longest period of sustained investment in public services for a generation. Social security bills for unemployment have been halved since 1997, saving £5 billion a year, and we are also saving £4 billion a year on debt interest payments. Over the ten-year period 1997-98 to 2007-08, real-terms investment per year in education will have risen by 4.8 per cent and in health by 6.5 per cent.

Every pound we invest goes further because of our drive for efficiency and reform. Labour will complete the implementation of Sir Peter Gershon's recommendations to improve public-service efficiency and root out waste, liberating over £21 billion for investment in front-line services.

Labour believes tax policy should continue to be governed by the health of the public finances, the requirement for public investment and the needs of families, business and the environment.

We will not raise the basic or top rates of income tax in the next Parliament. We renew our pledge not to extend VAT to food,children's clothes,books, newspapers and public transport fares. We will continue to make targeted tax cuts for families and to support work. As a result of personal tax and benefit measures introduced since 1997, by October 2005 families with children will be on average £1,400 a year better off in real terms. Living standards in Britain have been rising, on average, by 2.5 per cent per year since 1997 – a total increase of nearly 20 per cent.

We want a tax regime that supports British business. That is why we have cut corporation tax to its lowest ever level, introduced the best regime of capital gains tax in any industrialised country, and introduced a new Research and Development tax credit.

Full employment

Our goal is employment opportunity for all – the modern definition of full employment. Britain has more people in work than ever before, with the highest employment rate in the G7. Our long-term aim is to raise the employment rate to 80 per cent. And, as we move more people from welfare to work, the savings on unemployment benefits will go towards investing more in education.

We will make work pay. With Labour's tax credits a family with two children pays no net tax until their earnings reach £21,000.

We will implement the recommendations of the Low Pay Commission to raise the minimum wage to £5.05 from October 2005 and £5.35 from October 2006.

The New Deals and the creation of JobCentre Plus have made a major contribution to cutting unemployment. The active welfare state created since 1997 is working.

The Tories trebled the number on incapacity benefits. We will help people who can work into rehabilitation and eventually into employment, recognising the practical assistance to disabled people of the Access to Work scheme. We will build on the successful Pathways to Work programme and reform Incapacity Benefit, with the main elements of the new benefit regime in place from 2008. The majority of claimants with more manageable conditions will be required to engage in both work-focused interviews and in activity to help them prepare for a return to work. Those with the most severe conditions will also be encouraged to engage in activity and should receive more money than now. We will continue to welcome new independent and voluntary sector partners to provide job-seeking services.

Supporting enterprise

Government does not create wealth but it must support the wealth creators. That is why our priorities are the national infrastructure of skills, science, regulation and planning, and transport. The economy of the future will be based on knowledge, innovation and creativity. That applies both to manufacturing and services.

In a fast changing global economy, government cannot postpone or prevent change. The modernrole for government – the case for a modern employment and skills policy – is to equip people to succeed, to be on their side, helping them become more skilled, adaptable and flexible for the job ahead rather than the old Tory way of walking away leaving people unaided to face change.

Successful manufacturing industries are vital to our future prosperity. The Labour Government backs manufacturing: from launch investment for Airbus A380 Super Jumbo to the successful Manufacturing Advisory Service helping 13,000 of our smaller manufacturing businesses in its first year. In a third term we will continue to do so.

Public procurement is a big opportunity for business in Britain and the source of many jobs. We will promote a public procurement strategy that safeguards UK jobs and skills, under EU rules, to ensure that British industry can compete fairly with the rest of Europe.

Britain has some of the strongest capital markets in the world. We are determined they – and our financial services industry – should prosper. We will ensure that companies have the right framework of corporate governance and relationships with the institutions that invest our pension funds and savings in them.

Skills at work

Our reforms to 14-19 education will raise the quality and quantity of apprenticeships and vocational education. We are now putting in place a comprehensive and ambitious strategy to help everyone get on at work:

- All adults to get free access to basic skills in literacy,language and numeracy.
- A new national programme, working with employers, to ensure that employees who did not reach GCSE standard (level 2) at school will get time off for free training up to level 2.
- A new partnership between government and employers to fund workplace training at level 3 (technician level)
- A genuinely employer-driven training system – in every sector there will be a Sector Skills Council determining the training strategy and a leading edge Skills Academy.
- A nationwide system of advice – bringing together support on skills, jobs and careers – helping people to get on at work.
- A strong partnership with trade unions to boost workplace training including a new TUC Academy and continued support for Union Learning Reps.

Supporting science

The alliance of scientific research and business creativity is key to our continued prosperity.

Looking ahead, we are committed to a ten-year strategy on science and innovation that will continue to invest in our science and industrial base at least in line with trend GDP. Our ambition now is to raise the UK's total private and public sector investment in research and development, as a proportion of national income, from its current 1.9 per cent to 2.5 per cent by 2014.

Our pharmaceutical and biotechnology industries are world leaders. We have created one of the world's best environments for stem-cell research. We have now passed legislation to protect our researchers from the activities of animal rights extremists.

Across a range of environmental issues – from soil erosion to the depletion of marine resources, from water scarcity to air pollution – it is clear now not just that economic activity is their cause but that these problems in themselves threaten future economic activity and growth. We will continue to work with the environmental goods and services sector – which is already worth £25 billion to the economy to promote new green technologies and industries in the UK and internationally, and use the purchasing power of government to support environmental improvement.

Competition, planning and regulation

Competition is a driving force for innovation. Our competition regime has been toughened with independent competition bodies and stronger penalties.

To the benefit of business and household consumers we are liberalising the postal services market, while protecting the universal service at a uniform tariff.

As we said in our policy document Britain is Working, we have given the Royal Mail greater commercial freedom and have no plans to privatise it. Our ambition is to see a publicly owned Royal Mail fully restored to good health, providing customers with an excellent service and its employees with rewarding employment. We will review the impact on the Royal Mail of market liberalisation, which is being progressively introduced under the Postal Services Act 2000 and which allows alternative carriers to the Royal Mail to offer postal services.

We have reformed our energy markets to make them open and competitive. And we are a leading force in the campaign to make Europe's energy markets the same. Our wider energy policy has created a framework that places the challenge of climate change – as well as the need to achieve security of supply – at the heart of our energy policy. We have a major programme to promote renewable energy, as part of a strategy of having a mix of energy sources from nuclear power stations to clean coal to micro-generators.

We will only regulate where necessary and will set exacting targets for reducing the costs of administering regulations. We will rationalise business inspections. The merger of the Inland Revenue and Customs and Excise will cut the administrative costs of tax compliance for small businesses.

We will take further action in Europe to ensure that EU regulations are proportionate and better designed. We strongly support the creation of an EU single market in services to match the single market in goods – and want an effective directive to provide real benefits to consumers and new opportunities to British business. We will protect our employment standards. In developing the directive we will want to avoid any undermining of our regulatory framework.

We will continue to work to protect the rights of consumers, bringing forward proposals to strengthen and streamline consumer advocacy. We look forward to action from the banking industry to remove delays in processing cheques and other payments and, if necessary, will legislate to ensure this early in the next Parliament.

There are many bank accounts that are lying dormant and unclaimed, often because people have forgotten about them or because the owner has died. We will work with the financial services industry to establish acommon definition and a comprehensiverecord of unclaimed assets. We will then expect banks, over the course of the Parliament, to either reunite those assets with their owners or to channel them back into the community.

An effective planning regime protects the environment while promoting economic growth – and does so quickly and responsively. In the next term, we will ensure that our planning system continues to protect the sustainability of local and regional environments – and we will continue to develop a regime which is simpler,faster and more responsive to local and business needs including the need to create jobs and regenerate our cities.

Fostering entrepreneurship

There are 300,000 more businesses now than in 1997. We are tackling barriers to financing for small and growing businesses – especially enterprises in deprived areas. Through Business Links we will offer start-ups, social enterprises and small businesses access to tailored intensive support and coaching. To foster the entrepreneurs of tomorrow, by 2006 every school in the country will offer enterprise education, and every college and university should be twinned with a business champion.

Modern transport infrastructure

An efficient transport system is vital to the country's future, to our economy and to our quality of life. We welcome the freedom that additional travel provides and support the continuing development of a competitive and efficient freight sector.Investment,better management of road and rail, and planning ahead are vital to deal with the pressures on the system in a way that respects our environmental objectives.

We have doubled transport spending since 1997 and will increase it year on year – committing over £180 billion in public money between now and 2015 as well as private investment. The Eddington Review will work with the Government to advise on how this investment should be targeted – in particular, where transport is vital to underpin economic growth.

We are now taking charge of setting the strategy for rail to further raise the standard of service and reliability. We will examine options for increasing capacity, including a new generation of high-speed trains on intercity routes and a new life for rural branch lines as community railways. We are committed to continuing to work to develop a funding and finance solution for the Crossrail project; and will look at the feasibility and affordability of a new North-South high-speed link.

We will support light-rail improvements where they represent value for money and are part of the best integrated transport solution. To that end, we are working with cities across the country and have committed £520 million to Manchester for Metrolink. We will support the continuing upgrade of the London Underground and the extension of the East London line.

Major investment is planned to expand capacity on the M1, M6 and M25. We must also manage road space better. We are examining the potential benefits of a parallel Expressway on the M6 corridor. We will introduce car-pool lanes for cars with more than one passenger on suitable roads and explore other ways to lock in the benefit of new capacity. We will complete the introduction of Traffic Management Officers to keep traffic flowing. Because of the long-term nature of transport planning, we will seek political consensus in tackling congestion, including examining the potential of moving away from the current system of motoring taxation towards a national system of road-pricing.

We will give all over-60s, and disabled people, free off-peak local bus travel and give local authorities the freedom to provide more generous schemes. We will continue to support growth in bus provision including innovation in school transport, with greater opportunity for local authorities to control their bus networks where they are demonstrating value for money and taking strong measures to tackle congestion. To facilitate improved public transport provision, we will explore giving Passenger Transport Executives greater powers over local transport.

We will continue funding local authorities and voluntary groups to make cycling and walking more attractive. We are committed to reducing child deaths and serious injuries on the road by 50 per cent, and we will continue to work to reduce dangerous driving, especially drink driving and uninsured driving. We will work with industry to make travel on public transport safer and more secure.

Government will continue to support technological innovation to reduce carbon emissions such as the hydrogen fuel-cell buses in London. We will explore the scope for further use of economic instruments as well as other measures to promote lower vehicle emissions.

We will continue to support air travel by implementing the balanced policies set out in our aviation white paper. We are committed to using the UK's 2005 presidency of the European Union to promote the inclusion of aviation in the EU's emissions trading scheme.

For shipping, our introduction of the tonnage tax has led to a trebling in size of the fleet since 1997. We want more ships to fly the British flag, to boost jobs and training, and to increase shipping and port capacity.

Opportunity for all

We are determined to spread the benefits of enterprise to every com-munity in the country.Every regional economy has different strengths, and Regional Development Agencies now play an essential role in regional economic development.

We have given local authorities a direct incentive to promote local business creation, allowing them to keep up to £1 billion over three years of increased rate revenues to spend on their own priorities. The Local Enterprise Growth Initiative will work through local authorities to remove barriers to enterprise in the most deprived areas of England.

In 1997, many parts of our towns and cities were suffering from deeply entrenched and multiple disadvantage. To tackle this we established a ten-year programme, the New Deal for Communities, empowering local communities – and this is already delivering improvements in education outcomes and crime reduction.

No area in our country should be excluded from the opportunity to get ahead, to benefit from improving public services, and to be secure and safe. We will maintain our commitment to tackling issues of worklessness, low skills, crime, poor environment and health in our poorest neighbourhoods.

Fairness at work

Since 1997, the Labour Government has introduced new rights for people at work and new opportunities for trade unions to represent their members. We see modern, growing trade unions as an important part of our society and economy. They provide protection and advice for employees, and we welcome the positive role they have played in developing a modern model of social partnership with business representatives. The Labour Party has agreed a set of policies for the work-place (the Warwick Agreement) and we will deliver them in full. They will be good for employees and for the economy.

We have introduced, for the first time, an entitlement for every employee to four weeks' paid holiday, and we propose to extend this by making it additional to bank holiday entitlement.

Promoting equality at work

A strong economy draws on the talents of all. We have extended legislation to protect people from discrimination at work to cover not only gender, disability, race and ethnicity but also religion and sexual orientation and – from 2006 – age. Labour has transformed legal rights for disabled people. We will empower disabled people further by joining up services and expanding personalised budgets.

We will take further action to narrow the pay and promotion gap between men and women. The Women and Work Commission will report to the Prime Minister later this year.

We will implement the National Employment Panel's report on measures to promote employment and small business growth for ethnic and faith minorities.

We will take forward the Strategy for Race Equality to ensure that we combat discrimination on the grounds of race and ethnicity across a range of services. The Equalities Review reporting to the Prime Minister in 2006 will make practical recommendations on the priorities for tackling disadvantage and promoting equality of opportunity for all groups.

Thriving rural areas

Since 1997, Labour has made it more difficult to close rural schools, put in £750 million to support rural post offices and introduced a 50 per cent rate relief on village shops. Through our £51 million Rural Bus Subsidy Grant we have delivered over 2,200 new bus services in rural areas this year.

We set targets for the creation of affordable homes in rural areas,which we have now exceeded. We will explore how to ensure a proportion of all new housing development is made available and affordable to local residents and their families.

Because of our success in achieving extensive reforms in the Common Agricultural Policy (CAP),2005 will be the first year for decades when farmers will be free to produce for the market and not simply for subsidy. We will continue to push for further reform of the CAP in the next Parliament, starting with the sugar regime.

We will continue to promote the competitiveness of the whole food sector, and assure the safety and quality of its products. We will introduce an explicit policy for schools, hospitals and government offices to consider local sourcing of fresh produce. We will continue to improve the environmental performance of agriculture,rewarding every farmer in England for environmental protection and enhancement work through our new Stewardship schemes. We will also promote biomass, biofuels and non-food crops. We will work to tackle diffuse water pollution through addressing impacts across water catchments without the costs falling on water customers.

Under difficult circumstances, Labour is working with the fishing industry to create a sustainable long-term future for the fishing communities of the United Kingdom. We have reformed the Common Fisheries Policy and will continue to protect the marine environment and ensure fish stocks and their exploitation are set at sustainable levels.

We will introduce the Animal Welfare Bill as soon as possible in the new Parliament.

The choice for 2010

The Conservatives are the party of high interest rates,high inflation, mass unemployment and house repossessions. Their tax-and-spend promises do not add up; and they would cut £35 billion from public investment. With new Labour, Britain can seize the opportunities of globalisation, creating jobs and prosperity for people up and down the country. We can only do so if we build a clear sense of shared national economic purpose, not just around economic stability but also investment in infrastructure, skills, science and enterprise. The choice is to go forward to economic stability, rising prosperity and wider opportunities with new Labour. Or go back to the bad old days of Tory cuts, insecurity and instability.

EDUCATION

Education is still our number one priority. In our first term, we transformed recruitment, training and methods of teaching, with record results in primary schools. In our second term we have driven fundamental reform in secondary provision – more teachers and support staff, more money, specialist schools and the Academies programmes. Our plan now is to tailor our education system to individual pupil needs, with parents supporting teachers and support staff in further raising standards. That means music, art, sport and languages as well as English and maths in primary school; a good secondary school for every child, with modern buildings and excellent specialist teaching; catch-up support for all children who need it; the guarantee of a sixth-form place, apprenticeship or further education at 16; sufficient quality and quantity in higher education. At each stage we send a clear message – every child has a right to a good education, but no child has the right to disrupt the education of other children.

The new Labour case

For generations our country has been held back by an education system that excelled for the privileged few but let down the majority. Every child can and should be able to fulfil their potential. We will achieve this by uniting our commitment to equal opportunities for all children with a reform programme which gives every child and young person, from pre-school to sixth-form or apprenticeship and beyond, the personalised package of learning and support they need. In a third term, we will entrench high expectations for every child, ensure the flexibility of provision to meet all needs and make parents true partners as we aim for the highest ever school standards.

Every pupil with better teaching

There is no greater responsibility than teaching the next generation. Head teachers, teachers and support staff deserve support and respect. There are now over 28,000 more teachers and 105,000 more support staff than in 1997; graduate teacher applications are up 70 per cent; average salaries are up by more than 30 per cent. The remodelling of the school workforce is benefiting staff and helping to tailor provision to pupil need. We will now go further – to intensify in-service training for teachers, to widen further routes into teaching, to help more teachers and pupils get the benefit of the range of support staff now working in schools, from learning mentors to music and arts specialists. The goal is clear: every pupil with extra support in their weakest subjects and extra opportunities in their strongest.

We want to see every pupil mastering the basics. If they are not mastered by 11, there will be extra time in the secondary curriculum to get them right: schools will be judged on how pupils do in English and maths at the ages of 11, 14 and 16.

We want every pupil to be stretched, including the brightest, so we will develop extended projects at A-level, harder A-level questions to challenge the most able, and give universities the individual module marks – as well as overall grades – of A-level students.

Every school with more money and effective leadership

Since 1997, school funding has risen by £1,000 per pupil. Education spending that was 4.7 per cent of national income in 1997 will rise to 5.5 per cent this year. We will continue to raise the share of national income devoted to education. And we will continue to recognise the additional needs of disadvantaged pupils. We will also ensure funda-mental reform in the way the money is spent. Funding will be allocated on a multi-year timescale. There will be a dedicated national schools budget set by central government, with a guaranteed per pupil increase for every school. Heads and governors will be in control. Successful schools and colleges will have the independence to take decisions about how to deploy resources and develop their provision. Schools will work together to raise standards. New provision will be created where standards are too low or innovation is needed. Local authorities have a vital role in championing the parent interest and providing support services.

A strong, effective governing body is essential to the success of every school and governors must be given support to help them play this role. We will allow more flexibility in the structure of governing bodies, including the ability to have smaller governing bodies, of ten members or less, to streamline management while strengthening the position of parents.

Parents as partners

Our aim for the education system is to nurture the unique talents of every child. But children and schools do best with real and effective parental engagement. Parents should have the information and support they need to encourage their children, from the first reading book to the key choices they make at 14 and 16. And parents should be central to the process of assessing school performance and driving improvement, as well as their vital role in promoting good behaviour and raising the quality of school meals.

All schools should have good home-school links, building on the new school and pupil profiles. Some schools are using ICT to make contact between parents and schools easier and better for both sides. We will encourage all schools to follow suit.

Ofsted now actively seeks the views of parents when undertaking inspections. Ofsted will be given new powers to respond to parental complaints and where necessary to close failing schools or replace failing management.

Enriching primary schools

International studies show that our ten-year-olds are the third highest achievers in literacy in the world and the fastest improving in maths. Three-quarters of 11-year-olds now reach high standards in reading, writing and maths. We will intensify our literacy and numeracy programme to help an extra 50,000 pupils achieve high standards at age 11, reaching our targets of 85 per cent of pupils succeeding at the basics.

All primary school children will have access to high-quality tuition in the arts, music, sport and foreign languages. We have set aside funds for this purpose, working with head teachers to develop support programmes and modernise the school workforce.

We have abolished infant class sizes of more than 30, and almost all primary schools have gained improved facilities since 1997. We will now upgrade primary schools nationwide in a 15-year Building Schools for the Future programme, including under-fives and childcare facilities where needed. Primary schools will become the base for a massive expansion of out-of-school provision.

Foundation schools operate within the local family of state schools, and are funded in the same way as others, but manage their own assets and employ their staff directly. We will allow successful primary schools, like secondary schools, to become foundation schools by a simple vote of their governing body following consultation with their parents.

Every secondary school an independent specialist school

We want all secondary schools to be independent specialist schools with a strong ethos, high-quality leadership, good discipline (including school uniforms), setting by ability and high-quality facilities as the norm.

The way to achieve this is not a return to the 11-plus or a free-for-all on admissions policies. It is to ensure that independent specialist schools tailor education to the needs, interests and aptitudes of each pupil within a fair admissions system.

There are over 2,000 specialist schools – schools which teach the entire national curriculum and also have a centre of excellence. Their results are improving faster than those of non-specialist schools. We want every secondary school to become a specialist school and existing specialist schools will be able to take on a second specialism. Over time all specialist schools will become extended schools, with full programmes of after-school activities.

Every part of the country will benefit, over fifteen years, from the Building Schools for the Future programme. This is a once in a generation programme to equip the whole country with modern secondary education facilities, open five days a week, ten hours a day.

Good schools will be able to expand their size and also their influence – by taking over less successful schools. We will develop a system to create rights for successful schools to establish sixth-form provision where there is pupil and parent demand, extending quality and choice for local students.

Britain has a positive tradition of independent providers within the state system, including church and other faith schools. Where new educational providers can help boost standards and opportunities in a locality we will welcome them into the state system, subject to parental demand, fair funding and fair admissions.

We strongly support the new Academies movement. Seventeen of these independent non-selective schools are now open within the state system; their results are improving sharply, and 50 more are in the pipeline. Within the existing allocation of resources our aim is that at least 200 Academies will be established by 2010 in communities where low aspirations and low performance are entrenched.

We will encourage more small schools and boarding schools as ways of helping the most disadvantaged children. We will make sure schools in deprived areas receive the resources they need. To enable all young people to enjoy the opportunities previously enjoyed by the few,we are developing a nationwide week-long summer residential programme for school students. We support partnership between the state and private sectors to bridge the unhealthy historic divide between the two.

Good discipline

Every pupil has the right to learn without disruption;no teacher should be subject to abuse or disrespect. We have given head teachers the powers needed to maintain discipline and the highest standards of conduct.

Violent behaviour,including the use of knives will not be tolerated. We are also working with schools and teacher organisations to implement a zero tolerance approach to lower-level disruption. The number of places in out-of-school units has almost doubled, and the quality of provision has been enhanced. We will give head teachers within each locality direct control of the budgets for out-of-school provision, so they can expand and improve it as needed. We will encourage more dedicated provision for disruptive and excluded pupils, including by charities and voluntary groups with expertise in this area, and no school will become a dumping ground for such pupils.

Parents have a duty to get their children to attend school. We have introduced parenting orders and fines and will continue to advocate truancy sweeps.

Special educational needs

Children with special educational needs require appropriate resources and support from trained staff. For some this will be in mainstream schools; for others, it will be in special schools. Parents should have access to the special education appropriate for their child. It is the role of local authorities to make decisions on the shape of local provision,in consultation with local parents.

No more dropping out at 16

The historic problems of our education system at 14-plus have been an academic track that has been too narrow and a vocational offer too weak.

We are determined to raise the status and quality of vocational education. Beyond the age of 14, GCSEs and A-levels will be the foundation of the system in which high-quality vocational programmes will be available to every pupil. Designed in collaboration with employers, specialised diplomas will be established in key areas of the economy, leading to apprenticeships, to further and higher education and to jobs with training. We will review progress on the development of the 14-19 curriculum in 2008.

We will not let economic disadvantage stand in the way of young people staying in education beyond the age of 16. We have rolled out Educational Maintenance Allowances, providing lower income students with a £30-a-week staying-on allowance. We believe that everyone up to the age of 19 should be learning, so we will expand sixth-form, college and apprenticeship places, and ensure that all 16-to 19-year-olds in employment get access to training.

We believe that every 16- to 19-year-old should have dedicated supervision and support, including in the further education sector. We will support sixth-form colleges and expect FE colleges to have dedicated centres for 16- to 19-year-olds.

Further education is vital to vocational lifelong learning. Achieving a transformation of FE colleges requires both our increased investment and serious reform. Every FE college will develop a centre for vocational excellence, and we will establish new skills academies led by leading entrepreneurs and employers from the relevant skill sectors. Sir Andrew Foster's review will help shape the reform process.

Children's Trusts

Ofsted reports show that local government is continuing to improve the vital services on which schools and families rely. Education and social services should collaborate to help youngsters, especially the most vulnerable, achieve their potential. Local government should be the champion of parents and high-quality provision, including special needs education, school transport, and other support services. We are reforming local education authorities to form Children's Trusts to provide seamless support to children and families and work in partnership with the private and voluntary sectors.

World-class higher education, open to all

Universities are critical to Britain's future prosperity. We need a bigger, better higher education system. We are investing £1 billion more in the science base, and increasing public spending on higher education by 34 per cent in real terms. But graduates and employers must also play their part. Our funding reforms will generate £1 billion of extra funds by 2010; the abolition of up-front fees and the creation of grants will help poorer students. A quarter of the income from the new student finance system will go to bursaries for students from poorer families. The maximum annual fee paid by students will not rise above £3,000 (uprated annually for inflation) during the next Parliament.

As school standards rise we maintain our aim for 50 per cent of young people to go on to higher education by 2010. Two-year foundation degrees in vocational disciplines have a key part to play.

PhD students are vital to universities and the nation's research base.

The number of PhD students in the UK has risen by nearly 10,000 since 1997, and we are carrying through a 30 per cent increase in average PhD stipends to make doctoral research still more attractive to high-flyers.

We will incentivise all universities to raise more charitable and private funding for student bursaries and endowments.

The choice for 2010

Under their last government the Conservatives spent more on unemployment and debt interest than on education. Their priority now is to take at least £1 billion from state schools to subsidise private education for the privileged few. In addition they would allow a free-for-all in school admissions – including an extension of selection – for five- and 11-year-olds, cap the number of pupils who can succeed at GCSE and A-level, and reduce places in higher education. The choice for 2010 is forward with new Labour: pupils with quality and opportunity through the system from three to 18; parents with the confidence that where there is no improvement there will be intervention; teachers knowing that quality will be supported and rewarded; and employers with a system that gets the basics right and provides the skills that industry needs.Or back with the Tories to an education system designed to look after the few but fail the many.

CRIME AND SECURITY

Today, there is less chance of being a victim of crime than for more than 20 years. But our security is threatened by major organised crime; volume crimes such as burglary and car theft, often linked to drug abuse; fear of violent crime; and anti-social behaviour. Each needs a very different approach. We are giving the police and local councils the power to tackle anti-social behaviour; we will develop neighbourhood policing for every community and crack down on drug dealing and hard drug use to reduce volume crime; we are modernising our asylum and immigration system; and we will take the necessary measures to protect our country from international terrorism.

The new Labour case

The modern world offers freedoms and opportunities unheralded a generation ago. But with new freedoms come new fears and threats to our security. Our progressive case is that to counter these threats we need strong communities built on mutual respect and the rule of law. We prize the liberty of the individual; but that means protecting the law-abiding majority from the minority who abuse the system. We believe in being tough on crime and its causes so we will expand drugs testing and treatment, and tackle the conditions – from lack of youth provision to irresponsible drinking – that foster crime and anti-social behaviour. In a third term we will make the contract of rights and responsibilities an enduring foundation of community life.

A neighbourhood policing team for every community

Overall crime as measured by the authoritative British Crime Survey is down 30 per cent – the equivalent of almost five million fewer crimes a year. Record numbers of police – almost 13,000 more than in 1997 – working with 4,600 new Community Support Officers (CSOs), local councils, and the Crown Prosecution Service deserve the credit. But local people want a more visible police presence and a role in setting local police priorities. So our pledge is a neighbourhood policing team for every community. We will carry on funding the police service to enable it to continue to employ historically high numbers of police officers.

Hard-working police officers should be supported by professional and trained supportstaff.So a new £340 million a year fund will take CSO numbers up to 24,000 – to work alongside the equivalent of an additional 12,000 police officers freed up for frontline duties. And we will work with representatives of police officers and other police staff to develop a modern career framework for the whole police team.

Not all problems need a 999 response, so a single phone number staffed by police, local councils and other local services will be available across the country to deal with anti-social behaviour and other non-emergency problems.

Empowering communities against anti-social behaviour

People want communities where the decent law-abiding majority are in charge. The experience of almost 4,000 Anti-Social Behaviour Orders, nearly 66,000 Penalty Notices for Disorder, and the closure of over 150 crack houses shows that communities can fight back against crime. We are ready to go further.

Parish Council wardens, like those working for local authorities, will be given the power to issue Penalty Notices for Disorder for noise, graffiti and throwing fireworks.Victims of anti-social behaviour will be able to give evidence anonymously. Local people will be able to take on 'neighbours from hell' by triggering action by councils and the police.

We have reformed housing and planning legislation to ensure that councils plan for the needs of genuine Gypsies and travellers. But with rights must go responsibilities so we have provided tough new powers for councils and the police to tackle the problem of unauthorised sites.

Excessive alcohol consumption fuels anti-social behaviour and violence. The new Licensing Act will make it easier for the police and councils to deal with pubs and clubs that cause problems. Local councils and police will be able to designate Alcohol Disorder Zones to help pay for extra policing around city centre pubs and clubs, with new powers to immediately shut down premises selling alcohol to under-age drinkers, and bans from town and city centres for persistent offenders. Police will be able to exclude yobs from town centres for 24 hours when they issue a Penalty Notice for Disorder.

We will continue to overhaul our youth justice system and improve Young Offender Institutions. We will make more use of intensive community programmes, including electronic tagging and tracking to deal with the most persistent young offenders, and will increase the number of parents of young offenders getting help with their children's behaviour. We will increase, by at least a half, programmes targeted at young people most at risk of offending and will expand drug treatment services for young people.

Cutting crime through cutting drug dependency

Communities know that crime reduction depends on drug reduction. There are now 54 per cent more drug users in treatment and new powers for the police to close crack houses and get drug dealers off our streets. We will introduce compulsory drug testing at arrest for all property and drugs offenders, beginning in high-crime areas, with compulsory treatment assessment for those who test positive. Offenders under probation supervision will be randomly drug tested to mirror what already happens to offenders in custody.

From 2006, the Serious Organised Crime Agency will bring together over 4,000 specialist staff to tackle terrorism, drug dealers, people traffickers and other national and international organized criminals. And in consultation with local police authorities and chief constables we will restructure police resources in order to develop strong leadership, streamline all police support services, and focus upon national and regional organised crime.

Reducing the use of guns and knives

Dangerous weapons fuel violence. We have banned all handguns, introduced five-year minimum sentences for those caught with an unlawful firearm and raised the age limit for owning an air gun. Now we will go further. We will introduce a Violent Crime Reduction Bill to restrict the sale of replica guns, raise the age limit for buying knives to 18 and tighten the law on air guns. Head teachers will have legal rights to search pupils for knives or guns. At-risk pubs and clubs will be required to search for them and we will introduce tougher sentences for carrying replica guns, for those involved in serious knife crimes and for those convicted of assaulting workers serving the public.

Punishing criminals, reducing offending

As court sentences have got tougher, we have built over 16,000 more prison places than there were in 1997. The most high-risk violent offenders will now be detained in custody indefinitely and our 2003 Criminal Justice Act confirmed that life sentences must mean life for the most heinous murders. Where significant new evidence comes to light we have abolished the 'double jeopardy' rule so that serious criminals who have been unjustly acquitted can be tried again. And we will introduce much tougher penalties for those who cause death by careless driving or who kill while driving without a licence or while disqualified.

We will tackle reoffending. By 2007 every offender will be supervised after release; we will increase the use of electronic tagging; and we will test the use of compulsory lie detector tests to monitor convicted sex offenders. Our new National Offender Management Service will ensure that every offender is individually case-managed from beginning to end of their sentence, both in and out of custody – with increased effort targeted on drugs treatment, education and basic skills training to reduce reoffending. Voluntary organisations and the private sector will be offered greater opportunities to deliver offender services and we will give local people a greater say in shaping community punishment.

Making sure crime does not pay

Those who commit crimes should not profit from them. Already we have introduced laws that enable the courts to confiscate the assets and property of drug dealers and other major criminals. We will enable the police and prosecuting authorities to keep at least half of all the criminal assets they seize to fund local crime-fighting priorities. And we will develop new proposals to ensure that criminals are not able to profit from publishing books about their crimes. In addition we will support magistrates effectively in fighting crime and improve the enforcement of court decisions – including the payment of fines.

Where a defendant fails to turnup for courtwithout good excuse,the presumption should be that the trial and sentencing should go ahead anyway.

We will overhaul laws on fraud and the way that fraud trials are conducted to update them for the 21st century and make them quicker and more effective.

Backing the victim

The legal system must dispense justice to the victim as well as the accused. We have invested to create a modern, self-confident prosecution service. With new powers and new technology to bring more offenders to justice more speedily and effectively, we will improve the way the courts work for victims, witnesses and jurors by:

- Building a nationwide network of witness and victim support units that provide practical help.

- Expanding specialist courts to deal with domestic violence and specialist advocates to support the victims of such crime and of other serious crimes like murder and rape.

We will extend the use of restorative justice schemes and Community Justice Centres to address the needs of victims, resolve disputes and help offenders to make recompense to victims for their crimes.

Legal aid will be reformed to better help the vulnerable. We will ensure independent regulation of the legal profession, and greater competition in the legal services market to ensure people get value for money. We will tackle the compensation culture – resisting invalid claims, but upholding people's rights.

Following consultation on the draft Bill we have published, we will legislate for a new offence of corporate manslaughter.

Migration: The facts

Over seven million people entered the UK from outside the EU in 2003: of whom 180,000 came here to work and over 300,000 to study, with the rest coming here as business visitors and tourists. People from overseas spent almost £12 billion in the UK, and overseas students alone are worth £5 billion a year to our economy. At a time when we have over 600,000 vacancies in the UK job market, skilled migrants are contributing 10-15 per cent of our economy's overall growth.

Since 1997, the time taken to process an initial asylum application has been reduced from 20 months to two months in over 80 per cent of cases. The number of asylum applications has been cut by two-thirds since 2002. The backlog of claims has been cut from over 50,000 at the end of 1996 to just over 10,000. There are 550 UK Immigration Officers posted in France and Belgium to check passports of people boarding boats and trains, and Airline Liaison Officers and overseas entry clearance staff are helping to stop 1,000 people a day improperly entering the UK.

Building a strong and diverse country

For centuries Britain has been a home for people from the rest of Europe and further afield. Immigration has been good for Britain. We want to keep it that way.

Our philosophy is simple: if you are ready to work hard and there is work for you to do, then you are welcome here. We need controls that work and a crackdown on abuse to ensure that we have a robust and fair immigration system fit for the 21st century that is in the interests of Britain.

A points system for immigration

We need skilled workers. So we will establish a points system for those seeking to migrate here. More skills mean more points and more chance of being allowed to come here.

We will ensure that only skilled workers are allowed to settle long-term in the UK, with English language tests for everyone who wants to stay permanently and an end to chain migration.

Where there has been evidence of abuse from particular countries, the immigration service will be able to ask for financial bonds to guarantee that migrants return home. We will continue to improve the quality and speed of immigration and asylum decisions. Appeal rights for non-family immigration cases will be removed and we will introduce civil penalties on employers of up to £2,000 for each illegal immigrant they employ.

Strong and secure borders

While the Tories would halve investment in our immigration services, we would invest in the latest technology to keep our borders strong and secure.

By 2008, those needing a visa to enter the UK will be fingerprinted. We will issue ID cards to all visitors planning to stay for more than three months. Over the next five years we will implement a new electronic borders system that will track visitors entering or leaving the UK.

Across the world there is a drive to increase the security of identity documents and we cannot be left behind. From next year we are introducing biometric 'ePassports'. It makes sense to provide citizens with an equally secure identity card to protect them at home from identity theft and clamp down on illegal working and fraudulent use of public services. We will introduce ID cards, including biometric data like fingerprints, backed up by a national register and rolling out initially on a voluntary basis as people renew their passports.

Fair rules

We can and should honour our obligations to victims of persecution without allowing abuse of the asylum system. We will:

- Fast-track all unfounded asylum seekers with electronic tagging where necessary and more use of detention as we expand the number of deten-tion places available.
- Remove more failed applicants. We have more than doubled the number of failed asylum seekers we remove from the UK compared to 1996.By fingerprinting every visa applicant and prosecuting those who deliberately destroy their documents we

will speed up the time taken to redocument and remove people and will take action against those countries that refuse to cooperate.By the end of 2005,our aim is for removals of failed asylum seekers to exceed new unfounded claims.

Tough action to combat international terrorism

We know that there are people already in the country and who seek to enter the United Kingdom who want to attack our way of life. Our liberties are prized but so is our security.

Police and other law enforcement agencies now have the powers they need to ban terrorist organisations, to clampdown on their fundraising and to hold suspects for extended questioning while charges are brought. Over 700 arrests have been made since 2001. Wherever possible, suspects should be prosecuted through the courts in the normal way. So we will introduce new laws to help catch and convict those involved in helping to plan terrorist activity or who glorify or condone acts of terror. But we also need to disrupt and prevent terrorist activity. New control orders will enable police and security agencies to keep track on those they suspect of planning terrorist outrages including bans on who they can contact or meet, electronic tagging and curfew orders, and for those who present the highest risk, a requirement for them to stay permanently at home.

We will continue to improve coordination between enforcement agencies and cooperation with other countries so that every effort is made to defeat the terrorists.

The choice for 2010

Labour's goals for 2010 are clear. Overall crime down, the number of offenders brought to justice up, with a neighbourhood policing team in every community to crack down on crime and disorder and a modern criminal justice system fit for the 21st century. And to reduce threats from overseas: secure borders backed up by ID cards and a crackdown on abuse of our immigration system. The Conservative threat is equally clear.Savage cuts to our border controls, 'fantasy island' asylum policies and a return to the days of broken promises on police numbers and crime investment.

THE NHS

The NHS is being restored to good health: more doctors,more nurses, better facilities. Waiting times are coming down and the survival rates for the biggest killers are improving. The revolution in quantity of care must be matched by a revolution in quality of care. With equal access for all and no charges for operations. That means new types of health provision, more say for patients in how, where and when they are treated, and tackling ill-health at source.

The new Labour case

Healthcare is too precious to be left to chance, too central to life chances to be left to your wealth. Access to treatment should be based on your clinical need not on your ability to pay. This means defeating those who would dismantle the NHS. But it also means fundamentally reforming the NHS to meet new challenges – a more demanding citizenry with higher expectations, major advances in science and medical technology, changes in the composition and needs of the population.

So our aim is an NHS free to all of us and personal to each of us. We will deliver through high national standards backed by sustained investment, by using new providers where they add capacity or promote innovation, and most importantly by giving more power to patients over their own treatment and over their own health.

We promised to revive the NHS; we have. In our third term we will make the NHS safe for a generation.

New investment

NHS spending has doubled since 1997, and will triple by 2008; already we have an extra 27,000 doctors in post or in training and 79,000 extra nurses; over 100 new hospital building projects under way; 500,000 more operations a year. We are proud of the dedication and commitment of NHS staff. We have widened the responsibilities of nurses and pharmacists, paramedics and porters, creating health services more convenient for patients.

Together with our organisational reforms, the investment is paying off. The maximum time that people waited for operations in 1997 was well over 18 months. Now virtually no one waits longer than nine months,and this year it will fall further to six months.For a heart operation or for cataract removal no one is waiting longer than three months; 97 per cent of people wait less than four hours in Accident and Emergency before treatment,admission or discharge.And speedier treatment saves lives. Death rates from heart disease are down by 27 per cent since 1996; from cancer by 12 per cent.

We will do even better. For too long waiting times have only counted the time after diagnosis. We will be the first Government to include all waiting times in this calculation, including waiting for outpatient appointments and for test results. There will be no hidden waits. So:

- By the end of 2008, no NHS patient will have to wait longer than a maximum of 18 weeks from the time they are referred for a hospital operation by their GP until the time they have that operation. This would mean an average wait of nine to ten weeks.
- We will commit to faster test results for cervical smears.
- We will go further in improving cancer waiting times.

All this with equal access for all, free at the point of need with no charges for hospital operations.

We have tightened the rules on NHS operations so that 'health tourists' now have to pay for treatment.

We will deal with the challenge of MRSA. Infections acquired in hospital are not new. The time to destroy MRSA was in the early 1990s – when only five per cent of the bacteria were resistant to antibiotics. At that time the Tory government did not even keep records about the incidence of MRSA and were forcing hospitals to contract out cleaning services. We were the first government to publish statistics on the problem. Now, thanks to the tough measures we have already taken, including the end to a two-tier workforce for contracted-out cleaning services, MRSA rates are on their way down. But there is still some way to go. We all want clean hospitals,free of infection. We have already reintroduced hospital matrons and given them unprecedented powers to deal with cleanliness and infections in their wards; we shall reinforce this by consulting on new laws to enforce higher hygiene standards.

And by strengthening accountability and cutting bureaucracy, we shall ensure that the new investment is not squandered. We are decreasing the numbers of staff in the Department of Health by a third, and are halving the numbers of quangos – freeing up £500 million for front-line staff. Given the pace of change within medical services we will ensure that it is possible for the NHS to change the way in which it organises its services as quickly as possible.Further streamlining measures will allow us to release an additional £250 million a year for front-line services by 2007.

In the light of the findings of the Shipman Inquiry, we will strengthen clinical governance in the NHS to ensure that professional activity is fully accountable to patients, their families and the wider public. Following the recommendation of the Health Select Committee, we will require registration of all clinical trials and publication of their findings for all trials of medicinal products with a marketing authorisation in the UK.

Innovation and reform

To achieve our goals we need to expand and develop different types of provision. We will put more money into the frontline, develop practice-based commissioning, and so ensure that family doctors have more power over their budgets. We will create more services in primary care. We will build on our family doctor service with more GPs delivering more advanced services more locally; new walk-in centres for commuters; specialised diagnostic and testing services; comprehensive out-of-hours services; high-street drop-in centres for chiropody, physiotherapy and check-ups. And we will continue to expand the role of nurses. These changes will result in more quality, convenience and care.

Expansion in NHS capacity will come both from within the National Health Service – where we will develop the NHS Foundation Trust model and the new freedom for GPs to expand provision – as well as from the independent and voluntary sector, where specialist services are available at NHS standards to meet NHS need.

To help create an even greater range of provision and further improve convenience, we will over the next five years develop a new generation of modern NHS community hospitals. These state-of-the-art centres will provide diagnostics, day surgery and outpatients facilities closer to where people live and work.

We shall continue to encourage innovation and reform through the use of the independent sector to add capacity to, and drive contestability within, the NHS. We have already commissioned 460,000 operations from the independent sector, which will all be delivered free – with equal access for all based on need, not the ability to pay.

Whenever NHS patients need new capacity for their healthcare, we will ensure that it is provided from whatever source.

Empowering patients: choosing not waiting

One principle underpins our reforms – putting patients centre stage. And extending patient power and choice is crucial to achieving this. We shall be embedding both throughout the NHS. So:

- By the end of 2008, patients whose GPs refer them for an operation will be able to choose from any hospital that can provide that operation to NHS medical and financial standards. There will be the choice of a convenient time and place for a non-urgent operation for example a location close to relatives.

- We will expand capacity and choice in primary care too. Where GPs'lists are full we will expand provision by encouraging entrepreneurial GPs and other providers to expand into that location.

- By 2009 all women will have choice over where and how they have their baby and what pain relief to use. We want every woman to be supported by the same midwife throughout her pregnancy. Support will be linked closely to other services that will be provided in Children's Centres.

- In order to increase choices for patients with cancer we will double the investment going into palliative care services, giving more people the choice to be treated at home.

By October 2005 we will have recruited more than 1,000 new NHS dentists and will have increased the number of dental school places by 25 per cent. We will undertake a fundamental review of the scope and resourcing of NHS dentistry.

We will provide more information and advice. Through NHS Direct, Health Direct,interactive TV,print media and the internet we will give more convenient access to much better information about health and health services, including the performance of doctors and hospitals.

Empowering patients: long-term conditions and social care

We will promote the integration of health and social care at local level, so that older people and those with long-term conditions can retain their independence. We will continue to provide healthcare free in long-term care establishments, and provide the right framework for schemes such as equity release which make staying at home an attractive option. Wewill develop our policyof community matrons for those with severe conditions, helping to keep people out of hospital by providing better care at home.

- We will develop personalised budgets in social care where people can decide for themselves what they need and how it should be provided.

- We shall extend case-management for the 18 million people with long-term conditions. We will treble the investment in the Expert Patients Programme, and help many more patients take control of their own care plans.

- Almost a third of people attending GP surgeries have mental health problems and mental health occupies approximately one third of a GP's time. So we will continue to invest in and improve our services for people with mental health problems at primary and secondary levels, including behavioural as well as drug therapies.

- We shall provide safeguards for the few people with long-term mental health problems who need compulsory treatment coupled with appropriate protection for the public. We shall also strengthen the system for protecting the public from offenders who have served their sentence but may still pose a threat because they have a serious psychopathic disorder.

Living healthier lives

People want to take responsibility for their own health outside the NHS as well as within it. They have the right to expect help from government. The killer diseases of the heart and the many forms of cancer are often the product of poor diet, lack of exercise and above all smoking. By 2010 we aim to reduce deaths from coronary heart disease and strokes by 40 per cent from 1997. And we want death rates from cancer to be cut by 20 per cent.

Healthy choices for children

We will start the drive for better health early – at school. We have already extended the provision of free fruit to all 4- to 6-year-olds at school. We will invest more in renovating and building new kitchens as well as investing an extra £210 million in school meals, guaranteeing that at least 50p per meal is spent on ingredients in primary schools, and at least 60p in secondary schools. We are introducing an independent School Food Trust, better training for dinner ladies and Ofsted inspection of healthy eating. we will legislate for tougher standards of nutrition for school meals and will encourage schools to teach more about healthy eating. We will ban certain products that are high in fat/salt content from school meals and ensure that fresh fruit and vegetables are part of every school meal. We will encourage secondary schools to keep pupils on the premises to ensure that they have a healthy meal. We will ensure that all school children have access to a school nurse.

Healthy choices for all

We will put in place a simple system of labelling to make it easier for busy shoppers to see at a glance how individual foods contribute to a healthy balanced diet. We will help parents by restricting further the advertising and promotion to children of those foods and drinks that are high in fat, salt and sugar.

We recognise that many people want smoke-free environments and need regulation to help them get this. We therefore intend to shift the balance significantly in their favour. We will legislate to ensure that all enclosed public places and workplaces other than licensed premises will be smoke-free. The legislation will ensure that all restaurants will be smoke-free; all pubs and bars preparing and serving food will be smoke-free; and other pubs and bars will be free to choose whether to allow smoking or to be smoke-free.In membership clubs the members will be free to choose whether to allow smoking or to be smoke-free. However, whatever the general status, to protect employees, smoking in the bar area will be prohibited everywhere.

These restrictions will be accompanied by an expansion of NHS smoking cessation services to encourage and support smokers to improve their own health by giving up smoking.

Starting with the poorest areas of the country we will introduce health trainers to help people maintain their healthy choices. By 2010, through this activity we plan to reduce the health inequalities that exist between rich and poor.

All this will be free at the point of need.

The choice for 2010

Today's Conservatives want to do what not even Margaret Thatcher would countenance – introducing charges for hospital operations so that those who can afford to pay thousands of pounds can push ahead of those who cannot. As well as ending the founding principle of the health service, this would take more than £1 billion out of the system to subsidise those who can afford to pay. For the rest of us, the Tories would abandon waiting list targets and allow a return to the 18-month waits that were their NHS legacy. The choice is forward with new Labour to a health system with patients in the driving seat, free to all and personal to each of us.Or back with the Tories to longer waits, and to a health system where treatment depends not on your condition but on your bank balance.

OLDER PEOPLE

Our priority since 1997 has been to tackle pensioner poverty. Nearly two million pensioners have been lifted out of absolute poverty as a result of Labour's measures, which are now getting on average an extra £2,000 a year to the poorest third.Our priorities now are to build a national consensus for tomorrow's pensioners, combining public and private pension schemes to build security in retirement, and to extend the quality of life of older people.

The new Labour case

By 2020 there will be more people over the age of 80 than under the age of five. For a progressive government there can be no compromise of our duty to today's pensioners. But while we fulfil that duty we must also see old age as a time of independence and opportunity. On pensions, our aim is a system that provides security and decency for all, which encourages and rewards saving, and is financially sustainable. And because, more than anything, people need certainty to plan for the future we will seek a national consensus – cross-party, cross-generation – for long-term reform.

Tackling pensioner poverty

In 1997, 2.8 million pensioners were living in poverty – with the poorest expected to live on just £69 per week. Labour's Pension Credit now means that no pensioner need live on less than £109 per week. It rewards saving and helps over three million pensioners,with women in particular benefiting. We will increase Pension Credit in line with earnings up to and including 2007-08.

All pensioners have benefited from improved universal benefits like the state pension,the Winter Fuel Payment (now worth £300 per year for the over-80s), help with council tax and free TV licences for the over-75s. This year, all households expected to pay council tax that include anyone over 65 will receive £200 towards the cost of council tax,and the following year there will be free,off-peak local bus travel in England for the over-60s.

Millions of pensioners have benefited from our fuel poverty programme.Our goal is to eliminate fuel poverty for vulnerable groups by 2010, and for all by 2015.

Pensions for the generation of tomorrow

The generation retiring in the future will be different in many ways from its predecessors. Their jobs will have been different; the expectations of women will be transformed;their retirements will be longer and healthier. We have begun to lay the foundations for the pensions system of tomorrow, for example, by: introducing the State Second Pension to ensure carers, low earners and disabled people have a chance to build up a decent pension for the first time; encouraging automatic enrolment into company pension schemes; creating the Pension Protection Fund; enabling pensioners for the first time to work part time and draw down their occupational pension; as well as offering an increased state pension or lump sum for those deferring their pension. We will work to increase the proportion of pension fund trustees nominated by scheme members, along with access to proper training. We will keep this issue under review, with consultation in the expectation of further progress to 50 per cent member-nominated trustees.

We need to forge a national consensus about how we move from a pension system designed for today's pension problems to one that is right for tomorrow's. We appointed the Pensions Commission to look into the future of pensions and its second report is due in autumn 2005. We are clear about the goals of a reformed system. It must tackle poverty,provide everyone with the opportunity to build an adequate retirement income, and be affordable, fair and simple to understand. In particular it must address the disadvantages faced by women.

New rights, new choices

Many older people want to carry on working in their 50s and 60s. The welfare state should be there to help them. Older people with their skills and experience are potentially an enormous resource. That is why we set up the New Deal for the Over-50s,with over 150,000 older people helped back to work.

We also need to put the force of the law on the side of older people who wish to continue working. Companies will no longer be able to force people to retire before the age of 65 except where specifically justified. All employees over the age of 65 will have the right to request of their employer that they be allowed to carry on working. After five years we will review whether there should be any fixed retirement ages.

We will give older people greater choice over their care.For every older person receiving care or other support, we want to offer transparent, individual budgets which bring funding for a range of services, including social care, care homes, and housing support such as adaptations, maintenance and cleaners together in one place. We will pilot individual budgets for older people by the end of this year.

We will make the most of the opportunities of an older population by creating a new programme for older people to be mentors and coaches to gifted and talented young people. We will also work with voluntary organisations to help expand grandparent and toddler groups across the country.

Support across the generations

The challenge of balancing work and family applies to parents but also to people looking after an elderly or sick relative – now one in five adults. Since the introduction of the right to request from their employer flexible working arrangements, a million parents have changed their working hours. We are consulting on a similar right for carers of elderly or sick relatives.

The choice for 2010

The Tories are the party of pensioner poverty. When they left office in 1997, one in four pensioners was living in poverty and the poorest pensioners were expected to get by on just £69 a week. They would phase out the Pension Credit and abolish the State Second Pension, hurting most those most in need. When the one thing we all need is certainty, the Tories have admitted they have absolutely no plans for how to fund their pensions policy beyond four years. The choice is whether we go forward with new Labour with today's pensioners provided for and poverty falling, a national consensus on fair and sustainable long-term reformand the policies to give older people enhanced rights and choices. Or back with the Tories to rising levels of pensioner poverty and unending insecurity for tomorrow's pensioners.

FAMILIES

It is impossible to fulfil the potential of our country – never mind promoting social mobility and equality of life chances – unless every child gets the best possible start in life. Government does not bring up children, but it must support parents in their key role. We will help parents balance work and family, expand paid leave, deliver the biggest ever expansion in childcare and end child poverty in a generation.

The new Labour case

Strong families are the bedrock of a strong society. Children cannot be the forgotten constituency of politics; parents put their children first and they deserve support from government. Yet fear of seeming to 'nanny' has in the past meant British law and culture have not supported parents and children. Government cannot shirk its responsibilities. Our starting point is that for children to come first parents need to be given choices: a tax and benefit system to raise family incomes and tackle child poverty; legal changes to promote a healthy balance between work and family; and services built around the needs of children. Our third-term commitment – not a nanny state but a family-friendly government.

Tackling child poverty

We will end child poverty, starting by halving it – both in terms of relative low-income and in terms of material deprivation – by 2010-11.

Work is the best anti-poverty strategy. Tailored help, especially for lone parents, is key but we are also committed to making work pay – with a guaranteed income of at least £258 per week for those with children and in full-time work.

The benefits system needs to support all children, and those in greatest need the most. That is the rationale for universal child benefit and targeted tax credits, and why we have committed to increasing the Child Tax Credit at least in line with earnings up to and including 2007-08. By October 2005, families with children will be on average £1,400 per year better off, and those in the poorest fifth of the population on average £3,200 a year better off compared to 1997. Labour's Child Trust Fund creates a nest egg for newborns that they can access at age 18. It is the world's first example of a government ensuring that all children grow up with a financial stake. We are determined to see it grow and are consulting on making payments at age seven and at secondary school age, in addition to those made at birth.

We are supporting local authorities in the radical reform of children's services, above all to ensure there is one professional with lead responsibility for each vulnerable child. We will also ensure that services are designed to meet the additional needs of disabled children and their families.

Universal childcare

Since 1997, the Government has funded an additional 520,000 sustainable childcare places and now every family with a three- or four- year-old child has access to a free nursery place. By 2010, we will create 3,500 Sure Start Children's Centres for children under five years – five in every constituency – a universal local service that brings together childcare and services for families. By 2010, all parents of three- and four-year-olds will have increased rights to flexible, free, part-time nursery provision for 15 hours a week over the whole school year. Over the longer term we will increase free provision to 20 hours.

For older children up to the age of 14 extended schools, working in partnership with the private and voluntary sectors, will offer affordable out-of-school childcare from 8am to 6pm throughout the year, with a range of arts, music, sport and study support.

We will help families with incomes of up to £59,000 a year with their childcare costs through more generous Working Tax Credit, including help for those using a nanny or au pair. Parents using childcare supported by their employer will be able to get a tax break worth up to £50 a week each. We are working with the GLA and the Mayor to bring down the cost of childcare in London.

Creating time

Over 350,000 mothers and 80,000 fathers each year are using new rights to paid maternity and paternity leave. Parents consistently say their top priority is more choice of whether to stay at home with their baby in the first year of its life. We will therefore increase paid maternity leave to nine months from 2007 – worth an extra £1,400 – with the goal of achieving a year's paid leave by the end of the Parliament while simplifying the system for employers. We want to give fathers more opportunities to spend time with their children, and are consulting on how best to do this including the option of sharing paid leave. We have already introduced the right to request flexible working to parents of children under six and nearly a million parents have benefited. We need to balance the needs of parents and carers, with those of employers, especially small businesses. We are consulting on extending the right to request flexible working to carers of sick and disabled adults as a priority, and also on whether we should extend the right to parents of older children.

Supporting family life

Common sense, as well as research, says that children need to be able to depend on the love and support of both parents. The financial support we are giving families, along with new rights to flexible working and access to childcare, are all designed to support family life. Government can and should support those public and voluntary agencies that support families and parents. We are examining the development of a new information service – Parents Direct – to provide advice on all aspects of children's services and parental entitlements.

For those parents who do separate or divorce, both have a responsibility for a meaningful relationship with their children where that is safe. We are introducing reforms to minimise conflict and encourage conciliation by greater and early use of mediation. We stand by the principle that absent parents should make a fair contribution to the cost of the upkeep of their children, and we are committed to tackling the backlog of Child Support Agency claims as efficiently and fairly as possible. We also need to ensure court orders on access are enforced according to the best interests of the child, which ideally gives both parents an important role.

Increasing home ownership

A decent home is crucial to family well-being. Homeownership has increased by over one million with Labour and by the end of our third term we aim for it to have risen by another million to two million. Rising house prices in many areas of the country have made it difficult for people on lower incomes to get a foot on the housing ladder. So we have raised the stamp duty threshold from £60,000 to £120,000 for residential properties, exempting an extra 300,000 homebuyers from stamp duty every year.

We will continue to respond to the challenges of local housing markets across the UK. In the South we will invest in extra housing in London and the wider South East, with particular emphasis on the Thames Gateway and other growth areas. In the Midlands and North we will tackle the problems of low demand and abandonment that threaten communities.

We want to widen the opportunity to own or partown, especially for more young people and those tenants who rent in the private or public sector. Our comprehensive plan includes:

- A new Homebuy scheme offering up to 300,000 council and housing association tenants the opportunity to buy part of their home, increasing their equity over time if they wish.
- A First Time Buyers Initiative to help over 15,000 first-time buyers who could not own or part-own a home without extra help. We will use surplus public land for new homes, enabling the buyer to take out a mortgage for only the building.
- Strengthening existing home ownership schemes, such as the Key Worker Living scheme and Shared Ownership.

Social housing

The increased supply and quality of social housing is central to Labour's belief in mixed, sustainable communities.

Since 1997, we have cut the number of substandard social-rented homes by one million; installing 300,000 new kitchens, 220,000 new bathrooms and 720,000 new boilers and central heating systems into council homes. By 2010 we will ensure that all social tenants benefit from a decent, warm home with modern facilities.

For too long, tenants have had little say over where they live. In a third term, Labour will offer greater flexibility and choice for those who rent. We will increase the annual supply of new social homes by 50 per cent by 2008, an extra 10,000 homes a year, and give local authorities

Families: Choice and support at work and at home

the ability to start building homes again and bring empty homes back into use. And we will end the 'take it or leave it' approach to social renting by expanding choice-based lettings nationwide.

The choice for 2010

The Tories are all talk and no action on family policy. They opposed our increases in maternity and paternity pay and the introduction of flexible working rights. Even the measures they have proposed wouldn't come in until 2009, by which time the Tories are committed to making deep cuts in spending. The choice is forward with new Labour to a universal, affordable, good-quality childcare, a million more homeowners, more choice for all parents and an end to child poverty. Or back to the risky economic policies of a Tory government that would let families sink or swim whatever the pressures they face.

INTERNATIONAL POLICY

Globalisation means that events elsewhere have a direct impact at home. So we will pursue British interests by working with our allies to make the world a safer, fairer place. This means reforming Europe. It means fighting terrorism and stopping the spread of weapons of mass destruction. It means modernising our armed forces. And it means using our leading role in the G8, EU, the Commonwealth and UN to promote global action on climate change and poverty.

The new Labour case

Domestic interests and international action are entwined more than ever before. Action on drugs, terrorism, people trafficking, AIDS, climate change, poverty, migration and trade all require us to work with other countries and through international organisations. The best defence of our security at home is the spread of liberty and justice overseas. In a third term we will secure Britain's place in the EU and at the heart of international decision-making. We will always uphold the rule of international law.

Making Europe work better for Britain

We are proud of Britain's EU membership and of the strong position Britain has achieved within Europe. British membership of the EU brings jobs, trade and prosperity; it boosts environmental standards, social protection and international clout. Since 1997 we have gone from marginal players, often ignored, to leaders in the European Union. Working hard with Labour MEPs, we are determined to remain leaders. Outside the EU, or on its margins, we would unques-tionably be weaker and more vulnerable.

The EU now has 25 members and will continue to expand. The new Constitutional Treaty ensures the new Europe can work effectively, and that Britain keeps control of key national interests like foreign policy, taxation, social security and defence. The Treaty sets out what the EU can do and what it cannot. It strengthens the voice of national parliaments and governments in EU affairs. It is a good treaty for Britain and for the new Europe. We will put it to the British people in a referendum and campaign wholeheartedly for a 'Yes' vote to keep Britain a leading nation in Europe.

We will also work to reform Europe. During Britain's EU presidency this year, we will work to promote economic reform, bear down on regulation;make progress in the Doha development trade round;bring closer EU membership for Turkey, the Balkans and Eastern Europe; and improve the focus and quality of EU aid so it better helps the poorest countries.

We will continue to lead European defence cooperation. We will build stronger EU defence capabilities, in harmony with NATO – the cornerstone of our defence policy – without compromising our national ability to act independently. We will ensure the new EU battle groups are equipped and organised to act quickly to save lives in humanitarian crises.

On the euro, we maintain our commonsense policy. The determining factor underpinning any government decision is the national economic interest and whether the case for joining is clear and unambiguous. The fiveeconomic tests must be met before any decision to join can be made. If the Government were to recommend joining, it would be put to a vote in Parliament and a referendum of the British people.

Protecting British interests and British citizens abroad

We will continue to provide effective support to British businesses and trade unions abroad, and we will continue to improve our ability to respond quickly to international crises and disasters which affect our citizens. The Foreign Office already provides a wide range of services for British people in difficulty overseas, and we will consult widely before drawing up a comprehensive statement spelling out the rights and responsibilities of British travellers abroad. This will include the help that people can expect from their government in times of need.

Helping make you more secure

We have worked closely with the US and other nations to combat the threat of terrorism in Afghanistan and in Iraq. The threat of the proliferation of chemical, biological and nuclear weapons – and their use by rogue states or terrorist groups – is a pressing issue for the world today. We have worked with the US to ensure that Libya has given up its WMD, and we will continue with France and Germany to ensure that Iran does not develop nuclear weapons. In North Korea we will support the multilateral approach of the Six Parties talks. We will continue to strongly support the peace process between India and Pakistan, and back moves to resolve the long-running dispute over Kashmir.And we will work to put an end to the international network of trade in weapons of mass destruction. Labour has already introduced a strict regime to control the export of conventional weapons, and we led moves for EU-wide measures. We will work actively to secure an international treaty on the arms trade.

Promoting human rights, peace and democracy

We need to be tough on terrorism and its causes. The threat of terrorism and the danger to British citizens is proven, not just by September 11th but by repeated attacks in Europe and around the world. So we cannot sit back and hope that we will be unaffected. It is right that we do everything in our power to disrupt terrorist networks, and to challenge the conditions that help terrorism to breed.

The UN Charter proclaims the universal principles of human rights and democracy. In an uncertain world they are not only right in principle, they are important guarantees of our national security and prosperity too.

There have been major strides forward in recent years: in Indonesia, Afghanistan and many parts of Africa and Latin America, democracy is being extended.

We mourn the loss of life of innocent civilians and coalition forces in the war in Iraq and the subsequent terrorism. But the butchery of Saddam is over and across Iraq, eight million people risked their lives to vote earlier this year.Many people disagreed with the action we took in Iraq. We respect and understand their views.But we should all now unite to support the fledgling democracy in Iraq. British troops should remain in Iraq under a United Nations mandate as long as the democratically elected government there wants them. They will continue to train Iraqi security forces to take responsibility for their own future.

We welcome the wider process of democratic reform across the Middle East, and we will work with our allies to encourage and promote economic and political change.

We strongly support the peace process between Israel and Palestine. Resolution of the conflict is crucial to peace in the region and the wider world. The conference held in London in March 2005 has started the process of helping a democratic government in Palestine build security and prosperity. We will work tirelessly to bring about a peace settlement in which a viable and independent state of Palestine lives alongside a safe and secure Israel.

Supporting our armed forces

Britain's armed forces are among the best in the world. They are able to play a key role in advancing our interests and values. We want to keep it that way.

We are immensely proud of the bravery,skill and dedication our armed forces have demonstrated in Afghanistan, Iraq, Sierra Leone, the Balkans and elsewhere across the world. They are a force for good. We will never commit forces to battle unless it is essential; but when they are committed they will have the investment, strategy, training and preparation they need. That is one reason we have given the armed forces the biggest sustained increase in funding since the end of the Cold War. But we also know that modern demands on our armed forces are changing. That is why reform and modernisation are essential. A reduction in the number of infantry battalions, made possible because of the improved security situation in Northern Ireland, has allowed extra resources for the vital support services such as signals, engineers, intelligence and logistics units – the parts of the army most under pressure. This is essential to allow our infantry soldiers to be fully supported when they go into action on our behalf. We will continue with the investment and reform that make our fighting forces the most flexible and effective in the world.

We are also committed to retaining the independent nuclear deterrent and we will continue to work, both bilaterally and through the UN, to urge states not yet party to non-proliferation treaties, notably the Nuclear Non-Proliferation Treaty, to join.

Veterans

Labour has always recognised the sacrifice and bravery of our servicemen and women. That is why we were the first government to appoint a Minister for Veterans Affairs. This has enabled us to put veterans' affairs at the heart of decision-making at the Ministry of Defence. Labour has also put more money than ever before into veterans'issues, including £27 million of Lottery funding over the last two years. We will continue to give priority to veterans' affairs as we mark 60 years since the end of the Second World War.

Reforming the United Nations

The UN is crucial to our efforts to build a more secure and more prosperous world. We support the reform of the Security Council so it becomes more representative and has a stronger focus on conflict prevention. We support the recommendation of the Secretary-General's High-level Panel for a Peacebuilding Commission to assist countries emerging from conflict and to develop mechanisms to enhance conflict prevention. We will press for more radical reform of the UN humanitarian system, so it is better equipped to saves lives. We will also press for reform of the World Bank and IMF to improve transparency, give more say to developing countries and, with the EU better focus their efforts on the poorest countries, particularly in Africa.

Climate change and Africa

Britain has the chair of the G8 this year. We will use the summit for two particular purposes.

First, climate change is the one of the most pressing challenges that the world faces. We will continue to lead internationally on climate change, and to strive for wider acceptance of the science and the steps needed to combat the problem. We will look beyond Kyoto and promote an international dialogue to reach agreement on the long-term goals and action needed to stabilise the level of greenhouse gases in the atmosphere. We will also work for effective international action to adapt to the impacts of climate change.

The UK has already met its obligations under the Kyoto Protocol. We remain committed to achieving a 20 per cent reduction in carbon dioxide emissions on 1990 levels by 2010, and our review of progress this summer will showus howto get back on track.A60 per cent reduction by 2050 remains necessary and achievable.

We will continue to promote and develop renewable energy sources, to seek high standards of energy efficiency in the public and private sectors, and to support emissions trading in Europe and beyond.

Secondly we will focus on Africa and the global fight against poverty.

We have more than doubled aid since 1997. We have cancelled the debts of the poorest countries and are now pushing others to follow our lead and offer 100 per cent debt relief for the poorest. We are proud to have established a Department for International Development, with a clear mission to reduce poverty. Now, for the first time ever the UK has a clear timetable – 2013 – for achieving the UN target of 0.7 per cent of national income devoted to development. Globally we are pressing for a doubling of aid backed by getting international agreement to an International Finance Facility as supported by the Commission for Africa.

But aid will not be successful without conflict prevention, good governance and zero tolerance of corruption. We will work for faster repatriation of stolen assets from UK financial institutions, ratification of the UN Convention on corruption, and more open and accountable reporting of revenues from oil and mining – that so often fuel local conflicts. Our commitment is to the people of the developing world; our contract is with their governments for reform. But if poor countries are committed to good governance and poverty reduction we then believe they should be in control of their own policies. We will end the practice of making aid conditional on sensitive economic policy choices, such as trade liberalisation and privatisation.

With this leadership and extra money, we can now work to ensure all children go to school, and millions of people in Asia and Africa suffering from AIDS, tuberculosis and malaria have access to treatment. In particular, we will press for an international agreement on universal access to AIDS treatment by 2010 and for all people in poor countries to have access to free basic healthcare and education.

Our long-term aim is to help lift a billion people out of poverty.

Fair trade

We also know that without fairer trade rules and private investment, poor countries will not generate the growth needed to lift themselves out of poverty. We will press for the conclusion of an ambitious trade deal that will completely open markets to exports from poorer countries; for further reform of rich countries' agricultural subsidies, including the EU's Common Agricultural Policy and a 2010 timetable to end agricultural export subsidies. We do not believe poor countries should be forced to liberalise. We will allow them to sequence their trade reforms, so they can build their capacity to compete globally.

The choice for 2010

In 1997 the Tories had left Britain isolated in Europe, overseas aid had declined and we lacked any coherent vision of our place in the world. With Labour, a strong Britain will force international terrorism into retreat and help spread democracy and freedom around the world. We will be leaders in a reformed Europe, and, with others, make significant progress towards raising a billion people out of extreme poverty. We will fight for a new global agreement on climate change, an arms trade treaty, and a trade deal that makes trade work for the many, not just the few. Our armed forces will continue to be the best in the world. The alternative is to go back to the Tories with their record of cuts in aid and defence and their policies of tearing up the Social Chapter, and marginalising Britain in Europe and the world.

QUALITY OF LIFE

Arts, culture and sport are thriving around Britain – enriching individual lives and transforming communities, towns and cities. They are important in their own right – as nourishment for our imagination or a source of plain enjoyment and our local environment should be a source of pride. We will work to improve the quality of life of every community in Britain.

The new Labour case

We believe in the inherent value of arts, culture and sport. Our towns and cities are being energised by sports and culture and as they are regenerated the quality of life for all is transformed. As we build on this change, our progressive challenge is to broaden participation as widely as possible, making the links between sport and health, and culture and well-being. We must combine the broadest base of participation with the ability for the most talented to progress to the very top. Our third term will embed the expectation that every child and every adult have the maximum chance to develop their creative or sporting talents.

Creative cities

Art and culture are valuable for their own sake; they are also crucial to our national prosperity. Britain's cultural industries now make up over eight per cent of our national income; and from computer games to the fine arts, British talent is gaining global recognition and generating real wealth. This is one of the fastest growing and fastest changing areas of the economy. And the transformation of our great cities is, in great part, a story of culture-led regeneration. We are proud of the record of Labour-led councils in leading this transformation, from Gateshead to Greenwich.

To help young talent get the right start we will work to establish Creative Apprenticeships. Through the National Endowment for Science, Technology and the Arts (NESTA) we are funding the Creative Pioneer Academy which will develop the entrepreneurial skills of recent graduates with outstanding talents and original business ideas – and for some there will be the offer of up to £35,000 to start their own business.

From 2006 we will provide £12 million over two years to the Arts Council England to promote leadership and management in the cultural sector. We want to invest in high-flyers developing commercial and business skills, encourage the talents of leading ethnic minority figures and improve the links between arts and business.

Arts, culture and museums

Since 1997 we have increased funding for the arts by 73 per cent in real terms. We will continue to support our finest artists and institutions to achieve world-class standards.

Thanks to our policy of free admissions the number of people visiting formerly charging national museums and galleries has risen by 75 per cent over three years. Many are first-time visitors, with the biggest increases among children.

Victorian City leaders left us a legacy of great local and regional museums, and through our investment programme 'Renaissance in the Regions', we are recreating them as centres of excellence. By 2008 we will have invested £147 million in partnerships across the country, modernising museum collections, broadening access to new audiences and providing a comprehensive service to schools. We will explore further ways to encourage philanthropy to boost the quality of our public art collections.

We will legislate, as soon as time allows, to implement the findings of the Heritage Protection Review, which allows the public a greater say in listing decisions.

Creative Sparks

Our aim is that everyone should have the opportunity to participate in cultural life, and we want that involvement to start as early as possible. Creative Partnerships, our programme of support for art in schools in our most disadvantaged areas, has already reached over 150,000 children. We will build on this approach by rolling out our new programme Creative Sparks to guarantee that all children and young people will be given the chance to experience the very best of culture every year.

Sport for all

Our aim is to increase participation in sport year on year. Central to this is having modern, high-quality facilities close to where people live. £1.5 billion is being invested in sports facilities in every community. By 2008 our aim is that almost everyone will be within 20 minutes of a good multi-sport facility.

Grassroots clubs are the lifeblood of sports in Britain, and week in, week out, they are sustained by an army of volunteers. Reform of Sport England will continue, to reduce overheads and ensure that more money reaches the grassroots. We have put sports clubs at the forefront of our investment plans with the £100 million Community Club Development Scheme and mandatory rate relief at 80 per cent for registered Community Amateur Sports Clubs already worth about £5 million. As we review the operation of the new licensing regime we will ensure that there is not an unfair burden on local community groups, including sports clubs.

Investment in school sports will ensure that by 2010 all children will receive two hours high-quality PE or sport per week. Building on that, we pledge that by 2010 every child who wants it will have access to a further two to three hours sport per week.

Every child should have the chance to compete at school. We have clamped down on the sale of playing fields: 96 per cent of schools in School Sport Partnerships now hold at least one sports day or sports festival each year. All secondary schools will be expected to field teams in regular competitive fixtures. We will also establish individual and team rankings in all the main sports, with clear and transparent success criteria.

Sport in the community

To make it easier to get access to sports in your local area we will establish Sport Direct – a single point of access for sports in the UK. One website and one phone number will help you find out what's going on in your area. Together with £155 million from the Big Lottery Fund, the Government will ensure that children who have had little access to play facilities and those with a disability have much better access to safe, modern playgrounds.

Building on the lessons of the Football Foundation, we will develop a National Sports Foundation to bring resources from the private and voluntary sectors together with public money to invest in grassroots sporting facilities. We will work with the Premier League and the FA to find innovative ways of assisting community sport, including Supporters Direct. Having passed the necessary legislation, we remain committed to completing the sale of the Tote to a Racing Trust.

The Olympics

Britain's medal hauls at the Sydney Olympics in 2000 and in Athens in 2004 were the best for over 80 years, and we maintained our position as one of the leading nations in the Paralympics. Now we are supporting the bid to bring the Olympics to London in

2012.Our plans would bring regeneration to the East End of London and will leave lasting sporting, economic and cultural legacies. As we approach the Olympics we will continue to invest in elite athletes through the Talented Athlete Scholarship Scheme for young athletes. In addition we have launched 2012 Scholarships worth around £10,000 a year each for our most talented 12- to 18-year-olds.

Libraries in the information age

Where they offer new services like childcare, after-school education for pupils, and IT learning our libraries are successful. We will develop a strategy for the modernisation of our libraries which builds on the best, strengthens library leadership, sharpens customer focus and harnesses local popular support. We will encourage further cooperation in back-office functions and identify the best ways to improve our library infrastructure.

Public service broadcasting and the BBC

We support a strong, independent and world-class BBC with clearly defined public purposes at the heart of a healthy public broadcasting system. We will replace the BBC Governors with a BBC Trust to ensure that the BBC's governance and regulation is accountable to the licence-fee payers to whom it belongs. The licence fee will be guaranteed for the whole of the ten-year Royal Charter that will take effect on 1January 2007.Channel 4 will continue to be a publicly owned broadcaster providing distinctive competition to the BBC. ITV and Five will also be retained in our public service broadcasting system.

Digital switchover

The success of satelite and cable television in driving take-up of digital shows how changes in technology bring real benefits – in terms of greater choice, and increasingly, in access to services. Our aim is to make those benefits available to all. We will achieve digital switchover between 2008 and 2012 ensuring universal access to high-quality, free-to-view and subscription digital TV. This will happen region by region, and we will make sure that the interests of elderly people and other vulnerable groups are protected.

Digital challenge

We will deliver our cross-government strategy for closing the digital divide and using ICT to further transform public services:

- By 2006 every school supported to offer all pupils access to computers at home.

- A Digital Challenge for a local authority to be a national and international pathfinder in universal digital service provision.
- A new National Internet Safety Unit to make Britain the safest place in the world to access the internet.

Copyright in a digital age

We will modernise copyright and other forms of protection of intellectual property rights so that they are appropriate for the digital age. We will use our presidency of the EU to look at how to ensure content creators can protect their innovations in a digital age. Piracy is a growing threat and we will work with industry to protect against it.

Film

The strength of Britain's film industry is a source of pride, and employment. Wewill continue to make the UK the right place to invest in film production. We will legislate to provide new tax reliefs that will ensure support is delivered directly and efficiently to those who produce films.

We will work with the UK Film Council to achieve a higher priority for funding film festivals around the country, in particular for the Edinburgh Film Festival, the oldest in Britain.

The Lottery

Every single part of British life has been touched by the £15 billion generated for good causes by the Lottery.Labour has made the Lottery more inclusive and more in tune with people's priorities. We have created the Big Lottery Fund and given it an explicit mandate to involve people not just in setting strategy but also in awarding grants. Our Lottery Bill will give a duty and a power to every Lottery distributor to involve the public more radically in decision-making at every level.

By the end of 2005 we will put in place a new, national consultation on the way that the National Lottery good causes proceeds are spent after the new Lottery Licence is awarded in 2009.

The local environment

The quality of our local environment is vital to our well-being and our natural environment is a key part of our national heritage.

The environment starts at the front door, and we have made action to improve the cleanliness of public spaces and communities a priority. The 2005 Clean Neighbourhoods and Environment Act will give local authorities and regulators the powers they have asked for to tackle litter, graffiti, abandoned cars, fly-tipping, noise pollution and other environmental concerns. We will further crack down on environmental crime, minimising litter, cleaning up graffiti and tackling fly-tipping. We will extend kerbside collection of at least two types of recyclable materials to all households in England by 2010. Polluters will have the opportunity to invest in environmental remediation or new local environmental projects rather than just pay fines. Rather than 'polluter pays' this new system would mean the 'polluter improves'.

Britain's beaches, rivers and drinking water are now of the highest ever quality. We have added 30,000 hectares to the green belt while exceeding our target of building 60 per cent of new houses on brownfield sites. We have established the first National Park in England since the 1950s. To enhance our children's understanding of the environment we will give every school student the opportunity to experience out-of-classroom learning in the natural environment.

All newly developed communities – such as the Thames Gateway Development – will be built to high environmental standards on issues such as energy efficiency and water use, and we will develop a clear plan to minimise the impact of new communities on the environment. From April 2006, all new homes receiving government funding will meet the new Code for Sustainable Buildings and we will encourage local authorities to apply similar standards to private homes.

Through a Marine Act, we will introduce a new framework for the seas, based on marine spatial planning, that balances conservation, energy and resource needs. To obtain best value from different uses of our valuable marine resources, we must maintain and protect the ecosystems on which they depend.

The choice for 2010

The Tories have always neglected the arts, seeing them as an easy target for cuts. They do not understand the role that culture can play in the lives of individuals, in the futures of our towns and cities, and in the prosperity of our country. The choice is forward with new Labour to more sport in schools, arts for all children and young people,and continued investment in culture.Or back to the Tories and cuts of £207 million across culture, arts and sport.

DEMOCRACY

In our first two terms we enshrined a new constitutional settlement between the nations of the United Kingdom. In our next term we will complete the reform of the House of Lords so that it is a modern and effective revising Chamber. And we will devolve more power to local authorities and local communities, giving people real power over the issues that matter most to them.

The new Labour case

Widening access to power is as important as widening access to wealth and opportunity. National standards are important to ensure fairness. But the best way to tackle exclusion is to give choice and power to those left behind. Our political institutions – including our own party – must engage a population overloaded with information, diverse in its values and lifestyles, and sceptical of power. However, people are passionate about politics – when they see it affects them. So our challenge is to bridge the chasm between government and governed. Our third term will build upon our unprecedented programme of constitutional reform embedding a culture of devolved government at the centre and self-government in our communities.

Building from the neighbourhood up

People want a sense of control over their own neighbourhood. Not a new tier of neighbourhood government, but new powers over the problems that confront them when they step outside their front door – issues like litter, graffiti and anti-social behaviour. That is why we will offer neighbourhoods a range of powers from which they can choose, including:

• New powers for parish councils to deal with anti-social behaviour.

• Powers for local people to trigger action in response to persistent local problems.

• Community funds for local neighbourhoods to spend on local priorities.

• New opportunities for communities to assume greater responsibility or even ownership of community assets like village halls,community centres, libraries or recreational facilities.

Good parish councils engage communities and make a real difference, so we will extend the right to establish parish councils to communities in London.

A vibrant civil society

We believe that enterprises in the mutual and cooperative sector have an important role to play in the provision of local services, from health to education, from leisure to care for the vulnerable. As democratic, not-for-profit organisations, they can help to involve local people in shaping the services they want, unleash creativity and innovation, create jobs and provide new services – especially in neighbourhoods where traditional services have failed local people in the past.

We have introduced a new legal form – the Community Interest Company (CIC) – and want to support new enterprises. As a major stimulus to this sector, central government and local authorities will work with these 'social enterprises' wherever possible. Where services can be provided by mutuals,cooperatives or CICs to the required standards of quality and value for money,they should be positively encouraged to develop and be included in procurement policies. We will discuss with local authorities the best way to achieve this.

In a range of services the voluntary and community sector has shown itself to be innovative, efficient and effective. Its potential for service delivery should be considered on equal terms. We will continue to improve the context in which the gifting of time and resources to the voluntary sector takes place. We will reintroduce the widely supported reforms in the Charities Bill.

We understand that often the spark for local innovation and change comes from one or two dedicated, visionary individuals. These people, sometimes dubbed 'social entrepreneurs', deserve our full support. We will develop a framework of incentives and rewards, to recognise the special people in every community whose voluntary efforts transform the lives of others.

A better alternative for young people

We know that parents and young people think that there should be more things to do and places to go for teenagers. We will publish plans to reform provision in order to ensure that all young people have access to a wider set of activities after the school day such as sport and the arts. We are determined that better provision will be allied to a stronger voice for the young themselves in designing and managing local provision. We will establish the first ever national framework for youth volunteering, action and engagement – a modern national youth community service, led by young people themselves – with an investment over the next three years of up to £100 million with matched funding from business, the voluntary sector and the Lottery.

Councils: more freedom, less bureaucracy

Strong communities ultimately require strong local government. We will give councils further freedoms to deliver better local services, subject to minimum national standards, with even greater freedoms for top-performing councils. We will reduce unnecessary bureaucracy by cutting both the cost of inspection and the total number of inspectorates, and we will dramatically simplify the many funding streams available to local areas through new Local Area Agreements. We will also give councils greater stability by providing three-year funding. We will continue to deliver efficiency savings and improvements to local services through joint procurement, shared services, streamlining administrative structures while promoting decision-making at the level that will make a difference. We will continue to strengthen the community leadership role of local authorities working in partnership with public, voluntary and private bodies.

Stronger leadership

Strong local government requires strong leadership. We will ensure that councils are organised in the most effective way to lead and support local partnerships and deliver high-quality services. We will explore giving people a more direct opportunity to express a view about whether they would like to have a directly elected mayor. We will also consult with city councils on the powers needed for a new generation of city mayors. And we will examine the case for simplifying the current local government election cycle by moving towards 'whole council' elections every four years.

Council tax under control

Labour recognises the concerns that have been raised about the level of council tax. This year we have delivered the lowest council tax increase in over a decade through a combination of extra investment and tough action to cap excessive increases.

We will continue to invest in local services with year-on-year increases in grants to local councils, and will not hesitate to use our capping powers to protect council taxpayers from excessive rises in council tax.

We remain concerned that many council taxpayers are not claiming reductions in their council tax bills to which they are already entitled. We will therefore introduce measures to make it easier for pensioners and people on low incomes to claim Council Tax Benefit.

In the longer term, we are committed to reforming council tax and will consider carefully the conclusions of the Lyons Review into local government finance.

The nations and regions of the UK

In our first term, we devolved power to Scotland and Wales and restored city-wide government to London. Britain is stronger as a result. In the next Parliament, we will decentralise power further. In Wales we will develop democratic devolution by creating a stronger Assembly with enhanced legislative powers and a reformed structure and electoral system to make the exercise of Assembly responsibilities clearer and more accountable to the public. We will also review the powers of the London Mayor and the Greater London Authority. And we will devolve further responsibility to existing regional bodies in relation to planning, housing, economic development and transport.

Northern Ireland

The Belfast Agreement on Good Friday 1998, was a remarkable achievement. Life in Northern Ireland is immeasurably better as a result. A huge programme of reform in policing, justice and rights, together with the lowest ever unemployment has helped address the inequalities of the past and has created a new confidence.

It is unacceptable that seven years after the agreement there are still paramilitary groups involved in criminality and punishment attacks. This has to end. The period of transition is over. Unionist politicians have made it clear that they are prepared to share power with nationalists and republicans if violence is ended once and for all. It is time for all groups in Northern Ireland to make it clear they will only use democratic and peaceful means to advance their aims.

We will work tirelessly with the parties in Northern Ireland and with the Irish government to re-establish the devolved institutions. But this can only happen on an inclusive basis if the IRA ends paramilitarism and criminality for good and decommissions its weapons. Bringing this about so that normal politics can take over in the Province will be our principal aim.

Loyalist paramilitary violence and criminality is equally intolerable. We will ensure that it is dealt with severely while providing the assistance necessary to Loyalist communities to ensure that prosperity is spread throughout Northern Ireland.

Parliamentary reform

Labour has already taken steps to make the House of Commons more representative,through all-women shortlists.Labour will also continue to support reforms that improve parliamentary accountability and scrutiny led by the successful Modernisation Committee.

In our first term, we ended the absurdity of a House of Lords dominated by hereditary peers. Labour believes that a reformed Upper Chamber must be effective, legitimate and more representative without challenging the primacy of the House of Commons.

Following a review conducted by a committee of both Houses, we will seek agreement on codifying the key conventions of the Lords, and developing alternative forms of scrutiny that complement rather than replicate those of the Commons; the review should also explore how the upper chamber might offer a better route for public engagement in scrutiny and policy-making. We will legislate to place reasonable limits on the time bills spend in the second chamber – no longer than 60 sitting days for most bills.

As part of the process of modernisation, we will remove the remaining hereditary peers and allow a free vote on the composition of the House.

Labour remains committed to reviewing the experience of the new electoral systems – introduced for the devolved administrations, the European Parliament and the London Assembly. A referendum remains the right way to agree any change for Westminster.

Having been the first government to take action to clean up the funding of political parties, we will continue to work with the independent Electoral Commission to explore how best to support the vital democratic role of political parties while recognising that campaigning activity must always be funded by parties from their own resources.

Since 1997 there has been a flowering of innovative forms of public engagement, for example, the Citizens Council used by the National Institute for Clinical Excellence to advise on ethical dilemmas. With the growing importance of new public policy issues and dilemmas – particularly those arising from scientific advances – we will continue to explore new and innovative forms of public engagement raising their profile and status in policy-making.

A voice for all

A fully democratic society depends on giving everyone a voice and stake. Only Labour governments have ever introduced race relations legislation, and laws passed in 2000 are ensuring that all public bodies promote diversity and tackle discrimination against black and Asian Britons. We will continue to promote civil rights for disabled people, ensuring full implementation of the new positive duty on the public sector to promote equality of opportunity for disabled people. We will also introduce a similar duty to promote equality of opportunity between women and men, and will further extend protection against discrimination on the grounds of religion and belief. We are committed to improving the rights and opportunities of gays and lesbians, that's why we brought in legislation on civil partnerships, reducing the age of consent, repealed Section 28 and reformed the sexual offences legislation so that it was no longer discriminatory.

It remains our firm and clear intention to give people of all faiths the same protection against incitement to hatred on the basis of their religion. We will legislate to outlaw it and will continue the dialogue we have started with faith groups from all backgrounds about how best to balance protection, tolerance and free speech.

We are proud to have brought in the Human Rights Act, enabling British citizens to take action in British courts rather than having to wait years to seek redress in Strasbourg. But rights must be balanced by responsibilities. So we will continue to bear down on abusive or frivolous claims.

In the next Parliament we will establish a Commission on Equality and Human Rights to promote equality for all and, tackle discrimination, and introduce a Single Equality Act to modernise and simplify equality legislation.

The choice for 2010

The Tories have only one policy on democratic reform – opportunism. Arch centralisers when in office, they now claim to be localists. Having refused for decades to accept any reform of the archaic House of Lords, some of them now claim to support a fully elected House. The choice is forward with new Labour to modern institutions and more power than ever devolved to communities and successful local authorities. Or back with the Tories to a government indifferent to the health of our democracy and negligent of our institutions.

Conservative Party

ECONOMY: VALUE FOR MONEY AND LOWER TAXES

A strong economy is the foundation for everything we do. It provides higher living standards so that people can look to the future with optimism. It creates the jobs we all depend on – enabling families to build their financial independence. It should guarantee our pensions in old age. It provides a safety net for the least fortunate. It is essential in tackling poverty, including child poverty. It pays for our public services – our children's education and our parents' healthcare. And it allows us to invest in our nation's security – defence, the police and border controls.

Our economic success over generations has been built on the hard work, enterprise and creativity of the British people.

Today, government is spending too much, wasting too much and taxing too much. Britain cannot continue indefinitely to spend more than she is earning without higher taxes or higher interest rates – either of which will harm our economic prospects. If we are to secure our future prosperity, government must once again start to live within its means.

The consequences of Labour's profligacy are now plain to see. Last year, average living standards fell for the first time in over a decade – and the poorest 10 per cent of Britons became poorer.

We need to change direction.

The way in which a government allocates taxpayers' money demonstrates its values. By going to war on waste and ending ineffective public spending programmes, we will achieve three simple aims.

First, we will give taxpayers value for money. We will spend the same as Labour would on the NHS, schools, transport and international development, and more than Labour on police, defence and pensions. But we will save £12 billion a year by 2007-8 by cutting back other expenditure. We will freeze civil service recruitment, remove 235,000 bureaucratic posts, and cut or abolish 168 public bodies.

Over the period to 2011-12, we will increase government spending by 4 per cent a year, compared to Labour's plans (on current trends) to increase spending by 5 per cent a year.

Second, we will avoid further Labour stealth taxes by reducing government borrowing. Of our £12 billion savings, we will use £8 billion to reduce Labour's excessive borrowing, so that we can avoid the tax rises that would otherwise be needed.

Third, we will lower taxes. We believe that people should choose how their money is spent. They should be rewarded for their hard work and be given peace of mind in old age. We will use the remaining £4 billion of our £12 billion savings to cut taxes in our first Budget.

Lower taxes promote enterprise and growth. But they also promote the right values. Hard-working families have suffered from Labour's tax raids on mortgages and marriage, pensions and petrol, buying a home and having a job.

We will change direction. Whereas Labour want to make people more dependent on the State, we believe that lower taxes help families build their financial independence and security. For those on low incomes we will retain the minimum wage, together with proposed increases.

After a lifetime of paying taxes, we believe people deserve dignity in retirement. Rising council tax bills, which are up by 76 per cent since Labour came to power, have hit pensioners particularly hard. That is why our tax plans include halving council tax bills for millions of pensioners. Our new, permanent discount, reducing council tax bills by up to £500 for households where all residents are over 65 will be fully funded by central government.

A Conservative Government will increase the basic state pension in line with earnings rather than prices, reversing the spread of means-testing. Over four years, this will increase the value of the pension by around £7 a week for single pensioners and £11 a week for couples – on top of increases in line with inflation. We will also keep all the other benefits that pensioners currently receive, including the Winter Fuel Payment, free television licences for the over-75s, and this year's one-off £200 council tax payment.

The financial security of pensioners tomorrow will be vastly improved by encouraging more saving today. To get more people into the saving habit, we will create a new Lifetime Savings Account in which government contributions top up the money that people save themselves. And we will take a series of steps to strengthen company pensions. We will abolish the rules that stop firms promoting pension schemes to their staff, encouraging employers to make pension schemes 'opt-out' rather than 'opt-in'. We will also use the unclaimed assets of banks and other financial institutions to replenish the pension funds of people who lose out when a scheme fails.

The best guarantee of future prosperity is a dynamic economy. The growth of China, India and other Asian economies poses a direct challenge to our future competitiveness. New technology and the speed of global capital flows punish the inflexible and the sluggish. We need to reward risk-taking and innovation so that Britain becomes the best place in the world to start and grow a business.

As well as keeping taxes low, we must reduce the burdens on business through deregulation.

A Conservative Government will negotiate to restore our opt-out from the European Social Chapter and liberate small businesses from job-destroying employment legislation.

We will set regulatory budgets for each department, capping and then cutting the cost of the regulations that they can introduce in any one year. All new regulation will have to have benefits exceeding costs, and regulations will be given 'Sunset Reviews' to check that this remains the case. A Conservative Government will end the elaboration or 'gold-plating' of EU directives.

A Conservative Government will lock in economic stability. We will maintain the independence of the Bank of England in setting interest rates. We will not join the Euro. By keeping the pound as our currency, control of our interest rates will continue to be set to meet the needs of the British economy. As the other major parties are committed to joining the euro, only the Conservatives can make this pledge.

FLEXIBLE CHILDCARE AND SCHOOL DISCIPLINE

It's not easy bringing up a family in modern Britain. Parents who work hard to give their children the best start in life need a government that is on their side. That means access to flexible childcare and schools with good discipline and high standards.

Juggling work and family life can be a struggle. Under Labour, Britain has the most expensive childcare in Europe, and many working families receive no help.

Conservatives trust families to make the right decisions about childcare. We will reform the system to increase choice, flexibility and support for working families.

We will provide more flexible maternity pay – giving mothers a choice of whether to receive it over nine months, or a higher amount paid over six months.

During the next Parliament, we will ensure that all working families who qualify for the working tax credit will receive up to £50 a week for each child under the age of five, irrespective of the type of childcare they choose. We will end Labour's insistence on endless form-filling and enable families to choose between formal and informal childcare.

We will also give extra support for workplace nurseries and provide a new network of clubs for older children.

Education enriches lives and provides us all, whatever our background, with the tools to achieve our ambitions.

Providing good education costs money – and our plans provide for an extra £15 billion a year for schools by 2009-10. Even more important than extra money, we must get the fundamentals right.

Classrooms need to be disciplined environments where children can learn. Teachers must be free to follow their vocation and inspire young minds. Standards must be maintained so that pupils, colleges and employers have examinations they can trust. Our education system should encourage excellence and ambition.

Today, these basics have been completely neglected. Over one million children play truant each year. Head teachers have been denied the final say on expulsions, and good schools will be further punished by being forced to admit a quota of disruptive pupils.

Last year a third of children left primary school unable to write properly and more than 40,000 teenagers left school without a single GCSE. Examinations have been devalued so that it is possible to secure a 'C' Grade at GCSE maths with just 16 per cent.

A Conservative Government will put the right values at the heart of our education system. We will ensure proper discipline in schools by giving heads and governors full control over admissions and expulsions. We will not allow a minority to ruin the education of the majority. Instead of disrupting the education of others, difficult pupils will be given the chance to get their lives back on track in special Turnaround Schools.

The respect due to teachers will be enhanced by protecting them against malicious allegations of abuse and, most importantly, reducing the massive burden of paperwork.

Schools will be liberated to set their own priorities and budgets. The current proliferation of funding streams will be replaced by a simple system, with funds allocated on the basis of pupil numbers. Money will follow the pupil. Head teachers will then have the freedom to spend money in accordance with their school's own needs, without interference from Whitehall.

The examination system will be made more transparent and accountable. The targets which encourage examiners to award higher and higher grades for the same level of performance will be scrapped. Marks will be published alongside grades. And schools will be free to offer internationally-recognised qualifications alongside GCSEs and A-Level. We will slim down and improve the National Curriculum, root out political correctness, restore rigour and give teachers the scope once again to be creative and imaginative.

Many children leave school at 16 because they are bored and because vocational education does not have the status that it deserves. We will end the snobbery that has damaged vocational education. New grants will be made available to help pupils who wish to combine GCSEs with vocational study at a wide range of colleges, businesses and other enterprises. We will introduce 300,000 vocational grants of £1,000 each for 14-16 year olds.

Education should be about more than academic learning. Under Labour, sport has been squeezed out of the curriculum and child obesity has risen alarmingly.

Our schools should be places where children also learn other skills for life, such as healthy living, being part of a team and respecting others. We will give every child the right to two hours of after-school sport with our Club2School programme, at no cost to parents. We support improvements to school dinners, and will go further by banning junk food in schools.

Children need to be taught how to deal with risks in life. We will encourage learning outside the classroom and provide protection for teachers worried about school trips.

Parents know their children best and are increasingly frustrated at not being able to exercise more choice and control over their children's education. We will give parents the right to choose the school best suited to their child's needs, and our school expansion fund will provide an additional 600,000 places in our first term. This will ensure that in our first five years 100,000 more parents get their first choice of school.

Schools will have responsibility for admissions, good schools will be allowed to grow and support will be given to new schools set up to respond to parental demand. Parents will also be able to send their children free of charge to any independent school that offers a place at no more than the cost of a state-funded school.

We will pay particular attention to children with special needs. Under Labour, the dogmatic pursuit of inclusion has led to the closure of special schools and children have suffered as a result. A Conservative Government will introduce a moratorium on the closure of special schools and give parents proper information and choice so they can secure the best opportunities for their children.

Labour have ignored the further education sector. We will simplify funding, replace the bureaucratic Learning and Skills Councils, ensure that money follows the student and allow colleges to apply for "Super college" status with greater freedom to manage budgets, specialise and innovate.

We will restore real choice in higher education by scrapping fees and abolishing Labour's admissions regulator. University funding will depend on attracting new students and so excellence will be encouraged. We will also help universities move towards greater financial independence by building up their individual endowments.

BETTER HEALTHCARE AND CLEANER HOSPITALS

We believe that everyone has the right to high quality healthcare, free at the point of use, delivered when and where they need it.

Record amounts of taxpayers' money have been spent on the NHS. Yet over a million people are still waiting for treatment, and average waiting times have gone up. More people die each year from infections they pick up in hospitals than on Britain's roads.

Taxpayers have not received value for money because the NHS has not been reformed. It is too impersonal, too inflexible, too centralised and too bureaucratic to respond to the needs of patients.

Staff in the health service – from doctors and nurses to porters and cleaners – work hard to deliver world class healthcare. But the system lets them down.

We have a clear plan of action to cut waiting times and clean up hospitals. We will increase funding, reduce bureaucracy, empower local professionals to operate local services and give greater choice to patients.

We will increase the NHS budget by £34 billion a year during our first Parliament – at least as much as Labour – from £1,450 per head to £2,000 per head. And we will ensure that the money reaches the front line.

We will radically reduce the number of Primary Care Trusts, abolish the Strategic Health Authorities and cut the number of quangos, inspectorates and commissions.

Centrally set targets on hospitals will be abolished. Patients will be treated according to clinical needs, not government targets.

We will give power and responsibility to local professionals. All hospitals will have the freedom to hire staff, specialise and borrow to invest. In response to local demand, hospitals will have the flexibility to increase the number of individual rooms and invest in infection control teams. We will bring back matron, who will have the power to close wards for cleaning.

We will give patients and local GPs the right to choose the hospital or care provider that is right for them.

Funding will follow the patient and go directly to front-line care. Hospitals will be paid according to the treatments they deliver, rather than by Whitehall budgets. Small community hospitals which have the support of local patients and GPs will not be closed by bureaucrats.

Each year around 220,000 people without health insurance pay for important operations. We believe that providing a contribution based on the cost of half the NHS operation when people make these choices both recognises the tax they have paid towards the NHS and will help further reduce waiting lists.

Choice gives people power, a sense of purpose and control. It makes those who offer a service accountable to those who use it. It will give patients the clean hospitals and the shorter waiting times they want. Our policies will give everyone the kind of choice in healthcare that today only money can buy.

We believe that increased choice, combined with extra resources and freedom for local professionals, will end waiting lists as we know them during the life of the next Parliament.

As we live longer and expect more treatment and care to be available at home and in the community, social services will inevitably face greater demands. We will give people more control over their social care and introduce a partnership scheme so that no one is compelled to sell their home to pay for long-term care.

Carers who look after elderly or disabled relatives, including those suffering from long-term conditions, deserve more support. We will boost respite for carers and give them more choice and information about the support available.

We will ensure greater access to NHS dentistry by changing the way in which dentists are paid and offering patients a low monthly payment system to cover against large and unplanned bills.

We will introduce health checks for immigrants in order to curb the spread of diseases such as TB and to protect access to our NHS. It is, after all, a national health service not a world health service. People coming to Britain for over 12 months from outside the EU will be required to undergo a full medical test. And anyone settling permanently here from outside the EU will have to demonstrate that they have an acceptable standard of health and that they are unlikely to impose significant costs or demands on Britain's health system.

Public health is important – it affects every family in our country. That is why a Conservative Government will take action to tackle sexually transmitted infections (STIs). In Britain today we face an STI epidemic. Today's sexually transmitted infections are tomorrow's NHS bills. It's time for a clear, bold and very public health TV campaign – young people need to know the risks involved and the precautions they can take.

SAFER COMMUNITIES AND MORE POLICE

Ensuring order is the first priority of government. Crime blights lives and ruins communities: it should not be excused, but condemned and punished. That means drawing a clear distinction between right and wrong, and restoring respect, discipline and decent values.

Crime today is out of control. There is a gun crime every hour. A million violent crimes are committed each year. Fewer than one in four crimes are now cleared up.

Criminals have a better chance of getting away with breaking the law today than at any time in the last 25 years.

Anti-social behaviour – vandalism, graffiti, binge-drinking, threatening behaviour – is a growing concern in all our communities.

Too many of Mr Blair's responses have been gimmicks, some of which, like marching yobs to cash machines, were never even introduced.

It doesn't have to be that way. Crime can be cut. Anti-social behaviour can be confronted. Communities can and should be made safe for the law-abiding. It requires active community policing and a relentless focus on catching, convicting and punishing criminals.

Labour's centralised control of the police has sapped officers' morale, increased bureaucracy and undermined public confidence.

It is time to change direction. We will recruit 5,000 new police officers each year, radically cut paperwork and introduce genuine local accountability, through elected police commissioners.

Giving local people a say over police priorities will lead to genuine neighbourhood policing with officers based in the locality clearly focused on zero tolerance.

When criminals are caught they should be punished properly. If appropriate they should be sent to prison, and in any event encouraged to reform their ways. None of these things happens properly today.

So, we will end Labour's early release from prison scheme and provide 20,000 extra prison places.

We will introduce honesty in sentencing so that criminals serve the full sentence handed down by the court. They will be told, in open court, the minimum time that they will serve behind bars.

There is much that can be done to improve the justice system – the police, courts and the prison and probation services. But they only pick up the pieces of problems whose roots often lie elsewhere.

Our goal is to reverse the drift towards communities that are blighted by crime, where people live in fear. We will deliver safer neighbourhoods where the streets belong to the law-abiding.

We will start at school by ensuring proper discipline.

We will break the link between drugs and crime by massively expanding treatment programmes, including 25,000 residential rehab places (compared with fewer than 2,500 places today), and by giving all young users of hard drugs a straight choice – effective treatment or appearing in court. We will stop sending mixed messages on drugs by reversing Labour's reclassification of cannabis as a less serious drug, changing it from class 'C' back to class 'B'.

We will support the social institutions – families, schools, voluntary bodies and youth clubs – that can prevent crime and drug dependency before it starts.

A Conservative Government will place the highest possible priority on combating the threat from terrorism. This requires a co-ordinated response right across government, including funding for the intelligence services, training for the emergency services, robust anti-terror laws, controlled immigration and rigorous arrangements for the extradition and deportation of terrorist suspects. That's why we will appoint a Homeland Security Minister to co-ordinate our national response.

SECURE BORDERS AND CONTROLLED IMMIGRATION

Britain has benefited from immigration. We all gain from the social diversity, economic vibrancy and cultural richness that immigration brings.

But if those benefits are to continue to flow we need to ensure that immigration is effectively managed, in the interests of all Britons, old and new.

This Government has lost effective control of our borders. More than 150,000 people (net) come to Britain every year, a population the size of Peterborough. Labour see "no obvious upper limit to legal immigration".

Our asylum system is in chaos. Instead of offering a safe haven to those most in need, the current system encourages illegality. Desperate individuals are forced into the hands of people smugglers and when they reach Britain they are open to continuing exploitation in the underground economy. Only two out of every ten asylum seekers are found to have a genuine claim.

Britain has reached a turning-point. That is why a Conservative Government will bring immigration back under control. We have set out a series of practical and considered steps to restore control and fairness to our immigration system.

First of all we will take proper control of our borders. We will ensure 24-hour surveillance at our ports, and restore full embarkation controls. Border security is currently divided between seven different bodies reporting to three different cabinet ministers. We believe that the time has now come to establish a British Border Control Police, whose sole job will be to secure Britain's borders.

We will introduce a points-based system for work permits similar to the one used in Australia. This will give priority to people with the skills Britain needs.

On asylum, a Conservative Government will not allow outdated and inflexible rules to prevent us shaping a system which is more humane, more likely to improve community relations and better managed. So we will take back powers from Brussels to ensure national control of asylum policy, withdraw from the 1951 Geneva Convention, and work for modernised international agreements on migration.

Our objective is a system where we take a fixed number of refugees from the UNHCR rather than simply accepting those who are smuggled to our shores. Asylum seekers' applications will be processed outside Britain.

We will set an overall annual limit on the numbers coming to Britain, including a fixed quota for the number of asylum seekers we accept. Parliament will set, and review, that number every year.

We are committed to making a continued success of Britain's diversity. There should be popular consent for further demographic change. And the best way to secure continuing support for future migration is by showing that government has control of our borders. Refusing to set a limit on new migrants is irresponsible politics. Only the Conservatives take this issue seriously enough to insist on a limit, and will introduce the policies necessary to police it.

ACCOUNTABILITY

In the real world, if you say you're going to do something, you do it. And if you fail, you can lose your job. That is accountability. Accountability is at the heart of good government and a healthy democracy. We all know that when people think they can get away with it, they won't do things as well as they should.

That's why we've published a Timetable for Action that sets out clearly what we will do, and when we will do it. And Michael Howard has made clear that ministers who fail to deliver will lose their jobs.

Under Mr Blair, the way we are governed has become less accountable, more complex and, ultimately, less democratic. Ministers don't take responsibility for their failures. Unprecedented powers have been given to new, unelected and remote bodies, including regional assemblies for which there is no popular support. The House of Commons has been steadily undermined, and proper reform of the House of Lords has been repeatedly promised but never delivered.

Conservatives understand that people identify with their town, city or county, not with arbitrary "regions". We will abolish Labour's regional assemblies. Powers currently exercised at a regional level covering planning, housing, transport and the fire service will all be returned to local authorities.

The House of Commons needs to be made more capable of standing up to the executive. We will strengthen select committees and make time for proper scrutiny of all legislation. As part of our drive for efficiency across Whitehall and Westminster, we will cut the number of MPs by 20 per cent. We will seek cross-party consensus for a substantially elected House of Lords.

Conservatives believe that the Union of England, Scotland, Wales and Northern Ireland brings benefits to all parts of our United Kingdom.

We remain strongly committed to making a success of devolution in Scotland, so that it delivers for the Scottish people. In Wales we will work with the Assembly and give the Welsh people a referendum on whether to keep the Assembly in its current form, increase its powers or abolish it.

But devolution has brought problems of accountability at Westminster.

Now that exclusively Scottish matters are decided by the Scottish Parliament in Edinburgh, exclusively English matters should be decided in Westminster without the votes of MPs sitting for Scottish constituencies who are not accountable to English voters. We will act to ensure that English laws are decided by English votes.

We are committed to supporting Northern Ireland's position within the United Kingdom in accordance with the consent principle. We will continue to work for a comprehensive political settlement, based on the principles of the Belfast Agreement. We will not accept any party into the government of Northern Ireland linked to a paramilitary organisation that holds on to illegal weapons and is engaged in any criminal activity. In the absence of devolved government, we will make direct rule more accountable.

Communities, Transport and the Environment

Britain draws great strength from its diversity. We are a country of vibrant urban centres, historic towns and an evolving countryside. It is both inefficient and insensitive to local communities to impose uniform control from Whitehall.

We believe in devolving power down to the lowest level so that local people are given greater control over their own lives.

Local councils should be accountable to voters. But under Labour, people's priorities have taken second place to centrally imposed targets and Whitehall inspection regimes. The cost to local taxpayers has increased rapidly, with council tax levels up 76 per cent since 1997. It has been a vicious circle – less representation and more taxation.

The Conservatives will liberate local government.

Local communities will have a greater say over planning decisions. We will also give new powers to help local councils to deal with those incidents, such as illegal traveller encampments, which breach planning laws. Together with clear guidance for police and our review of the Human Rights Act, this will ensure fairness for all, rather than special rules for different groups.

With greater power for local people will come less interference from central government. We will radically cut the burdens on local councils.

A Conservative Government will support creativity and excellence in the arts. Instead of Labour's centralised bureaucracy and political interference, including in the National Lottery, we will devolve funding and decision-making while ensuring that the lottery supports the arts, heritage, sport and charities.

The most powerful form of devolution is to individuals and families. The Right to Buy for council tenants extended home ownership, transformed many of Britain's housing estates and expanded our property-owning democracy.

A Conservative Government will extend this right to tenants of housing associations. Our plans to boost shared ownership schemes, and give social housing tenants the right to own a share of their home, will also benefit first-time buyers.

Empowering individuals also means giving them the opportunity to get around Britain more quickly and safely. A modern economy depends on it.

A Conservative Government will end Labour's war on the motorist. We will modernise Britain's road network and review all speed cameras to ensure they are there to save lives, not make money.

We will bring stability to the rail network, avoiding further costly and inefficient re-organisation. Successful train operating companies will have their franchises extended to allow companies to invest in improved stations, car parks, facilities and rolling stock.

A commitment to safeguarding our environment lies deep in Conservative thinking. We instinctively understand the importance of conservation, natural beauty and our duty of stewardship of the earth.

A Conservative Government will call a halt to Labour's plans to concrete over our green fields. We will promote development on brownfield sites and establish more Green Belts with tighter development rules.

To ensure Britain plays its part in combating climate change, we will phase out the use of harmful HFCs and deliver greater incentives to make homes more energy-efficient. Through cuts in Vehicle Excise Duty and increased grants, we will significantly reduce the cost of cars with low carbon emissions. We believe that households and businesses should recycle an increasing amount of their waste.

A Conservative Government will guarantee the security and sustainability of Britain's energy supplies. We will do this by supporting the development of a broad range of renewable energy sources. We also recognise that energy efficiency must play an increasingly important role in our energy policy.

Conservatives understand the pressures on the livelihoods of those who work in rural areas.

We value the diverse nature of our nation and believe in defending traditional liberties. A Conservative Government will therefore introduce a Bill, and offer Parliament a free vote, to overturn the Government's ban on hunting with dogs.

Britain's farmers operate to some of the highest animal welfare standards in the world and help to preserve the countryside for all of us to enjoy. We will introduce a Bill to ensure honest labelling of food and stem the flow of expensive new regulation. We will support initiatives, such as farmers' markets and local food projects, that enable British customers to support Britain's farmers. The Little Red Tractor mark denotes high British animal welfare and production standards. We will insist that all publicly procured food carries this mark.

We will press for further reform of the Common Agricultural Policy, to make it less burdensome for farmers and taxpayers alike. And we will promote legislation to strengthen and update animal welfare.

DEFENDING OUR FREEDOMS

Britain plays a unique role in the world. We are the only nation that is one of the five permanent members of the United Nations Security Council, a net contributor to the European Union, a member of the G8, at the centre of the Commonwealth family of nations and a leading member of NATO. We are a global trading nation with interests in every continent. As the world's fourth largest economy, we have the potential to be a powerful force for good.

These durable strengths allow Britain to defend our interests and promote our values across the globe.

As a country, we have been in the vanguard of freedom's advance, a friend to the growth of democracy, an advocate of the rule of law, a defender of the oppressed and a robust protector of our people's security.

But, under this Government, Britain's ability to defend its interests and secure valuable freedoms has been undermined. Our Armed Forces, the vital muscle which allows us to punch above our weight, have been allowed to weaken. And our relations with the European Union have been mismanaged in a way which threatens not just British interests, but the capacity of the continent to adapt flexibly to the future.

A Conservative Government will strengthen our Armed Forces within NATO by spending £2.7 billion more than Labour on the front line by 2007-08.

Those serving in our Armed Forces are vitally important to us, so we must take care of the people most important to them. A Conservative Government will support service families. They deserve decent homes, good schools for their children, and the chance to spend as much time as possible with their families.

We will make the Army stronger. A Conservative Government will preserve the regiments Labour would abolish and improve the supply and procurement of weaponry.

We will save warships Mr Blair would scrap. A Conservative Government will support European co-operation on defence but we strongly believe that such co-operation should take place within the framework of NATO.

If a Conservative Government ever has to take the country to war, we will tell the British people why. Mr Blair misrepresented intelligence to make the case for war in Iraq, and failed to plan for the aftermath of Saddam Hussein's downfall. It is nevertheless the case that a democratic Iraq would be a powerful beacon of hope in a troubled part of the world. So we believe that Britain must remain committed to rebuilding Iraq and allowing democracy to take hold. And a Conservative Government will work to achieve peace in the Middle East based on the principle of Israel secure within its borders and a viable Palestinian state.

Conservatives support the cause of reform in Europe and we will co-operate with all those who wish to see the EU evolve in a more flexible, liberal and decentralised direction. We oppose the EU Constitution and would give the British people the chance to reject its provisions in a referendum within six months of the General Election. We also oppose giving up the valuable freedom which control of our own currency gives us. We will not join the Euro.

In a reformed Europe, the restrictive employment laws of the Social Chapter will have to give way to more flexible working. We will ensure that Britain once again leads the fight for a deregulated Europe by negotiating the restoration of our opt-out from the Social Chapter.

The common policies on agriculture and fisheries are unsustainable, damaging to free trade and conservation, and waste huge sums of money. The CAP needs further and deeper reform. And, because fisheries would be better administered at the national level, we will negotiate to restore national and local control over British fishing grounds. We are determined to ensure national control in this area.

We will also build on the success of enlargement, making Europe more diverse by working to bring in more nations, including Turkey.

We value Britain's membership of the European Union, but our horizons extend much further. A key element of British foreign policy under a Conservative Government will be fighting world poverty. We will support further action on debt relief and will work to meet the UN target of spending 0.7 per cent of national income on overseas aid by 2013. We believe that British aid programmes are among the best in the world, so we will negotiate to increase British national control over our international aid spending.

Above all, we recognise that there is a vital thread that links open markets, free trade, property rights, the rule of law, democracy, economic development and social progress. We will use our global influence to champion these principles in the interests of the developing world.

Liberal Democrat Party

GREEN ACTION

The environment features on every page of this manifesto – a strong green thread running through everything we do and promise.

HEALTH

Free personal care

Those towards the end of their lives deserve the best possible care. Liberal Democrats will provide free personal care for elderly people and people with disabilities, for as long as they need it, funded out of our new 50 per cent rate on that part of people's incomes over £100,000. In short, we will implement the recommendations of the independent Royal Commission on Long-Term Care. Liberal Democrats in government in Scotland have already achieved this for elderly people.

Quicker diagnosis for serious conditions – so your NHS treatment is not delayed

Your chances of surviving life-threatening and debilitating illnesses improve the swifter the diagnosis. When a GP considers you may have a serious illness we will make sure you are offered diagnosis by the quickest practical route, public or private, so that the NHS can treat you more quickly. More tests and scans will be available in places like GPs' surgeries and community pharmacies. We will tackle the scandal of expensive scanners being under-used by investing in training, recruitment and retention of the key staff needed to operate them. We will provide more scans at weekends and in the evenings. We will publish waiting times for tests and scans – figures which the Labour Government has refused to make public.

Cut unfair charges – free eye and dental checks, fewer prescription charges

To reduce the risk of illness going undetected we will end the charges for eye and dental check-ups which deter people from coming forward for testing. It is also unfair that some people living with long-term conditions pay no prescription charges, while people with other, equally serious, conditions (such as cystic fibrosis and multiple sclerosis) have to pay. We will extend the range of long-term conditions which qualify for exemption from prescription charges, based on an independent review.

Put patients first – more doctors and nurses, free from Whitehall meddling

We will complete NHS plans to recruit at least an extra 8,000 more doctors, 12,000 more nurses and 18,000 more therapists and scientists by 2008. That will cut waiting times and improve the quality of care. Doctors, nurses and therapists are highly trained and dedicated health professionals, while ministers and civil servants are not. Liberal Democrats will hack away the red tape and abolish the absurd targets set by government, and free frustrated health professionals from demoralising government meddling. Clinical decisions should be taken by health professionals and local investment will be determined by locally elected and accountable people who can be removed by local people if they get it wrong. Scrapping unnecessary centralised targets will mean that your local hospital will have the time and flexibility to put patients first, providing personalised care and cleaner hospitals and treating the sickest the quickest.

High-quality dental care

Many people can't find an NHS dentist to take them on. We will reform NHS dental contracts so that more dentists are encouraged to do more NHS work. This will rebuild the relationship between the dental profession and government which has been badly damaged under Conservatives and Labour. Personal Dental Plans will set out how frequently people should have a check-up, how better to look after their teeth and, for those with serious dental problems, their future course of treatment.

Give people more control over their healthcare

We will encourage regular health 'MoTs' tailored to individual patients' needs, with wider access to screening and blood pressure and cholesterol tests. Tens of thousands of patients die in the NHS every year without access to specialised care and pain management. We will prioritise extending choice and access to these services, including more support for hospices. People with long-term conditions should be entitled to an agreed Personal Care Plan, setting out their course of treatment, where and when they will be treated, and what other help, such as social care, they will receive. We will introduce new legislation to safeguard the rights and welfare of people with mental health problems, allowing them to exercise more control over their treatment. We will end inappropriate age discrimination within the NHS; for example, many older women are not currently invited for the routine breast cancer screening which could save their lives.

Prevention is as important as cure

We will concentrate on helping people stay healthy, as well as caring for them when they fall ill. According to the NHS report, Securing our Future Health, the Government's failure to tackle the unnecessary causes of ill-health will cost the NHS an extra £30 billion a year by 2022. If the causes of ill-health aren't tackled, the NHS of the future won't be able to cope – so we will give people the information and opportunities to make healthy choices, for example through clearer food and alcohol labelling. To improve children's health, on top of plans to increase funding for school meals, we will introduce minimum nutrition standards for school meals, as we already have in Scotland; we will restrict advertising of unhealthy food during children's television programmes; and we will require food and drink sold in vending machines on school premises to meet minimum health and nutrition standards. Because secondhand smoke kills, we will ban smoking in all enclosed public places. Our policies as a whole will help tackle other causes of ill-health, such as poverty, pollution and poor housing.

GREEN ACTION

Clean air and water

Pollution in the air, in water and in the food chain causes or aggravates many illnesses as well as destroying the environment. We support the adoption of the EU Registration, Evaluation and Authorisation of Chemicals (REACH) Directive. This will mean that information becomes available to the public on the consequences of exposure to all chemicals in daily use and that those of high concern are replaced by safer alternatives.

Promote walking and cycling

Fewer school-run car journeys means less pollution, less congestion and fewer road deaths. Children walking or cycling to school also get fitter – but the journey must be safe. Liberal Democrats will encourage and promote nationally what many Liberal Democrat councils already do locally, such as 'Safe Routes to School' with calmed traffic, safe pavements, good lighting and adults on hand to conduct 'walking buses'. We will also provide more cycle routes and reform planning rules to make sure that key services are more easily accessible by foot or bicycle. This will benefit adults as well as children.

EDUCATION AND SKILLS

No tuition fees, no top-up fees, fair grants – university affordable for every student

Labour broke their promise on tuition fees. The result: tens of thousands of able students are saddled with mortgage-sized debts or deterred altogether from going to university. Funded from part of our new 50 per cent rate on incomes over £100,000, Liberal Democrats will abolish all tuition fees and make grants available to help poorer students with maintenance costs. That will build on the achievements of Liberal Democrats in government in Scotland. No one will be denied the opportunity of a university education because of the fear of debt, while universities will receive the increased funds they need.

Cut class sizes – using the £1.5 billion Child Trust Fund

Expert opinion confirms what common sense tells us: children well taught and well-cared-for in their early years have a better opportunity to lead successful and rewarding lives. The Government has the wrong priorities, handing out a one-off cash windfall to 18 year-olds at taxpayers' expense through the Child Trust Fund. Liberal Democrats will use this money better by recruiting 21,000 more teachers to cut infant class sizes from the present maximum of 30 to an average of 20, and junior class sizes to an average of 25. We will extend before and after school provision from 8 a.m. to 6 p.m. for all children and complete 3500 Children's Centres by 2010. Building on our Maternity Income Guarantee, which will raise maternity pay for the first six months to £170 a week instead of £102.80 at present, these policies will give every child the best possible start.

Every child taught English, Maths, Science, Modern Languages, plus Information and Communication Technology, by suitably qualified teachers

The teacher recruitment crisis means that thousands of children are being taught key subjects by staff who are not trained specialists in that subject. Liberal Democrats will guarantee that all children will be taught the core subjects of English, Maths, Science, Modern Languages and ICT by suitably qualified teachers through funding secondary schools to provide the necessary high-quality teacher-training courses in these subjects.

School discipline

Children need to learn in a safe and orderly environment, where high standards of behaviour are upheld, where bullying is challenged effectively and where teachers are able to teach without disruption. Our smaller class sizes will help reduce discipline problems. To deal with more persistent disruption schools will agree externally-monitored 'positive behaviour plans'with parents and pupils. If necessary, local education authorities'Behavioural Support Units will tackle exceptional problems in particular schools. When all else fails we will guarantee that head teachers will have local education authority support for 'managed transfer'to other schools or special units for pupils whose behaviour remains unacceptable.

Time to teach

Children in England are now the most tested in Europe, yet there is little evidence that the Government's obsession with testing and targets has improved standards. Liberal Democrats believe that teachers should be given more time to teach and that testing should have a clear purpose: to improve learning for individual children. We will reduce the level of external testing, replacing compulsory tests at seven and eleven with a system of sampling against national standards. Teachers will regularly assess pupils'performance, using the results to inform teaching and give parents accurate information on their child's progress.

Special educational needs

Children with special educational needs should be schooled in an environment appropriate to their needs – usually in local schools with appropriate support, or in specialist schools for those who need them. Parents'wishes must be considered when making decisions about type of schooling. A designated teacher in each school will have responsibility to identify and plan for children with special needs, and act as a contact point for parents and other teachers. We will make sure that all teachers and teaching assistants working with children with special educational needs are appropriately trained. Special schools will act as resource centres to support local schools with their specialist provision. In turn special schools will be linked to research departments in universities so that they can benefit directly from, and be involved with, the latest research in special education.

Skills for work

School-leavers should be equipped with the skills they need to succeed in the workplace. We will combine GCSE, A-level and vocational programmes of study within a new diploma system, stretching the most gifted and engaging those previously turned off by schooling. We will give all students over the age of 14 the opportunity to combine vocational and academic learning, as Liberal Democrats in government in Scotland are already doing.

World-class skills for a world-class economy

We are committed to closing the funding gap between schools and colleges, starting by providing equal funding for equivalent courses, wherever they are taught. To deliver world-class skills, world-class facilities are needed. We will implement plans to invest in the modern, high-quality college facilities needed to deliver high-quality skills training.

School transport

We will maintain the right of children to free school transport when they live more than two miles from their designated primary school and three miles from their secondary school – a right which is being taken away by the Labour Government. For those who live nearer school, there still need to be safe alternatives to the car; we will promote 'Safe Routes to School', with calmed traffic, safe pavements, good lighting and adults on hand to conduct 'walking buses'.

GREEN ACTION

Green every school, college and university

All plans for new educational buildings must be good for the environment as well as good for education, for example by minimising the need for heating and using sustainable building materials. By putting the two together, children and students can learn about caring for the environment by seeing green projects in real action in their own school or college. We also believe that out-of-classroom learning is a key part of a good education, and will include the quality of out-of-classroom education in the criteria on which schools are inspected.

JUSTICE AND CRIME

10,000 more police on the streets – cut crime and the fear of crime

By getting rid of Labour's expensive, illiberal and ineffective ID card scheme, we will pay for 10,000 police on top of Labour's plans. We will also complete existing plans for an extra 20,000 community support officers to back them up. The average police officer today spends more time in the police station than they do on the streets. We will give the police the technology they need, and simplify the bureaucracy they face, to allow them to spend more time on patrol and less time tied to the desk. We will concentrate more police efforts on tackling drug traffickers and those drug users who resort to crime to feed their habits, rather than criminalising people possessing cannabis only for their own personal use.

Make offenders pay back to victims and their communities

Liberal Democrats will make more non-violent criminals, such as fine defaulters, shoplifters and petty vandals, do tough community work as an alternative to jail. Experience shows that this reduces re-offending, gives them skills for legitimate work, and means that they pay back to the community. Through Community Justice Panels, local people will have more say in the punishment offenders carry out in the community – for example, by making them clean off graffiti or repair damage to victims' property.

Get tough on anti-social behaviour

Many towns and cities are becoming no-go areas at the weekend. We will tackle excessive drinking by cracking down on licensees who serve people when clearly drunk or under-age. We will make big late-night venues contribute to the cost of extra late-night policing. Unacceptable noise and offensive behaviour will be tackled through Acceptable Behaviour Contracts agreed between the individual, their family, the police and the local authority. Where individuals do not co-operate we will use Anti-Social Behaviour Orders, plus appropriate measures to tackle underlying causes.

Give prisoners skills for work, not crime

With four out of five prisoners functionally illiterate, and over half of prisoners re-offending, it's time to make prison work. Prisoners will be subject to a tough working day, with increased resources for education and training a top priority so that they learn the skills to acquire a legitimate job. The effort a prisoner puts into their education and work-related skills will be one of the factors used when considering their release date, as part of our emphasis on tackling the causes of crime.

Quality investigations, safe convictions, fighting crime and terror

We will increase police resources to improve the detection and investigation of crime. We will create a co-ordinated UK Border Force to strengthen the country's borders against terrorism, people-trafficking and drug smuggling. We oppose moves to reduce or remove rights to jury trial, and the routine use of hearsay evidence or revelation of previous convictions. We opposed Labour's plans to allow the Home Secretary to order house arrest and other restrictions on personal liberty. A British citizen's liberty must only be removed through a fair judicial process, not on the command of politicians. Liberal Democrats achieved substantial amendment of the Prevention of Terrorism Act, but it still has serious flaws, and we will repeal it. Effective action against terrorism is vital, and our priority will be to extend the criminal law to enable terrorist suspects to be prosecuted in the mainstream courts. We will admit evidence from communications interception. If control orders are still required they must be granted by a judge, be time-limited and be subject to a high standard of proof.

Firm but fair on asylum

For centuries Britain has had a proud record of granting safe refuge to those fleeing persecution. In turn, refugees have enriched the UK's culture and wealth immeasurably. The Home Office has a record of delays and bad decisions on asylum, so we will transfer responsibility for assessing asylum claims to a dedicated agency to sort out the mess, ensuring that those who need help get it, whilst those who don't can't abuse the system. We will work within the EU to develop common standards so that all EU countries take their fair share of refugees. We will also end asylum-seekers' dependence on benefits, allowing them to work so they can pay their own way and use their skills to benefit everyone.

Strengthen the fight against discrimination

We will introduce a Single Equality Act to outlaw all unfair discrimination, (including on the grounds of race, gender, religion or belief, sexual orientation, disability, age or gender identity), thus giving equal protection for all. We will establish hate-crimes investigation units in each police force to co-ordinate information and action against racism, homophobia and other hate crimes. Liberal Democrats led the call for an amendment to the laws on incitement to racial hatred, to criminalise those who use religious words as a pretext for race hate. Our Equality Act will stop same-sex couples in civil partnerships being treated unfairly compared with married couples in pension arrangements.

GREEN ACTION

Tougher action to enforce high environmental standards.

The courts have struggled to enforce the rules in environmental cases that are often highly technical and specialised. We will improve the enforcement of pollution controls through a specialist Environmental Tribunal to deal with enforcing environmental rules. We will also make sure that the level of penalties that polluters have to pay are appropriate to the offence – at present they are often trivial compared to the profits from environmental crime.

THE ECONOMY

All our policies are costed and affordable

Unlike the other parties, we have consistently set out costings for our manifesto pledges, explaining how much money they will need and how they will all be paid for. So this manifesto includes a specific section outlining our main costings. Our package of tough choices on spending, and fairer taxes, means that most people will be better off. There is only one proposed net tax rise (to 50 per cent on the proportion of incomes over £100,000 a year, affecting just one per cent of tax-payers) which will pay for the abolition of student tuition fees, free personal care for the elderly, and lower local taxes. Most people's tax will be cut by replacing Council Tax with a system based on ability to pay, saving the typical household around £450 per year.

Tough choices in public spending

Liberal Democrats have different spending priorities from Labour. We believe that in order to concentrate resources on currently under-funded areas such as pensions, policing and early years education, funding should be switched from lower priority areas. That means reducing unnecessary subsidies to industry, and cutting wasteful new initiatives like the ID card and the Child Trust Fund handouts for future 18 year-olds. This will allow us to spend more on the things that really matter, like better pensions, more police and smaller class sizes.

A stable, well-managed economy

We welcome the greater economic stability that has been established since interest rates were set independently by the Bank of England (which the Liberal Democrats were the first party to advocate). Now, there needs to be more independent scrutiny and discipline in fiscal policy. We will give the National Audit Office the power to scrutinise the budget figures, including public borrowing, so that no Chancellor can fiddle the figures. We will make sure that the Office for National Statistics is independent and accountable to parliament, not subservient to ministers. We will tackle irresponsible credit expansion in mortgages and personal loans by curbing misleading advertising and anti-competitive practices by promoters of insurance for mortgages and loans, and of credit cards. We oppose the increasing complexity of business taxes and we will consult with business on a simpler and fairer system, giving priority to helping small businesses.

Fairer taxes

Under Labour, ordinary hard-working families pay more as a share of their incomes in tax than the very rich. Under Labour, the elderly have to sell their homes to pay for their care, while rising Council Tax and university top-up fees are making the system even more unfair. Taking all taxes together, the poorest 20 per cent of the population pay 38 per cent of their income in tax, compared to just 35 per cent for the richest 20 per cent. That's not what people expected from a Labour Government. Liberal Democrats will make the tax system fairer and simpler. As a first step towards reducing tax paid by low earners, we will axe the unfair Council Tax and replace it with a Local Income Tax based on people's ability to pay. This will cut the typical household's tax bill by over £450. To pay for our policies of abolishing student top-up and tuition fees, ending elderly and disabled people needing to pay for their care, and cutting Council Tax, the richest one per cent of the population will pay 50 per cent tax (up from 41 per cent) on that part of their income over £100,000 per year.

Cut stamp duty

People are increasingly struggling to afford their first home. We will raise the starting point for stamp duty from £120,000 to £150,000. This step will take 150,000 mainly first-time buyers out of paying stamp duty altogether, and cuts the cost of home ownership.

An outward-looking economy

Liberal Democrats support a liberal economic approach to trade, investment and migration in the national interest. We want Britain to be at the centre of a liberalised, reformed European Union. Liberal Democrats believe that Britain should work to create the right economic conditions to join the euro (subject to a referendum) in order to safeguard investment in the UK and reduce the cost and risk of trade with the rest of Europe. We will work to break down the trade barriers that prevent the poorest countries in the world selling their goods to the richer countries on fair terms.

Economic migration

Economic migrants have helped make Britain one of the richest countries in the world, both economically and culturally. There remains a positive economic benefit from managed immigration to fill the demand for skills and labour that are in short supply. We will consult with business and the public services to agree numbers of work permits for economic migration to make sure that Britain continues to prosper.

BUSINESS

Cut the red tape that stops businesses from growing. Liberal Democrats will slash the red tape, bureaucracy and over-regulation that are holding British businesses – especially small businesses – back. We will start with these three measures:

- No new regulation will be passed until a full assessment of its costs and necessity is published.
- New regulations affecting business will automatically be scrapped unless Parliament specifically approves their renewal after a period specified in a 'sunset clause'.
- Endless visits by all sorts of inspectors will be replaced in most cases by one all-purpose inspection.

Introduce small-business rate relief

Many small businesses pay a disproportionate amount in rates – as much as 35 per cent of their profits. We will help small businesses by reforming the business rates system to allow firms with a rateable value of less than £25,000 to claim a business rate allowance of up to £1,500. This would represent a saving of over £600 a year for the majority of small businesses. We will also reform the valuation system to base rates on site values, rather than rental value, which penalises businesses that invest in improving their premises.

Scrap the Department of Trade and Industry

There is no need for a big department that interferes in the economy and subsidises failing companies at taxpayers' expense. The DTI is irrelevant to most enterprises, so in abolishing it Liberal Democrats will cut away its bureaucratic and wasteful functions. We will transfer its useful roles to more appropriate departments, such as support for scientific research to our Department for Education, Skills and Science. The Chief Secretary to the Treasury will take on the role of advocate for business at the Cabinet table. Overall, this will save £8 billion of taxpayers' money over the life of a parliament. We will invest this saving in our priorities, including improving education and training – which are of far more real benefit to business.

Protect consumers from rip-offs

We will introduce a new legal duty on businesses to trade fairly, while cutting back unnecessary red tape and bureaucracy. Enforced by the courts, this will require less form-filling than Labour's complex rules, yet provide more effective protection for consumers, and promote free competition.

Boost tourism

We will promote domestic tourism opportunities, starting by creating an English Tourism Board to match those in Scotland, Wales and Northern Ireland, with increased resources for marketing England.

These measures will help reduce the 'tourism deficit'– the difference between the amount spent by overseas visitors in the UK and the amount spent by UK tourists abroad – which has quadrupled under Labour and now stands at £17 billion.

GREEN ACTION

Using economic instruments to benefit the environment

Green tax reforms and traded permits should be used to encourage people to act in a more environmentally responsible way. We will change the Climate Change Levy into a Carbon Tax, making it more effective at discouraging the use of the polluting fuels and energy sources that harm the environment. We will also strengthen tax incentives to use smaller and less polluting vehicles and create more energy-efficient homes. We will launch a Treasury-led Environmental Incentive Programme, examining tax reforms that will reduce pollution and protect the environment, on the clear principle of taxing differently, not taxing more.

Promote clean energy

Liberal Democrats will make sure that at least 20 per cent of the UK's electricity comes from a full range of renewable sources by the year 2020, by increasing and reforming the obligation on energy suppliers to use renewable energy. Liberal Democrats will not replace existing nuclear power stations as they come to the end of their safe and economic operating lives – instead we will use renewables and conserve energy. We will encourage the use of alternatives, such as hydrogen fuels, as technology develops.

PENSIONS AND BENEFITS

Over £100 more on the pension every month at 75 – a million pensioners off means-testing

Millions of elderly people are failing to receive the pensions they've earned – and deserve and need – because of demeaning and unworkable means tests. Liberal Democrats will simplify the system, immediately guaranteeing a basic pension at 75 of at least £109.45 per week, with future increases linked to earnings. That's over £100 a month more at 75 for every single pensioner. Every pensioner couple over 75 will receive at least £167.05 per week state pension – over £140 a month more than at present. This will abolish the need for means tests altogether for a million people.

Citizen's Pension

Many women who gave up work to bring up their children receive as little as a penny a week because they haven't paid enough national insurance. From the age of 75 we will give pensioners our increased 'Citizen's Pension'as of right, making sure that 2.8 million women pensioners have security and dignity in retirement.

Help pensioners by axing the Council Tax

Too often, pensioners are forced to pay huge Council Tax bills despite being on low incomes, and many will be faced with further massive increases due to revaluation. Replacing Council Tax with Local Income Tax means eight out of ten pensioners will be better off and six million poorer pensioners will pay no local tax at all. Unlike the other parties'proposals, no one will be denied help simply because of their age or who they live with – everyone will only pay what they can afford.

Help working parents spend more time with their children

Becoming a parent for the first time is a daunting and expensive task. Giving new working parents more support has benefits for them, their babies, their employers and the economy. Liberal Democrats will give working families having their first child increased maternity pay for the first six months at the rate of the minimum wage – that's £170 a week instead of £102.80 at present, a lot more just when parents really need it.

Reform the New Deal to get more people into work

The present New Deal leaves too many people on unnecessary or ineffective schemes rather than getting them into real jobs. Liberal Democrats will instead tailor the assistance so that jobseekers receive the package of support they need to get proper, permanent work. We will also scrap benefit sanctions which leave genuine claimants unable to feed and house themselves.

Scrap the Child Support Agency

The CSA is failing. Some parents are required to pay an unrealistic amount for maintenance, whilst other payments are never enforced. We would scrap the CSA and hand over its initial assessment and enforcement functions to the Inland Revenue so that payment is enforced fairly and effectively. Special circumstances would be addressed by appeal to a specialist tribunal able to take account of individual circumstances, instead of the present unfair rigid formula.

Provide more support for people with disabilities

Many severely disabled people feel the cold intensely and cannot afford to heat their homes adequately, despite the fact that the cold will often make their conditions worse. We will help severely disabled people of working age with their fuel bills by giving them the same £200 a year Winter Fuel Payment that pensioners receive. We will also implement the recommendations of the Royal Commission on Long-Term Care to guarantee free personal care for people with disabilities who need it.

Private and public sector pensions

More than 60,000 workers worked for companies that have gone out of business leaving insufficient money in their pension funds. We will bolster the government's compensation scheme to make sure that these workers are compensated at the same level available under the new Pension Protection Fund. Unlike Labour, we will give proper time for consultation before making changes to existing public sector pension schemes, and we will honour the entitlements already built up.

Beating fraud and error

Each year, around £3 billion is lost to the taxpayer due to fraud and error in the social security system – £100 for every taxpayer every year. The new tax credits could add a further £1.6 billion to that loss. We will reverse the spread of mass means-testing, simplify the benefits and tax credit system, and extend fraud prevention and detection activities to all benefits, reducing both fraud and error.

GREEN ACTION

Save energy and cut fuel bills

Thousands of people – mostly pensioners – die each year from preventable cold-related illnesses. On average, around fifty people die unnecessarily in each constituency every year. Poor home insulation and poor-quality housing lead to cold homes and high fuel bills, the main causes of this 'fuel poverty', while the average pensioner household spends £500 a year on energy. We will help pensioners and severely disabled people cut this bill by allowing them to take a year's Winter Fuel Payment as a voucher redeemable against insulation and energy saving materials. These would be made available at about half price through a partnership with fuel suppliers. A pensioner could save more than £100 from their energy bill every year by investing just one year's Winter Fuel Payment, and help the environment as well. In this way we will invest in cutting energy use and at the same time help pensioners and severely disabled people stay warm and save money.

LOCAL COMMUNITIES

Axe the unfair Council Tax – Local Income Tax is fair and affordable

On top of the Chancellor's plans to increase Council Tax yet again, Council Tax revaluation in England in

2007 threatens one in three households with huge and arbitrary rises, as is already happening in Wales. The Council Tax penalises pensioners and people on low incomes, who pay a far higher proportion of their income in Council Tax than the very rich. A Local Income Tax is based very simply on the ability to pay. It would be run through the existing Inland Revenue Income Tax mechanism, so saving hundreds of millions of pounds by abolishing Council Tax administration. The typical household will save around £450 per year, and eight out of ten pensioners will have lower bills.

Affordable homes

We will help tackle the affordable housing crisis by making available public sector land currently owned by the Ministry of Defence, the Department of Health and English Partnerships, sufficient to build 100,000 more homes both for rent and for affordable purchase through shared ownership schemes for local people. We will reform VAT to encourage developers to repair and reuse empty buildings and brownfield land, rather than building on greenfields and eroding the countryside. We will take 150,000 homebuyers a year out of paying stamp duty altogether, by raising the threshold to £150,000. In areas where second homes are overwhelming the local housing market, we will require people to get planning permission before turning another full-time home into a holiday home.

Art, heritage and sport

Liberal Democrats have a proud tradition of championing the arts, culture and heritage, which successive governments have undervalued. This Government's move towards greater state interference in the arts has threatened to stifle artistic freedom. We will restore the National Lottery funds'independence, requiring the Department for Culture, Media and Sport to separate clearly government spending from independently determined Lottery spending in its annual reports. We will end Labour's freeze in the core Arts Council budget, guaranteeing that growth in core arts funding at least matches inflation. We will help protect the built environment by reducing VAT on historic building repairs. We will increase grassroots sports funding, and support the UK's 2012 Olympic and Paralympic bid.

Set communities free from Whitehall

We will free local councils from many of the stifling controls of central government so that they can innovate and deliver services that meet local people's real needs. Councils will become genuinely accountable to their local communities rather than being agents of Whitehall. To cut bureaucracy and increase effectiveness we would go much further than Labour or the Tories to cut the burden of inspections, merging eight government inspectorates into one, a streamlined and independent Audit Commission.

Protect the post office network and universal mail delivery

Over 3,500 post offices have closed under Labour, and hundreds more are due to be axed. Thousands also closed under the Conservatives. Our priority is to secure a viable future for the post office network, by developing a business plan based on providing a combination of commercial services, benefits transactions and government information. This will help keep more post offices open. We will maintain the obligation on Royal Mail to provide universal same-price delivery of letters throughout the UK.

GREEN ACTION

Tackle waste

Liberal Democrats will set a long-term goal of zero municipal waste, through waste minimisation, reuse and recycling. As a first step, we will make sure that within seven years 60 per cent of all household waste is recycled and we will aim to offer every household regular kerbside recycling. Manufacturers will be held responsible for disposing of their products and materials that are difficult to reuse or recycle. We will not allow new incinerators for municipal waste unless they can be shown to be the best environmental option after considering all alternatives, including new technologies where waste reduction and reuse are not possible.

Planning for sustainability

We will reform the planning system to make sure that local authority development plans are sustainable. That means incorporating targets for CO_2 emission reductions to encourage the development of renewable energy facilities, and accounting for the climate change consequences of policies, including transport. We will also use building regulations to improve the environmental quality of new buildings.

INTERNATIONAL AFFAIRS

We should not have gone to war in Iraq

There were no weapons of mass destruction, there was no serious and current threat, and inspectors were denied the time they needed to finish their job. Thousands of soldiers and civilians have been killed and it has cost the UK over £3.5 billion. Britain must never again support an illegal military intervention. But by invading Iraq the Government has imposed on us a moral obligation to work towards a stable, secure and free Iraq. We welcome the recent elections. We will seek to strengthen and enlarge Iraqi security forces so that they can assume greater responsibility, include Sunni leaders in the political process, and ensure adequate provision of food, water, sanitation and health care for all the Iraqi people. We will support the transition to a fully democratic and legitimate government, aiming to withdraw British troops by the expiry of the UN mandate at the end of the year; the open-ended presence of coalition forces is destabilising and fuels the insurgency.

Build security at home and abroad

The best way to achieve security and to tackle the threat from terrorism is through international action. Britain must work through the United Nations, as a committed member of the EU, and with the US to promote international law, democracy and respect for human rights. We will work to reform the UN and the EU to make them more responsive to international challenges.

EUROPE

Make Europe more effective and democratic

Membership of the EU has been hugely important for British jobs, environmental protection, equality rights, and Britain's place in the world. But with enlargement to twenty-five member states, the EU needs reform to become more efficient and more accountable. The new constitution helps to achieve this by improving EU coherence, strengthening the powers of the elected European Parliament compared to the Council of Ministers, allowing proper oversight of the unelected Commission, and enhancing the role of national parliaments. It also more clearly defines and limits the powers of the EU, reflecting diversity and preventing over-centralisation. We are therefore clear in our support for the constitution, which we believe is in Britain's interest – but ratification must be subject to a referendum of the British people.

DEFENCE

Our troops protect the nation – we must protect them

Britain's armed forces protect the country and are a force for good in the world. But with increasing overseas commitments, they are overstretched. The Government should not be cutting the size of the armed forces while at the same time asking them to take on ever more difficult tasks. New equipment continues to arrive late and over-budget, so we will make military procurement more open and competitive. By switching funding from unnecessary programmes, for example by cutting the third tranche of the Eurofighter programme, we will be able to invest more in protecting the welfare of the armed forces, ensuring that they are well-trained and well-equipped. We will seek new ways of sharing the military burden, by working with allies through NATO and the EU. Liberal Democrats will be realistic about what Britain can, and should, take on, and British forces must always be able to deal with emergencies at home, such as terrorism or natural disasters.

Work for the elimination of nuclear weapons and tackle the arms trade

We will press for a new round of multilateral arms reduction talks, retaining the UK's current minimum nuclear deterrent for the foreseeable future, until sufficient progress has been made towards the global elimination of such weapons. Arms sales contribute to conflict, so we will establish a cross-party Parliamentary Arms Export Committee to monitor arms exports and scrutinise individual licence applications. We will require arms brokers to register under a code of conduct and revoke the licences of those who break the code. We will support the establishment of an International Arms Trade Treaty.

INTERNATIONAL DEVELOPMENT

Meet Britain's promise on aid

Liberal Democrats are committed to realising a world free from poverty. In order to achieve the UN Millennium Development Goals by 2015 (which include tackling extreme poverty and hunger, providing universal primary education, and combating HIV/AIDS) the UK needs to provide more effective international assistance. Liberal Democrats will increase British aid spending from 0.35 per cent of Gross National Income today to at least 0.5 per cent by 2007/08, and set out detailed plans for it to reach 0.7 per cent by 2011 at the latest.

Fair and sustainable trade and investment

Working through the EU and the World Trade Organisation, we will seek to remove the subsidies and tariff barriers that prevent the poorest countries in the world selling their goods on fair terms. We will work to end the dumping of subsidised agricultural exports by developed economies which is wrecking farming in Africa and other parts of the world. We will work to make sure that agreements to liberalise new sectors proceed on a genuinely voluntary basis, without undue pressure on developing countries. We will require companies benefiting from open markets to behave responsibly, and we will promote a new international agreement to encourage investment, particularly in the poorest countries.

GREEN ACTION

Promote environmentally sustainable development

We will make sure that development assistance, whether delivered from the UK, EU, or multilateral institutions, not only meets the needs of the poor, but does so in ways that contribute to environmental sustainability. This means, in particular, targeting aid on renewable energy, clean water and sustainable agriculture, and increasing market access for green products from the developing world. We will devote resources to protecting biodiversity in developing countries, where many species of rare plants and wildlife are seriously endangered.

Take effective action to protect the global environment

We will work through the EU to promote effective and enforceable international agreements to protect the global environment, such as the Cartagena Protocol (on GM products). We will support international agreements and activities designed to stop international environmental crime, such as illegal logging or illegal trade in endangered wildlife, and improve customs training to tackle these illegal activities more effectively. We will argue for reforms of the World Trade Organisation, World Bank and International Monetary Fund to make sure that trade and development policies support rather than hinder environmental sustainability.

Put Britain at the forefront of climate change negotiations

Catastrophic climate change is the major environmental threat to the planet. Urgent action is needed. Liberal Democrat plans will make sure that Britain achieves its targets from the Kyoto Protocol (the international agreement on the pollution that causes climate change) well before the deadline. Britain and the EU must take the lead on negotiations for the next set of targets for greenhouse gas emissions. It is vital that we include the US and Australia but we also need to work with developing countries. Our long-term goal is 'contraction and convergence'– which means agreeing for every country a sustainable population-related allowance for emissions.

RURAL AFFAIRS

Fair prices for food

Of every pound consumers spend on food in supermarkets just eight pence goes to the farmer. Liberal Democrats will introduce a legal duty to trade fairly, supported by a Food Trade Inspector within the Office of Fair Trading. This will protect farmers and consumers from unfair practices by supermarkets and processing companies.

Speed up reform of the Common Agricultural Policy

The CAP fails to protect the interests of rural communities, family farms and the environment. We will press within the EU to speed up reform so that the public funding available is used to provide public benefits. These should include improved access and environmental protection, support for traditional farming and organic systems and new opportunities for agricultural products and local markets. We will use the UK's CAP flexibility to support family farms and aid new entrants more effectively.

Save the UK's fish and marine environment

We will seek early further reform of the Common Fisheries Policy to give local fishermen and other stakeholders a real say in the management of their own regional waters. We will introduce a Marine Act to create a marine planning system to resolve problems of conflicting uses of the sea and sea bed. This would establish conservation zones for highly sensitive areas and strengthen protection of commercial fish stocks, dolphins, porpoises and other endangered marine wildlife.

Improve animal welfare

Liberal Democrats will establish an Animal Protection Commission, bringing all animal welfare matters under the responsibility of a dedicated, expert body, with the duty to make sure that animal protection laws are properly enforced and kept up to date. We will introduce a new Animal Welfare Act to guarantee high standards of animal welfare across the board for farm livestock, working animals and domestic pets, and will close the loophole in existing legislation which allows people who have been banned from keeping animals still to own them if someone else has 'custody'.

GREEN ACTION

No commercial GM crops unless we know they're safe for the environment

We support the right of communities to create GM-free zones. We will insist on rigorous schemes of labelling and traceability in food to guarantee consumer choice. At the same time we will introduce measures to promote organic farming.

TRANSPORT

Make the railways work again

Conservative privatisation left the railways in a mess, but Labour hasn't solved the problems. Whilst delays have doubled, bureaucracy has increased fivefold, while services are being cut. Liberal Democrats will streamline the system, with fewer, larger franchises, given longer contracts in return for more investment and better services. We will use savings from the roads budget to prioritise safety at stations, and to restore the key rail upgrades postponed or cancelled under Labour.

Reward owners of less polluting cars with lower taxes

For many people, particularly in rural areas, cars are a necessity and cannot be replaced by public transport. But they can be far less damaging to the environment when they use less fuel or alternative fuels. We will start by reforming the Vehicle Excise Duty system ('road tax') to cut tax altogether on cars that pollute least, funded by increasing it on those that pollute more. Congestion charging in London (first proposed by the Liberal Democrats) has cut pollution, cut traffic jams and paid for new investment in buses. We will encourage more cities and towns where traffic congestion is a problem to extend congestion charging, linked to up-front investment in better public transport to give millions real alternatives to the car and to reduce the need to drive. In the longer term, as technology allows, we will scrap petrol duties and VED altogether, replacing the revenue with a national road user charging system based on location, congestion and pollution (including the level of pollution of the particular vehicle). As a result, pollution and congestion will be better targeted, with no need for the present system of heavy taxes on every journey.

Free off-peak local bus travel for all pensioners and disabled people

Liberal Democrats were the first to make the case for giving all pensioners and disabled people free off-peak local bus travel, and have already done so in Scotland and Wales. We will implement this policy, and we will in addition provide all pensioners, disabled people, families and young people with their rail discount cards free.

Cut lorry traffic, reduce pollution, and make towns and villages safer

In office, Labour has now increased road building, while the Conservatives' plans would concrete over an area half the size of London with new roads. Both their approaches mean more traffic and pollution, not less. We will not proceed with major new road-building schemes unless the benefits are clear, including environmental and safety factors and a full assessment of alternative public transport schemes. Resources switched from the roads programme will be used to increase investment in public transport, and we will promote safer cycle and pedestrian routes throughout towns and cities. In addition, we will encourage the development of freight interchanges to facilitate growth in rail freight, and we will develop a shipping, ports and waterways strategy.

Reform aviation taxes

To encourage more fuel-efficient aircraft and discourage half-empty planes we will press for international agreement on extending emissions trading to aviation, while at the same time implementing per-aircraft rather than per-passenger charges. We will oppose the construction of international airports on new sites, and also the expansion of airports in the South East. We will end the regulation on busy national airports which results in retail rents subsidising landing charges and encouraging congestion and pollution. We will protect essential 'lifeline' routes to remote UK communities.

GREEN ACTION

Green transport policies

All our transport policies are designed to encourage more environmental transport options, including cutting the cost of using more environmentally friendly vehicles, boosting public transport, discouraging heavily polluting vehicles and reforming aviation policies to cut emissions.

BETTER GOVERNMENT

Curb the power of the Prime Minister

In recent decades Prime Ministers have exercised a growing domination over the political system, insufficiently accountable to Parliament or the people. We will curb this excessive concentration of power. We will cut back the powers of patronage, in particular through our plans for a predominantly elected second chamber. We will make the Royal Prerogative powers which the Prime Minister exercises – such as decisions over war and peace – subject to parliamentary accountability, including bringing in a War Powers Act to require parliament's authority before a government takes Britain to war. A Civil Service Act will introduce a barrier to politicisation of the civil service. We will also strengthen the powers of parliament to scrutinise the actions of the government, enhancing the Select Committee system.

Cut back central government

We will cut the excessive number of government departments and reduce the number of government ministers by over a third. We will also move government bureaucracy out of London, saving money on office rents and spreading wealth and jobs more equally through the UK. The savings will be ploughed back into better public services.

More power for local communities

Our priority is to make local services, like health and education, work better for people. That means that local communities need to have more influence and say over the major issues affecting them. So we will strengthen local democracy, taking power down from Whitehall and reducing central interference and the burden of inspection. The powers of many unelected regional and national quangos and administrators will be given to local cities and counties, including returning to County Councils their strategic planning role. The healthcare planning role of Primary Care Trusts will be given to elected local social services authorities. We will streamline remaining regional functions into a single agency, increasing accountability to the local community through an executive comprising councillors elected from the cities and counties, rather than appointed by the Secretary of State. Underpinning these reforms will be a new system for dividing up government funding fairly within the UK, so that the system is fair for the nations and regions according to their real needs.

A more democratic Britain

Liberal Democrats will improve and strengthen the UK's democratic systems. Liberal Democrats in government in Scotland are already bringing in the single transferable vote (STV) system for local elections, so that local councillors will genuinely represent their community. We will extend this fair voting system to all local elections in Britain, and to the House of Commons, Scottish Parliament and National Assembly for Wales. At the age people can marry, leave school and start work, they will have the right to vote. We will review the European electoral system so people can choose their MEPs personally, rather than just vote by party list as at present. Reform of the House of Lords has been botched by Labour, leaving it unelected and even more in the patronage of the Prime Minister. We will replace it with a predominantly elected second chamber.

Better government in the nations of the UK

Liberal Democrats have led the way in arguing for devolution to Scotland, Wales and Northern Ireland. We believe that people in those parts of the UK, rather than the government in London, should take the decisions on issues that affect them directly. We will therefore strengthen the powers of the Northern Ireland Assembly and extend primary legislative powers to the National Assembly for Wales. In consultation with the Scottish Parliament, we will consider how to extend its role.

Make the BBC more independent from government

The BBC has, over the last eighty years, made a major contribution to Britain's democracy, culture and standing in the world. The Liberal Democrats will make sure it remains the world's leading public service broadcaster – strong, independent, and securely funded. But the regulation of the BBC has been insufficiently independent of its own management, and of the government. Labour's proposals fail to address this. Liberal Democrats will scrap the current government-appointed Board of Governors, and introduce a new, independent external regulator appointed by parliament, to make sure that all public service broadcasters live up to their obligations to the public.

GREEN ACTION

Make government take the environment seriously

It is vital that government and business are made to take their environmental obligations seriously. We will strengthen reporting obligations for government and business as part of an Environmental Responsibility Act, holding government as well as business to account. We will use the purchasing power of government to boost the market for green products and services. We will unite those areas of government with the biggest impact on the environment in a single Environment, Transport and Energy department.

GREEN ACTION

Concern for the environment has always been a core Liberal Democrat value. Our policies are focused on three main areas:

Tackle climate change

Catastrophic climate change is the major environmental threat to the planet. Urgent action is needed. Liberal Democrat plans will make sure that Britain achieves its targets from the Kyoto Protocol (the international agreement on the pollution that causes climate change) well before the deadline. Britain and the EU must take the lead on negotiations for the next set of targets for greenhouse gas emissions. It is vital that we include the US and Australia but we also need to work with developing countries. Our long-term goal is 'contraction and convergence'– which means agreeing for every country a sustainable population-related allowance for emissions.

Cleaner transport and environment

Pollution and congestion have a major impact on people's health and quality of life, as well as on climate change. Many of the solutions to these problems involve transport and this document includes plans to promote public transport, especially the railways. However, pollution can also be cut by reducing domestic waste and promoting recycling. Pioneering Liberal Democrat controlled local authorities are leading the way in cutting unnecessary waste and we will expand these practices nationally.

Cleaner power

Energy use is the main source of greenhouse gas emissions and hazardous waste. We will introduce measures to reduce energy use overall – for example through better home insulation which will also tackle the 'fuel poverty'faced in particular by pensioners. We will make sure that at least 20 per cent of the UK's electricity derives from a range of renewable sources by the year 2020. Finally, given their long-term problems of cost, pollution and safety, we will not replace existing nuclear power stations as they reach the end of their safe and economic operating lives. We will use renewables and save energy instead.

Government Relations Directory

PARLIAMENTARY CONSULTANTS

YOUR CLOSEST PARLIAMENTARY COMPANION

Can you afford to leave your business decisions to the politicians?

Burson-Marsteller provides expert advice on Issues Management, Government relations and Community relations, through an unrivalled integrated network spanning 17 European countries.

Contact: Simon Elliott
Burson-Marsteller
24-28 Bloomsbury Way
London WC1A 2PX
Tel: +44 (0) 20 7300 6276
Fax: +44 (0) 20 7831 3690

www.bm.com

CONNECT PUBLIC AFFAIRS

Millbank Tower, Millbank,
London SW1P 4QP
Tel: 020 7222 3533
Fax: 020 7222 2677
E-mail: g.morris@connectpa.co.uk
Website: www.connectpa.co.uk
Turnover: £1,500,000
Established: 1998
Professional Associations: APPC, IPR
No. UK consultants: 22
Major Clients: Unison, Abbey, Orange
Delivers creative and innovative solutions to public affairs issues.
Provides a comprehensive range of political services including: campaign management, legislative programmes, high-level strategic advice, political monitoring, policy, analysis, conference and event management.

KEY SPECIALIST AREAS	%
Campaign Management	25
Legislative Programmes	20
Financial	15
Coalition Building	10
Policy Research and Analysis	30

GCI *POLITICAL COUNSEL*

GCI LONDON LTD
New Bridge Street House,
30-34 New Bridge Street,
London EC4V 6BJ
Tel: 020 7072 4000
Fax: 020 7072 4010
E-mail: awheeler@gciuk.com
Website: www.gciuk.com
Senior Staff: Adrian Wheeler, Chief Executive

GCI *Political Counsel* is the strategic public affairs arm of top-10 PR
consultancy GCI. Our team provides a complete range of public affairs
services from political monitoring and government relations to issues
management, corporate communications and stakeholder dialogue.

The strategies we develop with our clients are based on the realities of
modern politics and cover the diverse and complex influences on the
political process. We are driven by the business and organisational needs
of our clients, not by the process of communications itself.

Grayling Political Strategy

a network of experience

Westminster Strategy
1 Dean's Yard, Westminster, London SW1P 3NP
Tel: 020 7799 9811
Fax: 020 7976 8276
E-mail: michael.burrell@weststrat.co.uk
Website: www.westminsterstrategy.co.uk
Senior Staff: Michael Burrell

Whether you wish to influence Government thinking in a key policy area,
manage a crisis or achieve a campaign goal, making the right move at the
right time can often be the difference between success and failure.

We are knowledgeable, experienced professional consultants who know
how to make your voice heard.

We help define your issues, frame the debate and develop clear, consistent
and compelling messages.

We can advise on the channels of communication best suited to your goals
and build alliances to help achieve success.

And with a network of offices in London, Edinburgh, Cardiff, Brussels,
Paris and the US, we are able to provide a fully coordinated public affairs
programme.

KEENE PUBLIC AFFAIRS CONSULTANTS LTD

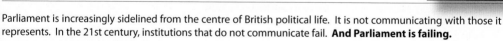

KEENE

Victory House,
99-101 Regent Street, London W1B 4EZ
Tel: 020 7287 0652
Fax: 020 7494 0493
E-mail: kpac@keenepa.co.uk
Website: www.keenepa.co.uk
Established: 1986
No. UK consultants: 8
Parent Company: Independent, with associate companies in Europe and North America

Established in 1986 as an independent consultancy, we specialise in government relations and public relations in the UK and Europe.

Through our London office and our European associate, we offer a professional, cost-effective service based on a thorough analysis of our clients' needs.

Our services include: Monitoring, research and strategic advice; Assistance in contact-making and campaigning; Government marketing; Public and media relations; Crisis communications and media training; Speech writing; Event and conference organisation.

KEY INDUSTRY SECTORS
Aviation, Transport and Travel
Energy and Utilities
Environment Regulations
Healthcare
Representational – Governments, Companies and Trade Associations

---

Members Only?
Parliament in the Public Eye

Report of the Hansard Society Commission on the Communication of Parliamentary Democracy

Members Only?
Parliament in the Public Eye

Parliament is increasingly sidelined from the centre of British political life. It is not communicating with those it represents. In the 21st century, institutions that do not communicate fail. **And Parliament is failing.**

WHAT THE REPORT COVERS...

★ How Parliament has gone wrong – how has it come to be perceived as remote and increasingly powerless?

★ What can be done to change this – ways in which the current system can be reformed to re-establish the crucial link between the people and Parliament

★ What role the media play – the media as a major contributor in reflecting the public's view on issues, policies and the work of Parliament.

Members Only? is essential reading for everyone interested in politics and the media. The recommendations are a blueprint for transforming politics as we know it.

Published: 24 May 2005	Over 120 pages	ISBN: 0 900432 77 2	Price £25	30% student and Hansard Society member concessions

Copies are available from *Dod's Parliamentary Communications* publishers on behalf of the Hansard Society

To order your copy - call 020 7091 7540 - Fax 020 7091 7515 - e-mail: hansard@dods.co.uk

DOD

TRADE ASSOCIATIONS AND PUBLIC AFFAIRS DEPARTMENTS

ADVERTISERS

ISBA

Tel: 020 7291 9020
Fax: 020 7291 9030
E-mail: iant@isba.org.uk
Website: www.isba.org.uk
Senior Staff:
Malcolm Earnshaw, Director General;
Dr Ian Twinn, Director of Public Affairs
ISBA is the authoritative source on all advertising matters from the advertiser's perspective. The social and economic contribution of our members makes us a crucial reference point for you on advertising and commercial communication issues.

The Voice of British Advertisers

DIRECTOR OF PUBLIC AFFAIRS	
Dr Ian Twinn	020 7291 9020

BUSINESS REPRESENTATION

INSTITUTE OF DIRECTORS

116 Pall Mall,
London SW1Y 5ED
Tel: 020 7451 3280
Fax: 020 7839 2337
E-mail: policy-unit@iod.com
Website: www.iod.com

The Institute of Directors is a non-party political business organisation, with around 53,000 members. It helps directors to carry out their leadership responsibilities in creating wealth for the benefit of business and society. The IoD represents members' interests to government and opinion formers in the areas of small business policy, corporate governance, employment, education and training, taxation, pensions, economic policy, environment, health, health & safety, regulation and EU issues.

DIRECTOR-GENERAL	
Miles Templeman	020 7451 3116
DIRECTOR OF PUBLIC AFFAIRS	
David Marshall	020 7451 3263
POLICY UNIT MANAGER	
Lisa Tilsed	020 7451 3280
CHIEF ECONOMIST	
Graeme Leach	020 7451 3366
HEAD OF BUSINESS POLICY	
Richard Wilson	020 7451 3284
HEAD OF CORPORATE GOVERNANCE	
Patricia Peter	020 7451 3113
HEAD OF EUROPEAN AND REGULATORY AFFAIRS	
James Walsh	020 7451 3282
HEAD OF HEALTH. ENVIRONMENT AND TRANSPORT POLICY	
Geraint Day	020 7451 3286
HEAD OF TAXATION	
Mike Templeman	020 7451 3212
SENIOR POLICY ADVISER – eBUSINESS AND eGOVERNMENT	
Professor Jim Norton	020 7451 3279

CONSTRUCTION

NHBC

Buildmark House,
Chiltern Avenue,
Amersham,
Buckinghamshire HP6 5AP
Tel: 01494 735262
Fax: 01494 735365
E-mail: ahoward@nhbc.co.uk
Website: www.nhbc.co.uk
Senior Staff: Andrew Howard, Head of Corporate Communications
Established: 1936

HEAD OF CORPORATE COMMUNICATIONS	
Andrew Howard	01494 735262

NHBC (National House-Building Council) is the UK authority on new home construction.

NHBC's expertise informs the industry through our Standards, inspection service, technical advice and guidance to house builders. Our primary purpose is to help raise the standards in the new house-building industry and provide consumer protection for new homebuyers.

NHBC has approximately 18,000 registered builders who agree to comply with our Rules and Standards and registers 85% of all new homes in the UK. Around 1.6 million homes are currently benefiting from our 'Buildmark' 10 year warranty and insurance cover.

DISTRIBUTION SERVICES

ROYAL MAIL GROUP plc

148 Old Street,
London EC1V 9HQ
Tel: 020 7250 2888
Website: www.royalmailgroup.com
Senior Staff: Mick Fisher, Head of Government Relations; Steve Newsome, Head of EU Affairs.

HEAD OF GOVERNMENT RELATIONS	
Mick Fisher	020 7250 2446
HEAD OF EU AFFAIRS	
Steve Newsome	00 322 286 1143

Royal Mail Group plc is the parent company for the well known brands of Royal Mail, Post Office® and Parcelforce Worldwide, which provide distribution services in the UK and internationally.

ENERGY

E.ON UK

53 New Broad Street,
London EC2M 1SL
Tel: 020 7826 2734
E-mail: chris.morritt@eon-uk.com
Senior Staff: Chris Morritt, Public Affairs Manager

PUBLIC AFFAIRS MANAGER	
Chris Morritt	chris.morritt@eon-uk.com

E.ON UK is the company that runs:
- Powergen, the UK's second largest domestic and small business energy supplier with over 8,500,000 customers;
- Central Networks, the UK's second largest domestic and small business energy supplier with over 8,500,000 customers;
- E.ON Energy, serving more than 10,000 industrial and commercial customers;
- operates a fleet of ten coal and gas-fired power stations generating enough power to meet 15% of the UK's needs;
- has a renewables business covering 17 wind farms, including the thirty turbine development at Scroby Sands, off the coast of Great Yarmouth.

INSURANCE

ASSOCIATION OF BRITISH INSURERS

51 Gresham Street, London EC2V 7HQ
Tel: 020 7600 3333
Fax: 020 7696 8999
Website: www.abi.org.uk
Senior Staff: Stephen Haddrill, Director General;
Stephen Sklaroff, Deputy Director General

DIRECTOR GENERAL
Stephen Haddrill
stephen.haddrill@abi.org.uk
DEPUTY DIRECTOR GENERAL
Stephen Sklaroff
stephen.sklaroff@abi.org.uk

ABI is the trade body for insurance companies. 400 members account for 97% of UK insurance business worldwide. ABI leads on issues affecting the industry's future and image; works with Government, regulators and other authorities, within and outside the UK, to benefit the industry; and communicates with the media and other stakeholders.

TELECOMMUNICATIONS

BT

BT Public Affairs, PPA5D,
BT Centre, 81 Newgate Street,
London EC1A 7AJ
Tel: 020 7356 5392
Fax: 020 7356 5610
E-mail: suzanne.masterton@bt.com
Website: www.bt.com
Senior Staff: Suzanne Masterton, Public Affairs Manager

PUBLIC AFFAIRS MANAGER	
Suzanne Masterton	020 7356 5392

For advice on enquiries from constituents, and for guidance on national and international telecommunications policy issues, please contact Suzanne Masterton.

If you have an enquiry about your own home or business lines, including new orders, please call the Parliamentary Helpline on 0800 200 789 (Monday – Friday 8am – 5pm).